BIBLICAL
WORLDVIEW

CREATION
FALL
REDEMPTION

TEACHER'S EDITION

bju press®

Greenville, South Carolina

Note: The fact that a given writer is cited or quoted in this textbook does not mean that BJU Press endorses that writer (or his or her book, article, etc.) from the standpoint of morals, philosophy, theology, or scientific hypotheses. The nature of a worldview book is such that we must cite and quote people with whom we have fundamental disagreements. In some cases we quote or cite positively people with whom we strongly disagree on other issues—because they do an excellent job saying what's true about the issue at hand. Part of developing a Christian worldview is cultivating the ability to discern between the good and problematic views even of other Christians. This textbook itself is not flawless; it was produced by fallen and finite human beings. It is the privilege and responsibility of every teacher and student to test the claims of *Biblical Worldview: Creation, Fall, Redemption*—and of the writers this book cites—against God's infallible revelation in Scripture.

BIBLICAL WORLDVIEW:
CREATION, FALL, REDEMPTION
Teacher's Edition

Lead Author
Kevin Collins, MDiv

Contributing Authors
Mark L. Ward Jr., PhD
Brian Collins, PhD

Editor
Dennis Cone, MA

Consultants
Bryan Smith, PhD
Brad Batdorf, EdD
Wesley Barley, MDiv

Project Coordinator
Matthew Ryan

Cover & Book Design
Michael Asire

Page Layout
Bonnijean Marley

Cover Illustration
Chris Koelle

Illustrators
Zachary Franzen
Chris Koelle
Del Thompson

Permissions
Sylvia Gass
Sarah Gundlach
Meg Jones
Carrie Walker

Photograph credits appear on page 473.

Unless otherwise noted, all Scripture quotations are from The Holy Bible, English Standard Version® (ESV®), copyright © 2001 by Crossway, a publishing ministry of Good News Publishers. Used by permission. All rights reserved. Quotations marked KJV are from the King James Version. Quotations marked NKJV are from the New King James Version®, copyright © 1982 by Thomas Nelson. Used by permission. All rights reserved. Scripture quotations marked NASB are taken from the New American Standard Bible®, copyright © 1960, 1962, 1963, 1968, 1971, 1972, 1973, 1975, 1977, 1995 by The Lockman Foundation. Used by permission. (www.Lockman.org)

Student Text: Excerpts on pages 385, 390, 391, 395, 398, and 399 are from *Art and Music: A Student's Guide* by Paul Munson and Joshua Farris Drake. Published by Crossway, 2014. Used by permission. All rights reserved. Excerpts on pages 50, 54, and 187 are from *Delighting in the Trinity* by Michael Reeves. Copyright © 2012 by Michael Reeves. Used by permission of InterVarsity Press, P. O. Box 1400, Downers Grove, IL 60515. (www.ivpress.com)

Teacher's Edition: Excerpts on pages 128–29 are from *Addictions: A Banquet in the Grave* by Edward T. Welch (ISBN 978-0-87552-606-3), pages 33–36. Used with permission of P&R Publishing Co., P. O. Box 817, Phillipsburg, NJ 08865, www.prpbooks.com. Excerpts on page 171 are from *What Is a Healthy Church?* by Mark Dever, © 2005, pp. 48, 91. Used by permission of Crossway, a publishing ministry of Good News Publishers, Wheaton, IL 60187. (www.crossway.org)

© 2016 BJU Press
Greenville, South Carolina 29614

Printed in the United States of America

ISBN 978-1-60682-815-1

15 14 13 12 11 10 9 8 7 6 5 4 3 2 1

CONTENTS

TO THE TEACHER

BIBLICAL WORLDVIEW: CREATION, FALL, REDEMPTION provides an overview of the biblical worldview and guides application of this worldview to multiple social institutions and disciplines. In the process, it introduces students to apologetic methods and guides them to discern and refute false worldviews. Particular attention is given to social institutions and disciplines so that students can contribute to rebuilding these disciplines from a biblical worldview.

The first unit lays the foundation for properly understanding worldview and its significance to all of life. The following three units present the biblical worldview in terms of Creation, Fall, and Redemption (CFR). The remaining five units of the book examine how to approach various social institutions and disciplines (marriage and the family, government, science, history, and culture and the arts) according to the biblical worldview.

This is a capstone text that brings together in one book the biblical worldview approach that is integrated into all of BJU Press's product lines. It is intended to give the high school student a solid foundation before moving on to university or vocational training.

General Course Objectives

By the end of the course, the students should be able to:

1. Define worldview and demonstrate how worldviews influence the way people think about all of life.

2. Analyze a biblical worldview in terms of Creation, Fall, and Redemption.

3. Apply Creation, Fall, and Redemption to analyzing and evaluating various real-life issues as well as to making Christian contributions to various aspects of culture.

Teaching Biblical Worldview

There are different approaches to teaching worldview, but the commonly used approaches are not all created equal. The four distinctives of our approach can be summarized as follows.

1. Focus on a biblical worldview

Our approach to worldview instruction is focused on the presentation of the correct worldview. False worldviews will necessarily be evaluated in the process, but the instruction is largely constructive so that biblical worldview thinking leads to biblical action. We want students to focus on the biblical worldview.

2. Bible-first perspective

Approaches to teaching worldview, especially as it pertains to apologetics, tend to follow one of two philosophies. The first philosophy asserts that evidence is what convinces people to take the positions they take, especially their worldview positions. It purports that people embrace secularism and evolution because these positions seem to have all of the important evidence on their side. For this reason, some Christians encourage students to follow the evidence wherever it leads, asserting that if, in all honesty, students find that it leads away from belief in the Bible, then they should feel free to go away from the Bible. We don't believe that Jesus reasoned this way with unbelievers or doubters. We believe that worldview precedes evidence and that only faith in the true authority source opens up understanding (Prov. 1:7; Heb. 11:3). As the saying goes, "believe to understand [the evidence]" rather than "understand [the evidence] to believe." The evidence looks different depending on what glasses you use for examining it. If you use the glasses of evolution to look at the stuff of biology, biology will seem to argue for evolution. But if you look at the stuff of biology through the glasses of God's Word, you will see that it all argues for God as the Creator. The right worldview takes God at His Word. It's the only thing that can stand as the authoritative foundation in place of autonomous human reasoning. This is the Bible-first perspective.

3. Emphasis on evaluation and positive response

One common criticism of worldview thinking is that it never goes beyond critique. It tends to deconstruct the false worldviews without actually compelling people to rebuild with the biblical worldview in the real world. We want students to be more than evaluators; we want them to learn to apply the truth as subcreators. Therefore, the Student Text emphasizes both evaluation and positive response.

4. Content that is both accessible and compelling

The Student Text was purposefully written in a style that's more enjoyable to read. Rather than introducing students to an encyclopedic overview of abstract philosophical concepts, our approach to worldview studies is designed to be engaging by being set in the context of the unfolding story of the world. A worldview isn't just a viewpoint; it's a narrative of God's interaction with His creation and its responses to Him. The overarching story allows people to orient themselves and then apply the beliefs and values, which grow out of that larger story, to the practical issues of life.

The Teacher's Edition

The teacher's edition (TE) of BIBLICAL WORLDVIEW: CREATION, FALL, REDEMPTION has been designed to help you carry out the instructional process. It includes reduced student pages (RSPs) ❶ for easy access to what students are reading. Each lesson begins with objectives that guide the instruction and assessments. Teacher notes ❷, parallel to the Student Text RSPs, suggest a variety of educational methods for accomplishing teaching strategies. The course is meant to interactively engage students; it's not designed for a lecture-only presentation. Answers for the Thinking It Through questions ❸ and Chapter Review answers ❹ are also located in the margins.

The flow of the teacher's notes begins at the top left column and continues seamlessly across the bottom margin and up to the top right column all the way to the bottom of the page in that right column. Some notes will continue to flow onto the next spread of pages.

Chapter and Section Objectives

Each chapter objective usually corresponds to a major section. The chapter objectives are not meant to be specific instructional strategies. Those should be accomplished through the TE notes with corresponding icons ❺. The chapter objectives ❻ are educational objectives that describe a specific student action in relation to the main point of the content in each major section. The section objectives ❼ will help you guide students to accomplish the chapter objectives.

Lessons and Scheduling

Each chapter generally consists of two to four sections that divide the information into convenient reading assignments. You may wish to have students read the section before teaching it in class. Refer to the lesson plan overview at the beginning of this book and the suggested lesson plan chart ❽ at the beginning of each chapter. Your students' abilities and your own interests will help determine how you schedule lessons. The schedule you choose to follow for your worldview class depends on time constraints, your perception of your students' needs and interests, and other variables.

Teaching Strategies (Icons)

- Teacher notes without an icon provide additional information that the teacher can use to further explain a concept to students. Some notes are written as "teacher talk" (i.e., the students are addressed directly as *you*); other notes are instructions or additional information addressed to the teacher.

Discussion sections provide teachers with prompts and suggested answers for in-class discussion to engage the students.

Group Activity sections suggest in-class exercises and activities for collaborative teamwork that will provide students opportunities to brainstorm ideas together.

Debate suggestions provide students with the opportunity to hone their skills of persuasion and to work through controversial issues.

Current Event activities encourage students to engage with the culture around them and to learn how to carefully analyze and evaluate the input from that culture with a biblical worldview.

Writing activities provide students with more time to distill their ideas and an opportunity to communicate their ideas clearly in an organized fashion.

Special speaker items suggest opportunities to hear from other voices with some personal and practical experience or some expertise in a particular institution or discipline.

Additional Resources notes point teachers to helpful sources to expand their own knowledge of the subject matter. Many of the topics are complex, and the TE note margins do not provide enough space for a comprehensive treatment of a difficult subject. Teachers may also point exceptional students to some of these resources for enrichment.

Student Activities sections remind teachers that there are corresponding activities in a separate book for students, which provides further reinforcement, more expansive explanations, and opportunities for application. Note that the vast majority of activities are simply identified in the chapter opener lesson plan charts; most don't have a specific TE note with an icon.

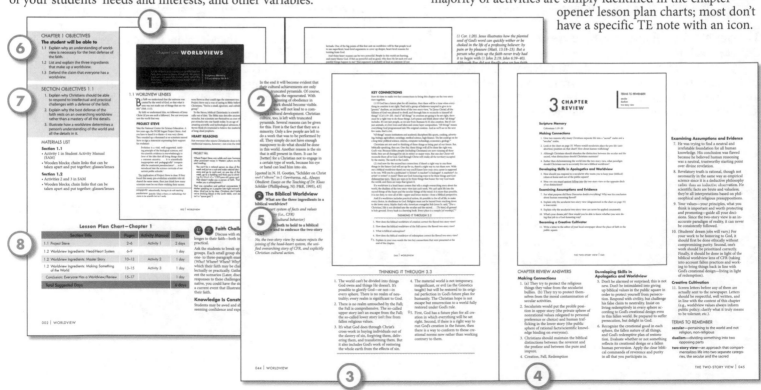

Additional BJU Press Materials

- The *Biblical Worldview Student Activities* manual includes activities that challenge students to creatively apply what they've learned and to analyze and evaluate biblical and nonbiblical worldviews in the culture. Also available is an answer key for the *Student Activities* manual, which provides additional tips for teacher guidance through the activities.

- Unit tests for *Biblical Worldview* may also be purchased. These include a variety of question types, such as true-false, multiple-choice, short-answer, matching, and essay. Each test covers one unit (three chapters) and has approximately fifty items. An answer key is available for the teacher.

Project Ideas

There are numerous Additional Resource sections throughout the TE. You may wish to assign to students some of these books and then have them present an oral or written report. While most of the books will not be found in a public library, many of the books will be available at a Christian university or seminary with a quality theological library. You may be able to utilize an interlibrary loan system to get access to these helpful resources.

Student Text Features

The textbook contains the following features:

- an engaging, conversational style of writing
- twenty-seven chapters divided into nine units with symbolic art to introduce each unit
- memory verses conveniently displayed in the chapter headings
- section headings and subsection boldfaced headings
- margin boxes to supplement material in the main text
- pullout quotes that highlight or reinforce significant points
- easily accessible definitions for starred words in the margins for students' better understanding
- boldfaced terms to remember for student assessment
- engaging pictures and diagrams to illustrate or reinforce concepts
- Thinking It Through review questions after each reading section; a higher-order evaluation (with a lightbulb icon)
- Chapter Reviews divided into sections that reflect Bloom's taxonomy of learning levels: Terms to Remember (remember); Making Connections (understand); Developing Skills in Apologetics and Worldview (apply); Examining Assumptions and Evidence (analyze and evaluate); Becoming a Creative Cultivator (create)
- endnotes that enable you to locate sources cited
- memory verse list compiled from the chapter opening pages
- Scripture index
- topical index including authors
- photograph credits

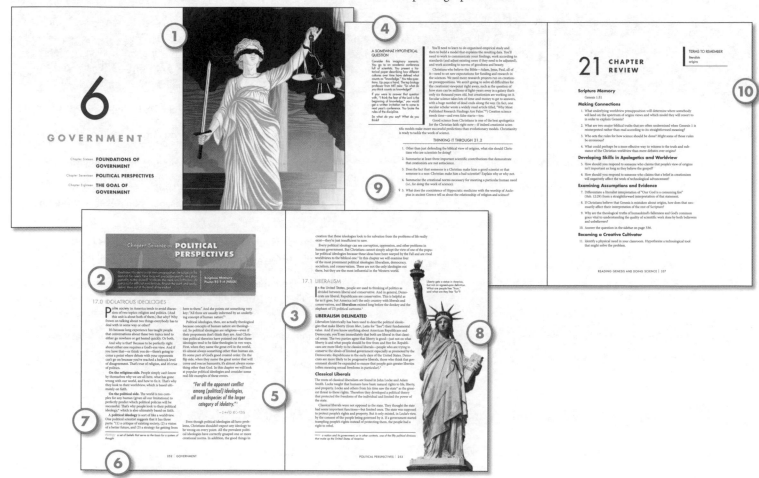

LESSON PLAN OVERVIEW

DAY(S)	PAGES	ACTIVITY	SECTION	OBJECTIVES
UNIT 1: WORLDVIEW				
Chapter 1: Worldviews			1.1 Explain why an understanding of worldview is necessary for the best defense of the faith. 1.2 List and explain the three ingredients that make up a worldview. 1.3 Defend the claim that everyone has a worldview.	
1–2	2–6		1.1 Project Steve	• Explain why Christians should be able to respond to intellectual and practical challenges with a defense of the faith. • Explain why the best defense of the faith rests on an overarching worldview rather than a mastery of all the details. • Illustrate how a worldview determines a person's understanding of the world and all the details in it.
3	6–9	1 and 2	1.2A Worldview Ingredients: Head-Heart System	• Explain how the basic beliefs of someone's head system (thinking/understanding) are grounded on his worldview faith pre-commitments. • Explain how the values of someone's heart system (desires/loves) influence his head system (thinking/understanding).
4	10–13		1.2B Worldview Ingredients: Master Story	• Define *metanarrative* and explain the scope of its influence. • Summarize the biblical metanarrative and explain its powerful influence.
5	13–15		1.2B Worldview Ingredients: Making Something of the World	• Apply the exhortation to be salt and light to real-life situations. • Analyze the implications of the creation mandate for creative cultivation in culture.
6	15–17		Conclusion: Everyone Has a Worldview/Review	
Chapter 2: Presuppositions			2.1 Compare and contrast worldview apologetics with evidentialism by analyzing the role of evidence in relation to presuppositions in each approach. 2.2 Defend the proper role of reasoned evidence even though it cannot provide proof apart from faith. 2.3 Explain why a Christian's desire for proof must ultimately rest on faith in God's authority and the fear of the Lord.	
7–8	18–22	3	2.1 Presuppositions	• Define *presupposition* and explain how presuppositions orient a person's understanding. • Summarize the evidentialist approach and explain why many people favor this approach. • Explain why the morality of knowledge, human finitude, and model-making all necessitate presuppositions. • Summarize and defend the worldview apologetics approach. • Explain why the evidentialist approach can never provide final certainty.
9–10	22–27	4	2.2 Proof	• Explain the value of using evidence in spite of its limits. • Explain why God's undeniable proof doesn't count in the unbeliever's mind. • Summarize three common faith-bases for proof: empiricism, rationalism, or revelation. • Defend the proper use of reason and evidence.
11	27–30		2.3 Doubt Your Doubts	• Determine the underlying biblical explanation for why people leave the faith—spiritual deadness and idolatry. • Explain why belief must precede understanding and why faith is the necessary means of finding certainty. • Define *belief*, and explain why it must rest on the fear of the Lord.
12	31		Review	

DAY(S)	PAGES	ACTIVITY	SECTION	OBJECTIVES
Chapter 3: The Two-Story View			3.1 Analyze the two-story view. 3.2 Explain why the two-story view fails. 3.3 Defend the claim that CFR is the best way to outline a Christian worldview.	
13	32–35	5	3.1 The Two-Story View	• Summarize what the two-story view is. • Explain why the two-story view seems attractive to many Christians. • Explain why the two-story view seems attractive to many secularists.
14–15	35–41		3.2 Critiquing the Two-Story View	• Explain why secularists are being inconsistent when they attempt to remove religious values from the public square. • Evaluate what happens when a person tries to isolate the sacred from the secular: failure to protect the faith and the faithful. • Evaluate what happens when a person tries to equate the secular with the sacred: failure to maintain reverence and purity.
16–17	41–44	6	3.3 Creation, Fall, Redemption	• Evaluate the claim that some aspects of human life are neutral, untouched by the biblical worldview under God's creational rule. • Explain that Christians must distinguish creational good from fallen perversions in every sphere of life since the Fall comprehensively taints God's good creational structures. • Explain the responsibility of all believers to live according to God's creational structures in every area of life.
18	45		Review	
19			Unit 1 Test	
UNIT 2: CREATION				
Chapter 4: God the Creator			4.1 Explain why the personhood of God—specifically, the mutual love displayed among the persons of the Trinity—must provide the basis for God's motivation to create the world and the human motivation to exist. 4.2 Explain how God's ultimate goal for all things, namely, the display of His own glory, is consistent with His love. 4.3 Defend the proper relationship between God and creation by contrasting the biblical portrayal of the unrivaled transcendent yet immanent God with four false views.	
20	48–51	7	4.1 God the Three in One	• Explain why every motivation for existence can be traced back to who or what a person loves. • Explain why your ultimate motivation of love ought to be expressed toward God and your neighbor. • Connect God's own ultimate motivation of mutual Trinitarian love to His design for all creation to share in His love.
21	51–55		4.2 God the Spring	• Identify God's ultimate goal as His own glory. • Explain how God's ultimate objective to display His own glory is consistent with His essence as a God of love. • Attribute God's creation of the world and of humans to the overflow of His glorious love rather than to His need for or lack of anything. • Identify humanity's ultimate goal as enjoyment in God's glorification.
22–23	55–60	8	4.3 God the Unrivaled, Yet God with Us	• Defend the idea that God is knowable because He revealed Himself to His creation. • Identify and explain the four false views of God's relationship to creation. • Explain the biblical view of God's unrivaled relationship to creation, defending His transcendent self-existence and immanence.
24	61		Review	

DAY(S)	PAGES	ACTIVITY	SECTION	OBJECTIVES
Chapter 5: Man and His Mandate				5.1 Defend human value by defining humans according to the image of God, distinguishing them from plants and animals. 5.2 Define the Creation Mandate and categorize it as a blessing from God for all humanity. 5.3 Defend the idea that the Creation Mandate is a command to create and cultivate culture.
25–26	62–66	9 and 10	5.1 Mirrors of God	• Critique evolution's inability to provide a basis for the unique value of human life. • Attribute the value of human life to the Creator's gift of the image of God. • Analyze the components of the image of God in humans. • Explain why failing to recognize humans as image-bearers leads to attributing human value subjectively, resulting in despair or contempt for others.
27	67–70		5.2 Man and Woman Given a Task	• Defend the foundational place of the Creation Mandate in the metanarrative of the biblical worldview. • Explain the two parts of the Creation Mandate, distinguishing them from fallen humanity's rebellious departures. • Explain why the Creation Mandate is a blessing from God for all humanity even after the Fall.
28–29	71–75	11	5.3 Man and Woman, Creating and Cultivating	• Explain how filling the earth and subduing it necessarily results in shared human actions of stewardship: culture. • Explain the power of culture to limit or open up horizons of possibility for cultural creativity and cultivation. • Summarize how engaging in cultural creativity and cultivation contributes to the positive formation of a more God-honoring culture.
30	76		Review	
Chapter 6: Everything God Made Was Very Good				6.1 Defend the goodness of God's creation. 6.2 Defend the existence of natural laws and creational norms. 6.3 Demonstrate that the good design of God's created world—in both the physical and social order—is the standard by which we must judge the way things ought to be.
31–32	77–81	12	6.1 And God Saw That It Was Good	• Recall God's own testimony about His creative work and clarify the meaning of that testimony. • Defend the goodness of God's creation even though it has been marred by the Fall and used in perverse ways by fallen humans. • Identify and refute various attempts to malign an aspect of God's good creation as intrinsically evil.
33–34	81–86		6.2 Laws of Nature and Creational Norms	• Defend the idea that the natural order of the universe is governed by laws of nature upheld by God's sovereignty. • Defend the idea that the social order of the universe is governed by creational norms fitting with God's design. • Explain how creational norms are discovered through personal application of biblical wisdom to real-life situations.
35	86–90		6.3 The Way Things Are Supposed to Be	• Defend the necessity of standards for evaluating the goodness of something. • Explain the twofold nature of the Christian standard: (1) special revelation of moral laws declared in Scripture and (2) general revelation of natural laws and creational norms built into God's design. • Recognize that there are differing consequences for violating both natural laws and creational norms. • Implement a knowledge of biblical morality to detect the trumped-up claims of supposed creational norms.
36	91		Review	
37			Unit 2 Test	

DAY(S)	PAGES	ACTIVITY	SECTION	OBJECTIVES
			UNIT 3: FALL	
Chapter 7: **Far as the Curse Is Found**			7.1 Defend the idea that every aspect of a human individual is touched by the Fall. 7.2 Defend the idea that the Fall includes cosmic effects on the physical world. 7.3 Defend the idea that every aspect of human culture is touched by the Fall.	
38–39	94–98	13	7.1 The Personal Effects of the Fall	• Describe the pre-Fall conditions of humankind as comprehensive perfection for fulfilling the Creation Mandate in right relationship with God. • Describe the process of the Fall, accomplished through Satan's deceptive questioning of God's Word and goodness. • Analyze the extent of both the physical and spiritual ramifications of the Fall as comprehensive corruption frustrating the fulfillment of the Creation Mandate due to a broken relationship with God. • Clarify that although each part of human nature is fallen, not every person manifests fallenness to the greatest possible extent or in the same way. • Explain how sin powerfully enslaves human nature through its deceptiveness.
40–41	99–102		7.2 The Cosmic Effects of the Fall	• Explain why all death and suffering is abnormal (i.e., not supposed to exist anywhere in this world). • Explain why Adam's sin led to the Curse not only on the whole human race but also on all of creation. • Demonstrate that the Fall resulted in physical consequences that correspond to each task of the Creation Mandate. • Conclude that the Christian's hope is in both a spiritual redemption and a physical restoration.
42	103–6		7.3 The Cultural Effects of the Fall	• Exemplify how a variety of societal institutions can reflect corruptness. • Recognize that fallen humanity produces fallen societal expressions. • Recognize that fallen cultural expressions are everywhere in both obvious and subtle ways. • Identify the biblical term for fallen cultural expressions—*worldliness*.
43	107		Review	
Chapter 8: Common Grace, **the World, and You**			8.1 Explain that much good can still exist in human culture because God's common grace restrains sin. 8.2 Defend the idea that the pervasive effects of the Fall demand the sanctified use of culture rather than uncritical consumption of culture. 8.3 Explain what "affection drives cognition" means.	
44–45	108–11	14	8.1 Common Grace	• Differentiate between the fundamental condition of all humans due to original sin and their actual behavior, restrained by common grace. • Define *common grace* and explain why God supplies it even to rebels. • Explain and demonstrate how common grace both restrains sin and promotes good in the individual. • Explain and demonstrate how common grace both restrains sin and promotes good in culture.
46–47	112–16	15	8.2 The World	• Critique the values of pop culture from a Christian worldview. • Recognize that Christians must renew their own minds because the flesh is naturally drawn to worldly culture. • Defend the idea that worldliness, even though it begins internally, is communicated externally. • Critique asceticism's denial of truth, goodness, and beauty in a fallen world. • Defend the need to refine one's tastes in order to recognize truth, goodness, and beauty, particularly in high culture. • Plan how to avoid worldliness and asceticism by living as a pilgrim and an ambassador, discerning light and darkness in fallen culture.

DAY(S)	PAGES	ACTIVITY	SECTION	OBJECTIVES
48	116–20		8.3 Affection Drives Cognition	• Define the fear of the Lord, and explain why this affection must guide a person's knowledge. • Explain how wrong affections lead intelligent people to suppress the truth and support foolish ignorance.
49	121		Review	
Chapter 9: Structure and Direction			9.1 Explain the concept of structure and direction and how it relates to the CFR story line of Scripture. 9.2 Apply structure and direction to the issue of sexual relations. 9.3 Apply structure and direction to the issues of materialism, technology, and language..	
50–51	122–25		9.1 Understanding Structure and Direction	• Describe the earth's condition through the lens of the CFR story line. • Define what *structure* means and what *direction* means, and explain how these terms describe the realities of CFR. • Illustrate structure and direction. • Explain why it's necessary to recognize that the world is structured according to God's good design. • Explain why it's necessary to recognize that every human use of creation is directed in conformity to or away from God's good design.
52	125–29		9.2 Sex in a Fallen World	• Recognize that secularism's denial of God's structure results in a rejection of any justifiable ethical standards. • Summarize God's structured design for sexual relations and explain the purposes for His design. • Explain why fallen direction away from God's structure always results in detrimental consequences.
53–54	129–34	16a 16b 16c	9.3 Other Structures Bent in Bad Directions	• Explain and exemplify how material goods can be directed toward or away from God's structure. • Explain and exemplify how technology can be directed toward or away from God's structure. • Explain and exemplify how language can be directed toward or away from God's structure.
55	135		Review	
56			Unit 3 Test	
UNIT 4: REDEMPTION				
Chapter 10: An Everlasting Kingdom			10.1 Trace the unfolding story line of Redemption: how God promises in successive covenants to establish His kingdom. 10.2 Trace the unfolding fulfillment of God's redemptive promises in the work of Jesus Christ. 10.3 Defend the idea that Redemption is the restoration of God's original creation.	
57–58	138–44	17	10.1 The History of Redemption in the Old Testament	• Explain why Genesis 3:15 is the thesis statement for the whole Bible. • Summarize the promises and explain the significance of the Noahic Covenant. • Summarize the promises and explain the significance of the Abrahamic Covenant. • Summarize the promises and explain the significance of the Mosaic Covenant. • Summarize the promises and explain the significance of the Davidic Covenant. • Analyze how the exile directly relates to God's covenants. • Summarize the promises and explain the significance of the New Covenant.
59–60	144–48	18	10.2 The Coming of the Kingdom	• Describe how Jesus began to fulfill the kingdom promises. • Explain how Jesus' death and resurrection fit in with kingdom fulfillment. • Conclude that the message of the gospel—proclaiming Christ's salvific work—makes sense in the larger context of the promised kingdom. • Summarize how Jesus will complete the fulfillment of the kingdom promises.

DAY(S)	PAGES	ACTIVITY	SECTION	OBJECTIVES
61	148–51		10.3 Restoring God's Good Creation	• Defend the idea that Redemption is restoration by explaining that resurrection brings restoration rather than replacement. • Defend the idea that Redemption is restoration by clarifying that the future kingdom brings restoration rather than replacement. • Plan specific activities to carry out the Creation Mandate, engaging in the culture in ways that are biblically faithful.
62	152		Review	
Chapter 11: **Redeemed for Good Works**			11.1 Determine the present place of Christians in God's unfolding kingdom story. 11.2 Explain the present role of Christians—to be salt and light during times of suffering. 11.3 Apply structure and direction for the purpose of bearing witness and living a life of good works in the midst of current culture.	
63–64	153–57		11.1 Our Place in God's Story	• Defend the idea that God's kingdom comes in two phases—the first of which has already come and the second of which is yet to come. • Compare and contrast what should and shouldn't be the mission of believers based on their place in God's kingdom story: living in the gap between salvation and judgment.
65–66	158–63	19	11.2 Witness and Good Works	• Explain that Christians are often called on to suffer because God's kingdom of salvation overlaps with Satan's kingdom of darkness. • Explain the Christian's task of bearing witness in word and works in every sphere of life. • Explain the Christian's task of living a life of good works as a kingdom citizen.
67	163–67	20	11.3 Pushing in the Right Direction	• Explain how applying structure and direction to the sphere of sex can help believers to be salt and light while living in a fallen culture. • Explain how applying structure and direction to the sphere of material goods can help a Christian to be salt and light in the context of a fallen culture. • Explain how applying structure and direction to the sphere of technology can help a believer to be salt and light in a fallen culture. • Explain how applying structure and direction to the sphere of language can help a follower of Christ to be salt and light in the middle of a fallen culture.
68			Review	
Chapter 12: The Mission of the **Church and Your Vocation**			12.1 Distinguish the specific mission of the institutional church from the organic church's broader social responsibility of doing good works. 12.2 Explain the importance of living a life of good works through one's vocation.	
69–70	168–76	21	12.1 The Mission of the Church	• Explain how the church fits into God's unfolding plan of redemption. • Define and relate the institutional church, the organic church, and the kingdom of God. • Summarize the six tasks identified in Scripture as the mission of the local church. • Explain how the institutional church and the organic church relate differently to the various tasks of cultural institutions. • Defend the value of the church and its specific God-given mission.
71–72	177–80	22	12.2 The Vocation of the Christian	• Explain both the reason work is a God-created good and the purposes for that work. • Evaluate how a person's Christianity should affect both how one does his work ethically and in accordance with creational norms. • Identify the proper motivation for work: redeeming the time by living in light of redemption. • Compare and contrast two faulty responses toward work: idolizing it due to its joy or neglecting it due to its frustration.

DAY(S)	PAGES	ACTIVITY	SECTION	OBJECTIVES
73	181		Review	
74			Unit 4 Test	
UNIT 5: GENDER				
Chapter 13: The Man and Woman in Creation			13.1 Defend God's creational design for gender roles in marriage. 13.2 Defend God's creational design for the family. 13.3 Defend God's creational design for gender roles in the church and society.	
75	184–89	23	13.1 Marriage and Family	• Explain why creational norms must eventually push back against secular culture's rebellion. • Analyze God's structured design for marriage: man and woman equal in essence but different in functional roles. • Compare and contrast the differing gender roles of husbands/fathers versus wives/mothers.
76–77	189–93		13.2 God's Design for Family	• Discuss how human selfishness undermines the primacy of the family. • Recognize that having children is God's intended purpose and blessing for most married couples. • Explain why the normal intended role for children is one of submissiveness to their parents. • Summarize the responsibility of parents to nurture and to train their children. • Clarify the biblical structure for family headship established in each family unit.
78–79	193–98	24	13.3 Gender Roles Beyond the Nuclear Family	• Explain why secularism's position on gender roles in society is inconsistent with its evolutionary metanarrative. • Explain and defend the complementarian position on gender roles in the church. • Explain and defend the complementarian position on gender roles in society.
80	199		Review	
Chapter 14: Marriage Twisted			14.1 Identify and give examples of fallen family relationships. 14.2 Evaluate and respond to the claims of the "Gay Christian" movement. 14.3 Explain why both cohabitation and divorce twist God's design for marriage. 14.4 Summarize the negative consequences of failing to recognize two distinct genders and varying roles for men and women.	
81	200–204	25	14.1 Dysfunctional Family Relationships	• Classify different ways humans twist God's creation of marital intimacy. • Compare and contrast the opposite extremes of a fallen husband (passive or domineering) and a fallen wife (resistant or manipulative). • Summarize how one would identify sins of parents against children and of children against parents.
82-83	205–9		14.2 Homosexuality	• Summarize the changing landscape of the approval/disapproval of homosexuality. • Apply CFR to the reality of homosexual temptation, and explain the responsibility of believers who face this temptation. • Explain why this particular temptation has recently been brought to the forefront of cultural discussions.
84	210–14	26	14.3 Cohabitation and Divorce	• Identify any cultural causes that may have contributed to the rise of both cohabitation and divorce. • Identify the two essential elements of a true marriage, and explain why cohabitation violates God's norms. • Explain how divorce distorts the purpose God created marriage for.

DAY(S)	PAGES	ACTIVITY	SECTION	OBJECTIVES
85	214–18		14.4 Gender Roles in a Fallen World	• Summarize the consequences of societal confusion over the roles and responsibilities of men and women in society. • Summarize the consequences of societal confusion over the recognition of the gender identity of men and women within that society. • Defend the responsibility of believers to endeavor to maintain loving compassion while remaining uncompromisingly opposed to destructive behavior.
86	219		Review	
Chapter 15: **Marriage Redeemed**			15.1 Connect the temporal pattern of a Christian marriage—love and submission—to its ultimate reality and goal: the eternal spiritual marriage of Christ with God's people. 15.2 Explain how the fellowship of the physical family ought to visibly reflect and cultivate God's redemptive work and purpose for His spiritual family. 15.3 Explain how the redemptive teaching of the New Testament elevates the roles of both women and men.	
87	220–24	27	15.1 Redeeming Marriage	• Distinguish the marriage of a husband and wife from the marriage of Christ to His people. • Explain why the wife's respectful submission pictures the church's relationship to Christ. • Explain why the husband's sacrificial love pictures Christ's relationship to the church. • Plan how to prepare for a marriage that will properly picture Christ and the church.
88–89	224–29		15.2 Redeeming Family	• Trace the spiritual family of God through biblical history. • Explain how children, by carrying out their responsibility of obedience, can better enable their parents to nurture them according to God's redemptive work and purpose. • Summarize the positive and negative responsibilities of parents that will better enable children to receive their parent's nurturing according to God's redemptive work and purpose.
90–91	229–34		15.3 Redeeming Gender Roles	• Compare and contrast the biblical concept of women's roles versus the world's concept. • Compare and contrast the biblical concept of men's roles versus the world's concept.
92	235		Review	
93			Unit 5 Test	
			UNIT 6: GOVERNMENT	
Chapter 16: **Foundations of Government**			16.1 Defend the idea that government is a God-given established good, not a necessary evil. 16.2 Demonstrate from Scripture that the main purpose of government is to ensure justice. 16.3 Compare and contrast the kinds of governments formed to carry out the biblical duties of government.	
94	238–41		16.1 What Good Is Government?	• Describe the origins of government. • Explain how the Creation Mandate and the kingship of Christ relate to human government. • Defend government as an institution that is good and necessary for humans to flourish in community.
95–96	241–45	28	16.2 Why Do We Need Government Anyway?	• Defend the claim that ensuring justice is the main purpose of government. • Critique unbiblical understandings of justice. • Formulate a biblical definition of justice.

DAY(S)	PAGES	ACTIVITY	SECTION	OBJECTIVES
97–98	245–50	29	16.3 What Should Government Do and How?	• Explain why a just government must defend its people, must promote morality, and should at times help the poor. • Evaluate the advantages and disadvantages of the major forms of government. • Defend the wisdom of a mixed form of government. • Defend limited government by demonstrating that each differing institution has its own sphere of authority.
99	251		Review	
Chapter 17: **Political Perspectives**			17.1 Evaluate the three kinds of liberalism from a biblical worldview. 17.2 Evaluate the rise of democracy from a biblical worldview. 17.3 Evaluate varieties of socialism from a biblical worldview 17.4 Evaluate three kinds of conservatism from a biblical worldview.	
100–101	252–57	30	17.0 Idolatrous Ideologies and 17.1 Liberalism	• Define *ideology* and relate it to the concept of idolatry. • Define *liberalism* as it is used in political science and distinguish this definition from popular usage. • Outline the development of differing conceptions of liberalism. • Evaluate the values, goals, and outcomes of classical liberalism, progressive liberalism, and libertarianism.
102–3	257–60		17.2 Democracy	• Distinguish between democracy as a political system and democracy as an ideology. • Trace the history of opposition to and acceptance of democracy. • Evaluate the strengths and weaknesses of democracy.
104	260–62		17.3 Socialism	• Identify the origins of socialism and explain its concerns and values. • Evaluate the goals and the effectiveness of socialism.
105–6	262–66		17.4 Conservatism	• Explain how conservatism differs from other ideologies. • Define the three strands of American conservatism. • Evaluate the strengths/weaknesses of each strand of American conservatism.
107	267		Review	
Chapter 18: **The Goal of Government**			18.1 Explain how the realities of Christ's present and future reign should shape Christian involvement in politics. 18.2 Evaluate the church and state positions described in this chapter. 18.3 Describe the methods and characteristics of proper Christian political involvement.	
108	268–70		18.1 The Coming King	• Compare and contrast right and wrong Christian responses to political victories and defeats. • Explain the differences between Christ's kingdom rule in His first and second comings and how that affects Christian political involvement. • Differentiate between Christians' task of advancing the kingdom of Christ under His authority and their political involvement.
109–10	270–74	31	18.2 Church and State	• Evaluate the state over church position. • Evaluate the church over state position. • Evaluate the civil religion position. • Evaluate the exclusion of religion from the public sphere. • Evaluate the church influencing the state position.
111–12	275–82	32	18.3 Christian Political Prudence	• Identify the primary objective of Christians living during a time of difficulty. • Contrast a biblical approach (preserving the good and reforming the evil) with theonomy and pluralism. • Evaluate contemporary political discussions and tactics in light of the Christian political virtues of prudence, boldness, humility, and respect. • Compare and contrast unrighteous rebellion with righteous resistance to a wicked ruler's demands.

DAY(S)	PAGES	ACTIVITY	SECTION	OBJECTIVES
113	283		Review	
114			Unit 6 Test	
UNIT 7: SCIENCE				
Chapter 19: Science Is Something God Created Humans to Do			19.1 Defend the idea that science is a God-established good and that it is made possible by three major Christian assumptions. 19.2 Determine the main purposes of science: to declare the glory of God and to make wise use of the earth for the benefit of others. 19.3 Structure scientific study according to the creational norms that govern science.	
115–16	286–91	33	19.1 Science Belongs to Christianity	• Critique the claims that Christianity is anti-science and that scientism is nonreligious. • Connect the work of the Creation Mandate to the work of science to explain why science is a God-established good. • Summarize the three major Christian assumptions, and explain why they justify the work of science. • Explain why it's not possible to separate the sacred from the secular in the work of science.
117	292–95		19.2 The Ultimate Purpose for Science	• Explain how science can be a tool for discovering the glory of the Creator. • Explain how science can be a tool for loving your neighbor.
118–19	295–300	34	19.3 Creational Norms for Science	• Attribute the discovery of creational norms for scientific work to the wisdom built into God's created order. • Outline the creational norms and explain why they must govern scientific work.
120	301		Review	
Chapter 20: Fallen Science			20.1 Explain how the work of science has been affected by the Fall. 20.2 Examine scientism's claims and values. 20.3 Detect the cause of scientism's faulty way of living: its inability to provide justification for meaning and morality. 20.4 Detect the cause of scientism's faulty way of knowing: its method dismisses all sources of knowledge other than empiricism and denies its own presuppositional interpretation of the empirical data.	
121	302–6		20.1 Science Is Fallen	• Understand that scientific work often produces unintended consequences rather than the promised benefits. • Summarize six ways that the Fall affects scientific work.
122	306–10		20.2 Scientism: Science Exalted	• Explain why many people hold to the claim that only scientific knowledge is legitimate. • Evaluate scientism as an idolatrous religious worldview that requires faith beyond its own empirical scientific knowledge. • Explain why naturalism is an appealing myth that must resort to the faulty two-story view.
123	311–14	35	20.3 Scientism: A Faulty Way of Living	• Evaluate scientism's approach to the meaning of life. • Evaluate scientism's approach to morality.
124–25	315–20		20.4 Scientism: A Faulty Way of Knowing	• Critique scientism's exclusive claim to knowledge by exemplifying two major ways its adherents must inconsistently resort to nonempirical knowledge. • Critique scientism's exclusive claim to knowledge by explaining why its adherents can't justify scientism's own claim to rationality.
126	321		Review	

DAY(S)	PAGES	ACTIVITY	SECTION	OBJECTIVES
Chapter 21: Reading Genesis and Doing Science			21.1 Defend the young-earth creationist position. 21.2 Explain why gifted scientists who are Christians, given the opportunity, ought to positively contribute to the good of others and this world.	
127–28	322–30	36	21.1 Reading Genesis 1–3 as Foundational to a Biblical Worldview	• Identify the underlying cause of the conflict between young-earth creationists and the wider culture. • Outline the major origins models according to their underlying worldview presuppositions. • Defend both the historicity of Adam and the absence of death before the Fall.
129–30	331–36	37	21.2 Christians in the Sciences	• Explain why some gifted scientists may find it harder to take advantage of certain opportunities in the scientific community. • Give examples of work done by some scientists who self-identify as Christians that has positively contributed to the advancement of science. • Recognize both the imperfection of Christian scientists because of the Fall and the abilities of non-Christian scientists because of God's common grace. • Explain why the biblical worldview provides a foundation for doing the work of science. • Use their own gifts to actively identify and solve real-life problems for themselves and others.
131	337		Review	
132			Unit 7 Test	
UNIT 8: HISTORY				
Chapter 22: Foundations for History			22.1 Connect the importance of history to the origin of God's created order and the advance of God's redemptive plan. 22.2 Explain the purposes for studying history. 22.3 Discern the creational norms for how historical study should be conducted.	
133	340–42		22.1 History Began	• Attribute the origin of history to God's created order. • Attribute the advance of history to God's redemptive plan. • Explain why properly understanding the Bible and how it connects to one's own context demands historical awareness. • Explain why the historical development of God's redemptive plan was necessary.
134	342–45	38	22.2 Why Study History?	• Explain the importance of interpreting the ways and works of God in all of world history through the lens of Scripture. • Explain the importance of inferring lessons for life for today by evaluating finite and fallen humans from the past through the lens of Scripture. • Explain the importance of understanding one's own and others' cultural identity, analyzing both positive and negative values through the lens of Scripture.
135–36	345–52	39	22.3 Christian Foundations for History	• Defend an approach to historical study that both maintains acknowledged basic commitments and also strives for thorough honesty. • Summarize and explain each creational norm for conducting historical study. • Explain why conducting historical research should expand the Christian's worldview grasp of the ways and works of God, lessons for life, and cultural identity.
137	353		Review	

DAY(S)	PAGES	ACTIVITY	SECTION	OBJECTIVES
Chapter 23: Fallen History			23.1 Critique four significant ideologies that distort the work of historians. 23.2 Evaluate how fallenness can affect a historian's selection and moral judgments.	
138–39	354–64	40	23.1 The Fall, History, and Ideologies	• Summarize the naturalistic view of history, and evaluate its views on determinism and morality. • Describe the characteristics of extreme nationalism and summarize its view of history, identifying problems with its demonization of others and minimization of its own shortcomings. • Summarize the postmodernist view of history, identifying problems with its skepticism of a larger unifying story, its denial of historical certitude, and its refusal to critique wrong perspectives. • Summarize the views of history that emphasize class, race, and gender, identifying problems with single-issue emphases, forced interpretations, and blindness to both good and evil in every race, every class, and every gender.
140	365–67		23.2 Selection and Moral Judgments	• Explain how selection can lead to errors in the presentation of history. • Compare and contrast the proper and improper uses of moral judgments in historical evaluation.
150	368		Review	
Chapter 24: History in Light of Redemption			24.1 Determine the appropriate means and motivations for establishing or refuting historical claims. 24.2 Explain why data from source materials should be humbly and honestly interpreted according to a viable model. 24.3 Defend the legitimacy of discerning divine providence in human history.	
151–52	369–72		24.1 Finding Reliable Source Materials	• Explain the appropriate means for establishing or refuting historical claims: scholarly study of legitimate source materials through the interpretive lens of a biblical worldview. • Summarize the appropriate motivations for establishing or refuting historical claims: God's glory and your neighbor's good.
153	373–75		24.2 Proposing Historical Models Humbly	• Explain why a model is necessary. • Compare and contrast faulty models with viable models. • Defend the necessity of humility and honesty in the work of model-making.
154–55	376–80	41	24.3 Seeing God's Hand in History	• Define providence and defend its reality in human history. • Explain the objections to discerning divine providence in human history (outside of specific biblical revelation). • Explain guidelines and limitations for properly discerning divine providence in human history.
156	381		Review	
157			Unit 8 Test	

DAY(S)	PAGES	ACTIVITY	SECTION	OBJECTIVES
			UNIT 9: ARTS & CULTURE	
Chapter 25: Truth, Goodness, and Beauty			25.1 Explain why a person with a biblical worldview must hold to an objective and transcendent standard for beauty just as he does for truth and goodness. 25.2 Defend the idea that a person's subjective apprehension of truth, goodness, and beauty must be developed according to the divine standard. 25.3 Use the creational norms of truth, goodness, and beauty to evaluate various artistic products.	
158	384–86	42	25.1 Beauty and Culture	• Detect the fallacies of both the scientistic and postmodern views of beauty. • Defend the idea that beauty, inextricably linked to truth and goodness, is objectively based on a transcendent divine order. • Analyze what art is, namely human subcreation that either imitates or twists God's divine order.
159–60	386–93	43	25.2 Truth, Goodness, and Beauty in the Eye of the Beholder	• Explain why some unbelievers embrace relativism with regard to truth, goodness, and beauty and why believers must reject relativism with regard to all three. • Refute the fallacies of both the scientistic and postmodern views of truth, goodness, and beauty. • Clarify that, although people's tastes need to be developed, their providential personal and cultural situations may lead them to explore different aspects of God's beauty. • Identify the ultimate purpose and standard of beauty.
161–62	393–99		25.3 Norms for the Arts	• Determine that the creational norms for evaluating a cultural product include truth, goodness, and beauty—and that they must all stand together in harmony. • Exemplify the necessity of joining truth to goodness and beauty in various artistic subcreations. • Exemplify the necessity of joining goodness to truth and beauty in various artistic subcreations. • Exemplify the necessity of joining beauty to truth and goodness in various artistic subcreations.
163	400		Review	
Chapter 26: The False, The Bad, and The Ugly			26.1 Evaluate cultural productions that fail to maintain the balance and unity of the truth, goodness, beauty triad. 26.2 Defend in light of human nature the necessity of keeping truth, goodness, and beauty a unified triad. 26.3 Explain how the sensibilities of pop culture, regardless of the content, tend to attack truth, goodness, and beauty.	
164–65	401–6		26.1 Unraveling Truth, Goodness and Beauty	• Explain how idolizing truth, goodness, or beauty above other elements in the triad distorts the creation order. • Explain how attacking truth, goodness, or beauty is rebellion against the creation order.
166	406–11	44	26.2 The Great Unraveling of Human Nature	• Defend the unity of the inner person as the receiver of truth, goodness, and beauty. • Explain why truth disconnected from goodness and beauty is irrational. • Explain why goodness disconnected from truth and beauty is immoral. • Explain why beauty disconnected from truth and goodness is ugly.

DAY(S)	PAGES	ACTIVITY	SECTION	OBJECTIVES
167–68	411–16		26.3 Pop Goes the Culture	• Judge which content is unacceptable for Christian consumption. • Summarize the sensibilities that pop culture produces within a culture. • Explain how pop culture powerfully reinforces a wrong definition of truth. • Explain how pop culture reinforces a wrong definition of what matters in the realm of goodness and beauty. • Explain that, while pop culture's sensibilities may be appealing, matured sensibilities are worthy of the effort in order to take dominion over God's world.
169	417		Review	
Chapter 27: Creative Cultivators			27.1 Summarize four possible responses to cultural artifacts and apply criteria for discerning which gesture is most appropriate. 27.2 Explain why the postures of creativity and cultivation should be the ultimate goals of Christians implementing a biblical worldview as they engage culture.	
170–71	418–25	45	27.1 Gestures and Postures	• Explain why discernment is necessary and how that wisdom can be gained. • Construct condemnations of some cultural artifacts or practices. • Construct critiques of some cultural artifacts or practices. • Evaluate the appropriateness of consuming some cultural artifacts. • Evaluate the appropriateness of copying some cultural artifacts.
172–73	426–33		27.2 Creating and Cultivating	• Construct a cultural artifact that displays love for God and neighbor. • Explain why the posture of cultivation is necessary: to hone skills for creativity.
174	434		Review	
175			Unit 9 Test	

UNIT 1: WORLDVIEW

CHAPTER 1

This chapter lays the foundation for worldview study by explaining what a worldview is, by showing that everybody has a worldview, and by showing how useful worldview thinking is for worldview apologetics. We claim that worldviews tell a big story about the world that generates basic beliefs, assumptions, and values, resulting in changed lives and the group action we call culture.

CHAPTER 2

Because everyone has a worldview, it's important to learn how to examine and challenge people's basic beliefs, assumptions, and values. This is necessary both to give students confidence in their own worldview and to give them the ability to defend the biblical worldview.

CHAPTER 3

As Chapter 1 argued, worldviews tell a big story (metanarrative) about the world. This chapter outlines competing metanarratives that are often adopted by Christians. The two-story view illegitimately separates the sacred from the secular; whereas the Creation, Fall, Redemption story of Scripture shows that God created everything good, the Fall has affected all that God has created, and that God intends to restore all things.

1

WORLDVIEW

Chapter One **WORLDVIEWS**

Chapter Two **PRESUPPOSITIONS**

Chapter Three **THE TWO-STORY VIEW**

CHAPTER 1 OBJECTIVES

The student will be able to

1.1 Explain why an understanding of world-view is necessary for the best defense of the faith.

1.2 List and explain the three ingredients that make up a worldview.

1.3 Defend the claim that everyone has a worldview.

SECTION OBJECTIVES 1.1

1. Explain why Christians should be able to respond to intellectual and practical challenges with a defense of the faith.

2. Explain why the best defense of the faith rests on an overarching worldview rather than a mastery of all the details.

3. Illustrate how a worldview determines a person's understanding of the world and all the details in it.

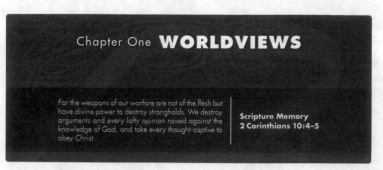

Chapter One WORLDVIEWS

For the weapons of our warfare are not of the flesh but have divine power to destroy strongholds. We destroy arguments and every lofty opinion raised against the knowledge of God, and take every thought captive to obey Christ.

Scripture Memory
2 Corinthians 10:4–5

1.1 WORLDVIEW LENSES

"By faith we understand that the universe was created by the word of God, so that what is seen was not made out of things that are visible" (Heb. 11:3).

By faith *we* understand this, we followers of Jesus Christ (if you are such a follower). But not everyone sees the world that way.

PROJECT STEVE

Take the National Center for Science Education. A few years ago, the NCSE began Project Steve. And you have to hand it to them—it was very clever. They rounded up a thousand or so scientists named Steve to sign a statement expressing their support for evolution:

> Evolution is a vital, well-supported, unifying principle of the biological sciences, and the scientific evidence is overwhelmingly in favor of the idea that all living things share a common ancestry. . . . It is scientifically inappropriate and pedagogically* irresponsible for creationist pseudoscience* . . . to be introduced into the science curricula of our nation's public schools.[1]

The implication of Project Steve is clear. If they found this many pro-evolution scientists who all shared the same name, then just think how many scientists must be out there wishing their names

were Steve so they could sign the statement too. Project Steve was a way of saying to Bible-believing Christians, "You're a small, ignorant, and cultish group."

To the Steves, biblical Christianity is scientifically out of date. The Bible may describe ancient miracles, but scientists see themselves as ones who put miracles into our hands today. In an age of amazing scientific and technological advances, the Steves think it's irrational to believe the mutterings of long-dead prophets.

HEART REASONS

Not everyone who rejects Christianity does so for intellectual reasons, however—not even the intel-

---

PROJECT BILL

Where Project Steve was subtle and even humorous, other prominent voices in Western culture are blunt and insulting:

> You can't be a rational person six days of the week and put on a suit and make rational decisions and go to work and, on one day of the week, go to a building and think you're drinking the blood of a 2,000-year-old space god. That doesn't make you a person of faith. That makes you a schizophrenic.[2]

That was comedian and political commentator Bill Maher speaking on a popular late-night network TV show. (And just to be clear, Christians don't believe we're drinking blood at the Lord's table, and Jesus isn't a "space god.")

---

pedagogically: *educationally, having to do with teaching*

pseudoscience: *(pseudo: false) a theory or methodology that claims to be scientific but isn't really*

Lesson Plan Chart—Chapter 1

Section Title	Pages	Activity Manual	Days
1.1 Project Steve	2–6		2 days
1.2 Worldview Ingredients: Head-Heart System	6–9		1 day
1.2 Worldview Ingredients: Master Story	10–13	Activity 1 Activity 2	1 day
1.2 Worldview Ingredients: Making Something of the World	13–15		1 day
Conclusion: Everyone Has a Worldview/Review	15–17		1 day
Total Suggested Days			**6 days**

  Faith Challenge

Discuss with students challenges to their faith—both intellectual and practical.

Ask the students to break up into small groups. Each small group should write a one- to three-paragraph example scenario (Who? Where? When? Why? How?) in which their faith may be challenged intellectually or practically. Gather back to present the scenarios (Later, discuss the three responses to these challenges.). As an alternative, you could have the students bring in a current event that illustrates a challenge to their faith.

Knowledge Is Constructed

Students may be awed and shaken by the seeming confidence and expertise that the

lectuals. One of the big points of this first unit on worldview will be that people tend to use superficial, head-level arguments to cover up deeper, heart-level reasons for turning from God.

And those heart reasons can be very powerful. People in this world are hurting, and many blame God. If He's so powerful and so good, why does He let such evil and painful things happen to me? That argument is probably at least as common (if not more common) among unbelievers than the pro-evolution arguments used by the Steves. In an age of deep despair, many victims of other people's sins find it offensive to be told that they are sinners too.

SMART PEOPLE

Western society (the "West" basically means the nations of Western Europe and some of the countries colonized by them, such as the United States and Canada) has a sometimes awkward, sometimes adversarial relationship with religion. Hurting people sense that they need "spirituality," but Christianity is too exclusive and too demanding for them. And among cultural elites,* religion—especially Christianity—is thought to pose a threat to the social order. Those elites will let you have your religion if you really must—as long as you keep it out of politics and the laboratory. But the boundaries around religion keep shrinking ever tighter, squeezing it out of journalism, the arts, and education (in a process called secularization*).

cultural elites: *the recognized leaders in all aspects of a culture, from politics to academics to the arts*

secularization: *the process of a society turning away from religion or faith in anything supernatural*

We might as well admit it because the Bible does. Many of the very smart people out there—smarter than you, smarter even than *Biblical Worldview* textbook authors—think that your religion is not just mere opinion, but mere foolish opinion. Paul admitted about the Corinthian Christians long ago, "Not many of you were wise according to worldly standards, not many were powerful, not many were of noble birth" (1 Cor. 1:26).

NOMA

One of the most famous scientists named Steve was Stephen Jay Gould (1941–2002), a paleontologist and evolutionary biologist who wrote many popular books about science. Dr. Gould is known for proposing an idea about the relationship between religion and science that he calls "NOMA"—Non-Overlapping Magisteria.[3] Gould is willing to grant some kind of authority (that's what *magisterium* means) to religion, but it's an authority that does not overlap with scientific authority.

But take heart because that's not where Paul stops. Instead, he continues, "God chose what is foolish in the world to shame the wise; God chose what is weak in the world to shame the strong" (1 Cor. 1:27).

How, then, do you respond to these smart people? There are three major options:

Option 1: Give in. Give up your faith completely.

Regarding this option, this whole book is one big "Don't do that." It's totally unnecessary, not to mention that it's an offense against your Creator.

Option 2: Give in a little—but only on the really disputed issues like evolution and homosexual marriage. Admit that the Bible may be wrong in just a few places.

Don't do this, either. Either God spoke clearly in His Word about these issues or He didn't. If He spoke clearly, giving in even a little will lead to giving in a lot anytime someone puts enough pressure on you.

Option 3: Don't give in at all if someone contradicts Scripture, no matter how smart or how numerous the Steves are. Instead, argue back—lovingly and graciously, but powerfully and confidently—knowing that God's reason for using the weak to shame the wise is "so that no human being might boast in the presence of God" (1 Cor 1:29).

majority of secularists purport to have in regard to the so-called brute facts. Students need to understand that knowledge is constructed—built on previous bits of knowledge that one has already been convinced to accept. In fact, students need to be careful when they are being led down a particular pathway of thinking (taught concepts which seem to be neutral "brute" facts but which are actually based on a system of thought not yet revealed to them) by a guide (a teacher who "knows" more than they do). Often, the pathway has actually been designed to lead students in a particular direction to reach a particular destination (a conclusion; "knowledge" or "fact"). It is not until they reach the end of the path that they may finally realize a conflict exists between what they thought they believed about life and what is now being presented as reality.

This is why students need to be thoroughly equipped with the correct worldview first. Then they can evaluate evidence and facts as they are presented to them.

Giving In

Prompt students to explain in more detail why Option 1 is biblically invalid.

Based on the faith-challenging scenarios the small groups constructed earlier, discuss with students their response to those pressures.

What kind of a person would choose Option 1—finally and firmly giving up his faith completely?

The Bible is clear that nobody denies God unless he is a fool with corrupt reasons for doing so (Ps. 53:1) no matter how shrouded in intellectual arguments his doubts may be

(1 Cor. 1:20). Jesus illustrates how the planted seed of God's word can quickly wither or be choked in the life of a professing believer: by pain or by pleasure (Matt. 13:18–23). But a person who gives up the faith never truly had it to begin with (1 John 2:19; John 6:39–40). Although Eve did not finally give up her faith in God, she exemplifies how a person can be intellectually deceived, blinded by the heart's desires. Driven by a desire for the fruit, she was deceived into believing Satan's intellectual reasoning rather than believing in God's declarations of reality (Gen. 3:1–6; 1 Tim. 2:14).

Another key reason for giving up the faith is fear. As a true child of God, you may be tempted to give in to your fears, but no one ought to bully you into denying your Father (Matt. 10:28, 32–33).

Present the gospel with fervency and pray that God will open the eyes of students who have already turned from the truth (Titus 1:16; 2 Tim. 2:25; 3:7; Jude 1:22–23).

Giving In a Little

Prompt students to explain in more detail why Option 2 is biblically invalid.

What kind of person would choose Option 2—compromising the essential, clearly declared truths stated in God's Word?

The Bible is clear that resorting to man's wisdom over God's wisdom leads to folly and destruction (1 Cor. 3:19). In contrast to Abraham, the man of faith, Lot is an example of one who looked to his own intellectual understanding to make the seemingly obvious wise choices for his life (cf. Prov. 3:7; Isa. 5:21). He was quickly led to compromise in the prosperous city of Sodom, only to be righteously vexed, barely escaping destruction (Gen. 18–19; 2 Pet. 2:7–9).

A person may also move away from his firm convictions when he becomes disillusioned through his own personal experiences. Job maintained his faith without compromise (Job 1:22; 2:10) even though he did question God's reasons. The antidote to disillusionment is to maintain a steadfast faith in God and the clarity of His Word (2 Pet 1:3; Jude 1:17–21; 2 Cor. 10:5; Col. 2:8) and to humbly submit to God and His working in your life when you don't understand your difficult circumstances (James 1:5; Job 28:28; 40:1–8; 42:1–6). Christians are not required to have all the counterarguments or answers (though hopefully they will learn some to equip themselves for Option 3); they are required to have faith (Heb. 11:1–3, 6).

Students Must Be Equipped

Even though students may be convinced that they ought to choose Option 3 to defend the faith, they may still be reluctant to try because they are not sure how to do it well. They may not even recognize when a defense is needed because faith is sometimes undermined in very subtle ways. (Teacher note: Look for a current event that could illustrate this). For example, what was our imaginary professor "Steve" doing for three weeks in biology class before he hit the evolution lesson? There's a good chance he was seeking to lead his students to a point at which they would be more susceptible to accepting his evolutionary conclusions. For example, he would probably be careful to demonstrate in detail that natural selection produces microevolution or adaptation so that three weeks later he could jump to the conclusion that, given enough time, natural selection is a mechanism capable of allowing macroevolution to take place. Of course, he wouldn't make any distinctions here between adaptation and macroevolution. This is why students must be equipped—so that they can analyze and evaluate presentations of knowledge.

Don't Give In

Christians must defend the faith. This is what is known as apologetics: a defense in answer to an accusation. There are three parts:

(1) Present the Scripture's explanation of reality, truth, and values.

(2) Answer the unbeliever's objections (defensive approach).

(3) Confront the unbeliever's false explanations of reality and truth (offensive approach).

Multiple Scripture passages exhort Christians to contend for the faith; Scripture presents the apostles as contending for the faith (2 Cor. 10:5; Col. 2:8; 1 Cor. 1:29; cf. Matt. 10:34–36; Acts 17:1–34; 18:4, 28; 19:8; 22:1; 24:10; 25:8, 16; 26:1–2, 24; Jude 1:3).

The faith ought to be defended (Titus 1:7–9) because the lordship of Christ warrants this defense (1 Pet. 3:13–17). Any imagination opposed to Christ must be cast down so that no one may boast (1 Cor. 1:29). In 2 Corinthians 10:4–5, Paul models a bold yet gracious manner to do that.

OPTION 3

Option 3 is, obviously, this book's recommendation. The Bible speaks about all of life—not just about morals and church. God speaks through Scripture in ways that ought to influence even a college biology class. So there's good reason to go for option 3.

But it raises some immediate practical problems.

Let's imagine a Steve-versus-You scenario: Dr. Steve at his lectern versus you in your fold-down, wooden seat in a massive lecture hall during your freshman year at college. Steve with his hard-earned PhD (give him some real credit for that) versus you with your hard-earned high school diploma.

Scene: Biology 101, State University in Dodge, Dakota. One-hundred thirty-six 18-year-olds (you're sitting on the tenth row) watching ugly but informative PowerPoints that Steve has put together to lead his young charges from ignorance to scientific light.

Dialogue: Not much, really. It's just Steve talking. And he's good at it. He's smart and engaging—nerdy but only in a cool way. He knows his phyla and his genera. You, as one who's always enjoyed science, are really liking this class.

Internal dialogue: But you're ready. You know he's going to deny the Bible's account of creation; you just don't know how or when. But you won't give in. No matter what. You promised Mom.

But three autumn weeks pass, and you haven't heard anything you believe you're supposed to disagree with. You're pretty overwhelmed by the vast store of scientific knowledge between Steve's two ears. And then, finally, Steve hits the evolution lesson.

Steve is very disarming. He's not nasty toward creationists. He doesn't make you stand up to proclaim your faith and then laugh derisively at you. He doesn't even know you're there. Nonetheless he makes you feel dumb, dumber than you already feel after almost a month listening to his intellect sing.

He simply points to the evidence: there those trilobites* are, sitting in exactly the sedimentary stratum* that the evolutionary model* predicts. Look at the picture. They're just hanging out, doing whatever it is fossilized trilobites like to do while they're waiting millions of years to be discovered by paleontologists. You can't deny your senses. Suddenly you can't think of a way to make the evidence fit Scripture.

You've got an immediate, practical problem.

OPTIONS 3.1 AND 3.2

As it turns out, Option 3 has two sub-options, each of which is valid in its own way.

Option 3.1: Argue back based on your own superior understanding of the evidence.

There are Christian geologists and biologists in the world (some of them are even named Steve) who can offer competing explanations of the scientific data—or who have access to additional data that might revise the picture described by your university professor.

This is part of why you have a high school science class: to learn these explanations and amass this data—and to learn how to come up with your own explanations and find your own data via scientific methodology.

But believing scientists haven't yet persuaded the non-Christian ones (or vice versa). And you? You're eighteen. Your professor has been teaching the evolutionary history of apes and men since the days when you were learning to make monkey

trilobite: extinct sea creature often found fossilized

stratum: rock layer

model: a simplified description of vast amounts of data

Special Speaker

Invite a Christian professor or businessman (knowledgeable in both Christian worldview and his particular field) to discuss the impact that worldview has in his sphere of work and his experience living out/defending the faith to a hostile audience.

sounds. You simply don't know as much as he knows. That's why you're sitting in his class. You're hoping he'll teach you.

Arguments based on evidence have a definite place, and we'll talk a lot more about them. But right now, as you're sitting in that class, they're not going to help you very much—even if you were the top science student in high school.

What do you need to help you answer the questions that Dr. Steve put into your head—so that you stay true to your Christian beliefs and live according to them when you reach college? You need the other sub-option.

Option 3.2: Argue back, perhaps initially only in your own mind, based on the concept of "worldview."

WORLDVIEW

It certainly seems like Dr. Steve has a mountain of evidence on his side. But if you look at what he says more closely, you'll find that evidence is not the only ingredient in his thinking. The evidence he cites sounds convincing only because he looks at that evidence in a certain way—in a way that is colored by his **worldview**.

What exactly is a worldview? Let's start with a few illustrations; a little later in this chapter, we'll move to a definition.

- A chain: Every chain of reasoning has to start somewhere.
- A building: Every brick of your knowledge has to be built on some ultimate foundation. It can't just be bricks all the way down.
- A lens: A worldview is like a set of lenses through which you see everything around you.

Lenses may be the most helpful illustration of what a worldview does. If you wear glasses or contacts, you might remember when you first put them on. The world looked sharper, but your new seeing apparatus felt awkward. You were very aware of it. Maybe the contacts made your eyes water or the frames on your glasses distracted you by their shape and color. But it's unlikely that this feeling lasted very long. By now, you're so used to your lenses that you don't see them at all. Instead you see through them.

That's what a worldview is like—a set of lenses through which you view the world. But because you got it so long ago and it grew on you so naturally, you may never have looked at your worldview at all.

And let's extend this metaphor a little bit: you really can't look at your glasses distinctly while they're on your face. At most you see a fuzzy rim and the very edges of the lenses. You can't look at the lenses themselves unless you take them off, and that is very difficult to do. They're stuck on there pretty well.

Dr. Steve, trained biology expert, wears glasses just like you do—except your glasses (if you're a Christian) are different from his, or at least they ought to be. Most scientists in Project Steve see the world through atheistic lenses in which every evidence for God's existence is twisted into an evidence for His absence. But it's not the evidence that's different. It's the lenses through which Dr. Steve sees it.

WORLDVIEWS | 005

COMING TO TERMS

The word *worldview* appears to have come into English as a translation of the German word *Weltanschauung*. *Welt* (velt) means "world," and *anschauung* (ON-shao-ung) means "point of view," "opinion," or "perception."

Christian thinkers have used or proposed different terms. The prime minister of the Netherlands at the turn of the twentieth century, Abraham Kuyper, was a strong Christian and strong proponent of worldview thinking. He liked to call the biblical worldview the "Christian world and life view." But that's unwieldy, like a couch being carried through a narrow door. Most people have settled on *worldview*.

FOR REAL?

A website publicizes a program for teaching science and claims that it is "the only worldview-neutral curriculum that supports both Christian and secular values."[4] Evaluate the claim this advertisement makes. Can a science curriculum be worldview neutral?

Facts Are Always Interpreted

Illustrate to the students that facts are always interpretations of data based on worldview.

All facts are discovered as such by means of interpretation. Therefore, if people's interpretations are wrong, then their understanding of what truly is factual will also be wrong. A person must demonstrate that his interpretations of the data are valid in order to claim that something is truly factual. There is no such thing as a brute, uninterpreted fact.

Use concrete objects (chain links, building blocks, lenses/glasses) to illustrate that a person must accept some authoritative criteria (a worldview) to guide his interpretations.

Use a scientific taxonomy as an example. The first link in the chain, the foundational building blocks, or the lens by which decisions are made to place the organisms into the taxonomy assumes that the slightest common feature means common ancestry rather than a common designer. [See Bodie Hodge, "A Biblically Based Taxonomy? Answers in Genesis (website), June 25, 2010.] The taxonomies are not just the organization of the brute facts, but are human conclusions based on interpretations guided by the criteria of one's worldview presuppositions. Claims are often made without explicitly relating those claims to their assumptions. Often there is a whole web of assumptions that undergird the more complex and controversial claims.

[Jason Lisle's book *Discerning Truth* (Green Forest, AR: Master Books, 2010) is a helpful resource for discussing logical fallacies in the creation versus evolution debate.]

You Need Superior Knowledge—or Do You?

Assure students that they can begin to develop the essential tools to defend the faith without having to have a comprehensive knowledge of everything.

When people confront your faith with contradictory "evidence," are you expected to or even able to defend the faith by always being a greater expert of the evidences (having a lot more data/evidence than they have and a greater intellect and use of logic than they have)?

While it is often beneficial to utilize logical arguments based upon some knowledge of the evidences, you must first have a clear understanding of your own foundational worldview from which to interpret and evaluate that evidence. You don't need to be an expert in every field of knowledge; you simply need to have the right worldview system of interpretation in which to place the evidence. The real issue is not a matter of who has the most evidence and detailed knowledge of that evidence; the real issue is who is interpreting the evidence according to the correct truth system. As long as you have a basic understanding of the foundational worldview starting points, you can evaluate another person's interpretations of evidence.

1. that most scientists affirm evolution as vital and well-supported; that it is inappropriate and irresponsible to teach otherwise

2. (1) giving in or giving up your faith completely (2) giving in a little (only on certain issues) (3) not giving in at all

3. presenting arguments based on evidence (Option 3.1) or based on worldview (Option 3.2)

4. (1) the first link in a chain, (2) the foundation of a building, (3) lenses

⚲ 5. Option 1 is biblically invalid because giving up the faith means that you denounce the God who created you (Ps. 53:1; Rom. 9:20) and prove that you are one of those who hear but never understand (Matt. 13:18–23). Although believers may struggle with doubts because of their limited understanding, by faith they need to "keep [them]selves in the love of God" (Jude 1:21).

Option 2 is scripturally invalid because giving in a little is a compromise, which often leads to further compromise. If you can be pressured to give up what the Bible says in one area, you can be pressured to give up on what it says in other areas. Instead, remain steadfast in the clarity of His Word even when you don't have all the answers or counterarguments (1 Pet. 3:15; 2 Pet. 1:3).

SECTION OBJECTIVES 1.2

Head-Heart System

1. Explain how the basic beliefs of someone's head system (thinking/understanding) are grounded on his worldview faith pre-commitments.

2. Explain how the values of someone's heart system (desires/loves) influence his head system (thinking/understanding).

Master Story

3. Define *metanarrative* and explain the scope of its influence.

4. Summarize the biblical metanarrative and explain its powerful influence.

Making Something of the World/Action

5. Apply the exhortation to be salt and light to real-life situations.

6. Analyze the implications of the creation mandate for creative cultivation in culture.

Look at the Grand Canyon through biblical lenses, and you'll see results of a world-wide flood. Look at the same 277-mile stretch of beauty through evolutionist glasses, and you'll probably see millions of years of erosion. But the canyon stays the same.

THINKING IT THROUGH 1.1

1. What claim(s) did Project Steve make in expressing its support for evolution?

2. List the three major options for responding when your faith is challenged.

3. Identify the two distinct approaches you can take when seeking to carry out the third option.

4. What are the three illustrations the book provides regarding how a worldview functions?

⚲ 5. Briefly explain why it is biblically invalid to respond with Option 1 or Option 2 to those who challenge your faith.

1.2 WORLDVIEW INGREDIENTS

This book will suggest that every worldview—whether Dr. Steve's or yours—has three ingredients:

1. A worldview contains a "head-heart system" of basic beliefs, assumptions, and values.
2. A worldview tells a big story about the world.
3. A worldview produces action.

INGREDIENT 1: HEAD-HEART SYSTEM

Most definitions of worldview start here: a worldview is a set of **basic beliefs**, a more or less organized (and most people's worldviews are less organized) system of assumptions and values. People's thoughts tend to develop patterns and fit into systems. Even if they are content with numerous inconsistencies, their thoughts are never completely random—none of us can bear to live in total mental chaos. God made us to be like Himself; that's what it means to be made in God's own image (Gen. 1:27). God thinks logically, and we can't help but want to as well.

There is a difference between functional beliefs and basic beliefs. You may believe that Reykjavik is the capital of Iceland, but this is not a basic belief. Worldview thinker Al Wolters suggests that basic beliefs answer questions like "Can violence ever be right? Are there any absolute, unchanging moral rules for human life? Is there a point to suffering? Do we survive death?"[5]

A Head System

Think again of that chain metaphor. Why do you think, if you do, that a mass murderer such as Hitler deserved death? Probably because you believe that taking numerous innocent human lives—like Hitler did—is wrong. That's one chain link back. Why is taking six million Jewish lives (and perhaps five million other civilians' lives) wrong? Because taking even one human life is wrong. That's one more chain link. But why is that wrong? Because human life should not be taken without just cause. Why? Because human life is intrinsically valuable.

The Head System and Basic Beliefs

The head system is simply a way of saying that one aspect of a person is his intellect. Intellectual perceptions are built on basic beliefs that help a person analyze and evaluate. Therefore, the validity of one's basic beliefs determines the validity of one's intellectual analysis and evaluation of evidence and claims. Basic beliefs are those beliefs which have significant ramifications on one's understanding of the reality of the world. Often, these basic beliefs are simply assumed or taken on authority (accepted by faith). Unbelievers often deny that their basic beliefs are based on faith or unsubstantiated authorities. They want to insist that their basic beliefs are just the facts about the way the world is (i.e., they assume their conclusion in their premise—faulty circular reasoning). The difference between believers and unbelievers is not that believers take some things by faith (on the authority of God's Word) and unbelievers don't take anything by faith. The difference is not that believers ignore evidence or have less evidence. The difference is that believers will *admit* that the foundation of their intellectual analysis of the evidence is based on faith pre-commitments while unbelievers will often deny that they have the same kind of pre-commitments.

That's the last link in the chain for most people like Steve. It seems totally obvious to them that this is the case. When American Founding Father Thomas Jefferson wanted to argue that every person has equal value, he wrote, "We hold these truths to be self-evident, that all men are created equal." But he added something: "They are endowed by their Creator with certain unalienable Rights." By saying that, Jefferson added one more link to the chain: humanity gets its value from its Creator.

So what if Steve's set of beliefs and system of assumptions includes no Creator? What if, when Steve looks through his worldview lenses at another person, he sees a fellow survivor of the evolutionary process rather than one who bears the image of the one true God? What if his chain of reasoning only goes as far as the big bang?

This is the Western (remember: European and American) world we live in, a world where every chain hangs, ultimately, from a large explosion 13.8 billion years ago. Suppose you ask, "What is the big bang hanging on?" You're likely to be told you're talking nonsense. As one famous scientist named Steve (Stephen Hawking) reportedly put it, asking what happened before the big bang is like asking what's north of the North Pole.

But Westerners don't tend to see their set of beliefs as a worldview precisely because they don't think they have any mere "beliefs"—not about what's important, at least. They frequently fail to recognize, as two particular worldview thinkers put it, that "world views are founded on ultimate faith commitments."[7]

Dr. Steve isn't a geologist, but he's pretty smart. What would he say about the Grand Canyon? How old is it? He might respond that there are several theories: 5–6 million years, 17 million, maybe even 70 million. The middle figure seems to be the most popular right now. And those numbers are arrived at via a combination of various "data sets." We know, Steve will say, how much erosion the Colorado River has created in the last hundred years or so—since records began to be kept. We can also locate fossils and study rock deposition layers.

WHAT'S NORTH OF THE NORTH POLE?

World-renowned scientist Stephen Hawking, a believer in macro-evolution,* reportedly commented, "What happened before the big bang? Well, what's north of the North Pole?"

But is this a legitimate comparison? We know there is a North Pole. You can go there and stand on it. But no one has seen the big bang. You can't go there. It seems like a necessary conclusion from the evidence only if you look at the evidence from a certain worldview—a strange worldview in which natural things (like big bangs) can happen without causes.[8]

macro-evolution: the scientific model which proposes that living species evolved from lower forms of life

Stephen Hawking (1942–)

Basic Beliefs Are Ultimate Faith Commitments

Explain the head system and define basic beliefs that make up the foundation of the head system.

What is a faith commitment? It is the way we answer four basic questions facing everyone: (1) Who am I? Or, what is the nature, task and purpose of human beings? (2) Where am I? Or, what is the nature of the world and universe I live in? (3) What's wrong? Or, what is the basic problem or obstacle that keeps me from attaining fulfillment? In other words, how do I understand evil? And (4) What is the remedy? Or, how is it possible to overcome this hindrance to my fulfillment? In other words, how do I find salvation? When we've answered these questions, that is, when our faith is settled, then we begin to see reality in some sensible pattern. Out of our faith proceeds a world view, without which human life simply cannot go on. [Brian Walsh and Richard Middleton, *The Transforming Vision* (Downers Grove, IL: IVP Academic, 1984), 35]

Can a person make decisions in life, from mundane things to monumental things, without relying on his basic beliefs about these fundamental questions?

No. Every decision people make goes back to assumptions about who they are, where they fit into the world, what they perceive to be right/wrong, and what they perceive to be the solution to a need or problem. A person must be committed to some kind of an answer, whether he consciously thinks it through or not.

Links in a Chain

Demonstrate to students how conclusions from one's intellect/head system must be examined based on one's assumed faith presuppositions. Bring in a series of chain links that can be put together or taken apart. Visualize the chain of thought illustrated in the textbook regarding people's evaluation of Hitler's actions. Hang the chain down from something. What happens when the first link (the starting point of a Creator) is removed? It falls to the floor.

Those who deny that they need a starting point for their conclusions end up with a jumbled mess of thoughts. Non-Christian worldviews will always fall apart because they are always false presentations of the reality God created. Therefore, Christians should always be confident that there is a way to critically evaluate any non-Christian worldview, pointing out how it does not fit with reality.

The problem is often located in the first link of the chain or the starting presupposition. Most non-Christians today immediately recognize the immorality of Hitler's actions, but they have an inconsistent set of basic beliefs if they believe in evolution. Those who supported Hitler in his day were seeking to be consistent in their Darwinian beliefs; that's what enabled them to justify the atrocities.

Infinite God or Infinite Matter

Pinpoint the distinct starting points for the two major systems of thought that influence the West. Believing in infinite matter or in the infinite God may be the most foundational belief. The reason why the debate over creation and evolution is so significant is that it is the foundational starting point for the two head systems that are the most popular in the West.

Stephen Hawking is admitting that he simply replaces the faith the Christian worldview uses as a starting point (faith in the infinite God) with the faith of the evolutionary worldview's starting point of infinite matter. But he wouldn't say it is by faith; he simply assumes his conclusion. In choosing this starting point, his perception of all reality is influenced by viewing it through that lens. Therefore, the way he analyzes and evaluates evidence is based on this basic belief—his worldview.

Man Replaces God with Himself

Demonstrate to students how intellectual conclusions must be examined based on one's assumed faith presuppositions.

Why would it be arrogant for a person to claim "I don't have ultimate faith commitments"?

When a person suggests that he does not have to have a faith commitment (a basic belief), he might as well claim that he has all knowledge (omniscience) because he must have observed all relevant data in all places at all times and done so with perfect interpretation (or must have received perfect information from all others who have done the very same thing). This is arrogantly making oneself into a god.

What is the consequence of trying to live as if one does have God's capabilities?

Eventually the arrogance will be shattered when one realizes the impossibility of this task. Such a person is left only with despair.

The Heart System and Values

Explain the heart system and define *affections*, which drive the Head System. The heart system is simply a way of saying that one aspect of a person is his affections (loves and desires of the soul). Affections are built on values, which drive a person to pursue certain ends. Often those pursuits can overshadow or dictate intellectual perceptions of reality and drive basic beliefs. Therefore, it is vital that the affections be properly shaped because the heart system typically drives the head system.

Thus Proverbs 1:7 declares that one must have a particular affection shaped by proper values (the fear of the Lord) in order to begin down the right path toward knowledge. Why would that be so? Before a person will be teachable and learn anything from a source/person, he has to first respect and accept that source/person as the knowledgeable authority over him. The mark of a fool is having no fear of God and thus being unteachable. It is dangerous to refuse God's revelation as the basis for knowledge, but God promises security if you rely on His revelation as the basis for knowledge (Prov. 1:20–33).

Putting all these data sets together is a very demanding and complex process. Let's focus on only one. If Steve studies just erosion, he can calculate how long it would take for the Colorado River to cut the canyon from top to bottom (though one theory, at least, thinks it was cut at different rates on either side of a divide).

But if Steve uses erosion rates to arrive at an age for the Grand Canyon, where's fact and where's assumption? Where's evidence and where's belief? Fact and evidence are limited to a mere century of data, and they tend to hide an essential layer of Steve's assumptions and beliefs: that erosion rates have been more or less constant—that no cataclysmic floods, for example, have come through town (but not all scientists assume this regarding the Grand Canyon).

Steve can't come to the Grand Canyon without any preconceived notions; we've all been conceiving notions since not too long after we ourselves were conceived, and we will necessarily carry them with us on our trip. All "facts" come with theories attached. Steve can't and won't ever see "facts" without his worldview lenses on.

In fact, as we'll discuss later, no understanding can ever happen without believing. The fear of the Lord (which certainly implies belief in His existence) is the beginning of all knowledge, according to Proverbs 1:7. It's the first principle. It's the ABCs, the basics, without which we don't have any knowledge worth calling knowledge.

A Heart System

This connection between the fear of the Lord and knowledge points to a key truth: a worldview isn't just a "head" system. One reason a person's worldview can be inconsistent, wrong, and even evil is that worldviews grow ultimately from the heart.

A man on the street in a downtown area (true story) once told a Christian who was handing out tracts, "I used to be a Christian. I went to church with my grandma pretty much all the time. But I wanted to have sex whenever I wanted it, and I couldn't see how a God who wants me to be happy would tell me to stop."

> PEOPLE WHO WANT FREEDOM FROM GOD ARE LIKE FISH THAT WANT FREEDOM FROM WATER. [9]

That was not a head system speaking—a careful, logical analysis of the benefits and detriments of sexual promiscuity. It was a heart system saying, "I want what I want [pleasure via immorality, in this case], and I'm going to adopt a belief system which allows it—and drop the belief system that doesn't."

The Bible speaks of the heart as the center of the person. Jesus said, "Out of the abundance of the heart the mouth speaks"—in other words, whatever fills your heart will tend to flow out of your mouth (Matt. 12:34). And right after that, Jesus said that the nature of your heart determines what kind of fruit you produce, good or bad (12:35). You say what you say and you do what you do because you love what you love—because of what's in your heart.

After Adam's Fall, the human heart became "deceitful above all things, and desperately sick" (Jer. 17:9). So one of the most precious promises of the Bible is that through Jesus' death and resurrection God not only cleanses our hearts (1 John 1:7) but also gives us new ones:

> I will give you a new heart, and a new spirit I will put within you. And I will remove the heart of stone from your flesh and give you a heart of flesh. (Ezek. 36:26)

Gospel-Transformed Thinking

The apostle Paul was a highly intelligent, well-educated member of one of the most prestigious religious sects in Israel. Yet his affections blinded him to a proper understanding so that his zeal was misdirected against the Christians. The testimony of his life is amazing because of the drastic change of his zeal. It was not that he became more intelligent; rather his affections were transformed when he submitted to Christ. As a result, his whole way of thinking was also transformed. Ask students if they know of any other biblical, historical, or modern-day examples of people like this.

This is a display of omnipotence; God can clean up and replace the dirtiest and most unredeemable thing in the universe, the human heart. God alone has the power to reach inside you and alter you at your very root, your innermost heart desires and loves. And by giving you a new heart, God sets into motion a lifelong process whereby He reshapes you into the image of Jesus Christ (Rom. 8:28–29). This is a process in which you must "make every effort," Peter says (2 Pet. 1:5), but in the end you'll find that only "divine power" can explain why you went from loving evil things to loving good (1:3).

Modern, rationalistic* humans tend to believe that what they love does not matter—that a soccer player, for example, who cheats on his taxes and sleeps around a lot can be just as good a goalie as the next guy; all that matters is that the neurons in his brain and the tendons in his arms are in proper working order. But the Bible points to a deeper reality underneath our reasoning and our cognitive* skills. Even non-Christian philosopher and public intellectual* Stanley Fish has said, "Sometimes the principled reasons people give for taking a position are just window dressing, good for public display but only incidental to the heart of the matter, which is the state of their hearts."[11]

Dr. Steve likes to say that he's just taking an unbiased look at the evidence. He'll believe in God when he sees God, like the Soviet cosmonaut who reportedly informed ground controllers that God didn't exist because He wasn't visible from space. But especially when it comes to life's significant questions, an unbiased view is not possible. If Steve doesn't love the loveliest Being in the universe, how can his head-heart system really be expected to lead him to truth?

rationalism: *the belief that reason, and not religion or experience, provides the only firm foundation for knowledge*

cognitive: *having to do with the mind and thinking*

public intellectual: *an academic or other member of the intelligentsia who takes his message public rather than keeping his debates stuck in places where only other intellectuals will read them*

THINKING IT THROUGH 1.2A

1. What are the three ingredients of *worldview* that are mentioned in the definition given in this section?

2. Why do humans seek to have systems of thought with logical consistency?

3. How does Proverbs 1:7 express the connection of basic beliefs with values in the head-heart system?

4. What is at the center of a person, determining beliefs and behaviors?

♀5. When evaluating the chain of reasoning for the most popular systems of thought (i.e., head systems) in Western culture, what is the first link in the chain (the ultimate faith commitment) for Christianity versus the first link for secularism?

THINKING IT THROUGH 1.2A

1. A worldview contains a "head-heart system" of basic beliefs, assumptions, and values. A worldview includes a big story about the world that interprets basic beliefs, assumptions, and values. A worldview produces action (culture) that stems from those basic beliefs, assumptions, and values.

2. because humans are created in the image of God

3. The values that accompany the fear of the Lord are fundamental prerequisites (the beginning) for a person's basic beliefs (knowledge).

4. the heart with its affections (loves and desires)

♀5. creation versus evolution; Creator versus big bang; eternal/self-existent God versus eternal/self-existent matter

---

What You Love Matters

Illustrate that although people may be intelligent and informed, their affections may still impair them. What's wrong with the idea that someone can live however he pleases personally as long as he remains productive and competent in his public life?

Briefly recount some well-known examples of people who have tried to live by a double standard, engaging in immorality in their private lives while presenting themselves as morally upstanding citizens in their public lives. By God's common grace an unsaved person may be skilled in performing particular tasks, but life is far more than the sum total of external tasks that a person performs. You can't compartmentalize your own life; it's impossible to segment off a part of your life so that it has no effect on the rest of your life. Some professions may make this more obvious than others, but only a naïve, myopic, or superficial examination of a person's life allows you to deny that the personal life affects the public life.

What Does Metanarrative Have to Do with Me?

Explain the term *metanarrative*. A narrative is a story; a metanarrative is the larger story that those smaller stories fit within. Every one of a person's individual experiences is like a smaller story, and together those stories add up to the larger story of life that is in the process of unfolding. Thinking about what the larger story of your own life will end up being can be exciting and scary at the same time. It could be disappointing; it most assuredly will be a surprise, turning out to be different from what you expect at this point in your life and different from the way it would turn out if you were in control.

Students must rest confidently in God as the sovereign, loving God who has a marvelous plan for the bigger story of their lives (Ps. 139:16–18). Not only that, but each short and perhaps seemingly insignificant life (cf. Ecclesiastes) does contribute to God's larger story of the whole history of the world. That's why history class is so significant. It helps place each person within the context of the larger story in which he's living his life.

Technically Speaking

In his classic definition of *postmodernism* as "incredulity toward metanarratives," French philosopher and literary theorist Jean-François Lyotard used the word *metanarrative* as a technical term meaning a legitimizing or justifying grand-narrative, namely the cultural myths of ongoing scientific progress, of Marxism, and of Enlightenment emancipation. [See James K. A. Smith's essay in Myron B. Penner, ed., *Christianity and the Postmodern Turn: Six Views* (Ada, MI: Brazos Press, 2005), 126.] This textbook uses the word metanarrative in a nontechnical (non-Lyotardian) way, the way it is most commonly used in popular discourse.

INGREDIENT 2: MASTER STORY

The second major element in worldviews is story. A worldview tells a *master story*, a big story that begins in the beginning (like Genesis 1:1) and tells what happened afterwards to shape the world into what it is. (Such a "big story" is sometimes called a **metanarrative**.)

The story of the world that Project Steve is promoting goes something like this: "Once upon a time, the big bang happened. We all evolved by random, undirected processes from non-life through lower forms of life to reach the top of the evolutionary heap (at least here on earth). Our problems exist because our evolution is incomplete. Our purpose is to evolve and progress still further toward . . . well, future extinction as the energy in the universe burns out."

Some scientists have recognized that this master story is, to put it mildly, uninspiring. It does little to bring purpose to individual cultures or peace to individual people who find themselves hurting on the bottom of the heap. Those on top might even use this story to conclude that survival of the fittest justifies whatever violent choices they make. So some scientists have worked to turn the results of modern science into what they call "a story for our times," a big story that will inspire us and guide us all morally on life's path.

Two of these scientists produced a PBS* documentary called *The Journey of the Universe*. Host Brian Swimme, an evolutionary cosmologist,* opens the film with the following comments, as stirring music plays in the background:

> Many of the world's greatest stories begin with a journey, a quest to answer life's most intimate questions: Where do we come from? Why are we here? From the dawn of time, all cultures have created stories to help explain the ultimate nature of things. And perhaps a new story is emerging in our time, one grounded in contemporary science and yet nourished by the ancient religious wisdom of our planet.[12]

In something of an odd twist, Swimme actually teaches at a Catholic university (the coauthor of the documentary, Mary Evelyn Tucker, is a scientist at Yale who also teaches at the divinity school there). But despite Swimme's apparent respect for "religious wisdom," God never shows up in this story of the universe's journey:

> The universe began as a great outpouring of cosmic breath, of cosmic energy, that then swirled and twisted and complexified until it could burst forth into flowers, and animals, and fish—all of these elegant explosions of energy. . . . These deep discoveries of science are leading to a new story of the universe: over the course of 14 billion years hydrogen gas transformed itself into mountains, butterflies, the music of Bach, and you and me. . . . The universe has a story: a beginning; a middle, where we are now; and perhaps in some far distant future, an end.[13]

PBS: *Public Broadcasting Service, a nationwide network that produces documentaries that are generally respected*

cosmologist: *a scientist who focuses on the big story of the universe*

The Power of Story

Swimme and Tucker recognize that human beings need stories to organize their lives and their ideas. The beliefs, assumptions, and loves found in Worldview Ingredient 1, the head-heart system, make sense because of the story into which they fit. It makes sense to believe that humans are valuable within a story that starts with God making them in His image—just like it makes sense for animal-rights activists to refuse to eat meat in a story that portrays humans as just another kind of animal.

The Power of Metanarrative

Connect worldview ingredient 1 to ingredient 2, demonstrating the powerful influence of metanarratives. Clarify that ingredient 1 (the head-heart system) necessarily depends on ingredient 2 (a big story about the world). These are not random ingredients; they work together—or at least they should. Therefore, these larger stories are very powerful in helping to determine (give a basis for) and make sense of beliefs, assumptions, and values. A metanarrative provides the interpretive framework that beliefs, assumptions, and values rest on. The question then is whether the larger story actually can provide the basis for one's beliefs and values or whether there is inconsistency between what someone says he believes or values and his story about this world and reality.

For example, a person may say that he believes lying to another person is wrong. But if his metanarrative comes from the teachings of an Islamist extremist, then he may believe that an infidel forfeits his rights as a person and becomes no better than an animal. Therefore, that kind of person may have no qualms about lying to you if you're a non-Muslim. A metanarrative has a powerful influence on the interpretation and application of one's beliefs and values.

Guide students through Activity 1 in the *BIBLICAL WORLDVIEW Student Activities* manual, which is sold separately.

On the other hand, it doesn't make sense to believe that this world is going to get better and better forever (an assumption if there ever was one) if the story you believe about the world begins with a big bang and ends with the dissipation of all matter and energy.

It doesn't make sense to call anything in this world "right" or "wrong" if we are all random atom collections. What does it matter if I hate my sister or I ate all your candy? Or if I love porn? So what? That's just what protoplasm does at this elevation above sea level.

It also doesn't make sense to get upset about injustice if your big story has only two characters, matter and energy. North Koreans are starving to death? Hey, their matter and energy will go back into circulation after they're done with it. Your dad screams at you or gets drunk (or both)? Hey, as long as the species survives, we can handle some collateral damage.*

It simply isn't true that atheists and evolutionists are all openly horrible people who use natural selection* as an excuse to rape and pillage. None of them would talk this way. But, given the story they tell about the world, how can they justify getting so publicly upset about rapists and pillagers?

The true story about the world will work. It won't tell you to believe what your everyday experiences tell you is false. It won't tell you that God doesn't exist when, in actual fact, "the heavens declare the glory of God" (Ps. 19:1). It won't tell you morals are up for grabs when, in actual fact, every "conscience also bears witness" that God's law has been written on the human heart (Rom 2:14–15). It won't tell you there's no hope when your whole heart knows that there is, somewhere (Eccles. 3:11).

collateral damage: *accidental, unintended negative consequences—such as civilians dying when a military target gets bombed from a drone*

natural selection: *the evolutionary process by which the "fittest" survive the clash of organisms, regional populations, or even whole species*

Death Is Wrong

In *Surprised by Oxford*, Carolyn Weber tells the story of how she became a Christian at an unlikely place: Oxford University in England. One experience that was instrumental in her conversion was a formal dinner party at which a renowned surgeon spoke of an experience he had while poised over a beating heart, scalpel in hand.

> "As I was standing there, all the uncertainty of my life, the absurdity of all this death, and all our attempts to ward it off, came down to a pinprick of light." His hands began to tremble—a serious problem for a surgeon—until something clicked. "When I see death, I know it is *wrong*," he said. "*Really, really wrong*. In-my-gut wrong. It was not meant to be. It was not meant for us. We were not built for it. Everything in my body . . . twists against it. Not just my death, but the death of every living thing. . . . I don't know how one can go to medical school and not be in greater awe of a Creator than ever before."[14]

You also know, as every atheist does on some level, that death was not meant to be. Don't ever believe a big story that tells you otherwise.

Alternate Stories

Swimme's is not the only big story that people in our world find persuasive. Many other stories have told whole nations and cultures where they came from, who they are, and where they're going:

• *Secularism* tells a story that goes like this: "However we got here, we're here now. And the one unchanging fact about humanity is that we won't all agree why we're here anyway because we all believe different things about the gods—or lack thereof. Our societal problems come from the way religion heats up simple, solvable conflicts

The Most Popular Metanarrative?

Summarize and discuss the metanarrative of secular humanism. The overarching story most people in the secular world believe in is founded on the evolutionary story. The documentary that the Student Text mentions serves as an example and may be accessed on PBS.com for the purpose of showing students excerpts.

Break the class into small groups. Have some of the groups construct a detailed summary of the evolutionary story. Have the other groups construct a critique of the evolutionary story, listing some ways it falls short of being able to explain the reality of this world. They should consider how it fails as a metanarrative (e.g., it can't explain the basis for morality or the basis of nonphysical realities such as logic).

[Resources: You may wish to present a video that gives a brief summary and critique of the evolutionary story. The Answers in Genesis website has many free videos (e.g., *Big Problems with the Big Bang*).]

Death Is Wrong

The larger story must comport with reality or it will have devastating effects. Metanarratives are falsifiable. The purpose of a metanarrative is to provide an overarching summary that explains the reality of what is going on in this world. When it fails to provide that explanation, it fails to provide a valid basis for one's beliefs, assumptions, and values and must be adjusted or thrown out.

A few examples of failed metanarratives include secularism, Marxism, and postmodernism. You may wish to do further research on why these are failed metanarratives.

Resources include the following:

Hunter Baker, *The End of Secularism* (Wheaton: Crossway, 2009).

David T. Koyzis, *Political Visions and Illusions* (Downers Grove, IL: InterVarsity Press, 2003).

Nancy S. Love, *Understanding Dogmas and Dreams*, 2nd ed. (Washington, DC: CQ Press, 2006).

Leszek Kolakowski, *Main Currents of Marxism* (New York: W. W. Norton & Company, 2008).

Heath White, *Postmodernism 101* (Grand Rapids: Brazos Press, 2006).

One of the most vital tests of the truthfulness of a metanarrative is how it handles the questions of death and suffering (significant realities in this world). You can never arrive at the correct answer regarding why death and suffering happen unless you view them from biblical creationist history—the proper metanarrative. For a brief explanation, see the Answers in Genesis website for the booklet by Ken Ham and Mark Looy, "Why Is There Death and Suffering?" When people try to explain the significant realities of this world based on a false metanarrative, they will fail to correctly evaluate problems and will pursue wrong solutions.

The Creation, Fall, Redemption Metanarrative

The Bible is the story of what God is doing to glorify Himself by redeeming His fallen creation. The basic beliefs/ultimate faith commitments and values of the head-heart system (worldview ingredient 1) all fit within the framework of CFR—the Biblical metanarrative (worldview ingredient 2).

Creation

1. Who am I? Or what is the nature, task, and purpose of human beings?

2. Where am I? Or what is the nature of the world and universe I live in?

Fall

3. What's wrong? Or what is the basic problem or obstacle that keeps me from attaining fulfillment? In other words, how do I understand evil?

Redemption

4. What is the remedy? Or how is it possible to overcome this hindrance to my fulfillment? In other words, how do I gain salvation?

[The above questions are adapted from Walsh and Middleton, *The Transforming Vision*, 35]

Creation, Fall, Redemption is an overarching interpretive system/metanarrative that answers all the key questions of life. Use Activity 2 to compare and contrast a Christian approach and secular approach to the question of death and suffering based on their respective metanarratives of creation and evolution.

 Evaluate According to CFR

Illustrate how the big story of the Bible can help students interpret everything they evaluate.

Choose an overarching topic (sports, business, politics, etc.). Break it down to evaluate it according to CFR:

C: How is it fundamentally good according to God's creation of it?

F: How has it been affected by sin?

R: How can it be restored to its original created purpose? How can a person participate in it in a way that is biblically faithful and pure?

POSTMAN ON POSTMODERNISM

Look at what public intellectual Neil Postman had to say about the effects of the postmodern worldview combined with the unbelievable amount of data spraying at us in this information age:

Like the Sorcerer's Apprentice, we are awash in information, without even a broom to help us get rid of it. The tie between information and human purpose has been severed. Information is now a commodity that is bought and sold; it comes indiscriminately, whether asked for or not, directed at no one in particular, in enormous volume, at high speeds, disconnected from meaning and import. It comes unquestioned and uncombined, and we do not have . . . a loom to weave it all into fabric. No transcendent narratives to provide us with moral guidance, social purpose, intellectual economy. No stories to tell us what we need to know, and especially what we do not need to know.[15]

proletarian: member of the proletariat (working class); a person who has no money and must therefore "sell" his labor

bourgeois: (boor-ZHWA) members of the middle class; owners of industrial factories

CFR: an acronym for Creation, Fall, Redemption

into holy wars. Because we just can't know who's right, religion should stay out of education, law, politics, and the marketplace. Humanity will improve if people can just learn to keep their religion private."

• *Marxism's* big story, which once ruled much of the world, goes like this: "As the proletarians* begin to notice that the bourgeois* are getting rich off their labor, they stage a revolt. This revolution ushers in a new socialist society in which everyone owns the means of production and benefits fairly from it."

• *Postmodernism* has a fuzzy big story which basically boils down to a deep skepticism that anyone can even tell big stories. How can we claim to view the whole world when each of us is rooted so firmly to the ground? Postmodernism's story is this: "Once upon a time, there were no big stories, only local ones. So don't pretend you know the big story of the world because you might start to believe yourself and therefore begin oppressing people who disagree with your story."

Like the story Brian Swimme tells, none of these stories works. Secularism's story can't be right: politics and education are always full of religious assumptions—neutrality is a myth. Marxism's story can't be right, either. Its record of mass murder, corruption, and poverty at least puts that story into grave doubt. And postmodernism's story can't be right. Some people are being oppressed by other people's big stories, but without the ability to tell a story about the way the world *really should be*, how can the oppressed people fight back?

The Christian Story

Christianity, of course, must be added to the list of powerful big stories (metanarratives) that people tell themselves about our world. The argument of this book is that biblical Christianity tells the only big story that works, the only one that is true. We'll talk a great deal more about the Christian metanarrative, but here's a short summary: *the Bible is the story of what God is doing to glorify Himself by redeeming His fallen creation.* This is the story of Creation, Fall, and Redemption—**CFR.***

Every little story in the world, from the Bible's stories to your own life story, makes the right sense only when seen within this big story. Choose anything God put in this world, and you can be certain that (C) it is fundamentally good because God created it, (F) the Fall of Adam has tarnished it in some way, and (R) it can be restored to its original purpose by Christ, the rightful ruler of this planet.

Take music. Music is, at its heart, good like its Creator. Notes are good. Tones are good. It's the same with pitches, timbres, and rhythms. Every one of these things was programmed by God into His "very good" creation. Every one of them will be present in the new earth, where the "glory and the honor of the nations" will shine (Rev. 21:26). But in between Creation and full Redemption, there's the Fall. And music, like every other good thing created by God, has been touched by the Fall. We

---

can still use it for good, but now it's often hijacked for all sorts of wicked purposes. Good things God created are twisted every day into things that dishonor Him.

The same is true of every subject you study in school, like science and history. It's true of sports, of business, of politics, of journalism, of marriage. If you don't have a Christian master story, a biblical metanarrative, to guide you in evaluating what you see, you'll tend to get confused about what's good and what's bad in this world. But with that story you will know who you are, where you came from, where you're going, what's wrong with the world, and who can fix it—all the basic worldview questions.

Every worldview contains a master story that answers questions about our world.

INGREDIENT 3: MAKING SOMETHING OF THE WORLD

If, after reading *Biblical Worldview: Creation, Fall, Redemption*, you start to see the power of our world's various head-heart systems, this book will have achieved only partial success. If you are skilled at seeing the importance of the Bible's metanarrative to a truly Christian worldview, success will still be incomplete. The goal of this book is to be God's tool to move you to live out the Christian worldview. This is the third aspect of our definition of worldview: action.

Worldview talk can sound like useless intellectual discussion to some Christians. But if you will use the Christian worldview to influence and shape your life—your job choices, your family size, your community involvement, your use of media—you can have an impact on your world.

Salt and Light

Jesus Christ Himself, a masterful teacher, used two metaphors to make this point. He urged His followers to be "salt" and told them to shine as "light."

> You are the salt of the earth, but if salt has lost its taste, how shall its saltiness be restored? It is no longer good for anything except to be thrown out and trampled under people's feet. You are the light of the world. A city set on a hill cannot be hidden. Nor do people light a lamp and put it under a basket, but on a stand, and it gives light to all in the house. In the same way, let your light shine before others, so that they may see your good works and give glory to your Father who is in heaven. (Matt. 5:13–16)

Light shines. That's its job. Jesus' disciples are supposed to shine a light through doing good works, a light everyone can see. There may be places of great influence available to you in this world, and it is not wrong to stand in those places: a taller lampstand can give light to more people. Film, education, journalism, sociology—all of these fields are open to Christians with the right knowledge and skills. All of them are powerful tools for spreading light. No Western nation, at least currently, bars Christians completely from positions of shining influence.

Light shines, but salt flavors. If salt loses its sharp, distinct taste, it's worthless. Some positions of influence will be available to you only if you are willing to diminish the unique taste of your biblical views. You can have the job only if you agree to be a little less salty.

> *"We should want to live our chapters well, but doing so requires that we know the chapters that led up to us in our time and our moment; it requires that we open our eyes and consciously begin to shape those chapters that are coming after."* [16]
>
> —NATHAN WILSON

Old Testament Backdrop

Jesus didn't invent a new truth when He called on His people to be salt and light. God gave His Old Testament people, the Jews, basically the same calling in Exodus 19:5–6. Israel was supposed to be a kingdom of priests—and what do priests do? They stand in between God and men, representing God to their neighbors. Israel was supposed to do that. They were supposed to be a light to the Gentile nations. But they were also supposed to be holy, distinctive, and different. They were supposed to be salt.

Salt and Light

Explain what it means to be salt (distinctive and sanctified) and light (impactful and making a difference). Members of the New Testament church are called on to follow the truths that Jesus enunciated in His Sermon on the Mount (Matt. 5:16–17). Christians must be distinctly set apart (1 Pet. 1:14–16) as well as distinctly visible as God's testimony of righteousness (2:9). They must participate in the culture even though they sojourn as outsiders in a worldly milieu (2:11–12). This participation must be characterized by conduct that is distinctly flavored by holiness and honorableness (salty) and that is filled with good works that are distinctly visible (light). The goal is never self-aggrandizement; rather it is to point people to the glory of the God they will one day stand before (Matt. 5:16; 1 Pet. 4:5). Don't consider it strange when persecution for distinctiveness comes (1 Pet. 4:3–4, 12). Believers were called to these things (2:21) so that they would obtain God's blessing (3:9, 13–14; 4:13–14; 5:10). All this context surrounds the injunction to defend the faith (3:15).

Making Something of the World

Introduce students to the Creation Mandate and explain its all-encompassing application.

What does the Creation Mandate command?

• *Be fruitful, multiply, and fill the earth.*

• *Subdue/have dominion (stewardship, not abuse).*

How can the Creation Mandate be applied?

any creative activity of stewardship/making use of God's creation and created order (not limited to gardening or farming)

How would you defend that the Creation Mandate still applies to us today?

It is what we do by nature of our creation in the image of God as humans. We long to be productive.

It is impossible to do anything in this world without making use of God's creation and created order—without an attempt at stewardship. The question is whether we are good or bad stewards not whether we are stewards.

We are still God's stewards because the Fall didn't remove our responsibility; it only damaged our ability to carry it out well (see the restatement of the Creation Mandate after the Fall/Flood in Gen. 9 and Ps. 8).

But Jesus says you have to be influential and distinct at the same time. You have to be light and salt. Don't drop your Christianity in order to gain more influence; then what will you be influencing people to do? And don't pass up opportunities for legitimate influence (state senator, TV journalist) out of some fear that it's wrong for a Christian to have influence.

Jesus' call here is, at the very least, a call to bring glory to God by living out the Christian worldview. Keeping your Christian worldview inside the class you're now taking will be like covering your headlights with duct tape. You won't see where you're going, and people won't notice your presence. So let this book be a call to you to go live out what you learn.

Dominion over the Earth

This call has deep roots in the Bible, going all the way back to the first page. God created Adam and Eve with several purposes, according to Genesis 1:

- be fruitful and multiply
- fill the earth
- subdue the earth and have dominion over it

We'll explore these commands in much greater detail in the next unit, but for now simply notice that powerful word *dominion*. Who has dominion? Kings, queens. God wanted mankind to be kings and queens over His planet, to fill and rule the world as His representatives. That's one reason we are, according to that same chapter, made "in God's image." We are, in other words, to be like God and to represent Him. He is a ruler, and so are we supposed to be.

But the territory God made man and woman to rule over is not merely spiritual; it is physical. To subdue the earth and have dominion over it is to press it toward its ideal, to maximize its usefulness for humanity. It means taking whatever little section of this world God gives you and making the most of it.

supernaturalism: *the idea that there is something above or outside of nature, such as a divine being*

apologist: *defender; often refers to one who commends and defends the Christian faith*

Interestingly, this kind of dominion is just what the scientists in Project Steve are good at. And in this they're really on to something. Many of them, even the most atheistic, admit having a certain eager awe that pushed them into science at a young age. Listen to what Dawkins, as a scientist and one of the world's most influential atheists, has said about his own response to nature: "The fact that I do not subscribe to supernaturalism* doesn't mean that I don't respond [to the discoveries of science] in an emotional way that one might almost describe as spiritual."[17] (This calls to mind a comment reportedly made by apologist* G. K. Chesterton: "The worst moment for an atheist is when he has a profound sense of gratitude and has no one to thank.")

A desire to obey Genesis 1:28 is not what motivates most scientists, but they are, in fact, subduing the earth and having dominion over it. They are making something of this world. They are living out their worldview, inconsistent though it may be, in such a way that it overlaps with the Christian faith. Scientists—along with musicians, artists, writers, engineers, chefs, and people in nearly any other profession—have inherited a tradition of doing their jobs a certain way. Previous generations have made advances and improvements in all these areas, and that's a good thing. That fits well with God's command to have dominion.

The call of the Christian worldview is for you to become a "creative cultivator," someone who takes the traditions of your calling (history, politics, literature, art, computers, or whatever) and cultivates those traditions in a faithfully Christian way. This book, then, will end up being something of a waste if you don't ever take your worldview into the real world.

What Is Culture Anyway?

How would you define *culture*?

a. anything pertaining to the arts done in a refined way

This is a narrow definition of culture that actually refers to high culture.

b. anything pertaining to what's popular and trendy in mainstream society; often unrefined

This is a narrow definition of culture that actually refers to pop culture.

c. anything pertaining to a specific people group or area of the world

This is a narrow definition of a specific kind of culture known as ethnic culture.

These are all definitions people usually think of when they hear the term *culture*, but they

Culture

One last note: You'll find that as you work out your worldview, you won't be alone. You will naturally find yourself aligned with (and influenced by) other people. You will be part of a "culture." **Culture** is what you and others together make of the world. Your worldview will unite you with others, and the things and ideas you all produce will change and develop the culture you've inherited from previous generations. Culture is a good thing. God built culture into this world.

But not everyone who fills the earth, subdues it, and takes dominion over it does so in a God-honoring way. Great artists and scientists take dominion, but so do dictators and mad Nazi doctors who experiment on living children. So let's end with two warnings about the work of creating and cultivating:

- "Engaging the culture" is a common catch phrase. If it means taking part in our God-ordained work of taking wise dominion over the world He gave us, then fine. But for some Christians it seems to mean going to sexually explicit movies in order, somehow, to gain a platform for telling others about Jesus (a platform that rarely seems to materialize). This is a world created by God, but it's also a world that has fallen into sin. Some elements of a given culture may be too twisted by sin for you to get involved in them. We will discuss this in much greater detail later on.
- "Changing the world" is another buzzword you might have heard. And again, if God lets you do some world-changing, then fine. But because of the sinful twisting the world has undergone, God warns you not to love it (1 John 2:15–17) and not to let it shape you (Rom. 12:2). It is naive to assume that you can change Hollywood without Hollywood changing you. Though you should make every effort to represent God as a creative cultivator who bears His image, there will be some aspects of nature, culture, and your own life that will not be made right until Jesus, God's Son, comes back to rule in person on earth (Rom. 8:23; Phil. 3:20–21; Rev. 19:11–16).

So be careful how you view your role in this world. God will one day triumph over all His enemies, but this triumph does not give Christians the right to be "triumphalist"—full of arrogance about our supposed virtue and future success compared to others'. Your life's calling may be a humble one that makes a difference that only God and your own family notices. That's up to God, not you.

Make it your life's ambition to be faithful to God's words in Scripture, and—despite all the ways every Christian is inconsistent with his or her own worldview—you will find that the Christian worldview will bring contentment. Only people who live God's way will feel satisfied with God's plan for the world He made.

EVERYONE HAS A WORLDVIEW

This all adds up to a definition of *worldview* that goes something like this:

A worldview is

1. a set of basic beliefs, assumptions, and values,
2. which arises from a big story about the world and
3. produces individual and group action—human culture.

All three of these things are visible daily in the lives of every human on earth. What do you say when you're at the graveside of a friend? How about when you vote? How will you respond when someone deeply wounds you? What set of values will guide you as you raise your children? Having a worldview is simply part of being an adult.

---

are all definitions of particular kinds of culture.

What is culture in general?

Culture is simply the carrying out of the Creation Mandate. It is the result of individuals sharing their stewardship of things in this world with others. When that stewardship of making or cultivating something in the world for one's betterment is passed on to the next generation, we call it that society's customs (whether it's technology, social structures, or religious institutions and philosophies). All of culture is rooted in the carrying out of the Creation Mandate.

Culture is making something of the world; it is maximizing the available materials in the world for mankind's most ideal use—creative cultivation.

 ### God Wants to Use You and Your Culture

Motivate the students by revealing the practical goal of worldview knowledge: making something of the world; participating in cultivating and creating culture; and taking action.

Students should live out a Christian lifestyle in every sphere of culture based on a full-orbed biblical worldview. They should develop and use their talents in a variety of spheres where God can use them to impact those spheres with a Christian perspective of creativity (not just in full-time Christian service roles).

In what sphere(s) could God use students to be salt and light now and in the future?

Examples include education, politics, sports, art, science, music, technology, agriculture, ministry and so on.

How could you make something of the world, as God intended, in one of those spheres?

Answers will vary

Foundation for Life

Motivate students to take part in culture based on a solid understanding of their worldview. Students will involve their lives in many different spheres: education, politics, art, science, music, sports, and so forth. The question is whether they will participate in the activities of life based on (a) their own wisdom, assuming the popular thinking of their culture, or (b) God's wisdom from a biblical worldview. This textbook is meant to equip them and to encourage them to participate in every one of those spheres without limiting themselves. But it is also meant to encourage them not to limit the Bible. The biblical viewpoint should guide their participation in every one of those spheres. The Bible is not limited to only a few explicitly religious spheres of their life. Students must be salt and light as they apply scriptural wisdom to everything they think and do.

 ### Everyone Has a Worldview

Discuss with students how all human thinking makes use of ingredients 1 and 2 and all human behavior makes use of ingredient 3. Everyone has a worldview. Have students review the three ingredients that make up a worldview and ask them the following questions:

Who doesn't have any beliefs, assumptions, or values in this life?

Who doesn't fit his beliefs, assumptions, or values into his larger understanding of the reality of this world (into a bigger story)?

Who doesn't actively participate in making something of the world?

There may be people who try to avoid these things, but they will quickly find that it is very difficult if not impossible to avoid them altogether. Elements of each ingredient are by nature a part of even the simplest everyday things of life. Students began shaping their worldview from the time they were toddlers, discovering things about their world. It's not long before they were asking why things were the way they were and then asking why things ought or ought not to be that way.

Dangers: Transformationalism, Triumphalism, and Power

Warn students about some of the pitfalls along the way as they seek to impact culture.

(a) Beware of Christians being transformed by culture rather than the culture being transformed by Christians. This is a significant danger when people get sidetracked by trying to engage culture or change the world by their efforts rather than simply being faithful testimonies to the world as God's stewards. While believers desire to creatively cultivate according to God's design so that others in the culture will be drawn to Christ, they must humbly realize that they are limited. The Christian responsibility is to simply shine as light in the midst of a crooked and perverse culture (Phil. 2:15–16).

(b) Beware of the attitude of triumphalism, which overestimates the cultural accomplishments of the church/believers and often diverts the mission of the church from its assigned task: the Great Commission.

(c) Beware of the trap of lusting for power in order to make a difference. Rather than assuming that one must pursue the power-broker positions in society to make a difference, recognize that one can also make a difference through service to others. God works through the powerless as well as the powerful to make cultural changes; the task of Christians is simply to be good and sanctified stewards of the talents and opportunities that God has granted to them.

THINKING IT THROUGH 1.2B

1. metanarrative

2. They allow us to organize and make sense of our lives and ideas (beliefs, assumptions, and values). The head-heart system (worldview ingredient 1) makes sense because of the metanarrative (worldview ingredient 2) that it fits into.

3. Creation, Fall, Redemption

4. The Creation Mandate in Genesis 1:28 indicates that we were created to naturally desire to be productive.

5. salt and light

♀6. A Christian ought to be salt by remaining distinct from the ungodly world around him as a sojourner (not conforming to the world). A Christian ought to be light by maintaining a witness in the midst of the ungodly world around him (not isolated from the world).

---

finite: *limited by space, time, and gifting; the opposite of infinite*

Many modern liberals, influenced by the secularist worldview, don't like to be upfront about their deepest beliefs, values, and commitments. They hide behind a veneer of neutrality that often deceives even those liberals themselves. But one reason Christians can see the world with clarity is that we can be upfront. In the secularist worldview, everyone's beliefs have equal value. There is no authority to appeal to apart from other humans—humans who disagree, who all have their own biases, who are finite.* But Christians have access, through the Bible, to the one Person who has a true worldview—He can see everything. By faith we understand.

This does not mean we know everything or that other worldviews are always wrong and Christians are always right. Christians are sinful and limited too. You are holding a "worldview" textbook in your hands because you need to know what God says to you about your world and what it contains. "The earth is the Lord's," after all, "and the fullness thereof"—that means everything in it (Ps. 24:1). God has a plan for this world. And He views it from a perspective that you're going to learn more about.

There have been times when Christians apparently understood God's viewpoint—and God's "big story"—a little better than they do now. It's always a mistake to think that some previous era in history was the ideal one (Eccles. 7:10), but there's no denying that Christianity used to be salt and light on a grander cultural scale than it is today. For all the sins and errors of the church through the centuries (times when its salt was way too bland and it hid its light under a basket), Christians still had a big impact on education, politics, art, science, and music. Christians truly made something of this world, just as God intended. They did heady, intellectual things like analyzing and evaluating, but they also acted. They did something with the biblical worldview. They proclaimed Christ's gospel, and they wielded great societal influence.

In fact, that influence is the very reason so many scientists are named Steve (did Project Steve ever think of that?). *Stephen* is a name from the Bible, and its popularity stems directly from Christianity's past cultural dominance in European countries. It's ironic that a thousand unbelieving scientists bear the name of the first Christian to die for his faith—all because Christians in the past were salt and light, used by God to influence the pagan world around them.

> **WHAT'S IN A NAME?**
>
> Why is *Stephen* (*Stefan, Etienne, Esteban, Steffen, Steponas*) such a common name throughout the modern West?

There's no reason that can't happen again.

And no reason you shouldn't take part.

THINKING IT THROUGH 1.2B

1. What is the technical term for the second worldview ingredient, a big or master story?

2. Why do humans need big stories?

3. What are the three main points of the big story of the Bible?

4. What biblical command should motivate you to be engaged as a creative cultivator in your culture?

5. What two metaphors did Jesus use to illustrate the third worldview ingredient (putting into action what you believe)?

♀6. Explain what it means for a Christian to be salt and light.

CHAPTER REVIEW ANSWERS

Making Connections

1. You ought to choose Option 3 (not giving in at all) and respond with a defense of the faith. This response demonstrates that you are committed to the truth of God's Word in all things (2 Cor. 10:5; 1 Pet. 3:15; 2 Pet. 1:3). Choosing either Option 1 (giving up your faith completely) or Option 2 (giving in a little) reflects a false or compromised faith.

2. The idea of a lens communicates that your worldview determines what you see or how you interpret everything.

3. A head system is a person's intellect—his basic beliefs. A heart system involves someone's affections—his loves and desires. Your heart system is intertwined with and even directs your head system.

1 CHAPTER REVIEW

TERMS TO REMEMBER

worldview
basic beliefs
metanarrative
CFR
culture

Scripture Memory

2 Corinthians 10:4–5

Making Connections

1. Which option does this chapter recommend you should take when your faith is challenged? Why should you respond this way?

2. Explain how the illustration of a lens communicates the way a worldview functions.

3. Explain the head and heart systems and how they are related.

4. How does Genesis 1:28 relate to culture?

Developing Skills in Apologetics and Worldview

5. If you were called upon to defend a biblical view of creation in a conversation with a non-Christian science professor, would you choose Option 3.1 or Option 3.2? Why?

6. How do you think telling the "big story" of Creation, Fall, and Redemption could help your non-Christian neighbor better understand your presentation of the gospel?

Examining Assumptions and Evidence

7. Are the scientists in Project Steve looking at the world through worldview lenses? How do you know?

8. How did the affections of the Soviet cosmonaut (page 9) influence his interpretation of what he saw in space?

9. Why are metanarratives necessary?

10. What is the danger of ignoring your responsibility to be salt? What is the danger of ignoring your responsibility to be light?

Becoming a Creative Cultivator

11. Brainstorm to come up with a list of three ways you can be salt and three ways you can be light in your community.

---

4. The Creation Mandate is the biblical directive that establishes our stewardship, the responsibility to creatively cultivate what is in this world. Culture is the result of that creative cultivation.

Developing Skills in Apologetics and Worldview

5. Option 3.2 (arguing back according to worldview) is foundational to Option 3.1 (arguing back according to evidence). The reason it is more helpful and effective is that it takes a lot of intelligence, time, and study to become a knowledgeable expert in the details of the evidence. In addition, in order to properly interpret any evidence, worldview guidelines must be established first.

6. The larger story provides the context to make sense of the specific truths. When people understand their place within the larger story, then they will begin to understand their need for the specific truths that you present to them.

Examining Assumptions and Evidence

7. Project Steve's brash claims are not built on irrefutable science but on faith-based worldview presuppositions. Only those who view the world through the lens of their metanarrative will accept their explanations as overwhelmingly convincing.

8. His affections misdirected his reasoning. Since he already assumed that God didn't exist (and didn't want God to exist), he refused to believe in God's existence as long as God didn't appear to him in a physical form when and where he demanded.

9. A metanarrative (the second ingredient of your worldview) provides the interpretive framework to make sense of your beliefs, assumptions, and values (the first ingredient). Without the foundation of the metanarrative, you are left without a basis for your beliefs, assumptions, and values.

10. The danger of ignoring the Christian's responsibility to be salt is that people will try to be highly involved in culture to influence it but in the end will become conformed to the world instead. The danger of ignoring the responsibility to be light leads believers to isolate themselves from the culture, which results in society becoming more and more anti-God since it has less and less Christian cultivation affecting it.

Becoming a Creative Cultivator

11. This could be a group project. You may wish to work in tandem with a church youth group to carry out the project.

TERMS TO REMEMBER

worldview—(1) a set of basic beliefs, assumptions, and values that (2) arises from a big story about the world and (3) produces individual and group action (human culture)

basic belief—a foundational understanding of the world and reality with significant ramifications based upon faith pre-understandings and commitments

metanarrative—a larger story that narratives (smaller stories) fit within to provide an overarching explanation of the reality of this world from the beginning

CFR—(Creation, Fall, Redemption) a shorthand way of referring to the story of what God is doing to glorify Himself by redeeming His fallen creation; the metanarrative of the Bible

Creation Mandate—the divine command given in Genesis 1:28–29 that lays out the stewardship responsibility humans have because of being created in the image of God

culture—the result of humans carrying out the Creation Mandate and making something of the world

The student will be able to

2.1 Compare and contrast worldview apologetics with evidentialism by analyzing the role of evidence in relation to presuppositions in each approach.

2.2 Defend the proper role of reasoned evidence even though it cannot provide proof apart from faith.

2.3 Explain why a Christian's desire for proof must ultimately rest on faith in God's authority and the fear of the Lord.

SECTION OBJECTIVES 2.1

1. Define *presupposition* and explain how presuppositions orient a person's understanding.

2. Summarize the evidentialist approach and explain why many people favor this approach.

3. Explain why the morality of knowledge, human finitude, and model-making all necessitate presuppositions.

4. Summarize and defend the worldview apologetics approach.

5. Explain why the evidentialist approach can never provide final certainty.

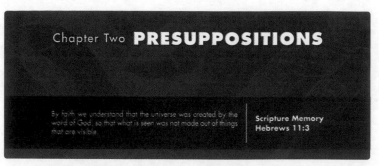

Chapter Two **PRESUPPOSITIONS**

By faith we understand that the universe was created by the word of God, so that what is seen was not made out of things that are visible.

Scripture Memory
Hebrews 11:3

2.1 PRESUPPOSITIONS

Whenever you go on a mission to prove something—to find the truth—you have to make a distinction between two different kinds of ideas. Some ideas will be new to you, things you discover on your truth mission. But other ideas will already be there in your head. You can't start a truth mission without them (every chain of reasoning hangs on something previous). In fact, you wouldn't seek truth if you didn't already have some ideas in your head (and some desires in your heart) motivating you to go seeking and letting you know where to begin.

PRESUPPOSITIONS MAKE IT POSSIBLE (AND IMPOSSIBLE) TO SEE

J. Warner Wallace was thirty-five years old before he ever realized that there was one idea in his head guiding and shaping all his other ideas—namely, the idea that "nature is all there is." It was then, he says, "I recognized how unreasonable it was for me to reject the possibility of anything supernatural before I even began to investigate the supernatural claims of Christianity."[1]

Wallace was an atheist at the time and a homicide detective. And he tells an interesting story about how **presuppositions** can influence someone's thinking. While training to figure out real-life whodunits, Wallace and his mentor* were investigating the murder of a woman in her own home.

"It was her husband," announced the more experienced detective. "Find him for me, and we'll have our killer." The older man pointed out to Wallace a picture of a man and the murdered woman that had been turned over on the bedside table. He pointed to men's clothes in the closet. In his mind, the evidence was conclusive. Mystery solved.

Or was it? Police later discovered that the woman had no husband or even a boyfriend. The picture and male clothing were evidence not of a spouse but of a brother. This brother lived in another country but visited occasionally, so he kept some clothes at his sister's home. The murderer, as it turns out, was a neighbor she didn't even know.

The older detective had what's called a "presupposition"—an idea you have in your head before you look at the evidence. He presupposed (and in many cases he would have been right) that murdered women were often killed by men they loved, and this presupposition guided his interpretation of what he saw. He didn't even consider other possibilities because the lenses he was looking through kept him from seeing them.

EVIDENTIALISM

The apparent solution to this detective's problem is to try to eliminate all presuppositions, attempting to come to the evidence with total neutrality, complete objectivity, no bias or opinion.

---

mentor: *a respected and experienced teacher or trainer*

Lesson Plan Chart—Chapter 2

Section Title	Pages	Activity Manual	Days
2.1 Presuppositions	18–22	Activity 3	2 days
2.2 Proof	22–27	Activity 4	2 days
2.3 Doubt Your Doubts	27–30		1 day
Review	31		1 day
Total Suggested Days			**6 days**

Presuppositions

The term *presupposition* is often used in both a technical and nontechnical sense. It can describe any prior knowledge already accepted to be true and on which new knowledge builds (this is actually just an assumption). Technically, *presupposition* is used to describe particular prior knowledge that is self-evidencing (for which no greater authority can be given). A biblical worldview presupposition is not an ignorant assumption (e.g., the other planets orbit the Earth). It is not an arbitrary statement (e.g., unicorns are pink). It is not merely a correct assumption (e.g., Tom assumed Kendra would like him). A biblical worldview presupposition is an informed basic belief that is self-evidencing (e.g., God exists because He has spoken to us in His Word).

And this is precisely how most modern defenders of the Bible operate. One philosophy professor, for example, says that when studying the claims of the Bible, the "subjective* element" needs to be "offset as much as possible." He admits that "biases can never be completely eliminated," but he insists that we can know what happened in the past if we follow the evidence of history according to the rules. This is the way he argues for Christianity when debating non-Christians.[2]

This viewpoint is called evidentialism. **Evidentialists** tend to think that the way to persuade unbelievers that Christ died for them or that God created the universe is to list all the evidence. If only unbelievers could be persuaded that there is a mountain of evidence for our position and very little, if any, for theirs, they'd believe. We need, they say, to get unbelievers to set aside their worldviews for just an hour and take an honest look at the evidence. Some evidentialists make it a policy not to use the Bible at all in public debates with non-Christians. An evidentialist may say to the unbeliever, "I recognize that you don't believe the Bible, so I'm going to set it aside and step onto some common ground, some neutral territory where we can both talk peacefully. Then you'll see that my position is the more reasonable one."

THE MORALITY OF KNOWLEDGE

Maybe that's good advice for a Sherlock Holmes working on a murder case. But when it comes to life's most important questions, is that even possible? Can you be neutral and objective about God?

The Bible says you can't. Early in his letter to the Romans, Paul says very clearly that unbelieving people "suppress" the truth about God that they can see all around them in creation—and inside themselves through the moral laws God has written on their hearts (Rom. 1:18–21; 2:14–15). Despite that knowledge, they have "exchanged the truth about God for a lie" (Rom. 1:25).

People who suppress their knowledge of God's existence and their innate knowledge of God's moral law are not neutral and objective. Paul says that "*although they knew God*, they did not honor him as God or give thanks to him, but they became futile in their thinking, and their foolish hearts were darkened" (Rom. 1:21).

People, in other words, don't start off neutral. We're all born knowing about God and His moral law at some level. Being an unbeliever requires many acts of willful suppression of the knowledge that God put inside us. People can't claim ignorance of Him. They are morally responsible for what they know. Paul says, "They are without excuse" (Rom. 1:20).

This is so true that Solomon is willing to say in Scripture, "The fear of the Lord is the beginning of knowledge" (Prov. 1:7). You don't have knowledge of the world as it really is till you have something else first—the fear of the Lord. Not just our actions,

---

A VERDICT THAT DEMANDS EVIDENCE

An apologist who has authored dozens of books summarizes well the evidentialist viewpoint: "I prefer a method that I call the 'minimal facts' approach. The major idea is to utilize data that have two characteristics: they are well-evidenced, usually for multiple reasons, and they are generally admitted by critical scholars who research this particular area."[3]

AS A MATTER OF FACT

Evidentialism is "a method of defending the Christian faith (apologetics) that assumes that data drawn from history and experience (facts) can demonstrate the reasonableness of Christian claims and can therefore help to prepare a person for faith in Christ by removing obstacles to belief. Thus evidentialism attempts to give as much 'evidence' as possible to substantiate crucial facts of the Christian faith such as the resurrection of Christ or the historical accuracy of the biblical accounts."

—*Pocket Dictionary of Theological Terms*[4]

subjective: based on someone's personal knowledge, opinions, and desires

---

- *Informed:* It's reasonable; it doesn't ignore evidence. The evidence correlates or fits when using the presupposition.
- *Basic belief:* It's foundational; it's a part of the head system of a person's worldview lenses and has significant ramifications for the rest of his thought.
- *Self-evidencing:* It's authoritative; further evidence can't be appealed to in order to justify the presupposition, but the presupposition justifies itself when it makes sense of all the evidence.

Starting Points Determine Reasoning

Presuppositions determine not only a person's conclusion but also his process of reasoning. Reasoning back (inductively) from the evidence to a conclusion (design implies a Designer) only works when someone is already willing to accept (deductively) the underlying starting presupposition (only a Designer could create designed-looking things). Until presuppositions are settled, opposing parties will simply talk past each other as they look at the same evidence.

Evidentialism in a Nutshell

Goal or purpose: (a) understand (evidence) in order to believe; (b) tentatively believe, but understand (evidence) to really believe

Means/method of using the evidence: (a) Evidence outright proves God and His claims. (b) Evidence verifies/confirms a tentative belief. Evidence must justify God/His claims. God is put on trial and acquitted by the evidence.

Basis of authority: The common, neutral ground of human reasoning (e.g., logic and science) is the authoritative platform on which faith must rest. You must play by the unbeliever's rules for evaluating the evidence; the only authoritative and reliable basis for obtaining knowledge is through natural rather than supernatural means.

Fairness Without Bias?

What is the perceived loss when neutrality is taken away and the gain when it's achieved? *fairness; a shared starting point of agreement*

What does bias supposedly hinder? *willingness to see things from another's perspective*

Should neutrality be the Christian's goal in order to get others to switch sides?

The goal of the believer isn't to get the unbeliever to become unbiased; unbelievers won't fairly assess the evidence (John 8:45; Rom. 3:18; Prov. 1:7; 26:4; Jer. 8:9; Col. 2:8). The goal is to persuade the unbeliever to submit his mind to thinking God's thoughts after Him (2 Cor. 10:4–5).

Neutral Knowledge?

Reasoning is a part of the image of God, marred by the Fall but not obliterated. While humans still have the capacity to reason, the content of that reasoning is always influenced by moral fallenness (1 Cor. 2:14; 2 Cor. 4:4; Eph. 2:1–3; 4:17–18; Ps. 10:4). Unbelievers are not unintelligent; they can have a detailed and expert knowledge of a lot of facts due to God's common grace. What unbelievers lack is (1) a proper ordering of those facts into a coherent truth system with (2) an authoritative basis. Van Til compared the intellect of fallen humans to a "buzz-saw that is sharp and shining, ready to cut the boards that come to it." However, instead of cutting straight lines, it can only cut slanted lines because of its faulty setting. [Cornelius Van Til, *The Defense of the Faith*, 4th ed. (Phillipsburg, NJ: P & R Publishing, 2008), 97]

It's not that unbelievers can never have correct knowledge; it's that they can never have neutral knowledge. Correct knowledge is always due to thinking God's thoughts after Him (whether or not one acknowledges doing so). The basic principle that leads unbelievers into darkness and foolishness is the principle of autonomous human knowledge. When they are consistent with their principle of autonomous knowledge, then their interpretations will be wrong. But when they are inconsistent with their own principle and think God's thoughts after Him (borrowing from the Christian worldview), then their interpretations are correct. [John Frame, *Cornelius Van Til: An Analysis of His Thought* (Phillipsburg, NJ: P & R Publishing, 1995), 198–99]

What Is a Model?

A model helps organize huge amounts of data into a coherent system; it's a simplified representation of reality. As the data is plugged into a system of thought, it can then be explained and understood. The facts follow from the interpretive system. For example, a model of the solar system helps people understand both its structure and planetary motion. However, the model simplifies reality by highlighting only certain truths while ignoring other aspects of that reality (e.g., the elliptical orbits are exaggerated, the sizes of the planets in relation to the sun are inaccurate, etc.).

Complex models also exist. Scientists have gathered data on temperatures from around the world in the last hundred years or so. However, that data is meaningless until a person finds similarities and differences, evaluates cause and effect, and so on. One scientist might take that data and plug it into one model or theory (increased carbon emissions from human development are the major cause for warming or cooling trends) while another scientist takes the exact same data and plugs it into another model or theory (warming and cooling trends are due to a multiplicity of influences that have always been a part of the cycles of earth's climate changes—including but not limited to solar flares and volcanic eruptions). These scientists arrive at different conclusions, not necessarily because the data or evidence is different but because their models are different.

That's why models are important. They influence what people will perceive to be the hard, undeniable facts. The complexity of data often makes it difficult to simply dismiss another person's model. Yet legitimate models are often dismissed simply because of the agendas that rule the day.

Information Overload

Explain the need for models due to human finitude. **Does the internet (with all its data at your fingertips) make it easier or harder to know what is true?**

Some things are easier.

It does provide access to a lot of simple answers to a lot of simple questions (from giving you step-by-step directions for making poached eggs to listing all the cities of all the countries in the world).

Some things are harder.

It has also introduced so much data and so many claims about that data that humans are drowning in a lot of confusion. The more data you have, the harder it is to fit all the pieces together into a consistent working model (e.g., from political and economic strategies to the historical origins of the date of Christmas).

Instead of being the solution to our finitude, computers magnify our finitude. What's easier—a ten-piece puzzle or a billion-piece puzzle? The internet has increased our access to data so astronomically, we must construct models that can make sense of billions of pieces of information rather than hundreds or thousands of pieces. Left to their own reasoning powers, humans are struggling more than ever to be sure about anything. This is because many unbelievers are trying to be more consistent with the principle of autonomous human knowledge by rejecting any authoritative declarations of knowledge.

---

not just our emotions, but even our knowledge is supposed to be submitted to God. As Paul puts it, we are to "take every *thought* captive to obey Christ" (2 Cor. 10:5).

According to the Bible, knowledge is moral; you know either obediently or rebelliously. The answer, then, is not to get rid of your presuppositions but to have good ones.

FINITUDE AND MODEL-MAKING

Even if you could be a neutral fact-evaluating machine, you'd still have to deal with your limits. Humans can't know everything, and they can't be everywhere at once. They can't travel back in time.

In the absence of firsthand eyewitness experience (and even that can get twisted in a person's memory, as any courtroom cross-examination can show you), you are stuck putting together a good theory—or **model**—with the available data. It's just like the way an aeronautical engineer might build a scale model of a new jet to test it in a wind tunnel. And it's not just engineers that make models. Economists and others do it too. The real-life facts about economics in a country of 320 million people are unbelievably complicated, so much so that only one Person can hold them all in His mind, let alone understand them. But economists at the US Federal Reserve still have to make decisions that affect every single one of those people (and, truly, countless more around the globe). So they simplify. They have to. They boil down trillions of facts—payroll numbers in Portland, sugar sales in Sarasota, the housing market in Hartford—into a much simpler "model" of all the data. Without a model to hang new facts on, the facts become an impenetrable jumble, like earbuds in your pocket.

That's why most scientists, when making new discoveries in the biological field, immediately attempt to fit those discoveries into the evolutionary model. For example, paleontologist Mary Schweitzer of North Carolina State University discovered something that captured the world's attention: she found soft tissue inside a *T. rex* bone—blood, cartilage. "What we found was unusual, because it was still soft and still transparent and still flexible," Schweitzer said.[5]

This find was unusual because the currently accepted scientific model says that (1) the *T. rex* became extinct sixty-five million years ago and (2) soft tissue doesn't last anywhere near that long.

When evolutionary scientists can't explain how soft tissue could have lasted millions of years, they have a conundrum, facts that don't fit well into their model.

But let's be clear: there's nothing wrong with trying to fit new facts into your model. It's a necessary process for all human knowing. If the new facts don't fit well, then the question is whether the model itself is accurate and self-consistent (and, as we'll see in the science unit, the evolutionary model is not).

After Schweitzer's discovery, researchers looked for soft tissue in other fossils, and they found a lot of it, in fossils going back (allegedly) as much as 200 million years. "The problem is, for 300 years we thought, 'Well, the organics [like soft tissue] are all gone, so why should we look for something that's not going to be there?' and nobody looks," she says.

In other words, paleontologists went on a truth mission with certain ideas (a certain model) already in their heads, and those ideas both guided and shaped their inquiry. Those ideas actually blinded them for decades to facts sitting right in front

> **THE IRONY OF IT ALL**
>
> Evolutionary scientists now think iron in a dinosaur's blood may explain the soft tissue's survival; they've preserved tissue in a lab for two years using iron. It's hard to call this proof of their view; two years is a good deal less than 65 million. More finds like this may someday overturn the evolutionary model, even among non-Christians.

Discussion: Talk with students about how much information hits their eyes and ears in a given day.

How can you make sense of it all?

How do you know what's true and what's false?

How do you know what's valuable and what's worthless?

You have to set up a mental "filter." That filter will be a function of your worldview made up of your presuppositions. If you already know that a particular news show spins every story too far to the left or the right, you can run what its host says through that filter. If you know that God created the world in six days, you can feed every science story through that filter, straining out the false and worthless and keeping only the true and valuable.

of them. Because they presupposed that these bones were countless years old, they never stopped to look for soft tissue inside. The solution is not for scientists to shove all their knowledge out of their heads and start over with complete objectivity; it's to start with the right model, the right presuppositions.

WORLDVIEW APOLOGETICS

The morality of knowledge, human finitude, and model-making all point us back to the value—actually, the *necessity*—of presuppositions. We can only take in so many facts at a time, so we build models. And those models are based on presuppositions. And those presuppositions are either submitted to God's Word or they are not. No one can serve two masters (Matt. 6:24).

Even homicide detectives can't set aside all theories and become completely neutral and objective while working on a murder case. And when it comes to life's most important questions, it's even more obvious that complete objectivity is simply not possible.

So evidentialists, despite all the good they do, are wrong about something very important. There is no neutral territory that believers and unbelievers can step onto for purposes of discussion. If a Christian says to an atheist, "I won't quote the Bible in my debate with you," the Christian has already given up the debate—because the main point being debated is whether or not people can know ultimate truth without God revealing it to them in Scripture. You can't build a ladder up to God made out of good reasons when, without God, there's nothing to put the ladder on.

There's got to be a way to debate the claims of the Bible with non-Christians that doesn't start with denying certain claims of the Bible, an approach that doesn't act like *God's* words are somehow proven true by *your* words.

There is a way, and it goes back to what we discussed in the previous chapter on worldview. Christians need to gently, graciously, but confidently show unbelievers their own lenses, their presuppositions. Christians—in reliance on the Holy Spirit who alone can open people's eyes—should use the claims of the Bible to help non-Christians see the role their head-heart systems and their master stories play in what they make of the world. (We'll call this **worldview apologetics**.)

We're back to the idea of worldview lenses. If you believe that the earth is billions of years old and that humans evolved by chance from lower forms of life, you will see all of the evidence you encounter through those lenses. If you believe, as some ancient cultures did, that men were created because the gods got tired of doing manual labor, your view of your own job will be distorted by that lens. Even if you believe that God was too weak or too uncaring to give you a better family—or body, or brain—it will be impossible for you to see the world as it really is.

A lot of people in the West (Christians included) talk as if the worldview with the biggest bucket of evidence wins. But it's not as if there is a bunch of evidence for Creationism in the world, a bunch of evidence for evolution, some for a spiritist/animist viewpoint, and a little for a cyclical Hindu worldview. Instead, everybody has access to the same data. Think of some of the simple facts of our experience: the salinity levels in sea water, the properties of aluminum, even the personality tendencies of kids with Down syndrome. These are not **proof** of anyone's worldview; no, they are interpreted by your worldview. You see these facts through the lenses made up of your beliefs about the world.

> "It seems to me that . . . the current orthodoxy about the cosmic order is the product of governing assumptions that are unsupported, and that it flies in the face of common sense."[6]
>
> —THOMAS NAGEL

Worldview Apologetics in a Nutshell

Remind the students about the evidentialist's goals, means, and basis (see the "Evidentialism in a Nutshell" note on page 19). Then explain the contrasting approach of worldview apologetics below.

Goal or purpose: believe in order to understand (evidence)

Means or method of using evidence: Presuppositions govern interpretations of evidence; evidence correlates/fits with the presupposition. Rather than being conclusive in itself without a presupposition, evidence can only be supportive of the presupposition in use. The presupposition justifies a person's interpretation of the evidence. Evidence is put on trial and accepted when submitted to God's authoritative declarations.

Basis or authority: God's declarations are the presuppositions. Scripture is the authoritative platform on which evidence (logic and science) must rest. There is no greater authority over God (Heb. 6:13). There is no common ground of interpretation. Don't play by the rules of the unbeliever's worldview, evaluating evidence based on his presuppositions (Prov. 26:4). Demonstrate the foolishness of his position by showing the inconsistency of the evidence if interpreted by his worldview rules (Prov. 26:5). The Bible is the authority not only in theology but also when examining the evidence in apologetics. Scriptural principles validate or invalidate all truth claims—whether explicitly mentioned in the Bible or not.

Investigating in the Right Direction

Compare and contrast worldview apologetics with the evidentialist approach.

The Bible declares that God is both sovereign and loving—without exception.

The evidentialist approach of using the evidence to critique this presupposition:

- Method: Look at the puzzle pieces (the evidence of the world/your life) without the bias of glasses/a picture.
- Reality: Millions or billions of pieces in this puzzle don't seem to fit no matter how hard you try to make them fit. Deception, disease, despair, and death have become devastating personal realities.
- Result: The more you judge God's claims according to the evidence of your circumstances, the more you are convinced that the claims can't possibly be true. The evidence just won't justify the presupposition that God is both sovereign and loving all the time.

The reason this approach fails is that the method of investigation is flawed (not the presupposition that God is loving and in control). It's backwards—like holding up puzzle pieces to examine your glasses (and griping about how useless your glasses are) instead of holding up the interpretive lens of your glasses to examine the puzzle pieces.

The worldview apologetics approach of using the presupposition to critique the interpretations of the evidence:

- Method: Put on your glasses and look at the picture on the box (get your bearings by understanding the correct presuppositions/the biblical metanarrative). Open your eyes when you put on your glasses by trusting that the Creator of the puzzle has provided all the right pieces to form a beautiful picture (trust the infallible God to work out all things for your good and His glory).
- Reality: You lack the wisdom to fit the millions or billions of pieces together yourself; go to the Creator of the puzzle for help.
- Result: Many of the pieces will fall right into place, but some of the pieces still won't make sense until the Creator comes and reveals the solution to you.

People who can't fit the pieces together have not put on the biblical worldview glasses, or they have closed their eyes to trusting the Creator even though the glasses are supposedly on. They won't admit that the puzzle pieces don't fit together because of their own inadequacy, so they blame or deny the Creator.

No Authority Means No Certainty

Which of the following statements better reflects the views of secular society?

- The facts speak for themselves; gather evidence; examine it according to the scientific method; prove truth claims.

- That's your interpretation; evidence is subject to one's perspective; there is no truth—only your own individual perceptions of it.

Sometimes secularists use the first statement for things they categorize under reason/science and the second statement for faith/values.

The first view is a simplified version of what is called modernism: the belief that humans have the intellectual ability to conclusively prove things—given enough intellectual effort and scientific examination. (Evidentialism tries to play by these rules.)

The second statement is a simplified summary of what is called postmodernism. Humans began to realize that their intellectual efforts could only produce relative probabilities even in the hard sciences. With the overwhelming flood of information and the myriad of competing models for making sense of all that information, many people have thrown up their hands and accepted relativity, deciding that "truth" simply depends on the person. (Fideism plays by these rules; this approach is discussed later.)

Neither view is right because they both resort to human autonomy—people searching for and determining knowledge on their own. They reject outside authority above themselves. Certainty can only be found in a trustworthy, authoritative source.

The Impossibility of Irrefutable Evidence

A smoking-gun piece of evidence is always elusive because it can't exist. Those in Jesus' day saw many miracles done right in front of them, but they still rejected His authority (Matt. 12:24; 16:1–4).

You shouldn't be surprised that there aren't any irrefutable pieces of evidence. You should understand that evidence is always interpreted to align with presuppositions. Presuppositions dictate the view of the evidence every time. You will never be able to place confidence in the Bible as long as you demand irrefutable evidence—not because the Bible falls short but because you fall short. Irrefutable evidence is beyond the grasp of anyone who is less than omniscient and less than infallible. Evidence can only provide probability. There will always be ways to refute a person's interpretation. The idea that an interpretive conclusion of evidence can be irrefutable is a false presupposition—an impossibility. Therefore, your quest

is an impossibility. The problem is not with the Bible. The problem is with the arrogance or naiveté of the quest.

Furthermore, if you try to verify God's Word by appealing to a higher authority, you deny that God is ultimate. Making evidence ultimate presupposes human autonomy.

The Possibility of Refuting Presuppositions

Presuppositions are falsifiable. The way to falsify a presupposition is to demonstrate that it is self-refuting or inconsistent. The presupposition invalidates itself when the evidence can't even be used in a supportive role to one's admitted presupposition.

For example, secularism usually presupposes an evolutionary metanarrative. The evolutionary metanarrative only allows for a material or physical world. But there's a problem

with the logic here. Logic itself is not material/physical. As a result, it can't be proven to exist by the scientific method. You can't do a scientific investigation in which you see it, touch it, taste it, smell it, or hear it. (You hear the arguments that result from it, but you don't hear logic itself.) The brain is material, but it is not logic; it only makes use of logic. That logic exists is self-attesting. One can't refute it without using it. Therefore, it must exist. But how can you explain the existence of this nonmaterial abstraction in a metanarrative that only allows for a material world? You can't. Since the presupposition can't explain the evidence (the reality of the world), it can't justify itself and therefore must be flawed. There must be an immaterial world in addition to the material world; there must be truths or realities that are beyond the grasp of natural, scientific investigations. There must be other sources of truth or

---

THINKING IT THROUGH 2.1

1. What must every truth mission start with and why?

2. Why do evidentialists attempt to set aside their worldview lenses when they interpret evidence?

3. What three realities point to the necessity and value of presuppositions?

4. What's wrong with holding to your Christianity loosely until all the evidence is in?

5. What is the worldview apologetics approach to using evidence?

2.2 PROOF

Evidence is important, because Christianity is a religion rooted firmly in history. Unlike, say, Buddhism, the life and teachings of the founder of our religion (Jesus Christ) would be worthless if He never really existed. It matters a lot whether a flesh-and-blood man named Jesus of Nazareth really lived and really died in Palestine two thousand years ago—and really lives again. If He doesn't live, we Christians should be pitied more than anyone (1 Cor. 15:19). Historical evidence for Christ's death, therefore, has real value.

But it has equally real limits. Many sites on the internet list a lot of evidences that Jesus really and truly rose from the dead, evidence such as ancient historians who mention Jesus.

But even if the valuable academic discipline of history were able to "prove" to everyone's satisfaction that Christ really died and lived again, could it ever demonstrate what Christ's death and resurrection *meant*? How can any historical or scientific evidence prove that Christ's crucifixion on a Roman cross in AD 29 paid for the sins of the whole world, the way the Bible claims (1 Cor. 15:3)? Evidence has limits. And "proof" is not as simple a concept as you might think.

WHAT COUNTS AS PROOF?

We often talk as if proof is obvious. We fight instead over evidence—whether or not the evidence really "proves" our assertions. But how often have you stopped and asked yourself, "What counts as proof?" And better yet, "Who says?"

The kind of proof demanded by a lot of people in the educated West is empirical,* scientific proof. "If I can't prove God's existence, I won't believe in Him!" Other people instead demand miracles: "If God gets me a new car and a new job, I'll believe." This is nothing new. Two thousand years ago Paul observed, "Jews demand signs, and Greeks seek wisdom." And what was Paul's solution? Miracles? Rational debates? He did use those things. But ultimately his solution was simple: "We preach Christ crucified" (1 Cor. 1:22–23).

empirical: *able to be seen, heard, smelled, tasted, or felt*

And notice what Paul says next: preaching Christ was "a stumbling block to Jews and folly to Gentiles" (1:23). Paul purposefully preached a message he knew most people would reject. He knew that his "proofs" would not be sufficient for them. But he also knew that there were some people who would listen: "To those who are called, both Jews and Greeks, Christ [is] the power of God and the wisdom of God" (1:24). Christ Himself was the sign the Jews were looking for; He is the wisdom that educated Greeks wanted to find—even if many refused to see it.

It is appropriate to use reason and argumentation and evidence when presenting the Christian faith to others—and when you are struggling with your own doubts. But the Christian message has at its heart the message, "Christ died for our sins and rose again," and many people won't accept any miracles or any argument as proof of that. Even within the pages of the Bible, miracles have a pretty poor track record of convincing people of the truth. Just think about the Israelites bitterly demanding to go back to Egypt very shortly after God parted an ocean to rescue them!

And what scientific or historical "proof" could possibly be offered for the assertion that Jesus died for our sins? Even if credible witnesses saw a man named Jesus of Nazareth die (and they did), how could they possibly know that His shoulders were truly bent by the weight of the world's sin? That's not something any human can see. And even if credible witnesses saw Christ resurrected (and they did), how could they possibly know that He was "raised for

PERSUADING OTHERS

The apostle Paul himself "reasoned in the synagogue every Sabbath, and tried to persuade Jews and Greeks" about the truths of the gospel (Acts 18:4). The art of persuasion was also of interest to the ancient Greek philosopher Aristotle, who defined rhetoric as "the ability in any particular case to see the available means of persuasion."

Whereas Paul's writing offers more warnings about evil means of persuasion than it offers suggestions on how to persuade, Aristotle outlined three major factors involved in persuading others through speech: *pathos*, *logos*, and *ethos*. Your *pathos* includes your feeling as well as your read of the audience. Your *logos* is your reason and your structure. Your *ethos*, lastly, is your character. Character is an especially important part of the defense of the Christian message because the gospel claims to save people from the power of sin. Anybody, Christian or not, can memorize a list of proofs for the existence of God. But Christians should make every effort to ensure that their *ethos* is as powerful an argument as their *logos* is.

methods for finding out truth other than science. There must be the possibility of discovering God's existence apart from science.

The presupposition is falsified. You falsify presuppositions by demonstrating that they fail when you seek to make use of them.

THINKING IT THROUGH 2.1

1. presuppositions; because it's impossible to approach evidence without ideas already in your head driving the investigation; Every chain of reasoning has a starting point.

2. because they want to present evidence with total neutrality or complete objectivity, setting aside worldview bias

3. the morality of knowledge; the finitude of humans necessitating the model-making nature of human knowledge

4. There will always be new evidence to consider; your faith will always be unstable and reinterpreted if its basis is founded on shifting evidence. Instead, faith in the unchanging authority of God's Word must be the foundation on which evidence gets interpreted.

♀5. The pivotal difference between evidentialism and worldview apologetics isn't whether proponents use or don't use evidence. The difference is that worldview apologetics affirms that (1) evidence can never be presented without the influence of worldview lenses interpreting that evidence and (2) the role of evidence in apologetics is limited—it supports truth claims rather than proving truth claims.

1. Explain the value of using evidence in spite of its limits.
2. Explain why God's undeniable proof doesn't count in the unbeliever's mind.
3. Summarize three common faith-bases for proof: empiricism, rationalism, or revelation.
4. Defend the proper use of reason and evidence.

Fideism in a Nutshell

Goal or purpose: experience (a personal encounter with God) in order to believe

Means or method: Evidence is irrelevant.

Basis of authority: a person's own subjective experiences and testimony

While Christians ought to share the testimony of a changed life by the Spirit (Rom. 8:15–16; Acts 22:1–21), their personal experience isn't the proof or basis of authority any more than a Mormon's experience would be. Experience follows belief; it's not what leads to it. The basis must be the Word of God, not another person's word of experience.

Just as evidentialists are wrong to throw out presuppositions in their search for neutrality, fideists are wrong to rule out evidence in favor of simply parroting presuppositions. Both presuppositions and evidence are necessary. The key is to place them in their proper roles. Presuppositions must be the authoritative foundation for critiquing the evidence—not the reverse. But evidence does need critique.

Supportive Evidence

Why does the evidence need to be consistent with the biblical truth claims?

The worldview apologetics approach doesn't ask you to blindly believe truth claims in spite of the reality of this world. Christianity is not meant to be some sort of social club to make you feel psychologically better (like a placebo). The Bible is not merely a bunch of theological or religious concepts. The Bible reveals the realities of God, His creation, and the nature of our relationship to Him and His creation. It recounts His historical interaction with mankind. Therefore, we don't just believe abstract concepts about sin and our need for a Savior; we believe in actual individuals named Adam and Eve, who really disobeyed God, bringing about a real curse and our need for a real God-man, who truly suffered, died, and defeated death by rising again. Evidence is used in a supportive role consistent with our presuppositions. Evidence can relieve believers from doubts when it is shown to be consistent with pre-suppositions.

Proving God's Existence

Two sources contribute to the human knowledge that God exists: general revelation and special revelation. Through general revelation (creation, providence, and conscience), God displays His deity and power. However, this revelation only brings about the wrath of God because this evidence from general revelation is always suppressed by the sinful nature (Rom. 1:18–32). Thus, rational arguments for the existence of God are at best tenuous from the unbeliever's perspective. Only submission to the second source of knowledge will make it possible for a person to accept the truth revealed in general revelation.

The second source of knowledge is God's special self-revelation. God has spoken, so He must exist. This is assumed from the very first verse of the Bible. Since humans suppress evidence from general revelation, they need the illumination of special revelation. Paul's discussion of general revelation rests on the need for special revelation in which God's righteousness is revealed to darkened minds (Rom 1:16–17). Since He has spoken and has even come in the flesh into human history (Heb. 1:1–3; Exod. 3:14), God has more than sufficiently demonstrated His existence.

God's non-existence can't be justified. God is in fact a precondition for the experiences that we have. He must exist in order for our life to be possible. To say God does not exist is to express something that is impossible. Why? The reality of this world can never support the idea of the nonexistence of an absolute being over all. Why? The absolutes that God has built into this world cannot be accounted for otherwise. This is demonstrated by the example of the existence of the laws of logic, science, and morality, none of which atheists can justify or account for even though they are trying to use them. The laws of logic, science, and morality are justified in Christianity because they are derived from God.

---

our justification" (Rom. 4:25)? Justification, one of the most precious realities in the Bible, is completely invisible, weightless, and odorless. You can't "prove" these things via the scientific method.

Are Christians stuck, then, when it comes to rational debate? Do we have no way to answer the demand to "prove it"?

GOD'S UNDENIABLE PROOF

Some evidentialists (not all) do talk as if the Christian faith can be rationally proved to the satisfaction of anyone who will listen. Many websites boast that they present "undeniable proof that the Bible is true!"

But these presentations typically ignore very direct statements of Scripture: Paul said in Romans that the truth about God's power and existence can be "clearly seen" in the creation (Rom. 1:20 KJV), and yet some people deny it every day of their lives. Paul says they "suppress" it:

> The wrath of God is revealed from heaven against all ungodliness and unrighteousness of men, who by their unrighteousness suppress the truth. For what can be known about God is plain to them, because God has shown it to them. For his invisible attributes, namely, his eternal power and divine nature, have been clearly perceived, ever since the creation of the world, in the things that have been made. So they are without excuse. (Rom. 1:18–20)

If you can't "prove" the Christian faith to your atheist aunt, don't assume the trouble is with your command of the evidence. She's already denying the best evidence there is, the evidence God gave her. Creation is "undeniable proof." But because people's minds and hearts are fallen, they do in fact deny it. Paul says so. One day God will bring a proof so undeniable that "every tongue [will] confess that Jesus Christ is Lord" (Phil. 2:11). But for now He allows His image-bearers—breathing air He provides using lungs He designed—to deny that He exists.

Christians should point to evidence; God does. But they shouldn't have high hopes that their evidence and their arguments will be successful in winning over people who are determined not to believe. And that's most people, most of the time.

So one answer to the non-Christian's demand that we "prove it" is that God is already doing it, right now, everywhere, and yet people aren't listening.

> **GOD PROVES GOD**
>
> Jesus talked to a gathering of Jews about proof: "The Father who sent me has himself borne witness about me. His voice you have never heard, his form you have never seen, and you do not have his word abiding in you, for you do not believe the one whom he has sent" (John 5:37–38). Even God in flesh, Jesus Christ, ultimately appealed to the Father's authority when arguing that He was telling the truth. If people believe God, they'll believe His Son.

BY FAITH WE ALL UNDERSTAND

Some of the central claims of Christianity are impossible to "prove" if science (including the historical sciences) is the only way to achieve proof. Christians ought to feel free to admit that no scientific or historical test could ever confirm that Jesus died for our sins. We know that He did, but it is "by faith we understand" (Heb. 11:3). Ultimately, however, faith is how everyone understands anything. It's not just Christians who must rely, ultimately, on faith. It's scientists, atheists, spiritualists—everybody.

Some people are **empiricists**. In their view, only experience, regulated by the scientific method, can discover truth. But how can empiricists prove this? What experiment can they run to verify that the scientific method is the only way to know anything? How can the scientific method prove the validity of the scientific method?

Acceptable Circular Reasoning?

Circular reasoning takes place when a person restates his presupposition (which is what the debate is about) as his defense. It's also circular reasoning for him to defend his presupposition using an interpretation of the evidence that already presumes the truthfulness of the presupposition. How else would you interpret the evidence though? You would never purposefully contradict your presupposition in interpreting the evidence because that would be self-defeating. So everyone must resort to circular reasoning when defending foundational beliefs.

Circular reasoning is considered to be a logical fallacy because the conclusion is considered to be arbitrary. Beliefs should have justifiable reasons. But what if the belief is foundational? There's nothing more foundational to appeal back to. Is this basic belief arbitrary? Not when you can demonstrate the necessity of using the basic belief in order to make sense of anything. Rather than looking for a reason for the basic belief, look for the impossibility of not having that basic belief. In apologetics, this is called the impossibility of the contrary argument. For example, it is not logically possible to argue against the existence of logic since you must use logic in order to argue against it. It's like arguing against the existence of the floor while you are standing on the floor to make that argument.

This is not to deny that science is useful; it's only to note that empiricists have a very definite faith lying at the foundation of their worldview. They believe that true knowledge comes only through the five senses, aided by scientific tools.

Or take a worldview we could call "rationalism." **Rationalists** trust reason. For them, reason is the bedrock that all human knowledge rests on. And if you ask them how they know that reason determines what counts as proof, all they can do is give you a reason. But how could reason ever prove that reason is the only way to prove things? How can reason prove reason? It takes blind faith to be a rationalist.

Christians are not alone in basing their worldview on faith, but at least Christians can be honest about it. Christians believe that God counts as His own proof, and that He has spoken in the Bible. In the end, the worldview approach in this book is only saying that God doesn't need character references. He's the ultimate foundation for truth, a foundation not resting on anything else. This is an argument the Bible itself uses. "When God made a promise to Abraham, since he had no one greater by whom to swear, he swore by himself, saying, 'Surely I will bless you and multiply you'" (Heb. 6:13–14).

Every worldview is based ultimately on a foundation that is taken by faith. If you appeal to reason but refuse to appeal ultimately to God, then reason is the faith-based foundation that God (in your mind) rests on. If you think that experience can prove God independently from His Word, then the five senses are more ultimate than God is. If God really did speak in Scripture, what higher authority can we appeal to in order to tell us that God really did speak and that what He said was true?

Philosopher Bertrand Russell was once asked what he would say if, after death, he was questioned by God about why he hadn't believed. The famous atheist's reply? "Not enough evidence."[7] But if every worldview is based on faith, even Russell's materialist view, then the demand for more evidence is an insult to our Creator.

THE ROLE OF REASON AND EVIDENCE

Does the role of faith in Christianity—and in every worldview—eliminate the need for reason and evidence? Definitely not.

Reason

Reason is an incredibly valuable tool that God has given us for better understanding His Word and His world. Human reason is only problematic when it tries to become a judge standing above God's Word.

But even people whose intellects are not submitted to God often use their powers of reason to spot falsehood. For example, agnostic* philosopher Thomas Nagel demonstrates several logical problems with Neo-Darwinism in his book *Mind and Cosmos*.[8] Nagel simply points out that materialist explanations for human consciousness and values actually undermine our ability to have confidence in our reason—including the reasoning for Neo-Darwinism.

agnostic: *someone who says he does not know whether God exists*

Empiricists and rationalists are guilty of a vicious form of circular reasoning. It's like they are looking in a mirror with a mirror behind them. They see an infinite regression, and in the end all they're looking at is themselves.

The Values and Limitations of Evidence

Discuss what evidence can and can't do.

	EVIDENCE CAN SUPPORTIVELY . . .	**EVIDENCE ALONE CAN'T CONCLUSIVELY . . .**
Field of reference	Speak to physical, historical realities	Speak to spiritual significance
Means of arguing	Negate false physical or historical claims and uphold true physical or historical claims	Negate or uphold spiritual claims
Example	Refute the claim that "Moses didn't write the Pentateuch because writing hadn't been invented yet" or uphold the claim that "Hittites existed"	Validate claims such as "Moses was inspired by God" or "the Hittites were wiped out due to God's judgment on them"
Purpose	Correlate/fit with presuppositions	Prove/confirm/verify presuppositions

Evidence, Proof, and Persuasion

How does a person determine what qualifies as proof?

It's determined by one's belief about how knowledge can be obtained and established as reliable.

Some people measure reliability empirically: they insist on having physical means to test that knowledge. Others measure it based on rationalism: they require logical means to test it. Still others measure it based on experience: they want practical means to test it. In the end, proof is based on what a person accepts as most authoritatively reliable.

The Christian should endeavor to point out how all of those means, though valuable, are limited and prone to human fallibility. The Christian's measure of reliability is based on revelation from an omniscient and infallible authority source—God (Prov. 1:7).

How can a person be persuaded to accept God's revelation as the most reliable and authoritative basis for knowledge?

Ultimately, the Holy Spirit is the one who persuades through illumination and conviction in tandem with the power of God's Word with its presuppositions properly interpreting the evidence (Acts 17:4; 18:4).

Don't get that backwards by claiming that the evidence leads to the illumination of the Holy Spirit and acceptance of the Word. While you may need to offer the alternative scriptural interpretation of the evidence first, your goal must always be to lead someone to the Word as the basis for properly understanding that evidence.

Recommended Apologetics Resources

John Frame, *Apologetics to the Glory of God: An Introduction* (Phillipsburg, NJ: P&R Press, 1994).

Greg L. Bahnsen, *Always Ready: Directions for Defending the Faith*, ed. Robert R. Booth (Nacogdoches, TX: Covenant Media Press, 1996).

Richard L. Pratt Jr., *Every Thought Captive: A Study Manual for the Defense of Christian Truth* (Phillipsburg, NJ: P&R Press, 1979).

K. Scott Oliphint, *The Battle Belongs to the Lord: The Power of Scripture for Defending Our Faith* (Phillipsburg, NJ: P&R Press, 2003).

Experience, Experimentation, and Authority

A major part of philosophy involves investigating how people can reliably discover knowledge/truth. This branch of philosophy is called epistemology. There are several major options for determining the ultimate source of knowledge or truth so that we can be sure of it.

- *Experience or subjectivism:* This is the philosophy of existentialism. Fideism takes this route.

- *Experimentation and/or logical thought:* This is the philosophy of empiricism and rationalism. Evidentialism takes this route.

- *Authoritative revelation:* This is biblical philosophy. Worldview apologetics takes this route.

Experience, experimentation, and logic can provide some valuable knowledge, but they are all limited and often misinterpreted. They can't comprehensively confirm truth. God's revelation makes use of experience, experimentation, and logic. In fact, it doesn't dismiss any of that, but it does rule over all of it. As long as we consult the right authority source (i.e., the genuine revelation of God), we have access to the only Being in the universe who can comprehensively confirm the truth because He is truth (John 14:6). Human knowledge is only reliably true as long as it is analogous to God's thoughts (i.e., thinking God's thoughts after Him, but note Isa. 55:9). Without this comprehensive authority, you are only left with probabilities (the end result of modernism) or skepticism (the end result of postmodernism). But God will teach you knowledge (Ps. 119:66; Prov. 2:5; 28:26; Col. 2:3).

The Role of Reasoned Evidence

The believer can use evidence to refute the attacks of the unbeliever. Kick out from under him the support for his own wrong interpretations of evidence used as an excuse for denying the Bible. Clear up any misunderstandings; burn any straw-man arguments. Although this doesn't prove the Bible, it can prove wrong the reasons for rejecting it. Instead of searching for common ground, look for foundational flaws in the unbeliever's worldview. Challenge his unbelief by showing the inconsistencies in his worldview's explanation of evidence. Then present a biblical worldview. Evidence should always be presented in a supportive role to the presupposed authority source of God's Word; evidence should never be presented in a conclusive, self-referential role presupposing human intellectual autonomy.

Nagel's critique of Neo-Darwinism does not prove that Christianity is true, but it does point out serious problems with a worldview that has been a powerful enemy to the biblical one.

A Christian is totally free to use his reasoning powers to step into another worldview like Neo-Darwinism and ask questions like Nagel's. How is it that you can feel such strong moral opposition to genocide or child labor given your worldview? How can you say, if the world is a closed system of cause and effect, that anything is "wrong"? You can say you don't like it. You can say it's not likely to help humanity win the great battle of the survival of the fittest. But how can you justify calling anything truly "evil"? Surely a worldview in which you can't call something evil is not a worldview you want to live in.

Then invite unbelievers to look at the world from the Christian point of view. Encourage them to see how human values and morality flow from the fact that God created us out of love. This is a biblically faithful way to use reason.

Evidence

There are biblically faithful ways to use evidence too. Christians should believe God's Word because God is trustworthy, not (ultimately) because the evidence points to it being true. That would make evidence an authority over Scripture. But Christians should expect the world to be full of evidence for Scripture and the Christian worldview.

For instance, critics of the Bible used to see Daniel's claim that Belshazzar was king of Babylon as an error. All the historical records, the critics said, indicated that Nabonidus was the last king of Babylon prior to the Persians' arrival. Belshazzar's name didn't even appear in any Babylonian records. But then in 1854 (as well as again in the 1960s), archaeologists discovered documents that identify Belshazzar as Nabonidus's son. These documents in the form of clay cylinders mentioned that he participated in governing Babylon. The critics were silenced, sort of. They came up with new objections to Daniel, but at least they dropped that one.

Notice three little things about the use of evidence that we can learn from this story (and many others like it):

1. Evidence can play an important role in defending Scripture against attacks.
2. Evidence does not "prove" that the Bible is true. The Bible was true in its statements about Belshazzar long before 1854. The archaeologists' discoveries made that truth easier to defend, but they didn't "prove" the Bible.
3. The Bible's critics are like moles in a whack-a-mole game. Bop one on the head and another one will pop up instantly. Bop that one, and the first one is back up again. Evidence alone cannot persuade those who want to disbelieve. Nonetheless, God's Holy Spirit sometimes uses evidence from archaeology or history to diminish a person's resistance to accepting God's Word.

PROOF AND PERSUASION

There isn't one single method of proving the truth to every person. Paul used more than one approach to preach the one gospel (compare Acts 14:13–52 with Acts 17:22–34). The arguments you offer for the truth of Scripture can differ depending on your situation. There will be times when it's appropriate to tell stories of Christ's power over alcohol addiction. That might be a wise "proof" to offer. And there will be

---

times—depending on your gifting, your training, and the situation—when it will be wise to mention the work of a contemporary historian or archaeologist. But ultimately, the best thing is just to let God speak. At the very least, don't agree to silence Him before a discussion even begins. Go ahead and quote Scripture to non-Christians. God's Spirit goes with His Word. He is the only one, in the end, who can really persuade. He can use you as His tool to defend the Bible, but ultimately He is the only one who can reach into a person's heart and "prove it."

THINKING IT THROUGH 2.2

1. Why is evidence important even though it is limited?

2. What evidence for God's existence are all atheists denying even before they ever hear the gospel?

3. Why is faith a necessary element in every worldview?

4. What positive role can historical and scientific evidence play in the defense of the Christian faith?

♀5. What might be a wise "proof" of the Christian faith to offer to a wealthy businessperson who has no time for God? Or to a lonely widow?

2.3 DOUBT YOUR DOUBTS

Do you ever find yourself having doubts about the Christian faith?

Like personal, emotional doubts: *How could a loving God let this happen to me? How could I possibly be a true Christian when I just can't ever seem to win the battle against my lusts or my anger?*

Or like intellectual doubts: *How could the Bible be true when most of the smart, influential people out there think it's a myth or out of date? How come I can't get answers to all my questions?*

One wise Christian author has this advice for doubters: "Doubt your doubts."[9] And here's why you should: If you could find out all the facts about the young adults who have left your church or Christian school and then abandoned the Christian faith entirely, you'd likely notice something about them. They tend to fit in pretty well with the outside world. They might be hipsters* instead of goth* or preppy* instead of grunge,* but not one of them would have adopted the ancient animistic* beliefs of the Uyghur people of northwestern China.

This is not an accident, so doubt your doubts. If Americans leaving the church find TV-saturated, pop-music-inebriated atheistic secularism to be more attractive than Christianity, it's not because that worldview is truly a more intelligent choice than a biblical one. It's attractive to young people in the American church because so many people around them find it attractive—and because a heart with an agenda to live its own way will find a way to throw off God's authority. If they had been born into a Christian family in the Tarim Basin, surrounded by those Uyghurs, they'd probably find Uyghur animism attractive and plausible. So doubt your doubts.

But the truth can't be determined by majority vote—there are too many competing worldviews out there. No single one would be the clear winner.

hipster, goth, preppy, grunge: *four different subcultures each with its own fashion style*

animistic (n. animism): *believing that inanimate objects such as rocks, trees, and rivers have souls or spirits*

THINKING IT THROUGH 2.2

1. Christianity is rooted in historical realities; it's not merely a system of moralistic living.

2. the preaching of the gospel/Christ

3. Everyone must assume the validity of his own starting point. A person's starting point is always used to interpret the evidence in defense of his assumed starting point. (Circular reasoning is inescapable.)

4. It can prove that many of the attacks on Christianity are unfounded, and it can prove that many of the claims made by unbelievers are false.

♀5. Presenting the gospel persuasively doesn't always result in positive responses, but tailoring it to the rich man's situation or objections might mean that you need to pinpoint his idolatry as Jesus did with the rich young ruler. Prove to him that wealth is a bad exchange for the soul. For the lonely widow you may need to present the biblical answer to death and suffering.

---

1. Determine the underlying biblical explanation for why people leave the faith—spiritual deadness and idolatry.

2. Explain why belief must precede understanding and why faith is the necessary means of finding certainty.

3. Define *belief*, and explain why it must rest on the fear of the Lord.

The Head-Heart System

Remind the students about the first chapter's discussion of the head-heart system. A person's intellect never independently guides him to reject the faith. Such a rejection always involves someone's affections as well (Prov. 14:6; 15:14). If a person's heart is alive toward God and His glory, then his intellect will be informed by that (2 Cor. 4:6; Eph. 1:17; Col. 3:10). But if his heart is unresponsive toward spiritual things, then his intellect will be informed by that (Prov. 28:26; 1 Cor. 2:14; Job 21:7, 14). The dead affections may be shrouded in intellectual hang-ups, but ultimately a person rejects the faith because his dead and deceived heart is blinding his intellectual eyes to the truth (Ps. 53:1; Eph. 2:1–3; 4:17–18; 2 Cor. 4:4; 2 Tim. 3:7). You can't separate the head (intellect) from the heart (affections). People leave the faith due to what's attractive to their natural affections, not due to the intellectual superiority or certainty of another worldview (Prov. 1:20–33).

Doubt Is Unbelief

Discuss with students whether or not the advice to doubt everything before accepting anything is biblical advice.

Ours is an age in which we are told to doubt everything before accepting anything. This idea can be traced back to Enlightenment thinkers such as Rene Descartes, who doubted everything except the fact that he doubted—and was therefore sure he was thinking and must exist. But the idea can be traced further back. Satan's first temptation was to get Eve to doubt what God really said and to doubt God's pure motivations (Gen. 3:1–6). Jesus' advice to us is the exact opposite. He tells us to believe Him. Unbelief is a manifestation of a person's desire to continue in darkness (John 3:17–18, 36). If you lack understanding, the solution is to ask God for wisdom in faith—without the characteristic of double-minded doubting (James 1:5–8). Where can wisdom be found? Only in the fear of the Lord (Job 28:28).

Intellectual Rejections

According to the parable of the soils, some people reject the Word of God because of hard hearts that don't/won't understand the gospel (Matt 13:4, 18–19).

The Pharisees rejected the truth because they understood its implications very well. They would not admit to the truth Jesus knew they understood (John 8:39–47; Hos. 4:6; Acts 26:27–28).

The Greek philosophers of Athens rejected Paul's presentation of the gospel because their worldview couldn't intellectually fathom the resurrection of the dead (Acts 17:18–21, 30–34; cf. 1 Cor. 15:20–25). The intellectual "problem" would have been immediately removed if they had simply admitted the existence of the all-powerful Creator that Paul was preaching about.

Every intellectual reason for rejecting the gospel has an unsubmissive heart behind it (Prov. 28:26; Jer. 8:9).

Just Believe . . . as Opposed to What?

Beliefs involve the mind, the affections, and the will.

Mind: Belief involves the content that your intellect understands.

Belief can't exist apart from a comprehension of some knowledge (1 Thess. 2:13).

Affections: Belief involves the bent of your spirit that accepts the content understood by the intellect.

Belief can't exist apart from embracing acceptance of that knowledge (1 Thess. 2:13).

Will: Belief involves the choice to submit to and depend on the content that your spirit has accepted and your mind has understood.

Belief can't exist apart from actions that demonstrate your comprehension and acceptance (James 2:14–26; Titus 1:16).

When you believe with biblical faith, you apprehend (mind), accept (affections), and act (will) on the authoritative content communicated to you. Biblical faith is not arbitrary, mystical, or irrational.

Many secularists assume that belief is just a blind emotional acceptance without an intellectual evaluation of content. Therefore, they often contrast science with faith. This is actually a straw-man argument because it misrepresents what faith truly is. It excludes the cognitive aspect of true biblical faith while pretending that science does not rest on assumptions taken on authority.

This observable fact—that people believe all sorts of different things about the world—can be unsettling when you first encounter it. But trust the truth and doubt your doubts. This is exactly the situation the Bible would lead you to expect: when people suppress their knowledge of the one true God, they come up with all sorts of other idols to replace Him (Rom. 1:18–32).

YOU WANT PROOF?

People who doubt want proof. But it's precisely what you presuppose about God that determines what counts as "proof" for you. Do you want proof that the Bible is true? Proof that God exists? The author of the epistle to the Hebrews wrote,

> By faith we understand that the universe was created by the word of God, so that what is seen was not made out of things that are visible. (Heb. 11:3)

This is the Christian way of knowing truth: "by faith we understand." Faith comes before knowledge.

counterintuitive: something that seems absurd at first glance

This seems totally counterintuitive* to most Western people. You believe and then you understand? Isn't that backwards? Don't we understand and then believe? We look for evidence, and then we believe what we see. It seems wrong, even, to believe something before we see the evidence and make a judgment for ourselves. Atheist Richard Dawkins said, "Faith is the great cop-out, the great excuse to evade the need to think and evaluate evidence."[10]

But as this chapter has tried to persuade you to see, Richard Dawkins has faith-based presuppositions just like everyone else. And, interestingly enough, that phrase in Hebrews 11:3—"by faith we understand"—follows shortly after another phrase in which we see the Greek word for "evidence," "demonstration," or "proof." It's in a sentence you may have memorized:

> Now faith is the substance of things hoped for, the evidence of things not seen. (Heb. 11:1 KJV)

Note carefully what this verse is saying: "faith is . . . evidence." Another accurate way to translate the Greek here is, "Faith is . . . proof."

WE WALK BY FACT

A secularist will typically say that Christians live by faith while he lives by fact. But everyone lives by faith—the difference is what they have their faith in. The secularist has his faith, ultimately, in human reason. The Christian sees reason as a valuable tool, but only if it's submitted to its Creator.

It's a fact that the universe was created by the word of God—a knowable fact we can have evidence and proof for. But, ultimately speaking, faith is the means by which we get this all-important knowledge. The experience of your five senses (the basis of the scientific method) is important, but it's not enough. Neither is mere logic. Your five senses are very useful in bringing you all kinds of data, but they can't build you a tower all the way to heaven and give you some kind of scientific "proof" that God exists. There does come a point at which you must simply believe what Romans 1 says you already know: that God exists. If you want to understand—if you want proof—the Bible says, "Believe." And the chapter that says "by faith we understand," Hebrews 11, is called "The Hall of Faith" because it lists dozens of people who bucked their cultures and maintained a rock-solid belief in realities they couldn't see.

Abraham lived in a day when belief in one God seemed implausible to everyone—as implausible as the idea that science is the only way to achieve certainty (almost certainly, *nobody* in Abraham's day believed that). Abraham moved into a tiny minority in his world when he decided to believe what just about no one else did: "the Lord, he is God" (Ps. 100:3). What proof of God's existence could Abraham offer that would satisfy all the idol worshipers around him?

How Can Faith Be Proof?

If you presuppose a wrong understanding about faith (thinking that it is arbitrary, mystical, irrational, or blind), then you'll immediately react against the idea that faith could be any kind of substantive proof of anything. But that indicates a problem with your presupposition about what faith is.

Faith is always dependent on the object of that faith. If the object of your faith is reliable, then your faith is valid. In addition, faith doesn't exclude a rational understanding of substantive content or evidence (unless you're a fideist). The choice of faith isn't about excluding reasoned evidence from the equation; it's about where you place it in the equation.

- The atheist pretends to exclude faith altogether, but he is depending on authority sources beyond himself (fallible ones). He actually lives by faith too.

- The evidentialist places faith as an add-on at the end (feigning neutrality, not admitting he had faith in something all along).

- One who practices worldview apologetics is honest enough to say that faith in God's declarations is and ought to be the ultimate starting point. Faith in God's declarations of reality proves out and tests the evidence (not the reverse), correlating that evidence with God's declarations.

No Other Option but Faith

Remember, a presupposition is a basic belief that is foundational. That means no further foundational evidence can be given to justify it. So you cannot escape circular reasoning. The basic belief or presupposition is self-justifying or self-evidencing. As a result, you're left with no other option except to

And what does it mean to "prove" that God is what He says He is, anyway? If He's omniscient (all-knowing) and omnipotent (all-powerful)—then how can this be proved? If such a being exists, humans are too limited to discover if there are any limits to His knowledge. We're too weak to even be able to find out if He has all power. We're just going to have to take His word for it. We're going to have to believe.

TAKING TRUTH ON AUTHORITY

Modern Americans (and other heirs of the European intellectual tradition) simply must recognize that, when it comes to many, many truths we accept, we are all believing without seeing. It isn't just Christians who have presuppositions; it's everybody.

Take climate change. Is the earth warming? If so, are people causing it to warm? If it's warming because of human activities, is that bad? If the earth is warming and if this is bad, can humans do anything to cool it back down—or are we in the middle of some big global cycle we didn't cause and can't stop?

Now another question (answer honestly!): are you qualified to judge?

Are you a climate scientist with extensive knowledge of the complex computer-based weather modeling necessary to speak with authority on global climate change? Are you even one of the small minority of people in the world who have enough scientific knowledge to follow and evaluate those experts' arguments?

There are educated people who make good-faith efforts to read credible publications and reach informed decisions on these issues. But that's probably not most of us. Most people's belief or disbelief in climate change does not come from careful reading and study. Instead, asking people if they believe whether humans are responsible for global climate change really boils down to asking, "Which authorities do you accept?" In the United States, for example, belief in global climate change tends to follow political party lines.

You can, of course, go to the library, do some intensive Googling, or even travel around the world and look at the evidence for yourself. And these are important research skills you're now learning in school. But how long will it take you to have a truly informed opinion? Probably a good while: years of schooling and lots of hard study on your own. No one person can do that kind of work for every major issue facing society. There's not enough time in the day.

C. S. Lewis has a classic paragraph about this in his influential book *Mere Christianity*.

> Ninety-nine per cent of the things you believe are believed on authority. I believe there is such a place as New York. I have not seen it myself. I could not prove by abstract reasoning that there must be such a place. I believe it because reliable people have told me so. . . . A man who jibbed* at authority in other things as some people do in religion would have to be content to know nothing all his life.[11]

jib: *to draw back like a harnessed horse that doesn't want to move forward*

C.S. Lewis

TRUSTING THE TRUTH

One of the authors of this textbook faced a crisis in his own faith during his senior year of college. He didn't doubt that, if the Bible is true, he himself was a child of God. He just began to doubt that the Bible is truly God's Word. It was largely Romans 1 that helped him to reestablish a firm faith in the God of the sixty-six books of the Bible. Romans 1 says that God's eternal power and divine nature are clearly visible in the creation. And indeed, it seemed obvious to this doubter that the beautiful, awesome creation—from the biggest redwood tree to the smallest microbe on its bark—simply could not have come from nothing as many modern scientists believe.

---

trust the authority that declared the axiomatic statement. There are, in fact, only two options for this bedrock of authority—God's authoritative testimony or humanity's collective autonomous thinking. That leaves only two ways to arrive at the surety of the truth: trust the infinite, all-knowing God who tells you what is true or trust finite humans who think they can figure it all out on their own without God. Believers choose the first option, and unbelievers choose the second. That doesn't mean that believers simplistically resort to blind faith while unbelievers rely on solid scientific evidence. Everybody must have faith—either in God or in humanity/self. Based on that starting point, the evaluation and understanding of the evidence commences.

The Will to Believe

If understanding requires belief and belief requires a submissive spirit and will, then how can you obtain that submissive spirit and will? Only through the fear of the Lord.

The beginning of knowledge is the fear of the Lord (Prov. 1:7). When you have the fear of the Lord, your spirit and will submit to Him. In that submission you are able to rely on Him as the trustworthy authority for interpreting all data/evidence. When you trust Him as the authoritative source of knowledge as you form your presuppositions, then you will properly understand the significance of the evidence.

The Lord must work in your heart system, which is intertconnected with your head system, before you can begin to really understand anything properly. You may be able to understand a lot of details without having the fear of the Lord, but you won't know how to understand those details properly (i.e., prioritizing them into a coherent worldview system).

The Relationship Between Faith and Reason

Demonstrate how faith can precede knowledge without dismissing the value of rational thinking.

What are the options?

• *Reason without faith*

Adherents: Many secular philosophers, atheists, agnostics

Problem: Truth is based on autonomous human thinking, but mankind is finite, fallible, and fallen.

• *Faith without reason*

Adherents: Fideists, Neo-Orthodox theologians, Mormons

Problem: Truth is subjectively based on personal, mystical experiences or "encounters" with God rather than the rational, objective content of God's revelation.

• *Reason over faith* (reason as the platform/ basis for faith)

Adherents: Evidentialists, many Roman Catholics, many interpreters of Aquinas

Problem: Truth may be rooted in God's revelation but must be confirmed as such by autonomous human investigations. But mankind is finite, fallible, and fallen. This approach presumes too much about people's ability to overcome their fallenness to come to faith; it downplays the effects of the Fall on the intellect. They think that examination and understanding of the evidence lead to a work of the Holy Spirit illuminating one's eyes to come to the faith, but this is backwards.

• *Faith over reason* (faith as the platform/ basis for reason)

Adherents: Christians who engage in worldview apologetics, Augustine

Solution: The ultimate standard for determining truth is God's Word (John 17:17). Only submission to its truth claims can open up the understanding of everything else. The moral fallenness of individuals prevents them from accepting the truth even when it is perfectly explained to them (1 Cor. 2:6; John 8:39–47). But the work of the Holy Spirit illuminating people's minds leads to a proper examination and understanding of the evidence.

[Jason Lisle, "Faith vs. Reason," Answers in Gensis (website), May 19, 2013]

THINKING IT THROUGH 2.3

1. whatever worldview is (1) most prevalent around them and (2) most pleasurable to their affections

2. Believing is seeing because faith opens the eyes of understanding. Certain knowledge of the truth comes only from faith in God's Word (Heb. 11:1–3).

3. Personally proven knowledge of every single issue in the world that's in question is beyond any single person's ability. Everyone must trust someone else's claims by faith.

4. He confronted Job with the fear of the Lord.

♀5. Answers will vary but may include the following:

- any historical accounts, especially from ancient times

- different kinds of technical knowledge (e.g., working scientific models of climate change, working economic models, etc.)

- knowledge of foreign places they've never been to

- medical advice from doctors

- literary critiques that determine what is good/classic literature/the classics

---

In the end, on many significant issues, you're going to have to look to some experts. You're going to have to take answers to important questions on someone else's authority. If we have to accept truth on authority all the time anyway, what is so strange about accepting God's authority?

You don't defend a lion. You just let it out of its cage. So said the eloquent preacher Charles Spurgeon. He was talking, of course, about the Bible.

Now this is a book defending the Bible. And the Bible itself calls on us to be ready to answer non-Christians' questions—and to be as persuasive as we can be (1 Pet. 3:15). But Spurgeon was on to something important. Quite frequently the Bible needs no defense; it just needs to be let out of its cage. The Bible carries the authority of its Author, and He can answer—or silence—objections as He sees fit.

When we have hard questions about the world, about our own pain, about truth, the Bible is not shy in giving us answers. And faithful men and women in the Bible were not too shy to ask God hard questions.

Think about Job. If anyone had good reasons to ask, "Why, God?" it was Job. As one author put it, "Job believes in the moral order, but in his case God has repaid good with evil, and this throws his worldview into crisis."[12]

God could have provided Job with reasons to trust His goodness and power. He does this, in fact, in many places in Scripture: "God is our refuge and strength, a very present help in trouble" (Ps. 46:1).

But God doesn't have to do this, or at least not in the way we demand. And in Job's case, He didn't. At the end of the book of Job, God basically said, "I am Creator; you are creature. That should be reason enough to trust My power and goodness." Then in the New Testament, Paul raises what is probably the most difficult question in theology: "[If God] hardens whomever he wills . . . , 'Why does he still find fault?'" (Rom. 9:18–19). And God's answer is similar to what He said to Job: "Who are you, O man, to answer back to God? Will what is molded say to its molder, 'Why have you made me like this?'" (Rom. 9:20). These are reasons to trust God, but they don't explain everything we might want to know—Job presumably died without ever knowing why he had suffered so much.

ULTIMATE AUTHORITY

"I'll believe it when I see it" may sound like a pretty defensible, unobjectionable thing to say. But as our Creator, God is allowed to determine what counts as proof. He's allowed to demand that we simply trust Him, that we take truth ultimately on His authority. He's allowed to expect us to make His words our starting presupposition. The fear of the Lord *is* the beginning of knowledge.

THINKING IT THROUGH 2.3

1. If young people in your church or Christian school abandon the Christian faith, which worldview do you think they're likely to adopt instead?

2. Biblically speaking, is seeing believing, or is believing seeing?

3. Why is faith in some authority unavoidable?

4. How did God confront Job's faltering faith?

♀5. List five things that most people in your culture believe on the authority of others rather than from their own direct experience.

CHAPTER REVIEW ANSWERS

Making Connections

1. bias or presuppositions; because they believe that neutrality is necessary for a fair examination of the data/evidence; they think that once common ground has been established as a starting point, they can then begin to persuade others to switch sides based on the evidence.

2. The morality of knowledge, human finitude, and model-making demand presuppositions for examining data.

3. You can't become an expert in everything. Ultimately even the experts are finite, fallen, and fallible, so the only possibility for a perfectly trustworthy authority is God.

4. by having faith rooted in the fear of the Lord

2 CHAPTER REVIEW

Scripture Memory

Hebrews 11:3

Making Connections

1. What do evidentialists seek to eliminate? Why?

2. Explain why presuppositions are inescapable.

3. Explain why truth must be taken on authority.

4. What's the first step, according to the Bible, in getting true knowledge?

Developing Skills in Apologetics and Worldview

5. How could sharing your personal testimony of the Holy Spirit's work in your life add to your conversation with an unbeliever?

6. How could you help friends who believe in evolution to recognize ways their worldview lenses are influencing their interpretation of the scientific evidence?

Examining Assumptions and Evidence

7. Why must all knowledge be moral?

8. What authority source do empiricists presuppose? What about rationalists?

9. What role does evidence play in the pursuit of truth? What can and can't it do?

10. Is there anyone who has merely intellectual objections to the gospel? Explain.

Becoming a Creative Cultivator

11. Listen to a debate between a Christian and an unbeliever. Write a one-page paper in which you do the following:

☐ identify the apologetic approach the Christian most closely exemplified

☐ evaluate the benefits of that approach

☐ evaluate the drawbacks of that approach

☐ offer any alternative or additional arguments the Christian could have used

true knowledge of God whenever they examine any data.

8. Empiricists ultimately rely on their own experience and the five senses; rationalists rely on their own reasoning.

9. Evidence can be used to falsify the attacks of unbelievers. It may be useful to defend some of the claims of believers. It can never definitively prove the Bible.

10. Fallen heart desires conform to mainstream fallen society (the world), influencing the intellectual evaluations to reject biblical interpretations of the evidence.

Becoming a Creative Cultivator

11. (See TE page 472 for a rubric.)

Here are a couple of debates that would work well for this assignment:

Bahnsen vs. Stein: The Great Debate (worldview apologetics example)

Ken Ham vs. Bill Nye (worldview apologetics example)

Gary Habermas or William Lane Craig debates (evidential examples)

TERMS TO REMEMBER

presupposition—an idea you have in your head before you look at evidence [simplistic definition from the Student Text, which is actually just an assumption]; an informed basic belief that is self-evidencing [the definition of a true presupposition from the Teacher's Edition]

evidentialists—those who attempt to defend the Christian faith without the bias of presuppositions, assuming that data drawn from history and experience can, by itself, demonstrate the reasonableness of Christian claims

model—a set of theories in which all data is made to fit for proper interpretation

worldview apologetics—a method that attempts to defend the Christian faith by forcing people to examine their own presuppositions, which influence their interpretation of all the data and their experiences

proof—an undeniable answer to those who question the validity of something

empiricists—those who hold the view that only experience, regulated by the scientific method, can bring truth

rationalists—those who hold the view that reason is the bedrock on which all human knowledge rests

Developing Skills in Apologetics and Worldview

5. Your testimony is a simple way to engage others with the personal nature of salvation, and it's a platform for sharing the simple gospel message. The truthfulness of the message is not based on your personal experience any more than a Mormon's testimony of a changed life proves Mormonism's truthfulness. Genuine salvation will produce a changed life, but moral reform doesn't prove genuine salvation. Gospel truths are self-attesting. Your life should not undermine those truth claims, but your testimony does not provide airtight proof that the Bible is true.

6. • Clarify what they mean by scientific investigations (i.e., observe, test, repeat).

• Clarify what they mean by evolution. Whereas macroevolution involves a change of kinds, microevolution occurs in adaptation.

• Clarify that young-earth creationists accept microevolution (adaptation within a kind) but reject macroevolution (a change of one kind to another kind).

• Challenge them to offer an example of macroevolution not microevolution.

• Challenge them to examine if any of those observations are actual direct observations, testable and repeatable with no outside designer manipulating things. Or are they all indirect inferences based on presuppositions?

Examining Assumptions and Evidence

7. Nobody begins neutral. Reasoning is part of the image of God, which is fallen; all people naturally suppress the

CHAPTER 3 OBJECTIVES

The student will be able to

3.1 Analyze the two-story view.

3.2 Explain why the two-story view fails.

3.3 Defend the claim that CFR is the best way to outline a Christian worldview.

SECTION OBJECTIVES 3.1

1. Summarize what the two-story view is.

2. Explain why the two-story view seems attractive to many Christians.

3. Explain why the two-story view seems attractive to many secularists.

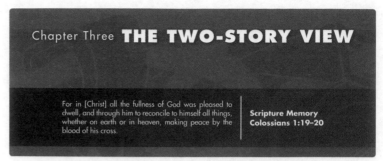

Chapter Three **THE TWO-STORY VIEW**

For in [Christ] all the fullness of God was pleased to dwell, and through him to reconcile to himself all things, whether on earth or in heaven, making peace by the blood of his cross.

Scripture Memory Colossians 1:19–20

3.1 THE TWO-STORY VIEW

There are various ways to win an intellectual debate. The good ways all involve diligently researching the topic and carefully listening to your opponent(s). But there are other ways to win—like diligently knocking your opponent down and carefully taking his lunch. Playground bullies typically employ the latter approach. And so, sometimes, do worldviews.

Minority worldviews are the ones that can expect to experience bullying, and right now, despite large numbers of people claiming to be Christians around the world, the biblical worldview is a minority pretty much everywhere. So, along with other minorities, it sometimes finds itself lunchless.

One example is Nathaniel Abraham, a Christian biologist (an expert on zebrafish) who says he was fired by Woods Hole Oceanographic Institute because he refused to admit that Darwinian evolution was scientific fact. In similar cases major universities have denied career advancement to Christians, and sometimes it can be difficult to figure out whether their belief in creationism was a factor or not. But Woods Hole, a federally funded research center, didn't deny Abraham's claim; they admitted that he was fired for his creationism. They simply alleged that belief in evolution was a necessary component of his job.

Don't get *too* alarmed. Christians in the Western world are not facing violent persecution, or at least not yet. Few are losing their jobs because of their faith. But the intellectual climate in most places is not friendly to biblical Christianity. If Christians aren't being fired from high-profile academic or political jobs, it may be because they're not getting them in the first place (or because they aren't working in a way that's distinctively Christian).

This is not new. Christians have always faced challenges to their worldview. The ancient Romans actually accused Christians of being atheists because they didn't believe in the gods of the Roman pantheon.* Greek philosophers laughed at the idea that God became man, died for human sin, and rose from the dead. Christians today should not be surprised when the biblical worldview creates friction with the popular worldviews around it—or when that friction makes sparks fly.

THE MORAL MINORITY

The biblical worldview is a minority position all around the globe (though not necessarily in all portions of history), even in so-called "Christian" nations since not all self-professed Christians have a biblical worldview. When pollsters ask Americans what they believe, only a small percentage give answers that really agree with what the Bible teaches. And most of the biggest names in academia, the media, politics, and entertainment—the influential people of this world—are not Christians. For example, 62 percent of philosophy professors are atheists.[1]

pantheon: *all the gods of a particular nation*

Lesson Plan Chart—Chapter 3

Section Title	Pages	Activity Manual	Days
3.1 The Two-Story View	32–35	Activity 5	1 day
3.2 Critiquing the Two-Story View	35–41		2 days
3.3 Creation, Fall, Redemption	41–44	Activity 6	2 days
Review	45		1 day
Total Suggested Days			**6 days**

 Expelled: No Intelligence Allowed

Ben Stein, a well-known conservative and eccentric humorist, hosted a documentary titled *Expelled: No Intelligence Allowed* that exposes the intolerance of academia, the media, and the courts toward any who refuse to embrace evolution—even supporters of the non-Christian intelligent design movement. If time permits, you may wish to show it to students.

 Lessons from the Persecuted

Students may learn a lot of practical wisdom from the real-life examples of Christians who have endured persecution. In addition to the biblical illustrations (Rom. 1:16; Heb. 11:24–40; 2 Cor. 4:7–18), *Foxe's Book of*

INTIMIDATION

Even if intellectual opposition doesn't come as a surprise, it's easy for Christians to be intimidated by the hostility they sense in the academic world. And the easiest way to avoid conflict is to just give the bully your lunch. When the most powerful force on the intellectual playground says religion doesn't belong there, some Christians hand over their baloney sandwich, apple, and juice box, and slink away from the slides and monkey bars where the bullies like to play.

COURTEOUS BULLIES

It's not that individual non-Christian scholars are all intellectual bullies; it's that most Western academics have accepted rules for their disciplines that exclude the influence of the Bible. Christian scholar Lesslie Newbigin, speaking at the University of Cambridge in England, told this story: "A Ph.D. student in this university recently wrote to me with the following problem: he had submitted the outline for his proposed dissertation. It had been accepted by his [academic] supervisor except for one chapter which he was told to remove, since it dealt with matters of faith, not of fact, and was therefore inadmissible. Faith is one thing, facts are something else."[2]

The student gave no indication that the supervisor was mean about it; Cambridge simply exists within a community that doesn't allow religion on certain parts of its playground. Western secular scholarship as an institution has therefore "bullied" Christianity, even if individual scholars do it courteously.

This climate of intimidation is one big reason why some Christians drift into thinking that the Christian life is only about spiritual things—such as Bible reading, prayer, helping those in need—and not about science, politics, and academics. It's easier to leave that territory to the secularist majority. And some Christians go a step further: they start seeing science, politics, and the intellect as part of a so-called **secular*** realm that should be kept separate from the sacred parts of life.

secular: *pertaining to the world and not religion, nonreligious*

Christians generally make this separation with some good motivations in their hearts. They do it in order to protect the sacred things they value. They think that by keeping their religion away from the playground where everybody else is, science and politics will play nice and let them keep their lunch.

Another big reason why some Christians leave the playground is that they see the moral corruption there. They feel that if they focus on spiritual things like Bible reading, prayer, and doing good to all people, they can avoid being contaminated by the moral mess of modern life. They see studying science or literature, engaging in politics, or writing for newspapers as dangerous. Secular activities, they feel, are best avoided because they are morally tainted by the influence of non-Christians. Such Christians divide the world in two not so much to protect their religion as to protect themselves.

But when you sort religion and science, or religion and politics, or religion and education into two separate compartments, you create some real problems. For one, you are guilty of applying an improper **dualism***—dividing in two what God has made one.

dualism: *dividing something into two opposing parts*

Some Christian worldview thinkers have used a two-story house as an illustration of this dualism. Dualists keep science, math, and everyday life in the lower story. For them, Bible reading, prayer, and the spiritual life go in the top floor, the upper story.

THE TWO-STORY VIEW | 033

Martyrs and many other biographies recap the lives of believers who had an exemplary commitment to Christ. You may want to read some excerpts.

The Intolerance of Tolerance

D. A. Carson, in his book *The Intolerance of Tolerance* [Grand Rapids: Eerdmans, 2013], distinguishes between two definitions of tolerance. The old definition allowed for different positions in the public square and vigorous debate among parties that hold firmly to their respective positions. The new definition demands that all parties concede the potential validity of all positions. Therefore, any position that takes an unequivocal stand on absolute truth tends to be excluded from the conversation. Defenders of absolute, transcendant, revealed truth can't even defend their position because, by definition, it violates the new tolerance. This contemporary perspective on tolerance is known as a defeater belief—a belief that, once popularized as common sense, makes other beliefs seem ridiculously implausible, ruling out by fiat any vigorous debate or the examination of assumptions.

Carson adeptly exposes the intolerance of this new tolerance with a multiplicity of illustrations. Under the guise of antidiscrimination laws and new social standards, religious truth is limited to the private sphere. The autonomous human reasoning of postmodern relativism bullies the religious revelation of truth out of the public square. It allows for the absolutes of modernism only in certain areas such as science and math.

So how should Christians respond? At the end of his book (161–76), Carson offers some practical tips for engaging the "new tolerance": challenge its false claim to neutrality and its claim of progress toward a higher morality; expose its arrogant claims about the unequivocal goodness of all diversity; "preserve a place for truth"; model civility especially in disagreement; evangelize; "be prepared to suffer"; and "delight in and trust God." More may be gleaned from this book by guiding students through Activity 5 in the student activity manual.

Responding to Persecution

Discuss the reality of persecution. Jesus said the world would hate and persecute believers just as it hated and persecuted Him. But He has not left believers alone; He provides them with the Holy Spirit (John 15:18–27; 1 Pet. 4:12–19).

What is God's purpose in persecution?

Persecution tests and refines all who claim to follow Him, purifying the church from pretenders (1 Pet. 1:3–9; 2 Tim. 4:10).

How should Christians respond?

Follow Jesus' example (1 Pet. 2:21–23). Do good to enemies (Rom. 12:14, 19–21). Be thankful for being counted worthy to suffer (Acts 5:41; 1 Thess. 5:18; Heb. 10:34). Strive against the wicked (Prov. 28:4), and obey God when pressured to give in to unrighteousness (Prov. 25:26).

Why does God's final judgment provide Christians with future hope?

Although the Christian should pray that his persecutors will repent and receive forgiveness (Matt. 5:44; Luke 23:34), God promises final justice (2 Thess. 1:5–12) and great reward (Matt. 5:10–12; James 1:12; Rev. 6:9–11).

Summarize the Two-Story View

Students should be able to summarize the three significant aspects that make up the two-story view.

The framework: The two-story view compartmentalizes life into two major floors—the secular bottom story of objective facts and the sacred upper story of subjective beliefs and values.

The furnishings: Different aspects of life fit on one floor or the other. For example, science, politics, and business fit on the secular public floor while church, scriptural revelation, and morality fit on the private sacred floor.

The blocked stairway: The sacred and secular floors seldom interfere with each other. In extreme cases, they don't even interact.

Why Conservative Christians May Be Attracted to the Two-Story View

Many conservative Christians have biblical concerns about the way unregenerate culture can influence proper worship and devotion to God both in the church and in everyday life. These concerns gain credibility from the reality that many Christians who have sought to be mission-minded and to contextualize the Christian faith in order to engage and infiltrate the culture have abandoned faithful Christian living or orthodoxy. This creates a temptation for many Christians to retreat, abandoning most of God's creational structures to the unregenerate culture. This response, however, is simply another way of conceding to secularization.

 ## Why Secularists Are Attracted to the Two-Story View

Since the time of Enlightenment humanism, man has been viewed as the measure of all things. That means that autonomous human reason stands as the authoritative standard by which all truth claims must be judged. Since revelation has been discounted as subjective and unverifiable, relativism reigns. Thus, religious beliefs, values, and morality must be partitioned off into one's own subjective personal inner life. The public square only tolerates objective scientific facts verified by what man himself considers reasonable. Biblical truth and values, since they often conflict with that which secular people deem reasonable, are removed from the public square. In a nation that guarantees religious freedom, some place must be reserved for that liberty. However, the only place reserved for the sacred is in the private realm. Thus, religion isn't allowed to make any substantive contribution in the public square unless it submits to secular aims.

[Hunter Baker, *The End of Secularism* (Wheaton, IL: Crossway, 2009)]

Descartes and Dualism

Descartes dichotomized revelation and reason in his *Discourse on the Method and Meditations* [trans. by E. S. Haldane and G. R. T. Ross (Mineola, NY: Dover Philosophical Classics, 2003), 7–8]. Though he spoke respectfully of theology, his approach indicated he did not believe it to be a reliable foundation for verifiable knowledge. Descartes's conclusions, and even some of his arguments, were not novel. But his method placed authority not in revelation or tradition but in one's own rationality. This was a radical innovation that resulted in creating

---

THE TWO-STORY VIEW IN THE SECULAR WEST

This two-story way of thinking about the world is popular not only with Christians. It is actually the dominant view of the secularized West in general. Simply put, secularists view post-Reformation (after 1520) Western European history as a bloody chronicle of religious wars. For example, the Protestants and Catholics who began the Thirty Years' War (1618–1648) both professed (as Abraham Lincoln would later put it about the American Civil War) to pray to the same God and read the same Bible. But that didn't stop them from slaughtering one another; it spurred them on.

intelligentsia: the politically influential and powerful intellectuals in any given group

The exhausted European intelligentsia* of the time began to look for a neutral way to solve conflicts before religion turned them into bloodbaths. When religion walks into the public square, everyone's temperature rises, and the guns and knives come out—or at least that's what Western elites thought. So, they concluded, it's better to just keep religion upstairs.

The two-story view places churchy and religious stuff on top and real-life stuff below. The implication is that real-life stuff can't be holy and that true Christians will spend as little time in the lower story as possible.

European intellectual René Descartes (reh-NAY day-KART) was one of these elites. In his quest for a neutral foundation for knowledge, he determined to doubt everything he couldn't know for certain, to dig down in his knowledge until he reached a bedrock level that no one could doubt or disagree with. His famous statement, "I think, therefore I am" (*cogito ergo sum*, sometimes called "the cogito") was the result. He was, in fact, a dedicated, churchgoing Roman Catholic. So it's all the more significant that he did not say, "God speaks, therefore I know." He started with himself: "*I* think."

Reason, he argued, could provide a neutral starting point for human knowledge. Subsequent Enlightenment philosophers believed that they could then build on that foundation and arrive at truth all humans could agree on. Religious disagreements could go on in the private world of the upper story, but religious wars—which happen in the public world of the lower story—could end.

aesthetics: "a set of principles concerned with the nature and appreciation of beauty, esp. in art" (New Oxford American Dictionary)

Secularists thus have their own **two-story view** of the world. The "lower story" is where most Western people put science, math, and the facts—stuff (they think) we can really know for sure. Everything else, stuff we can't really know, goes in the "upper story." That's where many people in our culture place religion, morals, and aesthetics*. It isn't just beauty (aesthetics) that's in the eye of the beholder; bioethics and Buddhism (morals and religion) have to go there too.

---

a fact/value dichotomy that distinguishes between what reason can verify and religious opinions. Dutch theologians objected to Descartes's method of systematic doubt as a violation of the first commandment and a suppressing of general revelation. [Theo Verbeek, *Descartes and the Dutch* (Carbondale: Southern Illinois University Press, 1992), 23].

 ## Evaluating the Presuppositions of the Two-Story View

Challenge students to identify the flawed presupposition of the two-story view that has especially permeated society since the Enlightenment. [Clue: The flaw concerns the nature of knowledge and how it is come by (called epistemology in philosophy).]

The flawed presupposition is the belief that there is a neutral starting point for at least some, if not all, human knowledge. That starting point is identified as one's own reason gained independently of any other outside authority source. If human reason is neutral and independent, then the disciplines of knowledge, such as science and literature, and spheres of knowledge, such as politics and education, will be treated as neutral and cut off from the authority of revelation.

Why is this a fundamentally flawed presupposition?

Humans are fallen and not neutral—this includes their reasoning faculties. Humans are limited and dependent on authoritative sources outside themselves to verify knowledge.

The two-story view of the secular West can be diagrammed like this:[3]

UPPER STORY

PRIVATE SPHERE personal preferences	VALUES individual choice	NONRATIONAL noncognitive

LOWER STORY

PUBLIC SPHERE scientific knowledge	FACTS binding on everyone	RATIONAL verifiable

This isn't all just theory. You've seen it. You know from experience that this is how most people in the West view the world. Suppose you are a senator in the Congress of the United States. You just know that "teens shouldn't have premarital sex because teen pregnancy is associated with lower high school graduation rates" is an acceptable argument to present in a debate in the Senate. Other senators may dispute the research you cite, but they won't dispute your strategy of citing it. But you also know that "God says sex before marriage is wrong" is *not* an acceptable argument in the Senate. Other senators won't dispute your Bible interpretation; they'll reject your argument simply because you cited the Bible or God. You know that as soon as you cite the Bible in any significant disagreement in the public square,* you'll be escorted up the stairs to the second story and told that you have to quit trying to impose your religion on the rational, scientifically verifiable facts downstairs in the living room. You're supposed to keep your religion private because it's not a public fact; it's just an unverifiable, unknowable personal preference.

> **public square:** a metaphor referring to all the many places (books, magazines, newspapers, the Internet, city halls, courtrooms, Congress) where issues are debated publicly

THINKING IT THROUGH 3.1

1. Summarize the two-story view.

2. Why do many Christians separate the "sacred" from the "secular"?

3. Why do many secularists separate the "sacred" from the "secular"?

4. How should Christians respond to bullying?

♡ 5. Provide two examples of two-story view thinking that you have observed. Include examples from both Christian and secular sources.

3.2 CRITIQUING THE TWO-STORY VIEW

The two-story view is wrong, but it isn't *all* wrong. There's something in it worth saving. To find out what it is, we'll have to look at two versions of the two-story view, the secular version and the Christian version.

THE SECULAR TWO-STORY VIEW

First, the secular. Every year on the first Thursday in February, American religion and politics get together for a prominent and well-attended event called the National Prayer Breakfast.

---

opposing religious organizations or religious morality in the public square while seeking to promote their own values in society.

THINKING IT THROUGH 3.1

1. It divides life into a secular realm of objective facts and a sacred realm of subjective beliefs and values. These realms should not interfere with each other or even interact.

2. They are intimidated by secularism but want to protect the sacred things they value and/or want to protect themselves from corrupting influences.

3. They think we can solve public conflicts by dismissing the "subjective" sacred realm in favor of "objective" human reason.

4. They should follow Jesus' example; bless their enemies; strive against the wicked; obey God.

♡ 5. Answers may vary.

SECTION OBJECTIVES 3.2

1. Explain why secularists are being inconsistent when they attempt to remove religious values from the public square.

2. Evaluate what happens when a person tries to isolate the sacred from the secular: failure to protect the faith and the faithful.

3. Evaluate what happens when a person tries to equate the secular with the sacred: failure to maintain reverence and purity.

Whose Values?

"We shouldn't leave our values at the door." Whose values? What values? The melting pot of the United States used to be composed of diverse people who shared similar values, informed by Scripture, even if the individuals were not believers. This morality seemed to be obvious—the commonsense laws of nature or of God's created order. But now the nation is a mosaic of peoples with few shared values. Laws of nature don't seem obvious. So what happens when divergent groups all bring their own conflicting values to the table? A society without shared values will fragment. Opposing value systems cause gridlock or the loss of individual freedoms as the powerful foist their own value system on others.

What's the solution? Many people believe that it's best to leave values at the door—sector them out of the public square into the privacy of individual lives. Libertarians try

---

What is the correct authority for human knowledge?

God's infallible revelation received in the fear of the Lord rules over all human reason, disciplines, and spheres of knowledge.

Clarify that this position doesn't reject the use of reason; it puts it in its proper place. Reason must not function as an authority, but it must be used as an instrument under the authority of Scripture.

In addition, clarify that the knowledge of the so-called upper story is rational, but the means of obtaining it is achieved through a different methodology from the knowledge of the so-called lower story. Beliefs and values often come through the rational use of deductive reasoning. This type of reasoning is categorized as philosophical or theological thinking; it is thinking that reasons from

general principles derived from a source of authority—divine revelation for the believer. Scientific knowledge is derived from inductive empirical experimentation that reasons back to generalizations. The generalizations are always influenced and interpreted by presupposed beliefs and values from philosophical/theological thinking. Secularists often hide their own philosophical presuppositions but criticize religious people for being honest about their starting points.

 The Two-Story View in Your Culture

Since the two-story view is a faulty paradigm of reality, we shouldn't expect it to work in real life. Those who would have us divide the sacred from the secular are always inconsistent. Students should look for current events that demonstrate secularists

to be the most consistent in this approach. But eliminating moral legislation is impossible because neutrality is a myth. This approach simply props up secular values as the only option. But secularism isn't religiously neutral. Every law, every policy, every fact must be based on interpretations that are guided by one's religious worldview values. A society that tries to function apart from moral values will of necessity smuggle another set of values back into the discourse.

The wedding of morality and freedom works when both are rooted in the norms of God's created order. Disjoining these can only lead to the tyranny of the majority (a pure democracy) or anarchy (everyone doing right in his own eyes). The book of Judges warns what the latter will be like. The Founding Fathers explicitly feared a pure democracy ("Federalist No. 10"); they favored rule by law. As long as secular pluralism retains its monopoly in the public square, any attempt to reunite around the transcendant values of creational norms will be impossible. But that's the only solution.

 ## Religious Values in the Public Square?

Have the students debate the legitimacy of legislating morality in the public square. The two opposing sides should address the following questions:

(1) Does legislating morality demand some kind of illegitimate religious coercion?

Points to consider: Every form of government legislates some kind of morality based on its understanding of what is right and what is wrong. God's purpose for government is to enforce justice (Rom. 13:1–8); governments must be informed by values to know what is just. Only biblical principles truly reflect the norms and design of God's created realities in this world. As a non-theocratic society, the United States flourished for two centuries guided by these biblical values under the older definition of tolerance. The possibility of a world free of any kind of coercion is a fantasy that only leads to anarchy. There are good and proper ways for a nation to set the tone for what is acceptable and what will not be tolerated in its culture. God designed people to submit to the authority of government, not to be free from any incentives toward righteousness.

(2) Is it possible to legislate anything without values or a moral standard?

Points to consider: Everyone has a worldview. Every worldview is made up of a head-

heart system of beliefs and values. Your values guide all your decisions; every decision a person makes reveals his worldview values. Values are inescapable. Conflicting worldviews are inescapable. Neutrality is a myth. For many years the secularist worldview has tried to hide its values, pretending to resolve all conflicts. Now the secularists are demanding a new morality, demonizing Christian values as immoral, and accusing those who hold to those values of committing crimes against humanity (e.g., hate speech). Secularism is now causing greater conflict. Secularism doesn't eliminate coercion; it introduces a new kind of coercion—persecution of Christians.

Values Can't Be Eliminated

Secular pluralism can only lead to inconsistency. Whenever it calls for the elimination of a religious moral value from the public square, it always enforces an opposite moral value. This reversal of values isn't new. Isaiah 5:20 comes in the middle of a culminating discourse that details God's many judgments on a rebellious people. In those devastating days in Israel, the land was filled with people who called good evil and evil good. Values did not disappear; they were simply turned upside down.

Every president since Eisenhower has attended the prayer breakfast, and when Barack Obama got his turn to speak to the large crowd in 2012, he chose to speak about the upper and lower stories. He seemed, in fact, to take direct aim at the two-story view. "We can't leave our values at the door" when it comes to political debates, he said.

> If we leave our values at the door, we abandon much of the moral glue that has held our nation together for centuries, and allowed us to become somewhat more perfect a union. Frederick Douglass, Abraham Lincoln, Jane Addams, Martin Luther King Jr., Dorothy Day, Abraham Heschel—the majority of great reformers in American history did their work not just because it was sound policy, or they had done good analysis, or understood how to exercise good politics, but because their faith and their values dictated it, and called for bold action.[4]

This statement is perceptive, both about American history and about politics in general. When Abraham Lincoln issued the Emancipation Proclamation, when he gave the immortal Gettysburg Address, and when he led his precious Union through a long and bloody war, he wasn't driven by nonpartisan* economic studies demonstrating that the GDP* would increase if slaves were freed. Lincoln said in his second inaugural address, as the Civil War still raged,

> Fondly do we hope, fervently do we pray, that this mighty scourge of war may speedily pass away. Yet, if God wills that it continue until all the wealth piled by the bondsman's two hundred and fifty years of unrequited toil shall be sunk, and until every drop of blood drawn with the lash shall be paid by another drawn with the sword, as was said three thousand years ago, so still it must be said "the judgments of the Lord are true and righteous altogether."[5]

Lincoln was clearly motivated not by economics but by his personal moral outrage, his belief in divine justice. And Lincoln, though not an orthodox* Christian himself, knew that this appeal would motivate the average Americans listening to him. No president in American history has spoken more freely and more eloquently about God than Lincoln.

But the president of the United States is not powerful enough to overturn the two-story view. And it's clear that President Obama did not really want the barrier between religion and politics to come down. The very week before he gave the address to the National Prayer Breakfast, the president left a lot of Christians' values outside the door when his administration insisted that Christian employers had to pay for their employees' abortions. The so-called HHS Mandate, later struck down by the courts, would have forced the Christian owners of Hobby Lobby, for example, to pay for abortifacient contraceptives* for their female employees—or pay a $1.3 million fine for every day they refused.

President Obama was the leader of the Democratic Party. Listen carefully to the wording in the official Democratic Party platform* on abortion:

> The Democratic Party strongly and unequivocally supports *Roe v. Wade* and a woman's right to make decisions regarding her pregnancy, including a safe and legal abortion. . . . Abortion is an intensely personal decision between a woman, her family, her doctor, and her clergy; there is no place for politicians or government to get in the way.[6]

The Democratic Party puts abortion squarely in the upper story. It is precisely because abortion is an "intensely personal" decision that government, they say, is not supposed to stand in a woman's way. Religion (notice the mention of "clergy") can play a role in advising an individual woman if she goes upstairs and asks for its advice, the platform says. But because abortion is so personal, religion is not allowed to come downstairs and outlaw abortions for all American women.

Democrats don't feel the same way about other murderous violations of human dignity. The Democrats are not opposed to using the power of government (or the influence of religion) to stamp out human trafficking.* A few paragraphs away from the abortion statement, they (rightly) call human trafficking "an affront to our fundamental values."[7]

So why are some values (such as opposition to abortion) supposed to stay private while others (such as opposition to slavery) are allowed to guide public policy? What makes Abraham Lincoln's values good and Hobby Lobby's bad?

The Democratic Party platform, it seems, is smuggling values from the upstairs to the downstairs through a laundry chute. And, to be fair, the Republicans do this too. Many American politicians talk as if they are guided solely by the facts and that their religion and personal values are not causing them to be biased. Their two-story view of reality leads them to *try* to keep religion and other private values upstairs—but without success. They can't do it. Their upper-story values still shape their lower-story policies.

The simple fact is that you can't live without values. Your values—your principles, what you think is important and worth protecting and promoting—guide all your decisions. You can try to shove all your values into the upper story, but they will always sneak downstairs. The Democratic Party is not making a neutral, valueless, fact-based decision on abortion. It simply values something else (perhaps sexual freedom or human autonomy?) over the lives of unborn children.

So it's commendable for President Obama to praise moral reformers like Martin Luther King Jr. It was right, too, for John the Baptist to shout downstairs, "King Herod, you can't have your brother Philip's wife!" (Matt. 14:3–4). It was a private sin *and* a public injustice for King Ahab to use his political power to steal Naboth's vineyard (1 Kings 21)—and it was right for God's prophet Elijah to say so.

But inviting us all to bring our values into politics forces us to answer this insistent question: whose values are going to win? Values have a way of clashing, and clashing hard.

THE RELIGIOUS TWO-STORY VIEW
Protecting the Faithful

That clash is what created the two-story view in the first place. When value systems clash, people can get hurt. Lunches can get stolen. Recognizing the danger, some Christians want to put significant distance between themselves and the rest of the world. They have created a religious version of the two-story view.

human trafficking: *the sale of human beings as either domestic or sexual slaves*

JUDGMENTAL JUSTICE

Harvard professor Michael Sandel writes in his book *Justice: What's the Right Thing to Do?* about how your values always impact your decisions:

> Justice is inescapably judgmental. Whether we're arguing about . . . surrogate motherhood or same-sex marriage, affirmative action or military service, [the size of] CEO pay or the right [of a disabled golfer] to use a golf cart, questions of justice are bound up with competing notions of honor and virtue, pride and recognition. *Justice is not only about the right way to distribute things. It is also about the right way to value things.*[8]

"The right way to value things" stands at the very heart of the Christian religion. What am I supposed to value or to love most? Jesus answers this very directly: I'm supposed to love God most, then God's image-bearers (Matt. 22:34–40). Without God standing at the appropriate place on my value scale, I won't know how to value other things. Justice is inescapably judgmental because we all make judgments every day based on what we value.

Antidiscrimination Policies That Are Discriminatory

A bank in Britain asked a Christian organization to close its bank accounts because the organization would not broadcast a show that it considered to be blasphemous. The bank insisted that its customers should conform to the bank's antidiscrimination policies. D. A. Carson notes that in doing this the bank itself was actually discriminating against one of its customers. It is, in fact, impossible not to discriminate in some way. Carson says, "The issue ought to be whether any particular act of discrimination is good, sensible, and proper, for there are both good and evil forms of discrimination." [*The Intolerance of Tolerance*, 21–22]

 Freedom, Equality, Moral Judgment

In 2014, Brenden Eich resigned as CEO of Mozilla under pressure because in 2008 he had donated a thousand dollars to a campaign to ban same-sex marriage in California. Those pushing for Eich's resignation believed he was morally unfit to be CEO because they found his views on marriage offensive. Those defending Eich worried about the obvious intolerance toward those holding traditional views on marriage. The company chairwoman noted that the controversy reflected conflicts between the two American core values of freedom and equality.

How can the conflict between these values be resolved?

The conflict between freedom and equality cannot be settled apart from moral judgment. Can marriage be redefined at will, or is marriage a creational structure that cannot be changed by majority vote? Is homosexual behavior moral or immoral? The answers to these moral questions determine whether Eich was treated justly or unjustly. The secular public rejects any religious contribution to this debate while necessarily smuggling in its own values to deal with these moral questions.

 Protecting the Faithful—Biblically

Which of the following is the appropriate biblical approach?

a. carelessly ignore how evil is presented (Eph. 5:10, 15)

b. permissively embrace all that is sordid for the sake of realism (Rom. 12:9; 16:19)

c. completely isolate yourself from every mention of evil even though the Bible discusses many instances of evil (e.g., in the book of Judges)

d. pragmatically accept the reality that evil is unavoidable; just live with it (Eph. 5:3–15)

e. carefully discern whether or not a presentation of evil is appropriate (i.e., whether it presents evil in the way the Bible does)

Of course, *e* is the correct answer. If a presentation depicts evil in an inappropriate way, it should be denounced and turned away from (Eph. 4:17–24). Gratuitous, explicit, and pervasive evil ought to be avoided—even when making a correct point (Phil. 4:8). The maturity of the believer must also be evaluated when determining the dosage for inoculation.

[See Ronald A. Horton, *Christian Education: Its Mandate and Mission* (Greenville, SC: BJU Press, 1992), 45–70.]

Those who call for cultural engagement often fail to appropriately guard their own minds and hearts (Prov. 14:16). But it's just as dangerous for Christians to disengage from the culture in favor of purely pietistic pursuits.

Why Abandoning Culture Is Not the Solution

Why shouldn't Christians abandon culture in an attempt to maintain purity?

God created the world, and He created humans in His image with the task of stewardship (Gen. 1:26-28). He designed humans to interact in community as they carry out that stewardship (implied in Gen. 4:12). Human cultures form as people work together to carry out that stewardship (Gen. 4:20–22). But the Fall has greatly corrupted human interactions so that cultures frequently produce perversion (Gen. 6:5; 11:1–9). Christians must not embrace those perversions, but they must not shirk their responsibility of stewardship in human culture (Gen. 9:1–3, 7). Rather than abandoning the God-given task of stewardship because others pervert it, Christians ought to model good stewardship instead (Matt. 5:13–16; 1 Pet. 2:11–12; Phil. 2:14–15).

Otherwise only perverse expressions of culture are left. Disciplines such as science and literature ought to be embraced with a desire to glorify God (1 Cor. 10:31). Christians may need to separate themselves from non-Christian organizations that insist on perverseness (Prov. 4:14–17; 15:9). But Christians ought to shine as lights of good stewardship—either in the middle of a pagan culture or in their own organizations that promote God's glory (Matt. 5:13–16).

Every Job Matters

Every field of work needs biblical worldview influence for two major reasons:

- to provide a basis for ethics, integrity, honesty, and so on

- to govern tasks according to the biblical norms God designed for the function of a particular task in a particular sphere with its roles and responsibilities

Figuring out the norms and how to operate according to them is the difficult task of life. [Ray Pennings and James Brink, "Sphere Sovereignty 101," *Comment* (March 1, 2004)]

For example, what might some of the norms be for government? *Justice.* For a family? *Loving discipleship.* For business? *Stewardship.* For healthcare? *Compassion.*

But when endeavors are abandoned to those with an unbiblical worldview, whole sectors of society are run contrary to God's design. For example, business and healthcare are run according to financial profits rather than stewardship and compassion.

A Comprehensive Worldview

Christians also betray a divide between the sacred and the secular when they treat so-

---

For example, if the study of literature is corrosive to good morals (kids may see obscenities or read about drug addiction), perhaps Christians should read only Christian books. If science attacks the existence of God, perhaps it is best to leave science to the atheists. These Christians would prefer as much as possible to live in the upper story. They might have to descend on Mondays to go to work, but they do it only as a necessary evil—to provide money for their families and to support missionaries.

Some Christians even see themselves as second-class citizens of the kingdom of God because they have to spend so much time in that lower story—because, in other words, they don't work in "full-time Christian ministry." One Christian school even made this view one of its stated goals: "To encourage each student to plan on full-time Christian ministry unless God clearly leads otherwise." For this group, staying in the upper story is the ideal.

But this view has its own dangers. Every Christian will have some view of science, politics, and journalism. You can't help it. If you don't work hard to construct a Christian view, you will probably absorb the default view of society around you—namely some form of modern secularism. If you try to do the impossible and stay in the upper story all the time, wrong ideas about the world will still get in through the air vents. And your own sinful flesh will be in the upper story with you, don't forget. These Christians want to protect themselves from the world, but the two-story view actually lets worldliness sneak in unnoticed.

Protecting the Faith

Another religious version of the two-story view attempts to protect the Christian faith itself, not just individual Christians. Prominent Christian worldview writer Nancy Pearcey tells the story of one Christian teacher who "strode to the front of the classroom, where he drew a heart on one side of the blackboard and a brain on the other." He told the class that "the heart is what we use for religion, while the brain is what we use for science."[9]

This teacher, it appears, was trying to protect religion from the power of modern science by putting religion and science out of each other's reach. But if secularists cannot live in the world without smuggling their values down into the lower story, then Christians certainly can't do it either. And shouldn't.

If God's Word speaks to all of life, the Christian is not free to ignore or be silent about what God says concerning science, mathematics, literature, ethics, and everything else in His world.

THE OTHER DITCH

If you haven't picked up on it by now, this book on biblical worldview takes a pretty negative view of the two-story mentality. And yet there's another ditch, too—on the other side of the road. If the two-story view cuts in two what God joined together, it's also possible to mix up things God keeps distinct.

Here's an illustration. In the movie *The Incredibles*, the super-fast-running boy Dash makes an insightful comment (especially for a ten-year-old) when he complains to his mom about not being allowed to use his super powers:

> **Dash**: But Dad always said our powers were nothing to be ashamed of, our powers made us special.
>
> **Mom**: Everyone's special, Dash.
>
> **Dash**: [muttering] Which is another way of saying no one is.[10]

---

called secular disciplines as if they're neutral, free from biblical critique. No knowledge is neutral; it either reflects an understanding of God's creative order from a biblical worldview or it conflicts. Therefore, Christians must carefully evaluate assumptions and biases in all their work. For instance, secular psychotherapy is filled with unbiblical concepts of humanity's origin, nature, motivations, and problems, and thus promotes unbiblical solutions. Through God's common grace, the unbeliever may observe and comprehend some truths. However, the structure of thought in psychotherapy is so fundamentally and thoroughly contrary to biblical teaching that its practical ramifications rarely correlate with biblical practices. A Christian psychologist who simply goes to church on Sunday to learn about his own personal spiritual life but then approaches

his job according to a secular model of humans Monday through Friday has compartmentalized Christianity to a useless upper story. Every discipline must be evaluated by God's norms. But the two-story view segments off disciplines as if they were neutral and thus beyond evaluation by Scripture.

Don't Compartmentalize Your Life

Nancy Pearcey tells the story of a committed deacon who was a lawyer. His job consisted of finding legal loopholes so people could break contracts. She says, "How can even committed Christian believers be so blind? Because they often undergo many years of professional training in a secular setting where they have no opportunity to develop a biblical worldview. In fact, they know that if they *did* express a biblical perspective, it

It is possible to treat everything as sacred until nothing is, but some things in this world *are* more sacred than others. Extra sacred.

Think of Sunday. God, who doesn't need rest, took a whole day off after creating the world, Genesis tells us. Why would He bother? In fact, why bother creating the heavens and the earth in six days instead of one nanosecond?

He did this not for Himself but for us, to set up a weekly rhythm for our lives. He explains this in one of the Ten Commandments: "Remember the Sabbath day, to keep it holy," He said to the Israelites, "for in six days the Lord made heaven and earth, the sea, and all that is in them, and rested on the seventh day. Therefore the Lord blessed the Sabbath day and made it holy" (Exod. 20:8, 11).

Monday is important. You've got to obey God on Mondays. Thursdays, too, require twenty-four hours of love and obedience to God. And don't forget Saturdays—Christians don't get days off from Christianity; all our work and study is therefore "sacred," set apart from the way we would act if we weren't believers. But one day a week is still supposed to be special, set apart from the other days of the week. On that day you get to rest and focus on the Lord. You get to fellowship in a special way with God's people when the church, Christ's body, gathers together.

And just like one day is more important than the others, distinct from them, so the spiritual life is more important than other good and necessary things.

Just ask Martha. The Gospel of Luke tells her story:

> Jesus entered a village. And a woman named Martha welcomed him into her house. And she had a sister called Mary, who sat at the Lord's feet and listened to his teaching. But Martha was distracted with much serving. And she went up to him and said, "Lord, do you not care that my sister has left me to serve alone? Tell her then to help me." But the Lord answered her, "Martha, Martha, you are anxious and troubled about many things, but one thing is necessary. Mary has chosen the good portion, which will not be taken away from her." (Luke 10:38–42)

There *is* a difference between washing dishes and sitting at the feet of Jesus. If these two activities ever truly come into conflict, it's clear that Jesus should take priority—just like He did in Mary's situation. You need a prayer room to retreat to. You need a sanctuary in this fallen world, a place to sit at Christ's feet while the dishes soak in the sink. You need a safe place where you go to recharge for the constant battles you face in a fallen world and to learn what God expects of you out there.

But the dishes do need to get washed. And though you can't take dishes into your prayer closet with you, the neat thing about prayer is that you can take it to the kitchen. The spiritual life gets to have special focus on Sundays and during your devotions, but the spiritual life is supposed to fill and cover your work life and your education life and your dating life and your sports life too.

THE SABBATH AND SUNDAY

The Jews celebrate the sabbath on Saturday, as God instructed in the Old Testament. The way the sabbath became Sunday for Christians is a longer story, but it basically boils down to four reasons:

- **Event**—The resurrection occurred on "the first day of the week" (Matt 28:1).
- **Example**—The early church met on "the first day of the week" (Acts 20:7).
- **Precept**—Paul commanded the Corinthians to gather and give "on the first day of the week" (1 Cor 16:2).
- **Designation**—John refers to "the Lord's day" as if it's something all Christians would recognize (Rev 1:10).

Admittedly, these verses stop short of giving an explicit command to move the sabbath to a different day. But Christians throughout the history of the church have met on Sundays.

---

would be a barrier to getting into most graduate schools. And so, most believers learn to compartmentalize their lives, absorbing the reigning secular assumptions in their field of study, while maintaining a devotional life on the side in their private time." [*Total Truth*, (Wheaton: Crossway Books, 2004), 98]. Beware of compartmentalizing your life.

✎ Constructing a Christian View

Assign students to write one-page papers to summarize a Christian view of the discipline of literature. Resources for research include Ronald A. Horton, *Christian Education: Its Mandate and Mission* (Greenville, SC: BJU Press, 1992), 45–70, 93–112; Tony Reinke, *Lit! A Christian Guide to Reading Books* (Wheaton: Crossway, 2011).

Protecting the Faith Is Biblical

The church shouldn't be sidetracked from its main mission: the Great Commission (Matt. 28:19–20). But what does carrying out the Great Commission include? It's far more comprehensive than merely getting a person to profess the name of Christ. The Great Commission is a command to make disciples who are publicly committed (baptized) and carefully taught to obey the commands of Christ (Matt. 5:13–16; cf. Gen. 1:26–28; 9:1–3, 7).

A problem develops when the teaching of the church fails to be all-encompassing because it only deals with inward spiritual piety and not application to living all of life in every sphere of labor. Those who attempt to grapple with cultural issues don't necessarily want to divert the church's attention away from its main mission; they desire to take the main mission of the church to every sphere because Christ is Lord of all. Nancy Pearcey says, "God is not just the Savior of souls, He is also the Lord of creation. One way we acknowledge His lordship is by interpreting every aspect of creation in the light of His truth. God's Word becomes a set of glasses offering a new perspective on all our thoughts and actions." [*Total Truth* (Wheaton: Crossway Books, 2004), 24]

Discipleship ought to change the whole person, including his cultural interactions and his intellectual thinking. The church fails when it allows ungodly thinking in the disciplines and ungodly behavior in culture to direct a person's life. While the church itself can't teach all the details of those disciplines on Sunday, it can challenge major presuppositions and it can extend its ministry through Christian education during the week. Faith must be integrated into all of life.

Spiritual Disciplines Are Foundational

While some people err by cultivating personal piety while neglecting cultural engagement, others err by trying to engage culture in contradiction to personal holiness. Prayer, Bible study, fighting inward sin, gathering with a body of believers, and serving God in ministry are all very important. The spiritual disciplines ought to guide and enable you to live Christianly in your culture with biblical faithfulness and purity.

🖥 Two Ditches and a Road

One ditch: Have you ever justified avoiding your homework by engaging in something "more spiritual" as if you had no spiritual obligation to do your homework well?

The other ditch: Have you ever justified skipping church so you could finish a school project?

The road: Glorifying God encompasses all of life including schoolwork. But this doesn't excuse you from properly managing your time. All things in life are important to God and to a biblical worldview, but some things still have priority over other things. You can know how to order your life by examining your role and responsibility in a particular sphere at a particular time (Heb. 10:25).

This applies to your future job as well. All vocations are worthy of honor when you serve God for His glory according to His design. But failure to order your life properly undermines that service. A person can't claim that since his job glorifies God through stewardship and service to others, he never needs to get together with the corporate body of believers in a local church. That person has landed in the opposite ditch (from those holding to the two-story view) by seeing no distinctions when God clearly distinguishes between the two ways of glorifying Him.

Not All Distinctions Are Wrong

Although we shouldn't divide the world into the sacred (what matters to God) and the secular (what doesn't matter to God), a person should recognize that some things are specially set apart by God. While the two-story view tends to be dismissive of certain aspects of God's created order, the opposite extreme tends to ignore the distinctive place for certain aspects of God's created order. While all of God's created order is important, not all things are equal. God has differing priorities, roles, and responsibilities for different spheres in culture. For example, a local body of believers shouldn't neglect the preaching of the gospel on Sunday in favor of picking up trash on the side of the highway in order to model good stewardship to the community. This would indicate confusion about its priorities, role, and responsibility. However, a local church can certainly encourage its membership to participate in community clean-up events and perhaps facilitate one in an appropriate context.

 ## The Right Kind of Distinctions

Should we be concerned about keeping the things of God from being profaned?

The Bible recognizes a distinction between that which is set apart unto God and that which is profane. This isn't just an Old Testament concern. In fact, a Christian has an even greater accountability in the New Testament age of grace (Heb. 10:26–31; Rom. 12:1–2; 1 Cor. 3:17; Eph. 2:21).

Should we be concerned about protecting ourselves from corrupting influences?

The Bible recognizes the need for keeping oneself unspotted from the corruption in this world (Prov. 14:16; Rom. 6:12–14; 1 Cor. 6:19; Eph. 1:4; Phil. 4:8; 2 Tim. 2:21; James 1:27; 1 Pet. 1:15–16).

Should we be more concerned about eternal things than about temporal things?

The Bible makes a distinction between the eternal and the temporal (1 Cor. 9:25; 2 Cor. 4:16–18; Col. 3:1–4). Any Christian who desires to be pleasing to God ought to be committed to these biblical truths.

As one great theologian put it, that prayer room

> remains the center, the heart, the hearth, out of which all [the Christian's] thought and action proceeds and from which it receives inspiration and warmth. There, in fellowship with God, he is strengthened for his labor and girds himself for the battle. But that hidden life of fellowship with God is not the whole of life. The prayer room is the inner chamber, but not the whole dwelling in which he lives and moves. The spiritual life does not exclude domestic and civic, social and political life, the life of art and scholarship.[11]

The dishes won't wash themselves, political crises won't solve themselves, and important books won't write themselves. But if you're going to do those "secular" things as a faithful Christian, that's all the more reason to protect the "sacred" things: going to church, praying, reading the Bible, evangelizing, maintaining a real and personal faith. Don't fall into the ditch on the other side of the road.

PURITY IS IMPORTANT

And we can't forget that the Fall has happened. Because of the Fall, some Christians in some situations simply cannot pursue certain vocations because it would damage them spiritually or diminish the light they are supposed to shine on the world. The ancient church father Tertullian pointed out, for example, that in his day it was pretty much impossible for a Christian to be a sculptor. There is nothing inherently wrong with sculpture, of course—God commanded sculptures to be made in His own temple (Exod. 25:18–20). And sculpture, like any art form, is a way of expressing the creativity given to us by God the Creator. But in Tertullian's day it was difficult or impossible to make a living as a sculptor if you refused to make idols.

It is also becoming more difficult in the Western world for Christians to have some jobs that seem totally innocent, like baking or photography. Why? Because if you refuse to provide a four-layer cake or take pictures for a same-sex wedding, you may be sued and lose your business. Such lawsuits are already being filed.

Or consider this true story: a gifted ballet teacher with an extremely successful (and lucrative) ballet school became a Christian. As she began to grow in her love for Christ and her desire to obey His word, conflicts began to erupt. It wasn't with her Christian husband; he had no objection to her running the school. It was with her students and her teaching partners.

SHOULD A CHRISTIAN BUSINESS TURN AWAY HOMOSEXUALS?

If you try to keep your business life and your spiritual life totally separate the way the two-story view would suggest, you will run into troubling questions. For example, if you are a Christian wedding cake baker or a Christian wedding photographer or a Christian screen-printer, what will you do if a same-sex couple or the organizers of a white supremacist rally try to hire you?

This is very different from owning a restaurant. There you can't check at the door to see if your customers are racists or homosexuals—or adulterers or gossips (and based on 1 Corinthians 5:10, you shouldn't).

You should serve with kindness everyone who's willing to maintain public decorum (that's why many restaurants post signs saying, "Shirt and shoes required").

But if you are asked to print an Aryan Nation (racist) T-shirt or bake a wedding cake with two men on the top, you are being asked to directly and obviously support what God condemns—racism (Gen. 1:27) and homosexual acts (1 Cor. 6:9–10). Our society happens to condemn one sin and not the other, so you'll only get sued if you refuse to serve the wedding. What you can't do in such situations is remain neutral.

Creation and Fall: Necessary Distinction

Although we shouldn't divide the world into the sacred (what God's Word speaks to) and the secular (what doesn't matter to God), we should make distinctions between what is godly and what is ungodly.

Some proponents of the holistic Christian worldview seem to ignore all the passages of the Bible that warn about the profane (Heb. 10:26–31; Jude 1:4; 2 Pet. 1:9; 2:1–22; 3:17–18). They sometimes argue from Romans 14:14 ("nothing is unclean in itself") and 1 Timothy 4:4 ("nothing is to be rejected if it is received with thanksgiving") that no aspect of culture is off limits to the Christian. However, considered in context, these passages simply encourage believers to participate in what God has created and not that which is condemned in God's Word

as perversions of God's creation. The Fall twists God's created order, and 1 Timothy 4:5 teaches that making use of God's good created order with thanksgiving is contingent on holiness, which is discerned through prayer and the Word (Eph. 5:10–11).

Some human activities are inherently a manifestation of the perversion of God's good creation. An obvious example is the way the pornography industry perverts human sexuality. Sex is part of God's created order, and the marriage bed is undefiled (Heb. 13:4). But the pornography industry could never be redeemed by creating "Christian porn." The pornography industry is a human endeavor that is inherently a perversion of God's created order. Christians act faithfully by seeking to eliminate porn and by promoting a biblical sexual ethic.

The conflict wasn't mainly about modesty, though that played a role. The Christian ballet teacher began to see that the real motivation for most of her ballet students was to glorify themselves, to make a name for themselves. So she began to make changes in the way she ran the school. She wanted to minimize this motivation.

The students weren't interested. They left. The non-Christian teachers couldn't understand what she was doing; they thought she'd gone crazy. One of them even sued (and lost).

In this fallen world, there are times when even good, God-honoring jobs aren't available to certain Christians because the fallen state of the culture puts those jobs off-limits, or at least makes them very difficult.

THINKING IT THROUGH 3.2

1. Why is it impossible for secularists to be consistent in keeping values out of the public square?

2. How does the two-story view fail to protect the faithful?

3. How does the two-story view fail to protect the faith?

4. The two-story view cuts in two what God joined together; give an example of mixing up things God intends to keep distinct.

♀5. What are you supposed to value or love most?

3.3 CREATION, FALL, REDEMPTION

The two-story view has some strengths. It tries to protect some things of real value. But it has some fatal flaws. We can see those flaws if we'll go back to the Christian worldview, the Christian story of Creation, Fall, Redemption.

CREATION

God created this world and therefore owns it, so the biggest flaw in the two-story view is this: the Bible just won't let us divide the world into things God owns and things He doesn't. The Bible makes big claims. It claims that the earth and all it contains are the Lord's (Ps. 24:1; 50:12; 89:11; Exod. 9:29; 19:5). God says to Job, "Who has first given to me, that I should repay him? Whatever is under the whole heaven is mine" (Job 41:11). And don't forget Paul's simple encouragement to the Corinthians: "Whatever you do, do all to the glory of God" (1 Cor. 10:31).

God owns everything He created, and it's possible to glorify Him (or not) with every decision we make. That has to include politics and scholarship, music and sports. So the two-story view tells a lie about the way the world is: it says there's a broad area of neutrality over which God is not King.

Some of the most famous and stirring words in theology come from theologian, pastor, teacher, journalist, and ultimately prime minister of the Netherlands (1901–1905) Abraham Kuyper:

> There is not a square inch in the whole domain of our human existence over which Christ, who is Sovereign over all, does not cry: "Mine!"[12]

Kuyper also said, "No single piece of our mental world is to be hermetically* sealed off from the rest." You can't put religion and science in separate ziplock bags.

hermetically: sealed so tightly that air cannot get in

1. Your values and principles—what you think is important and worth protecting and promoting—guide your decisions.

2. Christians assume worthlessness in vast areas of life, leading to the devaluation of work in many sectors. Christians assume neutrality in vast areas of life, leading to the absorption of secularist principles in their work. These assumptions may also give a false sense of immunity from sin in "sacred" areas of life.

3. It fails to uphold an intelligent and reasonable defense of the Christian faith by trying to separate the head system from the heart system.

4. We must distinguish between what's reverent and what's profane (e.g., loud cheering is usually appropriate at a ball game but not usually during a worship service). We must distinguish between what's pure and what's impure (e.g., immorality doesn't become acceptable just because it's portrayed artistically).

♀5. Fellowship with God in prayer. It strengthens and equips all other labor.

SECTION OBJECTIVES 3.3

1. Evaluate the claim that some aspects of human life are neutral, untouched by the biblical worldview under God's creational rule.

2. Explain that Christians must distinguish creational good from fallen perversions in every sphere of life since the Fall comprehensively taints God's good creational structures.

3. Explain the responsibility of all believers to live according to God's creational structures in every area of life.

⭐ God's Good Creation

God created every physical element on this earth. He created all the minerals, plants, animals, and humans. But God also designed orderly relationships for His physical creation. He created roles and responsibilities in many different spheres such as family, community, business, and government. God created humans in His image with particular abilities such as music and scholarship.

Everything ought to function according to His design. Nothing is outside of the realm of the lordship of Christ (Col. 1:19–20). The biblical worldview must comprehensively direct everything in every sphere. Not one function can claim neutrality, as being outside the control and standards of God's creative design. Not one of these realms

Justifying Discrimination?

As Christians try to apply a holistic worldview to all of life, their values will clash with the values of secular pluralism—especially the values of the new tolerance.

Under the rules of the old definition of tolerance, the Christian owner of a restaurant would have no problem serving homosexuals because that particular service has nothing to do with sanctioning, approving, or enabling the particular behavioral choices that the Christian deems to be immoral. The eating of food has nothing to do with their immoral choices, and the Christian ought to show civility to all people behaving civilly in a public business. In fact, under the rules of the older definition of tolerance, homosexuals would be considered intolerant of Christian business owners by trying to force them to sanction, approve, and enable their lifestyle. Demanding that Christians provide particular services that would implicate them with the homosexuals' immoral choices is intolerant. But the new definition of tolerance under the rules of secular pluralism demands the approval and enablement of every other person's values—except for a biblical Christian's values (Rom. 1:32; cf. 2 John 1:11).

As one blogger put it in proposing a workable principle, "Every business must serve any person, but it must not be required to serve every act." [Michael Wittmer, "Plea for Sanity" *Don't Stop Believing* blog, February 23, 2015]

should be dismissed or ignored in favor of exclusively pursuing personal pietistic endeavors. God designed us to steward His good creation; God designed us to interact in community while doing so. Therefore, Christians should not abandon God's creational structures in culture to the secularists.

Guide students through Activity 6 in the student activity manual. This activity is essential.

Common Grace in a Fallen Creation

The presence of God's common grace is the way the biblical worldview accounts for the valuable contributions of fallen humans contributing to the good cultivation of God's creation.

At certain times and certain places God restrains the extent of man's fallen expressions through His work of common grace (often mediated through the influence of His own people) so that sinful humans don't always manifest the worst possible evils (2 Tim. 3:13; 2 Thess. 2:7).

> Where evil does not come to the surface, or does not manifest itself in all its hideousness, we do not owe it to the fact that our nature is not so deeply corrupt, but to God alone, Who by His 'common grace' hinders the bursting forth of the flames from the smoking fire.

[Abraham Kuyper, *Lectures* (La Vergne, TN: Lightning Source Inc., 2001), 124]

Kuyper illustrates God's restraint and common grace with an analogy to a ferry boat driven along by swift currents (the powerful current of sinful human nature) but chained and so directed across the current to the other side (common grace).

How much more should regenerated Christians contribute to the good cultivation of God's creation by His grace?

> Not only *the church*, but also *the world* belongs to God and in both has to be investigated the masterpiece of the supreme Architect and Artificer. . . . [A Christian] who seeks God, does not for a moment think of limiting himself to theology and contemplation, leaving the other sciences, as of a lower character, in the hands of unbelievers; but on the contrary, looking upon it as his task to know God in all his works, he is conscious of having been called to fathom with all the energy of his intellect, things *terrestrial* as well as things *celestial*; to open to view both the order of creation, and the 'common grace' of the God he adores in nature and its wondrous character, in the production

of human industry, in the life of mankind, in sociology and in the history of the human race. Thus you perceive how this dogma of 'common grace' suddenly removed the interdict, under which secular life had laid bound, even at the peril of coming very near a reaction in favor of a one-sided love for these secular studies. . . . It was the 'common grace' of God, which had produced in ancient Greece and Rome the treasures of philosophic light, and disclosed to us treasures of art and justice, which kindled the love for classical studies. [Kuyper, *Lectures*, 125]

How to Live Faithfully in a Fallen World

Hiding out in the so-called sacred realm doesn't protect the faithful. One unbiblical view of sanctification teaches that a person can live on a plateau of pietistic perfection above a sinful world, but the biblical teaching of progressive sanctification pictures the believer doing battle in the midst of a fallen world, where he must continue fighting against his own flesh until glorification (John 17:18; 1 Cor. 10:12; 2 Cor. 3:18; Rom. 7; Gal. 5:16; Phil. 3:12–14; Col. 1:9–11, 23).

How does this battle rage in both the upper and lower story realms?

A few examples include prayer used as a prideful display, Scripture twisted to fit one's own agenda, ministry projects done for one's own advancement, education inculcating subtle antibiblical presuppositions, psychology misinterpreting sinful choices as mere sickness, and businesses and healthcare existing merely for profits.

FALL

But because the whole creation is in the same ziplock, it was all contaminated when Adam fell into sin. And that creates two more problems for the two-story view, particularly the religious version:

(1) It sometimes seems to forget that *sin* comes with us into the upper story. We won't ever get away from it until the day Christ finally gets it away from us.

(2) The Christian version of the two-story view also fails to recognize something about non-Christian worldviews. Those worldviews are opposed to Christianity in more than just upper-story things; they stand opposed to God's claims in the lower story as well. You won't escape conflict by heading to the lower story, as if it were neutral.

Journalism and education are fallen just as much as sex and speech are. Non-Christians don't want God ruling their newspapers or their high school curricula, but God isn't going to give up His claims on that territory. God speaks to every aspect of individual and cultural human life. We shouldn't get in the way of God's program but instead participate with it.

REDEMPTION

As one of today's greatest critics of the secular two-story view put it, "A religion deprived of the opportunity to transform the culture in its every detail is hardly a religion at all."[13] Christianity, biblical religion, does have a program for world transformation. It's called God's work of "redemption."

When Jesus Christ, God in flesh, died on the cross to satisfy God the Father's anger for your sins, He did it "to *redeem* us from all lawlessness" (Titus 2:14). Scripture says that Christians "are justified by [God's] grace as a gift, through the *redemption* that is in Christ Jesus" (Rom. 3:24). Jesus is the one who descended into the dirty slave market of sin where we were all in chains, and He's the one who paid the money to buy us out of slavery. That's what "redeeming" means.

If the Bible is the story of what God is doing to glorify Himself by redeeming His fallen creation, then this redeeming—the redeeming of fallen humans—is surely the culmination of that story. Christ's death on the cross for human sin, followed by His triumphant resurrection from the dead, is the most important redemption God accomplishes in Scripture.

But that's not the only redemption He'll ever accomplish. It's important to recognize that human souls aren't all that God redeems. The Christian story does *not* end with God redeeming humanity by pulling us out of our universe and taking us to live with Him as spirits in some nonphysical dimension called "heaven." The Christian story ends with Christians back in physical bodies living on the earth. These bodies and that earth will both be what the Bible calls "new." They won't decay and break because of sin like they do now. Eternity, according to the Bible, doesn't take place in heaven. God will one day redeem souls, bodies, *and the whole earth*.

All creation is waiting for this redemption, Paul says: "The creation waits with eager longing for the revealing of the sons of God" (Rom. 8:19).

But why? Why is it waiting for some future day? Why does creation care what happens in the future? Paul answers that it's because

the creation was subjected to futility, not willingly, but because of him who subjected it, in hope that the creation itself will be set free from its bondage to corruption. . . . For we know that *the whole creation has been groaning* together in the pains of childbirth until now. And not only the creation, but we ourselves . . . groan inwardly as we wait eagerly for adoption as sons, *the redemption* of our bodies. (Rom. 8:20–23)

This is a dense statement with a lot of truth packed into it. But simply notice what it says: The creation is awaiting redemption—not just humanity. The creation is waiting to be "set free."

The apostle John said, "I saw a *new heaven* and a *new earth*, for the first heaven and the first earth had passed away, and the sea was no more" (Rev. 21:1). And what John saw happening in that new earth is very interesting:

> And I saw the holy city, new Jerusalem, coming down out of heaven from God, prepared as a bride adorned for her husband. And I heard a loud voice from the throne saying, "Behold, the dwelling place of God is with man. . . ." And he who was seated on the throne said, "Behold, I am making all things new." (Rev. 21:3–5).

The Christian hope is not escape but resurrection (2 Cor. 4:14). God will dwell with us on this earth—that's why the new Jerusalem, God's dwelling place, is said to "come down out of heaven." At the end of the Bible's story, God restores the world to the way He originally created it to be.

One day, God is going to reestablish His rule over all creation (1 Cor. 15:28). And that's why no true Christian can view secularism, the main non-Christian form of the two-story view, as a good thing. Secularism tries to push God off the throne He established over His own creation. It tries to steal from God what He owns, like an art thief stealing a canvas directly from an artist's studio. And this particular thief has the gall to turn around and say to the Artist, "You didn't paint this! It just *is*."

Christians who live by the two-story view are subtly confirming the thesis* of secularism. That's because American secularists don't try to ban religion outright. Instead, they push it out to the margins of society. They say it is supposed to be private and to have no effect on government, the arts, and the life of the mind. And this is just what the two-story view does when Christians hold it; it keeps the Bible from having its proper influence on vast portions of their lives. But the truth of the Creation, Fall, Redemption story shows that we must not let this happen to us.

thesis: the point someone wants to prove

Why should we even bother with temporal things that seem vain (Eccles. 2:18–23) and will be remade by God?

Current interactions with temporal things still bring about God's blessing (Eccles. 2:24–25; 5:18; 9:9–10) and still have eternal implications (Matt. 25:14–30). While you shouldn't live for the sake of the temporal things themselves (Matt. 6:19–24; Col. 3:1–2), an eternal focus doesn't negate the work of stewardship here on earth (Eph. 4:28; 1 Thess. 4:11–12). Otherwise, humans should have stopped obeying the Creation Mandate as soon as Adam and Eve fell in the Garden of Eden. Humans have to try to fulfill the Creation Mandate not only because it is intrinsic to their created nature, but also because God clearly reaffirmed it after the Fall (Gen. 9:1–3, 7).

The New Heavens and the New Earth

Eternity is going to be anything but monotonous. God will restore the earth and humans to the perfection that existed before the Fall. If humans in their fallen state have been able to develop some limited cultural good, think of what they will be able to accomplish for the glory of God in a perfect world. Unhindered humans will be given the task of stewarding God's perfect earth for all eternity (Isa. 65:21–23; Joel 3:18; Amos 9:13–15).

What Faithful Living Looks Like

Christians ought to take an interest in a variety of disciplines and activities, such as science, agriculture, literature, cooking, math, politics, and carpentry because they desire to be good stewards of the resources and abilities that God has granted them. They should desire to model creation stewardship in all these things because unregenerate humanity tends to do it in tainted ways. By God's common grace, unbelievers often produce amazing stewardship results. But even those amazing results tend to be turned into idols or used in ways contrary to God's creational design. Christians who seek to live faithfully in all these categories attempt to develop these potential idols into God-honoring tools.

What Faithful Living Doesn't Look Like

Christians ought not to be conformed to the world (Rom. 12:1–2). Some Christians say they're seeking to redeem culture but are simply embracing fallen human expressions of culture. They emphasize the need for having a significant presence in the culture to the neglect of maintaining a faithfully pure and holy walk. What's redemptive about mimicking fallen expressions of perverted human culture for the sake of saying something about God to others? (See 1 John 2:15–17; James 4:4; 1 Cor. 10:6–14; Ezek. 20:1–32.) While the Bible commands us to be light, it also commands us to be salt (Matt. 5:13–16; 1 Pet. 2:11–12; Phil. 2:15). The emphasis in this textbook is on students being faithful to God's original creational design in every sphere of life, which is made possible because a person is redeemed. Be sure to distinguish between this emphasis and the erroneous view that Christians must triumphantly overtake the cultural centers and power-broker positions of this world for the purpose of transforming (redeeming) culture (i.e., Christianizing all of society or bringing in the kingdom of Christ). That perspective can feed into a postmillennial eschatology, theonomy, or dominion theology (i.e., promoting theocracy).

Beware of Triumphalist Attitudes

Klaas Schilder discusses the limitations faced by both Christians and non-Christians in their cultural work:

> All men should do their daily work as cultural work. They are all creatures made by God. While living on this earth, they should labor in God's service on God's earth. But many do not work in this way. This is one reason why cultural development, the development of this world, will never be completed. Those who reject God use the materials that God has created and work with the abilities that God has given them, but without obeying God. As a result of this disobedience much of their cultural work will be spoiled.

In the end it will become evident that their cultural achievements are only torsos, truncated pyramids. Of course, there are also the regenerated. With them a beginning of obedience in cultural work should become visible. But this, too, will not lead to a completed cultural development. Christian culture, too, is left with truncated pyramids. Several reasons can be given for this. First is the fact that they are a minority. Only a few people are left to do a work that was to be performed by all. They simply do not have enough manpower to do what should be done in this world. Another reason is the sin that is still present in them. It can be [better] for a Christian not to engage in a certain type of work, because his eye or hand can lead him into sin.

[quoted in N. H. Gootjes, "Schilder on Christ and Culture," in J. Geertsema, ed., *Always Obedient: Essays on the Teaching of Dr. Klaas Schilder* (Phillipsburg, NJ: P&R, 1995), 43]

The Biblical Worldview

What are the three ingredients in a biblical worldview?

• *Head-heart system of facts and values*
• *Master story (i.e., CFR)*
• *Action (i.e., cultural behavior)*

Is it possible both to hold to a biblical worldview and to embrace the two-story view?

No, the two-story view by nature rejects the joining of the head-heart system, the unified overarching story of CFR, and explicitly Christian cultural action.

KEY CONNECTIONS

Now it's time to make two key connections to bring this chapter on the two-story view together.

(1) If God has a future plan for all creation, then there will be a time when everything in creation is set right. Paul told a group of believers tempted to give in to "gnostic" dualism, an ancient form of the two-story view, "In [Jesus Christ] all the fullness of God was pleased to dwell, and through him to reconcile to himself all things" (Col 1:19–20). And if "all things" in creation are going to be set right, there must be a right way to do those things. Let's pause and think about what "all things" includes. It's not just people, as we saw from Romans 8; it's also creation. But it's not just animals, or even trees and lakes and ozone layer composition. "All things" means everything God programmed into His original creation. And as we'll see in the next few units, that's a lot.

"All things" means institutions and academic disciplines like sports, cooking, advertising, biology, agriculture, sociology, medical science, high finance. The list could go on for a long time: political science, cinema, computer technology, economics, geology.[14]

Christians are not used to thinking of these things as being part of our future. But, biblically speaking, they are. One day, these things will all be done the right way, God's way. Because fallen people (including Christians) are now running all these fields, they are all damaged by sin in minor or major ways. But one day Christ will reconcile them all to God. God through Christ will retake all the territory occupied by the enemy. The earth is the Lord's.

(2) And now for the second key connection: if there's a right way to run these things in the future God will set up for us, there's a right way to run them *now*. Without a biblical worldview there's no way you'll know how your own career is supposed to be run. Will you be a politician? A farmer? A teacher? A biologist? A marketer? An artist? A writer? A mom? There are God-honoring ways to be these things and God-dishonoring ways. There are ways to be these things that honor the way God made the world, and there are ways that ignore it.

If a worldview is a head-heart system that tells a single overarching story about the world, the dualism of the two-story view just can't work. We can't split life into the sacred things of the heart and the secular things of the mind. It is more than possible, it is our duty, to view all of life—upper and lower stories—from a biblical perspective.

And if a worldview includes practical action, it's possible to *live* all of life, to make every choice, in obedience to God. Religion must not be barred from reaching down to the lower story. Maybe that's why American evangelist Bob Jones Sr. said, "[For a Christian,] life is not divided into the secular and the sacred. . . . [To him] all ground is holy ground. Every bush is a burning bush. Every place is a temple [of worship]."[15]

THINKING IT THROUGH 3.3

1. How does the biblical worldview of creation correct the flawed two-story view?

2. How does the biblical worldview of the Fall correct the flawed two-story view?

3. What is biblical redemption?

4. How does the biblical worldview of redemption correct the flawed two-story view?

♀5. Explain in your own words the two key connections that were presented at the end of the chapter.

THINKING IT THROUGH 3.3

1. The world can't be divided into things God owns and things He doesn't. It's possible to glorify God—or not—in every sphere. There is no realm of neutrality; every realm is significant to God.

2. There is no realm untouched by the Fall; the Fall is comprehensive. The so-called upper story isn't an escape from the Fall; the so-called lower story isn't free from fallen religious values.

3. It's what God does through Christ's cross-work in buying individuals out of the slavery of sin, forgiving them, delivering them, and transforming them. But it also includes God's work of restoring the whole earth from the effects of sin.

4. The material world is not temporary, insignificant, or evil (as the Gnostics taught) but will be restored to its original perfection in God's future plan for humanity. The Christian hope is not escape but resurrection to a world fully restored under God's rule.

♀5. First, God has a future plan for all creation in which everything will be set right. Second, if there is a right way to run God's creation in the future, then there is a way to conform to those creational norms now rather than working contrary to them.

3 CHAPTER REVIEW

Scripture Memory

Colossians 1:19–20

Making Connections

1. Give two reasons why many Christians separate life into a "sacred" realm and a "secular" realm.

2. Look at the chart on page 35. Where would secularists place the pro-life (anti-abortion) position on that chart? How about human trafficking?

3. Although Christians should abandon the distinction between the secular and the sacred, what distinctions should Christians maintain?

4. Rather than dichotomizing the world into the two-story view, what paradigm should Christians use to accurately live out a biblical worldview?

Developing Skills in Apologetics and Worldview

5. How should you respond to a secularist who wants you to keep your (biblical) values at home and out of the public square?

6. How can you guard against falling into the two-story view or the opposite ditch of no distinctions?

Examining Assumptions and Evidence

7. For what purpose did Rene Descartes doubt everything? Why was his conclusion about human reasoning flawed?

8. Explain why the secularist two-story view (diagrammed in the chart on page 35) is inaccurate.

9. Explain why the secularist two-story view can never be applied consistently.

10. What's your dream job? How would you be able to know whether you were doing that job in a God-honoring way?

Becoming a Creative Cultivator

11. Write a letter to the editor of your local newspaper about the place of faith in the public square.

CHAPTER REVIEW ANSWERS

Making Connections

1. (a) They try to protect the religious things they value from the secularist bullies. (b) They try to protect themselves from the moral contamination of secular activities.

2. Secularists would put the prolife position in upper story (the private sphere of nonrational values relegated to personal preference or choice) and human trafficking in the lower story (the public sphere of rational facts/scientific knowledge binding on everyone).

3. Christians should maintain the biblical distinctions between the reverent and the profane and between the pure and impure.

4. Creation, Fall, Redemption

Developing Skills in Apologetics and Worldview

5. Don't be alarmed or surprised; this is not new. Don't be intimidated into giving up biblical values in the public square in order to protect yourself from persecution. Respond with civility, but challenge his false claim to neutrality. Insist on living redemptively in every sphere according to God's creational design even in this fallen world. Be prepared to suffer persecution, but delight in God.

6. Recognize the creational good in each sphere, the fallen nature of all things, and God's redemptive plan of restoration. Evaluate whether or not something reflects its creational design or a fallen human perversion. Apply the clear biblical commands of reverence and purity in all that you participate in.

Examining Assumptions and Evidence

7. He was trying to find a neutral and irrefutable foundation for all human knowledge. His conclusion was flawed because he believed human reasoning was a neutral, trustworthy starting point over divine revelation.

8. Revelatory truth is rational, though not necessarily in the same way as empirical science since it is a deductive philosophy rather than an inductive observation. No scientific facts are brute and valueless; they're all interpretations based on philosophical and religious presuppositions.

9. Your values—your principles, what you think is important and worth protecting and promoting—guide all your decisions. Since the two-story view is an inaccurate paradigm of reality, it can never be consistently followed.

10. (Students' dream jobs will vary.) For your work to be honoring to God, it should first be done ethically without compromising purity. Second, one's work should be prioritized correctly. Finally, it should be done in light of the biblical worldview lens of CFR (taking into account fallen practices and working to bring things back in line with God's creational design—living in light of redemption).

Becoming a Creative Cultivator

11. Screen letters before any of them are actually sent to the newspaper. Letters should be respectful, well written, and in line with the content of this chapter (e.g., worldview values always inform public policy; clarify what it truly means to be tolerant; etc.).

TERMS TO REMEMBER

secular—pertaining to the world and not religion, non-religious

dualism—dividing something into two opposing parts

two-story view—an approach that compartmentalizes life into two separate categories, the secular and the sacred

UNITS 2–4

Unit 1 introduced students to a basic understanding of worldview, argued for the best apologetic approach, and reinforced the necessity of applying that worldview to all of life. The next three units provide students with a positive presentation of the foundational biblical teachings of a Christian worldview. Each of these units explains the three parts of the Bible's CFR story.

CHAPTER 4

This chapter presents to the students who the Creator is, what His motive and goal in creating the world were, and how He relates to His world. Since man is patterned after His Creator (see chapter 5), understanding what God loves is essential for understanding who we are as humans and what our goals ought to be.

CHAPTER 5

The image of God in man and the Creation Mandate constitute the foundation for all the cultural activities that will be discussed in this book. The image of God also provides the only secure foundation for human value, grounding the Christian view of justice, gender, and other major aspects of human life.

CHAPTER 6

The Christian worldview affirms the goodness of God's creation. It also teaches that God built laws into His creation that govern how creation works and how we ought to live. False worldviews always underlie the world's problems in some aspect of God's good creation. Understanding the goodness of creation is necessary to identify the real problems in the Fall. Understanding creational norms is important because these norms are bent by the Fall and need to be bent back by redemption.

2

CREATION

Chapter Four **GOD THE CREATOR**

Chapter Five **MAN AND HIS MANDATE**

Chapter Six **EVERYTHING GOD MADE WAS VERY GOOD**

GOD THE CREATOR | 047

The student will be able to

4.1 Explain why the personhood of God—specifically, the mutual love displayed among the persons of the Trinity—must provide the basis for God's motivation to create the world and the human motivation to exist.

4.2 Explain how God's ultimate goal for all things, namely, the display of His own glory, is consistent with His love.

4.3 Defend the proper relationship between God and creation by contrasting the biblical portrayal of the unrivaled transcendent yet immanent God with four false views.

SECTION OBJECTIVES 4.1

1. Explain why every motivation for existence can be traced back to who or what a person loves.

2. Explain why your ultimate motivation of love ought to be expressed toward God and your neighbor.

3. Connect God's own ultimate motivation of mutual Trinitarian love to His design for all creation to share in His love.

Chapter Four GOD THE CREATOR

In the beginning was the Word, and the Word was with God, and the Word was God. He was in the beginning with God. All things were made through him, and without him was not any thing made that was made.

Father, I desire that they also, whom you have given me, may be with me where I am, to see my glory that you have given me because you loved me before the foundation of the world.

Scripture Memory
John 1:1–3

John 17:24

4.1 GOD THE THREE IN ONE

The Christian story doesn't actually begin at the beginning.

It can't because one of the distinctive claims of the Bible is that there was a "time" before the beginning of our universe—and we can know about it. If "in the beginning, God created" (Gen. 1:1), then God must have existed before the beginning. Just like your parents had a life long before you were born, there was a time in which God existed with His own purposes, purposes that didn't necessarily have anything to do with us or our planet.

In fact, it's this time before time that will help us dig down to the true bedrock of a Christian worldview and even the real meaning of life. There couldn't be any overall meaning or purpose for our world if it came into being by accident. Big bangs don't have motivations any more than volcano eruptions do; they just happen. Only persons have purposes. And if you are going to have a Christian worldview, you need to know what motivated God to make this world in the first place.

> "WHEN YOU SAY,
> 'IT'S ALL CHAOS, MAN,'
> YOU'RE ALSO SAYING,
> 'YOU'RE POINTLESS.'" [1]
>
> —N. D. WILSON

LOVE AND MOTIVATION

Motivations—whether God's or yours—are interesting, complex things. For example, why did you get up this morning? Was it because your mom made you, or because you wanted to?

Either way or both ways, the operative motivation at your house this morning probably boiled down to one word: *school*. Your mom was motivated by school because if you don't graduate from high school the chances are higher that you will still be living in her basement, adding to her laundry piles, and eating her meatloaf at age thirty-six. Perhaps *you* were motivated by school for a related but different reason: because you're planning to head off to college, and high school is a stepping stone toward that goal.

But this analysis doesn't go far enough because going to college isn't an end in itself. You go to college for deeper reasons. Have you ever traced your motivations all the way to their root?

Why, in fact, do you want to go to college? So you can get a good job and make money—to provide for your future family? There's nothing necessarily wrong with that. Or maybe to train for service in Christ's kingdom? Nothing wrong with that either, of course.

But can we stop here? Is this what you live for? Future spouse and future kids? Future church ministry? Are these the things that motivate you? Maybe, but we're still not down to bedrock.

Lesson Plan Chart—Chapter 4

Section Title	Pages	Activity Manual	Days
4.1 God the Three in One	48–51	Activity 7	2 days
4.2 God the Spring	51–55		1 day
4.3 God the Unrivaled, Yet God with Us	55–60	Activity 8	2 days
Review	61		1 day
Total Suggested Days			**6 days**

Introduce Unit 2

Unit 1 introduced students to a basic understanding of worldview, argued for the best apologetic approach, and reinforced the necessity of applying that worldview to all of life. The next three units provide students with a positive presentation of the foundational biblical teachings of a Christian worldview. Each of these units follows the outline of the Bible's metanarrative: CFR.

Purposeless Existence

Can there be meaning or purpose if the world came into being by accident without God? Most people with an evolutionary worldview seem to desire meaning and purpose in life. But can they simply make up their own purpose in life? How can they justify ultimate meaning beyond themselves when their master story is one of chaotic

If you dig and dig to the very bottom of all your motivations, the Bible tells you what you'll find: love. It's ultimately what and whom you love (like God, like a future spouse and future kids—or, sadly, just yourself) that determines what you think and do. Motivations are built on loves. That's why Jesus Himself named (1) loving God with your whole heart and (2) loving others the way you love yourself as the two most important laws there are (Matt. 22:34–40). A Jewish expert in the law of God asked Jesus a question "to test him."

> "Teacher, which is the great commandment in the Law?" And [Christ] said to him, "You shall love the Lord your God with all your heart and with all your soul and with all your mind. This is the great and first commandment. And a second is like it: You shall love your neighbor as yourself. On these two commandments depend all the Law and the Prophets." (Matt. 22:36–40)

Every one of the rules in the Bible, Jesus says, depends on love. In other words, if you really love God with all your heart and love the people God has placed in your life as much as you love yourself, you will obey God's laws. Because that's all the laws are: a description of what life looks like when your loves are all in the right order. That's true today, too, even with mundane things like traffic laws. If you really love other people, you'll be a careful driver.

GOD IS LOVE

If love lies at the very center of what we are, it's not a coincidence that it lies at the center of who God is too. But we need to flip that order around. God doesn't love because we do; we love because God does and because we are made in His image. First John 4:8 says this with brevity ("Love is from God") and with beauty ("God is love").

And the centrality of love brings us to a very important worldview question, the most important and foundational question in the Christian worldview: ultimately, what or whom does God love? In other words, what are God's motivations built on? We can't ask God why He gets up in the morning or why He wants to go to college! We can't find out what motivates Him the same way we find out what motivates you, but we *can* listen to Him speak in Scripture.

And this is what He says:

> "Behold my servant, whom I uphold, my chosen, in whom my soul delights" (Isa. 42:1).

When God speaks about His "servant" in Isaiah 42, one of Isaiah's servant songs, He is speaking of Jesus more than seven hundred years before His birth.

And He also says:

> "This is my beloved Son, in whom I am well pleased" (Matt. 3:17).

And this is what His Son, Jesus Christ, says about Him:

> "The Father loves the Son" (John 3:35; 5:20).

Each of these three statements from the Bible says the same thing in a different way: God the Father loves God the Son. God's soul "delights" in His Son, Jesus. He loved Him before the first Christmas ever happened. And it's this love that gives us a window into what happened even before the beginning because, three decades after the first Christmas, Jesus prays this:

> "Father, . . . you loved me before the foundation of the world" (John 17:24).

random chance? If we are just stardust originating from the big bang, molecules bumping into each other by chance, a psychological machine of hormonal reactions, then it follows that we can bear no personal responsibility for choices or actions—and there is no meaning or purpose.

Even though he's in the minority to admit such, Will Provine makes the case that a consistent evolutionary worldview doesn't allow for meaning and purpose in life:

> Let me summarize my views on what modern evolutionary biology tells us loud and clear. . . . There are no gods, no purposes, no goal-directed forces of any kind. There is no life after death. When I die, I am absolutely certain that I am going to be dead. That's the end for me. There is no ultimate foundation for ethics, no ultimate meaning to life, and no free will for humans, either. [W. B. Provine, quoted in Matthew B. Wincowski, *Crumbs from a Bum: Exploring the Intellectually Stagnant Impulses of an Inattentive Age* (Bloomington, IN: Westbow, 2014), 91]

Without the personhood of God there is no foundation for the personhood of humans—from which flow purpose and meaning.

God's Law Reflects God's Design

You can't live contrary to God's design and function successfully in life. You were designed to love God and others; God provided guidelines to help you know how to live according to this design. The law of Christ for the New Testament believer isn't a burden but a guideline for living the best way possible (1 John 5:3; Pss. 40:8; 119:70).

Living out of step with His design/law can only lead to the destruction of self and others. It's fruitless to live contrary to it (Prov. 1:20–33; Rom. 1:28–32). Yet, this has been the history of humanity—people raging against God's design by trying to go their own way (Ps. 2:1–6; Prov. 14:12).

Motives Are Desires

The Bible uses the terms *desire* and *delight* to describe a person's motives based on what he loves. The Bible has a lot to say about desires and delights. Ask the students to create a chart that compares and contrasts the desires of the godly with the ungodly.

Example verses for the godly: Pss. 1:2; 19:10; 37:4; 40:8; 73:25; 119:14, 16, 24, 35, 47; 145:19; Prov. 10:24; 11:23; Rom. 7:18, 22; 10:1; 13:14; 1 Cor. 10:6; Gal. 5:16–17, 24; Phil. 1:23; 1 Tim. 3:1; 2 Tim. 3:12; Heb. 11:16

Example verses for the ungodly: Gen. 3:6; 4:7; Ps. 10:3; Prov. 1:22; 2:14; 13:2, 19; 21:10, 25; John 8:44; Eph. 2:3; 4:22; Col. 3:5; 1 Tim. 6:9; James 1:14–15; 4:2; 2 Pet. 1:4; 3:3; 1 John 2:16–17; Jude 1:7, 16

Misplaced Loves

God summed up His requirement by telling us to love Him and others (Deut. 6:4–5; Matt. 22:36–40). Every sin is the result of misplaced loves.

What are some Bible verses that connect sin to a misplaced love?

Eccles. 5:10; Matt. 6:24; 1 Tim. 3:3; 6:10; 2 Tim. 3:2; Heb. 13:5—the love of money/gold

Phil. 2:21; 2 Tim. 3:2—the love of self/one's own glory

1 Kings 11:1-8; Prov. 7:1-2, 25—love for the wrong girls/guys

2 Tim. 4:10; 1 John 2:15–17—love of the worldly culture around you

Most people are tempted to live for gold, glory, or girls/guys rather than God.

God Is Love (1 John 4:7–12)

Why should we love one another? Where does this motivation come from?

We should love because we have been born of God and have inherited His love.

If you don't love what God does, what does it prove?

You don't have a relational knowledge of God because it's impossible to be born of God without inheriting His love.

How was God able to share His love?

He transformed those who were by nature unloving by sending His Son to pay for their sins.

What was God's goal in sharing His love?

spiritual life that manifests loving obedience

What results from our love for others?

Even though no one has seen God, people can be assured of His existence and what He's like when Christians love others—something that must constantly be perfected in us.

God's Ultimate Motivation

God is holy in His love and loving in His holiness. Each of these attributes complements the other rather than competing against each other. Every attribute of God is perfectly balanced by all of the other attributes. However, there's nothing wrong with emphasizing a particular attribute, just as Scripture does. Nothing God does can be done apart from the mutual love of the Father, Son, and Spirit. Thus, it may rightly be stated that God is ultimately motivated by love in all that He does.

Explaining the Trinity

The discussion of the Trinity in this context isn't meant to provide an exhaustive explanation or apologetic. Rather, it is meant to highlight a particular implication, which reinforces the importance and significance of the doctrine as it relates to the existence of the world. Therefore, do not feel obligated to conduct an extended discussion explaining the details of the doctrine. The discussion in this text is based on the assumption that students have already been taught the biblical data undergirding the doctrine.

[A pamphlet that gives a helpful summary of this doctrine is *The Trinity* (Torrance, CA: Rose Publishing, 1999).]

Islam's Denial of the Trinity

Surah 4.171: "People of the Book [Christians]...do not say: 'Three.' . . . God is but one God. God forbid that He should have a son!"

Surah 112: "Say: 'God is One, the Eternal God. He begot none, nor was He begotten. None is equal to Him.'"

[*The Koran*, trans. N. J. Dawood, rev. ed. (London: Penguin Classics, 1994)]

> *"BEFORE HE EVER CREATED, BEFORE HE EVER RULED THE WORLD, BEFORE ANYTHING ELSE, THIS GOD WAS A FATHER LOVING HIS SON."* [2]
>
> —MICHAEL REEVES

This is what God was doing before He ever let there be light. His Son and Spirit were the delight of His heart before there were any other beings to love. And the love didn't go in only one direction. Jesus also said,

"I do as the Father has commanded me, so that the world may know that *I love the Father*" (John 14:31).

There is little doubt that this love began before the world did.

THE INNER LOVE OF THE TRINITY

Digging deep into what the Bible says about God's loves brings us right into the middle of one of the most important doctrines of the Christian faith: the **Trinity**.

The doctrine is simple in a way but so profound that you'll never search it out completely. God is one and, in a different sense, God is three. The ancient Jews were taught to have no other gods before God, and they were told to say, "The Lord our God, the Lord is one" (Deut. 6:4). But when Jesus came, God revealed what He had hinted at in the Old Testament: there are three persons—Father, Son, and Spirit—in the one God. The Father is the director, the leader—the *father*. But this doesn't mean the Son is a second-place God, or the Spirit a third-place God. Since the earliest centuries of the Christian church, careful readers of the Bible have agreed that Scripture gives fully equal divinity to each of the three persons of the Trinity. Jesus, the Bible says, "is the radiance of the glory of God and the exact imprint of his nature" (Heb. 1:3; cf. Col. 2:9). John explains that "this was why the Jews were seeking all the more to kill [Jesus], because . . . he was even calling God his own Father, making himself equal with God" (John 5:18).

But why would God ask people to swallow such a difficult doctrine? Islam, in effect, makes *disbelief* in the Trinity one of its five doctrinal pillars. Most major splinter groups that have left Christianity—the Mormons and the Jehovah's Witnesses—have done so in part so they could avoid belief in the Trinity. It seems utterly irrational to them. Why hold on to this strange teaching?

Most importantly, Christians hold on to the doctrine of the Trinity because the Bible teaches it, and it's not up to us to teach logic to the owner of logic. But another big reason is actually *love*. Think about it: if God were one person, completely alone, there could not have been any love before He created other beings (whether angels, humans, or dogs). Love, then, couldn't be essential to God. Love could only be something else He created, a later add-on. Before creation, it wouldn't have been true to say that "God *is* love."

But the doctrine of the Trinity indicates that love existed before the world did—among the three persons: Father, Son, and Spirit. As one theologian put it, "When the love between . . . persons is happy, healthy and secure, they rejoice to share it. Just so it is with God. . . . Being perfectly loving, from all eternity the Father and the Son have delighted to share their love and joy with and through the Spirit."[3]

Christians have worked for a long time to understand the Bible's talk about the Trinity and the love inside it. We're past the limit of human capacities here. We have enough trouble understanding ourselves; what human could fully comprehend his or her Creator? Every illustration of the Trinity is a feeble attempt to describe a truth

---

 ## Why Trinity Is a Hard Concept to Understand

A brief but very helpful illustration regarding our difficulty in understanding the Trinity can be found in Lewis's *Mere Christianity*. He makes an analogy about a line (which is one-dimensional), a square (which is two-dimensional), and a cube (which is three-dimensional). Just as it would be difficult to understand a two-dimensional world if you lived in a one-dimensional world, it's hard for us to comprehend one Being as three persons when in our world one being is always one person. However, that world is not in

contradiction to our world; it is simply more complex than our world—just as a cube is still simply made up of the same straight lines that a square is but in a three-dimensional way rather than a two-dimensional way. [C. S. Lewis, *Mere Christianity*, rev. ed. (San Francisco: HarperCollins, 2001), 161–62]

Of course, the illustration breaks down because God is in fact more than just a more complex version of us (even though we are patterned after His image). He is in a category all His own.

Assign Activity 7, "Defining God Properly."

so big it can't fit in our minds, like one housecat trying to explain to another the literary themes of their owner's favorite novel. (See sidebar.)

But there's something here you do have to get: the love and joy and happiness of God is totally full. God is not and has never been lonely. Whatever motivated Him to create the world, it wasn't that He lacked something. He had in Himself—in the love and fellowship of the three persons—an infinite amount of everything He could ever need.

THINKING IT THROUGH 4.1

1. What is your ultimate motivation for everything in life?

2. What central biblical commands reveal that this is indeed the overarching motivation for all of life? What is the connection between God's law and your motivation for existence?

3. What is the ultimate motivation that caused God to create the world? Was His motivation to create the world due to anything that He lacked?

4. Why is the doctrine of the Trinity a necessary foundation for explaining God's ultimate motivation?

♦ 5. Why can't the evolutionary worldview truly justify any ultimate meaning and purpose in life? What is the necessary outcome of lacking ultimate meaning and purpose in life?

4.2 GOD THE SPRING

Just as human love is an echo of divine love, humans have goals because God does. In the last section we asked, "What does God love?" In this one we ask a similar but related question: "What does God aim at?" Since the Father loves the Son, who loves the Spirit, who loves them both—what goals grow out of this Trinitarian love?

GOD'S FINAL PURPOSE

The Bible answers this pretty directly. What is the end of all history, the overriding purpose the **triune*** God aims at in all He does? Put simply, it is His own **glory**—the display of His own amazing love, holiness, power, justice, and all the other things that make God God. When the apostle Paul described the culmination of the Bible's story, he described it this way:

> Then comes the end, when [Christ] delivers the kingdom to God the Father after destroying every rule and every authority and power. . . . When all things are subjected to him, then the Son himself will also be subjected to him who put all things in subjection under him, that God may be all in all. (1 Cor. 15:24–28)

"That God may be all in all." God's own uncontested rule and subsequent glory make up the goal He has aimed at in all His works throughout all time.

triune: three ("tri-") in one ("-une").

SECTION OBJECTIVES 4.2

1. Identify God's ultimate goal as His own glory.

2. Explain how God's ultimate objective to display His own glory is consistent with His essence as a God of love.

3. Attribute God's creation of the world and of humans to the overflow of His glorious love rather than to His need for or lack of anything.

4. Identify humanity's ultimate goal as enjoyment in God's glorification.

The Glory of God
What is the glory of God?

The glory of God is the display of all of His attributes, perfect character, and abilities.

What words describe why something is considered glorious?

Something is considered glorious due to its honor, splendor, majesty, dignity, and awesomeness.

What common scriptural metaphor pictures what viewing God's glory is like? (Exod. 34:34–35; Matt. 17:2; Heb. 1:3)

It's comparable to looking at the brightness of the sun. You can't look at it directly—even the indirect radiance is blinding.

How has God displayed His glory in creation, in His Son, and in the church? (Ps. 19:1; Eph. 3:21; 2 Pet. 1:17)

The intricate design and beauty of creation, the power and authority of the Son, and the new life of sanctified believers all display God's glory.

How are New Testament believers changed by God's glory? (2 Cor. 3:5–18)

The glory of the Old Covenant fades away and the veiled heart is done away with when a believer turns to Christ under the New Covenant. The glory of the Lord is revealed by the Spirit through the Word, progressively sanctifying the life.

THINKING IT THROUGH 4.1

1. Love—what and whom you love—determines everything you think and do.

2. You must love God with your whole being and your neighbor as yourself (Matt. 22:37–39). God's law is simply a description of what it would look like if you were living out that love.

3. What or whom God loves guides all His motivations. Thus, the mutual love of the Trinity caused Him to create the world. He didn't lack anything; He desired to share His fullness with those He created.

4. Love must be an uncreated attribute that has been a part of God's essence on display for all eternity; only the Trinity makes this possible.

♦ 5. Ultimate meaning and purpose is rooted in love, which can't exist without a person at the foundation of the world. The necessary outcome is despair because impersonal meaningless chance is at the foundation of an evolutionary world.

💬 God's Goal and Your Life

Discuss with students how their lives will either reflect a concerted effort to glorify God, as they were created to do, or a life pulled into the vortex of what comes natural to fallen beings—finding enjoyment in things other than God.

Is it possible to embrace God's love (His promises of justification) and live in constant disobedience to Him—contrary to sanctifaction? (John 14:15; Rom. 8:29; Gal. 5:25; Eph. 1:4; 2:10; 4:1)

No, beliefs ought to transform behavior. Sanctified living flows out of lives conformed to Christ and His law (1 Cor. 9:21).

If God's goal for your life is to glorify Him by enjoying Him, then how can you reach that goal? (Rom. 6:16; Phil. 3:12–14)

by yielding your life to and seeking after God

Ephesians 4:17–24 gives one description of the characteristic pattern of someone yielded to and seeking after God. It's not a formula or a twelve-step process. It's a description of characteristics that develop when you walk relationally with God. While it demands effort on your part, it's all due to the empowering of the Spirit (Eph. 5:18; Phil. 2:13).

What is the pattern of a godly person's thinking, desires, and actions as outlined in Ephesians 4:17–24?

- *Put off a hardened, calloused heart greedy for impurity and filled with corrupt and deceitful desires (change your desires).*
- *Put off the futility of a darkened mind and put on a renewed mind (change your thinking).*
- *Put off the practice of impurity, living like unbelievers do, and put on righteousness and holiness (change your actions).*

What motivates believers to do this?

Believers are people who have "learned Christ" (Eph. 4:20) through hearing and submitting to His teaching of the truth by putting off and putting on.

Renewing the mind is the lynchpin that holds together putting off and putting on (Eph. 4:23). How do you renew your mind? (Rom. 12:1–2; cf. Eph. 5:25–27)

Renewing the mind is in direct contrast to conforming to the world. The world influences you and always seeks to mold you into its image. But God, through the influence of Scripture (the washing of the Word), transforms you into the image of His Son.

How do you battle against corrupt and deceitful desires, which lead to impure actions? (Eph. 6:10–18; cf. James 1:13–15)

by putting on the full armor of God, every piece of which represents an aspect of the gospel

---

Paul says the same thing another way in his famous letter to the Christians in Rome. After finishing a massive section of intense theology about God's wise and gracious plan for the world, Romans 9–11, Paul just stops and marvels at the plan of God, quoting the biblical prophet Isaiah along the way:

> Oh, the depth of the riches and wisdom and knowledge of God! How unsearchable are his judgments and how inscrutable his ways! "For who has known the mind of the Lord, or who has been his counselor?" "Or who has given a gift to him that he might be repaid?" For from him and through him and to him are all things. To him be glory forever. Amen. (Rom. 11:33–36)

GOD'S GOAL: GOD'S GLORY

It's important to understand that these are not isolated verses. This goal—God's goal to display His own glory—is a pattern throughout the Bible. Have you ever noticed Bible statements like these? What motivates God in these passages?

- "The Lord will not forsake his people, for his great name's sake" (1 Sam. 12:22).
- "Our fathers, when they were in Egypt, did not . . . remember the abundance of your steadfast love, but rebelled by the sea, at the Red Sea. Yet he saved them for his name's sake, that he might make known his mighty power" (Ps. 106:7–8).
- "Bring my sons from afar and my daughters from the end of the earth, everyone who is called by my name, whom I created for my glory" (Isa. 43:6–7).
- "For my name's sake I defer my anger, for the sake of my praise I restrain it for you. . . . For my own sake, for my own sake, I do it, for how should my name be profaned? My glory I will not give to another" (Isa. 48:9, 11).
- "Father, the hour has come; glorify your Son that the Son may glorify you" (John 17:1).

We could list many, many more scriptural quotations that all say the same thing: when God makes a choice, He is motivated by His own glory, the honor of His own name, the display of His great power, the extending of His rule. God told Pharaoh, the king of Egypt who enslaved Abraham's family, "For this very purpose I have raised you up, that I might show my power in you, and that my name might be proclaimed in all the earth" (Rom. 9:17). God's goal in all He does is God's glory.

Glory and Love

The only way you can know God is for Him to reveal Himself to you. He has; the Bible says He's done it inside you by writing His laws in your conscience (Rom. 2:14–15). He has done it outside you through His creation, which shouts His glory all day (Rom. 1:20–21; Ps. 19:1–4). But conscience and creation can tell you only so much. You need words. And you have them. You've read a lot of them just now—words, of course, from the Bible.

And now you need to do an important piece of theological thinking with those words from the Bible, some thinking that you may never have been called on to do before. To have a right view of God, you need to notice an apparent problem with the two sets of Bible passages you've just read—the passages about God's love and the passages about God's goal, His own glory. The apparent problem is that these two groups of Bible statements don't seem, at first glance, to fit very well together. "God is love" and "God seeks His own glory in all He does"—how could both be true?

If it bothers you that God seeks His own glory above all else, it's probably because people you know who seek their own glory are offensively proud, arrogant, and

---

According to Ephesians 4:25–5:12, what are some of the practical applications that illustrate what it means to put off ungodliness and to put on righteousness and holiness?

Don't lie; rather, tell the truth.

- *Don't hold onto sinful anger; rather, do what's needed to diffuse it immediately.*
- *Don't steal; rather, labor to provide for your own needs and give to others.*
- *Don't speak corruptly; rather, edify others with graciousness.*
- *Don't grieve the Holy Spirit by being bitter, wrathful, angry, or slanderous; rather, be kind, tenderhearted, and forgiving.*
- *Don't be immoral and impure or even talk about such things; rather, shine as light on that darkness.*

Is it misapplying Scripture to connect the dots between these broad categories of sin and the actual concrete, practical actions of one's life? (For example, is it legalistic to identify a particular action, such as embezzlement, as fitting into the category of stealing? Or is it legalistic to identify particular words as vulgar metaphors that paint an uncouth descriptive picture, fitting under the category of corrupt communication?)

No, it's proper to compare the reality of your life to the principles of the Bible. The Bible would be absurdly useless if it were wrong for us to identify the actual practical actions of our lives with the broad categories listed above. Paul assumes that these things are identifiable with some common sense and careful discernment (Eph. 5:10, 15; cf. Prov. 14:8). In contrast, a fool refuses to be instructed or corrected (Prov. 1:7).

self-absorbed. What's more, they're wrong. They aren't the exalted beings they think they are.

But God is. The reason it's wrong for humans to seek their own glory is that they're humans—fallen, finite humans. Boxer Muhammad Ali was famous for shouting, "I am the greatest!"[5] Of course, his greatness faded. But God truly is the greatest, in every category and for all time. God is right to be focused on His own glory because He is not one of us. He is infinitely wiser, more powerful, and more righteous than any human could possibly be. To show others His preeminent glory is just to tell the truth about the way things are. If He loved and valued anything else more, He would be lying. Even if He loved you more than He loves His own glory, He would be an idolater—and you would be His idol.

We are offended by arrogant, selfish people because their self-love comes out in the way they act. They're hard to be around; they don't give; they don't love. But this kind of twisted self-love is not what we see in God. We know that in part because God Himself came to live among us in the person of Jesus Christ. Was Jesus selfish, arrogant, and hard to get along with? No, God's love for Himself translated into a love for us that sent Jesus to a cruel death and the ultimate sacrifice. And yet the Bible says that God sent His Son to die for our sins precisely for "the praise of His glorious grace" (Eph. 1:3–6).

The End for Which God Created the World

Now we're ready to ask again the questions we've been raising here and there throughout this chapter: Why did God create the world? Why is there something rather than nothing?

Search online for that second question and you'll find out that it's a very old one. The online *Stanford Encyclopedia of Philosophy* carefully lists the answers philosophers have given over time, and there's a lot of disagreement among them. The author of this encyclopedia's article about "Nothingness" even raises the Bible's answer as a major possibility:

> The Genesis creation story suggests that God made everything without relying [on] any antecedent ingredients. The story also suggests that God had a reason to create. If this account could be corroborated we would have an explanation of why there are some concrete things.[6]

JONATHAN EDWARDS ON GOD'S GOAL IN CREATION

Early American pastor, theologian, and evangelist Jonathan Edwards dedicated close attention to this question: Why did God create the world? He answered it in a richly scriptural and carefully logical book called *A Dissertation Concerning the End for Which God Created the World.* He wrote, "It appears that all that is ever spoken of in the Scripture as an ultimate end of God's works is included in that one phrase, the glory of God. . . . In the creature's knowing, esteeming, loving, rejoicing in, and praising God, the glory of God is both exhibited and acknowledged; his fullness is received and returned. . . . The refulgence shines upon and into the creature, and is reflected back to the luminary. The beams of glory come from God, are something of God, and are refunded back again to their original. So that the whole is of God, and in God, and to God; and he is the beginning, and the middle, and the end."[7]

Jonathan Edwards
(1703–1758)

Not the Reason God Created the World

God wasn't lonely or bored or unhappy. He wasn't just experimenting. God had a plan to share His love with us all along (Eph. 1:4; 2:10; Jer. 31:3). God didn't have to share His love with us, but He wanted to do so. The earth doesn't have to necessarily exist for God to exist. Creation is due to the mutual and everlasting love of the Trinity overflowing from His gloriousness to us—not because He lacked anything that He needed in us or the world (Gen. 1:26; Acts 17:24–25).

The Eternal Motivation: God's Love

The existence of Trinitarian fellowship from all eternity means that God's love preceded God's creation of the universe. God's love was the motivation for creating the world.

The answer to the question of why God created the world and humans is that it was done *by* God *for* God out of mutual Trinitarian love (Col. 1:16; Gen. 1:26). The reason God created the world provides a basis for the reason you live your life the way you do (the meaning for your existence).

How does this fundamentally impact a person's worldview? Compare and contrast the Christian and secular worldviews.

Christian Worldview

Basis: special creation due to God's Trinitarian love

Implication for living your life: live it so that you delight in your Creator and He delights in you

Secular Worldview

Basis: random chaotic evolution due to chance processes

Implication for living your life:
(1) live according to impersonal laws of nature (fatalism);
(2) live according to situation ethics (the end justifies the means), utilitarian pragmatism (the greatest good for the greatest number of people), or self-realization (might makes right); or
(3) live according to your own subjective desires (whatever makes you happy)

Jonathan Edwards on Trinitarian Love

The American theologian Jonathan Edwards said, "The happiness of God consists in the infinite love he has to and delight he has in himself; or, in other words, in the infinite delight there is between the Father and the Son. . . . The happiness of the Deity, as all other true happiness, consists in love and society."

[*The Works of Jonathan Edwards* in *Writings on the Trinity, Grace, and Faith,* ed. Sang Hyun Lee (New Haven, CT: Yale University Press, 2003), 21:186–87]

The concepts in this chapter are reflected in Edwards's somewhat difficult-to-read "Concerning the End for which God Created the World" in volume 8 of the Yale edition of his works. (Edwards's works are available for free online courtesy of the Jonathan Edwards Center at Yale University.)

Ben Stevens has written an adapted version of Edward's work in updated language: *Why God Created the World: A Jonathan Edwards Adaptation* (Colorado Springs: NavPress, 2014).

Creation and the Meaning of Life

If the very reason God created us was His desire to share the overflow of His love with us, bringing glory to His name, then it's a travesty to live life for something other than God's glory, refusing to share in His love. It's foolish to spurn your Creator's love because it's anti-normative (contrary to your creational design and purpose). Your meaning in life is wrapped up in God's motivation for creating the world and His end goal for the world. Your meaning in life is to glorify God by sharing in His love.

God's Self-Existence

What does it mean to say that God is self-existent, and why is it so foundational? It means that God is sufficient in Himself. He is totally full and not lacking anything. He is independent from the necessity of any created thing outside Himself. The absolute fullness of anything that He needs can be found within Himself—infinitely so. This is the foundation that distinguishes the Creator from the created, keeping Him in a unique category of His own. We are all dependent on things outside of ourselves in order to come into existence and to maintain our own life. In contrast, God's self-existence means that God wasn't brought into being by someone or something else. Thus, He is eternal because of His self-existence. Since He has always been, it's absurd to ask what caused Him to exist. He exists by nature of who He is (He's God) and not by the quality of some mechanism of nature outside Himself. God's Trinitarian self-existence means that God never needs something from the outside to bring Him joy or fellowship. This foundational attribute is the best way to identify who exactly God is—He is the I Am (Exod. 3:13–15). Out of Him flows all life (Ps. 36:7–9; John 5:26).

The Chief End of Man

What does the question about man's "chief end" mean? It's a question that asks what your primary goal in life is.

Your primary goal ought to be to glorify God. That goal is achieved when you share in His love—when you enjoy unhindered fellowship with Him. All of your God-given desires can be satisfied in your relationship with Him (Ps. 37:4). Therefore, longing for an enjoyment of God's glory should not just be prominent in your life; it should be preeminent. It is the whole purpose of your created life.

What does a longing to enjoy God's glory include? It includes a certain kind of God-driven emotion rooted in active obedience. Many are misled by an approach that seeks to work up an emotional high to feel spiritually connected. But this is backwards. Working up emotions to feel spiritually connected often results in a superficial counterfeit that also ignores obedience and holiness. Instead, one ought to be spiritually connected to God by seeking holiness and obedience. This will result in a proper fear and love of God and proper emotions. Remember, God's commands are simply the descriptions of what it means to love God and your neighbor in all the concrete details of life. If you long to enjoy God's glory, you will also love God's commands and long to obey them (Ps. 1:2; 119:70, 77, 97, 113, 163, 165, 174; Rom. 7:22; 1 John 5:3). Lawlessness is the manifestation of a lack of love for God and others—and a mark of false teachers and counterfeit Christians in the end times (Matt. 24:9–14; 2 Tim. 3:1–9; Titus 1:16; 2 Pet. 2:1–22).

But the author dismisses the Bible's view. He says it would mean that "the existence of God necessitates the existence of the Earth."[8] In other words, he thinks the Bible is saying God had to create the world. This is no answer, he thinks.

But does the Bible really say He *had to*?

If God had been lonely or unhappy—if there had been no gloriously joyful Trinity living in perfect unity with one another eternally—then maybe it would make sense to see our world as something God had to make. Without us, who would He have to talk to? To love? Maybe creating the world all those years ago was His last attempt at finally making Himself happy.

But God isn't unhappy. He isn't lonely. That's us, not Him. We're the ones who, because of sin, are often unhappy. We're the ones who can't find ultimate contentment even in the best things in this earthly life, even in falling in love. Many marriages end in unhappiness even if they don't end in divorce. And even the best Christian marriages do not provide the perfect love we were born to want.

But God doesn't need more love. He doesn't need more education. He doesn't need anything. You can't give Him something that doesn't come from Him already (Rom. 11:35–36). At the foundation of the Christian worldview is a self-sufficient, joyful, triune God.

So why *did* God create the world? If He doesn't need it, why make it? The Christian answer puts God's desire to share His own glory together with the inner love of the Trinity.

Theologian Michael Reeves points out in his book on the Trinity that "while the Father loves the Son and the Son loves the Father, there is a very definite shape to their relationship. Overall, the Father is the lover, the Son is the beloved."[9] The Bible does mention the Son's love for the Father, but far more often it talks about the Father's love for His Son. The flow of love in the Trinity starts with the Father.

And this matters because the wellspring of love that starts with the Father flows through the Son and onto us. "As the Father has loved me, so have I loved you," Jesus said (John 15:9). Just like the Father loves the Son, the Son loves the church.

> "WORTHY ARE YOU, OUR LORD AND GOD, TO RECEIVE GLORY AND HONOR AND POWER, FOR YOU CREATED ALL THINGS, AND BY YOUR WILL THEY EXISTED AND WERE CREATED."
>
> —REVELATION 4:11

God created the world for the same reason a spring keeps bubbling out water: it's God's nature to overflow. The mutual love of the Trinity has a tendency to spill over. It isn't lack but abundance that makes God, the spring, pour out His love on creatures He creates. There is something rather than nothing because it is the very nature of God to pour out His love on—and display His wondrous glory to—others.

Westminster Confession of Faith: *a widely used summary of Christian doctrine written by English theologians in the seventeenth century*

The classic Westminster Confession of Faith* says that the "chief end of man," humanity's ultimate purpose, is "to glorify God and enjoy him forever."[10] But again, these are not two competing goals. *One absolutely essential part of glorifying God is, in fact, enjoying Him forever.*

Because that's what you do with a spring. You drink. The strongest way to recommend the purity and refreshment of a spring is just to drink and drink and drink till others start to see how valuable a treasure you've found.

THINKING IT THROUGH 4.2

1. He is self-sufficient.

2. In contrast to a finite and fallen human, whose self-love is revolting, God's self-love and deserved glorification over-flows and translates into perfect love for our highest good and His own glory.

3. God is a self-sufficient, joyful, triune God. God didn't have to create the world for His own glory, to receive honor and love, in order to escape loneliness. God chose to create the world to share the overflow of His love and glory with us.

4. to glorify their Creator God by finding satisfaction and delight in Him in all that they do; Humans only achieve this through the revelation of Jesus, who is the fountain of living water, the source of all life.

♀ 5. The love and glory of God overflow through Jesus into our lives.

And in this case the treasure finds you. Because that's His loving way. Jesus is the source of living water (John 4:10), and He gives it away freely to the thirsty (Isa. 55:1–5).

4.3 GOD THE UNRIVALED, YET GOD WITH US

How do you get to know an orange? Tasting it is a good start. But there are lots of other ways. You could slice it thin and put it under a microscope. You could take infrared photographs. You could dissolve it in acid and see what compounds it contains. You have lots of options; you're in control.

But that's not how you get to know a person. For you to get to know people, they have to be willing. They have to decide what they want to reveal to you and when. And you will probably have to open yourself up, too, at least a bit, if you expect them to open up. They probably won't get under a microscope, and it wouldn't help you get to know them better if they did because personal knowledge doesn't come primarily through scientific tools.

Some people treat God like a fruit. They're in control; they decide how to investigate Him. They let God know what He's allowed to be like and when. They might even insist that He meet them through microscopes, or they won't believe He exists.

But if God is a person—and a kind of person far greater than we can imagine, a tri-personal person, a person in whose image you are made—you're not in control of how you get to know Him. He is. You meet Him on His own loving terms. He decides what to tell you, and you have to open yourself up to receive it.

It sounds arrogant to most people when Christians claim to know God personally. But He came and met us; what else can we say?

THE BLIND MEN AND THE ELEPHANT

People who find Christians arrogant sometimes use the blind men and the elephant story to explain their viewpoint. It goes like this: some blind men encounter an elephant. Each of them, feeling a different part of the elephant, perceives the elephant differently.

One blind man, holding the elephant's tail, insists that the elephant is a rope. Another, touching the feet, insists that the elephant is a thick tree. Another, touching the elephant's side, is certain the others are wrong: the elephant is a stout, tar-papered building.

SECTION OBJECTIVES 4.3

1. Defend the idea that God is knowable because He revealed Himself to His creation.

2. Identify and explain the four false views of God's relationship to creation.

3. Explain the biblical view of God's unrivaled relationship to creation, defending His transcendent self-existence and immanence.

The Elephant in the Room

First, help students to understand that the illustration itself doesn't prove the claim that every religion, *without exception,* evolved through fallible human investigation. This is an assumed presupposition based on materialism. Any illustration is simply a tool used to explain an assumed truth claim. Illustrations don't prove; they clarify.

Second, explain that the illustration is powerful because every religion but one is, in fact, a human invention. All human religions are the product of blind humans groping for their own desired truth system to make sense of the world (2 Cor. 4:4). By God's common grace they may have stumbled upon some truth. But they all twist the truth into a distorted understanding of reality. However, is there an exception to the rule? Is one religion actually based on truly divine revelation with an entirely accurate picture of the whole of reality? This illustration doesn't allow for that possibility.

Third, refute the illustration with biblical claims. The presupposition in the blind men and the elephant story is that we are all spiritually blind. This may sound like humility. But it denies that God can communicate through the light of His Word. Jesus opened the eyes of the blind; the Holy Spirit illuminates the mind to the truth He reveals. Without defense, the illustration rules out the possibility of any true revelation (1 Cor. 2:13).

Fourth, the illustration assumes that secular humanists *can* step back and see the whole reality with clarity. The elephant in the room is that the illustration is simply an arrogant disparagement of every religion except secular humanism, which illegitimately pretends to be above the fray.

  ## A Sure Knowledge of God

Discuss with students how they would defend their knowledge of God.

Is God knowable? Isn't He incomprehensible (Job 11:7; Is. 40:18)? What are two major reasons people often reject the possibility of knowing God?

the finiteness of humans

• the transcendence of God

[Louis Berkhof, *Systematic Theology,* 4th ed. (Grand Rapids: Eerdmans, 1939), 29–40]

How can you answer those objections? How can a transcendent God be known to finite humans?

He can be known through His revelation of Himself in creation (general revelation; Rom. 1:20), but more particularly in His propositional Word and His embodied Word (special revelation; John 1:1, 14; 17:3; Heb. 1:1–3; 1 John 5:20).

God desires to reveal Himself, and He will not be thwarted. He revealed Himself in history through His Son and in human language through objective truth statements that can be understood. His Word is accessible to everyone, but its significance is apprehended through the illumination of the Holy Spirit within believers (1 Cor. 2:9–10, 12–13). Even though we may not have a comprehensive, full knowledge of God, we can have an accurate knowledge of God.

• Materialism

What it teaches: All reality is purely physical or material (matter + energy), governed by scientific law with a mechanical explanation.

What it rejects: It denies that there is a non-physical or spiritual realm, including a person's soul, the afterlife, and God. It rules out spiritual explanations in favor of scientific explanations.

Proponents: Secular humanist atheists with an evolutionary worldview

Intrinsic problems: It can't justify the presence of personal and moral capacities. It can't account for any meaning in life if everything is just a long string of impersonal mechanical physical reactions beyond human control and oblivious to our personhood. It can't justify the goodness or evil of anything.

How God relates to the universe: He doesn't. The universe is all there is; God doesn't exist.

Idolatrous twisting of God's truth: Nature replaces God as the self-existent sovereign.

[James N. Anderson, *What's Your Worldview?* (Wheaton: Crossway, 2014), 69–70]

Materialism Is Religious

Materialism attempts to answer all the same philosophical questions that other religions seek to answer. It simply attempts to do so under the guise of impartial scientific inquiry.

Why is it illegitimate to limit scientific investigations by excluding theological input?

Observational science is descriptive. It can explain what has been observed and how things function. However, observational science is limited. It can't answer all the philosophical worldview questions. Scientific work must rest on philosophical or theological assumptions to provide those answers. Science has always included philosophical reasoning. Theology is simply philosophy done in such a way that God's Word is the source for those philosophical answers rather than autonomous human reasoning. The reasonable man of materialism is not so reasonable—he's a fallen rebel that needs to submit to God's revelation.

Sagan's Idolatry

Carl Sagan said, "Our contemplations of the cosmos stir us. There's a tingling in the spine. . . . We know we are approaching the grandest of mysteries. The size and age of the cosmos are beyond ordinary human understanding, lost somewhere between immensity and eternity is our home the earth." [Carl Sagan, *Cosmos*, episode 1]

Evaluate Sagan's statement that the cosmos stirs us. Based on his own materialistc worldview, can he provide any reasons why it should stir us?

Sagan tried to make it sound like the naturalistic mechanisms were powerful and glorious in themselves. But why should there be a spiritual high in those contemplations if there's no personal meaning or purpose behind it all? The hugeness of an impersonal universe doesn't inspire; it leads only to

despair. Without a personal Creator and a soul that can relate to Him, all such contemplations of an impersonal, random-chance world are vacuous. The fact that he was trying to find something to worship demonstrates he was created with that necessary capacity because he was made in the image of God. But he expressed idolatrous worship for the creation while rejecting the Creator (Rom. 1:25).

Evaluating the *Cosmos* TV Series

Answers in Genesis provides a full list of articles that critique each of the thirteen episodes of the new *Cosmos* television series hosted by Neil deGrasse Tyson.

Americans and Western Europeans often tell this story as a rebuke to anyone who claims to know the truth about God—like Christians. All religions have truth, they say, just different parts of it. They urge Christians to admit that, as limited human beings, we have only a partial view of God. Other religions know things about Him that we don't know.

But there's something ironic here: how do those who tell the story know that all world religions are blind unless they themselves can see? How can they know that those religions are seeing only part of the elephant unless they are standing back and looking at the whole pachyderm? They are offended by Christians' claim to be right about God while other religions are wrong. But that's just what they're doing.

And *what if the elephant talks*? What if he says to the blind men, "I'm an elephant. That's not a fan; it's my ear." Will we think the men humble if they ignore him and keep on arguing?

It's true that people are limited. Worse, we're fallen. God's prophet Isaiah therefore urged his hearers centuries ago, "Stop regarding man in whose nostrils is breath, for of what account is he?" (Isa. 2:22). People can be wrong about God. But God has spoken. And no matter how arrogant it sounds to other people, we can't deny the truth of what our Creator has said.

GOD'S RELATIONSHIP TO THE UNIVERSE

The major religions of the world couldn't possibly be blind men all offering their partial "view" of the same God. That's because world religions have mutually exclusive views of God. They disagree so fundamentally about who God is that if one of them is right, the others must be wrong.

The major views of how God relates to His creation can be boiled down to five: (1) **materialism**, (2) **pantheism**, (3) **dualism**, (4) **deism**, and (5) **biblical theism**.[11]

Materialism

Materialism isn't exactly a view of God's relationship to His creation; materialists argue that there is no God, and thus there's nothing that can be called "creation." That's why it's the one view of the five that most people wouldn't call religious. For materialists, the universe is all there is. The classic expression of this view doesn't come from a philosopher but from a TV series, the famous documentary *Cosmos*

• Pantheism

What it teaches: Everything, including you, is one piece of the whole pie labeled as "god." All those pieces become unified as one reality again when you become one with the universe, achieving peace or nirvana, by denying the desires of the illusory material self.

What it rejects: This philosophy rejects a personal God who is distinct from the universe.

Proponents: Certain versions of Buddhism, Hinduism, Taoism (primarily in the East); and New Age philosophies (primarily in the West)

Intrinsic problems: Pantheism is the flip side of materialism. Materialism says mind came from matter and the spiritual world is

by scientist Carl Sagan. Released in 1980, the series has been viewed by half a billion people around the world.

The very first words in *Cosmos* are spoken confidently by Sagan: "The cosmos* is all that is or ever was or ever will be."[12] That's materialism. Sagan proceeds in the thirteen-part series to display the wonders of science and of the universe—and they surely are wondrous. But *Cosmos* is like a documentary about *Hamlet* that fails to mention Shakespeare. There is no Shakespeare; the play is all there ever was.

Though this kind of atheism seems to be the very opposite of religion, religious overtones are far from absent in the statements of materialists. Sagan died in 1996, but his wife Ann Druyan has championed his causes since then. And in her introduction to a re-release of *Cosmos*, she said this: "*Cosmos* is both a history of the scientific enterprise and an attempt to convey the soaring spiritual high of its central revelation: our oneness with the universe."[13] "Soaring spiritual high . . . revelation . . . oneness"—these are words that Druyan used precisely for their religious resonances.

Sagan, Druyan, and other materialists mean to inspire people with their view of existence. Sagan also said in that same first episode of *Cosmos*, "The cosmos is . . . within us. We're made of star-stuff. We are a way for the cosmos to know itself." In other words, human consciousness is the only instance we know of in which the atoms bumping around our universe have ever chanced upon a mirror. Sagan wants to convince his hearers that our self-awareness and our consciousness allow us to play an exciting role in a cosmic drama.

But it's difficult to see how materialism can really be inspiring because materialists are forced to conclude that humans not only have no souls, but no desires, beliefs, or goals. And where's the drama in finding out that you're the product of an unbending line of cause and effect stretching back as far as scientists can see? In this view, choices are illusions. Right and wrong, freedom and equality—these are just labels we use because using them confers evolutionary advantages on our species. Behind it all is nothing but matter and chance.

Materialism has been around—over and over again—throughout human history,[15] and it has never successfully answered its challengers. It turns out that being made of star-stuff isn't quite as noble as Sagan believed.

Pantheism

Pantheism argues that we're all made of god-stuff instead of star-stuff. There is no "God" in pantheism—we are all part of "god." The god-stuff that humans are made of is also what animals are made of. And rocks. And comets and the stars, the whole universe. In other words, god is everything, and everything is god. That god isn't a person and, really, neither are we—at least in the way Western people (due to the influence of the Bible) are used to thinking of persons. We are not individuals but inseparable parts of a universal whole. A prominent pantheist website explains,

> Pantheists see their personal religion as a system of reverent behavior toward the Earth rather than subscription to a particular creed. Because Pantheists

---

cosmos: *a synonym for universe that emphasizes the orderliness and coherence of what exists*

THE NEW *COSMOS*

When a new version of the *Cosmos* documentary was made in 2014, host Neil deGrasse Tyson—a charismatic astrophysicist like his mentor Carl Sagan—expressed a hope in science that sounds religious, just like Sagan did. Science often takes over the role of religion for materialists. Tyson said, "Science is an enterprise that should be cherished as an activity of the free human mind, because it transforms who we are, how we live—and it gives us an understanding of our place in the universe."[14]

But if pure empirical science, the kind that by ideology or by implication admits the existence of nothing but nature, gives us any understanding of our place in the universe, it's a deterministic place that can by no means transform how we live—because we don't have free human minds. We have the pieces of star-stuff the universe gave us by accident.

---

illusory; pantheism says matter came from mind and the material world is illusory. Yet pantheism has the same problem materialism does in distinguishing good from evil since all distinctions are actually unreal or identical. If everything is one (god), then how can there be a distinction between good and evil?

How God relates to the universe: There is no personal being called God as such. Rather, the universe, including us, is all a part of a larger whole referred to as "god"—"god" is everything, and everything is "god."

Idolatrous twisting of God's truth: Nature is identified as self-existent, sovereign god.

[James N. Anderson, *What's Your Worldview?* (Wheaton: Crossway, 2014), 71–72, 81–82]

Pantheism's Influence in Everyday Life

It may seem like pantheism has little impact on students' lives. But some seemingly neutral practices actually stem from beliefs about how the reality of the universe works—that everything must be perfectly balanced in oneness. [*Hint*: These ideas have been imported from the Far East.]

- **Yoga:** While this type of physical exercise may seem healthy and beneficial, the practice is rooted in a desire to release the mind so as to experience your true self at one or at peace with the universe.

- **Martial arts:** While the athletic aspects of these sports may be quite innocuous, the mystical teachings they developed from are deeply rooted in Eastern mysticism (e.g., the

---

idea that mind is over matter since matter is an illusion).

- **Yin-yang:** This common symbol means that apparently opposite or contrary forces are actually complementary or interconnected. Everything in the world supposedly exists within this illusory duality.

- **Feng shui:** This Chinese philosophy teaches that humans need to be in perfect harmony with the surrounding environment. Everything needs to be perfectly balanced. It most often shows up in architecture (the alignment, angles, and placement of buildings, furniture, and even stairways). HGTV has featured this philosophy.

- **Karma:** "What goes around comes around," so "pay it forward." Since everything is connected as one in one big circle of life, whatever "good" or "bad" that you do must come back around to you. Some Christians ignorantly confuse this with the general biblical principle of sowing and reaping. The Bible, however, does not teach a strict retribution theology. Assuming that this is how God operates was the problem in the thinking of Job and his friends. The Bible's teaching of grace directly contradicts the idea of karma.

- **Radical environmentalism:** The influence of pantheism explains the purist attitudes of those promoting the preservation of a pristine earth untouched by humans. The earth (and everything in it) is elevated to the status of godhood, and we must learn to be at one with it in order to achieve peace.

Warn students to be careful not to mindlessly embrace practices that are rooted in false ideas. The pragmatic practices may seem innocent, but they should be careful of syncretism (combining paganism with Christianity).

Dualism

What it teaches: The physical realm is evil; the spiritual realm is pure. God exists, but you can't encounter Him in this material world. (Gnostics say this because they think the material world is intrinsically evil; existentialists say it because they see God as completely transcendent and humanity as finite). While pantheists seek to rise above the material world of illusions by being absorbed back into the oneness of it, dualists seek to rise above the material world of evil by finding release for their immaterial souls to a spiritual realm.

What it rejects: It rejects the idea that this universe is intrinsically God's good creation but fallen. It posits that God is in a struggle against the evil powers of the material world, a view that denies His complete sovereignty over it.

Proponents: Gnostics; existentialists (i.e., neo-orthodox liberals); some syncretistic religious secularists

Intrinsic problems: No truth about God can be verified. It's only available to a special elite who have personally encountered God. There's a possibility that evil will defeat God.

How God relates to the universe: The spiritual realm exists apart from and in opposition to the material realm of the universe. God is trying to overcome the evil material world.

Idolatrous twisting of God's truth: God's creation is identified as intrinsically evil, and His sovereignty is diminished by seeing Him as just one of two powerful forces battling for control over the universe.

[James N. Anderson, *What's Your Worldview?* (Wheaton: Crossway, 2014), 55–56, 73–74]

Early Gnosticism in the Church

Paul clearly taught believers to put to death the sinful deeds of the body (Col. 3:5; Rom. 8:12–13) even though he clearly recognized that the ultimate problem was spiritual and that it was completely taken care of in Christ (Col. 2:11–15). He combatted both ritualistic asceticism (Col. 2:6–23) and antinomianism (1 Cor. 6:9–20). Guide the students through Activity 8, "Gnostic Dualism", which explains and refutes both of these extremes.

• Deism

What it teaches: This philosophy argues that God exists but is distant from us. The Bible contains merely the best human wisdom and moral laws of nature. Jesus was the foremost human example of a good teacher of these morals laws built into the universe.

What it rejects: This philosophy doesn't accept the providential intervention of God in human affairs, directly sustaining the universe. Thus, it rejects all references to the supernatural or miracles in this world, seeking only naturalistic explanations. It rejects the revelation or communication of God with humans.

Proponents: Nominal Christians claiming the heritage of American civil religion

Intrinsic problems: Deists can't explain why a personal God would create humans in His image (with the personal and moral capacities to worship, communicate, judge morals, etc.) but would never communicate with them or guide their moral judgments. In fact, deism presupposes an evil god that allowed humans to fall but never engaged this world to do anything about it. Deism tends

---

anthropomorphic: *human-like; such as a cartoon bird given hands and a human voice*

anthropocentrism: *a humanity-centered perspective*

ethereal: *out of this world; heavenly; immaterial*

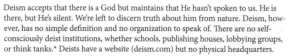

think tank: *a group of scholars who hold a particular political or religious viewpoint and conduct intensive research to promote it via academic papers, newspaper articles, books, and so forth*

identify God with Nature rather than an anthropomorphic* being, Pantheists oppose the arrogant world-view of anthropocentrism.*16

Pantheism purposefully downgrades God from a person to a thing—the universe. And it demotes man from ruler of creation to just another speck of stardust; they just call the stardust divine.

Dualism

There are multiple kinds of dualism. We talked about one kind of dualism in the last chapter: secularist dualism that says that even if there is a God, there's no reliable way of sorting out what's true about Him from what's false. This kind of dualism puts all the unknowable supernatural stuff in the "upper story" and lets people visit that upper story as long as they promise not to bring anything downstairs.

In another kind of dualism, God and the universe have always existed, but on parallel tracks that may or may not ever meet—depending on the particular view (since there are many species of dualism besides the one pictured in the diagram). Dualists think God and matter (the universe) make up the two major forces in existence.

People who have taken this view throughout history have tended to see these forces in opposition to each other. The goal of life, for this kind of dualist, is to escape the evil shackles of the material world and join the rational, eternal, harmonious, spiritual world in which God lives. Salvation becomes a way for the soul (the one part of humans that is not material) to escape from the world of flesh and blood into the ethereal* world of divine perfection. For dualists, the body itself is evil.

Since the early church, some Christians have felt attracted to this kind of dualism, but it isn't Christian. On the very first page of Scripture it is clear that God existed before His creation and that He views that creation as "very good."

Deism

Deism accepts that there is a God but maintains that He hasn't spoken to us. He is there, but He's silent. We're left to discern truth about him from nature. Deism, however, has no simple definition and no organization to speak of. There are no self-consciously deist institutions, whether schools, publishing houses, lobbying groups, or think tanks.* Deists have a website (deism.com) but no physical headquarters.

Nonetheless, you might be surprised to know that one of America's most prominent sociologists has said that deism is "the de facto dominant religion among contemporary U.S. teenagers."17 That sociologist, Christian Smith, conducted a massive survey of American thirteen-to-seventeen-year-olds about their religion, and he concluded that their views are best summarized by the label **moralistic therapeutic deism**, or MTD. This is how Smith summarizes the "creed" of MTD:18

1. A God exists who created and orders the world and watches over human life on earth.
2. God wants people to be good, nice, and fair to each other, as taught in the Bible and by most world religions.
3. The central goal of life is to be happy and to feel good about oneself.
4. God does not need to be particularly involved in one's life except when God is needed to resolve a problem.
5. Good people go to heaven when they die.

Point 2 is the *moralistic* part. Point 3 is the *therapeutic* part. Point 4 is the deism. But Points 1 and 5 are (sort of) taken from Christianity. Deism is parasitic; it takes

---

toward practical atheism, which often turns into full-blown agnosticism or atheism.

How God relates to the universe: God exists but doesn't interact with His created universe. He doesn't really care about us and leaves us to work things out for ourselves.

Idolatrous twisting of God's truth: The laws of nature replace God's self-revelation and relegate God to obscurity.

[James N. Anderson, *What's Your Worldview?* (Wheaton: Crossway, 2014), 61–62]

Moralistic Therapeutic Deism

Christian Smith writes, "No teenagers would actually use the terminology 'Moralistic Therapeutic Deist' to describe themselves. That is our summarizing term. And very few teenagers would lay out the five points of

its creed as clearly and concisely as we have just done. But when one sifts through and digests hundreds of discussions with U.S. teenagers about religion, God, faith, prayer, and other spiritual practices, what seems to emerge as the dominant, de facto religious viewpoint turns out to be some version of this faith."

[Christian Smith with Melinda Lundquist Denton, *Soul Searching: The Religious and Spiritual Lives of American Teenagers* (New York: Oxford University Press, 2005), 163]

American Civil Religion and Deism

Discuss with students the religious identity of the Founding Fathers. It is common for Christians to appeal to the Founders as Christians. They can point to references to God and morality in their writings. Secular-

a faith like Christianity and strips out the stuff that's offensive to human reason—or whatever passes for "human reason" at the time. Deism is to Christianity what a barbecue is to a snowman after sixty seconds. There's something left, but it's barely recognizable.

This category of deism is where we'd probably have to place MTD's cousin, American **civil religion**, a concept first named by sociologist Robert Bellah in 1967.[19] When US presidents say to disaster or accident victims, "Our thoughts and prayers are with you," when they put their hands on Bibles and solemnly swear oaths, when they end speeches with "God bless America," when they imply that Muslims and Christians worship the same deity—that's American civil religion. Its high priests are presidents. "God" in this civil religion is never defined, and he's mainly called in (as with MTD) to solve problems and benignly bless what we were all planning to do anyway. The god of American civil religion has been cut down to the size Americans like. As Voltaire reportedly said, "Ever since God made man in his own image, man has been trying to return the compliment."[20]

Biblical Theism

Our world is full of ideas about God. He's either nonexistent (materialism), or he's everything (pantheism). He's either at war with the universe (dualism)—or he doesn't really care about it much and just expects us not to mess up the furniture while He does His own thing (deism).

It's interesting how many of the views above are undercut by the Bible's opening statements. The very first words of Genesis reveal a personal God who stands above His creation but is deeply involved in it. And the rest of the Bible reveals, as Paul put it, "one God and Father of all, who is over all and through all and in all" (Eph. 4:6). If He's in all and through all, there's no room for materialism or deism. If He's over all, there's no pantheism.

God is distinct from His creation; He's not mixed up in it. He is what theologians call **transcendent**.* He transcends the limitations of time and space that apply throughout the universe He created. Wise potters don't get stuck in their pots (Isa. 64:8). God truly rules as King over His creation, even if there remains some yet-to-be-conquered territory (1 Cor. 15:25–26).

And God has no rivals in that exalted position. "I am God, and there is no other," He told Isaiah (46:9). God isn't in a fight with the universe, and even His conflict with Satan is one He could win in an instant if it served His purposes. One day, it will (Rev. 20:1–4).

But God isn't just transcendent; He is also what theologians call **immanent**.* He is deeply and lovingly interested in His creation, guiding its affairs from His sovereign throne. "In his hand is the life of every living thing and the breath of all mankind," Job says (Job 12:10). Jesus told us that not a sparrow (or even a human hair) falls without God's knowledge and consent (Matt. 10:29–30; Luke 12:6–7).

God once made the greatest ruler on earth eat grass for seven years. And when God mercifully restored Nebuchadnezzar to his exalted—but still earthly—dominion, he was compelled to confess that

> [God] does according to his will among the host of heaven
> and among the inhabitants of the earth;
> and none can stay his hand
> or say to him, "What have you done?" (Dan. 4:35)

GOD

GENERAL REVELATION   SPECIAL REVELATION

CREATION

transcendent: *so far above as to be in a different category*

immanent: *personally present, accessible*

GOD THE CREATOR | 059

---

the particularities of the Christian faith is inappropriate in a public setting. The civil religion does not profess to supplant Christianity; it simply relegates it to the arena of personal piety or private social good while reserving for itself all public roles.

Deism and Nominal Christianity

You may not have thought of deism as all that popular anymore, but you probably know lots of nominal Christians. Nominal Christians are people who say they're Christians because they grew up in a culture that's "Christian" in contrast to Islamic, Buddhist, Hindu, or animistic. They may know some biblical phrases, principles of morality, and Bible stories, but they know very little of what Scripture actually teaches. While some nominal Christians simply live in contradiction to their own intellectual knowledge of the right answers, many often get the most fundamental biblical worldview questions wrong (e.g., Is the Bible inspired? Is Jesus God? Is salvation by grace or works? Is there really a heaven and hell?). They certainly wouldn't understand the Bible's metanarrative (Creation, Fall, Redemption). Nominal Christians represent a broad mixture of people with a variety of beliefs, some of which are deistic. They tend to live their lives either ignoring traditional religious rituals or just going through the motions. They may assent to the existence of God but only tip their hats to Him once in a while when in need. A major difference between the deists of the Enlightenment—who believed God to be beyond humanity due to His complete transcendence—and the moralistic therapeutic deism of today is the influence of pop psychology, which points people inward to find "God" within themselves—making God completely immanent and indistinguishable from humanity or self. [Joe Carter, "Deists Who Love Jesus (and Talk Like Freud)," *The Gospel Coalition*, March 20, 2012]

Biblical Theism
Compare and contrast the four false views of how God relates to the universe with biblical theism by summarizing what biblical theism denies and what it teaches.

Biblical theism is a denial of materialism—that God is non-existent. It teaches that God does exist.

Biblical theism is a denial of pantheism—that god is everything and everything is god. It teaches that God is transcendent—separate from His creation in a category of His own (Creator).

Biblical theism is a denial of dualism—that God is at war in a struggle to subdue the evil

---

ists often try to minimize the religious side of the Founders, pointing out they were deists.

Some of the Founders and their supporters were dedicated, Bible-believing Christians. In this category we find Roger Sherman, John Witherspoon, Isaac Backus, and John Leland. Many others could be called theistic rationalists. By the time of the American Revolution, the effects of the Great Awakening had waned and the influences of deism were present but in a milder form than in Europe. Theistic rationalists believed in a god who created the world and who would answer prayers. But they were rationalists who rejected the deity of Christ and the inspiration of the Bible. They stressed the importance of morality but rejected the doctrines of Christianity. In this category we find Thomas Jefferson, Benjamin Franklin, and perhaps George Washington.

[Gregg L. Frazer, *The Religious Beliefs of America's Founders: Reason, Revelation, and Revolution* (Lawrence: University Press of Kansas, 2012)]

Discuss with students American civil religion. Help them to see that American civil religion is closely related to theistic rationalism. Its god is active and involved in American history but remains a generic god not identified with Jesus Christ or the Christian Trinity. American civil religion draws on biblical symbolism because of the Christian heritage of the American people. Common symbols are Americans as a chosen people, the United States as the Promised Land, and soldiers or presidential martyrs dying sacrificial deaths for the rebirth of the nation. This civil religion has emerged beause the diversity of religious belief in this country has led many to think that invoking Jesus Christ or

in the material universe. It teaches that God is transcendent—sovereignly ruling over His creation with no rivals.

Biblical theism is a denial of deism—that God is disinterested in the universe, doing His own thing. It teaches that God is immanent—personally involved with caring for His creation and His people.

How does Ephesians 4:6 refute all four false views?

If He's in all and through all (immanently involved with everything), there's no room for materialism or deism. If He's over all, there's no pantheism or dualism (transcendently distinct from creation and without rival).

Explain how Daniel 4:35 and Isaiah 46:9–10 display both God's immanence and transcendence.

Immanence: God's will/purposes certainly will be accomplished in the affairs of humans on earth.

Transcendence: God is in a category all His own; there is none like Him. He is outside of time. Thus, He can declare the end from the beginning.

💻 Is There Significance?

Seth MacFarlane and Steve Scheibner have almost identical 9-11 stories but diametrically opposite outlooks on their situation. Scheibner's story is recounted in his wife's book *In My Seat* and in a short video by the same title. Scheibner was scheduled to pilot American Airlines flight 11, which crashed in Pennsylvania, but was bumped from the flight by another pilot. He testifies to God's mercy and grace—ultimately in the substitutionary atonement of Jesus Christ, who took His place on the cross. All significance in life is attributed to the centrality of the gospel.

The Bible displays both God's transcendence and His immanence:

> I am God, and there is none like me,
> declaring the end from the beginning
> and from ancient times things not yet done,
> saying, "My counsel shall stand,
> and I will accomplish all my purpose." (Isa. 46:9–10)

GOD WHO NEEDS NOTHING

Seth MacFarlane, the somewhat infamous comedy writer who created the raunchy TV show *Family Guy*, was executive producer of the new *Cosmos* documentary released in 2014. MacFarlane is an ardent materialist.

On September 11, 2001, MacFarlane was scheduled to fly on the American Airlines jet that crashed into the World Trade Center. NPR interviewer Terri Gross said to MacFarlane, "You were late. Your travel agent gave you the wrong time, so you missed being on that catastrophic flight. Do you ever think of the rest of your life as being this kind of gift? . . . It could have all ended for you that day."[21]

MacFarlane replied, "One of my favorite quotes by Carl Sagan is that we are—as a species and as a culture—we are significance junkies. We love attaching significance to everything, even when there is really no significance and something is just a coincidence."

MacFarlane told the interviewer that the near-death experience hadn't changed him at all. "I'm living the same way . . . as I was in 1999."

In a materialist's world, there is no significance, no overall purpose. All the things that happen to us are coincidences, and so are we.

But the Bible tells us what we all already know in our hearts at some level (Rom. 2:14–15): when God created this universe out of nothing, He did so with an end goal in mind. He was working to glorify Himself. But His act of creation wasn't selfish. It was an overflow of Trinitarian love, an overflow that God has poured into your own soul if you have submitted yourself to His rule. Christian apologist C. S. Lewis wrote, "God who needs nothing, loves into existence wholly superfluous creatures in order that He may love and perfect them."[22]

THINKING IT THROUGH 4.3

1. How does God relate to the universe according to materialism?

2. How does God relate to the universe according to pantheism?

3. How does God relate to the universe according to dualism?

4. How does God relate to the universe according to deism?

5. How does biblical theism characterize God's relationship to the universe, offering a corrective to all of the above false worldviews?

💡 6. How could you refute someone who says the analogy of the blind men and the elephant shows that there's no possibility of accurate knowledge about the reality and truth of God?

THINKING IT THROUGH 4.3

1. He doesn't. The universe is all there is; God doesn't exist.

2. There is no personal God. Everything in the universe is a part of a larger whole referred to as "god"; "god" is everything and everything is "god."

3. God exists apart from and in opposition to the material realm of the universe.

4. God exists but doesn't interact with His creation. He doesn't care about us but leaves us to work things out.

5. God is both transcendent (ruling over the universe) and immanent (personally involved with His creation). He is a personal God who stands above His creation but is deeply involved in it.

💡 6. Illustrations clarify; they don't prove. The story arrogantly presupposes secularists can step back and see the whole while presuming everyone else is blind. It dismisses the possibility of one true source of revelation from God, which accurately communicates to humans so they can rightly understand truth.

CHAPTER REVIEW ANSWERS

Making Connections

1. motivation of what and whom you love

2. He was motivated to share the overflow of His love displaying His own glory. It was wrong to think He lacked anything or that He was lonely. The Bible teaches that He has always been self-sufficient.

3. Glorify God and enjoy Him forever. You glorify God by lovingly enjoying Him.

4. God is transcendent since there is only one God who rules over creation. He has no rivals, is distinct from creation, and is not limited by creation. God is immanent since He exercises loving control over all human affairs.

4 CHAPTER REVIEW

Scripture Memory

John 1:1–3; John 17:24

Making Connections

1. According to Scripture, what determines everything you think and do?

2. Why did God create the world—especially humans? What are some common incorrect reasons? Why are those reasons unbiblical?

3. According to the Westminster Confession, what is the main purpose of man? Explain how the two parts of the answer ought to work together.

4. How does Ephesians 4:6 demonstrate that God is both immanent and transcendent?

Developing Skills in Apologetics and Worldview

5. When you are evangelizing, some people may express the view that God's laws are burdensome obstacles that prevent them from having fun or a good life. What response would you give to this charge?

6. If you were witnessing to pantheists, what biblical truth about God would you want to impress on them (in contrast to their own concept of "god")? What would be some helpful Scripture passages?

Examining Assumptions and Evidence

7. Why does "God is love" (1 John 4:8) demand the doctrine of the Trinity?

8. How do God's love and glory work together?

9. Why is materialism a religious view?

10. Why is the analogy of the blind men and the elephant false?

Becoming a Creative Cultivator

11. Construct a philosophy of life—a statement that encapsulates your desired way of life. Then write a plan of action for your college years—a statement that enumerates how you are going to practically go about living out that philosophy.

The driving motivation behind my life is to worship my great God by glorifying Him as the one Lord over all: the Creator, Savior, and King of my life (Ps. 24). This driving motivation behind my life produces the two desires—to fear God (Eccl. 12:1, 13–14) and to love God (John 14:15). These two desires will produce obedience to God's commands due to my being truly most satisfied by God being most glorified—what every human was designed for by being created in God's image.

My plan of action is to seriously study God's Word as deeply as possible ("put on") and to do battle against my own inward sin ("put off"), always depending on God's power through prayer (Eph. 4:17–24; 6:18).

TERMS TO REMEMBER

Trinity—a term that summarizes the biblical teaching that God is three persons in one

glory—the display of God's love, holiness, power, justice, and whatever else establishes Him as God

materialism—an evolutionary worldview that assumes that the material or physical universe is all that exists

pantheism—a worldview that denies God (as an independent, personal being separate from His creation), teaching that everything is god and god is everything

dualism—a worldview that views the material or physical world as evil and God as standing in opposition to the material world

deism—a worldview that denies God's personal interaction with creation, viewing God as silent and uninterested in humans

moralistic therapeutic deism (MTD)—a nominal form of "Christianity"

civil religion—a vague and ill-defined moralistic ideology that is embraced by a majority of Americans (see **moral therapeutic deism**)

biblical theism—a biblical worldview that recognizes a personal God who stands above His good creation but is deeply involved in it

transcendent—so far above as to be in a different category

immanent—personally present, accessible

Developing Skills in Apologetics and Worldview

5. God's laws simply describe what a proper love for God and others looks like so that you can fulfill the meaning in life God designed and created you for.

6. God is an individual person not a thing that we are all a part of; the Creator is separate from His creation and rules over it. Refer to any Scripture passage that establishes a personal attribute of God and distinguishes Him from creation, ruling over it (e.g., Gen. 1:1; John 1:1–3; Rom. 1:18–24; Heb. 11:1–3).

Examining Assumptions and Evidence

7. Since love is part of the very nature or essence of who God has always been and true love (self-sacrifice for the good of another) always can exist only between two or more person, God must be Trinitarian.

8. God's love overflows onto us as a display of His glory so that we can glorify Him.

9. Materialism is a value system that makes claims about reality, truth, God, revelation, meaning in life, and so on.

10. It arrogantly assumes the secularist sees the whole of reality, knowing all religions are false in some way. It ignores the possibility of special self-revelation from God that makes Him truly knowable.

Becoming a Creative Cultivator

11. Each student's philosophy of life ought to reflect the ultimate motivation of love and the ultimate goal of glorifying God. Here's an example of a philosophy of life and plan of action:

CHAPTER 5 OBJECTIVES

The student will be able to

5.1 Defend human value by defining humans according to the image of God, distinguishing them from plants and animals.

5.2 Define the Creation Mandate and categorize it as a blessing from God for all humanity.

5.3 Defend the idea that the Creation Mandate is a command to create and cultivate culture.

SECTION OBJECTIVES 5.1

1. Critique evolution's inability to provide a basis for the unique value of human life.

2. Attribute the value of human life to the Creator's gift of the image of God.

3. Analyze the components of the image of God in humans.

4. Explain why failing to recognize humans as image-bearers leads to attributing human value subjectively, resulting in despair or contempt for others.

Chapter Five MAN AND HIS MANDATE

Then God said, "Let us make man in our image, after our likeness. And let them have dominion over the fish of the sea and over the birds of the heavens and over the livestock and over all the earth and over every creeping thing that creeps on the earth."
So God created man in his own image,
  in the image of God he created him;
  male and female he created them.
And God blessed them. And God said to them, "Be fruitful and multiply and fill the earth and subdue it, and have dominion over the fish of the sea and over the birds of the heavens and over every living thing that moves on the earth."

Scripture Memory
Genesis 1:26–28

5.1 MIRRORS OF GOD

Star Trek is America's top sci-fi franchise: 726 episodes in five TV series—plus twelve films—over fifty years (so far). Many of the episodes focus on moral questions, and these are often generated by the Starfleet "prime directive." This directive is a form of intergalactic multiculturalism;* Starfleet officers are not allowed to interfere with the cultures of other planets, especially primitive ones.[1] But nearly every time the prime directive comes up in the show, it does so because the principle is in conflict with some other value Starfleet officers hold dear. Usually that value is human or humanoid* life.

In one episode, an alien scientist offers advanced medical knowledge to a Starfleet doctor to help save a crewmember whose life is threatened by an ugly parasite. The starship's crew members slowly discover that the scientist gathered this information through deadly experiments on living subjects, people from a planet his species had subjugated.* The Starfleet doctor argues firmly that it is immoral

to use this knowledge. The alien points out in reply that "half the medical knowledge acquired on Earth came through experiments on lower animals!"

multiculturalism: *the idea that all cultures are not just different and valuable but equal in every respect; no culture is allowed to judge another*

humanoid: *in science fiction, an alien with human-like features (two arms and two legs, ability to walk upright, to speak, etc.)*

subjugate: *to violently bring someone else under your control*

PEOPLE FOR THE ETHICAL TREATMENT OF ALGAE?

People for the Ethical Treatment of Animals (PETA) proclaims its creed at the top of its webpage: "Animals are not ours to eat, wear, experiment on, use for entertainment, or abuse in any other way."[2] No Christian should ever abuse an animal, of course. The Bible says clearly, "Whoever is righteous has regard for the life of his beast" (Prov. 12:10). But God just as clearly gave humans the right to eat animals when He told Noah, "Every moving thing that lives shall be food for you" (Gen. 9:3).

But, given their evolutionary worldview, why should PETA supporters care more about animals than about insects or algae? Brian May (one of the few world-famous rock guitarists who also holds a PhD in astrophysics) was probably more consistent with evolutionary ethics when he said, "Human beings have no right to consider themselves any more special than any of our fellow survivors on the planet. And as far as being the dominant species, there is no question that bacteria, not us, are way out in front—in their numbers, in the number of environments they inhabit and even in total mass."[3]

Lesson Plan Chart—Chapter 5

Section Title	Pages	Activity Manual	Days
5.1 Mirrors of God	62–66	Activity 9 Activity 10	2 days
5.2 Man and Woman Given a Task	67–70		1 day
5.3 Man and Woman, Creating and Cultivating	71–75	Activity 11	2 days
Review	76		1 day
Total Suggested Days			**6 days**

Multiculturalism
Why is multiculturalism unbiblical?

If culture is understood to be the collective behavior of individuals in a group and if individuals can behave sinfully, then groups of people can agree to behave sinfully together. Every culture is a mixture: some aspects conform to the design of God's creational norms, and some rebel against them. Culture is never neutral.

Human Value Without God

Evolutionists may claim to maintain human value. But what is the basis for maintaining that value in their worldview? The only distinction they can make between humans and animals is a distinction of degree in abilities rather than a fundamental difference in essence or status. According to evolutionists,

"But not people!" the Starfleet doctor shouts angrily.

"It's convenient to draw a line between higher and lower species, isn't it?" replies the alien scientist.

The Starfleet doctor can only observe that the scientist is "barbaric."[4] The camera cuts to another scene. No reason is given in this episode, or in the whole *Star Trek* universe, for drawing a line of moral difference between animals and people. In fact, one episode (though admittedly not a well-regarded one) suggests that future evolution will turn people back into animals.[5]

SELF-PORTRAITS OF GOD

The Bible gives a reason to distinguish animals from people. It's on the very first page.

> Then God said, "Let us make man in our image, after our likeness. And let them have dominion over the fish of the sea and over the birds of the heavens and over the livestock and over all the earth and over every creeping thing that creeps on the earth."
>
> So God created man in his own image,
>   in the image of God he created him;
>   male and female he created them. . . .
>
> And God said to them, "Be fruitful and multiply and fill the earth and **subdue** it, and have **dominion** over the fish of the sea and over the birds of the heavens and over every living thing that moves on the earth" (Gen. 1:26–28).

When modern Western man chose a label for himself, it was *homo sapiens*, "wise man"—a thinking being.[6] That label certainly captures part of the truth. But the Bible's label is more satisfying, more complete: "image of God." When God took the dust of the ground and blew His living breath into it (Gen. 2:7), He made something unique in this universe. He made a kind of self-portrait.

That's what it means to be made in God's image, in God's likeness: we're images. *Image* and *likeness* are synonyms; the Bible doesn't draw any significant distinctions between the two terms. Both simply point to similarities between God and humans that no other creatures share, ways that we reflect God. But what similarities? What likenesses exist between man and the God he images?

At the very least, the image of God must include the abilities humans need in order to carry out the jobs assigned to them in the same verses that describe their position as image-bearers (Gen. 1:26–28). In order to fill the earth, subdue it, and have dominion over it, people need to have some of the capacities that God has: self-consciousness, rationality,* language, emotions, and the ability to form relationships with others. Without those capabilities, the work of dominion couldn't get done.

Animals have survival instincts, and they can respond in primitive ways to other creatures—dogs come when you call their names; they bark warnings to each other. But no one has ever caught a couple of them curled up in front of a fire conversing about the relative merits of rabbit and squirrel meat. Beavers haven't figured out how to use concrete in dam construction. Ancient gazelles never painted pictures of

> **THE TRINITY IN GENESIS 1**
>
> Who do the *us* and the *our* in "Let us make man in our image" refer to? God can't be speaking to angels because the Bible never says that humans are made in the image of angels or that angels worked with God to create the world. Christians through the centuries have often seen an indication of the Trinity here, and John 1:3 supports this interpretation of Genesis 1:26 by noting that Jesus was the agent of creation. Also, Colossians 1:15 says that Christ Himself is the **image of God**. And, of course, the role of the Spirit in creation is mentioned in Genesis 1:2: "The Spirit of God was hovering over the face of the waters." The whole Trinity has been active in creation ever since; perhaps the phrase "our image" is part of a conversation inside the Trinity.

rationality: *the capacity to think and reason logically*

humans share a single ancestor with the rest of the animal world. Humans can't be any more than a higher order of animals—the same in essence.

In the world's model, an individual's value is often measured by his larger benefit to the ecosystem or society. If an individual human or animal contributes positively, then value is granted. Positive contribution is tied to abilities. As scientific observation accumulates more knowledge about animal abilities, animals increase in value. However, this can also result in the devaluing of humans. If human value is granted only according to abilities that outstrip animal abilities, then old people and the mentally or physically disabled may be expendable. If it's based on self-awareness, then babies in the womb may be expendable. If based on the ability to feel pain, then animals are exalted to human status.

Who Am I?

Properly defining humankind is important because it reflects and informs your larger story of the world and it directs how you value humans. How you value humans determines the ethics of how humans ought to be treated. The evolutionary story of the world can't provide the basis for intrinsic human value necessary to protect justice and equity for every human life nor can it consistently distinguish humans from animals. The results can be devastating, as clearly illustrated in eugenics and genocides of the twentieth century.

Man's Label: *Homo sapiens*

Labels can reveal underlying worldview presuppositions. Compare and contrast secular modernism with secular postmodernism.

How does the label *Homo sapiens*, created in the early 1800s, reflect the secularist worldview rooted in the Enlightenment commitments of modernism?

Enlightenment modernists exalted human reason as the defining characteristic that made humanity possible. It's what made humans human.

However, a shift has taken place in the postmodern world.

How have secularists gone to the other extreme today?

Many secularists are prepared to blur the distinction between humans and animals by elevating animal intelligence as if humans are nothing special after all.

Andrew Lansdown, "Differences between Humans and Animals," Answers in Genesis (website), September 1, 1995.

The Image: Reflecting the Designer

What does it mean for humans to reflect or resemble the Designer? Humans are not clones of God; they aren't little deities. But they do share similarities or resemble certain characteristics of their Maker: communicable attributes. God created many things that reflect the wisdom and power of their Creator just like a painter can produce a beautiful landscape. But humans were designed to represent a likeness in character to their Designer just like a self-portrait. While self-portraits are superficial physical representations that are static and nonliving, God breathed life into His self-portraits, granting them a soul/spirit to actively represent Him here on earth as personal and moral beings. One scriptural analogy of what it's like to be created in God's image is what it's like to be born in the likeness of one's own parents (Gen. 5:1–3).

God's Label: Image/Likeness

The Bible uses two synonyms to define humans: *image* and *likeness*. Discuss with students what these descriptive metaphors communicate about humankind's resemblance to their Creator. Break students up into small groups to work on Activity 9.

The Answers in Genesis website has a topic index of articles about the question "Are Humans Animals?"

The Image: A Status with Capacities

The image of God is a bestowed status—the reality of who humans are in the essence of their being. The Bible hints at what this image entails when it relates God's creation of humans in His image to their carrying out the Creation Mandate (Gen. 1:26–30). This means that the capacities to carry out the Creation Mandate are bound up with the image. The unmarred human image was to reflect God's holiness, but in the Fall this holiness was lost and needs to be restored by redemption. Human capacities were also damaged in the Fall, most evident in humans with disabilities. Such people are still image-bearers because it is their nature to have these capacities even though they may struggle more than others to carry them out. Animals may have some capacities that overlap with those of humans, but the combination of capacities in humans is a whole that is greater than the sum of its parts, making humans unique from animals.

Components of the Image of God

Ask students to identify the capacities that seem to be a part of the image-bearing status of humans. Note that these qualities are inferred rather than directly identified in Scripture but are described according to (1) God's communicable attributes and (2) what humans need to carry out their purpose in fulfilling the Creation Mandate.

Personal capacities of the soul/spirit

The head-heart system of the mind, will, and emotions includes things such as

- self-consciousness/world-consciousness,
- self-determination/volitional freedom,
- rationality/intelligence,
- propositional language, and
- emotions.

Moral nature of the soul/spirit

The *bent* of the affections toward or away from God in the head-heart system (mind, will, and emotions) manifests itself through

- loves/desires (affections),
- conscience,
- morality/ethics (right and wrong),
- fellowship with God,
- worship, and
- eternality of the soul/spirit.

[Wayne Grudem, *Systematic Theology* (Grand Rapids: Zondervan, 1995), 445–49]

The Image: Marred but Not Lost

Why can't the image be lost?

It's a part of the structure of human makeup. It is something a human is *rather than something a human* has *or does. Losing the image would mean ceasing to be human.*

---

humans on cave walls.[7] Human capacities so far outstrip those of animals that people are in a different category of being than animals are. We're image-bearers.

But there's more to the image than human abilities. The New Testament suggests that man's moral nature—and not just his personal capacities—is part of the image. Every human has a conscience, a heart that loves, and a desire to worship someone or something. That's why Christians are told to "put off" immorality and idolatry and instead "put on the new self, which is being renewed in knowledge after the image of its creator" (Col. 3:10). True Christians experience a process of renewal toward the image of God.

The capacities that come with the image are deeply damaged by sin (Eph. 4:17–18), but the image is never totally lost, even in an Alzheimer's sufferer or a comatose patient. The image can, however, be "marred" because of the moral responsibilities tied to it. It can be defaced, like a vandalized portrait on a wall. Your forefather Adam's sins—and your sins—are darts thrown at God's self-portrait.

That's why Aslan told one prince of Narnia, "You come of the Lord Adam and the Lady Eve. . . . And that is both honour enough to erect the head of the poorest beggar, and shame enough to bow the shoulders of the greatest emperor on earth."[8]

HUMAN VALUE

Animals have value. Jesus said that not a single sparrow is forgotten by God. But He must have had something of a twinkle in His eye when He added to His disciples, "You are of more value than many sparrows" (Luke 12:6–7). In contrast, the *Star Trek* universe has no God to give humanoids more value than birds or even crabgrass. Famous scientist Stephen Hawking said,

> The human race is just a chemical scum on a moderate-sized planet, orbiting around a very average star in the outer suburb of one among a hundred billion galaxies. We are so insignificant that I can't believe the whole universe exists for our benefit. That would be like saying that you would disappear if I closed my eyes.[9]

The materialist worldview (matter is all there is) wants self-consciousness and personhood to be things that dawned on humanity gradually as evolution ran its erratic course. They aren't willing to receive their humanity as a gift from someone else.[10]

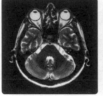

MRI of a man (left) and a dog (right)— are dogs people too?

But just as all love comes ultimately as a gift from God, so does all value and worth. Whatever God loves is valuable; God doesn't love worthless things. And the Trinitarian God's love flows to *you* in a special way because He has made you more valuable than any other part of His creation. He has made you in His own image. If you're unsure of your place in the world (join the club—a lot of teens feel that way), don't base your self-worth on being athletic, likable, or smart. You'll only be wracked with doubts whenever anyone comes along who exceeds you—and someone will. Instead, the image of God should be the foundation for your self-worth. Just rest your confidence in your Creator; your value is secure with Him.

Apart from the biblical concept of the image of God, our perception of human value will be flawed. You get neuroscientists proclaiming, as one did after analyzing a series of canine MRIs, that "dogs are people, too."[11]

Identify the biblical data that confirms that even fallen humanity retains the image of God.

Gen. 9:6—Murdering any human is wrong.

James 3:9—Cursing any human is wrong.

Rom. 8:29; 2 Cor. 3:18; Col. 3:10—Believers can begin the process of image restoration.

Morally Repugnant but Still Valuable

Clarify that Christ did not die on the cross for us because of our intrinsic human worth. The cross work of Christ is based on grace; nothing obligates God to redeem anyone since we're all morally reprehensible and spiritually bankrupt (Job 25:6; Eph. 2:1–10). The death of God's Son demonstrates the serious extent of human sinfulness and the

amazing extent of God's love. Yet God is buying back what He created in His own image. Humans are given as a gift from the Father to the Son (John 17:6); we become God's inheritance (Eph. 1:18).

Are Dogs Really People Too?

Assign students to read and evaluate an article, such as the one cited in the Student Text, that seeks to prove through scientific study that animals are essentially human. Identify the faulty presuppositions that lead to faulty conclusions (e.g., evolutionary materialism, behaviorism in psychology, a mechanical or chemical explanation for brain activity).

You hear NPR science journalist Robert Krulwich saying, "We're not different from other creatures, we're just more than other creatures."[12]

And you end up with the MTD we talked about in Chapter 4. Remember moralistic therapeutic deism—that watered-down form of Christianity in which God exists to make me happy and nice? Sociologist Christian Smith argues that MTD is the predominant religious belief of American teenagers today. One of the biggest truths that this view ignores is the status of humanity as being made in the image of God.

When MTD looks at the human self, it doesn't see a divine image-bearer, someone who gets his or her selfhood as a gift from above. It sees the self as the source, the originator, of all value and meaning. As fallen image-bearers, we're tempted to think that something is important and has value simply because we like it. Even when our parents are citing Bible verses and cautioning us to avoid certain friends or choices, we decide to follow our hearts. Smith writes that for adherents of MTD

> subjective, personal experience is the touchstone of all that is authentic, right, and true. . . . Right and wrong are determined not by external moralities derived from religious teachings, natural law, [or] cultural tradition. . . . Rather, clearly unaware that feeling itself is profoundly socially formed, individual subjective feeling establishes for individuals what is good and bad, right and wrong, just and unjust.[13]

People think their deism liberates them from all the rules of a religion or the commands of a god, but in reality their feelings about what is right and wrong are "profoundly socially formed." They exchange the glory of their Creator for the latest opinion polls. And public opinion offers no secure underpinning for the value of human life. Just ask the 44 million babies who are killed by their parents each year around the world.[14] Many people are appalled by the slaughter, but apparently they are too few to put an end to it.[15]

Ignoring Genesis 1:26–28 creates a vacuum, and what typically rushes into it is the concept of "self-esteem." Secularism has to find some way to increase human value without getting it from God. So a popular talk-show host's website offers articles with descriptions like this: "She spent years looking for validation in all the wrong places—until the day she discovered it was hers to give all along."[16] And many Americans dedicate their entire social-media presence to sharing platitudes* such as this one: "If you're still looking for that one person who will change your life, take a look in the mirror."[17]

Without a God to give them value and purpose, people are stuck creating their own. Despair is the result because we were designed to be dependent on our Creator.

And without a God to forgive—and pay for—their sins, people can never make up for any personal value they feel they've lost. The cross, in fact, shows how much God values His image-bearers; though we are undeserving of salvation because of our sin, Christ didn't die for utterly worthless beings but for His image-bearers (Rom. 8:32). Now that our vital connection to God is widely denied, it just can't be accidental that depression is so common in modern Western society and that suicide is one of the top ten causes of death in the richest nation on earth.[18] And, on the flip side, now that our dependence on God is widely denied, it's no accident that many people think of themselves more highly than they ought to think (Rom. 12:3). They worship creatures—namely themselves—rather than the Creator.

We are made in God's image. There's no other lasting means of finding self-worth and no other way to be truly humble.

platitude: *empty, inane, clichéd advice*

Human Value Without God's Image

Christians believe that human value is derived from being created in God's image. This value can't be removed because humans never cease to be image-bearers. It is a gift from God embedded in human nature. Students shouldn't doubt their value as special creations of God any more than they should doubt God's existence as a loving God. Self-value isn't something students need to search for; it is a gift of God that they can rest in as they pursue Him.

However, without the image of God, humans are left to grant value to other humans based on ability or likability. Since this approach is so fickle and causes so much hurt and even suicide, unbelievers try to find some intrinsic value within themselves. But they have no basis for doing so. Often the result is narcissistic selfishness. People become unteachable fools, resisting any reproof or correction (Prov. 16:18, 22). They muddle through life, leaving ruined relationships in their wake and ultimately end up in despair. The reality is that the "search for significance" is simply a ruse to live for self rather than for God (Rom. 1:18–32; 2 Tim. 3:1–2). Unsaved people don't really want to find value. It's offered to them by a loving Creator and Savior. By rejecting Christ, they pridefully choose godless autonomy.

Following Your Heart

Connect the cause to the effect. If human value is sourced in self-made purposes, then it follows that one ought to demand the liberty to express oneself without restraint.

If human value is sourced in the self, apart from the image of God and the purpose for which He created humans, then people are told to "be true to themselves." To do that they must "find themselves" by experimenting with their own abilities and desires. Any stifling of the expression coming out of them hinders them from discovering their own value and happiness and from creating their own purpose in life. They should only be encouraged and empowered to express whatever is inside of themselves.

What major biblical theme warns of the danger of this approach to life?

The Fall means that the human heart has been corrupted so that apart from the grace of God only evil pours out of it (Prov. 14:12; 28:26; Isa. 1:5; Jer. 17:9; Matt. 15:19; 1 Cor. 2:14; 4:3–4; Eph. 4:17–18).

What major biblical theme reflects the opposite approach to life?

Redemption makes possible our renewal into the image of the Creator, beginning with a teachable heart that puts to death the natural desires of one's own heart (Pss. 51:6; 86:11; Prov. 1:7; 3:1–8; 23:12, 17–19; Luke 9:23–24; Rom. 6:17–18; 8:5–14; Gal. 2:20; Eph. 4:23; Col. 3:10).

Finding Yourself

Christian students shouldn't be wandering into adulthood trying to "find themselves" until they mature. God has already told them who they are, why they're valuable, and how they ought to behave to grow into maturity in Christ. He's already told them what life is all about: glorifying Him by loving Him as they carry out the Creation Mandate and the Great Commission. God has given them all the guidance they need to accomplish those tasks (2 Pet. 1:3). Students shouldn't explore ways to contribute to this world by experimenting with life however they wish. Students should find their specific purpose by delighting to follow God's Word (Ps. 37:4).

Self-Esteem: A Biblical Critique

A biblical critique of the self-esteem movement: Jay E. Adams, *The Biblical View of Self-Esteem, Self-Love, and Self-Image* (Eugene, OR: Harvest House, 1986).

The self-esteem movement grows directly out of a materialist worldview, which replaces the spiritual aspect with a physical psychological explanation. Self-actualization is the supposed solution when humans are viewed as machines.

Human Rights and Social Justice

Compare and contrast the evolutionary worldview with the biblical worldview as it relates to providing a basis for ethics.

The evolutionary worldview is based on survival of the fittest. Therefore, consistency with that worldview would result in might or power driving all decisions related to the treatment of others. However, many unbelievers try to pursue the greatest good for the greatest number of people. Others value a pristine universe over people.

The biblical worldview is based on the image of God in humans. All of the law of God hangs on love for God and your neighbor. If Christians were consistent with their worldview, truth, justice, and mercy would drive all their decisions about how to treat others.

Ignoring Your Obligation

Does the social culture of your family need to change? Does sibling rivalry need to stop?

Does the social culture in your school need to change? Do cliques that revolve around despising one group of people or another need to stop?

Does the social culture in the church need to change? Do members slander and backbite one another?

Does the social culture of the nation need to change? Do citizens often resort to class warfare, pitting one group against another? Does their social attitude toward other nationalities need to change? Why do ethnic groups clash?

When James wants to force people to admit that everyone has broken God's law, he pinpoints the problem of showing partiality for external reasons. He challenges believers to view everyone as an image-bearer, deserving of love and mercy (James 2:1–13; 3:1–18). Warring hatred comes from selfish lusts (James 4:1–3). There is a wrong kind of judging that hijacks the position that is only God's (James 4:11–12). The solution is humility (James 4:6–10).

Ask students to brainstorm practical ways to positively contribute to the social culture of their home, school, church, or nation. Remind them of the biblical ethic and their obligation to be salt and light (Matt 5:1–16).

We all bear the divine image.

HUMAN OBLIGATION

And without the concept of the image of God, there's no firm foundation for the worth of others. If the world is built on the principle of "survival of the fittest," then some people are surely expendable. But the Bible poses love for your neighbor as the second most important commandment (after love for God; Matt 22:34–40) precisely because you aren't the only image-bearer in existence. Your sister's one too. The cranky people next door are too. And so are homeless people. Russians and Inuits and Kazaks and Tanzanians are as well. We're all portraits of God. We all bear the divine image. We didn't lose it in the fall of Adam. We know this because Genesis and James base moral commands on the image: you must not kill (Gen. 9:6) or curse (James 3:9) fellow humans because they are just as much God's image-bearers as you are.

Human rights (such as the right not to be forced to marry against your will) and social justice (such as the fight against South African apartheid and other forms of racism) must be firmly based on the image of God, or they will not be strong and lasting. They will come and go with public opinion. Remember the 44 million babies?

The secular metanarrative can't give humans their rights. It doesn't recognize who humans truly are, so how can we trust what it says about what we truly deserve? Personhood is a divine gift, and until we see it that way, we're just lucky animals.

THINKING IT THROUGH 5.1

1. What is the basis for human value in the evolutionary model of the world? What is the result of operating according to this model?

2. According to the biblical model, what is the transcendent and absolute basis for the value of every human regardless of that person's abilities, contribution, likability, and so on?

3. Why has the self-esteem movement developed? Why is it unbiblical? Why will it end in despair?

4. Where do "human rights" come from? What is the ultimate reason we should love our neighbors?

5. How does the image of God relate to the Creation Mandate?

THINKING IT THROUGH 5.1

1. There is no absolute basis. The subjective sensibilities of a particular society determine who's valuable and who's not.

2. the image of God within one's being

3. Without God-given value, value must be self-created. That idolatrously makes self the source of all value. Self-esteem can't overcome finiteness and fallenness; only forgiveness from God can.

4. As a gift from God; they are made in God's image, bearing His value.

5. Humans bear the status of uniquely reflecting God's likeness. That likeness includes personality (self-consciousness, rationality, language, emotions, relationships) and morality (conscience for right and wrong, affections, worship). It was given to enable us to carry out the job of dominion over the earth.

5.2 MAN AND WOMAN GIVEN A TASK

THE CREATION MANDATE

If you miss the first five minutes of a long movie, you may never catch up. You'll be spending the whole film whispering to your fellow movie-watchers, "Now who was that guy?" The things that happen at the beginning of a complicated story—the characters who are introduced, the conflicts that begin—are essential for understanding that story. And the Bible is no exception.

Genesis 1 introduces a character: man. It describes this character: man made in the image of God. And it gives this character a job: fill the earth, subdue it, and have dominion over it. So there are two major theological ideas in Genesis 1:26–28 that you simply must grasp if you are to understand the rest of the story of the Bible: (1) humans are image-bearers of God, and (2) humans are rulers over God's creation.

That second theological idea is called the **Creation Mandate**. It goes like this:

> God said to them, "Be fruitful and multiply and fill the earth and subdue it, and have dominion over the fish of the sea and over the birds of the heavens and over every living thing that moves on the earth." (Gen. 1:28)

These are foundational divine commands for all humanity, and they have never been taken away.

MANDATE PART 1: FILL

There are two parts to the Creation Mandate in Genesis 1:28. The first is, "Be fruitful and multiply and fill the earth." In other words, mushroom and move. Have babies and settle new territory. This first part of the mandate itself divides into three imperatives.

- The command to "be fruitful" is, in one sense, a command to be like God. God creates; humans procreate. Animals do this instinctually (they received this blessing, too, in Genesis 1:22), but men and women are privileged to do it purposefully. And enjoyably—sex was not invented by Satan. (As C. S. Lewis pointed out in *The Screwtape Letters*, no pleasures were.)
- The command and ability to "multiply" were given to the animals also (Gen. 1:22), but animals aren't very good at math. No dingo in Australia knows whether the dingo population has risen or fallen in the previous century. But humans can count; we can both enjoy and obey this command to increase in number.
- And mankind can navigate. We can know whether or not we are spreading out to "fill the earth." This third imperative seems to be the logical result—and the divinely intended purpose—of the other two. The earth is a big place, and a varied place. None of us knows quite what the world was like before sin and before the Flood, but we have no reason to believe that the planet was somehow smaller. Filling it would take Adam and his descendants a long time. But that was God's command.

And it still is. God's basic intent for mankind is still to increase in number and fill up the good planet He gave us. It is true that after the Fall, some men and women are called to singleness (1 Cor. 7:17, 32–35), and some couples are incapable of having children (Gen. 29:31). God also stops short of specifying a required number of children for a married woman. Nonetheless, to be what sociologists call a "DINK" ("Double Income, No Kids"; a husband and wife who refuse to have children) is

---

(Gen. 1:26–28; 2:18, 23–25). Selfish pursuits shouldn't trump this responsibility. Some Christians try to spiritualize their career ambitions. They interpret 1 Corinthians 7 as meaning that the truly spiritual should embrace celibacy for a higher ministry calling. Marriage is treated as a concession for the majority of unspiritual people who can't control their unworthy passions. But this runs contrary to the rest of Scripture's counsel on the matter (Prov. 18:22; 31:10; 1 Tim. 4:1–3; 5:14; Titus 2:4–5). "Paul would have none of this. For him both marriage and celibacy are gifts, and despite his own preference for his gift, he certainly does not raise it to a higher spirituality. That is to fly full in the face of the text itself." [Gordon D. Fee, *The First Epistle to the Corinthians*, New International Commentary on the New Testament (Grand Rapids: Eerdmans, 1987), 285]

Paul simply counsels that it is religiously irrelevant to think that you must change the status you may find yourself in due to the extenuating circumstances in the end times. Whatever state you find yourself in, minister with an eternal focus. In the church age, neither singleness nor marriage is superior; both have a role in God's work.

Prepare to Fill the Earth

Although the Fall has dramatically twisted God's good creation (thus, purity is most often stressed with teens), Christian teens ought to be encouraged to form proper friendships with the opposite gender.

Should guys and girls be friends?

The Bible never teaches that guys and girls ought to shun one another at any age; rather, God created all people in His image for sociability, especially in the church body.

What is the difference between friendships and serious relationships?

Friendships aren't exclusive or romantic like the relationships of those pursuing a marriage commitment.

What are some of the detrimental results of discouraging guy-girl friendships?

- *Young adults won't know how to interact. If they've never learned how to be friends at all, they can't just automatically know how to form a closer relationship later.*
- *Singleness can become epidemic because guys and girls have been taught (1) to view all attempts at friendship as an attempt at a romantic relationship and (2) to shun a friendship that may turn into a relationship if it won't contribute to their own self-referenced dreams—including spiritualized ones. Therefore, they reject even the first step toward getting to know someone even when there is no spiritual disqualification that should prevent the possibility of future marriage.*

SECTION OBJECTIVES 5.2

1. Defend the foundational place of the Creation Mandate in the metanarrative of the biblical worldview.

2. Explain the two parts of the Creation Mandate, distinguishing them from fallen humanity's rebellious departures.

3. Explain why the Creation Mandate is a blessing from God for all humanity even after the Fall.

Don't Miss the Creation Mandate

All the details throughout Scripture fit in with the overarching CFR storyline introduced at the beginning. For example, you might have assumed that the Creation Mandate plays only a minor role after the early chapters of Genesis. However, many details throughout the entire Bible simply describe how sin frustrates the human task of being fruitful and having dominion over the earth. Every curse in Genesis 3 directly corresponds to something that frustrates human fruitfulness and dominion. Redemptive benefits include not only the restoration of broken relationships with God and others but also the promise of future physical restoration: land, seed, and blessing for the Old Testament saint (Gen. 12:1–3) and reigning with Christ over a fully restored earth for the New Testament saint (Rev. 22:3, 5; Rom. 8:18–25).

Selfish Pursuits or Marriage (Plus Kids)?

The Creation Mandate presumes that men and women will marry and fill the earth

- *Separating the genders doesn't guarantee or produce purity.*

How should students form proper friendships now?

- *Biblical principles must direct them to form friendships with those of good character.*
- *Biblical principles must direct the manner of their friendship (how they act and what they do).*
- *Biblical principles must direct the limit or extent of their friendship (biblical standards of purity and modesty).*
- *They should embrace accountability and submit to parental authority. Friendships should revolve around family or group activities rather than solitary individual romanticism.*

Young people shouldn't be taught to completely avoid friendships with one another nor should they be encouraged to pursue romantic relationships too soon.

[Gerald Hiestand and Jay Thomas, *Sex, Dating, and Relationships: A Fresh Approach* (Wheaton: Crossway, 2012)]

 Population Control: Rebellious Disaster

What unbiblical motives drive population control?

- *fear based on evolutionary and environmentalist models that reject God's sovereignty*
- *selfishness*

What unbiblical methods are utilized?

- *abortion and abortifacient medications*
- *refusing conjugal rights (1 Cor. 7:3–5)*
- *forced sterilization and eugenics*

What are the devastating consequences?

- *Individuals face injustice and abuse because of forced abortions in some countries.*
- *World population is trending down toward replacement levels or less in many countries.*

What's the biblical emphasis rooted in God's design?

Procreation is a blessing (Pss. 127–28).

What Humans Are to Subdue

The language of Genesis 1:26–31 is all-encompassing (Ps. 8:6–8). Subduing the earth is exemplified from one extreme realm to the other: from the fish in the deep to the birds in the air; from the larger livestock to the minuscule creeping things. In summary, humans are to have dominion over every living thing on the earth and over all the earth itself. In addition to animals, God gave humans rule over all plant life. In an industrial world full of manufactured and synthetic materials, we may lose sight of the fact that everything we make is ultimately derived from the natural resources of God's creation.

to live contrary to God's command—and His blessing, as we'll see. God has told His image-bearers to spread out over the planet He gave us. This command means something for your future *and* for your present: prepare now to be a good spouse and parent someday. It is probably what you're called to, even if it seems far away at the moment.

MANDATE PART 2: SUBDUE

Many people in the West are so worried about population growth that they're willing to nix the first half of the Creation Mandate. Influential American scientist Nina Fedoroff told BBC news, for example, "There are probably already too many people on the planet."[23] But in the same interview she inadvertently appealed to the Bible's answer to that apparent problem: the second half of the Creation Mandate. "We're going to need a lot of inventiveness about how we use water and grow crops," she said. Filling the earth and having dominion over it work in tandem.

Not all the earth is well suited for human habitation (scientists still don't know how human life holds on in northern Minnesota). And that's where the second part of the Creation Mandate comes in: "Subdue [the earth] and have dominion . . . over every living thing that moves on the earth."

"FULFILLING THE CREATION MANDATE INVOLVES PRESSING GOD'S WORLD TOWARD ITS IDEAL AND MAXIMIZING THE WORLD'S USEFULNESS."[24]

—BRYAN SMITH

Some Bible readers assume this just means that humans have authority over animals—we can domesticate oxen for farm work and keep cats as pets (cats only *think* they have dominion). And that's part of the truth. But note two other things the passage says: we're supposed to have dominion over "the birds of the air" and, according to 1:26, over "all the earth."

Dominion over the birds of the air? How are humans supposed to do that? Fly?

Why not? The possibility has always existed, even if it took a few millennia till the Wright brothers figured it out. And flying is no harder than subduing and having dominion over "all the earth." Humans still aren't masters of the ocean depths, for example. There are marine species we know very little about. Who will our Wright brothers of deep-sea exploration be? Rich resources are still hidden all over the globe, untapped by its designated kings and queens. We have a lot of work to do because

How Humans Subdue

If humans are to properly take care of the earth, they must study the earth (the work of science) and then cultivate and develop it according to its best use (the work of technology). As knowledge increases and techniques become standardized, specific disciplines of study and fields of work spring up. Since Old Testament Israel was an agrarian society, that kind of dominion is most often emphasized in Scripture. But dominion is far more expansive than just the primary industries of agriculture, fishing, forestry, and mining. Secondary industries of construction and manufacturing should also be included. As a nation advances, it adds tertiary industries of infrastructure, trade, finance, general services, and government. In addition, the well-rounded person participates in the humanities and fine arts.

The New Testament assumes all of this labor is going on and provides principles for doing it in a godly (ethical) and Christian manner (following creational norms).

[Henry M. Morris, *The Genesis Record* (Grand Rapids: Baker Book House, 1976), 77]

[Dennis Bollinger, CULTURAL GEOGRAPHY, 4th ed. (Greenville, SC: BJU Press, 2015), 59–82]

 Why Humans Are to Subdue

What's the point of subduing the world?

Image-bearers were created to represent God by ruling over the earth under God's kingdom rule.

Humans still rule in their fallen condition. But that rule is often imperfect and corrupted. Redemption in Christ restores that

subduing means "to bring out the potential of everything in the earth so that it will be of service to human beings as they bring glory to God."[25] To subdue the earth is to press God's world toward its ideal and to maximize its usefulness for mankind. That ideal won't fully come until Christ brings it in a cataclysmic judgment, but we're still called to press toward it.

It's important to clarify here that the command to subdue isn't a license to exploit or destroy. A glorious national park like Yosemite is not a waste of space, and a fetid dump is not a "subdued" piece of ground. When Italian authorities failed to create new waste-management facilities several years ago in Naples, the streets of that iconic Italian city literally filled up with garbage.[26] That's not subduing. One of the solutions city officials found was to send 200,000 tons of trash to the Netherlands, where advanced treatment facilities recycle or incinerate all garbage rather than putting it in landfills. That's subduing.

But subduing and having dominion go far beyond the negative work of taking out the trash; they mean developing the world positively. Genesis 2 tells us that God put Adam in the Garden of Eden "to work it and keep it." That's the model. *Develop* the world—"work it." And *preserve* the world—"keep it." It may start with you stepping outside today and mowing your lawn. It may culminate some day with you working as a civil engineer on a city planning commission to create a beautiful, functional urban space for your family and your neighbors.

Paradise for Adam and Eve was joyous but very busy. They were blessed to go fill and rule a big planet. Said one writer, "Eden certainly is not a paradise in which man passes his time in idyllic and uninterrupted bliss with absolutely no demands on his daily schedule."[27] And Adam and Eve had to do this work while an enemy, the serpent, worked to destroy them.

Yosemite National Park is not a waste of space, and a fetid dump is not a "subdued" piece of ground.

TEEN DOMINION

Dominion is for teens, not just adults. However, it may not seem like that's true right now. That's because most of your dominion work is preparation. Faithfulness in today's seemingly insignificant tasks is the only way you'll ever achieve the advanced kinds of dominion that become possible as you mature.

It may not be scientific, exactly, but famous writer Malcolm Gladwell's "ten-thousand-hour" principle carries some real wisdom.[28] He has observed that true mastery of anything—from piano performance to engine repair—takes about ten thousand hours of practice. That's four hours a day, six days a week, for eight years.

Some five-year-olds know exactly what vocation taking "dominion" will mean for them and get their ten thousand hours in by age ten, and they're playing circles around other pianists or point guards their age. Or, like fifteen-year-old Flynn McGarry, they're cooking incredible gourmet meals and charging $160 a plate for them— and then getting profiled on the national news.[29]

But Flynn had to work fifteen-hour days at age twelve to accomplish this feat. And he still has a lot to learn. Flynn is a creative chef who has pushed the culinary arts to a higher level, but he made national news precisely because he's an exception. It usually takes many more years for someone to achieve what Flynn has.

And that's OK. God doesn't gift everyone to be a phenom. If you're not sure how to take dominion, you can start by subduing your locker, your homework, and your daily chores. Then you'll have some space to grow into the role God has called you to fill.

rule, especially when Christ returns as the King to take all dominion. Christians will be co-regents with Him over the earth.

Why does the earth need to be ruled over?

There are two goals:

(a) to press God's world to its ideal

(b) to maximize its usefulness

This means that the goodness of God's creational design must be both preserved and developed to maturity. Although God pronounced the world good at the time of creation, it will be fully developed to maturity in the future new heavens and new earth—millions of people will fill the earth in a city with civilization and culture (Rev. 21–22).

Connect the task of subduing the earth to the tasks of students at school and at work.

Why should students consider their schoolwork to be an important biblical command?

All academic fields are meant to equip students with the powerful tools needed for dominion and for the proper cultivation and creation of culture to the glory of God. Christian education seeks to teach students how to be salt and light (good works with purity) in every field of work for their future.

 Faithful Efforts to Preserve and Develop

How can you faithfully engage in preserving and developing the world now?

Endless opportunites are available in school and extracurricular activities in the home, church, and community.

A lot of the mundane tasks of life contribute to preserving and developing one's little corner of the world. It doesn't have to be extraordinary or mysterious. When more and more individuals fail to carry out their everyday responsibilities, cultures quickly become dysfunctional.

Why do people neglect that effort in favor of overindulging themselves?

Developing skills takes hard work; the lazy person will miss out. It requires opportunity, resources, perseverance, time, and maturity to develop.

Challenge students: If they spent the time and effort to master a profitable skill rather than wasting so much time on vacuous entertainment, what might they be able to accomplish?

What would you enjoy doing in the future to preserve and develop the world?

Answers will vary.

Why can it be dangerous for parents to push children to be the best and brightest, world-class professionals right now?

Cultures can be just as dysfunctional when children are placed under so much stress to perform at a certain level that they are forced into being workaholics. When success is elusive, discouragement and even high rates of suicide characterize that society. When success is achieved, arrogance characterizes that society. God's requirement is to put in the effort of faithfulness, not to reach a phenomenal level of success.

What Dominion Looks Like

The economic situation in an Indonesian village was not good. The men worked hard distilling sugar palm sap but didn't make enough money from selling the sugar to even send their kids to school. So people were stuck in grinding poverty. Charitable donations might have helped for a little while. But they needed a lasting source of income; they needed to produce more goods and services that other people would buy.

A Dutch engineer, Willie Smits, stepped in with his organization. He showed the people how to use simple industrial tools to maximize the benefits of sugar palm harvesting. The men of the village worked hard with him to set up a system in which not just palm sugar but all of its byproducts were put to good use. The distillery produces ethanol for cooking and for motorbike fuel. A retention pond turns other waste into feed stock for animals. An unsubdued plot of ground is subdued. Its potential is maximized. It becomes useful for mankind. People take dominion over their slice of God-given earth. Believers with a biblical worldview could align this kind of work more closely to biblical principles and be a testimony for God.

Enjoying God's Gifts

Caution students to avoid two unbiblical extremes: a philosophy of life that is pleasure-driven to the exclusion of labor versus a philosophy of life that is labor-driven to the exclusion of pleasure.

According to Ecclesiastes 2:1–11 and 18–23, what is elusive and why?

Finding ultimate satisfaction either in pleasure or labor because everything under the sun (in a fallen world) ends in perplexing futility.

According to Ecclesiastes 2:24–26 and 12:13–14, how should you live life then?

In all of life's perplexities and futility, the end of the matter is to be in a right relationship with God by fearing and pleasing Him as you both enjoy His good pleasurable gifts and work to subdue the earth.

Exploiting the Earth or Subduing It?

Brief students on a variety of current events from both radical environmentalists and Christians concerned about proper dominion. Have students evaluate each case and determine whether humans are truly exploiting the earth through ignorance and carelessness or whether humans are wisely pressing the earth toward its ideal, maximizing its proper usefulness for humans.

By what standard are students making their judgment calls? What presuppositions cause people to reject proper dominion, calling it exploitation? When students determine exploitation is real, how should it be addressed?

[Roger Scruton, *How to Think Seriously About the Planet* (New York: Oxford University Press, 2012)]

Life Without the Blessing

Imagine life without the blessing of the Creation Mandate. What would it be like?

There would be no marriage, intimacy, or family relationships; either humanity would quickly die out or the human race would just mindlessly reproduce like so many insects without any purpose or meaning. There would be no investigation or discovery, no technological advancements, nothing to do in life to accomplish anything lasting. Life would be boring and pointless. The gospel ought to restore you to a life that is driven by pursuing the glory of God as you properly fill and subdue the earth. In eternity you will be fully restored to this purposeful and satisfying work—done in perfect relationship with the Creator without sin hampering anything—just as humans were originally designed.

Dominion is an exciting task that blossoms into all the major vocations you can think of—forestry, scholarship, politics, graphic design, business. And God has never taken His Creation Mandate away. Your dad and mom are probably obeying it right now, and so are you as you prepare for whatever calling God has on your life.

A BLESSING IN DISGUISE

The divine command to fill the earth may seem like a burden to people who don't want to sacrifice time and income opportunities to bring children into the world. The command to subdue the earth may seem arrogant to people who believe humans are just successful primates. But there's something left out of the Creation Mandate that might help change their view. Three little words that come before the commands to fill, subdue, and have dominion. Those words are, "God blessed them." God gave us the glorious tasks of the Creation Mandate as a *blessing*.

Think of it like this: when you say, "Have a great day! Do well on your test!" you are, in a grammatical sense, issuing commands. God did the same in the Creation Mandate. *Fill* and *subdue* are both imperative verbs. But when you say, "Have a great day!" you don't really mean it as a command to be obeyed but as a wish, a blessing to be enjoyed.

This blessing, a blessing all mankind receives, explains why people who don't even believe in God end up living out His Creation Mandate anyway. Some people who care nothing for their Creator still develop incredible skills in astrophysics, architecture, athletics, and the arts. Everyone is an image-bearer blessed with the ability to rule over God's world. The things mankind can do with the raw materials of our planet are utterly astounding, from the ancient pyramids to genome sequencing, from Herod's temple to today's computers. God blessed His image-bearers to be exceptional subduers, powerful kings and queens. You're called to do eternally enriching and satisfying work.

Because we are fallen, however, so is the way we exercise dominion. Astrophysical calculations are sometimes mistaken; architectural choices are sometimes ugly; athletics can become an idol; art can be blasphemous. Some odd and bitter person could say to you, "I refuse to have a nice day no matter what you say!" In fact, there are many people who live against the grain of God's blessings. They pointedly refuse to marry or bear children. They throw all their potential for productive work into a hole and do nothing to preserve and develop God's creation.

THINKING IT THROUGH 5.2

1. What two major theological ideas are introduced in Genesis 1:26–28, foundational for the rest of the Bible's metanarrative?

2. Identify and explain the two parts of the Creation Mandate.

3. How do fallen humans rebel against both parts of the Creation Mandate?

4. In what way is the Creation Mandate a blessing?

5. How can you, at the present time, get involved in exercising dominion over the earth?

THINKING IT THROUGH 5.2

1. Humans are image-bearers and given the Creation Mandate to rule over creation.

2. First, humans are to be fruitful, which means they are to procreate, multiply in number, and spread out over the earth. Second, humans are to subdue the earth, which means they must learn to harness, manage, and cultivate the best development and uses of resources.

3. Humans oppose the first part of the Creation Mandate by promoting population control, abortion, and family breakdown. They oppose the second part by cavalierly exploiting the earth or by opposing appropriate uses of the earth's resources, seeking to maintain a pristine world.

4. Accomplishment and progress in pursuit of subduing the earth is meant to be enriching and satisfying—even within the context of frustrations from the Fall.

5. Examples may include anything they do to help the family or a job function at work. They can also get involved in community projects.

5.3 MAN AND WOMAN CREATING AND CULTIVATING

The food you eat is one of the most obvious results of human dominion. In ancient times, most people ate whatever was in season, ate it all season, and maybe even ate it without seasoning.[30] But the incredibly varied food on your table today has probably traveled from multiple climates and time zones. And it comes from multiple sources: you eat meat or cheese from kinds of animals that had to be domesticated by enterprising farmers many centuries ago. Those farmers also had to figure out that oxen could pull plows, but lions couldn't. And have you ever stopped to think that even the plants you eat—wheat, lettuce, bananas—had to be "subdued" by people? Noah didn't step off the ark into a cultivated orchard. Humanity has had to discover which plants could be grown on purpose and which among those were worth growing. In fact, one of the reasons certain cultures have developed further than others may be that they happened to find themselves in parts of the world where crop yields allowed many people to leave farming behind and form cities.[31]

ALL FOOD AS ETHNIC FOOD

People in cities still need to eat, of course. Cities, therefore, are impossible without the amazing work of dominion we call the "grocery store." Think of the store where your own family shops. Think of all the foods it contains. You've probably even got a whole aisle full of exotic foods; the sign over it reads, "Ethnic Food." There you'll see mysterious cans and jars with Arabic and Hindi labels, food with unfamiliar tastes and origins.

There's another lesson about dominion in that aisle—because why aren't the other aisles at the store called "Ethnic Food"? Don't the foods in those aisles come from a particular culture? Or are they just normal?[32] Believe it: to many of the people in this world, American hot dogs and peanut butter are not normal. They are just as ethnic (and perhaps just as inedible) as super-spicy Thai curry is to you. All food is ethnic. Most of it comes from a different *ethnos* than yours—a different people-group or nation.

The point of connecting dominion to the ethnic foods in your local store is this—the work of subduing and having dominion is done in groups.[33] And we call these groups "cultures." A **culture**, as we touched on briefly at the end of Chapter 1, is what a particular group of people make of the world. Those people tend to live near each other and, typically, speak the same language. They tend to share broad agreement about how to make something of this world—in two senses. (1) They take the raw materials of the world and make the same kinds of food, the same kinds of clothes, the same kinds of tools and art and music. (2) They also tend to see the world in the same way. What they make of it—in the sense of processing it or understanding it—looks similar across the culture. Remember that one of the three components of every worldview is action. Culture is a worldview in action within a group.

THE CREATION MANDATE AND CULTURE

Culture is good. It's part of God's design. It's one of the seeds in God's creation that He intended to grow into great trees. You can see this at the end of the Bible's story, as we've already noted. There we're told that "the glory and honor of the nations" is brought into the new Jerusalem (Rev. 21:26). The Bible doesn't spell out what that means in detail, but the glory and honor of nations (like Egypt and Assyria, which Isaiah 19 says will be in the new earth) would have to include cultural products—just like the glory and honor of the French today would have to include their cuisine.

SECTION OBJECTIVES 5.3

1. Explain how filling the earth and subduing it necessarily results in shared human actions of stewardship: culture.

2. Explain the power of culture to limit or open up horizons of possibility for cultural creativity and cultivation.

3. Summarize how engaging in cultural creativity and cultivation contributes to the positive formation of a more God-honoring culture.

The Creation Blessing and Culture

The mandate/blessing to fill and subdue the earth inevitably results in groups participating in tasks of stewardship together in their own unique ways. Carrying out the Creation Mandate naturally results in the creation and cultivation of culture. Food is only one example. Ask students to write two to three paragraphs about a cultural endeavor, connecting it to the blessing of filling and subduing the earth. They should describe the cultural endeavor and highlight the unique touch a particular people group's culture contributed. Then they should demonstrate how it exemplifies filling and subduing the earth. You may also ask them to evaluate whether any characteristics of the culture produced reflect the fallenness of humankind (even though this won't be addressed until Unit 3).

Blending Cultures and Subcultures

It may be difficult to distinguish one culture from another, especially as the world grows smaller due to transportation, communication, and the resultant mixture of cultures. Even people with radically different worldviews can both inhabit the same culture. Quite a lot of Republicans and Democrats in America, for example, would not want to admit how much they are in agreement with people on the other side of the political aisle. They could still share a lot of assumptions about democracy and capitalism. Compared to the average Afghani tribesman, they have a lot in common.

Culture, then, has levels. "American culture" is a reality, and it's a reality that differs from "French culture" even though within both America and France there are many different subcultures. America has its goths, who wear all black and are fascinated by heavy metal. It has its bluebloods, people born into wealth and privilege. It has its NASCAR fans, its hip-hop gurus, and its evangelical Christians. Quite often these subcultures, though recognizably distinct, also mix (for better or for worse). There is the occasional Harvard grad who enjoys NASCAR and hip-hop and goes to church on Sundays. But this is not the norm. Despite all the value Americans place on individual freedom, they tend to exercise their freedom by choosing to look and act just like the people they want to please (for better or for worse). Culture, even subculture, is a powerful force.

Spreading Cultural Dominion

Technology, produced because of humans taking dominion, has helped spread the cultivation of culture around the globe even more so than in ancient times (though their markets were abundant through trade too). For example, humans transformed society when they learned how to preserve and package food and transport it quickly around the globe, allowing people everywhere to enjoy a variety of fresh fruits and vegetables from other regions.

What are some other examples of the good cultivation of culture being shared and spread around the world?

Examples include medicine, infrastructure, and methods or philosophies of government.

The Glory and Honor of the Nations

What's the glory and honor of the nations in Revelation 21:26–27?

This phrase most likely refers to the fame or reputation of the people but could also include the things produced by those nations that brought them such acclaim.

Will this glory and honor be from this present age or created and cultivated entirely in the age to come?

Some continuity seems to exist both in national identities (e.g., Israel, Assyria, and Egypt in Isa. 19:24–25) and in existing kinds of human cultivation of the earth's goods (e.g., houses and vineyards in Isa. 65:21–22)—though the particulars will probably not carry over (2 Pet. 3:10–13). Revelation 21:27 makes clear that fallen aspects of culture will not exist on the new earth, assuring some discontinuity.

Culture Is Good, but Cultures May Not Be

Distinguish between culture and cultures. Culture is the result of filling and subduing. Those tasks were present before the world fell and will flourish in the world to come. Culture is not evil.

What is the fallacious worldview that shunning culture stems from? [*Hint:* Chapter 3 discussed this view.]

The dualistic two-story view, which separates the sacred from the secular, often is an attempt to protect the faith and the faithful from corrupting influences.

Identify practical examples of how this two-story view results in avoiding culture.

One common example is the disparagement of a liberal arts Christian education. Another is the Amish retreat from modern culture with its technology.

If culture shouldn't be rejected, then should any particular cultural expression be rejected?

Cultures are the actual human expressions of filling and subduing. The world system that bends cultural expressions away from God's design is what's evil (Eph. 2:1–3; 4:17–19). Therefore, there are indeed many cultural expressions and even entire subcultures rooted in humankind's fallen ideas and behaviors that ought to be shunned (Prov. 14:16). This will be discussed in more detail later.

A CFR View of Labor

Creation: Because of your created design, what should motivate your efforts at school and work?

Labor is more significant than just getting paid to provide you a comfortable standard of living. It is meant to accomplish something larger than yourself. Filling and subduing the earth to the glory of God is what you were designed for (Gen. 1:26–28).

Fall: What often hinders that motivation?

Working to create and cultivate culture is laborious because sin frustrates the fruitfulness

---

Various future nations might bring beautiful clothing, profound novels, or spicy curry into the new earth. (Hot dogs won't make it; there will be no death.) The last two chapters of Revelation speak of "nations" and "kings" as ongoing realities. Men and women "from every tribe and language and people and nation" will praise God at the end of time (Rev. 5:9). The point is that the nations don't go away in the eternal state, and nations always have cultures.

But it's not just the end of the Bible's story that reveals the value God places on culture. It's also the beginning. As the Garden of Eden is the seed of future cities, so the Creation Mandate is the seed that blossoms into multiple cultures. As soon as you start trying to live out the blessing of the Creation Mandate, you will start creating culture. The Creation Mandate is a command to create and cultivate our world: it's a command to build culture.

Imagine you are one of Adam's grandsons. As you grow up, your grandfather tells you about God's original blessing encouraging you to fill, subdue, and have dominion. The enormity of the project only adds to your excitement. There are precious secrets out there ready for you to find, like music and metallurgy* (whose discoverers are mentioned in Genesis 4:21–22). So along with your brothers and sisters and aunts and uncles, you work. You move some distance from your parents, subdue a plot of ground, and wrench as much bread out of it as you can by the sweat of your brow (Gen. 3:19).

You start to find real success after you manage to divert a nearby brook to irrigate your fields. You start to produce surplus grain—grain that your relatives across the ridge, who have no brook, are willing to barter for (they've got metal). But you can't get the grain to them without a cart, and you can't cart it to them without a bridge over that brook. So you work together with your relatives to build what you all need to facilitate trade.

A city begins to develop as more subsistence farmers adopt your irrigation practices and have food surpluses. A form of currency is invented and achieves widespread use. You gain enough of it to establish yourself within the city, and soon you become a leader there. The conflicts among various clans have to be adjudicated*, and someone has to pay for and manage the upkeep of roads and bridges the whole community uses—so a government is formed.

> *"Thousands of years after Genesis was written, we can see in a way its first readers could never have imagined just how much capacity . . . human image bearers had to fill the earth—just how much power was ultimately available to them, coiled in the physical elements' chemical and nuclear bonds, and emerging from the incredible complexity of the human mind and the fecundity [fruitfulness] of human culture."* [34]
>
> —ANDY CROUCH

This is all happening twenty valleys away too. And eighty. Over time whole nations develop, with their own foods, their own customs, their own architectural and artistic styles, their own folk songs, their own distinct clothing and pottery—their own

metallurgy: the study of metals and the technology for extracting them from ore to be made into useful objects

adjudicated: judged, resolved, decided, arbitrated

---

of your God-given task (Gen. 3:17–19; Eccles. 2:18–23).

Redemption: What hope is there?

Though the restoration is incomplete, you can begin to fulfill your God-given design with the tools and talents you've been equipped with because your God-given image is being renewed (Col. 3:10; Rom. 8:29) until the whole earth is restored (Rom. 8:18–25).

The Mandate and the Commission

The commands given in Genesis 1:28 and Matthew 28:19–20 don't conflict. There's no question that the Great Commission is the focus of the New Testament church. The New Testament is filled with commands that are moral and relational in nature. However, just as Paul rooted his theology in the created order, so must we. Neither

the Great Commission nor the moral and relational commands negate or supercede the command to fill and subdue the earth. The gospel brings fallen humanity back into increasingly greater conformity to the image of God. The moral and relational commands equip believers to carry out their God-given roles in a God-glorifying manner. One of those roles commended in the New Testament is our work—filling and subduing the earth. This task is and should be a major portion of a person's life.

Created to Cultivate and Create

Your laborious work at school is meant to open up the horizons of possibility for you. It's meant to enable you to engage in positively contributing to filling and subduing the earth by your labor for the rest of your

cultures. "Culture," says author Andy Crouch, is "the name for our relentless, restless human effort to take the world as it's given to us and make something else."[35] Different groups of people make different "something elses," but all humans make culture.

THE HORIZONS OF THE POSSIBLE

Crouch probes the Bible's teaching on culture with real insight, and his first chapter in *Culture Making* he entitled "The Horizons of the Possible." That's because culture, he points out, has a powerful effect on what any human being can do in obedience to the Creation Mandate. The culture you were born into makes some things possible and other things impossible, or nearly so.

It's now possible, for example, to have a blog—a personal Internet page where you write regular entries for all to read. In the whole history of the world, blogs were impossible until about the year 2000. Now anyone can publish blog posts, attract a following, sell advertising, and maybe even write full-time. Blogs have changed Western culture, introducing some amazing possibilities that didn't exist when your parents were born.

We're used to thinking about what new cultural products—especially those we call "technology"—make possible, but we rarely stop to ask what they make impossible or difficult. But new features of culture always take away as well as give. Blogging, for example, makes it more difficult to squelch rumors. And it's impossible now for major media outlets to command the following they used to have. Newspapers and network TV used to be the only significant sources for major breaking news. Now there are millions of sources, some high quality and many not.

Or take porn. It used to take real effort to find it. Now, thanks to technology, it takes effort not to. Or take phones. Cellphones, especially, make it difficult to live and work without interruption. They make it difficult to escape other people's demands and have quiet, undistracted time with God or a good book. They make it difficult to make firm plans with friends—friends know they can always text you and tell you they're running thirty minutes behind, so you'll need to wait for them. Cellphones bring many benefits and can be used wisely for God's glory, but they show that not all aspects of culture in this fallen world are good. "The bad part of culture" is, in fact, an accurate definition of that bad thing the New Testament calls "the world" (1 John 2:15–17).[36] We sinners can always find a way to twist good things for sinful purposes.

---

life. While few individuals can ever change the culture of the world, every believer should strive to be faithful, contributing to the formation of a more God-honoring subculture.

Understanding Your Culture

The accumulation of individual artifacts and ideas makes a culture what it is. Pick a specific, concrete object in your culture (e.g., a lamp, an e-book). To help you better understand your own culture, evaluate it through the following five questions, taken from Andy Crouch, *Culture Making: Recovering Our Creative Calling* (Downers Grove, IL: IVP Books, 2008), 29–30:

(1) **What does this cultural artifact assume about the way the world is?**

a lamp—you have a cheap source of power

an e-book—you have a literate, digital society

(2) **What does this cultural artifact assume about the way the world should be?**

a lamp—you should have light in order to do activities even after the sun goes down

an e-book—you should have a conveniently portable way to carry a whole library of information with you digitally

(3) **What does this cultural artifact make possible?**

a lamp—makes possible any number of activities when it would otherwise be dark

an e-book—quickly search content and record lengthy highlighted notes

(4) **What does this cultural artifact make impossible (or at least very difficult)?**

a lamp—most in society rarely go to bed early

an e-book—uninterrupted concentration; motivation to memorize

(5) **What new forms of culture are created in response to this artifact?**

a lamp—endless specialized varieties

an e-book—tablets exclusively for books without the distraction of other apps

  ## Your Cultural Approach

People tend to take one of five approaches toward culture: *consume it, copy it, critique it, condemn it,* or *creatively cultivate something new.* [Note: These categories are from Crouch, *Culture Making,* 65–77. We agree with his general analysis but significantly depart from some particulars in his analysis.]

Every approach, or *gesture,* can be deemed appropriate at one time or another based on a person's discernment of the particular cultural expression. But a tendency toward a particular approach to culture can develop into a pattern, or *posture* (Crouch, 78–98).

Pick a specific cultural good produced by your culture. How should you approach it? In what ways can you consume, copy, critique, condemn, or creatively cultivate it? What is your general posture toward it? What should it be?

Help students work through Activities 2 and 3 on the Teacher's Toolkit CD. They provide vital practical guidelines for biblical discernment in making these kinds of decisions.

Humility and Purity

Two guardrails must be set up to keep a person from going off the road into arrogance or impurity whenever he seeks to cultivate culture. First, a person must guard against the arrogant presumption that he or his group has the ability to change the world or transform culture. Those are monumental tasks! Rather, he should humbly and self-sacrificially seek to be faithfully obedient. He may contribute positively to the culture or subculture of his little corner of the world by conforming every action to biblical norms and morality. Second, rather than compromising with those aspects of culture that shouldn't be consumed or copied, a person must carefully critique them, condemning all fallen expressions, and creatively cultivate a biblical expression of culture when possible, in purity.

Faithfulness Not Triumphalism

An important warning and clarification: The description of what it looks like to carry out the blessing in the Creation Mandate—a blessing which naturally results in the creation and cultivation of culture—can be twisted, just like all good things. Christian reconstructionism, for instance, teaches that Christians should work to see governments enact laws in line with the Mosaic code. (Theonomy is discussed in Chapter 18.)

As postmillennialists, reconstructionists are optimistic that Christians will succeed in getting this to happen at some point. Despite having a high view of Scripture and its applicability to all of life, their interpretation of the law and of last things is inaccurate. The shift from the Mosaic Covenant to the New Covenant means that Israel's laws with their penalties are not directly binding today for God's people, let alone the nations. Nor should we expect Christ's kingdom to triumph over His enemies prior to the return of the King Himself.

We would expect from the Creation Mandate for Christians to be employed in every morally legitimate aspect of society. This would include the political realm. Christians are not called to a quietism that eschews all cultural and political involvement. Christians, however, must beware of triumphalism. Though Christ is reigning, He presently reigns in the midst of His enemies (Ps. 110:2). He promises His followers persecution in this present evil age (Matt. 5:10–12).

In addition, the Bible does not call the church as an institution to engage in cultural pursuits. The church is, instead, meant to disciple individuals in the godly use of those pursuits. The emphasis ought to be on faithfully stewarding individual opportunities, resources, and talents rather than on Christendom triumphalistically taking dominion over the cultural power-centers of the world. You may in fact end up influencing culture in a positive way as a natural result of being salt and light. But that's very different from a mandate for cultural takeover, bringing in the kingdom of Christ.

CULTIVATING AND CREATING

It's precisely because of the power of culture—for bad or good—that Christians should pay attention to it. And as one helpful author said, "The way to change culture is to make more of it."[37] Yes, in this fallen world, change must often include getting rid of some element of a particular culture. But generally it needs to be replaced with something else. So one key way to change the culture of your school is to add something that wasn't there before. Maybe just genuine love for the uncool. Or maybe tangible cultural "goods" like a new school logo, or a bake sale, or a charity bike race.

You might even create a new "institution" which can attempt to do more lasting good, like making that bake sale and bike race annual events. Think what personal growth and what unity could take place in your school if you cooperated to reach goals of fundraising, evangelism, or community service. That could change the culture of interactions in the lunchroom pretty fast. Your creativity, one of the most Godlike things about you, has power to improve your cultural world.

But you need to be careful not to become arrogant and impatient. The things God put within your power to do are important, but modest. Think again of how God described Adam's job: He put Adam in the Garden of Eden "to work it and keep it" (Gen. 2:15). *Develop* it and *preserve* it. Create and cultivate. And that's still your job with whatever aspect of this world God hands you. You can't develop if you don't preserve. There's simply no way you could start over, for example, with music. It's too late. You've already inherited a musical tradition—a tonal scale, a notational system, a collection of instruments, a huge number of brilliant compositions for orchestra, choir, string quartet, and so on. Your job is to preserve whatever is true and good and beautiful in the tradition of whichever academic or cultural discipline God calls you to, and then work to develop it.

And why would you want to start over with Western music when the existing structures provide so much room for rich development? Some of the most beautiful and innovative music today may actually be that of such composers as Arvo Pärt of Estonia and John Tavener of England, artists who have purposefully reached deep into musical tradition to write pieces of astonishingly fresh contemporary power.

Every scale you play in music practice—on an instrument you didn't invent, using a scale that not all cultures use—is one step toward preserving a particular tradition of music. Your teacher is handing it to you, as it was handed to her. Only if you preserve this tradition can you add to it.

The opposite of preserving and developing can be seen in composers such as John Cage, who wrote the (in)famous *4'33"*, usually called "Four Minutes Thirty-Three Seconds of Silence." Cage also wrote "aleatoric" (or chance-driven) music that sounds like a cacophony of random sounds with no identifiable melody or structure. Cage was purposefully turning the Western musical tradition backwards and blasting it to bits.[38] He was eliminating music's good and beautiful development. He was, therefore, going against the grain of the Creation Mandate.[39]

Far from limiting one's freedom, it's actually structure and order that provide space for creativity to flourish—in music, in sports, in business, in medicine, in woodworking, in homemaking, in automotive engineering, in whatever dominion work you find yourself called to do. Creativity is possible because of who we are—God's image-bearers—and because of the structured world God gave us to subdue.[40]

Rules for Culture

Because of relativism, pop culture tends to rebel against the rules that were once understood and cultivated for the production of something aesthetically acceptable and beautiful. Rules in aesthetics, or even in manners, are mocked as elitist high culture to be rebelled against. However, apply this same attitude in sports culture and what would you get? Body-slamming basketball players with a disregard for the rules of the game might be entertaining, but you wouldn't have much of a basketball game to watch for very long. Using handballs to play soccer would change the game. You can't just overturn the rules without overturning or changing the game. Having rules is not a hindrance to sports, art, or society; it's what makes such cultural activities possible.

DOMINION AND CULTURE

Humans have a nature given by God and a mandate from the same source. Take away Genesis 1, and we don't know who we are. Without Genesis, men and women have no ultimate identity. We don't know if we're accidental groupings of carbon atoms who only think we can think. We have no firm, ultimate foundation for human rights and social justice. We also have no purpose, no job to do, and no way to know whether our lives were spent well or wasted. We don't know if culture is good or bad. We don't even know if we're allowed to eat hot dogs.

But armed with God's original marching orders for mankind, you can know your place in the world. You don't have to know that your toddler will one day work for the woman who finds a cure for cancer. You just need to stay faithful filling the earth and teach the little image-bearers God gives you. You don't have to know that your job teaching autistic kids to communicate is going to result in important progress for the whole profession or that your thirty-seventh student will become a powerful Christian evangelist. You just need to take dominion over your little sector of the world and to put all the gifts of an image-bearer into that daily work.

Found your life on the foundational chapter of Scripture, Genesis 1. There you will find out who you are by finding out who you're imaging. You'll find your place in God's universe. You'll find your prime directive.

THINKING IT THROUGH 5.3

1. Explain how the formation of a cultural identity occurs.

2. As soon as you start trying to live out the blessing of the Creation Mandate, what will you find yourself doing?

3. How does the Great Commission enable people to better carry out the Creation Mandate?

4. Explain how Christians ought to involve themselves in a culture that is a mixture of both good and bad elements.

♀5. Name three ways your own culture affects the "horizons of the possible" for you.

THINKING IT THROUGH 5.3

1. Cultural groups form as people work together to fill and subdue the earth. They take action to make something of the world. They share the same way of understanding and doing things.

2. creating culture

3. The Creation Mandate is only impeded by fallen people exercising their fallen desires. But when people are saved, they seek to live in light of Redemption, carrying out the Creation Mandate according to God's creational design.

4. Christians must distinguish between the bad and good elements in their culture. They must humbly recognize that changing culture is often beyond their ability. Their focus must be on faithfully developing and preserving culture in purity.

♀5. Answers will vary. Advances in transportation and communication mean that we live in a global world; the digital world makes privacy difficult; a social media world can connect us with friends but can also hamper deeper relationships.

CHAPTER REVIEW ANSWERS (P. 76)

Making Connections

1. the personal capacities to carry out the Creation Mandate (such as self-awareness, rationality, language, and emotions) and the moral capacities (such as the conscience, affections, and worship)

2. the image of God in humans

3. Humans are created in the image of God and in the Creation Mandate are given the task of ruling over God's creation.

4. the formation of cultures

Developing Skills in Apologetics and Worldview

5. We have a great opportunity to demonstrate the failure of humans trying to live without God in this world. We have the answer for how the world was created to function under the direction of God's image-bearers (Creation), why it isn't functioning well now because of sinful humans who have marred the image of God (Fall), and what the hope is for renewed image-bearers in a restored world that will function properly again (Redemption).

6. Answers may vary. Older teens should set the tone for the rest of the school or youth group with how they treat each other

and those who are younger. Normal daily interactions that simply show the love of Christ, self-sacrifice, and self-control (e.g., refraining from picking on others) ought to be encouraged by positive peer pressure. Perhaps a structured mentoring, tutoring, or coaching program could be organized. Students should brainstorm and try tangible efforts to show care and compassion for one another.

Examining Assumptions and Evidence

7. When the image of God is eliminated, humans become fundamentally indistinct from animals and even plants—they are just another organization of chemicals in a completely material world, possessing certain skills that other animals don't have yet. When the image of God is eliminated, the source of value is no longer transcendent and absolute but pragmatically determined by subjective whims.

8. First, nobody merely follows his or her own heart. Your own personal feelings about what is good and bad or right and wrong or beneficial and detrimental are inescapably socially formed by one cultural group or another. To think that your ideas are original with yourself is simply naive or narcissistic. Second, trying to base value and fulfillment on the self is invalid since you were created in the image of God to be dependent on Him. It's foolish to try to live contrary to the Creator's design for His creation; it's impossible to find confidence, value, and fulfillment apart from Him. Third, because you are finite and fallen, you will always fall short of expectations—even the ones you have for yourself. The secular self-esteem movement only leads to disappointment and despair because it has no place for a God who forgives and loves you.

9. When God gave humans the task to fill and subdue, ruling over the world as His representatives, it was meant to be a blessing to be enjoyed. All people end up living it out because it is intrinsic to their design in the image of God to exercise their skills in creative cultural pursuits.

10. Although the tasks are distinct and the Great Commission is highlighted explicitly in the New Testament, the Great Commission commands believers to spread the good news that restores humans to a relationship with God so that they can begin to be discipled to obey God again, including carrying out the unavoidable task of the Creation Mandate in a God-glorifying manner.

TERMS TO REMEMBER

subdue/dominion
image of God
Creation Mandate
ethnos
culture
Great Commission

Scripture Memory

Genesis 1:26–28

Making Connections

1. What likenesses exist between humans and the God they image?

2. Rather than being based on survival of the fittest, what must human rights, social justice, and the worth of others be based on?

3. If you are to understand the rest of the story of the Bible, what two major theological ideas from Genesis 1:26–28 must you understand?

4. What necessarily results from groups of people carrying out the commands of the Creation Mandate?

Developing Skills in Apologetics and Worldview

5. How does the Christian worldview support human value in a world in which human life is often expendable—whether in school shootings or terrorist acts?

6. If your school is filled with cliques, how could you contribute to positive change in a way that honors all God's image-bearers?

Examining Assumptions and Evidence

7. Why do people cease to value others appropriately when the image of God is eliminated from their thinking?

8. Why can't you be liberated by simply following your own heart and being true to yourself? Why does the self-esteem movement fail to solve your need for confidence, value, and fulfillment?

9. Explain from Scripture why the Creation Mandate can also be called the Creation Blessing.

10. Why shouldn't the task of the Great Commission be viewed as a contradiction, replacement, or competitor with the task of the Creation Mandate?

Becoming a Creative Cultivator

11. Create a log that identifies and describes cultural activities you may already be involved in that positively contribute to the well-being of others. List one more cultural activity you could do that would make positive contributions to your school, church, home, or community.

Becoming a Creative Cultivator

11. Answers may vary. Students may be surprised to realize that they are already involved in cultural pursuits even though they may be in a learning stage of life. Examples may include participating in band or choir concerts, organizing a church outreach event to meet the physical and spiritual needs of others, spending time helping a brother or sister learn a hobby, fulfilling any number of job functions at work, volunteering for a political campaign, and so forth.

TERMS TO REMEMBER

subdue/have dominion—to press God's world toward its ideal and to maximize its usefulness for mankind; to care for and develop the world as stewards

image of God—God's likeness with particular moral and personal similarities that reflect Him and enable the activities of the Creation Mandate

Creation Mandate—the blessing given by God to humans to rule over His creation: be fruitful, multiply, fill the earth, subdue it and have dominion over it

ethnos—a different people group or nation

culture—what a particular group of people makes of the world; characterized by shared behaviors and ways of thinking about the world

Great Commission—Christ's command to make disciples, baptize them, and teach them to observe all that He commanded, which includes the whole of Scripture, beginning with the Creation Mandate

Chapter Six **EVERYTHING GOD MADE WAS VERY GOOD**

The Lord by wisdom founded the earth; by understanding he established the heavens.

Scripture Memory
Proverbs 3:19

6.1 AND GOD SAW THAT IT WAS GOOD

If you've ever created something you've been justifiably proud of (not sinfully proud of, but proud in that elusive *good* sense), you know that there's no other feeling quite like it. To sit back and look at a design you created or a speech you delivered or a project you completed or a car you fixed or a garden you planned or a meal you crafted, and to know *I made something good*—there's a particular kind of satisfaction there you just don't get anywhere else. To exercise your creative powers and make something new and useful and beautiful and true, for yourself and your neighbor, is to be like God as only an image-bearer can be. When you wake up the next morning, the first thing you want to do is go look at your creation.

VERY GOOD

After the first five days of the creation week, God looked at the work He'd done up to that point, and "God saw that it was good" (Gen. 1:21). Light (day 1), sky (day 2), land and plants (day 3), sun, moon, and stars (day 4), and birds and fish (day 5)—all good. And then on the sixth day, after sculpting His self-portrait, God is extra pleased. "God saw everything that he had made, and behold, it was very good" (1:31).

Nothing in God's original creation was out of place; nothing was lacking. When God pronounced His creation "very good," it was truly good, morally good. Brand new in all the best ways. (There was one respect in which God's world wasn't like new, of

course. He did create it with the appearance of age. There's no other way to create a grown tree, elephant, or man.)

There was only one exception to the creation's goodness, one thing in all of God's creation that, as He Himself said, was "not good," and that was that the man was alone (Gen. 2:18). But we shouldn't think this loneliness was an oversight on God's part, a mistake. Creating woman was something God intended to do all along. In any case, God fixed this one "problem" in creation very quickly and gave Adam a wife. God started us with a clean and beautiful slate. He made this world very good. The Fall didn't make a messy world worse; the Fall twisted a perfect world.

VERY VALUABLE

"God does not make junk," says one theologian, "and we dishonor the Creator if we take a negative view of the work of his hands when he himself takes such a positive view." God valued His creation so much that "he refused to scrap it when mankind spoiled it, but determined instead, at the cost of his Son's life, to make it new and good again." Not only does God not make junk, but "he does not junk what he has made."[1]

This is so true that even after the Fall of Adam, when the whole world was plunged into "bondage to corruption" (Rom. 8:21), the apostle Paul could give the following counsel to the young pastor Timothy:

Lesson Plan Chart—Chapter 6

Section Title	Pages	Activity Manual	Days
6.1 And God Saw That It Was Good	77–81	Activity 12	2 days
6.2 Laws of Nature and Creational Norms	81–86		2 days
6.3 The Way Things Are Supposed to Be	86–90		1 day
Review	91		1 day
Total Suggested Days			**6 days**

The student will be able to

6.1 Defend the goodness of God's creation.

6.2 Defend the existence of natural laws and creational norms.

6.3 Demonstrate that the good design of God's created world—in both the physical and social order—is the standard by which we must judge the way things ought to be.

SECTION OBJECTIVES 6.1

1. Recall God's own testimony about His creative work and clarify the meaning of that testimony.

2. Defend the goodness of God's creation even though it has been marred by the Fall and used in perverse ways by fallen humans.

3. Identify and refute various attempts to malign an aspect of God's good creation as intrinsically evil.

Very Good

Since God is omniscient, His testimony is sure to be completely and comprehensively true. He repeated His good pleasure each step of the way until the climactic completion—seven times (Gen. 1:4, 10, 12, 18, 21, 25, 31). This judgment applied to *all* that He had made, and everything was *very* good.

The goodness of creation necessarily follows from the goodness of its Creator. Since God is good, that perfection must also be reflected in the work of His hands (Rom. 1:20; Ps. 104:24; Prov. 8:22–31). Therefore, everything God created must have been created perfect and in harmony—nothing out of place or lacking but entirely fitting (Job 38–41).

"There could have been nothing that was *not* good in all creation: no struggle for existence, no disease, no pollution, no physical calamities (earthquakes, floods, etc.), no imbalance or lack of harmony, no disorder, no sin and, above all, *no death!* Even Satan was still good at this point; his rebellion and fall must have come later" [Henry M. Morris, *The Genesis Record* (Grand Rapids: Baker, 1976), 79].

Not Good?

Rather than interpreting Genesis 2 as an account of a second re-creation, it must be taken as a zoomed-in and more detailed account of day six. At the end of day six, everything was very good. Therefore, the creation of Eve (Genesis 2:18) must have taken place before the end of day six when

God made that pronouncement. Furthermore, the statement that Adam's aloneness was "not good" refers to incompleteness rather than moral degradation.

Paul's Advice to Timothy

Describe story line of Scripture should inform the reading of 1 Timothy 4:4–5.

Creation, Fall, Redemption

Read 4:1–16 for context (cf. 1:3–11).

Is Paul unconcerned about the practice of godliness according to 4:7b–8, 10a, 12, 16a?

No, Paul encourages Timothy to work hard for godliness and to carefully guard himself, rejecting anything impure.

What were the spiritual condition, character, and conduct of those who are described in 4:1–3?

They were apostates who had abandoned the true faith in favor of demonic teaching. They were lying hypocrites who contradicted Scripture (forbidding marriage) and added ascetic practices to Scripture (cultic dietary restrictions contradicting Mark 7:19; Acts 10:9–16).

These weren't sincere Christians simply applying scriptural principles of purity to the conduct of their lives. They followed myths (likely tied to the Gnostics or the Judaizers).

What two sources help true believers to discern the holiness of their practices so they can gratefully embrace them?

God's Word and prayer give discernment.

Discerning what is pleasing to God must be prayerfully searched out by a proper reading of God's Word (Eph. 5:10). Scripture is clear that God's creation is good (including food), not mystically cursed as in the cultic mythology of Gnosticism. The true gospel also frees believers from the dietary restrictions of the Judaizers.

Are recreational drugs and modern alcoholic beverages good creations of God to be received with thanksgiving?

No, they are twisted uses of God's good creation by fallen humankind. Modern alcoholic beverages are produced in a way that increases the intoxicating content (whereas wine in Scripture was diluted unless used for the purpose of drunkenness). Scripture warns against the use of substances that are controlling, preventing sober-mindedness (Prov. 23:29–35; Eph. 5:18; 1 Pet. 1:13).

[For more information on this point, see Randy Jaeggli, *Christians and Alcohol: A Scriptural Case for Abstinence* (Greenville, SC: Bob Jones University Press, 2014), 40–48.]

Everything created by God is good, and nothing is to be rejected if it is received with thanksgiving, for it is made holy by the word of God and prayer. (1 Tim. 4:4–5)

That doesn't mean that everything humans do with what God created is good. In fact, the goodness of God's creation often gets twisted and obscured in this fallen world. But it's still there; it never goes away. "Everything created by God *is* good," Paul said—not "*was* good." Like an inflatable beach ball shoved below the surface of a pool, you can suppress the goodness of creation for a while, but it always struggles to the surface. When Paul gave that counsel to Timothy, he was talking specifically about food. Like other things God created as good, food can be used for evil purposes: gluttons make food a god, and so sometimes (in a different way) do foodies.* Humans and human cultures can twist God's good gifts in evil ways, but those gifts are still good. Poppy seeds can be used to make deadly, addictive heroin—or killer lemon muffins.

foodie: someone with a special interest in food; a gourmet, an epicure

WHOSE FAULT IS EVIL?

Pointing out that all created things were originally good seems so simple and obvious. But it's crucial to mention it anyway because people are always trying to pin the blame for the world's problems on something other than their own insurrection.* And their chosen whipping boy* is generally something God made. Ultimately, then, they're blaming God.

Let's look at three things God created that people sometimes blame for the problems in our world: the body, authority, and emotions.

insurrection: organized rebellion against a rightful authority

whipping boy: an innocent party who bears the punishment for someone else's sin

Blaming the Body

Some people blame the body. A student at a Christian university once came to see his theology professor complaining that multiple health problems were making it difficult for him to study, and he wanted help discovering the spiritual source of those problems.

When the professor probed a little, it didn't take long to find out that the guy was consuming lots of junk food, getting little rest, and getting no exercise. The learned Bible scholar suggested to the young man that he needed a good diet, sufficient sleep, and regular physical activity.

The student was a little miffed; he was expecting a more theological answer. Anyway, he told his teacher, someday he'd get rid of his body when he died, so why bother taking care of it now?[2]

> *"WE ARE NOT MERELY PASSENGERS RIDING AROUND IN SKIN-TIGHT RACECARS; WE ARE OUR BODIES. THEY EMBODY US."*[3]
>
> —FREDERICA MATHEWES-GREENE

The body isn't really you; it's just a skin-and-bone cage the real you is stuck in temporarily—that's the view assumed by a lot of people, even some Christians. And some people go one step further. They start saying that the cage itself is evil. The ancient Gnostics actually hated the body; they felt that "the divine spark of the human soul must be freed from the material constraints of the world in order to attain salvation and unity" with god.[4]

The Temple of the Holy Spirit

According to 1 Corinthians 6:12–20, how were the Corinthian believers trying to justify their sin?

They claimed that they could do anything they wanted to with the body, including sexual immorality, because God gave us sexual appetites just as He gave us the desire for food and the ability to eat.

How does Paul counter that argument?

- *At the very least, not all things are helpful.*
- *Believers shouldn't be controlled by passions.*
- *The body is meant for the Lord; it will be raised up and restored; it is even now joined to Christ and is the temple of the Holy Spirit.*
- *What's physically done to the body has spiritual significance.*

The Sinfulness of Asceticism

Asceticism is the severe denial of the normal physical needs of the body, usually for the purpose of gaining spiritual merit. The Bible clearly teaches that our only merit is found in Christ. Therefore, this kind of activity is idolatrous (Col. 2:8–20; Gal. 3:1–3). Furthermore, God created physical things as gifts for human enjoyment (Eccles. 2:24–25) as long as they are used in a manner that glorifies Him (1 Cor. 10:31; 1 Tim. 6:17).

Body and Soul: Good but Fallen

The Bible treats the human person—body and soul—as a unity. When God created man, He formed the material body and breathed into it, so that man became a living soul (Gen. 2:7). Man—body and soul—was declared very good (Gen. 1:31). When humankind fell, both physical and spiritual

You could possibly come away from the New Testament with the mistaken idea that the body is evil—Paul does warn over and over again about the evil power of the "flesh." He even asks in Romans, after complaining bitterly about his sinfulness, "Who will deliver me from this body of death?" (7:24).

But Paul's answer is Christ—*and Christ has a body.* The teaching of the Bible is not that when we reach heaven we'll leave our bodies forever behind. The Christian hope is that "the dead will be raised imperishable" and that "this mortal body [will] put on immortality" (1 Cor. 15:52–53). Christ does not deliver us from our sinful bodies into a foggy world of floating spirits; He gives us our bodies back, just like He got His back—renewed, restored, transformed, perfect. When Paul speaks of "the flesh," he's talking about the sinful part of us, not our physical bodies. The human body is good. The Son of God Himself has one. You can't blame the problems in the world on the fact that people have bodies. Our bodies are deeply affected by the Fall, but they're not evil; they were created good and still are.

Blaming Authority

Sometimes authority and power get blamed for the world's predicament.* American culture, in particular, is suspicious of authority. Because of extreme individualism, says one Christian sociologist, there is "widespread American distrust of the government and other institutions of authority." This distrust, he says, is "incessantly depicted in television and movies, particularly those aimed at youth."[5] And this distrust has only increased with time.

predicament: *a difficult and unpleasant situation*

So, for example, the postwar-era Superman of the 1950s famously fought for "truth, justice, and the American way!"[6] But now, after the anti-authoritarian 1960s, it would be impossible for Superman to utter that phrase without a snicker coming from somewhere. The 1978 version of Lois Lane, for example, wisecracked after Superman used the phrase, "You're going to end up fighting every elected official in this country!" One of the most popular (and hyperviolent) action series of the 2000s, the Bourne trilogy, followed the odyssey of a CIA agent who discovers that his own government has betrayed him since his earliest days in their employ. This isn't to say that anti-authoritarian cynicism was nonexistent before the sixties, or that blind patriotism (*"My country can do no wrong"*) doesn't exist today. Humanity swings from one error to another. It's just to say that there's an overall antiauthoritarian tendency in US culture that you won't necessarily see in other cultures. (In fact, in some cultures, authority is revered to an unhealthy degree.)

But God put man and woman in authority over creation—and over their children (Gen. 1:28; Exod. 20:12). Think of the power mothers and fathers have over their kids. They could do any number of cruel things to them, especially when they're small, without anyone knowing (tragically, some parents do—this is a reason why authority itself gets a bad rap). If "absolute power corrupts absolutely," then why do the great majority of parents not treat their little kids with cruelty? Why, instead, do they sacrifice so much—like sleep, money, and time?

Because love turns authority into what it was created to be—a powerful force for good. As one author put it, "Love

The Superman of the 1950s fought for "truth, justice, and the American way." But after the anti-authoritarian 1960s, no one can say that phrase without a snicker coming from somewhere.

death resulted (Gen. 2:17; Rom. 5:12; 6:23). The Fall resulted in damage to the image of God as well as to the physical body. The Bible rejects the idea of a distinction between an evil material body and a good spiritual soul (2 Cor. 7:1). Each person can utilize his members for good or evil (Rom. 6:12–13). Man—body and soul—is fallen. The redemption of humans brings restoration to both the spirit (renewing the image of God) and the body (resurrected to immortality). Man—body and soul—will be fully restored (1 Cor. 15:51–55).

"Every act of man is seen as an act of the whole man. It is not the soul but man that sins; it is not the body but man that dies; and it is not merely the soul, but man, body and soul, that is redeemed in Christ." [Louis Berkhof, *Systematic Theology,* 4th ed. (Grand Rapids: Eerdmans, 1939), 192]

The Flesh

The Greek word meaning "flesh" (*sarx*) is used in a variety of ways. The meaning must be determined by the context: (a) the human body (Rom. 2:28; 2 Cor. 4:11; Gal. 4:13); (b) the physical realm or earthly things (Rom. 9:3; 1 Cor. 1:26; 2 Cor. 11:18); (c) humanity or national descent (Rom. 3:20; 1 Cor. 15:50; Gal. 1:16; Phil. 3:3–4); (d) sinful orientation (Rom. 8:13–14; Gal. 5:16). [Kittel and Friedrich, *TDNT: Abridged in One Volume,* trans. Bromiley (Grand Rapids: Eerdmans, 1985), 1004–1005] The physical body isn't evil but suffers from the Fall. The physical realm, earthly things, and national descent aren't evil, but relying on them is. Humanness isn't evil, but unregenerated humanity is enslaved to evil. Since the flesh is so tarnished by the Fall, the term became a metaphor for pervasive sinfulness.

Why the Body Gets Blamed for Sin

In today's secular worldview, which "science" blames what the Bible calls sinful behavior on our physical bodies?

Psychology generally takes a materialistic view of the human person. Thus, it applies a disease model whenever something goes wrong with a person's desires that results in damaging choices. [Edward T. Welch, *Blame It on the Brain* (Phillipsburg, NJ: P&R, 1998)]

The biblical model recognizes several categories of problems:

(a) purely physical issues (John 9:1–3)

(b) spiritually sinful choices (Gal. 5:21)

(c) physical difficulties that lead to temptations to sin (as in the case of Job)

(d) sins that lead to physical problems (Ps. 32:3–4)

Match the following scenarios to the above biblical model.

• constant and deeply distressing worry that leads to high blood pressure *(d)*

• a hereditary genetic muscle disorder *(a)*

• a lack of self-control resulting in disorderly disruptiveness *(b or possibly c)*

• pain from a broken bone that causes a person to grumble, complain, and lash out at others *(c)*

[Activity 12 provides a critique of the disease model as used by secular psychology.]

Authority: Good but Fallen

God is an authority, and He created humankind to be in authority over His creation as vice regents. God designed human relationships with authority: husbands (1 Cor. 11:1–3; Eph. 5:22–33); parents (Exod. 20:12; Eph. 6:1–4); governments (Gen. 9:5–6; Rom. 13:1–8); church leaders (Eph. 4:11; Heb. 13:7); masters (Eph. 6:5–9). However, husbands are commanded to love their wives, fathers are cautioned not to exasperate children, governments are not to punish good conduct, pastors are to be examples for their people, and masters are told to stop threatening. The Bible recognizes the fallen corruption of authority. Ultimately, all authority is given to Christ, who rules in the midst of His enemies (Ps. 110:1–2). One day, perfected believers will reign with Christ, the vanquisher of all enemies (Eph 1:20–23; Rev. 22:5).

Why Authority Gets Blamed for Sin

What are two major reasons for the human tendency to reject authority?

(1) Abuse of power: When trust has been repeatedly and thoroughly destroyed, people desire to be more independent and self-reliant,

free from any hold that a higher power might have over them.

(2) Selfish desires: When the flesh is set on doing its own thing, it doesn't want anyone hindering it from obtaining its lusts. It doesn't want oversight, accountability, or consequences.

What is the biblical response to both reasons for rejecting authority?

For people who have suffered under abusive authorities, the Bible's answer is to appeal to other God-given authorities (parents, church, government, employer) that can provide oversight, accountability, and consequences for the corrupt authorities (Acts 25; Rom. 13:1–8). However, the Bible recognizes that some societies become so corrupt that there is no avenue for redress. In that case, the oppressed must trust in the Lord and wait on Him to bring about justice either in this life or the next (Pss. 62; 72; 73; 2 Thess. 1:5–10; 1 Pet. 2:13–25; 3:12; 4:19).

For the second group of people, the Bible confronts their lawlessness and demands submission (Prov. 17:11; Heb. 13:17; 1 Pet. 2:13; 1 John 3:4).

Sphere sovereignty is a biblical model that guards against both tyranny and extreme individualism. (Refer to Activity 6 on sphere sovereignty in Chapter 3.)

Emotion: Good but Fallen

God has emotions. Examples include His loving delight and rejoicing as well as His hatred, anger, and grief (Matt. 3:17; John 15:11; Prov. 6:16; Rom. 1:18; Eph. 4:30). Humans were created in God's image to experience emotions as well (1 John 4:7–11; Rom. 5:2; Ps. 139:21–22; Eph. 4:26; Ps 119:136). Just as depravity darkens the mind (Isa. 1:3; Jer. 4:22; Rom. 1:21–22; Eph. 4:17–18) and perverts the inclinations of the will (Jer. 13:23; John 8:34; Rom. 8:7) so also it may corrupt the goodness of that which God created humans to feel (1 John 2:15; Prov. 2:14; Eph. 4:26; 2 Cor. 7:10). God's redemption will restore the whole human person to the original goodness of creation, including the emotions (Rev. 19:6–7).

Why Emotion Gets Blamed for Sin

Why are emotions so often disparaged?

(1) They are subjective and non-rational. Some unbelievers are so committed to scientific rationality that they reject other means of guidance; believers are rightly committed to the objectivity of Scripture for guidance.

2) They are powerfully corrupted. Unbelievers' passions often blind them to the truth; believers often struggle with passions that

---

transfigures power. Absolute love transfigures absolute power. And power transfigured by love is the power that made and saves the world."[7] Authority is a good thing God created. Paul goes as far as to say, "There is no authority except from God, and those that exist have been instituted by God" (Rom. 13:1). You can't pin the blame for human problems on something God made *good*. If you do, you're blaming God.

Blaming Emotion

Another thing God made that sometimes gets blamed for all the trouble we're in is emotions. But God didn't just make emotions; He has them. The big differences between God's emotions and the human emotions patterned after them are that (1) no one can make God feel something He doesn't want to feel[8] and (2) God's emotions aren't tied up with a physical body like ours are. But even given these differences, we can see God's emotions everywhere in Scripture. He loves (John 3:16; 1 John 4:8), He hates (Ps. 5:5; Rom. 9:13), He's angry (Ps. 7:11), He's sad (Gen. 6:6). It's impossible to imagine a *person* who doesn't have any feelings whatsoever. We are all portraits of God, after all.

And yet feelings are very commonly blamed for the troubles in our world. Hans Rosling, a prominent Swedish doctor and professor of international health, told *The Economist* magazine, for example,

> We can eradicate poverty, we can solve the energy and the climate issues but we have to make the right investments. . . . I know a good world is possible *if we leave emotion aside and just work analytically.*[9]

Dr. Rosling's snubbing of emotion is not an isolated instance in the Enlightened West. It's not uncommon for Western people—especially in discussions believed to be within the realm of science—to talk as if emotion is flawed and unreliable while reason is not. But as one former employee of an abortion clinic has found out (see sidebar below), your gut reaction might be right and your careful rationalizations may be wrong.[10] Reason and emotion are both fundamentally good, and yet both are twisted by the Fall.

Interestingly enough, *The Economist* saw a contradiction in Dr. Rosling's negative view of emotions. The article noted,

> [Dr. Rosling's] ability to set aside his own emotions remains to be demonstrated. Like Florence Nightingale before him, what gives his work its persuasive force is not just rock-solid data . . . but his personal passion and enthusiasm.[10]

EMOTION CAN LEAD TO TRUTH

Abby Johnson says she always had a strong desire to help needy women. This desire led her to Planned Parenthood, the nation's largest abortion provider. But her life was radically changed one day when she was brought in to assist with an abortion procedure. Her website says that she "watched in horror as a 13-week baby fought [for], and ultimately lost, its life at the hand of the abortionist."[11]

This emotional experience led to "the full realization of what abortion was." She became "desperate and confused"—

and soon, thankfully, she left Planned Parenthood and dedicated her life to the pro-life cause.[12]

The Bible provides the lenses necessary to see clearly what happened to Abby: her God-given conscience was violated (Rom. 2:14–15), and her emotional horror was the sign. Whatever her reasons for defending abortion in the past, it became clear to her that those were rationalizations obscuring the truth. Her God-given emotion actually led her back to the light.

---

conflict with what they know to be good and true.

While Scripture must always be upheld as the normative guide and source for truth through which the Holy Spirit guides the conscience, the emotions that result from that conviction and that are guided by the truth ought to be embraced.

  Primacy of Intellect, Will, or Emotions?

Many Christians, unwittingly influenced by secular philosophers from ancient times to the Enlightenment, emphasize the primacy of the intellect over the emotions in order to safeguard Christians from an emotionalism that bypasses the intellect. Have students evaluate the following quotations, which correct such thinking.

- Cornelius Van Til: "It is sometimes argued that unless one asserts the primacy of the intellect, one may justly follow any or every sort of emotion. But this would be true only in the non-Christian concept of the nature of man. Only in the non-Christian concept of man are the emotions inherently unruly; they have become unruly only because of sin. But, when sin has entered into the mind of man, the intellect is as unruly as are the affections. The whole man refuses to subject itself to the rule of God. When a saved sinner learns to control his passions, the reason is not primarily that he has understood the meaning of the primacy of the intellect as a psychological truth, but the primary reason is that in the whole of his being he is born of God." [*An Introduction to Systematic Theology* (Phillipsburg, NJ: P&R, 1978), 34]

- Jonathan Edwards: "I don't think ministers are to be blamed for raising the affections

Earthly authority and emotions were created, and created good, by God Himself. If either of them were evil, we would have no Dr. Roslings. He is, in fact, a scientific *authority* driven by a deep *passion* to improve the world, to maximize its usefulness for mankind. Authority and emotion are fundamentally good creations of God. No one should blame the good things God made for the mess we're all in.

HUMAN RELIGIOUS MUTINY

Other worldviews have blamed rationality or other good things God created. "All of these have been scapegoats,"* says worldview thinker Al Wolters, "that have drawn attention away from the real root of the trouble, human religious mutiny* against the Creator and his laws for the world."[13]

That Creator, it's true, gave Adam and Eve a creation that was undeveloped. Man was given the job to "subdue" it to better suit his needs (the Creation Mandate). In this sense, much of the good of creation was potential, not yet actual. But on that glorious sixth creation day "when the morning stars sang together and all the sons of God shouted for joy" (Job 38:7), when the world stood like an unopened present for God's second son, there was nothing deficient about the creation. When God handed the earth to Adam, it was everything a perfect Creator wanted it to be.

scapegoat: an innocent party who takes the blame for some sin

mutiny: rebellion against one's rightful authority

THINKING IT THROUGH 6.1

1. How did God assess His own creative work when He finished? What does this imply?

2. After the Fall, does God's creation become inherently evil? Why or why not?

3. Why do people tend to blame things such as the body, authority, or emotions for the world's problems?

4. Why aren't the body, authority, and emotions to blame for the world's problems? What is to blame?

♀ 5. Why might some people blame money, for example, as the source of evil in the world? What is wrong with such blame?

6.2 LAWS OF NATURE AND CREATIONAL NORMS

"Did God make the moon, kids?"

All the boys and girls in the Sunday school class shout "YES!" holding out the vowel for as long as they can.

"How do you know?" says the teacher, who usually teaches the high school class. The kids don't have any idea, but they've been in church long enough to catch on that the answer to most questions is either "Jesus" or "the Bible." Hailey quickly raises her kindergarten-sized hand and opts for the latter. "Right!" says the teacher. "The Bible says it right here in Genesis 1—God made the 'lesser light to rule the night.'"

"Did God make Saturn, kids?" Not all of them have heard of Saturn, so the chorus of yeses is not quite as loud this time. "How do you know?" asks the teacher. Hailey, who is very bright, figures she'll go for "the Bible" again. "Right!" says the teacher. "Genesis 1 says that God made the 'lights in the expanse of the heavens,' and that would have to include the planet Saturn."

1. He observed with satisfaction that it was very good, nothing evil or lacking.

2. Everything is pervasively marred and used perversely, but the Fall can only suppress, twist, and mar; it can't annihilate the goodness of God's creation.

3. Sinfulness can be clearly and thoroughly carried out in the abuses and perverted uses of the body, authority, emotions, and other such things.

4. These are all basically good things created by God; personal sin in a person's use of these things is to blame.

♀ 5. Some people suppose that the Bible says that money is the root of all evil rather than the love of money. They may be able to exemplify many cases of corruption involving the accumulation or use of wealth. But a system of commerce correlates with God's created order when people are free to own and trade possessions with one another.

SECTION OBJECTIVES 6.2

1. Defend the idea that the natural order of the universe is governed by laws of nature upheld by God's sovereignty.

2. Defend the idea that the social order of the universe is governed by creational norms fitting with God's design.

3. Explain how creational norms are discovered through personal application of biblical wisdom to real-life situations.

Defining Laws of Nature

Laws of nature are descriptions or models that humans have made based on the regularities of God's world. Natural laws exist because God has determined that His world will work in particular ways (Gen. 8:22; Pss. 104:14–23; 147:15–18).

Countering Laws of Nature

Through technology, humans may be able to "override" a law of nature. But we still can't break it in the sense of doing away with the law of nature altogether. The law is still operating even while the technology negates its effect. For example, flying an airplane doesn't break the law of gravity. The law of gravity is always operating while the plane is in the air. It's just that flying involves the use of other natural laws that enable lift.

of their hearers too high, if that which they are affected with be only that which is worthy of affection, and their affections are not raised beyond a proportion to their importance, or worthiness of affection. I should think myself in the way of my duty to raise the affections of my hearers as high as possibly I can, provided that they are affected with nothing but truth, and with affections that are not disagreeable to the nature of what they are affected with." [*The Great Awakening*, vol. 4 of *The Works of Jonathan Edwards*, ed. C. C. Goen (New Haven, CT: Yale University Press, 1972), 387]

• John Frame: "It is true, of course, that people sometimes 'follow their feelings,' rather than thinking responsibly. But it is also the case that people sometimes follow rationalistic schemes that run contrary to what they know in their 'guts' (feelings) to be true. God gives us multiple faculties to serve as a sort of internal system of checks and balances. Sometimes reason saves us from emotional craziness, but emotions can also check the extravagant pretenses of reason." [*The Doctrine of the Knowledge of God* (Phillipsburg, NJ: P&R, 1987), 336]

Emotionalism, not emotion, is the root problem. Emotionalism occurs when the emotions are disassociated from truth and inappropriately matched with situations.

It's impossible to divide the human soul into tidy compartments of the mind, the will, and the emotions and then decide which should always be the primary guide over the other. Instead, the human person is a unified whole, each "part" working simultaneously in harmony. [See also Mark L. Ward Jr., "Paul's Positive Religious Affections" (PhD diss., Bob Jones University, 2011), 98–118, 156–61]

Norms: Wisdom and General Revelation

Wisdom was the first principle and the blueprint, derived from God's own nature, by which God created the world (Prov. 3:19; 8:22, 30). Humans gain wisdom when they understand and conform themselves to the wisdom that God built into the world. The fear of the Lord is the beginning of that wisdom (Prov. 9:10). God's special revelation of His law makes explicit the wisdom built into the world for proper human functioning (Ps. 147:19–20); this law is just as integral to the nature of the world as are the natural laws (Ps. 147:15-18). Therefore, though suppressed to varying degrees by the unregenerate, general revelation provides a basis for the ethics of human behavior that ought to be understood by the consciences of those who lack the explicitness of special revelation (Rom. 2:14–15). These creational norms are built into God's design for both interpersonal relationships and societal institutions.

As Albert Wolters says,

> God's ordinances also extend to the structures of society, to the world of art, to business and commerce. Human civilization is *normed* throughout. Everywhere we discover limits and proprieties, standards and criteria: in every field of human affairs there are right and wrong ways of doing things. There is nothing in human life that does not belong to the created order. Everything we are and do is thoroughly *creaturely*. . . . Even without God's explicit verbal positivization of the creational norms for justice and faithfulness, stewardship and respect, people have an intuitive sense of normative standards for conduct. One word for that intuitive attunement to creational normativity is *conscience*. . . . An implication of the revelation of God in creation is that the creation order is *knowable*. . . . This fundamental knowability of the creation order is the basis of all human understanding, both in science and in everyday life. Again, this is generally admitted readily enough in the case of the natural sciences . . . , but it meets with skepticism and outright disbelief when it is applied to the social sciences and the humanities.

[Albert M. Wolters, *Creation Regained*, 2nd ed. (Grand Rapids: Eerdmans, 2005), 25, 29, 33]

The more the truth is suppressed, the more the conscience is seared and the more foolish, ungodly, and unnatural humans become in their interpersonal relationships, societal institutions, and cultural expressions.

God's Control over the Universe

Divide students into groups of two or three and assign them a section of verses from Job 38–41 (cf. Job 12:7–10; Ps. 148). Have them list not only the created things but also all the implications of natural laws (boundaries for and operations of those objects) that God says He rules over in His all-knowing wisdom—both now and since the beginning of creation.

"Did God make gravity, kids?" A few of the kids think she said "gravy," so they murmur, a little tentatively, "Nooo." (*Moms* make gravy, obviously.) Only Hailey says, "YES," but she's just going on her years of Sunday school instinct. The rest of the kids are quiet. "Right, Hailey!" says the teacher. "Genesis doesn't just tell us the things God made, but it tells us the jobs those things are supposed to do—like the sun ruling the day and the moon ruling the night. And those things are impossible without what we've come to call gravity. So God made gravity."

The kids are getting fidgety. But the teacher isn't picking up the cues. "Did God make marriage?" A feeble "yes" comes from Hailey, her instincts faltering. "Yes, God made marriage," the teacher says, "because God called humans to do jobs just like the sun and moon. He told them to fill the earth—and marriage is the first step God intends for that filling to be done."

The bored boys in the back are starting to poke one another, but the teacher goes on. "Did God make government?" Silence. The kids are lost. This is not a question for the five-year-old class.

LAWS OF NATURE

Saturn and the moon are obviously God's creations. Gravity is, too, once you understand how Saturn and the moon operate. Gravity is a "law of nature." Even the naughty boys in Sunday school know this. Or at least they find out when, in the deep devotion to Superman common to boys their age, they don a red cape and attempt to fly off the top of the living room couch. Every Superman-wannabe wearing a cast is testimony to the simple fact that gravity is an utterly unbreakable law.

But try as you might, you will never find a Bible verse teaching little kids to obey the law of gravity. The Bible never says we can't fly faster than a speeding bullet or leap tall buildings in a single bound.

Even so, it's right to use the word *laws* when talking about the laws of gravity, of motion, or of thermodynamics—all the "constants" described by the tools of science. It's right to use the word *laws* because, like all laws, they are issued by a lawgiver. We don't know those scientific laws like God knows them; since we don't have any Scripture that tells us exactly how they operate, our understanding will always be limited, subject to revision. But we do know that God's speech continually upholds the order we see around us. The apostle Peter points out not only that "the earth was formed . . . by the word of God" but that "by the same word the heavens and earth that now exist are . . . being kept" (2 Pet. 3:5–7). And Paul says that in Christ "all things hold together" (Col. 1:17). God through Christ actively commands the universe to act the way it does, all day every day. God's law ordains and upholds the orbits of planets and the orbits of electrons. God wouldn't have to do anything, exactly, to destroy the universe. He could merely relax His hands and let it fall.

Nothing (and nobody) disobeys the **laws of nature**. Soccer balls always come back down no matter how hard you kick them into the air. Water always boils at the same temperature at a given height above sea level. Animals always follow their instincts

> *Thus says the Lord, who gives the sun for light by day and the fixed order of the moon and the stars for light by night, who stirs up the sea so that its waves roar — the Lord of hosts is his name: "If this fixed order departs from before me, declares the Lord, then shall the offspring of Israel cease from being a nation before me forever."*
>
> —JEREMIAH 31:35–36

Natural Laws and Creational Norms

Albert Wolters writes:

> There is, however, a crucial difference between the laws of nature and norms. In speaking of the 'stormy winds that do his bidding' (Ps. 148:8), the psalmist does not ascribe responsibility to the wind. The wind cannot help but obey. But human beings do have responsibility: we are held to account for the way we execute God's commandments, and we are liable to punishment if we do not execute them at all. Norms are complex. They can be violated in any number of ways, and they also leave a good deal to the resourcefulness and responsible imagination of the human being who is called to

(even though, as we'll see in Unit 3 on the fall of mankind, animals have been damaged by human sin). Seasons always come and go (Gen. 8:22). God upholds all these laws of nature by His personal word. These laws are so certain that the King of the Universe Himself swears by them (Jer. 31:35–36).

CREATIONAL NORMS

So God didn't just make stuff, physical objects. He also made the laws that govern those objects without fail. Including human beings. And yet both experience and (more importantly) Scripture demonstrate that the laws of nature aren't the only divine laws governing humans.

There are other divine laws that, unlike gravity, are indeed breakable. At least by humans. We are God's responsible creatures. We can make choices, and quite often (after Adam's Fall) we have all chosen to break the laws God gives us freedom to break.

God's word governs creation in two different ways, then, and it will be helpful for us to add a label for the laws we are responsible to follow. We'll use the term *creational norms* because these norms have been present since creation. A truly Christian worldview recognizes that God put all the stuff He made into a *created order*. He made creational norms—divine laws that govern the way human individuals and cultures operate. There are right and wrong ways to fulfill your God-given earthly task, no matter what it is.

Marriage Norms

Marriage is a good example of a creational norm. Because it was instituted at creation (Gen. 2:24) and built into the way the world works, it's no surprise that marriage is an extremely important institution in virtually all human cultures.[14] But those cultures sometimes forget that marriage wasn't created by people. That's why Supreme Court justices can't reinvent it. No one can—at least not without turning marriage into something that no longer deserves the title. The way God made marriage is the standard by which all future marriages must be judged.

Jesus used this very argument when some Pharisees asked Him about divorce. They asked, "Is it lawful to divorce one's wife for any cause?" Jesus answered,

> Have you not read that he who created them from the beginning made them male and female, and said, "Therefore a man shall leave his father and his mother and hold fast to his wife, and the two shall become one flesh"? So they are no longer two but one flesh. What therefore God has joined together, let not man separate. (Matt. 19:4–6)

Jesus' words form the foundation of the scriptural argument against not just divorce but polygamy, same-sex marriage, and all other sexual sin. Humans can't create "same-sex marriage" any more than they can make "four-sided triangles" or "dry water." *One man and one woman become one for life*—that's the pattern.

Note, however, that you don't discover this norm of creation from Genesis alone. Other portions of Scripture have rich things to say about what God created marriage to be. In fact, God kept the preeminent truth about marriage as something of a secret (with hints) for thousands of years. Paul reveals that secret in his letter to the Ephesians, namely that marriage is a picture of Christ's relationship to His church (Eph. 5:31–33). This relationship is a "creational" truth because it has always been true, ever since the foundation of the world (cf. 1 Cor. 11:8–9). But it was only revealed after Christ's incarnation.* We know about creational norms from more than just Genesis.

incarnation: *Christ's taking on flesh to become human as well as divine*

implement them. . . . A falling stone has no comparable task in obeying the law of gravity, nor does an eagle in observing God's ordinances for raising its young. The stone obeys necessarily, the eagle responds instinctively, but a person must exercise personal responsibility: we are called to *positivize* the norm, to apply it to specific situations in our lives. All of human life, in all its vast array of cultural, societal, and personal relationships, is normed in this sense. The almighty Creator lays claim to it all.

[Albert M. Wolters, *Creation Regained*, 2nd ed. (Grand Rapids: Eerdmans, 2005), 17]

A Comprehensive Creation

According to Scripture, are societal institutions arbitrary or are they structured according to God's sovereign rule and design?

The clearest examples in Scripture include marriage and family (Gen. 1:26–28; 2:24; 1 Tim. 4:3–4), governmental authority (Rom. 13:1–2; 1 Pet. 2:13), and the church (Eph. 3:8–11).

While some principles may need to be inferred, every institution is sovereignly ruled over by God and ought to be run according to His design: agriculture (Isa. 28:23–29), business and labor (James 5:1–6), learning (Ps. 1:1), the arts (Exod. 28:3; 35:10, 35; Prov. 22:29), and so on. The broad principles of wisdom revealed in Scripture can be applied to everything in creation (2 Pet. 1:3).

Perversions Are Always Doomed

Like an inflated beach ball shoved below the surface of a pool, you can suppress the goodness of creation for a while, but it always struggles to the surface.

Illustrate how creational norms operate by bringing in a container with water and an inflatable object. Shove it under the water for a while and then let go, demonstrating that the inflatable object is designed so that it always comes back to the surface.

For instance, a particular human society can insist on labeling homosexual unions as marriage, but eventually that society will collapse because it contradicts God's design for filling and subduing the earth (Gen. 1:26-28). The creational norm will come back to the surface as other societies take over and proceed through world history.

What's Your Starting Point?

Remind students about presuppositions and the worldview apologetics approach.

Should you approach the marriage debate by trying to find neutral, common ground? That is, should your strategy be to throw out the Bible and argue from "undeniable" evidence back to your own view?

No, it's impossible to correctly interpret the evidence unless a person views that evidence through the correct lenses of a worldview presupposition. The authoritative starting point of God's Word must be established first.

How can God's Word be established as the starting point if unbelievers refuse its authority?

The truth of God's creational design must be unapologetically declared (deductive approach). If God's Word on the matter is rejected, the Christian should point to evidence that shows the damage that comes from violating God's creational norms. (Destroy the furniture in their worldview house.) In other words, use evidence to demonstrate the self-defeating nature of the secularist worldview. Then correlate the evidence with the biblical worldview's interpretation, demonstrating that life was designed to work accordingly. (Invite them into your worldview house.)

Should a Christian expect to be able to persuade non-Christians?

A Christian may sometimes succeed in persuading a non-Christian. God's law is written on the consciences of unbelievers, and God restrains sin in the world's cultures by opening people's understanding to these norms (Rom. 2:13–14). However, unbelievers are also blind to the truth apart from grace, which means even the most persuasive arguments and evidence may not convince them (2 Cor. 4:3–4; Rom. 6:16; 8:5).

The Mundane and Apparently Amoral

Divide the class in half to debate whether or not there may be activities that are amoral or so mundane that regardless of how you go about doing them, God wouldn't care.

It may seem as if creational norms are limited to the overt moral concerns of human interrelationships emphasized in Scripture. However, Scripture indicates that even the mundane activities of farming, for instance, are subject to God's creational design. It may not be sinful to trample over one's own crops, ruining them, but it is certainly unwise and anti-normative. Believers should strive to avoid not only what's normally recognized as sinful but also foolishness that is anti-normative.

Capitalism Versus Communism

While capitalism and communism are both subject to corruption by fallen humans, communism generally seems to be more anti-normative than capitalism. For instance, within capitalism, private property can certainly be stolen by means of a loophole designed for a rich and powerful elite with political connections. However, when something like that comes to light, the public has legitimate legal means for shutting down the cronyism. But within communism, private property for the masses is disallowed (to varying degrees) as the norm. A political elite always ends up having full control to distribute everything among the lower classes. Any dispute by the lower classes is squelched by force. So while it's possible to carry out capitalism in ways consistent with the biblical principles of private ownership and redress for injustice, there's no possibility of carrying out communism in a way that's consistent with those biblical principles.

Farming Norms

And we know about more than just marriage. There are other creational norms. Look, for example, at what the prophet Isaiah has to say about farming:

> Does [the farmer] who plows for sowing plow continually?
>   Does he continually open and harrow his ground?
> When he has leveled its surface,
>   does he not scatter dill, sow cumin,
>   and put in wheat in rows
>   and barley in its proper place,
>   and emmer as the border?
> *For he is rightly instructed;*
>   *his God teaches him.*
>
> Dill is not threshed with a threshing sledge,
>   nor is a cart wheel rolled over cumin,
> but dill is beaten out with a stick,
>   and cumin with a rod.
> Does one crush grain for bread?
>   No, he does not thresh it forever;
>   when he drives his cart wheel over it
>   with his horses, he does not crush it.
> *This also comes from the Lord of hosts;*
>   *he is wonderful in counsel*
>   *and excellent in wisdom.* (Isa. 28:24–29)

God teaches farmers how to do their job. But the Bible doesn't have an appendix listing wheat and barley cultivation practices. It doesn't include diagrams for crop-rotation or black-and-yellow stickers saying "WARNING: Do not use threshing sledges on dill." What Isaiah is saying is that a farmer who pays careful attention to the way his seeds and soil work together is actually listening to the voice of God. He'll only know it's God's voice, of course, if he reads his Bible. But once he does, he's discovering creational norms through his work that were put there by the Creator. God built certain "best practices" into the world of farming, and He'll teach them to people who are patient enough to listen.

Economic Norms

The Bible upholds the right of private property—otherwise many laws in the Pentateuch (including "thou shalt not steal") would make no sense. Scripture also teaches accountability for one's economic decisions—see the book of Proverbs, where the field of the lazy man gets overgrown with weeds (Prov. 24:30–34; cf. 1 Tim. 5:8). Both private property and economic accountability are cornerstones of Western capitalism. But the Bible stops short of specifying which economic system is best. Nonetheless, with the light of Scripture shining on God's world, we can discover truth—even economic truth. There are economic creational norms.

democratic capitalism: an economic system in which the free market determines the value of goods, and people elect their own leaders

Marxist socialism: an economic system in which government planners determine the value of goods, and leaders are not elected

As the twentieth century unfolded, it was not at all clear which of the two major economic systems would prevail. For example, North Korea became a nation in the mid-1940s when the forces of democratic capitalism* and the forces of Marxist socialism* in Russia and China divvied up the Korean peninsula. Russia and China fought the United States to a stalemate over North Korea shortly thereafter (1953). Russia soon became the first nation to launch a satellite into space (1957) and, more importantly, the first to put a human up there (1961).

What Are Some Economic Norms?

List some biblical principles that reveal creational norms in the realm of economics.

- *Laboring to supply your own needs or else suffering want if you don't; rewarding diligence (Exod. 20:9; Pss. 104:23; 128:2; Prov. 6:6; 10:4; 13:4; 21:25; 2 Thess. 3:6–15)*

- *Private ownership of property; guarding against stealing by requiring and enforcing restoration (Exod. 20:15; 22:1; Lev. 19:11; Deut. 5:19; Eph. 4:28; 1 Pet. 4:15)*

- *Designing an unjust system that cheats people into poverty and enriches oneself is condemned (Exod. 23:8; Deut. 16:19; Pss. 15:4–5; 26:10; Isa. 5:8, 23; Amos 5:11–13).*

- *Cheating includes breaching a contract or giving someone something other than what was promised (Gen. 31:7; Mal. 1:14; 1 Tim. 5:18; James 5:4).*

Guarded Optimism

Guarded: It would be wrong to say that the capitalistic system of modern-day America couldn't possibly be subject to cronyism and corruption. Biblical critiques of aspects of the free market system can and do reveal corruption and injustices that ought to be corrected. Every human system has flaws.

Optimism: Capitalism works far better than socialism at bringing people out of poverty, raising standards of living, protecting private property, and preserving individual freedom. Capitalism's success in this respect seems to indicate that it has gotten something right when it comes to creational norms that socialism has not—just as a farmer who's figured out the benefit of crop rotation has learned something about the way God's creation works.

But today there's only one nation's flag on the moon.[15] By the time it got there (1969), the seeds of the USSR's destruction were already beginning to germinate. The economic and political system of the old Soviet Union finally disintegrated as the century drew to a close (1991). The Cold War ended not with a bang but a whimper.

What did the world discover about economics in the last hundred or so years? Simply put, the lesson learned was that capitalism—though distinctly imperfect itself—is a better economic system than socialism.[16] And if the world needed any more proof, the fact that Chinese communism has successfully adopted capitalism should be sufficient. So did the world discover truth? Did it find some creational norms? No one should presume that any economic system is unaffected by the Fall. Capitalism often has significant downsides: people start to think that their greed is normal and even beneficial, the desires of the market drive art and leisure even when those desires are immoral, and so on. But one thing appears clear at the moment: no economic system in the history of the world has ever delivered so much poverty-ending wealth, so much subdue-the-earth opportunity, even so much physical height and health as capitalism. North Korean defectors say that one of the most eloquent arguments for capitalism was the standard of living they glimpsed (illegally) on South Korean television. In light of almost a century of socialism's disastrous and murderous failures, it's difficult to believe that Marxism fits within the creational norms set up by the Creator of economics. Capitalism can be improved upon,[17] but socialism is not the solution. It violates too many creational norms.

Capitalism and socialism are both affected by the Fall. But a simple look at their results suggests that the former fits better with creational norms than the latter.

DISCOVERING CREATIONAL NORMS

Discovering creational norms is like spelunking.* Spelunkers normally have powerful headlights on their helmets. Without them they'll almost certainly die, so they've got to pay some attention to the functionality of their lights. But they do that when they're on the surface. When they're actually in the cave, they don't spend time looking at their lights; instead they use the light to see the "path" in front of them, to light up their surroundings.[18]

spelunking: *cave exploring*

Likewise, the psalmist wrote, "Your word is a lamp to my feet and a light to my path" (Ps. 119:105). You've got to pay some attention to your light; learn it well. But the Bible will do you little good if you never take its truths out into the real world and let them light up your surroundings. You will never find the right path unless you pay close attention to those surroundings—using the light of God's Word. This is how you gain what the book of Proverbs calls wisdom.

Wise people put light and the world together to figure out the creational norms around them. And when a wise person discovers those norms, he or she is submissive to them. It's hard work to discover, like the farmer in Isaiah 28, the creational norms related to your calling. But it's not as if the Bible is unnecessary for you to be a good farmer. The Bible is a lamp illuminating whatever you're looking at—marriage, farming, economics, government, journalism, or education.

Caution: The Obscure and the Bizarre

Things go wrong when a person's knowledge of God's Word *or* the world is distorted and inaccurate. Sometimes Christians attempt to connect certain Scripture passages to life situations when no connection exists. When this happens, a Christian may mistake his own opinions for creational norms. The result is that human traditions can come to be equated with the inspired Word of God and cultish "Christian" counterfeits form (Gal. 3:1–3; 1 Tim. 1:3–11; 4:1–5; Col. 2:8–23). Pragmatic life principles and practical formulaic steps for success must never replace the foundation of sound biblical doctrine applied to life with sound biblical wisdom.

Discovering Creational Norms

Being convinced that God's world is ordered according to God's design of transcendent and absolute creational norms is only the first step. It's also necessary to accurately recognize these norms. While some norms are presented explicitly and extensively in Scripture, much of the path of life needs the light of principles from God's Word to illuminate it. This requires spiritual discernment— the application of accurate biblical knowledge about God's revealed principles to an accurate studied knowledge of the world or a field of study or labor (Col. 1:9–10; Rom. 12:1–2). Doctrine defines; right beliefs must undergird proper behaviors. But the Bible isn't a detailed textbook on every specific field of study that exists in the world. A person must study his area of expertise in detail, shining the light of biblical wisdom on that study.

Discovering Biblical Wisdom

When Christians need to make ethical decisions in life, there are always three major factors involved that must be clarified:

• What is the situation?

• What does God's Word say?

• How should you respond?

In other words, biblical wisdom is the application of God's revelation (normative) to a problem (situational) by a person (existential). This is what John Frame calls *triperspectivalism*. All three perspectives must always be considered. [John Frame, *The Doctrine of the Christian Life* (Phillipsburg, NJ: P&R, 2008), 131–32]

1. natural laws or laws of nature

2. creational laws or norms

3. Marriage: a permanent male/female one-flesh relationship

   Farming: patterns for plowing, rotation, sowing, threshing, and reaping

   Economics: ownership; work ethic

4. They're revealed through the moral lens of scriptural principles personally applied to the practical wise observation of real-life situations.

♀ 5. • Marriage: unstable family and society

   • Farming: failed crops and hunger

   • Economics: poverty and injustice

SECTION OBJECTIVES 6.3

1. Defend the necessity of standards for evaluating the goodness of something.

2. Explain the twofold nature of the Christian standard: (1) special revelation of moral laws declared in Scripture and (2) general revelation of natural laws and creational norms built into God's design.

3. Recognize that there are differing consequences for violating both natural laws and creational norms.

4. Implement a knowledge of biblical morality to detect the trumped-up claims of supposed creational norms.

🖥 Standards for a Fully Christian Ethic

John Frame writes:

Let me try to diagnose . . . the reason why secular ethics is regularly led down blind alleys. The main problem is not conceptual confusion, a lack of logical skill, or ignorance of facts, although such problems do exist in both Christian and non-Christian ethical systems. The chief problem is rather unbelief itself. Secular ethics . . . seeks to find an absolute somewhere other than in the Word of God. It therefore seeks its ethical standard in the most probable locations: human subjectivity . . . the empirical world . . . or logic or reason. . . . A fully Christian ethic accepts only God's word as final. That word is found preeminently in Scripture . . . but is also revealed in the world . . . and in the self. . . . A Christian will study these three realms, presupposing their coherence and

therefore seeking at each point to integrate each source of knowledge with the other two.

[John Frame, *The Doctrine of God* (Phillipsburg, NJ: P&R, 2002), 194–95]

A clear understanding of both special revelation (2 Tim. 3:15–17) and general revelation (Ps. 19) is absolutely essential for a proper Christian standard or ethic. The norms found in God's Word should correlate with the norms found in God's world.

Scripture: Sufficient and Authoritative

Scott Aniol identifies two major approaches to the application of Scripture and the formulation of a Christian ethic: the encyclopedic approach and the encompassing approach. The first approach assumes that

anything not explicitly commanded in Scripture is amoral and thus a person is free to pursue his own desires however he wishes. The second approach recognizes that there are norms even for things not explicitly commanded in Scripture. [Scott Aniol, *Worship in Song* (Winona Lake, IN: BMH Books, 2009), 1–22] The encyclopedic approach limits itself to mere prooftexting; the encompassing approach simply maintains that scriptural principles ought to be applied to every contemporary situation (2 Pet. 1:3).

Sola Scriptura was intended to affirm that the Bible is the Christian's ultimate and final authority. It was never meant to prohibit believers from applying Scripture to situations the Bible does not directly address (Eph. 5:10). In order to make such application, not only must the truth of God's Word be correctly understood, but the contempo-

---

1. What is the label we use for God's governance over the fixed order and operation of the physical objects He created?

2. What is the label we use for God's governance over the roles and responsibilities of humans carrying out their social tasks of filling and subduing the earth?

3. What are some possible examples of God's design for marriage, farming, and economics?

4. How are creational norms discovered?

♀ 5. What are some undesirable results of working contrary to God's design in marriage, farming, and economics?

6.3 THE WAY THINGS ARE SUPPOSED TO BE

Was Nolan Ryan the best baseball pitcher ever? Check his stats against other pitchers' stats. That's the standard. Did you get an A+ on your last exam? Check your answers against the answer key. That's the standard. Did we put that oil filter on the motorcycle correctly? Check what you did against the owner's manual. That's the standard.

If there are no standards, there can be no evaluation, no judgment. Not all judgments are as easy to make as those about pitchers, exams, and oil filters. But all judgment is pointless without a standard to judge by. Without a standard, it's meaningless to call something right or wrong, good or bad.

Followers of the Abrahamic religions (Christianity, Judaism, and Islam) all look to specific holy books for their standards, especially moral ones. So they have a definite idea of where their standards come from. But atheists and other people who claim no specific religion—and this is a growing group in the West[19]—also have standards. Everyone does because standards are part of a person's worldview.

A great many people in the West, however, are fuzzy on what their standards are, especially their ultimate standard. They have a vague notion that everything they believe has been scientifically proven and that their particular beliefs are normal and unobjectionable; but that's as far as they go in acknowledging their own standards.

Occasionally, however, a thinker will step out into the public square and speak with perfect clarity as to the source of his or her standards. Feminist philosopher Linda Hirshman is one such thinker. In an interview on Beliefnet, Hirshman measured stay-at-home moms against her standards and found homemakers to be off base:

Just because you choose to stay at home doesn't make it right; . . . you have to examine the decision for its worthiness up against some kind of standard other than what St. Paul told the Ephesians.[20]

Hirshman won't allow us to use the Bible as our standard—no Paul at all. The interviewer, naturally, asked her what standard she would offer instead: "You're asking what makes for a good life for women. How do you define 'good life'?" To Hirshman's credit, she was ready with an answer. She listed three replacement standards:

1. According to Plato and Aristotle, you've got to use your full human capacity.

2. According to Enlightenment thinkers, you've got to be independent, morally autonomous.

3. According to general human experience during European industrialization, you've got to do more good than harm.[21]

Hirshman called this set of standards "secular western goodness." And she told Beliefnet,

> I applied those standards to the decision [by women] to stay home and tend children and the household, and I found that they were, in fact, lacking. These women are not using their full human capacity. They are not independent, and they are not doing more social good than harm.[22]

Of course, Hirshman's standard hides the important questions about what counts as good and what counts as harm. And why pick Plato over Paul? Why, indeed, listen to Linda Hirshman? What gives any human being the right to define the good life (or morality) for any other? By what standard can we say that Hirshman is right and stay-at-home moms are wrong? It's her word against Mom's. She said, she said.

We need access to moral standards that transcend human disagreements, or all we'll ever be able to do is shout at each other louder (or shoot each other). Humans are all stuck on the same level, low to the ground; we need someone sitting above the fray to tell us who's right.

THE CHRISTIAN STANDARD

Every person raised in Sunday school knows that it's God's Word that provides the Christian standard. But the Bible is a big book full of all kinds of stories, and most of them contain a good deal of human sin—in what way can a bunch of stories and letters and prophecies and poems provide us a standard?

We need to be more specific. What is it in the Bible that reveals the standard by which we judge what we see in our world? The answer is rich and complex, but an important way you can summarize it is this: "Creation." The way God created the world is the standard by which we judge the way things in the world ought to be.

The Heavens Declare

The point of this chapter about laws of nature and creational norms is to show that God communicates truth outside of Scripture as well as through it. You can understand the truth outside the Bible only if you understand and obey and love the truth inside it. But if God's creation is fundamentally good, then it too must contain truth.

Just listen to David in Psalm 19. He talks about two ways God communicates truth to us. The first is nature:

> The heavens declare the glory of God,
>   and the sky above proclaims his handiwork.
> Day to day pours out speech,
>   and night to night reveals knowledge.
> There is no speech, nor are there words,
>   whose voice is not heard.
> Their voice goes out through all the earth,
>   and their words to the end of the world. (Ps. 19:1–4)

Nature is telling us something, but without audible voices and human words. Nature is telling us about the "glory of God" and "his handiwork."

In the second part of the psalm, David turns to the other major way God tells us truth: His written Word.

rary situation must also be understood accurately. This is what is meant by discovering truth outside of Scripture in general revelation. Rather than undermining Scripture's absolute authority, it is expanding the authority of Scripture into every realm of life.

Aniol presents abortion as a clear example to confirm the validity of the encompassing approach. Believers must logically connect what they know from extrabiblical information to the biblically authoritative principles of Scripture. While one may infer from Scripture that babies in the womb are humans who should not be killed, that's not explicitly stated. Believers must logically connect information from general revelation, discerning that the authoritative principles of Scripture apply to abortion.

Responding to Hirshman

Identify some flawed presuppositions in what Linda Hirshman says.

- *She assumes that past collective human wisdom should be authoritative over revelation.*
- *She is very selective in choosing which collective human wisdom to highlight.*
- *She wrongly assumes that homemakers don't use their full human capacity and don't do more good than harm. In fact, cultural upheaval has never been more apparent than when mothers fail to fully give themselves to properly training their children.*
- *She wrongly assumes that moral autonomy and independence bring fulfillment. In fact, this spirit undergirds destruction of families.*

The Biblical Appeal to Creation

Shouldn't God's character be the standard?

Creation is designed in accordance with the character of the Creator. Therefore, it is biblical to root the Christian ethic in creation with the understanding that creation ultimately reflects God's character. Both Jesus and Paul do this (Mark 10:6; 1 Cor. 11:14; 1 Tim. 2:13). The norms in the Bible aren't arbitrary; they are built into the design of God's world, which was made in accordance with God's character.

The Christian Standard and the Law

According to Matthew 5:17; Romans 7:12, 14; 8:4; and 1 Timothy 1:8, is the Old Testament law good or bad?

Even though it has never justified a person, the law still has a good and useful purpose.

Based on Romans 3:19-20 and Galatians 3:24, what was the purpose of the Old Testament law?

While the law often served to reveal sin, it also provided ethical guidance, as a guardian, by means of explicit moral norms for a particular situation (people, place, and time).

In light of Romans 3:28; 6:14–15; 10:4; 2 Corinthians 3:6; and Galatians 2:16, 19; 3:10–13, 24–25; 5:18, does the Old Testament law directly apply to believers today?

No. Even though many of the same moral norms are repeated in the New Testament, believers are under a new jurisdiction (a New Covenant system). Believers today rely on the internal guidance of the Holy Spirit, which can never be divorced from the objective principles of the New Testament; specific applications to one's own situation must be discerned from these principles. Explicit specificity for particular situations (people, places, and times) is no longer catalogued as in the Old Testament.

Do Romans 3:31; 6:1–2; 1 Corinthians 7:19; 9:21; Galatians 6:2; James 1:25; 2:12, 14–26; and Titus 1:16 indicate that believers are still under an ethical obligation to the law of God today?

Yes, believers are still obligated to evidence the righteousness of Christ in the fruit of their behavior; otherwise, they prove that they have a dead faith. This obedience is energized by the Spirit rather than an external written code.

In line with 1 Corinthians 10:6 and 1 Timothy 5:18, does the Old Testament law provide any direction for believers today?

Yes, although believers aren't under jurisdiction of the Mosaic Covenant system, the underlying norms are just as true today as they were in Old Testament times because they are rooted in the transcendent character of God. The underlying principles of the law are still applicable today. What has changed is the situation. Analagous situations in ancient times may serve as illustrations for today. The principles or norms still apply even though the particularities of the situation may differ.

In sum, the moral norms don't differ between the Old and New Testaments because they're rooted in God's character and the function of God's created order; what differs is the situational application of those creational norms.

How to Apply the Old Testament Law

One Bible scholar explains a four-step process for properly using the law in a modern-day context:

> I would suggest the following . . . procedure for applying any of the OT laws, whether the law be deemed ceremonial, judicial, or moral:
>
> 1. Remind yourself that this law is not my law, that I am not legally bound by it, that it is one of the laws God issued to ancient Israel as part of his covenant with them. When I look at this law I am looking over the shoulder of the Israelite. . . .

[To clarify, what he means is that the New Testament believer is under a new jurisdiction. Many of the Mosaic laws are repeated in the New Testament. But it's the new jurisdiction that is binding not the old with its situational context for those same laws. This is analogous to a law against murder that may be the same in different countries but can only be enforced according to the jurisdiction, with its penalties, in which someone committed the crime.]

> 2. Determine the original meaning, significance and purpose of the law. What was its point? Why did God issue it? What apparently were his motives in giving it? (Allegorizing, spiritualizing and typologizing here are counterproductive, succeeding only in obscuring the original significance and purpose of the law.)
>
> 3. Determine the theological significance of the law. What does this law reveal about God and his ways? A law, as mentioned, reveals a great deal about the lawgiver. What does this law reflect about God's mind, his personality, his qualities, attitudes, priorities, values, concerns, likes and dislikes, his teaching methodologies, the kinds

of attitudes and moral and ethical standards he wants to see in those who love him? In spite of the fact that these 613 laws were issued to another people who lived at another time under very different circumstances than ours . . . they come from the God whom we too serve, and they represent a vast reservoir of knowledge about him and his ways.

> 4. Determine the practical implications of the theological insights gained from this law for your own NT circumstances.

[David A. Dorsey, "The Law of Moses and the Christian: A Compromise," *Journal of the Evangelical Theological Society* 34 (September 1991): 321–34]

The law of the Lord is perfect,
reviving the soul;
the testimony of the Lord is sure,
making wise the simple. (Ps. 19:7)

We perceive God's moral law by reading the Bible. We perceive the laws of nature and creational norms by careful observation of His creation through the lens of the Bible's moral laws. All of God's laws reveal God's glory (Ps. 19:1, 7). Although only the Bible laws are written down—and that's very important to remember—the other laws are no less real. And they're no less good. If creation is fundamentally good, then creational norms are fundamentally good too. They lead toward fruitfulness and success in this created world.

In fact, the whole system of laws that God gave Israel through Moses can be seen as an application of creational norms to their situation. What did it look like in the Ancient Near East to follow creational norms? Read the Mosaic law, and you'll see. This is why Paul can say that the Mosaic law "is holy and righteous and good" (Rom 7:12).

Violating Creational Norms

When you violate a law of nature, your "punishment" comes quickly. You jump off the couch like Superman; you fall to the floor. You were never really flying.

But what happens when you don't care to follow creational norms for human behavior and society? When you violate a creational norm, it's like you're pushing hard against a powerful metal spring. You can push it down, but it's going to take a great deal of effort, and at any moment the coil may spring back into its original shape. That's why some worldview thinkers have pointed out that humanity is "coming perilously close to the point where the earth itself will impose certain norms on us."[23] They point to the example of industrial wastes:

> It is creationally unlawful to put chemical wastes into an ecosystem when they cannot be assimilated. If we persist in breaking such a law, eventually the ecosystem will break down completely and we will lose the resource essential to life. . . . Creation is law-bound.[24]

So you can't run your state like a dump. You can't run a family like an army, and you can't run an army like a family. You can't run a church or a school like a business. The basic elements of human culture fit into structures God has already set up. He has norms and expectations for them. If you violate those norms, eventually you'll face consequences.

So it's not quite accurate to say that you can't break the divine law of gravity, but you can break the creational norm of marriage. You can't break either divine law without consequences; it's just

RUNNING YOUR COUNTRY LIKE AN ARMY

What happens when you don't choose to follow creational norms? Ask North Korea. The leadership of North Korea runs that nation like an army instead of like a nation. Almost four out of every ten people in North Korea are either in the military or in the reserve, and they keep a million-man standing army. (The United States has a million-man military, too—but the US population is six times bigger than North Korea's.)

In part by running his country like an army, "Dear Leader" Kim Jong Il ended up starving millions of his people to death in the late 1990s. One North Korean pediatrician who escaped the famine stumbled into the courtyard of a Chinese home and couldn't understand why there was a bowl of rice with meat in it just sitting on the ground. Suddenly she realized that it was a food dish for the family pet. It hit her that dogs in China ate better than doctors in North Korea. The size of the military budget was not the only reason for this mass starvation, but it was a significant contributing factor.[25]

The Bible never says in so many words that it's wrong to have a huge army and buy expensive missiles when your people are starving to death. God hasn't chosen to reveal all His creational norms explicitly. It can take hard work to discover them, but that doesn't mean they aren't there. God has provided direction—standards, criteria, principles—for how to run nations, schools, families, and businesses. To discover them is part of the blessing and task of the Creation Mandate.

Political Opinion or Biblical Norm?

Christians may sometimes presuppose that a particular political perspective is a biblical position. They may read that political position back into the Bible (eisegesis) rather than formulating their political position from the Bible (exegesis). Christians must be careful to differentiate between clear biblical principles and preferred political opinions. Political opinions may or may not be clearly rooted in creational norms. This doesn't mean that those kinds of political opinions can't be defended. It just means that rooting that defense in an unchanging universal biblical or creational norm may not be possible. Trying to stretch the Bible or a creational norm to do so actually undermines the defense of one's political opinion.

that the consequences come immediately when you attempt to break a law of nature, but they may be delayed for a long while in the case of a creational norm.

Objections to Creational Norms: Baptizing Political Platforms

There are a few objections to the idea of creational norms that we should consider. The first has to do with political arrogance. People sometimes talk as if they've discovered the way God's world really is when all they're really doing is "baptizing" the positions of their particular political party—trying to borrow God's authority for their own ideas.

It is dangerous to join a political team and then go in search of all the creational norms (and Bible verses) you can twist to fit that team's views. Bumper stickers will tell you that God is in favor of or against all sorts of political positions and parties. Liberals and conservatives both do this: "Jesus would raise the minimum wage." "Guns are a God-given right."

A lot of people have it backwards; they're more concerned about getting God on their side than they are about lining up with His. They haven't worked hard to discern what God really wants—or whether He might possibly allow liberty on a given issue.

The existence of creational norms provides confidence that there is truth to discover in the world of politics and economics—and in every major field of human endeavor. God made this world. God made it *very good*. And whatever vocation you end up in—politics included—it will be a large part of your task to discover that goodness.

So some parties may indeed line up more closely with biblical views than others (issues such as abortion and same-sex marriage come to mind). But limited, fallen human beings should be very humble and careful in their search for norms outside of Scripture.

Objections to Creational Norms: Justifying Ethnic Prejudice

Another objection to the idea of creational norms comes from the way they have been used to justify ethnic prejudice. During South African apartheid,* there were plenty of Christian Afrikaners* who argued forcefully that since God created the races to be separate, they should stay that way.[26] US Christians have often used the same argument.

But in both nations, the idea that the races (whatever a "race" is—the modern concept of race as a distinct set of physical characteristics cannot be found in the Bible[27]) should remain separate often obscured what was really going on: oppression.

And that oppression tended to be used to further justify racial segregation. When a particular people group is oppressed—whether blacks in America and South Africa or Dalits in India—they lack the educational opportunities to improve themselves, and their oppressors begin to feel that they are racially superior to their lower-class neighbors.

> **GOD REVEALED**
>
> There are basically two ways God reveals truth to humans today: the Bible and creation. Theologians call the Bible **special revelation**, and they call truth in creation **general revelation**. The classic Scripture demonstrating the difference is Psalm 19, which starts out by saying that "the heavens declare the glory of God" (general revelation) and ends by praising God's Word: "The law of the Lord is perfect, reviving the soul; the testimony of the Lord is sure, making wise the simple" (19:7). God's Word and God's world are both revelations of God. But there's a key difference, as David's song shows. The heavens do declare the glory of God, but "there is no speech, nor are there words" (19:3).

> **apartheid:** "apartness," the policy of racial segregation that governed South Africa 1948–91
>
> **Afrikaner:** a white resident of South Africa, descended from Dutch settlers of the seventeenth century

Baptizing a Political Platform?

Debate illegal immigration. Is one's position based on biblical norms, or is it political opinion baptized with biblical language? Answer the following questions.

Is national sovereignty a biblical norm?

God ordained governments to enforce justice. This presupposes that each government has a known jurisdiction and citizenry with privileges and responsibilities (Rom. 13:1–7).

Should national sovereignty be undermined by open (or unenforced) borders?

Maintaining sovereign borders is a matter of wise discernment. Different time periods and situations may call for different responses. For example, survivors fleeing genocide ought to receive protection as an exception to the rules.

What biblical principles apply to concerns about illegal immigration?

It's anti-normative to demand that legal citizens shoulder all the responsibilities, such as paying taxes, while illegal non-citizens are free to enjoy and even demand the privileges. Citizens rightfully demand that the government protect them from those who would subversively enter in to do them harm. They rightfully demand equal justice against lying, cheating, stealing, and other unlawful activities involved in both illegal border crossing and long-term living. Legal immigrants rightfully demand that government reward righteous attempts to enter the land and punish unrighteous attempts. Immigrants should be protected from the unlawful activities of employers who find it advantageous to underpay and abuse employees.

Isn't compassion the higher duty?

The means of showing compassion can't violate other biblical norms. Compassion can be shown in other ways. Bob Jones Sr. was known for saying that it's never right to do wrong in order to get a chance to do right.

An analogy may help. If a criminal were to break into your home, stealing goods and endangering your family, it is illegitimate for that criminal to appeal to the biblical ethic of compassion to deter prosecution. The difference between this and illegal immigration is only a matter of scale; the principles are the same.

What's the best way to solve the illegal immigration problem?

It is a transgression of law and order to hamper attempts to truly secure the border and to refuse to enforce current immigration laws. If a believer doesn't like a law, he cannot support disobedience. He can only support the legal procedure for improving or changing the laws. Until then, current laws must be enforced.

Once the above matters are settled, then the real debate can begin. Christians may differ regarding what changes ought to be made (i.e., what exacerbates the problem by raising incentives for illegals and what serves as a proper deterrent to illegal activities). [James K. Hoffmeier, *The Immigration Crisis: Immigrants, Aliens, and the Bible* (Wheaton: Crossway, 2009)]

Status Quo or Biblical Position?

Sometimes the way things are becomes the standard rather than the way things ought to be. Christians must be careful to distinguish descriptive passages of the Bible from prescriptive directives in the Bible. For example, the story of the tower of Babel has at times been taken out of context in order to defend the status quo of racial segregation. This historical judgment was turned into a prescriptive directive (and the division of people by language was reinterpreted as division by skin color). The status quo of white supremacy was comfortable for many white Americans or South Africans, but their trumped-up creational norm was ultimately based on racism and selfishness rather than on Scripture.

Resources on Race

Ken Ham and A. Charles Ware, *One Race, One Blood: A Biblical Answer to Racism* (Green Forest, AR: Master Books, 2010).

Only One Race: The Scientific and Biblical Case Against Racism DVD (Answers in Genesis, 2002).

Why Bother with the Temporal World?

The implication that stems from God's restoration of all things is that there is an ideal to which it can be restored. It follows then that humans should be searching for that ideal while tasked with stewarding God's creation. That ideal may be more difficult to discern in a fallen world awaiting the eternal state of perfection. However, an ideal may be found when God's written Word is wedded to His created world. Even though the ideal may not always be clear in the natural world, Christians should continue striving for excellence. They shouldn't accept mediocrity as a way of life. This is just as unacceptable in one's cultural and vocational life as it is in one's spiritual life.

THINKING IT THROUGH 6.3

1. Worldview commitments are necessary for any moral evaluations.

2. moral laws; natural laws and creational norms

3. Usually the violation of a natural law has immediate physical consequences; the violation of a creational norm may not have recognizable physical consequences until later.

4. True creational norms will never violate scriptural morality. The agendas behind false claims to creational norms will reflect unbiblical attitudes (e.g., political arrogance, ethnic prejudice).

♀ 5. No, many of them can no longer use their full human capacity; they're usually not independent; some of them might do harm to themselves or others if they weren't being carefully watched.

The idea of creational norms should never make us conclude that *the way things are now is natural and good.* This world is so deeply fallen that we need the light of Scripture—telling us that all people are created in God's own image, for example—to help us discern when what seems "normal" to us (note the *norm* in that word) should not. The present state of the cosmos is *ab*normal, after all.

CFR

God made this world good, and both the stuff in it and the rules governing it are good too. The way God made this world is the standard by which we judge the way things ought to be.

This doesn't mean, however, ditching our clothes, razing our cities, and living in gardens like Adam and Eve. The Fall has happened since then, of course, and that has changed things drastically. But even if you set aside the Fall, the Bible shows that God didn't create the world static or stuck. He created it with a plan for what it would become—filled, subdued, and dominated—developed toward its ideal. And this isn't true only of visible, physical things like mountains and insects. In those six days of creation, norms for human culture were created too. When we create, we create within structures that God set up.

So boil anything in this world down to its basic elements, and you can say "CFR" about it. It was *created* good, but the *fall* has damaged it—and it only Christ's powerful *redemption* can restore it. This is true of marriage and economics and farming and ethnicity; it's also true of music, art, business, banking, communication, and all the things you're studying in school: history, science, math, and language.

Either the Creator is King over society and culture, or He is not. Either God has set up expectations for how farming and education are supposed to work, or you can just do what feels right and hope for the best. As one theologian put it, if God is not sovereign over every part of life, "we are then freed from trying to discern God's will in these places as well as any responsibility for following it."[28]

Humans can look forward to the day when Christ will truly rule over all aspects of human culture, conforming them to His will. We can't bring that day about. But we must not think to ourselves, "Why polish the brass on our sinking ship?" Christ cares about our ship, and we are blessed and called by the Creation Mandate to polish it for His glory. He will pull it out of the waves one day.

It's the work of a lifetime to see the created good in your vocation, to detect the sinful twisting that has marred it, and to work to push it in some small way back toward the biblical-creational standard. But if you use "secular western goodness" as your standard, creation will push back. It won't work. Use instead the light of God's Word shining on your path.

THINKING IT THROUGH 6.3

1. Why are standards necessary for all judgment?

2. What kinds of laws are given to us through special revelation? What kinds of laws are given to us through general revelation?

3. How might the consequences of violating a natural law and a creational norm differ?

4. How can you spot a false claim to a creational norm?

♀ 5. Think of a relative or someone else you know who lives in a nursing home. Does that person's life measure up to the standards of "secular Western goodness"?

CHAPTER REVIEW ANSWERS

Making Connections

1. the body, authority, and emotions

2. laws of nature; creational norms rooted in God's moral law

3. a standard that stems from your worldview, measuring right/wrong

4. special and general revelation; Special revelation must always be the light by which general revelation is understood.

Developing Skills in Apologetics and Worldview

5. Abusive sinfulness in a fallen world may be illustrated both by authoritarians and anarchists. God is good, and He set Himself up as an authority. He also designed human authorities. They are

CHAPTER REVIEW

TERMS TO REMEMBER

laws of nature
creational norms
special revelation
general revelation

Scripture Memory

Proverbs 3:19

Making Connections

1. List three aspects of God's good creation that are commonly blamed for the problems of the world.

2. What governs the operation of the physical universe? What governs the way human individuals and cultures ought to operate?

3. In order to evaluate or make judgment calls about anything in the world, what must you use?

4. What two forms of revelation should guide a Christian's judgment calls? Should one form take priority over the other?

Developing Skills in Apologetics and Worldview

5. How should you respond if someone who's complaining about the problems in the world proposes the solution of just doing away with all authority structures?

6. How should you respond when a well-meaning Christian blames emotion as the root of all sin?

Examining Assumptions and Evidence

7. Why should God's creation still be considered essentially good even in spite of the pervasive negative effects of the Fall?

8. Why should you heed the laws of nature even though the Bible doesn't directly command you to?

9. Evaluate the following argument: "Spotted hyenas are polygamous (males have multiple mates), so polygamy is natural and good."

10. Did God make government? Why or why not?

Becoming a Creative Cultivator

11. Pick one of the academic disciplines or cultural domains featured as a unit in this textbook: gender, marriage, and family; government; science; history; or culture and the arts. Make list of what you think might be some creational norms for that discipline or domain.

---

commanded not to abuse, and we are commanded to obey them (Eph. 6:1–9; Rom. 13:1–7).

6. God has emotions of love, sorrow, hate, anger, and the like. Emotions are a part of the image of God in man just as the intellect is. Emotions are a part of God's good creation even though they can often be used to direct us in sinful ways. But the intellect is just as fallen (Eph. 4:17–18).

Examining Assumptions and Evidence

7. According to 1 Timothy 4:4–5, sin didn't annihilate the goodness of God's creation. Since sin did mar and twist it, humans must be careful to discern through God's Word and prayer the proper and holy use of it and then embrace the pure use of it with thanksgiving.

8. The laws of nature are a part of God's design for the world. God designed you with the intellectual capacity to figure this out and respond accordingly or suffer the consequences.

9. The way God made marriage is the standard by which all marriages must be judged. The animal world is not a good standard because even nature has been affected by the Fall (and humans aren't animals).

10. Yes, it was instituted by God (Rom. 13:1) as an outgrowth of the created order that should be naturally discovered as multiple groups of humans form and need leadership, accountability, oversight, mediation, and so on.application as if it is directly from authoritatively inspired Scripture. Another godly believer with a biblical worldview may be able to dispute some of his supposed scripturally wise observations of the world.

Becoming a Creative Cultivator

11. Answers will vary. The norms are what one would expect, through wise discernment, would govern the tasks of each academic discipline or cultural domain.

Gender, marriage, and family: permanent, male/female, one-flesh covenant marriage; differing family roles— male leadership and breadwinner; complementary female enablement and nurturing; gender is granted according to biological creation not self-determined

Government: grant justice; provide defense; inculcate and reinforce morality

Science: observational study of the universe; interpreting data from observations; communicating findings; standardizing measurements

History: studying historical sources and artifacts; interpreting data from study; selecting what events are significant; mapping out chronology; deciding causes and effects; discerning the unfolding of God's plan; judging moral lessons to learn from and communicating it to others

Culture and the arts: reflecting truth, goodness, and beauty

TERMS TO REMEMBER

laws of nature—constants built into the design and operation of the physical universe

creational norms—the design of God's created order (the way things are supposed to be) translated into divine laws that govern the way human individuals and cultures ought to operate

special revelation—the testimony of God's written Word; the Bible

general revelation—the testimony to truth in God's created world

CHAPTER 7

Since the Fall extends to every aspect of creation and culture, the academic disciplines and cultural domains discussed in this book are not neutral but twisted by the Fall. This means that a Christian perspective on every aspect of life is necessary.

CHAPTER 8

Even though the Fall has twisted every aspect of creation and culture, the image of God and His common grace ensure that the goodness of creation is not completely destroyed. This means that even non-Christians can make useful cultural contributions. However, this reality must be balanced by the real danger of being conformed to the world. The reason intelligent people who contribute to culture hold false worldviews is that affection drives cognition.

CHAPTER 9

As noted in Chapter 6, God built creational norms into His world. These norms can be called "structure." The Fall bends these structures in various sinful directions. The goal of this book is to help students perceive how given disciplines have been bent, and how students might be God's tools to bend those disciplines back toward their created structures.

3

FALL

Chapter Seven **FAR AS THE CURSE IS FOUND**

Chapter Eight **COMMON GRACE, THE WORLD, AND YOU**

Chapter Nine **STRUCTURE AND DIRECTION**

The student will be able to

7.1 Defend the idea that every aspect of a human individual is touched by the Fall.

7.2 Defend the idea that the Fall includes cosmic effects on the physical world.

7.3 Defend the idea that every aspect of human culture is touched by the Fall.

SECTION OBJECTIVES 7.1

1. Describe the pre-Fall conditions of humankind as comprehensive perfection for fulfilling the Creation Mandate in right relationship with God.

2. Describe the process of the Fall, accomplished through Satan's deceptive questioning of God's Word and goodness.

3. Analyze the extent of both the physical and spiritual ramifications of the Fall as comprehensive corruption frustrating the fulfillment of the Creation Mandate due to a broken relationship with God.

4. Clarify that although each part of human nature is fallen, not every person manifests fallenness to the greatest possible extent or in the same way.

5. Explain how sin powerfully enslaves human nature through its deceptiveness.

Chapter Seven **FAR AS THE CURSE IS FOUND**

The creation waits with eager longing for the revealing of the sons of God. For the creation was subjected to futility, not willingly, but because of him who subjected it in hope that the creation itself will be set free from its bondage to corruption.

Scripture Memory
Romans 8:19–21

7.1 THE PERSONAL EFFECTS OF THE FALL

You probably have lots of dos and don'ts to keep track of—as a citizen of your nation, as a student in your school, and as a child in your family. Adam and Eve's "do" list was fairly short: fill the earth, subdue it, have dominion over it, and start by working and keeping the garden—the Creation Mandate. And yet inside that to-do list is a nearly infinite number of possibilities. Adam and Eve could pretty much do whatever they wished—because their wishes were aligned with God's.

Adam and Eve's "don't" list, by contrast, was just one item long:

Of the tree of the knowledge of good and evil you shall not eat, for in the day that you eat of it you shall surely die. (Gen. 2:17)

WHAT BEFELL ADAM AND EVE?

The perfect man and woman, with perfect loves, perfect bodies, and perfect minds were very unlikely to disobey their one "don't." But for reasons we cannot fully know (because God hasn't revealed them), God allowed a malevolent force to enter His creation. And as that serpent approached Eve with the first temptation in the history of our planet, he knew he had to overcome God's threat that Eve would die. His chosen strategy is one he hasn't ever tired of using: he questioned the authority and truthfulness of God's word, and at the same time, God's goodness:

He said to the woman, "Did God actually say, 'You shall not eat of any tree in the garden'?" (3:1)

That wasn't what God had said, of course. Even Satan's question twists God's speech. God said His image-bearers could freely enjoy the riches of every tree—every tree except one. But the serpent successfully wrested Eve's eyes away from that vast gift and got her to focus on the one thing she couldn't have. That's what all covetousness is, including yours.

God said, "You shall not eat of the fruit of the tree that is in the midst of the garden, neither shall you touch it, lest you die." (3:3)

The crafty serpent saw an opening in Eve's words. He became bold; he contradicted God directly and then snuck in a half-truth.

The serpent said to the woman, "You will not surely die. For God knows that when you eat of it your eyes will be opened, and you will be like God, knowing good and evil." (3:4–5)

Satan suggested again, without ever saying so, that God was not good, that God was withholding some pleasure from Eve—a life better than the one she had. Satan tricked Eve into seeking a good thing, but seeking it in an evil way. The serpent knew his prey: it was precisely because Eve was made in the image of God that she viewed being like God as a tempting prospect. Satan didn't create evil desires; he twisted good ones.

The Problem of Evil

Why did God allow the Fall? All orthodox Christians believe that God created this world knowing that Adam would sin. Why didn't God create a different kind of world, a world in which everyone willingly loved and obeyed Him? The biblical answer is that God has not chosen to tell us. We do know that the new earth will be such a world (Rev. 21:27) and that God hates sin (Ps. 5:4). God is entirely righteous (Hab. 1:13; 1 John. 1:5), and God tempts no one to sin (James 1:13). Furthermore, by allowing sin and planning for salvation, God determined that He would bear the full weight of suffering for sin by the Father pouring out His wrath for the sin of the world on His beloved Son (Rom. 3:25; John 1:29). And yet despite these realities, God allowed the Fall. And He was righteous in doing so (Lam. 3:37–38;

When the woman saw that the tree was good for food, and that it was a delight to the eyes, and that the tree was to be desired to make one wise, she took of its fruit and ate, and she also gave some to her husband who was with her, and he ate. (3:6)

Genesis 2 makes it clear that God had made trees for just the reasons Eve was attracted to this one. The text says that He made "every tree that is pleasant to the sight and good for food" (2:9). So food is good. As is delight. As is being wise like God. Eve's sin began, as all sins do, when good things were bent the wrong way. God's good creations were used against Him. God's creatures tried to make themselves *equal to* Him instead of merely *like* Him.

WHAT CONSEQUENCES DID THE FALL HAVE FOR EVERY PERSON?

By the third chapter of the Bible, God's highest creation has already plunged into sin. A sin that happened embarrassingly fast would now take millennia to undo. But this epic, world-shattering Fall was so stupid. Like all of our sins, the pleasure was so miniscule compared to the subsequent pain. Adam and Eve ate, but as a result they felt empty rather than full.

Naked

The serpent, of course, had wrapped the truth around a lie. Yes, God knew that when Adam and Eve ate from the tree their eyes would be opened. But what they got when that forbidden juice hit their tongues was not a better life. What they experienced was something only humans can experience, and only because of sin: the shame of nakedness.

Then the eyes of both were opened, and they knew that they were naked. And they sewed fig leaves together and made themselves loincloths. (Gen. 3:7)

It's a little awkward to say so, but you know this is true: to go without clothes around other people takes real trust. You trust a doctor when absolutely necessary, but only for a few minutes. You will likely one day trust a spouse because in a marriage two become one. And even in both of those trusting situations, you're never unaware that you're exposed. (Nobody ever forgets to put on clothes before going out.) The relationship Adam and Eve shared with each other and with their Creator must have been deeply rich and trusting if Adam and Eve never even realized they were without clothes. And now, with one act of defiance, that trust is shattered. The beautiful life they were given is gone.

Even the wickedest people on earth have not forgotten that they are naked. That barrier between humans and God, created by sin, remains. From Genesis 3 onward the Bible speaks of all people, all Adam's race, as being "dead in . . . trespasses and sins" and "by nature children of wrath" (Eph. 2:1, 3).

That is the sense in which Adam and Eve "died" on that dark day when man fell. Death is the loss of life. Since man is complex in his being—a spirit being and a physical being—the judgment of death is complex as well. Adam's inner man died immediately when he sinned; he was separated from God, the only source of spiritual life. But his outer man didn't die till he was 930 (Gen. 5:5).

> "Sin is irrational. Why would anyone turn from the beauty and joy of covenant life with God and embrace its opposite? Or why would anyone think he could succeed in opposing God's omnipotent power?" [1]
>
> —JOHN FRAME

Eph 1:11). To those who doubt this, God's reply is, "Yet you say, 'The way of the Lord is not just.' Hear now, O house of Israel: Is my way not just? Is it not your ways that are not just?" (Ezek. 18:25) and "Who are you, O man, to answer back to God?" (Rom. 9:20; cf. Job 38:2; 40:2; 42:2–3). In the end, the Christian is left with affirming all that the Bible teaches and humbly trusting God regarding the things that He has not revealed. This should be a matter of marveling praise rather than questioning doubt.

Twisting What Is Good

Just as darkness is simply the absence of light so also unrighteousness is simply the absence of righteousness. God didn't create evil and neither did Satan. Evil is simply the twisting of righteousness into its opposite. Satan couldn't create something new; only God can create. Satan could only twist God's good creation into a perversion. Therefore, whenever something is identified as evil, one must remember that it is simply a twisted version of what God created good. Thus, we must be careful not to reject God's good creation but only perversions of God's good creation.

Distorting God's Good Creation

First, students must be able to differentiate between what God made (governed by laws of nature and creational norms) and how that good creation is put to use by humans.

What God Made (general categories)
music, government, marriage and sex, etc.

Human Use (particular expressions)
music: classical, folk, country, pop, rock, etc.
government: communism, democracy, etc.

marriage and sex: adultery, monogomy, heterosexuality, homosexuality, etc.

(These particularities are all human expressions and sub-creations either more or less conformed to God's laws and norms.)

Second, students must discern whether the human expressions conform to or distort God's design and norms (Eph. 5:10).

While some things are directly condemned or condoned in the Bible, others are left to the wisdom of believers applying biblical principles—but no human expression is neutral or above critique. This demands an accurate understanding of both Scripture (CFR) *and* the cultural expression.

Lead a discussion, applying the Bible to one of the more controversial expressions.

The Root of Unbelief

Have students evaluate a news article or blogpost about someone leaving the faith. How do the given reasons boil down to doubting God's goodness and truthfulness? What would transform doubts into trust?

Have students summarize the biblical account of someone who doubted God's goodness or trustworthiness. Have them identify why the person doubted and what the biblical antidote is. Below are suggested passages and possible summaries:

Doubting God's Goodness

Sarah in Genesis 18:1–15: *When God's promises seem impossible, wait on His power.*

Job in Job 31:1-40: *When integrity doesn't seem to pay off, wait on God's reward.*

Solomon in Ecclesiastes 1:1–18; 12:13–14: *When everything in your life seems frustratingly worthless, fear God and keep His commands, waiting for God's final judgment.*

Doubting God's Authority and Truth

The unsaved people in Acts 17:16-34; 1 Cor. 1:18–29; 2:14: *Since the gospel seems foolish to the natural man, a person must submit his thinking to God's declarations.*

King Agrippa in Acts 26:1–32: *Since the gospel will usually get in the way of one's current pursuits, a person must deny self.*

The Extent of the Fall: The Human Body

Nakedness

While broken fellowship with God was the root problem, the symptom of shame because of nakedness was the first effect of sin perceived by Adam and Eve (Gen. 3:7–11). Adam's idolatrous obedience and commitment to Eve turned out to be destructive to the very relationship he tried to maintain by sacrificing obedience to God. Instead, it undermined the special communion of the one-flesh relationship, which was designed for fruitfulness and multiplying. But why was shame because of nakedness pinpointed as the key attribute of fallen humankind's now enlightened mind about evil?

What was lost: innocence and trust

What replaced them: guilt and fear

This is the result of every sexual abuse or immoral relationship. While some unsaved people's hearts may be so hardened and deadened that they become insensitive, those with a conscience still feel the loss of innocence and trust replaced with guilt and fear. Only maintaining moral relationships with God's approval will spare you from these consequences; only God can bring healing to the consequential heart-deep wounds.

Death and Disease

But shame because of nakedness was only an obvious side effect of the real issue. Because broken fellowship with God was the root problem, the most significant consequence would be death. Due to the Fall, both the inner and the outer person experience death (John 11:25–26; 2 Cor. 4:16).

⭐ Immodesty Is Idolatry

Guide students to think through a gospel-driven standard of modesty by reading an appropriate book and completing Activity 13.

There are two major mistakes that such a gospel-driven approach must avoid.

(1) The currently accepted forms of clothing in one's own culture should never be the starting point, trumping biblical norms for the function of clothing.

form = style; function = purpose

It is true that the precise form of clothing from an earlier culture shouldn't be conserved as the timeless standard (whether that of the ancient Israelites, the pioneers of the 1800s, or the businessmen of the 1950s). Those styles can be mistaken as the modest standard because they followed the biblical norms for the function of clothing (in their situational context)—standards largely lost in the status quo styles of our own culture. But it's not the style that must be returned to or maintained but the functional norms. While our situational context has changed and thus styles should be allowed to change, the function of clothing (to discretely cover rather than accentuate and uncover) shouldn't change with it. Thus, while we need not return to the same style of a previous generation, neither can we uncritically dress in such the same style of our own culture if such clothing functions

---

Jesus restores both kinds of life, spiritual and physical. He said, "Whoever believes in me, though he die, yet shall he live, and everyone who lives and believes in me shall never die" (John 11:25–26; cf. 2 Cor. 4:16). But just as Adam's physical death didn't occur till long after his spiritual death, perfect physical life will be restored (to believers) long after they get spiritual life. Until then, we face the effects of the Fall in our always-dying bodies.

Loving and Thinking

Adam's Fall flipped the world upside down. He was supposed to submit to God just as his wife submitted to him (Eph. 5:22), and as animals submitted to them both (Gen. 1:28). Instead an animal led Eve, who led Adam—who blamed God.

When Adam and Eve heard God coming, they did something image-bearers had never done before: they hid. When God found them, Adam explained, "I was afraid, because I was naked, and I hid myself." God replied, "Who told you that you were naked? Have you eaten of the tree of which I commanded you not to eat?" Watch how quickly Adam learns, serpent-like, to twist the truth: "The woman whom you gave to be with me, she gave me fruit of the tree, and I ate" (Gen. 3:10–12).

We're starting to see that the Fall has effects. Like a lie that requires a cover-up lie or like pollution that permeates an entire reservoir, sin spreads immediately through God's best creation. Adam's reasoning has been damaged: it is supremely irrational to make excuses to a God who sees all—and then to blame Him for the trouble you caused! The powers of logic given only to image-bearers have been damaged. The apostle Paul explains that, after the Fall of Adam, people are naturally "darkened in their understanding, alienated from the life of God because of the ignorance that is in them" (Eph. 4:18). *Understanding* and *ignorance*—these are words that focus on a person's mind or his thinking. Sin has twisted mankind's reasoning powers.

But it hasn't removed them. Adam actually uses exquisite logic in the three statements he makes to God. All three are true, and yet he manages to weave them together into a lie. He's not just listing off what happened; he's giving three reasons for the Fall. "First, there's *you*, God—you gave me this woman. Second, there's *she*—she gave me this fruit. (Then, last and certainly least, there's *me*—I ate.)" He admits to his

---

contrary to biblical norms (designs that uncover or are form fitting). Ethical standards must be based on what ought to be acceptable, not what is. Thus, a clothing style can't be defended simply because that style isn't conspicuous in one's own situational context or because it fits the status quo of what's acceptable to fallen humans with seared consciences who feel free to express their sinfulness. Therefore, a bikini on Miami Beach must still be considered immodest.

(2) The other mistake is to refuse to set any concrete standards in one's own situational context in order to avoid legalism. The biblical principles must be applied. Designs that uncover or are form fitting contrary to biblical norms for the function of clothes must be identified and repudiated. It's impossible to pretend there is no standard; that pretense only lowers the bar for what will be

acceptably tolerated—in clear violation of biblical norms. Unwritten rules only cause confusion and make enforcement impossible. Standards that are clearly thought out and agreed upon ought to produce unity and the ability to enforce expectations.

The Extent of the Fall: The Human Spirit

The Fall touches every person and every part of every person. First, no person escapes the corruption of the Fall; every person is born into sin (Ps. 51:5; Eccles. 7:20). Second, sin has penetrated and affected the whole of the human being: body, mind, will, emotion, and affection (Isa. 1:6; Rom. 3:10–18; 6:12, 17; 8:5–8; 1 Cor. 2:14; 2 Cor. 4:4; Eph 4:17–18; Titus 1:15). It is important to note that these aspects of human nature overlap and interact so much that they can't

role in the sin only after he condemns his Maker and his mate. The two beings Adam is supposed to love most, God and Eve, he throws under the bus.

So it isn't just his mind that's damaged. After Paul describes how Adam's heirs are all naturally "darkened in their understanding," he says quite clearly that their darkness is "due to their hardness of heart" (Eph. 4:18). Adam, deep in his heart, strayed from his purpose of loving God and neighbor, and he subsequently twisted his picture of reality to fit his wayward loves. This pattern still exists today: what you love drives what you think.

Those in the Flesh Cannot Please God

The Fall of man—mind and heart and spirit and body—is why people today go so wrong, both Hitler-wrong and *you*-wrong. Just as Adam hid from God's sight, people hide God from their own sight. People suppress their knowledge of God—knowledge that God says He gave them (Rom. 1:18–19). They have "exchanged the truth about God for a lie and worshiped and served the creature rather than the Creator" (1:25). Their thinking minds and worshiping hearts are twisted in wrong directions. "No one does good, not even one" (3:12). They do irrational, self-harming things. "No one seeks for God" (3:11).

> "THE IDEA THAT DESIRE EQUALS LICENSE COMES FACTORY-LOADED IN ALL OF US." [4]
>
> —JEFFREY KLUGER

In his book about **original sin**,* writer Alan Jacobs notes that "whatever the situation might have been for Adam and Eve, for us the devil on our shoulder is only truly dangerous because of the devil that's already inside us."[5] That's why, Jacobs says, a devil and an angel hovering over each shoulder of a cartoon character are usually pictured as miniature versions of that same character. There is good in every person because God's image is still resident in every person; but evil has touched every aspect of every man, woman, and child. God destroyed the world in Noah's day when He saw that "the wickedness of man was great in the earth, and that every intention of the thoughts of his heart was only evil continually" (Gen. 6:5). Even after He cleanses the earth with the Flood, He says, "The intention of man's heart is evil from his youth" (8:21). Nothing has changed.

The Bible teaches that the effects of the Fall are pervasive. They touch every aspect of every person. Your feeling, your willing, and your thinking are all damaged. But the Bible does not teach that all people are as bad as they could possibly be. Instead it says, "Those who are in the flesh cannot please God" (Rom. 8:8). And by "in the flesh" he means people who do not have spiritual life from God. Some non-Christians are incredibly generous and gracious; some are Hitlers. But the same spiritual death and ultimate rebellion runs through each group. No amount of good deeds can overturn the fact that, deep in their hearts, people are at war with God and not at peace with Him (Col. 1:21). Even if they do good, they refuse to do it for the only right reason there is: love for the loveliest Being in the universe.

original sin: the theological term designating the fact that all humans are guilty sinners at their conception because of Adam's first sin

---

actually be separated even though it is helpful to categorize them for discussion.

Humans still exercise every capacity of their nature. They can think, choose, respond emotionally, and so forth. But the Fall touches their thinking, willing, and desiring. This does not mean that people will act wickedly at every point. Common grace ensures that the image of God in man is not entirely effaced. Sinners still have God's law written on their hearts, and God restrains their sinfulness so that many people do right things even if not for the ultimate reason of glorifying God (Gen. 20:6).

Thoroughly Bad?

How to be deceived into believing that you're basically good:

- Be deceived by external pietism (1 Sam. 16:7; Matt. 15:7–20; Mark 10:17–22; Rom. 2:1–3; 1 John 1:8, 10). This lie says, "I haven't sinned like others."

- Be deceived by redefining sinful behavior (Isa. 5:20; Rom. 1:28, 32; Titus 1:16; 1 John 1:6; Jude 1:4). This lie says, "I'm not currently sinning."

- Be deceived by underestimating the potential for succumbing to any possible sin (Proverbs 16:18; 1 Cor. 10:12; 2 Pet. 2:20–22; 3:17). This lie says, "I won't sin."

Hitler and Your Neighbor

There's probably a striking difference between your average neighbor and Hitler. It's highly unlikely that your neighbor wants to exterminate millions of people.

Is it fair that the nice little old lady that served you lemonade when you were a kid could end up in hell with Hitler?

Condemnation is based on one's identity in the flesh rather than in Christ. No one is righteous, so everyone practices sin. Every sin reveals a God-rejecting heart worthy of hell (Mark 10:18; Rom. 3:10; 8:8–9; Eph. 2:1–3; James 2:8–11).

No amount of good behavior can save a person from condemnation as long as he continues to reject the content of the true gospel. Good works can never outweigh a person's original sin or commitment to a false religious system (Gal. 1:8; 2:16, 21; 3:1–3; 1 Thess. 1:9; 2:13). Moralistic goodness doesn't trump doctrinal soundness. The true faith is more than moralistic character. The true faith is a relationship with God on His terms. While true belief produces good behavior, good behavior doesn't necessarily produce or accompany true belief. Only salvation provides liberty from the law and its punitive judgment and condemnation. Only salvation provides liberty in the Spirit, empowering a believer to truly practice righteousness (Romans 8:1–5; Gal. 5:13–25).

Judgment is meted out based on one's actual practice of sin. Since all people do not practice sin to the same extent, Scripture seems to indicate that neither is their judgment to the same extent (Matt. 11:20–24; Luke 12:47–48; Rom. 2:6, 12–14; 2 Tim. 3:13; Rev 20:12–15).

The Enemy Within

Echoing the Puritan writer John Owen, Kris Lundagaard enumerates four key truths that define the nature of the battle.

(1) "Sin living in us is a 'law.'"

This law enslaves everyone under its power and authority (Rom. 6:17; 7:21). Its rule must be overthrown by Christ (Rom. 6:18; 7:25).

(2) "We find this law inside us."

It is a driving force waging war and seizing opportunity when confronted with decisions (Rom. 7:8, 11, 21–23).

(3) "We find this law when we're at our best."

The battle is strongest when we want to do good (Rom. 7:15–21).

(4) "This law never rests."

The believer has both the Spirit and a sin nature always waging war (Gal. 5:17). [Kris Lundagaard, *The Enemy Within: Straight Talk About the Power and Defeat of Sin* (Phillipsburg, NJ: P&R, 1998), 23–26]

Putting Sin to Death

Assign one of the following books and ask students to write a three- to five-page report that explains the mortification of sin by means of progressive sanctification.

Kris Lundgaard, *The Enemy Within: Straight Talk About the Power and Defeat of Sin* (Phillipsburg, NJ: P&R, 1998).

John Owen, *Overcoming Sin and Temptation* ed. by Kelly M. Kapic and Justin Taylor (Wheaton: Crossway, 2006).

Jim Berg, *Changed Into His Image* (Greenville, SC: BJU Press, 1999).

Jerry Bridges, *The Pursuit of Holiness* (Colorado Springs: NavPress, 1978).

Fallenness: Diagnosis, Symptoms, and Antidote

Both the root problem and its symptomatic results are significant aspects that should be addressed when discussing fallenness and what to do about it.

Cause

What is humankind's root problem?

a broken spiritual relationship with God due to misplaced loves within an idolatrous heart

As a symptomatic result of the broken relationship with God, what task, for which humans were created, gets impeded?

Every curse in Genesis 3 summarizes a frustration of fulfilling the Creation Mandate.

Why is a relationship with God necessary for fulfillment of the Creation Mandate?

Humans were created to fulfill this task under God's rule. But humans rebelled against their sovereign Lord. The consequences were fitting: both the physical creation and the spiritual nature of humans were thoroughly corrupted, rebelling through self-efforts to fill and subdue—impossible without restoration of God's lordship through His intervening grace.

Effects

Although all the constituent aspects of human nature simultaneously interact, it may be helpful to trace how fallenness generally operates within the spiritual nature of humans.

- **Affections:** Wrong desires in the heart produce idolatrous lusts. Thus, affections are bent in the wrong direction.
- **Mind:** Foolish thinking ensues, and the heart meditates on what it wants.
- **Will:** Sinful choices follow from the mind's meditations and the affection's lusts.
- **Emotions:** General emotional disruption is the consequence. Enticing lusts promise happiness and satisfaction, but the fruition of sin only brings pain, guilt, and death.

Remedy

The solution isn't Christianized psychological self-help and self-esteem. The solution isn't formulaic steps to reinforce moralism. The solution isn't to merely think positively—even about gospel truths. All of those efforts, at best, superficially address the affections, mind, will, or emotions.

Then how *should* you deal with an idolatrous heart?

The Holy Spirit must apply the sanctifying work of the gospel.

- The application of gospel truth and grace must first root out idolatrous lusts through repentance, which is a forsaking of idolatrous affections so that one loves God.
- Wedded to this is the renewing of the mind through the washing of the Word, reinforcing both a fear and love for God.
- This love and fear ought to produce willful obedience in one's choices.
- The end result includes a restoration of emotions such as joy in God's glorification.

Freedom and Slavery

As Frodo Baggins stands over the fires of Mount Doom at the climax of *The Lord of the Rings*, having reached the end of his quest to destroy the evil ring, he does the unthinkable. Instead of throwing the ring into the fire, Frodo puts it on and vanishes. But it's not clear whose decision it was, Frodo's or the ring's. Even Frodo avoids saying that it was his choice; he says only, "I do not choose now to do what I came to do. . . . The Ring is mine!"[7] In both book and film, Frodo speaks with a voice not quite his own—but yet his own. Tolkien doesn't tell us exactly what's going on inside the hobbit, but he does provide a picture of the power of sin that every Christian can recognize (Rom. 7:15–20).

Frodo's uncle, Bilbo, felt that power too. When Gandalf the wizard asks Bilbo about the ring, Bilbo snaps, "It is mine, I tell you. My own. My precious. Yes, my precious."

"It has got far too much hold on you," Gandalf warns Bilbo. "Let it go! And then you can go yourself, and be free."

"I'll do as I choose and go as I please," Bilbo replies obstinately.

But Bilbo's choosing and his pleasing are not free. While he still has the ring, Bilbo is in bondage, unaware that true freedom is not the liberty to do what you want, but the liberty to want what you should. Tolkien brilliantly pictures the tendency of sin to promise freedom and deliver slavery. That's the legacy of Adam's Fall—the enslavement of mankind. "Everyone who practices sin is a slave to sin," Jesus said (John 8:34). And no one in this sin-cursed world is exempt.

Thank God that God sent a second Adam, a sinless one, to set the captives free (1 Cor. 15:47).

THINKING IT THROUGH 7.1

1. Why does it seem unlikely that Adam and Eve would have disobeyed God if Satan hadn't been there to tempt them?

2. What did Satan's deceptive questions imply about God's word and character?

3. Describe the effects of the Fall on the whole person: the body, the affections, and the mind.

4. What does sin always promise? What is always its result instead?

5. Why aren't people as bad as they could possibly be? Why can't their good works compensate for their fallenness?

THINKING IT THROUGH 7.1

1. They had perfect loves, bodies, and minds in a perfect relationship with God in a perfect world.

2. that His Word was not authoritative and true and that God was not good

3. The Fall caused shame and began the process of physical dying. It broke a loving spiritual relationship with God and others. It darkened the understanding, making reasoning irrational and ignorant.

4. freedom; slavery or bondage

5. People still retain the image of God and benefit from His common grace. Those in the flesh can't please God because they are spiritually dead and rebelliously at war with God. The good they do is idolatrous.

It may surprise you to know that there were no twins born in the whole United States of America (including Puerto Rico and other U.S. territories) between 1987 and 2013. To giant pandas, that is.

On July 25, 2013, beautiful panda mother Lun Lun gave birth to cuddly twin boy bears Mei Lun and Mei Huan at the Atlanta Zoo, and the whole world said a collective, "Awww!" When the two tiny, wiggly, pink pandas were presented to the public, Mommy and little ones looked like try-outs for a cutest greeting card competition. A live, 24-hour-a-day PandaCam allowed panda enthusiasts from around the world to monitor the adorableness in real time.

Mei Lun and Mei Huan

But Lun Lun's keepers at the zoo knew that, for public relations purposes, they needed to handle this situation carefully. They prepared to rotate the babies, giving only one at a time to Lun Lun. Her public image—and that of all pandas—was at stake. That's because panda mothers typically keep twins alive only long enough to know if their chosen baby is healthy. Then they let the other baby die. [8]

If Lun Lun did that with either Mei Lun or Mei Huan, it would be bad for zoo business. Small children would be confused—"Mommy, why doesn't she feed that one?" Hallmark wouldn't come calling anymore.

But if Lun Lun had let one baby panda die, it would not have been unique—not among pandas, and not among mothers. Mother guinea hens walk so fast that they purposely leave some of their cute little chicks behind, weeding out the weak. Great black eagle moms regularly feed only one eaglet. [9]

THE HEART OF THE CREATION-EVOLUTION DEBATE

The conflict between creation and evolution may seem like it's all about radiometric dating, fossils, starlight, shale layers, and DNA analysis. It may seem like an epic war of science versus religion, reason versus faith. But it's really about dead panda babies. The real heart of the creation-evolution debate is a question: is the world the way it's supposed to be? In other words, is the present state of the cosmos normal or abnormal? [11] Are pandas supposed to let their babies die? *Are humans?* (About 20 percent of pregnant women had their unborn babies killed in a recent year. [12]) Are pain and death and terrible evil supposed to exist in this world?

The secular, materialistic, evolutionary worldview can't say anything is "supposed" to be. It just is. Material universes formed by random chance can't *suppose*. So when Alfred, Lord Tennyson, famously described nature as "red in tooth and claw" [13] in

> *"Are God and Nature then at strife,*
> *That Nature lends such evil dreams?*
> *So careful of the type she seems,*
> *So careless of the single life;*
>
> *That I, considering everywhere*
> *Her secret meaning in her deeds,*
> *And finding that of fifty seeds*
> *She often brings but one to bear."* [10]
>
> — ALFRED, LORD TENNYSON

SECTION OBJECTIVES 7.2

1. Explain why all death and suffering is abnormal (i.e., not supposed to exist anywhere in this world).

2. Explain why Adam's sin led to the Curse not only on the whole human race but also on all of creation.

3. Demonstrate that the Fall resulted in physical consequences that correspond to each task of the Creation Mandate.

4. Conclude that the Christian's hope is in both a spiritual redemption and a physical restoration.

Why Does Evil Exist?

How can an all-powerful God allow evil and still be good? There are four ways to answer this question:

1. There is no God because evil exists.

2. God is not all-powerful because evil exists.

3. God is not good because evil exists.

4. God is lovingly in control but has sufficient reasons for allowing evil to exist.

Only a proper metanarrative will lead you to the proper conclusion.

First, challenge the idea that the evolutionary story can even define or explain evil at all.

Second, challenge the ideas that God is powerless to stop evil or that He is evil.

Present the biblical claims to the contrary (Job 2:10; Ps. 34:8; Eph. 1:11; Dan. 4:35).

Third, lay the foundation for a true chronology of history. Death is an intruder—not the way the world was created to be. It's the fitting consequence of sin; it's a taste of what humans wanted: life without God.

Fourth, give the good news. God has already done all that is necessary to address evil in this world by providing salvation, sustaining grace, and promising future restoration—all by means of the infinite suffering of the Son.

Finally, explain why God doesn't immediately do away with evil. Immediate removal of evil would require immediate removal of all humans and the end of grace. Suffering reminds humans they have an indisputable problem and need restoration.

[Ken Ham and Mark Looy, *Why Is There Death and Suffering?* (Petersburg, KY: Answers in Genesis, 2001)]

Just the Way the World Is?

Discuss whether materialists must be fatalistic due to survival of the fittest.

The phrase *red in tooth and claw* encapsulates the idea of survival of the fittest. Survival of the fittest is a necessary operation for the evolutionary process to move forward. Since death is necessary to natural selection, it's the way the world is supposed to be according to evolution. But it's not a very pretty sight when you see it in action—especially when it's someone you love.

Materialists tend to sidestep the metaphysical questions about why the world is this way and whether it should be this way. They tend to view survival of the fittest as merely a mechanistic process that just is. But that response seems to be fatalistic or deterministic—everything that takes place in the world is inescapably caused by abstract laws of nature.

Not every evolutionist would claim to be deterministic. However, determinism seems to be correlative with a world formed by means of impersonal laws or chemical reactions determining the survival of the fittest. Therefore, while not every evolutionist is fatalistic about everything in life (an inconsistency with their own worldview, which doesn't fit with reality), the most common explanation of the survival of the fittest motif is that it's just the way the world is (which is fatalism).

Discuss whether or not Christians must be fatalistic due to God's sovereignty.

But aren't Christians fatalistic when they believe in a sovereign God who is in control of absolutely everything? Not if you properly understand the biblical teaching of God's sovereignty and human responsibility.

God is neither coercive nor a blind abstract force mechanically at work in the universe. He's a person upholding the design of His Creation and, in a fallen world, offering both common and special grace to humans otherwise constrained to choose consistently with their own fallen, rebellious nature.

Yes, God directs all of this in complete sovereign control. Yet, He never needs to coerce humans contrary to their own volitional free choices. God either chooses to allow humans to continue to freely act in accordance with their own fallen nature or God chooses to open blind eyes in such a way that humans freely choose to submit to Him. He's in complete control and humans choose in complete freedom in accordance to their own nature or in accordance with God's grace.

 ## The Imputation of Adam's Sin

What does *imputation* mean?

It's a legal term that means crediting something to another person's account.

In this context, it is the application of one person's merit or depravity to another person's account. Romans 5:12–19 explains the imputation of Adam's sin to the whole human race that descended from him. It does so by comparing and contrasting it to the imputation of Christ's righteousness on behalf of all those in Christ: "For as by the one man's disobedience the many were made sinners, so by the one man's obedience the many will be made righteous" (5:19).

The logic of this passage can seem confusing unless it is clarified that 5:13–17 is a parenthetical remark that interrupts the flow of thought introduced in 5:12. The first part of the comparison is introduced in 5:12 and then repeated and completed in 5:18–19.

How does it work that one person's merit can be applied on behalf of another?

representative headship

But how is that fair?

It's fair because we are legitimately and accurately represented by the one from whom we all extend.

Reality: Adam's sin *corrupted* the human race descended from him. We *are* corrupted.

Consequence: Since we *are* corrupted, *guilt* must be imputed to us at conception.

The Extent of the Fall: Physical World

Both Adam's race and Adam's realm became corrupted when he fell into sin. The Fall had spiritual consequences: a broken relationship with God and a ruined spiritual nature. But the Fall also had physical consequences: a

---

1844, it was a description of evolution that both evolution's critics and its believers have adopted. Atheist Richard Dawkins is one adopter of the phrase: "I think 'nature red in tooth and claw' sums up our modern understanding of natural selection admirably."[14] Evolutionists think the phrase accurately describes the way things just are: species kill each other off in the never-ending struggle toward survival of the fittest. "The secrets of evolution are time and death," said Carl Sagan, "time for the slow accumulations of favorable mutations, and death to make room for new species."[15]

But creationists (or at least Christian ones) use the "red in tooth and claw" phrase as a criticism: death is abnormal. *This is not the way things are supposed to be.* Death wasn't in God's "very good" creation. Paul says clearly, "Sin came into the world through one man, and death through sin" (Rom. 5:12). If there had been no sin, there would be no death. And Paul says "one man" is responsible. That man, of course, was Adam. And yet his sin didn't affect just himself.

Rep. Adam

The US Congress is divided into two houses—the Senate and the House of Representatives. Representatives of what? Of *you* (if you live in the United States). They represent the voters who put them into office in whatever district they hail from. If the congresswoman from the 12th district of California votes "no" on H.R. 253, then it's as if everyone in that district voted against that particular bill.

But there are most definitely people in the 12th district of California who would have voted *for* that bill. And there were children and others in the district who were unable to vote but who are nonetheless affected by the decision. There are, in fact, animals and rivers and trees that are affected by votes in faraway Washington, DC, that they know nothing about. Not everyone can vote on every bill, so that's the way the American governmental system works.

And it's basically the way God's system works too. God appointed one representative for the entire human race. When that representative voted against God in the Garden of Eden, God treated that vote as if we all voted. Adam voted for the "de-Godding" of God. That audacious act was recorded on the books as the vote of the whole of humanity.

But Adam wasn't just the representative for the human race. He was also the ruler of creation; his sin was a terrible distortion of the Creation Mandate. So when Adam sinned, it was like he jumped into a hole with all of creation tied to his waist by a rope—including animals, rivers, and trees. When its God-appointed ruler fell into sin, *all of creation* was plunged into the same pit. The Fall, in other words, had "cosmic effects"—it touched the whole cosmos, the whole created order.

Two major passages of Scripture, both essential to a biblical worldview, describe these cosmic effects: Genesis 3 and Romans 8.

IS THE FALL FAIR?

Is it fair that we face so many perverse effects from Adam's long-ago sin? Theologian John Frame offers several responses:

1. We all sin just like Adam did. There are no innocent human beings.

2. If you had been in the garden, are you certain you would have done better than Adam did?

3. Humans are always tied to one another. There is no such thing as a true loner. Parents, for example, don't just pass on eye shape and hair color to their kids; they pass on moral character.

4. If treating Adam as our representative is unfair, so is treating Christ as our new representative.

At some point we have to simply trust that God is good even if He doesn't seek to exhaustively prove it to us. And yet—what other proof is needed besides Christ's self-sacrificial death for us? Adam jumped into a pit with a rope tied to him, and he pulled us all in. But the rope tying believers to Christ is stronger than the one tying them to Adam.[16]

---

dying physical body and a frustration of the Creation Mandate. Neither the spiritual nor physical consequences should be ignored. In fact, the physical consequences make ignoring or denying the spiritual consequences impossible. The physical consequences testify to the need for spiritual restoration.

Furthermore, two factors necessitate the cosmic extent of the effects of the Fall. First it's a fitting consequence that God's punishment frustrates the efforts of His rebellious vice regents who try to usurp His authority. He gives humans a taste of what life would be like without His upholding rule. Second, the cosmic extent of the Fall is the necessary result of fallen humans rebelling against God's design. They pervert the way things are supposed to be when they do try to carry out the Creation Mandate. The only possible result is a world in ruin.

Grace Restores Nature

The pervasiveness of the Fall in the physical world has caused some to dismiss the physical world as unimportant. By limiting grace to spiritual realities alone, they end up veering toward monasticism, pietism, and asceticism. The physical world is vilified or ignored. However, nature is preserved because of common grace and will be fully restored in the consummation.

[Common grace is discussed in Chapter 8 and redemption in Unit 4.]

Genesis 3 on the Cosmic Effects of the Fall

God knows all. So His questions to Adam and Eve as they hide from His face ("Where are you?" "What have you done?") are not requests for information; they're opportunities for Adam and Eve to repent.[17] (He doesn't give such an opportunity to the serpent because Satan is beyond redemption.) But Adam and Eve don't express sorrow for their sin, and God is ready with consequences—but not just bad ones. It is so typical of our gracious God that He doesn't even tell Adam and Eve what their punishments are until He has already promised to save them—eventually—from those punishments. Listen to what He says to the serpent:

> I will put enmity
> between you and the woman,
> and between your seed and her seed;
> He shall bruise you on the head,
> and you shall bruise him on the heel. (Gen. 3:15, NASB)

We'll discuss this statement in much greater detail in the unit about redemption, but you need to know that this seed who will bruise the serpent's head is none other than Jesus Christ. A bruised heel hurts, but a bruised head can be fatal. God is promising that a redeemer will come and beat Satan.

Then God turns to Eve:

> "I will surely multiply your pain in childbearing; in pain you shall bring forth children. Your desire shall be for your husband, and he shall rule over you." (Gen. 3:16)

Now one of Eve's most important roles—bringing new image-bearers into the earth to fill it—will involve multiplied pain. And her most important role, helping and complementing* Adam (Gen. 2:20), will be damaged too. The verb used in the phrase "shall rule over you" appears to mean that Adam will dominate Eve harshly (cf. Gen. 4:7). Bible scholar Derek Kidner says, "'To love and to cherish' becomes 'To desire and to dominate.' While even pagan marriage can rise far above this, the pull of sin is always towards it."[18]

It's when God turns to Adam that sin's cosmic effects become most clear:

> "Because you have listened to the voice of your wife and have eaten of the tree . . . , cursed is the ground because of you; in pain you shall eat of it all the days of your life; thorns and thistles it shall bring forth for you; and you shall eat the plants of the field. By the sweat of your face you shall eat bread, till you return to the ground, for out of it you were taken; for you are dust, and to dust you shall return." (Gen. 3:17–19)

God was to rule over man, but man rebelled. Man was to rule over the ground; now it will rebel against him.[19] Work ("the sweat of your face") is not itself a punishment because God gave Adam work to do before the Fall. But the very blessings of the Creation Mandate are now cursed: Adam's work of dominion will now be frustrating; thorns and thistles will constantly fight to thwart Adam's labors. The ground will still be fruitful, but it will also be cursed—good but fallen. And at the end of years—centuries—of often frustrating work, Adam will return as ashes to ashes, dust to dust.

complement: to add to something in order to complete or perfect it

Genesis 3: A Cosmic Curse
Mandate Part 1: Fill

What judgments in Genesis 3 frustrate the first part of the Creation Mandate?

The woman's task to bear children will be frustrated by increased pain.

Both the roles of the husband and wife will be frustrated by the Fall. Wives face the temptation to be dissatisfied with their position in the family. Husbands face the temptation to abuse their authority in the family. The natural outcome of this is a frustration of fruitful multiplying for filling the earth.

Mandate Part 2: Subdue

What judgments in Genesis 3 frustrate the second part of the Creation Mandate?

The man's task to subdue the ground, especially for food to provide for his family, will be frustrated by toilsome labor because the ground will resist his efforts to make it productive.

All the efforts at subduing the earth will seem like a vicious cycle of endless futility until humans die (see Ecclesiastes).

Does the Curse of the ground only apply to farming? Explain why or why not.

Although the Curse specifies the particulars of agricultural work, it is simply the representative illustrative example of what follows from a world that has been thoroughly corrupted by the Fall. Every effort under the sun suffers under the larger reality of the curse (Eccles. 1:2–3, 8; 2:18–23).

In an industrialized world of synthetic materials, it's easy to disconnect products from the natural resources of the earth that they're made from and the hard work that goes into

manufacturing them. But it still takes a lot of diligence to earn enough money to trade for those products that were made by the hard work of others. The Curse hasn't disappeared because of modern technology.

Based on Proverbs 30:7–9 and Ecclesiastes 2:24–26, is it appropriate to seek a more comfortable life to reduce feeling the effects of the Fall?

Humans can enjoy benefits from their labor. It's even appropriate to pray for an enjoyment of God's blessing because of your toil (Prov. 13:4; 15:27; Matt. 6:19–21; 1 Tim. 6:10).

However, humans may be rebelling against their Creator through materialistic pursuits (overworking) or through unjust gain (stealing, lazy dependence) in order to idolatrously enjoy the comforts of life and ignore the Curse or the effects of the Fall.

Romans 8: A Cosmic Restoration

What passages of Scripture indicate that the future state will include physical restoration?

Isaiah 11:6–9; 65:17–25; Amos 9:11–15; 2 Corinthians 5:1–4; Revelation 21:4–5; 22:1–5

Should physical restoration be thought of as peripheral or as an integral part of the CFR storyline of Scripture? Explain why.

Physical restoration is an essential part of the very fabric of the kingdom of God established in the new heavens and earth.

The Scripture passages listed above are climactic promises predicting a future hope that reverses the fallen world back to what it was originally created to be. Physical restoration is a key part of the central theme of Scripture: redemption through the establishment of God's kingdom for His glory. A wrong position on the restoration of the physical world leads to bad theology.

Some theologians believe that differences among various Christian groups originate from this basic issue:

> Every Christian must take into account two factors: creation and re-creation, nature and grace, earthly and heavenly vocation, etc.; and in accordance with the different relationship in which he puts these to each other, his religious life assumes a different character. Man's relationship to God is determinative of his relationship to things in general. Whoever breaks the divinely appointed connection between nature and grace is led to sacrifice one to the other. Socinianism and Anabaptism, Rationalism and Mysticism are the resulting deviant paths into which the Christian goes astray.

[Herman Bavinck, quoted in Jan Veenhof, *Nature and Grace in Herman Bavinck,* trans. by Albert M. Wolters (Sioux Center, IA: Dordt College Press, 2006), 8]

In other words, if you get this wrong, you fall into opposite extremes. Aside from the cultish extremes listed in the above quote, true Christians may tend toward opposite extremes that are still out of step with a biblical worldview. An emphasis that disconnects nature from common grace leads to a contemplative quietism that fails to apply a holistic worldview for engaging with the world (earthly things are minimized). An emphasis that disconnects special grace from nature leads to a busy life of moralism in the affairs of the world that fails to be driven and energized by quiet communion with God (spiritual things are minimized).

Romans 8 on the Cosmic Effects of the Fall

The ground—including your own lawn—is still cursed today. Work—including your schoolwork—is still good but often frustrating. Childbearing is still painful, even dangerous.[20] Adam's terrible vote many centuries ago still counts, all around the world. The Christian hope is that one day God will put everything right.

But we're not the only ones hoping. "The creation waits with eager longing for the revealing of the sons of God," Paul says in Romans 8:19. That revealing is going to take place in the age to come, not in this time (8:18). There is a future glory that God intends to bring to His children. The important thing to note here is that the whole creation, not just people, is waiting eagerly for this day. The animals and rivers and trees are craning their necks, longing to be transformed into glory along with God's children—longing to escape the curse.

Paul explains that curse: "The creation was subjected to futility, not willingly, but because of him who subjected it, in hope that the creation itself will be set free from its bondage to corruption" (8:20–21). After Adam sinned, God subjected all of creation to "futility," to a frustrating inability to achieve its intended purposes. The thorns God sent as a judgment are always getting in the way. But He sent this judgment in a context of "hope"—the promise of Genesis 3 that one day the seed of the woman would bruise the head of God's enemy. It would be strange for creation to "hope . . . [to] be set free" if it's all going to be annihilated one day, as some Christians assume. No, when God's people are finally delivered from the effects of sin and gloriously transformed, creation will be too.

Humans are major characters in the drama of Creation, Fall, Redemption. Nature is our stage. But that doesn't make nature irrelevant. The nonhuman creation was deeply affected by the Fall too, and it will remain part of the drama God has written for all eternity. When the main characters are redeemed and restored (Rom. 8:19), so will the stage . . . lions and lambs, birds and beetles, rivers and trees, panda moms and panda babies. "The whole creation has been groaning," Paul says (8:22). Creation is stuck in the same hole Adam got us all into.

THINKING IT THROUGH 7.2

1. Which two chapters of Scripture are most important for the Christian doctrine of the Fall?

2. Since Adam was the representative of the human race, why does the rest of creation also have to suffer?

3. List each punishment and relate it to the corresponding task given in the Creation Mandate.

4. Is creation going to be completely annihilated one day? Why or why not?

5. Why isn't it unfair that we have to suffer the consequences of Adam's sin?

THINKING IT THROUGH 7.2

1. Genesis 3 and Romans 8

2. As the ruler over creation tasked with carrying out the Creation Mandate, Adam experienced consequences that affected the realm he ruled over too.

3. Pain in childbirth frustrates fruitfulness and multiplying. Wives will be tempted to rule over husbands, and husbands will be tempted to dominate wives. This disrupts the one-flesh relationship. The resistance of the ground frustrates subduing and taking dominion over the earth.

4. No, creation is awaiting the time of humanity's restoration for its own restoration for all eternity.

5. We aren't innocent; we sin just like Adam. We would have sinned in the garden just like Adam if we had been there. Our moral character goes back to Adam; we can't separate ourselves from him. If Adam isn't our representative then neither can Christ be.

Somalia became a "failed state" in 1991 as societal institutions completely broke down.

7.3 THE CULTURAL EFFECTS OF THE FALL

Somalia, situated on the Horn of Africa, has often been called a "failed state." In 1991, the institutions that normally provide governmental, educational, and other services in a smoothly functioning nation simply broke down as civil war engulfed the land. Warlords took over, fighting each other for territory.

One of the first Western Christians to spend significant time in Somalia after war broke out was a missionary in nearby Kenya. He goes by the pseudonym Nik Ripken because he still serves Christ's kingdom in dangerous places around the world.

Nik started making regular trips into Somalia as the situation there became more and more desperate. Dead bodies littered the roads, and it often fell to him to have to choose which towns got food and water and which didn't. One time he found out that the people he had just given food to the day before were being raped and tortured by the people of another village who felt they deserved the food more.[21] It was emotionally devastating work, but Nik plowed forward with the love of Christ and the help of his godly wife back in Kenya.

Nik longed to tell people about Christ, but he knew that to do so was to risk not only his own life but theirs as well. Islamists in Somalia had driven out nearly all Somali Christians. On one special day, Nik was able to meet in a top-secret location with the four—four—Somali Christians known to be left in the country. They had precious Christian communion together.

Days later all four were dead, killed in a coordinated attack at separate locations around the (former) capital city, Mogadishu.[22]

Once, Nik entered a hut in a village and discovered three dead bodies—including those of a girl with her brush still in her hair and a grandmother still appearing to stir a pot. Nik and his team fell silent until one of his Somali staffers said with anguish, "You know, Dr. Nik, they used to call Somaliland a third-world country. But now we are a pre-world country."[23]

1. Exemplify how a variety of societal institutions can reflect corruptness.
2. Recognize that fallen humanity produces fallen societal expressions.
3. Recognize that fallen cultural expressions are everywhere in both obvious and subtle ways.
4. Identify the biblical term for fallen cultural expressions—*worldliness*.

Social Institutions

A societal institution is a set of customs and laws for a social order. These customs and laws govern human behavior, shaping the society. Social institutions ought to grow out of and reflect the creational norms built into God's design for His creation. While social institutions are abstract realities (e.g., academia, marriage and family), they are developed and expressed through concrete cultural organizations (e.g., a particular school or a particular family unit). Those organizations may or may not carry out their institutional calling in conformity to creational norms because the humans that make up those institutions are fallen.

Effects of the Fall: The Family

Genesis 1:28 identifies the family unit as foundational to the human task on earth. The purpose of the family is clearly identifed by means of the numerous exhortations throughout Scripture to mothers, fathers, and their children. Both mothers and fathers are to nurture and disciple their own children (including teens), and those children/teens are to submit to that training (Deut. 6:6–7; Prov. 1:8; 4:1; 13:1; Eph. 6:4; Titus 2:5).

The family's purpose ought to dictate the family's priorities and structure. But that discipleship is undermined when parents abdicate their responsibilities. Anything that undermines this purpose or pushes it to the periphery must be identified. What are the things that prevent the father and mother from (1) being present in the home to organize/guide it and (2) being involved in the discipleship process at home? The reasons for a lack of presence and concerted discipleship effort may include busyness, laziness, carelessness, burdensomeness, lifestyle status, or comfort level.

All these factors must be addressed. Priorities must be adjusted to achieve goals for nurturing and discipling one's own family. No other purpose should be higher. Regardless of the home life they grew up in, students should strive to follow biblical guidelines. How are they going to counteract busyness, laziness, and so on? How are they going to build an open and loving relationship so that their children will love, respect, and communicate with them in the future? If their life becomes centered on their ministry or job instead of their family then their priorities will be misplaced. Since everyone grapples with these issues, students should show mercy to their parents.

Effects of the Fall: Marriage

What major symptoms reveal the decay of marriage in the fallen human social order?

immorality and divorce

What do societies do to discourage or encourage the decay (whether by biblical motivations and means or not)?

Customs and laws punishing or objecting to immoral people put social pressure on them to conform to a higher standard of conduct. Societies that remove objections no longer deem the behavior to be unacceptable, and it eventually becomes the new norm.

Which social order are students living in?

Postmodern secularism has worked to remove restraints, allowing individuals to behave as they wish without social stigma. Even as the erosion of society has become more ap-

parent, individual libertinism rules the day (regardless of one's political party or religious background). Social conservatism that favors moral legislation and conservative Christian living is now stigmatized instead.

What can individuals do to stem the tide of decay in the realm of marriage?

First and foremost, an individual Christian couple must exemplify a biblical marriage that conforms to God's design.

Second, Christians ought to enunciate and defend the biblical worldview in the public square and in moral legislation, balancing love and uncompromising compassion with a correct definition of immorality and a correct manner of punishment or social objection to perversions.

[The unit on marriage, family, and gender roles (Unit 5) will equip students to that end.]

Effects of the Fall: The Arts

Debate topic: Are creational norms built into God's design of the world for the arts: literature/movies, artwork, music, and so on? Can violations of those norms be identified?

First, students should conclude that God designed the world in a certain way to reflect His truth, goodness, and beauty (Phil. 4:8).

Second, students should conclude that every human expression has the potential for fallenness regardless of the medium of communication (Eph. 2:1–3; 4:17–19).

Third, students should recognize that identifying violations of truth, goodness, and beauty demands both an understanding of the objective guidelines provided by scriptural principles and an accurate understand-

---

FALLEN CULTURE

utopia: an imagined world in which everything is perfect

kitsch: excessively sentimental art, considered to be done in poor taste

schlock: cheap junk

Culture, intended by God as a blessing (a result of the Creation Mandate), can be twisted so far that it breaks. Government can fall apart. Education can just stop. Business and journalism and the arts can grind to a halt. Whole nations can effectively cease to be. Cultural institutions and laws and customs that took centuries to build can fall in a day. Developed and developing nations can regress to "pre-world" status.

But collapse usually takes longer than that; it's generally preceded by decay. And why do such failures happen anyway? Why haven't humans achieved utopia*? Because the Fall has touched everything God created. If, as the previous unit argued, God created family, sexuality, and all the institutions of society, then those things have been affected by Adam's Fall just like people have.

- Marriage: Consider that the out-of-wedlock birthrate among low-income American whites is 50%. Among the upper classes, that number is about 7%. Marriage as an institution is dying in the former group (and generally healthy in the latter).[24] Societies have always had to balance individual freedom to leave a difficult marriage with the responsibility parents owe to their children.[25] But now so little legal pressure is placed on parents to stay married (divorce is, legally speaking, quite easy) that America as a whole is undermining its most important institution.
- The family: Western families are under sometimes intense strain. The institutions and structures of society which used to support and protect them—church, school, even divorce laws—have been weakened. The important role parents are told to play in the spiritual formation of their children (Deut. 6:6–9) has been endangered by many cultural pressures.
- The arts: An occasional blasphemous piece of art makes the news (like the infamous painting of Jesus' mother dotted with elephant dung[26]), and pornographic art goes back at least to the time of Pompeii, where it was preserved by a volcanic eruption a mere fifty years after Jesus' resurrection. Blasphemy and pornography are obvious twistings of art. But so are kitsch* and schlock*; in other words, art unworthy of the name (though porn is obviously more morally degraded than a sentimental painting). Some music is evil, but some is just dumb—the musical equivalent of chocolate cheese in a can. The arts are fallen in numerous ways.
- Education: Academia is deeply damaged by the Fall. The more educated you are, the more humble you (should) become about what you don't know. There are a lot of smart people out there. But that doesn't change the fact that most of Western academia ignores the reality of God completely. "God" is only an object of historical study, if that. What happens when you build a whole discipline on a godless foundation? Much of this book is dedicated to answering that question.

Culture is what we make of the good creation. When we are twisted, we create a twisted culture. So everywhere you look in human culture you will see not just individuals but cultural products and institutions that are distorted, abnormal, sick, dysfunctional, corrupted, and vain. They have all been twisted by the Fall. Stable marriages, loving families, well-cared-for environments, beautiful art, and insightful academic study are still visible. But evil has entwined itself like invasive vines around the good, weakening it and in some cases even obscuring it from public view.

Genesis 4

We don't have to guess that culture is affected by the Fall. It shows up right away in the Bible's story. From the Fall in Genesis 3 come its effects in Genesis 4. Cain murders Abel, an example of the Fall's effect on individual humans (Gen. 4:1–16). And immediately after that, the most fundamental human institution takes a significant turn away from the pattern God gave when Lamech, one of Cain's descendants, marries two wives (4:19). The Bible text doesn't comment on this twisting of marriage; it just reports it. But this polygamy* is obviously a significant deviation from the one-man, one-woman pattern of Genesis 2:22–24.

Sons born of this polygamous marriage, we are told, became the "fathers" of "those who dwell in tents and have livestock" (Jabal), "those who play the lyre and pipe" (Jubal), and those who forge "all instruments of bronze and iron" (Tubal-cain; 4:20–22). These descendants of Cain are living out the creation blessing. They are taking dominion. Music and metallurgy are complex skills; these were not intellectually deficient cavemen.

But what were these early men and women making with their newfound cultural skills? We don't fully know, but the text hints that it wasn't all good. The passage includes the first post-Fall poem. And what is it about? It's a boast from Lamech (the husband with two wives) about how he took murderous vengeance:

> Adah and Zillah, hear my voice;
> you wives of Lamech, listen to what I say:
> I have killed a man for wounding me,
> a young man for striking me.
> If Cain's revenge is sevenfold,
> then Lamech's is seventy-sevenfold. (Gen. 4:23–24)

Add the right beat, and it sounds just like the violent gangsta rap of right now. As with a lot of other poetry and music throughout history, a sinful man was using artistic power in the service of sin.

Fallen Culture and You

There are no safe places where you can get away from the effects of the Fall. You can't join a local civic chorus or orchestra and escape it; sin will be there. You can't play in a softball league or take gymnastics lessons or join a book club or even help in a ministry to the homeless without running into the twisting power of the Fall. And not just in the people, but in the very structures of the groups, the shared expectations and practices that define them—because of the fallen human affection and thinking that pervade them.

Sports, like all created things, are fundamentally good, but the culture of a sports team (or a whole sport!) may be excessively macho—even among girls. A sort of competition will go on among the players in which each is trying to out-crass the others. If you don't participate, you'll be seen as opposed to the team. A ministry to the homeless may be willfully blind to the harm it's doing by handing out food to certain people whose real need is job training and counseling.[27] All the structures of the organization may actually be set up to make well-off people feel good about helping the poor rather than being set up to actually help those in need.[28]

polygamy: a marriage including more than just one man and one woman (typically "polygyny," a man having more than one wife)

---

ing of the objective realities of what is being communicated through the artistic medium.

Fourth, students should recognize that perceptions of those objective realities and applications of those definite guidelines must be filtered through one's own subjective personal apprehension of those objective realities.

Debates on this topic often end in stalemates. One side tends to emphasize subjectivity without admitting to any objective guidelines that ought to rule over one's perceptions. The other side tends to emphasize objectivity while minimizing subjective perceptions. Connecting the dots from the art form to what and how it seeks to communicate to guidelines or norms that it conforms to or violates is often difficult work that demands both a thorough grasp of theology and a level of knowledge of the art form. Therefore, many deny that critiques of art forms can or should happen. [Unit 9 will address these concerns more thoroughly.]

Effects of the Fall: Academia

Education isn't largely a neutral regurgitation of brute facts; that's a naive assumption from a superficial understanding of what goes on in the curriculum development of an educational system. Every educational system seeks to inculcate a particular system of thought. Facts are always interpreted according to presuppositions. Ideas are reinforced by means of certain teaching strategies that correlate with the purpose or aim of the curriculum. The purpose, presuppositions, and strategies are all directed by worldview commitments. If a person's worldview is fallen then his purpose, presuppositions, and teaching strategies grow-

ing out of that worldview will be fallen to one extent or another. The more divergent from the biblical worldview, the more twisted education becomes.

Ask students to write a purpose statement, in one or two sentences, for an educational system's curriculum development. What should be the overarching aim of all of the curriculum? What goals should it seek to accomplish in light of that larger aim?

[Resource: Ronald A. Horton, *Christian Education: Its Mandate and Mission* (Greenville, SC: BJU Press, 1992), 1–44]

Example: Curriculum development is

- the purposeful selection of knowledge content and student experiences
- that reflect a set of values and
- that seek to inculcate a comprehensive biblical worldview
- which will produce God-honoring citizens
- who can use their skills in society to further His kingdom.

Genesis 4: Effects of the Fall on Culture

Humans are thoroughly fallen. Culture results from the collective efforts of thoroughly fallen humans. Everything they do is the work of subduing the earth for their own purposes rather than working as God's vice regents under His direction. Therefore, every human culture must thoroughly reflect expressions of pervasive fallenness twisting God's design. Because of God's common grace and because of Christian influence, some cultures are more in line with God's design than others. But no culture is ever neutral or naturally good (despite multiculturalism's claims to the contrary). Darkness is the norm; the light of God's grace shines in the midst of it (Phil. 2:15). Believers are sojourners because their lives run contrary to the norms of surrounding culture (1 Pet. 2:11–12).

As the book of Genesis unfolds the story of the Fall, the corruption of cultural institutions, particularly marriage and family life, comes to the forefront (Gen. 4). Both the cosmic effects and cultural effects of the Fall drive the story forward (Gen. 5:29; 6:5, 11–13) until final and total judgment seems imminent. Only God's grace restrains Him from destroying all humanity. This will be the focus of the next chapter and the next unit.

Participation in Fallen Culture?

Discuss two extremes to avoid:

Isolation (failing to be light)

The Bible calls for distinctiveness within fallen culture, not isolation from it (John 17:15).

Isolationists tend to compartmentalize fallenness into certain sectors of society. But this discounts the pervasiveness of the Fall and leads to blind spots. Only certain segments of society are critiqued and condemned while others get a free pass.

What are some examples?

- *Pop culture is largely condemned; high culture is largely condoned without critique.*
- *Secular or work activities are largely condemned; pietistic or work activities are largely condoned without critique.*

Imitation (failing to be salt)

The Bible calls for holiness within fallen culture, not conformity to it (Rom. 12:1–2).

Imitators tend to minimize or deny that expressions of fallenness can be consistently prominent in certain sectors of society.

What are some examples?

- *Pop culture is largely consumed and copied.*
- *Secular or work activities are rarely critiqued.*

The Christian can't compartmentalize or conform. The Christian must maintain holiness and display Christ's love in the midst of the fruits of darkness around him (Eph. 5:1–18).

"THINGS FALL APART"

The Bible lays the blame for seemingly small, individual sins squarely at the feet of Adam and Eve. And the sins of big cultural institutions—the recording industry, university education, radio and television broadcasting—trace their roots back to Adam and Eve too. The effect of the Fall on cultures is why the Bible warns about the sinful power of the **world**, and not just of individuals in it (Rom. 12:1–2; 1 John 2:15–17).

The "world" in the Bible is "the totality of unredeemed life dominated by sin outside of Christ,"[29] says one theologian. Another simply defines the world as "the bad part of culture."[30] And after a chapter like this in which we've seen how far the effects of the Fall have traveled, it's apparent why God would use such an expansive word as *world*.

As the British poet William Butler Yeats wrote:

Things fall apart, the center cannot hold;
Mere anarchy is loosed upon the world.[31]

That's the way of our fallen planet, both the people and the cultures they inhabit. Without the gracious restraining hand of God, we would have all been like Somalia and become like Mogadishu (Isa. 1:9).

Missionary Nik Ripken's experiences in Somalia drove him to ask whether Christianity was capable of surviving in places of great persecution. When he began traveling to interview Christians who had been through terrible abuse for their faith—the former USSR, China, and places he didn't even dare name in his book—Nik discovered that the power of Christ's resurrection was able to give amazing life even in the deadliest of circumstances.[32]

This amazing spiritual life is one of the ways God shows His determination not to let the world crumble. He uses His children—you?—as lights shining in the darkness, as salt giving people a taste of the age to come.

THINKING IT THROUGH 7.3

1. Why does the Bible use the terms *world* and *worldly* to refer to fallen cultural expressions?

2. Can fallen humans make unfallen things?

3. Genesis 3 recounts the Fall and its consequences. What particular effects of the Fall does Genesis 4 exemplify?

4. Are fallen cultural expressions found only in certain segments of culture? Why or why not?

5. Give three examples of cultural institutions or products discussed in the chapter, noting at least one way the Fall has affected each example

---

THINKING IT THROUGH 7.3

1. because of the extent of the Fall (touching everything God has created and integrated into all of the cultures of the world)

2. Fallen humans can make things that are largely good (because they are still persons created in God's image), but whatever they make will be affected by their fallenness and finiteness.

3. the effects of the Fall on human culture

4. No, while fallen expressions may be more obvious or pronounced in a particular segment of culture, every segment of culture is touched by fallen humans and susceptible to fallen expressions.

5. *marriage*—out of wedlock babies, divorce, polygamy

family—failing to nurture children

the arts—blasphemy, pornography, kitsch and schlock

academia—elitist pride, godless foundation

CHAPTER REVIEW

TERMS TO REMEMBER

original sin
world

Scripture Memory

Romans 8:19–21

Making Connections

1. What details in Genesis 3 attest to the full extent of the Fall's effects on individuals: their relationship with God, their affections, their wills, their intellects, and their physical bodies?

2. Relate the curses God pronounced on the man and the woman in Genesis 3 to their corresponding elements in the Creation Mandate.

3. Describe how each of the following examples of a cultural institution has been touched by the Fall: marriage, family, the arts, education.

4. What cultural endeavors are noted in Genesis 4? How were those cultural institutions already suffering under the effects of the Fall?

Developing Skills in Apologetics and Worldview

5. If an unbeliever complains that it's unfair for all of us to have to suffer the consequences of sin because of Adam's representation, how would you respond?

6. Suppose a believer thinks all earthly things are temporary and irrelevant in the light of eternity. What if he said to you, "Why polish the brass on a sinking ship?" How would you respond?

Examining Assumptions and Evidence

7. Since every part of every person is touched by the Fall, can there be any social institutions, disciplines of study, or fields of work untouched by the Fall? Why or why not?

8. Since no aspects of individual humans remain untouched by the Fall, can there be any goodness manifested in the above-mentioned categories? Explain why or why not.

9. Provide one example of fallenness in popular culture and one example of fallenness in high culture.

10. Why is *worldliness* a fitting term to describe the bad part of culture?

Becoming a Creative Cultivator

11. What's one way you could align your wishes with God's and try to push back against the Fall by creatively cultivating something in line with the creation blessing of Genesis 1:26–28?

---

6. Although the things of this present age are temporary and fallen, the promise of future redemption includes the earthly realm according to Romans 8:18–23.

Examining Assumptions and Evidence

7. Since the effects of the Fall are pervasive, touching every aspect of a human being, all human institutions, fields of study, and occupations are also subject to fallenness.

8. Humans may still do some good things because they are made in the image of God. Even though humans are thoroughly fallen, they don't always manifest that fallenness to the furthest possible extent.

9. Answers will vary. Content and presentation should be evaluated according to biblical principles such as those explained in Ephesians 5:1–18.

10. *Worldliness* aptly captures the scope of the Fall's pervasiveness everywhere on earth.

Becoming a Creative Cultivator

11. (Answers will vary.) Students should be encouraged to put their worldview into practice in the social structures, academic disciplines, and fields of work they may be interested in participating in now and in the future.

TERMS TO REMEMBER

original sin—the theological term referring to the fact that all humans are guilty sinners at their conception because of Adam's first sin

world—"the totality of unredeemed life dominated by sin outside of Christ" or "the bad part of culture"
[Herman Ridderbos, *Paul: An Outline of His Theology* (Grand Rapids: Eerdmans, 1975), 91; John Frame, *The Doctrine of the Christian Life* (Phillipsburg, NJ: P & R, 2008), 866]

CHAPTER REVIEW ANSWERS

Making Connections

1. They hid from God and tried to blame God. They lusted after things that were contrary to God's will due to their own selfishness and pride. They chose to disobey and ate of the fruit (Adam did so presumptuously). They interpreted the facts in a dishonest way. They were ashamed of their nakedness. Eventually, they would die not just spiritually but also physically.

2. Pain in childbirth represents the frustration of being fruitful, multiplying, and filling the earth. Toiling in one's work because of thorns and thistles represents the frustration of subduing the earth.

3. *Marriage:* divorce
Family: neglecting child discipline/discipleship in favor of pursuing status and material goods
The arts: blasphemy and pornography
Education: pride and a godless foundation

4. Marriage, poetry, music, metallurgy; polygamy, using poetry to express pride and glorify violence

Developing Skills in Apologetics and Worldview

5. God is good; He is not unjust. He proved it when He sent Jesus to be our representative to free us from sin's consequences. No human is personally innocent or would have been personally innocent if he could have traded places with Adam.

The student will be able to

8.1 Explain that much good can still exist in human culture because God's common grace restrains sin.

8.2 Defend the idea that the pervasive effects of the Fall demand the sanctified use of culture rather than uncritical consumption of culture.

8.3 Explain what "affection drives cognition" means.

SECTION OBJECTIVES 8.1

1. Differentiate between the fundamental condition of all humans due to original sin and their actual behavior, restrained by common grace.

2. Define *common grace* and explain why God supplies it even to rebels.

3. Explain and demonstrate how common grace both restrains sin and promotes good in the individual.

4. Explain and demonstrate how common grace both restrains sin and promotes good in culture.

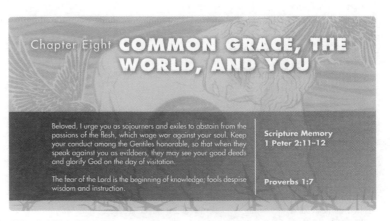

Chapter Eight **COMMON GRACE, THE WORLD, AND YOU**

Beloved, I urge you as sojourners and exiles to abstain from the passions of the flesh, which wage war against your soul. Keep your conduct among the Gentiles honorable, so that when they speak against you as evildoers, they may see your good deeds and glorify God on the day of visitation.

The fear of the Lord is the beginning of knowledge; fools despise wisdom and instruction.

Scripture Memory
1 Peter 2:11–12

Proverbs 1:7

8.1 COMMON GRACE

A group of sailors decides to push their good captain off the boat, take the cargo, and sell it in a distant port. The subsequent journey proves difficult until a leader arises to establish some order. He succeeds, and remarkably so. Soon the mutineers are the most courteous, hard-working, efficient crew on the high seas. They go out of their way to rescue the victims of damaged vessels. They obey all the maritime codes for international waters. They scrub up their ship, invent new uniforms for themselves—and politely neglect to talk about their origins as a group.

"How dare you question our morality!" the leader might say. "Anyone can see that we are honest men!"

> *"FALLEN MAN IS NOT SIMPLY AN IMPERFECT CREATURE WHO NEEDS IMPROVEMENT; HE IS A REBEL WHO MUST LAY DOWN HIS ARMS."* [1]
>
> —C. S. LEWIS

To which there is one appropriate response: *But you're all pirates!* Nothing they do—short of seeking forgiveness for their fundamental sin—can change that fact.

Our world is chock full of pirates, steering this beautiful planet away from its intended port. Stealing the good gifts of God and using them as weapons against Him—quite often while wearing a nice smile.

People can be outwardly very moral, but if their hearts are fundamentally oriented away from God, God cannot be pleased with them, or He Himself would be unjust.

GOD'S COMMON GRACE

Yet God loves even rebels, made as they are in His own image. He loves His enemies just as Jesus told us to love ours:

> Love your enemies . . . so that you may be sons of your Father who is in heaven. For he makes his sun rise on the evil and on the good, and sends rain on the just and on the unjust. (Matt 5:44–45)

This favor of God, given even to people who hate Him, is meant to be a sign pointing them back to their Creator. And His patience (1 Pet. 3:20) and

---

Section Title	Pages	Activity Manual	Days
8.1 Common Grace	108–11	Activity 14	2 days
8.2 The World	112–116	Activity 15	2 days
8.3 Affection Drives Cognition	116–20		1 day
Review	121		1 day
Total Suggested Days			**6 days**

Original Sin

What is the doctrine?

The term *original sin* was briefly mentioned and defined in the last chapter: all humans are guilty sinners at their conception because of Adam's first sin (Rom. 5:12; Ps. 51:5). In other words, the fundamental problem of every human goes much deeper than the sum total of each of his sinful thoughts and actions. Those are only the symptoms of the real disease that must be healed. Every human practices sin because of a sinful nature.

Why is this doctrine significant?

The gospel may be skewed and conversion counterfeited if original sin is denied or misunderstood. The gospel cannot be reduced to learning to live a moral life. When people believe they're converted simply because

THE MOST OFFENSIVE VERSE IN THE BIBLE

C. S. Lewis observed that even a professing Christian may "at bottom . . . still believe he has run up a very favourable credit-balance in [God's] ledger by allowing himself to be converted."[2]

So perhaps the most offensive line in the Bible is one we looked at briefly in the previous chapter: "Those who are in the flesh cannot please God" (Rom. 8:8). At the end of the day—at the end of all days—none of the things unbelievers do will truly and finally please their Creator.

No cancer research, no business integrity, no suffering on behalf of the innocent—nothing will ultimately please God

if it's done "in the flesh." Giving all your goods to feed the poor, even giving up your body to be burned for your ideals— it will all profit you nothing unless, at the center of your heart, there burns a love for the one true God (1 Cor. 13:1–3).

If you have no love for God, that love is precisely what the Bible promises God will give you if you accept the terms of the New Covenant instituted by Jesus: repent and believe the gospel. Turn from your sins, believe that Jesus died for those sins and rose again to give you new life, and you'll get a new heart that loves God as it should (Deut. 30:6; Jer. 31:31–33).

forbearance (Acts 17:30) with sinners is meant to do the same (2 Pet. 3:9). Paul told a group of pagans in the city of Lystra:

> In past generations [God] allowed all the nations to walk in their own ways. Yet he did not leave himself without witness, for he did good by giving you rains from heaven and fruitful seasons, satisfying your hearts with food and gladness. (Acts 14:16–17)

God makes good food grow even in the ground He cursed (Gen. 3:17), and He does this as a "witness" to His own goodness.

So there are people who, all the while they are receiving God's gifts, refuse to see them as the signs they are. They worship all sorts of things other than God and degrade* themselves in the process (Rom. 1:24–25). They don't deserve God's favor. No human ever does. But God still gives it to them.

degrade: to dishonor and disgrace through sin

What do we call God's favor, given even to people who deserve His judgment? "Grace." And yet, not all grace is saving grace because not all sinners are saved. When that divine favor is spread all around the world, given commonly even to unbelievers, we call it **common grace**.

Common grace, rightly defined, is an important component of a truly biblical worldview because it explains how fallen people who hate God can produce so much truth, beauty, and goodness for the rest of us to enjoy. Beautiful music, well-executed art, thoughtful films, smoothly operating cities, wise public policy, amazing medical advances—God's enemies regularly produce them all by God's common grace.

Restraining Sin

Common grace explains why the people the Bible calls "the wicked" aren't as evil as they could be: God's common grace restrains them from committing all the sin they would otherwise commit. Our good God pours His goodness on and through people made in His image, even if they are encamped with the rebel army. Consider some biblical examples:

- God stopped the tower-builders in ancient Babel from accomplishing their sinful purpose (Gen. 11:6–8).

they have reformed their behavior, then they deceive themselves (Gal. 1:6–10). They are in danger of legalism—seeking to earn favor from God by obeying a set of laws (Gal. 3:1–3).

Instead, a changed life must result from receiving a new nature (2 Cor. 5:17). This is what it means to be born again or regenerated. It can only happen when a person is united with Christ through the indwelling of the Holy Spirit through faith in the content of the gospel (John 3:3–16; Rom. 8:9). A new way of living results from receiving a new nature (Rom. 6:1–5; Eph. 2:8–10). Many false gospels teach the reverse of this, confusing truths about sanctification with justification.

Unsaved people can live moral lives. Some of them display remarkable generosity or compassion. But these actions don't save, nor are they evidence of salvation. Instead, they are displays of God's common grace.

 ### Condition and Character

Discuss Colossians 1:13–14, 20–22.

Core Condition

Before salvation, everyone is alienated from God as enemies.

After salvation, believers are reconciled to God and at peace with Him.

Consequential Character

Before salvation, everyone manifests hatred through both a hostile mind and evil deeds.

After salvation, believers manifest love for God through a blameless, holy lifestyle (John 14:15; 15:10).

Discuss the apparent inconsistencies in these truths:

Don't believers sin?

Yes, but continuous sinful practices should be out of character (1 John 2:1; 3:1–10).

Don't unbelievers do good?

Yes, God enables unbelievers to do good to one another. But since they don't act out of love for God and for His glory, their actions aren't ultimately good (Matt. 7:9–11; Mark 10:18).

Challenge students to examine themselves:

What is your core condition? What does your consistent character evidence?

[See 2 Cor. 13:5; 2 Pet. 1:5–10.]

 ### Which Do You Prefer?

Debate this proposition: An unbeliever who displays moral goodness because he's embraced good values is better than an unbeliever who displays his wickedness without restraint.

Guide students to answer the following questions as they debate:

- What is meant by *better*?
- How exactly would it be better—or not?
- For whom would it be better?

The debate can only be settled by differentiating the realms of common and special grace.

Common grace: The cultural life of both the believer and unbeliever will be better off with the morally good unbeliever. Believers benefit from cultures that are shaped by biblical ethics. Unbelievers benefit by avoiding the fallout from a destructive lifestyle. But this is only temporal, not eternal.

Special grace: The unbeliever is no better off and may be worse off because his self-righteousness blinds him to the light of the gospel (Matt. 7:21–23; 11:20–24).

Those in the flesh can't please God because nothing good dwells in them (Rom. 7:18; 8:8). They're thoroughly corrupt (Jer. 17:9; Mark 10:18; Eph. 4:18; Titus 1:15). And they are enslaved to sin and can't please God without faith in Him (Isa. 64:6; John 8:34; Heb. 11:6). Any good they do is incomplete; it's never ultimate because it springs from wrong motives and aims (2 Kings 10:29–30; Luke 6:33). And the relative good they do never originates from themselves but from the goodness of God—more specifically, from God's common grace working in all people (Luke 6:35).

Thus, the aim of Christian organizations shouldn't be to inculcate moralistic character building into the lives of unbelievers. Character building doesn't necessarily lead people to Christ. Leading people to Christ through the gospel inculcates character.

Common Grace and the Unbeliever

Theologian Wayne Grudem defines common grace as "the grace of God by which he gives people innumerable blessings that are not part of salvation." Christ's work on the cross not only cancels guilt for believers but also delays the full wrath of God, keeping Him from immediately casting into hell those who never believe. Grudem goes on to exemplify common grace in a variety of realms:

- physical (Gen. 39:5; Ps. 145:9, 15–16; Matt. 5:44–45; Acts 14:16–17)
- intellectual (Prov. 14:33; Matt. 16:3; Luke 16:8; Rom. 1:19)
- moral (2 Chron. 24:2, 17–25; Rom. 1:32; 2:14–15)
- creative/skill (Gen. 4:20–22; 11:1–9; 25:27)
- societal (Matt. 7:9–11; Rom. 13:1–4)
- religious (Rom. 10:18–21; Heb. 6:4–6)

Notice that the skill and goodness of the unsaved are intermixed with corruption.

[Wayne Grudem, *Systematic Theology* (Grand Rapids: Zondervan, 1994), 497–98; 657–68]

Common Grace All Around

Ask students to give examples of common grace that they have experienced because of the work of an unbeliever.

Recognizing common grace all around, even in the lives and work of unbelievers, should motivate students to express thankfulness and praise to God for His goodness.

Common Grace and Your Life's Work

What should be the Christian's aim in his life's work?

In addition to finding satisfaction by carrying out one's created purpose of subduing the earth, a believer's job should also give him plenty of opportunities to minister God's common grace by doing good to others. Your job should reach out to others in some way to help them physically, emotionally, intellectually, and so forth. That's ministering God's common grace as a tool in His hands.

But shouldn't all Christians be more concerned about declaring the special grace of the gospel in full-time Christian service?

Both full-time Christian work and the other vocations have an important role in advancing the message of the gospel. The spoken Word is vitally necessary for saving faith. But substantive deeds are just as vital. Why would someone listen to a message of the gospel that seems to consist of spiritual platitudes disconnected from a real-life demonstration of

the gospel (James 2:14–17; 1 John 3:16–18)? Removing deeds from the Word makes Christianity seem disconnected from the real world of people's daily lives. Separating the Word of the gospel from the deeds turns them into social work absent of spiritual transformation.

Both the Christians who try to witness in word only and those who try to witness in deed only end up being ineffective.

Working in the realm of common grace should open up doors to share God's special grace. Ministry in deed must be wedded to a ministry in word.

Discuss with students how they can minister in word and deed in a variety of vocations.

- God kept the unbelieving King Abimelech from committing adultery with Abraham's wife: "Yes, I know that you have done this in the integrity of your heart, and it was I who kept you from sinning against me. Therefore I did not let you touch her" (Gen. 20:6).
- God even put limits on the wickedness of Satan. He could do nothing to Job without God's permission. "The Lord said to Satan, 'Behold, all that he has is in your hand. Only against him do not stretch out your hand'" (Job 1:12; cf. 2:6). And Satan did exactly what God permitted, no more.[3]

Promoting Good

God, by His common grace, doesn't just restrain evil; He promotes good. Did you notice how God referred to the "integrity" of Abimelech? God is even willing to call some of the actions of His enemies "good."

But wait a minute—where did these enemies get this "good"? Does Satan have a little "good" to hand out to his children along with the "evil" he's so well known for? The Bible says that sin is like a disease—"The heart is deceitful above all things, and desperately sick" (Jer. 17:9). How could people desperately sick with sin ever manage to do something that isn't itself infected?

If there is good in anyone at any time, that goodness has to come, ultimately speaking, from God. This is why God can look on sinful people and see His goodness reflected in them.

- This is true even of King Ahab, one of the Bible's biggest scoundrels. On the one hand, Scripture says, "There was none who sold himself to do what was evil in the sight of the Lord like Ahab" (1 Kings 21:25). But a mere four verses later—after a divine rebuke—Ahab (temporarily) humbles himself and God notices: "Because [Ahab] has humbled himself before me, I will not bring the disaster in his days; but in his son's days" (21:29).
- Jesus said to one audience, "If you then, who are evil, know how to give good gifts to your children, how much more will your Father who is in heaven give good things to those who ask him!" (Matt. 7:11). In other words, "evil" people can still give "good" gifts.
- "If you do good to those who do good to you, what benefit is that to you? For even sinners do the same." (Luke 6:33) Jesus was saying that "sinners" can "do good."

> **TOTAL DEPRAVITY**
>
> An important theological term points to the pervasiveness of sin in people—**total depravity**. *Depravity* means moral corruption. But *total depravity* doesn't mean that people are as bad as they could be. Because of common grace they're not that bad. *Total* only means that moral corruption has touched every part of every person (e.g., there's no part—like the intellect, say—that has escaped the effects of the Fall).

A non-Christian can humble himself, give good gifts, and do good to others. Some unbelievers killed Jews in the Holocaust; others risked their lives to save them. But even the most self-sacrificial actions are not "pleasing" to God in any ultimate sense—because they're still the actions of *pirates* (1 Cor. 13:3). Nonetheless, these actions are still better than pride and selfishness. In that sense, they are "good." Not everything God's enemies do is completely wicked. They are still capable of goodness, even great goodness. God, who is the definition of good, says so.[4]

Cultural Discernment

Because of common grace, it's wrong and impossible for Christians to reject everything produced by unsaved people in the culture. Yet, because fallenness pervasively corrupts everything, it would be just as foolish to uncritically accept everything produced by unsaved people in the culture.

If you shouldn't reject everything but can't accept everything, then what are you supposed to do?

Believers are called to exercise discernment (Eph. 5:10–11).

But how do you discern what to accept and what to reject?

If something in the culture is a product of God's common grace then it must largely reflect a combination of truth, goodness, and

CULTURE AND COMMON GRACE

Now we arrive at the point of this section: what is true of individuals is true of the cultures they form and are formed by. Your favorite meal at your local restaurant was probably designed, cooked, and served by non-Christians—as a result of millennia of cultural traditions formed, mostly, by God's enemies. Some of the most beautiful music known to man was composed by wicked people who hated God. Even your favorite bedtime story as a kid was probably written, illustrated, published, shipped, stocked, and sold by people with no love for God at all, no desire to please Him whatsoever.

A few Christian families choose not to listen to any music or view any art by non-Christians. But this choice overrules God's verdict: He said that these people, made in His good image and given the blessing of His Creation Mandate, can do genuine good. Even groups of wicked people, working together, can produce real good along with their evil. Buildings, bridges, books; cars, companies, cookery—all these prove that lost people can make truth, goodness, and beauty.

The key here is to recognize the ultimate source of that truth, that goodness, and that beauty. And there's only one possible answer. All truth is God's; all goodness is His; all beauty is too. If we refuse a gift from God because of its faulty wrapping paper, we are insulting Him.

What does the beauty of India's Taj Mahal, built by a Muslim emperor in the 1600s, say about God's common grace?

THINKING IT THROUGH 8.1

1. Why can't those who are in the flesh, rather than in Christ, ever please God—regardless of all the good things they do?

2. Define common grace.

3. Identify several reasons God provides common grace to rebels.

4. Why is common grace an important component of understanding culture from a biblical view?

5. Do cultures show common grace, or just individuals? How do you know?

without asking questions. But don't eat something if another Christian does ask questions and his conscience would cause him to stumble.

How is that fair? Love for others always takes precedence over personal liberty (Gal. 5:13). Do you serve others out of love, or are you selfish—demanding your own enjoyment even if it damages others (Phil. 2:3–4)?

THINKING IT THROUGH 8.1

1. The particular good actions of unbelievers must be interpreted within the larger context of their rebellion against God.

2. Common grace is the undeserved favor of God given to all people.

3. All people were made in God's image. God loves even His enemies. Common grace points rebels back to a Creator who is patient and good.

4. Common grace explains why unsaved people aren't as wicked as they could be and can produce many good things.

5. Cultures show common grace because cultures are simply the result of a collection of individuals who form the shared characteristics of a culture.

---

beauty (Phil. 4:8). And it must be profitable (1 Cor. 10:23).

But how do you know what is true, good, and beautiful?

You have to bring together an understanding of Scripture with an understanding of a particular cultural expression or product.

[*Note*: This will be addressed further in Unit 9.]

Ask students to list practices or products accepted by most Christians within the realm of common grace.

Example: cell phone

Note that a cell phone isn't neutral. It's an acceptable tool when it can be used to reflect God's design of truth, goodness, and beauty due to His common grace.

Now evaluate how that product may be used in a twisted way.

Example: inordinate usage or sinful content on a cell phone

What kinds of things could many Christians debate?

Example: the wisdom of giving teens free access to YouTube on their smartphones

These kinds of issues aren't new. The prime biblical example is in 1 Corinthians 8–10.

Food is a part of God's good creation. But food sacrificed to idols and eaten a temple as a part of a religious ritual is off-limits to every believer because it involves them in idolatry. However, food sacrificed to idols and sold in the marketplace became a point of contention between well-meaning Christians. In the end, Paul's biblical, inspired advice was to buy food in the marketplace

1. Critique the values of pop culture from a Christian worldview.

2. Recognize that Christians must renew their own minds because the flesh is naturally drawn to worldly culture.

3. Defend the idea that worldliness, even though it begins internally, is communicated externally.

4. Critique asceticism's denial of truth, goodness, and beauty in a fallen world.

5. Defend the need to refine one's tastes in order to recognize truth, goodness, and beauty, particularly in high culture.

6. Plan how to avoid worldliness and asceticism by living as a pilgrim and an ambassador, discerning light and darkness in fallen culture.

Realms of Culture

Cultures are worldviews embodied in artifacts and manifested in collective actions. Cultures reflect systems of beliefs and practices. Cultures are sustained by institutions.

Folk culture emerges organically through the natural creativity of people in a particular region.

High culture is the result of centuries of refinement and development toward excellence. It often requires formal training for those who create it.

Popular culture is also known as mass culture or consumer culture. It is called mass culture because it came into existence through mass media. It is called consumer culture because the goal is to sell it to a large audience.

Pop culture is typically aimed at diversion, shaped by the latest fad, and targeted at youth. There is no sin in occasionally watching a diverting special-effects spectacle, just as there is no sin in eating fast food on occasion. But a steady diet of diversion and the continual celebration of novelty, immediacy, and personal gratification are destructive to spiritual growth. They're dangerous when they become the medium for worship.

A life of high culture or folk culture can be spiritually damaging and dead as well. High culture and folk culture are not exempt from the Fall. Recent high culture is often a manifestation of modern or postmodern despair. Often it has turned against the very idea of excellence and thus consumes itself. But sometimes the values of these kinds of cultures, especially respect for the wisdom and excellence of past generations, are more compatible with biblical values.

One of the most exciting stories in the book of Acts occurred during the apostle Paul's ministry in the city of Ephesus. Paul was busy turning the world upside down, and some of the idolaters who were shaken up in the process decided to launch a protest—a protest that quickly turned into a riot.

Most of the people in the huge crowd of rioters didn't know why they were rioting; they were just caught up in shouting, "Great is Artemis of the Ephesians!" (Acts 19:28, 32). Paul saw the ruckus as a great opportunity to evangelize the whole city; the local Christians knew that was a bad idea and wouldn't let him go into the amphitheater. Ignorant riots can easily turn deadly—and two of Paul's friends were in fact dragged into the brawl by the mob.

What finally stopped the crowd from hurting or killing someone? Common grace. These rioters were restrained from violence by the threat of greater violence—from a government that, as Paul said elsewhere, God had set up (Rom. 13:1–7). The town clerk managed to quiet the crowd and then sent them home by warning them that they might be charged with rioting. In some places in the world, the government itself is a mob, but this was one place where the mere existence of the government probably stopped a mob from murder.

COMMON GRACE THROUGH CULTURE

Cultures throughout history have existed at least in part for the purpose of restraining people from antisocial impulses. Cultures develop traditions, laws, and institutions in order to put pressure on people to serve whatever that culture believes to be the common good. Cultures, then, can be tools of God's common grace to restrain sin. Cultures also tend to bind generations together; older people take seriously their role of handing off beliefs and practices and stories to the young.[5] And it is in this way that a culture is preserved.

Beliefs and practices and stories can be false, of course—and yet they can still restrain sin. By God's common grace, even governments dedicated to the worship of false gods (like Rome was in Paul's day) still scare mobs away from sin.

But culture is fallen, and at different periods in different places, that fallenness may be especially obvious. The common grace in a culture may be nearly overwhelmed by a tide of sin. Think of today's Western **popular culture**, the mainstream culture of music, movies, and celebrities. It's impossible to avoid that culture if you live in the Western world; it's everywhere (1 Cor. 5:9–10). "More than any other cultural expression, [pop culture] reaches, embraces, enthralls, and influences the largest portion of the American public," says one Christian culture watcher.[6]

In *All God's Children and Blue Suede Shoes: Christians and Popular Culture*, Ken Myers writes that "popular culture . . . is a part of the created order, part of the earth that is the Lord's, and thus something capable of bringing innocent pleasure to believers."[7] Who doesn't like a great story, told with humor and insight through an entertaining movie? Christians are allowed to enjoy the good gifts of popular culture. Pleasure wasn't invented by the devil. "But," Myers says, "not everything that is permissible is constructive."[8] Myers says it's not necessarily the wicked content of the movies and top-forty hits that concerns him (although they are surely problematic); it's the whole mood that pop culture encourages. What does American popular culture value? It values what's now. It values pleasure, immediate gratification, the latest fad. It values what's young and new; older people are seen as tired or hokey, not wise.

Cultural Sensibilities

When evaluating culture, most people evaluate only content without evaluating how their own sensibilities are being shaped. That is, they fail to evaluate culture's effects on *how* they tend to think and feel. Such sensibilities can make a person more closed to certain *presentations* of information.

Discuss pop culture's effect on sensibilities and why that's a cause for concern.

"Popular culture encourages a mood of expecting everything to be immediate, a mood that deters greater depth and breadth in other areas of our lives, including our understanding of Christianity and our experience of obedient faith." [Kenneth A. Myers, *All God's Children and Blue Suede Shoes: Christians and Popular Culture* (Wheaton: Crossway, 1989), xv]

Decades ago Neil Postman wrote,

New technologies compete with old ones—for time, for attention, for money, for prestige, but mostly for dominance of their worldview. This competition is implicit once we acknowledge that a medium contains an ideological bias.

Postman goes on to contrast the world of the printed word with the world of television. The former is a world that emphasizes "logic, sequence, history, exposition, objectivity, detachment, and discipline." The latter is a world that emphasizes "imagery, narrative, presentness, simultaneity, intimacy, immediate gratification, and quick emotional response." His concern is that "new technologies alter the structure of our interests: the things we think *about*. They

Young people may indeed know things their grandparents don't, but what do you call a whole culture that assumes the superiority of youth wisdom as a kind of law? It's hard to even call it a culture because there's no way it can be passed on. Opinions from people who appear to be over thirty-five are automatically discounted. So Myers warns that dealing with pop culture can sometimes be as challenging for Christians today as confronting persecution and martyrdom was for first-century believers. Getting thrown to the lions is certainly not something anyone would want to face, Myers says, but at least it was a direct threat that was easily perceived. The danger in our era is that Christian character is eroded, ordinary enjoyments are ruined, and life itself is cheapened by the subtle influence of popular culture without our even being aware of it. [9] How can professing Christians—who are supposed to see culture as a good but fallen gift—live holy lives in a world like this?

Worldliness

A lot of them don't. They give in. They're worldly. There are many people who claim Christ's name who nonetheless refuse to take seriously the important biblical truth that the Fall has touched every aspect of human culture, just as it has touched every human. The "world"—the bad part of culture[10]—goes far beyond pop culture; **high culture** (like operas and fine art) and **folk culture** (like bluegrass and Mongolian throat singing) are touched by sin too. But opera and bluegrass stars don't typically make the evening news or the racy gossip magazines in grocery store checkout lines. Pop culture, precisely because it's everywhere, is perhaps uniquely effective in its effort to influence people toward the values of the world.

The "world" is like poison that has seeped into a pond. Fish aren't aware that they're swimming in water any more than humans stay conscious that they're breathing air. It takes deliberate effort not to be affected by something once it successfully passes itself off as a natural part of your environment. And the world's assumptions do seem so normal, so inevitable.

You may be used to thinking about individual sins like lying, cheating, and stealing. But **worldliness** is group sin. As one theologian aptly puts it, "Sin is not only personal but also interpersonal and even suprapersonal."[11] He means, of course, that sin goes beyond the merely human level: Satan is called "the god of this world" (2 Cor. 4:4). So, the theologian continues, "Sin is more than the sum of what sinners do. Sin acquires the form of a spirit—the spirit of darkness, the spirit of an age, the spirit of a company or nation."[12] Worldliness in Botswana or Kyrgyzstan can look different from worldliness in Bali or Karachi. Different cultures (and different eras) have different ways of expressing hostility and rebellion to God.

But they all do it. The world puts a constant pressure on all people. Including you. And that's why Paul's main comment about worldliness uses an image something like clay forced into a mold: "Do not *be conformed* to this world" (Rom. 12:2). To *be conformed* is to be passive, to let the world shape you with

CHIC VS. KITSCH

Many people are skeptical about the distinction between high culture and folk culture. To call opera and poetry "high" and bluegrass and romance novels "folk" (or worse, "low") sounds like elitist sneering. And in our postmodern world, people believe there are no real standards for beauty anyway—it's just different strokes for different folks. Some people like Shakespeare; some people like World Wrestling Smackdown.

But Christians know that because God created an ordered world, standards for beauty do exist—even if they are difficult to apply with perfect confidence. High and folk are proper distinctions to make. Christians, who are called to press God's world toward its ideal, ought to take part in the fine arts and to rise as high in them as God's gifting will allow.

But this doesn't mean folk culture should be shunned; folk music and art, regional novels, and other forms of "low" culture are appropriate in some settings (such as a state fair) where high culture isn't. Even pop culture carries some benefits for Christians. Pop culture can provide humor, relaxation, and entertainment—and these things weren't invented in hell. But those values are probably not enough to justify the amount of time and money many Christians spend on such things.

God's good creation there we find the "world." World here is the rottenness of the earth, the antithesis of creational goodness.

[Al Wolters, *Creation Regained* (Grand Rapids: Eerdmans, 2005), 64]

What is worldliness?

Worldliness is the desire to conform to the surrounding sinful human culture characterized by its hostility and rebellion against God (Deut. 18:9; 2 Kings 17:7–8; Ezek. 20:32; Eph. 2:1–3; 4:17; Phil. 2:15; Col. 1:13, 21; James 4:4; 1 Pet. 2:11–12; 4:3).

What is the extent of worldliness?

It is pervasive, threatening every aspect of life—including the parts often deemed sacred. Worldliness can't be compartmentalized into a secular realm. Sin is everywhere.

How does Scripture describe the world (in the negative sense)?

Evil (John 7:7; 16:9; Gal. 1:4; Eph. 2:2)

Hateful (John 15:18–19; 17:14; Titus 3:3)

Morally filthy (James 1:27; 2 Pet. 1:4; 2:20)

Arrogantly self-focused, self-indulgent, and self-assured (Titus 2:12; 1 John 2:16)
[Leedy, 50–56]

What's the source of the world's pull?

Satan, as the prince of the power of the air (Eph. 2:2 cf. John 12:31; 14:30; 16:11; 2 Cor. 4:4), lures the sinful human nature with his deception (James 1:14–15; 2 Cor. 4:4; John 8:44). [Leedy, 59]

How can worldliness be defeated?

Knowing God is necessary for overcoming the world (1 John 2:12–14; 5:4–5).

The grace of God delivers from sin (John 16:33; Gal. 1:4 Col. 1:13), and its sanctifying work teaches us to deny our worldly lusts (Titus 2:12; 2 Pet. 1:2–4).

"When some attraction can be discerned as manifesting the character of the world, true grace extends no smiling approval, permission, or tolerance. What grace is it that wishes a drowning child a pleasant swim?" [Leedy, 66]

Not only is worldliness a biblical concern; it's a watershed. Either you love God, or you love the world with all its lusts and arrogance (James 4:4; 1 John 2:15–17; Matt. 6:24; John 14:15). Either you love what God says is true, good, and lovely, or you love the perversion of those things by this world's system (Phil. 2:15; 4:8). The gospel of God's grace should not be perverted to justify partaking in such things (Prov. 8:13; 14:16; Jude 1:4; 2 Pet. 2:1–2). Regeneration (new life) produces sanctified living worthy of God's holiness (1 Cor. 6:11; Eph. 1:4; 4:1, 17–24).

alter the character of our symbols: the things we think *with*. And they alter the nature of community: the arena in which thoughts develop." [Neil Postman, *Technopoly: The Surrender of Culture to Technology* (New York: Vintage Books, 1992), 16–17, 20; see also Neil Postman, *Amusing Ourselves to Death: Public Discourse in the Age of Show Business*, rev. ed. (New York: Penguin Books, 2005)]

Note also sensibility problems in folk and high culture:

Folk: Disdains formal, educated analysis

High: Disdains "common" and "unrefined"

The World and Worldliness

When the Bible refers to the world in a negative sense, how should it be defined?

The world, in this sense, is "the totality of unregenerate persons living on the earth within some period of time, along with the habitual patterns of thought and behavior by which they express their ignorance of and insubordination to God."
[Randy Leedy, *Love Not the World: Winning the War Against Worldliness* (Greenville, SC: Bob Jones University Press, 2012), 50]

According to Herman Ridderbos, in Paul's usage it refers to "the totality of unredeemed life dominated by sin outside of Christ." In other words, *world* designates that totality of sin-infected creation. Wherever human sinfulness bends or twists or distorts

Worldliness Identified

Scripture identifies categories of sin that are prohibited along with the antithetical virtues God requires. Divide students into groups of various sizes and assign each group a passage of Scripture (Eph. 4:17–5:21; Titus 2–3; 2 Timothy 3:1–5; 1 Peter 2:11–18; 1 Peter 4:3–5; Matthew 6). Ask them to chart out the Scripture reference, the sin prohibited, and/or the virtue required. (Helpful charts are available in Leedy, 75–88.)

Once the groups have created their charts you may compile a master chart that categorizes them by topic: bodily appetites, attitudes, speech, relationships, material goods, religious ceremony, miscellaneous. (Such a chart is available in Leedy, 86–88.)

Note that worldliness can be manifested in both blatanty licentious living and hypocritical religious pietism.

Worldliness Discerned

Christians are called to apply the general categories found in the Bible to specific actions and attitudes in their own cultural and historical context (Eph. 5:10, 15–17). Scripture provides all the necessary principles for doing so (2 Pet. 1:3). You won't be able to find a proof text about every worldly activity possible. The lists in Scripture were never meant to be exhaustive (Rom. 1:32; Gal. 5:21; 1 Tim. 1:10) and even true liberties may be unacceptable in certain contexts (1 Cor. 8–10; Gal. 5:13; 2 Tim. 2:4–7).

Two extremes must be avoided. "The alternatives range from inferring from . . . silence a full personal liberty, at the one extreme, to constructing, at the other, detailed do-and-don't schemes based on a variety of applications and inferences. . . . Both extremes are guilty of presumption: one presumes liberty while the other presumes to speak for God" (Leedy, 90). The former extreme makes the Bible meaningless because it disallows any correlation between the specific issues of the day and the Bible's general principles (Gal. 5:13). The latter extreme turns the Bible into a rulebook of one's own making (Mark 7:5–13).

What's the solution? People who go to the first extreme must admit that applications must be made; people who embrace the second extreme must be taught how to make valid applications of the biblical text to specific situations.

Libertinism and Legalism

The basis of these two false gospels is an improper view of sanctification as it relates to justification. Guide students through Activity 15.

---

whatever force it exerts. Paul commands that you let another force mold you, a godly force: "Be transformed by the renewal of your mind" (12:2).

If you have come to think that your church or your parents don't see enough good in the surrounding culture, if you're constantly chafing under their expectations about your entertainment or clothing, then you need to take what Paul says in Romans 12:1–2 very seriously. Because he follows up his command not to be conformed to the world with a very practical promise: if you'll be transformed by the renewal of your mind, you will be able to "discern what is the will of God, what is good and acceptable and perfect" (Rom 12:1–2). Does that sound attractive to you? Do you want to do what is good, acceptable to God, perfect in His sight? Then start by admitting that your mind might need some renewing.

Do you have a category called "worldliness" in your own personal thinking as a Christian? Not just your parents' thinking or your church's thinking (though these are extremely valuable). Have you ever decided—on your own—not to do, watch, say, read, invest in, follow, or like something because you knew it was "worldly"? When was the last time you resisted the pressure of the world to press you into its mold?

"I rarely meet the young Christian who needs to be exhorted to engage their culture," says one American Christian writer. "They seem to consume what everybody consumes, and are in general agreement with the zeitgeist* that a steady stream of entertainment is the Fifth Freedom that our forefathers fought for."[13] Another leading Christian thinker said something similar:

zeitgeist: typical attitude or outlook of a particular generation

> When I am among evangelical Christians, I find that they seem to be more avidly consuming the latest offerings of commercial culture . . . than many of my non-Christian neighbors. They are content to be just like their fellow Americans, or perhaps, driven by a lingering sense of shame at their uncool forebears,* just slightly more like their fellow Americans than everyone else.[14]

forebears: ancestors

There are magnets so powerful they can lift semi-trucks, but they can't lift a twig. If you were perfect, you'd be like that twig. The magnetic pull of sin wouldn't affect you. But you're fallen. It's not a mark of holiness that you can "handle" worldliness and sin in your entertainment without being affected. It's a mark of blindness; you *are* being affected.

One more piece of advice on worldliness: don't make the mistake of believing that music and dress and other cultural "artifacts" (tangible goods produced by a culture) are meaningless. One of the authors of this book, as a small boy, once wandered around the first-grade lunchroom with his middle finger up, insisting, "It doesn't *mean* anything. It's not different from any other finger." Needless to say, his teacher (Miss Ferguson) kindly asked him to refrain from making that particular obscene gesture. Putting up your middle finger does mean something, at least in Western culture. You can walk around insisting that it means nothing—or that it means what *you* say it means, not what everyone else *thinks* it means. But your classmates will just stare at you (and then go tell Miss Ferguson). Yes, your heart is more important than your haircut. But your haircut, your hemline, and even your hand gestures are "texts"—messages you send to the world about what's inside your heart. (And if music, dress, and movies are meaningless, why do people care about them so much?) The heart is where worldliness begins, but it always shows up on the outside.

A Worldly Church?

Assign a passage of Scripture to each student to read and respond to (Lev. 11:45; 19:1–2; 20:7–8, 26; Deut 7:6; John 8:12; 1 Cor. 1:2; Eph. 4:1; 1 Pet. 2:16–17; etc.). **How are the lives of God's people supposed to be characterized in the Old Testament? Are they supposed to be characterized any differently in the New Testament?**

God's people, whether in the Old or the New Testament, are to be holy or set apart; this is how they are to be a light in a dark world of unrighteousness.

Should Christians be distressed by this unrighteous world (Phil. 2:15)?

Many true believers have raised concerns for many years about the cultural decline that has been taking place.

Is being distressed a sufficient response?

probably not

Based on the presentation of Lot in both Genesis 19 and 2 Peter 2:7–8, one author observes that "it is possible, then, for a believer to be distressed by the world while willfully clinging to the world." [R. Kent Hughes, *Set Apart: Calling a Worldly Church to a Godly Life* (Wheaton: Crossway, 2003), 13] Hughes is concerned about the huge disconnect that he sees between what Christians say they believe and the way they live their lives. "There has been a deficiency of cultural awareness and a resulting lack of discernment regarding how the world has overwhelmed the thinking and behavior of Christians" [Hughes, 10]. Evangelical Christianity, in his view, is on its way to "becoming a mere mirror of secular culture" [Hughes, 15].

Asceticism

Worldliness is a huge problem because cultures are fallen. But don't forget that every culture, by God's common grace, still retains some good. Some people *do* forget that. Ascetics* are such people.

There are comparatively few true ascetics in the Western world—and there's no one today quite like the ancient monk Simon Stylites, who lived on a tiny platform atop a pillar for thirty-seven years! But there are plenty of people who are missing some of the true good in human culture, high and folk.

If you view God as an ascetic, you're going to be confused (at best) when you find out that there's a lot of good in culture that you were missing. More than one Christian has come close to losing his faith because he grew up assuming that non-Christians couldn't produce truth, goodness, or beauty—only to find all three when he actually looked.[15] Instead, you need to expect to see good in your culture. And you need to see that goodness as a gift from a good God, an example of His common grace. "This is my Father's world," the old Christian hymn says, and "He shines in all that's fair." Ascetics miss this truth.

It is worth spending time and effort developing your ability to appreciate the finer things of culture—refined classical music, poetry, literature, high art, and architecture. One of the values of a good liberal arts education in high school and college is that it introduces you to good things in your cultural tradition that you never would have discovered on your own.

ascetic: person who practices extreme self-denial, giving up even normal everyday pleasures

Pilgrims and Ambassadors

The Bible offers two metaphors that might help you as you try to avoid the two ditches of **asceticism** on the one hand and worldliness on the other: Christians are both pilgrims and ambassadors.

Every Christian, the Bible says, is a pilgrim. John Bunyan titled his world-famous allegory *Pilgrim's Progress* because every Christian is on a sacred journey. We're traveling through a place that's not really ours in order to get to the day when the whole place really *will* be ours. This is our Father's world, but for right now "the whole world lies in the power of the evil one" (1 John 5:19). And that's why we don't belong. We're pilgrims, sojourners, exiles (1 Pet. 2:11).

Exiles from other nations move to the United States on a regular basis, and they're usually easy to spot—because they never quite lose the accent of their native tongue. And that's just what you want as a Christian pilgrim. If you fit in just fine with the world around you, the world ruled by Satan, either you're not a pilgrim in the first place or you've forgotten that you don't belong.

That's sort of like an ambassador—which is another metaphor the Bible uses (2 Cor. 5:20)—who goes to a foreign country to represent the interests of his nation. Yes, an ambassador needs to learn the local language, or he'll do little good. But you don't want him becoming so totally assimilated into the culture that he forgets what he's there for.

As the US Secretary of State represents his nation's interests abroad, so a Christian needs to represent the interests of Christ wherever he lives.

What should be the response of Christians in addition to being distressed?

to be salt and light (i.e., gospel witnesses)

Hughes believes the church has taken a wrong approach to witnessing: "A worldly church cannot and will not reach the world. The church must be distinct from the world to reach the world. . . . The only hope for us and the lost world is a holy church" [Hughes, 17].

A sanctified church avoids the ditch of legalism (pursuing mere moralistic and pietistic perfectionism), but it also avoids the ditch of license (apathetic and worldly carelessness). A sanctified church body exercises itself unto godliness because God's transforming holiness changes the discipline and pursuits of the body (1 Tim. 4:7–8; Phil. 3:12–14). The church body must say no to sin by putting sin to death (Rom. 8:12–13). This requires watchful steadfastness (Matt. 26:41). A sanctified church won't be liked by the world, but it will be a witness to the world (John 17:14–18).

Asceticism

"There is a good Biblical base for the practice of mortification (1 Cor. 9:27; Rom. 8:13), but the practice of asceticism in the church degenerated into making men hermits or recluses, with the idea of meriting God's favour by suffering." [Alan Cairns, *Dictionary of Theological Terms* (Greenville, SC: Ambassador Emerald International, 2002), 42]

Ascetics reject *all* culture. In contrast, biblical Christians should accept goodness and reject badness in culture. When a believer rejects the bad part of culture, he shouldn't be accused of asceticism. "Rightly motivated obedience based on wise understanding is not legalism" [Leedy, 9]. The error of asceticism is that it not only denounces worldly perversions of God's world but also God's world itself.

> Human rebellion ought not to exist; it does not follow, of course, that humanity ought not to exist. Certain aspects of the present, fallen scheme of human existence ought not to exist; it does not follow that there is no valid root for these things that is itself good and legitimate. For instance, the self-gratification of gluttony or sexual promiscuity ought not to exist, but food and sex are themselves good gifts of a gracious God to be enjoyed gratefully within the limits He has set for them [Leedy, 48].

"Strict isolationist sects go astray on this point, failing to distinguish between normal human behavior that interacts with God's world and His creatures consistently with His design and that which arises in rebellion against His holy character" [Leedy, 105].

Believers should recognize the work of God's common grace in the way unbelievers carry out their work in the world. Believers should depend on the grace of God, recognizing their own shortcomings. But the grace of God isn't meant to provide cover for participating in the bad part of culture. "According to Titus 2:11–12 and Romans 6:1, anything called grace that provides a safe haven for ungodliness and worldly lust, or that condones continuing in sin, is something other than the saving grace of Christ" [Leedy, 11].

Differentiating Asceticism from Mortification

What should mortification (putting sin to death) look like according to Romans 6:12–23; 8:12–15?

When a believer is putting sin to death, he will not participate in things that Scripture has identified as the works of the flesh. The Christian is no longer a slave to these things. A Christian should not allow himself to be an instrument used to display unrighteousness.

Describe what asceticism looks like according to Colossians 2:8–23.

Someone who is practicing asceticism is following a formulaic system of human traditions that doesn't allow the use of creationally good things or requires extrabiblical rituals. The system brings spiritual superiority rather than spiritual maturity in Christlikeness.

How can you discern whether a modern-day application is biblical mortification or unbiblical asceticism?

Discernment comes from a Spirit-renewed mind illuminated by the Word. You must discern what the Bible presents as a creationally good use of God's design versus a human distortion and corruption of God's design. You must accurately handle Scripture and accurately know the situation.

If someone tells you not to eat something, is it mortification or asceticism?

You can't simply say that it's asceticism according to Colossians 2:21. A discerning Christian will ask for more context.

If it's human flesh, you shouldn't taste it. If it's simply pork (and you're not obligated to apply 1 Corinthians 9:20 or 10:28), then go ahead and eat it.

Dwelling as a Pilgrim

When English speakers use the word *pilgrim*, they typically think of someone who is traveling from one place to another like Pilgrim in *Pilgrim's Progress* or like the Pilgrims who came to America on the *Mayflower*. But the biblical concept of a pilgrim or a sojourner is different.

Abraham is the representative sojourner in Scripture. He is a foreigner dwelling in a foreign land. Both the idea of dwelling or being at home and the idea of being a foreigner are part of what it means to be a sojourner. A Christian dwells within his culture. He buys his clothes from department stores, he drives his car to work, and he uses a computer just like his coworkers. But he's also a foreigner in his culture. Some clothing stores he won't patronize, some of the places where his coworkers hang out after work he won't go. But as Abraham lived as a foreigner in a land that would one day be his, so Christians live as foreigners in a world that will one day be theirs through Christ.

Psalm 119 is the longest chapter in the Bible—176 verses, almost every one of which mentions the Word of God in some way. But the Word is not the only theme in the psalm. Another major emphasis is sojourning. The psalmist says, "I am a sojourner on the earth" (119:19), and "Your statutes have been my songs in the house of my sojourning (119:54).

And the theme pops up over and over throughout the psalm. The psalmist, because of his love for the Word of God, doesn't quite belong. He prays, "Take away from me scorn and contempt" (119:22), and he prays for "an answer for him who taunts me" (119:42).

One really remarkable thing about this scorning and taunting is that the psalmist presumably lived in Israel. He was a sojourner, a stranger, a pilgrim, an exile—even within the land God had promised and among God's chosen people. Someone with a truly biblical worldview and a heart of love for the Lord and his neighbor will never be at home and at rest until God puts all things under Christ's feet.

DARKNESS AND LIGHT

There is darkness, and there is light. We must never confuse the two. There is sin, and there is grace. We must never confuse the two. But for now, darkness and light as well as sin and grace are found in the church and in the world. In the end, only Christ will be able to separate the wheat from the weeds, the good from the evil. God invites you to enjoy all His good gifts; because of common grace, there is a way to make holy use of human culture. But because of the Fall, you dare not participate in any aspect of culture (pop, high, or folk) uncritically. God warns us about the dangers that pervade culture after the Fall. A life well lived is one that stays constantly aware of the tension between common grace and the Fall; a Christian life well lived seeks to "test everything [and] hold fast what is good" (1 Thess. 5:21).

1. Why is all culture—pop, folk, and high—in need of critique? What makes popular culture in particular an effective vehicle for worldliness?

2. Explain what worldliness is and what you must do to discern it in real life.

3. How would you describe an ascetic? What's wrong with the ascetic view of the world?

4. Explain how Christians must behave as pilgrims (sojourners) and ambassadors in this world.

5. How would you describe folk, high, and pop culture? What are some illegitimate and legitimate reasons for rejecting some forms of each of these kinds of culture?

8.3 AFFECTION DRIVES COGNITION

Identical-twin studies are a fascinating branch of psychology, especially when those twins have been separated at birth. Watching them grow up helps researchers figure out the roles nature and nurture play in forming our personalities and habits. Some psychologists who specialize in studying twins have actually concluded that "identical twins raised apart are as similar in personality as are identical twins raised together."[16] Other psychologists think that nature and nurture have a roughly equal effect on shaping a person.

The Task of an Ambassador

Diplomats are supposed to properly represent their own country and head of state. They are also supposed to extend themselves to the host country they reside in by following particular protocols, preventing any unnecessary offense. This doesn't mean that the content of the message or loyalty to one's own country should be diminished. But the way the diplomats present themselves shouldn't be purposefully rude. Diplomats for the United States are trained to advance the interests of the country by taking courses through the Foreign Service Institute, which is like a college program for diplomatic service overseas. It provides more than six hundred courses. Ambassadors and other diplomats are expected to learn how to conduct themselves and perform at a high level in order to be successful in their representation of the United States.

What appropriate parallels apply to Christians taking the message of Christ to the world?

- *Christians ought to properly represent the church and Christ (1 Thess. 1:7–9).*

- *Christians ought to extend themselves graciously to unbelievers, giving no unnecessary offense (Matt. 10:16; Rom. 12:18; 1 Pet. 4:15).*

- *Christians must not change the content of their message or communicate any disloyalty to Christ by undermining that content through unworthy conduct (Eph. 1:4; 4:1; 2 Pet. 2:1–22).*

- *Christians would do well to undergo intensive training for the work of the gospel in every field (e.g., worldview training even at the college or university level) (2 Tim. 2:2).*

No matter who's right, the issue raises a fascinating question: why do two people (like twins, perhaps) respond differently to the same information? Two people listen to the same sermon about the resurrection of Jesus Christ. One believes, the other scoffs. It has always been this way. It was this way among the people of Athens when Paul visited their city:

> When they heard of the resurrection of the dead, some mocked. But others said, "We will hear you again about this." So Paul went out from their midst. But some men joined him and believed. (Acts 17:32–34)

But why only some? They all heard the same words. It's hard to believe that anyone could be a better evangelist than the apostle Paul himself. Why did some in his audience believe and not others?

PROVERBS 1:7 AND THE FEAR OF GOD

The key verse[20] of the book of Proverbs provides insight into why people respond differently to the truth. Solomon said, in the very first chapter of the book, "The fear of the Lord is the beginning of knowledge" (Prov. 1:7).

Notice the two key words in this key verse: fear and knowledge. *Knowledge* is a **cognitive** word. It refers to your mental processes, your thinking, your "cognition." But fear isn't essentially a cognitive thing. It's a heart thing. Fear does involve your mind—babies don't fear hot stoves because they don't realize, cognitively, that extreme heat brings pain. But *fear* is a more emotional word than *knowledge*; it's related to your "affections," the bent or inclination or direction of your inner being. This verse says that the "affective" thing comes before the "cognitive" one. The fearing comes before the knowing.

But it's not fear in general that Solomon encourages you to have; it's fear of one specific object: the Lord, the God of the Bible. If you look at how the Bible uses the phrase "the **fear of the Lord**," you start to get a picture of what it means. It means a trembling awe and respect before a vastly more powerful, perfectly holy, and utterly good Being. This is not a cowardly fear, like a soldier running away from a battle. This is a holy fear, one actually filled with love. The prophet Isaiah even predicted that the Messiah Himself—the Son of God—would "delight . . . in the fear of the Lord" (Isa. 11:3).

The whole thesis of Proverbs is that you're not going to be able to understand the world the way it really is till you're right with God, till your inner person is inclined toward God in the right ways. First fear, then knowledge. One way to summarize this is to say, "Affection drives cognition." What you love determines what you think and what you know.

The smartest kids in the class don't necessarily get the highest grades—or learn the most. It's the students who love history or science who do the best at them. Affection drives cognition.

BORN THIS WAY

Pop music isn't generally meant to be taken seriously, but pop star Lady Gaga tried to preach a serious message in her worldwide hit "Born This Way."

> No matter gay, straight or bi,
> Lesbian, transgendered life,
> I'm on the right track, baby.
> I was born to survive.
>
> . . . .
>
> I'm beautiful in my way,
> 'Cause God makes no mistakes.
> I'm on the right track, baby.
> I was born this way.[17]

Gaga herself believes some things are evil—"prejudice" and "judgment," for example.[18] So how does she know that moral judgment is evil but homosexuality is blessed by God? (And isn't that a moral judgment?) The only way we can know what is creational and good versus fallen and evil is to let our Creator tell us. And He says that "I was born this way" is never a valid excuse for sin. Because of Adam's Fall, we were all born in sin (Ps. 51:5). "If I am so bad that I can't delight in what is good, that is no reason God can't command me to love the good," wrote one theologian. "If I am so corrupt that I can't enjoy what is infinitely beautiful, that does not make me less guilty for disobeying the command to delight in God (Ps. 37:4). It makes me more guilty."[19]

THE FEAR OF THE LORD

Biblical scholar Bruce Waltke says that "fear of the Lord . . . involves both rational and nonrational aspects at the same time"—head and heart. It's rational because it can be memorized and taught (Ps. 34:11). But "'fear of the Lord' also entails a nonrational aspect," Waltke adds, "an emotional response of fear, love, and trust."[21]

---

1. Define the fear of the Lord, and explain why this affection must guide a person's knowledge.
2. Explain how wrong affections lead intelligent people to suppress the truth and support foolish ignorance.

Born This Way: Sinful

Orthodox Christianity has always maintained that people sin (behavior) because they are sinfully inclined to do so (nature/disposition).

> The sinfulness of that estate whereinto man fell, consisteth in the guilt of Adam's first sin, the want of that righteousness wherein he was created, and the corruption of his nature, whereby he is utterly indisposed, disabled, and made opposite unto all that is spiritually good, and wholly inclined to all evil, and that continually; which is commonly called Original Sin, and from which do proceed all actual transgressions.

[*Westminster Larger Catechism*, question 25]

Thus, an external angry act is rooted in an internal angry disposition. It's not just the external act that must change but also the internal disposition. This is true of every sin and was Jesus' point in Matthew 5:20–48. The command to be perfect as He is perfect is impossible (Matt. 5:48). That's the point. Christ must transform the inner person at conversion; that new life works itself out externally in progressive conformity to His image until glorification (Rom. 8:29). Internal dispositions should change (1 Cor. 6:11). Christians can be perfected—that is, made to be mature (2 Tim. 3:17; James 1:4). Even though this perfection isn't complete until glorification (1 John 2:1; Col. 1:22), it does begin at regeneration (2 Cor. 5:17) and continues in progressive sanctification (2 Cor. 3:18).

Understanding this biblical teaching helps clarify discussions about homosexual desires and actions. Christians should not be surprised or suspicious when people claim to have longstanding, deep-rooted same-sex attraction. Everyone has longstanding, deep-rooted tendencies toward certain sins. Sometimes people justify homosexual desires on the grounds that they are natural. The Bible, on the other hand, distinguishes between what is natural according to God's creational norms (Rom. 1:26–31) and what is natural according to human nature, which is fallen (1 Cor. 2:14). When it comes to sexual morality, what seems natural—physical passions, whether heterosexual or homosexual—are to be controlled (1 Thess. 4:3–8).

---

1. Every realm can express fallenness; pop culture is more influential and often expresses fallenness with less restraint.
2. Worldliness is the desire to conform to sinful human culture. It's discerned through a Spirit-renewed mind washed by the Word.
3. It's someone who rejects God's good creation because he fails to see God's common grace in God's world.
4. A sojourner participates in the community even though he's always an outsider who's different. An ambassador represents another country while residing in a foreign place. Christians must remain distinct, representing God, while living within a foreign culture.
5. See the TE note "Realms of Culture" on page 112. Folk and pop culture shouldn't be rejected simply because of an elitist arrogance that despises what's "common" and "unrefined"; high culture shouldn't be rejected simply because of a populist disdain for "educated analysis." Regardless of the cultural form, unbiblical values or moral content must be rejected.

When a person becomes a Christian, the Spirit gives him a new heart with affections that turn toward God. But until he is glorified, he will still have a flesh with affections that turn toward sin. This means that all Christians will struggle with sinful desires and that some Christians may struggle with same-sex desires. But they may also rejoice in forgiveness from all sin in Christ Jesus (Rom. 8:1) and the promise that they are no longer slaves to these desires (Rom. 6:12–14).

[Denny Burk, "Is Homosexual Orientation Sinful?" Canon and Culture website (February 18, 2014)]

Fear God: Affection Drives Cognition

Although the fear of the Lord certainly includes a cognitive element because some propositions must be known intellectually (Ps. 19:7–9; 34:11), the fear of the Lord is primarily an attitude of the affections (a submissive bent toward God).

People can be taught about reverence and submission owed to God; they can be taught a standard of conduct worthy of God. In that sense they are being taught the fear of the Lord. But the inner constraint by which a person does, in fact, fear the Lord is an affection that can't simply be taught; it must be instilled within a person by God as that person seeks to personally walk with God (Prov. 2:1–7). In the Old Testament, the fear of the Lord is conjoined with the affection of loving the Lord (Deut. 6:1–2, 5). It's more than merely a mental understanding of God's worthiness. "In Isa. 29:13 Israel's distorted 'fear of me' is rejected precisely because it is made up only of rules taught by men." [Bruce K. Waltke, *The Book of Proverbs: Chapters 1–15*, New International Commentary on the Old Testament (Grand Rapids: Eerdmans, 2004), 101]

Furthermore, the fear of the Lord is inextricably linked to faith because a person must believe who God is and what He says (promises and threats) in order to respond in humble submission. The term is used in the Old Testament to identify true believers.

Fear and Knowledge

According to Proverbs 1:7, all knowledge rests on the foundation of the fear of the Lord. Why must fear precede knowledge?

Bruce Waltke wrote: "What the alphabet is to reading, notes to reading music, and numerals to mathematics, the fear of the Lord is to attaining . . . knowledge" (Waltke, 181). This is not to say that unbelievers can't have any knowledge; it's that they can't justify the

---

A particular teenage guy might write very poor analyses of the literature texts he's assigned in class, but when he wants his dad's car keys on Saturday, he brings to bear his full powers of analysis, evaluation, and argument creation. His desires fire up his mental powers. Affection drives cognition.

When a guy's heart is turned toward a girl (perhaps one he has failed to notice in the previous twelve years as her classmate), his mental energies all become dedicated to thinking of creative ways to be near her and to please her and to win her affections. If he does win them, that girl's brain will be working on the same tasks as his. Affection drives cognition.

WHY SCIENTISTS ARE NERVOUS ABOUT THE BIG BANG

cosmology: the scientific field dedicated to explaining the origin of the universe

Affection doesn't always drive cognition in good directions. *Time* magazine interviewed scientist and popular author Brian Clegg after he wrote a book about various theories of how the universe began. He said scientists generally speak about the big bang as if it were a settled result of modern science. Clegg says it's not; it's a speculative cosmological* theory.[22]

The *Time* interviewer asked Clegg to mention the theory's major flaws, and Clegg responded that scientists have expected to find aftershocks from the big bang, changes in gravity rippling outward from the center of the explosion. Clegg pointed out that a great deal of cash has been expended in looking for those waves, and so far nothing has been found.

And then Clegg asked a simple question: why did the big bang happen in the first place? "There is no sensible answer . . . unless you move over into the religious side and say, 'Well, it began because God began it.' That's why quite a lot of scientists are nervous about the Big Bang."[23] They don't want a Someone outside the system telling the system to get going, Clegg said.

The interviewer said that he was troubled by Clegg's assertions that scientists won't question the big bang because that would unsettle their careers. Clegg replied that science is a club, a "social network" like any other: "In the end, there is almost a fashion in science—ideas that are in, ideas that are out."[24]

Affection drives cognition.

ROMANS 1 AND THE TRUTH OF GOD

"The fear of the Lord is the beginning of knowledge" is not the only verse in Scripture demonstrating that affection drives cognition. Think of this key passage in Paul's letter to the Roman Christians:

> The wrath of God is revealed from heaven against all ungodliness and unrighteousness of men, who by their unrighteousness suppress the truth. For what can be known about God is plain to them, because God has shown it to them. For his invisible attributes, namely, his eternal power and divine nature, have been clearly perceived, ever since the creation of the world, in the things that have been made. So they are without excuse. (Rom. 1:18–20)

What does it mean to "suppress the truth"? If someone doesn't want to admit to himself that his actions (getting drunk, say) have caused a tragedy, he may compress that truth into a dark corner in his heart. He lets himself believe that the fatal car accident he caused was really the fault of poor brakes in his truck. He never lets the truth out in the air long enough for it to be confessed. He starts living his life as if a lie were true, and any time the truth tries to get out he shoves it back into its tiny corner.

---

knowledge they do have. Any true knowledge that they do have is the result of God's common grace. When they do attain true knowledge it's because, ultimately, they must borrow from the Christian worldview; they must be inconsistent with their own false worldview. Van Til taught that all truth is God's truth; no true knowledge can be confirmed as such by the autonomous human mind. [Cornelius Van Til, *The Defense of the Faith*, 4th ed. (Phillipsburg, NJ: P&R, 1955), 62–67, 174–83]

Every truth claim is built on assumptions that must be traced back to an ultimate presupposition. That ultimate presupposition must rest on absolutely certain, declared revelation since there's no other way for finite humans to be absolutely certain of any presupposition. The only way to attain

certainty in God's revelation is by means of the fear of the Lord. Thus, the fear of the Lord is a foundational necessity for certainty in any true knowledge. Any knowledge that a Christian claims to have should fit into the framework of the truth system declared by God's Word. Any so-called knowledge that doesn't square with the truth claims of God's Word must be rejected. God's Word is the foundation and framework for all other knowledge claims because all truth is a harmonious unity in God's world. Accepting God's Word as such only happens to those who fear the Lord. [See Greg L. Bahnsen, *Van Til's Apologetic: Readings and Analysis* (Phillipsburg, NJ: P&R Publishing, 1998), 416–18.]

Follow Paul's logic: God is angry because wicked people He created suppress the truth. But the truth about God isn't just in our hearts (though it is there—God put it there, as Paul will later show). The truth is all around us. It's plain, evident, obvious. God has shown it to us. Truths about God that are invisible become visible in His creation. You can't see God's "eternal power," for example. But you can see its effects in every intricately designed flower on the planet. You can't see His divine nature (His "Godness") directly, but you can see it reflected in every human face around you. It is, indeed, "the things that have been made" by God that bear His stamp and point to Him. Some plastic toys say "Made in China" on the bottom. Stamped all over our globe, from the tropics to the ice caps, is another label: "Made by God."

So what? So truth-suppressers have no excuse. How can Amazonian tribal people who've never heard of Jesus be blamed for failing to become Christians? Well, it's true that they don't bear the same amount of blame as someone raised in church who denies the Christian faith. But from their earliest lies as children they—like every person on the globe—have suppressed the truth that is evident all around them.

The beautiful things "that have been made" point to God's "eternal power and divine nature" (Rom. 1:2–21).

"CREATION AS A WHOLE GIVES 'VISIBILITY' TO THE INVISIBLE GOD." [25]

—SINCLAIR FERGUSON

Every one of God's human creatures knows, at some level, that God exists and that He's eternally powerful. It takes a wicked act of willful suppression to become ignorant of God. Everyone—everyone—knows his Creator. That's why one Christian apologist* can say that any atheist has two basic beliefs:

(1) God doesn't exist, and
(2) I hate Him.[26]

apologist: *someone who defends his viewpoint from attacks (from Latin apologia, a defense)*

IGNORANT OF WHAT YOU CAN'T NOT KNOW

What does it do to people when they suppress and deny what they can't not know? Their thinking gets twisted, darkened. That's why Paul told the Ephesian Christians,

You must no longer walk as the Gentiles* do, in the futility of their minds. They are darkened in their understanding, alienated from the life of God because of the ignorance that is in them, due to their hardness of heart. (Eph. 4:17–18)

Gentiles: *non-Jews, but in this context "non-Christians"*

The Bible does not teach that non-Christians are stupid or uneducated. A non-Christian intellectual can be like a sharp, well-honed buzz saw—but one often sawing in the wrong direction. The Bible does not say that the one thousand Steves of Project Steve or the countless other college professors, mechanical engineers, biomedical researchers, artists, and writers in the non-Christian world are stupid.

And you are a Christian, if you are one, not because you are extra smart. In fact, God tends to choose "what is foolish in the world to shame the wise" (1 Cor. 1:27). You are a Christian because the hard heart you used to have has been replaced by the soft heart God gives to all His children (Jer. 31:31–34; Ezek. 36:25–26). And non-Christians see the world the way they do and know what they know "due to their hardness of heart."

If there seems to be confusion or disagreement, then ask this question:

Do all scientists hold to a particular master story of the world?

Yes, every person (whether he consciously thinks it through or not) presupposes something about the larger story of the world. Therefore, he must have interpretive bias.

Not all of his scientific work will be affected to the same degree, but the interpretive framework always exists nonetheless.

Secularists maintain an evolutionary story of the world with its presuppositions (e.g., the biblical God doesn't exist) and defeater beliefs (e.g., miracles could never occur). Since both creation scientists and secularists hold to presuppositions, neither of them can claim to be without interpretive bias. Both may observe the same evidence and make use of the same scientific processes in order to produce something. But neither can claim to be without a truth system framework.

> The clash between creation science and evolution science is thus not a clash between science and religion at all, but between two competing world views. . . . The Bible has never claimed . . . that it gives exhaustive truth, merely that what it does teach *is* the truth. There is a vast amount of room for real science within the boundaries of a biblical framework. Many varying hypotheses can be constructed and tested.

["Bias and Faith," *Creation* 15 (September 1993):50–51]

 Scientific Bias and Peer Review

Many secularists (postmodern or otherwise) are now willing to admit that scientific claims shouldn't be given the status of a sacrosanct inspired canon as many modernists would have had you believe in the past. *The Economist* reports, "Too many of the findings that fill the academic ether are the result of shoddy experiments or poor analysis. . . . A rule of thumb among biotechnology venture-capitalists is that half of published research cannot be replicated. Even that may be optimistic." ["How Science Goes Wrong," *The Economist* (October 19, 2013)]

The article goes on to explain why the peer review process (the practice of having fellow scholars within the same field fact-check papers, providing a safeguard against shoddy science) isn't working. In a test of the peer review system, many reviewers failed to flag errors placed in papers by the testers. Creation scientists and intelligent design scientists have long complained that they get locked out of the peer-reviewed scientific journals simply because the scientific

---

 ### Opening the Eyes of Understanding

Based on Scripture, why do unbelievers persist in unbelief even after the truth has been clearly explained?

Suggested passages: Prov. 1:29; Matt. 13:1–9, 13–15; John 3:10; 8:43; Acts 28:26–27; Rom. 3:11; 2 Cor. 4:4; Eph. 4:18

The soil of their heart is hard, rocky, or thorny; they don't want to understand because Satan has blinded them so they refuse to fear the Lord.

Based on Scripture, what must take place for a person to change from unbelief to belief?

Suggested passages: Prov. 1:7; Ezek. 36:22–32; Matt. 11:25; John 6:35–40; Acts 16:14; 1 Cor. 2:11–14; Eph. 1:18; Heb. 11:3; 1 John 5:20

The things of God must be revealed through the Son and the Spirit so a person can fear God and place his faith in God.

In summary, the Spirit must illuminate the mind so that a person can correctly apprehend the content of God's Word (Eph. 1:13, 17–18). But that person must also accept the significance of that truth for himself (Isa. 55:6–7; 2 Cor. 6:1–2). His affections (the bent of his inner person) must embrace and apply the reality of that truth to his own life.

This apprehension and acceptance are evident in a clear act of reliance—conversion, which includes both faith and repentance (Luke 13:3; 1 Thess. 1:9).

  ### Scientific Bias

Ask the students to debate whether all scientists have interpretive biases even if they don't admit it.

establishment rejects their worldview. But that doesn't mean that Christians should reject the peer review process entirely. They should embrace it when it promotes honesty, wisdom, accountability, and correction (based on correct presuppositions).

[For a thorough biblical assessment of the peer review process, see Todd Wood, Joe Francis, Kurt Wise, and Roger Sanders, "Toward a Practical Theology of Peer Review," *Answers Research Journal* 1 (April 9, 2008): 65–75.]

Living a Lie

The Fall into sin began with a lie about being able to function without God according to autonomous human wisdom (Gen. 3:1–5). Humans are still trying to live their lives according to this same lie when they suppress God's revelation (Rom. 1:18, 22) and rebuff every attempt to convince them of the truth (1 Cor. 1:18–25).

How should a Christian respond?

Christians must use discernment. You should patiently declare the gospel to people with whom you can gain a hearing (1 Thess. 2:1–13). But it's also acceptable to shake the dust off your feet; it's not necessary to continue to cast the pearls of the gospel before those who scorn it (Matt. 7:6; 10:14). Depend on the Spirit to break through the lie that unregenerate humans are believing and to convict them of sin, righteousness, and judgment (John 16:8).

What You Can't Not Know

There are certain things that everyone must know about God. Or we could say it's impossible for them not to know—they can't not know. Why? Because they *are still* made in God's image (and they can't change that) and God *has* revealed the truth to them in their conscience and in creation (and they can't change that). They're stuck with a true knowledge of God regardless of how much they wish to rebelliously suppress what they do know and refuse to admit.

These passages of the Bible are pointing to one of the key ingredients of a person's worldview: what we called earlier the "head-heart system." In these passages, the head-heart system appears to be the reason why your reasoning works the way it does. This is why people with the same intelligence, similar experience, and apparently equal amounts of common grace nonetheless disagree on basic issues of human existence. Thinking (head) and loving (heart) are tied closely together. You think what you think because you love what you love. Affection drives cognition.

THINKING IT THROUGH 8.3

1. What's the problem with trying to excuse sin by claiming you were just born that way?

2. Define the fear of the Lord.

3. Why is the fear of the Lord crucial for correct knowledge?

4. What does it mean to suppress the truth, and what is the result of suppressing the truth?

♦ 5. Explain how non-Christians can be both intelligent and foolishly ignorant at the same time.

Making Connections

1. It restrains sin and promotes good.

2. worldliness and asceticism

3. Worldliness begins in the heart but is always expressed in external behavior and symbols of identity.

4. The bent of one's affections toward or away from the fear of the Lord.

Developing Skills in Apologetics and Worldview

5. Truth, goodness, and beauty must be sourced in God. Since even unbelievers are made in God's image and influenced by God's common grace, they sometimes display these qualities while believers sometimes don't due to their own fallenness. Therefore, this rule of thumb

THINKING IT THROUGH 8.3

1. It blasphemously blames God for creating you with an identity that is contrary to His holiness. The truth is that sin results from our being born with a fallen nature.

2. One definition is "the awe and reverence left over when the frightening vulnerability before the greatness of God is mixed with the joy of security upon experiencing the goodness of God."

3. It's the only way to justify with certainty any truth claim, and all such claims must ultimately be rooted in what God has revealed.

4. It's when someone doesn't want to admit the truth even though he knows it, so he ignores it or argues against it in order to silence it. After a while he begins to believe his own lies.

♦ 5. Non-Christians may have sharp minds, but if they pursue truth in the wrong direction from the wrong source, they end up with the wrong answers. This is because the head-heart system of affections drives cognition.

 **CHAPTER REVIEW**

TERMS TO REMEMBER

common grace
total depravity
popular culture
high culture
folk culture
worldliness
asceticism
cognition
fear of the Lord

Scripture Memory

1 Peter 2:11–12; Proverbs 1:7

Making Connections

1. What are the two overarching benefits of common grace?

2. Identify the two responses to culture Christians must avoid.

3. Where does worldliness begin, and how does it manifest itself?

4. What ultimately determines the way people interpret the evidence they see?

Developing Skills in Apologetics and Worldview

5. Respond to the following claim: Christians ought to reject any cultural product created by an unbeliever and accept any cultural product created by a believer.

6. Evaluate the viewpoint that music is amoral or neutral.

Examining Assumptions and Evidence

7. Why can't you evaluate a person's goodness by outward morality alone?

8. Why are non-Christians "darkened in their understanding, alienated from the life of God" (Eph. 4:18)?

9. Why can't you excuse your sin by claiming, "I was born that way?"

10. If many non-Christians are intelligent (and they are), then why do they embrace falsehoods?

Becoming a Creative Cultivator

11. Keep a journal for one week, daily noting all your observations of both common grace and worldliness.

desires and sanctified by denying one's own natural desires.

10. They use their intelligence to suppress the truth and to support the blind assumptions of their own head-heart system.

Becoming a Creative Cultivator

11. Answers will vary. You may wish to have students sign a statement that they have completed this assignment rather than requiring them to turn it in to you. However, take advantage of any discipleship opportunities by engaging them in discussion.

TERMS TO REMEMBER

common grace—undeserved favor given to both the saved and unsaved alike

total depravity—the inherent moral corruption that affects every human and every aspect of human existence because of the Fall

popular culture—culture that results from quickly spreading mainstream and widely marketed media for the purpose of immediate gratification and pleasure

high culture—culture that results from centuries of human observation and analysis, that determines the best standards for the highest quality, and that usually involves formal training, producing experts who study why and how this quality can be produced

folk culture—culture that results from the organic, usually informally trained, natural creativity of a particular localized region

worldliness—the spirit of the age defined by the fallen affections of the heart that embrace (and pressure others to embrace) ungodly expressions of culture manifested in one's external behavior or identity

asceticism—the strict denial of any enjoyment of truth, goodness, and beauty in God's good creation

fear of the Lord—"the awe and reverence left over when the frightening vulnerability before the greatness of God is mixed with the joy of security upon experiencing the goodness of God"

[Jim Berg, *Created for His Glory* (Greenville, SC, JourneyForth, 2002), 28]

---

will be full of inconsistencies rather than providing an effective safeguard.

6. Music communicates and expresses emotions. Just as an emotion can manifest fallenness, so also can the music giving expression to that same emotion. While your critique of another person's emotions may involve a subjective element, some expressions are objectively undeniable; the same is true with music. Music is a part of God's good creation, but a particular musical form falls within the realm of a cultural good produced by depraved humans and affected by a comprehensive Fall. Those humans may produce truth, goodness, and beauty because of common grace. But they may produce lies, badness, or ugliness because of the Fall. What can't be defended is that music is above critique.

Examining Assumptions and Evidence

7. People can be outwardly very moral. But if their hearts are fundamentally oriented away from God, God cannot be pleased with them, or He Himself would be unjust. Those in the flesh cannot please God. Only submission to the gospel and union with Christ make a person good.

8. It takes time and effort to develop a refined and mature palate for that which is excellent. If you are given freedom to consume only what comes easily or naturally, then you will probably consume only that which is equivalent to junk food.

9. Every human was born into sin and its natural desires. Christianity is all about being saved from one's own natural

The student will be able to

9.1 Explain the concept of structure and direction and how it relates to the CFR story line of Scripture.

9.2 Apply structure and direction to the issue of sexual relations.

9.3 Apply structure and direction to the issues of materialism, technology, and language.

SECTION OBJECTIVES 9.1

1. Describe the earth's condition through the lens of the CFR story line.

2. Define what *structure* means and what *direction* means, and explain how these terms describe the realities of CFR.

3. Illustrate structure and direction.

4. Explain why it's necessary to recognize that the world is structured according to God's good design.

5. Explain why it's necessary to, recognize that every human use of creation is directed in conformity to or away from God's good design.

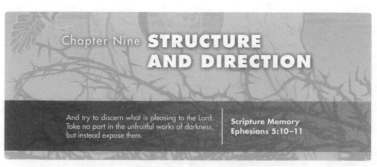

Chapter Nine **STRUCTURE AND DIRECTION**

And try to discern what is pleasing to the Lord. Take no part in the unfruitful works of darkness, but instead expose them.

**Scripture Memory
Ephesians 5:10–11**

9.1 UNDERSTANDING STRUCTURE AND DIRECTION

C. S. Lewis was one of the most influential apologists for the Christian faith in the last century, and part of his genius was that he used a variety of literary genres to advance Christian ideas, from children's literature to a science fiction trilogy. The second book in his sci-fi series, *Perelandra*, tells a creation story very similar to that of the Bible, but this one's not about Earth but about Venus. The Great Lord and Great Lady—the first two members of the human-like race God has placed on Venus, which they call Perelandra—have lost each other on the sea-covered planet's floating, shifting islands. And just as God told Adam and Eve not to eat of one tree, God has told the Lord and Lady of Venus that they must not sleep on the "fixed lands," the only "terra firma" in that world.

Satan arrives to tempt the Perelandran woman to break that simple command. While Earth's Eve seems to have taken only moments to fall into sin, Venus's first mother outlasts many mind-bending conversations with the devil.

Satan in Lewis's story focuses much of his energy on twisting the woman's love for God. He tries to get her to believe that living independent of her Creator is actually the best way to please Him. But she implicitly trusts and deeply loves her Creator, who is as real to her as the air and water—so what Satan says generally sounds ridiculous to her.

God sends her a helper, an English professor from Earth named Ransom. As a Christian, he attempts to explain to the unfallen woman just what breaking God's commands will do to her race and her planet. He knows from bitter earthly experience.

The lady is perplexed, and Ransom has a difficult task: How do you explain the seriousness of sin to someone who has never seen anyone disobey the Creator? Words like *sin* and *bad* and *wrong* mean nothing to the Great Lady. She has never seen such a thing. So he chooses *bent*. He describes those who disobey God as "bent ones," beings who have twisted, distorted, or perverted the good God put in them.[1]

Ultimately, Perelandra's first inhabitants do not disobey their Creator, and Satan is banished. A new world is born without sin, and God's creatures are free to flourish according to His perfect design. They aren't "bent."

BENDING THINGS BACK INTO THEIR PROPER SHAPE

Lewis's story about Venus is very different from what happened on Earth, of course. Our Great Lady gave in—and so did her husband. God actually permitted the sin within Satan to slink into our world without marring it; but as soon as God's appointed rulers sinned, they plunged the earth into ruin. "The earth and its condition is and remains a human responsibility," says one author. "[So] Satan can wreak havoc on the good earth only by first controlling mankind."[2] Every bit of perversion, sickness, and evil in this world can be blamed on the sin of the race God made to rule it. We have bent our world pretty badly.

122 | FALL

Lesson Plan Chart—Chapter 9

Section Title	Pages	Activity Manual	Days
9.1 Understanding Structure and Direction	122–25		2 days
9.2 Sex in a Fallen World	125–29		1 day
9.3 Other Structures Bent in Bad Directions	129–34	Activity 16a–c	2 day
Review	135		1 day
Total Suggested Days			**6 days**

The Condition of the World: Fallen

The world is no longer perfectly good as God originally created it. The world is not yet redeemed as God promises it will be. The *whole* world's current condition is fallen (Rom. 8:22). The Bible straightforwardly presents this CFR storyline. Most of the material in the Bible focuses on the present fallen condition of the world and how believers ought to live in it (Eph. 2:1–3; Phil. 2:14–15). Believers shouldn't disconnect the CFR story of the world from their day-to-day interactions with culture. Since humans have been touched by the Fall at every point of their personhood, their artifacts are not generally neutral but are shaped both by their image-bearing capacity and by their fallenness. This means social structures and cultural pursuits must be scripturally evaluated.

But by God's common grace—and His amazing grace, special* grace—all humans are capable of the opposite kind of bending. They're capable (*only* by the grace of God, the fountain of all goodness) of bending things back into their proper shape. What else do you call it when a school with terrible discipline problems gets cleaned up? Or when a rotten law—like the racist Jim Crow laws in the American South—gets scrubbed from the books? Or when society as a whole starts to praise exercise and condemn smoking? Or when slaves get freed, musical traditions become more beautiful, and technology progresses? Situations can and do improve in this world. They go from being bent to being less bent. And as we saw in the common grace chapter, that bending back pleases God.

Everything in this world is moving in one of two directions: it's either bending or getting bent back. Christians are called to join the bending-back operation that God is already engaged in. Of course, God is the only one powerful enough to bend the whole world back into shape, but that shouldn't stop us from doing hard de-bending work ourselves. (God is the only one who can completely sanctify us, but that doesn't stop us from pressing toward holiness till He does so.)

"Try to discern what is pleasing to the Lord," Paul said to the Ephesian Christians (Eph. 5:10). In any given situation, look for the things that are going in the right direction, the things that please God. But be careful; Paul adds, "Take no part in the unfruitful works of darkness, but instead expose them" (5:11). In other words, if you see "bent ones" bending God's creation away from God's purposes, expose the bad bending. Point it out to the world.

Biblical worldview thinker Al Wolters uses two labels to help Christians do this discerning of good and evil—**structure** and **direction**. "Direction" is the bending, whether bad bending or good bending. "Structure" is the way things are supposed to be before they get bent, the way things are supposed to be when they get bent back. Think of a flexible, springy metal pole sticking out of the ground. "Structure" is when the pole is perfectly straight. "Direction" is when the pole is getting bent, whether the bending is going away from its original structure or back toward it. "Structure" is good because God created everything good. "Direction" can be good or bad.

special grace: the grace of God given to regenerate fallen sinners; the grace that makes people Christians (1 Pet. 1:3).

DIRECTION: GOOD
Bending it back toward its intended order

STRUCTURE
God's created order

DIRECTION: BAD
Bending it toward fallen human nature

STRUCTURE AND DIRECTION | 123

If a Christian resists evaluation of his artistic, political, scientific, or sexual choices (to name just a few cultural categories), he disconnects his biblical understanding about the Fall from real life. The Fall affects all aspects of the human person. As a result, it affects all aspects of culture. Every human sub-creation is subject to fallenness and thus to evaluation. Some sub-creations should be rejected because they can only be expressions of human fallenness. Other sub-creations may only be tainted with fallenness—they may or may not be able to be cleaned up in a particular cultural context so as to be utilized in ways more consistent with God's original creational goodness.

If a Christian tries to refrain from any cultural participation, he fails to understand the balance of the Bible's teaching about the Fall. The Fall doesn't obliterate the goodness of God's creation. A person can't escape the effects of the Fall by isolating himself from others' contributions to culture. Fallenness resides within each human heart, but God doesn't command people to cease living lives that contribute to the activities of this world until they are perfected and glorified. Instead, Christians must be careful to be salt and light as they contribute to and participate in the culture of this present age.

Structure and Direction

Structure: the nature or essence of a created thing according to its God-given creational norms or design [see Chapter 6]

Direction: the use of a created thing either toward or away from its God-given creational norms or design [See Al Wolters,

Creation Regained: Biblical Basics for a Reformational Worldview (Grand Rapids: Eerdmans, 1985), 57]

These terms are simply another way of explaining CFR and applying it to cultural choices.

Structure is equivalent to creational norms (God's good design). Direction is equivalent to Fall or Redemption—depending on whether the directional use is counter to or conforming to God's creational design.

"The great danger is always to single out some aspect . . . of God's good creation and identify it, rather than the alien intrusion of human apostasy, as the villain in the drama of human life." [Wolters, *Creation Regained*, 61]

The Fall and God's Good Creation

"Sin neither abolishes nor becomes identified with creation. Creation and sin remain distinct, however closely they may be intertwined in our experience." [Wolters, *Creation Regained*, 59]

Why would it be important to distinguish between God's good creation and sinful distortions?

Failure to distinguish between the two can cause people either to reject God's good creation along with the distortion or to accept the distortion as part of God's good creation.

Sin and evil always have the character of a caricature—that is, of a distorted image that nevertheless embodies certain recognizable features. A human being after the fall, though a travesty of humanity, is still a human being, not an animal. A humanistic school is still a school. A broken relationship is still a relationship. Muddled thinking is still thinking.

[Wolters, *Creation Regained*, 58]

Common and Special Grace

Creation is like a leash that keeps a vicious dog in check. If it were not for the leash, the dog (fallen mankind) would go completely wild, causing incalcuable harm and probably bringing destruction upon its own head. Redemption in this image is the uncanny power by which the dog's master persuades it to become friendly and cooperative, so that the dog no longer strains at the leash but seeks guidance from it. It is because of the leash that fallen man is still man.

[Wolters, *Creation Regained*, 60]

The external curbing of sin because of creational restraints is common grace. The internal renewal because of redemptive transformation is special grace.

The Task of the Believer

Second Peter 3:10–13 teaches that, at Christ's return, the world in its present fallen state must be purged by fire. But it will not be annihilated; it will be fully *restored* as the new heavens and earth. Therefore, no current human effort to bend the fallen world back to its original creational goodness will totally succeed. This reality can be discouraging, leading some students to conclude that since the world can't be restored until Christ returns to transform it, it doesn't matter how Christians live.

What does 3:11 exhort believers to do?

Believers should live holy and godly lives.

Living a godly life means living faithfully according to God's creational norms. This faithfulness should lead to an attempt to bend cultural expressions back in line with creational norms. Exposing bad bending and working against it will often lead to persecution. But rather than becoming discouraged, Christians can take comfort that God's reward is based on faithfulness, not on effectiveness.

The Necessity of Structure

What is given up when absolutes rooted in creational norms (structure) are denied?

justifiable standards that apply to everyone

When a unified standard can't be appealed to, what inevitably results?

conflicting moral judgments

What is often lost when there is confusion over moral judgments?

justice and restraint

When justice and restraint are lost, what happens to society?

It devolves into chaos and destructive living.

Since the leading forces in secular societies presuppose philosophical materialism (which teaches that matter is all there is) and insist on tolerance, no one can appeal to a unified standard for moral judgment. Thus, justice and restraint continue to erode, and society breaks down because it continues to bend away from God's normative structure.

Why does structure, with its standards and moral judgments, actually liberate people?

Structure frees people from chaos and injustice. An absolute standard sets consistent expectations that are enforceable and that everyone is equally accountable to.

Metal poles can get bent in any direction—just like sin can twist God's good creation in numerous ways. There are political extremists on the left and the right; both sides have bent the pole of God's created structure, just in different directions. (And that doesn't mean political moderates are right, either—they have their own ways of bending the pole.)

Let's develop this pole metaphor just a bit further: no matter how much you bend a metal pole, if it is firmly anchored in the ground—in concrete, say—it's going to stay connected. Likewise, fallen humanity can bend creation only so far. Homosexuals will never be able to produce children on their own. Polluting factories will ultimately not get away with pumping endless chemicals into the water supply. Drug addicts and drunks will not be able to get their highs and still drive safely on their side of the road. Non-Christians are stuck in the world God gave us all, not in the one they want. That metal pole resists being pulled, and sometimes springs back into place. God's created structures endure all the abuse they receive.

Straight Structure

Of course, you can only know a pole is bent if you have some idea of what it looked like when it was straight. And that's why the Creation-Fall-Redemption metanarrative of Scripture is so important. It tells us that every created thing was originally good, and it gives us guidance as to what that good looked like (what we've called "creational norms"). This guidance is something that other prominent worldviews out there fail to give. Here are just two examples:

- Classic secularists (see Unit 6 about government) steadfastly refuse to describe what the ideal world would look like (what the pole looks like when it isn't bent). They point out that different cultures and religions disagree over the shape of the perfect world, and if you try to claim that your view is right, someone else will just come along and offer a different opinion. Then you'll have a fight on your hands. Better not to talk about the pole.
- In philosophical materialism, matter is all that exists. Who can say which states of matter are "good" and which are "bad"? They're just there. They're just obeying physical laws; they're not guided by any intelligence. Birthday parties happen, genocide happens. The big bang giveth, and the big bang taketh away.

But the Bible gives us the power to make moral judgments—in part because it tells us that the world has a structure, and a good one. It isn't just churchy, religious stuff that can be good (that's the way other religions tend to view the world).[3] No, the New Testament says that "everything created by God is good" (1 Tim. 4:4). Mere stuff can be good. Not neutral. Good.

By itself, no created thing is sinful. It's only when moral agents such as humans pick up creation and use it that it can get bent in bad directions. But God's people can pick up creation and use it for holy purposes too. In other words, they can "sanctify" it. Every God-created thing in this world can be "sanctified" by God's children, 1 Timothy 4:4–5 says. And this book has worked hard to show that good creational norms govern not just physical things but also institutions and disciplines such as marriage, government, academic research, and the arts. These nonphysical things can all be bent, but they can all be bent back too.

What happens in unstructured classrooms, homes, workplaces, and nations?

Chaos and injustice must eventually be checked by creational norms springing back into place. However, the process of readjusting may be long and painful.

The Myth of Neutrality

Is there anything in culture that is neutral?

The two-story view divides the world into categories of "sacred" and "secular." This division may lead people to categorize some good things in the secular category as neutral. (Good things in the sacred category are good.) But, as argued in Chapter 3, the two-story view is unbiblical. A biblical view of the world understands that anything that is directionally conformed to God's creational design (structure) is good—not neutral. Some things may be more or less good as they are more or less conformed to God's standard. But they are not neutral.

Can unsaved people do good things, or are the things they do that aren't sinful simply neutral?

That unsaved people are involved in good things doesn't make those things neutral; the things are positively good due to God's common grace.

Abandon Some Activities?

Debate the point first, not the example in the Student Text. Then discuss examples that would appropriately illustrate the point.

Issue: Is it ever legitimate for Christians to abandon a *particular* social activity if participation is no longer possible without compromise with corrupting elements?

Direction Detection

You have to know about something's structure before you can discern its direction. But make no mistake: every created thing has a direction. C. S. Lewis said, "There is no neutral ground in the universe: every square inch, every split second, is claimed by God and counterclaimed by Satan."[4] There is a spiritual battle going on *in* this world—and it's going on *for* the world. The creation is what each side is trying to win, with mankind as the ultimate prize. Satan is trying to destroy the creation; God is trying (and will, in His time, succeed) to restore it to the way He intended it to be.

Because of this tug-of-war over creation, you must not assume that anything in creation is amoral or neutral. Music and sports, cartoons and novels—they're all going somewhere, and sometimes two somewheres at once. Your local soccer league may be headed in a good direction: it may be increasing the players' skills while recognizing that family and church take precedence over sports. Meanwhile, the high school football culture may be headed in a bad direction: football may become a community god, and the players may goad each other into being arrogant and obnoxious. Your local downtown area may be headed in good and bad directions, revitalizing run-down buildings but enabling (and subtly encouraging) drunkenness on the weekends.

So when we say that every created thing in this world—even marriage, government, and the arts—can be sanctified, we don't mean that Christians should necessarily try to sanctify every particular expression of those things in their cultures. Some institutions or cultural systems are so bent that they are best abandoned for now. Drama and theater, for example, had become so corrupt in seventeenth-century England that the Puritans were probably right to put an end to them while they held political power. At the same time, students at Christian liberal arts colleges today can benefit from Shakespeare's insight into human nature by producing his plays. It would not be right for conservative Christians to abandon drama entirely. Different circumstances call for different applications of the same unchanging biblical truths. Wisdom is needed, and discernment.

BABIES IN THE BATHWATER

This chapter is dedicated to helping you discern what's created and what's fallen in the world around you. You know the cliché: Don't throw the baby out with the bathwater. Anywhere there are babies (created structure), there's bathwater (fallen direction). Let's learn to distinguish the two. In the next unit, we'll focus on saving the babies; in this chapter we're just going to spot them out there bobbing in the water.

THINKING IT THROUGH 9.1

1. What do the terms *structure* and *direction* mean?

2. Explain the illustration the textbook uses to picture how the concept of structure and direction works.

3. Why is it necessary to define structure? What should determine the definition of structure?

4. Why can't there be any neutral ground in the universe?

5. Even though Christians are to make sanctified use of God-created things (general categories), should they try to sanctify every particular human use of creation? Why or why not?

(nor did the Puritans argue that theater was inherently sinful). Tertullian's opposition was rooted in the reality that participation demanded partaking of elements that would force Christians to disobey clear scriptural morality that believers are obligated to obey and cannot ignore or minimize. He didn't oppose sports; he opposed idolatry. He didn't oppose drama; he opposed immorality (as did the Puritans).

THINKING IT THROUGH 9.1

1. Structure refers to the way things are before they get bent, the way things are supposed to be when they get bent back; direction is the bending, whether bad or good.

2. Structure is like a straight metal pole; direction can bend that pole in any number of ways away from or back toward its original straightness. Bending away has limitations; eventually the pole must spring back into place.

3. Without a defined structure it's impossible to make any moral judgments. A person's worldview (e.g., the CFR metanarrative) determines structure.

4. Everything is moving in one direction or another—either conformed to God's design (claimed by God) or contrary to God's design (counterclaimed by Satan).

5. No, some of the particular human sub-creations have departed so far from God's design (at least in a particular context) that they simply need to be rejected.

---

1. Recognize that secularism's denial of God's structure results in a rejection of any justifiable ethical standards.

2. Summarize God's structured design for sexual relations and explain the purposes for His design.

3. Explain why fallen direction away from God's structure always results in detrimental consequences.

More Than a Bodily Function

Our culture's attempt to justify freedom to participate in unbridled sexual pleasure without moral constraints isn't a new strategy. Some believers in Corinth compromised with Gnosticism's compartmentalization of the physical and spiritual realms (1 Cor. 6:12–13). But the biblical worldview can't countenance this physical/spiritual divide. What's done with the body is intertwined with the inner person (1 Cor. 6:13–18; Rom.

[Refer to the teacher's margin note "Distorting God's Good Creation" in Chapter 7.]

Students must be able to differentiate between the general categories of God's creation and particular human cultural expressions or products. The general categories of God's creation shouldn't be abandoned, but a particular human sub-creation may have become so corrupt that the only thing believers can do is abandon that particular corrupt human expression for a time. If believers can creatively produce their own sub-creations in their own institutions, then they should. If they can enter back into the public square later on without compromising holiness, then they should. But there are times when Christians themselves don't have the resources, and the public square won't allow faithfulness to God. At that point it is biblically legitimate for Christians to withdraw from a particular activity. The Bible clearly directs Christians not to get involved in activities that demand compromise and disobedience (Eph. 5:7, 11; Prov. 14:16). Christians are required to follow biblical morals; if a job or activity requires violation of those morals, then the activity is expendable. The Christian's duty is to obey God. Christians aren't required to always participate in every social activity. There will be plenty of opportunities elsewhere. Caution: Over time Christians may confuse opposition to the corrupting elements within a social activity with opposition to the social activity itself. This is often invalid.

Illustration: Tertullian's opposition to the Roman games wasn't rooted in a position of isolated withdrawal from society. Neither was he trying to argue that games are inherently sinful and directly were in Scripture

6:12–13). For the believer, the body is the temple of the Holy Spirit (1 Cor. 6:19–20). What's done with the body goes beyond the physical realm; it affects both spiritual and social relationships (1 Thess. 4:3–8; Prov. 6:23–35). Sex is inescapably a moral issue. People in today's culture desperately try to suppress their feelings of guilt (which are impossible to escape) when they engage in immorality. That's why they get so angry when anyone dares to judge (from any angle) the choices they make. Not even a secular feminist motivated by a desire to prevent self-hurt can get away with a critique.

Responding to Sexual Abuse or Assault

- Report it to the police immediately. This is a crime. Regardless of the complexity of the situation or who committed the crime against you, fearing negative responses from others shouldn't prevent you from going to the appropriate governmental authority. The sphere of government was designed by God to hold abusers accountable within other spheres of authority: family, church, business, and so on.

- Get spiritual counsel. Don't isolate yourself, trying to figure out how to respond to the hurt on your own. Even though trust may have been betrayed (perhaps even by someone in spiritual leadership), you need the restoration of your trust in other spiritual leaders who can help you. You will want to find support and help in dealing with this tragedy in a biblical way that will do you the most good and bring God the most glory.

Judging Destructiveness

A red herring is a tactic that is often used to divert a conversation to a point other than the one that has been raised.

Why is the response to Stepp (that she shouldn't judge) a red herring?

Rather than evaluating whether or not immoral actions have negative consequences, the respondent tries to sidestep that evaluation by turning people's attention to debate the appropriateness of any evaluation at all.

What kind of judgment does the Bible condemn and commend?

God condemns the following:

- *rigid and prideful judgments against others whose problems are less severe than our own (Matt. 7:1–5)*
- *the foolishness of presenting good and wise counsel to obstinately profane blasphemers (Matt. 7:6; Luke 9:5)*
- *slanderous judgments without mercy that presume upon God's position as the law-giver and punisher of sin (James 2:12–13; 4:11–12)*

Structure and direction are abstract concepts, and often the best way to understand difficult ideas is to see them worked out in real life. So let's get real practical. How do the labels "structure" and "direction" help us discern the good and evil in real-life situations?

Remember, in this chapter we're focusing on discerning fallen direction. The other direction—the redemptive direction—will have to come up soon, but it will take a back seat till we can explore it more fully in the next unit (Unit 4—Redemption).

In this section we'll discuss the fallen direction of a topic that can't and shouldn't be avoided: sex.

THE SITUATION WE'RE IN

What is sex like in our world? When you look out on the moral landscape of Western sexual life, what do you see?

Asking "what is sex like?" is akin to asking "what are people like?" Sex—like the people who engage in it—is different all over the place. But there are certain observable international trends. One of them is "hooking up," or sex without relationship and without commitment. It's not as if this has never existed before, but it has appeared only recently as part of the national conversation in America.

Washington Post reporter Laura Sessions Stepp wrote a book called *Unhooked: How Young Women Pursue Sex, Delay Love and Lose at Both.* She followed the lives of nine young women, ages sixteen to twenty-one, as they navigated the hookup culture in their high schools and colleges. This culture has developed, Stepp says, in place of the dating culture of earlier American generations. After Stepp befriended these girls, she interviewed them about how they had "hooked up" with varying degrees of eagerness. As a middle-aged feminist, Stepp wrote her book in part to help other young women who are hurt and confused by their own sexual choices.

Not all young women who read Stepp's work were appreciative. One challenged her in an online discussion of her book on the *Post* website: "Do you think that in your book you are making a judgment that hooking up is wrong? . . . As long as people are [practicing safe sex,] then why should they be judged for the choices they make?" Another young woman wrote, "I started hooking up because I felt it was healthier to have [my] physical needs met."[5]

This is the current worldly perspective on sex in the West: sex is not a moral issue at all. It's just a bodily function, like scrubbing dead skin cells off your hands with the right kind of soap. People think the only relevant moral issue is consent. Did the participants agree? Then no one else can say a word.

To people shaped by this view of sex, the Christian perspective sounds repressive—as if Christianity views sex itself negatively. And numbers of ex-Christians claim this is precisely the message they got while they were in church: "Sex is bad. It's a duty for married couples and necessary for the propagation of the species, but it's basically dirty."

CONSENT AND ABUSE

The University of California system has instituted a "yes means yes" policy for sexual activity among its students. This means that any sexual act is permissible as long as both partners explicitly say "yes" to it. Anything else can be called rape if one partner so chooses.[6]

Consent is a moral issue when it comes to sex. Rape and other forms of sexual abuse are horrific things, and one of their worst elements is the violation of human choice that they force on victims.

But consent is not the only relevant moral issue in a sexual act because people can consent to things that are wrong and self-destructive. Secularism reduces people to their physical impulses; the Bible sees people as embodied souls. Damage done to someone's body is a terrible thing, and so is damage done to someone's spirit, his or her "inner being" (Eph. 3:16). And illicit sex, consensual or not, inflicts precisely that kind of internal damage.

God commends the following:

- *prudent recognition of and wariness of corrupt influences (Matt. 7:15–20; Prov. 22:3)*
- *reproof and exhortation given with the intent to restore (James 4:4; 5:19–20)*

Ask students to synthesize these statements about what God condemns and commends and apply these principles to various situations.

Why can't immorality ultimately fulfill its promise of freedom and lasting pleasure?

Violating creational norms always leads to negative and destructive consequences.

What negative consequences commonly distress immoral people?

- *betrayal of friendships and trust of others*
- *deep wounds and scars of emotional hurt*
- *discouragement and confusion*
- *anger and hatred leading even to murder*
- *fear and anxiety because of a double life*
- *divorce, financial upheaval, and vicious child-custody battles*
- *objectification: feelings of being used by others for their own pleasures*
- *STDs and unwanted pregnancies*
- *church discipline for unrepentant believers; loss of fellowship with brothers and sisters in Christ and of life-giving corporate worship*
- *a hardened heart and seared conscience; more corruption and consequences*
- *guilt and condemnation apart from God's gracious forgiveness and restoration*

God's Design and Purpose for Sex

- Sex is a God-created good (Gen 1:28; 2:24–25).

On any number of ex-Christian websites, people testify that they have been liberated from the Christian view and now see sex as simply a pleasurable, healthy exercise. One convert to atheism—sadly, the daughter of a Christian leader—wrote,

> For a long time I couldn't have sex with my boyfriend (of over a year by this point) without crippling guilt. I had anxiety that I was going to Hell. I felt like I was standing upon glass, and, though I knew it was safe, every time I glanced down I saw death.[7]

"Christianity," such people often say, "guilted me into thinking that sex was bad, but I discovered when I tried it that I had been lied to. I just had to get past my inhibitions." To a culture that views sexual freedom as the highest good and sexual pleasure as the very definition of pleasure, Christianity's view of sex sounds downright sacrilegious.

THE STRUCTURE OF SEX

As you stand on the part of life's timeline before marriage, you're going to have to take someone else's word for what the best way forward is. You (hopefully) don't know from personal experience which sexual choices will bring you pain and which will bring you present and eternal joy.

So trust what the Creator of sex says: the world has everything backwards when it comes to sex (1 Pet. 4:3). The ultimately biblical concepts of structure and direction can help us get it straight. What's structural about sex, and how is it being bent in fallen directions?

The structure is clear in Scripture: God created sex, so sex is good. ("Sex is bad" is not the Christian view.) Sex's structure is revealed in many places in the Bible, but it can be boiled down to this—Enjoy sexual intercourse often—within the covenant bonds of exclusive, one-on-one, heterosexual marriage. (See Exod. 20:14; 1 Cor. 7:1–6.)

Paul is very clear that married couples should engage in sexual intercourse regularly (1 Cor. 7:4–5). And one of the reasons he says so is that sex has incredible spiritual power: it unites people. Sex is structured to unite a man and a woman on a deep level, and that created purpose doesn't go away even when the man is an adulterer and the woman is a prostitute. Paul said, "He who is joined to a prostitute becomes one body with her" (1 Cor. 6:16), and then to prove this point Paul quoted the Genesis 2:24 principle: "They shall become one flesh." The created structure of sex can't be avoided; it's present even in a wicked place like a brothel.

> *"Prostitution does not eliminate the goodness of human sexuality; political tyranny cannot wipe out the divinely ordained character of the state."*[8]
>
> — AL WOLTERS

Paul doesn't focus on the joy of sex, but other parts of the Bible do. God's main answer to worldly perspectives on sex is the promise of enjoyment. In fact, there's an entire book of the Bible dedicated to painting the "structure" of sex in beautiful colors. You may have been told that this Bible book isn't about sex at all, but about something "spiritual" (sex *is* spiritual, of course). But there's no way around it: God devotes a whole book of the Bible to sex. That book is Song of Solomon (or Song of Songs). And it doesn't take a clinical approach to sexuality, like an instruction manual; it's celebratory. The point is to praise profoundly, with intense poetry, the enjoyment God gives to married men and women so that you're enticed to follow God's plan. Why work at engaging in sex rightly? Because, when practiced according to its created structure, there is no joy quite like it.

Healthy Inhibitions and Fears

Evaluate the claims of "ex-Christians" by discussing the following questions.

Are biblical warnings about the danger of immorality actually guilt-tripping or are they loving and wise counsel leading back to God's design?

Are you safe because you enjoy something and can get away with it for some time?

What's the consistent evidence of the long-term effects of immoral relationships? Has sexual freedom brought happiness or chaos to cultures and families?

What's the biblical answer to the those who claim that they were lied to about the dangers of illicit sex? Is the danger of immorality real or imagined? Why do they think it's imagined?

Provide biblical answers by discussing the warnings in Proverbs 2:16–19; 5:5, 21-23; 7:1-27.

The warnings are motivated out of loving and wise counsel (Prov. 7:1–5).

Going down the immorality road may seem harmless in the first part of the journey, but the road inevitably leads to spiritual death as well as to eventual destruction (Prov. 5:5, 21–23; 7:26–27).

A wise person can observe many illustrations—in the culture at large and in one's own social circles—of the heartbreaking havoc and hurt that immorality causes (Eccles. 2:1–2, 8; Neh. 13:26).

The danger of immorality is real. People who believe they can play with fire (immorality) and not be burned (suffer the consequences) are either ignorant or foolish (Prov. 6:27–29).

People who think this is all imagination simply haven't experienced their demise yet (Prov. 7:26–27).

- Sex has God-designed creational boundaries: exclusive, permanent, and heterosexual (Exod. 20:14; Prov. 5:15–18; Matt. 5:32; 19:4–6, 9; Rom. 1:26–27; 1 Cor. 6:9; 1 Tim. 3:2; 5:9).
- God intends for married couples to procreate (Gen. 1:28; 9:1; Titus 2:4; 1 Tim. 5:14).
- God intends for married couples to be united in oneness on a deep level (Gen. 2:24).
- God intends for married couples to enjoy sex (Prov. 5:18–19; Song of Sol. 1:2; 7:6).
- God doesn't intend for married couples to consistently abstain from sex (1 Cor. 7:4–5).

Sex Is Good; Immorality Is Bad

A straw-man argument is an argument that carelessly (or purposefully) caricatures the position of one's opponent—a position he wouldn't ever actually consider trying to defend. Often, it's so ridiculous that anyone familiar with the true position will be able to spot it immediately. This is what a number of "ex-Christians" attempt to do with the biblical teaching about sex as presented by conservative Christians. The Bible never says that sex is dirty or bad. The Bible teaches that participating in sex contrary to God's creational design and structure is destructive. In other words, the Bible never condemns sex; it only condemns immorality, which distorts God's good creative design for sex. To say that the Bible is repressive or that it teaches that sex is bad is a straw-man argument. It's not what the Bible actually teaches.

Resources on Purity and Dating

Gerald Hiestand and Jay Thomas, *Sex, Dating, and Relationships: A Fresh Approach* (Wheaton: Crossway, 2012).

Joshua Harris, *Not Even A Hint: Guarding Your Heart Against Lust* (Sisters, OR: Multnomah Publishers, 2003).

Heath Lambert, *Finally Free: Fighting for Purity with the Power of Grace* (Grand Rapids: Zondervan, 2013).

Richard D. Phillips and Sharon L. Phillips, *Holding Hands, Holding Hearts: Recovering a Biblical View of Christian Dating* (Phillipsburg, NJ: P&R, 2006).

More Righteous than God

Does God approve of those who promote more rigorous standards than He has given?

No, you violate God's Word by constructing standards that condemn what God has approved. Ironically, this actually makes a person less sanctified (Matt. 23:1–39). Fearing God and keeping His commands brings life (Eccles. 12:13). The gospel liberates you from human traditions (1 Tim. 1:3–8; 4:1–7; Col. 2:8–23).

Are applications that put biblical principles into practice the same as extrabiblical standards people construct?

No, the Bible doesn't give an encyclopedic list of dos and don'ts for every situation. Believers must be able to apply the Bible, connecting the principles to concrete standards within their own context (Eph. 5:10).

How to Fight Sexual Sin

• Admit that it is sin.

The addictive nature of sin (especially sexual immorality) has caused some Christians to debate whether it is a matter of sinful choices or biological make-up. But the Bible recognizes the addictive control of our fallen selves over our choices; it describes this as slavery to natural desires (Rom. 6:12–13).

[Note: The following four excerpts are taken from *Addictions: A Banquet in the Grave* by Edward T. Welch, ISBN 978-0-87558606-3, pages 33–36. Used by permission of P&R Publishing Company, P. O. Box 817, Phillipsburg, NJ 008865, www.prpbooks.com]

Our slavery . . . may include actual physical dysfunction, but it goes much deeper than that. It is an infection of the human heart. Although voluntary, we are inclined to it. We want it. Our will is bent toward it. Indeed, we are powerless. Where we are powerless is in changing our inclination and desires. We cannot do it apart from God [Rom. 6:5–11, 14]. [Welch, *Addictions*, 34]

• Understand dominating sin.

While a person is responsible for his choices, he can't control his sin; sin controls him.

Sin is more than conscious choices. Like a cruel taskmaster, sin victimizes and controls us (John 8:34). It captures and overtakes (Gal. 6:1). In fact, there are times when we intend to do one thing but sin causes us to do things we don't want to do. Even though we may really want to change, it can seem like an overwhelming or impossible task to actually do so [Rom. 7]. . . . *Sin feels exactly like a disease.* It feels as if

Of course, we shouldn't forget the first purpose God gives in Scripture for sex: procreation. Part of the joy of sex is the privilege of being used by God to bring into existence more image-bearers. Bearing children after the Fall is painful; and that same Fall has poisoned male-female relations, making sex difficult for many couples. But the potential to bring children into the world and the joyful power of sex to unite a married couple are both precious values that need to be protected.

SEX IN ITS FALLEN DIRECTION

If sex had no created structure, you could do whatever you wanted and, if you played your hormones right, you'd get away with it. Sex couldn't be bent in wrong directions if there were no structure to bend. But when the author of *Unhooked* was told by a reader of her book not to judge the hookup culture, she replied wisely, "There are no condoms for the heart. Girls shouldn't fool themselves into thinking that just because they're enjoying a physical experience, they won't feel something afterward. Example: the number of girls who check their cell phones the day after a hookup, wondering why he hasn't called or messaged them."[9]

Sex—as part of its created nature—unites people, even if they say they don't care and don't want it to. And men can't escape that created structure any more than women can. Solomon asked this question about adulterers many centuries ago: "Can a man carry fire next to his chest and his clothes not be burned?" (Prov. 6:27). If Solomon were writing today, he might say, "Can you keep porn on your phone and never experience any negative consequences? Can you play the field for ten years with no adverse effects on your eventual marriage?" A man who uses a woman solely for her body is denying that she bears God's image. He's insulting her Maker. He's violating the most beautiful earthly picture of Christ's relationship to His church (Eph. 5:31–32). He's twisting a structure God made. Make no mistake: it's not just girls who face negative consequences for engaging in extramarital sex.

Sex, of course, gets twisted in a lot more ways than those mentioned here. Sexual abuse of minors, for example, is a horrendous sin with lasting consequences (Luke 17:1–2). The Bible says that "it is shameful even to speak of the things" that wicked

---

SATISFACTION, SEXUAL SINS, AND SINGLENESS

You're living in a unique time in world history. The internal pressure to give in to sexual immorality is just as intense as ever, but Satan now has more powerful and invasive weapons than he's ever had before. The internet is a great tool for many good purposes, but it's also the most efficient spreader of sexual immorality ever invented. You may be addicted to online porn—or trapped by a hundred other kinds of sexual sin, from graphic romance novels to sexting.

Get help. It's not too late for you. You're not meant to fight your battles alone. Seek out a trusted parent, pastor, or teacher. God, by His grace and the power of the Holy Spirit, can make sexual sin a thing of your past (1 Cor. 6:9–11). "The blood of Jesus. . . . cleanses us from all sin" (John 1:7).

There are many illicit sexual pleasures available to the singles in Western society. If you're a Christian, you must deny yourself—but not merely for the sake of denial. You must set before yourself a grand and holy motivation: one day God will very likely give you the pure sexual satisfaction found only in a spouse. The need for self-denial and the battle against lust won't end when your wedding day arrives.

But you will enter a very different phase. God's advice to singles of marriageable age is pretty blunt: "Because of the temptation to sexual immorality, each man should have his own wife and each woman her own husband. . . . For it is better to marry than to burn with passion" (1 Cor. 7:2, 9). God's normal answer to sexual temptation is a husband or a wife.

---

something outside ourselves has taken over. In fact, one of Scripture's images for sin *is* disease (e.g., Isa. 1:5–6). . . . In sin, we are both hopelessly out of control and shrewdly calculating; victimized yet responsible. All sin is simultaneously pitiable slavery and overt rebelliousness or selfishness. . . . Addicts genuinely feel out of control, but they are also making choices rooted in their own self-centeredness and pride. Since this is an apparent paradox, we tend to emphasize one or the other. Theology, however, keeps us balanced. Sometimes we will stress the in-control nature of our hearts; at other times we will emphasize the powerlessness and slavery of addictive behaviors. [Welch, *Addictions*, 33, 34, 36]

• Pursue change through the gospel and progressive sanctification.

If you deny the out-of-control nature of all addictions . . . then you assume that everyone would have the power to change himself. Change would be easy. . . . There would never be a sense of helplessness or a desperate need for both redemption and power through Jesus. [Welch, *Addictions*, 34–35]

There will be other problems if you ignore the in-control, purposeful nature of addictions. . . . If personal responsibility is ignored, addicts are ultimately helpless before their alleged disease. All they see in the future is the fear of passing it on to their children. Scripture counters these fears with 'and that is what some of you *were*' (1 Cor. 6:11). Where there is sin, God always

DIRECTION: BAD
hookup culture

STRUCTURE
within the covenant bonds of exclusive, one-on-one, heterosexual marriage

DIRECTION: BAD
forbidding marriage

people do "in secret" (Eph. 5:12). Because sex is such a powerful experience, people have dedicated immense energy to inventing ways to bend it away from God's structure.

And it's possible to bend sex in something other than a libertine* direction. Paul warned about those who "forbid marriage," and it was partly in response to them that he said, "Everything created by God is good, and nothing is to be rejected if it is received with thanksgiving" (1 Tim. 4:4). Some religious groups today have the reputation, at least, of being prudish.* Whether this is fair or not, the Victorian era is often thought to be one in which respectable people were much more eager to talk about death than about sex. (In our era, of course, it's just the opposite.) Perhaps some people do need to be exposed to Song of Songs and to verses such as Proverbs 5:18–19, where God tells husbands to be "intoxicated" with the love—and the bodies—of their wives. If people do exist who deny that sex ought to be pleasurable, that's what they need to hear. But there seem to be very few of them left in America.

libertine: *totally disregarding moral rules*

prudish: *excessively wary of any discussion of sexual topics*

THINKING IT THROUGH 9.2

1. What does the hookup culture insist you can do without? What's problematic with this viewpoint?

2. Why isn't it legitimate to claim that the Bible opposes sex? Why do some unbelievers say that the biblical position is repressive?

3. For what purposes did God design sexual relations?

4. According to 1 Timothy 4:1–3, what sexual deviation was being promoted by those who had departed from the faith?

♡5. Why is the created structure for marriage the only appropriate means for fulfilling God's purposes for sex?

1. It insists you can do without a committed relationship with moral constraints. Sex isn't just an external bodily function; it has moral effects on the whole person internally.

2. God created sex—not only for dutiful propagation of children but also for pleasure. Some people want complete freedom to engage in it however they wish but the Bible restricts it to monogamous marriage between a husband and wife.

3. Sex is meant to unite a man and a woman physically for procreation (Gen. 1:28) and enjoyment (Song of Solomon) and also spiritually for an intimate relationship (1 Cor. 6:16–18; 7:4–5).

4. forbidding marriage and by implication any sexual relationship

♡5. Only a covenantal, exclusive, one-on-one, heterosexual marriage can properly fulfill the one-flesh relationship that God designed; every deviation is labeled as perversion because it contradicts, in one way or another, the God-designed one-flesh relationship.

SECTION OBJECTIVES 9.3

1. Explain and exemplify how material goods can be directed toward or away from God's structure.

2. Explain and exemplify how technology can be directed toward or away from God's structure.

3. Explain and exemplify how language can be directed toward or away from God's structure.

offers forgiveness and the power to cast it off. [Welch, *Addictions*, 35]

Progressive sanctification denies that perfection can be achieved short of glorification; expect the fallen nature to always be present and never change (Gal. 5:17). However, progress can be made. Mature believers learn to stop feeding their sinful inclinations and to say no to their flesh (Gal. 5:16, 25).

Keep the Focus on the Gospel

What should prevent promiscuity—the fear of STDs, failed marriages, emotional confusion, or loss of reputation? Some of these may well be the inevitable fallout of a destructive life that bends God's designed structure in the wrong direction. But the central problem with promiscuity isn't the negative side effects (as significant and devastating as those can be); the central problem is spiritual. The one-flesh relationship of marriage is supposed to image the church's single-minded and wholehearted relationship to Christ (Eph. 5:31–32). Those joined to Christ and indwelt by the Spirit can't join their bodies to prostitutes without hindering their relationship with God (1 Cor. 6:15-20). Both physical adultery and spiritual adultery are reprehensible (Jer. 13:27; 29:23; Mal. 3:5; 1 Cor. 6:9; James 4:4) even to a loving, merciful, and forgiving God (Hos. 3:1; Matt. 21:31-32; Heb. 11:31). The gospel that heals the hurt caused by promiscuity should also be the means for preventing that hurt in the first place. The gospel refocuses one's vision on the truth behind what God created sexual relations to picture by the marriage covenant: the exclusivity of the spiritual oneness and intimacy that believers can have with God (1 John 3:3; Rev. 19:7).

 A Biblical Theology of Wealth

The Bible is replete with passages that pertain to wealth and poverty. A whole host of passages could be appealed to in order to try to support the health-and-wealth gospel that some promote: "God wants you to be prosperous and happy; and if you're not, then you must not be blessed by Him." On the other hand, a whole host of passages could be appealed to in order to try to support a monastic life of denial: "God only loves and blesses the poor who give up all their earthly possessions." The Bible's teaching isn't contradictory; it holds in tension two truths that must be harmonized and balanced (Prov. 30:8–9).

Here's how one theologian summarizes this tension as recognized in Psalms, Proverbs, and Ecclesiastes:

> Two of the themes of these three books stand in a certain tension with each other. On the one hand, the "prosperity gospel" of the Deuteronomist is preserved. Industry and faithfulness lead to God's covenant blessings, including material well-being (Pss. 112; 128; Prov. 12:11; 13:21; 21:5). On the other hand, continuing the theme of Job, these wisdom writers recognize that many of the poor and suffering in this life never find relief for their lot, while many wicked rich people continue to flourish (Ps. 37:16–17; Prov. 15:16–17; 16:8). Although it is debated to what extent these books envision a full-orbed future life, some resolution of this tension clearly appears in the theme of justice in a coming world (Ps. 49:10–20).

[Craig L. Blomberg, *Neither Poverty nor Riches: A Biblical Theology of Possessions* (Downers Grove, IL: InterVarsity Press, 1999), 60]

Symptoms of Materialism

What might be some common practical symptoms of materialism?

Open-handed symptoms: overspending, failing to stick to a budget, compulsive buying, and the like

Tight-fisted symptoms: hoarding wealth, refusing to give to others, and so on

What is the root problem underlying the symptoms?

It's covetousness—the lust of greedily desiring what we don't have, which is often a result of envying what others do have. This usually accompanies dissatisfaction with circumstances and acting independently of God.

List and summarize some of the Bible's warnings about covetousness.

- *Matthew 6:19–34; Luke 12:13–34: Beware of idolatrously hoarding possessions or anxiously worrying about a lack of possessions.*
- *Matthew 19:22–24: Beware of devoting your life to possessions rather than to God.*
- *1 Timothy 6:6–19: Beware of the love for money that tempts you to do evil to get it; beware of the love for money that tempts you to be discontented with the basic necessities of life; beware of the love for money that tempts you to place hope and security in the uncertainty of riches; beware of the love for money because it can lead to wandering from the faith to hell.*

How can you diagnose a materialistic attitude?

Ask yourself questions like these:

- *Am I content with my circumstances?*
- *Do I show gratitude for what I have?*
- *Can I trust God to take care of me?*
- *Do I envy others' blessings?*
- *Do my plans revolve around getting rich?*
- *Do I think happiness and security can be achieved with money?*

Work to Give

Read Ephesians 4:28.

What does the verse prohibit?

stealing

What does the verse commend?

laboring honestly with your own hands

Why does it commend labor?

Having met your own needs, you can share your abundance with others who are in need.

How should this affect current and future career plans and motivations as well as practical budgeting?

Students should plan to budget their money to cover their expenses. But they should also create a category for giving out of compassion to those in need—maybe even beyond simply giving to their local church. They can give directly to someone in need.

Technology Pitfalls

Any time a person critiques technology, he must make clear that highlighting dangers isn't meant to dissuade people from using the technology. Most technologies have appropriate uses. The critique is meant to encourage the careful use of the technology. It's meant to help people avoid pitfalls that come with it.

Have you ever seen a caricature? It's a picture of someone with purposefully distorted features. A large nose becomes a huge nose; a spacious forehead becomes a football-field-sized one. Presidents and other public leaders probably get caricatured more often than anyone else. A good caricaturist manages to hold on to enough reality that the leader is still instantly recognizable.

A good caricature exaggerates certain features but leaves enough reality to make the figure recognizable.

Sin is a caricature—a messed up, distorted image of the way things are supposed to be. But the image is still recognizable. Fallen people are still people; they don't become dogs after their one-millionth sin. Broken families are still families. Cussing is still language. Despite the fears of many English grammarians over the centuries, all the grammatical faults (and the cussing) of the masses have never succeeded in killing the capacity for linguistic communication. Sin has distorted every created thing to some degree, but never so much that the created order itself breaks down.

The previous section examined one created thing—sex—that people have twisted in sinful directions. But fallen sex, as we saw, is still sex. Sex still does the deep uniting of people that God created it to do. The created order never breaks down.

This section looks at several more examples of fallen direction twisting the created structure: materialism, technology, and language.

MISGUIDED MATERIALISM

Throughout most of this book, *materialism* is used to name the philosophical position that matter is all that exists. That's sense 1 for the word in most dictionaries. But listen to sense 2: "the tendency to treat material possessions and physical comfort as more important or desirable than spiritual values; a way of life based on material interests."[10] One clever person has called this "affluenza."[11] If matter really is all that exists, then you might as well get all the matter you can—especially the green paper matter with pictures of presidents on it. Have your best life now. He who dies with the most toys wins.

EPICUREANISM AND MATERIALISM

Most major ideas out there are not new. Materialism—the idea that matter is all there is—is a philosophy that can be traced back at least to Epicurus, a Greek philosopher who died almost three hundred years before Jesus was born. Epicurus stressed that pleasure was the only thing we know to be good. He doubted the existence of the gods and recommended that people not engage in crime not because it was wrong but because they might get caught—and might worry about getting caught, diminishing their pleasure. Ironically, *materialism* today often means trying to amass a lot of stuff since this world is all we get. But Epicurus took his philosophy of materialism in the opposite direction: the more stuff you have, the more worries you create. So live simply.

Materialism is, quite obviously, not a Christian point of view. Jesus said, "Do not lay up for yourselves treasures on earth, where moth and rust destroy and where thieves break in and steal, but lay up for yourselves treasures in heaven" (Matt. 6:19–20).

So what possible created good could lie at the heart of materialism? Matter. Stuff is intrinsically good because God made it. It's part of the structure of creation. That doesn't mean you should get as much as you can; that would be bending the acquisition of stuff in a fallen direction. God tells us to give some stuff away to the church and to poor people, and He warns us that stuff can be used for fallen purposes.

But God put us into a material world, and you're going to have to gather some of those materials if you hope to do God's will. "Everything created by God is good, and nothing is to be rejected if it is received with thanksgiving" (1 Tim. 4:4). Paul later tells the rich not to "set their hopes on the uncertainty of riches, but on God, who richly provides us with everything to enjoy" (1 Tim. 6:17). God gives us stuff, and He gives it to us for our enjoyment. But when we set our hopes on and organize our lives around that stuff, we're guilty of materialism. Materialism twists something good in an evil direction.

TWISTED TECHNOLOGY

Technology is a broad term for the tools humans develop to aid them in the work of dominion. If you're a Christian, you probably believe that materialism is wrong, but you may assume—at least in practice—that technology is all good.

And it is, at heart. God structured the world to require tools. We aren't Inspector Gadgets with built-in magnifying glasses, drills, and earth movers hiding in our hats. We need to invent and construct tools to help us do our work.

We don't usually think of all our tools—hammers, tape measures—as "technology," just those tools that have microchips in them. Tech gadgets are so useful. How can such amazing tools as these be twisted in fallen directions?

Simply put, when technology gets bent, we become the tools of our tools. Our tools become our gods, and we become their devoted servants. And that goes beyond the obvious things, like people who cannot stop texting even when they're driving. Technological tools, for all their power for good, also have the power to shape their users in negative ways they don't see.

It goes beyond the obvious fact that television, movies, and the internet are efficient spreaders of wicked content. No, technology itself has power regardless of what's on the screen, and tools themselves carry messages. Every piece of technology implies something about the way the world ought to be, and every piece of technology both gives and takes away. It makes some things easier and some things more difficult.

Let's take television as an example. TV is a well-accepted technology, one that is being transformed by the internet age but by no means destroyed. TV assumes that people need constant access to entertainment, and it makes nonstop diversion possible. It also makes it possible to tell certain rich stories that don't fit well in books or movies. At one time TV made possible a fairly united American culture: everybody watched the same shows because there were only three or four channels to watch across the nation.

money do you spend (or ask your parents to spend)? Log your time per day and per week. The goal shouldn't be to eliminate all entertainment and nonessential spending; the goal is to see whether or not a major imbalance can be easily identified.

How would you evaluate the positive and negative effects?

Is the quality of your schoolwork affected?

Does it affect time with God and family?

Can you profitably use technology for community service, church ministry, a job, or honing other worthwhile skills?

  ### The Pitfall of Distraction

Poll students to see how many believe multitasking is good and that they can do it well.

It's just so seductive to think you can multitask. But when the brain has to switch-switch-switch-switch-switch, each realignment from one task to another requires time and mental energy. . . . Is it possible to do A, B, C, and D? Yes, but if you monotasked, doing A, then B, then C, then D instead of A-B-A-C-D-B-A-C-D-C-B-D-C-D-B-A, it will probably take less time overall, be much less stressful, and result in a better product at the end. . . . Multitasking isn't about doing multiple things at once; it's about managing multiple distractions. Multitasking shatters focus and concentration.

[Gregory L. Jantz with Ann McMurray, *Hooked: The Pitfalls of Media, Technology, and Social Networking* (Lake Mary, FL: Siloam, 2012), 45]

  ### The Pitfall of Cognitive Decline

"Our digital gadgets are so smart that we don't have to be so smart ourselves. . . . We don't have to remember how to spell words, do math, or research a project. We can get any answer we need with the click of a mouse. . . . Rote learning has taken over what used to be reasoned learning." [Archibald D. Hart and Sylvia Hart Frejd, *The Digital Invasion* (Grand Rapids: Baker, 2013), 43]

This may sound attractive to the immature and lazy student. But it has massive downsides. Ask students what they are.

"This easy access to a lot of information is . . . reshaping our creativity, inventiveness, and ingenuity" [Hart and Frejd, 43].

In addition, people who can't analyze presuppositions will simply be skill-performing cogs within a larger political machine.

What are some technology pitfalls?

- *Idolatry: Secularists often look to technology as the savior of humanity and the key to a better future. New, innovative ways supercede older, outmoded traditional ways.*
- *Materialism: It amplifies covetousness. People always want new and improved.*
- *Corruption: It provides easy accessibility to pornography, ungodly music, and so forth.*
- *Self-absorption: It allows people to ignore the community around them.*
- *Self-importance: It lends status or becomes an image-maker.*
- *Unethical decisions: Whatever is possible becomes acceptable.*
- *Engrossing diversion: Rather than being a useful tool for people, people become its tool.*
- *Cognitive decline: Thought patterns are diverted from linear, analytical thinking and replaced with visual, emotional responses.*

Resources Regarding Technology

John Dyer, *From the Garden to the City: The Redeeming and Corrupting Power of Technology* (Grand Rapids: Kregel, 2011).

Neil Postman, *Technopoly: The Surrender of Culture to Technology* (New York: Vintage Books, 1992).

Nicholas Carr, *The Shallows* (New York: W. W. Norton & Company, 2010).

 ### Is Your Use of Technology Wise and Helpful?

We tend to underestimate how much time and resources get squandered. Chart it out. When you are using tech gadgets, how much time is spent on entertainment versus necessary tasks for school, work, or to accomplish a chore to help others? How much

Corrupt Language

Your Knowledge

It should be sufficient to know that a word is vulgar because it makes use of a picturesque comparison to excrement or sexual activity in order to add power to an exclamatory outburst. If you're ignorant of the particularities, you shouldn't feel the need to even look it up; being innocent in your knowledge of evil isn't necessarily bad (Rom. 16:19).

Your Own Speech

Legalists may feel that as long as they don't say the really bad words on the "forbidden list," frowned on by their circle of society, then they can feel comfortable using replacement words that also refer to excrement (*crap*) sexual activity (*freakin'*), or that covertly invoke the Lord's name (*gosh*) or spiritual things (*heck*). But you should care about the spirit behind what Scripture teaches about corrupt talk (Eph. 4:29). You should want to make sure that your *ideas* are clean as well as the particular words you choose to express them. If that's the case, then you will want to eliminate from your vocabulary even the replacement words that mean the same thing as the words on the "forbidden list."

Words in Context

Impure people like to twist pure things out of context (Titus 1:15) and then snicker at the evil connotations that they foist onto innocent subject matter. They also like to attribute impure connotations to otherwise innocent things. If someone confronts them, they accuse the person of having a gutter mind. But God doesn't play this game; He will judge the unrighteous (Prov. 10:23; 11:20).

But think of what the medium of television itself leads viewers to expect: entertainment or diversion. Like Twinkies, this isn't so bad taken in small doses. But some people leave the TV on all day (and eat Twinkies the whole time). American kids watch as much as thirty-five hours of television a week—the same number of hours French people are legally permitted to work.[12] What does that many weekly hours of diversion do to people—especially kids?[13]

A technology like television is very difficult to resist, no matter what it is you're watching. Humans were created by God to enjoy entertainment. That's part of our structure in this created order. But TV can easily bend that structure—actually, bloat it—into something monstrous.

CORRUPTED COMMUNICATION

Language is actually not a creation of God, or not exactly. But it's not a creation of humans either. Language may in fact be part of God's essence; the three persons of the Trinity appear to have used language before the creation of the world (Gen. 1:26). And even today they use it among themselves (John 16:13–15). When God made the first image-bearers, they were invited to share the divine privilege of language.

> "Language is wonderful and mysterious. It is so because it is a gift of God to us. It reflects and reveals him."[14]
>
> —VERN POYTHRESS

Individual human languages, however, do appear to be subsequent creations of God. English, Chinese, Urdu, and all other languages can trace their roots to Babel (Gen. 11). And what amazing creations they are! Do you realize that almost every sentence you speak, if it's long enough, is a brand new creation in the history of the world? No one has ever said exactly those words—and yet people understand you perfectly. The capacity for language is clearly hard-wired into human babies; animals can communicate (anyone with a dog or a cat knows this), but they don't have language. The complex rules of syntax that you grasped as a toddler are far beyond them.[15]

The created structure of human communication is evident all throughout the Bible. Words exist, most fundamentally, for the love of God and neighbor. And they have great power to accomplish these purposes. Words can praise God, sing to God, describe God, and pray to God. They can edify, encourage, and instruct people. Words don't just transmit information; they do things. They change our world.[16]

That's the structure of human communication. But what does language look like when twisted in fallen directions? Let's look at just two cases—too much language and bad language.

Too Much Language

On April 1 one year, National Public Radio posted a link to an article on its Facebook page with a big headline: "Why Doesn't America Read Anymore?" Only there was no article, just a short explanation that the whole post was an April Fool's joke. But the commenters weighed in anyway, ignoring the "article" and posting their thoughts after having read only the headline. One Facebook commenter blamed "I-Pads and smart Phones." Another complained, "People don't have the attention span or the patience to read."[17] They didn't get the joke.

The internet has made it possible to be slow to hear and quick to speak on a global scale. Quick speech is not all bad; Twitter and other social media have given a voice to oppressed people in nations run by tyrannical governments. But they've also given a voice to "trolls," people who troll around the internet looking for people to verbally

---

 ### Structure and Direction Applied to Other Spheres

Refer to the three-part activity that applies structure and direction in the realm of education (Activities 16a, 16b, 16c). You may also want to discuss a number of other spheres in relation to structure and direction: healthcare, journalism, music, and so forth.

abuse and conversations to ruin. And most significantly, the internet has provided a platform for so many voices that no one could possibly keep up with it all. For all the good it does, the internet has become something of a worldwide shouting match.

"Be not rash with your mouth," Solomon advised, "nor let your heart be hasty to utter a word before God, for God is in heaven and you are on earth. Therefore let your words be few" (Eccles. 5:2). James says Christians should be "quick to hear, slow to speak" (James 1:19). These verses reveal one way the amazing gift of language gets twisted in our fallen world. People use too much of it in the presence of others. They talk too much. The created structure of language is built on love for God and others. When you talk too much, you twist that purpose to your own ends.

Bad Language

Why are cuss words bad? Have you ever wondered that? Mom's "because I said so" is a sufficient answer for six-year-olds, but not for you. Try applying the concepts of structure and direction here. Bad words are bad, generally speaking, because they take some of the most personal and sacred things in the universe and twist them in the wrong direction, out of the structures they belong to.

Religious terms used for cursing—names and words such as *God*, *Christ*, *damn*, and *hell*—take some of the most powerful realities in all human existence and wrench them out of place. The existence of damnation is one of the most terrible realities we know; and the love and authority of Jesus Christ make up the most glorious reality we know. These words belong in serious and reverent places. Cuss words throw these realities in the dirt. Their power is still present, even in the dirt, but it's twisted. People want that power; that's why these words are used by so many—even atheists who deny that Christ condemns anyone to hell.

It's similar for words that describe sexual and excretory functions. Sex has intrinsic power, and using sexual words as curses twists that power out of the only place it belongs, the marriage bed. Song of Solomon does speak literally of sexual matters (e.g., 1:13)—but only to a point. Beyond that, it resorts to figurative language (2:3–4).[18] The most graphic sexual imagery in the Bible is reserved for intense divine denunciations of Israel's sins. (See Ezek. 16.)

"Modern thinking typically supposes," writes Christian thinker Ron Horton, "that the goodness of nature justifies the flaunting of nature and . . . that the impulse for concealment implies shame." This is a wrong idea, Horton says. "The divine view combines high respect and secrecy."[19] There are times to talk about sexual and excretory functions. There's a structure to human communication that creates safe spaces for each kind of talk. But those spaces are private. Far from shaming those things, it gives them the kind of respect and privacy they deserve (1 Cor. 12:23–24).

Right Language

Human communication, including language, gets twisted all day long all over the world. About the only people who don't misuse their tongues are infants—though some of them get so angry that you sense they would curse if they could. But let's make a simple CFR point: language is still a good thing, despite the twisting. "No human being can tame the tongue" (James 3:8); it's true, but taking a lifelong vow of silence is not the solution to twisted speech. Your goal in language isn't merely negative—to avoid talking too much or saying the wrong thing. It should be positive—using the right words to bless God and your neighbor.

1. The God-created structure of the world is material, which God designed humans to make use of and enjoy.

2. when the tool begins to control you or constantly divert you

3. The purpose is to love God and others. Words that praise, sing, describe, and pray to God and words that edify, encourage, and instruct people don't just transmit information but accomplish things that affect lives in the world.

4. too much language and bad language

♡5. Using religious words out of context demeans the realities as if they didn't really exist or hijacks them as if you had the power to make such serious pronouncements. Using words referring to bodily functions out of context ignores the respect and privacy reserved for these realities.

STRUCTURE STICKS AROUND

The existence of corrupt politicians doesn't eliminate the goodness of government. The existence of hatred doesn't eliminate the goodness of emotion. (In fact, it's our moral duty to hate certain things in a fallen world. David wrote in Psalm 139:21, "Do I not hate those who hate you, O Lord?") Everywhere you turn in your daily experience you will see created structures skewed in fallen directions. You will see good creations of God twisted, bent, bloated, and shrunken into caricatures of what God intended. But the Fall isn't the end of the story. Rest assured that God can untwist, unbend, unbloat, and unshrink His creation.

And He will. Read on.

THINKING IT THROUGH 9.3

1. Why would it be wrong (and impossible) to reject the use and enjoyment of all material goods?

2. At what point does a good tool become twisted in a fallen direction?

3. Identify the purpose and describe the power of communication.

4. What are two major ways in which communication can be twisted in a fallen direction?

♡5. Why shouldn't religious words and bodily functions be used as curses?

9 CHAPTER REVIEW

Scripture Memory

Ephesians 5:10-11

Making Connections

1. When humans bend God's good creation in a wrong direction, what should be the twofold response of Christians?

2. What's the only moral stipulation demanded by secularists for sexual relations? Why isn't this sufficient?

3. Does the Bible teach that sex is good or bad? Explain your answer.

4. How does consumeristic materialism follow from philosophical materialism?

Developing Skills in Apologetics and Worldview

5. How should you respond to someone who says that the way God made one particular marriage—Adam and Eve's—doesn't rule out the possibility that other arrangements (polygamous, homosexual, etc.) might be acceptable to Him?

6. If you were Miss (or Mr.) Ferguson, what would you say to the first-grader with his middle finger up?

Examining Assumptions and Evidence

7. Is there any created thing that is not being bent either toward or away from God's design?

8. Why is there a limit on how long and how far humans can bend God's creation in a wrong direction?

9. Why is God's structure for sex the only righteous means of sexual expression?

10. Why is technology good? Why is it so powerful?

Becoming a Creative Cultivator

11. In one or two paragraphs, briefly evaluate an additional created structure using the paradigm of structure and direction. (Topic ideas: art, literature, music, hunting, automotive design, journalism, engineering, or biology.)

CHAPTER REVIEW ANSWERS

Making Connections

1. Once the bending is discerned, it must be exposed and Christians must seek to bend it back toward God's good creation.

2. the consent of adults; because adults can consent to things that are wrong and self-destructive both to the body and to the soul

3. Sex is good because it was created by God for the purpose of procreation and pleasure in a one-flesh marriage. Only that which contradicts the God-designed one-flesh marriage is bad because it is destructive to God's purposes.

4. If the material world is all there is, then it only makes sense to put your hope in and structure your life around stuff.

Developing Skills in Apologetics and Worldview

5. Adam and Eve's marriage wasn't just one example of a marriage. According to Jesus, it was reflective of God's creational design for the operation of the world (Matt. 19:4). Everything else is contrary to God's design. Living contrary to the inherent design of the created order is self-destructive.

6. [*Note:* The illustration is from the previous chapter on page 114, but it is applied in this chapter on page 133.] A first-grader needs simple instruction that it's wrong to communicate in a way that everybody would assume is dirty regardless of his own inward intent.

Examining Assumptions and Evidence

7. Since the world is fallen, it is no longer in line with God's original design. Therefore, every use of God's creation in this fallen world must either press back toward or continue against His intended design. There's no neutral option.

8. Bending God's creation in a wrong direction is destructive; if it is done long enough and hard enough, then society will collapse and have to start over in closer proximity to God's structured design.

9. Any other way contradicts and destructively undermines the purposeful, God-designed one-flesh relationship.

10. Technology is good because humans need tools to help them accomplish or enjoy things; it's powerful because it makes possible what would otherwise be impossible or difficult and then it so influences the world that it makes other things impossible or difficult.

Becoming a Creative Cultivator

11. (Answers will vary.) Sample answer for the topic of hunting: Although God originally provided food for humans without the need to shed the blood of animals, in a fallen world God has given humans dominion over the lives of animals (Gen. 9:2–4, cf. Acts. 10:10–16). But humans are still required to be good stewards and to treat their domesticated animals with kindness (Exod. 23:5; Deut. 25:4; Prov. 12:10; 27:23, cf. Luke 12:6). In the Millennium animals will be at peace with each other and with humans once again (Isa. 11:6).

TERMS TO REMEMBER

structure—the way things are supposed to be before they're bent or after they're bent back

direction—any bending, bad or good

materialism—a practical way of life that is more interested in material goods than in spiritual values

technology—the tools humans develop to aid them in the work of dominion

UNIT 4: REDEMPTION

CHAPTER 10

In order for students to participate in God's plan of redemption, they need to know how God is unfolding the plan of redemption in history and where they are in God's plan.

CHAPTER 11

Since Christians now live in the gap between the kingdom coming in salvation and the kingdom coming in judgment, they should not expect success in every Christian endeavor. Instead, they should expect to face suffering and persecution. Nevertheless, Christians living in the gap should still live a life of good works and press culture in redemptive directions as they are able.

CHAPTER 12

This chapter helps students see that different institutions play different roles within the biblical worldview. It highlights the specific mission of the institutional church so that its mission is not diluted to become simply another cultural institution. It also teaches students to value the various vocational institutions in which many of them will live and work. This chapter aims to exalt the church's unique role while also emphasizing the importance of work outside the church.

4

REDEMPTION

CHAPTER 10 OBJECTIVES

The student will be able to

10.1 Trace the unfolding story line of Redemption: how God promises in successive covenants to establish His kingdom.

10.2 Trace the unfolding fulfillment of God's redemptive promises in the work of Jesus Christ.

10.3 Defend the idea that Redemption is the restoration of God's original creation.

SECTION OBJECTIVES 10.1

1. Explain why Genesis 3:15 is the thesis statement for the whole Bible.

2. Summarize the promises and explain the significance of the Noahic Covenant.

3. Summarize the promises and explain the significance of the Abrahamic Covenant.

4. Summarize the promises and explain the significance of the Mosaic Covenant.

5. Summarize the promises and explain the significance of the Davidic Covenant.

6. Analyze how the exile directly relates to God's covenants.

7. Summarize the promises and explain the significance of the New Covenant.

[*Note*: As systems of biblical interpretation, both dispensationalism and covenant theology recognize the role played by the biblical covenants in the unfolding of God's historical relationship with His people. This particular chapter is neither a defense of covenant theology nor a defense of dispensationalism. It simply recounts the unfolding of God's covenant relationships throughout history from a biblical worldview.]

Chapter Ten **AN EVERLASTING KINGDOM**

And I will put enmity between you and the woman, and between your seed and her Seed; He shall bruise your head, and you shall bruise his heel.

Scripture Memory
Genesis 3:15 NKJV

10.1 THE HISTORY OF REDEMPTION IN THE OLD TESTAMENT

Readers love to be swept up in epic stories. Science fiction writer Isaac Asimov's famous *Foundation* trilogy, for example, covers a thousand years and the fate of millions of planets. *The Lord of the Rings* is pretty epic by itself, but author J. R. R. Tolkien gave it a backstory going back centuries (which true fans can read in *The Silmarillion*), and he even invented languages for it. The *Star Wars* saga claims to be an epic that happened "a long time ago in a galaxy far, far away."

There is no story more epic than the one you personally are playing a role in right now, the great story that engulfs all stories—the story of what God is doing to glorify Himself by redeeming His fallen creation.

This big story of Scripture—the metanarrative of the Christian worldview—contains many highs and lows. God created us in His own image and honored us with the task of ruling His world—that's a height. But we have rebelled against His goodness—and there's nothing else as low as that. God's image within us is now twisted, and our calling to have dominion has been frustrated.

But this is not the end of the story. The Bible not only tells us what we have done to ourselves and our world; it also tells us the remedy for our predicament. The actual events of Creation and the Fall take up just a few pages of the Bible (though they remain important to all the pages that follow). But the Bible takes its time telling the history of **Redemption**. It begins in Genesis 3 and doesn't end until Revelation 22.

The Bible's heavy emphasis on Redemption presents us with a significant challenge that you may have already noticed: it's not easy to figure out the main point of a story that lasts many hundreds and hundreds of pages and covers thousands of years of history. But the purpose of this chapter is to identify that main point. We need to learn what Redemption is all about, and then we need to examine its implications for how we understand the world.

We can't tell you the whole epic story—that's what the Bible is for. But we can go over the high points to show how that epic story flows through the whole of Scripture.

THE SEED OF THE WOMAN

"In the beginning, God created the heavens and the earth" (Gen. 1:1) He gave man and woman, His highest creations, a unique status and a unique job—they were made in His image, and they were to fill and rule the earth for His glory.

One marvelous proof of God's grace is that the same passage that records the Fall of those image-bearers into sin also records the beginning of Redemption. While God is speaking a curse on the Serpent (Satan, according to Rev. 12:9), He gives a whisper of hope to the human race. In Genesis 3:15, God tells the Serpent that he is cursed to fight a long war he cannot win. A seed given to the woman will oppose Satan and frustrate his plans. There will be times when it appears that the Serpent is winning the war, but his victories will prove to be nothing

138 | REDEMPTION

Lesson Plan Chart—Chapter 10

Section Title	Pages	Activity Manual	Days
10.1 The History of Redemption in the Old Testament	138–44	Activity 17	2 days
10.2 The Coming of the Kingdom	144–48	Activity 18	2 days
10.3 Restoring God's Good Creation	148–51		1 day
Review	152		1 day
Total Suggested Days			**6 days**

Redemption and the Larger Story

The redemption of the individual from his own sin is significant. Each person must be individually converted by believing in Christ's work and repenting of his own sin when he himself hears the gospel (Luke 13:5; Eph. 1:13; 1 Thess. 2:13). However, there's a larger story that individuals are a part of—God's kingdom work to glorify Himself (1 Thess. 2:12). Christ's redemptive work is typically presented as His work for the individual to receive eternal life (Luke 18:18, 26), but it often seems disconnected from His larger kingdom work (Matt. 4:17; Luke 18:24–25). It would be more helpful if believers would present the simple gospel in the larger context of the biblical story (Acts 8:12; 28:31). Then the implications

more than bruises on the heel of the woman's seed. In the end, the seed of the woman will leave the head of the Serpent crushed.

Genesis 3:15 is the thesis statement for the whole Bible. It expresses in just a few poetic lines the whole history of Redemption. It's a verse thick with meaning. And it is possible to uncover this meaning, but you have to look at the rest of biblical history to do so. That is, after all, how a thesis works. But before we work through what Genesis 3:15 leads to, we need to consider where Genesis 3:15 came from.

Before the Fall, God had stated that man was to rule over the world while still under God's greater rule over him. But now man has sinned. So God promises to send another man into this broken world: the seed of the woman. This man will do what the first man was supposed to do: he will subdue and have dominion. And in order to do that, he has to crush the enemy's head. The dominion God commands humans to take in Genesis 1:28 will not be set aside. It will be restored—by a man, the seed of the woman.

But who is this Seed, and how will he subdue and have dominion? Those are the questions that the rest of the story answers. The authors of the Old Testament begin to answer them by unfolding a series of covenants.

SEED AND OFFSPRING

Some translations of the Bible use the word *seed* in passages such as Genesis 3:15. Some use the word *offspring*. Both terms have the advantage of being either singular or plural. You can say, "Hey, give me the last sunflower seed!"—that's singular. Or you can say, "I planted sunflower seed in my garden this year." That's plural because you're not talking about just one seed. Hopefully you planted more than one!

The same is true of the word *offspring*. It can be singular or plural. Your parents probably don't use that word to describe you unless they're trying to be a little funny. But if you're an only child, they can tell someone, "This is our offspring." Or if you're one of several children, they can say, "These are our offspring." Same word, but one use is singular, and the other is plural.

To make things even more interesting, *seed* and *offspring* can refer to an immediate descendant or a much later one—or a large group of later descendants. So think of your great-great-great-grandfather. You are his seed. So are lots of your cousins and aunts and uncles and people you've never met. And so was each of his children. The word *seed* is flexible.

All this is important because God used an ambiguous word—one that could mean either singular or plural, soon or much later—on purpose. There are good reasons for that choice, but you'll have to keep reading to find out what they are.

The Hebrew word for *seed* can refer to one seed (singular) or to a whole pile of seed (plural).

relationships with His people is the key to answering the question, "Why should I be concerned about obeying all of Christ's commands if I have been saved by grace?" [Jonathan Lunde, *Following Jesus, the Servant King* (Grand Rapids: Zondervan, 2010), 35]

The Bible's Thesis Statement

The Bible is one unified story that centers on God's restoration of His relationship with humans. The Bible isn't a random series of moralistic stories *merely* for instilling good behavior. Rather, its unified theological story is the bedrock for rightly relating to God. What is the biblical story and how does it unfold? The unified story is the unfolding of God's *redemptive* plan for His fallen creation. The redemptive story begins with God's establishment of a relationship with Adam and Eve. Each successive covenant traces the *promise* of the seed (Gen. 3:15) to its ultimate *fulfillment* by a specific Seed— the Messiah. The goal of biblical history is the *restoration* of the human-divine *relationship* that God set up for His own glory in the garden. Thus, each covenant is rooted in restoring the land, seed, and blessing first given to Adam and Eve so that humans will once again properly rule in God's kingdom as His vice regents over God's creation now and ultimately over the new earth.

The Beginning of the Redemptive Story

Lunde uses a paradigm to summarize God's redemptive ways: "God's demand of righteousness always comes to humanity in the context of prior grace." [Lunde, 44] He applies this to Adam and Eve:

- God extends His gracious blessing: their status in the image of God and their task of the Creation Mandate (Gen. 1:26–30).

- God places conditions on this blessing: rebellion means loss of blessing—the Garden of Eden and tree of life (Gen. 2:16–17).

- Humankind rejects God's conditions of gracious provision: the Fall (Gen. 3:1–13).

- God graciously responds to humankind in mercy: a promised Redeemer (Gen. 3:15).

- Humankind can respond in faith: restoration evidenced in obedience (Gen. 4:1–7).

"While the demand of righteousness is there at the beginning, Eden suggests to us that the *means* by which this demand is to be met is always to be found in the prior reception and experience of grace. . . . *Subsequent* grace then precedes subsequent obedience. All the way through, the gracious grounding of the divine-human relationship *never* diminishes God's demand of righteousness." [Lunde, 44]

---

of Redemption for all of life would become clearer (Eph. 2:10–13).

 ## Discipleship and the Larger Story

Not only should *salvation* be understood within the larger story of Redemption, but so should *sanctification* or discipleship as well. The responsibility of biblical discipleship must be understood within the context of the New Covenant—the fulfillment of God's unfolding plan of Redemption through the previous covenants.

What is biblical discipleship?

It is the practice of, by grace, following the teachings of Jesus—teachings that fulfill the intent of previous covenants (Matt. 5:17–18).

Is discipleship optional?

If you belong to Jesus, then you follow Jesus (John 10:4, 27). If you have life in the Spirit, then you walk in the Spirit (Gal. 5:25), bearing fruit and crucifying the flesh (Gal. 5:16–24). New life (2 Cor. 5:17) necessarily follows a person's union with Christ (Eph. 1:4; 4:1; Col. 1:21–23). Sanctification is simply the ongoing transformative work of God, begun at salvation, that restores believers into the image of His Son (2 Cor. 3:18; Col. 3:10).

How does the larger covenantal context affect biblical discipleship for today?

New Covenant living can only be understood when it's connected to the historical unfolding of the redemptive covenants fulfilled in Christ and to His teachings for believers today.

Jonathan Lunde argues that understanding the whole history of God's covenant

Even though the same relationship paradigm may be rooted in both conditional (Adamic, Mosaic) and unconditional covenant relationships (Noahic, Abrahamic, Davidic, New) with differing situational demands, faithful obedience always follows from God's gracious provision. True faith is always evidenced by obedience (James 2:14–26).

God's Covenant Relationships

What is a covenant?

A covenant is a mutual agreement—including promises, obligations, and commitments—between two parties in a relationship.

What's the difference between conditional and unconditional covenants?

- Unconditional: Promised blessings are made with no conditional obligations demanded for the covenant to be fulfilled. This doesn't mean that there are no obligations because every covenant includes obligations; the obligations are simply not conditional in nature. *Fulfillment* is the sole responsibility of God. But the person who entrusts himself to God's gracious promises *responds* in faithful obedience—proving faith in God.

Lunde illustrates this as an offer of a father to take his kids to an amusement park. If they believe his offer to be genuine, then they will get their homework done in grateful response to the offer. [Lunde, 39]

- Conditional: Promised blessings are made with conditional obligations demanded for the covenant to be fulfilled. Remaining faithful is the condition for receiving the promises. Obedience doesn't earn the promise, but it is the means for opening God's hand of grace to grant it.

Lunde illustrates this as a father's promise to take his kids to an amusement park as a reward for getting their homework done. Doing their homework doesn't pay for the tickets (only he can do that), but it is the requirement for opening his hand of grace to pay for those tickets. [Lunde, 40]

Both kinds of covenants are ultimately grounded in prior grace and both include obligations that follow from that grace.

The Noahic Covenant

Read Genesis 8:15–9:17.

Gracious Grounding:

Was the Noahic Covenant conditional?

It was unconditional. After saving Noah from the Flood, God unilaterally committed Himself to sustaining the created order for all humans. He said He would refrain from judging all of humanity in spite of its continued sinfulness (Gen. 8:21–22; 9:8–11).

"THE SCOPE OF REDEMPTION IS AS GREAT AS THAT OF THE FALL; IT EMBRACES CREATION AS A WHOLE." [1]

—ALBERT WOLTERS

The Noahic Covenant

By Genesis 6, serious problems are already evident in God's good creation. "The sons of God" (perhaps a reference to the seed of the woman) intermarry with the "daughters of men" (perhaps a reference to the seed of the Serpent). In time the two lines become impossible to distinguish. Eventually, mankind is so wicked that God sends a Flood that destroys the whole world. Only Noah and those on the ark that God commands him to build are saved. Even after this drastic (but righteous) punishment the basic problem still persists because "the intention of man's heart" remains "evil from his youth" (Gen. 8:21). As one early American theologian noted, "If [God] was to drown them as often as they deserved it, one deluge must follow another continually."[2]

Instead of continuing to rain down punishment on the earth, God makes a covenant with Noah, with his seed, with all the creatures on the earth, and with the earth itself. God promises to not further curse the earth, to preserve regular seasons, and to never again destroy the earth with a flood. In the course of the covenant, God reaffirms that fallen man still bears His image and that in spite of the effects of the Fall, mankind is still to carry out the Creation Mandate (Gen. 9:1–7).

The Noahic Covenant promises to make the earth a stable place while God works out His plan for redeeming mankind. But how can God withhold due punishment from people who never cease being wicked? In Genesis, God institutes the covenant in response to Noah's sacrifice (Gen. 8:20–22). And this has always been God's way: sin must be paid for by blood.

The Abrahamic Covenant

The next stage in God's plan to redeem the world occurs centuries later—God operates on a time scale we can't use, one beyond the individual human lifetime. God reveals Himself to an unknown idolater in the city of Ur (Josh. 24:2–3), a man named Abram ("exalted father"). God graciously calls him away from all that he has known, changes his name to Abraham ("father of a multitude"), and makes three solemn promises to him (Gen. 12:1–3).

Promised Blessings:

List God's promises.

- *no universal, final destruction; preservation of all normal cycles (Gen. 8:21–22; 9:8–11)*
- *Creation Mandate reaffirmed (Gen. 9:1–3)*
- *animals and plants given for food (Gen. 9:3)*
- *sanctity of God's image-bearers (Gen. 9:5–6)*

Faithful Obligations:

How were humans to gratefully respond in faith to their sovereign Creator?

- *be fruitful; exercise stewardship (Gen. 9:7)*
- *respect life (Gen. 9:3-6, cf. Acts 15:20)*

Sacrifice/Sign of the Covenant:

When was the covenant established, and how long will it last?

In response to Noah's sacrifice of thanksgiving (Gen. 8:20-21), God made His covenant and sealed it with the sign of the rainbow—a reminder of His everlasting promise (Gen. 9:12–17). This covenant continues to the end.

Genesis 8:22 indicates that God promised to preserve the cycles of the earth *as long as it remains*, implying that there will be an end to the earth *as we know it*. God will judge the earth at the consummation of human history (Joel 2:31). But this judgment won't annihilate the earth into nonexistence but instead purify it for its restoration (2 Pet. 3:9–13; Rev. 21:1, cf. Rom. 8:19–23).

The Abrahamic Covenant

Read Genesis 12:1–4; 15:1-21; 17:1–23.

Instead of destroying the people of Babel, God faithfully kept the Noahic Covenant. He scattered the idolaters across the earth but called Abram out from among them.

- First, God promises to give him a "seed"—offspring, people. From the body of Abraham will come a great and mighty nation.
- Second, He promises to give Abraham a land where this seed will live and thrive.
- Third, He promises to bless all the families of the earth through Abraham and his seed.

Seed, land, and blessing: God's epic story of Redemption now begins to take shape. God had told Adam and Eve to fill the earth—now Abraham's seed would "be fruitful and multiply" in fulfillment of that promise. God had told Adam and Eve to take dominion—now Abraham's seed would have a land over which they could rule. And these blessings are not for Abraham's seed alone—now every family of the earth will be blessed. It is through Abraham that the "seed of the woman" promised in Genesis 3 will come. But throughout the coming epic story, many threats will arise to these three promises.

The Mosaic Covenant

In obedience to God, Abraham's family moves to the land of Canaan. When famine later threatens to wipe out that family (putting at risk the seed promise), they move to Egypt under the leadership of Jacob, Abraham's grandson. There they remain for the next four centuries. During these years the family grows to become a nation—but a nation of slaves under cruel Egyptian pharaohs.

God raises up Moses to lead this new nation back to the land God promised to Abraham. As a motley group of slaves, they have managed to hold on to some of their traditions (Gen. 32:32), but they need to be molded into a true nation to fulfill God's promise to Abraham.

So the Hebrews have an appointment with their God at Mount Sinai. Here God makes another covenant, the Mosaic Covenant. Unlike the Abrahamic Covenant, this one includes a major condition: if the people of Israel will agree to live by God's laws, He will make them a kingdom of priests. They will stand above all the nations of the earth in glory and privilege. They will also serve the nations of the earth as a priest does, by showing the world how to approach God in an acceptable way.

The Israelites accept God's condition. They promise to obey God's rules so that they can become His kingdom of priests.

God is slowly working out His plan to redeem the world. The Mosaic Covenant clarifies the Abrahamic Covenant by telling us more about the land promise and the universal blessing promise. It tells Israel how to live in the land of Canaan, turning it into a place where godly dominion replaces the sinful dominion of the Canaanites. It also tells us how God will bring a blessing to all nations. Israel will spread God's blessing to other nations by serving as the priest nation. God has called these people to Canaan not so that He can save only them, but so that He can use them to bring the whole world back to Himself.

But the "seed" in the promise to Abraham (and to Adam and Eve) is still left unclear. Is the seed one or many? Like any good author, God leaves some questions to be answered in later chapters of the epic.

of the land promise would be delayed (Gen. 15:13–16). As the biblical story line continues to unfold, we are informed that each Abrahamic promise awaits full and final fulfillment (Heb. 11:13); it's through the work of the New Covenant that the promises will be finally fulfilled (Gal. 3:7–9, 14; 4:31). Even though the Abrahamic Covenant can't be annulled (Gen. 17:7–8; Gal. 3:15), God's plan is unfolding through the work of the New Covenant (Gal. 3:14, 29) until the promises will finally be realized in the consummation (Isa. 66:22). Thus, the sign of circumcision—which became a part of the Mosaic law (John 7:22) to remind God's people to be faithful to the Abrahamic Covenant—is no longer necessary for God's people (Gal. 5:6). Its promises are now fulfilled in the New Covenant.

Threats to Abrahamic Promises

After dividing students into small groups, ask them to read one of the following narratives and explain how the story illustrates a major threat to one of the promises that God made to Abraham. How was God faithful?

- Genesis 13:1–18—Lot's choice threatened the land promise, but God rescued Lot from destruction (cf. Gen. 14; 19).
- Genesis 16:1–16—Fleshly attempts to produce an heir threatened the seed promise, but God extended His blessing to Ishmael.
- Genesis 18:1–15; 21:1–7—Infertility threatened the seed promise; God showed that nothing is impossible
- Genesis 20:1–18—Abraham's fleeing to a foreign land, fearing for his life, and lying to protect himself all challenged the land, seed, and blessing promises, but God provided safety, land, and wealth.
- Genesis 21:22–25, 34—A dispute over water rights threatened their ability to live in the land, but it was settled peacefully.
- Genesis 22:1–19—The command to sacrifice Isaac threatened the seed promise, but God provided a substitute.

The Mosaic Covenant
Read Exodus 20:1–26; 21:1; 24:3–8.

Gracious Grounding:

Was the Mosaic Covenant conditional?

The means necessary for receiving the promised blessings of this covenant were clearly conditional—by means of works of obedience (Deut. 11:26–29; 27:1–28:68; Josh. 8:30–35; 24:14–28). This was true even though the basis for being a part of the covenant nation was still due to God's graciousness—His choice to deliver Abraham's offspring from Egypt for the sake of His own name (Deut. 7:7–8; 11:1–4; Josh. 24:17–18).

Gracious Grounding:

Was the Abrahamic Covenant conditional?

It was unconditional. God bound Himself to fulfill the promises when the covenant was ratified (Gen. 15:9–21, cf. Gen. 17:7; Gal. 3:18). In spite of Abram's disobedience (Gen. 16:1–16), God renewed the same everlasting covenant in Genesis 17. But unlike the common grace of the Noahic Covenant, the means for receiving the special grace of God's blessings must come through faith. So God told Abraham to walk blamelessly (Gen. 17:1–2) proving his faith (Gen. 15:6; 22:16–18; James 2:21–24).

Promised Blessings: List God's promises.

- *seed (Gen. 12:2; 15:5; 17:4–7)*
- *land (Gen. 12:1; 15:7, 18–21; 17:8)*
- *blessing (Gen. 12:2–3; 15:1; 17:16)*

The biblical narrative revolves around challenges to these promises and God's faithfulness to His original blessing (Gen. 1:26–28).

Faithful Obligations:

How were God's people to gratefully respond in faith to their covenant God?

- *walking blamelessly (Gen. 17:1; 18:18–19)*
- *keeping covenant and submitting to its sign (Gen. 17:9, cf. Rom. 4:7–13)*

Sacrifice/Sign of the Covenant:

When was the covenant established, and how long will it last?

God initiated the formal ratification of the covenant to assure Abram that He would surely fulfill His promises (Gen. 15:7–9). God alone passed between the pieces of the sacrifice, symbolizing that He alone was responsible for fulfilling the promises (Gen. 15:17). But He informed Abram that the fulfillment

Lunde explains that "the Mosaic Covenant should always be understood as subordinate to the promises made to Abraham." The basis for God's promised blessings remained tied to the gracious unconditional guarantee of the Abrahamic Covenant received in faith. Faith in the Abrahamic Covenant comes first. But that faith always had to be evidenced in faithfulness (James 2:14–26). So Lunde says that "the Mosaic legislation unpacks and clarifies for the nation what it means to walk 'faithfully' and 'blamelessly'" (Gen. 17:1, cf. Deut. 11:13; 18:13). Thus, faithfulness to the Mosaic Covenant proves faith in the Abrahamic Covenant. Without this contingent proof of a true faith, the people couldn't receive the unconditional promises of the Abrahamic Covenant as God's people because their unfaithfulness proved that they weren't God's people. Lunde describes the function of the Mosaic Covenant as one that "administers or mediates the Abrahamic blessings to the nation. As the nation responds to God's prior grace . . . with obedience . . . , they will continue to experience the Abrahamic blessings, restated in their Mosaic expressions (Deut. 28:1–14)." One must be careful not to misunderstand the function of the Mosaic Covenant—it didn't provide the basis for salvation but the means for evidencing true salvation. Lunde says that when the Mosaic Covenant is understood in this context, "the people's obedience does not . . . earn the blessings, for these have already been granted to Abraham's seed by means of gracious promises. . . . Works of obedience to the law . . . are simply the means by which the reception of these gracious covenant blessings is maintained . . . Where there is obedience . . . , faith is assumed." But what happened when there was disobedience? God still provided a means by which His people could evidence genuine faith and restore their covenantal relationship with Him—through the sacrificial system, which pictured the atoning work of Christ on their behalf (Rom. 3:25). [Lunde, 58, 79, 96]

Promised Blessings, Faithful Obligations:

Read Deuteronomy 27–28 (cf. Exod. 21–23).

List what God promised His people if they would respond in obedience to Him.

Numerous promises and obligations are listed (traditionally, 613 commands). All explain the will of God—what it looked like in that context to love God and others (Matt. 22:37–40), reflecting God's own character (Lev. 19:2).

Sacrifice/Sign of the Covenant:

When was the covenant established, and how long will it last?

The covenant was ratified at Sinai with sacrifices and a fiery display of God's glory (Exod. 24:5–8, 17–18). All of its requirements were fulfilled by the coming of the Messianic Redeemer. None of them can ever be thrown out or anulled (Matt. 5:17–20), but none of them can be perfectly fulfilled by any other human as required by God (Matt. 5:48; Heb. 2:17; 4:15; 7:11). Circumcision became the sign of the Mosaic Covenant (John 7:22, cf. Lev. 12:3; Josh. 5:2–9). The command was reinstituted in conjunction with Passover (redemption from Egypt) which fulfilled God's original promise to Abraham to redeem his offspring (Exod. 12:40–51, cf. Gen. 15:13–14; Ex. 2:24–25). Sabbath rest was also a sign of Redemption (Exod. 31:12–17).

A PRAYER FOR THE FUTURE KING

Psalm 72 is a Messianic psalm written by Solomon, and here's what he prays for the future King in that psalm:

"Give the king your justice, O God, and your righteousness to the royal son! May he judge your people with righteousness, and your poor with justice! Let the mountains bear prosperity for the people, and the hills, in righteousness! May he defend the cause of the poor of the people, give deliverance to the children of the needy, and crush the oppressor!" (Psalm 72:1–4)

"May he have dominion from sea to sea, and from the River to the ends of the earth!" (Psalm 72:8)

"May his name endure forever, his fame continue as long as the sun! May people be blessed in him, all nations call him blessed!" (Psalm 72:17)

Jesus is the only king who could ever be God's answer to these prayers.

The Davidic Covenant

God gives the land of Canaan to the people of Israel as He promised. But they repeatedly sin and rebel against His law. He punishes them but never abandons them.

In time He raises up a king for them, David the son of Jesse. David is the greatest king the nation will ever have—precisely because he loves the Lord his God with all his might. He has left us some of the richest poetry in our Bibles, the Psalms. And in the middle of his reign, God makes a covenant with David.

In the Davidic Covenant, God promises that David's dynasty will last forever. God's actual wording is especially significant:

I will set up your seed after you, who will come from your body, and I will establish his kingdom. . . . I will be his Father, and he shall be My son. . . . Your kingdom shall be established forever. (2 Sam. 7:12–16, NKJV)

David also wrote psalms exploring and elaborating the marvelous promise God had given him (see Pss. 2, 22, 45, 89, and 110). The Seed of David, says Psalms, will "rule in the midst of his enemies" (Ps. 110) and then "make the ends of the earth his possession" (Ps. 2).

We're getting more clarity on the seed promise: the seed of the woman—the seed promised to Abraham—will be, specifically, David's seed. David will have a great and mighty descendant who will defeat the enemies of God's people and rule forever. It seems that this seed will be a single person. But He will be a person like no one the world has ever known. He will be divine as well. God Himself, somehow, will be His Father. This **Seed** will be the Son of God.

A psalm by David's famously wise son, Solomon, reveals that this Seed will not rule over only Israel; He will rule over the entire world (Ps. 72:8), and his rule will enforce justice that will be a blessing to all nations (Ps. 72:1–4, 17).

Exile

David's reign is a bright spot in a long story of Israelite sin and failure. Thirty-two of the Jewish people's forty-two kings were bad, and the other ten all had plenty of faults. Readers of Kings and Chronicles may be excused for wanting to tear out their hair as they watch these kings and their people fall into idolatry over and over.

God's mercy lasts for many human lifetimes, but God did promise back at Mount Sinai that violations of the covenant would bring terrible judgment. In the end God sends the Babylonians to take His people captive—including the descendants of King David. And this isn't a random judgment: it targets precisely God's promises to Abraham and David about the land.

 ### The Davidic Covenant

Read 2 Samuel 7:1–16; 23:1–5; 2 Chronicles 7:18; 13:5; 21:7. See also Psalm 89:1–4, 28–37; Jer. 33:14–26.

Gracious Grounding:

Was the Davidic Covenant conditional?

It is unconditional. Not only did God graciously choose the unlikely David over his brothers and preserve him for the kingdom (2 Sam. 7:8–9), He bound Himself to fulfill this everlasting covenant (2 Sam. 7:13–16).

Promised Blessings: List God's promises.

Like the Mosaic Covenant, the Davidic Covenant continued to unfold the fulfillment of the Abrahamic Covenant's promises:

- *land (2 Sam. 7:10–11, cf. Gen. 17:8)*
- *blessing (2 Sam. 7:14–15, cf. Gen. 15:1)*
- *seed (2 Sam. 7:12–13, 16, cf. Gen. 17:6, 16)*

It even leads many people to call those divine promises into question. Aren't the people supposed to have the land "forever"? The Abrahamic Covenant promised a seed, a land, and a blessing for all the world. But now the land is gone, the seed is in exile, and the hope of a universal blessing seems all but impossible. Small nations just don't recover from mass captivity. (Where are the Hittites* today?)

Hittites: an ancient people who lived in the Promised Land before the Israelites did

The New Covenant

But even in judgment, God remembers mercy. It was to Jewish exiles in a faraway city that God gave the prophet Jeremiah a special message:

> Days are coming, declares the Lord, when I will restore the fortunes of my people, Israel and Judah, says the Lord, and I will bring them back to the land that I gave to their fathers, and they shall take possession of it. (Jer. 30:3)

And then came these even more precious and tantalizing words:

> I will make a new covenant with the house of Israel and with the house of Judah, not like the covenant I made with their fathers. (Jer. 31:31)

The Mosaic Covenant required God's people to obey God's laws. But their history demonstrates over and over again that this obedience was something they simply could not maintain. The fall of Adam had infected his descendants too deeply. Even with perfect laws and God on their side in battle, the Israelites were lacking something essential. Jeremiah revealed what that essential thing was:

> This is the covenant that I will make with the house of Israel after those days, declares the Lord: I will put my law within them, and I will write it on their hearts. And I will be their God, and they shall be my people. And no longer shall each one teach his neighbor and each his brother, saying, "Know the Lord," for they shall all know me, from the least of them to the greatest, declares the Lord. For I will forgive their iniquity, and I will remember their sin no more. (Jer. 31:31–34)

The people needed new hearts. They needed God to redeem not just their surroundings or their government but their innermost beings.

The New Covenant makes obedience not the condition of the covenant (as it was with the Mosaic Covenant) but the certain result. In the New Covenant, people don't obey God in order to be His people; they become His people, and they therefore obey Him.

God's people in the New Covenant need never fear His anger or His judgment. Their guilt is removed forever: "I will forgive their iniquity."

But how? How can this New Covenant ever take place? God's people are in exile at this point in the Bible's story. And more importantly, how could a just God forgive the sins of His people, let alone all the Gentiles? Being a just judge, He couldn't just let them all off the hook. A judge has to follow the law, and especially if He made the law.

AN EVERLASTING KINGDOM | 143

The Call to Covenant Faithfulness

The role of the prophet was to call the nation back to covenant faithfulness. The book of Amos illustrates this well. It opens with a series of charges against the surrounding nations (1:3–2:5) but climaxes with an indictment of Israel (2:6–16). After three succeeding covenant lawsuits detailing the charges against Israel (introduced by "hear this word": Amos 3:1–15; 4:1–13; 5:1–17), closing arguments are made, declaring Israel's guilt and sentencing—exile (5:18–6:14).

But God's judgment was not without mercy. In fact, all the instances of God's severe chastisement referred to in Amos 4 had a merciful purpose. The judgments were not random acts of disaster. When the people saw a specific instance of disaster that countered God's covenant promises related to the land, seed, and blessing, they should have immediately recognized that they were under God's covenant curse as had been promised: hunger (Amos 4:6; Lev. 26:26; Deut. 28:48); drought (Amos 4:7–8; Lev. 26:20; Deut. 28:24); crop failure and insects (Amos 4:9; Deut. 28:22, 38, 40); plagues and military defeat (Amos 4:10; Lev. 26:16, 25); and devastation like Sodom and Gomorrah's (Amos 4:11; Deut. 29:22).

The last section of the book of Amos envisions the merciful delay of God's wrath (Amos 7:1–6) until the Lord must insist on judging (7:7–9; 8:1–3) His corrupt leaders (7:10–17) and people (8:4–14). The Lord assures them that his judgment is inescapable (9:1–6) and indiscriminate (9:7–10). But none of this means that God will be unfaithful to His unconditional and eternal covenant promises—the Day of the Lord will restore all His promises: land, seed, and blessing (9:11–15).

The New Covenant

Read Jeremiah 31:1–40, where the prophet recounts Israel's failure to keep the Mosaic Covenant, leading to exile. But God's promises haven't failed because His people still belong to Him. The climax of the chapter explains how God will accomplish this restoration (Jer. 31:31–34).

Gracious Grounding:

Is this covenant conditional or not?

It's unconditional (Jer. 32:40). (Note all the times that God states "I will" in the chapter.)

Promised Blessings: List God's promises.

- *internalized law (Jer. 31:33; 32:38–40) for all, not just some of God's people (Deut. 10:16; 11:18; 30:6, 14)*

- *intimate knowledge (Jer. 31:34) due to a new work of the Spirit (Ezek. 36:26–27)*

The promised seed narrowed from general to specific: from the offspring of Adam and Eve to Abraham and Sarah to the line of Isaac to Jacob to the tribe of Judah to David.

Faithful Obligations:

How were humans to gratefully respond in faith to their sovereign Creator?

God rejected Saul and set up the Davidic dynasty because David was a man after His own heart (1 Sam. 13:14). Even though the dynasty would be unconditionally preserved, an unbroken line was conditioned on individual faithfulness to the Mosaic law (2 Sam. 7:14–15; 1 Kings 2:1–4; Pss. 89:38–39; 132:12). The king was responsible to lead the nation in faithfulness (Deut. 17:14–20), placing trust in the covenant God to deliver them (Ps. 20:7; Isa. 7:1–14). Solomon's prayer in Psalm 72 exemplifies the expectations for

the line of Davidic kings, but only the Messiah would fulfill these expectations (1 Kings 11:1–13; 12:1–17).

Sacrifice/Sign of the Covenant:

When was the covenant established and how long will it last?

The covenant was established with David and will last forever (2 Sam. 7:28–29; Ps. 132:11).

Only one passage implies that a sacrifice accompanied the ratification of the Davidic Covenant—2 Chronicles 13:5 mentions that it was a covenant of salt. This reference to salt indicates that a grain offering, which always included salt (Lev. 2:13), ratified the Davidic Covenant. The salt was a sign of permanence because of its preservative nature (Num. 18:19). This kind of sacrifice is fitting since God's promise to David was the permanence of his dynasty (2 Chron. 13:5).

AN EVERLASTING KINGDOM | 143

- *permanent atonement (Jer. 31:34) through the work of the Servant (Isa. 53:3–12)*

Faithful Obligations:

How are humans to gratefully respond in faith to their sovereign Creator?

It will not be like the covenant made with Moses (Jer. 31:32). While obedient holiness still matters (1 Pet. 1:16), God's demands of righteousness will be expressed differently (1 Cor. 9:21)—they will be heightened (Matt. 5:17–48). But righteousness will be embraced internally rather than externally (Rom. 3:31; 8:2), leading to willing faithfulness (Jer. 50:4–5; Heb. 10:26–31) to the Davidic King (Ezek. 37:24–26; Heb. 3:6–14, cf. 1:5; Ps. 2:6–7).

"This discontinuity lies not so much in the nature of the covenantal *demands*. Rather, it concerns mainly the nature of the covenantal *people* themselves." [Lunde, 81]

Sacrifice/Sign of the Covenant:

The Messiah is the sacrificial Lamb of the New Covenant (Isa. 53:7; Heb. 10:1–18).

The Lord's Supper signifies the New Covenant work of the Messiah (1 Cor. 11:25). Water baptism symbolizes the Spirit baptism of the New Covenant (Rom. 6; 1 Cor. 12:13).

THINKING IT THROUGH 10.1

1. God makes the earth a stable place until He works out His plan of Redemption.

2. seed, land, and blessing; Seed correlates with being fruitful, land correlates with taking dominion, and the blessing correlates with the Creation Mandate.

3. conditional

4. an eternal dynasty reigning over a blessed land

♡5. new hearts and final forgiveness; Obedience isn't the condition but the certain result of the covenant.

SECTION OBJECTIVES 10.2

1. Describe how Jesus began to fulfill the kingdom promises.

2. Explain how Jesus' death and resurrection fit in with kingdom fulfillment.

3. Conclude that the message of the gospel—proclaiming Christ's salvific work—makes sense in the larger context of the promised kingdom.

4. Summarize how Jesus will complete the fulfillment of the kingdom promises.

Unfaithful—Again!

What happened from the time of the exile until the coming of Jesus in the New Testa-

The Direction of The Epic

The covenants of Scripture all point toward the future because if God is going to keep them all—and He is—He has some glorious work left to do. Abraham is going to get a land, and not just any land but a very particular one: the land of Canaan. And David's Son needs to sit on a throne in that land. God can't utterly destroy this world and still keep His promises. In fact, the biblical covenants suggest that God doesn't plan to replace this world but to restore it.

THINKING IT THROUGH 10.1

1. Why was the Noahic Covenant necessary?

2. What three promises did God give to Abraham? How do those promises relate to the Creation Mandate?

3. What makes the Mosaic Covenant distinct from the other covenants?

4. What is the promise of the Davidic Covenant?

♡5. What does the New Covenant provide that none of the other covenants could provide?

10.2 THE COMING OF THE KINGDOM

It is hard to keep track of everything that a big book like the Bible is saying. The promises and stories and genealogies and poems and laws and songs and proper names come at you so fast that it's almost impossible to put them together in any sensible way—until you see them all as part of an epic story. Seeing all the little stories like Jonah and Noah and Joseph as part of one big story—what God is doing to glorify Himself by redeeming His fallen creation—is absolutely key to understanding the Bible.

This chapter on Redemption is not just repeating stories you already know; it's trying to put them together into that one big story so you can hold on to them. It's easier to catch a hundred M&M's if someone tosses you a bag containing that many than if he throws them at you a handful at a time. If you've been following the big story, you may (and should) find yourself curious about how it's going to turn out, even if you think you already know the answer!

THE GOOD NEWS IN THE NEW TESTAMENT

Repeatedly, the Old Testament tells us what God will one day do to fulfill the grand, sweeping promise of Genesis 3:15: the Seed of the woman will crush the head of the Serpent. When we turn the last page of the Old Testament to begin the New, we pass from the age of promise to the age of fulfillment. We meet the Seed.

Jesus of Nazareth

The New Testament opens with the account of an extraordinary birth. Before this birth, an angel appears to the baby's mother, Mary, and announces: "You will conceive in your womb and bear a son, and you shall call his name Jesus." The angel goes on to explain the greatness of His mission: "The Lord God will give to him the throne of his father David, and he will reign over the house of Jacob forever, and of his kingdom there will be no end" (Luke 1:31–33).

ment? Where was the happy ending with the New Covenant blessings? Those returning from exile rebuilt the temple under Zerubbabel (Ezra 5:2, 13–16; 6:14–15) and the walls of Jerusalem under Nehemiah (Neh. 6:15–16). Godly leaders sought to teach the people their covenant obligations to the Mosaic law (Ezra 7:10; Neh. 8:1–18) and called on them to recommit themselves to covenant holiness (Ezra 9:1–10:5; Neh. 9:1–3). They recounted their whole covenant history (God's faithfulness and their own unfaithfulness) from creation to Abraham to Moses to their exile and return (Neh. 9:5–38). But the Israelites soon continued their rebellion against God (Neh. 13:1–30; Mal. 1:1–2, 6–7, 12–14; 2:8, 17; 3:7) and once again faced His covenantal curse (Mal. 2:1–4, 9; 3:9). The return from exile was but a foreshadowing; four hundred years of silence would precede

the coming of the Messiah to establish the New Covenant (Mal. 3:1, cf. Isa. 40:3).

 Jesus: The Davidic King

Jesus is *the* King: "This is my beloved Son" (Matt. 17:5).

God's plan continues to unfold with Jesus' arrival (Isa. 40:3; Matt. 3:3).

Identify the pivotal events when Jesus was declared King/God's beloved Son.

- *Luke 1:30–35—birth (cf. Matt. 1:1)*
- *Matthew 3:17—baptism*
- *Matthew 17:5—transfiguration*

The angels' announcement (Luke 1:30–35) must be understood within the context of the Old Testament promises (Gen. 17:6; 1 Chron. 17:11–14; Mic. 5:3–4). A virgin will give birth to a son (Isa. 7:14; Matt. 1:21–23)

Mary is perplexed when she hears this news. She's not married. How could she have the child that would fulfill these promises? The angel explains that the Holy Spirit will cause her to conceive. She will indeed be the mother, but the boy will have no human father: "The child to be born will be called holy—the Son of God" (Luke 1:35).

This human child, David's descendant, will nonetheless be a Son of God. As a man, He fulfills the seed promise of Genesis 3:15. He is the seed of a real-live descendant of Eve. And as God's own Son, He fulfills the promise that David's great descendant would also be the Son of God (2 Sam. 7:14).

And Jesus is something else God promised to David: a king. The King. The very first thing Jesus announces, and the very center of His message, is "The time is fulfilled, and the kingdom of God is at hand; repent and believe in the gospel" (Mark 1:15). The turning point of world history has come, and He is it.

The Kingdom

All through the Old Testament, God had been promising the coming of a kingdom. One day a dominion—a rule—would come to earth, crushing the Serpent, saving God's people, defeating the enemies of God, and exalting God's people to rule and reign forever. Now at last the kingdom has drawn near.

The kingdom has drawn near because the King has arrived. This is the most important point made by the four Gospels. When Jesus teaches the crowds, they are amazed that He speaks with kingly authority. When He calms a storm, He rebukes the wind and the waves with a kingly voice, and immediately all is still. Creation itself knows that it's in the presence of the King.

Even the kingdom of Satan knew that the King had come. "What have you to do with us, Jesus of Nazareth?" said a demon to Jesus. "I know who you are—the Holy One of God!" (Mark 1:24). And when the King commanded those demons to get out, they obeyed. "If it is by the Spirit of God that I cast out demons," Jesus said, "then the kingdom of God has come upon you" (Matt. 12:28).

Death and Resurrection

Jesus could have cut a straight path to full kingship. He could have put everything under His feet two thousand years ago. He could have ended all opportunity for salvation and brought only judgment to the world.

But that was not His plan. He was seeking worshipers for the Father (John 4:23), so He came not to bring judgment but to bring salvation. In the verse right after the most famous verse in the Bible, Jesus explains, "God did not send his Son into the world to condemn the world, but in order that the world might be saved through him" (John 3:17).

That salvation required a price. For the kingdom to come fully, the King had to suffer. This, too, is something that the Old Testament had predicted. Psalm 22 revealed that the King would be forsaken by God (Ps. 22:1) and that the enemies of God would pierce His hands and His feet (22:16). And Isaiah 53 explained why: "He was pierced for our transgressions; he was crushed for our iniquities . . . and with his wounds we are healed" (Isa. 53:5). There could be no kingdom without kingdom citizens. And in this world of sin, there can be no kingdom citizens without forgiveness. How can a just and holy God forgive people who have rebelled against His rule? There is only one answer: the sacrifice of the one perfect man, the Son of God.

---

who will reign as the promised human seed on David's throne (2 Sam. 7:13; Heb. 1:8).

God's announcements must also be understood within the context of Old Testament promises (Ps. 2:6–9). Throughout His ministry Jesus proved Himself to be the promised Messiah/Christ (Matt. 16:16; 22:41–45) and claimed to be the divine Son of Man (Dan. 7:13–14; Matt. 26:64–65, cf. Ps. 110:1). At His death, His claims were mocked (John 19:21), but at His resurrection they were vindicated (Acts 2:22–35; 13:32–33).

Did Jesus accomplish some, none, or all of the Davidic promises?

While Jesus clearly continued to unfold God's covenant promises in His first coming, He just as clearly has not fulfilled all of those promises completely. Yet, it is still predicted that He will actually fulfill all of His promises to Israel (Rom. 11:1, 5, 11–15, 25–27).

For example:

He did originate from obscurity (2 Sam. 7:8–9; Matt. 13:55–57; John 1:46; Luke 2:7)

He does reign as King (2 Sam. 7:11–12; Acts 2:29–35; Rom. 1:3–4; Eph. 1:20–22)

He will judge, providing peace and rest (2 Sam. 7:10–11, cf. Ps. 2:8; Heb. 2:5–9; 4:1–11)

Jesus is King, but He must rule in the midst of enemies (Ps. 110:1–2; Heb. 2:8–9). One day all people and nations will bow the knee (Amos 9:11–12; Phil. 2:9–11) and willingly serve (Zech. 8:23; 14:9) the one who has already come as King (Zech. 9:9–10).

 Jesus: The Mosaic Prophet

Jesus is the Prophet: "Listen to Him" (Matt. 17:5).

Because Jesus is the divine King, He also possesses absolute prophetic authority. He is *the* Prophet (Deut. 18:15, 18–19, cf. Acts 3:19–26). Jesus taught and ministered with this authority (Matt. 13:54; Mark 1:22; John 8:28). For this reason most people expected Jesus to restore an earthly kingdom to Israel at that time (John 6:14–15), delivering them from their enemies (Isa. 40:1–5; 43:16–21; Luke 1:67–79). But they hadn't grasped the central topic of Jesus' prophetic teaching: the kingdom at hand (Matt. 4:17, 23; 9:35; 13:1–52; 16:28; John 18:36).

Ask students to search for the term, *kingdom*, only in the Gospels, using an online Bible program. **Approximately how many times does this theme appear?** *125*

Matthew 13 contains a whole series of kingdom parables. They aren't meant to be understood by everyone; only His illumined disciples who seek further explanation begin to understand (Matt. 13:10–17).

Divide students into small groups. Each group should read Matthew 13:24–30, 36–43 and then chart out each element of the parable and its interpretation. Each group should summarize the parable's main significance.

What was Jesus trying to emphasize?

The primary theme of these parables is that of the differing responses to Jesus' proclamation of the kingdom. This parable explains why the King delays judgment on those who reject the message (cf. John 10:20). But judgment will come (cf. Matt. 25:31–46; Ps. 110:1–2). Therefore, Jesus isn't ready yet to restore the earthly kingdom to Israel even though kingdom citizens are presently in the world.

 Jesus: The Suffering Servant

Jesus is the Suffering Servant "with whom [the Father is] well pleased" (Matt. 17:5, cf. Isa. 42:1; 52:13–53:12). Jesus identifies Himself as such in the parable of the vineyard.

After dividing students into small groups, ask each small group to interpret the parable found in Matthew 21:33–46. Provide them with the following questions and references.

What is the vineyard (Matt. 21:43)?

the kingdom of God

Who are the vineyard's tenants (Isa. 5:1–7)?

Israelites

What is the fruit (Matt. 3:8; 7:1–17)?

The fruit is repentance and the works of righteousness that accompany it.

Who are the servants (Neh. 9:26)?

The servants who are killed are the prophets.

Who is the son (Ps. 118:22–23)?

Jesus, the promised Messiah, the rejected Cornerstone (cf. 1 Pet. 2:6–10)

Who is the owner, and what will he do?

The owner is God the Father, and He will take the kingdom from that particular disobedient generation that stumbled over Jesus (Rom. 9:30–33; 11:1–11, 25–32).

Jesus: The Perfect Priest

Why did Jesus have to suffer rejection? Why didn't He just judge the world (Ps. 96:10)?

He had every reason to judge the world (John 12:37–43), but that wasn't His mission at His first coming (John 12:46–47, cf. Luke 4:16–21). It will be His mission at His Second Coming (John 12:48; 2 Thess. 1:5–10).

Jesus had to be the Suffering Servant in order to fulfill His role as the superior priest (Heb. 6:20; 7:17, 24–25; 9:24). His priestly work brings to an end the whole sacrificial system of the Old Covenant (Heb. 10:12) and institutes the New Covenant (Heb. 9:14–15), paying for the whole curse of the Mosaic law (Gal. 3:13). Only then could people receive full and final forgiveness and enter the kingdom (Acts 13:39; Gal. 3:21–23).

Jesus is also the sacrifice. Just as the Israelites had been redeemed out of Egypt by the substitute of a passover lamb (Exod. 11:5; 12:3–13), so also Jesus, God's firstborn Son (Heb. 1:6), redeems us by becoming the sacrificial Lamb for us (1 Cor. 5:7).

Jesus: The Resurrected Lord

The resurrection of Jesus was the event that established His reigning authority both in this age and in the age to come (Eph 1:20–22, cf. Rom. 1:3–4; 10:9; 14:9). All dominion has been given to Him (Matt. 28:18; Acts 2:36). However, the earthly kingdom has not yet been fully restored. (This is discussed in more detail in Chapter 11. See Acts 1:6–8; 1 Cor. 15:24; Rev. 12:10.) So believers suffer persecution (1 Pet. 4:12) from God's enemies until He makes them His footstool (Ps. 110:1; Acts 2:33–35; Heb. 10:13) at His return (2 Thess. 1:5–10; Rev. 6:10).

 Proclaiming the Gospel Is Proclaiming the Kingdom

What was the theme of Jesus' teaching after His resurrection (Acts 1:3)?

the kingdom

What was the consistent theme of the apostles' preaching (Acts 8:12; 14:21–22; 19:8; 20:25; 28:23, 30–31)?

the good news (gospel) of the kingdom

What were the apostles trying to convince people of when they preached the kingdom (Acts 28:23)?

If we think through the history of Redemption, we realize that this sacrifice—the death of the innocent to pay the penalty due the guilty—was God's plan from the beginning. The original promise was not simply that the Seed of the woman would conquer, but that the Seed would suffer. "You shall bruise his heel" was just as much a part of the prophecy as "he shall bruise your head." In fact, the bruising of the Seed's heel was the only way to bruise the Serpent's head. Only by Christ atoning for man's sin could creation be released from God's curse. Man was guilty of the same crime against God that Satan was. Man and his world could not be healed without atonement. There could be no kingdom without the cross.

But even the cross is not the end of the story. Jesus didn't come simply to die. He came to subdue and have dominion. So when He had completed His atoning work, God raised Him from the dead, and in doing so invested Him with the full authority of the great King. When Jesus speaks to His disciples after the resurrection, He speaks not as a prince, someone about to take rule, but as a newly crowned King: "All authority in heaven and on earth has been given to me" (Matt. 28:18).

And when the apostles proclaim the gospel, they proclaim the authority of the conquering King. Peter tells the Jews on Pentecost, "Let all the house of Israel therefore know for certain that God has made him both Lord and Christ, this Jesus whom you crucified" (Acts 2:36). When Peter proclaims the gospel to the Gentiles, he tells them, "[Jesus] is Lord of all" (Acts 10:36). And when John introduces his readers to the glorified Christ, he calls Him "the ruler of kings on earth" (Rev. 1:5). Jesus isn't waiting to be crowned. He is now King of all.

SPREADING THE GOSPEL OF THE KINGDOM

Much of the New Testament is devoted to telling how Jesus spread this good news "to the end of the earth" through His apostles.

The Acts of the Apostles

The preaching of the apostles in the book of Acts announced to all people that the kingdom of God had finally come. Christ, the apostles proclaimed, was the King and future Judge (Acts 10:42). The book describes Paul's ministry this way: "From morning till evening he expounded to them, testifying to the kingdom of God and trying to convince them about Jesus both from the Law of Moses and from the Prophets" (Acts 28:23).

To enjoy the benefits of the kingdom, according to the apostles' preaching, people had to repent and believe in Christ. These believers will escape the coming judgment of God, and they will rule and reign with Jesus forever.

The New Testament Epistles

Paul and other apostles continued presenting this message in the letters they wrote to various early Christians around the Roman world.

In letters (or epistles) such as Romans and 1 Peter, the apostles explain the significance of the great events in the history of Redemption. Paul in particular seeks to explain why Gentiles and Jews belong together in the church as brothers and sisters.

It's important to understand that Paul saw the gospel he preached as consistent not only with Jesus' message but with the Old Testament—including the seed promise of Genesis 3:15. Paul explained that when God promised to give Abraham a Seed, He was speaking specifically of Christ, not of a whole host of Jewish descendants: "Now

---

They tried to convince them that Jesus was the Messiah both from the law of Moses and from the prophets (i.e., Jesus was the fulfillment of the Messianic or kingdom promises).

When does a person become a kingdom citizen (Col. 1:13, cf. Acts 2:38; 8:12)?

at salvation when he repents and believes

Does Scripture indicate that the kingdom is present or that it is future?

Some passages indicate a present kingdom experience (Rom. 14:15–19; 1 Cor. 4:17–21; Col. 1:13; 4:11), and some are unclear (1 Thess. 2:12; 2 Thess. 1:5; Heb. 12:28). But others indicate a future kingdom inheritance (Acts 1:6–7; 1 Cor. 6:9–10; 15:24, 50; Gal. 5:21; Eph. 5:5; 2 Tim. 4:18; James 2:5).

The Church

The story of Redemption that has been unfolding through the covenants with national Israel now takes a new turn. Paul explains why Gentiles and Jews belong together in one new body (Eph. 2:11–22).

The New Covenant work of Christ brings together two groups of people once divided (Eph. 2:13). Without becoming a part of the Jewish nation (Exod. 12:48), the Gentiles had lacked a covenant relationship with God and thus missed out on all the privileges (Eph. 2:11–12). How did Christ bring peace to once hostile groups? The law of Moses—the wall of hostility—was broken down (Eph. 2:14–15) when Christ provided atonement through His sacrifice on the cross (Eph. 2:16). This work provides all the benefits that the Gentiles once lacked—brought about

to Abraham and his Seed were the promises made. He does not say, 'And to seeds,' as of many, but as of one, 'And to your Seed,' who is Christ." (Gal. 3:16, NKJV).

Paul neatly answers the question of who the Seed is: it's Jesus. The Seed, then, is singular, not plural.

But wait: all true believers are included in this Seed because they are considered to be "in Christ":

> There is neither Jew nor Greek, there is neither slave nor free, there is neither male nor female; for you are all one in Christ Jesus. And if you are Christ's, then you are Abraham's seed, and heirs according to the promise. (Gal. 3:28–29, NKJV)

Paul explains, then, how sometimes the seed seems to be one person, Christ, but at other times, it seems to be a whole company of people, all of the saved. The Seed who crushes the Serpent in God's promise to Adam and Eve seems to be singular (Gen. 3:15), and so does the Seed who sits on the throne in God's promise to David (2 Sam. 7:12–16). But the seed that fills the land of Canaan (Gen. 12:7) and rules the world (Dan. 7:27) includes all the people of God.

Paul didn't invent a new religion called Christianity (and neither did Jesus). The New Testament sends hundreds of anchors back into the Old Testament. It claims over and over to be the continuation of the story begun in the Garden of Eden. And it ends with a future look at the new earth.

THE END OF THE STORY
The Book of Revelation

The book of Revelation describes the events leading up to the restoration of the earth. The apostle John is given a vision of God's throne in heaven. He sees God on His throne holding a scroll filled with the judgments that God has determined to pour out on a world of unbelief and sin. But the scroll is sealed, and no one is found worthy to take the scroll and break open its seals.

Until Jesus steps in. "Worthy are you to take the scroll," the elders in heaven say to Jesus, "for you were slain, and by your blood you ransomed people for God from every tribe and language and people and nation" (Rev. 5:9). Jesus has brought the blessing God promised Abraham to every family on earth, and Revelation tells of the time when He will fully cleanse the earth from sin, destroying all the works of the Serpent (1 John 3:8).

The rest of the book of Revelation tells how God completes this work. Jesus takes the scroll, opens its seals, and judges the earth—purging it of all who have refused to repent. Satan himself, "that ancient serpent . . . the deceiver of the whole world" (Rev. 12:8), is driven from the earth and cast into the lake of fire—along with all who have followed him. Then the earth becomes what it was meant to be from the beginning: the kingdom of God, ruled by His Christ, the second Adam. "The kingdom of the world has become the kingdom of our Lord and of his Christ, and he shall reign forever and ever" (Rev. 11:15).

JESUS SAVES AND JUDGES

The twenty-four elders praise Jesus in Revelation 5:9, "Worthy are you to take the scroll and to open its seals [judgments], for you were slain, and by your blood you ransomed people for God from every tribe and language and people and nation." So . . . Jesus is worthy to judge because He saved? What's the logic here?

The idea is that Jesus is judging in a "restorative" way. He's not just obliterating an enemy planet; He's judging the world in order to purge it, and ultimately to restore it. In order for Him to restore it, He has to provide atonement for it. He can judge because He saved mankind.

---

by the New Covenant function of the Spirit (Eph. 2:17–18, cf. 1:13–14; 1 Cor. 12:13).

Believing Gentiles no longer need to become Israelites; both believing Gentiles and Jews enter into a brand-new body created by God: one new man in place of the two (Eph. 2:15, 19, cf. 1:22–23). This new body was founded by the apostles who built on the revelation of Christ, the Chief Cornerstone (Eph. 2:20–22). While it's a new entity, the church was always a part of God's plan (Eph. 3:10–11).

It may seem that with this one new body, God's work with Israel is over. But what about the everlasting covenants that God made with that nation (Gen. 17:7; 2 Sam. 7:16)? The church is something new and different—it's not a form of the nation. Elsewhere, Paul makes clear that God has a future plan for the nation of Israel in which He will continue to fulfill His everlasting physical promises. The church is not a replacement for the nation of Israel; it exists to make that nation jealous until the fullness of time. Then God will restore national Israel (Rom. 11:1–2, 11, 23–27, cf. Isa. 65:17–25).

One further clarification about the church. It is not synonymous with the kingdom; the kingdom is broader than the church. The people of God in the church are kingdom citizens ruled over by Christ (Eph. 1:20–23). But the fullness of the kingdom is still yet to come (Acts 1:6–8). (This will be discussed in more detail in Chapters 11 and 12.)

Jesus: The Second Adam

The message of the gospel must be traced from Adam through the covenants to Jesus, who is the second Adam (Rom. 5:12–21; 1 Cor. 15:22, 45). The seed promise to Adam and Eve (Gen. 3:15; 4:1) passed on down through the line of Abraham (Gen. 13:15; 17:8) and was fulfilled in Jesus (Gal. 3:16; 4:4–5). Jesus is the culmination of the grace in each one of the covenants: Noahic (1 Pet. 3:18–21); Abrahamic (Gal. 3:16); Mosaic (Rom. 8:2); Davidic (Matt. 12:23–28); New (Luke 22:20; 2 Cor. 3:6). As such, Jesus unites all believers in Himself (Gal. 3:25–29). This work of uniting all believers in Himself is a special work of the New Covenant accomplished through the New Covenant work of Spirit baptism (1 Cor. 12:13). Spirit baptism is the means by which believers are placed "in Christ" so that they become one with Him. To be in union with Christ means to share in all the benefits of Christ. Thus, if you're Christ's, then you also become Abraham's offspring (Gal. 3:29). Being "in Christ" is in direct contrast to being "in Adam." In Adam there is only death and condemnation (Rom. 5:15–19), but in Christ there is life and righteousness (1 Cor. 15:21–22; Gal. 2:20).

The Day of the Lord

Through the Old Testament prophets, God promised that there would be a specific time period when He will judge the kingdoms of the world (Obad. 1:15–16, 18; Joel 2:1–17; 3:1–17; Zeph. 1:1–3:8) and bless His remnant (Obad. 1:17, 19–21; Joel 2:18–32; 3:18–21; Zeph. 3:9–20). This time was referred to as *the Day of the Lord* or *that Day*. Many Israelites looked forward to *that Day* when God would judge the enemy nations—not realizing that they too would be judged if they continued in disobedience (Amos 5:18–20).

Divide students into small groups. Have students search for *the Day of the Lord* or *that Day* in one of the passages listed above. Then they should create a chart with one column listing the details of the judgments that will accompany *the Day of the Lord* and another column that details the restorative blessings.

Every passage above includes a terrible judgment that seems to indicate complete destruction or a final judgment (Zeph. 3:8, cf. 2 Pet. 3:10), but every passage follows up that judgment with a promise to restore the earth for God's people (Zeph. 3:20). The exile and return may have foreshadowed *the Day of the Lord*, but the ultimate consummation described in those passages is still yet to come (Ezek. 38:1–39:29, cf. Rev. 20:7–10). The New Testament church still awaits *the Day of the Lord* (1 Thess. 5:2; 2 Thess. 2:2; 2 Pet. 3:10). The book of Revelation is filled with these same themes, identifying *the Day of the Lord* with a whole series of events that will take place during the time of the Tribulation (judgment) and during the time of the Millennial Kingdom (blessing).

Jesus: The Worthy Judge

In stark contrast to His first coming, when Jesus did not come to judge the world (John 3:17; 12:46-49), Jesus *will* come to judge the world at His Second Coming (2 Thess. 1:5–10). The basis of His judgment on *that Day* will be the world's disobedience to the Word (2 Thess. 1:8; 1 Pet. 2:8) that He had spoken at His first coming (John 12:48). People's refusal to submit to Him as Lord—to do the will of the Father (Matt. 7:21)—proves their unbelief and persistent, unrepentant rebellion (John 3:18–21, 36; Eph. 2:2–3). The basis for Jesus' qualification as judge is His resurrection from the dead, demonstrating that His sacrificial payment was accepted by God the Father (Acts 17:31). Thus, Jesus is able to intercede on behalf of those who accept His payment (Heb. 7:25), but He will judge those who reject His payment and His kingdom authority (2 Tim 4:1; Rev. 6:16).

THINKING IT THROUGH 10.2

1. take the throne of David to reign forever as King; He is both human and divine.

2. He had arrived as the King; He exercised authority in His teaching and miracles over the realm of nature and of Satan.

3. Since Jesus came to bring salvation, He had to pay the price for sin so that there could be kingdom citizens.

4. God's people will reign over the earth; they will take dominion as God originally intended.

♀5. When the apostles preached repentance for salvation, they preached Jesus' redemptive work and how that work fit into His larger kingdom mission. Therefore, the larger story of the Bible should be presented as a part of the gospel.

SECTION OBJECTIVES 10.3

1. Defend the idea that Redemption is restoration by explaining that resurrection brings restoration rather than replacement.

2. Defend the idea that Redemption is restoration by clarifying that the future kingdom brings restoration rather than replacement.

3. Plan specific activities to carry out the Creation Mandate, engaging in the culture in ways that are biblically faithful.

The People of God

Jesus' judgment of the earth is something the martyred saints in heaven beg for:

> O Sovereign Lord, holy and true, how long before you will judge and avenge our blood on those who dwell on the earth? (Rev. 6:10)

From the very first murder in history, the blood of godly people has called out for God's vengeance. God's children are part of the seed of the woman, and they have suffered repeated bruisings from the Serpent and his seed. And yet they—we!—have been promised eternal triumph because we are in Christ. "If you are Christ's, then you are Abraham's seed, and heirs according to the promise" (Gal. 3:29, NKJV).

The story of Redemption ends with a promise of what will become of Christ's people: "And night will be no more. They will need no light of lamp or sun, for the Lord God will be their light, and they will reign forever and ever" (Rev. 22:5).

"They will reign." The story of the Bible begins with a divine command for men and women to take dominion over the earth. We failed in that task, but the Son of Man has received the kingdom on our behalf. In Him, all the saints of the Most High have subdued the earth and will enjoy an eternal dominion.

THINKING IT THROUGH 10.2

1. What larger mission did Jesus come to fulfill, and what qualified him to fulfill it?

2. Why did Jesus proclaim that the kingdom had drawn near? How did He demonstrate that the kingdom had drawn near?

3. How did the death and resurrection of Jesus fit in with the larger mission that He had come to fulfill?

4. What future promise does the story of Redemption give to God's people? How does that promise relate to the original Creation Mandate?

♀5. How is the message of the gospel connected to Jesus' larger mission?

10.3 RESTORING GOD'S GOOD CREATION

When you get a hole in the knee of your pants, you have several options. You can patch it, but that will look funny. You can pay to have it rewoven, but that's very expensive. Restoring something broken is often more costly, in fact, than just replacing it outright. But restoration is precisely what God has in store for His broken creation.

One of the main lessons to learn from the history of Redemption is that God is sparing no expense, not even the cost of the lifeblood of His Son, to restore His good creation. And it isn't just people that God plans to redeem. He has committed Himself to giving His people a particular land—in fact, to restoring the entire globe. All of God's creation will get restored, including our cultural life.

So the general picture of eternity that many people in America have is all wrong. When they think of heaven, they envision the apostle Peter standing at a gate, lots of dead people with wings sitting around on clouds strumming harps—a picture of, well, holy boredom. Eternal cloud-based harp-strumming isn't most people's idea of a desirable life.

 The Earth: Restored or Replaced?

Read 2 Peter 3:10–13. Divide the class in half and introduce the debate: Will the earth be restored or replaced in the eternal state?

The pro side should support the restoration of the earth and the con side should cross-examine to challenge that position.

Examples of questions that could be used for cross-examination.

1. How can you explain the references to both the heavens and the earth being burned up in 2 Peter 3:10–13?

2. Don't believers just live on the new earth during the Millennium and then go to heaven for eternity?

3. Even if the new earth is a part of eternity, doesn't the Bible identify it as brand-new—not the same earth but a replacement of the earth that we live on now?

Examples of answers that could be given for these cross-examination questions:

1. (a) Compare a variety of translations of 2 Peter 3:10. The interpretation of the Greek word translated *elements* is debated. There is some evidence for interpreting it as *heavenly bodies*, in which case only they pass away, not the earth (Isa. 60:19–20).

Next, there is a variant reading in the older Greek manuscripts, which says that the works that are done on the earth will be laid bare, exposed, or found out—not burned up.

Most conservative scholars recognize that minor variants do exist in the thousands of manuscripts. Yet, God has faithfully preserved His Word so that

Nothing in this popular image, however, can be found in the Bible. We have little scriptural description of heaven at all, perhaps because that's not where believers will spend eternity anyway. Heaven is a temporary stop-over. Eternity will take place on the new earth (Rev. 21:1–22:5). And on that new earth, Christians will not be airy angels with nonphysical spirit bodies. On the new earth, you will get your body back—completely restored.

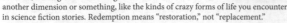

God does not plan to replace the created order with something entirely different, turning us all into beings from another dimension or something, like the kinds of crazy forms of life you encounter in science fiction stories. Redemption means "restoration," not "replacement."

Let's say that again: Redemption means "restoration," not "replacement." The new earth will be what this earth was always meant to be, not something entirely different.

The earth is like a four-year-old boy who contracts a serious disease. The disease saps his strength and deforms his limbs. But he still grows in many of the ways healthy boys do. His parents would be rightly insulted if a doctor said, "This boy is dying; we suggest you get a new boy." The parents love the boy they have, disease and all. But when he's twelve, doctors find a cure, and he begins the process of healing. The boy makes it to age twenty and by then no longer has any trace of that disease. He becomes what he was created to be—a healthy man.[3]

The earth has been progressing toward the purpose God intended for it despite the disease of human sin. And when sin is removed from the planet, the planet can be fully healed—restored to be what it was created to be. Not just people but environments, nations, cultures, academic disciplines—everything will be restored to its original purpose.

RESURRECTION

Popular symbolism and imagery about heaven have found their way into the church, so this idea of restoration may come as a surprise to you. And you shouldn't take a textbook's word for it. Let the Bible say it instead.

For example, Jesus repeatedly told His followers that after His death, He would be raised to life (Luke 9:22; 24:7). And when Jesus showed Himself to His disciples after His suffering, He proved that His physical life had been restored, not replaced. "Put your finger here," He told Thomas, showing him the wounds He received on the cross. "And put out your hand, and place it in my side. Do not disbelieve, but believe" (John 20:27). Jesus did not simply come back to life. He was restored to the same body He had lived in previously. And accepting this as true is essential to believing the gospel message.

The Bible teaches that what Jesus experienced is what every believer will experience. Paul says that the believers' resurrection bodies will be like Jesus' body: "We shall . . . bear the image of the man of heaven [Jesus]" (1 Cor. 15:49).

our copies are reliable. For a detailed treatment of this complex subject, refer to the following resources:

James B. Williams, *From the Mind of God to the Mind of Man* (Greenville, SC: Ambassador-Emerald, 1999).

James B. Williams, *God's Word in Our Hands* (Greenville, SC: Ambassador-Emerald, 2003).

According to the alternate reading from the older manuscripts, what takes place is a purging rather than an annihilation. Thus, the best of what is done on earth will come forth as gold, and the rest will be purged away. This isn't to say that particular physical goods that humans make right now will be transferred from this current time into eternity. Rather, the ideas behind them will continue on so that those same *kinds* of cultural products can be recreated: cities, houses, vineyards, and so on (Isa. 65:17–25).

(b) Peter preaches elsewhere that the earth will be restored just as the prophets had foretold—God hasn't changed His mind about the promised earthly kingdom (Acts 3:21, cf. Eph. 1:10).

2. After the thousand years on earth ends and Satan is finally defeated (Rev. 20:7–10), then the new Jerusalem comes down out of heaven to the restored earth so that God's dwelling place will be with humans—not the reverse (Rev. 21:1–4). This new earth includes all of the normal activities of human culture (Rev. 21:24–26, cf. Isa. 60:11).

3. The Greek word for "new" can mean new in quality rather than new in kind. Since there are many similarities between the new earth and the current

earth (nations, cities, houses, vineyards, etc.), replacement with something different doesn't make sense, but restoration does. It's still the earth even though it has been made new. The earth will be purged from sin (an ethical change), not destroyed and replaced by something different (an ontological change in the essence or nature of its existence). What's new is that the fallen direction has been removed; everything is structural—conformed to creational norms. Redemption is the reconciliation of people to God (1 Pet. 2:9), to others, (Gal. 6:10), and to their Creation Mandate labor on the earth (Col. 3:23–24).

Finally, any interpretation must take into account the promises of Romans 8:18–23.

Resources on Heaven

C. S. Lewis, "Learning in War-Time" in *The Weight of Glory and Other Addresses* (New York: Harper One, 1949).

Michael E. Witmer, *Heaven Is a Place on Earth: Why Everything You Do Matters to God* (Grand Rapids: Zondervan, 2004).

Randy Alcorn, *Heaven* (Carol Stream, IL: Tyndale House, 2004).

While the following resource is helpful overall because the authors defend a physical restoration of the earth in the eternal state, they spiritualize the reality of the new Jerusalem coming out of heaven in Revelation 21–22: Dan C. Barber and Robert A. Peterson, *Life Everlasting: The Unfolding Story of Heaven* (Phillipsburg, NJ: P&R, 2012).

What Is Heaven?

Heaven is often used to refer to both the intermediate state (where Christians remain until Christ's Second Coming) as well as to the eternal state. But the eternal state should not be confused with the intermediate state. So it is best to not use the same term to describe both realities. When the eternal state is confused with the intermediate state, it's assumed to be other-worldly (not on this earth). Thus, recent theologians, in an attempt to be clearer, distinguish *heaven* (the intermediate state) from *the eternal state* (the new heavens *and* earth). When that distinction is made, heaven is said to be temporary—between the time of Christ's first and second comings. (Before Christ's resurrection all people would abide in *sheol* or the grave: believers in paradise and unbelievers in *hades,* or hell. According to Revelation 20:14, hell is also a temporary abode for unbelievers until their final resurrection and judgment when they will be cast into the lake of fire.) However, it seems most accurate to view the intermediate state (heaven) as merging with the eternal state (the new heavens and earth). In John 14:1–3, Jesus affirms that He will go away to prepare a place for believers in which they will go to dwell with Him. In Revelation 21:1–3, this heavenly dwelling place prepared for believers (the new Jerusalem) comes down to earth, where God will then dwell with them.

Only a few other extended passages discuss the intermediate state. Both 2 Corinthians 5:1–9 and 1 Thessalonians 4:13–18 assure believers that when they or their believing loved ones die, they will be with Christ (cf. Phil. 1:21–24).

Restoration: Resurrected Bodies

Believers will be given resurrected bodies at Christ's Second Coming (1 Cor. 15:23). But what will those bodies be like? Paul addressed this question (15:35–38) for some people who doubted the resurrection. One of their reasons was that they doubted that the present mortal body could be resurrected and sustained for all eternity. Paul's answer was that they were foolish.

Why were they foolish? Do believers become disembodied spirit-beings?

Paul didn't deny a bodily resurrection. Humans don't wish to become "unclothed" nonphysical spirits (2 Cor. 5:2–4). Their future hope is to receive resurrected bodies of God's own choosing. Those bodies will be according to the kind of beings God originally created them to be (1 Cor. 15:38–41).

Do believers receive a replacement body?

Paul's answer was not that the mortal body would be replaced; rather, it would be transformed (1 Cor. 15:42–44).

Rather than returning to dust, the perishable body of flesh and blood becomes a transformed body—but it's still the same body (1 Cor. 15:50–54). According to 15:44, the transformation is a spiritual one. "It is 'spiritual,' not in the sense of 'immaterial' but of 'supernatural' . . . because it will have been recreated by Christ, who himself through his resurrection came to be 'a life-giving Spirit.'" [Gordon D. Fee, *The First Epistle to the Corinthians,* New International Commentary on the New Testament (Grand Rapids: Eerdmans, 1987), 786] Believers will bear the likeness of Jesus Christ (1 Cor. 15:45–49), who remained physical but was transformed (Luke 24:30–31; John 20:19–22, 26–27).

In addition, the house not made with hands in 2 Corinthians 5:1 doesn't mean that believers become nonmaterial spirit-beings but that God's work of transforming their resurrected *bodies* is a spiritual not material work (2 Cor. 4:14; 5:2–4).

Restoration: The Kingdom on Earth

The prophetic accounts of judgment on the Day of the Lord (Zeph. 3:8) are followed by the promises of a day of the earth's restoration for God's kingdom people (Zeph. 3:20). Peter preached about "the time for restoring all the things about which God spoke by the mouth of his holy prophets long ago" (Acts 3:21). Kingdom citizens (Rev. 1:5–6, 9; 12:1–17) are still waiting for Christ's return from heaven (Acts 3:20–21) when they will reign on a restored earth (Acts 1:6–7; Rom. 8:19–23; 11:1, 23–32; Eph. 1:10; Rev. 5:10). The kingdom of this world will become the kingdom of our Lord and of His Christ, and He will reign forever and ever at the blowing of the last of the seven trumpets (the seven bowl judgments are all contained within the last trumpet judgment) at the end of the Tribulation at Christ's Second Coming (Rev 11:15).

Divide students into small groups. Some groups should list all of the descriptions of the setting of the new heavens and earth (Rev. 21:9–23; 22:1–5, cf. Isa. 65:17–20, 24–25; Amos 9:13–15). The other groups should list all of the activities in the new heavens and earth (Rev. 21:24–27; 22:3–5, cf. Isa. 65:21–23; Amos 9:13–14).

Heavenly or Earthly Affections?

According to Colossians 3:1–2, what focus should Christians have?

a focus on the things that are above

And this isn't a minor subpoint tucked away in the appendix in a thick theology book. Paul says that this hope of resurrection is central to the whole Christian belief system. He tells the Corinthians that "if the dead are not raised," then "your faith is futile and you are still in your sins" (1 Cor. 15:16–17).

The Christian hope is not the ultimate weight-loss program—getting rid of our bodies completely. No, the Bible promises the "redemption of our bodies" (Rom. 8:23). We will be restored to the physical life we were designed for: free from illness, weakness, and any possibility of death or deterioration. As it was with Jesus, so it will be with us. We will live a glorious existence in our bodies. Just as Jesus left behind an empty tomb, so will every believer leave behind an empty grave.

THE KINGDOM OF GOD

Redemption does not put us on clouds forever. It puts our feet firmly on earthly ground.

The order that God intended for the universe was that humans should rule over the world, with God ruling over all. That's the point of the Creation Mandate (Gen. 1:28). That order, of course, was disrupted when we fell into sin. But God did not abandon this order. In Genesis 3:15, He revealed His plan to restore the human race to its original calling.

"HE WILL MAKE ALL THINGS NEW RATHER THAN MAKING ALL NEW THINGS." [4]

—BRUCE RILEY ASHFORD

If you prefer eternal cloud-sitting, the Bible's vision of eternal human rule over the earth may seem unattractive. But the Bible says in its last two chapters (Rev. 21–22) that the center of the new earth will be a city, the new Jerusalem. And what goes on in cities! All kinds of things have to happen to make a city run, and redeemed people will be running that city and its society. They'll be making human culture.

In some ways, this work will be very different from what has been known throughout the history of civilization. It will be different from Cain's city, a city built after he had strayed "from the presence of the Lord" (Gen. 4:16). And it will be very different from all of the Babylons in world history, cities renowned for their pride (Gen. 11:4), their cruelty (Jer. 50:15–16), their oppression and immorality (Ezek. 16:44–58), and their ill-gotten wealth (Rev. 18:6–8). In New Jerusalem, all of city life will be lived according to God's standards and expectations (Rev. 21:27)—according to creational norms.

But viewed from another perspective, New Jerusalem will look familiar. It will bear some resemblance to all of the great cultures—even the final Babylon. Just as the merchants of the earth carried on a prosperous trade in Babylon (Rev. 18:11–13), so the kings of the earth will trade with New Jerusalem (Rev. 21:24–26). Just as Babylon was a place of great wealth (Rev. 17:4–6) and was famous for its prominent situation (Rev. 17:9), so New Jerusalem will be wealthy beyond imagination (Rev. 21:18–21) and will be situated in a place of marvelous prominence (Rev. 21:15–17).

How will this trade be managed? Who will put this wealth to proper use? How will this prominence be maintained? This, we may infer, is the task of the redeemed—the ones who are called to reign forever on the earth (Rev. 22:5). Some will work in farming, some in architecture, some in the making of tools and musical instruments, some in engineering, some in government.

Viewed from a biblical worldview, none of this is surprising. This city is the final restoration of the Creation Mandate in Genesis 1:28. It is the restoration of the order God intended for the world from the very beginning.

IMPLICATIONS

God hasn't abandoned any aspect of human life, and neither should we. Marriage and family life shouldn't be avoided but should be restored to God's original intent. Scientific endeavors should not be abandoned as hopelessly secular; they should instead be engaged in from a Christian perspective so that God's glory may once again be declared in them. Politics ought not to be deemed forbidden for Christians but should be viewed as a legitimate place for Christian efforts of renewal. And the whole world of culture and the arts shouldn't be left to unbelievers but should be taken up by believers as a place for Christian witness.

It's true that many Christians have endeavored to live out Redemption in these areas in ways that are ineffective or, worse, in ways that compromise Christian belief and practice. But the failure of others doesn't mean that these areas should be abandoned. (Many Christians have compromised their beliefs in their attempts at evangelism or have proved ineffective in their attempts at foreign missions. But we don't give up on evangelism and missions.) The kingdom of God, the life and ministry of Jesus—the whole history of Redemption—tell us that seeking to live for Redemption in these areas is part of God's plan. Our duty is to figure out how to do this well, guided by biblical wisdom. And that's what the rest of this unit is about.

THINKING IT THROUGH 10.3

1. What does Redemption mean? What doesn't it mean?

2. How does the Christian hope of resurrection impact the overall Christian understanding of Redemption?

3. What will be at the center of the new earth and what activity will be taking place there?

4. Whether evangelizing or seeking to live redemptively, what must Christians always be wary of doing, according to the text?

♦5. Why shouldn't Christians abandon culture and its institutions?

Is Paul encouraging believers to set aside the physical world?

No, Paul had just warned the believers not to embrace the Gnostics' false philosophy of asceticism (Col. 2:8, 18–23).

How does Paul define what he means by earthly things in Colossians 3:5?

Rather than telling Christians to set aside the physical world, he is telling them to set aside sinful attitudes and actions that are common in this fallen world.

In 1 John 2:15–17, the "world" that believers are commanded not to love doesn't refer to the physical earth or to the mass of people on the earth but to an ethical system that is opposed to God. The context of Colossians 3:1–2 demands the same interpretation.

When Paul explains what he means by putting on the characteristics of a focus on things above (Col. 3:12–17), is he telling the believers to unplug from the present world?

No, he's telling them to engage in the present world's relationships in an ethical manner (as wives, husbands, children, servants; Col. 3:18–25).

Dominion in a Fallen World

C. S. Lewis asked his students whether it was worthwhile to begin their semester of academic studies when they would most likely be called up to war in the middle of the semester, leaving their work undone. Was it proper to engage in contemplation when their fellow-countrymen were sacrificing their lives? ["Learning in War-Time" in *The Weight of Glory and Other Addresses* (New York: HarperOne, 1949), 47]

Lewis addresses this question by paralleling their situation with the Christian life. He asks why we should ever engage in any of the disciplines of human culture when people are dying and going to hell. How can you go on learning when people all around you are going to their eternal damnation? He responds that this perplexity is nothing new—it has always been this way even though the realities of war make it more pronounced. The lesser matters of human culture are always overshadowed by greater matters of importance. But that doesn't mean that all culture must stop until the greater matters are resolved. Humans would never get started at all in their quest for knowledge and beauty. They would have to wait until the end of the world (Lewis, 49).

Lewis first defends the pursuit of culture, even in the midst of warfare, by arguing that to engage in culture is embedded in the nature of human life; a person's humanity can't be ignored because of a war. Ignoring knowledge and beauty would only lead a person to engage in those disciplines poorly (Lewis, 52).

Second, Lewis argues that everything we do contributes to God's glory. Knowledge and beauty are tools humans can use to help themselves and others see God's glory better (Lewis, 56). This is true even when we don't know how exactly our learning and cultural efforts will relate to advancing God's work.

Third, Lewis argues that Christians must not leave themselves defenseless because of their own ignorance in the face of unbelieving enemies. "Good philosophy must exist, if for no other reason, because bad philosophy needs to be answered" (Lewis, 58). And it will be more difficult to spot the errors of your own era if you are ignorant of the past, which reveals the erroneous thinking of both others in the past and ourselves in the present.

THINKING IT THROUGH 10.3

1. restoration not replacement

2. Resurrection restores our physical bodies; it doesn't replace them with something entirely new.

3. the city of Jerusalem; the creation of culture as the earth is subdued

4. compromising Christian belief and practice

♦5. God hasn't abandoned His creation, and He doesn't command His followers to abandon it in favor of heavenly piety; God plans to restore His creation, and Christians foreshadow this restoration when they work to steward God's Creation Mandate faithfully.

CHAPTER REVIEW ANSWERS

Making Connections

1. It's the story of what God is doing to glorify Himself by redeeming His fallen creation.

2. Genesis 3:15 not only records the Fall of Creation but also sums up the whole history of Redemption that the rest of the Bible's story is all about.

3. Noahic—God promises never to destroy the earth with a flood again; He will preserve the earth until He works out His full plan of Redemption.

   Abrahamic—God begins His plan to restore dominion through His promise of seed, land, and blessing.

   Mosaic—God gives conditional promises of blessing for obedience (and cursing for disobedience) and establishes a nation of priests to show the world how to approach Him in an acceptable way.

   Davidic—David's dynasty will last forever because a divine descendant will defeat God's enemies.

   New—God promises to forgive guilt once for all and to provide a new heart that will lead to obedience.

4. The kingdom has drawn near because the King/Jesus has arrived.

Developing Skills in Apologetics and Worldview

5. Start with Genesis 3:15, which predicts the suffering of the Messiah (Ps. 22; Isa. 53). Trace God's promises through the covenants, including the New Covenant promises. Then show how Jesus' death and resurrection fit into the larger story.

6. While Christians who engage culture need to be more aware of fallenness and more committed to faithful purity, they can't abandon God's good creation (which they have been mandated to steward) to corrupt unbelievers to do all the work of development.

Examining Assumptions and Evidence

7. Yes, Genesis 3:15 explains that the Seed of the woman would suffer (His heel would be bruised) in order to bring Redemption (He would crush the serpent's head).

8. He has been given all authority in heaven and on earth (Matt. 28:18); He is both the Messiah and the King (Acts 2:36).

9. He did the work of salvation and offered it freely to all who would believe; those who reject His offer receive His judgment (with the goal of purifying and restoring the earth).

---

10 CHAPTER REVIEW

TERMS TO REMEMBER

Redemption
Seed
kingdom

Scripture Memory

Genesis 3:15

Making Connections

1. Summarize the Bible's epic story in one sentence.

2. What Bible verse contains the thesis statement of Scripture? Explain why this verse is identified as stating the thesis of the entire Bible.

3. List the five major covenants outlined in the Old Testament and summarize their promises.

4. What is the most important point made by the four Gospels?

Developing Skills in Apologetics and Worldview

5. How could you explain the gospel to a Jewish person, connecting the New Testament to the Old Testament?

6. How would you respond to someone who says, "Every Christian effort to redeem culture has been fruitless or even damaging, so Christians should focus on evangelism and forget culture"?

Examining Assumptions and Evidence

7. Was Christ's suffering planned from the beginning? Explain why or why not.

8. Did Christ accomplish His larger mission (announced by the angel in Luke 1:31–33), or must He wait until His Second Coming before He can reign as King?

9. Why is Jesus worthy to open the seals to judge the earth?

10. Give two reasons Redemption should be interpreted as restoration rather than replacement.

Becoming a Creative Cultivator

11. What activities are you already participating in that could further contribute to stewarding God's original intent for His creation? Pick one activity and write out a vision statement (an attainable goal) and a mission statement (a variety of tasks that will help you attain your goal).

---

10. The resurrection and the future kingdom of God are both described as restorations of God's original creation.

Becoming a Creative Cultivator

11. Example: Playing an instrument

    Vision statement: My vision is to grow my current abilities and talents to better minister God's truths to others.

    Mission statement: My mission is to serve the church by providing God-exalting music that points the congregation to Him. I can do this by playing in the orchestra and ensembles on Sundays and providing accompaniment in youth group on Wednesdays. I can also do this by participating in the nursing home ministry and other outreach events.

[You may also want to ask students what values they will use as guidelines to keep their tasks in line with Christian beliefs and practices.

God-honoring not self-focused

Submissive to church's music philosophy

Excellent not unpracticed]

TERMS TO REMEMBER

Redemption—restoration not replacement

Seed—either a singular or plural referring to Jesus and Abraham's offspring in Christ

kingdom—Christ's rule/dominion on earth

Chapter Eleven: REDEEMED FOR GOOD WORKS

You are the light of the world. A city set on a hill cannot be hidden. Nor do people light a lamp and put it under a basket, but on a stand, and it gives light to all in the house. In the same way, let your light shine before others, so that they may see your good works and give glory to your Father who is in heaven.

Scripture Memory
Matthew 5:14–16

11.1 OUR PLACE IN GOD'S STORY

The author of *The Lord of the Rings*, J. R. R. Tolkien, once commented that stories like his, at their best, serve as "a far-off gleam or echo of evangelium [the gospel] in the real world."[1] Tolkien succeeded in echoing the gospel in his own story, and his trilogy is the number-two best-selling work of fiction in history.

One conversation in Tolkien's epic tale illuminates his comment. The main characters, Frodo and Sam, sit on the slope of Mount Doom contemplating their story. Sam speaks:

> We shouldn't be here at all, if we'd known more about it before we started. But I suppose it's often that way. The brave things in the old tales and songs, Mr. Frodo: adventures, as I used to call them. I used to think that they were things the wonderful folk of the stories went out and looked for, because they wanted them, because they were exciting and life was a bit dull, a kind of a sport, as you might say. But that's not the way of it with the tales that really mattered, or the ones that stay in the mind. Folk seem to have been just landed in them, usually—their paths were laid that way, as you put it. . . . I wonder what sort of a tale we've fallen into?[2]

Frodo admits he doesn't know but isn't bothered by that because "that's the way of a real tale. Take any one that you're fond of. You may know, or guess, what kind of a tale it is, happy-ending or sad-ending, but the people in it don't know. And you don't want them to."[3]

Sam agrees and starts recounting what happened to some other individuals in the story: "But that's a long tale, of course, and goes on past the happiness and into grief and beyond it. . . . Why, to think of it, we're in the same tale still! It's going on. Don't the great tales never end?"[4]

Frodo replies, "No, they never end as tales . . . but the people in them come, and go when their part's ended."[5]

Theodrama

"The tales that really matter" never end. That's truer of the metanarrative told by the Bible than it is of any other story. That's why enduring human tales like Tolkien's can point to the gospel. We can say of the people who played their parts in God's tale, from Adam to Ruth to Paul, that their "paths were laid that way" by a divine storyteller.

And when all their adventures and ours are over, we will begin—in the words of Tolkien's friend C. S. Lewis, the words Lewis used to draw his own famous tales about Narnia to a close—"Chapter One of the Great Story which no one on earth has read: which goes on forever: in which every chapter is better than the one before."[6]

SALVATION AND JUDGMENT

If you have a heart Jesus Christ has made new, that new heart thrills to hear that the big story isn't over. The story just can't be over—there are too many people who are suffering and too many who are rebelling. Many of God's image-bearers are doing

REDEEMED FOR GOOD WORKS | 153

Lesson Plan Chart—Chapter 11

Section Title	Pages	Activity Manual	Days
11.1 Our Place in God's Story	153–57		2 days
11.2 Witness and Good Works	158–63	Activity 19	2 days
11.3 Pushing in the Right Direction	163–67	Activity 20	1 day
Review			1 day
Total Suggested Days			**6 days**

The student will be able to

11.1 Determine the present place of Christians in God's unfolding kingdom story.

11.2 Explain the present role of Christians—to be salt and light during times of suffering.

11.3 Apply structure and direction for the purpose of bearing witness and living a life of good works in the midst of current culture.

SECTION OBJECTIVES 11.1

1. Defend the idea that God's kingdom comes in two phases—the first of which has already come and the second of which is yet to come.

2. Compare and contrast what should and shouldn't be the mission of believers based on their place in God's kingdom story: living in the gap between salvation and judgment.

Tolkien's Theology

Tolkien's *Lord of the Rings* critiqued modernism by reinforcing a larger epic story that reflects the gospel motif of Creation, Fall, and Redemption. That's the extent of what is meant by the Student Text when it says that Tolkien succeeded in echoing the gospel. His story is masterfully patterned after CFR.

However, it may be helpful to clarify to students that Tolkien was in fact a Roman Catholic. Therefore, evangelical Protestants would not agree with him about important aspects of the gospel even though they often view much of what he wrote as a largely positive reflection of some gospel truths.

One of those truths is that each one of us is playing a part in God's larger unfolding story of the world. We have a purpose. We have a role to play in God's larger plan.

The Mission of Believers

The verbal declaration of the gospel can't be pushed aside by engaging only in the work of the Creation Mandate. There's a danger in emphasizing cultural engagement to the neglect of giving out a clear *verbal* gospel presentation (Rom. 1:15–17; Eph. 1:13; Col. 1:5; 1 Thess. 2:13). But there is also a danger in emphasizing simple verbal witnessing to the neglect of contributing to the good of society (Matt. 5:16; James 2:14–16; 1 John 3:17–19). This neglect can make the message seem superficial. If persecution hinders Christians from influencing culture, then their good testimony in suffering gives their message substance (2 Cor. 6:1–11; 1 Pet. 2:12). Engaging in the Creation

Mandate should complement evangelism not compete with it. It shouldn't undermine it with impurity or wrongdoing (James 1:27; 1 Pet. 2:20).

Being a Verbal Witness
What makes verbal witnessing difficult?

• *ignorance*
• *fear*
• *isolation*
• *persecution*

What can you do to overcome such difficulties?

• *study God's Word; simply proclaim what you do know (Ps. 119:12–16)*
• *pray for boldness (Eph. 6:18–19; Phil. 1:20)*
• *go proclaim (Matt. 28:18-20; 1 Cor. 9:19–23)*
• *accept persecution (Matt. 5:10–12)*

How will you attempt to be a better verbal witness both as an individual and as a part of your church's outreach?

Guide students to brainstorm practical ways to engage others with a hearing of the gospel. What does their church do for outreach?

Sphere Sovereignty

The Christian version of the two-story view separates the sacred from the secular, encouraging believers to engage in endeavors that are sacred in nature (e.g., evangelism). "Higher level Christians" consecrate their lives to devotional pursuits or to full-time Christian service. They live primarily for spiritual endeavors, not temporal ones.

On the other extreme, Reconstructionism encourages believers or the institutional church to strive for a *Christian* society or even to "bring in the kingdom" or the Second Coming of Christ. These Christians seek to gain positions of significance in society, Christianizing the culture by exercising significant control in the main institutions of society. Of course, Christians should want to influence the culture for Christ, but the danger of triumphalism is that it fails to recognize the role of suffering in this present age.

The alternative to these views is sphere sovereignty. (Refer to Chapter 3 of the Student Activities Manual for an overview of this paradigm.) Every sphere is an important part of life that God has gifted to humans. Because of the Creation Mandate, all people should engage in the various spheres of life. However, two important warnings are in order. First, Christians must apply a biblical worldview to every sphere of life; no sphere is neutral. The institutions of society have been influenced by secularists and are normally governed according to models that

both. If Jesus Christ rose from the dead and ascended to heaven to be crowned King and Lord of all, why are there any sufferers or rebels left in His dominions?

Part of the answer lies in Jesus' final words to His disciples: "You will be my witnesses in Jerusalem and in all Judea and Samaria, and to the end of the earth" (Acts 1:8). Jesus is not content to have a kingdom with only a few citizens in it. He wants His Father's house to be full (Luke 14:15–24). And He has chosen to accomplish this mission by sending His followers into all the earth. Empowered by His Holy Spirit, they are to go everywhere announcing the good news that the King has come and has triumphed over sin, suffering, and death.

"The Son of Man came to seek and to save the lost," Jesus said of Himself (Luke 19:10). "Lost"—that's you. That's every person in every family on earth. Jesus came to find and rescue us. Is there any truth more precious?

And yet countless lost people refuse the King and His salvation. They—we—twist God's good gifts in wicked directions. Think of your good brain. Who or what are its incredible powers serving?

It's hard for us humans to feel the weight of sin because we're not God. Sin is the "de-Godding of God."[7] And sin "offends God not only because it assaults God directly, as in impiety or blasphemy, but also because it assaults what God has made."[8] Sin must and will stop, or God isn't God.

So Jesus didn't tell His apostles to preach only salvation. He told them to preach coming judgment. Said the apostle Peter, "He commanded us to preach to the people and to testify that he is the one appointed by God to be judge of the living and the dead" (Acts 10:42).

The King has ascended His throne. He is ruling, and He's a merciful monarch. But the opportunity for amnesty* will one day end. The King will eventually turn from salvation to judgment.

amnesty: the act of pardoning a group of people or setting prisoners free

Christian Reconstruction?

The story of Scripture tells how we failed to rule over God's world and how Jesus restores us to that rule. A cursory reading of this story may leave a person with the impression that Christians are called to rule the world right now. They're obligated to seek the top spots in media companies and the most influential positions in government. From these positions they are to exert a cultural domination that drives out sin and corruption while bringing in godliness and virtue.

But there's a problem with that kind of thinking—it's foreign to the New Testament. Jesus didn't try to climb the corporate ladder or take over the Roman emperor's palace. Likewise, the early church didn't try to co-opt the positions of power in first-century society. It is true that by the end of the story (Rev. 22), sin and corruption are driven out of God's world. But forcing sin out is not the church's role in God's story—or even Jesus' part while He walked the earth. He didn't try to use the power of cultural domination to bring about redemption, nor should the church.

CHRISTIAN RECONSTRUCTIONISTS

Christian Reconstructionism teaches that the moral and civil aspects of the Mosaic law are the standard of righteousness that should be incorporated into the law codes of all nations. Christian Reconstructionists are typically postmillennialists, and they advocate using democratic means to reconstruct US society according to God's law.

To some, these observations seem to contradict the whole idea of the kingdom of God. If that kingdom has come, why doesn't the New Testament present Jesus as a King with real power—the power to stop evil and overcome God's enemies? Why does it present the church as a persecuted community? Answering these questions requires us to take another look at how the Bible presents the coming of the kingdom of God.

are based on false presuppositions or faulty ethics. The manner of Chrisitan engagement must not only be holy (salt) but also shaped by a biblical worldview (light). Second, not every sphere is equal in every way. Different spheres have different tasks. Those tasks must be prioritized. Finally, both a biblical worldview and personal piety must remain at the center, primarily shaped through the ministry of the institutional church. It is only from the divine grace at the heart of all of the spheres that Christians will operate in those spheres faithfully.

Sphere sovereignty differs from Reconstructionism in *motivation*. The goal is not to bring in a Christian society but to live out the Creation Mandate faithfully in all areas of life. It differs in *tactics*. Since the goal is different, it's not necessary to take over power-broker positions. Christians may find

themselves in positions of influence, but faithfulness can take place on every level of society. It differs in *expectation*. Only Christ can set up the kingdom or a Christian society. Before His return Christians will suffer persecution.

[*Note:* Christian Reconstructionism (the approach to government called theonomy) is critiqued in detail in Chapter 18.]

A Vision of World History

Old Testament passages such as Daniel 7 provide orientation for understanding the theme of the kingdom of God in Jesus' teaching (Mark 1:14–15). Divide students into small groups. Each group should study the passage, answering the questions on their own. Discuss their answers and provide the additional information given below.

In the vision God gave Daniel about the rise and fall of the great kingdoms of the earth, each is presented as a vicious beast that comes to prominence and then fades (Dan. 7).

THE KINGDOM OF GOD: *ALREADY* AND *NOT YET*

The Old Testament is rich with prophecies concerning the coming of the Messiah—and with Him the coming of the kingdom of God. These prophecies make it clear that the Messiah's coming will be good news for some and bad news for others.

In the vision God gave Daniel about the rise and fall of the great kingdoms of the earth, each is presented as a vicious beast that comes to prominence and then fades (Dan. 7). When the last kingdom rises, Daniel sees "one like a son of man" coming "with the clouds of heaven" (7:13). He then sees Him approach "the Ancient of Days," from whom this Son of Man receives an everlasting kingdom, and with the power of this kingdom He saves His people and defeats God's enemies. For the "saints of the Most High," this is very good news because it means that they will be delivered from oppression and be allowed to "possess the kingdom forever" (7:18). But for those who oppose God's working in the world, it's the worst news imaginable. They will be "consumed and destroyed to the end" (7:26).

Some of those prophecies have been fulfilled already in Jesus. But many, especially the ones promising the destruction of God's enemies, have not yet been fulfilled. There is at the same time an *already* and a *not yet* in the rule of Jesus.

Already

The very first recorded sermon of Jesus was based on Isaiah 61. Standing in the synagogue of His hometown of Nazareth, He read,

> The Spirit of the Lord God is upon me, because the Lord has anointed me to bring good news to the poor; he has sent me to bind up the brokenhearted, to proclaim liberty to the captives, and the opening of the prison to those who are bound; to proclaim the year of the Lord's favor. (Isa. 61:1–2)

God and oppressive against the saints. His rule will seek to fundamentally change the ways and laws of God's norms in society.

- The Ancient of Days will intervene on behalf of the saints. Judgment will be meted out so that the saints of the Most High will possess the kingdom forever.

How should the kingdoms be identified?

- *The lion represents the kingdom of Babylon (Dan. 2:38; 4:28–37).*
- *The bear (ram in Daniel 8) represents the kingdom of Medo-Persia and its three great conquests: Lydia in 546 BC; Babylon in 539 BC; Egypt in 525 BC. (The parallel vision in Daniel 8 identifies some of the kingdoms by name; Dan. 2:39; 8:20.)*
- *The leopard (goat in Daniel 8) represents the kingdom of Greece (under Alexander the Great until 323 BC), which was divided into four parts under his four generals: Macedonia and Greece under Cassander; Thrace and Asia Minor under Lysimachus; Syria and Babylon under Seleucus I Nicator; Egypt and Palestine under Ptolemy I Soter (Dan. 2:39; 8:21–22). Subsequent to these four rulers, Antiochus IV Epiphanes (a type of the end-time Antichrist; Dan. 8:17, 25) came to power (175–163 BC), assassinated the Jewish high priest, set up an altar to Zeus in the temple, and persecuted the Jews (Dan. 8:8–14) until Judas Maccabeus overthrew his forces (celebrated by Hanukkah).*
- *The unique beast represents the kingdom of Rome (cf. Dan. 2:41–44). It will be revived during the Day of the Lord (Dan. 7:25; 12:11) when the Antichrist (the man of lawlessness) will be revealed (Dan. 11:36–37; 2 Thess. 2:3–12; Rev. 13:1–6).*
- *With the final destruction of the last kingdom (2 Thess. 2:8; Rev. 19:20), Christ will return (Dan. 2:44–45; 7:14, 27; Matt. 24:30; Mark 14:61–62) and His kingdom will be set up for a thousand years (Matt. 25:31–46; Rev. 19:11–21; 20:1–6) before merging into the eternal state (Rev. 21:1–22:5).*

Have some of these prophecies already been fulfilled?

Yes, world history can confirm the specific sequence of events—which took place long after the prophecy was given in 553 BC—from the rise and fall of Babylon to Medo-Persia to Greece to Rome.

Have all of these prophecies already been fulfilled?

No, not yet. The man of lawlessness has not yet been revealed (2 Thess. 2:1–3).

The *Already* and the *Not Yet*

Luke 4:21 isn't just a fulfillment of Jesus' *coming* as predicted in Isaiah 61. It's a fulfillment of Jesus coming *as the promised Messianic King*. As such, He performs the works of the kingdom, proving the genuineness of His Messiahship (Isa. 35:5–6; Matt. 11:2–6).

What is the general setting and topic of the vision (Dan. 7:1–3)?

In the first year of Belshazzar's reign (553 BC), Daniel had a dream of four beasts coming up out of a wind-blown sea.

What are the specific descriptions of the vision (Dan. 7:4-14)?

Daniel describes in detail the four beasts that come up out of the wind-blown sea:

- *A lion with eagle's wings was plucked of its wings, made to stand upright like a man, and given a mind to think like a man.*
- *A bear was raised up on its side with three ribs in its mouth; it was told to get up and to devour much flesh.*
- *A leopard with four wings and four heads was given dominion.*
- *A unique beast of fierceness with iron teeth, bronze claws, and ten horns devoured and*

trampled all that was left; a smaller horn with eyes and a mouth uprooted three of the previous horns.

Daniel describes a heavenly throne room in which judgment is meted out to each beast:

- *The Ancient of Days, His throne, and His servants are all described in detail.*
- *The court proceedings are described.*
- *The Son of Man's inheritance is described.*

What was the interpretation of the vision given to Daniel (Dan. 7:15–28)?

- *The four beasts represent four kings that will lose their worldwide dominions (the four winds may represent angels; the sea represents the earth with its nations).*
- *In particular, the fourth and greatest beast will successfully war against the saints. His kingdom will be unique because his rule will be worldwide, incontestable from competing kings, and particularly blasphemous against*

Since it has been revealed that Jesus' coming is actually split into two comings, then it should also be clear that Jesus' kingdom fulfillment has a two-fold character to it.

Because Israel killed the Son, the kingdom has been taken from Israel's oversight and given to the Gentiles until Christ returns. The *realm* (the kingdom) doesn't cease to exist just because the *ruler* has gone away for awhile. At His return, the kingdom will take on new characteristics, but the kingdom is currently being tended by tenants now (Matt. 21:33–46, cf. Rom. 11).

The Kingdom: Present and Future

What identity did Jesus accept? (Matt. 9:6, 27; 12:23; 15:22; 16:13-17; 21:9, 15; 22:42–46; Luke 1:32; John 1:48–50, cf. Dan. 7:13)

the Son of David; the Son of Man; the Christ—the Messianic King of Israel

He clearly established Himself as *Ruler*.

What were Jesus and His disciples constantly preaching? (Matt. 3:2; 4:17; 10:7–8; Mark 1:15; Luke 10:1, 9)

that the time was fulfilled—the kingdom was at hand or had drawn near

The time was *fulfilled* (at least partially)— not just impending—for the establishment of the *Realm* (at least in some form).

How did Jesus prove that the kingdom was present at His first coming? (Matt. 9:35; 12:22–28; Luke 11:20)

through miraculous works that fit the description of the works of the kingdom prophesied in the Old Testament (Isa. 35:5–6; 61:1–2)

Would the kingdom arrive in the observable form that the Jews expected—in accordance with the descriptions predicted in the Old Testament? (Luke 17:20–21)

No, the kingdom (in some form) was already in the midst of the unbelieving Pharisees, in the presence of Jesus, even though they didn't recognize the realm (in accordance with the Old Testament descriptions) and didn't submit to His reign (which won't be fully realized until His Second Coming; cf. Ps. 110).

How do people enter the kingdom? (Luke 18:18–30, cf. Acts 8:12; 28:23; Col. 1:13)

through salvation in Christ

This isn't teaching works salvation; rather, it teaches Christ's demand that people choose Him over everything or everyone else (Matt. 13:44–46; Luke 9:57–62).

This salvation is distinct from salvation in the Old Testament because it is a salvation in the context of the New Covenant's baptism in the Spirit—union with Christ (1 Cor. 12:13).

After reading the passage, Jesus sat down to teach and began by saying, "Today this Scripture has been fulfilled in your hearing" (Luke 4:21). Isaiah 61 wasn't just an important prophecy that He cared deeply about. Any scribe or Pharisee could have said that. Jesus claimed that He had been sent by God to *fulfill* Isaiah 61. He said that the promises of Messianic blessing in that prophecy were about *Him*. The poor, the brokenhearted, the captives—Jesus said that He had brought them good news. It was *already*; they needed to wait no longer.

Other statements of Jesus also stress the *already*. Throughout His preaching He said things like this: "The kingdom of God has come upon you" (Matt. 12:28). And the very title Jesus used for Himself, "the Son of Man," was a connection back to Daniel 7 and the vision of the Ancient of Days handing Him an everlasting kingdom. Every time Jesus called Himself by that phrase, He was making a claim: He was the ruler of that kingdom.

As the "Son of Man," Jesus had incredible kingly power: "The Son of Man has authority on earth to forgive sins," Jesus said (Matt. 9:6). And "all authority in heaven and on earth has been given to me" (Matt. 28:18).

Not Yet

But Jesus knew that His kingdom had not yet conquered all its enemies. In front of the Sanhedrin right before His crucifixion, He made a promise: "You will see the Son of Man seated at the right hand of Power and coming on the clouds of heaven" (Matt. 26:64). "You *will* see," in other words. The kingdom is not all here yet. It couldn't be— because many things the Old Testament prophets promised about the kingdom hadn't (and still haven't) come to pass.

The Old Testament predicted a kingdom of salvation, and that had already come in Jesus. But it also promised a kingdom bringing judgment—and that has not yet occurred. This fact confused some people, especially John the Baptist. It made John question whether or not Jesus was even the Messiah. He had introduced Jesus to the world as the one who would pour out the Holy Spirit on some and the fire of God's wrath on others (Matt. 3:11–12). But now John was in jail, imprisoned by an immoral but powerful king. So John sent messengers to Jesus to ask Him, "Are you the one who is to come, or shall we look for another?" (Matt. 11:3).

In Jesus' answer to John the Baptist, we find an important clarification: "Go and tell John what you hear and see: the blind receive their sight and the lame walk, lepers are cleansed and the deaf hear, and the dead are raised up, and the poor have good news preached to them. And blessed is the one who is not offended by me" (Matt. 11:4–6). With these words Jesus reminded John that His kingdom is what the Old Testament predicted. Jesus did not fail to do what He had come to do—all the things He said He would do in His first sermon.

Jesus did something very interesting in that sermon in Nazareth. He very clearly stopped His quotation before the end of the sentence. And what did He purposefully leave out? The prophecy says that the Messiah will come to proclaim not just salvation but also "the day of vengeance of our God" (Isa. 61:2). Jesus had brought God's kingdom to this world, but only in salvation and not yet in judgment and wrath on God's enemies.

Once you understand that the kingdom has *already* come in salvation but has *not yet* come in judgment, some of Jesus' most important parables begin to make much better sense. Jesus, for example, compares His kingdom not to a mighty warrior crushing his enemies but to a farmer scattering seed (Matt. 13:3–9). Most of the ground, in fact, rejects the seed, and in those places no crop is produced. But some

Have people been entering the kingdom since the time of Christ's first coming? (Matt. 11:11–12; 21:28–32; Luke 16:16)

Yes, every person who accepts Jesus as the Christ has entered the kingdom.

The least of those who accepted New Covenant salvation in Christ was greater than the greatest prophet of the Old Covenant.

Bible scholars interpret Matthew 16:28 as referring to Christ's transfiguration (a prefiguring of the Second Coming).

How would a person be prevented from entering the kingdom? (Matt. 23:13, 15)

by turning away from Christ in salvation to become a proselyte of the Pharisees

What does it mean to blaspheme the Spirit, and how is this unpardonable sin related to the kingdom? (Matt. 12:22–32; 13:1–3, 10–17)

Blaspheming the Spirit is rejecting the Messianic kingdom works of the Son, attributing them to Satan. It was a form of unbelief that rejected the direct manifestation of the Messiah's kingdom salvation in favor of maintaining the Old Testament law as the means to God (John 3:18, 36; 14:6).

The blasphemy of the Spirit in Matthew 12 is the turning point in Jesus' kingdom teaching. In Matthew 13, Jesus introduces a series of parables about the kingdom that indicate both present and future aspects of fulfillment. But the meaning of the parables is purposefully veiled, meant only for people who desire to understand and ask for an explanation.

What do the parables of the sower and of the wheat and the tares indicate about the kingdom of God? (Matt. 13:1–30)

ground receives it, and in those places a great harvest is reaped. Jesus later explains that the seed is the good news that the kingdom of God has come and that the different soils are the different people who hear the good news (13:18–23). Some receive the news and are transformed. But most reject it. What happens to those who reject it? Nothing—for now. The farmer in the parable doesn't try to obliterate the bad soil. He just lets it lie there.

And think about the next parable Jesus told. He compares the kingdom to a field where both wheat and weeds are planted (Matt. 13:24–30). The wheat are the people of God; the weeds are God's enemies. The point of the story is that both are allowed to grow together until "the end of the age" (13:37–43). Only in the final judgment will the weeds be dealt with.

Wheat / Tares

The wheat and the tares are allowed to grow together until the end of the age.

LIVING IN THE GAP

One of the great mysteries that Jesus' preaching explained was that the Old Testament prophecies speak of the kingdom in general terms, and in those general terms it seems that the kingdom of God and of His Messiah comes all at once—salvation and judgment in one great "Day of the Lord." But when Jesus begins teaching the crowds, He explains that the kingdom comes in two phases. First comes salvation—the forgiveness of sins, the gift of the Holy Spirit, reconciliation with God, and new life in Jesus Christ. Then, after a certain period of time has elapsed, there's judgment—the full destruction of God's enemies, the cleansing fire of God's wrath on the earth.

Christians today are called to live in the gap between kingdom salvation and kingdom judgment, between the *already* and the *not yet*. We're privileged to experience the blessings of God's salvation, and some divine wrath for sin does fall in this age (Rom. 1:18), but we must wait with patience for the full vindication that will come at the final judgment. So we're blessed now to see sinners repent and receive God's gift of forgiveness. We are also blessed to play a role in the advancement of Jesus' saving work around the world as the Holy Spirit empowers our prayers and our labors. But since now is not the time for judgment, our time is not the time for reigning. Now is not the time for us to seek cultural domination. Now is not the time for "winning."

THINKING IT THROUGH 11.1

1. How can we know that we aren't living after the time of God's completion of the big story of Scripture?

2. Even though Jesus has been crowned King, what mission has Jesus given to the church?

3. What is Christian Reconstructionism?

4. What part of the Old Testament Messianic kingdom promises did Jesus already begin to fulfill, and what part has He not yet begun to fulfill?

⚲5. What is it about the church's place between salvation and judgment that makes Christian Reconstructionism incorrect?

The kingdom comes in two phases: salvation and judgment. Now is the time for sowing the good news of the kingdom (salvation in Christ).

The two phases of the kingdom should not be a foreign concept. The epistles are clear that, in one sense, believers have their heavenly inheritance now; in another sense, believers will receive their heavenly inheritance later (Eph. 1:11, 14; Col. 1:5; 3:24; 1 Pet. 1:4, 11). The heavenly inheritance is synonymous with the believer's kingdom inheritance (Matt. 19:27–28; Col. 1:12–13).

How did Christ address the faulty understanding that the kingdom would fully arrive immediately? (Luke 19:11–27; cf. 18:31–34)

People were wrongly assuming that the kingdom would appear immediately—in its end-time fullness (Zech. 9:9; Luke 19:36–38). So Jesus told a parable that explained the responsibility of His disciples during the time between His resurrection and return. The parable explained the following realities.

- *Christ would go away from His servants to receive full kingdom reign in heaven (Eph. 1:19–23). After that, He would return.*

- *He delegated to His servants faithful stewardship in His realm until His return.*

- *While He was gone, His reign would be rejected by many on the earth (Ps. 110:2; Luke 20:17).*

- *At His return, His servants must give an accounting for what they had done.*

- *Some will be rewarded according to their differing abilities and deeds (1 Cor. 3:12-15).*

- *Some will be revealed as fakes—not truly knowing the King (Matt. 25:30; Titus 1:16).*

• *Others make their rejection of Christ clear, and they will also be judged on that Day.*

[See Darrell L. Bock, *Luke*, Baker Exegetical Commentary on the New Testament (Grand Rapids: Baker Books, 1996), 2:1525–1545.]

When will the kingdom fully arrive (Luke 21:7–32; Acts 1:6-7; 1 Cor. 15:24; 2 Tim. 4:1)?

No specific time is known, but it will come at the time of Christ's Second Coming after a time of great persecution.

Luke 21:32 should not be interpreted as meaning that the disciples' generation will see the end but that "the generation that sees the beginning of the end, also sees its end" (Bock, 1691).

Instead of revealing when the fullness of the kingdom would arrive, what mission did Jesus give to His disciples (Acts 1:6–8)?

They were to be witnesses of the good news of the kingdom—of New Covenant salvation in Christ (Acts 8:12; 19:8; 20:25; 28:23, 31).

Living in the Gap

The believer's identity as a pilgrim, sojourner, and ambassador

A sojourner temporarily settles into a foreign land (Heb. 11:8–10, 13–16; 1 Pet. 2:11). An ambassador represents and appeals on the behalf of another (2 Cor. 5:20; Eph. 6:20). See page 115.

The believer's task to be salt and light

Live a life of purity and righteousness (Matt. 5:13; Phil. 2:15; James 1:27).

Live a life of witness and good works (Matt. 5:14-16; 1 Pet. 2:12). See page 13.

THINKING IT THROUGH 11.1

1. people are still suffering and rebelling

2. to be witnesses (announcing the good news that the King has come and has triumphed over sin, suffering, and death), making more kingdom citizens

3. It teaches Christians that their mission is to rule over the culture by strategically taking over all of the key influential and powerful spots in government and society so that Christianity will dominate the world.

4. salvation; judgment

⚲5. The problem is not with Christian influence but with diverting the mission of the church from what Jesus tasked believers with in an attempt to bring in God's kingdom fully before Christ's Second Coming.

1. Explain that Christians are often called on to suffer because God's kingdom of salvation overlaps with Satan's kingdom of darkness.

2. Explain the Christian's task of bearing witness in word and works in every sphere of life.

3. Explain the Christian's task of living a life of good works as a kingdom citizen.

Persecution Today

Assign students to a particular region or country and ask them to bring to class one current event that represents the kind of persecution that takes place there. Students should give a brief summary of their region or country and the specific incident.

Organizations that keep track of the worldwide persecution of professing Christians include Voice of the Martyrs and Open Doors. General or specific keyword searches in a search engine will also turn up stories of persecution (e.g., Deborah Peter, Nigeria, Boko Haram; Christian churches or shops burned, Egypt or Malaysia; Christians imprisoned, China or Iran or North Korea; ISIS, beheadings; homeschooling, Germany, persecution).

You may also know of missionaries in a region that is especially prone to persecution. If it is prudent to contact them for information that they can share, then you may want to have students interview them. Or if a missionary is available locally, then you may want to invite that person as a special speaker.

Persecution in America

Are US Christians really being persecuted? They don't face violence or imprisonment like many other Christians around the world do. But Matthew 5:11 includes insults and slander along with other forms of physical persecution. Not only have American Christians been slandered for their beliefs, but some have also lost jobs or businesses for refusing to violate their consciences. Since *Obergefell v. Hodges* Christians are increasingly concerned that schools, organizations, and churches maintaining stances of biblical morality will face more governmental pressure (loss of accreditation or tax-exempt status, etc.). Keyword searches in a search engine will turn up stories of persecution in America against Christians or other people who don't wish to accept the new morality (Vanderbilt, non-discrimination, Christian groups; Ball State, Guillermo Gonzalez; Lamar University, Linda Ozmun).

11.2 WITNESS AND GOOD WORKS

In 2009, Manuel was a pastor in Colombia, in a region controlled by the Revolutionary Armed Forces of Colombia (FARC), a rebel group. FARC had closed many other churches in the area, but Manuel had spent eight years pastoring there despite the threats. One day when FARC guerillas made an appointment to meet Pastor Manuel, he thought they might actually be going to give him authorization to hold church services as he had asked.

Instead, they shot Pastor Manuel five times. One of the ringleaders who was inside the house with the pastor's family yelled, "Make sure that dog stays dead." The men shot the pastor again.

Pastor Manuel's wife cleaned his bloody face and dragged his body underneath a tree. In spite of her tears, she got her Bible and began to give the gospel to everyone who came by. Her ten-year-old son told her, "Mom, don't worry. Dad died for Christ, and now he is with Christ."[9]

For most American Christians, this story feels a million miles away. It almost sounds made up—would a ten-year-old really say such a thing? Could a brand-new widow possibly do what Manuel's wife did? But believe it: violent persecution is a daily reality for many believers around the world. And there are modern-day Christian martyrs.

FARC rebels have been heavy-handed in their treatment of fellow Colombians, including Christians.

Their stories ought to make you feel keenly a sense of violated justice, of righteous anger. John tells in Revelation how he saw in heaven "the souls of those who had been slain for the word of God and for the witness they had borne." And this is what they cried out to God: "O Sovereign Lord, holy and true, how long before you will judge and avenge our blood on those who dwell on the earth?" (Rev. 6:9–10).

John says, "They were each . . . told to rest a little longer, until the number of their fellow servants and their brothers should be complete, who were to be killed as they themselves had been" (Rev. 6:11).

Pray for the Persecuted

Divide students into small groups to pray for the persecuted (Heb. 13:3). Pray for

- the spreading of the gospel (2 Thess. 3:1)
- deliverance from evil people (2 Thess. 3:2); release (Acts 5:40)
- justice (Luke 18:7–8)
- steadfast faith (Luke 22:31–32)
- vigilence against temptation (1 Pet. 5:8–9)
- boldness (Acts 4:29; Eph. 6:19)
- a clear verbal testimony, given in the right manner (1 Pet. 3:15)
- wisdom and gentleness (Matt. 10:16).
- a clean testimony and patient endurence (1 Pet. 2:20–23)
- joy in God's blessing (Matt. 5:10–11)
- compassion in their loss (Heb. 10:34)

- love shown by actions of good will toward their enemies (Matt. 5:44; Luke 6:27–28)

These requests are according to God's will (1 John 5:14).

Love My Enemies?

Jesus' command isn't a command to feel the particular emotion of *endearment* toward people who are trying to hurt you. But it is a command to feel *pity* that strongly desires to do good rather than evil—to seek their well-being (Rom. 12:17–21, cf. Matt. 5:45) even if it means suffering loss (1 Cor. 6:7; 1 Pet. 2:19–23). However, loving one's enemies isn't inconsistent with seeking the protection of the law (Acts 16:37; 22:29) or with seeking justice (Prov. 18:5). Believers can still recognize evil people for who they are and seek to hold them accountable (Rom. 13:1–8).

SUFFERING FOR DOING GOOD

Jack (not his real name), a strong Christian, had risen through the ranks at his business over twenty years to become a high-ranking executive. The company was generating over $20 billion in annual revenue and had more than a hundred thousand employees worldwide. One day in a boardroom full of other executives, a new company policy was announced. "We are planning to provide marital benefits to same-sex couples. Does anyone have any objections?"[60]

"I do," Jack said, and he asked for time to put together his thoughts. In a later meeting he explained the biblical viewpoint on homosexuality, starting with these words: "I believe I am the worst sinner in this room." People listened respectfully. A few Christians told him privately that they were glad for what he did. One non-Christian said, "Diversity goes both ways." And Jack later got a promotion.

But not everyone was pleased. Jack was (and is) a faithful and winsome witness who has worked hard on the skill of asking people questions about their spiritual lives and then sharing the gospel with them. Jack's message—that Jesus is the only way to God (John 14:6)—ran right into the strong push for "diversity" at his company.

A canny political operator saw this as an opportunity to get rid of Jack. One day Jack was called into a meeting and summarily fired. His evangelism and his opposition to homosexuality were the stated reasons. Diversity went only one way in that room.

Jack has bills to pay like anyone else. He said, "I don't dare claim to be in the same category as people that have died for Christ . . . [but] when you take a person's livelihood away, and they've got four children, you are taking away their life in some senses of the term."

But then Jack said, "It was one of the greatest moments of my life. . . . I walked away from millions of dollars of income, and basically it was so clear to me at that moment that what really mattered [to me] was being right with God."[10]

SUFFERING

During this time between salvation and judgment, Christians are not to expect cultural triumph and a life of health, wealth, and prosperity. We're supposed to expect suffering. Early in Paul's missionary work, he told new converts in Lystra and Iconium, "We must through much tribulation enter into the kingdom of God" (Acts 14:22, KJV). Later, just before the end of his second missionary journey, Paul explained to believers in Rome that now "we suffer with [Christ] in order that we may also be glorified with him" (Rom. 8:17). And just before he was martyred, Paul told Timothy, "If we endure, we will also reign with him" (2 Tim. 2:12). Throughout his ministry, Paul taught that before we enter the triumph of the kingdom brought about by judgment, we must endure the suffering of the kingdom brought about by salvation.

Suffering is the unavoidable result of living in a world where the kingdom of Satan overlaps the kingdom of God. When salvation is proclaimed in Jerusalem, Ephesus, Rome, New York, Los Angeles, and Beijing, many people repent and enter God's kingdom. They enter the kingdom of forgiveness and holiness, but they also leave behind the kingdom of sin and darkness (Col. 1:13). And Satan will not accept their desertion without a fight.

This is the reason that all through its history, the church has suffered persecution. Think about Paul's experiences in the book of Acts. When the apostle came to Ephesus, he preached and persuaded people "about the kingdom of God" (Acts 19:8). A large number of people—both Jews and Greeks—believed and became part of the church in that city. But as the kingdom of salvation grew, so did the anger and hatred in the other kingdom.

Of course, the members of this other kingdom didn't think that they belonged to Satan or that they were fighting to recapture power for the king of hell. Satan prefers to keep people in the dark about such things. But it's clear from Acts 19 that many in

Doing good to someone and seeking justice are not contradictory responses.

Expect Persecution

Overtly sanctioned persecution in America seems strange. Americans have been used to religious freedom for hundreds of years. They have been largely protected from coercive cultural or governmental pressures against their moral stances. It has only been in recent years that Christians have started to see the loss of their First Amendment guarantee of the free *exercise* of their religion.

But the American experience is an unusual reprieve from the the normal course of the world (Eph. 2:3–4). The biblical expectation is that righteousness will be slandered (1 Pet. 4:4) and that the righteous will be persecuted (John 15:18; 2 Tim. 3:12; 1 Pet. 4:12; 1 John 3:13).

Even though persecution should be expected and may even be a Christian's calling to accept (1 Pet. 2:21), it's still proper and biblical for Christians to ask God to spare them from it (2 Thess. 3:2, cf. Acts 12:5). Christians may exercise the due process of the law, seeking justice (Acts 22:25–30).

Even though persecution should be expected, it's not something that Christians should look for. It is acceptable to flee (Acts 9:23–25; 17:10; 22:18).

Even though persecution should be expected, it's still natural to fear persecution. The natural human response is to be anxious because of the threats of others. But the Lord can provide strength for human frailties (1 Pet. 4:19); He promises that the Comforter will give the courageous words to say (Acts 4:8, 13, 19–20, 29, 31).

 Worthy of the Kingdom
Read 2 Thessalonians 1:1–12.

What should characterize believers' lives when they undergo persecution (1:3–4)?

Persecution provides an opportunity to showcase growth in faith, love for the brethren, and steadfast hope (Col. 1:23).

Why would God allow persecution (1:5–6)?

Persecution isn't a sign of God's rejection or wrath against believers. It's not a sign that God is neglecting believers or that things have gotten out of His control. It's all a part of God's plan of righteous judgment:

- *to prove the worthiness of believers' entrance into the kingdom (they're genuine)*
- *to prove the worthiness of the condemned for their repayment of affliction—eternal damnation in hell*

Suffering for Christ *reveals* who deserves destruction and who deserves salvation (Phil. 1:27–28). There really are wicked people in the world who deserve God's righteous wrath. Sometimes they manifest good works and moral respectability in the community, but their persecution of believers provides undeniable evidence of the real state of every wicked person's heart when they have the opportunity to display it. God allows persecution in order to demonstrate the justification of His wrath on the ungodly (2 Thess. 1:5–6).

Since Satan wants to protect his dominion (Job 1:7; 2 Cor. 4:4; Eph. 2:2; Col 1:13; Rev. 12:9), persecution is ultimately satanic—an attempt to destroy the believer's faith (Job 1:9–11; Luke 22:31; Eph. 6:12; 1 Pet. 5:8). But it's also God's way of proving Satan's accusations false (Job 1:8, 12; 42:5). It's God's way of proving the worthiness and genuineness of His people (Acts 14:22; 2 Tim. 2:12–13).

Should believers ever wish for the wrath of God to come down on their enemies?

While believers are required to love their enemies by desiring their well-being and not seeking vengeance (Rom. 12:17–21) and while God is merciful (Eph. 2:4; 2 Pet. 3:9), God is also righteous (Rom. 2:5; Heb. 12:29). He is jealous for His name and His people (Exod. 34:14; Ezek. 39:25). God's people are also jealous for God's name (1 Sam. 17:26; Ps. 139:21–24; Acts 21:13; Gal. 5:12) and for His righteous plan to be fulfilled on the earth (Acts 4:26–29). Therefore, it is fitting to cry out to God to avenge His name and the lives of His saints who have suffered for His name (2 Thess. 1:6-9; 2 Tim. 4:14; Rev. 6:10). Christians are to imitate God who hates both the wicked and their wickedness (Ps. 5:4–5). They are to imitate God who forgives those who show genuine repentance (Ezek. 33:11–20).

Suffering and God's Good Plan

If it's Satan's plan to destroy faith through suffering, it's God's plan to showcase the faith of His saints through their suffering (Heb. 11:32–12:4, cf. 1 Cor. 15:32; 2 Cor. 1:7–12; 4:7–17; 11:24–33). What Satan means for evil, God turns into good (Gen. 50:20) through His grace (2 Cor. 12:9). Responding to suffering with intense joy requires a correct perspective of faith—an unwavering faith that perseveres in trusting that God, who provided the greatest gift of all (salvation), unfailingly provides every perfect gift (James 1:1-18).

Writing assignment: Ask students to write one to three paragraphs describing a biblical incident in which God worked out for good what humans/Satan meant for evil.

Example passage: Joshua 24:1–15

Joshua recounts Israel's history from God's sovereign leading of Abraham to His guidance of the people out of Egypt, through the wilderness, and into the Promised Land. In recounting that history Joshua knows that the people are well aware of the many twists and turns that befell them. But he reminds them that "not one word has failed of all the good things that the Lord your God promised" (Josh. 23:14). It may have seemed to them that the only purpose of the wilderness wandering was punishment. But the historical reality was that Egypt was a dominant political power that had strong foreign policy interests in the land of Canaan when the Israelites first left. However, forty years later, Egypt's new ruler's focus was domestic—with little interest in defending the Canaanite city-states.

Culture Wars

Define *culture wars*.

They're the conflicts between groups (often religious conservatives and traditionalists versus secular progressives) with different worldview beliefs, values, and behavioral norms.

List examples of culture war issues (often social and political in nature):

- religious morality in the public square
- sanctity of life (abortion, euthanasia)
- sexual morality (cohabitation, homosexuality, feminism, pornography, censorship, sex education in public schools, etc.)
- recreational drug use
- violence in movies and video games
- evolutionary science
- environmentalism

Winning the Culture Wars

Cultures are not neutral. Since a culture is the way of life of a group of people, it will always reflect the beliefs and values of the majority of people in the group. Many foods, customs, and traditions don't violate a biblical worldview because every culture has much good in it preserved by common grace. But because people are sinners, all cultures have sinful aspects to them. When individuals receive the gospel, the gospel transforms their lifestyles (2 Cor. 5:17; Phil. 2:15). If enough individuals change, the culture of a society will be affected. But the changes demanded by the gospel often meet resistance (Prov. 9:7).

The goal of the Christian is not to win a culture war by triumphing over his political enemies. The goal is to love one's neighbor. This doesn't mean that Christians should be passive, allowing the wicked to have their way in society. Christians love their neighbors by doing what they can to strive against the wicked (Prov. 28:4) and to contend for justice (Isa. 1:17). Christians attempt to bend society back toward creational norms. A society may be able to spurn God's creational norms, but it can do so only for a limited time because living an anti-normative life is self-destructive (Prov. 11:10–11; 12:7; 13:6, 9; 14:11, 32). Eventually God's design must spring back into place. That snap back to reality often comes with a great deal of pain. To such people, Christians reach out in humble service to minister through sacrificial lives of witness and good works. Even when these good works are lived out in the political sphere, it should be clear that Christians are not out to destroy their enemies in a war. They're living lives of good works out of love for their neighbors.

Declaring Salvation and Judgment

Bridging the gap from what you know you should do (be a verbal witness) and actually

---

Ephesus wanted to stop what the church was doing. Here's how Demetrius, an idol-maker, spoke to his fellow Ephesians about Paul and the church:

> This Paul has persuaded and turned away a great many people, saying that gods made with hands are not gods. And there is danger not only that this trade of ours may come into disrepute but also that the temple of the great goddess Artemis may be counted as nothing, and that she may even be deposed from her magnificence, she whom all Asia and the world worship. (Acts 19:26–27)

The growth of God's kingdom directly threatened Demetrius's income. If Paul continued to persuade people to repent and believe the gospel, Demetrius might have to find a new career. But it also threatened his cultural pride. If Paul continued to see success, the pinnacle of Ephesian culture—the temple of Artemis—might become an object of scorn. So Demetrius was willing to do whatever it took to stop the growth of the church.

This was an early version of the very same culture war that exists in America today. And the "good guys" didn't win. God's judgment didn't fall on Demetrius because Jesus' authority is extended in this world to advance salvation, not to bring judgment. So Paul was left vulnerable. He was proclaiming a gospel that robbed Satan of his subjects. And when Satan fought back, divine judgment didn't strike Satan down. To be sure, Jesus didn't abandon Paul. He protected him and got him safely out of Ephesus (Acts 19:35–41). But it was Paul who had to leave the city, not Demetrius. And a few years later, when Paul's race had been run, history tells us, he was martyred for the kingdom of God.

We, too, are called to live vulnerable lives. We believe a gospel that the world finds offensive. When an alcoholic turns to Christ, he offends the pride of his old drinking buddies. When a concerned Christian writes an article about the evils of sexualized entertainment, those who provide that entertainment will do what it takes to protect their income. When government officials find that the preaching of the gospel makes them look corrupt, they will likely come down hard on the preacher instead of the corruption. And it may be that in the short term, evil seems to triumph. That's because Jesus now exercises His royal power to save, not to judge. So now is not the time for winning. Now is not the time for reigning.

Lives of Witness

When Jesus stood before Pilate, the governor asked if He was indeed a king. Jesus told him, "For this purpose I was born and for this purpose I have come into the world—*to bear witness* to the truth" (John 18:37). In His earthly ministry, Jesus was called to the task not of crushing His enemies but of testifying to the truth, the truth about Himself.

Witnessing is the task of Jesus' followers too. The book of Acts opens with Christ telling His disciples, "You will receive power when the Holy Spirit has come upon you, and you will be my witnesses . . . to the end of the earth" (Acts 1:8). In the story that follows, we learn that they are to bear witness to the fact that Jesus is exalted to God's right hand (5:31), that Jesus will one day judge the world (10:42-43), that people must repent and believe (20:21), that God is gracious to sinners (20:24), and that the kingdom of God has come (28:23). In other words, they testify to the kingdom salvation that has *already* come and to the kingdom judgment that has *not yet* come.

A significant portion of the church's witness in Acts was verbal. Paul spent countless hours preaching, discussing, debating, and explaining (Acts 19:9). Witnessing in the New Testament is never less than verbal. But it is often more. Our witness includes how we live. The church testifies to the kingship of Jesus by turning away from idolatry and sexual immorality (15:29; 16:4; 17:6–7). It bears witness to the kingdom of God when its members work hard at their jobs and then give generously to others (20:33–35). It testifies to Christ's triumph over sin and death as husbands love their wives, children obey their parents, and masters treat their servants with fairness and respect (Eph. 5:25–6:9). For the Christian, all of life is witness because, according to the gospel of the kingdom, Jesus has been made Lord of everything. As Paul taught the Ephesians, Jesus has been exalted "far above all rule and authority and power and dominion . . . not only in this age but also in the one to come" (Eph. 1:21).

This whole-life witness isn't all that different from what people everywhere do all the time. In every culture, people bear witness to some grand narrative by the way they live. People engage in predictable patterns of behavior based on the dominant story of their culture. For some cultures that story is about Zeus battling Hades; for others it's about species evolving in difficult environments. These stories guide and shape how people rear their children, pursue their education, view marriage, and seek justice in society. All people everywhere orient their lives by what they believe the world's grand narrative to be.

The difference with the church, of course, is that God has revealed to it the true grand narrative. Through the gospel we learn that Jesus has fulfilled the dominion that the first Adam failed to fulfill. He is exalted far above His enemies, and He now directs His followers, the church, to bear witness to this triumph in every part of life. We are to shine our light so people glorify God (Matt. 5:16–17).

The challenge for the church today is that it's hard to live out a grand narrative that people all around us don't believe. So believers are tempted to testify to God's story for just one day a week—and by default to embrace the story of their culture for the rest of the time. But this approach to life leaves the church ineffective and confused. Jesus is Lord not just of worship but also of marriage, of art, of business, of politics, of education. So believers must learn to engage in these aspects of their lives guided by God's narrative and not by the world's.

Lives of Good Works

The American culture war turns a lot of Christians into whiners. When non-Christians see something like *The American Patriot's Bible* sitting on the shelf in a bookstore (see sidebar), they get one clear message from Christians: "This is *our* country, and you're stealing it from us!"

And whining isn't the only sin Christians commit; sometimes Christians themselves become Machiavellian* political agents—they use underhanded tactics to defeat their political opponents, and they excuse themselves by pointing to their righteous goals. One Christian political leader reportedly walked around a gathering collecting sign-ups for her newsletter and then turned around and used those signatures on a petition.

Whining and underhanded political tactics are both terrible witnesses to the kingdom. The New Testament letters were written to Christians living in a pagan society but never recommend whining or cheating. Instead one of them says,

> **WORDS OF JESUS IN RED, WHITE, AND BLUE?**
>
> *The American Patriot's Bible* is a copy of the full text of the Bible (New King James Version) interspersed with pictures of George Washington, Frederick Douglass, Abraham Lincoln, Ronald Reagan, and other famous Americans. There are sidebars praising America's Christian heritage and urging Americans to return to their roots. The overall message is that the United States is, by all rights, a Christian nation and not a secular one.[11]

Machiavellian: *scheming, deceptive, unscrupulous*

doing it requires nailing down at least four planks. Then you can cross that bridge.

- The first plank is to learn a simple gospel presentation. Be prepared. Stay on track. Tell what you know. (Not every worldview objection to Christianity can be answered on the spot during the first exchange.)

- The second plank is to be compelled by bold love instead of fear (2 Tim. 1:7–12). This kind of passion must be fueled by heartfelt compassion that is stronger than fear (Ps. 119:136; Rom. 9:3; 10:1; Phil. 3:18, cf. Matt. 9:36). Such compassion comes through Spirit-filled prayer for the lost (Eph. 6:19–20).

- The third plank is to cultivate opportunities to share the gospel. Yield in obedience to the Holy Spirit with the sincere conviction of God's calling on every believer and His authority over all the earth (Matt. 28:18–20; Acts 1:8).

- The fourth plank is to accept any inescapable persecution for the sake of spreading the gospel (Phil. 1:12–18).

Verbal witness is difficult because of ignorance, fear, isolation, and persecution. But God has provided all that we need for life and godliness (2 Pet. 1:3). We have His sure Word (what to proclaim), His emboldening Spirit (why and how to proclaim), His authoritative commission to the ends of the earth (where to proclaim), and His promised reward (when to proclaim—even when persecuted).

The Third Plank: Opportunity

Because of the culture wars and the nature of a compartmentalized society, the hardest part of evangelism seems to be finding opportunities to personally share the gospel.

What solutions can you come up with?

- *community engagement (community service, hobbies, sports leagues, etc.)*

Before planting the seed, Christians need to till the soil. How? Christians should work harder at living a life of good works—reaching out in substantive ways to serve people in their community. First-century Christians were successful in winning others by their compassionate service even while they themselves suffered persecution. Community work isn't a waste of time; it's an opportunity to carry out the Creation Mandate *and* build relationships with others for evangelistic opportunities. Once a trusted relationship has been fortified, then Christians should find opportunities to share the gospel. It's only natural that people want to get to know others before they will open up to them in substantive conversations.

- *social networking or blogging*

In New Testament times, the marketplace was not only the place of trade, but also the general gathering place for social interaction and even for philosophical or religious discussions (Acts 17:17–18). In the twenty-first century the internet seems to be a fairly analogous place; it's normal for strangers to meet and to dialogue about a myriad of issues. It's not as if a person won't meet resistance or criticism on the internet. Paul also faced hostile crowds in Athens. But the people weren't upset by the fact that he was daring to proclaim at that *place*; they were disgruntled because of the *content* of his message. Sadly perhaps, in twenty-first century America, a person will rarely meet a stranger walking down the street or in the supermarket (or even on the doorstep of his home) who wishes to stop and chat, let alone engage in conversation about anything substantive. Although it may not be wrong to literally shout out the gospel on a literal street corner, it's simply not the normal venue for engaging the general populace with ideas anymore (1 Cor. 9:19–23). Methods such as door-to-door evangelism or street preaching shouldn't be denigrated. However, it seems clear that the expected platform for dialogue has shifted to the internet. However, there are drawbacks even there: it's often impersonal and uncivil. Personal blogs are also unlikely to draw much traffic.

Witnessing Tools
Helpful tracts and online presentations

- Two Ways to Live
- The Story (which uses a CFR approach)
- God's Bridge to Eternal Life
- Five Questions About Eternity
- Ultimate Questions
- 7 C's Evangelism Cube

Books and booklets

Ken Ham and Bodie Hodge, *Begin: A Journey through Scriptures for Seekers and New Believers* (Green Forest, AR: Master Books, 2011).

Christianity Explored (Purcellville, VA: The Good Book Company, 2011).

Thom S. Rainer, *The Unchurched Next Door* (Grand Rapids: Zondervan, 2003).

Will Metzger, *Tell the Truth*, 2nd ed. (Downers Grove, IL: InterVarsity, 1984).

Putting It into Practice

How can students get involved (or how are they already involved) in a local church ministry to share the gospel (children's church, weekly outreach efforts, etc.)? Church programs are a helpful starting point. But evangelism should especially take place when believers go out into their own community to build relationships.

Ask students to make a concerted effort to share the gospel personally in the next couple of weeks with a family member, a friend, a neighbor, a coworker, or even a stranger. Remind them that their primary objective is not immediate results. They must plant and water; God gives the increase (1 Cor. 3:6–7).

Lives of Good Works

Why isn't a verbal witness sufficient? (Phil. 2:15; James 1:27; 2:14–17; 1 John 3:17–18)

A living faith must be evidenced through practical actions of love that prove the substance of the faith. A living faith must not be undermined by a lifestyle of unrighteousness. (Believers follow the ethic of Matt. 5:13–48.)

What common accusation against Christians do unbelievers give as their reason for rejecting a hearing of the gospel?

While many may be turned off by the content of the gospel, unbelievers most often point to the hypocritical lifestyles of professing believers.

How can you respond to their accusations?

Before dismissing it as a simple excuse, you need to reckon with the reality of any ill treatment and with the public sins of well-known Christian leaders. However, your response must point them back to the truth of God's Word, which does reckon with all of these realities (1 Tim. 1:19–20; 2 Tim. 3:1–9; 2 Pet. 2:3, 14). Christians do behave sinfully, even in their evangelistic efforts (1 Cor. 3:1–9; Phil. 1:15). Your response must be to cultivate a trusting relationship over time that compassionately leads them away from doubt to the truth (1 Thess. 2:1–10; Jude 1:22–23).

Keep your conduct among the Gentiles [non-Christians] honorable, so that when they speak against you as evildoers, they may see your good deeds and glorify God on the day of visitation. (1 Pet. 2:12)

Peter, who lived in a culture both hostile to Christianity and ignorant of it—a dangerous combination now growing quickly in America too—repeatedly tells his readers that doing good works is one of their most important forms of witness:

For this is the will of God, that by doing good you should put to silence the ignorance of foolish people. (1 Pet. 2:15)

There's a famous verse in 1 Peter that Christian-worldview proponents like to point to. It instructs believers to always be "prepared to make a defense to anyone who asks you for a reason for the hope that is in you" (1 Pet. 3:15). But you need to realize this isn't a call to pick a fight. The verse goes on to call Christians to provide their defenses "with gentleness and respect." And in context, the reason non-Christians might even ask Christians about the reasons for their hope is precisely that those Christians are "zealous for what is good" even when they "suffer for righteousness' sake" (1 Pet. 3:13–14).

This emphasis on good works is found all throughout the New Testament. Paul said to the Ephesians that "we are . . . created in Christ Jesus for good works" (Eph. 2:10). We have been remade through the saving work of Jesus Christ so that now we can give ourselves to the lifelong pursuit of good works.

And Jesus Himself, in His foundational Sermon on the Mount, explains that Christians are supposed to be like light: "Let your light shine before others, so that they may see your good works and give glory to your Father who is in heaven" (Matt. 5:16).

Jesus' sermon describes what those good works are supposed to look like. When faced with the temptation to be angry and bitter, the person pursuing good works seeks forgiveness and reconciliation. When faced with the temptation to lust, the follower of Jesus does whatever it takes to have victory over that sin. When faced with the temptation to abandon his marriage obligations, the kingdom citizen chooses instead to stay true to his vows. When faced with the temptation to ignore the plight of the poor, the believer chooses to be generous. When faced with the temptation to hate those who hate him, the Christian chooses to love and to prove that love by praying for his enemies and seeking to do them good.

The follower of Jesus does all of these things because this is how he would want others to treat him if the tables were turned—and this is how he shows that Jesus Christ is worthy of trust and obedience no matter what. By living this kind of life, he bears eloquent testimony to the fact that God's appointed King has come, has triumphed, and now offers salvation to all. If He hadn't triumphed over sin, could anyone live in this world as His kingdom citizens now live?

THE HEALTH, WEALTH, AND PROSPERITY GOSPEL

Some television preachers talk about God as if He's aching to get you a new car, if only you'd have a little more faith (and if only you'd donate a little seed money to that preacher's "ministry"). God is certainly permitted to provide new cars for His children. Every car owned by a Christian is, in a real sense, a gift from God. And God cares about our needs, even for transportation. But making sure we have sufficient stuff is not the top item on God's agenda for His children. What we need is "holiness without which no one will see the Lord" (Heb. 12:14). And a new car isn't going to get us to that destination. Like all things worth having, holiness is going to take some suffering. Promises of health, wealth, and prosperity are not a gospel because they're not truly good news.

The Prosperity Gospel

At its foundation, the prosperity gospel is a human religion that turns God into someone who serves humans rather than someone humans must serve. Christianity is twisted into a religion of formulas where "God can be coerced, cajoled, manipulated, controlled, and exploited for the Christian's own ends." [John MacArthur, *Charismatic Chaos* (Grand Rapids: Zondervan, 1992), 324] Its "theology teaches that God is bound by spiritual laws that govern health and prosperity. If we say the right words, or believe without wavering, God is forced to respond in whatever way we determine" (MacArthur, 329). We become sovereign over God. Physical, financial, or other material blessings are guaranteed if only the right techniques are followed. Do the right motions or send the check to the evangelist, and you'll get whatever your heart desires—your best life now! These ministries minimize biblical doctrine; they don't teach an entire passage verse by verse in context, and they don't teach the whole counsel of God. They ignore major themes of Scripture that present poverty and suffering as the norm for believers. They ignore passages that warn the rich, greedy, and covetous. They're often characterized by smooth words of deceit, false prophecies, and immoral character (1 Tim. 6:5, 9–11; 2 Pet. 2:1–19; Jude 1:11–16).

1. Instead of cultural triumph, what must Christians expect to experience during the time between salvation and judgment? Why?

2. What caused the cultural conflict described in Acts 19, and why didn't Paul win?

3. According to the book of Acts, what specifically must believers verbally bear witness to when giving the gospel?

4. Explain one reason why witnessing must be more than verbal.

♀5. What, ideally, should impel unbelievers to ask Christians about the reasons for their hope in Christ?

11.3 PUSHING IN THE RIGHT DIRECTION

Teenagers should know what it's like to be placed between the *already* and the *not yet*. You're already capable of doing a lot of things (such as driving, working, or perhaps even getting married), but some of them may be things that your life circumstances don't allow you to do. There can be a lot of tension between the abilities you already have and the opportunities that have not yet come your way. Part of your calling right now is to wisely navigate this time of tension.

And that's the calling of all Christians, no matter their age, in between Christ's salvation and His judgment. How can you wisely navigate this time of tension when Christ really rules but hasn't yet brought all things "under his feet" (Ps. 8:6)?

The concepts of structure and direction should be a help to you in this. Everything has a God-given, created structure, and everything is pushed at least a little bit in the wrong direction by the Fall. Everything is moving either in a fallen direction or back in a redemptive direction.

If you really take hold of these biblical concepts, they'll liberate you from a misleading but common question. In a consumer culture overflowing with options for how you can spend your money, your time, and your life, it's tempting to ask yourself merely, "Is this thing good or bad?" But understanding structure and direction allows you to ask a wiser and more helpful question: "What is structural about this thing, and what is directional?" Once you answer that, you can ask the more practical question, "What's the proper redemptive response for me?"

In Chapter 9, we talked about the structure and direction of sex, matter, technology, and language. Given the way those things are viewed and used in our fallen world, what's the proper redemptive response for you? How can you witness to the power of Christ's salvation and live a life of good works in each of these areas?

SEX

First consider human sexuality. Right now in the United States of America, four out of ten children are born to unmarried mothers. Among some subgroups in society the number climbs as high as seven out of ten.[12] This doesn't necessarily mean that these kids' dads are absent, but it does mean that their dads have chosen not to make (and their moms have chosen not to insist on) the only public promise of family stability in existence: a wedding.

One of the most important tools of countercultural witness Christians have right now—and one of the most important defenses of the Christian faith—ought to be our

THINKING IT THROUGH 11.2

1. suffering and persecution; Satan's kingdom overlaps with God's kingdom.

2. The growth of God's kingdom threatened things such as income and cultural pride; Paul had to leave because Jesus' authority is extended in this world to advance salvation not to bring judgment.

3. They must testify to the kingdom salvation that has already come and to the kingdom judgment that has not yet come (Acts 5:32; 10:42–43; 20:21, 24; 28:23).

4. The way a person lives testifies to Christ's kingship—that He has been made Lord of everything; behavior betrays the larger narrative of one's true beliefs; life can't be compartmentalized into the sacred and the secular; good works substantiate the genuineness of words.

♀5. because Christians' lives are zealous for good works even when suffering for righteousness

SECTION OBJECTIVES 11.3

1. Explain how applying structure and direction to the sphere of sex can help believers to be salt and light while living in a fallen culture.

2. Explain how applying structure and direction to the sphere of material goods can help a Christian to be salt and light in the context of a fallen culture.

3. Explain how applying structure and direction to the sphere of technology can help a believer to be salt and light in a fallen culture.

4. Explain how applying structure and direction to the sphere of language can help a follower of Christ to be salt and light in the middle of a fallen culture.

 ### Should I Kiss My Girlfriend/Boyfriend?

In regard to sex, how can you live in light of redemption now even before you can be a countercultural witness through your own godly marriage? Remain pure. But what does that look like? How comfortable would you be sharing with parents and pastors the extent of your physical relationship with your girlfriend/boyfriend? Would you be embarrassed if you told the truth? Why? Would you defend kissing, caressing and cuddling, or more? How do you determine where the line is and when you've crossed it? Is the standard based on your own comfort level? Is it possible to control yourself and not be drawn across that line if you do engage in some sexual contact? Should kissing even be considered sexual contact? What is God's design for sex, and what direction do your actions take you in? Objective answers can be determined based on the norms of God's design. And it isn't legalism to insist on appropriate applications of biblical principles.

What's structural about sex?

It's designed to bind two people together in intimacy only within a marriage relationship (1 Cor. 6:16, 18; 7:1–9; Heb. 13:5). It's condemned in every relationship outside of marriage (1 Thess. 4:3–8; 2 Tim. 2:22). There is no biblical category for a serious dating or engagement relationship before marriage that excuses partaking in sex.

Should kissing be considered sexual?

Kissing your grandma isn't, and the "holy kiss" of first-century Christian wasn't either (Rom. 16:16; 1 Cor. 16:20; 2 Cor. 13:12; 1 Thess. 5:26). But kissing is sexual in nature whenever it stirs up hormonal arousal for sexual intimacy (this is its structural design). It's meant to allure; it's supposed to break down barriers, drawing you into more intimacy (Prov. 7:13).

If kissing were not sexual in nature, then coworkers could do it to each other without facing charges of sexual harassment, other men at church could make out with your mom and your dad wouldn't get upset, secular psychologists wouldn't have guidelines for how to kiss to heighten the sexual experience, and you wouldn't be so fixated on it because of the "buzz" that you get from doing it. You can't redefine romantic kissing as if it were not sexual in nature.

Is sex limited to "going all the way"?

No, the Bible condemns all sexual contact (before going all the way) by condemning the lust in the mind and heart that is the impetus for any contact, such as kissing (Matt. 5:27–28). Getting onto the road leads to the destination of going all the way. Thinking you can get off that road any time you want is arrogantly naive (Prov. 6:27–28; 14:16). Instead, you're urged to set up roadblocks (Job 31:1; Prov. 5:1–23).

You shouldn't try to redefine any form of sexual intimacy before marriage (including kissing) as if it's not sin. And you shouldn't tolerate sin just by trying to limit how far you sin. You shouldn't be subjective ("I prayed about it"; "Other good Christians I know did it without going all the way"; "I know good pastors that approve of it;" etc.). Such arguments aren't *biblical* arguments. They show a lack of discernment. Proverbs 7:1–27 describes the characteristics of immoral relationships: naivete, being in the wrong place at the wrong time, immodesty, dirty talk, kissing, flattery, and being alone.

See Gerald Hiestand and Jay Thomas, *Sex, Dating, and Relationships* (Wheaton: Crossway, 2012), 32–48.

Being Light in a Sexually Deviant World

How's the light in your neighborhood, in your Christian school (the cafeteria, the locker room, the bus on rides to and from activities), in the break room at work, at your best friend's house when the TV or the computer is on or when texts and pictures get passed around on cell phones? Do you feel the pressure of the darkness pressing in on you—even from professing Christian kids (Prov. 14:9; Rom. 1:32; Titus 1:15–16)? Are you a part of the darkness or the light (Col. 1:13)? How many innuendos or immoral one-liners from the latest TV show do you and your group of friends tolerate before someone will speak up or you leave (Eph. 5:3–16)? Do you think that participating in this atmosphere of darkness will leave your future marriage unaffected (Gal. 6:8)?

Becoming a godly husband and father or a godly wife and mother won't happen automatically. Your character is being estab-

---

loving, stable families. Sex binds a man and a woman together, but that bond is not an end in itself. Ideally, sex binds the husband and wife for a further reason: a stable bond is what their children need in order to thrive. The Bible doesn't promise every Christian sexual satisfaction in a perfect marriage. But it sets up guidelines and creates a (church) community in which loving, strong marriages can grow.

Do you want this? Do you really? It will take participation in that community, it will take intense effort, it will take suffering—ultimately, it will take divine grace—for you to survive the sexual onslaught of Western culture and to create a beautiful family. If you are as fallen as the Bible says you are, it matters what music courses through your earbuds. It matters what the cheerleaders wear and what the guys let each other say about the cheerleaders. It matters what internet filter you have—guys and girls.

One of your goals should be to become the kind of person whose marriage makes other people say, "Their light has so shined before others that we have seen their good works and give glory to their Father who is in heaven." Never underestimate the power that your own inconspicuous family has as a light in darkness.

What does a life of witness and good works look like when it comes to stuff?

MATTER

Materialism—not the philosophical kind, but the shopping-mall and storage-unit kind—is another powerful force in Western culture that is pushing people in sinful directions. Plenty of people seem to live by the bumper-sticker motto, "He who dies with the most toys wins."

What does a life of good works, a life of witness, look like when it comes to "matter," to stuff? What is the proper redemptive response for a Christian living in a culture of consumerism?

One of the most countercultural things you could do would be to give up your "rights" as a Western consumer and start being generous with your money and your time. Generally speaking, you can always make more money if you're willing to work more hours. And sometimes you may need to do just that. But a Christian can be salt in his or her neighborhood and shine like a light in his or her workplace by opting out of overtime pay and sales bonuses and dedicating time instead to evangelism or orphan care or Meals on Wheels or a million other ways to give. Christians can afford to be generous because God won't forget so much as a cup of cold water given in Jesus' name (Matt. 10:42).

One of the things that should motivate Christians in their work is precisely the opportunity to earn income so they can turn around and give some of it away.

TECHNOLOGY

Many people, almost all of them adults, are raising alarms about the power of technology in society. Adult readers are complaining that technology distracts them and shortens their attention spans. Politicians are complaining that the internet has polarized public discourse. Moms are complaining that smartphones have ruined the family

---

lished, and your way of life is being formed now. Pursuing purity involves not only speaking up against the immorality of the majority but also forming godly friendships with the opposite sex now, so that you form good habits for how you treat the opposite sex. Readying yourself for a potential spouse is a legitimate basis for purity. But preparing for a future spouse isn't a sufficient basis for purity because, whether or not you currently expect you will have to, some people have to remain pure as single adults. Purity has to be founded on the fear of God and His glory.

Being Light in a Materialistic Culture

Divide students into small groups. Provide each group with just the verse references from one of the descriptions listed below without revealing the description. Ask them

---

to summarize the common principle from their group's verses.

God's structure for material wealth:

- Give to God and to His work through other believers first (Prov. 3:9; 1 Cor. 16:2; 2 Cor. 9:5–9; 1 Tim. 6:17–18; Heb. 13:16).

- Work to provide for yourself and your family (Prov. 6:6, 9; 12:27; 13:4; 18:9; 19:15, 24; 20:4; 21:25; 22:13; 26:14; Eccles. 10:18; Eph. 4:28; 2 Thess. 3:10–12; 1 Tim. 5:8).

- Be content with basic necessities (Ps. 128:2; Matt. 6:25–32; Luke 3:12–14; 12:22–23, 29–31; 1 Tim. 6:6–8; Phil. 4:11; Heb. 13:5).

- Don't seek ultimate satisfaction (or expect to find it) through material gain (Eccles. 2:10–11, 17–26; 5:15; 6:7; Matt. 6:19-21, 24, 33; 1 Tim. 6:9–10, 17).

- Instead of hoarding wealth, discern when to give compassionately to those who can't responsibly provide for their own basic

dinner hour. And tech has created problems in lots of other cultures around the world; there's a summer camp in China to help teens who are addicted to the internet.

Where are the teens who are concerned about the power of tech? It's so easy to go with the flow, to never question the way your culture deals with technology. You don't do right so that others will notice, but others *will* notice if you push back against the Fall's effects in the area of technology. Human beings can make it to age eighteen without owning the latest smartphone or having unrestricted internet access.

What could you do (or not do) with your cellphone in order to witness to the power of Christ's salvation? What do "good works" look like on the internet? The call of Christ to be salt and light may not be very dramatic. It may mean tossing your phone into your room before family dinners without being asked. It may mean looking for people to encourage online rather than people to bash. Christians are called to be salt, to be different. And we're called to be light, to be different for the purpose of displaying the truth.

LANGUAGE

Language is one of the most powerful tools God has given to humans—powerful enough, James says, to "[set] on fire the entire course of life" (James 3:6). James marvels about the tongue: "How great a forest is set ablaze by such a small fire!" (3:5).

The tongue can ruin in a moment a good reputation that took a lifetime to build. But not all forest fires are bad. Some clear out underbrush to make way for future growth. The tongue can also comfort in a moment a pain that's been building up for a lifetime.

A lot of English speakers, and not just Christians or even conservatives, think that English is disintegrating, that it's getting worse and worse as time goes on. That's highly debatable; in fact, people have been making similar complaints for hundreds of years, and somehow English hasn't died. The Fall has damaged our messages far more than it has damaged the medium of English itself. Writers can still use English to create powerful, beautiful, enduring prose. And they do, in the service of all kinds of messages and ideas. Shouldn't Christians, who have been given the task of teaching the nations everything Jesus commanded, care deeply about the power of their words? Paul warned us not to trust in the power of our own words, but he himself used eloquent speech and powerful rhetoric to deliver that very warning (1 Cor. 1:17). Christians have the gospel. We have something to say. We should care deeply about how to use language to glorify God and to testify to His truth.

STRUCTURE AND DIRECTION

Christian missionaries face structure-and-direction questions every day. They seek to live in solidarity with the culture where they minister because the gospel of Jesus Christ is for every culture. Christianity is not—as North Korean, Iranian, and Chinese government leaders like to say—a Western religion. It's a global one. Every culture has beauty and value all its own. And yet part of the missionary's job is to view the surrounding culture through biblical lenses. And, inevitably, some things will look dark. Parts of every culture are headed in the wrong direction and need to be resisted and pushed back toward God's structure.

This will always be the case until Christ comes in judgment. Till then, a Christian will never fully belong in this world even though God owns it and Christ rules it.

- Are you receptive to the mentoring of parents and pastors? (Prov. 1:8; 10:21, 23; 13:10; 14:6, 8; 15:5; 1 Thess. 2:11–12)
- Do you grumble, or do you submit to the standards set up for you? (Prov. 13:10; Phil. 2:14–15)
- How many in your culture are more concerned about privacy (code for license to be ungodly) than they are with accountability with nothing to hide from godly leaders? (Prov. 3:32; 11:20; 23:26)
- Do you know of others using their tech savvy skills to get around accountability measures? (Prov. 14:2) What should you do about it? (Eph. 5:11–13)
- Are you being devious yourself? Can you get away with secret sin? (Prov. 9:17–18; Eccles. 12:14; 1 Cor. 4:5)
- What do Facebook photos communicate? (Prov. 7:10; 21:4)
- What about your Snapchat comments? (Ps. 64:1–10; Prov. 10:31–32)
- How about your "likes"? (Prov. 2:14; 8:13)
- What could Facebook photos (Col. 3:12), comments (1 Thess. 5:14–18), and "likes" communicate to build others up (Gal. 6:10)?

List all of the ways that you are using or could use technology or social media positively for the good of others:

- *cultivate uplifting friendships*
- *share Scripture verses each day or what you're learning in your devotions (but don't spiritualize your pride)*
- *share quotes and book recommendations from good (Christian) literature*
- *send an encouraging word (but don't reinforce others' narcissism)*
- *keep in touch with missionaries*
- *share church and community activities*
- *express love for Mom, Dad, and siblings on your page (rather than complaining about them)*
- *stay in touch with grandparents or other relatives that are far away*

necessities—when you have the means after you have already taken care of your own primary responsibilities (Prov. 19:17; Eccles. 2:18–21; Matt. 6:3–4; 19:21; Luke 12:33–34; Acts 3:6; 4:32; 1 Cor. 13:3; Gal. 6:10; Eph. 4:28; James 1:27; 1 John 3:17–19).

- Enjoy what God has given you with thankfulness! You can enjoy all good things (Gen. 1:28–30; Eccles. 2:24; 3:13; 5:18–19; Isa. 65:22; 1 Tim. 4:4; 6:17).

Supporting God's Work Matters

The context of Matthew 10:42 (cf. Matt. 25:31–46) specifically refers to the support of disciples or brethren—fellow Christians or missionaries in need. True Christianity is evidenced by love in deeds (1 John 3:17–19). True Christians won't support false teachers, but they will support the brethren and missionaries (2 John 1:5–11; 3 John 1:5–11). You can do good to unbelievers (you just can't support them in the capacity of spreading a false gospel), but believers spreading the gospel must have priority (Gal. 6:10).

Being Light in a Tech Savvy World

In your own church, school, and family culture, do the majority of the social media interactions build others up in Christ? (Eph. 4:25, 29)

Answers will vary. Discuss specific examples (without allowing students to personally attack other people by name), and test their assessments with the following questions:

- Would others outside of your favorite group of friends agree with your assessment? (Rom. 12:14–21)
- Would the mature spiritual leaders God has placed over you agree with your assessment? (Prov. 3:21; 5:1; 8:12–14; 10:13; 11:2, 12)

Being Light in Edifying Communication

Divide students into small groups. Assign each small group several chapters from the book of Proverbs. Each small group should create a chart with three columns for godly speech, ungodly speech, and the corresponding verse references.

Here are some examples of verses that refer to both godly and ungodly speech: (Prov. 10:32; 12:18; 13:1, 3, 10, 18; 14:3, 25; 15:1)

Next, have the small groups read James 3 and answer the following questions.

What motivates godly or ungodly speech?

human value/the image of God (9); jealousy and selfishness (14)

What generates the differing motivations?

character that is wise and meek (13) or that is worldly, fleshly, and even demonic (15)

What atmosphere results from godly or ungodly speech?

one of purity, peace, gentleness, reasonableness, mercy, good fruits, impartiality and sincerity (17–18); disorder and all kinds of vile practices (16)

List different kinds of ungodly speech with verse references.

lies (John 8:44), gossip (Prov. 16:28), slander (Eph. 4:31), anger (Eccles. 7:9), perversity (Prov. 6:12), seduction (Prov. 7:21), et al.

Which atmosphere do you want to be in? What kind of atmosphere do you foster?

Through God's common grace most people desire peace. But your fruit reveals what you're actually sowing. You may need to reexamine the motivations behind your treatment of people and the reasons your motivations are what they are (Phil. 2:3–5).

Appropriate Words of Boldness

American culture suffers from several conflicting sinful distortions in the area of speech. Check the web, the radio, or cable news, and you'll hear a great deal of abusive speech. People are called names, opposing ideas are dismissed as stupid, and people give full vent to their anger. On the other hand, certain speech is carefully policed. Arguments for biblical positions are called "hate speech" or "not nice."

The starting place for the Christian is to be slow to speak and to be gracious when speaking. "When words are many, transgression is not lacking, but whoever restrains his lips is prudent" (Prov. 10:19, cf. 17:28; 21:23). Christians should desire to say things that are wise and that will bless others (Prov. 10:21, 31; 15:7). Especially as the Christian speaks with unbelievers, his words should be gracious and winsome (Col. 4:6). Because the Christian has been mercifully saved out of a foolish, disobedient, malice-filled life, he should be careful "to speak evil of no one, to avoid quarreling, to be gentle, and to show perfect courtesy toward all people" (Titus 3:2, cf. 3:3–4). Part of devoting oneself to good works is to avoid "foolish controversies." A person who stirs up such controversies is to be avoided (Titus 3:8–11). The Christian should be very careful about becoming angry and expressing anger. "Whoever is slow to anger is better than the mighty" (Prov. 16:32). "The fool gives full vent to his spirit, but a wise man quietly holds it back" (Prov. 29:11). To lash out at someone and call him a "fool" is worthy of damnation (Matt. 5:22). Even enemies are to be spoken to with respect (Matt. 5:47).

Paul's gospel message brought change to Ephesus, as we saw. Likewise, the Wesley brothers (John and Charles) and their gospel message brought great change to Britain. William Wilberforce was salt in the wounds of that same nation until it stopped the slave trade. John Calvin, with his extremely careful and attentive Bible teaching, brought reform to Geneva, Switzerland. And the Puritans founded all sorts of prominent Christian institutions in New England. All of these people, based on their Christian beliefs, brought about great change. And yet that change was always disappointing in some ways. Most of it didn't really last. And some of it ended up paving the way for new distortions to come along. That's just the nature of living in the gap between salvation and judgment.

We need the prayer Paul prayed for the Colossians. He prayed that those believers would be "filled with the knowledge of [God's] will in all spiritual wisdom and understanding, so as to walk in a manner worthy of the Lord, fully pleasing to him, bearing fruit in every good work and increasing in the knowledge of God" (Col. 1:9–10). We need that discernment in order to be salt, to be light, and even to suffer in this time between the times.

THINKING IT THROUGH 11.3

1. As a teen, what kinds of activities could hinder not only the stability of your future marriage but also your witness for Christ?

2. How could you be a countercultural witness with your material things?

3. How could you be a countercultural witness with your use of technology?

4. How could your use of language be a witness to the culture?

5. Why would instability in your marriage and family life make it more difficult to testify about your Christian faith?

On the other hand, Jesus, the prophets, and the apostles could be scathing in the judgments they rendered. Jesus pronounces woes on the Pharisees, calling them hypocrites, whitewashed tombs, broods of vipers, and fools (Matt. 23:24–33; Luke 11:40). John the Baptist preached against Herod for taking his brother's wife (Mark 6:18). Paul calls on elders to rebuke with authority those who contradict God's Word (Titus 1:9; 2:15). Paul didn't mince words with those who spread destructive heresies, saying, "I wish those who unsettle you would emasculate themselves!" (Gal. 5:12). Rebuke isn't incongruous with patient love; it is evidence of it (1 Tim. 1:3–7).

At first it may seem that the Bible's teaching is contradictory. Jesus says that a person who calls someone "fool" is in danger of hellfire, but Jesus Himself calls the Pharisees fools. Paul says, "Let your speech always be gracious" (Col. 4:6), but then he excoriates false teachers. In reality these passages require Christians to draw distinctions. Christians must distinguish between personal offenses and offenses against God. They may not speak in anger for the first (1 Pet. 2:23), but they ought to for the second (Titus 1:9). The harsh language used by Christ and His representatives is the language of judgment. Christians must be sure that if they speak likewise they speak with clear scriptural authority. Second, Christians must distinguish between wicked people who can be won and wicked people who are incorrigible. The former are to be spoken to graciously (Col. 4:6) while the latter are to be condemned (1 John 2:22). Finally, the Christian should consider that the harshest judgment language in Scripture is rare. It cannot be used to defend common crudeness in speech. Doing good though speech requires wisdom to make these distinctions.

11 CHAPTER REVIEW

Scripture Memory

Matthew 5:14–16

Making Connections

1. Since Jesus Christ rose from the dead and ascended to heaven to be crowned King and Lord of all, why are there any sufferers or rebels left in His dominion?

2. Should a verbal witness be replaced by a life of good works?

3. What are the four major areas mentioned in the chapter in which Christians can bear witness to their pagan culture by pressing things back toward God's created structure?

4. What is the proper redemptive response for a Christian living in a consumeristic culture?

Developing Skills in Apologetics and Worldview

5. How would you respond to someone who claims that the kingdom of God has not yet come at all in any form?

6. How would you respond to someone who claims that the kingdom of God has already fully come before Christ's Second Coming?

Examining Assumptions and Evidence

7. Compare and contrast Christian Reconstructionism with the two-story view that you learned about in Chapter 3. Which view is correct?

8. Why must Christians live vulnerable lives?

9. Is the story of Adam and Eve in Genesis 2:18–25 descriptive or prescriptive? What evidence within the passage can you point to for your answer?

10. Why are so many people concerned about the negative impact of technology on society?

Becoming a Creative Cultivator

11. List one piece of technology that you use. In what ways can that device be used for good? In what ways can it be used for bad? Write out a plan for combatting any temptation it may pose to you:
   • What specific problem can you identify and describe?
   • What makes this problem tempting?
   • How often and how long have you been struggling with the temptation?
   • How does this problem affect you and others?
   • What "fences" can you set up to keep you from the problem?

REDEEMED FOR GOOD WORKS | 167

---

promised to this Messianic King had been given to Him (Matt. 28:18).

6. The suffering and rebellion that still exist in the world can't be a part of God's future promised kingdom. The kingdom won't fully come until Jesus comes in the clouds and conquers His enemies (Matt. 26:64).

Examining Assumptions and Evidence

7. Christian Reconstructionism encourages Christian cultural domination in every sphere of life while the two-story view encourages personal piety compartmentalized off from the secular world. Neither view is correct. They are opposite extremes that are both unbiblical. As *humans*, we must be faithful to the Creation Mandate, but as Christians our mission isn't to take over and Christianize the world.

8. The gospel they proclaim will offend the people of the world because it exposes their corruption and opposes their sinful way of living.

9. Since it describes God's created order, it also prescribes universal norms for all people. Verse 24 makes a clear application that is generalized to all people.

10. Technology, like any other good thing, can be twisted into fallen uses, which are most evident to those people who lived in a time when that technology did not exist to provide that particular avenue of fallenness.

Becoming a Creative Cultivator

11. Answers will vary.

   Example: Cellphone

   It can be used for good by providing security in times of emergency, a way of efficient communication between parents and children, setting up get-togethers with friends, and so on. But it can also bring problems.

   • Specific problems: gossip, porn, and so forth

   • Reasons for temptations: private, unaccountable texting; unfiltered and unaccountable internet connection

   • Answers will vary.

   • Answers will vary.

   • Fences: submission to parental controls and guidelines for use of the phone

---

THINKING IT THROUGH 11.3

1. listening to sexualized music, watching sexualized media, wearing sexualized styles, taking part in sexualized conversations with friends, and so on

2. being generous with time and money, sacrificing for the good of others

3. using technology to share Christ and encourage others; not being so self-absorbed in technology that it hurts personal relationships with others

4. instead of using words to destroy others, using them to build others up; using writing skills to create powerful, beautiful, enduring prose or poetry

5. People judge the truth claims of Christianity, not just Christians, when professing believers live a hypocritical lifestyle that contradicts the Bible.

CHAPTER REVIEW ANSWERS

Making Connections

1. The current mission is to make more kingdom citizens before Christ returns in judgment to fully set up His kingdom.

2. No, while behavior reinforces the verbal witness, witness in the New Testament is never less than verbal.

3. marriage and family (or sex), materialism, technology, and language

4. being generous with money and time

Developing Skills in Apologetics and Worldview

5. Jesus announced that He had fulfilled the promise of the coming Messianic King (Luke 4:21), and He declared that the kingdom had come on the people of His day (Matt. 12:28). The authority

TERMS TO REMEMBER

Christian Reconstructionism—the belief that the moral and civil aspects of the Mosiac law are the standard of righteousness that should be incorporated into the law codes of all nations

The student will be able to

12.1 Distinguish the specific mission of the institutional church from the organic church's broader social responsibility of doing good works.

12.2 Explain the importance of living a life of good works through one's vocation.

SECTION OBJECTIVES 12.1

1. Explain how the church fits into God's unfolding plan of redemption.

2. Define and relate the institutional church, the organic church, and the kingdom of God.

3. Summarize the six tasks identified in Scripture as the mission of the local church.

4. Explain how the institutional church and the organic church relate differently to the various tasks of cultural institutions.

5. Defend the value of the church and its specific God-given mission.

Chapter Twelve **THE MISSION OF THE CHURCH AND YOUR VOCATION**

And they devoted themselves to the apostles' teaching and the fellowship, to the breaking of bread and the prayers. | **Scripture Memory Acts 2:42**

12.1 THE MISSION OF THE CHURCH

Epic stories have heroes—whether they are modern epics like *The Lord of the Rings* and *Star Wars* or ancient epics like *The Odyssey* and *The Aeneid*. The hero is the focus of the epic. He overcomes the odds, he succeeds in his quest, and he achieves great victory. Jesus, of course, plays that heroic role in the drama of Scripture, the story of redemption.

And yet it isn't wrong for a Christian, when he learns of this great story, to want to play a "heroic" role too. It's natural, even godly, to have the ambition to live out your portion of the story of redemption by doing something of significance for the kingdom of God.

Some believers think that to be a Christian hero a person has to be a "full-time Christian worker." In this view, the most important and heroic role a Christian can play is pastor (or pastor's wife), missionary, or Christian school teacher—a job in which you're doing "ministry" all day.

These are certainly important callings—and sometimes the people God calls to fill these roles are positively heroic. But to think that such people are the only ones who serve God in their work is to buy into the two-story view.

We want this book to help you think in a Christian way about every part of your life. The Christian life and God's plan of redemption aren't limited to the church, Christian education, and mission work. When you graduate and get a job, you should do that job, whatever it may be, in service to Christ as a Christian. This thought is liberating for many

Christians. They come to realize that they're not second-class Christians in a slot below "full-time Christian workers." They can live lives of service to God in their jobs as well.

Sadly, important truths are often misused. Some people who have gotten excited about living as Christians in all of life have lost their excitement for the church. Others have decided that since Christians are to be involved as Christians in all of life, the church's mission includes not only evangelism and discipleship but also running food pantries, working to save endangered species, providing clean water in impoverished parts of the world, and much more. These are good, necessary, and excellent things for Christians to do—but are they the mission of the institution called the church?

The church has a vitally important mission. When Christians neglect the church and its mission, they damage God's work in the world. The same is true when Christians load the church down with other missions so that its true mission is lost in the clutter. On the other hand, the church is not all of life. God never intended it to be. Six days are for working, and God does not call most Christians to work for the church. Both church and the work that God calls Christians to do are important parts of God's plan of redemption.

WHAT THE CHURCH IS FOR

What is the church *for*? Why does the church exist in the first place? Can't people be saved without it? In order to know these things, we've got to look at

---

Lesson Plan Chart—Chapter 12

Section Title	Pages	Activity Manual	Days
12.1 The Mission of the Church	168–76	Activity 21	3 days
12.2 The Vocation of the Christian	177–80	Activity 22	2 days
Review	181		1 day
Total Suggested Days			**6 days**

A Distinctly Noble Sphere

People often swing from one error to the opposite extreme. In the past few generations, work in churches and Christian ministries was viewed as superior to work in other vocations, but this isn't a balanced biblical view. However, the current generation must be careful to affirm that serving the Lord *is* a distinctly noble task, demanding a person who is an exemplary model of the character and conduct expected of all believers (1 Tim. 3:1–13; 4:12). Pastors and missionaries who are dedicated to oversight and preaching full-time are to be specially regarded and supported (Acts 6:4; 1 Thess. 5:12–13; 1 Tim. 5:17; 1 Pet. 5:1–5; 3 John 1:7–8). In addition, the institutional church shouldn't take on the tasks of other institutions; it has its own distinct tasks (Acts 2:42; 1 Tim. 3:15; 4:13).

how the church fits into God's plan of redemption. As we saw in Chapter 10, God works out His plan of redemption through a series of covenants. The final covenant in God's plan—the New Covenant—is the one that gives us the church.

The Mosaic Covenant that God made with Israel had a flaw. Actually, the problem was with the people in the covenant—they couldn't keep the requirements of the covenant. Though individual Israelites could be saved by calling on God in faith (Deut. 30:6; Rom. 10:9–10), the covenant couldn't ensure that the people of Israel would love and trust God. This, of course, didn't surprise God. He predicted it when He made the covenant (Deut. 30:1). God used the persistent failures of His people throughout the Old Testament, culminating in exile from their land, to show that some other covenant was needed.

The prophets Jeremiah and Ezekiel were given the exciting message that this New Covenant was in fact coming. Here are the words of God that Jeremiah recorded:

> Behold, the days are coming, declares the Lord, when I will make a new covenant with the house of Israel and the house of Judah, not like the covenant that I made with their fathers on the day when I took them by the hand to bring them out of the land of Egypt, my covenant that they broke. . . . For this is the covenant that I will make with the house of Israel after those days, declares the Lord: I will put my law within them, and I will write it on their hearts. And I will be their God, and they shall be my people. And no longer shall each one teach his neighbor and each his brother, saying, "Know the Lord," for they shall all know me, from the least of them to the greatest, declares the Lord. For I will forgive their iniquity, and I will remember their sin no more. (Jer. 31:31–34)

Under the Old Covenant, the Mosaic Covenant, some Israelites had to tell other Israelites, "Know the Lord!" because they didn't know Him. But Jeremiah says that everyone who is part of this New Covenant will know God.

Ezekiel helps clarify these promises by recording God's intent to actually change even the affections and desires of His New Covenant people—from the inside out:

> I will give you a new heart, and a new spirit I will put within you. And I will remove the heart of stone from your flesh and give you a heart of flesh. And I will put my Spirit within you, and cause you to walk in my statutes and be careful to obey my rules. (Ezek. 36:26–27)

Anyone who's familiar with the dismal failures of the Old Testament Israelites (and who knows his or her own sinful heart) should be glad to read such a wonderful New Covenant promise. The Old Testament story ends with Nehemiah literally tearing out the hair of the Jewish men who had returned from captivity only to commit the very same sins that got their grandparents exiled in the first place.

And we don't have to wonder whether the New Covenant is yet to come. Jesus launched it when He shed His blood on the cross. Presiding over the Last Supper on the night He was betrayed, Jesus said, "This cup that is poured out for you is the *new covenant* in my blood" (Luke 22:20).

And the New Testament (a title that simply means "New Covenant") shows that the promises of Jeremiah and Ezekiel have begun to be fulfilled. Jesus' sacrifice made it possible for God to remember the people's sin no more. And the Spirit's arrival on the day of Pentecost (Acts 2:4) meant that God Himself lived in every New Covenant believer.

The New Testament does reveal something that was only hinted at in the Old Testament, however. Though God originally promised the New Covenant to Israel

 ## A New and Better Covenant

The whole argument traced through the book of Hebrews is meant to prove that Christ's provisions through the New Covenant are better than the provisions of the Old Covenant. Hebrews 8:1 introduces readers to the author's climactic point.

What specific role of Christ has the author been discussing? (Heb. 8:1)

His high priesthood

How has the author contrasted Christ's priesthood with the Old Testament Aaronic priesthood? (7:16–17, 21, 24, 26–27)

It's permanent and perfectly pure.

What is the beneficial consequence of this distinction? (7:18–19, 22, 25, 27–28)

Christ can guarantee a better covenant relationship, in which He is able to permanently atone for sin, perfecting His people and interceding for them so that they can draw near to God.

Now that the author has established who this better Priest is (the eternal Son of God) and the benefit of His better work (permanent atonement), he can make his climactic point in chapter 8.

Where is Christ now, and why is He there? (8:1–2, cf. Ps. 110:1)

He is seated (His work completed) at the right hand of God. He is there to minister in heaven on behalf of His saints (interceding as High Priest) until it is time for His return (time to conquer His enemies).

As High Priest, He must have something to offer to God in order to minister.

What is the basis of His ministry in heaven? (Heb. 8:6–9)

the better promises of the New Covenant prophesied in Jeremiah 31:31–34

What are the better benefits of Christ's New Covenant ministry? (Heb. 8:10–12)

- *internal, willing obedience*
- *intimate fellowship with God*
- *full and final atonement for sin*

After listening to the author's climactic point in Hebrews 8, what should be your conclusion? (8:13, cf. 10:12–18)

The Old Covenant is obsolete.

The redemption of humankind can only be made possible through the superior *person* of Jesus Christ who fulfills His superior *promises* to mankind through His superior *work*. Jeremiah prophesied that the day was coming when the New Covenant would be inaugurated (Heb. 8:8); the author of Hebrews declares that that day has come (Heb. 8:1–7, 13). The New Covenant work of the Messiah, inextricably connected to the establishment of the kingdom, has begun.

Doctrine should inform so as to compel application. What application does the author of Hebrews make in 10:19–31?

The application in this passage and in the rest of the book of Hebrews, in light of this understanding of Christ's work, is to have faith (cf. Heb. 11), demonstrated by your faithful obedience (cf. Heb. 12–13). The New Covenant provides no cover for sinning so that grace may abound (Rom. 6:1–2).

The Holy Spirit and the New Covenant

Students may wonder why they're reading a page on the superiority of the New Covenant over the Mosaic Covenant. The goal is for them to understand the marvelous privilege they have if they are part of Christ's church.

Though the Holy Spirit ministered to Old Testament saints, New Covenant saints receive a greater ministry of the Holy Spirit. Not only does He impart spiritual life (John 1:12–13; 3:3–5; Titus 3:5) to those who are spiritually dead (Eph. 2:1, 5), Christians are baptized in the Spirit into the body of Christ (Rom 8:9; 1 Cor. 12:13; Eph 2:13). This work of the Spirit began with the establishment of the church at Pentecost (Matt. 3:11; Acts 1:5; 2:1–4). To be in Christ by the Spirit means to share in all that Christ has accomplished—to share in the New Covenant blessings of the gospel (Rom. 5:19). But Christians don't have Christ apart from the church. The church is Christ's body, and when Christians are united with Christ through the New Covenant work of the Spirit, they are united with His body.

Church Membership

Begin by asking students to debate the main question: **Is church membership necessary?**

Ask them to answer the following questions in order to come to the right conclusions:

What does the Bible teach about the local church and its constituency?

The church formally gathers with a recognizable constituency (Acts 2:42; 1 Cor. 14:23).

Is it possible for a lone individual to carry out all of the functions that God has purposefully designed for the church?

Lone believers can't carry out the ordinances of baptism (which presupposes the giving of a public testimony to others) and the Lord's Supper (which presupposes coming together to remember). Nor can they teach, edify, or submit without leaders or other believers (Eph. 4:11–16; 1 Tim. 4:13; Heb. 10:24–25; 13:17).

What are some common reasons people give for refusing church membership?

abusive leaders; corrupt church practices; hypocrisy of other people

What is the biblical response to such reasons?

Although the Bible recognizes various expressions of corruption in different kinds of churches, it never recommends that people leave all churches entirely (Rev. 2–3). Corruption must be addressed within the institution of the church (1 Tim. 1:3; Titus 1:13). But the institution itself shouldn't be abandoned because abandoning Christ's body means abandoning the faith (1 John 2:19).

The Kingdom and the Church

Psalm 8 (cf. Genesis 1:26–28) defines the extent of the kingdom that the Messiah, as the perfect man, will reign over.

What is the extent of this kingdom?

God's kingdom encompasses the whole world.

According to Matthew 28:18, what is the extent of the authority that Jesus, as the Messiah, was given?

all authority in heaven and on earth

According to Psalm 110:2–3, why isn't all the world submitted to the reign of Christ at present?

At present, the Messiah reigns over His people who offer themselves freely, but this reign is in the midst of His enemies who reject Him.

The church is made up of people who have offered themselves freely to the Messiah. They have been transferred "from the domain of darkness . . . to the kingdom of his

---

ORGANISM

INSTITUTION

(Jer. 31:31), He poured out His Spirit on Gentiles as well as Jews (Acts 10:44–48). Gentiles, too, have God's law written on their hearts (2 Cor. 3:3). The New Covenant creates a new group of people, including both Jews and Gentiles, who get God's grace in a new way (Eph. 2:11–15).

That group is the church. The church is the New Covenant people of God. Under the Mosaic Covenant, the people of God formed a nation that included believers and unbelievers. But in the New Covenant, the people of God come from every nation, and every one of them, by definition, is a believer. As a result all true Christians can be said to be part of Christ's church (Eph. 2:8–15). But the church exists in specific locations (Acts 9:31; 11:22; 13:1; Rom. 16:1; 1 Cor. 1:2; Philem. 1:2). In these locations it has leaders (Acts 14:23; 20:17; Titus 1:5) and members (1 Cor. 5:4–5; 2 Thess. 3:14–15). Because of this, some theologians distinguish between the church as an *organism* and the church as an *institution*. As an organism, the church is the entire body with Christ as its head. But as an institution, the church gathers into local assemblies. This distinction will be important for understanding the mission of the church.

THE CHURCH AS THE KINGDOM OF GOD?

As you learned in Chapter 10, God made covenants with humans throughout biblical history for the purpose of establishing His kingdom on earth. At the heart of God's plan of redemption is the establishment of His kingdom, ruled by the perfect Man. But in Chapter 11, you also learned that Christians live in the gap between the coming of the kingdom in salvation and the coming of the kingdom in judgment. In this gap people are to prepare themselves for the coming of the kingdom in judgment by entering the kingdom by faith now (Luke 17:20–18:30). The church proclaims "good news about the kingdom of God" so that people can enter the kingdom by faith (Acts 8:12; 14:22; 19:8; 20:25; 28:31). It is for this reason that Jesus said, "On this rock I will build my church. . . . I will give you the keys of the kingdom of heaven" (Matt. 16:18–19).

Don't dismiss church as matter of routine weekly attendance. The church is a vital part of God's plan for establishing His kingdom and redeeming His world. The church is the outpost of God's kingdom in the present evil age. On the other hand, the church is not the fullness of that kingdom. The church's mission is not to conquer kingdoms by force and to ensure by force that Christendom encompasses the entire world. To say that the church *is* the kingdom is a dangerous and damaging idea. That misconception led the church of the Middle Ages to become a political and even military power.[1] Some of the popes in those days even had their own armies. When the church believes it is the kingdom, it begins to do what it ought not to do and neglects its true mission.

So what is the true mission of the church? For what purpose did God establish the church as an institution?

> **SHOULD EVERY CHRISTIAN JOIN A LOCAL CHURCH?**
>
> Some form of church membership is demanded by the New Testament. The logic of church membership is simple: both Jesus (Matt. 18:17) and Paul (1 Cor. 5:5) command Christians to excommunicate from the church any who refuse to repent of their sins (after making loving appeals to them, of course). You can't be kicked out of a group you're not part of in some recognizable way. Whether that means signing a form or publicly giving your salvation testimony and getting voted in, you need to join a church. If you're a Christian, you need—and should want—the pressure other Christians put on you to do right. You need to be "kickoutable." And you need encouragement; the members of a church are supposed to "stir up one another to love and good works" (Heb. 10:24).

---

beloved Son" (Col. 1:13). Because of this, the church has been rightly described by some as the outpost of the kingdom.

Why is the institutional church not to be equated with the kingdom of God?

The sphere of authority given to the church is limited, whereas the kingdom that the Messiah rules over encompasses all of creation.

Diverting the Church's Mission

Doctrine matters; it directs practice. A church's doctrine of the kingdom will affect the church's practice of its mission. The church's mission can be completely derailed just by making some seemingly minor adjustments to the biblical teaching. Dismissing the distinction between the church as institution and organism leads to a violation of sphere sovereignty. All of the good Creation Mandate tasks of the outer spheres swallow up the central sphere (see Kloosterman's chart and footnotes in Activity 6 about sphere sovereignty). When this happens, the distinctive work of the church is often left undone. Identifying the church as *the* kingdom (with all of its responsibilities) also leads to the cultural approach of Reconstructionism (discussed in Chapter 11) or the more specific governmental approach of theonomy (critiqued in Chapter 18).

The Importance of the Institutional Church

Going to church each week can become routine. But something marvelous is happening week after week if only we have eyes to see. A church is a gathering of believers in Christ. All who gather as members profess to be regenerated by the Spirit and baptized into the body of Christ. They're transformed

THE INSTITUTIONAL CHURCH IN ACTION

Jesus tells us what the church's mission is in Matthew 28:18–20. The basis of that mission is His own kingly authority. Before Jesus presented the church's mission to the apostles, He declared, "All authority in heaven and on earth has been given to me" (Matt. 28:18). And then Jesus used the little word *therefore* to draw a conclusion from that authority:

> Go therefore and make disciples of all nations, baptizing them in the name of the Father and of the Son and of the Holy Spirit, teaching them to observe all that I have commanded you. (Matt. 28:19–20)

At the beginning of Acts, Luke records the first sermon preached after God established the church. The apostle Peter proclaimed that Jesus was the exalted King, seated at the right hand of the Father (Acts 2:33–36). Luke goes on to tell what the early church did. Those who submitted to Jesus as King engaged in four activities:

> They devoted themselves to the apostles' teaching and the fellowship, to the breaking of bread and the prayers. (Acts 2:42)

These passages from Matthew and Acts outline the primary activities the institutional church should be doing even today. It can all can be summed up in a single phrase: *making disciples* (i.e., mobilizing followers of Jesus). But there are six ways the institutional church is to do this: evangelizing, baptizing, teaching, fellowshiping, participating in the Lord's Supper, and praying.

Evangelizing

This mission is very different from that of Israel under the Old Covenant. The number of Israelites didn't grow as a result of Israelite missionaries going out to invite the Gentiles in; the nation grew from the inside, the way families do, by having children. Christians, heirs of God's command to "fill the earth," also have children, but those children don't automatically become part of the New Covenant. In order for the church to grow, evangelism has to happen—and Jesus told us to make it happen all over the globe.

From the earliest days of the church, as recorded in the book of Acts, citizens of God's kingdom have done just what Jesus told them to do: they have been witnesses to Him around the world (Acts 1:8). The apostle Paul asked the Ephesians to pray that He would be a bold witness (Eph. 6:19). Acts includes some pretty amazing stories that record God's answer to that prayer (Acts 16:25–30). And Paul was not alone. Christian evangelism was happening all over the ancient world, especially after God sent a wave of persecution that drove most of the original Christian church out of Jerusalem (Acts 8:1–2). This work of evangelism has continued throughout the history of the church. During some periods, this part of the mission has seemed to all but disappear. At other times, it has flamed up and burned brightly around the world.

Baptizing

Most people are on the broad road to destruction, Jesus said (Matt. 7:13–14). Most of God's image-bearers, because of the blindness brought on by the Fall, don't consider the good news to be all that good. They reject it and keep on skipping or trudging toward doom.

But some people do listen, and some do repent (Acts 17:34). When people turn from sin to Christ, Jesus commands them to take the very first step of discipleship—

works of charity, though all three of these things may accompany evangelism. Nor should evangelism be confused with the results of evangelism, as if to say we've only successfully evangelized when a conversion follows. No, evangelism is speaking words. It's sharing news. It's being faithful to God by presenting the good news . . . that Christ, by his death and resurrection, has secured a way for a holy God and sinful people to be reconciled. God will produce true conversions when we present this good news (see John 1:13; Acts 18:9–10). [Dever, 91]

Whatever approach Christians take, they must be sure that their testimony, apologetics, or good works lead them to a verbal declaration of the gospel message set in the context of the larger biblical story of CFR. In that larger story, the benefit of salvation (heaven) must not be confused with the real need and motivation for salvation (reconciling sinful people with their holy Creator).

By now students should be equipped to share the overarching message of the Bible. Divide students into pairs and have them practice explaining the gospel in terms of CFR. They may use one of the witnessing tools suggested in the Teacher's Edition on page 162. You may also set up a role play in which they respond to your questions. They may choose to include their personal testimony or some apologetics along with the CFR presentation of the gospel.

Baptism and Forgiveness

Should passages such as Acts 2:38 be interpreted to mean that a person must both repent and be baptized for the purpose of receiving the forgiveness of sins?

This verse can be understood as giving two commands. First, repent. Then (after you have done that) be baptized on the basis of the forgiveness of your sins.

The phrase *on the basis of* is another legitimate way to interpret the Greek preposition translated with the word *for* in English.

Scripture must be compared with Scripture to clarify particular verses. In general, the Bible clearly teaches that salvation is not by works (Eph. 2:8–9). Specifically, Matthew 3:7–8 makes clear that repentance was the required basis of a baptism "for" repentance (Matt. 3:11).

What visible testimony did God design for making a public confession of the decision to identify with following Christ?

The first response of a true convert is to identify with the body of Christ through baptism (Acts 8:35–38). The biblically given visible

---

and brought into a unity that is unique on the earth. By gathering they manifest the bond that they have with one another as the temple of God (1 Cor. 3:16–17; Eph. 2:21–22; 1 Pet. 2:5), the body of Christ (Rom. 12:4–5; 1 Cor. 12:12–27; Eph. 4:15–16), and the family of God (Col. 4:15; 2 Thess. 3:15; 1 Tim. 3:15; 5:1–2).

In addition, no other institution can carry out the functions of the institutional church because only it was designed to fulfill God's distinct purposes for the church. These purposes all come together to serve the chief goal of all Christians, the glorification of God.

God created the world and humankind to display the glory of who he is. . . . God sent his Son to image his holy and loving character. . . . Now the church, which has been granted the life of Christ and the power of the Holy Spirit, is called to display the character and glory of God to all the universe, testifying in word and action to his great wisdom and work of salvation.

[Mark Dever, *What Is a Healthy Church?* (Wheaton: Crossway, 2005), 48]

Evangelism in Action

There are so many approaches to evangelism that many Christians feel overwhelmed. Which approach should they take?

Mark Dever shares some sound advice.

Evangelism is not the same thing as sharing a personal testimony. It's not the same thing as presenting a rational defense of the faith. It's not even doing

testimony of making the decision to follow Christ in salvation isn't raising a hand or walking an aisle; it's the biblical picture of baptism, which is simply the means by which a person appeals to God based entirely on Christ's work to remove sin (1 Pet. 3:21).

What does water baptism picture?

the believer's union with Christ (Spirit baptism) and hope of resurrection because of His death, burial, and resurrection (Rom. 6:3–4)

Teaching the Truth

The proclamation and explanation of the text of Scripture is the central pillar of the church's task to uphold the truth (1 Tim. 3:15; 4:13; 5:17; 2 Tim. 4:2; Titus 1:9). This central pillar must not be removed or replaced by entertainment-driven or social gospel programs. God's method for winning the lost is through preaching the powerful Word (Isa. 55:11; 1 Cor. 1:21–25; Heb. 4:12). It is both necessary (1 Cor. 9:16) and sufficient (Ps. 19:7; 2 Tim. 3:17). That it's a stumbling block or folly to unbelievers doesn't mean we should change the method. Only through this method will the intricacies of the unsearchable riches of Christ be made known (Eph. 3:8). Other human methods fall short; they can only provide a superficial understanding of the gospel. At worst, the other methods are manipulative (1 Thess. 2:3–6). God's method for equipping and discipling the saints is also through the teaching of the Word (John 17:17; Eph. 4:11–15).

[See Steven J. Lawson, "Sola Scriptura: The Sufficiency of Scripture in Expository Preaching," *Preaching* (website), September 1, 2002.]

Fellowshiping

How will true discipleship be demonstrated to others? (John 13:34–35)

by love for one another

What does that love look like? (1 Cor. 13:1–8; 1 John 3:17–18)

It's demonstrated in deeds driven by care.

What will fellowship require? (Phil. 2:1–5)

Self-sacrificial, encouraging friendships unified around the same thinking and goals.

It's disheartening when believers are absorbed into friendly crowds at church, but are never able to develop true friendships.

What undermines local church fellowship? (1 Cor. 3:3; 2 Cor. 12:20; Gal. 5:15)

The ungodly actions of leaders and fellow church members have disheartened many believers and turned away professing believers.

The effort to develop deeper friendships with others is destroyed by consistent experiences of betrayal by supposedly trusted

---

baptism (Matt. 28:19). At Pentecost, baptism was the response of those who received the Word. When people were baptized, they were added to the church (Acts 2:41).

Baptism is a public means of confessing that a person is a follower of Christ (1 Pet. 3:21). It can become commonplace for American Christians, but in many parts of the world, publicly confessing Christ through baptism is a difficult and dangerous thing to do. Yet few things are of greater importance or bring greater joy than confessing to be a follower of the Savior.

Baptism is also a symbol that the new Christian is now united with Christ (cf. Rom. 6:4). It's through the believer's union with Christ that he receives Christ's righteousness. Baptism is also a symbol that the Christian has received the Spirit and is united to other believers in the body of Christ (1 Cor. 12:13). Baptism is the visible sign of the New Covenant.

Teaching

But baptism is only the beginning of discipleship. Teaching people to observe all that Jesus commanded is a huge job because He really said a lot! Christ's phrase, "all that I have commanded you" includes the entire Bible. The Bible is a big and sometimes complicated book. So teaching is a key component of disciple-making.

The very first description we have of what the newly established church did after Pentecost shows that the believers took Jesus' words quite seriously: "They devoted themselves to the apostles' teaching" (Acts 2:42). That teaching is such an important part of the church's work that Christ marks out particular believers and gives them the necessary gifts to teach (Eph. 4:11). The ability to teach is a requirement for church leaders (1 Tim. 3:2).

And yet pastors and other church leaders are not supposed to be the only people who teach truth in your church. They teach so that *all* Christians can learn to "speak the truth in love" (Eph. 4:15) and even sing the truth to one another (Col. 3:16). Preaching and teaching the content and application of Scripture is the key means by which Christians are taught to be disciples of Christ, are guarded against false teaching, and are drawn together in unity with each other (Eph. 4:14–16).

Christians do lots of important things in their lives. This book talks about many of them. But nothing the Christian does will be done well if it is not informed by Jesus' teaching. For Christians to live like Christ in every other area of life, they need to know the teaching of Scripture. Listening to the preaching and teaching of God's Word is also an important act of worship. It's a way of showing that you recognize Jesus as your King and that you will obey all that He commands.

Fellowshiping

Church is not simply a school where people come to learn theology. Nor is it a motivational seminar that provides Christians with advice about issues that interest them. Teaching theology is an important part of the church's mission. Applying that teaching to everyday life is also important for the church. But the church is made up of people who have relationships with each other. This is why the earliest Christians "devoted themselves to . . . fellowship" (Acts 2:42).

Fellowship refers to the unity of believers. Christians hold Christian things in common with each other. Believers are truly one in Christ. They are united to Him as one body to its head. The teaching of apostolic doctrine has unified their view of the world. So teaching is an important part of fellowship, but it's not the totality.

---

friends in the leadership or body of numerous churches who refuse to repent. This pattern must change so that the saints can minister effectively (Heb. 3:13; 10:24–25).

It's also undermined when people become secondary to programs and buildings because all of the provisions are used up in endeavors of self-interest.

The Greek word for "fellowship" is related to the phrase "had all things in common" in Acts 2:44. When the first Jewish Christians saw other Christians in need, they sold their own possessions to provide for other Christians in need. By Acts 6, deacons were chosen to oversee a daily distribution to those in need. Christians should share in fellowship with one another financially. Churches should set aside money from the offerings to help families whose breadwinner loses his job or widows who are in need.

Paul uses the Greek word for "fellowship" in Philippians 1:5 to refer to the financial and prayer support that the Philippians extended to him. Doubtless, the ministry of Epaphroditus was included in this fellowship as well. When you give to missions, pray for those who carry the gospel on your behalf around the world, and encourage them through email or phone calls, you are fellowshiping in the New Testament sense.

Making the Lord's Supper Meaningful

Whenever you observe the Lord's Supper keep in mind four dimensions: looking back, looking inward, looking around, and looking forward.

First, Jesus said, "Do this in remembrance of me" (1 Cor. 11:24, cf. 11:25). When you eat the bread, remember that Jesus died on

The unity of fellowship works itself out in practical ways. Becoming a Christian in first-century Israel was a costly thing to do. It meant losing friends. Losing friends meant losing business partners and customers. It may have meant that many would experience real poverty. In the face of this, Christians provided material support for each other (Acts 2:44–45). Today when a church member loses a job, often others in the church help out with food and money. When a family member becomes very ill, other Christians are there to help. This kind of unity was so important to the early church that a group of godly leaders was selected to make sure that Christians in need were provided for by the church (Acts 6:1–6).

Participating in the Lord's Supper

Luke also says the earliest Christians devoted themselves to "the breaking of bread" (Acts 2:42). "The breaking of bread" in this context includes the Lord's Supper. The Lord's Supper is the eating of bread, which symbolizes the body of Christ that was broken on the cross, and the drinking of the fruit of the vine, which symbolizes the blood Jesus shed on the cross.

The Lord's Supper was frequently observed by the early Christians for several purposes. Jesus commanded that His followers observe the Lord's Supper in remembrance and in proclamation of His establishment of the New Covenant by the sacrifice of His body and His blood (1 Cor. 11:23–25). Frequent participation in the Lord's Supper should result in frequent personal examination and confession of sins (11:28). Partaking together of the Lord's Supper is another sign of believers' unity in Christ (10:16–17). On top of it all, by doing this act of worship, Christians look forward to the return of Christ (11:26). Regular observance of the Lord's Supper is one of the ways Christ intends for His church to remain focused on the central aspects of the Christian life.

Praying

Finally, the early Christians devoted themselves to prayer (Acts 2:42). Prayer in church can take many forms. Often the psalms and hymns that are sung by the church are praises and prayers to God. In many churches the pastor will lead the church in prayer. Sometimes believers gather in smaller groups to share prayer requests and to pray for each other. Paul often begins his letters with prayers for the churches he's writing to, which shows that Christians should pray for others beyond their local assembly.

Many times Christian prayers focus on the health needs of people Christians know. Health is an important thing to pray about, but it isn't the most important subject for prayer. A look at the prayers of Paul gives some insight into the kinds of prayers Christians should pray. First of all, Paul's prayers are full of thanksgiving. Paul is thankful that fellow Christians grow in faith and love. He's thankful that they persevere in persecution (2 Thess. 1:3–4). Second, Paul asks the church to pray for the salvation of people and for the opportunities that others will have to share the gospel (1 Tim. 2:1-3; Eph. 6:18–20). Third, Paul prays for Christians to become holy. He prays that God would count believers worthy of entering His kingdom. He prays that whatever desires these Christians have for doing good and for working out their faith in lives of good works will be fulfilled (2 Thess. 1:11–12). He prays that Christians will be "pure and blameless" as they await Christ's return (Phil. 1:10). Paul prays that Christians will overflow with love for each other (Phil. 1:9; 1 Thess. 3:12). Fourth, Paul prays that God will protect Christians so that they can live their lives as God intends (1 Tim. 2:2). Fifth, Paul recognizes that what he prays for can only be

---

disciplinarian. God is both holy (set apart from sin) and good. Therefore, Christians can approach God knowing that He desires to grant to them every good thing that's in conformity to His will—in accordance to Jesus' name or character (John 14:14; James 1:5, 17; 1 John 5:14). Praying in this manner is clearly modeled by the apostle Paul. His numerous prayers in the epistles provide themes that we ourselves should use in praying for each other.

Divide students into small groups. Assign each group a different model prayer from the apostle Paul and ask them to identify the themes (Rom. 15:14–33; Eph. 1:15–23; 3:14–21; Phil. 1:9–11; Col. 1:9–14; 1 Thess. 3:9–13; 2 Thess. 1:3–12).

Those themes include thanksgiving, faith, love, holiness, knowledge, the return of Christ, the benefits of the gospel, the need for the power of God, the glory of God, regularity in prayer, and others.

You may also assign each group the particular model prayer in 2 Thess. 1:3–12 and ask them to outline it.

I. Mindset or approach (3–10)
  A. Thankfulness (spiritual growth in trials)
  B. Confidence (God's sovereign justice)
  C. Hope (Christ's return)
II. Requests (11)
  A. Worthy walk (spiritual growth)
  B. Fulfillment of every godly desire
III. Goal (12a)
  A. God's glory
  B. Believers' sanctification and glorification
IV. Basis (12b)
  A. The grace of God
  B. The grace of Christ

[See D. A. Carson, *A Call to Spiritual Reformation* (Grand Rapids: Baker Books, 1992)]

 ### The Institutional Church in Action

Mark Dever and Paul Alexander, *The Deliberate Church* (Wheaton: Crossway, 2005).

Mark Dever, *What is a Healthy Church?* (Wheaton: Crossway, 2005).

Wayne A. Mack & David Swavely, *Life in the Father's House* (Phillipsburg, NJ: P&R Publishing, 1996).

The Social Gospel and Reactionism

In order to clarify the right approach to carrying out the mission of the institutional church and the broader mission of the organic church, it's necessary to distinguish the approach outlined in the Student Text from two opposite extremes.

---

the cross for your sins. He gave up His body in place of yours and poured out His blood so that you could be brought into the New Covenant. Look back to what Christ did.

Second, Paul said, "Let a person examine himself" (1 Cor. 11:28). A person who eats or drinks unworthily "eats and drinks judgment on himself" (11:29). This is a sober warning to observe the Lord's Table reverently according to its purpose. But it's also a blessing because it gives you a regular opportunity to examine yourself and confess your sin. The Lord's Supper is a reminder of the Spirit's New Covenant work to overcome the power of sin. Look inward.

Third, Paul said, "Because there is one bread, we who are many are one body, for we all partake of the one bread" (1 Cor. 10:17). Christians don't take Communion at home by themselves. The Lord's Supper is an ordinance for the gathered church. It testifies to the unity of the church as the body of Christ. Look around and recognize your unity in the body of Christ.

Fourth, Paul says that when you partake of the Lord's Supper you "proclaim the Lord's death until he comes" (1 Cor. 11:26). The Lord's Supper is not only a time of remembrance, it is also a time of anticipation. Christ is returning. Each time we observe the Lord's Supper we are anticipating that return. Look forward to the return of Christ.

Modeling Right Praying

The right kind of praying needs to be modeled corporately. Right prayers grow out of a right concept of God. He's not a vending machine, Santa Claus, or a doting grandfather. He's not your servant. Nor is He distantly aloof. He's not an ungracious

The Social Gospel

The so-called Fundamentalist-Modernist Controversy erupted in the 1920s across all the major US denominations. The controversy entailed disputes over the fundamental doctrines of the faith. Those who embraced the social gospel approach were characterized by two major problems.

- Despite still believing in the need for personal evangelism and conversion, they denied fundamental orthodox doctrines such as the inspiration of Scripture, the virgin birth, and substitutionary atonement. As a result, they had no true gospel to offer. They continued evangelicalism's emphasis on social reform but without the gospel that could actually transform sinners into righteous people.

- They confused the progress of technology and democracy with the inbreaking of the kingdom of God. And while they rightly identified some social sins, their solutions— such as the embrace of socialism by some— were often theologically problematic.

Isolationism

Not all Evangelicals or even Fundamentalists embraced isolationism. For instance, Fundamentalists sought to address social issues through rescue missions and by pressing for legislation that would lead to Prohibition. But a tendency did develop in reaction to the social gospel. An approach that is more reflective of the two-story view developed among some. This approach largely ignored physical or temporal needs in favor of an emphasis on spiritual needs or evangelistic efforts. In some cases the institutional church became the hub of the Christian's life with numerous programs operating every night of the week. Rather than helping believers go out into the culture to apply a biblical worldview, this often inhibited church members from living out their faith on an everyday basis in the culture.

A Path Forward: Sphere Sovereignty

Sphere sovereignty recognizes that the institutional church and various cultural spheres have their own distinctive tasks. Christians, who make up the organic church, gather in the institutional church and then disperse into various cultural institutions throughout the week. The mission of the institutional church is found in Matthew 28:18–20 and Acts 2:42. This means that the church has the responsibility of discipling Christians to live out the Creation Mandate in various cultural spheres. This means the church is to teach Christians how to recognize the design of God's creational norms in their vocations. Part of the Christian life involves works of compassion in society. Disconnecting the Great Commission from compassion undermines the gospel, which is meant to restore humanity to its task of ruling well over the earth.

WHAT ABOUT SINGING?

Singing is a major part of Christian worship. It's not listed alongside teaching and prayer as part of the church's mission because it's actually included in both. Many psalms and hymns are praises to God, and praise is a kind of prayer. Other songs are requests addressed to God. Finally, some psalms, hymns, and spiritual songs are opportunities for Christians to teach each other. This is why Paul writes that Christians should be "teaching and admonishing one another in all wisdom, singing psalms and hymns and spiritual songs" (Col. 3:16).

accomplished by the power of God (2 Thess. 1:11–12), so he prays that the Spirit will bring about what he's asking for (Col. 1:9–11; Eph. 3:16).

Prayer is difficult work, but imagine what would happen if God's people really devoted themselves to praying that God would fulfill whatever desires Christians have for doing good. For every other part of the Christian life to succeed, prayer is the essential foundation.

A GOSPEL THAT'S TOO SMALL?

Evangelism and discipleship are never-ending tasks. New people are always being born who will need to be evangelized and then discipled. The challenge is great; the task is vast. And yet some people think this biblical vision of the church's mission is too limited. If God's goal is to redeem and restore the entire created order, shouldn't the mission of the church be as broad as the mission of God? Christians who think this way wouldn't deny that the church's mission includes verbally preaching the gospel. They would simply say that the church's mission also includes creation care, the arts, care for the poor, political action against social injustice, and more.[2]

This discussion is not merely academic. You may soon have to choose a church for the first time in your life, and it matters a great deal what that church sees as its mission. Creation care, the arts, the poor, social justice—these are all good and important things. But a church that sees them as its mission is in danger of missing its real mission.

This is where the distinction between the **church as organism** and the **church as institution** becomes important. All Christians are part of the body of Christ. This body doesn't move in and out of existence every Sunday morning as the church gathers and scatters. The church as organism carries out all manner of good works in the name of Christ in a wide variety of vocations, as we'll see in the next section. But this is not the case with the church as institution. The institutional church focuses on the mission of making disciples through evangelism, baptism, teaching, fellowship, the Lord's Supper, and prayer.

This distinction between the organic church and the institutional church can be seen clearly in that the commands God gives to the institutional church and the organic church, though overlapping at points, are distinct. Two pastors who wrote a book about the mission of the church say:

> There are some commands given to the local church that the individual Christian just should not undertake to obey on his own. An individual Christian, for example, can't excommunicate another Christian; but the local church is commanded to do so in certain situations. Nor should an individual Christian take the Lord's Supper on his own; that's an activity the local church is to do "when you come together" (1 Cor. 11:17–18, 20, 33–34). In the same way, there are commands given to individual Christians that are clearly not meant for the local church as an organized group.[3]

🖉 Discerning the Mission

For further enrichment, you may wish to assign some students to read chapters from the following book and then give an oral or written report on what they learned:

Kevin DeYoung and Greg Gilbert, *What Is the Mission of the Church?* (Wheaton: Crossway, 2011).

🖉 Involved in the Right Way

Once individuals have decided to get involved by loving their neighbors in their own communities or around the world, then individuals must decide which organizations are doing things that are right and helpful. Many approaches are unbiblical and contrary to creational norms or simply unhelpful despite the best of intentions. Christians need to be careful to get involved in the kinds of organizations that won't conflict with their biblical worldview or hinder their opportunities for evangelism. They may need to start their own organizations with a clear mission and philosophy.

In conjunction with some students reporting on the book by DeYoung and Gilbert, assign some students to research organizations that are meant to help people in the local community. How will they determine which organizations are doing things right and helpful? They should give an oral or written report on which organizations they think are most appropriate for Christian involvement. Or they should offer alternatives. What can individuals do by themselves to reach out? Could a small group of people in a local church organize their own initiative?

Husbands, for example, are told to love their wives, and children are told to obey their parents. The church as a whole can't do those things.

God didn't give the church the gifts or the power to bring justice to the world. He ordained government for that purpose. Churches shouldn't have electric chairs, militias, or income tax forms. When the church tries to claim the authority of government, as it sometimes has in the past, bad things happen. Likewise, when the church as an institution seeks to provide solutions to intractable environmental issues or to resolve the problem of inner-city joblessness or to bring about the end of malaria—problems occur. There are other institutions that God has ordained to see to those tasks.

The institutional church, nonetheless, does have an important role to play in all of these areas. Prayer for righteous and just government should be a regular part of gathered church worship (1 Tim. 2:1–2). The church should preach against unjust and unrighteous laws. It should set a vision for what a righteous society would look like. The church also has a responsibility to disciple Christians to live biblically in the vocations God has called them to. And some believers are, in fact, called to government service, job-creation initiatives, or malaria prevention. They need to be taught by the institutional church how to be the organic church—how to do their work for love of God and neighbor in obedience to the Bible. Pastors ought to include in their sermons biblical counsel for engineers, lawyers, teachers, doctors, marketers, plumbers, and construction workers.

The church as institution and its mission to fulfill the Great Commission are central to how the church as organism participates in the Creation Mandate.

WHAT THE CHURCH CAN DO

Sometimes the church can do things outside its direct mission in order to further that mission. For instance, sometimes a church will establish a community outreach for the purpose of both evangelizing the lost and discipling its own members. A church may find that its members are evangelizing many people suffering from addictions. It may start an addiction ministry both to reach out to these people and to train its own people how to more effectively minister to those in need of help. Similarly, medical missions seeks to minister to people's health needs as a way of showing the love of Christ and gaining a hearing for the gospel, but the church is not given the mission of providing healthcare. Imagine the distraction from the church's real mission if local churches were also expected to manage all of the area hospitals. Yet

medical missions is still a legitimate avenue for ministry.

Similarly, the church is not given the task of helping neighborhood children with their homework. That is, of course, an excellent thing for Christians to do, especially in communities where students struggle academically. A church may choose to participate in a public school tutoring program because it gives the opportunity both to help students academically and to present the gospel.

When churches consider such ministries, they need to ask the right question. The question is not whether this is a good thing to do. There are many good things that Christians should do that the church is not commissioned to do (such as running hospitals). The right question is: will this further the church's mission?

Local Church Community Involvement

The role of the institutional church—as it relates to creation care, the arts, care for the poor, political action against injustice, and so on—is to inform believers of the biblical worldview as it relates to these matters. The institutional church may need to warn against or correct unbiblical approaches. But it should be constructively equipping and encouraging its people to get involved. The organic church needs to discover or create the avenues through which members can get involved—whether in their own vocations or through volunteer work in the community.

There are also some programs through which a local church can reach out to the community. The church must be careful

that these programs neither overwhelm the church's time, resources, and mission nor replace individual and family community involvement. Nonetheless, carefully constructed, such programs provide an opportunity for a church to disciple its members and to minister to the community. When churches reach out through community service, they do need to be sure that they're reaching out through genuine care for their community and not merely using the service as evangelistic bait. If people feel that the church has employed a bait-and-switch approach, the attempt at evangelism will be undermined. But if genuine concern for their well-being is expressed, and the evangelistic intentions of the church are made clear up front, such ministries can be beneficial to both church and community.

Valuing Christian Higher Education

Do you think that the institutional church alone can sufficiently teach its members how to thoroughly carry out their specific job functions in conformity to creational norms and biblical ethics?

Since the local church is limited in time and resources (and must stick to its mission), the biblical counsel from the pulpit specifically for engineers, lawyers, teachers, doctors, marketers, plumbers, or construction workers will be limited. Sermons can apply broad ethical principles and creational norms to real life, but specific nuanced advice for difficult decisions in a specialized discipline may not be possible.

Is there a resource for thoroughly teaching church members how to apply a biblical worldview to their job functions?

Yes, Christian educational institutions exist for this very purpose. Whether vocational training or higher education in the liberal arts from a biblical worldview perspective—these kinds of schools should be prioritized and valued by the majority of believers. Christians are always in danger of compartmentalizing their lives into the sacred and the secular— especially when all of the training for their jobs has been based on the status quo philosophies of secularism.

Are Christian schools immune from approaching the disciplines incorrectly?

Even at a Christian university, both students and teachers must constantly examine whether they have embraced a syncretistic approach to their discipline. What principles have they embraced from secular sources that presuppose a wrong metanarrative, a wrong view of man's nature or sin problem, a wrong view of God and His creation, and so forth? These assumptions are not always obvious. What principles, from unbelieving sources, can they embrace that conform to a biblical worldview due to God's common grace and a recognition of the natural laws of God's creational norms?

Does Christian education undermine the sufficiency of the local church?

Christian professors who specialize in a particular field and who have a biblical worldview that wrestles with the substantive issues are invaluable to a person's higher educational pursuits. Most often, the resources in a local church are not sufficient to provide all of the needed guidance for students attending a local community college or a distant secular university. But this view of Christian education doesn't undermine the primacy of the local church; the local church must stay on its own mission in its own sphere. Christian education comes alongside to support the local church and its mission.

God-Centered Worship

What is God-centered corporate worship?

Gathered believers actively participate in the six tasks given to the local church for the purpose of focusing on exalting God's worth because of who He is and what He has done (Pss. 95–96).

How could you better prepare your heart to focus on God before a service?

- *Approach Him without the hindrance of sin—obey Him throughout the week and make things right with other believers (Ps. 139:23–24; Matt. 5:23–24)*
- *Fellowship with friends before the service in such a way that would reflect God's work of growing your faith and love for others (2 Thess. 1:3–4)*
- *Quiet your heart in prayer for His powerful work in your life and in the life of the church (Eph. 3:14–21)*

How could you better reflect in your heart in response to the service?

- *Constructively discuss the biblical truth in the car and over lunch with family and friends*
- *Spend a quiet moment on Sunday afternoon in the passage that was preached and in prayer*
- *Approach your new week with a concerted effort to specifically apply what was preached in at least one way*

Churchless Christians?

According to Ephesians 2:16, what necessarily results from individuals being reconciled to God?

Hostility between people should be taken away as they unite in one body (the church).

Your Christianity is more than a personal relationship with God. It's a commitment to God's entire family. Being reconciled to God means being reconciled to each other.

According to 1 John 2:9–11, 19 (cf. John 13:35; 1 John 3:14–16; 4:20), is it ever possible for true Christians to disown all their brothers and sisters? Why?

No, disowning other believers who are walking in the light is evidence of rejecting the light. Hating other Christlike people is evidence of hating Christ. A person who loves Christ loves Christlike people.

According to Rom. 15:14 (cf. 1 Thess. 5:14–15; 2 Thess. 3:15; Heb. 3:12–13; Jude 1:20–23), what job do Christians have in relation to one another?

to admonish and exhort one another to remain faithful

The Church's Unique Role

The church should focus on the mission God gave it rather than trying to add more job skills to its résumé. God has given to the church, and the church alone, the ministries of the Word and the ordinances (baptism and the Lord's Supper). It is through the church that week by week God's Word is proclaimed to His people. It is through the church that week by week Christians gather to praise, thank, and petition God together. It is through the church that Christians regularly commemorate the death of Christ and look forward to His return. It is through the church that week by week Christians share together their common fellowship in Christ. This is how they meet to encourage each other and to meet each other's needs. It is through the church that the kingdom of God has an outpost on earth. The wider world should be able to look at the church and be attracted to Christ.

With a comment the apostle Paul makes in one of his letters, God draws back the curtain to give us a glimpse of what He's doing through the church. Paul wrote to a small group of believers in the ancient city of Ephesus that it is "through the church" that "the manifold wisdom of God [is] made known to the rulers and authorities in the heavenly places" (Eph. 3:10). Very few people in Ephesus in the first century knew or cared what a small group of Christians was doing on some back street. But angels were watching. What God is doing in His church is something that heavenly beings look at and marvel. Through the church, God is accomplishing His eternal purposes.

Paul makes a beautiful statement of those purposes in that same letter to the Ephesian church:

> [God] put all things under [Christ's] feet and gave him as head over all things *to the church*, which is his body, the fullness of him who fills all in all. (Eph. 1:22–23)

Incredibly, God's work of putting the world under the rule of Christ is for the church's benefit. The church is the body of Christ, the King of Kings. This is an esteemed position.

THINKING IT THROUGH 12.1

1. What is it in Jeremiah 31 and Ezekiel 36 that makes the New Covenant church most different from the Old Covenant people of God, Israel?

2. What are the two different aspects of the church, and what is their significance?

3. What six tasks are included in the biblically defined mission of the local church?

4. List at least two reasons given in this chapter that church is not optional for Christians.

♀5. How might a neighborhood medical clinic further a church's mission? How might it possibly undermine that mission?

THINKING IT THROUGH 12.1

1. Social involvement may cause some people to neglect or replace the church entirely; others redefine the church so that its missional focus shifts toward mainly social work rather than gospel ministry.

2. Local assemblies function as the institutional church with specific tasks, but all true believers function as an organism in everything that they do regardless of the sphere with its tasks.

3. evangelism, baptism, teaching, fellowship, the Lord's supper, and prayer

4. It is uniquely important in that it's the only God-designed body for carrying out the specific mission outlined in question 3.

♀5. Social involvement should primarily take place as individual believers get involved in their own communities and other spheres of society (not directly linked to their church). Some limited social activities may reinforce the local church's efforts at evangelism and discipleship, but these activities won't be the central focus that defines the church or its mission.

12.2 THE VOCATION OF THE CHRISTIAN

The institutional church has a limited, though very important, mission, but the organic church spreads out each week into the many institutions that exist in our world. The mission and calling of Christians as they work in the world is as broad as the creation itself.

In the Middle Ages the idea developed that certain Christians had a special **vocation**, or "calling," from God. People with vocations were priests, monks, and nuns. All other work was mere "secular" work, worldly work that was lower than that of those who had a "calling."

Many contemporary Christians know that the Protestant Reformation recovered and clarified the Bible's emphasis on justification by faith. But another very significant challenge the Reformers made against medieval Christianity was in this area of vocation. Martin Luther in particular argued that God calls people to work in many different areas. Every legitimate job is a vocation. All people can serve God in their work. This is a powerfully biblical idea, but even today the old medieval concept of two levels of spirituality in work has a stronghold.

The medieval concept of "secular" work being on a lower level than the "sacred" still influences the thinking of many.

THE GOODNESS OF WORK

Everything God created is good, and all legitimate jobs are, in a very real sense, created by God. So all legitimate jobs are good. A "legitimate job" is one that flows out of the Creation Mandate, God's command to fill the earth, subdue it, and have dominion over it. Some jobs are sinful and simply exist to help others sin. Those are jobs that have twisted the Creation Mandate.

This mandate is too big for one person to fulfill. And many of the skills needed in the work of the Creation Mandate are so specialized that, in order to do them well, you have to dedicate yourself to years of study. We need each other to get the job done; every vocation is a calling by God to obey a slice of the Creation Mandate.

It's true that the Fall complicated our work. Every vocation now involves elements of frustration, dreariness, and waste. But Genesis shows that God created a world that needed human work. God planted the Garden of Eden, and yet He "had not caused it to rain" (2:5). Yes, "a spring was going up from the land and was watering the whole face of the ground" (2:6, marginal reading). But this river that watered the garden (2:10), perhaps by flooding it as the Nile still does in upper Egypt every year, would only be beneficial to the kinds of plants that require farmers to cultivate them. That's the only way to make sense of Genesis 2:5, which says that "no bush of the field was yet in the land and no small plant of the field had yet sprung up—for . . . there was no man to work the ground." From the very beginning, God built a world that needed human work.

Not only is work rooted in the Creation Mandate and the nature of the creation itself, work is also a way of fulfilling the two great commandments. Good work can display love for God: "The gardener makes nothing, but rather gathers what God has

THE MISSION OF THE CHURCH AND YOUR VOCATION | 177

SECTION OBJECTIVES 12.2

1. Explain both the reason work is a God-created good and the purposes for that work.

2. Evaluate how a person's Christianity should affect both how one does his work ethically and in accordance with creational norms.

3. Identify the proper motivation for work: redeeming the time by living in light of redemption.

4. Compare and contrast two faulty responses toward work: idolizing it due to its joy or neglecting it due to its frustration.

All Work Matters

Spreading the gospel and discipling believers is an important work. It's a special work that is distinct from all other work. It has an exalted role in God's plan of redemption to restore the world. But all other work that grows out of the Creation Mandate has an important part in God's plan for creation. None of it should be disregarded as inferior.

Ask students which sphere of work they might be interested in for their future. Why are they interested in it? How would it contribute to the development or dominion of God's creation? What do they think they can accomplish for God's glory and the good of others?

The CFR Paradigm of Work

Creation (Gen. 1:26–30; 2:15)

God's created design for humans included work. God commissioned humans to rule over the world as His vice regents. This rule was expressed by keeping and cultivating the earth—by working it. Before the Fall ever occurred, the overarching task that defined the mission of humanity was work—the Creation Mandate. Work is a created good.

Fall (Gen. 3:17–19)

But the Fall brings frustration to work. Not only is work hindered, but some people are hindered from being able to work, bringing about an unavoidable feeling of emptiness. It is dehumanizing because humans were designed to work. Wishing to not have to work is anti-normative. Everybody wants to feel significant—that they matter because they can accomplish something substantive for the good of others. Meaninglessness kills the spirit. Christians must always be careful to maintain human value; it never disappears because it is tied to the image of God in humans regardless of their capabilities or contributions to society. But feeling needed is inextricably tied to purposeful and constructive work for others' well-being.

Redemption (Rev. 21:24–26)

On one extreme, some people imagine eternity to be a place of fun-filled recreation. On the other extreme, some people imagine eternity to be a place of holy boredom—one never-ending singspiration. Instead, eternity will be filled with the variety that God designed in the original created order—a cycle of work and rest. Perfected humans will be restored to creatively cultivate in a world free from the curse of sin. As such, believers will work but without the curse of toil. Thus, the promise of rest in Hebrews 4:9–11 fits with the description of the nations bringing the fruit of their labors to the new Jerusalem in Revelation 21:24–26.

Working for Others?

Work is usually thought of in terms of individual advancement. It's a means to support—if not to enrich—oneself. But the biblical purpose for work reaches far beyond self-interest—though supporting one's own family is of first importance (1 Tim. 5:8). Not only should believers strive in their labor to give to others financially (Eph. 4:28; 1 Tim. 6:17–18), but they should also labor in work that in some way supports the human flourishing of others. In other words, work becomes more than a job to make money; it's a vocational calling for the good of others. It's an avenue to demonstrate love to your neighbor. Different work functions provide different opportunities to directly or indirectly influence the lives of others. With such an approach, God will be glorified as the culture is enabled to thrive according to the direction in which He structured it to function.

Excellence

What does it mean for a person to carry out his work with excellence?

A person reflects God's character (ethics) and works (creational norms) through diligent efforts to produce something of quality or to provide a service of value for others' good.

What kinds of virtues will be displayed in this pursuit of excellence?

diligence, courage, passion, restraint, creativity, eloquence, integrity, fidelity, wisdom, grace, humility, interdependence, and love

For further definition and description of each virtue, refer to Andreas J. Kostenberger, *Excellence* (Wheaton: Crossway, 2011).

A Distinctively Christian...

Ask someone from your church community to speak to the class about their job and how exactly they approach their job functions as a Christian (with excellence, ethics, and from a biblical worldview perspective). How can they recognize God's common grace in allowing unsaved coworkers to do their job according to excellence, ethics, and even according to the creational norms of a God-designed world? How might the Christian approach the job differently?

Example: A Distinctively Christian Engineer

A Christian engineer who works on vehicles should be mindful of loving his neighbor. He will be careful to meet the highest safety standards. He will follow company protocols for any changes made in a design so that any introductions of new problems can be traced back to the source and properly resolved. (It will also save the company money and reputation by limiting the size of any recalls.)

Redeeming the Time

The straightforward rendering, "redeeming the time" (Eph. 5:16, KJV), makes good sense when placed in Paul's eschatological contrast between the present evil age and the age to come. Because the days are evil, Christians must buy back their time from the service of evil to the service of the Lord—in the church, in the home, and at their work (Eph. 5:15–16; 6:5–8). Because the days are evil, Christians must strive to use their abilities in service to righteousness (Rom. 6:13). This will bring a taste of the age to come into the present.

WORK OUTSIDE OF WORK

Christians aren't always paid for the work that God has called them to do. Some Christians might coach in a youth sports league for the opportunity to be a Christian mentor to some young people. Others might volunteer at a local school to help struggling students with homework. Another might volunteer at community events both to benefit the community and to build redemptive relationships with an eye toward sharing the gospel. This volunteer service doesn't bring a paycheck with it, but God calls some Christians to this work too.

made and shapes it into new and pleasing forms. The well-designed garden shows nature more clearly and beautifully than nature can show itself."[4] Work fulfills the command to love God with all of one's being because work, ideally, takes what God has created and uses the abilities that God has given to humans to show off the beauty of God's creation "more clearly and beautifully."

Good work also fulfills the second great commandment, "Love your neighbor as yourself."[5] Martin Luther pointed out in Reformation era Germany that when Christians pray, "Give us this day our daily bread," they are praying for the work of the baker, the work of the farmer, and the work of government in preventing war or fraud in the marketplace.[6] We all need bread, and when the farmer, baker, soldier, and police officer do their jobs, they are serving the rest of us. Ideally, that service should be done out of love.

DISTINCTIVELY CHRISTIAN WORK

Work that is done in obedience to God and out of love for God and neighbor is work that is pressing toward redemption. But Christians press toward redemption not only in how they do their work but in what they do. Work presses toward redemption when it is done in a distinctively Christian way, in a biblical way.

Not all Christians like this idea, however. Some argue that there really is nothing distinctively Christian about the vocations of carpenter, cashier, firefighter, plumber, landscaper, or goat breeder aside from the virtues of diligence, respect, and honesty that all people recognize as good. It's true that by common grace, and through attention to the creational norms governing these vocations, non-Christian people often do them just as well as or better than Christians.

Even in these very practical vocations, other things being equal, there will prove to be a difference between those who do their work out of love for God and neighbor and those who don't. But what if you expand the list of vocations to include research biologists, philosophers, historians, bioethicists, educators, and legislators? In these vocations the distinctions between the Christian perspective and non-Christian perspectives are often stark. A consistent, godly Christian philosopher simply could not do his work without sounding very different from his non-Christian colleagues at academic conferences. A Christian research bioethicist will have divine guidance in Scripture for his or her work on stem cells or cloning.

Christians are obligated to think about how being a Christian affects their work as scientists, teachers, elected officials, or artists. Much of the rest of this book is designed to help Christians in this way. When Christians attempt to do their work from a Christian perspective, they press that work in a redemptive direction, toward its created structure.

REDEEMING THE TIME

One of the reasons that the old medieval distinction between monks and miners, pastors and printers is still popular is that Christian service seems to have an eternal dimension. When you preach or evangelize, you are laying up treasure in heaven, aren't you? But secular work seems to fade. If you're a house painter, that fading is

---

How can you make the best use of your time now to contribute to the good of others or to equip yourself to contribute to the good of society in the future?

• School

Give yourself entirely to your work as a student rather than giving yourself entirely to entertainment and squeezing in enough effort at schoolwork just to get by for the time being (paying for it later in college or limiting your opportunities in your future work).

• Family

Look for opportunities to serve your family. How can you make life easier for your mom and dad by engaging in work around the house? How can you give time to your siblings, playing with them instead of taking for granted the limited time you may have with them? How can you mentor them and love them?

• Church

Look for opportunities to serve your church. What kinds of things never get done simply because there's a lack of manual labor? How can you use your youthful energy to make life easier on older members of the church body?

• Community

Look for opportunities to serve your community. What would make your community look nicer? What kinds of things or people are being neglected?

What kinds of things can be a waste of time?

It is possible that watching TV, playing video games, and surfing the web by yourself could serve a legitimate (very limited) purpose. But it's probably negligible compared to the huge number of hours most teens or young adults spend in these activities.

quite literal. And as Mr. Incredible once said, "No matter how many times you save the world, it always manages to get back in jeopardy again. Sometimes I just want it to stay saved! You know, for a little bit! I feel like the maid: I just cleaned up this mess! Can we keep it clean for . . . for ten minutes!"[7]

The only work worth doing, therefore—some Christians think—is the kind that gets people truly saved, like spiritually saved. Such Christians argue that only human souls will last forever, so work that focuses on souls is more important than other work. Working, in this view, is something of a necessary evil because we all have to eat in order to evangelize.

True Christians who love the Lord with all their hearts have often struggled over the issue we're discussing. Here's a point that may be helpful: remember that Christians don't actually redeem anything. They don't redeem people when they share the gospel. They don't redeem culture or science or education. They can press toward redemption or live in light of redemption in evangelism *and* in their "secular" work. But ultimately, redemption is brought about by Christ Himself.

There's one interesting exception. One verse in the Bible tells Christians to redeem something. Paul told the Ephesians that they should be "redeeming the time, because the days are evil" (Eph. 5:16, KJV). Paul had just been urging the Ephesians to "take no part in the unfruitful works of darkness, but instead expose them" (Eph. 5:11). And the conclusion he drew from the reality of darkness and the power of divine light was that believers should "redeem the time."

Like those first-century Christians, we live in a "present evil age" (Gal. 1:4). And precisely "because the days are evil," Paul says we should make the best use of these days that we can. Christians can redeem evil time by living righteously. They can redeem the time by walking wisely (Eph. 5:15). It's as if we can bring some part of the age to come into the present.

When Paul spells out what "redeeming the time" looks like in Ephesians 5, he doesn't focus on a bunch of holy, monkish, spiritual practices. Instead he makes a few comments about life in the church body but then devotes most of his letter to explaining how Christians ought to function in their normal everyday relationships. He talks about husbands, wives, children, *and workers* (Eph. 5:15–6:9).

Evangelism is quite obviously important to Paul, who was a missionary himself, but his examples of "redeeming the time" never mention it. Paul apparently saw no contradiction between the importance of work and the importance of evangelism. The two do not have to be in competition.

WORK AS JOYFUL VEXATION

As Christians, we do good work, we do hard work, not because it will bring in Christ's kingdom or establish some kind of permanent redemption in our corner of the world. All work is still frustrating and temporary. A Christian in government may spend a lifetime working hard to get righteous laws enacted only to see them swept away by injustice after the next election. A Christian businessman may see great success squandered by his heirs. Or a financial crisis or natural disaster may turn decades of hard work into dust.

Ecclesiastes is blunt about these fallen realities of life. Life in a fallen world is unsubstantial, transitory, and unsatisfying. "What has a man from all the toil and striving of heart with which he toils beneath the sun? For all his days are full of sorrow, and his work is a vexation" (Eccles. 2:22–23). Yet throughout Ecclesiastes, Solomon

- *micromanagement or perfectionism based on unrealistic expectations*

Idols can be hidden because workers simply conform to cultural expectations (in a particular company or country). But the status quo expectations may have been formed from the idolatrous focus of a collective group of people over decades or centuries. Christians must examine the foundation of their country's cultural "norms."

Idleness

Divide students into small groups. Each group should search for the words *sluggard*, *slothful*, and *slack* in the book of Proverbs using an online Bible program. They should chart out a column for each verse reference, a column for the characteristics of such a person, and a column for the consequences of such a lifestyle. Students could also note the characteristics of the diligent and the *general* promise of reward.

Frustration

Why don't riches always signify God's blessing? (Luke 12:16–21; 1 Tim. 6:9–10; James 5:1–6; Rev. 3:17)

The pursuit of riches leads to the temptation to abuse other people in order to achieve those goals. The gaining of riches may blind people to their true need for God.

Why don't diligent workers always receive the just fruits of their labors? (Lev. 19:13; Deut. 24:14–15; Prov. 22:16; Jer. 22:13; Mal. 3:5; Col. 4:1; James 5:4)

Ungodly people sometimes hold back wages from people who labor for them.

What is a common complaint of godly people and what is God's answer? (Job 12:6; 21:7; Ps. 37:7, 35–36; 73:1–17; 92:7; Jer. 12:1–2)

that wicked people prosper while God's people suffer helplessly; be patient for God will bring the wicked to a just end

Why won't riches bring ultimate satisfaction? (Eccles. 2:17–26)

The toil necessary to actually obtain riches seems like futility most of the time. Even if riches are finally obtained, they're quickly passed on to undeserving people who waste them.

Rest and Recreation

Rest from work is also a part of God's created design; it's not a part of the Fall. It's a part of the cycle of days and weeks built into the world by God (Gen. 2:1–3). Overwork is just as anti-normative as idleness. It leads to detrimental consequences: physical weariness, mental stress, neglect of family, inability to be involved in church or community,

---

Should recreation always be considered a worthless waste of time?

No, recreation can be purposeful and healthy just like eating sugar is necessary in limited doses. Recreational pursuits should be encouraged in moderation. Some people and societies have resorted to overwork in response to other people's and society's gluttony for relaxation. Neither extreme is proper.

Idols

What is an idol?

whatever takes the place of God—whatever someone depends on in place of God

Why do jobs become idols?

Jobs become a means for fulfilling lusts for money, material goods, status, power, achievement, or comfort. A job function becomes the measure of success—the essence or purpose of

one's entire life at the expense of every other sphere of one's life. But the ultimate purpose of a Christian's life (glorifying God) should encompass other broader cultural and family pursuits in addition to one's job.

How do employees reveal that their jobs have become idols?

- *driven to overwork for non-essentials*
- *unending anxiety or worry over pleasing others*
- *resorting to anger and manipulation to climb the corporate ladder*
- *discouragement due to unfulfilled lusts*

How do employers reveal that their businesses have become idols?

- *concern for efficiency and profit at the expense of the well-being and fair treatment of employees (treating them as cogs in a machine rather than as people)* and so forth. Laboring so much that there is no time to enjoy the fruit of one's labors by sharing it with others is anti-normative (Prov. 12:14; Eccles. 2:24–26; 3:13, 22; 5:18–19; 8:15; 9:7; 1 Tim. 6:17–19). A well-rounded life includes embracing downtime instead of renouncing it as a waste of time. God created a world with all the variety in it for humans to enjoy (1 Tim. 4:4–5).

 ## Summarize the Biblical View of Work

What is the reason or basis for work?

fulfilling the Creation Mandate

What are the purposes for work?

to demonstrate love for God and others

In what manner should work be carried out?

with excellence according to ethical standards of conduct and according to creational norms or a biblical worldview

What should motivate one's work?

redeeming the time or living in light of redemption (with the hope of your work's lasting value in the new earth)

What are the two wrong attitudes toward work on opposite extremes?

being idolatrous or being idle

THINKING IT THROUGH 12.2

1. obedience to God in carrying out the Creation Mandate
2. to love God and your neighbor
3. doing the work itself in accordance with a biblical worldview perspective
4. to live righteously in light of redemption in every task that they engage in
♀5. Work is a gift from God for which every person was designed, but the Fall makes work into an unsatisfying idol and/or frustrates its success and durability.

counsels the reader to find joy in this life—especially in work. "There is nothing better than that a man should rejoice in his work, for that is his lot" (3:22).

But many people make their work an idol. They look to it to bring them not just wealth but something they crave even more—prestige, power, or ultimate satisfaction. If that's what you want out of your career, your idol will most certainly let you down. Worse, instead of looking to God as your greatest source of satisfaction and security, you have replaced Him with something from His creation. But if you can simply accept the pleasure of a hard day's work as a gift from God, you'll be redeeming the time and bringing praise to God as the giver of the gift.

Whether God allows your work to help reshape your society in positive ways, or whether He allows your influence to shrink and your life to be threatened, you must be faithful—and keep an eye on the return of Christ to set things right.

THINKING IT THROUGH 12.2

1. What is the ultimate reason for engaging in any legitimate work?
2. What are the primary purposes that should orient how all legitimate work must be done?
3. In addition to the way Christians carry out their work, what should make their work truly distinctive?
4. What does Paul mean when he instructs Christians to "redeem the time"?
♀5. Why is work both joyful and full of vexation at the same time?

Scripture Memory

Acts 2:42

Making Connections

1. Compare and contrast the New Covenant people of God and the Old Covenant people of God.

2. List the six tasks involved in the mission of the institutional church. What are the two key passages that define the mission of the church?

3. Pick a job—your father's job, your job, or your dream job—and explain how (or whether) it flows out of the Creation Mandate of Genesis 1:26–28.

4. Referring to that same job (question 3), explain what it would look like if the person doing it were truly motivated by love of God and neighbor. How might that make the job different than if the person were motivated solely by money?

Developing Skills in Apologetics and Worldview

5. What guidelines should a local church establish in order to make sure that its work in its local community supports the primary tasks of its mission?

6. What guidelines should a person establish in order to make sure that work does not become an idol?

Examining Assumptions and Evidence

7. Why is church membership necessary for believers?

8. Why is it dangerous to view the church as completely synonymous with the kingdom?

9. Why is it important to understand that everyone working a legitimate job works in service to God?

10. When Christians do their work, are they actually causing the world to progress toward final redemption? Explain why or why not.

Becoming a Creative Cultivator

11. What is one thing you think your church could do to reach out to the community?

CHAPTER REVIEW ANSWERS

Making Connections

1. By definition, the New Covenant includes only saved people while the Old Covenant includes both saved and unsaved people. The New Covenant includes people from all nations within the church while the Old Covenant was primarily for ethnic Jews and secondarily for people who became a part of the Israelite nation.

2. evangelism; baptism; teaching; fellowship; Lord's Supper; prayer; Matt. 28:18–20; Acts 2:42

3. Particular jobs that students mention should be somehow connected to the larger endeavor of taking dominion.

4. Some people might carry out tasks well with a wrong motivation, but carrying out tasks with the right motivation should increase the quality of the work and satisfaction of the person doing the work.

Developing Skills in Apologetics and Worldview

5. Answers will vary; the needed time and resources for such endeavors can't displace the church's main mission; they should not replace individual involvement in the community; they must not involve bait-and-switch tactics; they must support the evangelistic and discipleship mission of the church but also genuinely arise out of compassionate care for people as humans.

6. Answers will vary; determine and prioritize necessary family, church, and other social needs with which work hours must not interfere; determine to be content with the basic necessities of life rather than resorting to overwork for greater comforts in life.

Examining Assumptions and Evidence

7. There must be some way to identify who is a part of a local church assembly so that both privileges and discipline may be properly exercised.

8. That confusion leads to granting the church authority and tasks that are reserved for other spheres, such as the government.

9. to avoid the two-story view that disparages "secular" work and portrays "spiritual" work as the preferred option for obedient, godly Christians; to reinforce the value of all jobs and to encourage a biblical approach in all jobs (rather than assuming neutrality)

10. No, only Christ redeems both people and creation. Christians can live righteously in light of redemption as they await Christ's Second Coming, but they can't fully and finally transform the world themselves before that time.

Becoming a Creative Cultivator

11. Answers will vary.
   Example: A summer sports camp can present an opportunity for evangelism to the community, provide coaching and mentoring in a variety of sports, and provide discipleship and service opportunities for church members. The once-a-year opportunity does not turn the church into a sports/recreation club, but it does build a bridge to the community.

TERMS TO REMEMBER

church as institution—the specific local gathering of believers in a particular assembly

church as organism—all believers everywhere under the headship of Christ

vocation—work as a calling of God, which can include every legitimate job not just full-time ministry

Now that we have laid the groundwork of what a biblical worldview is and outlined it in terms of Creation, Fall, Redemption, the following units examine various institutions in light of a biblical worldview.

UNIT 5: GENDER

This unit examines the institution of the family and gender roles in church and society. We begin with the family because it is the foundational institution in society.

CHAPTER 13

This chapter examines the creational norms for family and gender roles in church and society.

CHAPTER 14

This chapter examines the way that the Fall has twisted the gender norms that God has instituted and how the Fall has damaged the institution of the family.

CHAPTER 15

This chapter encourages students to press against the Fall and toward a restoration of God's creational intentions for family and gender roles.

5

GENDER

The student will be able to

13.1 Defend God's creational design for gender roles in marriage.

13.2 Defend God's creational design for the family.

13.3 Defend God's creational design for gender roles in the church and society.

SECTION OBJECTIVES 13.1

1. Explain why creational norms must eventually push back against secular culture's rebellion.

2. Analyze God's structured design for marriage: man and woman equal in essence but different in functional roles.

3. Compare and contrast the differing gender roles of husbands/fathers versus wives/mothers.

Chapter Thirteen **THE MAN AND THE WOMAN IN CREATION**

Then the Lord God said, "It is not good that the man should be alone; I will make him a helper fit for him."

Scripture Memory Genesis 2:18

13.1 MARRIAGE AND FAMILY

Chris Milloy, a writer for the popular online magazine *Slate* (one of the top websites in the United States and Canada[1]), is angry at doctors for committing one simple sin: telling parents the gender of their children at birth.

> Why . . . must this person be a boy and that person be a girl? . . . As a newborn, your child's potential is limitless. The world is full of possibilities that every person deserves to be able to explore freely, receiving equal respect and human dignity while maximizing happiness through individual expression.[2]

Milloy feels strongly about this, apparently, for personal reasons: he now calls himself "Christin" and dresses and identifies as female. His opinions don't sound nearly as extreme to Western ears now as they did a very, very short time ago. Even if they haven't reached Milloy's conclusions, many Westerners share his presuppositions. Milloy has only taken his worldview to its logical end with regard to gender. And he urges others to follow:

> Infant gender assignment is a willful decision, and as a maturing society we need to judge whether it might be a wrong action. Why must we force this on kids at birth? . . . What could be the harm in letting a child wait to declare for themself who they are, once they're old enough?[3]

Activist Sarah Wright, writing for another prominent online source, the *New York Times*, takes a view of marriage much like Milloy's view of gender: she denies that it really exists.

> We believe the arbitrary nature of elevating some relationships above others is unethical, and we advocate for fairness and equality among all caretaking relationships.[4]

The institution of marriage, Wright thinks, should probably be discarded. Or society should at least be open to "more choices for more people"—three people, eight people, people of the same gender, people of any gender on the LGBTQ* continuum, people of genders yet to be invented. How about identical twins? Elderly siblings? The definition of marriage, in her worldview, becomes so large and inclusive as to be meaningless.

Gender-deniers and marriage-deniers aren't like Holocaust-deniers and moon-landing-deniers (such people do exist); they're like gravity-deniers. They're not lunatics; they're rebels.

But creation is stubbornly resistant to change, and all of us, Christians and non-Christians, have to live in it. Even smart people with graduate degrees who write in major news sources can't be gravity-deniers for long. God's creation has a way of bouncing back when people suppress it. And the Western world is in the act of suppressing one of the hardest truths in the world to deny: the God-created realities of gender, marriage, and family.

LGBTQ: *lesbian, gay, bisexual, transgender, queer*

Lesson Plan Chart—Chapter 13

Section Title	Pages	Activity Manual	Days
13.1 Marriage and Family	184–89	Activity 23	1 day
13.2 God's Design for Family	189–93		2 days
13.3 Gender Roles Beyond the Nuclear Family	193–98	Activity 24	2 days
Review	199		1 day
Total Suggested Days			**6 days**

 Are All Options on the Table?

Jean Lloyd writes about her personal experience of gender identity confusion in her teens—in the 1980s. ["The Girl in the Tuxedo: Two Variations on Sexual Orientation and Gender Identity," Public Discourse (website) February 5, 2015] As she considers the options available back then contrasted with those available today, she concludes that, thankfully, thirty-five years ago she had the option *not* to switch genders. She's thankful because she wasn't forced to embrace her own destructiveness. In contrast, today the option not to switch is almost completely closed off because of the social climate and civil laws that prevent anyone from questioning or counseling against gender changes. But gender changes do have

GOD'S DESIGN FOR MARRIAGE

On the sixth day of creation, God created a man. And He didn't provide any other options for self-definition. "Man" was it. "Man" was his very name ("Adam" means "man"). God also created a woman. She didn't get to choose her sexual identity either. And her name, "Eve," given to her later by her husband, was chosen precisely because she is the "mother of all living" (Gen. 3:20). Gender is not arbitrary; it is a given—a God-given.

The same is true of the first marriage. God didn't bring Adam and Eve together as debate or tennis opponents. He brought them together to be "one" (Gen. 2:24), to be husband and wife.

The same God-givenness is true of the family: the very first thing God told Adam and Eve to do was to "be fruitful and multiply," to have kids. From the very beginning, gender, marriage, and family were central to God's design for creation. And it's safe to assume that He knows how they should work better than writers on popular news websites do.

A great number of those writers don't like what God has to say about the family because it puts limits on the freedom they demand. The apostle Paul describes the authority structure God instituted this way:

> The head of every man is Christ,
> the head of a wife is her husband,
> and the head of Christ is God [the Father]. (1 Cor. 11:3)

The authority structure in a marriage is like the one in the Trinity. (Have you seen enough examples now to understand why the Trinity is so fundamental to the Christian faith?) That's what *head* most naturally means in a context like this one: "authority." [5]

But note that the Father is not greater than the Son or more God-like somehow. The members of the Trinity—Father, Son, and Spirit—are all equal. They're equal in power, in wisdom, and in glory. So when Paul says that "the head of Christ is God," he's not denying their equality; he's speaking of the different roles they have in relationship to one another. Among the members of the Trinity, God the Father takes the lead, and Jesus obediently follows. Often during His earthly ministry Jesus insisted, "I have come . . . not to do my own will but the will of him who sent me" (John 6:38). No person of the Trinity is more important or necessary than another. But in their glorious work of creation (Col. 1:16) and redemption (John 3:16), they fulfill distinct roles. The Father, Son, and Spirit are all equal in essence, but each is unique in function.

And that's just the way it was with the first two created humans. From the earliest pages of Genesis we can discern this same kind of distinction between the husband and the wife: equal in essence, different in function. Neither is more important or better than the other; God has simply assigned them different roles in order to accomplish what is best for the good of the human race and for His own glory.

THE TRINITY

Essence
Father
=
Son   Spirit

Function
Father
Son   Spirit

HUSBAND & WIFE

Essence
Husband = Wife

Function
Husband   Wife

---

destructive consequences that result from struggling against both the reality of your design and your Designer.

Gender Recognition

Gender isn't chosen; it's established even before conception by God's creational design (Gen. 1:27; Psa. 139:16; Matt. 19:4). That God-created identity should remain easily recognizable. Human efforts to decrease this distinction are condemned (Deut. 22:5). This Old Testament law is rooted in universal creational norms that ought to be applied by New Testament believers in their own situational context (1 Cor. 11:14–15). God also repeatedly addresses some specific commands to men and others to women, presupposing that the genders exist and are distinct (Titus 2:1–8). Thus, a gender-neutral position undermines God's comple-mentary design for men and women (Gen. 2:18–24).

Freedom or Bondage?

Actually, the gender identity crisis is simply the fruit of secularism's belief that people should be free to express their own individuality however they wish—so that they can become whatever they want to be. In psychological terms, this is often described as self-actualization—unleashing or activating one's full potential by meeting a hierarchy of needs. Maslow's teaching about self-actualization can be summarized in this statement: "What a man can be, he must be." [Maslow, *Motivation and Personality* (New York: Harper, 1954), 92] In popular parlance, this is often called finding or discovering oneself. The popular secular idea of self-discovery or self-realization has simply been applied to the realm of gender.

The worldview problem that must be addressed is the mistaken idea that humans can find freedom and happiness by fulfilling all of their natural (sinful) desires. The reason that secularists base freedom and happiness on self-fulfillment is that they root human value in self-accomplishment [see TE notes on page 65]. Furthermore, this pursuit is ultimately founded on the desire for human autonomy. People want freedom from God and His structural design. But the Bible teaches that violating God's creational norms leads only to bondage (Rom. 6:16–18; Eph. 2:1–5; Titus 3:3; 2 Pet. 2:19). Eventually, the push against God's creational norms will result in the breakdown of society until creational norms spring back into place again.

True freedom may be compared to two skydivers—one with a parachute and one without a parachute. Which one is free of a burden while free-falling? Which one is free after reaching the ground?

> Many women (and men) . . . judge [freedom] on the basis of immediate sensations of unrestrained license or independence. But true freedom takes God's reality and God's purpose for creation into account and seeks to fit smoothly into God's good design. . . . True freedom is not giving in to our every impulse. It is the sometimes painful and exhilarating discovery of God's power to fight free from the bondage of our sinful selves.

[John Piper and Wayne Grudem, eds., *Recovering Biblical Manhood and Womanhood: A Response to Evangelical Feminism* (Wheaton: Crossway, 1991), 38–39]

Head Means Authority

Wayne Grudem provides a helpful analysis of the term *head*, defending the interpretation that *head* means "authority" (rather than "source" or "origin") but arguing that subordination doesn't mean inferiority. [*Recovering Biblical Manhood and Womanhood*, 424–76]

Imaging the Trinity

Ray Orlund Jr. Writes:

> If our Creator exists in this manner [as fully equal persons in a loving authority/submission structure], should we be surprised and offended if His creaturely analog on earth exists in paradoxical form? . . . I see this fallacy again and again in feminist argumentation. 'Subordination = denigration' and 'equality = indistinguishability.' . . . Is the Son of God slighted because He

came to do the will of the Father? . . . Feminists seem to be reasoning that, because some subordination is degrading, all subordination must necessarily be degrading.

[*Recovering Biblical Manhood and Womanhood*, 93–94]

The lie that Satan told Eve was that subordination (to God) was bad. That's the same struggle nearly every woman today has in relation to her husband (Gen. 3:16). The prevalence of spousal abuse in our culture also contributes to the perception that subordination is always degrading.

Equal in Essence; Different in Function

What do secularists see as the source of human value?

self-fulfillment, which usually comes through self-accomplishment

What do Christians see as the source of human value?

the image of God granted at creation

Why can't secularists accept the distinction between equal essence and different function? [*Hint:* It's rooted in their presupposition about the source of human value.]

Since secularists see self-accomplishment (function) as the source of human value, they can't distinguish equal value from equal function. Their problem is a faulty presupposition.

Mature Masculinity and Femininity

Assign outside reading to students from the first chapter of *Recovering Biblical Manhood and Womanhood*. The Council for Biblical Manhood and Womanhood (CBMW) offers this book in PDF format for free on its website. Then direct the students to do Activity 23.

It's important at the outset to distinguish the biblical position from two opposite extremes: an abusive patriarchal position that supports male domination versus an egalitarian position that fails to distinguish the roles of men and women.

Men and Women: Equal in Value

Based on Genesis 1, list all the reasons why men and women should be considered equals.

- *Both men and women bear the status of God's image—individually. By nature, they share the same capacities (Gen. 5:1; 9:6).*
- *Both men and women are blessed by God, serving as vice-regents over God's world and tasked with fulfilling the Creation Mandate.*

- *Both men and women have a special relationship with their Creator, distinct from all other creatures.*

These truths are sufficient to safeguard full respect and value for all men and women.

Men and Women: Unique in Function

If there isn't supposed to be a distinction between men and women, then why did God create humans male and female?

The very existence of two sexes argues that some kind of distinction must exist.

What was God's purpose in creating the woman after He had already created man?

According to Genesis 2:18 and 23, the woman was created to fit with Adam. She is his equal—unlike any of the animals God brought before Adam. She's made of the same stuff Adam was made from, but she was created to be Adam's helper. She has a distinct, complementary function.

The exalted, God-given role of a wife shouldn't be lost in a skepticism that questions God's good design. Adam lacked something that only Eve could provide and fulfill. His life, even in a perfect world, was incomplete without a companion to love. (Remember, as pointed out in Chapter 4, love is the ultimate motivation in life.) God created husbands to love and wives to be loved. His design is beautiful and perfect.

What happens when one role or the other is relinquished in a relationship?

If the man fails to lead or the woman fails to help then things become disorderly and eventually dysfunctional.

Consider what Ortlund has to say:

He let his wife lead him. (This doesn't mean husbands shouldn't listen to their wives, of course.)

The apostle Paul reads Genesis the same way. To prove his statement that "the head of a wife is her husband" (1 Cor. 11:3), Paul offers this argument: "For man was not made from woman, but woman from man. Neither was man created for woman, but woman for man" (11:8–9). We must not miss the importance of this. In order to explain the roles of husband and wife during his own day in the middle of the first century AD, Paul appeals to the way God ordered His creation at the very beginning. Fatherly leadership was not a result of the Fall. God created the man to lead the family.

Husbands and fathers do have final authority (under God) within their homes (Eph. 5:22; 1 Pet. 3:1). But if you've never been an authority or a leader, you may have the wrong idea about leaders. You may think of them as bossing other people around, getting to do things the way they want. But leadership in a fallen world mostly means giving up time you'd rather spend on something else to help others. Men (especially husbands) should run *to* problems, not *away from* them. A biblically faithful man doesn't sit passively by while the family blows up. Neither does he abuse his authority or throw his weight around; the wife is an authority in the home too, just one arranged underneath her husband (Paul speaks of women "managing their households" in 1 Timothy 5:14). And on practically the first page, the Bible says a husband should "hold fast to his wife" (Gen. 2:24). That doesn't mean to keep a tight rein on her; it means he persists in showing her faithful love (Eph. 5:25, 28–31) and honor (1 Pet. 3:7). The man is also to be primarily responsible for providing for his children, both their physical needs (cf. 2 Cor. 12:14) and their spiritual nurturing (Heb. 12:6–11). He is not to "provoke them to anger" with ungracious sternness but to train them "in the discipline and instruction of the Lord" (Eph. 6:4). There is joy in fatherly leadership—both in spite of and because of the difficulty.

In short, as a husband and father, the man has the unique and primary role as loving leader, spiritual nurturer, protector, and provider.

The Role of the Woman as Wife/Mother

Although both the man and the woman were created equal by God, the wife holds the unique position of being created for her husband (1 Cor. 11:9). God perceived that Adam's aloneness was "not good," and took the initiative to fashion the woman with whom he could share his life.[9] God created the woman to be a "helper fit for him" (Gen. 2:18, 20), a partner specifically designed by God for Adam's benefit, to share life with him and to fulfill God's will together.

> **LOVE IN THE TRINITY AND LOVE IN MARRIAGE**
>
> Michael Reeves writes,
>
> Therein lies the very goodness of the gospel: as the Father is the lover and the Son the beloved, so Christ becomes the lover and the church the beloved. That means that Christ loves the church first and foremost: his love is not a response, given only when the church loves him; his love comes first, and we only love him because he first loved us (1 Jn 4:19).
>
> That dynamic is also to be replicated in marriages, husbands being the heads of their wives, loving them as Christ the Head loves his bride, the church. He is the lover, she is the beloved. Like the church, then, wives are not left to earn the love of their husbands; they can enjoy it as something lavished on them freely, unconditionally and maximally. For eternity, the Father so loves the Son that he excites the Son's eternal love in response; Christ so loves the church that he excites our love in response; the husband so loves his wife that he excites her to love him back. Such is the spreading goodness that rolls out of the very being of this God.[8]

Must the male headship side of the paradox be construed as an insult or threat to women? Not at all, because Eve was Adam's equal in the only sense in which equality is significant for personal worth. Woman is just as gifted as man "with all the attributes requisite to attaining wisdom, righteousness and life." In a parallel sense, a church member has as much freedom and opportunity to achieve real significance as does a church elder; but the elder is to lead, and the member is to support. There is no cause for offense. . . . Genesis 2 supplements Genesis 1 by showing that God's commission that we "have dominion over the earth" (1:26, 28) as male and female works out practically through marriage. And in marriage the man heads the home for God, and the wife helps him to fulfill the divine calling.

[*Recovering Biblical Manhood and Womanhood*, 91–92]

 What Men Are Meant to Be

Break students up into small groups. Provide each group with the verse references from one of the following responsibilities. Ask each group what responsibility is indicated by the verses assigned to them.

Responsibilities of a husband

- give spiritual guidance and responsible leadership, representing Christ, under His authority (1 Cor. 11:3, 8–9, cf. Gen. 3:9; Eph. 1:21 with 5:21–23)
- love, cherish, and respect his wife (Gen. 1:27; Prov. 31:28; 1 Cor. 13:1–8; Eph. 5:25, 28–29, 33; 1 Pet. 3:7)

- provide financially and protect (Gen. 3:17–19; Exod. 21:10; by implication Deut. 24:19 and 1 Tim. 5:8; Eph. 5:25)
- engage in faithful intimacy (Gen. 1:28; 2:24; Prov. 6:23–24; Song of Sol. 1–8; 1 Cor. 7:2–4; Eph. 5:31; Heb. 13:4)

Responsibilities of a father

- seek children (Gen. 1:28; Pss. 127–128)
- give spiritual leadership and discipline (Exod. 12:3; Deut. 6:4–9; Josh. 24:15; Prov. 1:10; 2:1–5; 13:24; Eph. 6:4)
- reinforce his wife's headship over the children as their mother (Exod. 20:12; Prov. 1:8; 30:17)
- promote harmonious relationships and nurturing support (Ps. 103:13; Prov. 23:26; Eph. 6:4; Col. 3:21; 1 Thess. 2:11–12)
- provide financially and protect (Gen. 2:15; by implication Deut. 24:19; Pss. 127–128; Matt. 7:9–10)

Fathers Must Be Fathers

Since students come from different kinds of home situations, remind them that God is both good and sovereign even in a fallen world with fallen parents who sometimes make hurtful decisions that affect their children. Various kinds of difficult home situations may be a part of God's plan, testing students' faith. This doesn't excuse the sins of authorities, but it should provide comfort to those who are suffering. [This will be discussed further in the next chapter.] But students need to embrace God's creational norms and desire to build their own future homes in accordance with them.

Young men need to think correctly about their possible future role as fathers and plan accordingly. It might be tempting to relegate all responsibility to the mother to take care of the children. But fathers are called by God to be fathers (Prov. 23:26). Their presence in the home is as much a part of God's design for the home as the mother's presence is. The absence of a loving husband and father leading and disciplining his wife and children will result in a distressed household. His wife and children need his attention—they need his Christlike sacrificial servanthood in the home.

What Women Are Meant to Be

Divide students into small groups. Provide each group with the verse references from one of the following responsibilities. Ask each group what responsibility is indicated by the verses assigned to them.

Responsibilities of a wife

- be a fitting and complementary counterpart (Gen. 2:18; Prov. 31:11–12, 23, 28)
- be wise in counsel (Prov. 31:26; 1 Sam. 25)

- love, respect, and submit to her husband (1 Cor. 11:3, 8–10; 13:1–8; Eph. 5:21–24; Titus 2:4–5)
- engage in faithful intimacy (Gen. 1:28; Song of Sol. 1–8; 1 Cor. 7:3–4; Eph. 5:31; Heb. 13:4)

Responsibilities of a mother
- seek children (Gen. 1:28; Ps. 113:9; Pss. 127–128; 1 Tim. 2:15)
- provide spiritual leadership and discipline for children (Deut. 6:4–9; Prov. 1:8; 6:20; 29:15; 31:1; 2 Tim. 1:5; 3:14–15)
- support her husband's leadership over the children as their father (Exod. 20:12; Prov. 31:11–12 in contrast to Gen. 27)
- give nurturing support (Ps. 131:2; Prov. 4:3; 31:28; 1 Thess. 2:7)
- care for home and family needs (Prov. 31:13–22, 27; 1 Tim. 5:9–15; Titus 2:5)

The Wrong Question
Should a wife/mother have a job?

This is the wrong question to ask.

The right question to ask is whether a wife/mother can, in her particular situation, be wholehearted in fulfilling her God-given responsibilities so that all her work fits in with those duties rather than competing with them.

Following John Frame's triperspectivalism, analyze the three factors that affect this issue. [See note on "Discovering Biblical Wisdom," p. 85.]

First, what are her God-given responsibilities (normative principles)?

- *As a fitting helper, she should contribute to that which accomplishes the mission of the family, complementing her husband's leadership.*
- *She is the keeper of the home—she manages everything that revolves around the household. (This doesn't mean she stays inside the home all day.)*
- *She is the spiritual teacher of her children—she spends a great deal of her time mentoring and discipling her own children. (She can't be replaced by the Christian school teacher or youth pastor.)*
- *She is a spiritual guide and example for younger mothers—she takes time to make a concerted effort to pass on the wisdom of how to be a good wife and mother (or to learn this from older women).*

Second, what is her situation (situational context)?

A single mother, a wife with no children, and a mother with children will each face different situations in which to fulfill their God-given responsibilities. Regardless of the situation, a woman must ask herself whether she's living as if the God-given role and responsibilities of a wife and mother are honorable. Those re-

---

"Wives, submit to your own husbands" is taken by secular women to be Exhibit A proving that the Bible is not just outdated but hateful. But maybe this attitude says more about secular men than about anything else.

The very passage in which Paul tells wives to submit also includes much longer instructions to husbands, leading off with, "Husbands, love your wives, as Christ loved the church and gave himself up for her" (Eph. 5:25). Yes, Scripture tells a wife to submit. And the true test of submission comes when a wife disagrees with her husband; that can be difficult to swallow in a culture that values autonomy (self-rule) so highly.

But the Bible also calls for a husband to love, honor, and cherish his wife as Christ does the church. Christianity encourages husbands through positive means (Christian fellowship, Bible teaching) and negative means (the threat of church discipline) to stay faithful to their wives and children.

Christianity isn't just a set of rules and principles; the Bible creates a community—the church—in which the truth is supposed to be lived out. If secular women had husbands who loved them like Christians are supposed to love, would they still consider submission such a dirty word?

LOVE
HUSBAND · WIFE
SUBMIT

Just as the man as husband/father was created to be a loving leader, the woman as wife/mother was created to be a submissive partner, responsible to fulfill roles unique to her. As a "fit helper" for her husband, her function is to help him to fulfill the calling God has given him. Wives are instructed to "submit" to their husbands "as to the Lord" (Eph. 5:22; cf. 1 Pet. 3:1). In other words, it is the wife's role to place herself under her husband's authority; he is never told to make her submit. This is a fallen world, so no submission to any other human may be absolute. But that didn't stop Paul and Peter from telling wives to submit.

The woman has also been created by God with the special role of bearing children, a position of great honor (Gen. 3:20; Prov. 31:28). In fact, when Paul says that the woman will be "saved through childbearing" (1 Tim. 2:15), he's most likely referring to the fact that a woman shows her faith in God by fulfilling her God-ordained role, which significantly includes (but is not limited to) childbearing.[10] Furthermore, if giving birth to children is essential to God's command to rule over the earth, then the role of the woman is indispensable to God's divine plan.

But the wife's role does not mean she has second-class status. Her responsibilities are incredibly important. She is called by God to love her husband and her children (Titus 2:4), to manage the home (1 Tim. 5:14; Titus 2:5), and to participate in the spiritual nurture and discipline of her children (Prov. 1:8–9; 1 Tim. 5:10). The beautiful portrait of the wife and mother held as the crowning example in Proverbs 31:10–31 depicts a woman who honors and supports her husband (31:11–12) and who works sacrificially, wisely, and diligently to care for the daily needs of her family (31:13–27). She is praised and honored by her children and husband (31:28–29) and is referred to as one who "fears the Lord" (31:30) because she is honoring the role for which God created her.

In short, as a wife and mother, the woman has the unique and equally important role of submissive partner, companion, child-bearer, and homemaker.

CREATIONAL NORMS

In this chapter we're talking about gender at Creation, not after the Fall or in Redemption. So we'll talk about objections and exceptions in Chapter 14 about the effects of the Fall on gender. What about the issues of divorce, child abuse, and mari-

---

sponsibilities shouldn't be sidetracked by a job motivated by materialism or a selfish desire for status, freedom, and independence. However, some wives may be able to work outside the home without neglecting responsibilities or following wrong motivations.

Third, what does it mean for her to be wholehearted in fulfilling those responsibilities in that situation (personal conscience)?

The husband is the head of his own household and should work out with his wife convictions for applying her God-given responsibilities within her situational context. If the husband is absent, then the wife/mother will need to be convinced of God's will for her life in that context. While other Christians are called on by God to admonish others when they perceive a disconnect between God's Word and another member's life (Rom. 15:14), Christians must

also recognize the liberty that other Christians have to apply the Scripture differently because of different situations (Rom. 14:4–12).

 ## Mothers Must Be Mothers

Young women need to think correctly about their possible future role as mothers and plan accordingly. It might be tempting to think that time-saving technology allows a mother to spend more time in pursuits other than that of being the keeper of the home. However, this ignores the true reality of what has been happening to the family in this technological world.

> We may be watching the death of the germ-cell of all civilization, the family. Signs of the family's demise are abundantly clear all around us. Numerous facts confirm the grim prognosis. . . . For the past forty years or more the

tal conflict? Those things can only be called good or bad in relationship to a standard, and Genesis 1–2 sets the standard.

You can also see that standard in yourself, to a degree. Men and women simply are different, beyond (but including) mere anatomy. A culture that's reluctant to say so—like elite American culture—is pushing against creational norms.

THINKING IT THROUGH 13.1

1. What makes gender, marriage, and the family objective realities rather than arbitrary social constructs?

2. How do you know that men and women are equal in their created essence?

3. How do you know that men and women are given different roles?

4. Describe what the key functions are for a husband/father and for a wife/mother.

♀5. Why is it both rebellious and ultimately fruitless to try to redefine gender, marriage, and the family?

13.2 GOD'S DESIGN FOR FAMILY

An infamous phrase in the American culture war over abortion showed up in the *New York Times* when a Planned Parenthood activist told her personal abortion story. Amy Richards was in her early thirties; she had a boyfriend and lived in a walk-up apartment in New York City. And she found out she was having triplets.

"My immediate response was, I cannot have triplets," she wrote. "I would have to go on bed rest in March. I lecture at colleges, and my biggest months are March and April. I would have to give up my main income for the rest of the year."[11]

And to make matters worse, she thought, "I'll never leave my house because I'll have to care for these children. I'll have to start shopping only at Costco and buying big jars of mayonnaise."[12]

Costco mayonnaise. That's the infamous phrase. Amy Richards murdered two of her unborn children—stopping two heartbeats—in part because she didn't want to have to join the embarrassingly large families who often shop at warehouse stores like Costco.

So she glanced at her boyfriend and asked her doctor, "Is it possible to get rid of one of them? Or two of them?"[13]

Of course, it was possible; she was eight weeks along. Her boyfriend wondered aloud if they should keep the triplets, but Richards dismissed the idea. And two shots of potassium chloride later, she was carrying only one child.

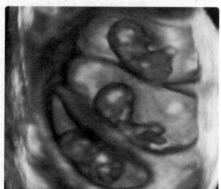

"My immediate response was, I cannot have triplets."

THE MAN AND THE WOMAN IN CREATION | 189

THINKING IT THROUGH 13.1

1. Gender, marriage, and family were created to function according to God's purposeful design.

2. Both are created in God's image (Gen. 1:26–27), are commanded to be fruitful and have dominion (Gen. 1:28), and are mutually dependent (Gen. 2:18, 20–23).

3. The Bible prescribes the different roles at creation and reinforces them at the Fall.

4. • The husband/father is a loving leader, spiritual nurturer, protector, and provider. The man was created to tend the garden (Gen. 2:7–8, 15) and after the Fall was told that he had to work by the sweat of his brow to sustain his family (Gen. 3:17–19).

   • The wife/mother is a submissive partner, companion, and keeper of the home. The woman was created to be a helper (Gen. 2:18, cf. 1 Cor. 11:8–9)—specifically, to bear and to raise children—and after the Fall was not to usurp Adam's headship (Gen. 3:16, cf. 1 Tim. 2:15; Titus 2:5).

♀5. These are created realities that God designed, and no amount of human effort can completely overturn the realities of God's created design before society will break down and/or be forced to operate according to God's design again.

SECTION OBJECTIVES 13.2

1. Discuss how human selfishness undermines the primacy of the family.

2. Recognize that having children is God's intended purpose and blessing for most married couples.

3. Explain why the normal intended role for children is one of submissiveness to their parents.

4. Summarize the responsibility of parents to nurture and to train their children.

5. Clarify the biblical structure for family headship established in each family unit.

When Does Human Life Begin?

In an Answers in Genesis video ("New Life, Stem Cells, and Cloning: When Does Life Begin?"), physician Tommy Mitchell explains why science can't answer this question; it's a theological question. Science can only describe stages of physical development. But the Bible is clear that, at conception (that is, at fertilization), the human nature (including sinfulness) has already become a reality

signs of the family's collapse have been paraded before us continually: divorce, the sexual revolution, abortion, sterilization, delinquency, infidelity, homosexuality, radical feminism, the "children's-rights" movement, together with the normalization of the single-parent home, the decline of the nuclear family, and other similar signs.

[John MacArthur, *Successful Christian Parenting: Raising Your Child with Care, Compassion, and Common Sense* (Nashville: Word Publishing, 1998), 5–6]

Biblical Submission or Unbiblical Abuse?

While Christians must be wary of role reversal, they must be just as wary of unbiblical distortions that turn submission into abuse.

Submission isn't just for women. All believers are obligated to submit to authorities in a variety of relationships (Rom. 13:1; Eph. 5:21; 6:1–8; Heb. 13:17).

Submission isn't slavery. If a husband is fulfilling his obligations to his wife, then enslavement won't be the result. A godly husband will sacrificially serve his wife. He will exalt his wife. He will enable his wife to use her talents and abilities (Prov. 31:10–31). Furthermore, a wife ought to appeal to other spheres of authority that God has placed over the husband if he is being abusive (both government and church authorities).

Submission doesn't mean that the wife is silenced from providing godly, wise advice. A godly husband seeks his wife's scriptural advisement; he sets the tone and creates an atmosphere so that his wife is encouraged to help him in this way.

THE MAN AND THE WOMAN IN CREATION | 189

(Ps. 51:5). Even before all the developmental stages have fashioned and knitted together the physical body, God acknowledges human value (Gen. 25:21–22; Ps. 139:13–16; Isa. 44:2; Jer. 1:4–5; Luke 1:41–44).

Other Resources on Abortion

Archives of helpful articles on the topics of abortion and the sanctity of life can be found at Albert Mohler's blog, on *World* magazine's website, and on the Answers in Genesis website.

Murder Is Being Justified

Christians must continue to maintain that abortion is murder and to urge people to reconsider taking steps to end a human life. But recent justifications for abortion are far more troubling than those used in the past. Rather than trying to argue against the overwhelming evidence that babies in the womb are humans, pro-choice activists are now ready to admit that. Unfazed by the argument that babies are human, they blatently defend the choice to murder humans in the womb simply because they have no personal desire to keep their babies alive (for any number of selfish reasons). It used to be assumed that everyone would value human life. Now, many people in the culture believe that some humans are expendable—and that they should have the power and freedom to end the life of another human. [Sarah Terzo, "Abortion Activists Admit: 'I Knew It Was a Baby,'" *Life News* (January 22, 2013)]

See also Al Mohler, "A Lot of People Want Intact Hearts These Days—Planned Parenthood, Abortion, and the Conscience of a Nation," albertmohler.com (July 15, 2015).

Children: Blessing or Burden?

Normative principle

God's original creational design and thus intent for married men and women is to attempt to be fruitful and multiply.

Situational applications

Of course, the principle shouldn't be turned on its head. A married couple who refuse to have children can't claim to be carrying out their particular discernment of the principle.

But on the other extreme, nobody can dictate to another couple to have a certain number of children in order to fulfill the principle. Descriptive Bible stories should not be made into prescriptive standards. The Bible mentions families of various sizes.

However, Christians can be legitimately encouraged not to make their decisions purely based on their status quo comfort or cultural or economic selfishness. When making the

---

If this were an isolated case, it would be tragic enough. But many educated Western people seem to have chosen to have fewer children for the same reason Richards used to justify her abortion—avoiding Costco and the other inconveniences and expenses of a large family. You may already know this from personal experience. Big families are considered odd. They get mocked. Parents with lots of kids hear snide remarks from strangers at the grocery store.

THE GIFT OF CHILDREN

Before you can even get close to answering the question "How many children should I have?" you have to acknowledge that in the Bible children are, quite literally, a blessing and a gift. "God blessed them. And God said to them, 'Be fruitful and multiply and fill the earth and subdue it'" (Gen. 1:28). Throughout the Bible, the ability to bear children is a sign of God's favor (33:5, but compare 30:2; Deut. 28:4; Ps. 113:9).

Psalm 127:3–5 sums up the attitude that God's people had toward their children:

> Behold, children are a heritage from the Lord,
>   the fruit of the womb a reward.
> Like arrows in the hand of a warrior
>   are the children of one's youth.
> Blessed is the man
>   who fills his quiver with them!
> He shall not be put to shame
>   when he speaks with his enemies in the gate.

The Bible stops short of saying how many children count as "multiplying." And different married couples may have different-sized quivers—some can handle ten kids (financially, emotionally, physically), and some can't. So most Christians in America have not prohibited "family planning"—controlling when and how many children a couple has. But the biblical attitude toward children is still noticeably positive in a world in which that perspective isn't always appreciated.

THE ROLE OF CHILDREN

Genesis says that Adam "fathered a son in his own likeness, after his image, and named him Seth" (Gen. 5:3). Do you recognize that language from Genesis 1? It's there so we make no mistake: the image of God passes from generation to generation. Image-bearing didn't cease with Adam and Eve (cf. Gen. 9:6; Ps. 8:3–8). Neither did human dominion. Adam and Eve couldn't have filled the earth without being fruitful and multiplying, of course. The blessing and task of dominion passes to all children.

But children exercise dominion (as people in general do) under the authority of others—namely their parents, in most cases. "Honor your father and your mother, that your days may be long in the land that the Lord your God is giving you" (Exod. 20:12). Paul explicitly commands children to "obey" their parents (Col. 3:20), but note that the context indicates that this applies primarily to children in the home. There may possibly be times in the life of an adult child when he honors his parents without obeying them (Gen. 2:24), but the command to honor parents for both young and old is treated as so important in all of Scripture that those situations ought to be rare. Under Old Testament law, extreme violations of this command to honor one's parents could carry the death penalty (Exod. 21:15; Deut. 21:18–21; Prov. 20:20; 30:17). In the New Testament, not only is the command to honor and obey repeated

---

decision to apply the principle for themselves, Christians need to view children as a blessing rather than a burden.

Abusive Extremes

While Christians most often recognize the dangers of groups that oppose biblical principles altogether, Christians must also recognize the dangers of groups that misapply biblical principles. The abuses that take place under the guise of following biblical principles do great damage to the name of Christ. Because extremist movements genuinely abuse biblical principles, some opponents have left Christianity and embraced false worldviews. However, these opponents fail to recognize that the abusive movements that they may have suffered under were misapplying Scripture rather than carrying out biblical principles. While

Christianity can't be separated from the biblical principles, it *can* be separated from the erroneous applications.

How can you discern the difference between biblical applications and extremism? Extremists tend to magnify the minute details of a human's (debatable) conclusions. Then they conflate those applications with the inerrant Word of God (as if they were one and the same). Another dangerous sign is when doctrine and sequential exposition of the Word are downplayed or replaced with behavioral mandates that aren't robustly connected to a solid doctrinal foundation within the larger theological context of the whole of Scripture. A healthy Christian who has a sound theological grasp of Scripture should be able to spot the extreme applications that are scripturally indefensible and that originate only from the mind of a

(Eph. 6:1–2), but disobedience to parents is listed as one of the extreme sins that marks the degradation of humanity (Rom. 1:30) and is a sign of unbelief (2 Tim. 3:2).

One of the marks of a godly person is his willingness to believe that God knew what He was talking about when He made honoring and obeying parents such a strong command. Yes, parents can be wrong. But when they're not clearly wrong, and when you (as a high school student in their home) have exhausted reasonable appeals, whatever they say is God's will for you. Just rest in the submissive role God has given you—life decisions won't always be so easy. If they don't like a particular boyfriend or girlfriend or television show or activity or college choice, God's word to you is "obey." Most parents won't micromanage you till you're thirty, but even if they do, they deserve your honor whenever biblically possible.

THE NURTURING OF CHILDREN

Before God's people entered the Promised Land, He gave them specific instructions regarding the nurturing of their children. First, they were to keep the words of God always before their children (see Gen. 18:19):

> These words that I command you today shall be on your heart. You shall teach them diligently to your children, and shall talk of them when you sit in your house, and when you walk by the way, and when you lie down, and when you rise. You shall bind them as a sign on your hand, and they shall be as frontlets between your eyes. You shall write them on the doorposts of your house and on your gates. (Deut. 6:6–9)

Second, they were to keep the works of God before their children:

> When your son asks you in time to come, "What is the meaning of the testimonies and the statutes and the rules that the Lord our God has commanded you?" then you shall say to your son, "We were Pharaoh's slaves in Egypt. And the Lord brought us out of Egypt with a mighty hand. And the Lord showed signs and wonders, great and grievous, against Egypt and against Pharaoh and all his household, before our eyes. And he brought us out from there, that he might bring us in and give us the land that he swore to give to our fathers. And the Lord commanded us to do all these statutes, to fear the Lord our God, for our good always, that he might preserve us alive, as we are this day. And it will be righteousness for us, if we are careful to do all this commandment before the Lord our God, as he has commanded us." (Deut. 6:20–25)

The future of the nation lay in the hands of these children, and God had two basic instructions for parents to protect that future: keep repeating what God had said and keep repeating what He had done. Israel ultimately failed to show forth God's glory in the land in part because they neglected to nurture their children (Ps. 78:5–11).

Today, Christian sons and daughters don't automatically follow the words and works of God out of love for Him any more than ancient Hebrew kids did. Children must be trained—ideally by parents who will nurture them "in the discipline and instruction of the Lord" (Eph. 6:4). God intended for the family to be a protected and loving environment where kids can learn the appropriate affections and skills necessary to love and follow God with their lives, to be a blessing to their families and to their society. The home is where parents encourage their children to develop talents, critical thinking skills, a strong work ethic, and ministry abilities that they will employ in the service of God and others. This includes preparation for their life's

domineering and misleading person. One last sign of extremism is a ritualistic or formulaic approach to sanctification—primarily motivated by a desire to achieve a greater spirituality or higher status over others (Col. 2:8–23).

Here's a concrete example. Some people have taught that since pain in childbirth is a God-given curse resulting from the Fall (Gen. 3:16), it is therefore sinful for women to diminish that pain at all. But such reasoning would also mean that humans should never try to diminish the effects of the Fall at all in any other area (such as using machines to make labor by the sweat of the brow easier).

"To suggest that there is anything unbiblical about relieving pain in childbirth as much as is safely possible makes about as much sense as refusing to ease the suffering of the sick and dying." [Elizabeth Mitchell, "Is it Wrong to Interfere with the Pain of Childbirth?" Answers in Genesis (website) January 28, 2011]

Patriarchal abusers are known to twist biblical truths about the sin nature (Jer. 17:9) and the Fall (1 Tim. 2:14–15)—wrongly applying those principles (only to those under them) in order to coerce and control wives into an unbiblical submission. Tyrannical dictatorship in the home over wife and (adult) children is scripturally indefensible. Tyrannical dictatorship is making absolute demands that are *nonbiblical* in precept and stretched in application (as if those demands are *the* biblical mandates), micromanaging every minute detail of other people's lives. Certainly, every family will have its own opinions on how to do some things that aren't explicitly detailed in the Bible. Young children do need to obey whether they

understand or not. But some people have presented their own extreme opinions as gospel in order to manipulate grown family members.

Why Obedience Is Hard

One Christian leader has said:

> The *corruption* all around our kids tends to defile them; the *curse* inside them tends to steer them the wrong way; and their own *childishness* makes them susceptible to many dangers.

[John MacArthur, *Successful Christian Parenting: Raising Your Child with Care, Compassion, and Common Sense* (Nashville: Word Publishing, 1998), 110]

Are you dead or alive?

Read Ephesians 2:1–3.

If obedience is hard for you, the first thing you need to ask yourself is whether or not you have really been made alive by Jesus Christ. A dead heart will be unresponsive and unteachable. For obedience to become easier, you must first be made alive, as evidenced by growth in virtue (Matt. 11:30; 2 Pet. 1:3–12; 1 John 5:3).

Have you been influenced by the rebellious culture around you?

If obedience is hard for you, the second thing you need to ask yourself is whether you have been influenced by this rebellious age that spurns authority in favor of autonomy (driven by selfish pride). The input from peers and pop culture certainly affects what you may consider to be normal and acceptable (Prov. 1:8–10; 24:21). Stop demanding that the world (your parents) revolve around your selfish desires. You may need to rebuild a relationship with your parents and seek to be discipled by them.

Can you admit that you may still need to grow out of childishness?

Even a person who fears God and is submissive must still grow in maturity, guided by his parents' wisdom (Prov. 19:27; Luke 2:52).

Unteachable = Foolish

Divide students into small groups. Assign each small group several chapters from the book of Proverbs. Have them find the word or concept that relates to being unteachable. Then have them look for the corresponding word or concept of the fool in that same context. They should make a chart showing the verse references and the descriptions or warnings.

In addition, you could have them look up every reference to the fool and the wise in Proverbs and what characterizes each.

Anger Is the Roadblock to Obedience and the Pathway to Rebellion

"This anger-to-rebellion process often can be traced through five distinct steps. These five steps on the stairway to destruction are hurt, bitterness, anger, stubbornness, and finally rebellion."

[Lou Priolo, *Keeping Your Cool: A Teen's Survival Guide,* rev. ed. (Phillipsburg, NJ: P&R, 2014), 13]

If there has been a perceived offense by an authority over you (regardless of whether it is real or not), but you have decided not to cover it with love or to address it (forgive and reconcile), then you have taken the first step toward rebellion.

If you continue to mull over the offense so that everything in life is viewed through that lens, then you have taken the second step toward rebellion.

If others begin to recognize that you are constantly at odds with an authority in your life, then you have taken the third step toward rebellion.

If you believe you have the right to rule yourself without anyone telling you what to do (like a mule that refuses to budge regardless of all the efforts to coax it), then you have taken the fourth step toward rebellion.

"A rebel is someone whose characteristics have gone beyond that of an *angry man* and have taken on the characteristics of the proverbial *fool*" (Priolo, 15).

The way to prevent rebellion (or move away from it) and to cultivate submissive obedience is to solve any anger problems you have (Eccles. 7:9). But it's important to understand that any effort put into this must be grounded in God's empowerment given to those who fear Him. If you fear Him, then He will give you both the volitional desire and the work ethic to do His good pleasure (Phil. 2:12–13).

Changing Obligations

Children, even adult children, ought to honor their parents. Adult children still have an obligation to love and care for their parents. Just as the parents once gave of themselves to support their children, sons and daughters ought to give back (with thankful hearts) to support elderly or widowed parents. Someone who fails to do so is marked out as worse than an unbeliever (1 Tim. 5:4, 8).

However, it is just as anti-normative for parents to try to continue to exercise unchanging, absolute authority over children who have grown to adulthood—especially after marriage has established a new one-flesh relationship, making the husband (not the

father or mother) the head of the wife and God (not the father or mother) the head of the husband (1 Cor. 11:3). It's not normative for married children to be under the dictates of their parents (Gen. 2:24).

Christians sometimes make two diametrically opposite errors. On the one hand, they may try to conform to their own cultural practices (often rooted in false worldviews), reinterpreting scriptural principles to fit. For example, Eastern cultures tend to promote strong parental dominance over adult (married) children rather than recognizing that the parents' role changes to that of wise advisers. This cultural tendency is probably influenced by the backdrop of pagan religious influences, such as ancestor worship. Christians in those cultures must recognize the differing motivations for and applications of respecting one's elders and ancestors

in the biblical worldview versus the pagan worldview. They must recognize that seemingly innocuous cultural traditions may have been influenced by and developed according to a pagan worldview. They may need to realign their practices with the Bible.

On the other hand, some Christians elevate the particular Jewish cultural practices of ancient Israel, making the *descriptive* practices prescriptive or normative for Christians in today's situational context. (Christians in a highly individualistic, secular Western culture may be tempted to embrace this reactionary approach to the vices of their culture.) Instead, Christians are obligated to follow the principles and precepts of God's Word, applying them to their own situational context (following neither their own cultural norms in the East or West nor the ancient Jewish practices described in Scripture).

---

callings as husbands/fathers or wives/mothers. Parents are not rearing mere children but "future child-rearers" who will, by God's grace, repeat this whole process in their own families in the future. The home is also where parents both teach and model for children the right kind of love they should have for others, so that children learn to serve one another. Preeminently, the family is where children learn to love God.

EXTENDED FAMILY

Moses, the author of Genesis, draws an interesting theological conclusion from the story of Eve being given to Adam: "Therefore," he says, "a man shall leave his father and his mother and hold fast to his wife, and they shall become one flesh" (Gen. 2:24). So a man changes his relationship with his parents when he gets married; the husband and wife start their own family unit that is in a definite way separate from what has gone before.

This doesn't mean, however, that grandparents and great-grandparents are to be shut out. In Deuteronomy 4:9, God instructs His people to make His words and works known to both their children and their children's children (cf. 2 Tim 1:5). Grandparents (and aunts, uncles, and other extended family) do not share the father's immediate responsibility for his home, but they should not cease to be consistent spiritual examples and an encouragement to both parents and children.

Christians do bear some responsibility for their relatives, especially aging parents.

And though each family unit—father, mother, and children—is distinct, the Bible does call on children to care for aging parents who can no longer help themselves. Jesus had extremely harsh words for the Pharisees who were neglecting their responsibility to provide for their parents (Matt. 15:3–9). And Paul says, "If anyone does not provide for his relatives, and especially for members of his household, he has denied the faith and is worse than an unbeliever" (1 Tim. 5:8).

1. Why should married couples try to have children?

2. What does widespread disobedience to parents in a society indicate about that society?

3. What is the normal obligation of children in the home when their personal opinions are at odds with their parents' wishes?

4. What two things of God must parents keep before their children as they nurture them spiritually to be leaders for the next generation?

♀5. How should adult children treat their parents?

13.3 GENDER ROLES BEYOND THE NUCLEAR FAMILY

In the grand story of life as told by evolution, the strong dominate the weak, and males in particular are most successful when they produce as many offspring as possible with as many females as possible. Evolutionists can and do resist this reasoning when applied to humans, but it's difficult for them to justify why they do. The evolutionary metanarrative gives mankind no higher purpose than procreation, and if male domination leads to more kids, then mankind is achieving that purpose. Women who spend their key childbearing years climbing the corporate ladder instead of having babies are violating the purpose for which evolution has made them: gene transmission.

The Bible, of course, gives women and men a higher purpose than procreation—though it certainly makes procreation a high purpose. Men and women are both image-bearers, and are both called by God to exercise dominion for God's glory whether or not He grants them children, and whether or not they are married.

This chapter has argued that men and women live out their dominion with different God-given roles. But unless you've been raised in a cave with no Wi-Fi (and perhaps even then), you must be aware that not all Christians agree that men and women are given different roles. Two major positions are influential: (1) **complementarianism**, which sees the sexes as serving in complementary roles, and (2) **egalitarianism**, which sees every role in home, church, and society as equally open to women and men (see sidebar on next page for more information).

The previous section discussed gender roles in marriage and the family; this section will discuss gender roles in church and society.

GENDER ROLES IN THE CHURCH

We'll start with gender roles in the church, an issue which should be less controversial than gender roles in society because the Bible speaks more directly about the qualifications for church leadership than it does about those for societal leadership.

But controversy has only increased over time; the argument between complementarians and egalitarians on this issue has been worn into grooves, with both sides saying the same things for decades. We'll follow the argument with a point-counterpoint. Egalitarians will get the first word, complementarians the last.

The basic reasoning of the egalitarians, those who think pastoral roles should be open to women, is very simple. They say that all people of either gender should be allowed to "exercise their God-given gifts with equal authority and equal

THINKING IT THROUGH 13.2

1. Children are meant to be a gift; they're part of God's intended blessing and purpose in the Creation Mandate.

2. Things are getting worse and worse (more anti-normative) because of unbelief.

3. submissive obedience

4. the words and works of God—what God said and did

♀5. As adults, they are obligated to honor their parents and to care for them. However, they are not obligated to strict, absolute submission and obedience once they have become independent adults and/or have established their own family units.

SECTION OBJECTIVES 13.3

1. Explain why secularism's position on gender roles in society is inconsistent with its evolutionary metanarrative.

2. Explain and defend the complementarian position on gender roles in the church.

3. Explain and defend the complementarian position on gender roles in society.

💬 Opportunities for Service Abound

Women should be encouraged to use their gifts and abilities in the service of the church. First, they must develop the right kind of character to qualify for that service.

Scripture paints a picture of what godly women serving in the church will look like (1 Tim. 5:9–16; Titus 2:3–5).

What should a godly woman's character be like (manifested in actions)?

• reverent in behavior
• not a slanderer, idler, or busybody
• not a slave to wine
• self-controlled
• pure and faithful to her husband
• kind
• submissive to her own husband

What should her ministering involve?

• teaching what is good; sharing her wisdom
• training the young women to love their husbands and children
• working at home and managing the household
• bearing and training children
• being dedicated to prayer
• having a reputation for good works: showing hospitality; serving the saints; caring for the afflicted

Complementarians encourage ministry by women in the local church with this kind of character and commitment. Complementarians don't stifle women from using their talents and abilities to minister. There are countless ways godly women can teach and serve without violating the biblical principle of male leadership.

💬 Galatians 3:28

What is the theological context of Galatians 3:28? (What doctrine has Paul been discussing earlier in the chapter?)

Paul has been discussing the doctrine of justification. The whole book of Galatians is a powerful discourse on justification by faith apart from works (Gal. 3:1–3).

More specifically, Paul is discussing the role of the Mosaic law as it relates to the promises given to Abraham 430 years before (Gal. 3:17). Paul explains why God gave the Mosaic law even though it would never bring an inheritance of God's blessing (salvation) or remove a person from God's covenant blessing (Gal. 3:18–19). The law wasn't given to provide life (salvation) but to provide external constraint and guidance until the Holy Spirit would provide internal constraint and guidance (Gal. 5:21–25). This internal constraint by the Holy Spirit became a reality only after Christ came to establish the New Covenant, placing a new heart within Spirit-baptized believers (Gal. 3:26–27; 1 Cor. 12:13, cf. Jer. 31:31–34; Ezek. 11:19; 36:26).

What was Paul's motivation or purpose for writing Galatians 3:28?

He was concerned about Christian unity in general. (Nothing in the context suggests that he was concerned about opening up church leadership roles or offices.)

What point was Paul trying to press home in Galatians 3:28?

the unity of all believers because they all share God's inheritance originally promised to Abraham

Since salvation is available to everyone through Christ—regardless of ethnicity, gender, or social status—all Christians without exception are heirs of Abraham through Christ. Since all believers have been unified, all believers have been made Abraham's heirs. There is no dividing wall to exclude anyone (cf. Eph. 2:11–22).

Paul simply recognizes that different kinds of distinctions do exist in the world. But when it comes to a person's salvation and heavenly inheritance, no distinctions can be made. Nothing further can be implied. Paul wasn't crusading for the end of all distinctions within society or the church (1 Cor. 7:20–22). (Galatians was an early Pauline letter; later Pauline letters clearly distinguish the roles of men and women in the church.)

[S. Lewis Johnson Jr., "Role Distinctions in the Church," *Recovering Biblical Manhood and Womanhood,* ed. John Piper and Wayne Grudem (Wheaton: Crossway, 1991), 148–60]

The Manner and Means of Service

Since all believers are one in Christ (regardless of ethnicity, gender, or social status), all may serve Christ (Matt. 28:19–20). Paul never excluded women from ministering in the work of the church (Rom. 16:1–16; 1 Cor. 11:5; Phil. 4:3). However, this doesn't mean that all may serve Christ any way they want (1 Cor. 12:12; Rom. 12:4–5). The rest of Scripture's guidelines must be followed. The Bible clearly distinguishes separate roles for men and women in the church (1 Cor. 14:34; 1 Tim. 2:12; 3:2). Jesus valued women in His ministry (Matt. 27:55; Mark 15:41; Luke 23:27, 49; Acts 1:14), but no women were among His twelve disciples or became apostles.

What are the complaints against the complementarian approach rooted in? They're rooted in two *false* presuppositions: (1) Worth is established by what someone *does* (e.g., exercising leadership and authority) rather than by who someone *is* (created in God's image and redeemed as one in Christ). (2) Leadership means one person lording it over another person rather than sacrificial servanthood. Fix the false presuppositions, and the problem with differing gender roles ceases to exist.

On the other hand, egalitarians have a difficult time defending themselves from charges that they undermine the inerrancy of Scrip-

CHRISTIANS IN CONFLICT

Christians, particularly American ones, disagree about gender roles. There are two major perspectives and two major organizations representing them: The Council for Biblical Manhood and Womanhood (CBMW) represents complementarianism, and Christians for Biblical Equality (CBE) represents egalitarianism.

CBMW believes that "distinctions in masculine and feminine roles are ordained by God as part of the created order."[15] In other words, God created the sexes to complement one another.

CBE believes "that the Bible, properly interpreted, teaches the fundamental equality of men and women of all ethnic groups, all economic classes, and all age groups" and "that women and men are equally created in God's image and given equal authority and stewardship in God's creation."[16] CBE argues that God gifts women to be pastors, leaders, and breadwinners just as He gifts men to fill these roles.

Labelling this second view as "egalitarian" implies that complementarians don't see men and women as equal, but the very first words in the CBMW doctrinal statement are, "Both Adam and Eve were created in God's image, equal before God as persons and distinct in their manhood and womanhood."[17] The real issues dividing the two groups are whether men and women can be considered equal while fulfilling different roles and (more importantly) whether the Bible in fact limits certain roles (particularly in church and family leadership) to men.

Which side do you fall on? If you want to earn the right to an opinion on the issue, studying the Scripture passages dealt with in this unit is the place to start.

responsibility in the church, the family, and society."[14] In other words, if a woman has the spiritual gifts, the speaking gifts, and the administrative gifts necessary for pastoring, where did she get those gifts? And if God gave her those gifts, doesn't He expect her to use them?

Egalitarians base much of their thinking on Galatians 3:28: "There is neither Jew nor Greek, there is neither slave nor free, there is no male and female, for you are all one in Christ Jesus." If there's no more male or female now that we're all one in Christ, they say, then what point is there in telling women not to teach in church?

But complementarians respond by pointing out that this isn't all Paul says about gender roles in church. He told Timothy, "I do not permit a woman to teach or to exercise authority over a man" (1 Tim. 2:12). He also said to the Corinthians, "The women should keep silent in the churches" (1 Cor. 14:34).

Since God inspired Paul's words, all Christians have a duty to read their Bibles in such a way that the two statements ("there is no male and female" and "I do not permit a woman to teach") fit together harmoniously—and both complementariness and egalitarians attempt to do so.

Egalitarians tend to harmonize the passages by arguing that Paul was speaking only to the very narrow situation faced by Timothy or the problems of the church in Corinth. They think Paul didn't mean to forbid all Christian women everywhere and at all times from taking leadership and teaching roles in church.[18] They propose various hypothetical situations in which there were a lot of boisterous women in Timothy's particular church who were perhaps even trying to teach doctrinal error. It's *those* women who were supposed to be quiet.[19] (Some egalitarians also attempt to invalidate the teachings of the Pastoral Epistles by denying that Paul wrote these books.)

Complementarians respond by noting what Paul argues in 1 Timothy, the most direct passage on the qualifications for pastoral leadership:

> Let a woman learn quietly with all submissiveness. I do not permit a woman to teach or to exercise authority over a man; rather, she is to remain quiet. For Adam was formed first, then Eve; and Adam was not deceived, but the woman was deceived and became a transgressor. (1 Tim. 2:11–14)

194 | GENDER

ture, the harmony of Scripture (not conflicting with itself), and the timeless application of New Testament biblical commands to the church for this present church age.

1 Timothy 2:11–15

[For help on this passage, refer to William Mounce, *Pastoral Epistles*, Word Biblical Commentary (Nelson Reference and Electronic, 2000), 120–49.]

What is the contextual setting?

Paul wrote 1 Timothy to provide universal guidelines for the oversight of the New Testament assembly.

What does Paul command?

Women are not to teach or to exercise authority over men in the church (1 Tim. 3:1–7). Rather, they are to learn quietly and submissively (1 Cor. 14:34).

What are the reasons given for these commands?

(1) the created order and (2) the Fall

Wasn't Paul just addressing a specific situation rather than giving a universal norm?

There's no indication that women (and not men) were teaching false doctrine. Even if that had been the case, then only certain women would have been rebuked for false doctrine. First Timothy 5:13 refers only to gossiping congregants, not to leaders teaching false doctrine.

Isn't this passage limited to the cultural assumptions of Paul's day rather than setting forth a universal norm for our day?

The idea that women were not educated and that Paul was simply telling them to conform to their culture is another imagined argument from silence. Paul's reason was given; it was

Complementarians point to the word *For*. They say there's a logic in Paul's words: "Women can't teach or lead men because Adam was formed first." That logic doesn't sound very specific to Ephesus, they say. It sounds universally applicable.

Egalitarians, in turn, respond that what Paul prohibited was women who took authority they weren't supposed to take—women who "usurped" or "seized" authority. Women who get authority in the appropriate way are acceptable.

Complementarians, at this point, tend to throw up their hands and say, "Isn't God allowed to tell men and women what to do in church, even if American culture hates it?" They point out that only men are invited to seek the office of pastor (1 Tim. 3:1–7; Titus 1:5–9); that Paul says pastors are supposed to be good fathers, faithful to their wives, having obedient children (1 Tim. 3:2, 4–5; Titus 1:6); that deacons must also be "the husband of one wife, managing their children and their own households well" (1 Tim. 3:12).

In response, egalitarians also tend to throw up their hands and say, "Does it make sense for God to give gifts to women that He won't let them use?" Egalitarians are, then, taking the argument back to the beginning of the groove. They complain that complementarians are wiping out the usefulness of half the church.

Complementarians have recognized that their whole message can't boil down to "No!"—a list of all the things women can't do in church. So they point out that the Bible honors women both young and old as examples of piety and good works as they serve others, rear their children, and keep their homes (1 Tim. 2:9–10, 15; 5:4–15; Titus 2:3–5). And they admit that God does gift women to be teachers. Paul specifically instructs older women "to *teach* what is good, and so train the young women to love their husbands and children, to be self-controlled, pure, working at home, kind, and submissive to their own husbands, that the word of God may not be reviled" (Titus 2:3–5). Christian women are free to teach children (just not men) and to share the gospel with anyone, man or woman, boy or girl. In the complementarian view, both men and women serve in unique and vital roles in the church, and young Christian men and women should learn to fulfill these roles also. Just like in the home, men take the lead in giving spiritual direction, in providing for the church, and in protecting the church against error.

GENDER ROLES IN SOCIETY

When *The Lion, the Witch and the Wardrobe*, written in 1950, was made into a movie half a century later, there was one line in the novel that was sure to get the ax. When Lucy Pevensie meets Father Christmas, he gives her a small cordial of magical healing medicine—and a small dagger. But he instructs her, "The dagger is to defend yourself at great need. For you . . . are not to be in the battle."[21]

"Why, sir?" Lucy asks. "I think—I don't know—but I think I could be brave enough."

"That is not the point," Father Christmas replies. "Battles are ugly when women fight."

Notice how gently C. S. Lewis, the author of the Narnia tales, states his point. He and Father Christmas don't question whether the little girl could be brave. Lucy is, in fact, the most "spiritually gifted" person in the series. She loves and trusts the lion Aslan—representing Jesus Christ—so much that she would surely rush into battle if Aslan commanded her to, but "that is not the point."

In the movie Lucy also says, "I think I could be brave enough." But Father Christmas's reply is subtly different: "I'm sure you could. [But] battles are ugly affairs."[22]

---

was not to teach as an elder over men, she took part in indiviual discipleship alongside her husband (Acts 18:26).

"There is not one example in the entire Bible of a woman doing the kind of congregational Bible teaching that is expected of pastors/elders in the New Testament church." [Wayne Grudem, *Systematic Theology* (Grand Rapids: Zondervan, 1995), 941–42, cf. 937–44]

1 Corinthians 14:34–35
Clarification

Paul is not forbidding all public speech in the church by women since in 1 Corinthians 11:5 he allows them to pray and prophesy.

"Most solutions to the perceived tension between these verses and Paul's position in chapter 11 have been based on understanding the silence or lack of speaking to entail refraining from a particular type of speaking." [Roy E. Ciampa and Brian S. Rosner, *The First Letter to the Corinthians*, Pillar New Testament Commentary (Grand Rapids, Eerdmans, 2010), 720]

Context

Paul wants three types of people to stop disrupting the orderliness of the public corporate gathering of the church: (1) the one who speaks in another language without interpretation from someone else (14:28); (2) the one who tries to prophecy after others have already begun to reveal God's revelation—people shouldn't be talking over one another (14:29–30); (3) women who are taking over the headship prerogative of their husbands or other leadership to explain to the congregation God's Word or to critique and evaluate the prophecy (14:34–35).

Paul's Teaching

When spoken prophesy took place it was supposed to be interpreted and judged, but women were not to take the leadership position in the church that judged and interpreted the prophesied proclamations in the church (1 Cor. 14:29). Women were allowed to speak and even prophesy truth (i.e., report or state the truth—testifying not preaching), but they were not allowed the leadership position of evaluating and critiquing prophecy—a ruling or governing function.

Most agree that Paul's directives are contextually nuanced in 14:34–35 so that he does not intend to prohibit women's speech absolutely, but rather calls for the constraint of certain kinds of speaking in order to maintain the integrity of the husband/wife relationship and/or the peace and order of the church gathered for worship. . . . One

---

rooted in the universal norms of the created order. Furthermore, Paul had no problem teaching countercultural doctrine and practices. In addition, formal education wasn't a qualification for elders; not even all of the apostles had formal education (Acts 4:13; 18:26; Rom. 16:1; 1 Tim. 2:11; Titus 2:3–4). An accurate study of ancient history reveals that there were many well-educated women. Regardless, Christianity elevated women's status, counter to the culture of the time.

What about women mentioned elsewhere in Scripture as prophesying and taking leadership?

There is a consistent pattern of male spiritual leadership throughout the Bible. Female leadership is the exception. Although it isn't always explicitly condemned, it's usually a negative sign of the abdication of male leadership. For example, Athaliah reigned as sole

monarch (2 Kings 11:1–20), but she's not a positive example. She illustrates a time of great wickedness in Israel. While Deborah is favorably commended for her judgeship, the historical context is in a time of chaos (Judg. 21:25, cf. Isa. 3:1–12). Barak is condemned for abdicating his leadership (Judg. 4:8–9).

In the Old Testament, the scriptural teaching responsibilities were limited to the priesthood (restricted to males); religious observances were led by Levites (restricted to males). Huldah's prophecy was private counsel and not public national leadership (2 Kings 22:14).

In the New Testament, women certainly prophesied as a part of the corporate body (Acts 21:8–9; 1 Cor. 11:5; Eph. 5:19–20; Col. 3:16). But they had to do so in a manner that didn't undermine male headship.

Priscilla was trained under Paul's teaching (Acts 18:18–19, 21; 2 Tim. 4:19). While she

of the more popular interpretations is that Paul forbids women from the oral weighing of prophecies as indicated by the context of the preceding verses.

[Mark Taylor, *1 Corinthians*, New American Commentary (Nashville: B&H Publishing, 2014), 358–59]

Paul's Reason

The concern is rooted in the law of God and not simply a culturally shameful practice for women to ask men questions instead of allowing their husbands to do so. Women were not to cross-examine and offer different interpretations because that would overturn the teaching and authority of male leadership. Criticism of the prophet's teaching through questions was forbidden (cf. Num. 12:1–15).

[D. A. Carson, "Silent in the Churches," in *Recovering Biblical Manhood and Womanhood,* ed. John Piper and Wayne Grudem (Wheaton: Crossway, 1991), 133–47]

Biblical Commands and Humble Opinions

It is vital at the outset of this section on gender roles in society to differentiate it from the preceding sections. The differing roles of men and women in the church and home can be defended dogmatically with certainty as the biblical position. But the differing roles of men and women in society can't be defended as dogmatically—at least not with as much specificity. It's an opinion. That being said, opinions aren't as inconsequential as our highly individualistic Western culture may devalue them to be. Some opinions may be worthless; other opinions may have sufficient warrant to make them persuasive even though they're not scripturally binding.

Christians are obligated to differentiate opinions from definitive biblical principles (with valid correlating applications). Presenting one's own personal opinions as Scripture (or as *the* interpretation of Scripture) only leads to dishonesty and perhaps even cultishness. The modern patriarchal movement tends to move beyond the complementarian position regarding women's roles in society. Complementarians believe that the Bible's teaching on the responsibilities of the wife and mother should naturally incline women away from participation in some jobs or roles in broader society. The reason is that to fulfill her role as wife and mother most likely would be indirectly sidetracked or directly undermined. However, complementarians don't formulate absolute, detailed rules and regulations about women's specific roles in society, while the modern patriarchal movement will insist on dogmatic specificity.

(And in the book, Father Christmas also tells Lucy's sister not to fight, while in the movie he leaves that possibility open to her. Neither girl ends up fighting, but "that is not the point.")

What happened in fifty years to make it impossible to say "Battles are ugly when women fight" in a major motion picture? The film's director, Andrew Adamson, told *USA Today*, "I had just come off two films that I hope are empowering for girls. I didn't want to turn that message around." Adamson said that he instead wanted to send a message that "applies to boys and girls equally." [23]

Western culture often seems to believe that the way to "empower" girls is to tell them women can be just like men. And let's remember, that's partly right: women are divine image-bearers just like men; they are given gifts by God just like men; they share equally in the glory of being human.

But they also have distinct glories, glories men don't have (and vice versa). "Nature itself," Paul says, teaches that a woman's "long hair . . . is her glory," to give just one example (1 Cor. 11:14–15). It is not empowering to erase the distinct glories God has given to women. And their role in society, as this section will argue, is one of those glories.

Mature Masculinity and Femininity

First, we must begin with an admission: the Bible simply doesn't say much about how women's roles in society differ from men's. Whether or not women are "allowed" to become CEOs of Fortune 500 companies—or senators, or heads of state—is probably not the right question to begin with. The complementarian view doesn't claim to have found ironclad scriptural rules about female gender roles outside home and church.

Instead complementarians make an inference: if God tasks men with ultimate (though not sole) authority in the home and in the church—and if He does so based, ultimately, on the order in which they were created—then shouldn't male leadership be the default in society, too? As Christian writer Marvin Olasky said, "God does not forbid women to be leaders in society . . . , but when that occurs it's usually because of the abdication of men. As in the situation of Deborah and Barak, there's a certain shame attached to it" [24] (Judg. 4:9).

Not all Bible-believing Christians find this reasoning persuasive. But there are other hints within Scripture that the inference is accurate.

One of the hints is that very story of Deborah. Egalitarians are eager to point to Deborah as an example of a God-approved female leader in Scripture. And she is that—sort of. The Bible never says a single negative thing about her. She was truly godly, and she did not sin in taking leadership. But her story appears in the book of Judges—and the whole point of that book is that God's people were getting the leaders they deserved because of their sin. There are many hints in the story that female leadership was an indictment* of the males for not stepping up to the plate. When the military leader Barak refused to meet the enemy without Deborah at his side, Deborah declared, "I will surely go with you. Nevertheless, the road on which you are going will not lead to your glory, for the Lord will sell Sisera into the hand of a woman" (Judg. 4:9; cf. Isa. 3:12).

An egalitarian may immediately say, "But that was a very different culture!" And he or she would be right. But the complementarian case for gender roles in society is "cumulative"—it doesn't rely on one absolutely clear proof text. So think of another

indictment: *an expression of strong disapproval; serious criticism*

Is Feminism the Answer?

Why are oppression and abuse biblically indefensible?

- *Women are made in God's image (Gen. 1:26).*
- *Husbands must sacrificially serve and love their wives (1 Cor. 13:1–7; Eph. 5:21–33), understanding, honoring and protecting them (1 Pet. 3:7).*
- *Christian women are heirs of salvation alongside their husbands (Gal. 3:28; 1 Pet. 3:7).*

How have women been devalued and degraded in male-dominated societies?

- *treated as property instead of people*
- *physically beaten as slaves*
- *sexually assaulted and then blamed*
- *unreasonably commanded at the whim of authoritarians*

Feminism began as a response to real problems in a fallen world and society. The opposition to feminism can't be to the neglect of opposition to patriarchal abuses.

However, does feminism offer the right answers to solve the problems, or does it twist God's good design to the opposite extreme?

In order to answer these questions intelligently, a person needs to understand feminism's historical development (i.e., the sociopolitical milieu and the theology/philosophy that the movement (the second wave) grew out of in the 1960s and continues to rest on even today).

- Sociopolitical milieu: socialistic, revolutionary rebellion

scriptural hint: if women are to be bearing children (1 Tim. 2:15) and "working at home" (Titus 2:5), when exactly are they going to climb the corporate ladder?

Of course, many women are called to singleness—or, though feeling called to marriage, they nonetheless haven't been asked to be in one. Complementarians stop short of saying that single women should not take leadership positions in society, because the Bible doesn't say that. Instead, the (complementarian) Council for Biblical Manhood and Womanhood prefers to speak of the characteristics of masculinity and femininity as "dispositions" or tendencies—not "rules." Listen to how CBMW defines maleness and femaleness:

> At the heart of mature masculinity is a sense of benevolent responsibility to lead, provide for and protect women in ways appropriate to a man's differing relationships.
>
> At the heart of mature femininity is a freeing disposition to affirm, receive and nurture strength and leadership from worthy men in ways appropriate to a woman's differing relationships.[25]

Men and women have "differing relationships." No sound complementarian will ever claim that all women must submit to all men. There's room in definitions like these for fully feminine supervisors standing in authority over fully masculine employees. But these definitions, if in fact they reflect divine creational norms, show that in general men are to lead and women are to support that leadership. Some women can lead men while receiving and nurturing those men's own leadership capacities. But complementarians tend to doubt that such is the norm.

In most cultures the men take the lead in the workforce and government, and the women serve in supporting roles, caring for family and keeping the home. And the Bible, at the very least, doesn't question this tendency. This does not mean that women can never make contributions to what the men are doing; precisely the opposite. Wives are not "helpers" unless they make contributions. So we have wonderful New Testament examples such as Priscilla, a woman who takes a major role alongside her husband, Aquilla, in strengthening the early church, even helping to train one of its most effective early preachers (Acts 18:24–28). There were many women invested in the ministry of the first-century church (for example, Phoebe in Rom. 16; Lydia in Acts 16; Euodia and Syntyche in Phil. 4:2–3).

Your Role

When world-famous Olympian Bruce Jenner declared that he was a woman (changing his name to *Caitlyn*) and was featured in a photo shoot and on a *Vanity Fair* cover, he was loudly applauded all over American culture. There's a terrific amount of cultural pressure on Christians to drop the whole idea of gender, let alone any idea of gender-specific roles in church, home, and society. But God is the Creator; He has a right to tell us how to live our lives. And He loves us. When God says something as clear as "male and female he created them" (Gen. 1:27), we must listen. When He says, "Wives, submit to your own husbands" (Eph. 5:22), then an attack on gender roles in the home becomes an attack on the Bible, a denial of God's goodness, love, and wisdom as well as a challenge against His authority.

"What makes men men, or women women, is intrinsically connected to the majesty of the God in our design. We each exist as we do in order to display that glory."[26]

—JONATHAN PARNELL

The movement developed from women like Simone Debeauvoir and Betty Friedan calling on women to join together in revolt. But it wasn't until the unrest of the 1960s that such revolt became possible. Handing over the responsibility of home and family to the state ("It takes a village") would free women to fulfill their utopian dreams outside the restrictiveness of keeping the home and raising a family.

As feminists redefined themselves, feminism first sought to change the structure of society; then it started making progress in changing the structure of the home and the church. Thus, the complementarian position about women's roles in society should be taken seriously (even though it is a more flexible opinion).

• Theology/philosophy: a rejection of the authority of God's Word and His created order in favor of existentialism and autonomy

Feminism argued that in order to have equal value, a woman must achieve fulfillment through finding herself and unleashing her full potential by what she does: self-actualization.

Remind students about the information in the teacher's note "Freedom or Bondage?" (page 185 of this chapter).

Simone Debeauvoir was influenced by the philosophy of existentialism, which she applied to women's sociology. "Women . . . were autonomous beings with the need to 'transcend' self, but this need was being suppressed by men . . . robbing women of autonomy."

[Mary A. Kassian, *The Feminist Gospel: The Movement to Unite Feminism with the Church* (Wheaton: Crossway, 1992), 18]

[Mary Kassian, "Leave it to Beaver, Sex and the City, and a Woman's Happiness," True Woman website (March 9, 2015)]

[Trevin Wax, "Who Should Raise Your Children: When G. K. Chesterton Debated Bertrand Russell on the Ideal Family," Gospel Coalition website (March 9, 2015)]

Women's Liberation

What are women being liberated from? What are they being liberated to do? Students need to be careful that they're not mindlessly being influenced by movements and agendas that are at odds with a biblical worldview. What hidden presuppositions motivate the social and political agendas to liberate women to follow their hearts?

Feminists complain that women (must) lead unhappy and unfulfilled lives that squelch their full potential as long as they focus their lives on the family and the home. No doubt, many women feel bored and unfulfilled staying home all day long doing nothing (but housework). Biblical Christianity would concur that this isn't the fulfilling role that God gave wives and mothers (Prov. 31). Godly women are never bored or busybodies; they are busy serving others: God, husband, children, church, and community (1 Tim. 5:5, 9–16; Titus 2:3–5).

Divide students into small groups. After reading Proverbs 31:10–31, 1 Timothy 5:5–16, and Titus 2:3–5, students should create a chart with the verse reference, the activity illustrated in the verse, and a modern-day application of that activity. Then they should explain how that activity fits with the role and responsibility of a wife acting as a helper and a mother acting as a nurturer (rather than undermining those roles). What would her schedule be like if she gave herself fully to all of these activities? In what ways could someone misapply those verses in a way that would undermine her roles and responsibilities as wife and mother?

The complementarian position can be caricatured as a negative position that merely tells women what they can't do. Although it's often explained defensively to guard against upending gender roles, complementarianism positively affirms the importance of the woman's role and the multiplicity of activities essential to that role. (However, husbands shouldn't demand that their wives wear themselves out either—she ought not to be treated like a slave.) Although all the activities must bolster her job of being a keeper of the home (rather than competing with it), her role doesn't curtail the labor of selling merchandise or planting a field.

Rejecting the God-given roles and responsibilities of a wife and mother isn't the means to a happy, fulfilled life. Using one's own talents and creativity to contribute productively to one's husband, children, church, and community is the means to a happy, fulfilled life blessed by God. If a woman is sitting around home feeling bored and useless, the solution isn't to throw off her roles and responsibilities as a wife and mother but to better engage in them—creatively and productively.

Exemplary Women

You may want to further reinforce the positive uplifting of women that the biblical, complementarian view promotes by assigning students a chapter or section from the following books.

John Macarthur, *Twelve Extraordinary Women: How God Shaped Women of the Bible and What He Wants to Do with You* (Nashville: Thomas Nelson, 2005)

Diana Lynn Severance, *Feminine Threads: Women in the Tapestry of Christian History* (Fearn, Scotland: Christian Focus Publications, 2011)

What If I End Up Single?

Being single isn't a curse; it's a blessing (1 Cor. 7:7–8). God created both men and women to take dominion over the earth (Gen. 1:28). Singleness shouldn't confine women to lifelong servitude in their parents' home; it shouldn't disqualify men from service in the church either. While the patriarchal movement often restricts single young ladies to the confines of their parents' household, complementarians encourage women to pursue education and to participate in society, using their talents and abilities in multiple spheres. However, godly, single women still do so through the lens of a complementarian worldview—not purposefully neglecting marriage or rebelling against God's creational norms for the roles of men and women.

[Katie Van Dyke, "Complementarianism and the Single Woman," 9 Marks (website) March 9, 2015]

And as for Christians in the egalitarian/complementarian debate (which is pretty well all of us), the only thing we can do is keep going back to Scripture. We can't do what one blogger did when she said, "No one seems to know for sure what [1 Timothy 2:12] means, and frankly, I've just about given up on figuring out exactly what's going on with it."[27]

Are the Bible passages mentioned in this chapter so unclear that it's impossible to understand them? What do you think? You don't have the option of being noncommittal. You will likely choose a church and a mate in coming years. God's Word about gender roles needs to guide you as you make these life-altering choices.

Simply put, in most cases a man should expect to marry, become a father, and lead and protect his home. In most cases a woman should expect to marry and become a mother, supporting her husband's calling and caring for her home. Godly young men and women should pursue this course first. And if along the way God makes His will plain that someone is called to singleness instead, each should be willing to follow God's leading. At the very least, Christian men and women should willingly raise up the role of wife, mother, and homemaker as an honorable and important calling. That calling demands incredible creativity and may necessitate considerable education. It does not demean women. To demand absolute equality in the functional roles of the sexes is to deny men and women the special glories God gave them.

THINKING IT THROUGH 13.3

1. What do you think women's roles in society would look like if people lived out the evolutionary worldview with consistency?

2. Contrast the complementarian and egalitarian positions.

3. How do egalitarians attempt to harmonize Paul's instructions about male leadership roles in the home and church?

4. The Bible specifically mentions that a woman's long hair is her glory (1 Cor. 11:14–15). Can you list another feminine glory suggested by Scripture? How about a masculine one?

♀5. Explain the real issue that divides complementarians and egalitarians.

THINKING IT THROUGH 13.3

1. In an evolutionary view of nature, the strong are supposed to dominate the weak, and the best males are supposed to produce as many offspring as possible with as many females as possible for gene transmission. The evolutionary worldview can't justify why women shouldn't be treated like animals.

2. • Complementarian: God designed men and women with distinct functional roles in the created order.
   • Egalitarian: Since men and women are equal, they should equally exercise their authority and talents in the home, church, and world regardless of their gender.

3. They claim that Paul was speaking only to the very narrow situation faced by Timothy or the church in Corinth.

4. tender care (1 Thess. 2:7; 1 Pet. 3:4, 7); strength and leadership (Prov. 20:29; 1 Thess. 2:11–12)

♀5. Both believe that men and women are equal beings. The real issues dividing the two groups are whether men and women can be considered equal while fulfilling different roles and, more importantly, whether the Bible in fact limits certain roles (particularly in church and family leadership) to men.

13 CHAPTER REVIEW

TERMS TO REMEMBER

complementarianism
egalitarianism

Scripture Memory

Genesis 2:18

Making Connections

1. Based on the realities of the Trinity and God's created order, how should and shouldn't *equality* be defined?

2. Was the father made the leader of his family before or after the Fall? Why is this significant?

3. Summarize the roles and responsibilities of parents and children in the family.

4. According to 1 Timothy 2:11–14, why is male leadership the norm in the church?

Developing Skills in Apologetics and Worldview

5. How should you respond to someone who presupposes that a woman's submission to her husband is outdated and oppressive?

6. How should you respond to someone who argues that denying women certain leadership roles in the church implies that women are not equal to men?

Examining Assumptions and Evidence

7. Why can't humans adjust and redefine gender norms?

8. Should parents expect their adult children to obey them? Why or why not?

9. Why are complementarians required to "make an inference" when it comes to gender roles in society?

10. What biblical support exists for generally expecting men to lead in society?

Becoming a Creative Cultivator

11. Suggest a specific family activity that can bring you, your siblings, and your parents together socially and spiritually.

CHAPTER REVIEW ANSWERS

Making Connections

1. *Equality* should be defined according to essence or identity, not according to identical functional roles. All three Persons of the Trinity are equally God but with different roles; all humans are made in God's image, and all Christians are one in Christ, but God has given equally important but different roles to men and women.

2. It was before the Fall; ruling over someone isn't inherently sinful or bad—it's the manner of the rule that can be twisted by sin.

3. Married couples are encouraged to have children because it is a blessing of the Creation Mandate they ought to fulfill; they must nurture their children physically and spiritually by guiding them in the Word and works of the Lord. Children must submissively obey and (even as adults) honor and care for their parents.

4. Based on the created order, man was created first, and woman was created to be his helper. In the Fall, Adam wasn't deceived (he sinned willfully), but Eve was deceived. Thus, Adam is charged with greater responsibility.

Developing Skills in Apologetics and Worldview

5. Submission is something we all must do in one relationship or another in life; it's not just something wives must do in relation to their husbands. People hurt by abuse may be reactionary, assuming that all submission must be just as hurtful. But in a good marriage with a loving, self-sacrificial husband, submission is not hateful or degrading.

6. The tasks that God has given to women in the home and the church are extremely important. When godly women fulfill those tasks thoroughly and excellently, then the home, church, and even society are markedly better.

Examining Assumptions and Evidence

7. Whether people want to admit it or not, God has revealed that He has established and designed these things according to His own creational norms. Any redefinition by humans can only be vain imagination rather than reality and leads to destruction rather than freedom.

8. The God-established norm is for children to leave their parents' family unit of authority and form their own independent family units of authority (Gen. 2:24). Adult children are obligated to respect and care for parents but are no longer under their absolute ruling authority.

9. Unlike the explicit and clear biblical directives for the roles of men and women in the home and church, there are no explicit and clear biblical directives for distinct roles for men and women in society.

10. The order of creation, the precepts for male leadership in the home and church as well as the responsibilities given to women to manage the household well all lead to the inference that a woman's taking leadership roles in society is antinormative or distracts from her God-given role as a manager of the home.

Becoming a Creative Cultivator

11. (Answers will vary.) family devotions, dinner together, reading together, conversations about society, and so forth

TERMS TO REMEMBER

complementarianism—the view that says men and women are equal in essence but different in function or roles; with "distinctions in masculine and feminine roles . . . ordained by God as part of the created order"

egalitarianism—the view that says men and women are equal in essence and can and should carry out the same function and roles, and that "all believers—without regard to gender . . . —must exercise their God-given gifts with equal authority and equal responsibility in church, home and world"

The student will be able to

14.1 Identify and give examples of fallen family relationships.

14.2 Evaluate and respond to the claims of the "Gay Christian" movement.

14.3 Explain why both cohabitation and divorce twist God's design for marriage.

14.4 Summarize the negative consequences of failing to recognize two distinct genders and varying roles for men and women.

SECTION OBJECTIVES 14.1

1. Classify different ways humans twist God's creation of marital intimacy.

2. Compare and contrast the opposite extremes of a fallen husband (passive or domineering) and a fallen wife (resistant or manipulative).

3. Summarize how one would identify sins of parents against children and of children against parents.

Chapter Fourteen **MARRIAGE TWISTED**

To the woman he said, "I will surely multiply your pain in childbearing; in pain you shall bring forth children. Your desire shall be for your husband, and he shall rule over you." And to Adam he said, "Because you have listened to the voice of your wife and have eaten of the tree of which I commanded you, 'You shall not eat of it,' cursed is the ground because of you; in pain you shall eat of it all the days of your life."

Scripture Memory Genesis 3:16–17

14.1 DYSFUNCTIONAL FAMILY RELATIONSHIPS

You probably don't remember American sitcom *Murphy Brown*. The show, about a successful female TV journalist, ended its run in 1998. And only the politics junkies among high schoolers are likely to recognize the name of Dan Quayle, who was vice president of the United States under George H. W. Bush (1989–93).

But the fact that Dan Quayle criticized Murphy Brown in one line of an otherwise forgotten political speech is something you do need to know. Quayle was discussing the absence of "mature responsible men" from the lives of too many American boys. And then he made this one-sentence observation:

It doesn't help matters when prime-time TV has Murphy Brown—a character who supposedly epitomizes today's intelligent, highly paid, professional woman—mocking the importance of fathers by bearing a child alone and calling it just another "lifestyle choice."[1]

Quayle touched off a media firestorm. To this day he is mocked and derided for his comment.[2] The sitcom writers saw the controversy as an opportunity and managed to weave video of Quayle's speech into the show. The Murphy Brown character delivered this tart response to Quayle:

Perhaps it's time for the vice president to expand his definition [of family] and recognize that, whether by choice or circumstance, families come in all shapes and sizes.[3]

In one sense, Ms. Brown was right. Not all single parents choose to be single parents, and families of two are indeed a different size than families of twenty.

But Brown was wrong overall. No one can expand—or contract—the very definition of *family* because the right concept of the family is something humanity discovers in the Bible and creation, not something it invents.[4]

For some people in Western culture, family has come to mean any grouping of people who love each other enough to share a relationship. Marriage and the family are no longer governed by the design of a Creator.

God's design for marriage and family was twisted mere moments after Adam and Eve ate the forbidden fruit: the very first casualty of the Fall was the openness Adam and Eve had enjoyed. "Then the eyes of both were opened, and they knew that they were naked" (Gen. 3:7). The Fall immediately began bending the first family out of shape even further when Adam blamed Eve (and ultimately God) for the sin he'd committed (Gen. 3:12). In the next chapter of Genesis, Cain murdered Abel. The world's very first family was dysfunctional.

This section will focus on how the Fall has twisted the family, including the intimacy and the roles of husbands and wives as well as the roles of parents and children.

Lesson Plan Chart—Chapter 14

Section Title	Pages	Activity Manual	Days
14.1 Dysfunctional Family Relationships	200–204	Activity 25	1 day
14.2 Homosexuality	205–9		2 days
14.3 Cohabitation and Divorce	210–14	Activity 26	1 day
14.4 Gender Roles in a Fallen World	214–18		1 day
Review	219		1 day
Total Suggested Days			**6 days**

Redefining Family
How should the concept of "family" be defined?

Family must be defined according to God's creational norms. God designed the union of one husband and one wife to form a one-flesh relationship (Gen. 2:24). Marriage establishes the most basic family unit. That family unit can expand as the union produces its own offspring (or graciously adopts children who need a family, e.g., orphans). The family line can be traced back to grandparents and great-grandparents along with all of their other children and grandchildren, making aunts, uncles, and cousins a legitimate part of a larger family unit.

TWISTED MARITAL INTIMACY

God, for our own good and His own glory, instructs us, "Let marriage be held in honor among all, and let the marriage bed be undefiled." And Scripture goes on to warn that "God will judge the sexually immoral and adulterous" (Heb. 13:4). "Among all" nations, "among all" cultures, "among all" people reading this book, marriage and the "marriage bed" (meaning sexual relations) should be "held in honor" (considered precious). The Bible allows only one man and one woman in that bed, and they are to be one for life.

But humans have invented many ways to twist the precious gift of sex:

- **Fornication** means sexual relations between unmarried partners. The Bible doesn't need to get into a lot of specifics;; it just condemns sexual immorality in very general terms.[5] Christians are supposed to "flee youthful passions" (2 Tim. 2:22) and "abstain from sexual immorality" (1 Thess. 4:3).
- **Adultery** is sexual relations between a married person and someone else outside the marriage. Over 90 percent of Americans actually agree, at least verbally, with biblical morality here, telling pollsters that adultery is wrong.[6] But remember Jesus' warning: adultery can be internal, not only external (Matt. 5:27–28).
- **Polygamy** violates the scriptural norm for marriage too.[7] God gave Adam only one wife (Matt. 19:5). The extreme troubles brought on by all of the prominent polygamous marriages in Scripture (Abraham, Jacob, David, Solomon) support the point: polygamy does not fit God's design for marriage. All the positive biblical instruction about marriage presents one man, one woman as the ideal (Prov. 12:4; 18:22; 19:14; Eph. 5:22–23).[8]

Child sexual abuse (and subsequent cover-up), date rape, incest, bestiality, prostitution, homosexuality, immodesty, porn—the list of twistings could go on and on. And all around the world, it does. Mankind has been pretty creative and energetic in its efforts to dishonor marriage and corrupt the precious gift of the marriage bed. And we've created books, movies, magazines, and internet sites to celebrate and promote every single corruption. All of these sins (and more) may be placed in the categories named in Hebrews 13:4—"sexual immorality" and "adultery." The Bible doesn't have to get very specific about which sexual acts are immoral; it's everything outside of the marriage bed.

Illicit sex is (often) pleasurable, maybe very pleasurable. The Bible doesn't deny that sin brings pleasure, but it's fleeting (Heb. 11:25). And you probably know at least some of the pain that the twisting of sex has caused people: addiction, guilt, broken relationships, disease. Poverty, too, is often one result of illicit sex, particularly when teenage pregnancy is involved.

One of the most moving stories in the New Testament is about a prostitute (Luke 7:36–50). Sexual sins can be forgiven and cleansed like all others. But the negative consequences of illicit sex display to the world that immorality runs counter to creational norms. It violates the way the world was made to work.

If people reject the creational norm,

🧍+🧍

then anything goes.

🧍+🧍🧍

🧍+🧍+🧍

🧍+🧍/🧍+🧍

🧍+?

SINGLENESS AND CHILDLESSNESS

Singleness and childlessness are not sins. Yes, God blessed marriage and childbearing in the Creation Mandate, and they are encouraged and celebrated throughout Scripture as the normal life pattern for most believers. But there are godly people mentioned all through the Bible who were unmarried or childless. And, as the New Testament teaches, God actually calls and gifts some men and women for singleness (1 Cor. 7:7), freeing them to devote themselves more completely to the Lord (1 Cor. 7:32–34) and to accomplish a unique mission in His name. Paul purposefully gave up the privilege of marriage so that he could have greater flexibility in his mission to preach the gospel (1 Cor. 9:3–27). John the Baptist was also single for his special calling. And Jesus Himself, who referred to singleness as a gift (Matt. 19:11), remained single. By implication, since it is God who is the giver of children in the first place (Ps. 127:3; 139:13), childlessness may also be the will of God for married believers who share an exceptional calling.

MARRIAGE TWISTED | 201

What are the consequences of redefining the family?

It leads to immorality through relationships/activities that are contrary to the one-flesh union (Heb. 13:4):

- *cohabitation (fornication)*
- *serial monogamy (a lifestyle of adultery; multiple divorces and remarriages)*
- *homosexuality*
- *polygamy*
- *familial sexual abuse (incest)*
- *designer babies/breeding babies as a product of professional surrogate mothers*

How should the Christian community treat people who are a part of a "family" structure bent in the wrong direction?

Upholding the truth of God's creational norms is the only basis for lovingly offering the help and healing of the transforming grace of the gospel. But Christians must be careful not to allow the mischaracterization of their position as hateful bigotry to be bolstered by wrongly responding with ridicule toward those in broken family relationships.

Twisting God's Design

If God designed marriage and family to function successfully in accordance with the good creational norms of His perfectly created world, then fallen perversions of that design can only lead to destruction. But the world, the flesh, and the devil blind the eyes of fallen humans to the destructiveness of their own behavior. How can a child molester assure himself that his actions won't really scar (his own) children? How can an adulterer become convinced that the fallout will be inconsequential to spouses and children (or that there won't be any fallout)? How can a teen dismiss the human trafficking that supplies his porn addiction? Or do any of these people really even care at all? Selfish autonomy—defying accountability and denying the consequences—lurks at the bottom of every one of these sins.

Covenant Companionship

The marriage relationship is so significant because of the kind of relationship it is—a covenant agreement of companionship for life. The sexual perversions that twist marital intimacy are all symptoms of a more foundational problem—a rejection of God's divine foundation for marriage: covenantal companionship.

Marriage is a sacred covenant.

In Chapter 10, students learned about the importance and permanence of God's covenants. A covenant is "a mutual agreement—including promises, obligations, and commitments—between two parties in an existing relationship." Since marriage establishes a divine covenant relationship between a man and a woman, it must not be entered into carelessly. It's a promise made to God, not just a civil contract with each other.

Recall that covenants can be conditional or unconditional. Which kind is marriage? It's supposed to be an unconditional covenant—it's for life because it makes two people into one person (Gen. 2:24). Divorce is the breaking of an unconditional covenant—that's what makes divorce anti-normative, that is, contrary to creational norms (Mal. 2:13–17). Even though Jesus acknowledged that the Mosaic law permitted divorce, He made it clear that the provision was made because of the people's hardness of heart. It was definitely contrary to God's creational intention (Matt. 19:1-12).

Marriage establishes companionship.

In a biblical marriage, sex is a significant privilege and purpose within the marriage relationship, but it's not the foundation. The foundation is faithful companionship with one another (based on unity in Christ—for Christians; Eph. 5:21-33; 2 Cor. 6:14).

When eroticism becomes the basis for marriage, sex becomes the focus, and faithful companionship becomes peripheral. Or worse, sex becomes the end-all to the neglect and ruin of faithful companionship. When sex becomes the raison d'être, then illicit attractions lure people to depreciate faithful companionship. But in the end sexual promiscuity leaves a person empty (2 Sam. 13:1–17). That's because God designed men and women to find substantive satisfaction in a faithful companionship commitment—even after the physical beauty

MARRIAGE TWISTED | 201

fades and sexual excitement grows dull to the senses (Prov. 31:10–31).

Compatibility or Christlikeness?

Secular sources that provide dating and marriage advice for a successful, long-lasting relationship emphasize compatibility (similar interests and goals, socioeconomic backgrounds, temperaments, etc.). Not only is this approach typically superficial, but it can also set up unrealistic expectations. The reality of life in a fallen world with fallen people is that there will always be differences that will cause tension. Difficulties in life will expose new differences never imagined before marriage. The only thing that can resolve these tensions is a unified pursuit of growth in Christlikeness in the middle of the difficulties and disagreements.

Pursuing Christlike Growth

Identify major character qualities vital to preventing tensions between spouses.

- *trust*
- *love (self-sacrifically pursuing the highest God-defined good for another)*
- *communication*
- *humble selflessness*
- *self-discipline and responsibility*
- *managing priorities and money*
- *confession and repentance*

Students may identify many more.

In each area listed above, what is the foundation for bringing about Christlikeness?

a proper relationship with God

It might be tempting to work at resolving tensions on a horizontal plane (husbands and wives working to change themselves and each other). But none of the interpersonal difficulties can be substantively resolved until the vertical plane is addressed first.

> What does give you reason to continue when the little problems have gotten under your skin or the big problems have left you devastated? What does produce a marriage with sturdy love, unity, and understanding? . . . *A marriage of love, unity, and understanding is not rooted in romance; it is rooted in worship.*
>
> [Paul David Tripp, *What Did You Expect? Redeeming the Realities of Marriage* (Wheaton: Crossway, 2010), 33]

Worshiping God as the Creator will remind you that God created your spouse and all his or her intricacies. Worshiping God as sovereign will remind you that God directs all your circumstances. Tripp concludes:

TWISTED SPOUSAL ROLES

Statistically speaking, ten years from now, most readers of this book will be married. And it's sad to say so, but God promised long before you were born that the results of the Fall would put negative pressures on your marriage. "Your desire shall be for your husband," God told Eve in the Garden of Eden, "and he shall rule over you" (Gen. 3:16). In other words, "You will desire to rule over your husband, and he's going try to lord it over you instead." Common grace means not all marriages fall apart, but the gravity of the Fall pulls spouses into these behavior patterns: women will be tempted to rule their husbands, and men will be tempted to be domineering over their wives.

Adultery and porn are perhaps more obvious sins, but they tend to start with simpler, subtler ones like those God mentioned would come in Genesis 3:16. Sexual sins are outward signs of other sins that are present at the very core of the marriage relationship: a failure of the husband and the wife to live in harmony according to the unique roles God has assigned to them.

Twisted Husbands

Look around at the marriages you see. Those that aren't doing well tend to fall into the two categories God listed in Genesis 3: either the wife rules the (hen-pecked) husband or the husband is overbearing, angry, and bitter toward his wife. But the Bible is clear: "Husbands, love your wives, and do not be harsh with them," Paul says in Colossians 3:19.

Have you ever picked some large, juicy-looking blackberries from a bush by the side of the road? They can be extremely tasty. Or they can be spit-it-out-right-now bitter. And you can't tell just by looking at them. So it is with husbands. A man may look like he's fulfilling his role as leader, but his leadership has actually wrenched out all the sweetness of love and grace God calls for. Some husbands think biblical leadership means wives don't get to offer their opinion, rebuke their husband's sins, or make any decision—or income—whatsoever. That's foolish; God gives men their wives to help them. And wives are authorities within their families.

On the other hand, of course, you've got your La-Z-Boy, leave-me-alone husbands who don't step up and provide any leadership at all. Some men have actually lost their marriages because of their devotion to video games (many grown men do more gaming than high schoolers).[9] Biblically faithful men run to the problem, not away—whether it's a mouse, a toddler Armageddon, or an angry outburst for which a man needs to ask forgiveness of a quietly crying wife or child. Some husbands force their wives to take leadership in the family because they never find the energy to do so themselves. But husbands are called to take the lead in spiritual nurturing, protection, and provision for their wives and children. Husbands have to make the final call on controversial matters, yes, but husbands must also, like Adam, take final responsibility if things go wrong.

Twisted Wives

God gave wives the role of submissive partner, companion, childbearer, and homemaker—and these responsibilities can also be twisted through the Fall. For example, a wife can give in to the fallen urge to dominate her husband or even to live in rebellion against his authority (Gen. 3:16). And rebellion can take many forms, from outright resistance to her husband's leadership to subtle strategies of manipulation. Either form is a refusal on her part to trust in the divinely created order of marriage.

Where will you find the reasons to continue working on your marriage in those disappointing moments when those reasons are most needed? . . . You will only find your reasons to continue by looking up. (Tripp, 40)

What is the goal of most married people?

to be happy by living out the planned dreams of one's own life

In that case, a spouse becomes a means to that end; actions and circumstances that block those dreams bring unhappiness.

What should be the Christlike goal?

Christlike marriages find happiness in fulfilling another person rather than self.

Paul Tripp tells spouses to ask themselves whether their anger stems from their spouse's violation of God's kingdom rules or their own self-made kingdom dreams and

rules (Tripp, 51). It isn't until your pursuit of your own kingdom dreams ends that true love for your spouse can begin and the cultivation of Christlikeness can begin.

"Marriage is not an end to itself. . . . Marriage has been designed by God to be a means to an end" (Tripp, 52). That end is Christlikeness; the means is God's gracious introducing of difficulties that expose selfishness.

Marriage Resources

Andreas J. Kostenberger, *God, Marriage, and Family* (Wheaton: Crossway, 2004).

Jay E. Adams, *Solving Marriage Problems* (Grand Rapids: Baker Books, 1983).

Lou Priolo, *The Complete Husband* (Amityville, NY: Calvary Press, 1999).

TWISTED FAMILIES

Families get twisted by the Fall too. The "nuclear family" is an accurate description of some homes because everybody's got a finger poised over the red button, just waiting to blow up at each other.

Sins of Parents Against Children

Sometimes it's the parents' fault. One of the main parenting instructions the New Testament gives is "Fathers, do not provoke your children to anger" (Eph. 6:4). Through the writings of author Charles Dickens people get a taste of the exasperation and bewilderment of a child whose caregivers mistreat him. Little Pip in *Great Expectations* is brought up being beaten for the slightest perceived infraction, and it's heart-wrenching to listen to the boy's confused reactions.

Sadly, child abuse didn't go away after Dickens wrote novels exposing it. And in a full 80 percent of child abuse cases, the parents are the abusers.[10] Physical and sexual abuse of children still occurs—even murder. That, of course, is what abortion is—mothers murdering their own children.

But the more common form of childhood exasperation comes from angry dads. Dads (like moms) may be impossible to please, sometimes insisting that their children follow petty rules. Some parents punish their kids severely, speak to them rudely, or make them fearful.[11]

Sins of Children Against Parents

The Ten Commandments tell children very simply, "Honor your father and your mother" (Exod. 20:12). Most children seem to have this desire innately. And yet it's still a responsibility—and not just because kids get pretty much everything they have from their parents; they must honor them because it is the way God has designed the family to function.

But you're not a young child. You're a teen. Teenagers have brains, skills, talents, and ideas. In more and more ways, they tend to feel ready to take charge of their lives, but Western culture subtly encourages them not to do so, even though that may sound odd. The world wants teens to have freedom, not to be held back by their parents. But the kind of freedom Western culture encourages teens to have is not an adult freedom but a teenage one.

Teenager is a comparatively recent invention. The word first showed up in English in the 1940s.[13] Before that, a thirteen- to nineteen-year-old's place in society was based not as much on age as on his or her ability to function as an adult. Girls tended to marry at much younger ages. Young men would go to work when they were strong enough. Or if they learned their Latin and could pass a college entrance exam, they might go to college at fourteen—age didn't really matter. More recently, several factors in our society—including good things like the development of secondary education (high schools) and laws regulating the legal work age, and not-so-good things like the rise of the teen subculture of entertainment and fashion—have detained a lot of young people in a sort of holding pattern where they're not encouraged to mature or allowed to be "grown up." Instead they're expected to "live it up," consuming as much as they can the offerings of popular culture.

> #### SEXUAL ABUSE
>
> There is one especially damaging sin that parents sometimes commit against their own children: sexual abuse. Children may not want to get their parents in trouble, but sexual abuse and physical abuse need to be reported both to church leadership and law enforcement. What an abuser does to one child may be repeated with younger siblings. And an abused child will have great difficulty finding healing if his or her abuser is never brought to justice. The best way to protect children is to expose the offender. And every teacher, principal, and pastor should be aware of relevant mandatory reporting laws for suspected child abuse and neglect.[12]

Martha Peace, *The Excellent Wife* (Bemidiji, MN: Focus Publishing, 1999).

Paul David Tripp, *What Did You Expect?: Redeeming the Realities of Marriage* (Wheaton: Crossway, 2010).

Richard D. Phillips and Sharon L. Phillips, *Holding Hands, Holding Hearts* (Phillipsburg, NJ: P&R Publishing, 2006).

Stuart Scott, *The Exemplary Husband* (Bemidiji, MN: Focus Publishing, 2002).

Parenting Resources

John Macarthur, *What the Bible Says About Parenting* (Nashville: Thomas Nelson, 2000).

Lou Priolo, *Teach Them Dilligently* (Woodruff, SC: Timeless Texts, 2000).

Martha Peace and Stuart W. Scott, *The Faithful Parent* (Phillipsburg, NJ: P&R, 2010).

Paul David Tripp, *Age of Opportunity: A Biblical Guide to Parenting Teens* (Phillipsburg, NJ: P&R Publishing, 1997).

Tedd Tripp, *Shepherding a Child's Heart* (Wapwallopen, PA: Shepherd Press, 1995).

Responding to Sinful Parents

The life-shaping experiences of the home and society in a child's formative years certainly influence a person (Prov. 22:6; 29:21). But a negative experience is never an excuse for wrong behavior because the experience itself doesn't determine behavior. Behavior is always a reflection of the heart (Prov. 4:23; Mark 7:21; Luke 6:45). It's one's response from the heart to the experiences that determines behavior. (This summary is based on Tedd Tripp's *Shepherding a Child's Heart*.)

What must orient the heart's response in spite of negative circumstances?

the fear of God (Prov. 9:10; Eccles. 12:13, cf. Gen. 50:20)

How can someone fear God in spite of negative circumstances?

only by faith (Heb. 12:2)

How should a child who has a heart of faith that fears God respond to a sinful parent?

A God-fearing child should respond with grace but also seek appropriate justice.

A response of pursuing grace or justice (with graciousness) must be discerned according to the severity of the sin. The underlying reasons for pursuing grace or justice will help the child to discern what to do.

For what reasons should a God-fearing child pursue grace when sinned against?

- *Parents are finite, so they'll be inconsistent and sometimes misjudge disputes between siblings.*
- *Parents are fallen, so they won't always display the fruit of the Spirit or walk uprightly.*
- *Parents struggle with responding correctly to their own pressures in life.*
- *Maturity changes one's perspective.*

The foundation for all the other reasons is that parents are God's ordained authority in the home (unless disqualified by egregious criminal activity). The children's role is to submissively accept the training of their parents (imperfect as it may be).

For what reasons should a God-fearing child pursue justice when sinned against?

- *criminal activity (such as verbal, physical or sexual abuse, child neglect) for which God has ordained governmental authorities*
- *spiritual problems (such as lack of loving leadership, nurturing) for which God has ordained spiritual authorities in the church*

A Matter of Worship

There are many reasons children sin against their own parents: thoughtlessness, anger and bitterness, exasperation, worldliness, and so on. But, fundamentally, rebellious disobedience stems from a heart that is idolatrous. What's most important becomes the worship of self, material things, friends, activities, freedoms, and the like. The world revolves around fulfilling one's own desires. Secularists view such idolatry as self-actualization, say it is necessary for self-esteem, and heartily approve of children who behave in such self-serving ways (Rom. 1:29–32; 2 Tim. 3:1–2, 14–15, cf. Prov. 29:15). But God calls on children to give up their idolatry and to worship Him. Children aren't supposed to to worship their parents. Their parents are fallen and fallible. But if children worship God, they'll give heed to their God-ordained parents (Gen. 18:19; Deut. 6:1–7; Eph. 6:4). They will seek to uphold their parents' God-given task, making it easier for their parents to do their job well (Prov. 10:1; 15:20; 23:15, 24–25; 27:11). Only then will they enjoy God's blessing of peace (Prov. 6:23). "Freedom is not found in autonomy, it is found in obedience. (Psalm 119:44–45)." [Tedd Tripp, *Shepherding a Child's Heart*, 27] Parents who love will discipline (Prov. 3:12; 13:24). Children who love will accept discipline (Prov. 15:5).

Teen Responsibility

The book of Proverbs was probably not written for a younger elementary-aged child. Much of its reasoning, content, and wisdom seems more appropriate for an older child or even a young adult (Prov. 5:20; 6:1–3). It was written for the age group that was transitioning from the sphere of parental authority into the sphere of parental advice.

Divide students into small groups. Assign each group several chapters from the book of Proverbs. Each group should list the responsibilities of children and parents with the corresponding reference.

Example: Proverbs 1:7–19

• *fear God because of accountability to Him*
• *hold fast to wise and godly instruction*
• *turn away from wicked companions*

Becoming mature young adults doesn't mean that people no longer need to fear God, listen to parents, or be concerned about who they hang out with. In fact, if they are maturing in godliness, they'll be even more careful about these things.

Hope in the Gospel

In a broken world full of broken marriages and families—even in your own home—what hope is there? God has provided all that you need for living this life in a fallen world (2 Pet. 1:3). While the hope of the gospel is ultimately future—when the earth is fully restored—the hope of the gospel also enables believers to respond properly now to their difficult circumstances in a fallen world.

> Each of these experiences is an opportunity to *do redemption*, that is, to bring [yourself] to the one place of hope and help, the Lord Jesus Christ. . . . This world is not a place of unmitigated chaos. Over all the brokenness rules the risen Christ, who reigns over all things for the sake of his people. He is bringing an end to all of the sin, sorrow, and suffering. What we face here is not comparable to the glories of eternity. There is hope! . . . There is more and better to come.

Patricia Hersch describes this social phenomenon in her book about teens, *A Tribe Apart*.

> Somewhere in the transition from twelve to thirteen, our nation's children slip into a netherworld of adolescence that too often becomes a self-fulfilling prophecy of estrangement. The individual child feels lost to a world of teens . . . notorious for what they do wrong, judged for their inadequacies, known by labels and statistics that frighten and put off adults.[14]

The trends, styles, language, and technology in our culture change so quickly that parents can appear hopelessly out of date to their teenage children because of seemingly outmoded ideals and traditions.

Teen culture is a departure from God's creational norms. While not all teens openly rebel against their parents, many are tempted to keep Mom and Dad ignorant of whatever they're up to.

Just because society considers teens as not quite adults, that doesn't exempt you from the command to children to honor their parents. Even if all of Western culture refuses to enforce this norm, God through His acts of providence will. The person who "mocks a father and scorns to obey a mother" (Prov. 30:17) is warned that he will come to a terrible end. Rebellion against parents leads to a life of dysfunction that ends in tragedy.

HOPE FOR WHOLENESS

Cultural pressure has never in history pushed people consistently toward holiness. God placed you into this culture in this part of history—your job is to live out your Christian life in the middle of these unique challenges and opportunities. Twisted sex, in various electronic forms at least, is easily available to you. And the sexual choices you are making right now may hurt your future marriage. On top of that, you've got to live as a fallen child of fallen parents and with fallen siblings.

Why not give up? Because your conscience and your Bible agree. Because sex has a created structure you will not be able to violate forever. Because God is in charge of you and your body. Because the reward is as great as the dangers are intense.

THINKING IT THROUGH 14.1

1. List at least three kinds of sin that according to the Bible are a corruption of God's design for intimacy.

2. List some scriptural reasons why it is wrong to look down on unmarried people.

3. What two types of husbands cause antagonistic relationships with their wives? What two types of wives cause antagonistic relationships with their husbands?

4. What do parents do to sidestep (and even abandon) their God-given responsibility? What do children/teens do to frustrate their parents' God-given responsibility?

♀5. How should and shouldn't the family be defined? Explain why.

There is reason to continue. [Tripp, *Age of Opportunity*, 68–70]

What can you do to help your siblings and parents to rely on Christ's redemption in the midst of their struggle against sin?

Answers will vary.

THINKING IT THROUGH 14.1

1. fornication, adultery, polygamy, child abuse, rape, incest, homosexuality, and so on

2. God's sovereign plan for certain people is for them to be devoted to Him without a helper or without children.

3. domineering or passive; resistant or manipulative

4. Parents provoke in anger or physically/sexually abuse children; children rebel, dishonor, and disobey.

♀5. The family should be defined according to God's revelation of His created order.

The family should not be defined according to human social constructions (e.g., any grouping of people who love each other enough to share a relationship) that twist God's created order, violating God's purposes for the family.

14.2 HOMOSEXUALITY

Rosaria Champagne Butterfield was everything some Christians fear: a successfully tenured* university professor of queer theory,* a pro-homosexual activist, and a practicing lesbian. Rosaria, for her part, viewed conservative Christians through the haze of a massive cultural divide. They were to her an object of fascination, disgust, and academic study. She writes,

> The closest I ever got to Christians during these times were students who refused to read material in university classrooms on the grounds that "knowing Jesus" meant never needing to know anything else; people who sent me hate mail; or people who carried signs at gay pride marches that read "God Hates Fags."*[15]

So when she wrote an op-ed piece attacking Christianity for the local newspaper and it yielded a stack of nasty letters from Christians and kudos from fellow liberals, Dr. Champagne was not surprised. She separated the letters neatly into boxes on opposite sides of her desk: fan mail and hate mail.

Except there was one letter that didn't fit. It was from a conservative Christian pastor in her town. It hovered between the boxes because it was a letter of disagreement—but not of hatred. It asked probing questions and invited further contact. It actually found its way into and out of her trash can more than once before Rosaria, intrigued, decided to meet its author.

After two years of friendship with this gracious pastor and his wife, Rosaria became what she calls an "unlikely convert" to the Christian faith. She is now everything that some homosexuals fear: a married homeschool mom who submits to her husband (a pastor) and lives to follow God's Word.

Because of her remarkable story and her obvious gifts as a thinker and communicator, Dr. Butterfield is in high demand as a speaker at churches, schools, and conferences around America. She's become a leading spokeswoman for the orthodox* Christian perspective on homosexuality.

Rosaria provokes strong reactions. Nine pro-**LGBT*** students at the University of South Florida stood in front of her with their backs turned during her entire speech there.[16]

Then there was the large evangelical Christian college that invited her to speak in chapel. Around a hundred students (all of whom had previously signed a community covenant promising to abstain from "homosexual behavior and all other sexual relations outside the bounds of marriage between a man and woman"[17]) staged a demonstration regarding Rosaria's visit. They sat silently on the chapel steps and held signs saying things like "We're all loved by God" and "I'm gay and a beloved child of God."[18]

tenured: achieving a permanent job as professor; a mark of academic success

queer theory: the study of homosexuality

fag: a demeaning and offensive term for male homosexuals

orthodox: the established, traditional, mainstream view

LGBT: lesbian, gay, bisexual, transgendered

Rosaria Champagne Butterfield

SECTION OBJECTIVES 14.2

1. Summarize the changing landscape of the approval/disapproval of homosexuality.

2. Apply CFR to the reality of homosexual temptation, and explain the responsibility of believers who face this temptation.

3. Explain why this particular temptation has recently been brought to the forefront of cultural discussions.

 Resources on Homosexuality

Adam T. Barr and Ron Citlau, *Compassion Without Compromise* (Bloomington, MN: Bethany House, 2014).

Denny Burk, *Transforming Homosexuality* (Phillipsburg, NJ: P&R, 2015).

Kevin DeYoung, *What Does the Bible Really Teach About Homosexuality?* (Wheaton: Crossway, 2015).

Peter Hubbard, *Love into Light* (Greenville, SC: Ambassador International, 2013).

Robert A. J. Gagnon, *The Bible and Homosexual Practice* (Nashville: Abingdon Press, 2001).

Rosaria Champagne Butterfield, *The Secret Thoughts of an Unlikely Convert* (Pittsburgh, PA: Crown & Covenant, 2012).

Sam Allberry, *Is God Anti-Gay?* (Purcellville, VA: The Good Book Company, 2013).

The Power of the Gospel

Rosaria Butterfield's book doesn't begin with the transformation of a political ideology but with the transformation of a person through the power of the gospel.

She says, "I often wonder: God, why pick me? I didn't ask to be a Christian convert. I didn't 'seek the Lord.' Instead, I ran like the wind when I suspected someone would start peddling the gospel to me" (Butterfield, *Secret Thoughts*, xi). But when the gospel was shared over the course of many years "in an organic, spontaneous and compassionate way," her resistance against God was transformed into friendship with Jesus (Butterfield, 1).

She met a pastor who kindly challenged her presuppositions by asking her to defend them: "How did you arrive at your interpretations? How do you know you are right?" (Butterfield, 8). For the first time she began to realize that her (materialist) worldview lenses of interpretation were fundamentally different from Christians' worldview lenses. "The Bible makes it clear that reason is not the front door of faith. It takes spiritual eyes to discern spiritual matters" (Butterfield, 8). The persistent witness of the pastor finally brought her to the crux of the matter: authority—biblical revelation versus humankind's collective reasoning. She was confronted with whether there was indeed truth or merely truth claims proposed by humans. But ultimately she was confronted with whether she would give up living her life her way—whether she could give up her whole identity. She didn't feel like repenting; she didn't feel like she wasn't a lesbian. Her turning point came through the preaching of John 7:17.

"Obedience comes before understanding" (Butterfield, 22). If you want to understand then you must be willing to submissively obey. (By faith we understand.) The power of the gospel was in convincing Rosaria to give up her pride and follow Jesus even if that meant taking up a cross (Matt. 16:24). "How did the Lord heal me? . . . The word of God got to be bigger inside me than I. . . . And eventually instead of resisting, I surrendered" (Butterfield, 25). Butterfield goes on to testify that her conversion didn't automatically make life easy. "What I faced at work following my conversion was the rubbish of my sin, forgiven by God, but still there to be cleared away. This required a newer and even more intense understanding and application of Scripture" (Butterfield, 26).

The Historic Rulings of June 26

Although the issue of homosexuality is primarily an issue of sin that must be addressed by the gospel, it can't be ignored as a political issue that must be addressed in the public square. From a biblical perspective, June 26 is a date that will live in infamy because of the historical magnitude of various attempts to overthrow God's creational norms for marriage. On June 26, 2003, the Supreme

Court struck down state laws prohibiting sodomy. [*Lawrence vs. Texas* overturned *Bowers vs. Hardwick* from seventeen years earlier. See Thomas Jipping, "In Brief: Lawrence Aftershocks," *World* (Aug. 9, 2003).] Ten years later, on June 26, 2013, the Supreme Court struck down a key part of the Defense of Marriage Act. [Emily Belz, "Back to the States," *World* (July 13, 2013).] Two years later, on June 26, 2015, the Supreme Court ruled in favor of legalizing gay marriage in all fifty states (*Obergefell vs. Hodges*). Each of these rulings was made in spite of the vigorous dissent of serveral of the Supreme Court justices [Emily Belz, "Excerpts from the Marriage Ruling and Dissents," *World* (June 26, 2015)].

Responding from a CFR Perspective

A person could get lost in all of the specific debates over the interpretation of Greek words or the relationship of the Levitical laws to the New Testament believer (Lev. 18:22; 20:13; 1 Tim. 1:6–11). But looking at the issue through the lens of CFR should settle the debate with simplicity and clarity.

What does the Bible reveal to be God's created order for marriage?

- *Genesis 1:27–28; 2:18, 23–24—God created humans to intimately unite according to their created, God-given, and patently recognizable complementary genders.*

- *Matthew 19:4–6—Even after the Fall, God's recognizable created order still remains.*

- *Malachi 2:14–15—Marriage is a covenant witnessed by and ratified by God to make a husband and wife one for the purpose of procreating.*

- *Ephesians 5:31–32—Marriage was designed to picture two distinct entities: Christ and the church. The picture can't be portrayed by two entitites that are the same.*

What does the Bible reveal to be the Fall's effect on sexuality?

- *Romans 1:24–32—Any same-sex sexual intimacy is fallen because the act itself contradicts God's design of the natural order. Natural refers to God's design not to the natural desires of fallen humans contaminated by original sin (Eph. 2:1–3).*

- *1 Corinthians 6:9–10—People can't claim to be saved with the hope of inheriting God's kingdom if they persist in unrepentant sin (1 John 3:3–10).*

- *1 Timothy 1:8–11—Homosexual practice (the underlying Greek word clearly reflects the wording of Leviticus as translated in the Septuagint) is one example of lawless rebellion that is contrary to sound doctrine and to the gospel of Christ (which fulfills God's law).*

THE "GAY CHRISTIAN" MOVEMENT

In 1988, almost 60 percent of Americans thought homosexuality itself should be illegal; the idea that homosexuals would be allowed to marry was, to say the least, unpopular. Less than a generation later, over 60 percent of Americans think homosexuality should be legal, and almost that many think gays and lesbians should be allowed to marry.[19] (Another relevant statistic is that only about 2.3 percent of Americans call themselves gay, lesbian, or bisexual.[20]) In 2015, the Supreme Court of the United States legalized gay marriage in all fifty states in a bitterly contested decision.

The SCOTUS decision didn't surprise anyone; America's commitment to empty concepts of "liberty" and "equality"[21] made it all but inevitable. What's surprising is that the tidal wave of support for homosexuality in America has swept up so many Christians—and not just theological liberals.* A growing movement of "gay Christians" argues that the Bible is God's holy Word and that it has nothing negative to say about faithfully monogamous* homosexuals. They make some intellectually demanding arguments; they're not ignorant of Scripture. The pro-gay protestors at the Christian college drew their slogans straight from the "gay Christian" playbook.[22]

One of the signs read, "Rosaria's story is valid, mine is too." "Gay Christians" are happy enough for a person to come to Christ and leave a same-sex partner; they simply want the freedom to keep theirs. Rosaria met with these protestors privately and was not persuaded by their arguments. Nor were they persuaded by hers.[23] Should everyone just agree to disagree?

theological liberals: *professing Christians who deny that the Bible is completely trustworthy and tend to go wherever the culture does*

monogamous: *marrying and staying sexually faithful to only one partner*

CFR and Homosexuality

This is a confusing time. That's why you need Bible study skills and a biblical worldview. You need Bible study skills because the "gay Christians" use sophisticated arguments about the meaning of New Testament Greek words, about Bible interpretation in general, and about the relationship of the two testaments in Scripture. This is not the place to enter those detailed arguments (see the sidebar on page 209 for recommended books).

This is the place, instead, to remember Creation, Fall, Redemption. If you don't see the Bible as the story of a good creation twisted by Adam's Fall and then restored to its purpose, you'll miss the most important argument in the whole homosexuality debate, which is this: the way God created the world is the standard by which we should judge the way things ought to be.

What is the created structure of marriage? It's what we saw in the previous chapter: a man and a woman (Gen. 1:27) being put together by God for life (Mark 10:9) so the wife can help her husband (Gen. 2:18), so the husband can love his wife (Eph. 5:25), and so the two of them can become one (Gen. 2:24) with the result that they multiply (Gen. 1:28). Homosexual relationships can never meet this standard.

Homosexuality is a worldview issue because to defend homosexual acts as acceptable to God is to deny that the design of our bodies implies anything about their purpose.[24] And that strikes at the heart of the Creation, Fall, Redemption worldview. Read your Bible and your body: homosexuality is a sinful twisting of sex.

At the same time, fallenness is not limited to unbelievers. It is to be expected that some of God's children will experience unwanted homosexual feelings. The Bible never promises that Christians will be immune to certain temptations. It also never says that homosexual desires are purposefully chosen or that therapy (or heterosex-

---

What does the Bible reveal to be God's redemptive transformative work in regard to the sexually immoral?

- *1 Corinthians 6:11—Believers in the church were once characterized by the practices mentioned in the previous verses. But they no longer practice those sins.*

- *1 Thessalonians 4:1–8—Believers must pursue sanctified living by saying no to their own immoral sexual passions. They must put sin to death (Rom. 6:12–19; 8:13).*

Responding to Specific Arguments

Students should read a concise treatment of the specific "gay Christian" arguments and a biblical response. Then they should write a report that summarizes at least one of those arguments and provides the biblical response. The following resources are rec-

ommended as exemplifying the most appropriate, concise, and lay-friendly theological responses.

Edward T. Welch, *Homosexuality: Speaking the Truth in Love* (Phillipsburg, NJ: P&R, 2000).

Kevin DeYoung, *What Does the Bible Really Teach about Homosexuality?* (Wheaton: Crossway, 2015).

Mike Riccardi, "Gagnon on *Arsenokoites*: The Bible on Abusive vs. 'Committed' Same-Sex Relationships," The Cripplegate (website), May 1, 2015.

Properly Defining Same-Sex Attraction

Same-sex attraction (SSA) should be carefully defined as "any erotic or romantic attraction to someone of the same gender."

ual marriage) will "cure" anyone of same-sex desires. The Bible does promise, however, that true Christians will grow in holiness. And it demands full repentance from all sexual immorality (1 Cor. 6:9–10).

The "gay Christian" movement regularly points out that Jesus never said anything about homosexuality.[25] But He didn't have to mention it explicitly to condemn it. What He did was appeal to the way God created the world (as did Paul in Romans 1:26–27). When asked about divorce, Jesus showed that he considered God's original design for human sexuality to be authoritative: "Have you not read that he who created them from the beginning made them male and female?" (Matt. 19:4).

Jesus puts His divine finger on the real issue: "Have you not read?" Multiple times

---

DID JESUS AND PAUL KNOW ABOUT SEXUAL ORIENTATION?

One of the arguments of the "gay Christian" movement that has proven very useful for them is that the apostle Paul simply didn't know about homosexual orientation—and therefore never considered the possibility of faithful, monogamous gay unions.[26] What Paul condemned (they say) was homosexual relations that exploited other people, like men sexually abusing boys. It takes some familiarity with ancient Greek literature to answer this argument, and here's the answer of one of the world's major New Testament scholars:

> When I read the accounts from the early Roman empire of the practice

of homosexuality, then it seems to me they knew just as much about it as we do. In particular . . . they knew a great deal about what people today would regard as longer-term, reasonably stable relations between two people of the same gender. This is not a modern invention, it's already there in Plato.[27]

We should not act as if the modern concept of sexual orientation (invented in the nineteenth century[28]) is a stable reality to which the Bible needs to adjust. The Bible is the reality to which our concepts need to adjust. Our Creator has the right to tell us what to do with our bodies.

Jesus held the Jews of His day responsible for how they read Scripture, and He will hold us responsible too (Matt. 12:3, 5; 22:31). And this is what Paul says: "Do not be deceived: neither the sexually immoral, nor idolaters, nor adulterers, nor men who practice homosexuality . . . will inherit the kingdom of God" (1 Cor. 6:9–10). And "The law is . . . laid down . . . for the lawless and disobedient, for the ungodly and sinners, for . . . men who practice homosexuality, enslavers, liars, perjurers, and whatever else is contrary to sound doctrine" (1 Tim. 1:9–10).

The real effect of the "gay Christian" movement's arguments is to cast doubt on whether or not God is capable of communicating moral expectations clearly through His Word. One prominent "gay Christian" leader, who left his wife for a male partner, just shrugs his shoulders when he reads the passages where Paul most clearly condemns homosexuality. "Greek scholars don't know exactly what [Paul] means," he claims.[29]

The work of biblical scholars is extremely valuable, but scholars have worldviews just like the rest of us—worldviews that can cause them to misread the scriptural text.[30] Listen to the honest admission of Luke Timothy Johnson, a liberal New Testament scholar:

> I think it important to state clearly that we do, in fact, reject the straightforward commands of Scripture, and appeal instead to another authority when we

---

SSA should not be confused with legitimate affections of love toward a good friend, sibling, or parent of the same gender. Deep friendships, including deep affection, should be encouraged as a normal part of life. What once was considered natural friendship (e.g., David and Jonathan in 1 Samuel 18:1; Anne Shirley and Diana Barry in *Anne of Green Gables*) has been misconstrued as SSA by those trying to legitimize homosexuality. The result could be the ruin of good God-honoring friendships of deep commitment, loyalty, and self-sacrificial love because nobody wants to be accused of having a wrong kind of erotic love. But God has not restricted friendships from being loving in any possible way except the erotic love reserved for marriage. Christians must learn to cultivate deep, God-honoring, and loving friendships with one another. God didn't design

humans for loneliness or simply superficial acquaintances outside of marriage.

Furthermore, SSA should not be confused with superficial cultural traditions (e.g., men love sports and hunting; men play trumpets; women love sewing and cooking; women play flutes). While there are legitimate cultural symbols that signal inappropriate identifications (e.g., men wearing earrings, makeup, or dresses and carrying purses), not every cultural tradition must symbolize gender-specific identification. Not every male must be equally masculine, nor must every female be equally feminine. Variance within genders exists.

 ### Responding to SSA Temptation

If a believer experiences SSA (as defined above), what should he or she do?

Should Christians self-identify as homosexuals because of this temptation? (Rom. 6:1–11; 1 Cor. 6:11; 2 Cor. 5:17; Gal. 2:20)

No, temptations do not determine identity. It would not be valid biblically to identify oneself as a Christian adulterer, thief, liar, wife-beater, or the like. Regardless of believers' continuing temptations, Christ defines and transforms their identity. The desires of the flesh that remain are no longer approved and satisfying; they are foreign to the new identity.

Should Christians continue to accept their own same-sex desires as long as they don't carry out those desires in their behavior? (Prov. 4:23; Matt. 15:19; James 1:14–15)

No, if this is what is meant by celibacy, then it is unbiblical. Both inward desires and external behaviors are subject to God's condemnation as sinful. When temptations are coddled or accepted rather than battled against, they become sinful desires of the heart. Sin begins not with behavior but with desires, which will certainly bear fruit in behavior if left unaddressed.

[Denny Burk, "Is Homosexual Orientation Sinful?" *Journal of the Evangelical Theological Society* 58 (2015): 95–115]

Why would Christians be subject to this kind of temptation? (Rom. 8:13; 1 Cor. 10:12–13; Gal. 5:16–17; Col. 3:5–10)

The flesh remains with the believer until glorification. Christians never attain the kind of perfection that entirely eradicates the sin nature in this life. Every believer is always capable of being tempted by any possible sin. But every believer has been given all that is necessary to resist every possible temptation. Believers can't totally eradicate the flesh, but they can render it inoperative as they grow in maturity. They can respond with increasing consistency in putting the flesh to death.

Responding to the Tempted Person

Wrong ways to respond

1. Persecute and belittle

   It is true that God hates sin (Lev. 20:13; Ps. 34:21; Prov. 3:33; Rom. 1:18). Surprisingly to some people, while God unequivocally loves the sinner (John 3:16; Rom. 5:8; 2 Pet. 3:9), He also simultaneously hates the sinful *person* too (Ps. 5:5–6; 11:5; Prov. 6:16–19; 15:29; 17:15; John 3:36; Rom. 2:5; 9:13–15). God calls on believers to discern how to simultaneously respond to unbelievers this way as well. [D. A. Carson, "God's Love and God's Wrath" *Bibliotheca Sacra* 156 (October–December 1999): 387–98] On the one hand, believers must not give support or approval to hardened sinners (Pss. 1:1; 26:5; 97:10; 139:21–22;

Prov. 4:14; 1 Cor. 15:33; Eph. 5:11). But on the other hand, Christians live and work and go to church with sinners (1 Cor. 5:9–10) and must seek to sacrifically love and minister to them (Phil. 2:14–15; 1 Thess. 3:12; 5:15; Titus 3:1–3). Thus, scorning the unrighteous is never justified.

2. Accept and enable

Due to societal pressures, it will probably be more tempting to approach the matter with acceptance and enablement. However, this approach not only undermines God's other attributes (such as holiness) but it also contradicts the true meaning of God's love, which is to deliver sinners from destructive behavior that's contrary to their created design. Love doesn't lead to the affirmation of self-destruction (Prov. 3:11–12); it leads to keeping God's commands (John 14:15). The grace of God doesn't lead to accepting someone's ungodliness but to turning away from it (Rom. 6:1–2; Titus 2:11–12).

The right way to respond

1. Show compassion

The church is for broken people who need to be forgiven and built up in the Lord (Luke 15:17–24; Gal. 6:1–2; 1 Thess. 5:14).

2. Don't compromise

The church is for repentant people who forsake their sin (Matt. 5:29–30; Luke 3:8; Gal. 5:19–21). Unrepentant sin shouldn't be given approval in the name of compassion (1 Cor. 5:1–13; Rev. 2:14–16, 20–23).

Responding to Specific Situations

Divide students into small groups to formulate an application of "compassion without compromise" to the following scenarios:

- **Should Christians attend same-sex weddings?**

No, never. The congregation is there to witness and approve of a holy covenant—whether the people getting "married" understand or admit to that inherent reality of marriage or not.

- **Should Christian businesses bake wedding cakes, sell wedding rings, or participate as a photographers for same-sex marriage ceremonies?**

No, they shouldn't. While Christians aren't opposed to providing general services to homosexual people, they shouldn't be required to service homosexual activities, which would imply that they support that behavior. [See TE note on "Justifying Discrimination," p. 41.]

- **Should Christians welcome homosexual relatives to holiday gatherings?**

Maybe; the circumstances will differ. Will they be a detrimental influence on other

family members (especially young children and teens) through obscene dress and erotic displays? But there's nothing inherently wrong with sharing a holiday with sinful people who are unsaved. The Bible doesn't hold relationships with unbelievers (1 Cor. 5:9–10) to the same standard as relationships with professing believers (1 Cor. 5:11–13; 2 Thess. 3:13–15).

- **Should Christians speak up in opposition to companies' diversity training?**

If interactive responses are required, discerning answers of truth should be expressed.

Responding in the Public Square

First, Christians need to understand the societal upheaval taking place. Young people, especially, must not be deceived into thinking that the conflict is about equality or nondiscrimination. Christians aren't opposed to doing business with homosexual people; they dispute being forced to service homosexual activities (implicating themselves in the support of homosexual behavior). In contrast, for example, few would support requiring a business owner to screen print Bible verses on T-shirts if he chose not to for personal reasons. Discrimination against religious convictions is taking place, violating the First Amendment rights to freedom of speech and to the free exercise of religion. New moral norms are being forced onto society, and religious opposition is being eliminated.

Students should read the following or other relevant articles from either conservative or Christian news services:

Jamie Dean, "Losing Their Shirts," *World* (May 2, 2015).

---

declare that same-sex unions can be holy and good. And what exactly is that authority? We appeal explicitly to the weight of our own experience and the experience thousands of others have witnessed to, which tells us that to claim our own sexual orientation is in fact to accept the way in which God has created us. By so doing, we explicitly reject as well the premises of the scriptural statements condemning homosexuality—namely, that it is . . . a symptom of human corruption, and disobedience to God's created order.[31]

What's the point of having a divinely revealed book if it isn't allowed to tell us we're wrong? Jesus Christ, the Judge of all the earth, will be justified in saying to the "gay Christians" on judgment day, "Have you not read . . . ?"

WHO'S "HUNG UP"?

One Christian public intellectual was being interviewed by a secular journalist. The first question was about homosexuality. So was the second. Then the third question was, "Why is it that we're talking about homosexuality?" The Christian thinker replied, "Because you called me and asked the questions!"[32] It is possible to harp on an issue. Is it excessive to spend a whole section of this textbook on homosexuality? Are we targeting homosexuals for special hatred just by talking so much about homosexuality?

No. The secular world is insistently bringing it up. And Christians need to have biblical answers ready, or what good is our Bible and our Christianity? Christians have begun, here and there in America, to pay fines for refusing to bake cakes or take photos for gay weddings. One case, *Elane Photography v. Willock*, went all the way to the U.S. Supreme Court.[33] The Christians lost. That's one reason to study what Scripture has to say about homosexual acts. You may be called upon to pay a price for your view, and you'll want to be sure you're really standing on the Bible and not just your own gut reaction to gay sex.

> *"Many of the advocates of unqualified acceptance of homosexuality . . . seem to be operating with a simplistic [theology] that assumes whatever is must be good: they have a theology of creation but no theology of sin and redemption."*[34]
>
> —RICHARD B. HAYS

But fighting the culture war or convincing "gay Christians" they're wrong should not be your primary reason to study this issue. Investigate what Scripture says so you can walk alongside fellow Christians at your school or in your church who experience this particularly difficult temptation. In doing so, you'll learn something about the power of your own sin and the power of Christ's salvation. Many, many practicing homosexuals testify that they did not choose their sexual desires—in fact, they were desperate to get rid of them. Some looked to psychological therapies, and some went "straight" but eventually gave in to their homosexual desires again.[35] But Christ can redeem someone from even the strongest sinful desires, gay or straight, or He is not

God in flesh. It may take a lifetime, but He can do it. And He doesn't leave anyone to face temptation alone. Christians have His Holy Spirit, we have His Word, we have prayer, and we have the church, including both fellow Christians and pastors (Heb. 10:24). Heterosexual marriage may, in God's providence, eventually be God's provision for a Christian struggling against unwanted same-sex attraction. And yet celibacy is also a legitimate option (1 Cor. 7:8, 17).

The fight against sin isn't easy for anyone; Christians aren't guaranteed easy lives or freedom from sinful desires (in this life). But "God is faithful" to His children, "and he will not let you be tempted beyond your ability" (1 Cor. 10:13). He'll give grace.

Rosaria Champagne Butterfield always asks to meet with the protestors who show up at her talks on homosexuality. "And even if I don't have people demonstrating, after a chapel message or an open lecture, I make sure that students know what coffee shop I'll be at, and for how many hours, and I've never been alone."[36] There are sound, biblical answers to whatever questions you may have about homosexuality, and there are Christians willing to provide them in a loving and personal way.

THINKING IT THROUGH 14.2

1. What makes the "gay Christians'" rejection of the biblical worldview even more perplexing than other homosexuals' rejection of it?

2. What should be the standard by which we judge the way things ought to be in this world?

3. What is the created structure of marriage?

4. Why shouldn't it be surprising that even Christians face homosexual temptations?

♀5. How should Christians respond to homosexual temptation?

Kiley Crossland, "Denver Bakers Cleared of Bias for Refusing to Make Bible Cakes," *World* (April 7, 2015).

Mike Wittmer "Plea for Sanity," Don't Stop Believing (blog), February 23, 2015.

Rod Dreher, "Heads LGBTs Win, Tails Christians Lose," *American Conservative* (May 21, 2015).

Second, Christians need to carefully prepare themselves to respond to persecution correctly: bold resistance with meek respect. Jesus is both a Lion and a Lamb. "Whenever Jesus' followers exclusively reflect Lion-ness or Lamb-ness, the 'admirable conjunction' dissolves into ugliness. . . . Real Christianity is characterized by both love and truth" (Peter Hubbard, *Love into Light*, (Greenville, SC: Ambassador International, 2013) 124–26).

Is Homosexuality an Extra-Bad Sin?

It has become popular to equate homosexuality with any other sin. It was once popular to claim that homosexuality was the worst possible sin. Which is it? Neither.

All sin is sin—from simply showing partiality to unlawfully taking someone's life. If you violate God's law in just one point, you're guilty. It's who you have scorned that's more significant than what you've done (James 2:8–11). That said, different sins do bring about different consequences (Matt. 11:21–24). And different sins can reflect hearts that have gone from bad to worse (Rom. 1:21–32; 2 Tim. 3:13).

But homosexuality *is* uniquely heinous because, unlike many other sins (even sexual sins), it goes against the fundamental nature of God's created order. All sins violate God's law, but not all sins so radically violate the fundamental nature of God's design.

As one recent book puts it: "Many pastors and theologians are arguing that if the act of homosexuality really is sinful, it is about as bad as gluttony. It might not make us friends, but someone needs to speak the tough truth: Homosexuality is different. Eating too much pie is not the same as same-sex sexual activity. Who we are as sexual beings and what we do with our bodies affects us in unique, eternal ways" [Adam T. Barr and Ron Citlau, *Compassion Without Compromise* (Grand Rapids: Bethany House, 2014), 52]. However, it may be argued that there are worse sins than homosexuality: blasphemy of the Holy Spirit and unbelief, for example (Matt. 11:21–24; 12:31).

See also Rick Phillips, "Should We Equate Homosexual and Heterosexual Sin?" Reformation 21 (website), June 4, 2015.

A Difficult Battle

Sexual sin is difficult to defeat (see the TE note, "How to Fight Sexual Sin," p. 128). Behavior changes only when the underlying meditations of an idolatrous heart change. The whole weed must be rooted out (not just chopped off at the surface). That means that Christians must battle their idolatrous desires and not just attempt superficial behavior modification. But don't be confused. The flesh can never be eradicated with its sinful desires (Rom. 7:25). It's the coddling of desires that can change. Christians are no longer slaves—obligated to the flesh (Rom. 6:16–22). Don't be either overconfident or discouraged. There are no formulas for success, but there are basic practices that Christians must follow (Eph. 4:20–24). These practices are necessary (but not sufficient). Ultimately, our sufficiency is in Christ and His power to enable both willing and doing what is right (Phil. 2:13). Ask yourself:

1. Am I really putting on what's right (feeding my heart with the Bread of Life)?

   Am I *studying* the Word out of loving *devotion*? Am I *communing* with God and not just flippantly praying? Am I renewing my mind? How consistent and deep is it really? Don't wait for God to draw near to you first. You are invited to submit yourself to Him in repentance (as dirty as you are), and He will draw near to you (James 4:6–10).

2. Am I really putting off what's wrong (no longer feeding the flesh)?

   What media am I refusing to watch or read? What friends will I no longer hang out with? What places will I no longer go?

Have I given up the kind of internet access that feeds my flesh (Matt. 18:9)?

3. Am I really being accountable to spiritual leaders (parents, pastors, teachers, friends)?

What guardrails have been set up? What spiritual help have I established? Are my accountability partners doing their job seriously (both challenging and encouraging)? What have I done to rectify it if they aren't doing their job well?

Half-hearted practices bring about failure. Don't blame God or say the Bible doesn't work. Humble yourself.

THINKING IT THROUGH 14.2 (P. 209)

1. their professed belief in and use of the Bible to defend their views

2. God's created order/design of the body

3. a man and a woman (Gen. 1:27) being put together by God for life (Mark 10:9) so the wife can help her husband (Gen. 2:18), so the husband can love his wife (Eph. 5:25), and so the two can become one (Gen. 2:24) with the result that they multiply (Gen. 1:28)

4. Christians are fallen, and the flesh never goes away (only obligation to it does).

♀5. Christians must repent, fight to put sin to death, and live a pure lifestyle, identifying themselves according to that pure lifestyle (1 Cor. 6:9–10; 1 Tim. 1:10, cf. Rom. 1:26–27; Gen. 19:5–8 with Judg. 19:22–26; Eph. 4:17–24; 5:3–6; 1 Thess. 4:3–8; Rom. 8:12–13; Gal. 5:16–17, 25).

SECTION OBJECTIVES 14.3

1. Identify any cultural causes that may have contributed to the rise of both cohabitation and divorce.

2. Identify the two essential elements of a true marriage, and explain why cohabitation violates God's norms.

3. Explain how divorce distorts the purpose God created marriage for.

Justifying Cohabitation

Are the biblical commands undeniably clear that sex outside of marriage violates God's will? List some of the commands.

Yes, numerous commands make the matter straightforward and clear for Christians (Rom. 1:29; 1 Cor. 6:18; 7:2; Gal. 5:19; Eph. 5:3; Col. 3:5; 1 Thess. 4:3; 2 Tim. 2:22; Heb. 13:4; Rev. 2:14, 20–21; 21:8).

"The relations between men and women have changed more in the past thirty years than they did in the previous three thousand,"[37] says marriage researcher Stephanie Coontz.

Until the late eighteenth century, most societies around the world saw marriage as far too vital an economic and political institution to be left entirely to the free choice of the two individuals involved, especially if they were going to base their decision on something as unreasoning and transitory as love.[38]

Romantic love is, biblically speaking, supposed to be part of marriage (again, see Song of Solomon). But marriages based solely on love are indeed problematic. Coontz has observed that the very feature which makes marriage-for-love so attractive has "an inherent tendency to undermine the stability of marriage as an institution."[39] That is, if a marriage is formed and based solely on romantic love, then once that love dies so does the marriage. If that idea doesn't sound so bad to you, you're not thinking like the dependent child you (probably) are. Marriages produce children, and divorces hurt children.

The prevalence of the love-based marriage has also contributed to another cultural trend: **cohabitation**. More than 50 percent of America's engaged couples live together before the wedding. And that percentage doesn't include couples who live together without ever getting married at all.[40] Living together before marriage is now the most typical path to marriage in the United States.[41]

A recent study showed, however, that 60 percent of first premarital cohabitations do not result in marriage after three years.[42] And for cohabiting couples who do marry, that particular path into marriage doesn't seem to have helped Americans avoid finding the pathway out of marriage a few years later. Divorce rates rose in the twentieth century to staggering heights, and they appear to have decreased now only because fewer people are actually getting married.[43] "This is the generation so afraid of divorce that it is also afraid of marriage," according to two family researchers.[44]

About half of young people ages fifteen to nineteen claim to be sexually active,[45] and around 70 percent of all high school seniors agree that it is a good idea to live together before marriage.[46] Cohabitation and divorce are far more likely to affect you—and tempt you—than homosexuality is. Let a biblical worldview shape the way you look at these sins before your choices make it difficult for you to listen to God's instruction.

SHACKING UP

There never was a golden age in which all the people in any nation followed God's ways and hated evil. Public morals always go up and down. Cultures trade new sins for old ones. There was a time, for example, when a US president could get away with racism but not adultery; now it's the opposite (it would be best if he could get away with neither, of course).

So there was a time in American society, a time your grandparents probably remember, when cohabitation was frowned upon. As a PBS special about the twentieth century pointed out, "Cohabitation was almost impossible in the United States prior to the 1960s. Laws prevented unmarried couples from registering in hotels, and it was very difficult for an unmarried couple to obtain a home mortgage." Only a tiny percentage of Americans cohabited in 1960. But in the forty years after that, "cohabitation moved from disreputable and difficult to normal and convenient."[47]

What do you think is the most common justification for cohabitation (fornication), even among professing Christians?

Many professing Christians believe that their sincere "love" for another person overrides obedience to the clear commands of Scripture. They're assuming that God will graciously overlook an unrepentant sinful lifestyle.

What's wrong with that view of grace?

God's grace doesn't provide cover for presumptuous sin (Ps. 19:13; Prov. 7:14; Rom. 6:1–2; 2 Pet. 2:1–22; Jude 1:4). God's grace leads to the repudiation of sin (Titus 2:11–15). True salvation regenerates and sanctifies (Matt. 7:21; 2 Cor. 5:17; James 2:14–26). Persisting in willful sin proves a false faith (Eph. 5:5; Titus 1:16; 1 John 3:3–10).

What's wrong with that view of authority?

They dismiss God's will (1 Thess. 4:3, cf. Matt. 7:21) and spiritual wisdom (Prov. 5:1–23) because sinful passions rule them rather than the fear of God (2 Pet. 2:10, 12–14, 18–22).

What's wrong with that view of love?

Erotic love is necessary but not a sufficient basis for marriage. While even true love may be present in a cohabiting relationship, as described in 1 Corinthians 13:4–7, lust drives and twists its expression (2 Sam. 13:1–20).

The Popularization of Cohabitation

Contributing factors include:

• Marriage based on erotic attraction
• Countercultural rebellion of the 1960s
• Birth control pill, which enabled "free sex"
• Promotion of the idea of testing out compatibility before risking a lifelong covenant

Cultural pressure wasn't the only factor. Before the birth control pill came along in America in the 1960s, those having sex risked pregnancy. But the pill joined other cultural forces in the "sexual revolution" to twist the sexual morality of American culture (and that of most other developed nations).[48]

Worldview and Cohabitation

The Bible condemns cohabitation when it condemns fornication, and perhaps little more needs to be said. But cohabitation, like homosexuality, still provides a good opportunity to use the lenses provided by Creation, Fall, Redemption. We are led to ask again, "What was the original marriage like?" There was no preacher around to conduct that first marriage, no flower girl, no ring bearer, and no photographer. But the essential elements of a true marriage were there: a covenant and a (hetero)sexual union.

Friends make covenants—Jonathan and David did (1 Sam. 18:3). But without sexual union, it's not marriage.

Unmarried people form sexual unions—that's what cohabiting is. But without a covenant, it's not a marriage.

Couples become truly "married" only when they vow before a witnessing community to join together in a covenant bond—and to remain faithful to one another, sexually and in every other way. They also agree to "sanctions"—negative consequences if they violate their vows.

There's something about romantic love that inspires promises of eternal devotion. But when a fourteen-year-old boyfriend whispers "I'll love you forever" in the ear of his thirteen-year-old girlfriend, that's not a covenant. It's sweet nothings (emphasis on the nothings) because he almost certainly can't (and won't) keep such a promise.

But when that young man and young woman, with a few more years of maturity, stand tall at a church altar "before God and these witnesses" and solemnly promise "till death do us part"—then, and only then, do they have a covenant. Some cultures use rings to symbolize this union; others use an exchange of pigs. The symbols can differ, but the covenant and the sexual union both have to be there for a relationship to be called a marriage.

When a couple takes covenant vows and enters a sexual union, they're aligning themselves with God's intent for creation. They're choosing to participate in an institution created at the foundation of the world.[49] In contrast, cohabitation removes one of the essential elements of marriage, thereby dishonoring the marriage bed (Heb. 13:4).

One secular defender of cohabitation disagrees: "If you wait until marriage to have sex, you're taking an enormous risk. What if you're not compatible? Or what if you regret not having shopped around?"[50] Cohabitation is an attempt people make to avoid risk. They are demanding that God not put them through any pain that, to them, seems unnecessary. So they test the waters.

BISEXUALITY AND MARRIAGE

The most persuasive pro-LGBT argument in the Western world may well be what leading Supreme Court lawyer Ted Olson has said: "Allowing people of the same sex to marry the person that they love . . . does no damage to heterosexual marriage."[51]

But think about what it means for the institution of marriage when public opinion affirms the morality of the LGBT movement. Think, in particular, about the B in that abbreviation. If we're celebrating the sexual identity of bisexuals, we're inviting them and encouraging them to have multiple sexual partners. The presence of bisexual neighbors may do no direct harm to the heterosexual marriages in adjacent homes, but cultural expectations at a broader level do exert a pressure on marriage.

If the major symbolic powers in a culture—the president,[52] the Supreme Court, entertainers, experts—all acknowledge bisexuality as a distinct sexual identity, what reason can they give to limit marriage to two people? Heterosexual monogamy just becomes one more sexual identity on the menu. Adults are encouraged to express themselves sexually even if it gives unstable lives to their children.

It may be tempting to think that cohabitation is simply the same arrangement as marriage—only informal. However, substantive distinctions are built into the very nature of cohabitation, making it a more appealing arrangement to some people.

Cohabitation tends to promote:
• a contingent bond (the union's nature)
• autonomy (the union's character)
• self-serving motives rather than sacrificial ones (the union's motivation)
• dismissal of family (the union's approval)

"The fact that couples choose to cohabit rather than marry indicates there is a difference between the two relationships. Marriage involves things the cohabiting couple . . . would rather not deal with. This is why cohabitation even exists." [Glenn T. Stanton, *The Ring Makes All the Difference* (Chicago: Moody, 2011), 43]

The test-drive approach promises to prevent getting stuck in a bad relationship—one that would "require" divorce. But statistics show that cohabiting couples, once they do marry, have a higher rate of divorce by as much as 80 percent (Stanton, 60). Test-driving only reinforces the ambiguity and contingent nature of the commitment. This is the worst path to choose if a person wants to avoid divorce. Spouses aren't consumer products to be tested and then discarded if they don't work or are no longer pleasing.

Cohabitation Consequences

Aside from the certain spiritual destruction declared by God (Prov. 7:26–27; 1 Cor. 6:9; Rev. 22:15), cohabitation leads to recognizable destructive patterns commonly pointed out by even unsaved traditionalists. You can't live contrary to God's creational norms without suffering the practical consequences. The "benefits" of cohabitation can be proven to be false (by a statistical analysis of the social experience of many over decades of trial). Less commitment and sacrificial effort for the good of the other person will lead to the following tendencies:

• Single-parenthood (and the resultant impetus to resort to abortion)
• Family instability (and the resultant prevalence of drug and alcohol abuse)
• Childhood insecurity (and the resultant academic and behavior problems)
• Financial difficulties (and the resultant complications from shared financial burdens and legal rights)
• Permissive sexuality (and the resultant prevalence of STDs as well as jealousy because of betrayal)
• Emotional instability (contingency makes one unsure about the relationship; disagreements and manipulation are more pronounced, leading to more distrust, anger, and domestic abuse)

The test-drive approach undermines the very nature of marriage—its unconditionality and self-sacrifice for better or for worse. The test-drive approach doesn't prevent a bad relationship; it begins the relationship badly. Without both commitment and relational skills grounded in self-sacrifice for the good of the other person, such an arrangement will not only likely fail but also sets up conditions for failure in future relationships.

A Better Way?

Divide the class in half and allow the two sides to debate which of the following options is better.

• The divine design: an unconditional covenant

It may demand sacrificial self-denial, but it guards against negligence. As such, it provides stability and security.

• The human construct: a conditional arrangement

It may allow more "freedom," but it does so at the cost of fickle unpredictableness. As such, it leads to instability and insecurity for both spouses and children.

Preferring the human construct implies that God's design is unwise and imperfect.

Be Prudent, Self-Controlled

Most people don't make a conscious, intellectual choice to cohabit and then act on it. They simply follow their hearts into sexual promiscuity and end up cohabiting.

Foolishness can be avoided by discerning your ways now and avoiding the deceitful cohabitation path with its false promises (Prov. 14:8, 15, 18; 22:3). Parental rules and accountability are set up to prevent falling into this pit (Prov. 2:1, 16–20; 5:1–13; 7:1–5; 15:5). Foolishness can also be avoided by committing yourself to self-denial until love should be awakened for a spouse (Song of Sol. 2:7; 1 Thess. 4:3–8; 2 Tim. 2:22, cf. Gen. 39:7–13).

"Falling" into promiscuity usually reveals that the love-based relationship is really lust-based. And the counterfeit won't last. "The old Puritans used to counsel young people not to marry because they were in 'love.' . . . Instead, they counseled that young people should marry *in order to love*." [Jeff Van-Goethem, *Living Together: A Guide to Counseling Unmarried Couples* (Grand Rapids: Kregel Academic, 2004), 67]

Marriage: A Formal Covenant

What is meant by *formal*?

witnessed by appropriate authorities in the spheres of the family, church, and/or state

What is meant by a covenant?

an unconditional commitment by two parties, including both promises and obligations

Couldn't two individual lovers just privately agree to declare themselves to be married without having a religious or civil ceremony?

No, they have no sovereign authority to bind the covenant or penalize violations. They fail to establish accountability with witnesses to a definitively made obligation.

Resources on Cohabitation

Glenn T. Stanton, *The Ring Makes All the Difference* (Chicago: Moody, 2011).

Jeff VanGoethem, *Living Together* (Grand Rapids: Kregel Academic, 2004).

Rationalizing Divorce
Common Unbiblical Justifications

- I no longer love him/her (biblical response: Prov. 5:18; Eccles. 7:10; 1 Cor. 13:5–7; Eph. 5:25; Phil. 2:3–4; Titus 2:4); I'm tired of trying to make it work; he/she will never change; the situation/spouse is unbearable (biblical response: 1 Cor. 7:10–17; Gal. 6:9; James 2:13; 1 Pet. 3:1–4; 5:7–10, cf. Ezek. 16:59–63; Hosea 3:1–5)

- I have peace because the Holy Spirit confirmed that it's right for me; good friends/family members support divorce (biblical response: Prov. 17:4; 30:5–6; John 17:17; 1 Cor. 4:3–4; 1 John 2:4, cf. Jer. 42:5–6)

- It's for the children (biblical response: Rom. 12:18–21; 1 Cor. 7:14; Eph. 4:26–27; 1 Pet. 3:1–4)

But cohabiting brings its own terrible risks. It produces insecurity in both partners, especially the woman, who may waste her best opportunity to bear children (it's harder for women to conceive as they get older). Men may leave the "union" at the time they're most needed, namely when children come along, and when it's most difficult for a woman to find another mate. Cohabitation may steal from someone his or her only chance to share the joy of raising children to adulthood with one special person. Cohabiting is not a shortcut to a happy marriage; it's a short-circuit.

GLOBAL ATTITUDES TOWARD DIVORCE

	Not a moral issue	Acceptable	Unacceptable
Ghana	10%*		80%
Pakistan	5	10%	73%
India	10%	18%	53%
El Salvador	9%	30%	48%
China	18%	45%	25%
Brazil	10%	62%	24%
Israel	34%	33%	23%
Russia	13%	46%	22%
United States	36%	33%	22%
Japan	27%	55%	13%
Britain	42%	41%	9%
France	52%	43%	5

*2% of people in Ghana believe divorce is not a moral issue.

SPLITTING UP

Cohabitation is union without the safety net of a lifelong, public pledge of faithfulness. Divorce, on the other hand, breaks that union, rips apart that safety net, and violates that pledge. Divorce is one of the ultimate twistings of marital roles, the very opposite of God's original instruction that a man should "hold fast" to his wife (Gen. 2:24; cf. Matt. 19:3–5; Mal. 2:16).

The rate of American marriages ending in divorce grew to an unprecedented high in the twentieth century. In 1900 the divorce rate was only 7 percent, but by 1940 the percentage had almost tripled. In 1965 the rate reached 25 percent and in 1970 jumped to 35 percent. The numbers continued to climb. In only five more years, the divorce rate stood at 49 percent! This dramatic increase was due in large part to the **no-fault divorce** laws states began to adopt starting in 1969, eliminating the legal requirement to prove one partner's wrongdoing in order to obtain a divorce.[53] In the 1970s, the divorce rate continued to climb, and recent research shows that it "increased substantially after 1990 and is now at an all-time high."[54] One opportunistic jeweler even tried to cash in on the brevity of marriages by offering wedding rings for rent.[55]

In a fallen world, marriages will always be far from perfect. Sometimes they will break apart. God in Scripture recognizes this reality. When marriages break apart, people get hurt. Women and children especially are put at risk—financially and in many other ways.

NO-FAULT DIVORCE

A no-fault divorce is one in which you get a judge to end your marriage for nothing more than alleged "incompatibility." In the United States, says one writer, "you can come home from work and tell your spouse the marriage is over and he or she can do nothing but cry, and fight for the best financial payout possible. Try doing that with Verizon. Or while under contract to buy a home. Or with your gym membership. You'll get laughed at."[56] Eight in ten divorces in America are one-sided—the other spouse doesn't want the divorce.[57]

Feminists fought for the freedom to leave their marriages in the 1960s and '70s. Prominent feminists such as Betty Friedan, author of *The Feminine Mystique*, were ecstatic when no-fault divorce swept America. But decades later, they've noticed that it tends to hurt rather than help women.[58] Women are left financially vulnerable and without support in the exhausting and difficult job of raising children alone.

God Himself set up legal structures in Israel to handle divorce. It can't be wrong for modern governments to do the same. But for the sake of all the people who are harmed by divorce, laws should put pressure on people to uphold their vows rather than making it easy to abandon them.

There is no debate; all these excuses are unbiblical.

[Lou Priolo, *Divorce: Before You Say "I Don't"* (Phillipsburg, NJ: P&R, 2007)]

The Possible Biblical Justifications

- adultery (Matt. 5:32; 19:9)

- abandonment (1 Cor. 7:15)

There is debate among believers over whether these exceptions are legitimate.

[H. Wayne House, *Divorce and Remarriage: Four Christian Views* (Downers Grove, IL: InterVarsity Press, 1990)]

Remarriage

Even believers who accept the possible biblical justifications for divorce may still disagree over whether a biblically justified divorce also justifies remarriage since both Matthew 19 and 1 Corinthians 7 are silent or inconclusive on the matter (1 Cor. 7:11, 15).

[Mark L. Strauss, *Remarriage After Divorce in Today's Church: Three Views* (Grand Rapids: Zondervan, 2006)]

The Old Testament is clear that a husband and wife can't divorce one another, marry new spouses, divorce those new spouses, and then return to and remarry their original spouses—that would be a devious way to attempt to legalize adultery (Deut. 24:1–4).

God's Design and Hard Hearts

What is God's attitude toward divorce?

God hates divorce. It is contrary to His design. Marriage was created to be permanent (Mal. 2:14–16; Matt. 19:3–6).

HITCHING UP . . . AGAIN

Faithful Christians who don't deserve it may end up in the ranks of the divorced. No serious interpreters of Scripture are saying that such people—the "innocent parties" in a divorce—are sinning merely by finding themselves in that category. (Of course, there isn't always an innocent party in a divorce; sometimes both stubbornly refuse to forgive.) The real question, and one that genuine Christians admittedly disagree about, is whether or not remarriage after divorce is ever permitted.

Getting into all the details about the Bible's teaching on divorce is something you should certainly do (see sidebar for a recommended resource). You need to study the issue and come to a conclusion before you get married, or even before you meet your future spouse.

Worldview and Divorce

But this is a book on biblical worldview. So focusing on the insight on divorce provided by a Creation, Fall, Redemption perspective, there are two points to make:

First, marriage was created to be an unbreakable bond. When the Pharisees challenged Jesus about His view of divorce, He explained to them, "Because of your hardness of heart Moses allowed you to divorce your wives, but from the beginning it was not so" (Matt. 19:8). Jesus appealed to Genesis—to creation—to undermine divorce. He began by saying,

> Have you not read that he who created them from the beginning made them male and female, and said, "Therefore a man shall leave his father and his mother and hold fast to his wife, and the two shall become one flesh"? So they are no longer two but one flesh. What therefore God has joined together, let not man separate. (Matt. 19:4–6)

God made marriage, and God makes marriages. No one has the authority to terminate a marriage, not even the two people in it. If there had been no Fall, there would be no divorces.

Second, marriage is a picture of an even deeper reality, the relationship between Christ and His church (Eph. 5:32). One day, when Christ redeems the world, He will fully purify His bride and marry her for all eternity (Eph. 5:25–27). Divorce, even divorce among non-Christians, shatters this precious picture (as does a homosexual relationship or cohabitation). It tells a lie about Christ's undying love for His people.

When husbands and wives cheat on each other, they are also damaging the picture God created. That's why throughout the Bible marital infidelity (adultery) is consistently used as a picture of spiritual infidelity, as in Ezekiel 16 and many other passages.

FORGIVENESS FOR THE FALLEN

The point of having a biblical view of divorce, cohabitation, and homosexuality—and all other twistings of the purposes of sex and marriage—is not to cause anyone to be discouraged or to despair. Some teachers teaching this material are divorced. Some students reading it have had premarital sex. No sin places someone beyond the reach of God's grace.

You can't know now all God's reasons for bringing this topic to your attention right now. But you can trust that the God who created marriage knows best how to set up yours.

STUDYING DIVORCE AND REMARRIAGE

One excellent resource on the issues raised in this unit is a book by Andreas Köstenberger and David W. Jones called *God, Marriage, and Family: Rebuilding the Biblical Foundation* (Wheaton: Crossway, 2010). The chapter in the book on divorce and remarriage provides a concise summary of Christian viewpoints on the question.

Why might God allow divorce in some instances?

While God may allow divorce in very limited circumstances, it's always due to a hard heart (Matt. 19:7–8). Otherwise reconciliation would take place, even in the case of sexual immorality (Hosea 3:3).

What is the biblical responsibility of church leadership when a church member's divorce is clearly unbiblical?

The church should call the person to repentance (make things right by reconciling) and exercise church discipline if the person remains unrepentant (Matt. 18:15–18; 1 Cor. 5:1–13; 2 Thess. 3:14–15; 2 Tim. 4:2).

What should be the biblical response of Christians toward divorced church members who are either innocent parties or repentant?

Church members are obligated to build each other up through love and encouragement (Eph. 4:1–3, 11–16; 1 Thess. 5:11–15). There is no excuse for despising others because they are suffering from the consequences of either their own sin or the sin of others (Gal. 6:1–6, 10; James 2:13).

How could you demonstrate compassion to a classmate whose parents are divorcing (regardless of whether you think divorce is biblical)?

You can always weep with those who weep without taking sides or legitimizing the divorce (Rom. 12:15). Don't shun your classmate; be a friend (Prov. 17:17; 27:6, 9–10).

Forgiveness: Getting It Right

Getting forgiveness right is vital. But cheap forgiveness is destructive. Christians are obligated to *offer* forgiveness, even for heinous sins, just as Christ offered them forgiveness (Matt. 6:14–15; Eph. 4:32; James 2:13). But God doesn't forgive unrepentant sinners; they face judgment and hell (Luke 13:27–28; John 3:36). True forgiveness requires that the guilty repent and ask for forgiveness (Luke 17:3). That's why Paul praised the Corinthians for a godly sorrow that manifested itself in repentance (2 Cor. 7:9–11). If a person will not repent, he isn't able to receive forgiveness.

These truths need special attention when being applied to the matter of sexual abuse. Requiring someone who's been abused to extend forgiveness to an unrepentant offender would be destructive to the one who was hurt. The consequences for sexual sins were serious in the Old Testament. In cases of rape, the abuser could face the death penalty (Deut. 22:25). Note carefully that Scripture never condemns victims of a sexual crime (Deut. 22:26). It teaches that the abuser, not the abused, is disgraced (Prov. 6:33). For the New Testament era the principles remain the same even though nations may frame their laws differently (Rom. 13:1–7).

In addition, forgiveness doesn't cancel justice (Isa. 26:9–10). No person can pardon the guilt of another person; only God can do that (Mark 2:7). Nor can personal forgiveness pardon someone from the consequences of criminal actions. When a person forgives someone who has sinned against him and repented of that sin, he is forgiving the offense on a personal level. It's a step in bringing about reconciliation between two persons. But this personal reconciliation doesn't remove legal penalties. Abusers still must face the criminal penalties demanded by law. If they hide what they've done from the appropriate authorities, they're indicating that they're not really repentant. Forgiveness also doesn't remove all other consequences for sin. For instance, certain sins disqualify a man from holding church office—even after those sins have been forgiven (1 Tim. 3:2). Even on the divine-human level, God's forgiveness removes a person from bearing God's wrath, but it doesn't remove the Christian from God's fatherly discipline (Heb. 12:5–12, cf. 2 Sam. 12:10–14). While forgiveness begins the restoration of a relationship, and though the one who forgives doesn't hold the sin of the sinner against him any longer, forgiveness doesn't move everything back to the way it was before the sin.

What if the person won't repent?

Although restoration may not be able to occur without restitution (making amends for wrongdoing) and reconciliation (renewal of trust and love), that doesn't mean that the Christian allows himself to grow bitter and angry over the offense. Though forgiveness itself is conditioned on repentance, the offer of forgiveness is unconditional (Col. 3:13). Christians must be willing to forgive and must forgive those who repent. People who refuse to forgive won't be forgiven by God for their own sins (Matt. 6:14–15; 7:1–2; 18:34–35). Christians don't earn forgiveness for themselves by forgiving others, but Christians are those who forgive. God has forgiven us for so much that we must, in turn, be willing to forgive others.

When the sin is deep and vile and the sinner is unrepentant, this is a hard saying. But it also frees the Christian from the destructiveness of bitterness. Romans 12:17–21 provides a biblical model for escaping bitterness toward a sinner who won't repent. First, don't seek revenge (12:17, 19, 21). Second, show love to your enemy (12:17, 20). Third, trust that God will bring justice by bringing His wrath on the unrepentant (12:19). Again, the pain that some sins bring makes this counsel difficult in many cases. But it is counsel designed to free people from the greater pain that bitterness brings.

[These notes summarize the teaching found in Chris Brauns, *Unpacking Forgiveness* (Wheaton: Crossway, 2008).]

Other helpful resources:

Edward T. Welch, *Shame Interrupted* (Greensboro, NC: New Growth Press, 2012).

Layton Talbert, "To Forgive, or Not to Forgive," Rooted Thinking (website), August 21, 2014.

Phil Johnson, "The Proper Ground of Forgiveness," Pyromaniacs (website) September 17, 2015.

THINKING IT THROUGH 14.3

1. When romantic love dies, then so does the marriage. Cohabitation is also based on fickle romantic love—with less of a commitment binding the relationship.

2. heterosexual union and a binding covenant

3. Yes, God allowed divorce due to hard hearts, but He put restrictions on it to manage fallenness; laws should pressure people to keep their vows not violate them.

4. the unbreakable bond between Christ and His bride, the church

♀5. marriages based on erotic feelings; the 1960s countercultural rebellion; the birth control pill, which allowed "free sex"; the promotion of the idea of testing out compatibility before risking a lifelong covenant

THINKING IT THROUGH 14.3

1. Why do marriages based solely on romantic love often disintegrate? Why doesn't cohabitation solve this problem?

2. What are the two essential elements in marriage?

3. Should a nation have laws allowing for divorce? What should those laws promote?

4. What did God originally create marriage to picture?

♀5. What cultural factors may play a role in the rise of cohabitation?

14.4 GENDER ROLES IN A FALLEN WORLD

In 2012, a high-ranking member of the Obama administration, Anne Marie Slaughter, decided to quit her job for "family reasons." Such resignations happen all the time, and "family reasons" is usually a euphemism* indicating that someone was fired. But this case was different: Slaughter was a mother, and when she said she was quitting for family reasons, she meant it. She explained in a much-discussed article in *The Atlantic* that "juggling high-level government work with the needs of two teenage boys was not possible."[59] Slaughter admits that women of her generation were taught the "feminist credo" that they could "have it all"—marriage, children, and career. But constant shuttling between New Jersey (she taught at Princeton) and Washington, D.C., just wasn't working for her family even though her husband had agreed to take over parenting duties so she could further her career.

euphemism: *an indirect or vague expression used in place of one that is considered offensive*

Slaughter is a highly educated, thoughtful, dedicated, and articulate woman, whose expertise is in high demand. She's an academic. She's a card-carrying member of the American elite. She wrote her *Atlantic* article both to defend her choice to leave her government job (many feminists criticized her for it) and to push society to adjust its expectations so that other working moms would not be forced to make the decision she did.

The American dream is that you can be anything you want to be. And Western individualist societies do provide a level of freedom for their citizens that is certainly not available to many other people in the world. But social expectations do and will play a role in what you—man or woman—can become. Those expectations will arise out of the major worldviews represented in a society. Will women be expected, in general, to be the primary caregivers for children? Will men be expected, in general, to be the primary breadwinners for their families? These are inescapably worldview-ish issues. Your view of where the concepts of "male" and "female" came from will necessarily determine your answers to these pressing questions.

And thanks to the Fall, people are very confused about such questions at the moment. (The comments in response to Slaughter's article online demonstrated this quite clearly.) The landmark book about complementarianism observes that

> confusion over the meaning of sexual personhood today is epidemic. The consequence of this confusion is not a free and happy harmony among gender-free persons relating on the basis of abstract competencies. The consequence rather is more divorce, more homosexuality, more sexual abuse, more promiscuity, more social awkwardness, and more emotional distress and suicide that come with the loss of God-given identity.[60]

SECTION OBJECTIVES 14.4

1. Summarize the consequences of societal confusion over the roles and responsibilities of men and women in society.

2. Summarize the consequences of societal confusion over the recognition of the gender identity of men and women within that society.

3. Defend the responsibility of believers to endeavor to maintain loving compassion while remaining uncompromisingly opposed to destructive behavior.

Gender Roles in Society

Why did God create humans with distinct genders? If He had wanted humans to be completely indistinct, then He would have made them that way. The answer is that God designed distinct *functional roles* for men and for women. Men and women are equal in essence, but they are not the same. Men and women both take part in fruitfulness and dominion. But men and women are *designed* differently to *function* differently. "In the Scripture, there is an organic connection between biological sex and gender roles." [Denny Burk, *What is the Meaning of Sex* (Wheaton: Crossway, 2013), 167]

As image bearers, man and woman would have different vocations in their callings as vice regents and rulers. These different assignments—which are rooted in God's good creation—do nothing to undermine the fundamental equalities. . . . But they are nevertheless differences, and they do involve a hierarchical ordering of roles. . . . Man and woman are equal in their essence as divine image-bearers, but

Without the Bible, it's anyone's best guess what society should look like. People can make gender roles into whatever they can get other people to agree to. (That's precisely what they've been doing, of course.) But with the Bible, any effort to build a society must be based on a certain foundation. And man and woman, equally created in God's image but called to different roles, are part of that foundation. Complementarity is meant by God to be a building block of human society.

There's a certain amount of flexibility in a complementarian approach. If a man is paralyzed and can't work, the Bible does not forbid his wife from becoming the family breadwinner. And the Bible contains few strict rules—mainly general principles—when it comes to men's and women's roles in society (their roles in family and church are more precisely delineated).

But a culture intent on pushing past even flexible boundaries will experience some resistance from the creation. Mrs. Slaughter's teenage sons needed their mom; they were created that way. The foundations of society will crumble if people ignore the creational norms of gender.

WHERE OUR SOCIETY IS HEADED

Of course, the Fall has twisted the gender roles God gave us, so there are cultures in which women are stifled and left uneducated and men are allowed (or even encouraged) to be overbearing or distant. But the created order is still visible everywhere you go even though sin has damaged it deeply.

Western individualist societies seem to be twisting the created order of gender roles in a new direction. There are women of course, who get stifled (simply because they're women) in America, and there are men who are harsh and violent toward their wives. Those sins are old. But leading Westerners are also pushing something relatively new—or at least rare—in world history: the idea that all differences between men and women are mere social constructs, false ideas built by society. In this view, men's and women's respective body parts may have some obvious differences, but all roles and identities for men and women in society (and in the family) are interchangeable. Proponents of this view say there's no good reason for women to do more housework than men or to stay home with the kids. There's no good reason why women generally grow their hair longer than men or why some sports or pastimes are more associated with men than women.

Our society doesn't yet know what to do with people who bend previously accepted categories of gender. Wellesley College, an all-women's school in Massachusetts (founded in a day when, sadly, women were not generally allowed to go to college), now has a few dozen students who were born female but no longer identify as women. A small number of them identify instead as men; the rest simply reject the idea of gender or want to position themselves somewhere in between "male" and "female."[61] What do you do when a "trans man" wins Wellesley's hoop-rolling contest, an annual tradition begun in 1895? Do you check for testosterone injections?

Even the liberal students of an elite institution such as Wellesley weren't sure what to do when that happened in 2013. A number of them sheepishly told a journalist that they went to a women's college to be in a place full of and led by, well, women. Letting some of those women become men seemed wrong somehow—but they didn't want to give their names after expressing that opinion. They feared being shouted down with cries of "discrimination."

they are unequal in their social roles. The first man Adam acts as the leader in this first marriage, and Eve is called to follow his leadership. . . . Though the primary orientation of Scripture is on the church and the home, the Bible's teaching on gender roles has application outside those spheres as well. Because man's relation to woman is a creation ordinance, it defines what the ideal is for all of humanity. . . . To the degree that men and women depart from those norms, frustration, disorder, and pain find their way into the human condition. (Burk, 162–63, 168)

When God is at the center, then who you want to be and what you want to do will align with who God designed you to be and what He designed you to do. Because of feminism's massive influence on social norms, Christians have been influenced to accept as normal ever-expanding career pursuits for women. Remember, it's not wrong for women to work (see TE note "The Wrong Question," p. 188). But since the home and society interrelate, some career pursuits in society would undermine a wife's and mother's role in the home. (Single women may be free to pursue these jobs, but they shouldn't normally prioritize a job over God's blessing of marriage.) Discerning this conflict of interests has become more difficult in our anti-normative society that has normalized conflicts of interest between society and the home. Christian girls must beware of being myopic—deciding what to pursue based on what *is* currently acceptable without regard to what *ought* to be acceptable (see TE note "Example of the *Is-Ought* Problem," p. 224). Boys aren't immune from

evaluation either. [Men's role in society will be evaluated in in Chapter 15.]

The Exaltation of Womanhood

Elizabeth George, *A Woman After God's Own Heart* (Eugene, OR: Harvest House, 1997).

Mark Chanski, *Womanly Dominion* (Lincroft, NJ: Calvary Press Publishing, 2008).

Nancy Leigh Demoss, *Becoming God's True Woman* (Wheaton: Crossway, 2002).

The Need for Male Leadership

Dan Doriani, *The Life of a God-Made Man* (Wheaton: Crossway, 2001).

Jim George, *A Man After God's Own Heart* (Eugene, OR: Harvest House, 2002).

Mark Chanski, *Manly Dominion* (Lincroft, NJ: Calvary Press Publishing, 2004).

Richard D. Phillips, *The Masculine Mandate* (Lake Mary, FL: Reformation Trust, 2010).

Women Are Given Dominion Too

Being a wife and a mother (God's highest calling for women) need not be incompatible with taking dominion (or with pursuing higher education). However, priorities must be set, and conflicts must be eliminated. Some vocations may not fit well with the priority of God's high calling (or they may not fit well at certain times in life). But the biblical calling is not for women to be ignorant. Even motherhood is enhanced by higher education. The biblical calling is not for women to be inactive outside the home. A wife and a mother may engage in numerous activities in the community that do not undermine her role as wife and mother. But as soon as a vocation or activity does undermine the role of wife and mother, then that activity should be deemed expendable. The role of wife and mother is not expendable. Each family, in its own sovereign sphere of authority, will have to discern for itself when conflicts of interest exist.

There are two important principles that should lead to wise discernment.

- Being a wife and a mother is not an inferior vocation.
- Being a wife and a mother is itself a full-time vocation when all that it entails is taken seriously. Most people can't take on two full-time vocations at once and be equally successful at both.

Womanly Dominion in Society?

One pastor illustrates the difference between following a clear biblical command

and using biblical discernment by referring to the helmet laws in Nebraska and Iowa. The law in Nebraska is for cyclists to wear helmets, but as soon as you cross into Iowa, there is no helmet law. That doesn't mean that the wisest action would be to take off the helmet. Therefore, he urges wisdom when considering the woman's roles in society. She may decide for more liberty, but she may also thereby risk devastating consequences. [Mark Chanski, *Womanly Dominion* (Lincoft, NJ: Calvary Press, 2008), 207–8]

Should women be political leaders?

The Bible recognizes the able rulership of women (1 Kings 10:1–10). Esther's boldness and discernment guided her husband (Esther 5:1–4; 7:2–6). Deborah's leadership preserved Israel in a dangerous time, but it was necessitated by the failure of male leadership in a time characterized by moral backwardness (Judg. 4:1–5:31). Isaiah 3:12 confirms that a lack of male leadership is anti-normative—a sign of shameful times in a nation.

Since the biblical pattern is for men to lead and since political leadership often requires a wife and mother to set aside her primary vocation, it's not the biblically recommended norm. Nonetheless, female leadership may be a legitimate providence.

Should women be in combat?

God designed men with greater strength to protect women (1 Pet. 3:6–7); the Bible exemplifies this norm (Num. 1:2–3; Deut. 20:1, 8; Josh. 1:14–15; Isa. 19:16; Jer. 51:30). As anti-normative as it may be, God providentially sometimes uses a woman to accomplish His plan (Judg. 4:9, 17–22). Women fight when survival demands it, but it should not be a pursuit or norm.

Furthermore, the recognizable normal physical strength differences between men and women can't be erased. Even with the intense effort to minimize these differences, controversy still abounds in the training of women for combat. The situations that require mixing men and women together in combat also give rise to practical and moral problems. It's imprudent to introduce these situations into military life.

Are there any other roles in society that a godly woman might be reluctant to pursue but may providentially engage in without violating clear biblical commands?

Godly women need to decide which job functions or situations might be more likely to compromise male leadership or moral boundaries. Discerning these applications has grown more difficult because of the normalization of anti-normative relationships in a gender-bending society.

Denny Burk, "Thin Completmentarianism?" dennyburk.com (blog), September 17, 2015.

---

lesbian: *"Their women exchanged natural relations for those that are contrary to nature" (Rom 1:26).*

gay: *"The men likewise gave up natural relations with women and were consumed with passion for one another, men committing shameless acts with men" (Rom 1:27).*

bisexual: *one who is sexually attracted to both men and women*

transgender: *self-identity that blurs gender lines*

transsexual: *a person who feels he or she belongs to the opposite sex*

queer: *homosexual [referring more to political views than sexual desires]*

questioning: *someone who questions traditional norms for gender and sexuality*

intersexual: *physically sexually ambiguous*

asexual: *a person without sexual desires*

pansexual: *someone who has given up all sexual and gender distinctions*

WHEN TO DISCRIMINATE AND WHEN NOT TO

Life is discrimination. You can't be a rational adult unless you choose pie and reject poison and, daily, choose the right path and discriminate against the wrong one. And you can't help discriminating against certain people—we don't hand out driver's licenses to the blind, no matter who cries discrimination.[62]

It would be wrong, of course, to refuse to give a voter registration card to a blind man because of his blindness. That's illegitimate discrimination because blindness is irrelevant to voting in presidential elections. But it is relevant to driving.

Someone's sex is irrelevant to his or her citizenship, to gasoline prices, to membership in an online computer-coding forum. But sex is relevant when it comes to admission into an all-girls school—or a marriage. An all-girls school with a few guys is no longer an all-girls school, and an all-girls relationship is not a marriage.

God made some women more athletic and some more delicate (Deut. 28:56–57). He gave some men artistic and academic gifts, and He gifted some of them to be middle linebackers and firefighters (Exod. 31:1–5). Christianity doesn't force every person into some ideal personality type. But there is a limit to allowable variation: men are men, and women are women. A society that allows people to bend gender past the breaking point will lose out on the unique values each sex provides.

L G B T T Q Q I A P ...

WHAT WE'RE LOSING OUT ON

Years ago, before anyone thought gay marriage was coming to the United States but after homosexuality began to be portrayed widely on television, one of the authors of this book was a camp counselor at a Christian camp. He noticed two seventh-grade girls, both homeschooled, and both very sweet, godly, and feminine (as they are to this day as young adults), who were holding hands as all the campers took a hike down a nature trail. Soon other campers, who were not so sheltered, began to point and snicker. "Lesbians!" they whispered loudly. It was a slander, not true in the least.

But what if it were true? Still, no Christian should be hateful toward homosexuals. All the way down to seventh grade (and below!), Christian students should not bully "queers." In fact, name-calling is where bullying starts. And all the way up to the level

---

DO CHRISTIANS PROMOTE HATE?

Is opposition to homosexuality an act of hatred? Not all homosexuals think so. One gay activist wrote, "Just because someone doesn't support gay rights doesn't automatically make them a hateful bigot. I have immediate family members who . . . believe my sexual orientation is sinful, but I've honestly not once questioned their love for me. I understand that they have deeply held beliefs about morality, which they would argue are born out of love and concern for me, not hatred. I certainly want to challenge their thinking on this, but their unwavering agreement and support for my position is not a prerequisite for our relationship."[63] If you have gay relatives or friends, you should act in such a way that they would be able to write something like this about you. They need to know both that the Bible names their sexual desires as sinful and that you love them.

John Piper, "Should Women Be Police Officers?" Desiring God (website), August 13, 2015

David Talcott, "A Sexual or Asexual Public Square," *First Things* (website), September 17, 2015.

Which Definition?

Look up the word *discriminate* in a good dictionary and you'll find a variety of definitions. One use of the word is to simply make distinctions or to differentiate between things. But of course, some of those differentiations lead to treating people unfairly. Differentiating isn't inherently bad; doing it unfairly is what's bad. So how do you determine when the differentiation is unfair? You have to have an absolute standard of morality to determine justice. D. A. Carson's book, *The Intolerance of Tolerance*, exemplifies how modern secular culture (without an absolute standard of morality) struggles to consistently apply its absolute standard of "no discrimination." Sooner or later secularists discriminate against (in the unfair sense) those who refuse to accept the new morality. Have students search for current events that demonstrate unfair discrimination or that purport to report on unfair discrimination when there is none.

Gender: Defined and Recognized

Gender is something you *are*. God designed and created humans to be male or female—two distinct genders both equally made in God's image (Gen. 1:27). There is no spectrum—God made humans male and female. (If you have a Y chromosome, then you're male. If you have only X chromosomes, then you're female.) Gender is not something you

of church leadership, a truly Christlike pastor will not be nasty toward the transgendered. A godly person's heart will ache for the pain all confused people experience because of the Fall, and for all the hardship they cause themselves and their families.[64]

But Christians are not being bigoted or hateful to insist on distinctions between the sexes. We are trying to preserve something precious in the created order and to help people live in a way that is best for them.

Why does it matter to you if someone else wants to cross-dress? Because people hurt themselves when they violate creational norms. And when people "come out of the closet" and into a new sexual identity, says one writer, they "hustle a lot of good and natural feelings back in."[65] Public gender-bending and homosexuality make close male friendship, especially, very difficult. It's hard to have a Jonathan-and-David or Sherlock-and-Watson friendship when people are snickering at you behind your back.

When the BBC rebooted the Sherlock Holmes stories (yet again) in a series called *Sherlock*, confusion over Sherlock and Watson's sexuality became a running joke. On screen, the two men's close relationship and intense loyalty to one another just felt weird. Gay jokes were brought in to relieve the tension. This didn't happen in the 1930s screenplays of Sherlock Holmes. It didn't have to. Gay jokes didn't occur to anyone. That innocence is one thing society loses when gender lines are crossed.

Society also loses fathers who walk out on their children for gay lovers. Another thing that's lost is the very possibility that children can grow up without the burden and confusion—and possible temptation—of seeing men kiss men and women "marry" women. Society may also lose the very definition of marriage; if gender is only a social construct, there's no good reason to forbid homosexual marriage and no good reason to limit marriage to two people—or even two humans. Homosexual activists call this argument "scaremongering," but when asked what marriage is, they struggle to find an answer that doesn't open the definition so wide that it's meaningless.[66]

THE THREE WAVES OF FEMINISM

Western feminism has come in three widely recognized waves over the past two hundred years. The first wave (1840–1920) was largely a helpful revolution overturning unfair laws that kept women from things like voting, receiving equal pay for the same job, or pursuing the same level of education as men. So the result of the early feminist movement was generally to release women from an unbiblical application of male authority that was dominating them instead of recognizing their shared rule over God's creation.

But feminism did not stop there. In the second wave (1960–1990) feminists continued to fight for the things that they did in the first wave but centered their efforts largely on overturning the biblically legitimate authority of male leadership, which they argued was patriarchal and relegated women to second-class citizenship. This wave resulted in many societal changes—more women in the workforce, the rise of child-care centers, and laws giving women a right to abortion.

The third wave (1990–present) has aggressively attacked creational norms of gender and the whole idea of distinctions between maleness and femaleness.

MURPHY BROWN AND DAN QUAYLE

Popular entertainment both reflects and shapes American values. There is a progression from *I Love Lucy* and other 1950s sitcoms in which even husbands and wives slept in separate beds, through *The Brady Bunch* (1970s) in which two families blended after (apparent[67]) divorce, to *Ellen* (1990s) in which the title character came out as a lesbian, to *Modern Family* (2010s) in which a gay couple adopts a child.

Murphy Brown and Dan Quayle belong in that story. Remember them? Quayle criticized the TV character's decision to bear a child out of wedlock, and Brown (in her TV role) responded with indignation. But what did Quayle actually say?

---

learn or decide for yourself; it's not a social construct foisted on you. The chromosomes don't change regardless of superficially cosmetic, external changes. Furthermore, the body and the soul are united in oneness. They don't contradict. One must presuppose a kind of Gnostic dualism, separating the material from the immaterial, in order to reject the *objective* biological markers of one's gender in favor of *subjective* psychological emotions. But such an approach only reinforces emotional caricatures and fallible cultural paradigms.

For clarification, psychologists and sociologists often distinguish sex, a biological reality, from gender, a socially or culturally constructed reality. Though this distinction is especially now being twisted for sinful purposes, the distinction isn't entirely wrong. God is masculine but not male.

There are cultural expressions of gender that appropriately differ from culture to culture. That is, what distinguishes male and female in dress and behavior can legitimately differ from culture to culture. Nonetheless, *gender* is sometimes used synonymously with *sex*. In the present-day society, the conflation of these two different uses of *gender* is being used to justify claiming that one's gender is not connected to one's sex and that one can attempt to change one's sex or appearance to match a self-chosen gender.

Close Friendships

People need friends—real friends. One of the underlying problems of our culture is a dearth of deeply committed friends. That hole needs to be filled. Many people try to fill the vacuum with eroticism instead of filling it with genuine and pure friendships.

The prevalence of homosexual and lesbian relationships complicates genuine friendship between people of the same sex. Now eroticism is alleged in any manifestation of closeness. But a reactionary response will only leave people lonely, searching for love. It's not enough to combat wrong kinds of same-sex erotic attraction. People need to develop good, godly, deep friendships—with both the same and opposite genders.

What is friendship?

Friendships are formed through mutual love (self-sacrificially seeking the best interest of another). Souls are knitted together in faithful commitment and personal investment—hopefully for the well-being of the other person (Deut. 13:6; 1 Sam. 18:1; Mark 12:31). Such a friendship requires fellowship—sharing the experiences of life, thinking, and goals.

Don't confuse biblical love with same-sex attraction. Having deep affection for someone is not the same as having same-sex attraction (erotic desires for sexual behavior).

Why should godly friendships be valued?

Godly friends encourage you as you bear life's burdens and strengthen you in Christ as you carry out the tasks that He has given to you. No person was designed to do life alone (Prov. 17:17; 27:6, 9, 17; Eccles. 4:9–12; Gal. 6:2).

What principles lead to good friendships?

- *Loving God leads to loving your neighbor (Matt. 22:37–39). Christian friendships aren't for their own sake (for approval, control, prestige, mere pleasure, or other selfish ends) but for building others up in Christ. No friend can replace God (Col. 3:4).*
- *Friendship requires time and sacrifice. Busyness and selfishness kill friendships.*
- *You can't force someone else to be your friend, but you can strive to be a friend to others—especially to the friendless. You can also ask God to provide for your friendship needs.*
- *Choose wisely; you can't join with everyone (Prov. 1:10–19; 22:24)—especially in dangerous times of wickedness (Mic. 7:5–6)—and you should avoid being used by others (Prov. 19:4, 6–7).*

What are some practical steps you can take to develop a friendship?

- *Engage in substantive conversation.*
- *Be an interested, empathetic listener.*
- *Serve God and others together.*
- *Share joyful experiences of life together.*
- *Sharpen one another's thinking.*
- *Spend time; be there for the other person.*
- *Prove trustworthiness through faithfulness.*
- *Cultivate the spiritual disciplines together.*
- *Exercise grace and forgiveness.*
- *Encourage hope in one another.*

[Michael A. G. Haykin and Joel R. Beeke, *How Should We Develop Biblical Friendship* (Grand Rapids: Reformation Heritage Books, 2015)]

How many close friends can you expect to have?

If you're developing friendships as you should, then you'll only find a few individuals who will be your genuine friends at all times (Prov. 17:17; 18:24).

This doesn't mean you lock everyone else out of your little group. Reach out to everyone as acquaintances. Seek to be a friend to people in lowly circumstances who are abandoned by others (Prov. 19:4, 6).

When should you give up a friendship?

Giving up a truly close friendship should only be very cautiously. In general, if you're a true friend, you will love at all times through the good and the bad. If a friend has sinned against you, seek reconciliation (Prov. 17:9). If a friend is in sin, then you must confront (Prov. 27:6) and, in the case of church discipline, may have to withdraw fellowship until restoration can take place (1 Cor. 5:11). But those actions demonstrate true friendship.

Should Christians Bully Sinners?

Sometimes an accusation of bullying is simply a pretext for defending the political correctness of the new morality. However, launching a hateful personal attack, as opposed to disagreeing with sinful behavior, is biblically indefensible (Col. 4:6; 2 Tim. 2:23–26; 1 Pet. 3:15).

Not all homosexuals show hostility toward Christians, but even if some do show hostility, Christians still shouldn't respond in kind (Prov. 26:4). Not only are Christians to love their neighbors as themselves (Matt. 22:39), but they are also to love their enemies (Matt. 5:43–44). In response to personal affronts that God-given authorities can't or won't resolve justly (Rom. 13), Christians are to turn the other cheek (Matt. 5:39–40; Rom. 12:14, 17–21).

Furthermore, if a homosexual were being harassed and called names, then the Christian should take the responsibility to put a stop to it (James 3:9–10). Christians ought to be hospitable to unsaved homosexuals whenever possible (1 Cor. 5:9–10). If substantive efforts to care for homosexuals are shown, then perhaps we may have the opportunity to gently share our understanding of the biblical norms without being personally offensive (Eccles. 10:12).

Christians can't shy away from speaking the truth, but they must seek to do so in love (Eph. 4:15). Characteristics of that love would include fairness, kindness, respect,

and honesty. In general, Christians are to be bold (Prov. 27:5; Acts 4:29, 31; Eph. 6:19–20; 1 Thess. 2:2; 1 Tim. 5:20; Titus 1:9–13) but not defamatory (Prov. 10:12; 12:18; 16:24; 17:27; 29:20; Eccles. 9:17; 2 Tim. 4:2). However, even the most gracious words of truth may cause dissension with those who are hardened against righteousness (Prov. 9:8; 23:9; Eccles. 12:11). In cases like that, both Jesus and Paul confronted with firmness and forthrightness (Matt. 21:13; 23:33; 2 Cor. 7:8–9; 10:1–3; 11:1–33; Gal. 5:12; 2 Tim. 4:14). Christians must use discernment when declaring God's truth to hardened people (Prov. 26:5; Matt. 7:6).

Christians are called on to be gentle *and* bold (and even sometimes harsh). Emphasizing only one side of the biblical tension or the other causes righteousness to fall to the ground.

We cannot be embarrassed out of our belief that two parents, married to each other, are better in most cases for children than one. That honest work is better than handouts—or crime. That we are our brothers' keepers.[68]

Murphy Brown the TV character was offended that Quayle would prescribe what families should look like, but the real-life actress who played her responded somewhat differently. Years later Candice Bergen told the Television Critics Association, "His speech was a perfectly intelligent speech about fathers not being dispensable, and nobody agreed with that more than I did."[69]

THINKING IT THROUGH 14.4

1. What determines the answers to societies' questions about gender roles and responsibilities? What should determine the Christian's answers?

2. What new idea or view about gender is Western society pushing for?

3. What happens to a society that allows people to bend gender away from God's creational norms to the breaking point?

4. What is the goal of the current (third) wave of feminism?

♥5. What does society lose as a result of gender-bending?

THINKING IT THROUGH 14.4

1. whatever society can convince or force people to approve of; a biblical foundation of the created order in which God designed complementary roles and responsibilities for males and females

2. All differences between men and women are merely social constructions. All roles and identities should be interchangeable.

3. chaos and devaluing the unique contributions of each gender

4. to erase the fundamental distinctions between maleness and femaleness

♥5. a clear recognition of marriage as God designed it; close, pure friendships with the same gender without questions being raised or jokes being made; clarity of gender recognition

14 CHAPTER REVIEW

TERMS TO REMEMBER

fornication
adultery
polygamy
LGBT
cohabitation
no-fault divorce

Scripture Memory

Genesis 3:16–17

Making Connections

1. What must govern the definition of marriage and family?

2. Which temptations are Christians immune to? Why?

3. What essential element does cohabitation remove from the union of a man and a woman?

4. How does gender-bending result in a loss of innocence?

Developing Skills in Apologetics and Worldview

5. How can you be as wise as a serpent and as innocent as a dove in expressing your opposition to homosexuality (Matt. 10:16)?

6. Is it illegitimate discrimination for a Christian restaurant owner to refuse to cater a banquet for the Ku Klux Klan (an overtly racist and violent group)? Is it illegitimate discrimination for a boy to refuse to wrestle a girl at a junior-high wrestling meet?

Examining Assumptions and Evidence

7. Why should polygamy be considered a violation of God's scriptural and creational norms for marriage?

8. Why must abuse be reported both to law enforcement and to spiritual leadership?

9. Why should homosexuality be considered a sinful twisting of sex, according to Genesis 1–2?

10. Why did God permit divorce in the Mosaic law?

Becoming a Creative Cultivator

11. Write three to six paragraphs to

(a) describe teen culture,

(b) evaluate any positives or negatives of teen culture, and

(c) propose alternatives to teen culture (e.g., ways teens should strive to be mature, contributing members of their families).

MARRIAGE TWISTED | 219

CHAPTER REVIEW ANSWERS

Making Connections

1. the design of the Creator who made marriage and family

2. none because salvation never removes the fight against the flesh; it only empowers the believer to fight

3. a binding covenant vow of committed faithfulness and purity before witnesses

4. Two people of the same gender used to be able to have close friendships without any questions of impurity being raised.

Developing Skills in Apologetics and Worldview

5. Simply and straightforwardly declare God's truth, and stand for righteousness without hatred. Be willing to be maligned for Christ's sake.

6. Christians shouldn't support, enable, or approve the sinful behavior of the KKK. It would be legitimate to refuse to service such an event. A Christian should discern that mixed-gender wrestling undermines both moral and chivalrous values.

Examining Assumptions and Evidence

7. God's original creation standard was one man and one woman (Matt. 19:4–6). The descriptions of polygamous marriages in the Old Testament usually describe negative examples (Gen. 4:19, 23–24) or include a larger story of difficulty in spite of God's forbearance (Gen. 30:1–24). All biblical instruction about marriage is in the context of one man and one woman (Eph. 5:22–23; 1 Tim. 3:2).

8. Abuse is not only a sin; it is also a crime—both God-given authorities have jurisdiction. The abuser needs to be brought to justice for the sake of the abused and to prevent any further abuse.

9. The way God created the world is the standard by which we judge the way things ought to be. God created sexual unions to produce offspring. This only works in the union of a man and a woman, whose complementary bodies make procreation possible.

10. God allowed divorce because of the hardness of sinful hearts in a fallen world; it's never His ideal for anyone.

Becoming a Creative Cultivator

11. Answers will vary.

TERMS TO REMEMBER

fornication—sexual relations between unmarried partners

adultery—sexual relations between a married person and someone outside the marriage

polygamy—more than one man and one woman within a marriage relationship

LGBT—Lesbian, Gay, Bisexual, Transgendered

cohabitation—couples living together before marriage

no-fault divorce—ending a marriage for nothing more than alleged incompatibility

The student will be able to

15.1 Connect the temporal pattern of a Christian marriage—love and submission—to its ultimate reality and goal: the eternal spiritual marriage of Christ with God's people.

15.2 Explain how the fellowship of the physical family ought to visibly reflect and cultivate God's redemptive work and purpose for His spiritual family.

15.3 Explain how the redemptive teaching of the New Testament elevates the roles of both women and men.

SECTION OBJECTIVES 15.1

1. Distinguish the marriage of a husband and wife from the marriage of Christ to His people.

2. Explain why the wife's respectful submission pictures the church's relationship to Christ.

3. Explain why the husband's sacrificial love pictures Christ's relationship to the church.

4. Plan how to prepare for a marriage that will properly picture Christ and the church.

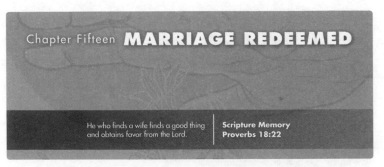

Chapter Fifteen **MARRIAGE REDEEMED**

He who finds a wife finds a good thing and obtains favor from the Lord.

Scripture Memory
Proverbs 18:22

15.1 REDEEMING MARRIAGE

There's something about romantic love that leads two people swept up by it to promise to love each other forever.

Forever? Like, for eternity? Who could possibly be certain about being able to keep such a promise? Eternity is a long time. A lot of things could happen between now and forever, and they probably will.

The traditional English wedding vows are a bit more realistic, asking partners to promise love only "as long as you both shall live." Those vows are also more biblical because not only does the Bible give widows and widowers the right to remarry, but Jesus actually taught that marriages don't continue beyond the grave. "When [believers] rise from the dead, they neither marry nor are given in marriage, but are like angels in heaven" (Mark 12:25).

WE'LL BE LIKE ANGELS?

Christ's comment that believers will be "like angels in heaven" (Mark 12:25) seems to be one of the reasons people tend to envision eternity as full of winged people sitting on clouds strumming harps. The fact is, we know very little about what the angels do. The Bible doesn't have a lot to say about them. We know that humans are of an order higher than angels; we will "judge angels," Paul says (1 Cor. 6:3). And as you learned in Unit 4, we do know that humans in the new earth will have plenty of enjoyable and enriching work. We also know that eternity is not a long enough time to ever explore all the depths of an infinite God.

If you're tracking with the CFR argument of this textbook, this ought to raise a big question in your mind. If Christ's work of redemption restores the world to the way God created it to be, where in the world is marriage? Marriage was certainly there at creation. Why does it go away when we get to eternity?

The human race will be complete in the new earth, of course; the globe will be fully populated with the offspring of Adam and Eve. Human marriage won't be needed for procreation anymore.

But actually, the testimony of the Bible is that marriage will not, in fact, cease to exist. It will be fulfilled—in another marriage, the one between Christ and His people.

In the new earth, marriage will be redeemed. Revelation 19 speaks of "the marriage supper of the Lamb." The climax of the complete restoration of all things on the new earth is the coming of Christ to receive His bride. This bride includes all those who have put their faith in Him and have been cleansed from their sins by His death in their place (Rev. 19:7–8). Christ will openly and visibly unite in full fellowship with everyone He has made righteous—both Jews like Abraham and Gentiles like Augustine—and they will know indescribable joy with Him forever.

In short, we could say that there will be no more marriages on the new earth because the ultimate marriage between Christ and His bride will have already taken place.

220 | GENDER

Lesson Plan Chart—Chapter 15

Section Title	Pages	Activity Manual	Days
15.1 Redeeming Marriage	220–24	Activity 27	1 day
15.2 Redeeming Family	224–29		2 days
15.3 Redeeming Gender Roles	229–34		2 days
Review	235		1 day
Total Suggested Days			**6 days**

Turning Marriage into Idolatry

What are the results when marriage becomes an idol?

• *widespread singleness*

While secular society has so sexualized friendships that it has damaged marriage, some Christians have overreacted by cutting off all guy/girl friendships in an attempt to preserve purity. Instead, young people should engage in the hard work and practice of forming good, godly friendships with the opposite sex. A variety of good friendships will provide the options for building a good marriage relationship in the future. But when marriage is idolized, some parents set impossibly high standards for any potential spouse their son or daughter might consider.

THE GOAL OF CHRISTIAN MARRIAGE

It's this ultimate marriage of Christ and His bride in the book of Revelation that helps us make sense of the most important New Testament passage on marriage and family—Ephesians 5:22–6:4. Only by seeing marriage as part of the grand story of Creation, Fall, and Redemption can you understand your own future marriage, if the Lord gives you one. Marriage and family play key roles in God's plan to redeem the earth.

But to understand Paul's words to husbands and wives in Ephesians, you have to understand what Paul meant earlier in his letter where he says that, through the death of Christ, God has united two of the most incompatible people groups in human history—Jews and Gentiles—bringing them together into fellowship and actually "creating" one new family (Eph. 2:11–22).

Jews and Gentiles in Paul's day were not one. They were deeply divided. Jews in the New Testament era didn't even eat with Gentiles (Gal. 2:11–14).

But God used the death and resurrection of Christ to bring the human family back together again into fellowship, both with one another and with Himself—as if an old-time family feud between two sets of outlaws miraculously ended in peace with each other and with the government. Paul says that the purpose of this newly united family of believers is to grow in unity with one another as they grow in Christ (Eph. 4:1–16).

It's after all this important theological background information that Paul mentions the topic of marriage to the Ephesian believers. Even the unnoticed marriages of ordinary people living in that city in ancient Turkey were sending messages, Paul said, about the unity God plans to bring to the earth. Every marriage, then and now, is supposed to be a picture of intimate fellowship and union with Christ.

The Redeemed, Submissive Wife

Paul ties his instruction to wives—"Wives, submit to your own husbands"—directly to the great reality marriage is portraying. Submit, Paul says, because "the husband is the head of the wife even as Christ is the head of the church, his body, and is himself its Savior" (Eph. 5:22–23). Just as the church submits to Christ, wives are supposed to submit to their own husbands.

Wives are commanded to submit to their husbands (not to all men) in several other places in the New Testament (Col. 3:18; 1 Pet. 3:1; Titus 2:5). But those husbands are themselves commanded to submit to God (1 Cor. 11:3) and, to a lesser degree, to church leadership (1 Pet. 5:5) and even to other Christians, including their wives (Eph. 5:21). These other authorities and influences should help make sure that a wife's submission is given to a man worthy of such a gift. The Bible doesn't tell women (or men) to stick around if they are being beaten or otherwise abused.

Paul's summary word to wives at the end of his discussion about marriage in Ephesians is not about submission, per se, but about respect: "Let the wife see that she respects her husband" (Eph. 5:33). Many wives are afraid to submit to their husbands because they do not trust them, but there is redemptive power in a wife's respect and honor toward her husband. Husbands get better at husbanding when they sense their wives respect them. When a woman waits for her husband to get his act together before she'll give him respect, she loses an opportunity to bring healing to their marriage as a whole. A gracious, submissive wife can even be God's means of winning an unconverted husband to Christ:

Marriage idolatry is also revealed in the way that singles are often treated. They feel ignored and shunned when they don't fit in anywhere in the life of the church or in the friendships of others their own age who have families. They feel disparaged when they're badgered about marriage (with little understanding of their circumstances or past experiences). Often they're treated as immature simply because they're not married.

• *unrealistic expectations*

If young people do get married, they soon find out that idealistic dream marriages never happen. Spouses aren't saviors, and they're not perfect. Life will be full of trials and disappointments. The unbiblical reasons for rejecting a potential friend (potential spouse) will be tested in marriage. Beauty will fade, and strength will fail. Are you willing to care for an invalid for thirty years? Are you ready to lose your spouse to cancer—five years into marriage? It's not a matter of *if* but *when* these kinds of trials will come.

• *desire for human marriage to be forever*

Those who lose spouses may remarry (1 Cor. 7:8–9; 1 Tim. 5:14). But in heaven humans will be like angels in this one way— they won't have marriages with other beings like themselves (Matt. 22:30). If this is a disappointment, then it's because the picture has been idolized over the reality.

• *confusion in regard to eternal marriage*

The idolatry of marriage can really be the idolatry of sex. The idea of being married to God sounds strange. But sex is not synonymous with marriage itself; it's only one part of *human* marriage. Marriage is the joining together of two parties in intimacy. Intimacy is the closeness of the *persons*. Sex is only one *means* to the deepest kind of *human* intimacy. But not all intimacy is sexual in nature. Marriage with God is the deep intimacy of believers with God.

Appreciating the Ultimate Reality

Only after the idolatrous worship of the temporal picture is dealt with can a person fully appreciate the ultimate reality of God's grand story. God created humans to fellowship with Him (Gen. 1:27, cf. Ezek. 16:1–14). That fellowship was broken in the Fall (Gen. 3:8–10, cf. Ezek. 16:15–59). But God's full and final redemption restores that fellowship through the marriage of God's people to the Lamb (Rev. 19:7–9, cf. Ezek. 16:60–63). The intimacy of personal fellowship that God had originally intended as the foundational purpose for human creation will be accomplished through that marriage. Nothing can be more ultimate than the fulfillment of humankind's fundamental created purpose: perfect fellowship with God.

Picturing Ultimate Reality as a Wife

Respect is the pathway to submission just as the fear of God is the pathway to obedience.

What is the basis of a wife's respect?

A wife's respectful submission pictures the church's relationship to Christ (Eph. 5:21–24, 32–33). But every husband will fall short of Christ's perfection; he will never be able to merit respect. Therefore, the basis of a wife's respect must be the husband's God-given position (1 Cor. 11:3). Of course, a husband's criminal activity or sinful demands invalidate his appeal to his position of authority. But exceptions can't redefine God's fundamental pattern.

How is respect manifested in submission?

A wife will be careful not to be condescending and contentious (Prov. 14:1; 21:19), impatient and selfish (1 Cor. 13:4–5), or inattentive and indifferent to her husband's wishes (James 1:19; Prov. 31:11). Instead, she will seek to be supportive and uplifting (Prov. 31:12, 23).

Blame Shifting

It's never right for a husband to claim that the reason he's a bad husband (unloving and not sacrificial) is that his wife is a bad wife (unsubmissive and disrespectful). As long as two people both stubbornly demand that the other person change first before they take responsibility for their own attitudes and actions, their opportunity for healing their marriage is blocked. The biblical instruction for a wife is to do her part to remove any of her husband's excuses by modeling excellence (1 Pet. 3:1–6). Even an unspiritual—but good—husband will notice and be inclined to live in a more understanding way (1 Pet. 3:7). But responding by backbiting only continues a cycle of viciousness. If the goal is healing, the response toward an offender can never be to up the ante by offending him out of revenge (Rom. 12:21).

 Character Qualities

Invite a pastor's wife to speak to the girls about developing the character qualities of a godly woman. The focus should be on application. Invite the pastor to speak to the boys about identifying the character qualities of a godly woman. The focus should be on forming the right kind of friendships.

Clothing Communicates a Great Deal About Character

In 1 Timothy 2:9–10, the idea of *adorning* with clothing means to put it in order. People are responsible for how they present themselves to others. Putting one's clothing in order implies that the presentation would not be disheveled or unattractive. Orderly attractiveness is marked by respectability or appropriateness.

Paul gives two principles to develop what respectability entails. First, a person must be modest. That is, people should present themselves to be decent, avoiding anything that ought to cause them to be ashamed. Second, a person must be self-controlled or discreet. That is, people must use good judgment and avoid extremes. (Rebellion has often been marked by making statements through deportment and clothing.) In Paul's context, the obvious examples of seductive dress and excessive ornamentation included elaborate hairstyles, piled-on pearls or gold, and manifestly costly attire. In contrast to drawing attention to externals, Christian women should showcase their good works.

 Picturing Ultimate Reality as a Husband

A husband's faithfulness requires his sacrifice to prove his love (Prov. 20:6). Sacrifice is the pathway to love.

What is the basis of a husband's sacrifice?

A husband's sacrificial love pictures Christ's relationship to the church (Eph. 5:25–33). But just as every believer falls short of being worthy of Christ's sacrifice, every wife will fall short of meriting the worthiness of her husband's sacrifice. Therefore, the basis of a husband's sacrifice must be grounded in his own unconditional choice to establish this special relationship (Deut. 7:6–9). Even if she is unfaithful, a husband who mirrors Christ will pursue his wife to win back her faithfulness (Hos. 3:1–5). This is the extent of his sacrifice.

Why should sacrifice lead to love?

Sacrifice is necessary to prove love, but it is not sufficient. You can't have love without sacrifice, but you could have sacrifice without love. Sacrifice should lead to love, but if the sacrifice falls short of love, then it turns out to be futile (1 Cor. 13:3). A husband must realize that he has to do more than simply provide things for his wife. He must be a certain kind of relational being toward his wife.

First Corinthians 13:4–8 (cf. Col. 3:19; 1 Pet. 3:7) describes such a relational being. "Love is patient and kind; love does not envy or boast; it is not arrogant or rude. It does not insist on its own way; it is not irritable or resentful; it does not rejoice at wrongdoing, but rejoices with the truth. Love bears all things, believes all things, hopes all things, endures all things. Love never ends."

 Learning to be Understanding

In the future, boys will need to be understanding husbands. That characteristic won't come naturally or automatically; young men need to learn how to treat young women with respect and sensitivity now. Graceless coarseness is unacceptable. Young men are to treat girls as *sisters* in Christ—with purity and protection (1 Tim. 5:2; Song of Sol. 8:8–9). A godly girl will be honored by courteous manners. These manners don't put girls down as unequals; they lift them up on a pedestal of esteem and honor.

A young man should become knowledgable about what is annoying and uncouth in the eyes of most young women and avoid annoying them. Forming friendships with girls involves both observation and commu-

---

NO JEWELRY? NO BRAIDS?

Newsweek magazine often publishes provocative attacks on Christian doctrine around Christmas and Easter. The job recently fell to journalist Kurt Eichenwald, who made this charge against the Bible (among many, many others): "[First] Timothy is one of the most virulently anti-woman books of the New Testament, something else that sets it apart from other letters by Paul. . . . It says women must dress modestly, can't embroider their hair, [and] can't wear pearls or gold."[1]

Eichenwald is one for four in those claims. Yes, Paul said women must dress modestly (1 Tim. 2:9). But careful readers will note that he didn't say women can't braid their hair or wear jewelry (and Paul isn't "anti-woman"). Paul said that women's real "adorning"—the things that display their personal glory to others—must not be merely external (see also 1 Pet. 3:3). "Modesty and self-control" (or "decency and propriety," as another translation puts it) ought to be a woman's true and ultimate adorning. Women with no earrings who have never cut their hair can nonetheless lack modesty and self-control. And women with jewelry and a contemporary hairstyle can have those godly qualities. Externals do matter, but the heart matters more. The outside reflects what's on the inside.

Wives, be subject to your own husbands, so that even if some do not obey the word, they may be won without a word by the conduct of their wives, when they see your respectful and pure conduct. (1 Pet. 3:1–2)

Respectful, pure, gentle, quiet—these traditionally feminine qualities seem quaint to many in the twenty-first century. Women today are more apt to be told, "Let it go," "Be yourself," and "Follow your heart." Biblically informed femininity is still countercultural in much of the world. It means developing those graces and character traits needed in a submissive partner, companion, child-bearer, and homemaker. Girls should grow into women of grace and dignity, kindness and inner beauty, having compassion and tenderness, modesty and strength of conviction, and a strong sense of their own purpose as first surrendered to God and later, if God so leads, to a husband.

The Redeemed, Loving Husband

The main responsibilities of wives are to submit to and respect their husbands, but the main thing God repeatedly tells husbands to do is to love their wives (Eph. 5:25, 28, 33; Col. 3:19). And the standard for "how much" a husband is to love his wife is set immeasurably high: "as Christ loved the church and gave himself up for her" (Eph. 5:25). Jesus didn't have an escape plan. He gave His bride the last full measure of devotion.

The New Testament elsewhere fleshes out what manly love for one's wife looks like. Colossians 3:19 likewise tells husbands not to be "harsh" with their wives. And 1 Peter 3:7 instructs husbands, "Live with your wives in an understanding way, showing honor to the woman as the weaker vessel." A wife with a biblical worldview isn't offended by this verse, and a husband with such a worldview doesn't expect his wife to be one of the guys. He treats her with the loving care a "weaker vessel" requires. A loving husband pays attention to his wife's emotions, her stamina, and even her preference that all the doors be locked at night.

Biblical masculinity is simply the collection of attitudes and character traits that one would expect to see developing in a male, if indeed his role is to serve as loving leader, spiritual nurturer, protector, and provider. When he reaches manhood, he's going to be called on to shoulder the ultimate responsibility for family finances, for discipline of children, and possibly for spider assassination. So boys should grow into

---

men who are strong, courageous, hard-working, able to take responsibility, able to lead, able to defend others, yet kind and gentle toward those they are called to protect. And to whatever extent a young boy does not manifest these qualities or value them, he must be nurtured and challenged in this direction. This is God's calling for him as a man.

A truly loving husband takes an unconditional delight in his wife and makes her feel safe. He's patient with multiple outfit changes on Sunday morning while the clock ticks. He does household chores without being asked. He has a flower budget. If a husband thinks, "I'll show her affection when she's worthy of it," he's got the cart before the horse. A woman will become worthy of affection when her husband showers her with it. Doing what you are supposed to do has a redemptive effect on your spouse. If you insist on waiting for your spouse to start the process of redemption, you may be waiting for a long time—maybe "until death do [you] part."

> ## "I HAVE YET TO MEET A WIFE WHO DIDN'T WANT TO FOLLOW A HUSBAND WHO WAS SACRIFICIALLY LOVING AND SERVING HER."[2]
>
> —DAVID PLATT

Love doesn't mean treating a wife as incapable or even protecting her completely from all harm (as if any human could do that). Christ in the New Testament led His church, His bride, into deep waters. Christians under Christ's care had their goods stolen and were mocked, reviled, and imprisoned (Heb. 10:34; 1 Pet. 3:9). But Christ asked them to do only those things that He Himself was willing to do. And all that they did was to their own honor and joy: they were carrying out the work of redemption on earth and felt privileged to play a part, even if it involved suffering. When the apostles were arrested and beaten, they "rejoic[ed] that they were counted worthy to suffer dishonor for the name" (Acts 5:41).

A loving husband will need to lead his wife through difficult times—every couple faces trials, especially if they have children. Read about pioneer men and women of the American West, such as Ma and Pa in *Little House on the Prairie*. These people were tough, and they went through terribly frightening and difficult times. And yet there is an irrepressible joy in the stories Laura Ingalls Wilder tells—these pioneers felt privileged to play a part in the expansion of the American frontier. In addition, Ma was a *woman* and one who saw it as her duty to bring up her little prairie girls with feminine civility. Pa was a *man* and one who treated his wife with tender care. He relied on her heavily for simple survival, but there were certain jobs he never asked her to do.

The Redeemed Marriage

The best way to redeem your own marriage is to learn to follow God's ways long before you reach the altar. But Christ is such a powerful Redeemer that He can restore failed or failing marriages. And He can restore immoral people to sexual purity. Slavery to sexual sin is one of the more common chains people

LOVE

SACRIFICIALLY

HUSBAND ← HONOR → **WIFE**

RESPECTFULLY

SUBMIT

have a clear conscience and when they follow after the sole rule of Christ's law. They can be bold because they can embrace suffering and persecution, trusting in God's providence over all of life's circumstances.

> There has got abroad a notion . . . that if you become a Christian, you must sink your manliness and turn milksop. . . . You are to take out your backbone and become [soft]; you are to be sweet as honey toward everybody, and every atom of spirit is to be evaporated from you. . . . [But, when] the heart knows itself to be set upon integrity and established in the right, the Christian man is not afraid to go anywhere. . . . When we become the servants of Christ, we cease to be the servants of men. When Christ's yoke is upon you, then are you free to do the right, whoever may forbid.

[C. H. Spurgeon, *A Good Start: A Book for Young Men and Women* (Morgan, PA: Soli Deo Gloria Publications, 1995), 16–18]

Leadership

Al Mohler outlines twenty-five principles of leadership in his book *The Conviction to Lead* (Bloomington, MN: Bethany House, 2012). He argues that true leadership begins with the right purpose (before a plan can be established). The plan of action is driven by beliefs. Those convictions, set in the context of a larger worldview story, drive the passion to communicate intelligently to people willing to follow somebody with integrity and competence. All the other characteristics and functions of leadership are based on that foundation.

The Other Ditch: Authoritarianism

Authoritarianism twists the biblical teaching. But it takes biblical wisdom to discern what qualifies as an unbiblical application of male authority and protection. Physical, verbal, or sexual abuse is never justified. In addition, restrictions that prevent a wife from having normal social interaction with other people aren't biblically defensible. A good husband trusts a good wife.

 Offering the Hope of Redemption

The biblical view (with its creational norms and high ethical standards for marriage and family) doesn't leave people in their fallen state and sinful mess. It doesn't leave people to be irreparably damaged. Yes, a person's own sinful choices bring consequences that are sometimes lifelong, but the gospel doesn't leave people to face those

---

nication—asking informational questions to better relate to them. A young man should become knowledgable about what kinds of attitudes, words, and actions are hurtful. And then he must respond by being careful to be gentle. Harshness is unacceptable. In 1 Peter 3:7, Peter isn't saying that women are weak; he's saying that men are responsible to treat women with carefulness the way someone would treat something that is delicate (e.g., a beautiful flower). Something that is delicate is of high value (e.g., a vase).

Put the girls into one group and the boys into another. Have the girls list all the things that they think boys should do to treat them with understanding. Have the boys list all the things they think they do to treat the girls with understanding. Bring them back together to compare their lists and to evaluate the reality of how they treat each other.

What can change and how can they model relationships for younger students?

 The Need for Bold Leadership

Immaturity is the bane of today's society. The result is a lack of male leadership and the destruction of marriages and families. [See "Missing Men" note on page 232.] Boys need to be challenged to be real men by being bold leaders. This doesn't mean that guys must be extremely macho and aggressive. Brashness is superficial and contrary to gentle understanding. But it does mean that men need to be steadfastly courageous and responsible.

Boldness

Spurgeon encourages young men to be bold because they are ultimately responsible to God alone. They can be bold when they

consequences in hopelessness. The gospel brings healing. It can provide restoration.

But gospel grace is not cheap. The key to restoration is repentance. Restoration flounders when offenders refuse to try to make things right and refuse to endeavor to renew trust and love. A good marriage is one in which both the husband and wife have learned how to humbly and truly repent. Husbands and wives will always struggle with offending and being offended by each other's attitudes and actions. But their marriage will still flourish if they can learn to demonstrate change in their attitudes and actions toward each other after an offense.

It's only by walking in step with the Spirit through the Word in God's powerful grace that a believer will have both the desire and the ability to change (Phil. 2:13).

Have students write a letter to a hypothetical future friend who has either failed terribly (watched porn, committed adultery or fornication, initiated an unbiblical divorce, etc.) or is on the receiving end of a spouse's sin. Students should consider these questions: *How would I minister the grace of the gospel to my friend? What would I say?* They need to write a letter that is full of grace but also full of an uncompromised gospel that encourages genuine repentance and forgiveness. They need to make sure that their counsel is rooted in scriptural advice and not in their own wisdom or trite worldly thinking.

THINKING IT THROUGH 15.1

1. Widows and widowers are allowed to remarry another person; there is no human marriage in eternity.

2. One of the main purposes of human marriage (procreation) will be fulfilled when the dead in Christ are restored to fill the earth, making further procreation (and human marriage) unnecessary. The only kind of marriage will be the one that human marriage was meant to picture: Christ will take the people of God for His bride.

3. respect

4. As the head, a husband lovingly and sacrificially honors his wife and serves his children. This means that he takes the ultimate responsibility for caring for her and the children.

♀5. Every marital problem can be traced back to either a husband who is not loving his wife sacrificially or a wife who is not submitting respectfully to her husband (or both); the core of a successful marriage is to follow the pattern of Christ and the church.

---

are bound by. Christ can free them. Divorce, adultery, pornography, and guilt from all three—Christ died to destroy them.

In a book such as this we cannot address in detail all the issues that arise in a marriage relationship. But at the core of every marital problem is either a husband who is not loving his wife sacrificially, as Christ loved the church, or a wife who is not submitting respectfully to her husband, as the church is to submit to Christ. Often we find both. A harsh, unloving husband makes it difficult and even grueling for his wife to follow his leadership. Or a wife distrusts her husband or tries to take the authority in the marriage, making it strenuous for a husband to lead. When these root sins go unchecked, they lead to the symptoms others can see: neglect or despondency, loneliness, verbal or physical abuse, hunger for gratification outside of the marriage, and ultimately divorce.

The biblical solution to marital sins is the same as it is for all other sins: repentance and faith. A man must turn from his sin, confess it to his spouse, and seek cleansing and change from the Lord in faith. A woman must do the same. The changes a man undertakes must prompt him to love and lead his wife. The changes a woman makes must lead her to respect and submit to her husband. This may sound overly simplistic. And there is certainly more than this to learn and to do, but never less. The husband's love and the wife's submission are at the core of the New Testament teaching on marriage. These are the roles that make the marriage a reflection of the unity of Christ and His church, and therefore they represent the pathway of redemption apart from which no marriage can be restored.

THINKING IT THROUGH 15.1

1. Why is it more biblical for couples to vow to love each other as long as they both shall live rather than vowing to love each other for eternity?

2. How will marriage be fulfilled in the new earth?

3. What necessary character quality makes a wife's submission to her husband possible?

4. Why should the husband shoulder the ultimate responsibility for the family?

♀5. What is at the core of every marital problem? Explain why.

15.2 REDEEMING FAMILY

The *New York Times* asked teenagers to comment on a scientific study surveying attitudes about the family. "Joey" said that he thought the "normal family" doesn't exist since everybody does something different. In our culture no one can precisely define *family* anymore because people just take life as it comes. "There isn't anything wrong with that though," he said. "A lot of the times different is better."[4]

"Walker" agreed that the definition of *family* is hard to pin down, but he thinks the problem is that families don't spend much time together. Both parents (if they haven't

---

SECTION OBJECTIVES 15.2

1. Trace the spiritual family of God through biblical history.

2. Explain how children, by carrying out their responsibility of obedience, can better enable their parents to nurture them according to God's redemptive work and purpose.

3. Summarize the positive and negative responsibilities of parents that will better enable children to receive their parent's nurturing according to God's redemptive work and purpose.

Example of the *Is-Ought* Problem

[Students will learn about the naturalistic fallacy on page 312.] The *is-ought* problem arises because the basis for morality in an evolutionary worldview (with no transcendent authority) can only be determined by observing what *is*; science can only describe. Morality can't be determined by what *ought* to be unless a transcendent, outside authority reveals the moral standard. In the biblical worldview, only revelation can prescribe.

The teenagers (in the *New York Times* article) who are finding it difficult to define the family have unknowingly presupposed a descriptive approach to defining it. It used to be easy to define the family that way because the traditional family was clearly the majority and the normative approach. But as the characteristics of society changed, the descriptive definition became so muddled by various practices that people can no longer come up with a definition unless it is expansive enough to describe everything (which in the end describes nothing). Although

split up) have jobs, and the kids are stuck at home alone or in daycare. Mealtime is no longer an occasion for togetherness. He concluded that *family* means "both parents and their children coming together and being with each other."[5]

Which vision of the family do you want, Joey's or Walker's? And more importantly, which vision is most similar to the one we see through biblical lenses? Do you want everybody (including your own future spouse) defining "family" the way that suits him or her, or do you want "both parents and their children coming together and being with each other"? Christ, through His redemptive power, offers you the latter vision.

FAMILY VALUE

Family is a good thing, something of great value. But it is not an ultimate thing. It is a means to an end. That end, that purpose, is that the glory and knowledge of the Creator would spread throughout the world. Families are the temporary means by which God is bringing about that larger purpose. Families are God's way of filling the earth with those who are in full fellowship with Him and with one another.

So when we order our marriages and order our families according to the principles God has set forth in Scripture, we are not obeying random, made-up rules. We are participating in redeeming something God has made for His glory, and we're doing it by fulfilling His original plan.

Since the Fall, God has been always about the business of bringing His true family back into fellowship with Him. There has always been a true **family of God** throughout history, comprised of all those who know God through faith. And ever since the first members of that family (Adam and Eve) were put out of the garden, God has been about the business of restoring that family to a place of peace with Him and with each other. The final meeting place of that restored fellowship is the new earth.

Adam and Eve's first two sons were Abel, who "did well," and Cain, who did not "do well" (see Gen. 4:4–7). And so it has always been ever since Eve picked fruit from the forbidden tree. Cain's family, Genesis shows, proved wicked (Gen. 4:23). His brother Seth's family, by contrast, was marked by people calling on the name of the Lord (Gen. 4:26).

By the time we reach Genesis 5, there are already two distinct people groups living on the earth: those who have rejected God and those who cling to God— the members of God's true family. God saves this true family by sparing Noah and his lineage in the Flood. After that, the Bible records a remarkable history

What results when the family becomes an idol?

• *undermining the local church*

The sphere of the family is important. But so is the sphere of the local church. Neither sphere should degrade the other. Pulling out of the life of the body of the local church (or even entirely replacing the local church with family worship) is contrary to the biblical instruction regarding church fellowship. If a family can no longer in good conscience participate in a particular local church, they don't have the option of completely abandoning gathering with other believers. They must find a local church in their community that they can participate in, move to another community, or start a church plant.

• *undermining marriage*

The relationship of a father to his daughter is special. He is supposed to protect her from the wrong kinds of boys. But God designed girls to grow up into women who leave their fathers to be joined to a husband. That husband becomes the new head of the family. Daughters can't idolize their fathers or mothers to the point that they undermine their own husband's headship. A daughter who talks to her parents for hours about every minute detail by calling them five times a day every day in college or after she's married probably has a problem with letting go of her parents. This issue also applies to sons and their mothers. (No wife wants to be married to a mama's boy.)

What are some other ways that people demonstrate that they have turned their families into an idol?

pride, perfectionism, hypocritical emphasis on external appearances or reputation, and so on

The Family of God and God's Larger Purpose

There is one family of God, but there are distinct expressions of that one family, and these must not be confused with one another. Israel and the church remain distinct entities with differing characteristics, roles, and responsibilities in the unfolding of God's plan of redemption. But the family of God encompasses those distinct entities as well as the God-fearing people in the era before the nation of Israel was ever established.

God's larger purpose for His people is for them to fill the earth. In order for God to fill the earth with His people, He must accomplish His plan of redemption. This plan is traced through the families of the earth from Adam to Seth to Noah and from Abraham to Isaac to Jacob until the promised Messiah, Jesus, is born. It is through Christ that the family of God supercedes the physical

---

the teens were not confident about a definition, they were confident that whatever was practiced shouldn't be considered wrong. Again, this is because they presupposed that the standard of morality is descriptive. The standard is whatever society embraces. Their evolutionary education affected their logical reasoning in other disciplines (in this case, sociology).

Christians shouldn't have any difficulty in defining the family. God designed it. A father and a mother produce children to form the most basic family unit (expanded to include grandparents, aunts, uncles, cousins, etc.). Christians shouldn't have any difficulty determining right and wrong approaches.

Qualities of a Good Family

By God's common grace Walker recognized some of the characteristics that make a good family. But can students identify the underlying biblical principles that give rise to the practical applications of togetherness?

How did God design parents to interact with their children?

• provide caring love (Prov. 4:3; 1 Thess. 2:7)
• provide stability (especially the mother) by being in the home for the children (Prov. 31:28; 1 Tim. 5:10, 14 ; Titus 2:5)
• provide counsel and instruction (Prov. 1:8; Eph. 6:4; 1 Thess. 2:11-12)
• provide discipline and correction (Prov. 13:24; Heb. 12:6–11)

In other words, fathers and mothers are not to be distant. They are to be there to direct and to care for their children.

descent of Israel (Gal. 3:26–29). And He's not ashamed to call us brethren (Heb. 2:11).

God's Special Relationship with His People

The depth of God's unconditional love for His chosen, but wayward, children is one of the most astounding realities at the core of the biblical story as it unfolds. It is this reality that should affect the reality of a believer's own familial bond.

"Our own love stories are really echoes of the far greater story of God's love for the world. That is why it's especially important for us to get our biblical theology of love right." [Michael Lawrence, *Biblical Theology in the Life of the Church* (Wheaton: Crossway, 2010), 141]

Divide students into small groups, and assign one of the following bullet points to each group.

- Adam and Eve and the serpent
- Abel or Seth and Cain
- Noah and those outside the ark
- Shem and Ham
- Abraham/Sarah and the Canaanites
- Isaac and Ishmael
- Jacob and Esau
- David and Saul
- Abigail and Nabal
- Esther and Haman
- The tax collector and the Pharisee
- The good Samaritan and religious leaders
- Judas and the rest of the Twelve
- Saul/Paul and King Agrippa
- The church and the world

(1) What are some ways God showed His love to His wayward people? (2) How does God's love differ in regard to His own covenant people and those outside the covenant? (3) What drives God's love?

Each group should identify a Scripture passage and answer the three questions listed above in order to explain how their passage exemplifies the pattern of God's love.

Michael Lawrence's answers to the three questions can be summarized as follows (Lawrence, 14–152).

(1) In answer to how God loves, the specific details in each passage will reflect that God shows His love in ways that providentially provide for the well-being of His covenant people—and sometimes for those outside of His covenant (Matt. 5:45–48). God also shows His love in ways that are sacrificial; God's love is free but it's not cheap (John 3:16). Sin costs and must be paid. God's perfect love also perfects His people (1 John 3:1–3).

---

of how God continued to preserve His family, particularly through Abraham and his descendants, the nation of Israel. God even referred to the nation of Israel as His family, often calling them His sons and daughters (e.g., Exod. 4:22; Isa. 43:6; Jer. 31:9; Hos. 1:10; 11:1).

But not all Israel was true Israel (Rom. 9:6–7). Being born as Abraham's seed didn't make you a member of God's true family. And on the flip side, God never intended for Israel to be His whole family. He made them, instead, a "light" to all the nations, calling all people to come back into fellowship with God and His family. One of God's first promises to Abraham was, "In you all the families of the earth shall be blessed" (Gen. 12:3).

Hidden in that last sentence is Jesus Himself. He was the Seed of Abraham, who blessed all the families of the earth by offering a way back to God. And Jesus made the "family of God" concept clear. One day, as he was teaching in a house, someone told Him, "Your mother and your brothers are outside, seeking you." Jesus paused and asked, "Who are my mother and my brothers?" Then, looking around the room at those who were listening, He said, "Here are my mother and my brothers! For whoever does the will of God, he is my brother and sister and mother" (Mark 3:31–35).

The church—which Jesus Christ brought about through His death and resurrection—is a visible expression of this same family. The church is "the household of God" (1 Tim. 3:15), and Christians are spiritual "brothers" and "sisters" to one another (cf. 1 Cor. 4:14–15; 1 Thess. 2:7, 11; 1 Tim. 5:1–2). The church is full of people who enjoy oneness with God because they have embraced God's Son, Jesus. The church is a "foretaste of glory divine," a big sign pointing to the day when the whole world will be reconciled to God.

I do not write these things to make you ashamed, but to admonish you as my beloved children. For though you have countless guides in Christ, you do not have many fathers. For I became your father in Christ Jesus through the gospel. (1 Cor. 4:14–15)

But we were gentle among you, like a nursing mother taking care of her own children. For you know how, like a father with his children, we exhorted each one of you. (1 Thess. 2:7, 11–12)

---

(2) In answer to who God loves, His love is offered and provided for everyone (2 Pet. 3:9; 1 John 2:2), even while they are still sinners (Rom. 5:8). But God also chooses to especially love His own special people by establishing a covenant relationship with them (John 6:44; 15:16; Rom. 9:18; Eph. 1:4–5). God's eternal love for His Son overflows in His provision of love for His people (John 17:24) so that they can also become God's children (Rom. 8:16).

(3) In answer to why God loves, we must understand that His love is based on His own character not on our loveliness or merits (Deut. 7:6–8; Eph. 2:4–10). He loves us because it brings praise to the glory of His Son (Eph. 1:6, 12, 14).

How should this undergirding theology of love be applied to the love of a Christian family?

The love of fathers, mothers, and children should reflect God's love. Although Christians are to love everyone, a husband and wife choose to especially love each other because of the covenant relationship established between them. Parents and children should love each other sacrificially, providing for each other's needs, with a desire to seek each other's highest good. The love of parents and children should be driven by and rooted in their family bond and not in merits or the duty the members owe each other.

What are some of the specific ways that your parents have sacrificially provided for your highest good?

How have you returned that kind of love to your parents?

Do not rebuke an older man but encourage him as you would a father, younger men as brothers, older women as mothers, younger women as sisters, in all purity. (1 Tim. 5:1–2)

What does all of this mean for us? It means that when the world looks at the church, it ought to see a family of people in fellowship with one another because they have been brought into fellowship with God through a common family member, the Lord Jesus. And just as the marriage union is a way to demonstrate that fellowship, the other relationships in the family prove it too. When parents fulfill their God-given role in the lives of their children, and children respond to their parents as God intended, it is a visible sign that God is indeed redeeming the world, reconciling the families of the earth to Himself one family member at a time, until all believers are united with God as one family on the new earth.

REDEEMED, OBEDIENT CHILDREN

Paul instructs children,

Children, obey your parents in the Lord, for this is right. "Honor your father and mother" (this is the first commandment with a promise), "that it may go well with you and that you may live long in the land." (Eph. 6:1–3)

In the previous chapter, we noted how difficult it is for children—especially teenagers—to obey their parents cheerfully, quickly, and completely. From birth, our natural tendency is not to get *under* authority but *around* it. And the struggle to obey often gets harder during the teen years.

To make matters worse, the trends, styles, language, and technology in our culture change so quickly that your parents can appear to you to be hopelessly out-of-date, with their outmoded ideals and traditions. You may not openly rebel against your parents, but increasingly you're tempted to keep them out of your business, trying to live a life of your own.

A word of encouragement: your ability to honor and obey your parents—or any authority—is really a matter of whether or not you're trusting God. God gave you the authorities you have (Rom. 13:1–7). You may wrestle with godly obedience, but you can trust that God has given you the parents He wanted you to have and the family and the experiences He wanted you to have. Even sinless Jesus had to "learn obedience" as He was growing up (Luke 2:51–52; Heb. 5:8).

And another encouragement: there's something redemptive about living in submission to your parents. Submissive teens receive better parenting—usually. By doing what they're supposed to do, they encourage and help their parents to do what they're supposed to do. But a rebellious teen can trigger a downward spiral of fallenness.

When you obey your parents, you are aligning yourself properly under God's authority, and you're declaring to the world that you can live in harmony with Him and with those He has placed in your life. You are playing a role in Christ's work to redeem the world back into fellowship with Him.

REDEEMED, NURTURING PARENTS

Paul also gives this instruction to parents:

Fathers, do not provoke your children to anger, but bring them up in the discipline and instruction of the Lord. (Eph. 6:4)

The Church as God's Picture of Ultimate Reality

Divide students into small groups according to a book or section of the New Testament letters. Students should search for the terms *brother*, *brothers* (or *brethren*), *sister*, and *one another* using Bible software. They should determine which verses apply to the life of the church family and answer the questions.

What responsibilities do church members have toward one another because of their familial bond as brothers and sisters?

greet one another; build up and encourage; love; admonish; exhort and bring back to the truth; discipline; forgive; confess sins; fellowship; be patient; be humble; be gentle; be kind; be grateful for one another; do good; sacrifice for one another; support one another financially; provide for physical needs; show hospitality; serve; esteem and put others first; rejoice with one another; comfort; care; give a good testimony; bless with your words; be honest; instruct; submit; worship with one another; look for the Lord's coming together; live in harmony, not grumble; not unjustly judge; not be a stumbling block; not provoke

What are some of the specific ways that your church family has modeled this kind of family love?

How have you participated in demonstrating this familial love to others in your church body?

How could the church be a better testimony to the world?

Entrusting Yourself to God

Children in a human family should live like children in God's family. Just as the children of God (including adults) are obligated to respect and obey the Father, so also are children in human families (including teens) obligated to respect and obey their fathers and mothers. Just as children in God's family respectfully obey because they're *trusting* that God is driven by a desire to uphold their greatest good, so also children in human families should usually be able to trust that their parents want their children's greatest good.

One of the evidences of growing up into maturity is an *increased* respect and love for one's parents because of an *increased* trust in their biblical and practical wisdom. Such maturity should usually manifest itself in abiding by their wishes as long as it's biblically possible. That kind of respect is willing to embrace the sacrifice of one's own personal opinions and desires. If you're walking in the Spirit, personal freedom is always placed under your first obligation to lovingly serve others (Gal. 5:13–14). A refusal to live sacrificially for others, simply for the sake of exercising personal liberties, is a refusal to be Christlike (1 Cor. 8:9; 10:23–24; Phil. 2:3–5). The reason why your liberty can be determined by someone else's conscience is that God's glory is more important than your own liberties (1 Cor. 10:29–31). A refusal to live for others' good and God's glory is proof that you're still immature and not ready to be treated as an adult (or mature Christian).

Obstructions to Submission

Why does peer pressure make submission to parents more difficult? (Prov. 1:10)

Bad friends entice others to please them.

How can you alleviate that peer pressure? (Ps. 1:1–2; Prov. 4:14–15; 13:20; 29:25; 1 Cor. 15:33; Gal. 1:10)

Choose wise friends; don't hang out with fools. Determine not to be driven by a desire to please people.

What marks a wise friend? (Prov. 9:9; 10:1)

Unwise friends consistently undermine parental instruction; wise friends receive it.

Why do people keep hanging out with unwise friends? (Prov. 22:3; Luke 6:45)

The naive foolishly refuse to be instructed by wisdom; they reveal their own evil hearts.

Will one-time submission bring about better parenting or more liberty?

No, you must establish a pattern of trust so that parents will learn to respond differently to you.

Responding to Provocation

If the provocation is criminal in nature, then governmental authorities *must* be contacted. Shielding a parent from accountability prevents God's servants from doing what God designed them for (Rom. 13:1–7). Protecting parents from accountability only increases their own self-destruction. And it gives them further opportunity to do harm.

If the provocation is not criminal, but it is clearly unbiblical (e.g., harsh, demeaning, unreasonable expectations, etc.), then church authorities certainly should be contacted. Ask for personal and family counseling. But make sure your approach is one of teachable submission that desires to be united to your family and under your parents' authority. Make it clear that your end goal is not to be at odds with your parents in rebellion, but to lovingly respect and obey them. Be willing to recognize your own failures and areas to change in this process.

Responding to Discipline

Read Hebrews 12:5–11 (cf. Prov. 3:11–12), which explains God's pattern for discipline.

What is chastening? What is its purpose?

It is training. It does not convey that God is condemning or rejecting you. It's the means by which God trains, through discipline, to bring a person to maturity.

Is it possible to undergo this kind of discipline without any pain or discomfort?

No physical discipline seems pleasant at the time; instead, it always brings about some measure of pain to be endured (Heb. 12:11).

Who gets chastened by God?

all God's children but only God's children

What should be your attitude toward it?

Instead of being discouraged by questioning God's love or being angry by despising God's correction, embrace God's gracious counsel.

What should be its end result?

what's best for us; righteousness

What does this passage assume about parental discipline?

The norm for good parents includes this kind of physical discipline.

To Spank or Not to Spank

The following articles thoroughly and accessibly examine the arguments.

Andy Naselli, "Training Children for Their Good," *Journal of Discipleship & Family Ministry* 3 (Spring/Summer 2013): 48–64.

Paul D. Wegner, "Discipline in the Book of Proverbs: 'To Spank or Not to Spank?'" *Journal of the Evangelical Theological Society* 48 (December 2005): 715–32.

In these brief words are the seeds for redeemed parenting: what to do and what not to do.

The Negative and the Positive

First, fathers in particular—and parents in general—are told what not to do: don't create strife in the home. Children begin their lives weak and vulnerable, under their parents' complete control, at their parents' mercy. Redeeming the parent-child relationship means eliminating all physical and emotional abuse. It means there's no cold authoritarianism under which children can never do anything quite right. Parents who are harsh with their kids create an atmosphere in which the marks of redemption are not able to flourish.

Second, however, parents are told what to do instead of provoking their kids. They must "bring them up," or train them. Applying the kind of discipline and instruction that's "of the Lord," they are to model their behavior on the way the Lord deals with His own children.

Discipline

In Ephesians 6:4, the word *discipline* includes both training and corporal punishment. "For the moment all discipline seems painful rather than pleasant," Hebrews 12:11 says, "but later it yields the peaceful fruit of righteousness to those who have been trained by it" (cf. Prov. 3:11–12). If discipline isn't painful, it's not the kind of godly discipline the Bible speaks of.[6]

Many countries around the world—forty-one by last count—ban spanking. Sweden was the first in 1979. There is now an organization called "Global Initiative to End All Corporal Punishment of Children."[7] And from a secular standpoint it's completely understandable. How else can secular governments be expected to react when so much violence against children occurs in their nations? But misuse of physical discipline isn't a good reason to eliminate its proper use. Biblical discipline requires different levels of response from parents, starting with teaching, then warning, then enforcing.[8] Proverbs is clear about that last level: "Whoever spares the rod hates his son, but he who loves him is diligent to discipline him" (Prov. 13:24). Discipline should not arise out of anger but out of love. Parents who love their children discipline them in wise and measured ways, as God instructs. And when they do, they redeem discipline.

Instruction

In Ephesians 6:4, the word *instruction* refers to the careful, consistent teaching that God directs parents to give to their children (Deut. 6:7–25; Ps. 78:5–8; Prov. 22:6). That is, parents are to keep before their children in all areas of life both what God says in His Word and what God has done for them. Parents may be tempted to neglect their responsibility to instruct by only disciplining their children for wrong behavior but never taking the time to offer positive instruction. Or their church may provide wonderful instruction for their children so that they do not feel the urgency of instructing in the home. But parents should take personally God's command to instruct their children because they're ministering to the world by preparing godly children who will enter the world, helping to fill the earth with the light and knowledge of God as we come nearer the final redemption.

Responding to Instruction

Divide students into two groups. Have one group brainstorm answers to question (1) while the other group brainstorms answers to question (2).

(1) What do children and teens commonly do to make themselves unapproachable so that their parents have difficulty instructing them?

They avoid spending significant time with their parents—being present but plugged in doesn't count. Their conversations are substanceless and answers to questions are elusive. Their body language communicates a closed-off attitude. Their lives are kept private; struggles are kept secret.

(2) What can you do to make yourself approachable so that your parents are invited to instruct you?

Spend significant time with your parents. Have conversations of substance, and ask and answer questions with depth. Be hospitable and inviting in your body language to communicate an open attitude. Be accountable, and ask for their wisdom to work through struggles.

Evaluate the answers of the two groups. How much do the answers to the second question mirror the answers to the first?

Discuss why children have so much difficulty communicating with their parents when God perfectly designed the structure of the family. God's norms are that parents and children get along (Mal. 4:6). God's norms are for children to find security and guidance in their parent's wisdom. Why is it not wise to sacrifice the parent-child relationship in order to have temporal childhood friends?

THE HEARTS OF THE FAMILIES

The very last promise of the very last book of the Old Testament is that God will, at the end of time, "turn the hearts of fathers to their children and the hearts of children to their fathers" (Mal. 4:5–6).

How can families know this blessing while we await the final redemption? Through repentance and faith. If the other people in your family won't repent and believe, seek God's grace and do it yourself anyway. Pray that the Lord would bring a taste of the new earth to your own family.

THINKING IT THROUGH 15.2

1. What is the ultimate goal of the earthly family?

2. How did Jesus define the true family of God?

3. What should motivate obedience of children to their parents?

4. What two major tasks are given to parents, and what is one major error parents are warned against?

♀ 5. Why is "neutral" parenting an impossibility?

15.3 REDEEMING GENDER ROLES

One Christian apologist tells the story of a boy named Ezekiel Bulver, who learns a useful but false lesson. He hears his parents arguing, and his mother says to his father, "Oh, you say that because you are a man."[9] Ezekiel is a very bright boy, and he realizes in a flash, "I don't have to refute anybody's arguments; all I have to do is show that my opponent's background or situation gave rise to his idea, and then I can dismiss it."

The apologist called this "Bulverism." And it's actually quite similar to "postmodernism." Postmodernism isn't really an ism, then. It's a destroyer of isms. It's an acid, a solvent that breaks down other people's claims.

Postmodernism (going back to Friedrich Nietzsche) sees arguments not as true or false but as power grabs. Suppose a tenured professor of literature says that the writings of Charles Dickens are classics and ought to be taught in class. Of course, he

---

THINKING IT THROUGH 15.2

1. to spread the knowledge and glory of the Creator throughout the earth by entirely filling it with people (children) who have been taught and nurtured to know and serve their Creator

2. Rather than a physical lineage, His family consisted of all those who do God's will.

3. Redeemed children desire to be submissive to God and the authorities He has placed over them. They desire to make their parents' job easier and effective.

4. discipline and instruct; don't provoke

♀ 5. If parents raise their children as if God is optional, then they're teaching their children a false religious view that still influences how their children think.

SECTION OBJECTIVES 15.3

1. Compare and contrast the biblical concept of women's roles versus the world's concept.

2. Compare and contrast the biblical concept of men's roles versus the world's concept.

Postmodernism: Might Makes Right

Bulverism is another example of an *ad hominem* argument, an attack on someone's person rather than an evaluation of that person's logical or reasonable position on an issue. The reason it's often effective is that it powerfully puts one's opponent on the defensive, deflecting the conversation from reasoning through the issues to attacking or defending the character of the person.

Postmodernism makes a logical leap in saying that *all* arguments are mere power grabs and that no position is ultimately or inherently authoritative or reasonable. Instead of employing legitimate ways to reasonably evaluate issues, postmodernism denies that any issue can be reasonably weighed against another to come up with an absolute conclusion of right or wrong, truth or falsehood. Every issue becomes a mere perspective or opinion. There is no ultimate authority to settle a matter. There is no ultimate hope that humans can, through logical reasoning, make progress to solve the problems of the world—the promise of modernism. Convenience or self-interest *always* determines one's position on an issue. Ironically, most postmoderns don't seem to recognize that their postmodern approach might be due to their own self-interest. To postmoderns, any profession of certainty in absolutes— whether sourced in authoritative revelation or in human reasoning—is tyrannical.

The biblical worldview makes use of reason, but it always does so under the authority of God's Word. It is a rejection of the premodern approach—superstitious trust in authority, which is contrary to and dismissive of reason. It is a rejection of modernism's approach—overconfident trust in human reasoning and its promised progress. It is a rejection of the postmodern approach, which is overly skeptical of any authority, including human reason. In contrast, postmoderns propose that freedom will flourish if only everyone agrees that there are no ultimate answers—at least that we have access to—and that the only thing that matters is that we all just coexist. The abuse of moral authority leads postmoderns to reject one absolute moral authority. But allowing depraved people to live however they wish with no moral norms to restrain them leads only to anarchy. Without any arbitrator or a rule of law by which one can objectively determine justice, society is only left with might makes right. The loudest or strongest group is able to dominate the weak minority. [See Heath White, *Postmodernism 101* (Grand Rapids: Brazos Press, 2006), 39–51.]

Postmodernism and the Gender Wars

Ideas have consequences. The philosophical underpinning of postmodernism directly affects sociology. One clear example is seen in the gender wars. Based on a postmodern worldview, there are no absolute standards to prevent or restrain power (might makes right). Postmodernism actually causes the tyranny that it wants to prevent. Anarchy always follows the path of toppling one tyranny only to replace it with another tyranny. Anarchy is never sustainable.

Ask students to look for news items about current events that exemplify the gender wars in society. What prevents people from just coexisting? How can justice be determined without any standards? What biblical standards should be applied in each situation?

Women in the Ancient World

Compare and contrast the status quo of the ancient world with the biblical norms that God directed His people to follow. Which attitudes and practices were contrary to biblical norms? Which were deceptive or excessive—going beyond the creational norms?

Treatment of Daughters

It wasn't criminal to kill an infant or to marry off a twelve-year-old girl to an older man.

> Roman fathers greeted the birth of an infant boy with more joy than the birth of an infant girl. Indeed, infant girls were sometimes unwanted and therefore exposed [to the elements and left to die]. Daughters who were allowed to live were often married at a very tender age to men chosen by their fathers. It was not uncommon for girls to be engaged at twelve and married at thirteen, and few were asked their opinions about prospective bridegrooms.

[Jo-Ann Shelton, *As the Romans Did: A Sourcebook in Roman Social History,* 2nd ed. (New York: Oxford University Press, 1998), 19]

Treatment of Wives in Ancient Rome

It wasn't a criminal offense for a husband to beat his wife. Public opinion sometimes applauded it, and the laws allowed it.

> Egnatius Mecenius beat his wife to death with a club because she had drunk some wine. And not only did no one bring him to court because of this deed, but no one even reproached him, for all the best men thought that she had deserved the punishment for her example of intemperance. For assuredly any woman who desires to drink wine immoderately closes the door to all virtues and opens it to all vices.

[Valerius Maximus, *Memorable Deeds and Words,* 6.3.9, quoted in Shelton, 47]

Attitude Toward Educated Women

Although it's meant to be sarcastic, this satire makes a point that many ancients would have agreed with—that society was better off with less educated women.

> Don't marry a woman who speaks like an orator—or knows every history book. There should be some things in books which she doesn't understand. I hate a woman who reads and rereads Palaemon's treatise on grammar, who always obeys all the laws and rules of correct speech, who quotes verses I've never even heard of, moldy old stuff that a man shouldn't worry about anyway. Let her correct the grammar of her stupid girlfriend! A husband should be allowed an occasional "I ain't."

[Juvenal, *Satires* 6.434–56, quoted in Shelton, 299]

Attitude Toward Women in Politics

> If each of us men, fellow citizens, had undertaken to keep the right and the authority of the husband out of the hands of the women of the family, we would have less trouble with groups of women. But as it is now, at home our freedom is trampled on by feminine rages, and here in the Forum it is crushed and trod underfoot. Because we were unable to control each woman as an individual, we are now frightened by women in groups. Indeed, it was with some embarrassment that I came a few minutes ago to the Forum right through a crowd of women. . . [I felt like saying,] 'What kind of behavior is this, running around in public and blocking streets and talking to other women's husbands? Could you not have asked your own husbands the same thing at home? Are you more persua-

---

would say that; he wants to preserve the privilege of other white males like himself and Dickens. Or imagine that a head of state says that the threats to his nation are dire and he needs to declare martial law. Of course, he would say that; he wants to preserve his own power.

Professors and presidents do make power grabs. Postmodernism is right about that. And someone needs to "speak truth to power" by telling powerful people they're wrong and standing up for the little guy.

But postmodernism is such a powerful acid that it melts the bottle it's in. Maybe women in a society can tell men, "You just say that because you're men and want to hold on to your power!" But then who's to stop the men from telling the women, "You just say that because you're women and you want our power for yourselves!" Postmodernism leaves us with "might makes right."[10]

The only way weak victims can get strong oppressors to stop is to appeal to an authority above those oppressors—ultimately, God Himself. Not all truth claims are just claims or power grabs. All people, both victims and oppressors, both men and women, really are made in God's image and really do have an essential equality. It's a biblical worldview that restores all people—and both genders—to their proper places of dignity.

WOMEN IN THE NEW TESTAMENT

How would men and women function in the world if the Creation-Fall-Redemption story were not true? What if humans were not created by a loving God, if marriage and family were not ordained by His design, if the relationships we share in the home were merely the results of purposeless evolution? Nothing in this "big story" about the world could stop the strong from dominating the weak. When it came to gender roles, the physically stronger sex would probably dominate the other. Male-dominated cultures would be the normative mode, and women would always be subservient to men, treated as second-class citizens or worse.

But an authority far above men has told them not to exploit their physical strength: "Husbands, live with your wives in an understanding way, showing honor to the woman as the weaker vessel" (1 Pet. 3:7). The Bible recognizes the slighter physical frame God gave women and urges husbands not to take advantage of them, but to be sensitive to their needs and to treat them with the understanding and respect they deserve as fellow image-bearers.

This honor that the Bible gives to women is even more pronounced when we consider the typical male domination over women in the ancient cultures back when the Bible was written. The well-documented restrictions on women in the first century, for instance, show that they were subject to the same types of strictures we see today in most Muslim countries. Roman women were confined mainly to the home. Typically, women in Roman culture were poorly educated, and they were not given equal access to the benefits of Roman law.

Even in Jewish society, women were poorly educated, had little or no authority in decisions, were not considered reliable enough to testify in legal matters, were restricted in the activities of the temple and synagogues, could not go out unveiled or talk to strangers, and were mainly confined to the homes of their fathers or husbands with little or no say in the matter. (The Bible, specifically Proverbs 31, does not support all these restrictions.)

Christ redeems women by raising them to the height of honor they were originally given at creation. The attitudes Jesus and the New Testament apostles demonstrated toward women—and what they taught about women—were countercultural in key ways. "Jesus treated women with dignity and respect and he elevated them in a world where they were often mistreated."[11] Jesus was surrounded by female supporters (Luke 8:2–3) and was close friends with women (Luke 10:38–42; John 11:1–44). Jesus accepted sincere, emotional worship from women (Luke 7:36–50; Matt 26:6–13). He commended women (Mark 7:24–30; 12:41–44; Luke 10:42), spoke of women in His parables (e.g., Matt. 13:33; 24:41; 25:1–13; Luke 15:8–10; 18:1–8), and taught women as well as men (Mark 6:34; Luke 10:39). Women were the first to arrive at the empty tomb, becoming the first-ever witnesses of Jesus' resurrection (Matt. 27:57–28:10).

Jesus' conversation with a Samaritan woman (John 4:1–42) is a major event in John's Gospel—an occasion when Jesus was willing to break several social norms.[12] Jesus conversed with the woman personally in broad daylight, showed concern for her soul, answered her questions, and offered her salvation. This incident doesn't seem that striking to us today only because we don't understand how unusual it was for a Jewish male to show equal respect to a female, especially in public, especially to a divorced-five-times-and-currently-cohabiting Samaritan female (4:16–18). But the disciples understood; "they marveled that he was talking with a woman" (4:27).

The apostles later followed Jesus' lead in their attitude toward women. Women were greatly involved in the ministry of the early church.[13] Although men took the lead—as they were instructed to do by the apostles—women were cared for and commended in the New Testament, and they ministered alongside men, filling important roles. Women were present in the upper room (including Mary the mother of Jesus)

In the New Testament, Jesus countered the Roman culture of His day.

- He, as the rabbi (teacher), included women as His disciples (Luke 8:1–3); He even prioritized learning at His feet over domestic duties (Luke 10:38–42).
- His encounter with a Samaritan woman was the first recorded instance of His openly declaring His Messiahship (John 4:25–26).
- He never rejected outcasts who came to Him for healing and forgiveness (Matt. 9:20–22; Luke 7:12–15; 37–50; 18:15–16; John 8:4–11).

In the early church, women were influential and involved in church life.

- Women were included in the prayer meeting with the Twelve (Acts 1:12–14).
- Women prophesied in the church (Acts 21:8–9; 1 Cor. 11:5).
- Women provided meeting places for the church (Acts 12:12–15).
- Women were commended for their hospitality, service, and financial support (Acts 9:36; 16:14–15; Rom. 16:1–6).
- Women participated in personal discipleship because they were well-versed in the teachings of God's Word (Acts 18:26; 2 Tim. 1:5).
- Women helped Paul in his missions labors to spread the gospel (Phil. 4:3).

[John MacArthur, *Twelve Extraordinary Women* (Nashville: Nelson Books, 2005), xi–xiv.]

As the influence of Christianity was felt more and more, women were less and less vilified or mistreated as objects for the amusement of men. Instead, women began to be honored for their virtue and faith. . . . One of the measurable early results [of Constantine's legalization of Christianity] was a whole new legal status for women. Rome passed laws recognizing the property rights of women. Legislation governing marriage was revised, so that marriage was legally seen as a partnership, rather than a virtual state of servitude for the wife. . . . New laws made divorce more difficult, while giving women legal rights against husbands who were guilty of infidelity. [MacArthur, xv–xvi]

From Constantine on, the rape of consecrated virgins and widows was punishable by death. Constantine abolished penalties against celibacy and childlessnesss. . . . Marriage was protected by laws restricting divorce, forbidding concubinage, and punishing adultery as a gross crime. . . . In 390, Theodosius I allowed mothers

sive in public than in private, with others' husbands than with your own?

[Livy, *A History of Rome* 34.2.1, quoted in Shelton, 298]

The ancients were blind to heinous cultural norms, just as many moderns are. Without question, in the biblical worldview, girl babies are certainly not to be killed as if they're less important. It's unthinkable to marry off young girls to older men—in a sort of master-slave relationship. Must it even be said that an unpleasant wife shouldn't be beaten to death at her husband's whim? If a husband lovingly exalts in his wife, he wouldn't pridefully detract from her use of intelligence. The closest parallel to a biblical norm is the advice to wives to ask their husbands questions at home (1 Cor. 14:34–35). God's norm is for male leadership in the church and the home. Some Christians

think it's likely that God's norms are the same in the public square.

Social Norms for Women in the Bible

The social order of the Bible, beginning with the Old Testament, stands in stark contrast to the rest of the ancient world. Women in Israel were allowed to participate in the life of the nation far more than women in the nations around them.

- in the worship of the nation and learning from God's Word (Deut. 16:14; Neh. 8:2–3)
- in managing the household, owning land, and receiving an inheritance (Num. 27:8; Prov. 14:1; 31:16)
- in the authority structure of the home (Lev. 19:3; Prov. 1:8; 6:20)
- in not being required to wear a veil in public (Gen. 12:14; 24:16; 1 Sam. 1:12)

certain guardianship rights previously entrusted only to men."

[Diana Lynn Severance, *Feminine Threads: Women in the Tapestry of Christian History* (Geanies House, Scotland: Christian Focus Publications, 2011), 67]

Missing Men

Ask students to search for current events that discuss the social ills that generally result from fatherless homes.

Helpful organizations that track these kinds of issues include the Heritage Foundation and the Family Research Council.

Discuss their findings.

Why have so many fathers abandoned their own families (evaluate it through the lenses of spiritual, social, and political catalysts)?

Selfish sinfulness leads to a society filled with immorality, drug and alcohol abuse, laziness—or, on the other extreme, workaholism or dedication to sports or hobbies. All of those activities undermine the faithful care and responsibility of fatherhood. Politically, no-fault divorce has made it easier for men to abandon their families to pursue individualistic selfish desires.

What kinds of consequences often trouble fatherless families?

poverty; kids who struggle morally, socially, and academically; higher rates of crime and gang involvement, and so forth

What can be done (spiritually, socially, politically, etc.) to encourage fathers to remain faithful and to take responsibility for their own families?

The sins that are rampant in society need to be combatted through both the gospel and political incentives or penalties. For instance, Christians need to work against no-fault divorce in favor of divorce laws that pressure spouses to work things out.

How can Christian young people overcome the statistics if they find themselves in a broken home?

find appropriate support or mentoring from godly men; rest in a personal relationship with God the Father, who promises never to leave or forsake His children and who designed the church to care for widows and orphans

Mature Manhood

What should be the goal of manhood?

fulfilling responsibilities courageously

What are some obstacles to that goal?

trials, opposition, temptations

How are men derailed from the goal?

---

when the Holy Spirit was given to the church (Acts 1:14). Lydia and a group of faithful women helped Paul to launch his ministry to Philippi (Acts 16:13–15). Priscilla worked alongside her husband to instruct Apollos in the way of God (Acts 18:26). A great number of the apostle Paul's coworkers were women.[14] For example, Paul spoke of two women in particular who "labored side by side with [him] in the gospel" (Phil. 4:1–3).

> *"People in our culture have a great need to see role models of biblical manhood and womanhood that flesh out God's design for men and women."*[15]
>
> —ANDREAS AND MARGARET KÖSTENBERGER

When a woman lives redemptively, she rejoices in the design of God and attempts to develop herself in accordance with a woman's position as an image-bearer of God, a disciple of Christ, and usually, a helper to her husband. Sometimes girls get the impression that unless they're just like boys, they're missing out. That's simply not true. God has different plans for boys (in general) than for girls (in general). If you're a girl, don't try to be a boy. Run track if you want to—but not just because the boys are doing it. Take a computer programming course if you want to—but not because there are too few women in the tech field. The cultural push to get all professions to a fifty-fifty gender split implies that women can't have glory until they match men. That's clearly not biblical thinking.

As a girl, you don't merely want to think rightly about God and His design yourself. You want to help others to think rightly as well. This means taking a hard look at what you're communicating to others through your words, your clothes, and even your Instagram account. Living redemptively means looking at the way you act in a group of people and avoiding those behaviors that don't communicate femininity. It means looking at your career options and choosing to pursue something that won't get in the way of your following God's design for men and women at home and in the church. Since God hasn't given us specifics in these areas, we have to pray and use the wisdom God provides. Whatever we choose, our goal should be the same—to hold up the truth that God has revealed in the Bible.

A biblical worldview doesn't demean women or relegate them to second-class citizenship. Rather, Christ redeems women from domination and raises them to their original status of co-regents infused with dignity and treated with distinct honor.

MEN IN THE NEW TESTAMENT

But women are not the only gender whose roles are mentioned in the New Testament. The roles of men are also addressed and often in a way that instructs men how to manage their strength and position rather than abuse them. When Paul addresses the male leadership of Corinth, he says, "Be watchful, stand firm in the faith, act like men, be strong" (1 Cor. 16:13), recognizing the role of strong leadership and protection that men are to exercise in the church. But men in particular are also exhorted to be loving, faithful, pure (1 Tim. 4:12), patient, kind, peaceable, and gentle even when facing those who oppose the truth (2 Tim. 2:22–26)—virtues that are not always associated with the dominant male. When Paul recounts his ministry to the Thessalonian believers, he likens himself to both a nursing mother caring gently, lovingly, and

---

by being compromised and passive or ungracious and angry

What is needed to strive toward the goal?

guidance from biblically minded fathers or mentors to pass on biblical wisdom, model biblical living, and enforce biblical discipline

How can men begin to make progress?

by being spiritually disciplined and motivated to take responsible initiative, overcoming fear and uncertainty

Fulfilling responsibility requires disciplined initiative. In the face of difficulty, it will take courage to fulfill one's responsibility when a virtue is being tested.

Ask students to write an essay on one of the following marks of mature manhood. What kind of young man should a godly young lady be looking for? How would she identify the particular character quality as

she observes his practical life at school, at church, and at home? What kind of man should a godly young man be striving to become for his future wife? How would he cultivate the character quality as he is challenged in his practical life in the school, church, and home?

• fulfills his responsibilities
• acts courageously in facing difficulties
• has been biblically mentored
• shows disciplined initiative
• exercises godly leadership

Beware of Macho Egotism

Mature manhood must not be confused with egotistical machismo. A godly man will be bold, but he will not be a bully. A man with a physically strong body and a domineering personality may reflect the latter rather

sacrificially for her children (1 Thess. 2:7–9) and to a nurturing father, exhorting and encouraging those in his care (2:11–12). This analogy is significant; while Paul still delineates specific roles for men and women, he's willing to define his own ministry in terms that elevate and honor both roles, recognizing that fathers and mothers serve alongside each other as they minister to their children.

If you're a guy, you need to understand true manliness. When a man lives redemptively, he rejoices in the design of God and attempts to live in accordance with his position as an image-bearer of God and the leader of his family. He will try to develop the skills and character of a leader. It's your responsibility to take care of others, particularly women and children and those who are weaker than you. You have a responsibility to lead people in the right direction. And you're supposed to be known as a man who can work. By upper high school, *play* should phasing out of your vocabulary. You should be thinking of your chores, your schoolwork, and even your basketball team as work that God has called you to do right now. In your work you're developing skills that you'll need as God calls you to more and more responsibility.

You can promote the truth by the way you act and talk. One idea you have to fight against is the idea that there's no such thing as masculinity. Some people think that's just something people make up. But as one pastor pointed out, "The reason people can cross-dress is because clothing communicates masculinity and femininity."[16] Living redemptively means taking a look at what you wear and avoiding those things that don't clearly communicate masculinity. It also means evaluating what you say and the way you treat others by asking yourself, "Does this help others think rightly about God and His design for men and women?" That kind of thinking isn't simple, and it isn't always the same—when Paul wrote the New Testament epistles, he probably wasn't wearing blue jeans. But in every culture Christian men should embrace the symbols that communicate that they have adopted the role God designed for them.

Some theologians argue that redemption through Christ erases gender roles. After all, they say, Paul declares in Galatians 3:28, "There is neither Jew nor Greek, there is neither slave nor free, there is no male and female, for you are all one in Christ Jesus." But Paul is referring to the fact that there is complete equality when it comes to receiving Christ and being welcomed into the family of God. Oneness in Christ transcends all other human relationships because those who are in Him belong to Him equally.[17] This was revolutionary in the New Testament era. In the church, men no longer have special privilege of closeness to God, as the Jewish men had been given in the temple. Slaves and free persons worshiped in the Chris-

SIMPLE EXAMPLES OF BIBLICAL MASCULINITY

Scenario 1: During a well-attended Thanksgiving service at a local church, a number of people found themselves in a crowded overflow room watching the service on a closed-circuit TV. The church had prepared to recite Psalm 103 together as part of the service, but when the time came, the audio inexplicably went off. Someone had to "lead" the recitation of Psalm 103, and fast, or no one would know when to start. People looked around nervously for a few moments, not sure what to do. No formal church leadership was in the room. What does a true man do? He speaks out loud and clear: "Bless the Lord, O my soul, and all that is within me, bless his holy name." He doesn't lead so he can enjoy the spotlight for a moment—most people won't even know who spoke up. He does it to serve others, so they don't have to be embarrassed in an awkward situation.

Scenario 2: A young man likes a girl but isn't sure she likes him back. He could find a sneaky, non-risky way of making her reveal her feelings before he reveals his. But a truly masculine young man does not do this. He puts his neck out and leads. He risks being embarrassed and hurt so she doesn't have to. He makes the phone call (to the girl or maybe even her dad!) and he does the asking out. He pays for the hamburgers. He has an end goal in mind for the relationship; he isn't just playing around.

---

than the former. A small, quiet, but steadfast young man may reflect mature manhood by courageously doing right and carrying out his responsibilities. A godly man will lead, but he will not elevate himself as a celebrity to be followed or push people beyond reasonable expectations. A godly man will be disciplined, but a disciplinarian may not always be godly. Discerning the pathway between the extremes requires biblical wisdom that synthesizes all of the biblical data.

Discipline

Divide the class in half to debate whether disciplined living is appropriate for New Testament believers in the age of grace.

After students debate it for a few minutes, ask them to provide scriptural support for their position.

If discipline is correctly understood, then it is certainly a New Testament concept. Discipline isn't about punishment (Heb. 12:1–13); it's about what it takes to succeed in any worthwhile endeavor. The greatest athletes, writers, and musicians embrace discipline instead of squandering their talents. Soldiers and farmers embrace it too (2 Tim. 2:4–6).

The age of grace (Phil. 3:8–11) doesn't remove the responsibility of obedience (Phil. 2:12; 3:12–17), which requires a denial of what comes naturally to the flesh (Phil. 3:18–21; cf. Titus 2:11–12). The Christian life is empowered by God (Phil. 2:13; cf. Gal. 2:20; 2 Pet. 1:3–4). But those who do have spiritual life will engage in the effort to walk in the Spirit (Gal. 5:25). Believers will train or discipline themselves for godliness (1 Cor. 9:24–27; 1 Tim. 4:7; 2 Pet. 1:5).

"For many men, spiritual discipline suggests putting themselves back under the law. . . . But nothing could be further from the truth. . . . The difference is one of motivation: legalism is self-centered; discipline is God-centered." [R. Kent Hughes and W. Carey Hughes, *Disciplines of a Godly Young Man* (Wheaton: Crossway, 2012), 24]

One pastor wrote, "The gospel that frees us *from* self-justification also frees us *for* obedience. In fact, 1 Corinthians 6 and Galatians 5 and 1 John and Revelation 21 and a dozen other passages make clear that when we have no obedience to show for our gospel profession, our conduct shows we have not understood the gospel. . . . When it comes to growth in godliness, trusting does not put an end to trying." [Kevin DeYoung, "Make Every Effort" *The Gospel Coalition* (June 7, 2011)]

A New Testament Model

Divide students into small groups to examine Paul's example as a mature man of influence. Have each group look up each passage and identify what characterized Paul's life.

- Acts 9:20–21; Eph. 2:4–5—*a life of rebellion against God transformed*
- Acts 22:10; cf. 9:6; 26:19—*a life of obedience*
- Rom. 7:21–24; 1 Cor. 2:3; 2 Cor. 11:5, 23–28; Gal. 2:11–13—*a life of adversity and trials, opposition (even from other Christian leaders), and temptation*
- 2 Cor. 10:1–2; Gal. 5:12; Eph. 6:19; 1 Thess. 2:2—*a life of boldness*
- 1 Cor. 9:24–27; Phil. 3:13–14—*a life of discipline*
- Phil. 1:21–24; 3:10—*a life with godly goals*
- Gal. 1:10—*a life of service*
- Col. 3:17—*a life of excellence*
- Phil. 4:9; 2 Tim. 2:2—*a life of discipling*
- 2 Cor. 11:6; 12:7; 1 Thess. 2:3–6—*not a life of celebrity; not known for his eloquence; burdened by a thorn in the flesh*
- 1 Cor. 4:1–5; 2 Cor. 8:21; 1 Tim. 1:5—*a life of integrity*

Warn students of falling prey to the mantra of wanting authenticity or transparency. Such a desire can be just as bad as hypocrisy if the authentic life is detached from character and integrity.

[Jim George, *God's Man of Influence* (Eugene, OR: Harvest House, 2003)]

Masculinity Manifested

What are some specific ways the culture undermines mature masculinity in men?

Some of the cultural symbols, styles, and trends that are purposefully designed to feminize boys include the following:

- *media: commercials that glorify the value of raising boys to play with dolls; sitcoms that try to normalize transgendered roles*
- *toys: removing gendered identifications from toys*
- *dress: clothing that looks feminine, makeup, nail polish, earrings, and so on*
- *mannerisms and speech: purposeful communication techniques (or badly formed habits) that are markedly effeminate*
- *attitudes: passivity*

How should a Christian young man respond to these trends in his culture?

Rather than simply adopting current styles, he must be careful to evaluate and embrace only that which will symbolize masculinity in his culture.

How should a Christian young man relate to other young men who seem to be embracing more effeminate trends in the culture?

It's wrong to bully, shame, or shun anyone. It's also wrong to attempt to change someone's habits by force or pressure. But it is appropriate to gently challenge someone, as a friend, to have a new outlook on life that is more biblically masculine, not to be confused with machismo. Styles and mannerisms should follow from an inner change in outlook based on biblical principles. New behaviors should follow from new beliefs and commitments.

---

tian assembly alongside each other, and amazingly, so did even Jews and Gentiles—and men and women.

Nevertheless, the oneness that men and women share equally in Christ does not negate their God-given, unique roles. Nor does Paul ever suggest such a thing in his other writings; he only puts those roles in the context of redemption, which unites men and women to the Lord and to each other in new ways.

Therefore, in Christ both men and women should still pursue the God-given roles assigned to them from the beginning of creation. Salvation does not release men and women from their responsibility to fulfill God's design but rather energizes them to do so, leading them to redeem their roles to function in the way God originally intended. Various cultures, including church cultures, have struggled to maintain the proper biblical balance between the redeemed roles of men and women, sometimes allowing men to be abusive and uncaring with their power and authority and at other times encouraging women to throw off their God-given role in the name of equality. Nevertheless, by carefully following the instructions given in Scripture in light of the redemption that is in Christ, men and women can be examples of the kind of peace and harmony God is restoring on earth as they humbly take up the roles that God has assigned to each.

CULTURAL DIFFERENCES

Different cultures will have different ways of expressing the biblical principles that men and women are equal in essence but unique in function. A given cultural practice—like men opening doors for women—may not be strictly necessary. But a young man who wants to be masculine, as well as a young woman who wants to be feminine, will work to discover the culturally appropriate ways to show respect to one another as male and female beings. They won't try to break down the distinctions between men and women but will attempt to honor them because they know that men and women play special roles alongside each other in the redemption of the world.

THINKING IT THROUGH 15.3

1. What kind of justice are you left with if you follow Bulverism?

2. Provide two examples that demonstrate that Jesus exalted women's roles in His ministry.

3. Provide two examples that demonstrate that the early church exalted women's roles in ministry.

4. What virtues ought to define biblical male leadership in contrast to domineering male leadership?

◊5. How should you relate to the applications of gender norms made by your particular culture?

THINKING IT THROUGH 15.3

1. Might makes right: an oppressed group tries to gain power to overturn an oppressive group only to become the new oppressor.

2. Jesus surrounded Himself with female supporters (Luke 8:2–3).
   Jesus was close friends with women (Luke 10:38–42; John 11:1–44).
   Jesus accepted sincere worship from women (Luke 7:36–50; Matt. 26:6–13).
   Jesus commended women (Mark 7:24–30; 12:41–44; Luke 10:42).
   Jesus spoke well of women in His parables (Matt. 13:33; 24:41; 25:1–13; Luke 15:8–10; 18:1–8).
   Jesus conversed with an immoral Samaritan woman (John 4:1–42).
   Jesus taught women as well as men (Mark 6:34; Luke 10:39).
   Women were the first to arrive at the empty tomb, becoming the first ever witnesses of Jesus' resurrection (Matt. 27:57–28:10).

3. There were women present in the upper room, including Mary the mother of Jesus, when the Holy Spirit was given to the church (Acts 1:14).
   Lydia and a group of faithful women helped Paul launch his ministry to Philippi (Acts 16:13–15).
   Priscilla worked alongside her husband to instruct Apollos in the way of God (Acts 18:26).
   Paul spoke of two women in particular who "labored side by side with [him] in the gospel" (Phil. 4:1–2).

4. loving, faithful, pure (1 Tim. 4:12), patient, kind, peaceable and gentle even when facing those who oppose the truth (2 Tim. 2:22–26); likened to both a nursing mother caring gently, lovingly, and sacrificially for her children (1 Thess. 2:7–9) and to a nurturing father, exhorting and encouraging those in his care (1 Thess. 2:11–12)

◊5. Young men who want to be masculine and young women who want to be feminine will work to discover the culturally appropriate ways to show respect to one another as male and female beings. They won't try to break down the distinctions between men and women but will attempt to honor them because they know that men and women play special roles alongside each other in the redemption of the world.

15 CHAPTER REVIEW

TERMS TO REMEMBER
family of God

Scripture Memory

Proverbs 18:22

Making Connections

1. In what one specific way will believers be like angels in their resurrected bodies?

2. According to Ephesians 5:21–32, what mystery is human marriage patterned after?

3. What should the parent-child relationship picture when parents and children fulfill their God-given roles?

4. According to 1 Peter 3:7, how should a godly husband treat his wife?

Developing Skills in Apologetics and Worldview

5. How should you respond to parents who may feel reluctant to raise you with bias toward their own Christian beliefs or ethical values?

6. How would you respond to someone who claims that Galatians 3:28 teaches that gender roles no longer exist?

Examining Assumptions and Evidence

7. When God restores the world, why will human marriage no longer be needed? Restate both reasons given in the chapter.

8. What underlying character quality is necessary for a wife to be submissive? What underlying character quality is necessary for a husband to be loving?

9. Why do submissive teens typically get better parenting?

10. How should salvation affect the ways husbands and wives live out creational norms about gender?

Becoming a Creative Cultivator

11. Different cultures have had different ways of showing respect and honor between the sexes. Evaluate several such recommendations from a recent book on etiquette and write a brief paragraph summarizing your evaluations.

CHAPTER REVIEW ANSWERS

Making Connections

1. They will not marry or be given in marriage.

2. the reality of the church submitting to Christ and Christ loving the church

3. God is redeeming the world, reconciling the families of the earth to Himself one family member at a time until all believers are united with Him as one family on the new earth.

4. Rather than dominating her, he must honor her by seeking to understand her needs and then caring for and protecting her.

Developing Skills in Apologetics and Worldview

5. Don't rebuke them but plead with them to guide you with biblical wisdom and counsel (as the father and mother in the book of Proverbs counseled).

6. You should have the person read the chapter to understand the context. Then explain that the point of the chapter is that there is complete equality in the context of receiving Christ as Savior and being welcomed into the family of God. Salvation transcends all other existing human relationships, but it doesn't erase the existing human relationships with their differing roles. A relationship with

Christ wouldn't erase the delegated roles given by God; it would restore God's creational norms that He designed for men and women at creation. The equality relates to the restoration of the image of God in both men and women and not to flattening out the creational roles given to them.

Examining Assumptions and Evidence

7. First, God's creative purpose in the goal of human marriage was that a righteous human population would be procreated to fully fill the earth. That will have been already fulfilled so that human marriage is no longer needed. Second, the reality that human marriage pictured (the union of Christ and God's people) will have been fulfilled.

8. humble respect; selfless sacrifice

9. Sinful living often triggers sinful responses from others; parents are fallen and struggle with sinful responses when they're consistently and constantly sinned against by their children.

10. Salvation doesn't release men and women from their responsibility to fulfill God's design but rather energizes them to do so, leading them to redeem their roles to function in the way God originally intended (neither allowing men to be abusive and uncaring nor women to be disrespectful and controlling).

Creative Cultivation

11. Although etiquette practices from the past are not inerrant or unchangeable, they may provide some helpful guidelines from a time period when cultures generally recognized that men should respect and honor women. Provide students with excerpts from an appropriate etiquette book. Students should then explain and apply appropriate etiquette guidelines that they could implement in their day-to-day interactions at school. For example, boys can allow girls to go first, hold the door for them, carry their books, and the like. Rather than dismissing such acts of chivalry or rebelling against them, girls should embrace the honor being shown.

TERMS TO REMEMBER

Family of God—all those who know God through faith, Jews and Gentiles alike, made one in Christ, the seed of Abraham

CHAPTER 16

This chapter argues that government is a divinely created institution that has the primary purpose of ensuring justice. The final section evaluates modes of government and examines the proper sphere of government's authority.

CHAPTER 17

The Fall has led to a number of problems in government and society. It has also affected the solutions that people have proposed to deal with these problems. Instead of identifying sin as the main problem, political ideologies assign the problem to some part of God's good creational order. Instead of looking to God for wisdom on how to deal with these problems, political ideologies typically look to another aspect of the creation order as a savior.

CHAPTER 18

Government will ultimately be redeemed in Christ's return as King. But Christians are still to live in light of redemption in the present age. This chapter looks at how church and state should relate to each other and discusses the activities that Christians should be involved in as citizens and the virtues they should cultivate.

6

GOVERNMENT

The student will be able to

16.1. Defend the idea that government is a God-given established good, not a necessary evil.

16.2. Demonstrate from Scripture that the main purpose of government is to ensure justice.

16.3. Compare and contrast the kinds of governments formed to carry out the biblical duties of government.

SECTION OBJECTIVES 16.1

1. Describe the origins of government.

2. Explain how the Creation Mandate and the kingship of Christ relate to human government.

3. Defend government as an institution that is good and necessary for humans to flourish in community.

Chapter Sixteen **FOUNDATIONS OF GOVERNMENT**

When one rules justly over men, ruling in the fear of God, he dawns on them like the morning light, like the sun shining forth on a cloudless morning, like rain that makes grass to sprout from the earth.

Scripture Memory
2 Samuel 23:3b–4

16.1 WHAT GOOD IS GOVERNMENT?

The 1960s-era bumper sticker "Question Authority" appeared on millions of cars for a reason: it resonated deeply with US culture.[1] Individual autonomy—making your own rules—has come to be the American way. You know that American distrust in government runs deep when even the president of the United States himself says, "Government is not the solution to our problem; government is the problem."[2] When Ronald Reagan said that in his first inaugural address, he was complaining about his predecessor; he didn't mean government is inherently bad (he was a politician after all). But plenty of people today seem to think it is bad. Americans from all points on the political spectrum are deeply suspicious about the goodness of government—and about institutions in general.

Christians, too, may think of government as a necessary evil. They may assume that government exists only because of the Fall. After all, there were only two humans living in the pre-Fall world, and presumably they had no tax forms to fill out.

But Christians who view government through a biblical lens will see—as with so many other things we've discussed—that government was a good institution created by God, that it is now fallen, and that it will be redeemed. One of the most important themes in Scripture is, in fact, the "government" of God—what we generally call God's "kingdom." God has, of course, always ruled (no one has ever toppled Him from His heavenly throne, not Hitler, not Satan). So when the Bible talks about the **kingdom of God**,

it's actually speaking of the rule of God *through a human that God appointed.*

God's original intent was that mankind would have godly dominion (a kingly word) over the earth, and God didn't give up this plan when Adam fell (Gen. 1:26–28; 9:1–7). Instead God appointed a different man to rule the earth, a son of David. He told King David, "Your house and your kingdom shall be made sure forever before me. Your throne shall be established forever" (2 Sam. 7:16).

KING JESUS

That son of David was, of course, Jesus. And it was the good news about His divine kingdom that made up Jesus' central message. He traveled all over Israel proclaiming "the good news of the kingdom of God" (Luke 4:43). His disciples did too. When Peter preached at Pentecost, he proclaimed that Jesus had been enthroned at the Father's right hand (Acts 2:30–36). When Paul preached from prison in Rome, his subject matter was the kingdom of God (Acts 28:31). And Revelation tells us that when Jesus returns to this earth, He will come as a judge and a conquering king (Rev. 19:15–16). He will "establish justice in the earth" (Isa. 42:4).

This King promises that He will set up his government on the earth. Isaiah 9:6 says of the Messiah that "the government shall be upon his shoulder"—He will carry the weight of authority. Jesus really will rule. Government is not a necessary evil but part of God's Creation Mandate.

Lesson Plan Chart—Chapter 16

Section Title	Pages	Activity Manual	Days
16.1 What Good Is Government?	238–41		1 day
16.2 Why Do We Need Government Anyway?	241–45	Activity 28	2 day
16.3 What Should Government Do and How?	245–50	Activity 29	2 day
Review	251		1 day
Total Suggested Days			**6 days**

 Thinking About Government

Solicit students' opinions about government before they read this chapter.

What do students think about government? What are their overall feelings about government? What do they think the purpose of government is? How well do they think governments have fulfilled those purposes historically? What kinds of things does government do that exceed its intended purpose? Will government exist in eternity?

Record, or have students record, the answers given to these questions. Have them compare their initial thoughts to their thoughts after having read this chapter or the entire unit. How has their thinking changed? In what areas have their views been reinforced?

God laid the foundation for government as He laid the foundation for the earth. Government, then, is not a patch put in place to manage the damage caused by the Fall. Government has been part of God's good and glorious plan from the beginning.

Interestingly, Jesus' kingship doesn't mean that humans no longer have any ruling to do. Psalm 8 speaks of fallen man as "crowned with glory and honor," and the passage says that God "put all things under his feet." That's king language. And Revelation 22:5 says that the redeemed will one day reign with Jesus over all the earth. All humans are blessed with the capacity to rule over God's creation, and one day some of us will.

THE RIGHT TO RULE

Human authority to rule benevolently over creation is clear. Birds, animals, and fish were placed under our dominion. But what about people? Does any human have a right to rule over another human? All people are made in God's image. Every one of us has been given dominion over the earth. So why do some people rule over others?

First, you must understand that equality and authority are not opposites. Within the Trinity, the Spirit submits to the Son, who submits to the Father (John 4:34; 14:24; 16:13). This order of authority within the Trinity doesn't mean the Son is less God than the Father. They are equal; they simply have different roles. Equality and authority can live peacefully together.

Hopefully, you already know this from experience because you see it in your parents. In a good marriage—like in the very first marriage—the husband and wife are equally image-bearers, but each plays a different role in the household. The father has final authority, but also final responsibility. The wife is his helper, as Eve was created to be (Gen. 2:18). Paul says that this fact established an order of authority between husband and wife (1 Tim. 2:12–13).

This order, this institution we call marriage, began in the Garden of Eden as part of God's command to be fruitful and multiply. Like all other institutions, marriage is a set of customs and laws that has endured in society. And some institutions, like marriage, have endured so long that they powerfully define the rules and roles for human behavior.[3] The institution of marriage provides rules and roles for husband, wife, and children.

Marriage is, of course, not the only institution in our world. As humans carried out the Creation Mandate, more institutions naturally developed. For instance, when Abel became a keeper of sheep he began to develop patterns of behavior for shepherds. If he hired others to work for him in keeping the sheep, then the roles of employer and employee—another structure of authority—would have been created. If Jubal not only invented the lyre and pipe but organized groups of musicians to play them together (Gen. 4:21), he would have created another institution with its own roles and structure of authority (somebody has to decide the tempo).

There were no employers and employees, conductors and players when only Adam and Eve existed. But by the end of Genesis 4 roles like these were developing as society grew in complexity. And out of this process of development government probably emerged.

Even if the world had remained unfallen, the increasing complexity of human life would have meant that institutions like government had to come. Imagine that two cities have developed along the Pishon River in the land of Havilah (Gen. 2:11). One of the cities wants to divert most of the Pishon for irrigation. The other city, down-

King Jesus

Why is talk about Jesus as king not just spiritual talk that doesn't really have anything to do with government?

To think this way would be to fall back into the two-story view. The reign of Jesus will be an earthly reign that brings justice to the earth.

How does Isaiah 51:4–5 indicate that the reign of Christ has to do with government?

The justice that the world longs for and that Christ will bring is not merely "spiritual." It is attained when a righteous king rules over the earth and establishes just law.

 The Creation Mandate and the Messiah's Rule

Ask students to turn back to Chapter 10 and skim and summarize "The Davidic Cov-enant" (p. 142), "The Kingdom" (p. 143), and "The Kingdom of God" (p. 150). Can they trace the basis or origin of the promises about Jesus' kingship?

Why is it essential for Jesus to be human for Him to be king?

As God, Jesus has always been sovereign over all things. But when Jesus announced that a kingdom was drawing near in His ministry, He was announcing something new. He is the promised Davidic king.

How are the Abrahamic Covenant and the Creation Mandate the foundation for the Davidic Covenant's promise of a king?

The promise of a Davidic king is built on even earlier promises. God had told Abraham "kings shall come from you" (Gen. 17:6). God also promised Abraham a great name, offspring, land, and the opportunity to bless others (Gen. 12:1–3, 7). As one bib-lical scholar notes, these are *kingly* blessings. [Gordon J. Wenham, *Genesis 1–15*, Word Biblical Commentary, ed. David A. Hubbard (Waco, TX: Word, 1987), 275]

The kingly blessings of land, seed, and blessing have roots even deeper than the Abrahamic Covenant. The promises that form the foundation of the Davidic Messiah's rule stretch back to God's first promises to humanity. At the very beginning of creation, God blessed the first man by declaring that his seed would be fruitful and multiply. God also blessed mankind with dominion over the earth, a promise of land (Gen. 1:26–28). The Abrahamic and Davidic Covenants were steps in restoring these blessings to humans. Hebrews 2:5–9 reveals that Jesus, as the perfect man, will indeed restore the blessing of the Creation Mandate.

What Is an Institution?

The Student Text defines *institution* as "a set of customs and laws that has endured in society." This is a definition of *institution* that is probably unfamiliar to students. When they think of an institution, they might think about a particular organization that has a building somewhere, such as the National Institutes of Health. The definition used here is the one used in the social sciences. Consider these examples: "Institutions are the rules of the game in a society or, more formally, are the humanly devised constraints that shape human interaction." [Douglass North, *Institutions, Institutional Change, and Economic Performance* (New York: Cambridge University Press, 1990), 3] Institutions are defined as "rules, design, and structures." [R. A. W. Rhodes, Sarah A. Binder, and Bert A. Rockman, *The Oxford Handbook of Political Institutions* (New York: Oxford University Press, 2006), xiv] "An institution is a relatively enduring collection of rules and organized practices, embedded in structures of meaning and resources that are relatively invariant in the face of turnover of individuals and changing external circumstances." [J. G. March, and J. P. Olsen, *Rediscovering Institutions* (New York: Free Press, 1989), 3]

By these definitions, an institution is not merely an organization but, for instance, the way that medicine is practiced in given parts of the world. Hospitals, ambulances, research centers, the methods of treatment—all of these together form an institution.

Some institutions, such as the family and government, are ancient and foundational to society. Others, such as the symphony orchestra are relatively recent. Institutions develop as the Creation Mandate is carried out and knowledge and practices become specialized.

Students should understand that many Americans are highly skeptical of institutions. Notice the recurrence of the word *rules* in the definition of an institution. Whether these are codified or established by custom, rules are an integral part of institutions. The sense that we're bound by rules or social customs runs contrary to the individualistic sensibilities of many Americans. Many pride themselves on their nonconformity. Others oppose institutions for philosophical reasons. They claim that institutions serve the interests of those with power. Some claim that since the institution of marriage strengthens the power of heterosexuals and disempowers LGBTQ persons, it should be dismantled. In the 1960s some argued that the institutions of government and police empowered white Americans and disempowered minorities. As a result, some have pressed for the dismantling of institutions, and sometimes this takes the form of violent protest movements.

Students need to understand that while institutions *can* become oppressive and that while some customs *do* need changing, destroying a culture's institutions is a "cure" that is worse than the disease. For example, ask students how they would go about buying a gallon of milk. Then ask them how they would perform the same task in South Sudan. They might end up confused and frustrated in trying to perform what is at home a simple task when in a foreign country. Why? The institutions are different. From this example it should be clear that institutions facilitate human interactions. They're necessary for a society to function smoothly. In addition, when an institution embodies wise rules, the institution ends up being a conduit of common grace that preserves a society from many evils.

While institutions sometimes need to be radically reformed because their rules and structures have been deformed by the Fall, anti-institutionalism is not a Christian stance. Far less Christian is the flouting of institutional customs for the sake of self-expression. This stands diametrically opposed to the command to love one's neighbor as oneself. This doesn't mean, however, that individual creativity is condemned. Far from it. Students should realize that the greatest artists and athletes and others exercise a great deal of freedom and creativity within the bounds of their tradition or their game.

How Governments Began

Ask students how they think the first government was formed. Some answers could include:

All the people voted on matters that affected the community as a simple democracy.

---

stream, wants the water level to remain high enough for its ships carrying bdellium and onyx stone up and down the river to trade with other cities. Each of the two cities is pursuing good goals: subduing the earth, taking dominion. But they have to figure out a way to work together in this endeavor. The two cities might send representatives who can meet with each other to work out a mutually agreeable solution. The Creation Mandate doesn't explicitly give humans the authority to rule other humans, but for the mandate to be carried out, authority structures such as those in the family and in government would need to emerge.

In order for humanity to maximize the use of God's world (including conflicting claims over water resources as in the picture), human government must develop.

Even in a world with no sin, people would need government. Government is not a necessary evil but a natural outgrowth of the Creation Mandate. Of course, since the Fall occurred so early in human history, the earliest statements about government in Scripture occur as the Creation Mandate is applied to a fallen world, not a perfect one (Gen. 9:1–7).

INVENTED VERSUS INSTITUTED

The Bible never tells us anything about the first human governments. The family groupings in Genesis—and the nations that arose from them—suggest that human government emerged from the family. Perhaps a patriarch began ruling over his growing clan. Or perhaps leaders were selected according to ability as Moses later did after the Israelites' Exodus from Egypt (Exod. 18:21–22). The latter may be more likely since government is fundamentally different from family.

God has not told us how government came about or what exactly it should look like. So God's people have some liberty when it comes to the forms of government they participate in. Christians should not think that only democracies or only monarchies are approved by God. Israel itself existed under various forms of government that God Himself set up. Israel was first led by Moses and the elders of their tribes; later it was led by the elders alone; later by judges (who were primarily military leaders, not judicial officials) and then kings.

Government emerged from the family structure, with the patriarch of the clan becoming the king.

The heads of households came together to rule as representatives of their families.

[Students may suggest other possibilities.]

Political philosophers have speculated about how government may have originated. Some of them set forth what they think may have actually happened. Others, such as John Locke (1632–1704), treat it as a thought experiment that can justify methods for establishing new governments in the present.

What biblical evidence exists for claiming that government emerged from the family structure?

Abraham had an army, and Judah had the power to sentence Tamar to death for her adultery. When God scattered the people after

Babel, he allowed them to remain in family groupings. Each family grouping had its own language. This allowed the father to continue to rule over his family.

[These are the arguments of philosopher Robert Filmer (1558–1652), who supported absolute monarchy and the divine right of kings.]

What biblical evidence exists against the position that government is based on family structure?

The kingship of fathers is nowhere affirmed in the Bible, but the Creation Mandate grants dominion over the world to every human being. Since every person is given dominion over the world, every person is born free. Children who reach adulthood aren't bound to obey their fathers in the same way that subjects are bound to obey their sovereigns. When children take care of aging parents with failing mental capacities, the child honors his

But Scripture is clear about one thing—government is God's creation, not a mere human invention. Peter says, "Be subject for the Lord's sake to every institution ordained for people" (1 Pet. 2:13, ESV marginal reading). Somebody had to do the instituting of the institution we call government; this verse shows that it was God. Peter is saying that government is a creation of God for humans that they must submit to. And in Romans, Paul says that the individual rulers who are in power "have been instituted by God" (Rom. 13:1). God's purpose for rulers is that they be servants for our good (Rom. 13:4, 6).

TWISTED POWER

Governments have power from the Highest Power. But governments are made up of fallen people who twist that power in various ways. Many governments have twisted that power so far that they use it to kill the people God intends them to serve. Many more twist that power just enough to shake some money into their own pockets. No wonder so many people (Americans included) have an anti-institutional and anti-governmental bias.

THINKING IT THROUGH 16.1

1. How do you know that government is more than just a patch put in place to manage the damage caused by the Fall?

2. Is the authority of one human over another a consequence of the Fall? Why or why not?

3. Why must authority structures emerge as humans begin to carry out the Creation Mandate?

4. List two Bible verses that declare that government was ordained and instituted by God.

◊ 5. Why do many Christians believe that government is a necessary evil?

16.2 WHY DO WE NEED GOVERNMENT ANYWAY?

In Dickens's *Great Expectations*, the narrator Pip observes that "in the little world in which children have their existence . . . , there is nothing so finely perceived and so finely felt as injustice."[4] There is nothing more frequently on the lips of kids than "That's not fair!" When you were a kid and someone treated you unjustly—whether they took your turn on the swing or swiped the slightly bigger piece of orange—your little heart cried out for justice.

And as you've grown up and learned about how viciously unjust people in this world can be, your now bigger heart has cried out for justice too. The dozens of Holocaust museums around the world are dedicated to telling searing stories of injustice—Jewish children hanged and gassed, old rabbis beaten, women treated like animals. And the museums tell these stories precisely so that we feel deep in our consciences that what we're seeing is terribly wrong.

Assuming you are not the one guilty of creating the injustice, there are three basic ways to achieve justice in this sin-cursed world:

(Exod. 18:13–27). Yet the people and their representatives seem to be involved when Saul and David came to the throne (1 Sam 10:20–25; 2 Sam. 5:1–4). The New Testament simply says that the existing authorities "have been instituted by God" (Rom. 13:1). Whether rulers arise by righteous or unrighteous means, God's providence stands behind their rise.

Interpreting Peter's Command to Be Subject to Every Institution

An alternative translation of 1 Peter 2:13 is "Be subject for the Lord's sake to every (divine) creation among mankind." Many versions translate the word for "creation" as *institution* (ESV), *authority* (NIV), or *ordinance* (KJV). The problem with these translations is that the Greek word is never used to mean "institution," "authority," or "ordinance." It's simply means "creation" or "creature." Some commentators have suggested translating the verse, "Be subject for the Lord's sake to every human creature." But subjection cannot be of everyone to everyone because an authority structure is implied. In context Peter is clearly talking about being subject to governing authorities, so translators choose words such as *institution*, *authority*, or *ordinance*. But instead of changing Peter's wording, it is better to understand the point Peter is making, namely that the institution of government, like the institution of the family, is a creation of God.

THINKING IT THROUGH 16.1

1. God's rule over the earth was first delegated to Adam at creation (before the Fall), and after earth's restoration human dominion will continue for all eternity through Jesus Christ, the promised Seed of the woman, the Son of David.

2. No. This is proved by the equality of the three persons of God in the Trinity. That equality isn't diminished by the differing roles of authority in the Trinity.

3. As culture becomes more complex, direction for working together must be given for orderliness and decision-making.

4. Romans 13:1; 1 Peter 2:13

◊ 5. They reason that since government's main purpose in a fallen world is to restrain evil by granting justice, government wouldn't exist otherwise—it's only necessary because of the Fall. Others point out the consistent abuse and corruption of power throughout history perpetrated by governments.

---

father by caring for him and even by guiding and instructing him. Further, while a son is always bound to honor his father when in the sphere of the family, the father may be bound to obey the son in the sphere of the state if the son holds a civil office.

[These are the arguments against Filmer used by John Locke. Locke's ideas are also mentioned in Chapters 17 and 18 on pp. 253, 273, and 281.]

In Locke's view, since everybody is free, and since someone is still needed to enforce the natural laws that God built into the world, the need for a government arises. There are two ways in which a government could arise in such a situation: by force or by consent of the governed. Locke objects to the former idea as inconsistent with each individual's free status. He promotes the idea of government by consent of the governed.

What is a major problem with Locke's view that government exists by the consent of the governed?

The people who are born under an existing government have never given consent to that government. Locke says they consent by continuing to live under that government as adults. If they don't consent, they move somewhere else. However, this answer has proved unsatisfying to many people.

[John Locke, *Two Treaties of Government* (London: Whitmore and Fenn, 1821), 234–35; Greg Forster, *Starting with Locke* (New York: Continuum, 2011)]

The Old Testament doesn't provide an answer to the question of how the first government formed. When God established Israel's government, He appointed Moses, who appointed leaders to serve under him

1. Defend the claim that ensuring justice is the main purpose of government.

2. Critique unbiblical understandings of justice.

3. Formulate a biblical definition of justice.

The Bible and Just Government

The Bible's teaching about just government will impress itself on the student's thinking more if they read these texts themselves. Consider assigning Deuteronomy 1:16–17; Psalm 72; 82; Jeremiah 22; Amos 1–2 to different students to read aloud to the class.

Translating *Elohim* in Psalm 82

"In the midst of the gods [*elohim*] he [God] holds judgment" (Ps. 82:1). The interpretation of this verse and its translation are frequently debated. The issue is the identity of the *elohim* that God judges. These have been variously identified as angels, the gods of the heathen (or demons), Israel, or human rulers. Despite the variety of suggestions, a closer look at the text makes several options unlikely. Limiting the *elohim* to the nation Israel seems inconsistent with the universal scope of 82:8. The claim that the *elohim* are gods or fallen angels falters in the face of the faults recounted in 82:3–4: judging unjustly, being partial to the wicked, and failing to give justice or deliverance to the vulnerable. These are the responsibilities of rulers.

The most likely interpretation is that the *elohim* of this psalm are human rulers. They're called *elohim* because they're entrusted by God with their responsibilities (there may be precedent for this use in Exod. 21:6; 22:9; Deut. 19:17). The major objection to this view is the statement, "You will die like men" (82:7, NASB). If they are men, why would they be told that they will die like men? Most likely this is a response to the inflated view these rulers have developed of themselves. The psalmist here reminds them that they are only men and that they'll die like all men. All things considered, therefore, the best interpretation of this psalm is the one that understands *elohim* to refer to human rulers. This interpretation is adopted by the NASB.

Mill's Defense of Utilitarianism

John Stuart Mill (1806–1873) answered the objections that (1) utilitarianism trampled on individual rights and (2) pleasure is not a sufficient standard for what is valuable.

In response to the first objection, Mill developed the harm principle. This principle stated that individual freedom should only be limited when it is used to harm others.

Justice Option 1: Achieve justice yourself by taking revenge. There have been at least thirteen movies in eight languages titled *Revenge*[5] because, let's face it, this option feels so right. Revenge is such a powerful and common human emotion because injustice bothers us all so much that we want to do something about it right away. But in our angry hands, such a reaction often creates more injustice.

Justice Option 2: Let God bring about justice. This is the very direct, very specific advice of the Bible. God takes complete ownership of all revenge: "Vengeance is *mine*," He says. "*I* will repay" (Rom. 12:19). God is a just, all-powerful King who will one day judge the world. We are commanded to leave justice in His hands.

Justice Option 3: Let God do it *through government*. Paul explains carefully in his letter to the Romans that every legitimate ruler "is the servant of God, an avenger who carries out God's wrath on the wrongdoer" (Rom. 13:4). Injustice makes God angry too. And though some injustices will not be made right until the whole world is, some will be corrected in this life by God's tool, government.

Options 2 and 3, then, are not in conflict. Or at least they need not be. (Romans 13:4 comes right after Romans 12:19, after all.) Correcting injustice is something humans care about because we are made in the image of a God who also cares about injustice. And promoting justice turns out to be the most important function of government.

JUSTICE: GOVERNMENT'S PARAMOUNT PURPOSE

In the first chapter of Deuteronomy, Moses tells the people of Israel as they stand at the border of the Promised Land how they have grown into a nation in need of a government. The first thing that Moses charges these leaders in Israel to do is to "judge righteously" (1:16). In other words, "do justice" (Mic. 6:8). Moses then specifies one characteristic of justice: judges are not to show any favoritism toward the rich and powerful (Deut. 1:17).

God made Solomon king precisely so that he could "execute justice" (1 Kings 10:9), and Solomon praises justice highly as one of the very purposes for having a king: "By justice a king builds up the land, but he who exacts gifts tears it down" (Prov. 29:4); "If a king faithfully judges the poor, his throne will be established forever" (Prov. 29:14).

Martin Luther King Jr. (1929–1968) called for justice to "roll down like waters."

Three Hebrew prophets—Jeremiah, Isaiah, and Amos—rebuked Jewish rulers for failing to live up to Solomon's standard. And those prophets still speak today through their words in Scripture. Martin Luther King Jr. used a beautiful line from Amos in his famous "I Have a Dream" speech: "Let justice roll down like waters, and righteousness like a mighty stream!" (Amos 5:24).

King was right to use those words on the National Mall in Washington, D.C., because this ideal of the just ruler is not only for Israel; it's for today's rulers too. Psalm 72 speaks of how the Messiah will treat the "poor with justice," saving "the lives of the needy" from "oppression and violence" (72:1–3, 12–14). Psalm 82 says that God judges all rulers (82:1). He condemns them with a biting question: "How long will you judge

---

Further, harm should be thought of in a limited sense rather than an expansive sense.

Why is the harm principle not a sufficient protection against oppressing others for the sake of the greater good?

Those with power may justify their actions toward those without it on the grounds that they are doing what is best for them. Mill himself justified British rule over India on the grounds that bringing British civilization to India led to the most happiness for everyone.

In response to the second objection, Mill argues that the quality of a pleasure is an important factor in the calculus of what brings the most pleasure. Mill thought he could determine quality on utilitarian grounds: "Of two pleasures, if there be one to which all or almost all who have experience of both give a decided preference, irrespective of any feeling of moral obligation to prefer it, that is the more desirable pleasure." [John Stuart Mill, *Utilitarianism* (London: Parker, Son, and Bourn, 1863), 12] He thought that because people were humans, and not pigs, they would find greater pleasure in things of higher quality.

How does Mill's response to the second objection smuggle in ideas that are contrary to utilitarianism?

Utilitarianism says whatever brings the greatest pleasure to the most people is just, but now Mill is granting that some pleasures are of a higher quality than others. To say this Mill is either smuggling in another "standard other than pleasure itself," or he isn't really escaping from the problem that not all pleasures are equally good. [Frederick Copleston, A History of Philosophy (London: Burns and Oates, 1966) 8:11–42]

unjustly and show partiality to the wicked" (82:2). Gentile kings will also be judged for their injustices (Amos 1). God expects all kings to rule justly..

Whose Justice?

It's good that one of the purposes of the US Constitution, set out in the preamble, is to "establish justice." The major biblical purpose of government is indeed to build a solid foundation for justice.

But whose justice? People don't always agree on what counts as justice. Harvard professor Michael Sandel has noted that the deep disagreements in our society over what is true and good have pressed many people to search for neutral, nonjudgmental definitions of justice. One of the most popular and enduring attempts to find such a definition is utilitarianism.[6]

Utilitarian Justice?

Utilitarianism, a philosophy developed by philosophers Jeremy Bentham and John Stuart Mill, is based on the seemingly simple, unobjectionable principle of "utility." It teaches that whatever brings the greatest happiness to the greatest number of people (and avoids the greatest amount of pain) is good. It's moral. It's just.

And utilitarianism does sometimes deliver justice. Most economic policies in America are defended via utilitarianism. Politicians argue that a particular tax cut will help millions of people get jobs while costing the wealthy only a tiny tax increase. That's maximizing utility.

But Sandel tells the story of four British sailors stuck on a raft way out in the ocean; three of them decided to eat the cabin boy, seventeen, in order to keep themselves alive. One unmarried young orphan gets zero happiness, but the others all get to keep their lives; their kids get to keep their fathers.[7] That's maximizing utility too.

So most teenage cabin boys in drifting lifeboats object to utilitarianism for reasons that should now be obvious. The same goes for ancient Christians who got thrown to lions in Rome. Sandel says,

> Yes, the Christian suffers excruciating pain as the lion mauls and devours him. But think of the collective ecstasy of the cheering spectators packing the Coliseum. If enough Romans derive enough pleasure from the violent spectacle, are there any grounds on which a utilitarian can condemn it?[8]

Or if framing an innocent person would prevent a violent, deadly riot—doesn't it become the utilitarian's duty to frame that person?[9]

People know in their God-given consciences (Rom. 2:14–15) that framing innocents, tossing Christians to lions, and eating cabin boys can't be right. We all know, then, that utilitarianism is wrong—at least if it tries to portray itself as a complete explanation of morality.[10]

Most people, at least sometimes, assume that certain actions *really are* right and others *really are* wrong—whether they appear to "maximize utility" or not. But that assumption only forces us back to the question of *whose justice*: Which actions are right? Whose idea of justice is the correct one?

ANOTHER PROBLEM WITH UTILITARIANISM

If the goal of utilitarianism is "maximizing utility," or bringing the greatest happiness to the greatest number of people, who could possibly have enough wisdom to know what would do that? Are all of your individual decisions successful in bringing you the joy and pleasure you desire? Probably not. Then who can be trusted to know what choices and policies will bring the greatest happiness to your whole nation, or to all mankind?

There is an answer: God. Our Creator knows best how to make us happy. He Himself is a happy God. But utilitarians don't generally consult Him. They want to define happiness their own way.

Is Mill right that most people who experienced both higher and lower pleasures will prefer the higher instead of the lower?

Consumer culture has demonstrated that Mill's standard of majority choice is not a reliable guide to the quality of a pleasure.

We are thus still left with a system with a high cost—a system in which some people may be oppressed for their own ostensible benefit or for the benefit of others—without the gain of actually achieving a nonjudgmental process by which to achieve justice.

Other sources: Richard Norman, "Happiness," *The Oxford Companion to Philosophy,* ed. Ted Honderich (Oxford: Oxford University Press, 1995), 332–33; Alan Ryan, *On Politics* (Liverlight, 2012), 2:696–721; Michael J. Sandel, *Justice: What's the Right Thing to Do* (New York: Farrar, Strauss,

and Giroux, 2009), 34–54; Michael Slote, "Utilitarianism," *The Oxford Companion to Philosophy,* 890–92; Robert C. Solomon and Kathleen M. Higgins, *A Short History of Philosophy* (New York: Oxford University Press, 1996), 230–31.

Neutral Justice

John Rawls has developed the most influential recent attempt to establish a neutral approach to justice. He begins with the assumption that justice is fairness. How is a fair society established? Rawls answers through a thought experiment. He asks his readers to imagine that they, along with all others in their society, were asked to design a binding social contact. But they must design this contract behind a "veil of ignorance." They would not know their own religion, their economic or social status, their abilities or

disabilities, their gender or anything else. The veil of ignorance ensures that the social contract is fair to society's least advantaged since the framers of the contract don't know whether they will fall into that category.

Consider having students attempt this thought experiment to see what social contract they come up with.

Rawls proposes that two principles will emerge. First, people will want to have as much liberty as possible, limited only by the reality that others will want the same. Second, equality in society is the ideal except when people will be better off by inequality (this exception is what Rawls calls the difference principle). For instance, if paying people in certain professions more than others benefits the least well off in society because it creates an incentive for producing goods and services that raise their standard of living, the resulting inequality would be just. If such a benefit is not created, then the inequality is not just. [John Rawls, *A Theory of Justice*, revised ed. (Cambridge, MA: Belknap, 1999), 53]

Critique Rawls's view that character and work ethic are a result of "happy family and social circumstances" (Rawls, 64). Is it therefore not fair to reward people for their better work ethic unless the least well-off person is also benefited?

While the Bible does teach that good or poor parenting can affect the character of children (Prov 29:15), it doesn't teach that it determines character (Ezek. 18). In addition, the Bible also teaches that people are to receive the consequences or rewards for wise and unwise choices (Prov. 6:6–11; 10:4–5).

How does Rawls smuggle in a view of what the good life is when he claims that the difference principle should be based on what is to "everyone's advantage."

Rawls's discussion presumes that this advantage is related to economic and social standing. But this presumes a view of what the good life is—an issue that Rawls's view is supposed to be neutral about.

After surveying several attempts to come up with neutral ways to determine what is just, philosopher Michael Sandel concluded rightly, "It is tempting to seek a principle or procedure that could justify, once and for all, whatever distribution of income or power or opportunity resulted from it. Such a principle, if we could find it, would enable us to avoid the tumult and contention that arguments about the good life invariably arouse. But these arguments are impossible to avoid. Justice is inescapably judgmental" (261).

Sources: John Rawls, *A Theory of Justice*, revised ed. (Cambridge, MA: Belknap, 1999);

Hunter Baker, *The End of Secularism* (Wheaton: Crossway, 2009), 115–19; Thomas Nagel, "Rawls, John (1921–)," in *The Oxford Companion to Philosophy*, 745–56; Ryan, *On Politics,* 2:972–76; Sandel, *Justice*, 140–83; Nicholas Wolterstorff, *Justice: Rights and Wrongs* (Princeton, NJ: Princeton University Press, 2008), 13–17.

The Christian Vision of the Good Life and Justice

The Christian has a view of what the good life is. The Bible teaches that the good life is the transformation of God's fallen image-bearers into the image of God's Son for His glory (Rom. 8:29; Phil 1:10–11).

Given this scriptural vision of the good life, on what basis can a Christian discern what justice is?

One way to get at an answer to this question is to ask why we must obey God's law. The answer is that because God is our Creator, He has the right to our obedience, and we have the duty to obey Him. It's because of who God is and who we are that it is righteous for us to obey God's commands and unrighteous for us to disobey them.

In a similar way humans have rights and duties toward each other based on their nature as image-bearers of God. This insight is at the basis of the two Great Commandments. God is worthy of love because of who He is and our neighbors are worthy of love because of who God has made them to be.

The Proliferation of Rights

The rights humans claim could be multiplied far beyond what is noted in the Student Text. For instance, the United Nations Universal Declaration of Human Rights contains thirty articles enumerating rights that it says are inherent to all humans. Some of the rights, such as life and freedom from slavery, match the biblical rights listed in the bullet points on this page. Others seem consistent with the rights of image-bearers: "No one shall be subject to torture or to cruel, inhuman or degrading treatment or punishment" (Art. 5). But others are questionable: "Everyone has the right to rest and leisure, including reasonable limitation of working hours and periodic holidays with pay" (Art. 24). A biblical case can certainly be made for a weekly day of rest (Exod. 20:10), but it would be hard to biblically justify "periodic holidays with pay" as an inherent human right. What about cultures without the concept of "periodic holidays with pay"? Were they unwittingly violating human rights? It is more likely that in this case one modern way of working out the right to periodic rest from work has been codified as a human right.

This example shows that defining justice in relation to rights can easily go astray. One danger is the tendency to multiply the rights that we claim for ourselves. Anything that we really want becomes a right. Another danger is focusing on our rights without considering that we also have responsibilities to those in community with us. A final danger is the tendency to make rights absolute regardless of the moral content of our actions.

For this reason, it is important to have a conception of what is good and what's not. It isn't enough to say that humans have a right to personal liberty. Personal liberty to do what? Does the right to liberty confer the right to own slaves, to have an abortion, or for a man to "marry" a man? All of these have been claimed as rights by Americans.

Stephen Douglas argued that the American way to handle such conflicts was for the people to vote on the matter (in his case, the spread of slavery into the territories). Abraham Lincoln replied to Douglas that a "just application [of popular sovereignty] depends upon whether a negro is not or is a man. If he is not a man, why in that case, he who is a man may, as a matter of self-government, do just as he pleases with him. But if the negro is a man, is it not to that extent, a total destruction of self-government, to say that he too shall not govern himself?" [Abraham Lincoln, "Peoria Speech," October 16, 1854] If something is wrong, it is no virtue to allow it to flourish.

Thus, as Sandel noted, justice must be judgmental. It is necessary to ask whether slaves and the unborn are humans with human rights in order to decide whether the right to own slaves or the right to kill the unborn can be granted. It is necessary to determine

3. What philosophy teaches that whatever brings the greatest happiness to the greatest number of people (and avoids the greatest amount of pain) is good? Why is this philosophy wrong?

4. How does the Bible *promise* that this yearning (identified in question 1 will be satisfied?

5. Throughout Scripture, when God addresses the task of government, what is His chief concern that government carry out?

16.3 WHAT SHOULD GOVERNMENT DO AND HOW?

The Great Famine in China (1958–61) killed an estimated 45 million Chinese, a death toll roughly equivalent to the number of civilians who died worldwide as a result World War II.[12] The Chinese government long referred to this deadly time as "Three Years of Natural Disasters." Drought did play a role, but the bigger truth is that Chairman Mao Zedong's Great Leap Forward program took away the private property of farmers, gave them unwise mandates about how to farm, mismanaged and stole their crop yields, and then blamed the resulting famine on the farmers—millions of whom then died of starvation. Mao may not have pulled a trigger or ordered a bombing run, but he (along with his government) still ended up being one of the worst butchers in history.[13] Uneducated Chinese farmers, with no political representation and no free press to put pressure on the government, were completely at Mao's mercy.

To be killed in a war by an unjust enemy is bad enough; to be killed in peacetime by your own government is certainly worse. How did things go so wrong? We can't know unless we know what things look like when they go right. And how will we know that? The Bible gives us God's view of the duties of government.

Mao Zedong (1893–1976)

JUSTICE AND THE DUTIES OF GOVERNMENT

Government is ordained by God to provide justice for the governed—justice based on their rights as image-bearers. This justice, according to Scripture, includes duties regarding defense, morality, and the poor.

Defense

Ensuring the defense of the nation is one of the ways that a government ensures justice—since wars almost always create injustices. God gave government the power of the sword, according to Romans 13. And if another nation threatens a people, their government has the right and responsibility from God to defend them. Throughout the Bible, and especially in the Old Testament, God expects those of His people who have any power to oppose injustice and oppression, to protect the weak.

Mao's "Great Leap Forward" yielded a great famine; governmental injustice claimed the lives of millions of Chinese.

1. justice

2. let God achieve it in His time or let God do it through the instrument of human authorities, such as the government

3. Utilitarianism seeks the greatest good for the greatest number, but it allows injustice toward an individual as long as the majority of people benefit.

4. The Bible promises that justice will be satisfied when Jesus comes as King.

5. God intends for government to maintain justice by rewarding the good and punishing the wicked.

SECTION OBJECTIVES 16.3

1. Explain why a just government has to defend its people, must promote morality, and should at times help the poor.

2. Evaluate the advantages and disadvantages of the major forms of government.

3. Defend the wisdom of a mixed form of government.

4. Defend limited government by demonstrating that each differing institution has its own sphere of authority.

Three Uses of the Law

When God gave the law to Israel, He knew that it could not save individuals (Gal. 3:21–24). Nonetheless, the nations could see that a nation that lived according to God's law would excel in comparison to other nations (Deut. 4:5–8). This is because the law served three functions. First, it served as a mirror to reveal to people their sin. Second, the law is like a fence that prevents people from acting unjustly or wrongly, not because of right motives but because of fear of the consequences. Third, the law teaches about Christ and can lead sinners to Christ. The first two purposes of God's law can be served to some extent by the laws of a variety of governments. A just law can cause people to realize their own tendency to act unrighteously, and it can serve as a fence to restrain people's tendency to act unrighteously. For instance, when various manifestations of racism were made illegal, racism in personal and non-legal settings became socially unacceptable. On the other hand, laws that give legal recognition to drug use or homosexual behavior will contribute to allowing those behaviors greater social acceptance.

Sources: The three uses of the law come from Calvin, *Institutes of the Christian Religion*, 2.7.6-12. The application to the civil

what marriage is and ought to be in order to determine whether it is even possible for a man to marry a man.

Why would it be just for a property owner to refuse to rent an apartment to an unmarried couple but unjust for him to refuse to rent to a white man and his African-American wife?

Scripture clearly condemns sexual activity outside of marriage (Exod. 20:14; Matt. 5:27–30; Gal. 5:19). It cannot be right for unmarried couples to demand housing or unjust for an owner to deny it. On the other hand, Scripture does not contain the category of race but instead affirms the unity of the human race (Acts 17:26). It would be unjust, therefore, to deny housing to a married couple because they have different skin colors or cultural backgrounds.

Moral judgments are necessary. This is why the basic human rights enumerated in the Student Text were ones based on direct scriptural statements. The Bible doesn't make direct statements about every situation, but the statements that it does contain can guide us regarding areas where Scripture seems silent. The problem comes when a society is composed of people who operate from different religious and moral frameworks. In this case, the solution cannot be to ignore these moral frameworks. The solution must include civil discourse in which people can openly appeal to their own moral frameworks and work out a way to function together in society.

sphere comes from J. Budziszewski, *Evangelicals in the Public Square* (Grand Rapids: Baker Academic, 2006), 48–50.

Discuss the Three Uses of the Law

Discuss with students how the three uses of the law show up in our national laws. For instance, discuss how a law against pornography or price gouging during a natural disaster can cause a person to see his or her own sinfulness. For example, a man who is tempted to profit from another's devastation might think little of it. But the law forces him to consider what he's doing because he has to break a civil law in order to violate a moral law.

Discuss how the law serves as a fence to limit unjust behavior. For instance, note that making recreational drugs illegal doesn't prevent drug use, but it does lower the rate of drug use. If something is legal, more people will be willing (even eager) to do it, but because it is illegal they are less likely to do it. Discuss some other behaviors that are immoral or unjust but accepted because they're legal.

Third, discuss with students the two levels on which Christians think about public policy. On one level, Christians want public policy that serves the common good, whether people are Christian or not. On the other hand, the Christian knows that civic goodness will count for nothing at the final judgment. The Christian desires for people as sinners to recognize their ultimate need for a righteousness not their own.

Legislating Morality

Ask students to informally debate whether governments should "legislate morality." Some have probably heard this phrase before and have been told that it's something a government cannot do. So you may have some students take the negative side.

Acknowledge that if to legislate morality means to make someone virtuous in his inner person, this lies outside the ability of governments. But note that if to legislate morality means to legislate from a particular moral viewpoint, legislating from morality is actually inescapable.

Ask students what kinds of laws governments enforce. They may mention some more mundane laws such as traffic laws or tax laws. They may also note laws against murder and theft, environmental and financial services regulation, and others.

Challenge the students to identify the moral basis for these laws. Grant that some laws are primarily to smooth the interaction of large numbers of people. There is no moral issue at stake between driving on the right or left side of the road. Yet even here there is a moral duty to have and obey traffic laws that best preserve life. Environmental regulations presume that preserving a diversity of species and habitats and not polluting the human environment are duties. This is a moral stance. Likewise, financial regulations are designed to prevent some people from defrauding others. It presumes that fraud is an injustice. Likewise, laws against murder and outright theft are based on moral claims.

Guide students to the conclusion that if the government's chief role is to ensure justice, legislating morality is inescapable.

Limits on Legislating Morality

Since government inescapably legislates morality, does this mean that every sin should be made a crime?

The permission for divorce, polygamy, and perhaps a few other matters in the Old Testament law means this question should be answered negatively. Jesus said that God permitted divorce because of the people's hardness of heart (Matt. 19:8).

In other words, in certain cultures some sins are so prevalent that the best the law can do is to restrain the worst abuses that arise from the sins.

Police protection against criminal activity is another way the government ensures justice. So is a judicial system that upholds the rule of law—no bribes or favoritism. And, of course, such a system depends on lawmakers to pass just laws.

Morality

Most people in the West would agree that a government is responsible to defend its people, but they do not always agree about a second responsibility of government: promoting morality and discouraging its opposite. But promoting a particular vision of morality is impossible to avoid because justice always requires moral judgments. As one writer put it, "Laws represent . . . the moral aspirations of a given society."[14]

That's obvious when we're talking about laws against murder and theft. It's obvious when we talk about laws against racism. In the civil rights era, America woke up to (at least some of) its moral obligations to African Americans, a group it had first enslaved and then relegated to second-class citizenship. Civil rights laws helped teach America that racism was wrong not just in formal, legal ways, but in personal ones.

But the right and moral way is not always so easy to see. It can't be found in popular slogans, even slogans as respected as ones about "freedom" or "equality." We must always ask, "Equality in what respect? Freedom to do what?" The great politician Edmund Burke said, "The effect of liberty to individuals is, that they may do what they please: we ought to see what it will please them to do, before we risk congratulations, which may soon be turned into complaints."[15]

Liberty means nothing without some moral vision of what you're free from—and free for. A great number of Americans who clamor "Liberty!" and "Equality!" when they want gays to be able to marry are silent when Christian businessmen wish to have the liberty to refrain from funding abortions in their employee healthcare plans. Freedom and equality aren't usually what either side in a big debate is really after; they're both after a particular kind of society.

And it will always be this way because God's image-bearers are moral creatures. We seem to have a drive to shape the world with our moral visions. God, in fact, despite being all too aware of the evil that rulers are capable of, says He has sent rulers "to punish those who do evil and to praise those who do good" (1 Pet. 2:14; cf. Rom. 13:3). Even modern secular societies will never escape the moral purpose of government, no matter how often they insist that they are worldview-neutral. As Solomon says, "Righteousness exalts a nation, but sin is a reproach to any people" (Prov. 14:34).

So Christians ought to advocate for truly moral laws—such as laws restricting divorce (Matt. 19:1–12), pornography (Matt. 5:27–30), child abuse (Eph. 6:4; Mark 9:42), prostitution (1 Cor. 6:18), and abortion (Exod. 20:13). And we ought to promote family unity (Gen. 2:24), hard work (2 Thess. 3:10), and ethical business dealings (Prov. 11:1).

Politics is the art of the possible, as Otto von Bismarck said.[16] Even the laws God wrote for His chosen people allowed for the ugly reality of divorce; God hated it but regulated it. God knew that hardened sinners would leave their spouses no matter what the law said, so He regulated divorce to constrain it and minimize its negative impact (particularly on women and children) in Israelite society. And Christians may have little power in society to do any legal advocating for anything. The first Christian to enter India could probably do no more than pray and evangelize in the face of the terrible practice of widow-burning called *suttee*. And even when Queen Victoria of England outlawed it in all India in 1861, Christians were a distinct minority in that land. They most definitely imposed their morality on the majority, but surely they did right.

There are plenty of Christians in America today. Surely it is right for us to try to protect the unborn, for example, from the injustice of being slaughtered. We will never succeed in banishing all sin from the world, but that is no excuse for doing nothing about it till Christ returns.

Poverty

Reasons. The government also has duties concerning the poor, and the Bible offers rich wisdom for this issue. Scripture gives several reasons why people are poor.

(1) Sometimes a disaster—such as a famine or a death in the family—plunges people into poverty (Ruth 1:1–5; Job 1:13–19).

(2) Other times people are poor because they're lazy (Prov. 14:23; 24:30–31) or unwise in the way they use their money (21:17).

(3) Finally, some people are poor because they are oppressed by corrupt governments or selfish employers (cf. Amos 5:11).

Responses. These different causes for poverty demand different responses.

(1) If a disaster comes, governments may need to join nongovernmental organizations such as the Red Cross to send help when people in far-flung places need it, which is *right now*. "Relief*" is what you do when tsunamis or hurricanes or sieges have suddenly displaced thousands of people, cutting off their supply of food, water, and jobs.

(2) But not all people with inadequate food need relief. The lazy poor should not receive a handout. Paul told the church in Thessalonica, "If anyone is not willing to work, let him not eat" (2 Thess. 3:10). These poor should be told to work and be given help to find jobs since the Bible presents work as the appropriate way of getting income (Prov. 10:4; 12:27; 22:29). A government that gives money to a man on the street is not necessarily being kind; it's actually being unjust—to him and to taxpayers—if he can work for himself. It's paying for him to continue in his sin without as many consequences. And it's paying him with money taken from other people's taxes. That's unjust.

(3) It's not always possible to know quickly, however, whether someone is poor through laziness or because of oppression. So the Old Testament made provision for all poor people. God encouraged individuals to be generous, of course, but He designed a role for government too. Individuals were required by law to leave the corners of their fields unharvested so that the poor could, through their own hard work and not through a handout, get some food (Lev. 23:22). And on a government level, Israelite towns levied a 10 percent tax every three years for those in need (Deut. 14:28–29). People with unpayable debts were also given a legal way to pay off those debts through their labor (Deut. 15:12–15).

Christians today are not bound by these Mosaic laws, but we are wise to use them as guidelines for our own situations—just as Gentile nations in Moses' day were supposed to do (Deut.

relief: aid given to help people affected by wars, disasters, and so on

LIMITS ON ENSURING JUSTICE

Not every sin is a crime. The difference between the two is not always easy to see. Some actions may be wrong but don't fall within the jurisdiction of the governmental sphere of authority; they fall under another sphere's authority. A brother may act unjustly toward his sister, but typically this is handled by the parents not the sheriff. However, if an aspect of that sin calls for penal justice (domestic abuse, for instance), then, in addition to the other authority's response, the government should also be called in to address the issue.

For example, God Himself permitted the ancient Israelites to divorce, Jesus explained, because of their "hardness of heart" (Matt. 19:8). A government that makes no provision whatsoever for divorce, such as the Philippines, can't keep it from happening—some men there just leave their wives without signing any papers. Laws are needed to contain the damage.

Christians in governmental positions must strain toward the ideal while being fully aware how far short the possible will always fall until the world's true King fully reigns.

What are other reasons civil law doesn't address everything that's a sin?

Some things are beyond the ability of civil law to detect. A civil law can punish adultery, theft, or murder, but it cannot detect lust, covetousness, or hatred (unless these attitudes result in overt actions).

Other sins are best handled by other spheres of life. A school rather than the police handles students who cheats. A business handles an employee who comes to work late every morning.

Addressing Poverty

Various proposals for addressing poverty are made, especially during an election year. Divide students into groups and ask each group to find a policy for addressing poverty from the present year or an earlier election cycle. Ask them to evaluate the program in light of the principles laid out in the text.

They should acknowledge that government does have a role in ensuring that the poor are taken care of. They should also be willing to allow the government some role in taxing and directly providing benefits. From a biblical worldview perspective, they should prefer programs that encourage individuals and businesses to provide assistance to the needy and which require those in need to work for the assistance they receive if possible.

Students should also prefer programs that don't create dependencies but that enable people work their way out of poverty. The goal should be to provide opportunities for people to carry out personal responsibility.

Creating the Conditions for Battling Poverty

The best way for governments to help the poor is not through money transfers. Often governments keep people in poverty or help people rise from poverty by the laws they have and by the enforcement of those laws. In fact, the governments most concerned about their duty of justice are the ones best positioned to address poverty.

Have students consider the following scenarios:

In an unspecified country people who have connections in government can have onerous requirements on their businesses waived. Someone with lots of money can likewise get an exception with some well-placed gifts. But a poor person starting a business will have to meet every single requirement to the letter.

By permitting bribery and corruption and by not ensuring that the law is applied equally to all, such a nation prevents poor citizens from starting businesses that would enable them to rise from poverty.

In a particular neighborhood the crime rate is high. An entrepreneur is thinking of starting a fresh produce market in this part of town, but he knows he has to take into account the likelihood of it being robbed. His margins are going to be thin enough as they are.

By not controlling crime, the government has made it difficult for business owners to profit in certain places. People in the community who might wish to start businesses may find they don't have the capital to do so, and those they would borrow from may not wish to risk their money in such a location. The lack of businesses in a crime-ridden location also deprives residents of potential jobs.

In a certain nation there is no real enforcement of patents. A company could invest in developing a new product or process, but there's no guarantee that someone else won't take the idea and be the one who makes the money from it.

Certain laws encourage innovation. The innovator may better his own financial situation, and he may create jobs for others. But if the laws discourage innovation, that wealth and those jobs are not created.

Terms for Forms of Government

Traditionally, rule by the many for the common good was called *polity*, and rule of the many in self-interest was called *democracy*. However, since *polity* in this sense is likely a term unfamiliar to students and since *democracy* now has positive rather than negative connotations, these labels were adjusted in the Student Text to *commonwealth* and *pure democracy*.

The term *aristocracy* also needs some explanation. Students probably think it means people who are born into wealthy and powerful families. In some countries these individuals had titles such as *duke* or *earl*. This is not the meaning of aristocracy as a form of government. The *Oxford English Dictionary* defines *aristocracy* as used on this page this way: "In the literal sense of the Greek: The government of a state by its best citizens."

Evaluating Shifting US Views About Modes of Government

Tune into political discourse today, and you'll hear people on the right and the left rail against the elites who run the country. These complaints are not entirely without merit. It's a problem when the wealthy and connected lean on legislators to craft laws that help them at the expense of average working Americans or when powerful media groups decide to place a finger on the scale when covering issues such as abortion or same-sex marriage.

But too often these complaints degenerate into railing against elites as elites and trumpeting the goodness of the people. In contrast, a biblical view understands that in their desires the people are often as misguided and depraved as the elites. The Bible also recognizes that while all the members of a church have governing responsibilities (1 Cor. 5:4), overseers and deacons are called to lead the church, not least by holding themselves to a high moral standard (1 Tim. 3:1–13). It also recognizes that certain skills are necessary for carrying out the duties of certain offices (Titus 1:9).

The same realities in church government apply in civil government. The American founders were influenced by this more biblical view of government. They recognized that the people play an important role in government, but they tried to devise a government that was weighted toward aristocracy in the old and best sense of the term. This is why the president was elected

4:6). The one earthly government that God has so far set up played a limited but definite role in taxing to help the needy. But the most significant thing God's system did for the poor was to safeguard opportunities for them to work to provide for themselves without being exploited.

THE MODES AND MOTIVES OF GOVERNING

How can we best structure government to deliver justice? We have to wisely use our experience viewed through a biblical lens in our attempt to formulate the best kind of governmental structures. The ancient Greek philosopher Aristotle offered a helpful outline naming six forms of government. He considered three of them good and three bad, based on the motivations of those who ruled.[17] Over the centuries Christian thinkers have refined Aristotle's ideas (as reflected in the chart) to make them consistent with biblical principles.

	MOTIVATIONS OF RULERS	
	THE COMMON GOOD	SELF-INTEREST
RULE BY ONE	monarchy	tyranny
RULE BY A FEW	aristocracy	oligarchy
RULE BY THE MANY	commonwealth	pure democracy

(row label: **FORMS OF GOVERNMENT**)

Rule by One

Monarchy is a familiar example of rule by one. This form of government has the advantage of decisive leadership. A truly powerful king doesn't have to wait to act until groups with different opinions can agree about what to do. And a virtuous monarch is able to set the moral tone for the nation.

On the other hand, a ruler can be a tyrant or a dictator who's treated like a god (or a powerful president who's seen as being above the law). Since he doesn't have to wait for Republicans and Democrats to agree, he can do evil without anyone standing in the way.

Rule by a Few

Aristocracy is rule by a select group of wise citizens. An aristocracy can be a great way to run a country because it can tap into the collective wisdom of the wise and virtuous, which is likely to be superior to the wisdom of a single monarch. And a small group may find it easier to come to agreement than a whole society will. Sometimes decisions do need to be made fast, and putting things to a national vote takes too much time.

But small groups of elites can also be as wicked, immoral, and tyrannical as any dictator.

Rule by the Many

Commonwealth is rule by the many for the good of all. It has the advantage of gaining widespread support for its policies. It also may benefit from gathering wisdom from many sources. But it can be terribly inefficient.

Aristocracy: commonly viewed as people of inherited wealth; here it means merely the wise citizens

through the Electoral College and why senators were originally chosen by state legislatures. This is why Supreme Court justices were appointed by the president with the consent of the Senate. The original intention was to set up a government in which the best citizens—the wisest and most virtuous people—were selected to govern.

In the course of history, whether Christians favor systems that lean toward monarchy, aristocracy, or commonwealth largely depends on the worldview and values that those wielding the power hold. Virtue is absolutely necessary for government to succeed in God's eyes no matter what the form.

What's worse is when all have the right to vote and they vote for the immediate gratification of their own selfish desires. A majority can be worse than a tyrant in its treatment of a minority it doesn't like. What if the majority of people in a given nation think that those with mental disabilities should be put to death (as happened in Germany under Nazi rule)?" should be replaced with "What if the majority of people in a given nation think that those with mental disabilities should be sterilized (as happened in America in the 1920s)? One of the most powerful arguments against rule by the many is demonstrated by certain comments about news articles or blogs you read on the internet—you know, the ones that make you wonder, even if they agree with you, "Are these people legally allowed to vote?"

Mixed Reviews: Which Form Is Best?

Many thinkers over the centuries have concluded that a good system will try to mix the three basic forms of government in a way that limits their defects and promotes their virtues. For instance, the American founders gave the United States a single president who could be active and decisive in executing the laws of the land and providing for the defense of the nation. They also brought in the commonwealth approach through the election of legislators to the House of Representatives. But many of the founders deeply distrusted pure democracy. They believed that the mass of people needed wise and virtuous leaders to guide them. For this reason the president is not selected by direct vote but through the Electoral College. Senators also were originally chosen by state legislatures, and Supreme Court justices were (and still are) appointed by the president with the consent of the Senate. This is a kind of aristocracy, though not one of birth but (hopefully) one of wisdom and virtue.

Is this mixed form of government a good idea when viewed through a Christian worldview? Basically, yes, it is; this framework tries to take human fallenness and finiteness into account.

- It acknowledges the truth that people are **fallen** and cannot be trusted to act unselfishly unless there are checks and balances. Absolute power corrupts absolutely. If you somehow find a benevolent dictator, chances are that his son will not be so benevolent (like Rehoboam in 1 Kings 12:12–14).
- Also, a government structure that draws insight from people in all walks of life recognizes that humans are **finite**. We need each other's perspectives and knowledge. We need intellectuals, and we need factory workers; all classes of people have been called to dominion over God's world. And humans will always be finite—heaven won't make us gods. So we will always need each other's wisdom, even in the new earth.

SPHERES OF AUTHORITY

Ronald Reagan may have been right when he said in 1981 that the US government was creating more problems than it was solving. And the "Question Authority" slogan isn't necessarily bad if you add two little words: "*Sometimes* question *an* authority." Human authorities are far from perfect; at times they need to be questioned. But to question authority in general is to dishonor the great Authority who has invested His authority in all other authorities. God instituted government. It is a good thing we all need.

Nonetheless, government is not the only institution that God has granted authority to. That's why this unit on government comes after the one on marriage, family, and gender roles. Fathers have authority whether a government says they do or not. Like-

Devising a Government

Divide the class into groups and assign each group the task of framing a government based on the different forms of government outlined in the Student Text. Then have the groups evaluate each other's suggested plans so that all the groups critique the strengths and weaknesses of the proposed governments. Use these proposals and critiques as the basis for a discussion about forms of government.

Sphere Sovereignty

As people carry out the Creation Mandate, it soon becomes clear that one person or group of people is unable to do everything necessary to subdue the earth. That's why being fruitful and multiplying is necessary! Lots of people are needed if the Creation Mandate is to be lived out.

As a result of the complexity of the Creation Mandate, a process of differentiation occurs in which different spheres of responsibility emerge. Some spheres are God-ordained institutions. For example, the family, the church, and the state are explicitly identified in Scripture as God-ordained institutions with distinct functions and structures of authority. Other spheres emerge organically as humans try to live out the Creation Mandate according to creational norms. For instance, what humans learn needs to be passed on from generation to generation, so schools are established. Study of the natural world develops some distinctive methods to ensure greater accuracy, so a sphere of science develops that is distinct from philosophy.

The same person often functions within multiple spheres. For instance, a man may be a father, a deacon at his church, a citizen of his nation, an employee, and the coach of his daughter's soccer team.

The spheres also interact with one another, but each should recognize the sovereignty of the other spheres. For instance, the church ought to disciple parents in raising their children. But the leaders of the church are not to take over the authority for childrearing from the families. Theologians should disciple scientists in how to approach science from a Christian worldview. But they should not lay out the standards for determining whether a medicine is safe for public consumption. They can point out the moral issues involved in ensuring safe medicines. But the standards and processes for ensuring safety lie within the scientific sphere.

Government is a unique sphere. God established government to exercise authority and prevent injustice in other spheres such as the family or business. But there are also limits on governmental authority. The role of the state is not to operate within or take over the tasks of any other sphere but to prevent injustices within or between other spheres of authority.

This pattern of sphere sovereignty has biblical roots (in addition to the argumentation given above, consider Jesus' exhortation to render to Caesar the things that are Caesar's). But it doesn't answer all questions. Sometimes discerning what constitutes a sphere and where its boundaries are can be fuzzy. This shouldn't be surprising. If spheres develop as the complexity of carrying out the Creation Mandate demands further specialization, then it would seem that apart from core spheres such as family, government, and church, the various spheres are dynamic rather than static.

1. defend its people; promote morality; help the poor

2. Only government has been given the power of the sword to protect its people from threats and oppression from within and from without.

   God instituted government to pass laws to restrain evil and to uphold good. Therefore, moral judgments must be made in order to decide what ought to be considered right or wrong behavior.

   Government has the responsibility to prevent injustice, and this means ensuring that people who are poor as a result of corruption or a disaster (whether catastrophic or unfolding slowly) have others provide for their basic needs until they are able to provide for themselves again.

3. Good: monarchy (decisive leadership), aristocracy (collective and decisive wisdom of the well-trained), commonwealth (widespread support and wisdom of the common folk)

   Bad: tyranny, oligarchy, pure democracy: each one becomes corrupted when an individual, small group, or majority become self-interested and unjust toward an individual or minority

4. A mixed form of government is best because it checks the defects and promotes the virtues of each of the other forms limited by finite humans and corrupted by fallen humans.

♀5. Each sphere of authority ought to carry out its own tasks without overstepping its bounds to carry out the tasks of another sphere of authority. However, the government's task of upholding justice must be enforced in every sphere.

---

wise, God has given genuine authority to the church and its leaders, even if a government says that no churches are allowed.

Government, family, and church are parallel authorities. Ideally, they would never need to reach into each other's realms. Churches shouldn't be setting speed limits on interstates, and governments shouldn't be telling churches who they can and cannot hire to pastor them. God seems to have set limits on the authorities He instituted. To give just a few more examples, most people would sense that something is wrong if the state took children to court for not eating their vegetables or if the government fined an employee of a local business for being perpetually late to work.

Every authority has its proper sphere. Children who break family rules should be disciplined by parents; employees who fail to meet company expectations should be dealt with by their managers; and congregations who hire pastors shouldn't have to check with a government official first.

totalitarianism: *a form of government in which the totality of life comes under the government's control or oversight*

When a government tries to reach into spheres where it doesn't belong, we have totalitarianism.* When that happens, the other institutions of society tend to wither rather than flourish.

And yet, among these various institutions, the state has a unique role. God established government to exercise authority and prevent injustice in other spheres. If a father fails to feed or clothe his children or if a business defrauds its customers, the state should intervene. However, the role of the state is not to operate within or take over the tasks of the many other institutions that exist.

THE FUTURE OF GOVERNMENT

Government is not a necessary evil; it is a good institution ordained by God to ensure justice. And government will always be with us. When our true King comes, we'll still have government. Jesus told His disciples that they would one day "sit on twelve thrones, judging the twelve tribes of Israel" (Matt. 19:28). Evidently, Christ's rule won't be so absolute that no other rulers will be needed. He will rule through lower-level rulers.

> For to us a child is born, to us a son is given; and the government shall be upon his shoulder, and his name shall be called Wonderful Counselor, Mighty God, Everlasting Father, Prince of Peace. Of the increase of his government and of peace there will be no end, on the throne of David and over his kingdom, to establish it and to uphold it with justice and with righteousness from this time forth and forevermore. The zeal of the Lord of hosts will do this. (Isa. 9:6–7)

THINKING IT THROUGH 16.3

1. Identify three major duties of a just government.

2. Explain why a just government ought to carry out each of the three major duties.

3. What are the three basic forms of government? Identify the ways in which each one can be good or bad.

4. Which system of government is best suited to uphold justice and why?

♀5. How should the sphere of governmental authority function alongside other spheres of authority such as the family and church?

16 CHAPTER REVIEW

TERMS TO REMEMBER

kingdom of God
utilitarianism
monarchy
aristocracy
commonwealth
tyranny
oligarchy
pure democracy

Scripture Memory

2 Samuel 23:3–4

Making Connections

1. Tell a brief story of how you think government would have emerged in an unfallen world.

2. Why do humans care so much about correcting injustice?

3. What's wrong with a utilitarian view of justice?

4. Explain the limited role of government in society. How can you know when government has overstepped its bounds?

Developing Skills in Apologetics and Worldview

5. If someone tries to argue that government would not be needed in an unfallen world, how would you respond?

6. If someone tries to argue that Christians shouldn't try to legislate anyone's morality, how would you respond?

Examining Assumptions and Evidence

7. What role does the image of God in man play in our understanding of justice?

8. Are Justice Options 2 and 3 (page 242) contradictory? Why or why not?

9. Is there only one biblically legitimate governmental structure? What factors should good government seek to balance?

10. Why shouldn't every sin be criminalized by the laws of a government?

Becoming a Creative Cultivator

11. Choose one of the following issues: abortion, same-sex marriage, legalizing marijuana, aid for the poor, or racism. Write a one-page plan for how a Christian should discuss this topic in the public square. What challenges should you anticipate? How will you respond effectively?

CHAPTER REVIEW ANSWERS

Making Connections

1. Some students may suggest that the first governments emerged as patriarchs ruled over extended families. Others may suggest that as the need for government arose, people selected leaders to fill that role.

2. Although some self-interest may be involved, in many cases the right kind of caring is due to the fact that all humans are made in the image of God.

3. It allows injustice toward an individual as long as the majority of people benefit.

4. Government is only one sphere of authority among many. While it is obligated to ensure justice, guarding against abusive authorities in each of those other spheres, government shouldn't seek to carry out or take over the tasks of those other spheres.

Developing Skills in Apologetics and Worldview

5. Governing roles were given to humans before the Fall and will be given to humans in eternity after final redemption. Governance is needed simply for structure and order in a complex society so that humans can work together effectively as they carry out the Creation Mandate.

6. It's impossible for the government to legislate anything without a moral compass guiding the lawmakers regarding how to reward righteousness and punish evil. Every law is based on someone's worldview beliefs and values and is meant to encourage or discourage certain kinds of behavior in society.

Examining Assumptions and Evidence

7. The value people have as God's image-bearers places certain obligations on us. Our neighbors, because they're made in God's image, have a right to be treated in certain ways and not treated in other ways.

8. No, God established government to carry out His justice right now, but if it fails, He guarantees us that eventually He will establish justice on earth someday.

9. No, monarchy, aristocracy, and commonwealth are all valid as long as they promote the well-being and common good of others. A good government will seek to balance the rule of virtuous and wise humans while also recognizing that the people themselves have been given rule over the earth and should have a say in government.

10. Some things that are wrong don't fall within the sphere of governmental authority but pertain to another sphere of authority. However, if the wrongdoing is not dealt with by the other authority or if it is of such a serious nature that laws have rightly been passed to ensure justice, the government has a role to play.

Creative Cultivation

11. Answers will vary, but students should demonstrate some facility in determining the different spheres involved, their limits, and the kinds of justice issues that demand government involvement.

TERMS TO REMEMBER

kingdom of God—the rule of God through a human appointed by God

utilitarianism—the view that whatever brings the greatest happiness to the greatest number of people (and avoids the greatest amount of pain) is good

monarchy—rule by one for the common good

aristocracy—rule by the wise and virtuous for the common good

commonwealth—rule by many for the common good

tyranny—self-interested rule by one

oligarchy—self-interested rule by a few

pure democracy—self-interested rule by the many

The student will be able to

17.1 Evaluate the three kinds of liberalism from a biblical worldview.

17.2 Evaluate the rise of democracy from a biblical worldview.

17.3 Evaluate varieties of socialism from a biblical worldview.

17.4 Evaluate three kinds of conservatism from a biblical worldview.

SECTION OBJECTIVES 17.0 & 17.1

1. Define *ideology* and relate it to the concept of idolatry.

2. Define *liberalism* as it is used in political science and distinguish this definition from popular usage.

3. Outline the development of differing conceptions of liberalism.

4. Evaluate the values, goals, and outcomes of classical liberalism, progressive liberalism, and libertarianism.

Chapter Seventeen **POLITICAL PERSPECTIVES**

God takes His stand in His own congregation; He judges in the midst of the rulers. How long will you judge unjustly and show partiality to the wicked? Vindicate the weak and fatherless; do justice to the afflicted and destitute. Rescue the weak and needy; deliver them out of the hand of the wicked

Scripture Memory
Psalm 82:1–4 (NASB)

17.0 IDOLATROUS IDEOLOGIES

Polite society in America tends to avoid discussion of two topics: religion and politics. (And this unit is about both of them.) But why? Why frown on talking about two things everybody has to deal with in some way or other?

It's because long experience has taught people that conversations about these two topics tend to either go nowhere or get heated quickly. Or both.

And why is that? Because to be perfectly right about either one requires a God's-eye view. And if you have that—or think you do—there's going to come a point where debate with your opponents can't go on because you've reached a bedrock level of disagreement. That's true of religion, and it's true of politics.

On the religious side. People simply can't know by themselves why we are all here, what has gone wrong with our world, and how to fix it. That's why they look to their worldview, which is based ultimately on faith.

On the political side. The world is too complex for any human (given all our limitations) to perfectly predict which political policies will be successful. That's why people look to their political ideology,* which is also ultimately based on faith.

A **political ideology** is sort of like a worldview. One political scientist suggests that it has three parts: "(1) a critique of existing society, (2) a vision of a better future, and (3) a strategy for getting from

here to there." And she points out something very key: "All three are usually informed by an underlying concept of human nature."[1]

Political ideologies, then, are actually theological because concepts of human nature are theological. So political ideologies are religious—even if their proponents don't think they are. And Christian political theorists have pointed out that these ideologies tend to be false theologies in two ways. First, when they name the great evil in the world, it's almost always something other than human sin. It's some part of God's good created order. On the flip side, when they name the great savior that will come and rescue humanity, it's almost always something other than God. In this chapter we will look at popular political ideologies and consider some real-life examples of these errors.

"For all the apparent conflict among [political] ideologies, all are subspecies of the larger category of idolatry."[2]

—DAVID KOYZIS

Even though political ideologies all have problems, Christians shouldn't expect any ideology to be wrong on every point. All the prevalent political ideologies have correctly grasped one or more creational norms. In addition, the good things in

ideology: *a set of beliefs that serve as the basis for a system of thought*

Lesson Plan Chart—Chapter 17

Section Title	Pages	Activity Manual	Days
17.0 Idolatrous Ideologies	252–53		½ day
17.1 Liberalism	253–57	Activity 30	1½ days
17.2 Democracy	257–60		½ day
17.3 Socialism	260–62		½ day
17.4 Conservatism	262–66		2 days
Review	267		1 day
Total Suggested Days			**6 days**

Government Is Fallen

This chapter focuses on how government is fallen by looking at political ideologies. But the Fall itself was a failure in government, since Adam and Eve should have served as God's representatives in the world. They should have used their God-given authority to rebuke the serpent.

After the Fall, sin affected government in many ways. The powerful oppress the weak (Isa. 10:1–2; Jer. 5:28), officials accept bribes (Prov. 17:23; Isa. 1:23), and taxes are levied for the ruler's benefit rather than the people's (1 Sam. 8:11–18). As a result, political ideologies try to root out evil. But the complexity of the fallen world as fallen and fallible humans try to fix it means that their best efforts lead to idolatry—trying to find salvation by idolizing one ideal and condemning others.

creation that these ideologies look to for salvation from the problems of life really exist—they're just insufficient to save.

Every political ideology can see corruption, oppression, and other problems in human government. But Christians cannot simply adopt the view of one of the popular political ideologies because these ideas have been warped by the Fall and are rival worldviews to the biblical one.[3] In this chapter we will examine four of the most prominent political ideologies: liberalism, democracy, socialism, and conservatism. These are not the only ideologies out there, but they are the most influential in the Western world.

17.1 LIBERALISM

In the United States, people are used to thinking of politics as divided between liberal and conservative. And in general, Democrats are liberal; Republicans are conservative. This is helpful as far as it goes, but America isn't the only country with liberals and conservatives, and **liberalism** existed long before the donkey and the elephant of US political cartoons.[4]

LIBERALISM DELINEATED

Liberalism historically has been used to describe political ideologies that make liberty (from *liber*, Latin for "free") their fundamental value. And if you know anything about American Republicans and Democrats, you'll see immediately that both are liberal in that classical sense. The two parties agree that liberty is good—just not on what liberty is and what people should be free from and free for. Republicans are more likely to be classical liberals—people who are trying to conserve the ideals of limited government especially as promoted by the Democratic-Republicans in the early days of the United States. Democrats are more likely to be progressive liberals, those who think that government should be expanded to ensure that people gain greater liberties (often meaning sexual freedoms in particular).[5]

Classical Liberals

The roots of classical liberalism are found in John Locke and Adam Smith. Locke taught that humans have basic natural rights to life, liberty, and property. Locke and others from his time saw the state* as the greatest threat to these rights. Therefore they developed a political theory that protected the freedoms of the individual and limited the power of the state.

Classical liberals were not opposed to the state. They thought the state had some important functions—but limited ones. The state was supposed to protect people's rights and property. But it only existed, in Locke's view, by the consent of the people being governed by it. If a government started trampling people's rights instead of protecting them, the people had a right to rebel.

---

state: *a nation and its government; or in other contexts, one of the fifty political divisions that make up the United States of America*

Liberty gets a statue in America, but not an agreed-upon definition. What are people free "from," and what are they free "for"?

it as evil, they begin to live in a way that is contrary to the way God made the world to work. Second, instead of looking to God as Savior, they look to something in His creation for salvation. That part of creation may be good, but it is not God. Treating it as a god is idolatry.

The three-part definition of *ideology* parallels Koyzis's analysis. Part 1 is the identification of what is fallen in the world. Part 2 is a vision for what the world ought to be. Already, it should be plain that these are theological questions: What is wrong with the world? What would a world set right look like? Part 3 of the definition is a secular soteriology. Ideologies have a plan for transcending the Fall and reaching their eschatological vision.

Ideologies and Human Nature

Every ideology depends on a particular view of human nature. This is another indication that ideologies are theological by nature. Students shouldn't identify with political ideologies without recognizing the theological and worldview implications of their choice.

What are a few theological principles about human nature that ideologies get wrong? [Students should be alert for these as they study the ideologies that follow.]

- *Humans are basically good.*
- *People do wrong because of societal conditions, oppression, poor education, and so on.*
- *People are at their best when freed from almost all constraints.*
- *People are corrupt because of corrupt power structures. Greater democracy would lead to less corruption.*
- *People act out of self-interest, but this can be good if we allow that self-interest to be directed by the market.*

Defining Terms

In popular political discussion in the United States, a liberal is usually considered to be a progressive, someone on the political left. American liberals are typically contrasted with American conservatives. However, as students begin to study political science and political philosophy, they will learn that liberalism has a much broader meaning and conflicting variations. A substantial part of the heritage that American conservatives wish to preserve is actually an older form of liberalism, now called classical liberalism. In Europe the term *liberalism* is still used to describe classical liberalism. The center-left in Europe is often termed social democracy. Though the term *liberal* is used differently than in popular media, the usage described

Once these problems have been outlined, lead a class discussion about how the students think these problems should be fixed. Document their answers. At the end of your study through this chapter, see if the answers align with the ideologies discussed here. See if students wish to adjust any of their views in light of what they learned in this chapter.

Ideologies as Idolatry

Over time the term *ideology* has taken on a neutral meaning, and it is used by some as merely equivalent to a political philosophy. However, historically, the term has had negative connotations. When originally coined, it referred to a kind of secular natural law. In the political realm an ideology is a kind of secular political religion, having identified a Fall, an eschatological goal, and a plan of salvation (see the three parts of an ideology mentioned on page 252 in the Student Text). For an explanation of how ideologies are idolatrous, see David Koyzis's work *Political Visions and Illusions* (Downers Grove, IL: InterVarsity, 2003). Koyzis operates within the same framework of structure and direction that we outlined in Chapter 9. He notes that ideologies function with a kind of Fall and Redemption structure. Ideologies recognize that the world has gone wrong. But instead of recognizing God's creational structure as good and seeing the bent direction of that structure as the problem, those who framed these ideologies identify some part of the creational structure as the problem and some other part of the creational structure as the solution. Thus, proponents of ideologies fail in two ways. They fail to recognize the goodness of God's creational order. When they identify part of

above is important for students to learn if they're going to follow more advanced discussions of political philosophy. This usage also helps students see that many of the debates between American conservatism and liberalism are often intramural debates among different kinds of liberals.

Different Types of Progressive Liberals

The Student Text simplifies the different kinds of liberals discussed by Koyzis and other political theorists. More than three distinctions could be made.

For example, Koyzis sees the 1960s as a new stage of liberalism, a development he calls "the choice enhancement state." In this form of liberalism, everyone chooses the good life that he or she wants. There is no common good that people should agree on. In fact, no one has the right to judge anyone else's choice. It is this stage of liberalism that demands that extramarital sex not be stigmatized, that abortion be widely available, that divorce be easy, that drugs be legal, that entertainment be uncensored. Of course, this liberalism pushes against the norms that God has built into His world. Pushing against these norms will have consequences.

Koyzis notes, "When these undesirable consequences do occur, rather than acknowledge that the quest to validate all lifestyle choices equally is a utopian one doomed to failure, [these] liberals increasingly call on government to ameliorate, if not altogether eliminate, such consequences so they can continue to engage in this fruitless quest. This inevitably leads to an expansion in the scope of government that is difficult to contain within any boundaries whatever."

[David T. Koyzis, *Political Visions and Illusions* (Downers Grove, IL: InterVarsity, 2003), 63–64]

What Is a Libertarian Approach?

Libertarianism and Government

There is some disagreement among libertarians about the precise role of the state. Jeffrey Miron writes "Under libertarianism, government would take part in national defense, criminal justice, and contract enforcement, but little else." [Jeffrey A. Miron, *Libertarianism, From A to Z* (New York: Basic Books, 2010), 1–2] Murray Rothbard goes further: "Libertarians regard the State as the supreme, eternal, the best organized aggressor against the persons and property of the mass of the public." He says this is true of "all States everywhere." [Murray Rothbard, *For a New Liberty: The Libertarian Manifesto*, rev. ed. (New York: Collier, 1978), 56]

Classical liberals believed that all men were created equal, but that in everyday life people don't live equally. In a free society, some people are going to become wealthy through a combination of hard work, wisdom, and social advantages. Others are going to become poor, whether through unchosen difficulties such as physical injury or through personal failures such as laziness and foolishness.

Progressive Liberals

Inequality is precisely what resulted from the industrial revolution. Wealth came to some, and with it came power. At the turn of the twentieth century, many began to think that the wealthy (and their big businesses), not the state, were the greatest threat to liberty.

People who found themselves trapped in dangerous, low-wage, long-hour jobs didn't seem to be free in the fullest sense of the term. This led to a new form of liberalism, called progressivism. The progressives thought that government regulation could be used to ensure freedom for those who were not wealthy or powerful. Large businesses would be broken up by trustbusters to give smaller businesses a better chance. Regulations about wages and worker safety would provide benefits that the workers desired but did not have the power to achieve. Progressive liberals also developed the welfare state—food stamps, low-income housing ("the projects"), and so on. They thought that government needed to take an active role in providing people enough money to have freedom of opportunity.

Liberty is the key idea here—but as Christianity's power in the West faded and ideological secularism grew, the concept of liberty among progressives expanded. By the 1960s, progressives began to insist that people should have the freedom to decide what the good life is. To say that there's a "common good" that people should agree on violates the liberty of individuals. All moral judgments of others are suspect. This kind of liberalism wanted to open up liberty for sex outside marriage and (therefore) for abortion. They wanted freedom for easy divorce, recreational drugs, and uncensored entertainment.[6]

Progressives have in many ways won the cultural battle for freedom in these areas. But whether they care to admit it or not, they have run into a divine wall. God sometimes gives people over to the sins they desire (Rom. 1:24). These freedoms go against God's created order, and so freedoms have become slaveries. Sex outside marriage has led to family breakdown and subsequent poverty, particularly within already vulnerable communities. Use of recreational drugs (including alcohol) has also wreaked havoc in countless lives and in the society as a whole.

Progressives have an answer, however: use government to take away the consequences of people's negative choices. Put a big financial pillow at rock bottom so it's not so hard for people. Government then gets bigger to the point of being difficult to contain.[7]

Libertarians

welfare state: *a state in which the government takes responsibility for aspects of citizen's financial security and health*

This expansion of the scope of government by the welfare state* provoked a response, at least in America. In the decades after World War II, libertarianism was born. Libertarians are similar in many ways to classical liberals, but libertarians want to see an even more minimal role for government—or no role at all.[8] Libertarian writer Murray Rothbard holds that even the police, the military, and the courts should be owned by private companies, not run by government and funded by tax dollars. Each individual should pay for whatever amount of service he desires.[9] Others see some

---

That's why he believes that even the police, the military, and the courts should be privatized with each citizen paying for whatever amount of service he desires.

Miron's position seems more typical.

Libertarianism and Morality

The scare quotes around "victimless crimes" in the quotation by Rothbard on page 255 are present not because Rothbard doesn't think these crimes are victimless but because he doesn't think they're crimes. According to Rothbard "a 'crime' [is a] violent invasion of someone else's person or property" (Rothbard, 27). Thus voluntary immorality should never be criminalized.

Agreeing with Rothbard on this issue, Miron writes, "In broad brush, libertarianism is socially liberal and fiscally conservative, so libertarians want government out of people's bedrooms and out of their wallets. . . . The principles of libertarianism point toward legalizing drugs and prostitution, replacing public schools with vouchers, eliminating farm subsidies, trade restrictions, and middle-class entitlements. Libertarianism opposes regulation of guns, child labor, campaign finance, unions, financial markets, and more. Libertarianism would leave abortion policy to state governments, terminate foreign policy interventions, and get government out of the marriage business" (Miron, 1).

What's the Difference Between Classical Liberalism and Libertarianism?

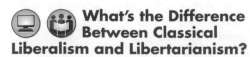

Have students create a chart that compares and contrasts classical liberals and libertarians based on the following information.

role for government. Libertarian David Boaz says, "Individuals have the right to do whatever they want to, so long as they respect the equal rights of others. The role of government is to protect individual rights from foreign aggressors and from neighbors who murder, rape, rob, assault, or defraud us."[10] For the libertarian there is no "society." There are simply individuals who have entered into agreements with other individuals. The libertarian holds that all these agreements should be free; none should be forced by the government.

Libertarians tend to agree with progressives about moral freedom. Rothbard argues for the freedom "to engage in such 'victimless crimes' as pornography, sexual deviation, and prostitution."[11] But unlike progressive liberalism, libertarians insist that people must live with the consequences of their choices.

Liberalism has a long history of development. It comes in many forms, and the older forms don't necessarily go away when the newer forms emerge. This means that several varieties of liberalism exist today, and they're not all compatible. But there is a common denominator; they all hold to the core value of liberty.

LIBERALISM EVALUATED

When you evaluate a political ideology, you must remember that it is "informed by an underlying concept of human nature."[12] At the heart of each form of liberalism is an emphasis on liberty as the great good which must be defended. For liberalism this liberty, or self-rule, is often overemphasized and out of balance with other norms that God built into the created order.

Classical Liberalism

Classical liberals (and libertarians) place a high value on the free market.* And, in fact, there seems to be something structurally right about giving businesses the freedom to excel, about allowing competition to drive innovation, and about creating a situation in which people must strive to better themselves and the world around them. The greatest force for reducing poverty around the world has been the free-market system.

> free market: *a market in which the government does not interfere in the competition between private companies*

But everything is fallen, including the market. Some classical liberals speak as if whatever the market does or drives must be right. Nineteenth-century classical liberals objected to safety regulations and child labor laws. Though classical liberals today accept such laws, some will argue that they were unnecessary. They think the market would have moved away from child labor on its own. Similarly, the classical liberal is not likely to grant that people can be paid unfair wages in a free market system. The market determines what is fair. But the Bible is clear that powerful people do oppress the poor by not paying them a fair wage (Deut. 24:14; Prov. 3:27; 29:7; Jer. 22:13–17; Mal. 3:5). The government has a mandate from God to ensure justice, even if classical liberals (and libertarians) call it "meddling." It is therefore right for the government to insist on safe working conditions and to prohibit businesses from employing young children at low wages while depriving them of the opportunity to get an education.

Another danger classical liberals (and libertarians) face is reducing everything to markets. Instead of talking about inculcating morals, some speak of creating the right incentives for desired behavior. So parents provide financial incentives for their children to earn good grades, or churches are organized to market their religion to consumers. When everything is seen as a market, moral considerations get sidelined.[13]

Both emphasize individual liberty, both seek limited government, and both favor a free market. The fact that market forces result in losers as well as winners doesn't justify government intervention. But there are differences, as Richard Epstein explains:

> This emphasis on freedom of choice and freedom of contract shows that close parallels between libertarian and classical liberal thought. But one must also attend to the differences, while noting that the Constitution is unambiguously in the classical liberal camp. The pure libertarian finds it difficult, perhaps impossible, to accept any forced exchanges initiated by the state for the common good. Hence, all forms of taxation and condemnation [related to eminent domain] are categorically ruled out of bounds. At this point, the classical liberal departs from the pure libertarian on the ground that some form of state power is needed to preserve the liberties that both groups believe should be protected. . . .
>
> The classical liberal position goes further in two key aspects. First, it argues that one function of tax revenues is to pay for infrastructure in the form of highways and public utilities, although these are often privately owned but subject to rate regulation. With respect to such private entities, the classical liberal position looks to limit the economic power of businesses that hold monopoly positions without confiscating their invested capital. Second, the classical liberal position accepts the proposition that certain forms of market failure require, or at least allow, some form of government intervention. Thus, government may restrict the acquisition, under the rule of first possession, of forms of wildlife and natural resources that a subject to premature dissipation through the standard common-pool problem.

[Richard A. Epstein, *How Progressives Rewrote the Constitution* (Washington, DC: Cato Institute, 2006), 16–17. See also Epstein, *The Classical Liberal Constitution: The Uncertain Quest for Limited Government* (Cambridge, MA: Harvard University Press, 2014)]

Judging Pros and Cons

None of the ideologies evaluated in this section gets every particular concern or solution wrong. They have all taken aspects of the creational structures that God put in place and bent them in various directions. Some have bent these structures in more unbiblical directions and others are less unbiblical. So with each evaluation there will be elements of approval and elements of critique.

The Free Market and Creational Structures

Why can't Christians simply assume that the free market system is a part of the structure of creation?

While we may discern some elements within that system to be creational, we have no special revelation for the particular complex structure that the market should take. Instead, concluding that the free market brings about more success than other systems is based on observations of how the world seems to work. But such claims must be made with humility and openness to critique.

Why might Christians suggest that a generally free market may well be part of the structure of creation?

Certain aspects of the free market system, such as private property, align with Scripture (Exod. 20:15). Other aspects produce results that are good from a biblical point of view, such as the reduction of poverty.

Unfair Wages

Classical liberals have made the case that there can be no such thing as an unfair wage. The market sets wages. If the worker is able to work somewhere else for a better wage, he can always leave for better employment, and if the employer wants to retain him he will raise his wage. On the other hand, if certain kinds of laborers are easily found, then the amount they'll be paid will naturally be low. This isn't unjust because it reflects the true market value of work.

Discuss with students Scripture passages that speak to the problem of oppressing the poor in their wages.

Deuteronomy 24:14–15: *The employer needs to take into special consideration when his employees are poor and needy. In ancient Israel, poor workers were to be paid every day because they depended on what they earned each day to survive.*

Proverbs 3:27: *In a highly competitive labor market, an employer may be able to make a lot of money while paying his workers very little. But if he has the power to do good to diligent workers, he shouldn't be stingy about paying them.*

Proverbs 29:7: *The poor are often deprived of their rights because they're too poor to have them defended. A righteous man, in contrast to a wicked one, doesn't deprive the poor of what is owed them.*

Jeremiah 22:13–17: *The Lord judges even kings who don't pay their laborers what they are owed. It may be that the king was forcing laborers to literally work for him for nothing, or that may have been a hyperbolic way of stating that he wasn't paying a just wage. In this passage God contrasts "dishonest gain" and "oppression" with bringing about justice for the poor and needy.*

Malachi 3:5: *This passage explicitly condemns oppression with regard to wages. One commentator notes that this includes "paying a nonliving wage to people who were so desperate for food that they would work anyway."* [Douglas Stuart, "Malachi," in *The Minor Prophets*, ed. Thomas Edward McComiskey (Grand Rapids: Baker, 1998), 3:1358]

Do these passages support the classical liberal view?

No, the Bible indicates that it's possible to take advantage of people by paying them too little for their work even if the market allows it.

Creational Norms and Progressives

The great folly of progressive liberals is their denial of creational norms, including a standard morality that ought to be enforced by government (Rom. 13:3–4).

What are some examples of the results of trying to live apart from creational norms?

Certain poverty programs disincentivize work, rewarding laziness over diligence. This exacerbates poverty because it destabilizes the fundamental structure that holds society together: a disciplined family.

Brainstorm with the class regarding other progressive policies that may deny the reality of creational norms.

Progressive Liberalism

Progressive liberalism must be severely criticized for often working to free people from creational norms. Most recently these freedoms have centered on freedom from sexual norms. At the foundation of God's plan for the world is mankind made in the image of God, male and female, with the commission to "be fruitful and multiply" (Gen. 1:28). So it should be no surprise that those who want freedom from creational norms want freedom from gender roles, freedom from sexual morality, freedom to choose one's own gender, and more. The Creation Mandate also teaches that work is good, yet many progressive poverty programs reward people for not working. The Bible places such a high value on work that Paul actually says that people who can work but don't shouldn't get to eat (2 Thess. 3:10).

Life in God's world doesn't work when people try to live apart from God's laws. It's like fish trying to be free from water or people trying to be free from oxygen. So progressives appeal to government to mitigate the consequences their freedoms bring. This only distorts the purpose of government. Government's primary purpose is to ensure justice. But a government that aids the effort to seek freedom from creational norms will be bound to perpetuate injustice. In addition, God has designed the world to work with multiple institutions, each with its own structures. God designed the family to nurture and raise children, and businesses to buy and sell products, and the state to ensure justice. If the state attempts to run a business, oversee worship in a church, or manage how families raise their children, it will likely carry out those functions poorly.

This is not to say that progressives are wrong about everything. The Old Testament law demanded safe working conditions (Exod. 21:29), provided a basic safety net for the poor from tax revenues (Deut. 14:28–29), and established laws that required individuals to provide for the poor (Lev. 19:9–10; Deut. 24:21). Individuals provided the aid, but the law required them to do so.[14] Laws like these ensure justice as God defines it. They stand in contrast to attempts to live contrary to creational norms.

Libertarianism

Libertarianism is wrong because it grabs on to the creational norm of individual accountability and turns it into an idol: individual autonomy. Individual accountability means that people have to live with the consequences of their choices. Their laziness does not obligate others to ensure that the lazy have all the comforts of life. But individual autonomy asserts that the government should never force anyone to do anything. Most libertarians wouldn't get rid of the government altogether, but they would give it the sole role of protecting individual autonomy.

The Bible teaches, however, that individuals are meant to be part of communities. Sinners will be held accountable as individuals (Ezek. 18:4), and people are saved as individuals (Rom. 10:12–13). And yet God places individuals in groups that are meant to work together—in the family (Gen. 2:18, 24), in nations (Gen 12:2; Rom. 13:1–7), and in the church (Eph. 4:16, 25). It is good for us to be accountable to others and obedient to our God-given authorities, even and especially when they contradict us.

Look at the places in the world where people are free to do what is right in their own eyes without government intrusion, such as Somalia. People there are not truly free. They're caught among the gears of a country grinding to a halt. Of course, this is an extreme example, and most libertarians would want a basic government to maintain order. But it does confirm the observation of the early American theologian

---

The Bible and a Basic Safety Net

Jonathan Edwards applied the biblical passages that teach that a basic safety net for the poor is an important part of a just society:

'Tis not fit that persons that are reduced to that extremity should be left to anything so precarious as voluntary charity. They are in necessity of being relieved, and, therefore, 'tis fit that there should be something sure for 'em to depend upon. But a voluntary charity in this corrupt world is an uncertain thing; and therefore the wisdom of legislators did not think fit to leave those that are so reduced upon such a precarious foundation for a subsistence. But I don't suppose it was ever the design of the law to make such a provision for all that are in want, as to leave no room for Christian charity. [Jonathan Edwards, *Sermons and Discourses, 1730–1733*, ed. Mark Valeri, in *Works of Jonathan Edwards*, ed. Harry Stout (New Haven, CT: Yale University Press, 1999), 17:403.]

The Bible passages noted in the Student Text and Edwards's statement indicate that it is an appropriate role for the state to provide a basic safety net for those in need. But the word *basic* remains a significant qualification for both Scripture and Edwards.

Interpreting *Tithe* in Deuteronomy 14:28–29

Tithe in these verses shouldn't necessarily be understood as a strictly religious term. The Hebrew word simply means "a tenth." In this case the tenth wasn't taken to the sanctuary but to the gates of the city. The gate of a

Isaac Backus: "It is so far from being necessary for any man to give up any part of his real liberty in order to submit to government, that all nations have found it necessary to submit to some government in order to enjoy any liberty and security at all."[15]

Government is not a necessary evil; it is a God-established (though fallen) good.

LIBERTY TO EXCESS

Liberalism overemphasizes liberty. It looks to freedom as a savior from many problems. But liberals easily get carried away with cries for liberty while not stopping to ask themselves, "Liberty to do what?" Liberty, like justice, must be based on moral judgments. Will those moral judgments be shaped by individual desires or by Scripture?

THINKING IT THROUGH 17.0 AND 17.1

1. What is an ideology? List the three parts of a political ideology.

2. Why are all political ideologies religious?

3. How is the term *liberalism* used in political science? How is the term used differently in American politics?

4. What key problem is common to all three kinds of liberalism?

♀5. Create a chart showing the three kinds of liberalism and identifying any biblical or unbiblical concerns, values, and approaches.

17.2 DEMOCRACY

For many Americans, **democracy**—like liberty and equality—has achieved the status of an unquestionable good. Rule "of the people, by the people, and for the people" is right up there with "God helps those who help themselves" among the sayings most likely to be mistaken for Bible verses.

But democracy needs the CFR treatment like everything else does: what's creational about it, what's fallen, and how do we push what's fallen back toward creational norms?

HISTORICAL PERSPECTIVES ON DEMOCRACY

Judging by the root words underlying *democracy*, you would think it simply means "people power" (Greek, *demos* = people, *kratia* = power). But democracy isn't a simple idea. It tends to include the right of all citizens to vote for their leaders, freedom of speech, and freedom of the press.[16] Most Americans, Christians included, believe that democracy is the best form of government. US foreign policy frequently pushes for or defends democratic elections in other nations—Americans tend to trust that democracy will work because they assume people will vote according to their own best interests.

But not all Christians throughout history have felt this way. As democratic

The gathering of democratically elected representatives in one room is a powerful symbol of democracy for Americans.

1. It's a kind of secular political, economic, or sociological worldview with its own conception of the Fall, eschatological hope, and plan of salvation. The three parts include (1) a critique of society, (2) a vision of a better future, and (3) a strategy for getting from here to there.

2. because they are all based on a theology of human nature

3. In political science *liberalism* is used for ideologies in which liberty is the fundamental value. Political scientists distinguish between classical liberalism and various later forms of liberalism. In US politics, classical liberals are typically identified as conservatives, and *liberalism* is used as a synonym for progressives.

4. a wrong view of human nature—specifically, an overemphasis on individual freedom, which erodes the value of responsibility and accountability in a community

♀5. Classical liberals are properly concerned about protecting liberty and property from tyranny, protecting freedom of exchange, and limiting government. Classical liberals run into trouble, however, if they conceive of the market as being above moral critique. Progressive liberals are properly concerned about demanding safe working conditions, fair wages, and a safety net for the poor. Progressive liberals run into trouble because their programs in practice often don't achieve their goals. In addition, progressive liberalism has tended to deny creational norms and to use the power of government to protect people from the consequences of acting anti-normatively. Libertarians are correct in recognizing the dangers of expansive government, but they go wrong by failing to account for the reality that individuals are enmeshed in community and that freedom from morality is damaging to society at large.

city was its seat of government. The elders of the city would likely have overseen these ten percent taxes. The tenth was paid every three years, but it may have been that different people brought their tenth on different years so that something was given each year. Levites, sojourners, widows, and the fatherless were the recipients of what was given. The Levites were beneficiaries because they did not receive a land inheritance. This passage teaches or implies several things: (1) It's appropriate for some taxes to be used to provide a basic safety net (food) for the economically vulnerable. (2) This provision imposed a minimal tax burden (10 percent every three years) and would not eliminate the need for individual aid. (3) This provision was paired with other provisions, such as permission to glean, that required work

from those who were able to work if they were to receive such aid.

John Winthrop on Liberty

John Winthrop, the early governor of the Massachusetts Bay Colony, makes a distinction regarding liberty much like Backus did. One of the great defects of libertarianism is an inability to distinguish between what Winthrop calls "liberty of corrupt nature" and "liberty for that only which is just and good." Libertarians minimize the reality that there are certain liberties for which "we are all the worse." [John Winthrop as cited in Cotton Mather, *Magnalia Christi Americana* (Hartford, CT: Silas Andrus & Son, 1853), 1:127]

[See also Activity 6.]

1. Distinguish between democracy as a political system and democracy as an ideology.

2. Trace the history of opposition to and acceptance of democracy.

3. Evaluate the strengths and weaknesses of democracy.

The Novelty of American Democracy

The disintegration of national morality was one of the major concerns Christians prior to the American experiment shared about democracy. Many thought that an external authority was needed to mandate or at least model morality for the populace. Religious authority and democracy were often seen as antithetical. In early America, however, religion and the growth of democracy went hand-in-hand. This was a new thing, as Alexis de Tocqueville observed in the early 1800s. This combination was also what allowed democracy to work. Though Americans did not have an established church, the churches of the United States did have a shared morality. This shared Christian morality prevented the moral degeneration of the population. The influence of the Christian religion enabled Americans to govern themselves morally.

[More information about this topic can be found in Hugh Helco, *Christianity and American Democracy* (Cambridge, MA: Harvard, 2007).]

The Founders and Limits on Democracy

As a result of the Founding Fathers' concerns about democracy, the president of the United States is chosen by the Electoral College, senators were originally elected by state legislatures, and Supreme Court justices are appointed by the president with the consent of the Senate. The people had a voice through the election of their Congressional representatives and state legislators. But democracy was checked by not allowing direct election for these other offices. Though many of the founders were not orthodox Christians, most did accept the Christian view of human sinfulness. They wanted the people to be a check on governmental tyranny, but they also wanted checks placed on the people themselves.

These checks have worn down over time, first through the reshaping of American politics by Andrew Jackson and later through changes brought about during the Progressive Era.

Two Reasons for Supporting Democracy

Evaluate the two opposite reasons that C. S. Lewis gives for supporting democracy.

What problems do you see with the first possible reason?

The Bible teaches that humans generally are neither good nor wise. The intention of the human heart is evil from infancy (Gen. 8:21).

---

ideas developed at the end of the medieval period, many Christians remained suspicious and concerned about democracy.[17] Early American theologian John Cotton (1585–1652) said, "I do not conceive that ever God did ordain [democracy] as a fit government either for church or commonwealth. If the people be governors, who shall be governed?"[18]

Cotton had good reasons for his concerns. The biggest champions of democracy were often Enlightenment thinkers who were very critical of biblical Christianity.[19] Like Cotton, many Christians worried that democracy placed too much emphasis on human freedom and not enough on righteousness. Democracy, they feared, would allow fallen people to define "the vision of the good" that society was supposed to aim for.[20] Christians also wondered if the people determined the laws that govern morality, what would keep a society from moral self-destruction?[21]

American Christians began to favor democracy, however, around the time of the War for Independence.[22] But even then the embrace of democracy was not total. Some early Americans, both Christians and others, did not trust the people to rule. They worried that the majority could become tyrants just as much as kings could. For this reason, the American constitutional system was a system of representative government that placed checks and balances on the people as well as on the elected officials.[23]

In God's providence, Christian morality was strong enough throughout most of nineteenth-century American culture to keep democracy from eroding public morals.[24] Democracy even gained moral authority as the champion of the rights of slaves and laborers in the 1800s and as the opponent of totalitarianism in the 1900s. When both Christianity and democracy saw a common enemy in godless communism, the link between Christianity and democracy was practically cemented.

EVALUATING DEMOCRACY

Democracy, does have a basis in God's creational design (as do the other political ideologies we're looking at in this unit—liberalism, socialism, and conservatism). Most obviously, God created all people as image-bearers who are given the responsibility of ruling over the world (Gen. 1:26–28). Since all people are fundamentally equal and are given divine authority to rule the world, it seems appropriate for all citizens to have a say in the political process.

Christians can also rejoice in democracy because it gives them a voice. Christians in a democracy are actually invited, along with all other groups, to shape the culture and governance of their nations. This is a solemn opportunity which should not be wasted. Also, along with democracy there usually comes a measure of religious tolerance and respect for the individual conscience. This tolerance gives Christians the space to live out their faith privately and publicly.

C. S. Lewis saw "two opposite reasons" for supporting democracy: "You may think all men so good that they deserve a share in the government of the commonwealth, and so wise that the commonwealth needs their advice.... On the other hand, you may believe fallen men to be so wicked that not one of them can be trusted with any irresponsible power over his fellows."[25] You can easily hear both justifications for democracy in the evening news. Lewis firmly adopted the second point of view.

But democracy commits the same kind of error other political ideologies do. It tends to find the source of evil in the world in a part of God's good creation order. Democracy tends to see authority itself as the source of evil—and equality as the

---

No one is righteous and does good in an ultimate sense (Rom. 3:10–12). Even those who do good in a relative sense are identified as fundamentally evil by Christ (Matt. 7:11). Wisdom comes from God (Prov. 2:6). Wisdom is something valuable that not all gain and should be treasured and guarded by those who possess it (Prov. 3:13–18). Since a great number of people are neither good nor wise, entrusting government to the populace in general is a dangerous thing.

What role would democracy play in a governmental system based on Lewis's second possible reason for supporting democracy?

Democracy would likely function as one part of a mixed form of government. If no one can be trusted with "irresponsible power over his fellows," then there must be some check on majority rule as well.

Help students to see that one of the struggles in framing a government is ensuring that wise and selfless people are the ones who rule and that dishonest, self-serving people don't gain power. However, the lure of power often attracts the latter. In a fallen world no form of government will fully achieve this goal, but some forms of government will restrain the worst abuses, and virtuous societies will not tolerate the latter kind of ruler if they have the power to remove him from his position. This is the reason democracy and virtue in society are both necessary for good government.

The Disease of Democracy

Americans value equality. We like presidents who grew up in log cabins or whose fathers worked in factories. We like commercial titans who started out on the

solution. As they say in Australia, "Cut down the tall poppy." In other words, don't let one person rise above anyone else. This is understandable given how people throughout history have abused their authority. But authority is a part of God's good created order, so opposition to authority leads to evils of its own. For instance, disrespect for the creeds and confessions of orthodox Christianity led to a proliferation of unorthodox religions in the United States in the 1800s. Unitarianism, Mormonism, Jehovah's Witnesses, Christian Science, and many other sects could flourish because Americans thought that everyone could choose whatever understanding of the Bible was right in his own eyes.

Another evil that can result from democracy is that its push for equality and resistance to authority can act as acid that dissolves a society's values. People who point the way toward higher values—higher art, higher aspirations—are mocked and shouted down. They're "elitists" who "put on airs." Lewis warns, "When equality is treated . . . as an ideal we begin to breed that stunted and envious sort of mind that hates all superiority. That mind is the special disease of democracy, as cruelty and servility are the special diseases of privileged societies."[26]

Sexual morality has also been a casualty of the acidic work of democracy. In the past, Western morality was deeply formed by (though not perfectly consistent with) a biblical worldview. So Westerners frowned on sexual activity outside of marriage. It is true that those who struggle with immorality—especially women—didn't always get the compassion, help, or forgiveness Jesus would have shown them. You can't blame a child for being born out of wedlock. But today democracy has joined other factors to reverse this situation. Our culture is in a rush to affirm immorality, whether heterosexual or homosexual. "Judge not lest ye be judged" has been twisted by democracy into a rejection of all moral judgments.

> **JUDGE NOT?**
>
> When Jesus said, "Judge not, that you be not judged" in the Sermon on the Mount (Matt. 7:1), did He mean that no one is allowed to make a moral judgment about anyone else's behavior? No, He not only makes such judgments Himself throughout that sermon, but He encourages others to make them. He called some people "hypocrites" (Matt. 6:16), and He told His followers, "First take the log out of your own eye, and then you will see clearly to take the speck out of your brother's eye" (Matt. 7:5). Jesus' point was that you are to be willing to be judged by the same standard you use in judging other people. In other words, don't be hypocritical.

When Saddam Hussein's Iraq fell to US forces in 2003, many Americans naively believed that kicking out the dictator and setting up fair elections would solve Iraq's problems in short order. President George W. Bush expressed the sentiments of many Americans in his second inaugural address: "It is the policy of the United States to seek and support the growth of democratic movements and institutions in every nation and culture, with the ultimate goal of ending tyranny in our world."[27]

But what actually happened in Iraq was that the majority Iraqi religious group (a version of Islam called Shia) used democracy to dominate the minority religious group (a version of Islam called Sunni). The result has been a lot of bloodshed. Democracy was not a salvation for the people of Iraq. Similarly, democracy in Gaza brought the terrorist group Hamas to power. Some analysts have wondered if Afghanistan would have achieved greater stability under a king than it has under a democracy.[28] The success of democracy is dependent on the values of a nation. Without Christian morality, a democratic structure will not itself produce justice. Yet democracy's egalitarianism can be an acid that eats away at the Christian concept of authority.

people like the latest movie but only the educated or those desiring to be educated will sit through Shakespeare, then a diseased democracy draws an equivalency between the two or, worse, denigrates the esteemed works of the past with the label elitist. This is especially the case if those who have studied the great works of art try to make an argument for their superiority. This artistic egalitarianism has moral consequences since art carries moral messages and mass media is one of the most effective moral educators in American culture.

How might this attitude affect morality?

Some people reject any concept of moral authority. They claim the right to determine their own morality and reject anything that would claim authority over them in the moral arena. They deny any objective aspect to truth, goodness, and beauty.

Given the answers above, how might democracy's egalitarianism act as an acid that eats away at the morality necessary for democracy's success.

Christian morality is a necessary condition for democracy's success. Democracy was feared until the United States showed how morality and democracy could function together. Democracy has failed in situations where it has been implemented as majority rule but where the values that make it successful were absent. But as Americans dismiss the very idea of moral authorities they undermine the preconditions for the success of democratic government.

Democracy and Elitism

Show students a segment of Leonard Bernstein's Young People's Concerts. Ask them what their impression of the music is. What do they think about music that requires explanation for them to better enjoy it—or to enjoy it at all? How would they respond to the claim that the music they just listened to might be better quality than the latest movie soundtrack or pop song? If students object to calling one better than the other, inquire why. See if the objection is based on a democratic idea that to claim that one form of art is better than another—especially a form of art that requires education—is elitist. Help students to see that such a response erodes what is good in a society by bringing all down to the lowest common denominator. Also help students see that such a response affects not only art but other areas of life as well, including morals.

Point out, on the other hand, how the Young People's Concerts also demonstrate a positive side of democracy. Bernstein was using television to spread a better understanding of classical music to many people who

shop floor and worked their way up. So students may need help appreciating Lewis's claim that equality is "the special disease of democracy."

In what way are all humans equals?

All people are image-bearers of God and have been blessed with the Creation Mandate (Gen. 1:26–28).

Give biblical examples of ways one person can be legitimately superior to others.

Exodus 31:1–7: God gifted certain men with the skill and ability to craft the tabernacle, its furniture, and its elements.

Proverbs 22:29; 1 Samuel 16:18: Proverbs teaches that the skillful man will stand before kings. David was a prime example of this since he was brought before Saul because of his skill in playing the lyre, his prudent

speech, his ability in warfare, and his dignified bearing.

Ezra 7:6, 10; Nehemiah 8:8: Ezra was skilled in his understanding the law of the Lord because he had devoted himself to its study. He, along with some others, was therefore qualified to teach the people the meaning of God's law.

These verses teach that certain people are more gifted in certain areas, both because of the gifting of God and the effort they have put into developing skill in a particular area.

How does a diseased democracy respond to this truth?

It attempts to deny that certain things are superior to others. Bach's music can't be declared better than the latest bubblegum pop phenomenon. A Shakespeare play can't be declared better than the latest movie. If lots of

probably could never afford to attend a concert at Carnegie Hall.

Caveats

Lewis singled out the "mind that hates all superiority" as the special disease of societies that make equality the ideal. But he also noted that other kinds of societies have their own special diseases. Students who grasp the importance of pursuing excellence and developing discernment between the good and the best, need to also remember the virtue of humility. As Paul cautioned the one group of first-century Christians, "What do you have that you did not receive? If then you received it, why do you boast as if you did not receive it?" (1 Cor. 4:7). Some students may also need the caution that not all wisdom comes through formal education. An older godly man or woman with little formal education typically has more wisdom than the brightest of students or teachers (Ps. 119:99).

THINKING IT THROUGH 17.2

1. people power
2. the right of all citizens to vote for their leaders, freedom of speech and the press
3. They were concerned that the masses governing themselves would pass laws that removed moral restraints on society.
4. Christian morality tempered the concerns about morality in a democratic system. Christians have a voice and opportunity to promote their beliefs and values in a democratic society. Their faith can be lived out privately and publicly.
♀5. It may promote rebellion against any kind of authority and an egalitarianism that does not recognize the superiority of certain ideas, cultural artifacts, or moral positions. It may seek to overthrow traditional structures and morality.

SECTION OBJECTIVES 17.3

1. Identify the origins of socialism and explain its concerns and values.
2. Evaluate the goals and the effectiveness of socialism.

Democracy and Socialism

Socialistic ideas existed in various forms all the way back to Plato, but attempts to actually practice socialism began in the late eighteenth and early nineteenth centuries when the ideals of democracy with its vision of fundamental equality for all people had begun to take root. In the middle of the French Revolution with its slogan,

---

1. What do the root words that make up the term *democracy* mean?
2. What kinds of freedoms does democracy often allow?
3. Why were some early Americans concerned about a purely democratic system?
4. Why have American Christians typically favored their democratic system?
♀5. How can a democratic system go wrong?

17.3 SOCIALISM

Socialism is generally viewed negatively in the United States by both conservatives and liberals (though not necessarily by progressive liberals). But the basic idea of **socialism** may seem pretty attractive to many readers of this textbook: the whole society—and not just the elite—should share in that society's wealth. In many forms, the entire country should own the factories and industries which earn money for the nation. Instead of enriching a select few with obscene wealth, the profits of oil companies and mattress factories and farms and automobile assembly plants should go to everyone, even and especially the workers who keep them running. There are different socialist systems employing different ideas about the roles of government, the market, and economic planning. But all of them view eliminating economic inequality as fundamental to creating a **utopia**.*

utopia: *an ideal society*

EXPERIMENTS IN SOCIALISM

Socialistic ideas existed in various forms all the way back to Plato, but attempts to actually practice socialism began in the late 1700s and early 1800s.[29] The oppression of the poor by wealthy landowners led some to propose an end to private property and an end to money. Instead, they believed that all people should share in common the benefits of their work by having necessities distributed to all as they need them.

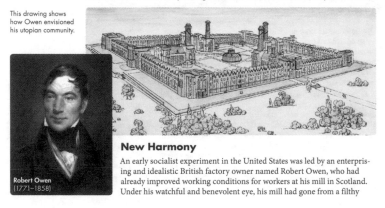

This drawing shows how Owen envisioned his utopian community.

Robert Owen (1771–1858)

New Harmony

An early socialist experiment in the United States was led by an enterprising and idealistic British factory owner named Robert Owen, who had already improved working conditions for workers at his mill in Scotland. Under his watchful and benevolent eye, his mill had gone from a filthy

---

Liberté, égalité, fraternité, one of the earliest socialist voices arose. The oppression of the poor by wealthy landowners distressed François-Noël Babeuf as well as many other revolutionaries. He called for an end to private property, an end to money, a sharing in common of the benefits of all work, and an equal distribution of all necessities by the state. Babeuf planned to achieve this egalitarian vision by setting up boarding schools in which family and religious ties would be weakened and loyalty to the state would be strengthened. The state would ensure a moral population through the training of children. Babeuf also thought that by abolishing cities and requiring people to live in villages, vice could be reined in. Babeuf's activities against the revolutionary government, however, led to his execution.

Why Did New Harmony Fail?

Owen believed that the major problem was that the people hadn't been properly educated or formed for the project to succeed. Some concluded that for socialism to work, state coercion would be needed after all. Coerced reeducation is a common tactic by those who are legitimately called the elites. Those who disagree just aren't smart.

Less noticed was the fact that religious socialists, such as the Shakers, proved more enduring. Perhaps this is due to the religious emphasis they placed on hard work. However, this fact reveals the difficulty of moving from a self-selected community with shared religious values to a nationwide economic system.

place staffed by equally filthy people (in every respect) to a model of efficiency and good manners. Owen basically invented daycare for small children. He reduced work hours from fourteen a day to eight, and children under ten were not allowed to work at all but were sent to school.

Owen decided he could do more good by setting up an entire community in America according to socialist principles. All that was needed was proper social conditioning, Owen felt, and a harmonious society would develop. In his Indiana town of New Harmony, he abolished private property and money, and he called for the sharing of all things in common.

But the people of New Harmony, although they had come there at Owen's invitation, balked. Owen's system for distributing the common goods was complex and inefficient, and the people set up a black market. Too many of the people were idle anyway, and not all the kinds of workers needed to make the community work were interested in joining Owen's experiment. The community split and eventually failed.

Karl Marx

Karl Marx scorned the failure of "utopian socialists" like Owen. He believed that socialism would arise through class warfare that would break out into revolution. Marx believed that the upper-class employers (the bourgeoisie) that hired the workers and owned the factories (the means of production) were in a fatal conflict with lower-class workers (the proletariat). Marx believed that conflict would arise between workers and owners because the capitalist system* is inherently unjust.

Karl Marx
(1818–1883)

Capitalist manufacturers of locomotives, for example, always charge more for their train engines than they cost to produce, so Marx thought they were unjustly taking profits they didn't work for. Marx didn't think managing or investing in a business counted as real work at all.[30] Therefore, he said, managers and investors should not share in the profits created by the workers. Marx thought that economic crashes would get worse and worse. He predicted that as more workers became unemployed or recognized the failures of capitalism, they would rise up in revolt. The revolution would eventually culminate in socialism.

But the bottom-up revolution never came. Some socialists responded by forcing a revolution from the top down—that was Vladimir Lenin's approach. Others, those we now call "social democrats," have argued that instead of pushing for a revolution, socialists should work democratically to continue to help workers by promoting the redistribution of wealth or government ownership of certain businesses.

capitalist system:
a system in which businesses are privately owned and operated for profit

EVALUATION OF SOCIALISM

Like other political ideologies, socialism has grasped some significant truths.[31] It emphasizes the equality of all people. Christians, because of their belief in the image of God in man, agree. Socialism perceives that those with wealth often use it to oppress others. The Bible, again, agrees that such actions are unjust and wrong. Many passages in Scripture condemn the oppression of the weak by the powerful. Socialists also perceive that humans live in communities, and the Bible supports certain kinds of communal ownership. Families and churches are good examples.

Utopian Socialism Evaluated

Princeton theologian James Alexander highlighted in a letter one of the chief Christian concerns with utopian socialism: "These Fourier-systems would make every one live in public, and obliterate little family-circles, and all that we call Home." [James W. Alexander, *Forty Years' Familiar Letters*, (New York: Charles Scribner, 1870), 1:376] Alexander recognized that socialist experiments in the United States tended to be hostile to the idea of marriage, separated children from their parents, or in other ways undermined the institution of the family. The socialists argued that this was necessary either to reeducate the youth into more productive and harmonious ways or to eliminate religious mores that had no rational basis.

What Did Socialism Get Right?

Should the Christian expect socialism to get anything right?

Yes. Ideologies that attract wide followings do not get everything wrong. If they did, they would not seem plausible. Sin, including idolatrous ideologies, is not creative; it merely twists the already existing creation.

Are ideologies all equally right or wrong?

No, some ideologies are more off-base than others. In addition, some implementations of ideologies are more damaging than others. For instance, Soviet Russia in the second half of the twentieth century brought about more damage than the British Labour party.

The Tragedy of the Commons

The "tragedy of the commons" is the label given to the observation that something owned or shared by a group of people is often treated with less care, or even abused. One reason for this is the reality that individual interests may be different from the communal interest. Another reason is the reality that when everybody is supposed to care for something, nobody cares for it.

Why does communal ownership seem to work in some situations, such as with a church or public library or park?

In successful instances of communal ownership, certain people bear the responsibility of managing and caring for the property.

Why has communal ownership not worked well on a nationwide basis?

In a socialist society, the commons ideally extends to everything. But a manager is needed, and this manager ends up being the state. The state is always less efficient than the market in determining people's wants and needs and how to meet them. A state-run system is therefore not able to rescue people from poverty as expected. Nor does the state-run system bring about equality. Managers in government end up being better off than others.

Feminism and Marxism

Marxism has affected more than just economic movements. It has also affected various other ideologies. For instance, many contemporary feminists think that early campaigners for women's rights (a classical liberal approach) misunderstood the nature of their oppression. They have now adopted an approach in which the Marxist ideology is applied to gender rather than class. [See Nancy S. Love, *Understanding Dogmas and Dreams*, 2nd ed. (Washington, DC: CQ Press, 2006), 178–81]

Interpreting Acts 2:44–45

Some Christians have argued that Acts 2:44–45 supports voluntary Christian-based communal ownership. The passage does talk about believers selling their possessions, holding what they have in common, and providing from that store for the needs of others.

Nonetheless, it's important to read these verses in context. Acts 5:4 clearly teaches that the early Christians weren't opposed to the possession of private property. It wasn't less Christian for a believer to continue to own property. Rather, in the context of the early church, Jews converting to Christianity may have been excluded by family, friends, and patronage networks. It may have been very hard for people to survive under such circumstances, so the believers banded together, voluntarily, to help each other by sacrificially selling property to care for other Christians. Acts 2:44–45 is not presenting a model national economy.

THINKING IT THROUGH 17.3

1. The whole society—and not just the elite—should share in that society's wealth.

2. an ideal society; economic inequality

3. Robert Owen tried to set up the factory town of New Harmony without private property or money. All was shared in common. It resulted in an inefficient method of distributing goods. Many people were idle and lazy. People had to resort to a black market to keep the community functional.

4. Karl Marx

5. No one should be oppressed by rich and powerful people who know how to use the system to their own advantage and the disadvantage of others.

Socialists consider owning any private property as theft from the state. Since the state manages and owns everything, almost everyone is in poverty except for those with high positions in the state.

SECTION OBJECTIVES 17.4

1. Explain how conservatism differs from other ideologies.

2. Define the three strands of American conservatism.

3. Evaluate the strengths/weaknesses of each strand of American conservatism.

But at its core, socialism calls evil something that God calls good: the right to private property. Socialists sometimes go so far as to say that "property is theft." In pure socialism, all land is owned by everyone. All businesses are shared too.

Many of the laws God gave Israel through Moses protected property rights (Exod. 21:33–33:14). Would the eighth commandment—"You shall not steal" (Exod. 20:15)—make any sense if God didn't recognize the value of private property? The early church in Jerusalem did voluntarily share its goods, but even in that sharing, the apostle Peter affirmed that it was the right of all the Christians to keep their property if they wanted to (Acts 5:4). No authority, in the government or the church, was forcing them to give it away.

So socialists run up against God's law—and therefore against creational norms—when they reject private property. And whenever humans do that, things fall apart. Here's what happens with socialism. The goal of socialists is to arrange society so everyone owns everything. But "everyone" is too nebulous a group to run a business or to manage land. So a particular institution—the state—has to step in and run businesses and manage lands. Where does that leave the vast majority of the citizens? They end up working for the government, often in abject poverty. There is a great irony here. Socialism has roots in the democratic ideal of equality, but state-enforced socialism tends to become very undemocratic. Another irony is that property ownership under socialism really just moves from the hands of common people to the hands of the elites. Socialism emerged in part out of concern for the plight of the poor and oppressed. That's a good concern. But it ends up making people even poorer by taking away from them one of the few things of value that they own—their land.

You shouldn't demonize the good things in God's creation (such as private property) or idolize them (such as equality). When you do, the inconsistencies and tensions in your ideology mess up your society. Very few people flee from capitalist nations to strictly socialist countries such as Cuba and Venezuela.

THINKING IT THROUGH 17.3

1. What is socialism's basic idea?

2. What is a utopia? According to socialism, what must be overcome in order to achieve that utopia?

3. Who tried a socialist system in America, and why did it fail?

4. Who believed that the only way to achieve a utopian restructuring of society was through class warfare?

5. What legitimate concerns does socialism have? What is fundamentally wrong with socialism?

17.4 CONSERVATISM

Conservatism usually refers to belief in the value of traditional practices, values, and institutions in politics and society. American conservatives typically value hard work, honesty, individualism, freedom, and the traditional family—precisely because that's what American culture used to stand for. Conservatives in other nations value their own culture's language, values, and social hierarchies. **Conservatism**, then, isn't really one easily identifiable set of views. It's relative to the situation.

Is Conservatism an Ideology?

David Koyzis, whose *Political Visions and Illusions* provides the framework for this chapter, opens his chapter on conservatism by acknowledging that conservatism is not a single position and that certain conservatives are expressly opposed to ideologies.

On what grounds, then, can conservatism be critiqued as an ideology? Koyzis mentions two. First, as a broader philosophy, conservatism lacks a standard by which to judge whether a tradition is worth conserving or not. Second, conservatives can be averse to progress whereas the Creation Mandate demands that progress be made in fulfilling the command to fill and to subdue the earth.

Traditional conservatives, being more influenced by Christianity, tend to have the same concerns about ideology that this chapter has raised. Yet there remains an awareness that American conservatism can become an ideology. Russell Kirk, a traditional conservative registers his opposition to ideology, opening one of his books on conservatism with the line: "This small book is a defense of prudential politics, as opposed to ideological politics." Yet he grants, "There exists some danger that conservatives themselves might slip into a narrow ideology or quasi-ideology." [Russell Kirk, *The Politics of Prudence* (Bryn Mawr, PA: Intercollegiate Studies Institute, 1993), 1]

Is it possible, someone might ask, that conservatives and Christians could have a right ideology, identifying the problem of the world to be sin and salvation to be in Christ? The answer is "no" because the third aspect of ideologies is a plan to move from the fallen condition to salvation. But even if the problem and the goal are defined by Scripture, there is no political strategy that can move the world, or even a nation, from Fall to Redemption. This doesn't mean Christians disengage politically. It simply means they take a more realistic view of what they can accomplish politically: seek to preserve what is good and seek to reform what is bad. This is what Kirk means by "prudential politics."

Ideology as Soteriology

Kirk's understanding of ideology as a soteriology parallels Koyzis's. Kirk writes:

Ideology, in short, is a political formula that promises mankind an earthly paradise; but in cruel fact what ideology has created is a series of terrestrial hells. I set down below some of the vices of ideology. 1) Ideology is inverted religion, denying the Christian

CONSERVATISM IN THE ABSTRACT

An intelligent observer looks for the substance behind the labels people like to wear. If someone says he's a "liberal," you'd better find out what he wants to be free from and to be free for (and whether or not your freedom is any concern of his). Someone else might claim to be a "conservative," but a conservative in Saudi Arabia is likely to be conserving something very different from what a conservative in Japan wants to conserve. A Russian conservative in the 1990s would have wished for a restoration of the Soviet system while American conservatives of the same time period were rejoicing in its collapse. The label *conservative* means nothing until you know what the person wants to conserve.

It ought to be fairly obvious to Christians that conservatism in the abstract has the capacity to go very wrong. What if the cultural tradition it's trying to conserve is a wicked one? Sometimes evil gets so woven into a cultural tradition that violence is the only way to get rid of it. For instance, the antebellum American South had many noble qualities worth preserving, but it took the horrendous bloodshed of the Civil War to deal with the terrible sin the entire Southern economy was based on. Race-based chattel slavery might have eventually withered away without the war, but that would have been no consolation to the slaves who would have been parted from their wives, denied education, and not given the freedom befitting image-bearers of God until another century had passed.

There's another reason conservatism by itself can go wrong. The Creation Mandate calls for growth and change. God intended for Adam and Eve and their descendants to move forward in the work He had given them—build, change, and grow.[32] When Jubal invented musical instruments (Gen. 4:21), it would have been wrong for Adam to say, "Our culture doesn't do that."

THREE STRANDS OF AMERICAN CONSERVATISM

American conservatism exists in three strands: traditional conservatism, laissez-faire conservatism, and neoconservatism.[33]

Traditional Conservatism

In America, *conservative* probably most often refers to a loosely organized movement often traced back through twentieth-century American public intellectual William F. Buckley to eighteenth-century British statesman Edmund Burke. Buckley and Burke and other traditional conservatives shared a reverence for exactly that: tradition. They felt that tradition preserved the wisdom of the ages, and that's what they were trying to conserve in the face of progressive liberals who were working

Edmund Burke (1729–1797)

William F. Buckley (1925–2008)

hard to undermine and jettison that wisdom. One of the most valuable elements of the tradition has been the Christian idea of **natural law.*** Traditional conservatives

natural law: *the moral structure that God has revealed to humans in creation and which is discerned through reason and experience (equivalent to what this book labels norms)*

doctrine of salvation through grace in death, and substituting collective salvation here on earth through violent revolution. . . . 2) Ideology makes political compromise impossible: the ideologue will accept no deviation from the Absolute Truth of his secular revelation. . . . 3) Ideologues vie one with another in fancied fidelity to their Absolute Truth; and they are quick to denounce deviationists or defectors from their party orthodoxy. Thus fierce factions are raised up among the ideologues themselves, and they war mercilessly and endlessly upon one another. . . . [Kirk, *The Politics of Prudence*, 5–6]

Kirk notes that American conservatives would be most tempted to accept the ideologies of democratic capitalism or "an ideology of Americanism, or perhaps of the Free World." Kirk isn't opposed to democracy or to reducing government involvement in the markets. Nor is he opposed to the idea of absolute truth or firm principles that should not be compromised (see below).

Rather his concern is that when these ideas are embraced as ideologies, a new civil religion is born. "A trouble with this civil-religion notion is that the large majority of Americans think they already have a religion of their own," and they do not need yet another civil religion hostile to their belief. [Kirk, *Politics of Prudence*, 8]

Conservatism and Original Sin

At the beginning of the chapter in the Student Text, a political scientist was quoted as saying that ideologies are "informed by an underlying concept of human nature."

Koyzis notes how this understanding of human nature informs a traditional conservative view:

> Conservatives have a heightened awareness of the fragility of human undertakings and the tendency of human beings to fall into evil and chaotic ways. Christians have labeled this tendency 'original sin.' . . . It is for this reason, in the face of these chaotic forces, that conservatives value every small achievement on behalf of the community. But it is precisely the achievements they value, and not the abstract proposals for reform or revolution that promise much but deliver little. Hence Edmund Burke's (1729–1797) preference for the rights of the English, with their time-tested guarantees, to the abstract notions of the rights of man, as preached by the French revolutionaries. Better an imperfect law offering some genuine protections than a law perfect on paper but without effect in the real world. [David T. Koyzis, *Political Visions and Illusions*, 76.]

 ### Ten Conservative Principles

Russell Kirk outlines ten principles that describe the traditional conservative. (*Politics of Prudence*, 17–24). Encourage students to evaluate these principles according to Scripture either through class discussion or by dividing the class into ten groups with each working on a particular principle. [Students can access the principles online by searching for "Ten Conservative Principles" on the website of Russell Kirk Center for Cultural Renewal. They may also download a PDF of "The Ten Conservative Principles of Russell Kirk" from the Heritage Foundation website.] You will probably need to provide each group with the relevant Scripture references to consult for each point.

1. Existence of a Lasting Moral Order

Students should readily see that Kirk's "enduring moral order" parallels the creational norms that this book has identified and the concept of natural law (Rom. 1:32; 2:14–15; 1 Cor. 5:1, cf. Gen. 20:9).

2. Adherence to Custom, Convention, and Continuity

For the Christian, agreeing with this principle hinges on nature of the custom and conventions. If the convention is good, then a great deal of what Proverbs says about children walking in the ways of their parents would apply (cf. Prov. 10:1). If the custom or convention is bad, then reform is necessary.

3. The Principle of Prescription

While appropriately humble about the wisdom of the present, this principle places too much confidence in the wisdom of the human race. If Romans 3 is true, the ancients were as foolish as moderns are, and the crowd is as foolish as the individual is.

4. The Principle of Prudence

Proverbs 22:3; 27:12 confirms this principle. (See also Proverbs 14:8, 15–18.)

5. The Principle of Variety

The Bible warns against the rich and powerful oppressing the poor (Deut. 24:14–15; Prov. 14:31; Amos 4:1–3), but it doesn't say all must be economically equal, nor are cultural differences bad in God's eyes (Rev. 5:9).

6. The Principle of Imperfectibility

This principle is built on the teaching of human sinfulness expressed in passages such as Genesis 8:21 and Romans 3:9–20.

7. The Link Between Freedom and Property

Money brings no lasting satisfaction (Eccles. 5:10), and the Bible warns against covetousness and the love of money (Col. 3:5; 1 Tim. 6:10; Heb. 13:5). But one of the great promises of God to His Old Testament people was land, and the Mosaic law protected people from permanent loss of land (Lev. 25:10). There were theological reasons for this, but the idea of making ownership widespread was also present in the society God created for Israel.

8. Voluntary Community Versus Involuntary Collectivism

The idea of voluntary community can be seen in the church (Acts 2:42–47). However, the Christian also recognizes that he has been placed in communities apart from his own choosing (he is born into a family; he does not necessarily choose his neighbors, and even the church is not simply a matter of consumer choice).

9. Restraints on Power and Passions

This principle also rests on the Christian view of man noted above.

10. The Balance of Permanence and Change

This principle reconciles affirmation of the improvement necessitated by the Creation Mandate (Genesis 1:26–28) with the recognition that fallen humans live out that command in twisted ways.

---

believe that there is a created order and that society will collapse if it violates that order. That order includes social hierarchies; it is good for some segments of society to set high moral and cultural standards that other segments of society can aspire to. Lastly, traditional conservatives approve of many of the benefits of the free-market system, but they aren't afraid to critique the morality of players in the market.

Laissez-Faire Conservatism

laissez faire: the philosophy that people should be allowed to do as they please; a "hands-off" approach to something

Because a conservative is defined by what he or she is trying to conserve, the **laissez-faire*** conservative is something of an irony because he's trying to conserve liberalism—either classical liberalism or libertarianism. It's a bit confusing, but laissez-faire conservatives are a recognizable group. And they *are* conservatives in one sense: they're trying to preserve the mutual toleration practiced at America's founding. Laissez-faire conservatives may or may not believe in natural law, but they do believe in freedom. In contrast to traditional conservatives who want the government to ensure justice on moral issues, laissez-faire conservatives tend to think that the free market will rein in people's vices—or even turn them into public goods. They often get impatient with the traditional conservative view when it appears to them that moral issues are getting in the way of good politics. However, some religious Americans seek to combine traditional moral values with classical liberal economics.

Neoconservatism

Neoconservatives were at first Democrats who supported Franklin Roosevelt's New Deal as morally necessary to help the poor and the civil rights legislation as morally necessary to protect the rights of black Americans. However, the next generation of neoconservatives became skeptical about the effectiveness of Lyndon Johnson's welfare vision (the Great Society). Neoconservatives were also concerned about the moral decay and lawlessness of the counterculture of the 1960s and 1970s. Defenses of Marxist dictatorships by the New Left struck them as naive and morally problematic.

Over time, neoconservatives transitioned from the Democratic Party to the Republican Party. They found themselves able to work with conservatives in a number of areas while retaining some distinctiveness. For instance, rather than blocking social welfare legislation, they were more inclined to offer alternative reforms that they thought would be more effective.

When evangelical Christians became more politically involved, they found allies more readily among neoconservatives than among laissez-faire conservatives. Though most neoconservatives were not evangelical Christians, they were rooted in the classical philosophical tradition and concerned about moral issues.

internationalism: a political ideal that seeks to overcome nationalism by uniting people above the bonds of loyalty they feel to their individual countries

In foreign policy, neoconservatives reject isolationism as impractical for a large nation with global interests. They are also nationalists and are suspicious of internationalism.* They believe that America should take an active role opposing oppressive regimes and in promoting democracy around the world.

EVALUATING THE THREE STRANDS

American conservatism is a complex phenomenon that is made even more complicated because most American conservatives don't fit neatly into one category or another. They may have been influenced by ideas from all three strands.

The strengths and weaknesses of the laissez-faire approach and certain aspects of neoconservatism have already been evaluated in the sections on liberalism and

---

Evaluating Laissez-Faire Conservatism

The main problem that the Christian has with laissez-faire conservatives is that if they believe in a natural law, they believe that it applies to social situations but not economic. The market ends up being the determiner of right and wrong.

This is problematic for the Christian because it exempts one part of the creation order from the effects of the Fall. As Chapter 7 has already established, the effects of the Fall are pervasive. No part of the created order has escaped its effects. Nonetheless, many traditional conservatives and Christians do wish to limit governmental interference in the economy for the reasons of economic growth because government intrusion into the economy can result in restriction of freedoms in other areas of life (e.g., the Affordable Care Act mandated that employers provide contraceptives and drugs that could induce abortions), and for philosophical reasons, such as belief in sphere sovereignty.

democracy, but traditional conservatism deserves closer attention. In the United States, this group has been highly influenced by Christianity. The conservative understanding of natural law is similar to this book's teaching about creational norms: God built the world to work in a certain way, and when in the name of freedom people go against these norms, consequences for society follow.

The traditional conservative also recognizes that humans are inclined to do wrong. In biblical terms, humans are sinners. The Christian and the conservative both know that this sin will infect whatever utopia people can come up with. It is for this reason that conservatives prefer small changes worked out over a long period of time rather than changes that are massive and potentially disruptive. This is also why conservatives favor reforms on the local or state level. If something goes wrong, as surely it will, the effects will be limited. Whatever goes right can spread gradually to other places. For instance, conservatives champion charter schools and private schools rather than across-the-board reforms imposed by the federal Department of Education. The leadership at some private and charter schools may make poor decisions. Those decisions, however, only affect a small portion of the population. Successes, on the other hand can spread naturally to other schools. But nationwide reform has to get everything right for everyone across the nation, or the consequences will be wide-ranging and difficult to fix.

> *"MEN OF INTEMPERATE MINDS CANNOT BE FREE. THEIR PASSIONS FORGE THEIR FETTERS."* [34]
>
> —EDMUND BURKE

Not all forms of conservatism are good. It depends on what they're conserving, and that has to be measured by Scripture. There has emerged in the United States a kind of conservatism that has been influenced by Scripture, and it does provide a good model for Christian political activity. But even traditional conservatism must beware of turning tradition into an idol and making change of any sort the great evil. God intends for His world to develop, and that means change. Furthermore, the past is a mixed bag of good and evil. Traditional conservatives sometimes appeal to Western culture as if it were an infallible standard, but Scripture—the only infallible standard—is what's needed in order for anyone to accurately judge what should be preserved and what should be relegated to the ash heap of history.

POLITICS AND YOUR FUTURE

Social media is a platform for promoting various causes. For some people, the hot-button issue is eating organic. For others, it's running or Christianity. But for many, it's politics.

If you read the comments on political posts, you know they often get excessively nasty. People don't write as if others are mistaken; they write as if their opponents are Satan's spawn. Few people, it seems, recognize that other people's political opinions tend to form a consistent pattern. Most of the American political opinions you are likely to encounter are described by the ideologies in this chapter. If you can see that truth with clarity, you will be able to add some light to discussions sadly lacking in both clarity and light.

Evaluating Conservative Sources

Provide for students articles from sources representing these three strands of conservatism and ask them to evaluate each of the articles, identifying what strand of conservatism it represents.

Sources could include:

The American Conservative, First Things, The Freeman, Modern Age, National Review, The Weekly Standard, and online articles posted by the Acton Institute, American Enterprise Institute, Intercollegiate Studies Institute, or Heritage Foundation.

Uncomfortable Fits

The text lays out the three stands of conservatism in a sharply defined manner, but in the real world not everybody fits into nice neat categories. Various thinkers coming from different backgrounds influence one another. People listen to commentators and read columnists from various perspectives without necessarily ensuring that their own thinking is rigorously consistent. Nonetheless, the three strands of conservatism are identifiable positions that help students make sense of some of the differences that exist among American conservatives.

Evaluating Neoconservatism

In some ways neoconservatives and traditional conservatives are closer together than traditional conservatives and laissez-faire conservatives. Neoconservatives do have a strong moral component in their political philosophy, which often allies them with traditional conservatives.

However, unlike traditional conservatives, neoconservatives do not reject the concept of ideology. They identify as a foreign policy goal the ideological aim of spreading democracy around the globe. It is at this point that traditional conservatives get uneasy. To transition other nations from traditional forms of government to democracy usually involves some kind of revolution of the sort that traditional conservatives find problematic as a matter of principle. At the same time, traditional conservatives are happy to benefit from the scholarship of neoconservatives who analyze issues of domestic and foreign policy.

1. Conservatism is the belief in the value of traditional practices, values, and institutions in society and politics.

2. It all depends on the context of what a society is trying to conserve. Are the things good or bad that they are trying to conserve, or are there needed reforms that should be promoted?

3. the philosophy that people should be allowed to do as they please; a "hands-off" approach

4. Traditional conservatism is rooted in the belief in an enduring moral order and the corruption of human nature. As a result, conservatives are suspicious of utopian promises and ideologies that act as secular religions. They believe in the wisdom of the past and of the fragility of the good that past generations have bequeathed to the present. They may hold to a free market system but also believe that system should come under a moral critique.

   Laissez-faire conservatives are either classical liberals or libertarians. While classical liberals may believe in a natural law, they don't see it as operative in the marketplace. This often puts them at odds with traditional conservatives.

   Neoconservatives have strong moral concerns in their political theory. They supported civil rights for moral reasons and rejected liberalism because of the New Left's inability to recognize the moral failings of communism. Unlike traditional conservatives, neoconservatives aren't opposed to ideology but instead embrace democracy as an ideology.

♀5. No, the three strands are at points philosophically at odds with each other. But the three stands of American conservatism share enough policy goals that they are often able to work together in practical ways to achieve them.

And if you can also see that no government or political system will be perfect until Christ reigns from the new Jerusalem, you can contribute even more light. Every major political system has something good to offer, but each one is also twisted in some way. Perhaps it will be your calling to serve your community, your state, or your nation as a politician. Getting a broad and clear understanding of politics now will help you greatly as you pursue that calling. Whatever your calling, that understanding will help you to press for a government that preserves creational norms, especially as they are revealed in Scripture.

THINKING IT THROUGH 17.4

1. What is conservatism?

2. Why is conservatism, as a general idea, sometimes good and sometimes bad?

3. Define the term *laissez faire*.

4. Describe the beliefs and values of the three kinds of conservatism by comparing and contrasting them.

♀5. Some conservatives have advocated "fusionism," an attempt to unite the three strands of American conservatism. Is a fusion of these three strands possible? Explain why or why not.

CHAPTER REVIEW ANSWERS

Making Connections

1. Political ideologies are soteriologies: they identify what is wrong with the world and how salvation can be achieved. In addition, they are based on presuppositions about human nature, a theological matter.

2. Liberalism
   Evil: various limitations on individual freedom
   Savior: liberty, individualism, or human autonomy

   Democracy
   Evil: hierarchy authority
   Savior: self-rule and equality

   Socialism
   Evil: private property
   Savior: equality through communal ownership

   Conservatism
   Evil: change
   Savior: tradition

3. Individual accountability means that people have to live with the consequences of their choices. But individual autonomy asserts that the government should never force anyone to do anything.

4. Strengths: It recognizes that society was designed to function according to natural laws or creational norms. It has been influenced by Christianity to conserve social morals based on biblical principles. It recognizes that humans are morally depraved and inclined to do wrong. Thus, safeguards must be put in place: small changes should come over a long time at the local level; power shouldn't be concentrated into one person; checks and balances are necessary.

17 CHAPTER REVIEW

Scripture Memory

Psalm 82:1–4

Making Connections

1. What makes every political ideology religious?

2. Identify both the great evil and the great savior in liberalism, democracy, socialism, and conservatism.

3. Explain the difference between individual accountability and individual autonomy.

4. What are the strengths of traditional conservatism? What are its weaknesses?

Developing Skills in Apologetics and Worldview

5. How should you respond to someone who argues that socialism is the political system that is most compassionate, fair, and consistent with biblical values?

6. How should you respond to a neoconservative who argues that spreading democracy and free elections around the world is an important way of making the world a better place?

Examining Assumptions and Evidence

7. What turns a political ideology into an idolatrous false theology?

8. Why do Christians tend to favor limited democracy?

9. Why did Marx think that managers and investors were acting unjustly by not returning all profits to the workers?

10. Why is a laissez-faire approach incompatible with biblical Christianity?

Becoming a Creative Cultivator

11. Choose a political topic that is currently under debate (e.g., immigration reform, renewable energy, legalization of recreational drugs, etc.). Explain your position on the issue and identify which political ideology it most closely aligns with (or explain how it combines the concerns and values of several ideologies). Defend your position from the accusation that it violates creational norms or that it elevates a creational norm as the savior.

Weaknesses: Traditional conservatism may be slow to recognize when traditions are in error and thus slow to rectify long-standing injustices. It may not subject ancient thought to scrutiny the way it does contemporary thought. It may not explicitly acknowledge Scripture to be the standard by which all ideas must be measured.

Developing Skills in Apologetics and Worldview

5. Christians ought to oppose oppression and embrace a social community larger than themselves. But under socialism, as opposed to equality of ownership for all, most people typically own very little. Instead, the government elites take over the management of everything. People are impoverished and given no incentive to work. Historical precedent demonstrates the corruption of that system. Furthermore, private property is a biblical norm, and revolutionary unrest is anti-normative.

6. Democracy alone and in general doesn't guarantee freedom from tyranny. Pure democracy may institute the tyranny of the majority over the minority through unjust laws. The success of democracy is dependent on the values of a nation. Without Christian morality, a democratic structure will not itself produce justice. It may also undermine a proper hierarchy of authority.

Examining Assumptions and Evidence

7. It may blame something that is creationally good as the great evil in the world and try to root that out completely instead of sin; it may exalt something else that is creationally good into being the great savior of the world.

8. Democracy grants freedom so Christians can live out their faith, but Christians want democracy to be limited to prevent the tyranny of the majority and moral self-destruction.

9. Marx didn't consider investing or managing to be work. Thus he thought managers and investors shouldn't share in the profits.

10. People cannot simply do as they please without degrading the social community as a whole. Injustice and immorality will be the result, but God has given government the role of restraining evil and maintaining justice. It should not take a hands-off approach to these matters.

Becoming a Creative Cultivator

11. Answers will vary, but students should demonstrate a good understanding of their topic and how various positions on that topic relate to various ideologies.

TERMS TO REMEMBER

ideology—a kind of secular political, economic, sociological worldview with its own conception of the Fall, eschatological hope, and a plan of salvation

political ideology—a view that includes three elements all informed by one's conception of human nature: (1) a critique of existing society, (2) a vision of a better future, and (3) a strategy for getting from here to there

liberalism—a political philosophy in which the chief value is liberty

state—a nation and its government

welfare state—a system in which the state bears the responsibility for the basic physical wellbeing of its citizens

free market—an economic system that is free from intervention or control by the government

democracy—a political philosophy in which power is vested in the people

socialism—a political philosophy in which inequality is addressed though society's ownership of the means of production

utopia—an idealistically perfect society or world

conservatism—belief in the value of traditional practices, values, and institutions

natural law—the created social order designed by God by which the world must function [This book uses the equivalent concept of creational norms.]

laissez-faire—philosophy that people ought to be allowed to do as they please; a hands-off approach

CHAPTER 18 OBJECTIVES

The student will be able to

18.1 Explain how the realities of Christ's present and future reign should shape Christian involvement in politics.

18.2 Evaluate the church and state positions described in this chapter.

18.3 Describe the methods and characteristics of proper Christian political involvement.

SECTION OBJECTIVES 18.1

1. Compare and contrast right and wrong Christian responses to political victories and defeats.

2. Explain the differences between Christ's kingdom rule in His first and second comings and how that affects Christian political involvement.

3. Differentiate between Christians' task of advancing the kingdom of Christ under His authority and their political involvement.

Chapter Eighteen **THE GOAL OF GOVERNMENT**

The kingdom of the world has become the kingdom of our Lord and of his Christ, and he shall reign forever and ever.

Scripture Memory
Revelation 11:15b

18.1 THE COMING KING

It happens every four years in America: Christian leaders take to their blogs on Election Day to remind a flustered Christian community that no matter who wins, God won't be unseated from His throne. He won't be surprised. God is still the supreme Ruler; Christ is still the King of Kings. God can't lose an election.

But a lot of Christians do seem to forget this most ultimate reality of their faith. They betray their lack of confidence in God's control when they go to school and work the day after the election utterly despondent, angry, and disbelieving because their candidate lost.

They also betray their failure to trust in a sovereign and all-wise God when their side wins and they are elated, certain that the future will be brighter because their candidate triumphed. When then-Senator Barack Obama ran for election as president of the United States, a striking popular poster pictured him above four block letters: HOPE. Many Americans placed a great deal of hope in President Obama, as others placed hope in a long line of politicians before him. But no politician ever quite lives up to the hype—and yet people get swept away by it every election season, all over the world.

Christians need not be pessimists; world leaders can do true good. George Washington, Winston Churchill, and others are revered for good reason. But read a biography of any great man or woman of political history—Queen Victoria, Caesar, even King David of ancient Judah—and you'll see a distinctly imperfect person. The Fall doesn't skip over

heads of state. No mere human is a safe place for all your hopes. There's only one Messiah. "In him will the Gentiles hope" (Rom. 15:12).

THE REIGN OF CHRIST IN THE PRESENT AND THE FUTURE

The title "Messiah" was first used in Scripture by an obscure Israelite woman during a period when God's people had no king and everyone did what was right in his own eyes. It was Hannah, the mother of Samuel. How did this (probably) uneducated but (obviously) godly woman, living over a thousand years before Christ, know that "the Lord will judge the ends of the earth; he will give strength to his king and exalt the horn of his anointed" (1 Sam. 2:10)? She was seeing with the eyes of a prophet. And what did she see? The word translated "anointed" is the Hebrew word *Messiah*—Hannah saw Jesus.

Two Comings of One King

What did she see Jesus doing? Repeatedly throughout her prayer (much like a famous prayer many years later from another young mother, Mary of Nazareth), Hannah saw this king, this Messiah, bringing justice to the world. She saw Him putting down the arrogant and powerful and raising up the humble and oppressed. The Old Testament consistently predicts a king and Messiah who "will reign in righteousness, and . . . justice" (Isa. 32:1).

This promised justice is why John the Baptist urged people to repent in preparation for the Messiah's

268 | GOVERNMENT

Lesson Plan Chart—Chapter 18

Section Title	Pages	Activity Manual	Days
18.1 The Coming King	268–70		1 day
18.2 Church and State	270–74	Activity 31	2 days
18.3 Christian Political Prudence	275–82	Activity 32	2 days
Review	283		1 day
Total Suggested Days			**6 days**

 How Relevant Is Christ's Kingship?

Some students may wonder at the relevance of Christ's kingship to politics. There may still be some two-story view thinking that considers the reign of Christ to be about spiritual things and politics to be about the messiness of this life.

The Hebrew word for "Messiah" is first used in 1 Samuel 2:10 (translated as *anointed*).

What are the problems that Hannah believes the Messianic king will solve?

The problems center on arrogant, powerful people who oppress the poor so that they are hungry or in danger of losing their lives.

What does the prophet Isaiah promise that God's servant will bring to the world? (Isa. 42:1–4)

People commonly put a great deal of hope in political leaders, but fallen humans are not a safe place for hope.

coming. The coming of the Messiah's kingdom wasn't good news for anyone opposed to His rule. For the unrighteous and the unjust, the coming of the Messiah meant judgment.

But something unexpected happened when the King actually came. Jesus taught that He was splitting His kingly work into two comings to earth. The first coming would bring mercy and salvation. He was holding off judgment till the second time He would come. Jesus left a lot of wrongs unrighted when He ascended to heaven nearly two thousand years ago. His miracles and healings were signs of what His coming kingdom would be like, but only signs. Jesus left a lot of sick people unhealed and a lot of dead people unraised when He returned to heaven. (And those He did heal and raise eventually all died.) Jesus did not then—and has not yet—put all wrongs right in this world.

Jesus could have judged the world as its rightful King at that time, but instead the climax of Jesus' first coming was His laying His life down under the judgment of God for all mankind's sin. But Jesus was, of course, not defeated. The cross was His greatest triumph. It enabled Him to "seek and to save the lost" (Luke 19:10) because it opened the only entrance into heaven with the only key in existence: blood sacrifice.

But you already read all about this in Unit 4. Why are we reviewing it here? Because we can't understand our present unless we understand our future. Jesus will one day come in judgment and will "put all things under his feet" (Eph. 1:22; cf. 1 Cor. 15:25–28). But even in this age, Jesus said, "All authority in heaven and on earth has been given me" (Matt. 28:18).

All Authority

It's important to notice what Jesus as the Messianic king does and does not command His disciples to do after He stakes this claim to universal authority. He doesn't tell them to take over the government of Israel and shake off the shackles of Rome. He doesn't tell them to seize power and to impose justice on the world. Instead He tells them to go throughout the world making disciples of the King—people who will do all that He commands in every area of their lives.

Psalm 110 is the psalm Jesus quoted most often in His earthly ministry. It begins with God the Father saying to the Messiah, "Sit at my right hand, until I make your enemies your footstool" (110:1). Jesus is on that throne now (Acts 2:32–36), but He's got enemies. The psalm says that, for now, the Messiah must "rule in the midst of" those enemies (110:2). So Christians, even though they're citizens of the kingdom of

---

The Messianic king will bring justice to the nations of the world.

Redemption as Restoration

Redemption is restoration. But it's not just a restoration to the way things were when God created the world. Redemption is a restoration that improves on the original creation.

According to Genesis 1:26–28, who did God originally intend to rule over the earth?

God intended for mankind to rule over the earth.

Redemption in government happens when mankind rules over the earth as God intended from the beginning.

According to Hebrews 2:5–9, who is the human king who will rule over the earth when the world is redeemed?

God will place Jesus as the human king who will rule over the world.

Jesus is a human king, but he is also fully God. So in the end God and man in the person of Jesus will rule over the earth.

Signs of the Kingdom

In what way were Jesus' actions of healing the sick, raising the dead, and cleansing the temple signs of the kingdom?

Sickness, death, and corrupt worship are all results of the Fall. When the Messiah establishes His kingdom, He will reverse the effects of the Fall.

How do we know that Jesus' actions were just signs of the kingdom and not its full arrival?

Jesus didn't heal all the sick, raise all the dead, or put all wrongs right.

The Kingdom Coming in Salvation and in Judgment

Why is it good news that the kingdom came first in salvation rather than being established all at once?

If Jesus had come to earth the first time as He will in the Second Coming to fully establish His kingdom, He would have judged the world—bad news for sinners.

Instead of ruling from Jerusalem, what did Jesus come to Jerusalem to do at the end of the Gospels? (Matt. 20:28)

to give his life a ransom for many

Has Jesus been enthroned as king or not? (Matthew 28:18; Acts 2:34-36)

Yes, all authority has been given to Him, and He has been enthroned at the right hand of God.

How are the present aspects of Jesus' reign and the future aspects distinguished in Psalm 110:2, 5?

Now He rules in the midst of his enemies, but in the future He will "shatter kings on the day of his wrath."

What does Jesus command His followers to do now that He is enthroned with all authority?

He commands them to make disciples of all nations and to teach them to submit to all that He has commanded.

Making Disciples of All Nations

Students may be so accustomed to Christianity that they have given little thought to the difference that Christ's coming made to God's work in the world.

From the time of Abraham to the time of Jesus, God worked in the world through Abraham and his seed, the nation of Israel. Israel was given a law that applied creational norms to that nation's particular time and place. By living according to this law, Israel was to draw other nations to worship God (Deut. 4:6–8). If people wanted to worship the true God, they would come to Israel's temple at Jerusalem (1 Kings 8:41–43). The king played a large role in whether his people lived lives that pleased God.

Now Jesus is the king, and the nations are not drawn to the twelve tribes of Israel. But the twelve apostles and other Jewish followers of Jesus move out to tell the Gentiles that Jesus is the king they must submit to before

He returns in judgment (Matt. 28:19–20; Acts 28:31).

Christ's Kingdom and Christian Kings

Jesus didn't tell the apostles to spread His kingdom by taking over governments. He told His followers to make disciples in all nations. But once Jesus' disciples make up a large percentage of the population, or once kings and rulers are saved, then Christians are faced with the question of what it means to observe all that Jesus commanded in the political realm.

THINKING IT THROUGH 18.1

1. He will judge the world in righteousness and bring justice to the oppressed.

2. In His first coming Jesus came to sacrifice Himself, bringing mercy and salvation rather than judgment.

3. Since Christ's kingdom is not of this world at this time (John 18:36), believers shouldn't seek to take over the governments in this world in the name of Christ's kingdom; they should take the gospel to the world. But as citizens involved in this world who are able to influence their respective governments, believers should seek to align government with biblical principles of morality and justice.

♀4. When Christ asks believers to trust in His sovereign control, He doesn't ask them to be indifferent to the realities in this world that affect them positively or negatively. Believers can cry out to Him with complaints of distress, and they can rejoice when oppression is overturned.

YOUR KINGDOM COME

When Jesus taught His disciples to pray "Your kingdom come" (Matt. 6:10) in the Model Prayer, what did He mean? There seem to be basically two options: He meant either something future or something present. Either that kingdom will come someday, or it's already here.

Or both. The kingdom of God is simply God's rule through Jesus Christ. And is that rule here? Yes, in Psalm 110 the Father tells Christ to "rule in the midst of [His] enemies," and that's happening right now. And yet that rule is not complete; He's still got enemies.

"Your kingdom come" is a prayer that Christ's rule would spread even now, broader and deeper. It's also a prayer that Christ's rule would become complete. When you pray that phrase, you're asking that Christ's rule would extend to more people and that it would go more deeply into the people (like you?) who are already under Christ's rule. We should also pray that Christ will achieve the ultimate triumph over all His enemies.

an all-powerful King, are often persecuted and even killed by lesser kings. It is also for this reason that powerful people still act unjustly. But Christ's kingdom will not be defeated. His kingdom, like yeast permeating dough, is always spreading (Matt. 13:33).

Christ rules, and Psalm 110 says that He will one day "shatter kings" and "execute judgment among the nations" in "the day of his wrath" (110:5–6). The king-shattering and other judgments are His job, not ours. We have other work to do.

None of this means that Christians are to abandon government and focus only on evangelism. The first thing we must do is pray for our rulers (1 Tim. 2:1–4). But we also get to promote true justice and the claims of the true King within government—while remembering that only Christ has the authority to advance His kingdom by violent force (John 18:36).

THINKING IT THROUGH 18.1

1. How does the Old Testament describe the reign of the Messiah?

2. Why has injustice continued to be a problem in the world even after Jesus came as the Messiah?

3. What are the roles and responsibilities of believers as citizens of Christ's kingdom and as citizens of nations within this world?

♀4. Based on Scripture, explain how believers can trust in Christ's sovereign judgment and also express joy or sorrow in response to righteous or wicked rulers (Pss. 42:9; 43:1–2; Prov. 11:10; 14:34; 21:1; Eccles. 3:16–17; 4:1–3; 5:8–9; 7:14).

18.2 CHURCH AND STATE

Most Americans assume that there's supposed to be a "wall of separation between church and state," but after that the details get murky. Where is the wall supposed to be exactly? And how high? Low enough to talk over, or high enough to create a prison for one side or the other?

Biblically speaking, the church and the state have to have some sort of relationship because both government and the Christian religion claim similar roles in society. One writer observes that both the church and the state are

about governing people. Both lay down rules for doing so. Both regard these rules as expressing moral values, the way things ought and ought not to be. Both insist that these normative rules are authoritatively binding on people. Moreover, any religion is a comprehensive worldview which necessarily includes the political, social, and all the other dimensions of human life.[1]

How can two institutions that make such sweeping claims possibly get along?

---

1. Evaluate the state over church position.
2. Evaluate the church over state position.
3. Evaluate the civil religion position.
4. Evaluate the exclusion of religion from the public sphere.
5. Evaluate the church influencing the state position.

Similar Roles of Church and State

Discuss the Hugh Heclo quotation at the bottom of page 270. Students may need help understanding some of the parallels since the church and the state function differently despite their similarities. The church doesn't govern in the same way the state governs. The church exercises a teaching ministry that guides people to become followers of Christ.

In addition, the quotation may in some ways overstate the similarities. For instance, the church does not lay down rules for people, but Christ in Scripture does give His followers commands that they are to obey: "Make disciples . . . teaching them to observe all that I have commanded you" (Matt. 28:19–20).

Nonetheless, the parallels remain significant. As this book has argued at length, the Christian faith is "a comprehensive worldview" that touches every aspect of life. We have also argued in this unit that laws inescapably reflect a particular moral viewpoint.

The end result is that both church and state give people guidance about how they ought to live. In some cultures the relation between church and state has been one of opposition because the worldviews they operate from are opposed to each other. Consider ancient Rome, communist dictatorships, or Islamic states. But when Christians have influence in the state, a more constructive relationship can be forged between Christianity and government.

Sphere Sovereignty

We argued earlier that different cultural institutions have their respective spheres of authority under the sovereignty of Christ. Thus, the church should not run a business, and a business should not run the state. And family authority is different from church authority, and so forth.

This principle should guide in church-and-state discussions as well. Any arrangement in which one sphere is claiming sovereignty over another is problematic.

State over Church

At some points in history, the state has claimed authority over the church. Roman emperor Constantine set this precedent by convening church councils—and thereby claiming the authority to do so.

This view—often called **Constantinianism**—misunderstands the nature of Christ's present reign. The kings of the earth are required to pay homage to the Messiah and to obey His word (Ps. 2:8–12). Kings (and presidents and prime ministers) are appointed by God (Rom. 13:1), but their failure to submit to Him doesn't automatically remove them from power (Dan. 2:21–23). Nor does their appointment by God give them authority over the church or its doctrine. Instead Christ, the Head of the church, appoints evangelists as well as pastors and teachers over that church (Eph. 4:11).

STATE *CHURCH*

Church over State

The medieval Roman Catholic Church flipped the state-over-church position on its head, claiming a church-over-state view instead. If the pope is Christ's representative on earth (Christ's "vicar"), then of course the pope has authority over any other human leader. The Roman Church recognized that the state had its own rightful sphere in which it functioned, but when Charlemagne was crowned Holy Roman Emperor in 800, it was the pope who did the crowning—implying that he had authority over the emperor. Four hundred years later, another pope put all of England under an interdict* when the English king didn't like the pope's appointment of an English archbishop. And it was the English king who had to give in in the end. Also, the Inquisition carried out by the Roman Church punished heretics with the sword of the state.

But simply put, nowhere in Scripture is the church given the power of the sword or legal authority over the civil government.

CHURCH *STATE*

interdict: *a restriction imposed by the pope barring a nation from participating in the sacraments*

Civil Religion

America has never, since its forming as a nation, had either a state-over-church or a church-over-state system. One alternative we have had is **civil religion**, "the appropriation of religion by politics for its own purposes."[2] People in public pray to and praise god (with a lower-case *g*), a god they never bother to describe in any detail. Does this god have a son, Jesus? Does this god send anyone to hell or express preferences about sexual ethics? If politicians answered these questions, the god they refer to wouldn't unite the nation anymore. Protestants, Muslims, Catholics, and Jews can all sing "God Bless America" only if everyone glosses over sticky theological questions.

Civil religion grew out of a compromise between the "theistic rationalism" of many American founders and the traditional Protestant Christianity practiced by much of the American populace.[3] Leaders such as Thomas Jefferson believed in god, in the moral teachings of certain parts of the Bible, and perhaps even in some final judgment. But they felt it was against reason to believe in the deity of Christ, the Trinity, and salvation by grace through faith in the death and resurrection of Christ.[4]

Because the civil religion of the United States is so closely tied to Christianity, it is sometimes difficult for Christians to discern the differences between the two. A Christian can pledge allegiance to "one nation under God" while standing next to someone who means something very different by the phrase.

S✝ATE

State over Church in History

This position was followed most extensively in the Byzantine Empire. In the medieval West it was followed in certain areas when the rulers appointed the bishops. This led to the investiture controversy in the eleventh and twelfth centuries between the popes and rulers of Europe. England adopted this position during the Reformation when the monarch was made the supreme head of the Church of England.

 State over Church: Arguments from Scripture

Some defenders of the state over church view pointed to the reign of Christ as justification for this position. Christ reigned over all the world. He also ordained government (Rom. 13:1). Rulers are therefore rulers under Him. Since rulers are representatives of Christ, the church is under these representatives. Supporters of this view noted that fearing God and honoring the king are linked by Peter (1 Pet. 2:17). Some also appealed to God's promise to His people: "Kings shall be thy nursing fathers, and their queens thy nursing mothers" (Isa. 49:23, KJV). This was taken to mean that the rulers were to protect and care for the church.

Use the following questions to evaluate these arguments with the students:

Who was emperor when Paul wrote Romans 13? How should this fact influence the claim that the ruler is Christ's representative and thus a head of the church?

Nero was the emperor when Paul wrote Romans 13. Since Nero wasn't a Christian, it's illogical to claim that Paul was asserting that Christ had ordained Nero to be head over the church as His representative.

Why does 1 Peter 2:17 not prove that the king is appointed by God as head over the church?

Fearing God and honoring the king are linked because God has appointed the king to rule in civil matters. The passage says nothing about the king's jurisdiction over church teaching, the appointment of church leaders, and so on.

What does Isaiah 49:22–23 teach in context?

This is a prophecy given to Zion (Israel) that the nations of the world will be transformed from antagonists to submissive benefactors.

Arguments for Church over State

The medieval Roman Catholic Church had many arguments for asserting authority over the state. One argument was founded on the "Donation of Constantine," a document purporting to be from the Emperor Constantine, granting secular power to the pope.

The Roman Church also claimed that it was more important than the state the same way the spirit is more important than the body (according to medieval Catholic theology). Thus, the pope could claim the right to grant power to the rulers to rule, to dictate how the spiritual affairs of the nation were to be run, and to use the sword of the state to punish heretics.

The "Donation of Constantine" was proven to be a forgery during the Renaissance. The argument from the analogy of spirit and body is based on a faulty theology of the body. The Bible doesn't teach that the spirit is more important than the body. In fact, Paul says that Christians wait eagerly for their body's redemption (Rom. 8:23) and that the Christian faith is in vain without bodily resurrection (1 Cor. 15:12–19).

 The American Founders and Civil Religion

Some Christians wish to make many of the Founding Fathers out to be Christians due to their references to God in public statements. They are wary of secularists who want to strip American history of its religious heritage. This is a legitimate concern.

But pointing out that not all of the founders were orthodox Christians is not secular revisionism. Conservative Christian historians who reject the secularist narrative have pointed out that a number of the Founding Fathers stand somewhere between orthodox Christianity and the stronger forms of deism. These Christian historians are concerned about distinguishing orthodox Christians, such as Samuel Adams and Roger Sherman, from theistic rationalists, such as Washington,

Adams, and Jefferson, because of their desire to maintain a clear definition of Christian orthodoxy. Religious views that deny the deity of Christ or the atonement through His blood cannot be classified as orthodox.

One of the best studies of this topic by a conservative Christian is Gregg L. Frazer, *The Religious Beliefs of America's Founders: Reason, Revelation, and Revolution*, [ed. Wilson Carey McWilliams and Lance Banning (Lawrence: University Press of Kansas), 2012]. Other conservative Christians who have written on this topic include Daniel Dreisbach and Thomas Kidd.

Civil Religion Discussion

Lead a discussion with students about how Christians can promote distinctively Christian involvement in the public square while avoiding the dangers of civil religion.

Secularism and the Interpretation of the Bible

Seventeenth-century Dutch philosopher Baruch Spinoza is considered the originator of modern liberal Bible interpretation. He laid the groundwork for liberal interpretations of the Bible with the express goal of secularization. J. Samuel Preus's study of Spinoza reveals the goal of Spinoza's work in its title: *Spinoza and the Irrelevance of Biblical Authority*. Spinoza made a case for the "irrelevance of biblical authority" in his 1670 *Theological-Political Treatise*. Spinoza argued that the Bible shouldn't be interpreted as the Word of God. Instead, it must be interpreted as a historical book. Once the different parts of the Bible are placed in their own historical contexts, the interpreter must recognize that they're bound to these contexts. That means different authors of Scripture can disagree with one another. The goal of the interpreter of the Bible was no longer to determine philosophical or theological truth that would guide life. Instead, the interpreter of the Bible now had a historical task. The interpreter must discover the historical meaning of the text. That historical meaning is an artifact. It is not a divine message with enduring relevance for life today. [J. Samuel Preus, *Spinoza and the Irrelevance of Biblical Authority* (New York: Cambridge University Press, 2001)]

Spinoza believed that such an approach to the Bible would secularize the state. That's precisely the approach to the Bible this textbook is opposed to. It's our hope that by the end of this course students will see that the Bible is no mere historical artifact but is instead relevant to every part of life.

A Secular Parable

Hunter Baker relates a parable in which Zarathustra, a character in a story by the

This places American Christians in an awkward spot. While we don't want to see God's name, prayer, or the Ten Commandments banished from public life, civil religion twists all of these things into something in service of a god-puppet telling us what we want to hear. American Christians shouldn't render homage to the god of American civil religion any more than the early Christians could offer incense to the supposedly divine Roman emperor.

In the end, civil religion has proved to be a step toward secularism. When largely Protestant nineteenth-century America searched for a common denominator of belief, what resulted was a generically Christian civil religion. But as the United States became more religiously diverse, the number of cultural values all Americans could agree on shrank considerably. Opposition to divisive and controversial religions in public life became opposition to religion in public life, period.[5]

CHRISTIANS AND AMERICAN CIVIL RELIGION

Christians need discernment to spot civil religion since in America it often makes use of Christian rhetoric and symbols. Civil religion was in play when Americans progressively moved from speaking of "Protestant morality" to "Christian virtues" (which included Roman Catholics) to "Judeo-Christian" values (Jewish and Christian) to the values of the "Abrahamic faiths" (meant to include Islam). When you separate the morality of several religions from the doctrines of those religions and then put that morality in service of the nation, you've got civil religion.

Civil religion also links piety and patriotism, and it promotes a manifest divine destiny for the nation. Some people speak of those who die in service of the nation as if they're therefore guaranteed a place in heaven. When representatives from multiple religions are gathered together to pray in the face of a national tragedy as if they are all praying to the god of the nation, this is civil religion.

While Christianity has influenced American civil religion, civil religion has also influenced American Christianity. When US Christians are suspicious of theology and creeds in favor of a practical religion, they are being influenced by civil religion. When they think the style of worship in church doesn't matter to God (but matters a lot in how to attract people to the church), they are being influenced by civil religion. These are major breaks from Christian orthodoxy and alignments to rational religion that have widely infected American evangelicalism.

STATE

CHURCH

Excluding Religion from the State

Western nations have over time developed a proposed solution to the shattering of political-religious unity: secularism, yet another version of church-state relations.[6] During the process of secularization, the wall of separation between church and state becomes an ever-tightening circular wall, with the church inside and the state outside. People can go in and out pretty freely as long as they leave their religion inside.

The story of secularism's rise has already been told in Chapter 3 on the two-story view. A brief recap: The Reformation shattered the religious unity of Europe. A growing cultural and intellectual force began to collect behind the idea that banishing religion from public life would restore unity and keep the peace. If religious reasoning could be excluded from politics, law, education, or anything that a society does together, then religious conflicts would cease. Religious people could still attend their places of worship, and they could talk about their religions among themselves, but only among themselves. Why is it so hard to talk about your faith to non-Christians today? Because the force of secularism is strong in America—and even stronger in many other Western nations.

Secularists assume that they shut religion up for its own good; they think their "neutral" viewpoint is the only way to keep the peace. But secularism doesn't really

philosopher Nietzsche, is traveling around bringing people the news that God is dead. "When he encounters a hermit who sings, laughs, weeps, and mumbles so as to praise God, Zarathustra 'leaves the old man to worship in peace.'" If, however, the hermit had come into town and talked about his belief in God, he would have been informed that God is dead. Baker notes that this reflects the view that "religious freedom is to be protected, strongly protected—so long as it is irrelevant to the life of the wider community." [Hunter Baker, *The End of Secularism* (Wheaton: Crossway, 2009), 111]

Secularists aren't concerned in the least if Christians make use of the Bible in a privatized, religious way. If the Bible is used in the way that some people use beautiful poetry or nature walks, the secularist doesn't mind. As long is the Bible is irrelevant to

public life, the secularist is happy for the Christian to do with the Bible what he will. But when the Christian brings the Bible to bear on public issues, the secularist objects.

The Relevance of Biblical Authority

What are some contemporary issues that the Bible speaks to and that governing authorities have to deal with?

- *abortion and embryonic stem cell research*
- *capital punishment*
- *gambling*
- *immigration*
- *LGBTQ issues*
- *pornography*
- *poverty programs*
- *racism*
- *recreational drugs*

resolve societal conflict. It just adds a new competitor to the list of groups seeking political power—a competitor that thinks it's a referee. That referee has handed out a simple rulebook to the other players in the game. (When those players ask, "Who made you the ref?" they are politely ignored.) The rule is that no religious or metaphysical* assumptions are allowed in the public square.

For example, a few years ago the Supreme Court of the United States considered two important cases on euthanasia* and refused to legalize doctor-assisted suicide. Six prominent philosophers filed an official legal brief with the court—"The Philosopher's Brief," it was called. One of the authors, New York University professor Ronald Dworkin, wrote,

> Denying [doctor-assisted suicide] to terminally ill patients who are in agonizing pain or otherwise doomed to an existence they regard as intolerable could only be justified on the basis of a religious or ethical conviction about the value or meaning of life itself. Our Constitution forbids government to impose such convictions on its citizens.[7]

In other words, the only justifications for stopping someone from committing suicide are private "convictions" that ought never to show their faces in public. Only neutral, secular reasons are allowed out in the sun.

Legal scholar Steven D. Smith wrote a book on secularism in which he demonstrates that Dworkin and other secularist referees can't abide by their own rules.[8] Dworkin—and numerous US judges writing legal opinions on euthanasia—defended euthanasia only for terminally ill patients, not healthy young people. But if we allow a terminally ill eighty-three-year-old to end her physical pain with a doctor's help, why would we not let an otherwise healthy twenty-three-year-old end her emotional pain the same way? Smith showed that Dworkin and the judges kept arguing that there's a "normal life span" that shouldn't be violated. Dworkin said it was a "cosmic shame" for healthy young people to take their own lives.[9]

But this is a religious and ethical assumption! Why should the fact that most people live to seventy or eighty force me to stay alive that long if I don't want to? How does Dworkin know what the cosmos thinks? And why should the cosmos care if I don't want to live in it anymore? Nature can teach us how to live our lives only if nature has a Creator. Secularism denies that we can know what this Creator says—but then it smuggles in religious assumptions anyway. It has to. You can't have a society with no ethical commitments.

When secularists exclude religious conceptions from even being considered in public discussion, they are being just as coercive* as the religious groups they view as intolerant. Harvard professor and moral philosopher Michael Sandel summarizes the problem:

> Asking democratic citizens to leave their moral and religious convictions behind when they enter the public realm may seem a way of ensuring toleration and mutual respect. In practice, however, the opposite can be true. Deciding important public questions while pretending to a neutrality that cannot be achieved is a recipe for backlash and resentment.[11]

metaphysical: *related to unseen realities*

euthanasia: *killing a person who is terminally ill to prevent further suffering*

> *"Men being all the workmanship of one omnipotent, and infinitely wise maker . . . are his property, . . . made to last during his, not one another's pleasure."*[10]
>
> —JOHN LOCKE

coercive: *compelling someone to do something by use of force or intimidation*

Choose one of these issues and discuss how it should be treated in relation to biblical norms by Christians in governing positions.

Example: gambling. The Christian should raise concerns about it based on the Bible's teaching on the ethical treatment of others— to promote others' best interests (Phil. 2:4). This is the Christian's presupposed moral concern. Gambling violates that norm, which the Bible simply enunciates. By common grace, non-Christians can see the value of this norm too. The Christian can support this biblical norm by making use of whatever social scientific evidence that might exist for demonstrating that gambling has various adverse effects. But he should not leave out his biblical basis for the ethical reasons for opposing gambling.

Example: embryonic stem cell research. Interestingly, President George W. Bush stated his opposition to embryonic stem cell research in explicitly Christian terms in his memoir. He wrote: "My faith and conscience led me to conclude that human life is sacred. God created man in His image and therefore every person has value in His eyes." [George W. Bush, Decision Points (New York: Crown, 2012), 112]

Discuss with students how secularists would react to introducing biblical reasoning into these discussions. Using embryonic stem cell research as an example, consider having students interact with the following statement by President Barack Obama on the occasion of lifting the ban that President Bush had instituted:

> This order is an important step in advancing the cause of science in America. But let's be clear: promoting science isn't just about providing resources—it is also about protecting free and open inquiry. It is about letting scientists like those here today do their jobs, free from manipulation or coercion, and listening to what they tell us, even when it's inconvenient— especially when it's inconvenient. It is about ensuring that scientific data is never distorted or concealed to serve a political agenda—and that we make scientific decisions based on facts, not ideology.

[The full text of this speech, including Obama's remarks about the role of religion, can be found at whitehouse.gov. Search for "stem cell executive order."]

Discuss with students that in these debates the issue is not with facts, but with how these facts are placed within moral frameworks. Earlier in the speech President Obama expressed his opposition to human cloning as "dangerous [and] profoundly wrong." But on what grounds is cloning humans "profoundly wrong" while opposition to killing embryos is merely ideological?

The goal of this exercise is to help students see that in these major policy decisions some moral viewpoint is shaping the discussion. It is not a matter of facts versus ideology or science versus religion. The problem with secularism is that these moral viewpoints have to be hidden away under the guise of neutrality.

The Failure of Secularism

The promise of secularism was peace. It claimed that if people left behind religious ideas and came to the neutral public square, old religious conflicts would melt away.

But as Steven Smith demonstrated, secularists don't play by their own rules. They have to smuggle in moral views that aren't neutral. This fact leads to Sandel's conclusion: "Deciding important public questions while pretending to a neutrality that cannot be achieved is a recipe for backlash and resentment." [Michael J. Sandel, *Justice: What's the Right Thing to Do?* (New York: Farrar, Straus, and Giroux, 2009), 243] The reason for the resentment is found in the phrase "pretending to a neutrality." It would be like a basketball team finding out that the referees were actually on the opposing team.

In a society with multiple religious and nonreligious moral viewpoints, a much better approach would be to allow each side to make its own case. Since, as Sandel says, "it's not always possible to set aside competing conceptions of the good life," public discourse would actually be enhanced by each party making its own case for what the good life is and how it ought to be lived.

How Can the Church Influence the State?

The state has the responsibility to praise the good and punish evil (Rom. 13:3–4; 1 Pet. 2:14).

But how can governmental officials know what is good and evil?

They may know through general revelation and the law of God written on the heart, but this is suppressed by the ungodly and only rightly understood when viewed through the lens of Scripture.

What are some ways Christians may be able to help governmental leaders understand what is good and evil from God's perspective?

In the institutional church, a pastor can make application of texts on both individual and societal levels. He influences members of his congregation, some of whom vote and work in government, to govern well and hold governors accountable. Moving beyond the institutional church to the organic church, Christians could work for think tanks that enable them to allow their Christian views to shape policy recommendations.

Why Should the Institutional Church Not Craft Public Policy?

While the institutional church is able to outline the moral guidelines that should shape particular policies, the institutional church doesn't have a biblical mandate to formulate public policy. In fact, there are significant dangers if it tries to do so:

First, researching issues and formulating workable policies takes a great deal of experience, time, and resources. The institutional church should be using its time and resources on the mission explicitly given to it in Scripture.

Second, if the institutional church is formulating public policy and presenting it as the Christian position, the dynamic between church and state has shifted from influence to a "church over state" position.

Third, while Christians can unite around a broad moral framework for public policy, they have liberty to disagree about which particular policies are best.

Differences in Influence

Christian influence on government will differ from one culture to another. In a culture largely shaped by Christian thought and morals, the influence of the Christian faith on public policy will be natural and extensive. In a pluralistic culture Christians will have to make the case that their viewpoint really is correct and for the common good.

CHURCH

STATE

Church Influencing the State

If Christians were allowed to bring their moral and religious convictions into the public realm, what would that look like?

We saved the best model of church-state relations for last, one in which the church influences the state. "All authority in heaven and on earth has been given" to the Messianic King (Matt. 28:18). But what should be clear by now is that Christ has not delegated all of His authority to any one sphere of human life. God has authorized fathers to rule their families as fathers. He has authorized congregations and their leadership to exercise rule in their churches. He has authorized kings and presidents, parliaments and congresses to rule over nations. He has not authorized the state to rule over the doctrines and practices of the church or the church to begin parenting the children of its members or the church to impose policy decisions on the government. God has created different institutional spheres, each with its own authority under Him.

And yet God has called for all of these authorities to submit to the authority of His Messianic King (Ps. 2:8–10). This means that the church has the responsibility to speak about all of life, including governmental life, just as the Bible speaks to all of life. The biblical prophets applied Scripture to the rulers of their day. When the secular ruler Herod took his brother's wife, John the Baptist told him it was "not lawful" for him to have her (Matt. 14:4). According to whose law? Not Roman law, but God's law. When King Jehoiakim cheated workers of their wages so that he could have a magnificent palace built, God sent Jeremiah to confront his wickedness (Jer. 22:13–23). Micah denounced the unjust rulers of Judah (Mic. 3:1–3).

All legislation is related in some way to moral issues. Someone's moral view will be legislated. It is therefore appropriate for churches to speak to the moral issues raised by legislation. This does not mean that churches are to craft public policy—they aren't. That responsibility lies beyond the church's authority. However, as they carry out their ministry of preaching the Word, it is right for churches to apply that Word to all of life. If politicians become Christians—or if young Christians are called to political work—how will the church disciple them? It is right for churches to disciple Christians who hold public office not only about aspects of personal character but also about the content of their political and governmental work.

Historically, Christians have spoken out against governmental injustice in significant ways. Churches and mission agencies spoke out against US president Andrew Jackson's removal of Indians from their own lands.[12] Many Christians—with British parliamentarian William Wilberforce as the leading example—spoke out against the international slave trade.

THINKING IT THROUGH 18.2

1. Why shouldn't the state be allowed to rule over the church or the church over the state?

2. Define *civil religion* in your own words.

3. What motivated Western secularism to exclude religion from the operations of the state?

4. Can secularism eliminate all religious assumptions from debates in the public square? Why or why not?

5. How should the church relate to the state?

In other cultures Christians simply may not be allowed to have political influence.

THINKING IT THROUGH 18.2

1. God established different spheres of authority with different leadership roles for the church and for the state.

2. Civil religion is an attempt to make use of religion for political purposes. Such a religion is deliberately generic enough that it can be embraced by a wide variety of people.

3. Secularists believed that sectoring religion off from public life would allow for only neutral argumentation and tolerance leading to peace and unity.

4. No, every debatable issue requires presuppositions that are built on beliefs and values stemming from a religious worldview; pretending to be neutral only misleads and coerces the naive.

5. Separate spheres of authority with different roles and responsibilities ought to be clearly defined. But the church should work to influence the opinions of the government leaders by providing a solid foundation for individuals' beliefs and values as they seek to carry out the work of the state.

A Christian business owner commented on an online news article about the First Lady of the United States. He wrote, "Get this trash out of Washington! I may have to respect her husband, but she was never elected to anything."[13]

What do you think of that comment? Is it right? He means that Romans 13 tells him to honor the governing authorities. The First Lady isn't an authority, so he doesn't have to honor her.

But he didn't read his Bible carefully. Paul actually said, "Pay to all what is owed to them: taxes to whom taxes are owed, revenue to whom revenue is owed, respect to whom respect is owed, honor to whom honor is owed" (Rom. 13:7). Average citizens don't owe the First Lady obedience, but they surely owe her respect.

So it isn't right to make such comments. But is it effective? Well, sort of. If your goal is to debase national political discourse, degrade public trust in national institutions, and make your political opponents feel justified in dismissing your concerns—then it's effective. But if your goal is to lead a peaceful and quiet life, godly and dignified in every way (1 Tim. 2:2), then it's simply wrong to call the First Lady "trash" online.

People who see the world through CFR lenses will choose not to demonize their opponents because they know that every politician, every politician's wife, every voter, and every voter's wife is created and fallen. As dissident Soviet intellectual Alexander Solzhenitsyn famously said, "The line separating good and evil passes not through states, nor between classes, nor between political parties either—but right through every human heart."[14]

What does Christian politics—politics that recognizes that line between good and evil—look like? Truly Christian politics presses for God's will to be done, but in a prudent way backed by prayer. And Christian politics is full of Christian virtues such as humility, respect, and boldness.

PRAYING FOR ALL PEOPLE

Christians in first-century Rome didn't have much if any political power—especially the many Christian slaves. Even today, not all Christians live in countries where their participation in government is allowed. No matter what their situation, however, Christians can do two things: pray for all people and press for God's will to be done.

Praying is something that all Christians may do under any form of government at any time in history. Paul makes prayer for those in authority a duty for all Christians.

> I urge that supplications, prayers, intercessions, and thanksgivings be made for all people, for kings and all who are in high positions, that we may lead a peaceful and quiet life, godly and dignified in every way. (1 Tim. 2:1–2)

Pray for all people, but specifically for governmental authorities. And why? In order that we might lead peaceful lives. When rulers rule well, that's what we get—peace.

And hopefully we get even more. We are to pray that government would permit us to live lives that are also "godly." One Christian goal for government is that it would allow Christians to practice their faith "in every way," in every area of life. Persecuted Christians around the world don't have this freedom. We ought to pray that God, through their governments, would give it to them—and that Christians in Western nations would get to keep their existing religious freedoms. There's no guarantee that this will happen. We should pray.

SECTION OBJECTIVES 18.3

1. Identify the primary objective of Christians living during a time of difficulty.

2. Contrast a biblical approach (preserving the good and reforming the evil) with theonomy and pluralism.

3. Evaluate contemporary political discussions and tactics in light of the Christian political virtues of prudence, boldness, humility, and respect.

4. Compare and contrast unrighteous rebellion with righteous resistance to a wicked ruler's demands.

The Danger of Political Worldliness

Christians are sometimes in danger of becoming so accustomed to the status quo that they fail to realize that the way things work is worldly in the negative biblical sense. But worldliness isn't limited to entertainment or dress. Worldliness can be found in every aspect of life, including political activities. It is possible for worldliness to be present in political discourse—even the political discourse of people who are right about the issues.

Paul admonished Christians to render to Nero the honor that God said he was due (Rom. 13:7), and Paul himself determined to render the biblically required honor to a corrupt high priest (Acts 23:4–5). So today Christian citizens ought to render the honor their leaders are owed by virtue of their office.

Honoring leaders doesn't mean they're above critique, even searching critique. If they're acting unlawfully (by God's law or just human laws), then the Christian, like John the Baptist, can forthrightly state this even if it results in being jailed. But Christians should be able to deliver these critiques in a way that still renders due honor.

Even if the political opponent could be considered an enemy in the fullest sense of the term, Christians are to love their enemies. This means that the Christian should treat his political opponents with kindness (1 Cor. 13:4). He shouldn't rejoice when political opponents are caught in wrongdoing (13:6). Believers shouldn't be arrogant or rude when dealing with political opponents (13:4–5). Nor should they be irritable or resentful when their opponents win (13:5). The Christian shouldn't believe every negative assertion made against his opponents, nor should he dismiss negative reports about his own side. The Christian should be scrupulous about being fair and truthful to all parties (13:6–7).

None of this means that believers shouldn't be bold in taking political positions, particularly positions that are clearly based on scriptural principles. But it does mean that Christian involvement in politics should be distinctively Christian.

What Should We Pray For?

Paul is specific about what Christians should pray for in 1 Timothy 2:1–2. First, he says that Christians should pray that rulers will rule in such a way that believers can lead "peaceful and quiet" lives. This may be a way of praying that governments would live up to their obligations as laid out in Romans 13:1–7 and 1 Peter 2:13–17. Rulers who are a terror to those whose conduct is evil but a blessing to those whose conduct is good will lead to peaceful and quiet lives for all, including Christians. But this prayer goes beyond praying merely that government would fulfill its responsibilities. Paul is praying that the government will permit believers to fulfill theirs. He prays that Christians might live lives of *eusebia*, a Greek word that means a life lived in the fear of God or a life that seeks to please God in every aspect. He also prays that Christians would be able to live "dignified" lives. A dignified person is not flippant about life; he knows that every moment is lived before God. Life is to be enjoyed, but it is enjoyed with due recognition of the duty to live always before God and a watching world. Finally, Paul indicates that Christians should pray for all people because God desires everyone to be saved. This means that Christians should pray for the salvation of those in government.

Prayer Project

[Note: If your students are also taking government or civics this semester, consider coordinating with that teacher on this project.] Have the class compile a list of the people who hold the positions of president, vice president, speaker of the House, Senate majority leader, Supreme Court justice, governor, representatives on the national and state levels, and local elected officials. (A larger class might expand this list by including cabinet members and/or minority party leaders; a smaller class may select only certain officeholders from the list.)

Invite students to select a person on this list to pray for until the end of the course. Each student should research that leader to ascertain (if possible) whether he or she is a believer. If the official is unsaved, students should pray for his or her salvation. Students should also research the major policy issues that these officials need to make decisions about or on which they have taken positions. If these are matters on which a clear biblical viewpoint is present, the students should pray for the scriptural position to succeed. In all of this, the students should pray that God's people would be able to live peaceful, quiet, godly, and dignified lives.

Consider having students open class in a prayer that includes their assigned official.

Thinking About Theonomy

In discussing the errors of theonomy it must be noted up front that it is praiseworthy for a group of Christians to determine that they're going to take seriously everything that the Bible teaches—even principles that are out of step with prevailing cultural norms.

It is also important to note that even though theonomists emphasize that the Old Testament law as a whole is still in force, they do recognize some discontinuities between the Old and New Testament eras. For instance, Greg Bahnsen notes that "localized imperatives" such as the conquest of Canaan by Joshua are not applicable to anyone today. In addition, "cultural details" need to be taken into account. He suggests that "faulty car brakes" would be covered by the same accidental manslaughter law that covered a "flying axehead." Bahnsen also grants that "administrative details," such as the location of a nation's capital, are not binding on other nations. Finally, fulfilled types, such as the sacrificial system, are no longer in force because they have been fulfilled. [Greg Bahnsen, *By This Standard* (Tyler, TX: Institute for Christian Economics, 1985), 3–6]

Thinking About the Old Testament Law

The relationship of the Christian to the Mosaic law is one of the most important and most difficult Bible topics to master.

We should pray, for example, that Christian businesses such as Hobby Lobby and Elane Photography would be free to do their work in accordance with their Christian principles. Hobby Lobby is a massive multibillion dollar corporation owned by Christians. Elane Photography (which was mentioned in Chapter 14) is a mom-and-pop small business, also owned by Christians. Both have come under legal pressure because the owners have tried to run their businesses consistently with their Christian values. Hobby Lobby faced a court case because it would not provide abortifacient contraceptives* to employees (employees who are already paid nearly double the minimum wage, along with generous health insurance). Elane Photography faced a court case because the owners, a married couple, refused to do the photography for a homosexual wedding. (They were willing to serve homosexual customers but felt that supporting a same-sex marriage ceremony was not compatible with their beliefs.)

A society that won't allow Christian businesspeople to do business in a Christian way is not a society at peace or a society in which people—including businesspeople—can live "godly" lives "in every way." So we should pray for change.

abortifacient contraceptive: *a means of birth control that causes an abortion*

PRESSING FOR GOD'S WILL TO BE DONE

Prayer is the most powerful thing Christians can do because God is the most powerful force in human politics. "The king's heart is a stream of water in the hand of the Lord; he turns it wherever he will" (Prov. 21:1). But when we pray, God isn't required to operate directly, as it were—changing individual politicians' minds or sending hurricanes to block certain legislators from participating in important votes. God can do that if He wants to, of course, but more often His pattern seems to be to use "means." That's us. We can be instruments in God's hands. While we pray, we can vote, we can protest, we can organize, we can write, we can debate—and most readers of this book can (one day) run for office. Under our great King, Christians have a responsibility to press for the King's laws to be obeyed in every nation.

Theonomy

The idea of "pressing for the King's laws to be obeyed" makes many people, including Christians, uncomfortable. They object that it will lead to **theocracy** (God-rule) or **theonomy** ("God's law"). So some careful distinctions need to be made. Theonomists believe that the Old Testament law as a whole, including penalties like stoning, is still in force today unless the New Testament has explicitly stated otherwise. Theonomists want Gentile nations to use the Old Testament to establish their laws.[15] Leading theonomist Greg Bahnsen has written, "We must recognize the continuing obligation of civil magistrates to obey and enforce the relevant laws of the Old Testament, including the penal sanctions specified by the just Judge of all the earth."[16]

But theonomists have made a grave mistake: not even Christians, much less the unsaved, are bound by the Mosaic law today as their covenant. The Mosaic law has been replaced by the New Covenant (see "Free from the Law" on page 77; cf. Rom. 7:4–6; 1 Cor. 9:21; 2 Cor. 3:3). It is therefore wrong to seek to impose the Mosaic Covenant with its penalties on Gentile nations. Theonomists are also too optimistic about Christians' ability to transform the world. The New Testament promises suffering and persecution for God's people in the present age (cf. 2 Tim. 3:12).

Even though theonomists have made some significant errors, we shouldn't overreact. Christians should not be afraid to say publicly what the Bible says about public matters.

Is the Old Testament relevant to the Christian life? (2 Tim. 3:16–17)

Yes, all Scripture, including the Mosaic law, is profitable for equipping Christians to live righteous lives full of good works.

Is the Christian bound by the Mosaic Covenant? (1 Cor. 9:19–21) What covenant is the Christian under? (2 Cor. 3:2–6)

No, the Christian is not under the Mosaic Covenant. The Christian is under the New Covenant.

If the Christian is not under the Mosaic law, does this mean that he is under no law? (1 Cor. 9:21; Jer. 31:31–34)

No, the Christian is still under God's law. In the New Covenant that law is written on the Christian's heart (James 1:25; 2:8).

Are some laws from the Mosaic Covenant directly applicable to the Christian? (Rom. 13:8–10; 1 Cor. 10:14)

Yes, laws about having no gods other than the true God and the basic moral statutes laid out in the Ten Commandments and similar passages are directly applicable.

Are other laws from the Mosaic law only indirectly applicable to the Christian? (Deut. 22:8; Mark 7:14–23; 1 Cor. 9:9–12)

Yes, some laws contain specific applications of general principles, and those applications are not relevant to every culture. In other cases, the laws themselves were designed not for their own sake but for the sake of teaching other truths. So some situations call for reducing the application back to the general principle so that it can be reapplied in a different context. Others call for discerning the

Pluralism

Other Christians feel uncomfortable appealing to the Bible in matters of public policy because they think there's no point. Most people in the public square don't believe the Bible is God's Word, and if we appeal to it, they'll immediately cry foul: "You're trying to impose your religious beliefs on us!"

Influential legal theorist John Rawls (one of the authors of the "Philosopher's Brief" quoted above) argued that in a pluralist society (one containing multiple belief systems), everybody should leave "comprehensive doctrines" out of public discussion. He said that people should make their arguments on reasonable, nonreligious grounds. In other words, you can't say, "We should limit divorce because God disapproves of it in Scripture." You must say instead, "We should limit divorce because it has a statistically negative impact on high school test scores, teen pregnancy rates, and future economic outcomes." Those are "secular" reasons.

But Rawls's view fails. First, as this book has pointed out repeatedly, there is no neutral moral ground where we can all live in peace. Everybody has a worldview, a viewpoint. To tell Christians that they can't bring up the biblical one is to stack the deck against us before we get to say a word.

Second, everybody knows that Scripture is the Christian's ultimate authority. So when Christians try to argue against abortion or same-sex marriage in a secular way, other people will see through the attempt. They'll call us out for trying to smuggle our Christian beliefs into the debate, and they'll criticize us for hypocritically pretending to be secular. That's precisely what has happened with the intelligent design (ID) movement.* Not all ID proponents are even Christians, but their whole effort is still seen by secularists as a way to sneak biblical creationism into public schools.

It would be much better for Christians—as graciously and carefully as they can—to mount arguments against secularism, appealing to Scripture as their final authority. When little boys want to identify as female at their public school, using the girls' restrooms and joining girls' sports teams (this is happening),[17] we can say, "God made us male and female, and the way God created the world is the standard by which we judge the way things ought to be."

Christians don't have to tear down the entire established order to root out secularism. Secularists, by God's common grace, are right about a great number of things. And Christians should not attempt to persecute (or exile, or stone) secularists; that's not how Christ's kingdom advances in this age. We should work for the good of secularists—even Muslims and other non-Christians of all sorts. Our love for those neighbors

intelligent design: *the view that evolution could not have produced the orderliness and complexity of the universe, indicating that there was an intelligent cause*

FREE FROM THE LAW?

In 1 Corinthians 9:20, Paul indicates that as a Christian he was not under the Mosaic law. Hebrews 8:13 teaches that the New Covenant made the old Mosaic Covenant "obsolete" and "ready to vanish away."

But neither Paul nor the author of Hebrews (if he was someone other than Paul) is teaching that the Christian is free from all law. Paul hastens on to say that he wasn't "outside the law of God, but under the law of Christ" (1 Cor. 9:21). And the New Covenant in Hebrews quotes God's promise, "I will put my laws into their minds, and write them on their hearts" (Heb. 8:10).

The Mosaic law was a particular application of God's law to a specific people in a particular culture at a particular time in a particular stage in redemptive history. This means that we should expect strong similarities between God's expectations then and now as well as some differences. For instance, laws against murder and adultery are rooted in God's eternal will. Murder does not become acceptable under the New Covenant. But modern governments that seek to conform their laws to God's laws do not need to set up cities of refuge, nor do modern penal codes need to prescribe stoning for adultery (cf. Lev. 20:10; Deut. 22:23–24). Instead the Mosaic law serves, in part, as an example of how to apply God's law to people who live in many different cultures and at different times in God's plan of redemption. It is still a source of guidance even though Christians are under a different covenant.

---

symbolism so that the truth can be learned and applied.

The Mosaic Law as an Application of Creational Law

In the sidebar "Free from the Law," the Student Text says, "The Mosaic law was a particular application of God's law to a specific people in a particular culture of a particular time in a particular stage in redemptive history." There's a lot packed into that little statement.

This book has placed a great deal of emphasis on creational norms. It's very helpful to see those norms applied in a concrete way. This is what the Old Testament law does.

However, it's also important to note that the creational law is applied to a particular culture at a particular time. Caring for the poor by allowing them to glean from the fields worked in an ancient agricultural society. A different application of the underlying creational norm is needed, however, to address modern urban dwellers.

It's also important to note that the Mosaic code was given to a specific people in a particular stage in redemptive history. Israel was a nation in covenant with God. "The Jews were entrusted with the oracles of God" (Rom. 3:2). To them were given the "covenants of promise" (Eph. 2:12). For this nation certain offenses against God were punishable by stoning. Since the church is not a nation, and since even nations with large Christian populations and Christian leaders are not in that type of covenant with God, these kinds of penalties are not guidelines for the laws of Gentile nations.

The Two-Kingdoms Approach and Natural Law

In contrast to theonomists, some Christians argue that Christians shouldn't appeal to Scripture in public political discussions. And they even claim there are good theological reasons not to appeal to Scripture in public.

These Christians argue that Christ rules over two kingdoms. One of these kingdoms is the common kingdom in which both Christians and non-Christians live together. The other kingdom is the church. Christ is the ruler of both kingdoms, but He rules over the two kingdoms differently. Christ rules over the common kingdom through the authority of natural law. The Bible is a covenant book, and it's the authority for God's covenant people in the sacred kingdom. Christians can better understand natural law and what ought to be done in the common kingdom by studying Scripture. But Scripture is not the authority for that kingdom.

These Christians are especially concerned that Christians recognize the distinction between the mission of the church and the responsibilities of politically engaged citizens. They're also concerned about claims that Christians should live distinctively Christian lives in the common kingdom. They argue that the Christian should instead be looking for ways to live in harmony with non-Christians in submission to natural law. They like to point out that there's nothing really distinctively Christian about the vocations of carpenter, firefighter, plumber, landscaper, or goat-breeder aside from the virtues of diligence, respect, and honesty that all people recognize as good.

 ## Evaluating the Two-Kingdoms Approach

Perhaps the most significant weakness in the two-kingdoms approach is the lack of scriptural evidence for the kingdoms. The church is not in itself identified in Scripture as a kingdom, and the Bible doesn't say anything about a common kingdom. The Bible does speak a great deal about Christ establishing the kingdom of God, but the kingdom of God extends to all areas of life and is not limited to the church.

The second critique has to do with the two-kingdom view of natural law.

Does the Bible teach the existence of natural law? (Rom. 1:19–20, 32)

Yes, the Bible does teach the existence of natural law, or law known through general revelation. [In this book we have used the term creational norms to describe this reality.]

Does natural law account for when un-saved people and nations act in morally correct ways (Rom. 2:14–15)?

Yes, Romans reveals that the natural law testified to by the conscience does enable non-Christians to act rightly sometimes.

Is natural law a sufficient standard for nations (Rom. 1:18)?

No, natural law was never intended to operate apart from special revelation. Even in the Garden of Eden, God's special revelation provided the framework by which Adam and Eve were to make sense of the general revelation in the creation. The need for special revelation is doubly present now that mankind has fallen and humans suppress the truth revealed in natural law.

Could it be true that in the common kingdom Christians live by commonly accepted morality and not by a distinctively Christian morality?

Certain vocations do not seem to raise large-scale worldview differences. But what if the vocations under consideration were to include research biologists, philosophers, historians, bioethicists, educators, and legislators? In these vocations the distinctions between the Christian perspective and non-Christian perspectives are often stark. In addition, the commonality between Christians and non-Christians in some vocations is sometimes due to the influence of Christianity on the culture. An artisan such as a carpenter or sculptor may be able to work together with non-Christian craftsmen or artisans in the United States at present, but in a culture where idolatry and idol temples are big business, he would face larger challenges. Similarly, for many generations Americans could agree on what made up a virtuous family. Now that consensus is vanishing. Christians who maintain a biblical view of the family are increasingly going to find themselves living in contradistinction to rather than in harmony with the larger culture.

What Did They Get Right?

Both theonomists and two-kingdoms proponents have made some missteps. But both groups get some things right too.

What do they get right?

The theonomist dedication to applying Scripture to every area of life is right, and the effort of the two-kingdom approach to keep the institutional church focused on its scriptural mission is correct.

WHY CAN'T WE JUST GET ALONG?

As religious (and irreligious) diversity within nations increases, standards of morality are no longer shared. "Culture wars" are the result, battles that haven't yet resulted in the shedding of blood.[18] Why can't people agree to disagree? Where is the tolerance that Americans, at least, used to practice with one another?

Tolerance itself has become a battleground in America. Theologian D. A. Carson argues that a new definition of tolerance is overtaking the old one. Under the old regime, Protestants, Catholics, Jews, and rationalists all accepted the rights of their neighbors to hold their beliefs—even though they firmly believed that their neighbors were wrong and they were right. Under the new tolerance one may no longer hold firmly to his own beliefs or morality; he must concede that all beliefs or morality are potentially true. To say someone is wrong is intolerant. Of course, this view cannot be lived out consistently. Usually the morality of the powerful ends up being smuggled in.[19]

For the Christian, tolerance cannot be an ultimate value. In the end Christ will tolerate no false belief or immorality. But at present Christians walk a fine line. On the one hand, the Christian has no confidence that rulers are going to embrace true religion, so tolerance is a good that enables Christians to live and worship around the world. Christians can champion religious freedom because without it many Christians would not be free to live and worship God as they should.

On the other hand, Christians recognize that the gospel is something that must be received, not enforced. It is impossible to force someone to have faith. This is another reason to champion freedom of religion. And yet, certain religious practices cannot be tolerated. It is good to not tolerate the burning of widows, polygamy, human sacrifice, or conversion by the sword even though all these have been claimed as religious practices by various religions. Even tolerance is judgmental. In making these judgments, Christians have no obedient option except to articulate God's viewpoint.

will make our efforts at political renewal harder to criticize.

Preserve the Good, Reform the Evil

Christ is King, but for now He does His work in a fallen world. Government and citizenry alike are full of sinners. A perfect utopia, therefore, simply won't happen in this age. Christians are right, then, to be skeptical about revolutions that promise utopia, as the French Revolution did. Those revolutionaries had lofty goals for the new society that they wanted to create, but their push for change degenerated into a reign of terror.

A little bit at a time. Because of sin, some "solutions" only make problems worse. Wise Christians will want assurances that a proposed solution will really be a net positive in the end. Small changes worked out over a period of time are often best. And, generally speaking, reforms are most effective when tried first on a local level before being rolled out on a large scale. If something goes wrong, as surely it will, the impact will be limited. Whatever goes right can spread gradually to other places.

This means that a Christian political program will have two prongs. It will seek to preserve what's good while seeking to reform what's evil. Christians should recognize "that no existing social, political or economic arrangement is ever completely without redeeming features."[20] The reason for this is clear: cultures are built by God's image-bearers working with God's good creation. Even in a fallen world, good remains in every culture. These are the features that the Christian wishes to conserve and protect from revolutionary policies that may sweep away the good with the bad. Since cultures extend in time as well as place, Christians value the insights of tradition, realizing that tradition contains a great deal of wisdom and practical life experience.

And yet the people of earlier generations were no less prone to sin and error than people in our times. While appreciating tradition, Christians recognize that the past was not uniformly better than the present. The Creation Mandate implies that humans will always be working to improve creation and culture; Christians also need to press for the righting of injustices. This is one of the purposes of government.

Slavery as an example. The tiny New Testament book of Philemon provides a key example of preserving the good and reforming the evil. In it, the apostle Paul counsels a Christian slave-owner, Philemon, on what to do with his runaway slave, Onesi-

---

Why Pursue Political Reform Rather Than Revolution?

Ask students what the three components of a political ideology are according to the previous chapter?

(1) a critique of existing society
(2) a vision of a better future
(3) a strategy for getting from here to there

What is the Christian view of the better future?

The return of Christ will establish justice on the earth and reverse the effects of the Fall.

What is the Christian's political strategy for getting from here to there?

The Christian has no political strategy for getting to the Millennium and new earth.

This is why the Christian has little hope in political ideologies, revolutions, or governments to bring in a utopia. Nonetheless, Christians who are able to be politically active should press towards the ideal through pressing their governments to live up to the task given them in 1 Peter 2:14 to punish evil and praise good.

Though the Christian knows that the reforms he presses for won't result in a utopia, sometimes the reforms do carry weighty, long-lasting significance, such as William Wilberforce's efforts to end the slave trade and slavery across the British Empire.

mus. Onesimus had become a Christian during his flight, and he had connected with Paul in Rome. Paul loves Onesimus as a son and wishes for him to be able to stay. But he still sends him back to his master. Some people look at this fact—along with New Testament instructions that tell slaves not to be too concerned about their status as slaves (1 Cor. 7:21) and to obey even cruel masters (1 Pet. 2:18)—and they wonder if the New Testament supports slavery.

It doesn't. This becomes clearer when you realize that the Old Testament permitted only certain types of servitude in Israel. No one was to be made a slave against his own will. Israelites who became slaves typically did so to work off debts. But they could be held only for six years, and in the seventh the master was not only to free them but was also to provide for them generously, so they could set up an independent life again (Deut. 15:12–14). Only if the slave requested it—perhaps because he valued the financial security of working for a good master—could he be someone's slave for life. In contrast, kidnapping someone or buying, selling, or possessing such a stolen person was a capital crime in Israel (Exod. 21:16). The Bible cannot be used to justify the kind of slavery that existed in the United States, a kind of slavery that began with man-stealing and continued as a permanent, race-based institution.

Turning back to the New Testament, many Bible interpreters have recognized that Paul sowed the seeds of slavery's demise in his dealings with Philemon and Onesimus. Paul instructed Philemon to receive Onesimus back not merely as a slave, but as a brother (Philem. 1:16). Paul forbade Christian masters to intimidate or threaten their slaves (Eph. 6:9)—which makes beating absolutely out of the question. Further, masters are told to remember that they are slaves to their heavenly Master; earthly masters don't have a status higher than their slaves in the eyes of God:

> Masters, . . . stop your threatening, knowing that he who is both their Master and yours is in heaven, and that there is no partiality with him. (Eph. 6:9)

Advising a slave revolt in the first century would have been unwise. It would have made conditions for the slaves worse, not better. Thus the New Testament preserves the good (a stable, functioning social order) and begins to reform the evil (slavery). Furthermore, planting the seeds of slavery's demise actually worked. It led to the virtual elimination of slavery in medieval Europe—though sinners, being sinners, found other means of oppression. And when slavery was revived among Europeans during the Enlightenment, Christian arguments again played a large role in this second demise.

FOUR CHRISTIAN POLITICAL VIRTUES

After the Supreme Court legalized elective abortion in 1973, Christians began to organize politically to end abortion . . . or at least limit it. But the defeat-versus-limit question has caused consternation for some Christians: "How can you compromise with baby-killers?" The answer is that baby steps aren't necessarily compromise. Compromise happens when you give up the long-term goal for a short-term gain, or when you assume that the end justifies the means. The long-term goal of the pro-life movement—ending all abortion—can be achieved slowly. In fact, the movement has seen remarkable success in restricting abortion. If the pro-life movement had taken an all-or-nothing approach, many people would not be alive today. Instead, pro-lifers have worked assiduously and creatively to come up with legal ways to protect unborn children. Some laws call for abortion doctors to have admitting privileges at local hospitals. Others require parental consent or a waiting period. And some prohibit abortion after "viability," the point at which babies can possibly survive outside the

THE GOAL OF GOVERNMENT | 279

Slavery and the Bible

Discussing slavery in the Bible can be complicated, but having this discussion is important from an apologetics standpoint. As Christians find themselves taking culturally unpopular positions on marriage and sexuality, critics of Christianity point to the fact that many American Christians used to argue that the Bible supported Southern slavery as a way of demonstrating that the Bible can be used to support positions that few Christians would publicly support today. The implied message is that Christians changed on the slavery issue, and they should change on the same-sex marriage issue too.

It would be easier from an apologetics standpoint if the Christian could simply say that the Bible doesn't support slavery and leave it at that. Yet the fact of the matter is that the New Testament doesn't tell Christian masters to simply free all of their slaves immediately. So how should the Christian work through this matter?

Slaves in Israel

In the first place, it's important to distinguish slavery as it was regulated under the Mosaic law from Greco-Roman slavery or antebellum race-based slavery in the United States. In general Israelites could indenture themselves for up to six years to work off a debt (Deut. 15:12). During this time those they were indentured to had to be sure not to treat them as other than hired workers: "If your brother becomes poor beside you and sells himself to you, you shall not make him serve as a slave: he shall be with you as a hired worker and as a sojourner" (Lev. 25:39–40). After the six-year period was up, the indentured worker was to be richly provided for by his master so that he would not find himself starting off again impoverished (Deut. 15:13–14). From these instructions, it's clear that the primary kind of slavery in Israel was designed as a means of handling bankruptcy, and it was designed to be beneficial to both parties.

There were two other kinds of slavery in Israel that weren't limited to six years. First, if after the six-year period the slave decided that he was better off remaining a slave, then he could voluntarily choose to remain so for life (Deut. 15:16–17). Why would anyone do this? First, according to the law even though he was a slave, he couldn't be treated as one. He had to be treated as a hired worker. Second, there was greater financial security if he was working for someone wealthy who guaranteed that his needs would be met for life. For similar reasons, a foreigner could sell himself to work for an Israelite for life (Lev. 25:44–45). But Israelites could not participate in the trade of stolen persons. People who engaged in stealing and selling stolen people faced the death penalty (Exod. 21:16).

Slaves in Greece and Rome

Greco-Roman slavery, however, was different. Why didn't the New Testament writers simply condemn it? Part of the reason is the complexity of Greco-Roman slavery. As Murray Harris notes, "[Slaves] served in a wide variety of roles. In fact, one scholar has drawn up a list of over 120 different duties and occupations! For example, some served as employees of a city or of the state, being salaried executives with heavy responsibilities. Others were employed in business as managers of shops or of ships. Others worked the land as farm labourers, often in chain gangs in the case of condemned criminals, and sometimes in appalling conditions. Or again, many worked in city households as cooks or cleaners, as tutors or doctors, or as sexual partners." [Murray J. Harris, "Slave of Christ," *New Studies in Biblical Theology*, ed. D. A. Carson (Downers Grove, IL: InterVarsity, 2001), 35] Given this wide diversity of situations, commanding that Christians free all their slaves would have met with mixed results for the slaves themselves. Many would have found themselves worse off. Thus, following the golden rule wouldn't necessarily mean that Christian masters should simply free their slaves. Given the way society operated, that might not have been most beneficial for each individual.

This doesn't mean that Greco-Roman slavery was benign. Slaves in the Greco-Roman world were considered property, and they had few if any rights. For instance, the master could beat his slaves if he wished, and if he beat a slave to death, there was no penalty for murder. Greco-Roman slavery was a societal structure that needed to be abolished. Christians in the first century had no political power to do this, so the New Testament instructions seek to mitigate the evil (since Eph. 6:9 forbids masters to even threaten—much less beat—their slaves) by laying the seeds for the destruction of the system (since Col. 3:11 and 1 Cor. 7:21 proclaim the equality of slave and free).

Slaves in the United States

It should be clear then that Americans could not rightly appeal to the Old Testament to justify stealing Africans away from their homeland and enslaving them and their posterity forever in a race-based system of slavery. The Old Testament penalty for participation in such a system would have been death (Exod. 21:16). In the New Testament the policy was guided by the golden rule. American Christians who attempted to defend Southern slavery using the Bible were actually misinterpreting Scripture in order to conform to an unbiblical culture.

Thus, some say that just as the church has changed its position on slavery, so the church should change its position on issues of gender and sexuality, but that's exactly backwards. In the past the church conformed to its culture against Scripture on the matter of slavery. That error brought about great cultural and personal damage. If the church conforms to its culture against Scripture on matters of gender and sexuality today, consequences for individuals and society will be just as grave.

Practicing Prudence

[Note: If your students are also taking government or civics this semester, consider coordinating with that teacher on this project.] Have students select a controversial issue that Christians should care about and set an end goal for how they'd like to see that issue handled in the law. Then have them write a bill that they think could pass their state legislature or the US Congress. Have students look at the voting records of the sitting members of their legislature or Congress to see whether their bill is likely to pass or whether it would die. Remind them to take into account whether governor (or the president) would be likely to sign the measure, and if not, whether they have enough votes to override a veto.

If they conclude that their measure would not pass, have them see if they can find an aspect of their plan that could pass and thus move them closer to their goal. If they do come up with a bill that would pass, have them evaluate it to see if it included any feature that would prevent them from reaching their overall goal in the future. Note that the

womb (twenty-two weeks). Some pro-life legal efforts have been unsuccessful, but overall progress on the issue in America has been undeniable.

Prudence

Prudence means understanding your situation, seeing what good can be accomplished in it, knowing what options are both morally legitimate and likely successful—and then pursuing the wisest goal in the wisest way. Prudence is a key virtue for Christians involved in politics (Prov. 8:12–16). The Bible does not provide specific revelation about how to frame laws, manage campaigns, or even who to vote for in a presidential election. But the Bible was written to help Christians live wisely in every aspect of their lives. Prudence is knowing the best way to get from here to wherever you ought to be.

For example, Christians and radical feminists fundamentally disagree about the structure of the family and the roles of men and women in society. But they both see pornography as degrading, and both oppose domestic abuse of women. A politically prudent Christian can reach across the aisle and cooperate with someone who wants the same biblical things even if their motivations are ultimately different.

Boldness, Humility, and Respect

Of course, some fundamental disagreements will always remain. Cooperation is sometimes impossible. On these matters the Christian should state the Christian position boldly, but not brashly. Repeatedly, Scripture urges Christians to engage their opponents humbly and respectfully. As the apostle Paul told one pastor,

> Remind [Christians] to be submissive to rulers and authorities, to be obedient, to be ready for every good work, to speak evil of no one, to avoid quarreling, to be gentle, and to show perfect courtesy toward all people. For we ourselves were once foolish, disobedient, led astray, slaves to various passions and pleasures, passing our days in malice and envy, hated by others and hating one another. (Titus 3:1–3)

If Christians participated in political life with these virtues, they would stand out in a positive way. Sadly, too often Christians speak with the same harshness, quarrelsomeness, and sometimes even untruthfulness about their political opponents as the lost world does. Even under a ruler such as Nero, who had starkly unchristian policies, Peter says to "honor the emperor" (1 Pet. 2:17).

THE RIGHT TO REVOLT?

What if a government gets to be so bad that people begin to talk about revolution? Should Christians join in? Should they lead the effort?

Opinions on Revolution

Christians have historically disagreed over this matter.[21] Martin Luther said no. Christians have a duty to disobey the government only when it requires them to disobey God. They should pray and speak out against injustice, but they should not revolt. Luther gave four reasons for this position. First, rulers are accountable to God, and God will judge those rulers who are disobedient. Second, rebellions rarely bring the benefits that people want. Luther says, "For insurrection lacks discernment; it generally harms the innocent more than the guilty." Third, God has explicitly forbid-

latter is the kind of compromise they don't want to make.

Practicing Boldness

Some people are averse to the virtue of prudence because they think that it signals a lack of boldness. They would prefer to take a stand and plant their flag even if they know their legislation will fail rather than move toward a goal incrementally. But prudence and boldness aren't antithetical virtues.

Have students develop a media campaign to support the issue they're trying to advance in the previous activity. The campaign could use print, audio, or visual media. It should make a case for their position not only to motivate like-minded voters but also attempt to persuade voters who might be undecided on the issue.

What Does Humility Mean?

Sometimes Christians speak and act as though the United States is a Christian nation. They think that secularists have stolen it away for a time but that Christians can rally and take their culture back from secularist invaders. Sadly, this approach to politics can result in Christians seeing other people not with compassion because of their need for the gospel but as enemies to be destroyed in political battle.

The reality is that God hasn't promised Christians a nation or a culture that is theirs to keep, at least not in the present evil age. This is not to say that Christians should give up on their political efforts to oppose secularism and policies that are contrary to Scripture. But the virtue of humility should steer the motivation away from getting back

den rebellion in Scripture (Deut. 32:3–5; Rom. 12:19). Fourth, when Christians rebel, it undermines their gospel witness.[22] Luther concurred with church fathers such as Justin Martyr—and most of medieval Christendom—in this opinion.[23]

Reformer John Calvin agreed with Luther, but he was willing for lower-level officials to actively oppose a tyrant. And some of Calvin's followers took that a step further. They argued that rulers and their people were bound together by a covenant. A ruler who violated the covenant lost the right to rule, and political leaders under him could ensure that he left office.[24]

Enlightenment philosopher John Locke built on this idea in his discussion of a social contract and a right to rebellion.[25] A tyrant ceases to be a king, he argued—so rebellion against him ceases to be true rebellion.[26]

The problem with Locke's view is that the concept of a covenant or contract between the ruler and the people is not found in Scripture. Babylon and Rome didn't get their rule over Israel through a social contract; God gave it to them directly (Ezra 5:12). The Bible even recognizes the rule of kings who got it by immoral means (for example, Jehu in 2 Kings 9:14–37). Romans 13 could hardly be more direct:

> Let every person be subject to the governing authorities. For there is no authority except from God, and those that exist have been instituted by God. Therefore whoever resists the authorities resists what God has appointed, and those who resist will incur judgment. (Rom. 13:1–2)

When Israel started demanding a king, God warned them about what life under a king would be like. And He never made provisions for a coup d'état*(coo day TAH) (1 Sam. 8:11–17). Even David, who had been designated by God as the next king of Israel, would not fight against the reigning king because he was the Lord's anointed (1 Sam. 24:9–11).

coup d'état: *a sudden and usually violent attempt by a small group of people to overthrow the government*

History of Revolutions

Luther's concern that revolutions typically do more harm than good is borne out by modern history all over the globe. This does not mean Christians must submissively do whatever a government asks. Sometimes, Christians must obey divine authority rather than human authorities (Acts 5:29). In these cases, Christians must hope that God will deliver them, or they must simply suffer whatever punishment comes (Dan. 2:18; 6:22). Shadrach, Meshach, and Abednego got the balance just right:

> Our God whom we serve is able to deliver us from the burning fiery furnace, and he will deliver us out of your hand, O king. But if not, be it known to you, O king, that we will not serve your gods or worship the golden image that you have set up. (Dan. 3:17–18)

What would've happened in Nazi Germany if all the Christians—and there were many—had been Shadrachs, Meshachs, and Abednegos? What if they had spoken boldly against Hitler's tyranny? What if Christian businessmen had insisted on continuing to serve Jewish customers? What if Christian soldiers had refused to fight an unjust war? What if Christian owners of chemical plants had declined to supply Zyklon B for the gas chambers? There are ways to resist evil government apart from outright rebellion and insurrection.

"WHILE HISTORY DOES NOT EXACTLY REPEAT ITSELF, IT DOES TEND TO RHYME."[27]

—ED PANOSIAN

a culture that is rightfully ours and toward love for our neighbors. Christians really believe that a culture that lives contrary to creational norms is a culture that will cause a great deal of harm to others. Christians really believe that a culture in which religious viewpoints and arguments for policy positions can be expressed openly is better for everyone than a culture that's supposedly neutral.

In the hardscrabble political world, even Christians who are demonstrably humble and loving in motivation and actions may be portrayed as heartless and bigoted by political opponents. But the Christian should strive to please God by his humility, and it may well be that the practice of this virtue may make the Christian message attractive even to political opponents.

What Does Respect Mean?

Within the context of government, Paul tells Christians to "speak evil of no one, to avoid quarrelling, to be gentle, and to show perfect courtesy toward all people" (Titus 3:2).

This sounds unrealistic. Is Paul really saying that a Christian can't say anything negative about a political opponent? Can he not argue with his policies or expose his corruption? That isn't what Paul means when he says, "Speak evil of no one," but he's still saying something that serves as a sharp critique of American political practice. The Greek word that underlies "speak evil" is the verb from which we get the word *blaspheme*. Paul is prohibiting angry or abusive speech, insults, slander, and defamation.

Practicing Respect
Present students with some sample political discourse by playing recordings and/or providing transcripts from cable or radio programs about political topics. Have the students evaluate whether the participants on those programs align with Titus 3:1–5 and with the passages discussed in the note "Danger of Political Worldliness" on page 275.

Have students pick a selection from one of the participants who generally represents their viewpoint, and have the students rewrite the dialogue in a way that would align with the virtue of respect as described in these passages.

What About Jesus and the Prophets?

Jesus and the Old Testament prophets rebuked leaders in Israel with strong language. For instance, Jesus called the Pharisees "fools," "hypocrites," and "whitewashed tombs" (Matt. 23:13–36). The prophet Amos called powerful women who oppressed the poor "cows of Bashan" (Amos 4:1). How does this match up with Paul calling on Christians to avoid insulting speech and to "show perfect courtesy toward all people"? How does it fit with Jesus' own warning that "whoever says, 'You fool!' will be liable to the hell of fire" (Matt. 5:22)?

First, it's important to note that Jesus and the prophets rebuke based on divine authority. It seems that they're rendering a judicial sentence in some cases. So if a Christian is going to launch this kind of critique, it can only be in condemning policies that Scripture condemns with the utmost clarity. It should never be used concerning policies or tactics over which Christians legitimately disagree.

Second, the Bible does distinguish between righteous indignation, which Jesus exhibits in Matthew 23, and sinful anger, which He condemns in Matthew 5. The Christian who thinks he's filled with righteous indignation needs to be careful that he's not actually sinfully angry.

Third, it may be that language that could be used of private citizens who have done wrong shouldn't be used of elected or appointed officials. Jesus called the Pharisees (who held no official position) "whitewashed tombs," but Paul retracted his statement that the high priest was a "whitewashed wall" (Acts 23:3–5) on the basis of the Exodus 22:28 prohibition of speaking evil of a ruler.

Finally, Jesus was characterized by the virtues that Paul lays out in Titus 3:2

(cf. Matt. 11:29; 21:5). His denunciations should not cause us to forget that the pattern the New Testament holds out for Christians is boldness coupled with gentleness and respect.

Final Redemption at Last: The Creation Mandate Fulfilled

Redemption involves the complete reversal of the Fall. When God pronounced curses in Genesis 3, they touched on different aspects of the Creation Mandate. That mandate, however, is restored in redemption. The man Jesus Christ rules over all the earth, and His people rule under Him. In fact, since Revelation 22:6–21 forms the conclusion to the book of Revelation, the final words of the body of the book are "and they will reign forever and ever" (Rev. 22:5). We have come full circle to Genesis 1:26–28.

THINKING IT THROUGH 18.3

1. Pray and press for God's will to be done.

2. *Theocracy* means "God-rule," and *theonomy* means "God's law." Theonomists believe Old Testament law with its penalties should still be enforced unless the New Testament directly overturns something specifically. The entirety of the Old Testament law system has been replaced by the New Covenant system, and the church wasn't set up to govern the world.

3. Every belief and value is rooted in religious worldviews. Ruling out the Bible and its authority from the outset unfairly establishes human reason as the ultimate authority.

4. preserve good and reform evil

♀5. prudence, humility, respect, boldness

Example of respect and boldness: Rulers who stand for unbiblical policies should not be called "trash," but they can be clearly identified for who they are—sinful people who oppose biblical morality.

FINAL REDEMPTION

Right now our job as Christians is to press for prudent reforms that push the world in small ways toward what it will look like one day when Christ redeems it. Despite the frustrations and setbacks that will most certainly come, we must continue to work. As with every other cultural activity mentioned in this book, our belief in the future coming of Christ doesn't remove our responsibility to submit to Christ's rule now in every way we can, even in politics and government. But only Christ's coming can achieve final redemption.

In the dark days of the judges, Hannah sang a song that proclaimed the power of God to exalt the humble and to humiliate mighty oppressors. Realizing that only the Lord could do this, Hannah closed her song with an appeal for Yahweh to "give strength to his king and exalt the power of his anointed [Messiah]" (1 Sam. 2:10). Hannah's prayer comes at the beginning of the story of King David. And it's through David's descendant, the Messiah, that God promises to "shatter" the nations that oppose Him (Pss. 2, 110).

The prophet Isaiah predicted that this same Messiah—called "Mighty God"—would sit on the throne of David (Isa. 9:6–7). This Davidic king, the Bible says, will rule the world in righteousness (11:3–5; 16:3–5). But Christ will not abolish human government. The climactic verse of the climactic book of the Bible is, "The kingdom of the world has become the kingdom of our Lord and of his Christ, and he shall reign forever and ever" (Rev. 11:15).

The government of God on the renewed earth will be eternal. But interestingly, the government of God will work through the same human dominion God blessed mankind with in Genesis 1:26–28 (cf. Ps. 8:6; Heb. 2:5–10). Daniel prophesied that God's people would themselves have dominion in God's future kingdom (Dan. 7:18, 22, 27). And John says that under the Messiah, the saints "will reign forever and ever" (Rev. 22:5). The twelve disciples in particular, Jesus said, will "sit on twelve thrones, judging the twelve tribes of Israel" (Matt. 19:28).

Revelation 21:24 reveals that there will be "nations" and "kings" throughout all eternity. These kings will bring "the glory and the honor of the nations" into the new Jerusalem (21:26). Kings and their citizens will still have a role to play—as kings and as citizens—for all eternity. This is government redeemed.

THINKING IT THROUGH 18.3

1. What two tasks should Christians engage in regardless of their political situation?

2. What do the terms *theocracy* and *theonomy* mean? Summarize the political philosophy behind them, and explain why it's wrong.

3. Why shouldn't Christians refuse to appeal to the Bible in order to defend their political positions?

4. What should be the two prongs of a Christian political program?

♀5. What are four Christian political virtues? Choose one virtue and give an example of how it should affect Christian political discourse.

Scripture Memory

Revelation 11:15*b*

Making Connections

1. List the five positions on church and state relations.

2. If Christ has assigned different realms of limited authority to the state and church, then how should the church relate to the state?

3. Why is praying the most powerful thing Christians can do in their political involvement?

4. Why can two Christians who have the same basic beliefs and values still disagree about what is a prudent political tactic or appropriate cooperation?

Developing Skills in Apologetics and Worldview

5. Explain whether or not you should participate or how you should participate in the following civil religious activities in the American public square: (a) saying the Pledge of A-llegiance, (b) observing a moment of silence, and (c) praying an interfaith prayer.

6. How should you express a biblical dissatisfaction with corrupt political policies or wicked rulers?

Examining Assumptions and Evidence

7. Why should Christians participate in government even though their task as citizens of Christ's kingdom is to spread the gospel?

8. Why is the secularist exclusion of biblical authority not a neutral position?

9. Differentiate the theonomist position from the position endorsed by this book.

10. How would you differentiate between rebellion and appropriate Christian resistance to wicked rulers?

Becoming a Creative Cultivator

11. Find a news article that opposes Christian moral values. Write a response that is characterized by the Christian virtues of prudence, humility, respect, and boldness. After it's reviewed by your teacher, you may want to submit it as a letter to the editor of the publication or website that published the news article.

THE GOAL OF GOVERNMENT | 283

---

6. Christians can boldly speak out against corruption and wickedness, but they do so with humility and with respect for the office. Their forthrightness is not marred by rudeness, slander, or incivility.

Examining Assumptions and Evidence

7. While Christians have been called to evangelize for Christ's kingdom, they have also been given the responsibility to participate in human society, carrying out the Creation Mandate.

8. Insisting that human reason is the only legitimate standard of judgment excludes all worldviews except secularism.

9. Theonomists claim that the specific commands and punishments from the Old Testament law directly apply to the nations today. This book recommends that Christians discern the creational norms being applied in the Old Testament and reapply those creational norms or principles in appropriate ways to today's cultural contexts.

10. Rebellion seeks to overthrow government authorities while appropriate Christian resistance simply refuses to participate in or carry out unrighteous demands given by those authorities.

Becoming a Creative Cultivator

11. Answers will vary.

TERMS TO REMEMBER

Constantinianism—the political position that the state should rule over the church because God appointed them to rule

civil religion—making use of generic religion in order to gain politically

theocracy—God-rule

theonomy—God's law; the belief that the Old Testament laws and penalties should be enforced today unless specifically overturned in the New Testament

prudence—understanding your situation, seeing what good can be accomplished in it, knowing what options are both morally legitimate and likely to be successful—and then pursuing the wisest goal in the wisest way

---

CHAPTER REVIEW ANSWERS

Making Connections

1. State over church; church over state; civil religion; excluding religion from the state; church influencing state

2. The church shouldn't try to craft and implement governmental policies, but it should try to disciple people who have beliefs and values based on a biblical worldview to apply them to all of life.

3. God is in control of all things. We have no ability to affect the world apart from Him.

4. They may understand the situation differently, causing them to disagree about approaches. Both may be seeing legitimate aspects of a situation. Or it may be that some people have greater political wisdom than others.

Developing Skills in Apologetics and Worldview

5. Most Christians who recite the pledge apply "under God" to the true God in recognition of the Christian influence on the nation, but they should realize that the pledge can be used to further civil religion.

A moment of silence: Christians should recognize that they're not a part of a true corporate prayer that unites them with those of other faiths. They may pray to the one true God individually during this time.

An interfaith prayer: Christians should make it clear that they cannot participate in an interfaith prayer without violating the fundamental tenets of their own faith.

7

SCIENCE

The student will be able to

19.1 Defend the idea that science is a God-established good and that it is made possible by three major Christian assumptions.

19.2 Determine the main purposes of science: to declare the glory of God and to make wise use of the earth for the benefit of others.

19.3 Structure scientific study according to the creational norms that govern science.

SECTION OBJECTIVES 19.1

1. Critique the claims that Christianity is anti-science and that scientism is nonreligious.

2. Connect the work of the Creation Mandate to the work of science to explain why science is a God-established good.

3. Summarize the three major Christian assumptions, and explain why they justify the work of science.

4. Explain why it's not possible to separate the sacred from the secular in the work of science.

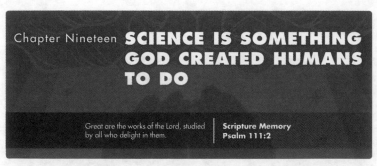

Chapter Nineteen **SCIENCE IS SOMETHING GOD CREATED HUMANS TO DO**

Great are the works of the Lord, studied by all who delight in them.

Scripture Memory Psalm 111:2

19.1 SCIENCE BELONGS TO CHRISTIANITY

Scientism is "excessive belief in the power of scientific knowledge and techniques."[1] That's kind of funny—the very definition of *scientism* is "belief," not "knowledge." And yet adherents of **scientism** commonly claim, "Faith is the great cop-out, the great excuse to evade the need to think and evaluate evidence."[2] But scientism is a faith, a worldview, like any religion.

Atheistic, materialistic scientism even has saints and martyrs, just like other belief systems. Watch the most recent incarnation of the *Cosmos* documentary, and you'll meet one: Giordano Bruno (c.1548–1600). As *Cosmos* presents it in a series of animations, Bruno was persecuted by cartoonishly wicked Christian clerics for daring to suggest that the universe might be infinite and that the stars might have their own planets. The way *Cosmos* tells it, Bruno was burned at the stake for his crimes against Christian dogma, becoming one of the first people to die for the one true science.[3]

Bruno and Galileo—as well as others—are often made to fit what science historian Lawrence Principe calls a "widespread myth," namely that "during the 16th and 17th centuries and during the Middle Ages, there was . . . a camp of 'scientists' struggling to break free of the repression of 'religionists.'" Principe calls stories like the one *Cosmos* tells about Bruno "folkloristic fabrications."[4]

Instead of "religion" and "science" being at war in the Renaissance period, Principe says, "the investigators of nature were themselves religious people,"[5] and many clergy members were among them. In

fact, "theological motivations—the desire to read [divine] messages in the Book of Nature—provided the single greatest driving force for scientific inquiry throughout the entire early modern period."[6]

Principe shows in his book *The Scientific Revolution* that Christianity didn't hinder science; it propelled it. As well it should have—and still should—because science is something God created humans to do.

SCIENCE AS SOMETHING GOD CREATED HUMANS TO DO

You might be called by God Himself to study the "book of nature" by becoming a working chemist, botanist, geologist, or one of the countless other scientific callings. Don't let the myth of a necessary conflict between science and religion stop you from answering that call.

And don't let any other secularizing ideas about science stop you either. The only truly good reasons to be a scientist are, in fact, *Christian* reasons—and that doesn't mean merely using science as a witnessing tool (although you can and should do this). Your actual day-to-day work with chlorophyll, hydrofluorocarbons, computer models, and DNA sequencers ought to be motivated precisely by your Christianity.

Once there was a Christian chemist who worked at Milliken, a major textile manufacturing company, who put his head on his pillow every night wondering whether he was doing any good. Christ's kingdom wasn't expanding in any obvious ways because

286 | SCIENCE

Lesson Plan Chart—Chapter 19

Section Title	Pages	Activity Manual	Days
19.1 Science Belongs to Christianity	286–91	Activity 33	2 days
19.2 The Ultimate Purpose for Science	292–95		1 day
19.3 Creational Norms for Science	295–300	Activity 34	2 days
Review	301		1 day
Total Suggested Days			**6 days**

Scientism

Scientism is a term students may not be familiar with. And there's no doubt that it's a term of criticism; many words ending in *-ism* are. Few if any of scientism's proponents would wish to own the label, and it should therefore be used carefully. Christians shouldn't be known for their quick resort to name-calling. But Christians aren't the only ones who have found the label useful because it isn't mere name-calling. It identifies a very specific critique: scientism is the idolizing or worshiping of science. That's what makes it an *-ism*. And the non-Christian contributors to *Scientism: The New Orthodoxy* (a book the Student Text references) can see that just as well as the Christians can. Christianity isn't the only modern Western opponent of scientism.

Out of love for their lost neighbors, Christian chemists should strive to develop better carpet fibers.

of his work. All the carpet fibers he refined and all the pipe casings he developed didn't seem to have anything to do with Jesus Christ.[7] He began considering a job change—maybe he was called to full-time ministry?

But look at the public relations material on the Milliken website that describes the work of scientists at the company:

> Deep Science at Milliken combines the structure and order of the scientific method with immense curiosity and creativity. It penetrates the surface to get to the underlying physics and chemistry that constitute our world. Science extends our understanding of the fundamental nature of things, enabling us to benefit humanity by creating new technologies that are both more effective and friendlier to nature.[8]

This paragraph borrows and relies on multiple Christian ideas: (1) Only the Christian worldview guarantees that the scientist will find "structure" and "order" in creation. (2) Curiosity is an essential quality for obeying the Creation Mandate. (3) Creativity is part of our nature as God's image-bearers. (4) Science, though it doesn't actually get down to "the fundamental nature of things," surely does enable us to "benefit humanity" through technology. Science is a key way to love our neighbors as ourselves.

Lying hidden in his own company's promo materials are some hints to the Milliken chemist that his work *does* have everything to do with his faith. Science is a major tool helping us to obey the Creation Mandate. We are supposed to "fill the earth and subdue it." In fact, the only way we *can* fill it is by subduing it. Population growth is a good thing that nonetheless brings challenges: where will all these people get sufficient food, clean water, and adequate shelter? The chemists at Milliken get to focus on one important element of the shelter question: how can a growing population get affordable, durable, clean flooring for their homes and workplaces? Science—along with politics, economics, and other fields—helps provide good solutions to those problems.

Christianity is not a threat to science. Why would God threaten something He created us to do? Science is just the label we give to some of the most useful methods of subduing creation and ruling over it. Those methods didn't get invented in 1900—or 1600. They began, in seed form, in the Garden of Eden before the Fall.

> God blessed them. And God said to them, "Be fruitful and multiply and fill the earth and subdue it, and have dominion over the fish of the sea and over the birds of the heavens and over every living thing that moves on the earth." (Gen. 1:28)

Most jobs have a larger mission. The majority of those missions could probably be understood in light of loving one's neighbor by taking part in a task that demands some kind of human dominion over the world's resources. The work of science often underlies such dominion tasks. Christians just need to make the connection between the mission of their job and God's larger purpose for the world so that they can approach their particular job function with the motivation to make a meaningful difference for God's glory and their neighbor's good.

Doing Science Christianly

Invite a scientist who's also a Christian to address your class about the role Christian faith plays in his or her work. (First, make sure that this person understands how a biblical worldview should be applied to all of life.) You could also interview the scientist in front of the class, asking whether he or she ever struggled with that role. Here are a few questions you could ask the scientist:

Have you seen other professing Christian scientists succeed at living out their faith? How did they apply their faith to their field?

Have you seen them fail? How did they compartmentalize their faith from their field?

How do you think your daily work in science would be different if you were not a Christian?

What would modern science look like if it were run according to God's laws or creational norms?

In what ways do your unsaved colleagues reflect God's common grace in their work?

A Definition of Science

Point out to the students that a kind of definition of science appears near the bottom of page 287. It's not a traditional definition; instead, it's a theologically practical one. Science is "the label we give to some of the most useful methods of subduing creation and ruling over it." (A more formal definition appears on page 300.) The definition is theological because it draws from the Creation Mandate of Genesis 1. But it's practical because it aims at usefulness, not specificity. Who is to say which methods of dominion count as "science" and which deserve some other label (such as "sports" or "child-rearing")? "Science" in the West tends to focus on those methods of investigation that are repeatable, testable, and empirical. But our definition of science must never imply that empirical ways of knowing are the only ways. That would be scientism.

Critiquing *Cosmos*

Clips from *Cosmos* are available on the internet, and the entire series may be available on loan from your local library. It might be instructive for your students to view the entire section about Bruno. Ask them in advance to look for evidence of scientism, a quasi-religious devotion to science.

Meaning Through Mission

Have your parents—or you yourself—ever expressed the kind of dissatisfaction with their jobs that the Christian chemist at Milliken felt. Have you ever felt your job was meaningless?

Describe the mission of a secular company or organization that you feel you could get behind.

Examples could include the mission of a hospital or nonprofit organization for people with various diseases, a food services company, an automotive company—any company that provides for others' well-being or an organization that promotes others' well-being.

Describe the mission of a company that you feel you could not get behind.

Examples could include the mission of a predatory lending institution, a casino, or a deceptive multi-level marketing scheme.

What makes one secular company's mission acceptable and another's not?

A mission must be guided by a vision that's based on legitimate goals and applied according to ethical values. Legitimate goals are consistent with the task of the Creation Mandate and directed by creational norms. Values are determined by biblical norms.

The Deep Conflict Between Science and Naturalism

Highlight the pull-quote from Christian philosopher Alvin Plantinga, which is the opening line of his book *Where the Conflict Really Lies: Science, Religion, and Naturalism*. Many of the supposed conflicts between science and theology can be resolved without undermining true science or compromising orthodoxy. It logically follows that there would be concord between God's Word and God's world. But, despite the wide acceptance of philosophical naturalism, it is fundamentally flawed. When its claims are examined closely, it becomes clear that they conflict with true science (e.g., the Second Law of Thermodynamics). Naturalism's claims are more philosophical than scientific. Scientific work simply presupposes this philosophical lens of interpretation. This is the point to press on students who still assume that, when it comes down to it, science (as a naturalistic lens) is the only way to "prove" something.

How has philosophical naturalism been so effectively passed off as synonymous with science? The forces of scientism have pretty successfully defined the argument over science in the public square (at least in secular Western thinking). And Christians need to admit that they have questions to answer about biology, geology, and other issues. There are far more non-Christian scientists than Christian, and they've raised a lot of valid questions. But as this unit repeatedly argues, the forces of scientism manage to claim the high ground in the culture by outlawing the fundamental philosophical question: where does everything come from, including the laws of science? Laws come from lawgivers, as any theist can tell you.

What Conflict?

What does Plantinga mean by saying there is "deep conflict between science and naturalism"? What are some of those conflicts?

Naturalism has a difficult time answering the following questions:

- *Why is there something rather than nothing?*
- *Why did the big bang occur, what caused it, where did the exploding material come from, and how does order come from disorder without an external mechanism directing it?*
- *Why would it make sense to trust brains that were supposedly formed by blind processes of natural selection?*
- *Where do the laws of logic or the laws of science come from, and what ensures their consistency?*
- *How does life come from nonlife?*
- *What is the reliable standard for justifying something as right or wrong?*

Mankind cannot possibly take dominion over the wide array of created things—fish, birds, insects—without a set of skills we have come to call "scientific." Science is something God created humans to do.

THREE CHRISTIAN ASSUMPTIONS THAT MAKE SCIENCE POSSIBLE

Christianity isn't merely compatible with science; it is essential to it. The religion of the Bible is the foundation that makes science possible. Consider three assumptions, drawn straight from a biblical worldview, without which science would be impossible.

Assumption 1: Nature Is Orderly

The first assumption is that **nature is predictable, orderly, and governed by laws**. God said to Noah,

> While the earth remains, seedtime and harvest, cold and heat, summer and winter, day and night, shall not cease. (Gen. 8:22)

"There is superficial conflict but deep concord between science and theistic religion, but superficial concord and deep conflict between science and naturalism."[9]

—ALVIN PLANTINGA

He told Jeremiah that He had made a "covenant with day and night and the fixed order of heaven and earth" (Jer. 33:25).

There was a time in Western history—in that portion of the premodern era called the Middle Ages—when it was actually difficult being an unbeliever. It wasn't just that you were surrounded by people who believed in God or that social pressure was put on you to believe (though that was all true), it was that your whole thought world was structured in and in God. Other views seemed utterly implausible. The word *atheist* didn't even enter the English language until the late sixteenth century. God was a given.

It was, in fact, the order and rationality of Western civilization's God that became the major basis for modern science. As Lesslie Newbigin, a Christian thinker and missionary to India, put it,

> Historians of science have devoted much thought to the question why the marvelous intellectual powers of the Greeks, the Chinese, the Indians, and the Egyptians, in spite of their achievements in science and mathematics, did not give rise to the self-sustaining science which has dominated our [Western] culture for the past two hundred years.[10]

A big part of the answer seems to be this: Christianity provided assurance that the apparent contradictions of our experience can be resolved. If my body temperature is 98.6° F one day and 99.3° the next, there's a rational explanation to be found. So while Western alchemists, astrologers, and naturalists were poking around God's world and discovering its open secrets—while they were becoming what we today call "scientists"—other worldviews around the globe kept equally intelligent people in their armchairs. Why should someone who believes that "all that exists is emanation from primal being"[11] (Newbigin's description of Hindu philosophy) bother to perform experiments? Why should animists work to discover the properties of granite, when everybody knows that the granite spirit controls those properties at his whim?

It's Christianity that allows chemists at Milliken to do their work with the confidence that the processes they perform in a lab in 2019 will yield the same results when they hit the manufacturing floor in 2021.

Is Western Science Really "Self-Sustaining"?

Modern Western science isn't the only science that has ever existed. Other views of science have held sway at earlier times in other places. But it's important for students to understand what sets modern Western science apart—positively speaking—from its predecessors. Simply put, it has produced results and maintained a good degree of coherence. That is, modern science and technology have brought more innovations and improvements to human life than other "sciences" of the past, and those improvements have been produced at an ever-increasing rate throughout the history of the tradition. These are (mostly) good things worth celebrating; the Christian critique of scientism need never deny this.

An Orderly World

Ask students to write about three things scientists assume about the orderliness of nature in order to do their work. How would their work be affected if they didn't assume this orderliness? For example, they assume that the scientific elements pretty well hold together under normal circumstances, that the external world really exists, and that "seedtime and harvest . . . shall not cease" (Gen. 8:22).

World Religions and Science

Divide students into small groups. Each group should do a different keyword search for a religion's "view of science": Hindu, Muslim, animist, ancient Greek, medieval Christian, and so on. Do they find evidence

The Roman Catholic Jesuit order produced numerous mathematicians, scientists, and educational institutions in the early modern era. Whatever their theological errors, they did have a sound motto: "To find God in all things." Science historian Lawrence Principe comments, "While Jesuits emphasized this incentive, it was not unique to them—it undergirded virtually the entire Scientific Revolution." [12]

One clarification is needed here: the Christian view of divine order in creation is not "uniformitarian." Christians do not believe that God set up the laws of the universe, wound it up, and let it go. (That's deism, remember.) God still rules over His own natural laws, and He can suspend them or stretch them if He desires. That's what we call a "miracle." Non-Christians may see the supernatural miracles in the Bible and conclude that Christianity does not teach an orderly universe. But the miracles are viewed in the Bible as remarkable happenings precisely because they are exceptions to the general rules of God's action in the world.

There are Christians who step into the deistic ditch, however. Says theologian Vern Poythress,

> Christians have sometimes adopted an unbiblical concept of God that moves him one step out of the way of our ordinary affairs. We ourselves may think of "scientific law" or "natural law" as a kind of cosmic mechanism or impersonal clockwork that runs the world most of the time, while God is on vacation. God comes and acts only rarely through miracle. But this is not biblical. "You cause the grass to grow for the livestock" (Ps. 104:14). "He gives snow like wool" (Ps. 147:16). Let us not forget it. If we ourselves recovered a robust doctrine of God's involvement in daily caring for his world in detail, we would find ourselves in a much better position to dialogue with atheist scientists who rely on that same care. [13]

God acts directly to sustain the order He created. This is the foundation on which every chemist at Milliken stands—and at least one of them should know it.

Assumption 2: Humans Are Capable

The second assumption drawn from Christianity and without which science could not exist is that **the human mind is capable of creatively describing the predictable natural order in useful ways** (Gen. 1:27). We're able to study our world and imagine future possibilities. There are some problems with wood floors—so we invent rugs, then carpets, then Scotchgard. There are some problems with our maternal survival rates—so we invent antiseptics and train obstetricians. There are some problems with our commute times and our fuel costs—so we invent superhighways and efficient vehicles.

Because we are made in God's image, we can approach nature the same way a mechanically minded kid approaches a lawnmower engine. He's thinking, "A human being like me designed this thing and put it together, so I should be able to take it apart, put it back together, and figure out how it works."

Likewise, cells and galaxies are complicated. But, ultimately, an Engineer with a mind like ours put them together. In principle, we should be able to figure out how they work. Human minds are patterned after the divine mind, so God's creations should be understandable and usable by the people made in His image.

From the atheistic viewpoint of scientism, whatever produced the universe is something totally different from us. It's an impersonal force or a huge bang. Imagine a lawnmower engine "built" by a tornado blowing stuff around a junkyard—it would

that any of these other views of reality account for the order observable in nature?

Uniformity vs. Uniformitarianism

See page 8 for a prior discussion of uniformitarianism (though that term was not used) with regard to the dating of the Grand Canyon. This is probably one of the most accessible illustrations of the Christian critique of uniformitarianism. Jason Lisle affirms "uniformity"—the idea that nature is orderly—but not uniformitarianism. He distinguishes the two this way:

> Uniformity . . . asserts a consistency in the way the universe operates (*if* conditions are the same, one can expect the same outcome). In other words, the laws of nature are constant, but conditions and specific processes may

be quite different in time or space. Conversely, uniformitarianism asserts that there is a consistency of conditions *and* processes. Uniformitarianism, as it pertains to geology, asserts that the geological past must be understood in light of present conditions and processes.

[Jason Lisle, "Is the Present the Key to the Past?" *Answers in Genesis* (website) (April 4, 2008)]

The Jesuit Order

The mention of the Jesuit order is not an endorsement of all of their beliefs and practices. While the Jesuits' desire to "find God in all things" is laudable, and while it has led to the founding of hundreds of educational institutions around the world, many of those institutions are theologically liberal

(i.e., they reject foundational tenets of the Christian faith). This is so because the Jesuits don't ascribe proper authority to Scripture.

[In his book, *Bad Religion: How We Became a Nation of Heretics* (New York: Free Press, 2013), Catholic *New York Times* opinion columnist Ross Douthat critiques the theological liberalism in the modern Jesuit order.]

Miracles

One of C. S. Lewis's larger works was *Miracles* (San Francisco: HarperOne, 2015 [originally 1947, rev. 1960]). Lewis argues in this book that the modern refusal to believe in biblical miracles is explainable only by an anti-supernatural bias—such a refusal cannot be derived from the evidence alone. Lewis argues that miracles aren't incompatible with natural law but instead go beyond it.

Whatever Produced the Universe Is Something Different from Us

What logical impossibility do evolutionists end up embracing when they claim that humans are nothing more than stardust?

Stardust is impersonal; it has no intelligence. Humans are personal and have intelligence. Explaining how personhood and intelligence came about from that origin through the naturalistic mechanisms of evolution has never been adequately explained. Thus, the evolutionary worldview has no basis for explaining why humans are capable beings.

How could evolutionists solve the conundrum inherent in their worldview?

Atheistic scientism could (sort of) solve its philosophical conundrum—the question of how it is that intelligent and self-aware beings arose from impersonal causes, how it is that mind came from matter—by denying that humans have intelligence and self-awareness, by saying that these apparent traits are only illusions created by physical forces operating untiringly on our evolutionary shape over billions of years. But oddly enough, few thinkers wish to deny the reality of their own thoughts.

How does the biblical worldview resolve the conundrum?

The Being who created the universe is different from us. But He's also like us in key ways—or rather we're like Him. Humans aren't little deities; we're different from God. But humans are image-bearers; we are patterned after God's likeness in some respects (according to His communicable attributes). The Designer is able to masterfully accomplish such a feat in His work. Humans were designed to fulfill a purpose—to carry out the Creation Mandate.

Human Creativity and Science

There are only two self-consistent ways of looking at Fleming's creative discovery of penicillin. Either the inescapable chain of cause and effect bumped into an evolutionary useful coming together of two species of flora and fauna (*homo sapiens* and *Penicillium notatum*), or a person created in God's image exercised the powers latent in that image and became yet another notable example of God blessing His creation.

Evolutionary Justification for Animal Experimentation

Ask students to debate the following:

Should humans experiment on animals? If they should, what basis is there for doing so? What values should guide it?

Students should conclude that humans should experiment based on their God-given task of dominion. After allowing the students to debate the questions, explain the ultimate justifications given by evolutionists and creationists. Ask them to evaluate which ultimate justification is ethically superior.

The ultimate justification a naturalistic evolutionist must give for experimenting with animals is power: *homo sapiens* is more advanced than *mus musculus*, so we can do what we want with them. But the ultimate Christian justification for animal experimentation is love—we must use the tools given to us in the natural order to express our love for God and for our fellow image-bearers. Power surely figures in—God gave us explicit authority over the animals.

Which view is more likely to lead to the abuse of animals? Is it the one based on power (naturalistic evolution) or the one based on love (the biblical worldview)?

the evolutionary view based on power

What negative effects follow from the view that there should be no experimentation?

The sanctity of human life is hindered because humans are hindered from receiving the benefits discovered through experimentation. But the animal world also suffers when it is allowed to grow out of control like a garden that is never weeded or pruned.

A Biblical View of Food

Most new diets that hit the bestseller list forbid one food or another, and freely choosing not to eat something is not wrong. Just because God created something doesn't mean that He created it to be ingested. (God created arsenic.)

What bearing do Genesis 9:2–3, Acts 10:9–16, and 1 Timothy 4:4–5 have on whatever diet is popular right now? Is that diet forbidding something God created to be received with thanksgiving?

"Christian" diet plans that put a guilt trip on people or promise higher spirituality through following Old Testament dietary laws or through eating a vegetarian diet are actually unbiblical (Col. 2:20–23). Becoming obsessed with subjective standards of healthy eating can lead to idolatry. Some Christians even become health zealots, trying to evangelize others to buy into their system as if it is inerrant. But God doesn't expect Christians to micromanage every bite of food or to deny themselves normal kinds and normal amounts of food (Eccles. 5:18).

What bearing should Proverbs 23:20–21 and 1 Corinthians 6:19–20 and 10:31 have on a person's diet?

Eating inordinate amounts of junk food or being gluttonous is also unbiblical. Christians are to take care of their bodies.

---

be unreasonable to expect anyone to be able to understand how it works. Adding in the "deep time" that modern science relies on doesn't change that fact. Even a billion tornadoes blowing stuff around a billion junkyards for a billion years can't "design" anything.

Science relies on the predictability of the natural world, and yet it thrives on something unpredictable: human creativity. Alexander Fleming discovered the first antibiotic (penicillin) by accident while pursuing the somewhat odd task of making small paintings using microbes in petri dishes. Fleming noticed a fungus growing in one of his little pieces of petri-dish art that was killing bacteria. Other researchers had seen the same thing and thought nothing of it. But "Fleming's discovery of the effects of penicillin, the compound produced by the fungus, was a function of his eye for the rare, an artist's eye."[14] It was his God-given creativity that gave us penicillin, a life-saving drug without which you might never have been born. (The great-grandmother of the author of this chapter died of an infected tooth in 1935 because penicillin hadn't yet been introduced.)

Humans are capable of discovering new ways to use the predictability of the natural order.

Assumption 3: Humans Have a Right to Use Nature

The third (ultimately Christian) assumption without which science is not possible is that **human beings have the right and the responsibility to rearrange nature in order to meet their needs.**

What gives humans the right to capture or kill an animal, or to cut down a tree?

It's not *what* gives us the right, but *who*. God did. He gave humans dominion over the earth, even over animals that don't deserve to die. If this point seems obvious to you, it shouldn't. Not today, when people as prominent as England's Prince Phillip can say, "In the event that I am reincarnated, I would like to return as a deadly virus, in order to contribute something to solve overpopulation."[15] Many people are openly questioning whether or not humans have a right to change the environment or even to kill animals.

Humans do not have a right, of course, to destroy our planet or to commit cruelty against animals (Prov. 12:10). But if you're going to take a strictly rigorous approach to science, especially experimental biology, you will have to put bacteria and lab mice into positions they did not choose to be in. The relationship between humans and the rest of creation, even and especially living creation, is one the Bible calls "rule" or "dominion" both before the Fall (Gen. 1:28) and after it (Gen. 9:2–4). Anyone who's excited about science has to be able to justify that relationship. And unbelievers have to borrow from a Christian worldview to do so.

God said to Noah,

> The fear of you and the dread of you shall be upon every beast of the earth and upon every bird of the heavens, upon everything that creeps on the ground and all the fish of the sea. Into your hand they are delivered. Every moving thing that lives shall be food for you. And as I gave you the green plants, I give you everything. (Gen. 9:2–3)

The Bible clearly gives mankind the right to kill and eat animals. And beyond that, every living thing is "delivered" into our hands. This is a privilege and a responsibility.

 ## Assumptions That Make Science Possible

Have students search for news stories online related to "science and faith" or "science and religion." They should examine the claims of mainstream scientists, looking for evidence that they rely on the orderliness of the cosmos. (*Cosmos* comes from the Greek word for "order" and, in English, still carries the idea of an ordered realm.) They should look for evidence that these scientists assume that humans are capable of describing that ordered realm in useful ways and that humans have a right to use nature to meet our needs. Not all scientists will share all of these assumptions, especially the last one. But those who do are unlikely to justify them, only assume them.

Without a Christian worldview, the only authority we have over animals is the unstable position we get by being temporarily on top of the evolutionary heap.

NON-OVERLAPPING MAGISTERIA

Many educated people in Western society have accepted the idea that science and religion will stop bickering and get along only if each stays on its own side of the back seat. Scientist Stephen Jay Gould called this **NOMA**—Non-Overlapping Magisteria (see page 3). In other words, religion gets morality; science gets the physical world. What seems to be a tidy division really isn't, says physicist Paul Davies in a *New York Times* op-ed piece:

> Science has its own faith-based belief system. All science proceeds on the assumption that nature is ordered in a rational and intelligible way. You couldn't be a scientist if you thought the universe was a meaningless jumble of odds and ends haphazardly juxtaposed.[16]

Davies points out that physicists and astronomers who manage to look deeper into the atom or outer space "expect to encounter additional elegant mathematical order. And so far this faith has been justified."[17]

Davies, an atheist, says he has often asked other physicists why physical laws work the way they do. Some reply that it's not a matter of science, and others claim the reason is unknown. Davies finds that the most common response is, "There is no reason they are what they are—they just are." But as Davies says, that's faith![18]

Both science and religion have to believe that something exists beyond the cosmos—such as an inexplicable deity or an array of principles of physics that likewise cannot be explained. Davies doesn't believe that in the beginning, God created the heavens and the earth. But, he says, science cannot claim the "reasonable" high ground: "Until science comes up with a testable theory of the laws of the universe, its claim to be free of faith is manifestly bogus."[19]

It's easy to think that science is a secular field that Christians are trying to break into, perhaps so they can use some of the cultural power science has gained. And secularism is only too happy to tell this version of the story over and over. But it's simply not true. Science requires faith, in two senses: (1) science has to start with some kind of presupposition taken on faith, and (2) the present tradition of science didn't take off until Christian presuppositions allowed it to do so. The Bible reveals that science is a God-created good.

THINKING IT THROUGH 19.1

1. Define *scientism*.

2. Science is a God-established good because it is a tool that enables someone to do what?

3. When did scientific work begin?

4. Summarize the three Christian assumptions that justify scientific work.

♀5. Why can't science and faith be separated?

People for the Ethical Treatment of Animals

Christians ought to be people for the ethical treatment of animals—who's for the *un-ethical* treatment of animals? But the line between ethical and unethical treatment is not always an easy one to draw. Is it permissible to do vivesection (perform operations on live animals) for research purposes? Is it OK to purposefully put the shampoo you're testing into the eyes of a rabbit to see how its tear ducts react? It's easy enough to set up the poles of this debate: (1) we have dominion over animals (Gen. 1:26–30; 9:2), and yet (2) we shouldn't be cruel (Prov. 12:10). Perhaps it will be the calling of one of the students some day to contribute in a distinctively Christian way to the conversation about how humans should treat animals.

Ask students to decide which of the following scenarios align with good human stewardship, cruelty, or a lack of wisdom. Sometimes no context is needed. Other times the larger context may change one's answer.

• dog fighting or cock fighting (cruelty)

• getting rid of rattlesnakes in a campground (stewardship)

But what contextual factors would justify just killing the snakes versus trapping and removing them?

• outlawing any hunting of wolves (unwise)

If there's an overpopulation problem that threatens the well-being and survival of humans, domesticated animals, or even other wild animals, such laws would be counter-productive.

• kicking or beating an animal out of anger (cruelty)

• implanting body cameras in rhinos' horns to prevent poaching (stewardship)

• capturing animals, tagging them, and releasing them to track migration and to gather other information about their habits (stewardship)

 NOMA

Smart people on both sides of the debate between Christianity and naturalism have questioned whether it is truly possible to divide reality into the provinces of religion and science, faith and reason.

Discuss with your students whether the following items fit in the "science" category or the "religion" category:

• prayer

• academic study

• childrearing

Students should conclude that every topic could include both scientific and religious dimensions.

The reality is that both science and religion have things to say about each of these things. Empirical methods of study can make genuine contributions, but every empirical method of gathering data is influenced by a lens of interpretation for understanding that data. That means that the work of science can never be done apart from a larger interpretive system—apart from philosophy, which includes theology. For the Christian, his interpretive system is primarily theologically informed. Religion—including the Bible—has to be allowed to influence the understanding of the data.

When secular scientists insist that Christian scientists draw conclusions without any influence from their biblical worldview, they are unfairly insisting that Christians draw conclusions only from the influence of a secular philosophical system of interpretation (empiricism, rationalism, etc.). Many secularists are unaware of their own systems of interpretation (called epistemology); they are even unaware that other legitimate lenses of interpretation exist. (Refer to Chapters 1–3 of the Student Text if students' memories need to be refreshed.)

THINKING IT THROUGH 19.1

1. Scientism is "excessive belief in the power of scientific knowledge and techniques."

2. to carry out the Creation Mandate

3. What we now label as science has been going on ever since the beginning when God created humankind to subdue the earth.

4. Nature is predictable, orderly, and governed by laws—since laws govern everything, there is normally a rational explanation.

Humans are capable of describing the natural order in useful and predictable ways—humans can use their knowledge to solve problems and to creatively produce beneficial tools.

Humans have a right and responsibility to use nature to meet needs—God gave humans dominion.

♀5. (1) Science has to start with some kind of presupposition taken on faith, and (2) the present tradition of science didn't take off until Christian presuppositions allowed it to do so.

SECTION OBJECTIVES 19.2

1. Explain how science can be a tool for discovering the glory of the Creator.

2. Explain how science can be a tool for loving your neighbor.

 Experiencing Outer Space

Search the internet for video interviews of Gene Cernan or *In the Shadow of the Moon*. More than once, Cernan has offered thoughtful and moving reflections about his experience in space.

 Awe and Insignificance

One theologian mentions an ad for granola bars. There were two people at the top of a mountain looking out over an amazing scenic view spread out before them. The caption said, "You've never felt more alive; you've never felt so insignificant." That feeling of awe or wonder is common to people who love the outdoors. And it's such a short step from that to worship of the Creator that Paul is right to say that truth-suppression is the only explanation for why people don't take that step. But that feeling of awe need not be limited to outdoor experiences. It can happen in any field of human endeavor that brings people into contact with God's glory in creation. And that's every field.

Ask students whether they have ever had that kind of experience. Ask them to describe it for their classmates.

Ask students if, in addition to their understanding of the gospel through Scripture, the display of God's overwhelming power and beauty in creation played a part in their experience of conversion. Ask them to share their conversion story with the class.

19.2 THE ULTIMATE PURPOSES FOR SCIENCE

Every American past a certain age remembers where he was when the Twin Towers in New York were struck by terrorists in jetliners on 9/11. Every American past *another* certain age remembers when man first set foot on the moon on July 20, 1969. Nowadays, space launches don't always make much news. Today's high school students did not experience 9/11, let alone the moon landing. So it may be hard for them to grasp how culturally momentous the Apollo 11 mission was—and not just for Americans. Half a billion people watching around the world felt that the human race itself had accomplished something.[20] That is, of course, why astronaut Neil Armstrong said as he set foot on the lunar surface, "That's one small step for a man, one giant leap for mankind."[21]

Armstrong composed those words not on the long trip to the moon but after his spacecraft had successfully landed. He wasn't sure he would make it, he said, and it seemed presumptuous to compose the words before that moment.

Armstrong wasn't alone among astronauts in being personally moved and humbled by the experience of space. Astronaut Gene Cernan later offered his reflections in a documentary on the moon landings:

I felt that I was literally standing on a plateau somewhere out there in space, a plateau that science and technology had allowed me to get to. But now what I was seeing, and even more important, what I was feeling at that moment in time—science and technology had no answers for it, literally no answers. Because, there I was—and there you are, there you are, the earth: dynamic, overwhelming, and I felt that the world was just . . . There's too much purpose, too much logic. It was just too beautiful to have happened by accident. There has to be somebody bigger than you, and bigger than me. . . . There has to be a creator of the universe.[22]

Cernan got the message the apostle Paul says humans are supposed to get: "[God's] invisible attributes, namely, his eternal power and divine nature, have been clearly perceived, ever since the creation of the world, in the things that have been made" (Rom. 1:20).

A TOOL FOR DISCOVERING THE GLORY OF GOD

It took the airless clarity of space for Cernan to see one of the two major purposes of science, the glory of the Creator (we'll get to the other one in a moment). God's eternal power and His divinity—His "Godness"—are visible to the naked eye in the beauty of the stars. "The heavens declare the glory of God, and the sky above proclaims his handiwork" (Ps. 19:1).

That glory is also visible every day at the powerful Iguaçu Falls in Brazil, in the majestic Himalayan Mountains, in the stark beauty of the Canadian tundra, in the swaying palms of Hawaii. And God apparently enjoys creating beauty whether others will experience it or not. "There are beautiful things in this universe we have never seen and never will—sunsets on faraway planets and a thousand other splendors known only by their Creator—that have no apparent evangelistic purpose."[23] These beauties simply declare God's glories, even without a human audience (though angels may be watching!).

Zoom in on creation a bit closer, and God's glory is there too. When British evolutionary biologist and geneticist J. B. S. Haldane was asked what nature taught about its Creator, he came up with a mildly mocking response: "God has an inordinate

Alternatively, you may ask students to write half a page describing such an experience.

Creation and Perversion

It's not politically correct to call anything in our modern Western world "perverted" because that implies that there is a moral standard that sexual desire and activity can be judged by—and there are very few such standards left in the West (the necessity of consent and the stigma against incest and pedophilia more or less remain). But in an article on Salon.com that can only be called perverted (and therefore will not be cited here), a columnist offers four reasons why monogamy is so difficult for people. She points to the design of human bodies and to the (supposed) sexual practices of our (supposed) hunter-gatherer ancestors as reasons why monogamy is unnatural. Her basic

message is "lighten up" and stop insisting on strict sexual standards such as monogamy. Why bring up this article here? Because it shows that people have a sense that the explanation of present norms, including even morality, is to be found to some degree in our past. Whatever forces made us what we are have significant bearing on who we're supposed to be. That's why it's so important to allow the Bible to influence your interpretation of your surroundings. Sinful, twisted humanity is adept at misinterpreting the truths that creation is constantly shouting at us. What should be the plain testimony of creation is suppressed and twisted (Rom. 1:18–19). That's why the book of creation (general revelation) must always be examined and interpreted through the lens of the Word of God (special revelation). Human observation and conclusions from the book

Iguaçu Falls

Himalayas

Canadian tundra

Hawaii

fondness for beetles."[24] His intent was to suggest that the four hundred thousand beetle species seem like overkill if God created the world. Couldn't God have been satisfied with, you know, ten different kinds of beetle? Haldane wanted to make the God hypothesis look ridiculous.

But what if Haldane was, strictly speaking, right? What if God does have an exuberant affection for His creation, so much so that He had to sort of make Himself stop after four hundred thousand beetle species? (This is true even though many of these species have developed providentially over time through speciation.) We know from Scripture that God created the world out of an overflow of the love and joy within the Trinity. Why shouldn't God lavish some of that love on beetles?

The tools of science are marvelous in their ability to reveal and describe the gloriously creative and unfathomably wise work of God. One study used scientific tools to examine the flight of various kinds of birds. Pigeons made tons of noise as they passed over the highly sensitive microphone; peregrine falcons made substantially less. Owls made almost none, barely a blip. The mice they prey on never hear them coming. Advanced optics and increasingly sensitive and accurate instruments allow us to look closer, listen harder, and even feel more keenly the truths God has placed into His creation. You can't help but marvel when you watch slow-motion footage of an owl in flight.[25] What a design!

SCIENCE IS SOMETHING GOD CREATED HUMANS TO DO | 293

---

of creation are not inerrant. Only God's Word reveals the inerrant standard of righteousness (Rom. 1:16–17).

God's Love for Beetles

If *inordinate* means "out of order," then God can't have a truly inordinate fondness for anything—all His loves are ordered properly; the order of God's loves is the standard by which all loves ought to be ordered. But *inordinate* typically means "unusually large," and compared to most people's fondness for beetles, God's may very well be—and likely is—unusually large. His eye is on the beetle as well as on the sparrow, we can safely presume (Matt. 10:29–31).

Another clarification is that although young-earth creationists believe in adaptation, they don't believe in macroevolution (a change between created kinds); even if

it were possible, the world isn't old enough for macroevolution to have occurred if the Bible is right about the age of the earth. [See Benjamin Shaw, "The Genealogies of Genesis 5 and 11 and Their Significance for Chronology," PhD diss., Bob Jones University Seminary, 2004.] Genesis 1 indicates that God created certain species directly. But *speciation* is a term that conservative Christians such as those at Answers in Genesis have been willing to own: "We do not deny that species vary, change, and even appear over time. The biodiversity represented in the 8.7 million or so species in the world is a testament, not to random chance processes, but to the genetic variability and potential for diversification within the created kinds that God built into the genomes of the originals 6,000 years ago." [Elizabeth Mitchell, "Number of Estimated Species Reaches 8.7

Beetles that Glorify God

Divide students into small groups of three or four. You can choose to hand out encyclopedia articles about beetles to each group, have each group search the internet for scientific articles on beetles, or have students watch a short documentary about different kinds of beetles. Ask students to form a list of ten to twenty ways beetles, in whatever species, bring glory to God by reflecting His masterful and wise design. (Asking for this many ways will force them to be specific.)

Examples may include:

- Beetles are highly adaptive as they move through the stages of grub and pupae to adulthood.
- Certain beetles are specially equipped for the land, air, and/or water.
- Certain beetles have escape or defense mechanisms that are quite ingenious, demonstrating God's own ingenuity.
- Exoskeletons are designed to withstand comparatively great forces, also demonstrating God's wisdom in making such tiny things so powerful.
- Some beetles are camouflaged to protect them from predators.
- Some beetles are comparatively massive in size, and some of them are tiny—but all are marvels of engineering.
- Highly sensitive antennae enable beetles to detect elements in their surroundings.
- Beetles play an important role in the ecosystem by cleaning up waste materials, which may explain the need for so many of them.
- Beetles seem to be able to communicate with each other.
- Unlike most insects, some beetles can see in 3D.

[Gordon Wilson, "Beetles—Go Anywhere, Do Anything," Answers in Genesis (website), April 1, 2013, and Don DeYoung, "Fire-Chasing Beetles," Answers in Genesis (website), April 1, 2011]

Clarify that due to speciation, even if beetle species have developed subsequent to creation, they're demonstrating the power latent in the genetic code God originally provided them.

A Clue to Your Calling

Some students are deeply concerned about what to major in when they attend college. They wonder what they're called to do in this world. A good clue comes from bringing together the major points of this section:

- Where do they perceive the greatest *opportunity* to bring their love of God together with their love of neighbor?
- Do they see possibilities to bring God glory and bring good to their neighbor from working with the raw materials of the world—through scientific work?
- Where do their own gifts and the opportunity to meet human needs through the work of science meet?

The question of vocational calling is a hard one for many teenagers to answer. They must realize that the educational process is meant to aid in their discovery of the answer to that question. Education is designed to expand their opportunities, giving them freedom to choose what they want to do.

Stuck in a Mindless Job?

Teenagers who have jobs often end up with mindless ones; they haven't yet necessarily developed the skills that make them suitable candidates for more challenging—and therefore more satisfying—work.

What are the specific tasks involved in your job?

What are the very best motivations for flipping burgers, babysitting kids, weeding gardens, restocking grocery store shelves, or other jobs teens typically have?

Every answer should ultimately reflect a motivation of love for neighbor.

If students work in fast food, they should think about how excited they were when they were little kids coming to a fast-food restaurant. They should recognize the hectic schedules of working adults who need to grab a quick bite between stressful meetings and deadlines. They should think of their own experiences at fast-food restaurants. What makes the experience better or worse? Are they being friendly, quick, sanitary, and accurately filling orders?

If students babysit, they should think about the fun they had when they were younger and got to hang out with an idolized teen. They should think about the happy opportunity they provide the parents to get a little break. They should realize the important part that they can play in helping those parents have the time they need to rekindle the romance in their marriage. They can relieve the stress of those parents by demonstrating responsibility and care for the little ones.

Each job has a larger context in which the minute responsibilities can be set. The duties can seem boring or tiring, but the bigger picture of serving others makes it worthwhile.

There is no "evidence" for a godless, materialistic, evolutionary view of the universe. Make no mistake: the primary truth found in every created thing is the glory of God. It takes willful suppression to deny it (Rom. 1:18).

We live in a fallen world, of course, so science also reveals the insidious effects of human sin on the cosmos. But those effects can never fully cover up the glories. God's eternal power and divine nature are still visible in the creation, and they always have been.

Scientists who love their Creator can take special delight in that glory, and they ought to. One of the marks of a calling to science is the feeling of wonder and joy that even a sixth grader can get when doing a project for the science fair. But we should all have that delight in whatever aspect of the creation our calling leads us to explore. Our world is as beautiful as it is amazing. Science is a God-created good because nature is meant to be, among other things, a pathway straight to the Creator.

A TOOL FOR LOVING YOUR NEIGHBOR

The first major purpose of science fits together with the greatest commandment in the Bible: love the Lord your God with all your heart. But, of course, there's also a second greatest commandment: love your neighbor as yourself. And in the day-in-day-out, rinse-and-repeat process that a Milliken chemist goes through as he searches for the best carpet fiber recipe, his neighbor may be the easiest motivation for him to keep in mind. His neighbor needs flooring, and his neighbor just had a third child and a blown minivan transmission. The chemist can make soft, beautiful, affordable carpet fibers simply because he wants a paycheck, or he can make them for that new neighbor baby who's going to learn how to crawl on that carpet.

The command to love your neighbors is not a command to love them *more* than yourself, but *as much as* yourself (still an extremely difficult command to obey with any consistency). Wanting to earn money isn't necessarily bad, but it's a mark of good character when the neighbor baby motivates a chemist as much as his paycheck does. Many people find it more satisfying to do a significant job—a job that matters to other people—than to do a mindless job, even if it pays better.[26] Work can be absolutely mind-numbing and even dehumanizing, especially if all you're making is more junk for future yard sales.

Science and the technologies based on it are capable of meeting so many genuine human needs. "Love your neighbor as yourself" can carry you very far in scientific work, as it can in most vocations. The second major purpose of science, then, is making wise use of the world for the benefit of your neighbor.

For example, back in the 1950s, concern for the needs of others took the work of one female chemist into every home in America. Ruth R. Benerito was aware of a problem that her male colleagues probably didn't care as much about: the cotton clothing of the day required lots of ironing, a job which fell mostly to women. Dr. Benerito and her team developed the chemical processes for making cloth wrinkle-free. Her work also made clothing resistant to stains and fire. Not so incidentally, this development also revitalized the post-war cotton industry and saved countless American jobs.

Benerito was inducted into the National Inventors Hall of Fame for her work. Certainly she and the dozens of other scientists on that list had various motivations for their work. Perhaps they did their work just for money or prestige, but—at least the way their biographies tell it on the website—it's hard to come to that conclusion.

How might your experience at work be different if you were motivated by love for customers and clients—or even for coworkers and supervisors? What specific things would you do differently? What corners wouldn't you cut?

If a student weeds the garden for his mom to earn some extra cash, he should think about the beauty of the garden that weeding necessarily enables. He can also have sympathy for an older person whose muscles and joints actually make bending over or getting on the ground difficult—probably a primary reason Mom is willing to pay money to get rid of those weeds.

If students bag groceries or restock shelves, they should think of the customer's shopping experience. Should you really load up a paper bag full to the brim with canned goods for the little old lady? What happens when the stocker is too lazy to rotate the produce or dairy items? Cutting corners reflects badly on your boss and business if customers receive spoiled dairy products or poor quality produce.

What do coworkers do or say to make it clear that they don't care about customers?

They focus on how hard they're having to work. They gripe about customers who want to be serviced well. They cut corners. They're motivated only by getting a paycheck.

Mostly, according to the site, they were fascinated by the potential of their innovations and did their work to meet human needs.

This is the Creation Mandate of Genesis 1:28. This is subduing and having dominion. This is cellulose fibers saying like toddlers at naptime, "I don't want to lie down!" and chemists coming along and making them do it for the sake of homemakers everywhere. This is pressing God's world toward its ideal. This is maximizing the usefulness of the creation for the benefit of others. This is science.

HOW YOUR WORK CONNECTS TO GOD AND NEIGHBOR

Loving God and loving your neighbor are the ultimate purposes of every academic discipline and cultural domain, not just of science. The connection between your work (whatever it is) and God's glory is one you must be always exploring, and the connection between your work and the good of your neighbor must also be strong. The work of science generally makes those connections obvious. Science, rightly done, focuses relentlessly on God's creation, and it generally serves some useful purpose for mankind—or it wouldn't get funded. Science is a God-created good that points people to God's glory and makes wise use of the creation for the benefit of other people.

The vast majority of the work of day-to-day scientists, even the non-Christian ones (remember the 1,642 Steves who believe in evolution?), is good. The conflict between "religion" and "science" shouldn't blind us to this fact. But that conflict does matter because it lies at the very foundation of science. Did God make the stuff of creation or not? Is the world fallen, or is there some other explanation for the red teeth and claws we can see in nature? The way you answer these questions will make a difference in your view and practice of science. Your love for God and others must fuel your work, or else your science—no matter how much good it does—will be ultimately immoral.

> "Science is increasingly seen as a fully human activity, involving a variety of social, cultural, and religious factors that go beyond mere reason and the senses."[27]
>
> —PETCHER AND MORRIS

THINKING IT THROUGH 19.2

1. How do the tools of science reveal God's glory?

2. What is one of the marks of a calling to scientific work named in this section?

3. How do the tools of science enable humans to love and serve their neighbors?

4. What are the ultimate purposes for every academic discipline and cultural endeavor?

19.3 CREATIONAL NORMS FOR SCIENCE

The story of the Bible runs from a garden to a city. And there are no cities without science. Even the earliest cities, those showing up in Genesis 4, had to use the basic sciences to build dwellings and appropriate water sources (and sewage systems). No modern city could possibly survive without science. Take just that one essential element of a city: plentiful fresh water. Geologists may find the water. Engineers pump the water across the city. Chemists purify the water. Botanists test the water. Entomologists examine the city reservoir for mosquito larvae. Ichthyolo-

• *stewarding (or developing alternatives for) natural resources that aren't replenishable*

The text says that love for neighbor can carry you far, not only in science, but also in other vocations.

How would you relate your parents' vocations to love for neighbor?

Can you explain how your own planned vocation could be based on love for your neighbor? Specifically, how would you be serving your neighbors?

If students can't think of an answer, perhaps they ought to doubt whether they're really called to that vocation. It's vital that, at some point (hopefully early on), Christians grasp the connection between what they do each day and the Great Commandments of love for God and neighbor. These two commands are meant to govern *everything* we do.

THINKING IT THROUGH 19.2

1. Science is a tool that reveals the gloriously creative and unfathomably wise work and design of God.

2. the feeling of wonder and joy when exploring the intricacies of creation

3. Science is a tool that enables you to love your neighbor by making wise use of the earth for the benefit of others.

4. loving God and loving your neighbor

SECTION OBJECTIVES 19.3

1. Attribute the discovery of creational norms for scientific work to the wisdom built into God's created order.

2. Outline the creational norms and explain why they must govern scientific work.

Science: A God-Created Work

It's absolutely key that students grasp the basic argument here—that science is in a very real sense created by God. It is, therefore, structured by divine norms—because there is no way for humans to live out the Creation Mandate/Blessing without running into those norms and resorting to the work of science. Science isn't a surprise to God. It's one of the fruits on the tree of creation that God intends for us to find and pick. That doesn't mean that our conception of science is always the purest and most accurate one. That cannot be because this is a fallen world. The work of science can be corrupted (its direction). But science itself is a God-created good (its structure).

A Small Contributor with a Larger Purpose

Most people aren't in the history books for making a world-changing discovery. But that doesn't mean that their jobs are pointless. The world operates more smoothly when each person is content to engage in his work each day as a small contributor to the good of others even in the mundane tasks.

How long would be too long to spend on a scientific task like discovering an effective treatment for heart disease, muscular dystrophy, multiple sclerosis, or cancer?

It's worth spending a lifetime on such a worthy goal, which is exactly what scientists have done to solve many other problems. Scientists may have to do research for several generations, building on the knowledge from previous generations, before they'll make a

breakthrough. Hundreds or thousands of people may be involved in detailed tasks or in support roles. They may not be credited with the final breakthrough, but every person plays a significant role in making the final breakthrough possible—maybe even after they themselves have passed on.

Describe other human needs that the tools of science could possibly help solve.

Some general categories that modern technology focuses on includes transportation, communication, collaboration, and logistics.

Some specific examples of problems that need to be solved might include

• *cost-effectively purifying salt water so that it's drinkable*

• *cost-effectively equipping all vehicles with Bluetooth technology to prevent accidents caused by people who text while driving*

Living Contrary to Creational Norms

It would probably be best not to name the specific movie (*Idiocracy*) in the following illustration. It's a film which is most certainly not recommended and has never actually been viewed by this writer—only read about.

In a 2006 satirical comedy, America gets dumber and more vulgar over several centuries. People are so wrapped up in their mind-numbing, salacious entertainment and so beholden to their commercialized culture that they forget the basics of civilization. A crisis develops because, instead of using water to irrigate their crops, they use a sports drink called Brawndo. In the face of overwhelming evidence to the contrary, they all believe and repeat the corporate slogan that Brawndo is "what plants crave" because "it's got electrolytes." Thankfully, real-life farmers have rarely if ever been this dumb. But humanity has shown a marvelous ability to deny equally clear wisdom available in creation, starting with God's "eternal power and divine nature" (Rom. 1:20).

Identifying the Norms in a Simple Scientific Activity

Even the simplest activity of scientific analysis demands organized empirical study—using the senses of observation, organizing the data from the observation, analyzing, and evaluating the data by comparing and contrasting it with a standard. It will also require making use of all of the other norms: model-making, communication, standardization, and combining truth with goodness and beauty. Organized empirical study inevitably leads to drawing conclusions and making use of those conclusions.

Ask each student to measure his or her own height. (Students may do this at home to save time in class.) They should use a variety of measuring tools (tape measure, yard stick, ruler, and random object), writing down the data of each measurement according to each measuring tool in a chart. Students should bring their charts to class so that the whole class can combine all of the data into one larger chart that lists all of the students' names with their differing measurements.

Which senses did you have to use in order to measure your height?

sight and feeling

Was it possible to do this simple scientific analysis without empirical observation? Was it possible without organization?

No, organized empirical observation is inherent within even the simplest activities of science.

How do the charts illustrate the necessity of the third norm?

Proto-Indo-European: the hypothetical language that gave rise to one of the largest language families in our world

gists study the fish in the reservoir for bloodstream contaminants. (And, of course, astrophysicists *drink* the water and linguists tell us where the word *water* comes from in Proto-Indo-European.* What would the modern city be without *them*?)

As with government and other aspects of human culture, science is not an accident. If the Fall had never happened, science would still have developed. It would have developed differently—and sooner. There would be no conflict between faith and science. But the human race wouldn't have gone on living in gardens forever.

Science is part of the created structure of the cosmos, and it is governed by creational norms—laws God built into His creation. Bend those created structures in the wrong direction, and your science may break. This chapter will suggest five creational norms governing science.

Determining what these creational norms are is not as straightforward as determining the norms for marriage and family life. In that realm, the Bible lays out explicitly what many of the norms are. Science, however, is more like farming (in fact, farming uses the tools of science extensively). The Bible doesn't give instructions for farming, but God has designed a world in which crops grow well under certain conditions and not under others. When the farmer learns how best to grow his crops, it's because "God teaches him" (Isa. 28:26).

The Bible explanation for this is that wisdom was the first of God's creations. Wisdom personified says, "The Lord created me at the beginning of his work, the first of his acts of old. Ages ago I was set up, at the first, before the beginning of the earth" (Prov. 8:22–23, ESV margin). This means that wisdom is closely linked to the creation event. In the verses that follow, Wisdom claims that she existed before the world began, and that she observed God as He ordered His world. The point is that God created wisdom to be built into His world. Those who find wisdom find out how to live in the world.

> **"WISDOM IS . . . THE FIRST PRINCIPLE OF THE WORLD AND THE PATTERN BY WHICH IT WAS CREATED."** [28]
>
> —DUANE GARRETT

God doesn't teach only Christian farmers. And Christians aren't the only ones who do good scientific work. So believers can learn a great deal from the science of non-Christians. And yet, "The fear of the Lord is the beginning of knowledge" (Prov. 1:7) as well as "the beginning of wisdom" (9:10). Wisdom is God's creation, and it is *God* who teaches, through the general revelation of His creation. Those who reject God are going to miss some of the basics for how life works. Thus, science done by Christians should always be similar to and yet different from science done by those who deny their Creator.

FIVE CREATIONAL NORMS FOR SCIENCE

The creational norms for science can be summarized in five principles.

Norm 1: Organized Empirical Study

The first creational norm governing science arises out of the regularity and predictability of God's rule over the created order (Gen. 8:22). The norm is this: humans need to perform organized **empirical** study of the created order in order to find ways to maximize its usefulness. *Empirical* just means "using the five senses." Empirical truths are those things you can know by observation or experience. But science goes

---

Recording the information allows the data to be preserved and passed on to others for analysis.

What standards of measurement did you use? Which measuring tool was most accurate? Were the miscellaneous objects helpful tools to compare and contrast students' heights?

Answers will vary.

What do the variations in measurements suggest?

that the fourth norm (standardization) is necessary

What is the average height of students in the class? Compare that to the national average. Compare it to the national averages of other countries around the world. How does age, gender, or ethnicity impact the national averages? Is there a model for determining which height is most beneficial for particular activities (e.g., military, sports, particular jobs, etc.)?

Answers will vary.

Which norm is involved in answering these questions?

Drawing conclusions from the data after analysis and evaluating the conclusions make the second norm necessary.

Would it be right to use this data to manipulate the height of people through medicine? Would it be appropriate to create a designer baby through the potential of modifying the genes of a person since scientists are currently making progress toward this goal?

These ethical concerns involve the the fifth norm. We must carefully evaluate the difference between what humans can *do with their*

beyond common-sense experience by using technological tools that have demonstrated their usefulness over time and by demanding "organized" study.

Any kid can perform the experiment of touching the inside of the refrigerator and then touching the back of it and discovering that one is cold and the other is hot. But it takes a thermometer—a technological tool—to determine the precise difference in temperature. It takes a microscope to see microbes. It takes litmus paper to determine pH. Tools help humans gather information through physical experience.

And science takes things a step further by insisting on "organized" study. It isn't enough for that Milliken chemist to show that a certain carpet fiber holds its color even after exposure to ultraviolet light. He will have to test it rigorously at different temperatures and for different time periods—anything he can think of that may be relevant (remember that creativity is a necessary part of science).

Things you take completely for granted reveal astonishing hidden layers of complexity when you subject them to the light of empirical investigation. Language, for example, is something (almost) every human uses all day every day. But how many language users have any idea about how the Great Vowel Shift affected the pronunciation and spelling of modern English? How many of them understand the actual source of the grammar rules they learn about in English class? Organized, empirical study (sometimes using tools such as spreadsheets, digital recorders, etc.) has proven itself to be the most useful way to answer many specific questions about language.

Norm 2: Model Making

Modern scientists, along with modern Western culture in general, tend to see science as a record of more or less unbroken progress, hindered here and there by religious or economic interests. This is a powerful myth because the current pace of technological and scientific change is obvious to nearly everyone in the world.

But scientists must not fall into the trap of talking as if their ways of viewing atoms and electrons and quantum mechanics are the best and most ultimate descriptions of reality. It is God's Word that defines reality at its most ultimate level. It is that Word that gives order to the creation. We need to step back and admit some of the limitations on our knowledge.

As Thomas Kuhn argues in *The Structure of Scientific Revolutions*, science proceeds through a series of "paradigm shifts," revolutionary changes from model to model. But any claim to have arrived at the final "truth," the bedrock reality, the world "as it truly is in itself," is premature because a new model may be right around the corner. Even a very good model cannot be a complete and perfect representation of the truth. There will always be unanswered questions. "To be accepted as a paradigm, a theory must seem better than its competitors," Kuhn said, "but it need not, and in fact never does, explain all the facts with which it can be confronted."[29]

Kuhn says that models tend to build up "anomalies" over time—inconsistencies, like those that ultimately overturned the Ptolemaic model of the solar system. That geocentric model actually explained some important observations in a very satisfactory way. It explained why the earth seems, to anyone standing on it, to be immovable. It explained why the sun rises and sets. It's a great deal easier, for most human purposes, to say, "What a beautiful sunrise" than to say "The morning appearance of the sun as my location on the earth rotated to reveal it was gorgeous!"

Over time, however, anomalies were found in the geocentric model. Thinkers had to invent more and more complexities to explain away the facts that didn't fit and

technological advancement and what they should do.

Organized Empirical Study of Language

Language provides an excellent example of something that the tools of organized, empirical study can shed light on. Gifted linguist and teacher John McWhorter has an entire course called "Myths, Lies, and Half Truths About Language" (The Learning Company, The Great Courses). There's no end to the silly and baseless things people believe about language—especially their own—that even a little empirical study can dispel. For example, it is commonly said that the reason proper English doesn't use double negatives—such as "I don't got no money"— is that the second negative cancels out the first one. "Ah," says the person who hasn't subjected his language to empirical study, "You *don't* have *no* money, so you *do* have *some*!" What this person could see with a little of that organized study is that there are other languages in the world, such as French and Spanish, which get along fine with their double negatives. And in addition, no English speaker is ever confused when someone says "I don't got no money." If someone says that, none of his hearers will come up quietly afterwards and say, "Now, you mean you *do* have money?" What's actually going on in an example like "I don't got no money" is that language exists in different social registers and subcultures. But the way we talk— and the way other-people-who-are-not-us talk—is so ingrained in us that it takes organized, empirical study to give us the personal distance to see the truth: the way we talk is different from the way others talk, but not necessarily intrinsically better. Highly educated, respectable Spanish-speakers say, "No hay nadie aqui" ("There is not nobody here") all the time, and who are we Standard American English speakers to proclaim that they have broken some immutable law of language?

Model Making and the Spirit of the Age

As various thinkers have observed, the person who marries the spirit of the age today will become a widower tomorrow. The models Christians are feeling pressure to adopt today will be replaced at some point, and our grandchildren will get pressured to adopt *those* models.

 A Vital Bridge from Observation to Conclusions

In his book about the scientific revolution, Lawrence Principe explains that early modern philosophers viewed the world as a well-organized *cosmos*, to use the Greek meaning of that term. In their worldview, the various elements of creation were all closely interrelated with each other as well as with humans and God, and every aspect of this interconnected network of phenomena had purpose and meaning, Therefore, observing and analyzing nature was for them not just a matter of discovering and documenting what existed but also involved bringing to light its unseen patterns and veiled meanings. Today's scientists, in contrast, work in ever more specialized disciplines and thus concentrate on precisely delineated areas of study and isolated phenomena. They're more adept at breaking things down into constituent parts than in seeing how varying approaches dovetail. Such a perspective practically excludes scientific inquiry into the meaning or purpose of anything. [Lawrence Principe, *The Scientific Revolution: A Very Short Introduction* (Oxford, England: Oxford University Press), 2011, 21]

In other words, scientists are less aware of their *philosophical* commitments—commitments that are a necessary part of synthesizing conclusions. Science has been reduced to utilitarian purposes (only for practical uses), disconnected from the broader meaning provided by philosophy. (Theology is philosophy from a biblical perspective with biblical answers.) They leap from their organized empirical study to their conclusions and to making use of those conclusions without being aware of or admitting to the model-making lens that filters their interpretation of the data. When their interpretive lens is assumed, it's protected from evaluation.

Many secular scientists still don't understand that Christians using the biblical worldview are no more biased and no less scientific. Christians simply recognize their model-making lens as they connect their organized empirical study to their conclusions and to making ethical use of their conclusions.

An Important Clarification

The Student Text carefully explains that while the earth really does revolve around the sun, we should be careful what kind of label we give to the heliocentric model. Note that the writers of this textbook don't doubt that the earth revolves around the sun! It is devotion to truth and not rejection of it that leads us to give thought to exactly what we're saying when we affirm a scientific postulate.

Truth and Model-Making

There are two parts to a Christian's model or interpretive lens as he goes about doing the work of science. The first part of his model is informed by the biblical worldview. The biblical worldview can provide Truth with a capital T—but only when something is specifically revealed in Scripture (special revelation). But all of our supposed human wisdom gathered from the book of nature (general revelation) is subject to revision. That part of model-making is what is referred to when it is said that we only discover usefulness rather than inerrant truth. Only special revelation can provide inerrant truth. God has provided humans with the capacity for reasoning, and we live in a world that is objectively ordered. Therefore, the usefulness of a model may in fact be considered the truth at some level, but humility demands refraining from declaring that humans have perfectly discovered an inerrant, unalterable principle for explaining all of that reality in comprehensive fullness.

An Architectural Model

The model-making character of knowledge is something discussed early in the Student Text (see page 20). But it isn't easy to grasp, so another illustration may help.

When the client of an architectural firm is spending $20 million on a building, the architect wants to make every effort to make the client happy. And one of the ways they have long done this is to build scale models. They may do so for their own purposes, to get an impression of how their proposed design will look from various angles; or they may do so for the benefit of their clients, to help them visualize a particular design. Models can help construction workers as they set out to construct the building, and they can help teams of civil engineers as they examine the impact a new building may

keep the model working. For example, it would be one thing for the sun to orbit around the earth, but as astronomers began to realize how far away the stars are, they began to see how impossible it was for the stars to be orbiting the earth too.

When Copernicus came along with a new model, the heliocentric model, it was not immediately accepted with open arms. But after Kepler modified it, thinkers began to see how many things it explained well. The heliocentric model became the new paradigm—the new set of assumptions governing astronomers in their work.

However—and this may seem odd at first—the heliocentric model doesn't explain everything. From our perspective on earth, we do revolve around the sun. But what about from the perspective of the Milky Way Galaxy? From that vantage point, both sun and earth are moving. And what about from a standpoint outside the Milky Way? Our whole galaxy is moving. Which vantage point is the "correct" or "ultimate" one?[30] Does the current scientific model explain *all* of the physical forces operating on the earth, from that ultimate vantage point?

No. The heliocentric model has proven useful for predicting sunrises, solar and lunar eclipses, and the "movement" of stars across the heavens at night. Usefulness, not Truth with a capital T, is what we look for in models. The earth really does orbit around the sun, but it would be arrogant of us to think that the heliocentric model is a complete explanation or that this model will never be tweaked. Think of how foolish previous generations of scientists look because of some of their confident predictions. Models change. They go through paradigm shifts. Even the scientific laws we make use of every day are not laws in the same sense that the Ten Commandments are. They're models. They're explanations of the data. Only what God says counts as a universal law.

Solomon noted that humans "cannot find out what God has done from the beginning to the end" (Eccles. 3:11). Not "all the work of God" is comprehensible to us. "Even though a wise man claims to know, he cannot find it out" (8:17). God is the one with the ultimate viewpoint. He's got the whole world in His hands, and He knows all the stars by name. We don't.

So the second creational norm governing science is that science is about "modeling" the natural order. You can never see everything at the same time; there will always be more things outside your view than in it, and humans have no "ultimate" vantage point to stand on. Good science uses models as summaries or packages of the data. These models set the rules and pose the questions that guide scientific inquiry, but they are subject to change.[31]

Norm 3: Communication

In 1982, Buckminster Fuller wrote a book in which he estimated that the sum total of human knowledge doubled between 1500 and 1750. It doubled again, he said, by the beginning of the twentieth century.[32] Today, thanks to computers and the internet, human knowledge is said to be doubling every year or two.[33]

But this deluge of technical data and scientific information isn't worth very much if people don't know about it and can't access it. The work of science, in every scientific field, relies on the work of communication. That's why scholars in various fields have conferences and publish journals; that's why they help make documentaries and why they write books for the general public.

have on existing infrastructure. Models are useful. But they aren't, strictly speaking, true. An architect would be foolish to use real wood, real wire, real brick, real glass—all in miniature—to build his model. Cardboard facades with Matchbox cars parked out front are all he needs. In one sense, his model misrepresents reality: the real building will not be made of cardboard. It won't lack wiring, ventilation, and a thousand other things models fail to include. And yet a model is not less useful because of that. Just like an architectural model, an intellectual or scientific one is meant to place important truths into a more manageable size. Now to press this illustration a little further, what would a "paradigm shift" or revolution look like in the case of an architectural model? It may be that, without changing the design of the final building, an architect decides that a differ-

ent way of constructing his model will better communicate to his client the reality of the future building he has in mind. He may use different materials, he may use a different medium such as a 3D model in a computer, he may build a cutaway that shows the inner rooms. But no one who has seen this model should say he "knows" the building it represents until he has gone through that actual building, used it, and looked at it from external vantage points.

Only God's knowledge is comprehensive, perfect, and complete. Truth is that which corresponds or coheres with the mind of God (making truth absolute and inerrant). In a biblical worldview, human thinking is only accurate inasmuch as humans are thinking their thoughts after God's. (Cornelius Van Til explained this as analogical knowledge. Human knowledge must meet

polymath: someone who has in-depth knowledge of a variety of subject areas or disciplines

God's knowledge for human knowledge to be true.) Since human knowledge is finite, it must be modeled after God's. A model can be accurate even if it's not comprehensive.

[See John M. Frame, *Cornelius Van Til: An Analysis of His Thought* (Phillipsburg, NJ: P&R Publishing, 1995), 89–95.]

Knowledge versus Data

If it's true that human knowledge is doubling every year or two, what kind of knowledge are we talking about?

Not the kind that humans painstakingly hammer out. We aren't that quick. No, this "knowledge" would probably better be termed "data," which isn't really the same thing.

Data isn't knowledge. Data is the temperature in the permafrost on January 13, 1996 twenty-two miles north of Ittoqqortoormiit,

Greenland. But that data doesn't mean anything; it isn't *knowledge*—until the mind of a person puts it together with other data points to form *ideas*. Ideally, those ideas are good and the scientist shares them with others in appropriate venues. This is one job of the scientist.

Of the Making of Many Books

If students were to type into a search engine (or Amazon) any academic specialty that they could think of—from "New Testament" to "engineering"—and they surfed through the books, the pages would be virtually endless. This illustrates the specialization necessary for the mastery of a particular field. No one could possibly exhaust a specialty that broad. People have to specialize in order to gain any kind of mastery. Specialization

necessitates collaboration. One person from a particular specialty must depend on another person from another specialty. They must work together. Collaboration demands communication. Specialists in different fields need to be able to clearly, simply, and concisely help others understand their findings.

The Breakdown of the Peer-Review Process

The peer-review process is meant to prevent dishonesty and promote quality. Christians should support a peer-review process. [Todd Wood, Joe Francis, Kurt Wise, and Roger Sanders, "Toward a Practical Theology of Peer Review," *Answers Research Journal* (April 9, 2008)] But the peer-review process can also break down. The assumed conflict between science and religion has so biased the secular fraternity of scientists that contributions from scientists outside the fraternity never get a voice. This might make someone think that Christians take an unnecessarily skeptical or even adversarial stance toward science since they never hear from them or learn about their significant findings.

But Christians aren't the main critics of the peer-review process. Recently, the process has been under scrutiny because of other issues. Peer-reviewed scientific papers published in major journals have been re-examined by later scientists and found to be deficient. Simply put, later scientists have regularly been unable to duplicate the results of experiments done by their fellow scientists in an earlier time. [John P. A. Ioannidis, "Why Most Published Research Findings Are False" *PLOS* (website) (Aug. 30, 2005)]

According to one news site,

> In 2003, researchers writing in the *American Journal of Medicine* [reported] something that should change how you think about medical news. They looked at 101 studies published in top scientific journals between 1979 and 1983 that claimed a new therapy or medical technology was very promising. Only five, they found out, made it to market within a decade. Only one (ACE inhibitors, a pharmaceutical drug) was still extensively used at the time of their publication.

[Julia Belluz, "This Is Why You Shouldn't Believe That Exciting New Medical Study," *Vox* (website), August 5, 2015]

The motivations for publishing and giving a positive peer review to bogus research findings vary: money, prestige, favors, and so forth. Whatever the motivations, the peer-review system is far from foolproof.

Standardization

Standardization is often taken for granted today. But figuring out how to provide precise measurements shared by all people is a monumental task. Even today there are different systems (e.g., metric units and British units of measurement). Switching back and forth between the systems in your head takes some practice. No human measurement system was inerrantly handed down to us from God. But some systems are easier, more useful, or provide for more accurate collaboration.

An Unbreakable Triad

Scientific work isn't complete until the observations are put to use in dominion over God's world. It's not enough simply to gather data through observation. The work isn't over when you've analyzed the data and drawn conclusions. The goal of science hasn't been achieved when you've shared your findings with others. Ultimately, the work of science culminates in putting your discoveries to good use. It is for that reason that the "truths" discovered in scientific work must be combined with goodness and beauty. How will the work be put to *good* use? Just because something can be done doesn't mean it should be done.

What are some examples of things our technology allows us to do (or could allow us to do in the future) even though we shouldn't do it?

selective pregnancies (choosing to keep or abort babies in the womb due to disabilities), altering genetic makeup in order to make designer babies, cloning humans, and so on

How might beauty play a pivotal role in putting scientific findings to work?

Designing a transportation system not only for utilitarian purposes (traffic flow) but also with beauty in mind (landscaping) can transform the inner city. Another example might be designing computer software that not only has a user-friendly interface but also looks inviting to use.

---

to say that the current standard always deserves its place—the meter is, ultimately, an arbitrary measure. More useful systems of measurement could possibly be invented. But the existence of a standard is itself a necessary part of science.

The use of international standards is, in part, a humble recognition that the Creation Mandate is given to all mankind, not just wealthy nations—and not just scientists. We humans need each other—everyone, in every field—to carry out the work of subduing and having dominion.

Norm 5: No Truth Without Goodness and Beauty

In the final unit of this book, Culture and the Arts, we'll talk a great deal about truth, goodness, and beauty. We'll argue that these three realities are most themselves when they are together. But that's not just true of the arts; it's also true of every domain of human culture, including science.

Science must stay within moral and ethical boundaries. The pursuit of "truth" becomes a lie if it takes a shortcut past goodness. If stem-cell research kills human beings—even tiny, unicellular human beings—it's not worth doing. The serpent was right: Adam and Eve managed to learn some new things they never could have known except by tasting the forbidden fruit. But how much better our world would be if we didn't know those terrible things!

On the positive side: sustainable forestry is a marriage of truth, goodness, and beauty. Totally denuded hillsides, covered in stumps, are ugly. And they're generally useless for any practical purpose. It isn't *good* to use up a resource like trees when it's more than possible to just plant more. Scientific truth isn't worth having at all costs. Some moral costs are too high.

WHAT IS SCIENCE?

No authoritative definition of science exists because there's only one person who knows what science truly ought to be—and He hasn't told us what science is. At least, He hasn't told us in so many words. The Bible contains no "definition" of science. Nonetheless, the elements of this chapter build up to a definition something like this:

> **Science** is the collection of observations, explanations, and models produced through an organized study of nature for the purpose of enabling people to exercise good and wise dominion over God's world for the glory of God and the good of mankind.[36]

Non-Christians have grabbed the cultural mantle of the "scientist." But it belongs to Christians. Science is a biblical calling. Science is a God-created good.

THINKING IT THROUGH 19.3

1. Since the creational norms for science are not explicitly stated in Scripture, what is needed to discover the pattern (the norms) by which the world was created?

2. Because the created order operates with regularity and predictability, which norm governs scientific study?

3. Because of the limitations on human knowledge, which norm governs scientific study?

4. Why is communication an important norm for science?

5. Why is standardization an important norm for science?

THINKING IT THROUGH 19.3

1. wisdom

2. Humans need to perform *organized empirical study* of the created order in order to find ways to maximize its usefulness.

3. Model-making is the norm that governs scientific study because science is about modeling the natural order—generating a representation of reality that is often incomplete and imperfect (i.e., not absolute, unchanging, and ultimate truth) but useful in many respects.

4. Scientific work stalls or must be redone countless times if people don't know about the scientific work already done or the progress made in discovering new things.

5. Humans need to communicate clearly so that everyone is on the same page in order to make use of others' work.

19 CHAPTER REVIEW

Scripture Memory

Psalm 111:2

Making Connections

1. What general tool provides the necessary skills for exercising expert dominion over a wide variety of created things?

2. Give the reference for a Bible verse in which God assures humanity that the earth will remain orderly until the end of time.

3. What are the two main purposes for science (and any other academic discipline or cultural endeavor)?

4. Science is not the best source for understanding the ultimate reality of this world. What is?

Developing Skills in Apologetics and Biblical Worldview

5. How should you respond to someone who challenges the human right to make use of natural resources at all?

6. How should you respond to someone who justifies a scientific endeavor because it will provide answers even though it ignores the sanctity of human life?

Examining Assumptions and Evidence

7. Why is it historically misguided to say that Christianity is a threat to science?

8. What divinely ordained reality, named in this chapter, makes organized empirical study possible?

9. Why can't science provide humans with absolute truth?

10. Why are communication and standardization necessary for scientific work?

Creative Cultivation

11. Suppose you're a member of a team of scientists and engineers that has been assigned the goal of developing a more efficient way to irrigate fields so as to minimize waste through evaporation and runoff. Briefly describe how creational norms would influence the different aspects of your work.

CHAPTER REVIEW ANSWERS

Making Connections

1. Science provides the necessary skills and tools needed for dominion.

2. Genesis 8:22; Jeremiah 33:25

3. to love God by learning about His gloriousness through His creative design and to love your neighbors by making wise use of the earth to benefit them

4. God's revealed Word

Developing Skills in Apologetics and Worldview

5. First, clarify that Christians believe that the earth should be taken care of with wise stewardship. Then stand on the foundation of the larger biblical story of creation, in which God created the world for humans to use for their livelihood.

6. The cost for discovering some truth is too high if it must be separated from moral goodness and beauty.

Examining Assumptions and Evidence

7. Religious people were scientists, and scientists were religious. The conflicts were due to differing theologies not religion against science; scientific discovery was advanced during the early modern era

8. The regularity and thus predictability of the way the world operates allows humans to examine the world and draw conclusions about how it operates.

9. Finite humans who do the work of science make the best models they can to explain reality, but their models often change or don't completely answer all the questions.

10. Without communication and standardization the work can't proceed beyond the time and place of the original discovery so that others can use the knowledge and build on it.

Creative Cultivation

11. Suggested answer: Since the conservation of water is important for maximizing the production of food, especially in drought-prone places, this project has an important and good dominion purpose (Norm 5: No truth without goodness and beauty).

The project will first require understanding what kinds of research and technology have already been done and developed to deal with this question. So a review of professional journal articles written by experts in the fields of hydraulics, agronomy, pedology, chemistry, materials science, and so on will need to be done (Norm 3: communication).

Your team should strive to assemble several potential solutions that can be first evaluated based on theoretical considerations and then be tested by developing working prototypes of the hardware and processes that will most likely be successful (Norm 2: model-making; Norm 1: organized study).

Finally, when your team settles on the technology and hardware that meet the project's objectives, they need to be translated into a design that will be economical and nonpolluting to manufacture and be documented with useful and complete instructions on their use (in foreign languages, as applicable) (Norm 4: standardization).

TERMS TO REMEMBER

scientism—the "excessive belief in the power of scientific knowledge and techniques"

NOMA—Non-Overlapping Magisteria, the idea that religion can deal only with the realm of morality while science deals with the realm of the physical world

empirical—using the five senses; said of things you can know by observation or experience

science—the collection of observations, explanations, and models produced through an organized study of nature for the purpose of enabling people to exercise good and wise dominion over God's world for the glory of God and the good of mankind

CHAPTER 20 OBJECTIVES

The student will be able to

20.1 Explain how the work of science has been affected by the Fall.

20.2 Examine scientism's claims and values.

20.3 Detect the cause of scientism's faulty way of living: its inability to provide justification for meaning and morality.

20.4 Detect the cause of scientism's faulty way of knowing: its method dismisses all sources of knowledge other than empiricism and denies its own presuppositional interpretation of the empirical data.

SECTION OBJECTIVES 20.1

1. Understand that scientific work often produces unintended consequences rather than the promised benefits.

2. Summarize six ways that the Fall affects scientific work.

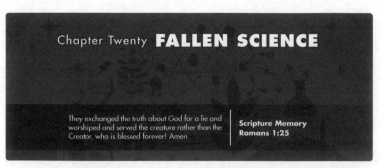

Chapter Twenty FALLEN SCIENCE

They exchanged the truth about God for a lie and worshiped and served the creature rather than the Creator, who is blessed forever! Amen.

Scripture Memory
Romans 1:25

20.1 SCIENCE IS FALLEN

A fascinating book titled *Yesterday's Tomorrows: Past Visions of the American Future* is full of pictures of what people once envisioned the future would be like. The things people in 1950 thought we'd have by now are sometimes silly: flying cars, hose-washable indoor furniture, robotic servants. Those dreams often tell us more about the people who had them than they do about us. But people in the past sometimes predicted the future pretty well: computers in your pocket, videophones, online shopping.

One thing that strikes any reader of *Yesterday's Tomorrows* is the sheer optimism of American culture. Americans shot for the moon, and they made it. Not only did they make it, but they did it at a time when even the vision of the computers of the future (as seen, for example, in the original *Star Trek*) was primitive. The moon landing was an incredible accomplishment, perhaps the crowning achievement on the huge list of US scientific and technological successes.

No one alive in America can ignore those successes. They take us—and go with us—everywhere. A Frenchman actually coined the phrase, but it is a very American thing to say: "Every day, in every way, I am becoming better and better."[1]

Americans are, by constitution, not as interested in thinking about the dark side of their scientific and cultural advances. The announcer on pharmaceutical commercials rhapsodizes about the drug's

benefits, but he races through the side effects in a muted voice. We like to trumpet our success in curing childhood diseases, but we may fail to mention that geriatric* diseases (such as Alzheimer's and Parkinson's) are on the rise.[2]

Virtually all scientific advances have unintended consequences. We need to train ourselves to ask not only what science and technology give, but what they take away. Technological advances have given us cars with multiple computers and dozens of sensors to prevent and diagnose failures. Whereas cars of a previous generation started to falter when the odometer hit 40,000 miles, now they often don't begin having trouble until 150,000. But there's a downside even to this technological success: cars are now so complicated that they experience bizarre failures that are expensive to fix; most people can't fix their own cars anymore. Scientific and technological gains generally come with some kind of loss, a loss that often goes unnoticed.

The wealth of information at our fingertips still hasn't overcome the downsides of scientific progress. It's like the imaginary animal in the Dr. Dolittle stories, the "pushmi-pullyu."[3] It was a rare two-headed llama, with one head on each end. (This allowed the pushmi-pullyu to eat and talk at the same time without being rude, a valuable skill.) But both heads couldn't walk "forward" at the same time. There is something stopping us from the leap forward we may have expected science to provide.

---

geriatric: *related to older people or the aging process*

Lesson Plan Chart—Chapter 20

Section Title	Pages	Activity Manual	Days
20.1 Science Is Fallen	302–6		1 day
20.2 Scientism: Science Exalted	306–10		1 day
20.3 Scientism: A Faulty Way of Living	311–14	Activity 35	1 day
20.4 Scientism: A Faulty Way of Knowing	315–20		2 days
Review	321		1 day
Total Suggested Days			**6 days**

 Technology = Improvement?

What do you imagine life will be like a hundred years from now?

[Most students will probably give a preponderance of positive, even glowing, descriptions of improvements—especially technological ones. If they do, ask them to factor the Fall into their suppositions about the future.]

What are some of the downsides of the technologies you use every day? For instance, what do you lose with today's mode of transportation possibilities?

In spite of expanded opportunities in a larger world, people today tend to miss out on the life of stability within one small community of neighbors and friends who would rarely leave. That kind of world had its unique challenges, but it also had its unique joys.

SCIENCE AND THE FALL

From a biblical worldview perspective, we don't have to guess what that hindrance is. We know what's frustrating our science and technology, and it's not Murphy's Law. It's the Fall of man.

> And to Adam [God] said, "Because you have listened to the voice of your wife and have eaten of the tree of which I commanded you, 'You shall not eat of it,' cursed is the ground because of you; in pain you shall eat of it all the days of your life; thorns and thistles it shall bring forth for you; and you shall eat the plants of the field. By the sweat of your face you shall eat bread, till you return to the ground, for out of it you were taken; for you are dust, and to dust you shall return." (Gen. 3:17–19)

After the Fall, all work is at least a little bit frustrating. Farmers can never get rid of all pests and weeds. Editors can never eliminate all typos. Teachers can never produce perfect SAT scores among their students. Piano recitals, plays, and concerts never go exactly right. Moms never have perfect kids (despite what their Facebook profiles portray). Instant riches aren't really . . . instant.

The price of a loaf of bread around the world is the same it has always been: sweat. And in the end, all your hard work doesn't win the battle against the decay of creation. All the bread you eat can't fend off death, the final curse.

That curse affects science in particular in at least six major ways:

1. Science Is Frustrated

The work of science has become frustrating; "thorns and thistles" of all sorts continually get stuck in the gears. Science carries risks and side effects; it encounters speed bumps.

Untold money has been poured into cancer research, but a cure is still highly elusive. Countless other human problems are crying out for solutions. Science in a fallen world doesn't fully deliver on its promise. Science will never sweep us into "the next phase of human evolution," let alone into heaven on earth.

2. Science Is Diverted

A second problem with science in a fallen world is that false and even idolatrous ideas can lead science astray, distracting us from more fruitful scientific work. Adam and Eve didn't know about electrons, and even in an unfallen world it likely would have taken time for the human race to progress toward organized, empirical study of such tiny things. And they wouldn't have accomplished a moon landing the first year.

But an unfallen human race would have avoided certain scientific dead ends. They never would have gotten sidetracked into thinking that one must appease the barley god in order to guarantee a good harvest. They might have tested many ultimately erroneous hypotheses, but the barley god would never have played a role. And unfallen people would not have dabbled in the occult or superstition (Deut. 18:10) by, for example, using divining rods ("dowsing") to locate underground water sources. Bad religious ideas can mislead science.

Bill Nye, a pro-evolution scientist and television personality, has made precisely this complaint about creationists:

> If you want to deny evolution and live in your world that's completely inconsistent with everything we live in the universe, that's fine. But don't make your kids do it, because we need them. We need scientifically literate voters and taxpayers for the future. We need engineers that can build stuff, solve problems.[4]

What might a smartphone take away?

In spite of the benefits of always being able to stay in touch, it manifestly dominates people's lives when they feel obligated to text back immediately—even while driving or in the middle of a conversation with somebody else. The possibility of reading a book without interruption or the possibility of living a life in which you are never exposed to unwanted porn has grown much more difficult.

What might the internet take away?

In spite of its many benefits, it tends to take away the possibility of living a life of privacy off the grid. It also tends to turn conversations about religion and politics into personal attacks because of the impersonal nature of online relationships.

Frustrated Science

The creation functions very well despite the Fall. But we have the Bible's testimony that it doesn't work the way it's supposed to. And as soon as we delve into the rigorous work of science, we have personal experience to support the biblical record. What are some hindrances ("thorns" and "thistles") in scientific work? If you have access to a special speaker who can speak about science from personal experience, ask him or her to describe how the Fall frustrates scientific work. Ask for stories illustrating the way specific studies are hindered because of unforeseen difficulties. What kinds of problems do scientists encounter, why is it difficult to overcome the problems, and how can those problems be overcome?

[As an alternative, you could ask a scientist to e-mail some anecdotal illustrations of these kinds of problems and you can read them to the class.]

Diverted Science

There may be some areas of study that don't generally interest secular scientists but might yield major insights if just a little of the billions of dollars in global research money were devoted to them. Creationists make unique contributions to scientific work by studying things according to biblical worldview presuppositions. They study flood geology, research how distant starlight can be observed on earth within a matter of only thousands of years, and align fossil evidence with the created kinds.

What Could Have Been?

Aslan told the Pevensie children that he never revealed what could have been. But in Scripture, God actually does do this at least once (2 Kings 13:18–19). It isn't mere speculation to ask what would have happened if the world had never fallen under the Curse. Certainly, humans would have engaged in scientific investigations without being frustrated by the Fall or diverted by useless investigations. It's likely that Adam and Eve would have accomplished astounding technological improvements fairly soon. (This is one reason theologians infer that the Fall happened relatively quickly.) Asking people to imagine what could have been is also a helpful way of revealing their assumptions about God's purposes for mankind and all of creation. Do they believe creation would have remained stagnant or that it would have been developed into a city? Their speculations also often reveal what they believe eternity will be like.

Studying a Fallen World

Humans in an unfallen world would have used the work of science to further develop the world in fulfillment of the Creation Mandate. However, for finite humans in a fallen world, the work of science has become almost synonymous with the work of solving the problems that plague us because of our fallenness.

Ask students to find current events that describe particular scientific efforts for the express purpose of solving a problem that could only exist in a fallen world with finite humans.

Science Mistrusted

There are plenty of opinions floating around on social media about vaccinations, essential oils, naturopathic remedies, and genetically modified organisms (GMOs).

Ask students to debate the merits of any of these items and how personal liberties should be balanced with love for one's neighbor.

Most of the claims about the effectiveness or mortal danger of any given item on the list come from personal experience: "My toddler got perpetual colds until I started putting a dab of wintergreen oil ($19.95 an ounce, click here to buy) behind her ears every six hours." The mere fact that people who are anti-vaxxers or anti-GMOs live on the fringe of American medicine doesn't mean any particular person's claims are wrong. But the fundamental question that always needs to be answered is this: How can you *know* whether a given treatment will help or harm someone in particular? The fundamental answer to that question must rest on something more substantive than anecdotal evidence. Causation and correlation have to be confirmed or at least hypothesized and then corroborated before certainty can be proclaimed. What appeared to work or not work on your own child is irrelevant; that's an insufficient sampling. Many such claims are subjective and impossible to verify.

Of course, the scientific community isn't infallible. Some health issues are idiopathic (of unknown cause). Scientists are also fallen. They may have special interests, or they may fail to examine anecdotal evidence that they should investigate.

Nonetheless, for all of science's flaws, empirical methods tend to be the most reliable way to know, with some measure of certainty, the things God hasn't addressed in Scripture—such as the best medicines for given maladies.

Science Exalted

The social sciences are indeed sciences because they use scientific tools of observation and analysis. Christian Smith, an eminent US sociologist, has used these tools to write landmark studies of the religious views of American youth. (He's the one who, along with his coauthors, coined the term *moralistic therapeutic deism*.) He is a recognized member of the sociological guild. But after many years in the field, teaching at Duke University and engaging in major research projects, Smith did precisely what Christians in a given field are supposed to do—he questioned the fallenness of his discipline and suggested a way to put it back on track. He titled the book in which he did

If Nye were right about evolution, then he would probably be largely right about the negative effects of creationism on science. But since he's wrong, the tables are turned: belief in evolution is what's negatively impacting science, not belief in biblical creationism. Wrong models of the origin of the world can't help but have an impact on someone's scientific work (and on whether someone goes into science in the first place). Evolutionists can do good scientific work by God's common grace, and creationists sometimes do bad work because of their own fallenness. But, other things being equal, the CFR perspective will help rather than hinder good science.

3. Science Has to Study a Fallen World

mitigate: *lessen or reduce*

The work of science is often dedicated to mitigating* the effects of the Fall. If there had been no Fall, there would be no need for cancer research or for sleep studies for apnea patients. Presumably, no one would ever have heard of seismology, and there would be no need for Doppler radar to spot tornadoes. This is another sense in which science is diverted from its original intent. Science is very useful in a fallen world, but just think what it could have done—and will do—in an unfallen world.

4. Science Is Mistrusted

People in the general public who hear about science on the news and read about it on the web or in magazines have been affected by the Fall too. Prejudice may keep such people from acknowledging the value of scientific work. Certain ideas may be so far ahead of their time that it will take two generations before people accept them. In other words, the Fall leads some people to resist the truth or usefulness of a certain scientific model.

When an Ebola outbreak struck West Africa, cutting a deadly path through villages and cities alike, many Westerners clucked to themselves: "If those primitive people would just trust the doctors and accept their preventive measures, they'd save their own lives." Western people often look down on cultures that distrust Western medical science.

But America and Europe have strong pockets of that same distrust, and it isn't limited to hyper-conservatives. Those who call themselves "very liberal" have the highest distrust of genetically modified organisms (GMOs) such as corn and soybeans,[5] and "anti-vaxxers" (people who believe that childhood immunizations are responsible for autism and other maladies) are found at similar rates among liberals and conservatives.[6]

How can someone "know" that childhood vaccines cause autism or that GMOs are dangerous? God hasn't ruled on either matter in Scripture, so it would seem there's only one way to know: organized, empirical study. A nonscientist who has never done or even read such a study would need to have a pretty strong reason for distrusting them.

5. Science Is Exalted

Distrust of science does not seem, however, to be a big problem among educated Western people. Rather, the primary problem is an exaggerated faith in science. People commonly hand science a scepter and a crown that don't belong to it and then ask it to do a job it can't do. Science has become almost a religion in its own right. True science has been largely replaced by "scientism," the belief that the scientific method is the only way to truly know anything. In this view, things that can't be measured can't be truly known.

this *The Sacred Project of American Sociology* (New York: Oxford University Press, 2014).

In an interview with Ken Myers, Smith made the point that sociologists often assume that they're making "value free, just-the-facts-ma'am" scientific observations about society. But all the while, these same sociologists are "highly committed—politically, ideologically, [and] morally." They resist evidence-based challenges or alternative interpretations of their own "revered" positions.

Smith doesn't think the whole "sacred project" of sociology is bad; parts of it are good, and he supports them, he says. But the part where sociologists all agree among themselves that their particular view of what it means to be human is neutral and unobjectionable—that part is bad. Smith says his colleagues get very impatient with any suggestion that they should consider the philosophical underpinnings of their discipline.

Smith goes on to point out that sociologists gain credibility by claiming to be objectively scientific; "it's not just an opinion." But at the same time, these sociologists have subtly assumed "value commitments . . . very particular ideas of human nature, human interests, human goods, human motivations, human flourishing, and all the implications of that for what a good society would look like." Since this is all subtly assumed, they draw conclusions that they believe are objectively scientific without admitting that other people might validly disagree with their conclusions because of a differing worldview for interpreting all the evidence.

Smith says his goal is to reveal unrecognized assumptions (which tend to escape any evaluation) to students who are unaware of

"We come to know what is real," says prominent atheist and Oxford biologist Richard Dawkins, "in one of three ways."

> We can detect it directly, using our five senses; or indirectly, using our senses aided by special instruments such as telescopes and microscopes; or even more indirectly, by creating models of what might be real and then testing those models to see whether they successfully predict things that we can see (or hear, etc.), with or without the aid of instruments. Ultimately, it always comes back to our senses, one way or another.[7]

Science is something God created humans to do. But not when defined this way. This is science exalted to a status above its Creator. It's a complete reversal of the emphasis of the Bible. "The fear of the Lord"—of a God you cannot see—"is the beginning of knowledge" (Prov. 1:7). Scientism says that seeing is believing. The Bible says that believing is seeing.

> By faith we understand that the universe was created by the word of God, so that what is seen was not made out of things that are visible. . . . And without faith it is impossible to please him, for whoever would draw near to God must believe that he exists and that he rewards those who seek him. (Heb. 11:3, 6)

People commonly hand science a scepter and crown that don't belong to it and then ask it to do a job it can't do.

6. Scientists Are Fallen

Non-Christian intellectual and novelist Kurt Vonnegut once spoke to the graduating class at the Massachusetts Institute of Technology (MIT), a prominent American university. He knew that sitting before him was

> a full house of young people who could do what the magician Merlin could only pretend to do in the Court of King Arthur, in Camelot. They could turn loose or rein in enormous forces (invisible as often as not) in the service or disservice of this or that enterprise.[8]

"In order to survive and even prosper," he told the budding graduates,

> most of you will have to make somebody else's technological dreams come true. . . . My brother got his doctorate [from MIT] in 1938, I think. If he had gone to work in Germany after that, he would have been helping to make Hitler's dreams come true. If he had gone to work in Italy, he would have been helping to make Mussolini's dreams come true. . . . He went to work for a bottle manufacturer in Butler, Pennsylvania, instead. It can make quite a difference not just to you but to humanity: the sort of boss you choose, whose dreams you help come true.[9]

Vonnegut gave an A+ to the scientists and engineers who built Hitler's concentration camps. "They surely solved all the problems set for them."[10] Obviously, excellent scientific work can be given as a service to a violent and even murderous ideology.

But scientists don't just serve fallen people; they *are* fallen people. Ernst Haeckel, a nineteenth-century Darwinist, produced a famous series of drawings of the embryos of various vertebrates. He attempted to validate evolutionary theory by showing that "ontogeny recapitulates phylogeny"—in other words, that embryos go through stages resembling the evolution of their ancestors. But Haeckel deliberately misrepresented

them when they learn in the classroom from these sociologists.

What might some of those assumptions be?

- multiculturalism: neutrality of all cultures
- hyper-individualism: human autonomy and the freedom from institutionalized authority structures or social structures (e.g., marriage)
- antinomian view of liberty: no law
- egalitarianism: no gender role differences
- self-actualization: living out whatever personal desires bring self-fulfillment
- hedonism: seeking pleasure
- sexual gratification

Christian Smith told Ken Myers that, "as a project, sociology belonged at the heart of a movement that self-consciously and intentionally displaced Western Christianity's integrative and directive hold on society. It was a key partner in modernity's world-historical efforts to create a secular, rational, scientific social order."

Smith compares this to the control that the Roman Catholic Church once had over society. But now secularism, through the work of sociology, mandates the accepted social order of Western culture. Smith says that "sociology was not merely about piecemeal reforms but world transformation, guided by a radically new sacred vision of humanity, life, society, and the cosmos."

Smith takes pains to clarify that he isn't simply claiming that "American sociology is predominantly liberal," although that may be true. Neither is he saying that sociologists are conspiring together in any way. Instead he's pointing out that unacknowledged— and highly contestable—philosophical and theological biases rule the discipline, and

this state of affairs is not conducive to good sociology.

[*Mars Hill Audio Journal*, Vol. 126, July 15, 2015]

Drawing Conclusions from Myers's Interview of Smith

What assumptions about human nature might lead American sociology to its particular "sacred" mission?

(1) that we are uncreated and therefore have no nature to follow and no creator to obey and (2) that humans create their own identities

What loves may be driving sociologists to adopt their particular sacred project?

Like all fallen people, they love themselves and don't want their personal, financial, sexual, and other choices to be questioned.

Like all fallen people, they love autonomy; they don't want their freedom to be curtailed by any authority.

Of course, like all fallen people, they retain God's image and creation blessing and their work does a lot of genuine good. But it's not accidental that a field twisted so deeply by the Fall ends up validating sin by using specious reasoning.

Science Is Broken Because Scientists Are Fallen

In an article titled "Science Is Often Flawed. It's Time We Embraced That," authors Julia Belluz and Steven Hoffman [*Vox* (website) May 13, 2015] discuss the same topic raised in the previous chapter: the failure of scientific studies to be reproducible by other scientists (see p. 299). They don't believe that science should be mistrusted as if people are purposefully trying to mislead; they admit that that's rare. Fraud is intentional error; but some errors, though not intentional, still leave the responsible scientists culpable to some degree.

For example, researchers may "run badly designed and biased experiments. . . . That ultimately distorts the evidence base—and what we think we know to be true in fields like health care and medicine." [Belluz and Hoffman] And the very real competition for funding may drive scientists to look the other way when university press releases promise more real-world value for their studies than is truly justified.

The publisher of *AAAS/Science* complains that "science today seems increasingly interested in 'other things' [beside the pursuit of truth], from academic advancement to financial rewards. And the scientific publishing process seems more and more geared to abetting these practices as the number and capacity of outlets has exploded over the past decade." [Kent Anderson, "Measuring the Wrong Things—Has the Scientific Method Been Compromised by Careerism?" The Scholarly Kitchen (website) (December 15, 2011)]

People have always been good at rationalizing sin; perhaps those whose powers of rationality exceed the norm don't always apply those powers to good ends. Richard Horton, editor of *The Lancet*, one of the world's most prominent medical journals, said, "Afflicted by studies with small sample sizes, tiny effects, invalid exploratory analyses, and flagrant conflicts of interest, together with an obsession for pursuing fashionable trends of dubious importance, science has taken a turn toward darkness" (quoted in Belluz and Hoffman). One possible partial solution to the problem of bad science is "meta-research," examination of published studies by independent teams of scientists.

The authors of the *Vox* article conclude that science shouldn't be given a status of perfection with absolute and unchanging infallible answers. Nor should science be dismissed. It should be used with an understanding that its work is done by people who make mistakes and that it takes a lot of hard work, including revision, to get things right.

Of course, without a standard above the human level, it's impossible to judge whether science has found the "truth" in its groping. It can only claim to have found something "useful."

THINKING IT THROUGH 20.1

1. First science can't ultimately save because the human problem and the difficulties in the world ultimately are due to sin. In addition, the work of science is frustrated by the unintended consequences that often accompany the advances; instead of solving all problems, science often just shifts the problems around.

2. false and idolatrous ideas

3. lessening the effects of the Fall, solving problems introduced by the Fall

4. totally mistrusting scientific work or totally exalting scientific work

♀5. They may end up using their skills to promote a horribly fallen agenda.

certain embryonic lines in order to overstate the similarities; in other words, he lied through his drawings. Haeckel's work has now been discredited, but his illustrations are still used in some secular science textbooks.

It's impossible to say whether scientists are any more or less ethical than people in other professions. And Christians themselves are not free from all temptation to stretch the truth. But this fact must be kept in mind: scientists are fallen.

FRUSTRATED, DIVERTED, MISTRUSTED, EXALTED, AND FALLEN

The tools of science are pointed at a cursed world and put in the hands of fallen people, who create technologies used by other sinners. Add in human limitations—we're not omniscient—and there's a lot of room for error in science.

But God blessed us at creation to fill the earth, subdue it, and have dominion over it. The Fall frustrates that blessing but doesn't remove it. And one day, of course, it will be fully restored.

THINKING IT THROUGH 20.1

1. Why won't science ever be the ultimate savior of humankind?

2. What distracts science from fruitful work?

3. What kind of work must science focus on because the world is fallen?

4. What two extremes represent wrong responses to scientific work?

♀5. Why must scientists carefully choose the boss for whom they work?

20.2 SCIENTISM: SCIENCE EXALTED

Christians aren't the only people who've noticed how scientism has risen to the status of a new Western religion. One recent book, written largely by non-Christians, is entitled *Scientism: The New Orthodoxy*.

What are the doctrines of this new faith? We can't answer that till we establish the big story (the metanarrative, remember?) out of which those doctrines arise.

> *"It is a tenet of scientism that only certifiably scientific knowledge counts as real knowledge. All else is mere opinion or nonsense."* [11]
>
> —RICHARD N. WILLIAMS

Scientism's story is substantially the same as the story of scientific naturalism (or metaphysical naturalism), the idea that matter is all that exists. So once upon a spacetime,* BANG! This particular cycle of existence began. A long, long time later, a few motley planets scattered around the cosmos were in temperate zones around their stars, and life was able to form. An unbelievably long series of minor genetic changes in that life killed most of it off but left enough of it to make us. As the first and only beings with consciousness and language, we can take charge of our environment, and we therefore have a responsibility to do so. Science is the only reliable tool we have for understanding ourselves and our world. One day in the distant future, this cycle of

spacetime: a mathematical model in physics, combining time and space into a single continuum

SECTION OBJECTIVES 20.2

1. Explain why many people hold to the claim that only scientific knowledge is legitimate.

2. Evaluate scientism as an idolatrous religious worldview that requires faith beyond its own empirical scientific knowledge.

3. Explain why naturalism is an appealing myth that must resort to the faulty two-story view.

🖱 Implicit Assumptions

Where have you observed the implicit assumption that science is the only way to "prove" or "know" something?

Answers will vary. This occurs every time any proposition is dismissed as not being knowledge simply because it is derived from revelation.

Remind students that the assumption that man is the measure of all things (that is, humans are the judge of all knowledge through their own intellect) is a presupposition derived from René Descartes, who doubted everything except his own thinking. In that view, humans become the ultimate judge of everything rather than God. This is a faulty presupposition from modernism. It's easy for present-day humans to disdain premoderns for their superstitions, but

the universe will run down and all energy will dissipate. Then, maybe, it will all begin again.

This is the big story of scientism, which generates its own creed: "I believe that matter is all there is, undirected evolution got us here, and only religious bigotry and time stand in science's way as it speeds up the process of human development."

Scientism has done a fairly good job of catechizing* people with its creed. Make any kind of controversial comment on a public news website—maybe something like "Jesus died for our sins and rose again three days later"—and other people will, understandably, respond with variations of "Prove it!" But what do they mean by "prove it"? What, in their minds, counts as proof?

If you respond with some variation of "God said so in the Bible," you'll soon find out how much influence scientism has. You'll very often hear, "That doesn't count as proof! Show me the science!"

One Christian was engaged in just such a discussion with a friendly atheist about the moral status of homosexuality. The Christian objected, on moral grounds, to homosexual acts. The atheist got right to the scientistic point: "By all measurables, children raised by homosexual parents have the same potential as children raised by heterosexual parents. . . . There are no demonstrable effects [from living in a gay household]."[13]

The atheist simply could not see the scientism hidden in his word *demonstrable*. He couldn't even conceive of a way to "demonstrate" something that wasn't a scientific way. Throughout the conversation, he kept coming back to that scientism: "I would [have] to see some research showing two same-sex couples kissing to be psychologically damaging to someone."[14]

Organized empirical study is useful in moral debates (and how children fare in gay households is relevant to that debate[15]). But science isn't ultimate. There are truths—facts—that the scientific method can't see but God can. If Christians implicitly agree to let science be the final court of appeal for truth, they have let their Bibles slip from their hands. They have given science an authority God never gave it. They have exalted science to the status of an idol.

WORSHIPING THE CREATION RATHER THAN THE CREATOR

Steven Pinker, a prominent atheist and a Harvard psychology professor, is the chair of the *American Heritage Dictionary* usage panel. Pinker has said that "the worldview that guides the moral and spiritual values of an educated person today is the worldview given to us by science."[16] And he's right.

But that's wrong. God has given this world natural laws that make science possible. It's idolatrous to believe in these

---

A FULL DEFINITION OF SCIENTIFIC NATURALISM

Scientific naturalism is "a worldview which holds that there is nothing but natural elements, principles, and relations of the kind studied by the natural sciences, i.e., those required to understand our physical environment by mathematical modelling."[12] This view can also be called "physicalism," which is distinguished from "materialism" by including spacetime, dark matter, and forces and physical energies in its category of "all that exists."

catechizing: giving formal religious instruction in the dogma of a particular religious group

---

THE RELIGION OF REASON, THE CREED OF SCIENCE

Well-known nineteenth-century orator and agnostic Robert Ingersoll actually wrote a "creed of science":

Superstition is not religion. Belief without evidence is not religion. Faith without facts is not religion. What is religion? To love justice, to long for the right, to love mercy, to pity the suffering, to assist the weak, to forget wrongs and remember benefits—to love the truth, to be sincere, to utter honest words, to love liberty, to wage relentless war against slavery in all its forms, to love wife and child and friend, to make a happy home, to love the beautiful; in art, in nature, to cultivate the mind, to be familiar with the mighty thoughts that genius has expressed, the noble deeds of all the world, to cultivate courage and cheerfulness, to make others happy, to fill life with the splendor of generous acts, the warmth of loving words, to discard error, to destroy prejudice, to receive new truths with gladness, to cultivate hope, to see the calm beyond the storm, the dawn beyond the night, to do the best that can be done and then to be resigned—this is the religion of reason, the creed of science.[17]

Association for Psychological Science wrote, "Science is not immune to lying and cheating." But he noted that "it was the suspicions of his colleagues and students that exposed [the Dutch professor]. Scientific inquiry is guided by laboratory conventions and publishing rules that promote integrity and minimize the publication of false conclusions." [Alan Kraut, "Despite Occasional Scandals, Science Can Police Itself," *Chronicle of Higher Education*, December 3, 2011]

There's truth in what he's saying, but there's an implicit scientism in it too—an assurance to the general public that science is still the best way to know truth (bad eggs notwithstanding). Science, in other words, is every day, in every way, getting better and better.

The reality is that, beyond the scientific discipline itself, scientists must also hold to a philosophy that they ought to be truthful.

Where do scientists' suspicions come from? Where do their lab conventions and publishing rules come from? Where does the idea that integrity matters come from?

The basis for all these commitments stands outside of science. Integrity is a universal absolute rooted in ethical convictions.

Where are those convictions derived?

They can't be derived from science alone. Science can only explain and describe what is, not what ought to be. They're derived from a worldview that stands above the discipline.

But what is the basis for that worldview?

They must borrow from the biblical worldview—from God's revelation. By God's common grace many scientists do borrow from the biblical ethic even though they'll never admit its basis.

---

postmodernism is just as wrong in its idea that humans are capable of discovering truth through their own rationality. The problem with postmoderns is that they also reject revelation as a source of truth.

How should Christians respond to such assumptions?

We should get into the habit of asking: "Who determines what counts as proof?"

That question challenges other people to defend the presupposition of modernism. Students should go on the offensive by asking people how they can know for sure that human rationality or empirical observation can be the only reliable authority source for truth. If people respond with a reason or with empirical evidence, then students should point out their circular reasoning, their fallibility, and their finiteness. Students

should point out that they might be able to show how their rationality or empirical evidence is able to reliably provide humans with *some* knowledge. But students must point out that it is a logical leap, based on circular reasoning, to insist that *all* knowledge can *only* be derived from those sources alone. It's a logical leap motivated by idolatry—making humans the final authority rather than God and His revealed Word.

  ## Self-Correcting Science?

Science does have its bad eggs, and when one of them gets caught—for example, the professor at a Dutch university who admitted to making up data—there may be a small round of public soul-searching among scientists. After that particular professor's story hit the headlines, Alan Kraut of the

Missa Charles Darwin

You can search online for *Missa Charles Darwin*. Let students listen to the skilled singers of New York Polyphony praising science with the ancient musical form of the mass. The composer of this mass, Gregory W. Brown, posted the Kyrie movement with subtitles so students can listen, see the singers, and read the *libretto* (the text of an opera or other long vocal work). It is quite an experience to hear the best of human singing intone the words, "Let the strongest live, and the weakest die."

Why it is that wealthy, largely secular audiences across the Western world still pay good money to hear sacred choral music sung?

Most of these secularists recognize the expertise of the musicians and the quality of the classics even though they don't believe the message. They simply view the message as a cultural expression from a past group of people. And as good multiculturalists, they try to accept all cultures (as long as they remain nonthreatening to their own secularism).

Provide students with specific examples and raise these questions:

Can you explain why nonbelievers would be drawn to sacred music with a biblical message?

Why do most educated Westerners have some familiarity with Handel's *Messiah*?

Why do secular choral groups sing, "We fear and love the living God"? Why do they sing about their own damnation? ("And I will shake all nations" is just one line of *Messiah*, a lengthy oratorio full of Scripture.)

Accomplished choral singer and Anglican priest Jonathan Arnold has written an entire book exploring this question. It's called *Sacred Music in Secular Society* (Surrey, England: Ashgate Publishing, 2014).

Why has atheist Ralph Vaughan Williams produced some of the best sacred music in English church history, such as "For All the Saints"?

Why are the works of John Rutter (a nonbeliever) sung in churches the world over?

Gregory Brown himself, the composer of *Missa Charles Darwin*, produced a beautiful arrangement of "Sweet Hour of Prayer" and put it up on YouTube after it was sung by an excellent, and apparently secular, choir.

One possible answer offered by Arnold is that secular people feel the loss of transcendence in their worldview, and they look for it in the beauty of the arts.

---

laws and yet not believe in the Lawgiver they come from. It's idolatrous to believe in a "cosmos"—an ordered realm—in the first place without believing in the God who gave it order. Humans have always been worshiping created things rather than the creator (Rom. 1:18–31). For most of human history, it was the sun or the moon or the Nile or the eagle that people worshiped; now it's often the cosmos as a whole.

Atheist Richard Dawkins defines biology as "the study of complicated things that give the appearance of having been designed for a purpose."[18] That little word *appearance* is a direct denial of what God says everyone can see if they have the hearts to look (Rom. 1:20). Scientism is an alternate belief system, a radically different worldview.

Christian philosopher Alvin Plantinga comments that scientific naturalism (or scientism)

> plays many of the same roles as a religion. In particular, it gives answers to the great human questions: Is there such a person as God? How should we live? Can we look forward to life after death? What is our place in the universe? How are we related to other creatures? Naturalism gives answers here: there is no God, and it makes no sense to hope for life after death. As to our place in the grand scheme of things, we human beings are just another animal with a peculiar way of making a living.[19]

Science is something God created humans to do, but scientism is an idolatrous twisting of that good gift.

MISSA CHARLES DARWIN

The term *mass* can refer not only to a Roman Catholic ritual but also to an ancient musical form used by both Protestants and Catholics. Bach's *B-Minor Mass*, for example, is a cultural treasure. The classic mass form features multiple movements: *Kyrie* ("Lord"), *Gloria* ("Glory"), *Credo* ("I believe"), and *Agnus Dei* ("the Lamb of God"). The lyrics, in Latin, are taken either from the Bible or (in the case of the *Credo*) from a biblically rich ancient Christian creed.

Scientism now has its own mass, the *Missa Charles Darwin* (*missa* is Latin for "mass"). The piece was written by composer Gregory W. Brown for the very capable men's group New York Polyphony.

"Unlike traditional Mass settings, however, the sacred texts have been replaced with excerpts from *On the Origin of Species*, *The Descent of Man*, and Darwin's extant correspondence."[20] Brown said the texts "represent a modern secular approach to explaining how we've come to be as a species."[21]

Scientism shows up clearly in the Alleluia movement: "It is those who know little and not those who know much who so positively assert that this or that problem will never be solved by science."[22] The mass celebrates "one general law, leading to the advancement of all organic beings namely, multiply, vary, let the strongest live and the weakest die."[23]

GIVE THEM ONE FREE MIRACLE

Scientism and naturalism aren't exactly the same thing. Scientism focuses on how you know anything and says *it's through the scientific method*. Naturalism focuses on the nature of the universe and teaches that there is no supernatural. But the two views tend to go together in the modern West. Both clubs have a sign on the door: No gods allowed. No divine revelation. No miracles . . . except one.

These secularists worship the transcendence of the art form rather than the transcendent Creator it points to (Rom. 1:25). Every major worldview feels the need to reach outside the system of our current order for something or Someone who may have pressed the start button on our current reality. Every worldview reaches for something above or outside of nature. Even naturalism does this. Worship of the Creator is a built-in aspect of the image of God in humans; it's inescapable. The void must be filled, but it can only satisfactorily be filled by the one true God.

Big Problems with the Big Bang

Answers Academy has a helpful two-part video on the Answers in Genesis website. In "Big Problems with the Big Bang," Jason Lisle demonstrates that the big bang theory lacks supporting evidence. Students need to understand how shaky the evidence is regarding the possibility of the big bang. They need to understand that it really is a hypothetical event that can't be scientifically proven or even defended. Honest evolutionary scientists admit the problems with this theory.

Have the students take notes on each problem with the big bang. Students could create a neatly written chart to refer to in future conversations to challenge the faith of people who hold to the big bang theory.

The Meaning of Myth

As pointed out on this page, there are two meanings of the word *myth*. In its first sense, the word is sometimes used for the purpose of denouncing a widely believed but false idea. The second sense is used

The big bang is allowed into the clubhouse through the backdoor. Countercultural intellectual Terrence McKenna was a sharp critic of scientific naturalism; he observed that it requires what he called a **singularity**, an unrepeatable, unexplainable event. "In order to kickstart the . . . engine," McKenna said, "you have to go outside the system."[24] In other words, said McKenna, "Science is saying, 'Give us one free miracle and we'll explain the rest.'"[25] McKenna, a non-Christian, observed that

> the dominant and virtually unchallenged myth of our origin is either that God created us in seven days along with all the rest of creation or that the universe was born out of nothingness in a single moment for no reason. These are the two choices on the menu.[26]

McKenna described the myth of scientific naturalism this way:

> Give me the first ten-to-twelve nanoseconds, and if I can do smoke and mirrors in that, then the rest will proceed quite in an orderly fashion. Now that's orthodoxy.[27]

Naturalism clearly crosses over into the realm of religion, as McKenna argues. It requires faith. It isn't pure empirical science. Even naturalism needs a miracle.

THE MYTH OF NATURALISM

Naturalism has proven over the centuries to be a powerful myth. Lucretius, a Roman philosopher who died half a century before Christ was born, wrote an epic philosophical poem called *On the Nature of Things* in which he argued for a naturalistic view. Centuries later, scientific naturalism has proven to be a **myth** in both senses of that term:

> **myth** 1. A widely held but false belief or idea: *he wants to dispel the myth that sea kayaking is too risky.* 2. A traditional story, especially one concerning the early history of a people or explaining some natural or social phenomenon, and typically involving supernatural beings or events: *the heroes of Greek myth.*[28]

Naturalism is appealing as a traditional story because it quite literally puts us humans at the top of the heap. We're the most advanced beings we know. And that gives us a power and an authority to make the world into whatever we want it to be.

Naturalism doesn't allow any supernatural beings into the clubhouse, only natural ones. But the dictionary says it can still count as a myth since supernatural *beings* are only typically part of the definition. The myth of naturalism gets along fine with just one supernatural *event*, the big bang.

SCIENTIFIC NATURALISM AND THE TWO-STORY VIEW

Genuine Christians are sometimes influenced by naturalism. One of the authors of this textbook was on a flight to deliver a paper on presuppositions and worldview at an academic conference. He wound up sitting next to a bubbly high school science teacher who had a double-major degree in science from Duke University. She had enrolled in Duke as a young-earth creationist but left professing to believe in evolution as well as the Bible. As they discussed the possibility of squaring the Bible with evolutionary theory, the author asked, "What role does the Fall of man play in your scientific work?"

"None," she replied.

"Why not?"

"Because you can't prove it."

more positively as a literary term to refer to any traditional story—even stories that are true (or at least have a seed of truth). The second sense is often connected with the first sense because most people today recognize that most of these old stories were made up by humans and believed by superstitious premoderns. But the second sense isn't intended to emphasize the falsehood of a story; it's simply used to identify a larger unifying story. So metanarratives are often called myths, but it's not meant to be derogatory.

These two senses of *myth* are important at a few junctures in this book. Make sure students understand both uses of the word. Students will likely be more familiar with the first denotation, and they may not initially see a distinction between it and the second. They may think that since the heroes in

Greek myths didn't exist, sense two means the same thing as sense one. But that is to pick out one incidental (not essential) truth about Greek mythology and make it the whole of the meaning of *myth*. The second denotation focuses on something different— the power of a story to unite people.

This is the power of modern-day myths— superhero stories. How many times and in how many media over how many years has the origin story of Spiderman been retold? How about Superman or Batman or Luke Skywalker? These stories have such a hold on American culture because they impart meaning and value. Spiderman learns a lesson about youthful impulsiveness through his uncle's death and responds the right way: with a self-effacing willingness to serve others. Batman likewise turns a childhood tragedy and adolescent angst into a powerful

force for good in Gotham. Luke Skywalker interrupts his training, despite the warning of his authorities, to save his friends. Whether these stories teach good morals or not (they're a mix), they are "myths" because they exert a powerful moral force on society. People take them seriously, as box office receipts and fan conventions and even fan fiction indicate.

But what if one of these myths really were true? That's the question that will be raised on page 318. Can there be a "true myth"—a story that involves supernatural beings that really exist and whose actions were determinative for the nature of our own morals and existence? The answer is, of course, yes. The biblical story that is often considered a myth (in the first sense of the word) by modernists is in fact a traditional, unifying history involving supernatural beings that is actually true (a myth in the second sense).

Evangelistic Encounters

Encourage students not to be afraid of engaging in evangelistic conversations with smart people.

If you had been talking with the teacher on the plane, how could you have presented evidence of the Fall?

The universal behavior of humans throughout history regardless of class, ethnicity, gender, or any other contextual social factors supports the biblical metanarrative. Nature also shows itself to be fallen. "Red in tooth and claw" isn't the way it's supposed to be. Animals have adapted to their environment to kill.

Why don't those realities count as proof to an evolutionist?

Evolutionists try to explain away the causation of this universal phenomenon through naturalistic explanations or by minimizing and redefining sin. They tend to blame abstract society rather than the particular individuals who make that society what it is.

What must change for evolutionists to accept evidence of the Fall?

their worldview lenses of interpretation

God won't call every student to a mastery of the topics people argue about. But He will call some students to rigorously answer the intellectuals of their day. God does call us all to love, to have compassion, and to have patience. God also calls us to have courage and boldness. All of us can learn some basic worldviewish questions such as "Who determines what counts as proof?" We must learn to stand firmly on the final authority of God's Word and to declare it lovingly to unteachable people who do not fear God (Prov. 1:7).

Poor Reasoning or Different Lenses?

Students should learn to ask another question whenever someone claims that Christians are anti-intellectual for rejecting scientism: "Who determines what counts as intellectualism?"

The accusation of anti-intellectualism is usually just a lazy retort that fails to actually analyze the thinking of a person someone disagrees with. Steven Pinker resorted to a similar *ad hominem* argument when Thomas Nagel disagreed with a foundational tenet of Pinker's worldview. It's not that Nagel's IQ had gone down or that his conclusions could be objectively shown to be logically disconnected from his major and minor premises. It's not that his handling and evaluating of evidence could be incontrovertibly refuted. Rather, Pinker had a worldview lens through which he viewed everything and by which he demanded that everyone else view things.

Most people just assume that their opponents can't think—instead of understanding why other people disagree with them and challenging their foundational presuppositions. Christians should be careful not to assume that non-Christians can't think. Instead, try to show non-Christians that they have a worldview lens, demonstrate some evidence of the problems with their worldview lens, and offer them a look at the evidence through the biblical worldview lens. God's truth can't be obscured by intellectuals who refuse to look at the evidence in God's general revelation through a biblical worldview lens. Ultimately, Christians must declare "thus says the Lord" to the unteachable person.

Paul's Approach in Athens

It's important to see that Paul *reasoned* with the philosophers of his day; it's also important to correctly identify *how* he reasoned (Acts 17:17–18). Among others, his audience included Epicureans, who were materialists (i.e., they didn't believe in a Creator or the supernatural). In his audience were also Stoics, who were pantheistic dualists (i.e., they believed that they were all representative pieces of the universe). In 17:22, Paul notes that they are very religious or superstitious. (His audience may not have known if that was a compliment or a criticism.) He enters into their worldview and critiques their inconsistency by using the example of their altar to an unknown god (17:23). He doesn't identify his God with their unknown god, but he does use their openness to the unknown god as leverage to introduce them to the true God they didn't know. He was attempting to show them that

---

MIND AND COSMOS

Thomas Nagel, well-known atheistic philosopher and New York University professor, dropped something of a bomb on scientism in his book *Mind and Cosmos: Why the Materialist Neo-Darwinian Conception of Nature Is Almost Certainly False*. He argued that non-material aspects of life such as consciousness, reason, morality, and experience—are really real even though not material. Nagel was attacked by prominent defenders of scientism such as Steven Pinker, who tweeted about "the shoddy reasoning of a once-great thinker."[29]

Philosopher Alva Noë of the University of California (partially) defended Nagel from such attackers: "He is questioning a certain kind of orthodoxy, and they are responding in the way the orthodox respond."[30] Noë said in a piece on NPR, "One reason we may feel inclined to react in this way is that we don't want philosophers washing science's dirty laundry in public in a way that runs the risk of allowing anti-naturalistic religious dogmatism to get a foothold."[31]

The author replied, "Who determines what counts as proof?"

Tension shot up between seats 9A and 9B. The science teacher felt the challenge of that question. She blushed a little—and changed the subject.

This young woman would never deny that God exists. She's not a naturalist in that sense. But scientism had successfully pushed her into a two-story universe where significant things God has said can't be "proven."

If you leave God out of your scientific work, you're giving in to the pressure of naturalism. It's also a form of idolatry because it turns something other than God into an absolute.

Even other non-Christian thinkers have concluded, as Terrence McKenna did, that "we are blinding ourselves to the intentionality present in our world."[32] Thomas Nagel, an atheistic philosopher, has also famously searched for what he calls a "mind," which he thinks may be responsible for creation.

It has been God's intent all through history that people "should seek God, and perhaps feel their way toward him and find him" (Acts 17:27), as Paul said to a group of Greek philosophers. He continued,

> Yet [God] is actually not far from each one of us, for "In him we live and move and have our being"; as even some of your own poets have said, "For we are indeed his offspring." Being then God's offspring, we ought not to think that the divine being is like gold or silver or stone, an image formed by the art and imagination of man. The times of ignorance God overlooked, but now he commands all people everywhere to repent, because he has fixed a day on which he will judge the world in righteousness by a man whom he has appointed; and of this he has given assurance to all by raising him from the dead. (Acts 17:28–31)

In their search for something absolute, for a miracle to explain our existence, scientific naturalism has stumbled into truth: the universe is not a closed system of merely physical causes. But we must not make gold or silver or stone—or dark matter or the big bang—into a god. In the beginning, it was God who created the heavens and the earth.

THINKING IT THROUGH 20.2

1. What's the only kind of knowledge that counts as proof if a person presupposes the worldview of scientism? Explain why.

2. How does scientific naturalism define "good"?

3. What's the one miracle that scientism can't escape? Why must it be taken by faith?

4. Why do many people find the naturalistic worldview appealing?

♀5. Where was the scientific naturalism in the Duke University graduate's comments on the plane (pages 309–10)?

---

their rejection of the biblical God (because He was a foreign, unknown deity to them) was inconsistent with their own worldview (17:18–20). Instead of resorting to common ground to demonstrate that God was their unknown god, Paul contrasts God with their idolatry. He presents God as the Creator, distinct from the creation (17:24–26). God is personal, not a piece of the universe (17:27). Paul argues his case by pointing out to them that their own respected poets borrowed from the biblical worldview by recognizing that human life was reflective of a living, personal God who was not merely a part of the universe (17:28). The true God is absolute and self-existent and not created by humans (17:29). As such, God has a claim on everyone and will judge everyone on the basis of His own standard of righteousness. People must respond with repentance (17:30–31). The ultimate proof of God's supernatural

nature (distinct from and ruling over the material universe) is the resurrection of Jesus. This was in stark contrast to the worldview of the philosophers of Paul's day; it was not an attempt to win them through common ground. Their response confirms that Paul's approach was confrontational but that his reasoning was effectively used by God's Spirit to convince some (17:32–33).

Christians can use this approach as a model. It is effective to use the words of atheistic scientists who question scientism to introduce the contrasting biblical worldview. Christians need not give in to evolutionary naturalism to prop up the gospel in order to gain a hearing.

20.3 SCIENTISM: A FAULTY WAY OF LIVING

Intelligent Life magazine asked seven prominent writers for their take on the questions, "What's the point? Does life have meaning?" Author and *New Yorker* reporter Elizabeth Kolbert responded:

> Most of us would . . . prefer to believe our lives have a higher purpose than those of *E coli* [bacteria]. The very capacity to aspire—to truth and beauty, fame and fortune, intimacy and immortality—is one of the characteristics that sets modern humans apart from other species.[33]

But Kolbert thinks it's wrong for us to impose the way we think on nature itself, to try to make the world fit our ideas of it. As Darwin put it, "Endless forms most beautiful and most wonderful" have evolved.[34] Kolbert emphasizes that they've done it without our help and will go on evolving when we're no longer here.

"Perhaps the wisest thing we could try to do is to make peace with pointlessness,"[35] Kolbert said. She agrees with Darwin that the point of our lives is to pass on our DNA. Since that plan went along fine for billions of years before the human species ever appeared, Kolbert says, nature can hardly be expected to change its methodology merely because some people today don't consider it meaningful.

THE MEANING WE CREATE

Scientific naturalism is the major worldview alternative to Christianity among thoughtful Western people. Do you find its vision satisfying? Are you prepared to make peace with pointlessness?

Prominent atheistic cosmologist* Lawrence Krauss thinks you should do both: "The two lessons I want to give people is that, you're more insignificant than you ever thought, and the future is miserable. And those two things should make you happy, not sad."[36]

cosmologist: a scientist who focuses on the origins of the cosmos

Why would anyone want to make peace—and even be happy—with such a worldview? What could possibly make such a bleak vision of the world attractive? Listen carefully to Krauss as he answers that objection:

> We should rejoice [that] this remarkable accident that led to our existence and that . . . consciousness evolved on a random planet in the middle of a random galaxy in the middle of nowhere. Four billion years into that time, consciousness evolved. . . . It's amazing, and the meaning in our lives is the meaning we create, and we should enjoy it and make the most of our brief moment in the sun.[37]

That's precisely it. If there is no God, the meaning of our lives is up to us. We rule ourselves. To many people, this is a liberating thought. Well-known atheist Thomas Nagel himself noted that the "scientific world view . . . owes some of the passion displayed by its adherents precisely to the fact that it is thought to liberate us from religion."[38]

Materialism's story can't be right.

THINKING IT THROUGH 20.2

1. empirical evidence because their meta-narrative insists that the material world is all that is real

2. only through demonstrable scientific evidence that can measure what seems to be beneficial

3. The so-called big bang must be taken by faith because it's a singularity that can't be repeated by empirical means or even explained scientifically.

4. It puts humans at the top of the heap as the most advanced beings with the authority to do whatever they want, totally excluding God and His authority.

5. It was assumed in her refusal to factor in the Fall in her analysis of the world and in her acceptance of the two-story view.

SECTION OBJECTIVES 20.3

1. Evaluate scientism's approach to the meaning of life.

2. Evaluate scientism's approach to morality.

Peace with Pointlessness

This is an insight worth hammering home—with grace and care but with pointed firmness—to students who are looking out of the corner of their eye at the joys of the irreligious. If they jump into the secular world with both feet, rejecting their Christian upbringing, they aren't just getting rid of a worldview they don't like; they're adopting one they may not understand. Materialism (the philosophical position that only the natural world exists) and materialistic greed for more stuff are just the intellectual and

popular versions of the same idea—that stuff is all that exists. Are students who just want to be rid of all the moral constraints religion puts on them really prepared to trade Christianity in for a worldview in which their lives have no meaning? Are their shoulders strong enough to carry the burden of creating their life's meaning for themselves (which is usually elusive and often leads to despair and even suicide)? Yes, materialism appears to liberate individuals from the seemingly unreasonable sexual constraints and other strictures of religion, but it shackles them with a purposelessness they won't be able to shake. Remind students that they can't *not* have a worldview. Rejection of one means adoption of another.

Of course, there are positions that try to stake out middle ground between theism and materialism. There is liberal mainline Protestantism in the US (and equivalents in other countries). And it appears that a relatively stable number of Americans are interested in this liberalized echo of Christianity—a religion that uses the familiar names and tunes of orthodox faith but vacuums out their meaning until they are weightless, easily blown about by the winds of culture. But most people who found themselves in theologically liberal congregations in the twentieth century either left for conservative ones or finally said to themselves, "I'm getting up early and missing the NFL pre-game show for this?" Mainline Protestantism has lost members at a precipitous rate. There is pointlessness at the heart of materialism and of religion without anything substantial to believe in.

Are Humans Really "Significance Junkies"?

Section 4.4 (p. 60) recounts how atheist Seth McFarlane describes his brush with death on September 11, 2001. He insists he didn't learn anything from his experience and that it didn't change his life at all. He quoted Carl Sagan, complaining that we are "significance junkies."

Another writer has said the same thing concerning her own close call with death. She somehow managed to contract flea-born typhus, landed in the ICU, and could have experienced brain damage if not death. She didn't die, however, and ended up with only minor hearing loss. Instead of being thankful for surviving—a miracle according to her doctor—she complained about the minor side effects. And she didn't like the word *miracle*. She rolled her eyes when a Christian friend told her that her family, Bible study group, and church were all praying for her. When she visited that friend and her husband after her recovery, they asked her if the experience had caused her to reevaluate her agnostic views. She mumbled something and excused herself to leave the room. But here's the interesting part: she also said that even her other friends who were secularists wanted to know about any transforming significance that might have taken place in her life. One unbelieving colleague told her that it was her choice to learn something positive or nothing at all—implying that it was better to take away something significant from the situation. [Meghan Daum, "I Nearly Died. So What?" *New York Times* (website), November 14, 2014]

Most secularists, who profess to live as if there is no higher power, can't live consistently with that view. They know, at some level of their being, that life is a gift, that life has meaning.

The *Is-Ought* Problem, or the Naturalistic Fallacy

The *is-ought* problem is a major, important defensive weapon in the hands of Christian philosophers, but it's readily accessible to regular Christians, including students. The basic idea is simple, and people violate it every day. For example, evolutionists in the mainstream press and in daily online chatter regularly say something like this: "Our ancestors evolved to be meat eaters, so we ought to eat meat too." Strip away all of the debate about evolution; strip away all of the debates about vegetarianism; simply look at the logic of this common argument. If something is, does that mean it ought to be? If it is true that we evolved to be meat eaters, does that have any bearing on whether we ought to eat meat today? How can a simple observation of the facts of experience or history tell us what, morally speaking, ought to be? There is an ultimately unbridgeable gap, in other words, between fact and value—unbridgeable, that is, by mere people. People try to bridge the gap all the time anyway, of course. They connect the eating of meat (or any one of a countless number of other issues) to their value system and make a determination as to what to do with the burger they've been offered. But you can't know what ought to be through science. Science by definition is observational and empirical. Moral conclusions are philosophical and determined through worldview lenses.

🖥️ Smuggled-In Assumptions

Provide students with some articles in which the authors are pressing for a moral agenda based on their scientific research. Ask students to analyze the logical leaps from pure empiricism (what can be described and observed, what is) to the moral imperatives (what ought to be according to someone's philosophical worldview standards). One example of this can be found on pages 224–225 of the Student Text. Note that scientific evidence can be used to support a moral imperative, but the ethical commitments must be presupposed based on a philosophical worldview.

Atheistic Morality

Christians ought to be ready to give every person a reason for the hope that is in them, Peter says. And they ought to do so with "gentleness and respect" (1 Pet. 3:15). Since atheists deserve that gentleness and respect, Christians ought to know that atheists find one particular argument against atheism highly offensive. That's the argument that goes like the one mentioned on this page under "Naturalistic Morality." It's easy to see how "Atheism leads directly to immorality, and all atheists are wicked" would be an offensive thing to say. But a Christian with a biblical worldview should also be able to see why such an argument is false. Atheists don't give up God's image when they deny His existence, any more than a coin loses George Washington's head because it can't understand the historical evidence for the existence of the first president. Since atheists have God's image and since they have the benefit of His common grace, they're restrained from evil at times and pushed toward good. However, even though plenty of Christian apologists have clarified to atheists that they are not saying all atheists are overtly wicked (only that atheists must *justify* their morality), atheists persist in misunderstanding them.

NATURALISTIC MORALITY

"Aha!" some Christians will say. "Atheism and scientism lead directly to immorality, and all atheists (and maybe even all scientists) are wicked!" That's exactly what atheists (and some scientists) think Christians say about them. But it isn't the Christian view. By God's common grace, atheists can be nice uncles, faithful taxpayers, and successful scientists (Matt. 5:46–47).

"I DON'T BELIEVE IN GOD, BUT I MISS HIM."[39]

—JULIAN BARNES

A biblical worldview doesn't demonize atheists; its challenge to atheism and scientific naturalism is more subtle than that. We're not saying atheists can't have morals; the Bible, in fact, says they do. What we're saying is that they can't explain their morality in a satisfying way.

Popular astrophysicist Neil DeGrasse Tyson nonetheless insists, "Science . . . transforms who we are [and] how we live—and it gives us an understanding of our place in the universe."[40] And atheistic Harvard professor Steven Pinker says that science "illuminates . . . the deepest questions about who we are, where we came from, and how we define the meaning and purpose of our lives" and goes on to declare that "the moral worldview of any scientifically literate person . . . requires a radical break from religious conceptions of meaning and value."[41]

But there is a fundamental problem here. Science, in the naturalistic view, can only describe what *is*. It has no authority to tell us what *ought to be*. Science can observe, "People typically behave like this." It cannot command, based on purely scientific grounds, "People ought to behave like that."

THE IS-OUGHT PROBLEM

British philosopher David Hume—although a materialist and religious skeptic himself—noticed that in a naturalistic worldview, there is an unbridgeable gap between what *is* and what *ought to be*. This has become known as the "is-ought problem" or the "naturalistic fallacy."

For example, it undoubtedly *is* that some eagle chicks kill their younger siblings.[42] *Ought* they to stop? Or *ought* human siblings to follow their example?

Those who use the tools of science can tell us (at least to a degree) what *is*, but they can't tell us what *ought to be* unless they smuggle in assumptions from somewhere outside science.

IF HUMANS WERE REALLY JUST ROBOTS

Skeptical humanist writer Kurt Vonnegut wrote an experimental novel in which the main character, Dwayne Hoover, is told that "everybody on Earth [is] a robot, with one exception—Dwayne Hoover." When Dwayne finds out that he lives in a mechanistic universe, his morality goes haywire. He explains his wife's suicide to himself (she drank Drano) by saying, "She was [just] that kind of machine!" He violently attacks two women because "he honestly believed that they were unfeeling machines." Dwayne says, "I used to think the electric chair was a shame. I used to think war was a shame—and automobile accidents and cancer." But not after finding out that other people are entirely physical: "Why should I care what happens to machines?"[43]

Atheistic philosopher John Gray, former professor at Oxford and visiting professor at Harvard and Yale, has demonstrated the disconnect between atheism and morality with a simple point: there have been many atheisms, and they have been associated with many different moralities. Why assume that the current crop of influential atheists (many of them scientists) have picked the right one?

> The racial theories promoted by atheists in the past have been consigned to the memory hole—and today's most influential atheists would no more endorse racist biology than they would be seen following the guidance of an astrologer. But they have not renounced the conviction that human values must be based in science; now it is liberal values which receive that accolade.*[44]

accolade: *praise*

The idea modern atheists seem to have is that "liberal values can be scientifically validated and are therefore humanly universal." But Gray asks,

> How could any increase in scientific knowledge validate values such as human equality and personal autonomy? The source of these values is not science. . . . It's not that atheists can't be moral. . . . The question is which morality an atheist should serve.[45]

What Gray says of atheism is true of scientific naturalism as well. And therein lies the trouble. As Gray says, you can't get a "universal morality" that isn't "borrowed from theism." The whole idea that man is making some kind of moral progress toward an evolutionary goal is actually "a hollowed-out version" of the Christian story.[46]

The big story of scientism doesn't portray human beings as moral agents struggling for a more just future society. It turns us into very complex "rocks" that do what our electrons and protons tell us to do. Rocks fall when dropped; people feed babies, help little old ladies across the street, and lie and murder. Whatever spreads our genes is "good." Scientific naturalism turns morality into "evolved herd survival instinct (nonbinding, of course, and as easy for us to outgrow as our feathers were)."[48]

> *"More than anything else, our unbelievers seek relief from the panic that grips them when they realise their values are rejected by much of humankind. What today's freethinkers want is freedom from doubt, and the prevailing version of atheism is well suited to give it to them."*[47]
>
> —JOHN GRAY

So scientific naturalism leads directly to **determinism** or **fatalism**—the idea that human freedom is an illusion, that we don't have "wills" at all, that we just do what we were programmed by evolution to do. As we observed in the very first chapter of this textbook, a person who believes that will tend to think,

> It doesn't make sense to call anything in this world "right" or "wrong" if we are all random atom collections. What does it matter if I hate my sister or I ate all your candy? Or if I love porn? So what? That's just what protoplasm does at this elevation above sea level.[49]

All Thunder Comes from On High

In one sense, we ought to be grateful that today's leading atheists are so dedicated to a moral vision. That vision isn't *completely* wrong. The work they do for the poor and even to fund scientific labors no doubt does a lot of genuine good. Some of the most prominent atheists, such as the late Christopher Hitchens, have sounded like old-time barnstorming tent-revivalists as they preach with holy passion against the moral evils of the day.

We should be grateful for their inconsistency because the truly consistent atheist would be more like the most influential atheist of the nineteenth century, Friedrich Nietzsche (1844–1900). He was an existentialist and **nihilist*** who believed in a "will to power" that crushes anyone in its way. Or they'd be more like Elizabeth, a twenty-two-year-old college student with a major tanning-salon habit. "If I get skin cancer, I'll deal with it then," she told a reporter. "I can't think about that now. I'm going to die of something."[50] *That* kind of morality is consistent with atheism.

nihilist: a person who believes life is pointless and that moral values have no basis

As with all human disagreements, once the best minds for each position have had their say, you might as well boil down their arguments to "Nuh-uh!" vs. "Yes-huh!"—and follow that up with a "Says who?" If a large number of people, educated and uneducated, find a particular worldview satisfying and compelling, it's meaningless to them to say, "Your worldview has been proven wrong!" They won't accept your definition of "proof."

Large numbers of people from all walks of life find atheism compelling. Yes, their view has been "proven" wrong from a Christian perspective. But the goal of a Christian evangelist speaking to an atheist should be persuasion, not necessarily proof. The worldview arguments presented in this book may provide helpful challenges and questions that Christian students can use with atheist friends to persuade them.

The Need for Meaning

You may be able to find a video online discussing C. S. Lewis's conversion from atheism to theism and then to Christianity. Or get a copy of Lewis's autobiography, *Surprised by Joy*, and read excerpts of his own testimony of conversion to the class. The absence of meaning in a materialistic world was a leading feature of his conversion.

Can Morality Be Culturally Determined?

The next section in the Student Text will briefly discuss Jonathan Haidt, a prominent and engaging non-Christian moral philosopher. Haidt is looked to by secularists and liberals (he is a liberal-moderate) for moral justification of their views. Secularists often rely on him in online debates, appealing to him as if his answer to the difficulty of establishing morality in a materialistic universe is no difficulty at all. What is his answer? As pointed out on page 318, Haidt's basic answer to the question of "What is morality?" is that it's a group-level adaptation. In other words, a group that evolves a moral code that is more successful than another group's will have a greater advantage in the survival of the fittest. Morality is simply the greatest good for the greatest number, and that's determined by majority vote (might makes right).

But does Haidt's hypothesis really work in the real world, or is the real world inconsistent with his evolutionary hypothesis? Give examples that contradict "survival of the fittest" morality.

Answers will vary. One major example of inconsistency is the nearly universal position that sati *(the Hindu practice of burning widows) is immoral. Yet the evolutionary position of survival of the fittest doesn't have any basis for condemning the practice.*

People in India have been burning widows for over two millennia. By the time the British outlawed the practice in 1829, they estimated that five to six hundred widows per year were being burned on funeral pyres next to their dead husbands. Sati lasted almost another century in Nepal. As recently as 1987, the Indian Parliament passed the Sati Prevention Act.

How, in Haidt's terms, can British people justify their culturally dominating self-righteousness in banning sati? If group survival is the standard by which morality is judged, isn't it possible that sati helped Indian culture survive and grow by ridding it of members who no longer had any contribution to make (or whose dependent status would have dragged everyone else down)? Who are Westerners to complain if another culture's morality seems inferior to their own? Manifestly, India as a superculture has lasted, even thrived—at least numerically. Its population is four times that of the US. The problem with atheism is not that it promotes widow-burning; in the Western world, running on moral fumes left over from Christendom, it doesn't. The problem with atheism is that it has no ground to stand on to say that widow-burning is wrong.

Even if morality *could* be culturally determined with justice for all, *should* it be culturally determined? Atheists run into the *is-ought* problem again. Can atheists justify why survival of the fittest should be the highest standard of morality?

More Lyrics and Analysis

A further analysis of the lyrics (use a lyrics site to find them) of "Take Me to Church" exemplifies additional moral assumptions (or the lack thereof). In contrast to the song, make the moral argument for Christianity: without a divine Person standing above human moral disagreements, the best we can hope for is a majority that rules in a way that happens to please us.

Hozier makes other charges, not mentioned in the Student Text, against Christianity in his song.

Lines 15–16 are a reference to a Christopher Hitchens article that criticized the Ten Commandments:

> One is presuming (is one not?) that this is the same god who actually created the audience he was addressing. This leaves us with the insoluble mystery of why he would have molded ("in his own image," yet) a covetous, murderous, disrespectful, lying, and adulterous species. Create them sick, and then command them to be well? What a mad despot this is, and how fortunate we are that he exists only in the minds of his worshippers.

[Christopher Hitchens, "Moore's Law: The Immorality of the Ten Commandments" *Slate* (website) August 27, 2003]

Despite the late Hitchens's considerable wit and intellect, that's a bad misreading of the Torah—a reading that completely skips over a rather prominent passage: Genesis 3. God did not create us sick. We did that to ourselves. And something else we did ourselves is on sad display in Hozier's lyrics. We have worshiped the creature rather than the Creator in our love for our sin (Rom. 1:18–31). And what has that got us?

In lines 51–55, Hozier appears to be saying that illicit sex is the moment when he feels most like himself, and the moment when his burdens—yes, even his guilt—fall away. The sexual act is the closest thing Hozier has to transcendence. (This is why our culture is prone to idolize sex.). But that act is not one that gets him very high above six feet: it only makes him "human"; nothing more.

The sad reality is that sexual perversion makes people inhuman not human. Fornicators and adulterers don't tend to treat their lovers with human value but as sex objects to fulfill their own lusts. People are no longer people; they're commodities to be thrown away and replaced. Why do you think divorce rates are so high?

Christians ought to feel how much more satisfying life lived according to a Christian

worldview is. We're more than merely highly developed animals; we bear the image of God. And through faith in Him, we get a cleansing that really lasts—one that's not over when the worship high is.

TAKE ME TO A CHURCH WITH NO ABSOLUTES

"Take Me to Church," a pop song by Irish musician Hozier, became a viral global hit, reaching the number-one slot in twelve countries and the top ten in twenty-one others.[51] In it Hozier complains about the Christian church's restrictive view of sex. By contrast, he sings, "My church offers no absolutes—/She tells me 'worship in the bedroom.'/The only heaven I'll be sent to/Is when I'm alone with you."[52] The worldview Hozier offers, at least within the limits of his song (and public comments he's made about it[53]), is only-sex-is-real-ism. There are no absolutes in his church (um, *absolutely* no absolutes?) except this one: sex feels good.

This may be great for Hozier—he gets what he wants out of his idol. But is it great for the woman he worships? In a "church" with no absolutes, how long will his worship last? Will he stick around when a more attractive idol presents herself? And what about any children Hozier's worship produces? Sexual freedom sounds like a good deal to a lot of adults, but few people stop to ask kids whose dads have left their families what they think about it.

Consistent atheism doesn't produce moral crusades. When an atheist does thunder about some injustice in the world, he stands "in the boots of forefathers who knew that all thunder comes from on high."[54]

MORAL ABSOLUTES

Richard Dawkins, perhaps the leading public atheist in the English-speaking world, has actually admitted that absolute right and wrong are hard to derive from scientific naturalism, or as Steven Pinker puts it, "Scientific facts do not by themselves dictate values."[55] But, with a quick sleight of hand, Dawkins turns this admission into a defense of his view: "It is pretty hard to defend absolutist morals on grounds other than religious ones."[56] Dawkins' trick is in that word *absolutist*. He knows his readership: people don't want to give anyone else, even and especially God, "absolute" rule over their choices.

But if morality isn't absolute, what is it? It's relative and debatable. It's whatever people more or less agree to. And if you find yourself a Jew in 1940s Germany or an African slave in nineteeth-century America, you'll just have to wait till the opinion polls go your way, if they ever do. That's why atheist John Gray says, "Anyone who wants their values secured by something beyond the capricious human world had better join an old-fashioned religion."[57]

Christianity offers "conversion"—a total remaking of someone's life that will give him freedom from sin. Atheistic scientism also promises that a conversion to unbelief will remake someone—and free him from "sin" by changing the definition.

THINKING IT THROUGH 20.3

1. Although atheists have morals, why can't they use science to justify their morality?

2. How does morality operate in scientific naturalism?

3. What is a nihilist?

4. Why is it dangerous to deny absolute morality?

♀5. Who determines the meaning of life according to the scientistic worldview? Why must that approach be doomed to failure?

Resource
Paul David Tripp, *Sex and Money* (Downers Grove, IL: InterVarsity Press, 2013).

THINKING IT THROUGH 20.3

1. Science can only describe what is and can never authorize what ought to be (the claim of morality).

2. In scientific naturalism, morality operates according to an evolved herd instinct to survive. Therefore, humans do whatever nature programs them to do to survive and spread their genes. Extreme forms of this view lead to a denial of the human will—fatalism or determinism.

3. a person who believes in a will to power that crushes anyone in its way

4. Morality that changes according to majority opinions in certain places and at certain times will eventually lead to the victimization of certain people.

♀5. Individuals determine it for themselves; people are finite and will always be frustrated in their quest to make life work according to their own dreams.

20.4 SCIENTISM: A FAULTY WAY OF KNOWING

John Nash, a brilliant mathematician who received a PhD from Princeton in 1950, wrote his dissertation on what's now called game theory, an extremely complex field. In 1994, Nash won the Nobel Prize for mathematics. But in between those two events, he was insane. Diagnosed as a schizophrenic, he heard voices and believed that people from outer space were attacking his work.[58] He emerged into sanity again after a decades-long period of madness, and his reflections on that experience are very interesting:

> People are always selling the idea that people who have mental illness are suffering. But it's really not so simple. I think mental illness or madness can be an escape also. . . . If things are not so good, you maybe want to imagine something better. In madness, I thought I was the most important person of the world and people like the Pope would be just like enemies, who would try to put me down in some way.[59]

Madness can be a refuge from the truth. In one sense, that can actually work pretty well for people. And who has the right to tell a John Nash, "Snap out of it and live in the real world!"—if the world he's created for himself gives him more pleasure than the mad, mad world the rest of us live in?

(Although Nash acknowledges that he chose mental shutdown as an escape, not all mental dysfunction is a choice. Dementia, blunt trauma injuries, fetal alcohol influences, infections, and many other truly physical problems can wreak havoc with brain function. Whether the dysfunction is chosen or not, the suffering is real, and it calls for compassionate understanding and care.)

WHAT A FOOL KNOWS

It's the fool who "says in his heart, 'There is no God'" (Psalm 14:1). The God-denier lives in an irrational world of his own foolish creation. And it can actually work pretty well for him—from one perspective (Ps. 37:35; 73:3–9). That world gives him more pleasure (at least temporarily) than the one that actually exists, the one that God made.

But God says that the very beginning of knowledge is fear of the Lord (Prov. 1:7), and we've given some attention to that claim in previous units. If scientism—scientific naturalism—says in its heart, "There is no God," then we can expect that it will not merely be a faulty way to live (the topic of the previous section) but a faulty way to *know*. Even in his madness, John Nash knew a great deal. He knew there was a pope; he continued to speak English and to eat and drink; still resident in his brain was a wealth of mathematical skill. But very few people would be satisfied with Nash's method of knowing.

Even in its madness, scientism knows a great deal. But Christians should not be satisfied with its method of knowing.

SCIENTISM AND KNOWLEDGE

Proponents of scientism make their view of knowledge perfectly clear. As Steven Pinker says, religion is *out*:

> Most of the traditional causes of belief—faith, revelation, dogma,* authority . . . —are generators of error and should be dismissed as sources of knowledge.[60]

As Richard N. Williams says (in a critique of scientism), the scientific method is *in*:

dogma: *a truth claim made by a religious authority*

This next section makes not a moral argument but an epistemological one—that is, an argument focused on knowing. Without God in your worldview, how can you say you *know* anything? This is a demanding argument to understand but a necessary one. One of the major trump cards educated secularists use against Christianity in the West is that religious knowledge isn't real knowledge, only scientific knowledge is. Most people don't clearly understand or acknowledge that that stance is the same as Steven Pinker's. His quote near the bottom of this page is absolutely clear that he rejects God's authority and God's Word. Secularism stands absolutely on this foundation as well. Thus, in the public square, Christians are pressured to capitulate and play by these rules. Evidentialists comply. Worldview apologetics challenges this as a faulty presupposition—one that is unfairly biased so that Christians lose the debate before it even starts if they agree to play by those rules.

The Great Debate

In a classic debate between Greg Bahnsen and Gordon Stein, Bahnsen illustrates how to challenge the presuppositions of scientism by demonstrating that it has no justification for the laws of logic or morality. He argues that only biblical Christianity has justification because it accepts that humans were created in the image of God and God has revealed what He is like, which humans ought to image. This is the basis for rationality and morality in the biblical worldview. It would be well worth students' time to listen to the whole debate.

[Greg L. Bahnsen and Gordon Stein, "The Great Debate: Does God Exist?" (Irvine: University of California, 1985), MP3 available for free online]

The Bedrock of Your Knowledge

Christians are doing to materialistic scientists exactly the same thing they do to us. Scientism says the Bible is all interpretation. We say the world is all interpretation. We say the Bible has a fixed meaning that everyone is morally obligated to hear and acknowledge. They say the world has a fixed meaning that everyone is morally obligated to hear and acknowledge. We say that the Bible tells us how to view the world. They refuse those lenses.

Scientism in the Humanities

In a remarkably arrogant article, Armand Marie Leroi (professor of evolutionary developmental biology at Imperial College, London) complains that the humanities are

---

SECTION OBJECTIVES 20.4

1. Critique scientism's exclusive claim to knowledge by exemplifying two major ways its adherents must inconsistently resort to nonempirical knowledge.

2. Critique scientism's exclusive claim to knowledge by explaining why its adherents can't justify scientism's own claim to rationality.

Arguments from Morality and Knowledge

Make certain students understand the basic thrust of the argument in this and the previous section. The prior section makes the *moral* argument against scientism—a closed system of purely physical causes cannot explain the reality of morals (nonphysical abstract standards that stand above the phys-

ical world). Atheists can't simply sidestep this problem by claiming that morals are preferences held by the majority of people in a culture. Some *so-called* morals may indeed be preferences on the order of one person's preference for chocolate ice cream over vanilla. But to oppose the enslavement and torture of small children is not a preference. All people have a sense, a God-given sense, that this moral standard should be applied to all people everywhere at all times. That is so because that moral standard reflects something real about the world. Therefore, it should be enforceable on all people everywhere at all times. It is a fact, not merely an opinion, that toddler-torture is wrong. And yet without God in your worldview, how can you explain the reality of this nonphysical reality—this morality—this fact?

resistant to employing scientific tools. Leroi singles out literary critics such as Harold Bloom for refusing to use the tools of science in their work. Leroi quotes Bloom saying in 2012, at the end of his long career, "I am an Epicurean literary critic, reliant upon sensations, perceptions, impressions." Leroi comments, "But scientists know that impressions lie; that they tell us what we want to hear, not what is." Science, Leroi thinks, tells us what is! And Leroi wants literary and art critics to use science to tell them what Mark Rothko paintings and Jane Austen novels mean. He derides people like Bloom for being unable even to understand the results of empirical study of literary texts. [Armand Leroi, "One Republic of Learning: Digitizing the Humanities," *New York Times* (website), February 13, 2015]

But Leroi is surely wrong: the dry, numbers-based approach to Mark Twain's humor or Picasso's artistic intentions can complement but never replace the very analog work of human critics. (The humanities are both a science and an art.) Leroi seems to believe that because humans are nothing but molecular machines, their cultural products are fundamentally readable by other machines. Machines can gather data more effectively (and may correct some false conclusions), but humans interpret that data. And not all of that interpretation will be purely scientific. Some of it will be philosophical or anecdotal. And it should be if you want life and heart to remain in the study. The study requires more than data analysis; it requires applied wisdom based on the fear of the Lord.

Evidence-Based Empiricism

Professor Rolf-Dieter Heuer, director of the prominent CERN nuclear research center in Europe, recently expressed concern that Western society as a whole is skeptical about science. And he admitted that "science is not about absolute certainty; it is about degrees of certainty. The better the evidence, the more certain you can be." Heuer says that "every decision we [as humanity] make will be better made through a rational evidence-based approach." He says that even the "complex ethical issues" of modern society are best addressed through "the rational, evidence-based approach that is the hallmark of science." [Rolf-Dieter Heuer, "The World Needs Scientific Rationalism," *Huffington Post* (website), May 9, 2015]

No one, least of all the Bible, is advocating an irrational, evidence-ignoring approach. Make it very clear that Christians have no problem embracing scientifically evidenced arguments—if the field of study or subject matter warrants it. Christians don't argue for the abandonment of observational sci-

Only certifiably scientific knowledge counts as real knowledge. All else is mere opinion or nonsense. Scientific knowledge is defined in terms of the method by which it is obtained. . . . There is a certifiable and specifiable method (or manageable set of methods) that counts as scientific.[61]

Scientism even attempts to exert control over academic disciplines that haven't generally been regarded as scientific. Scholars and teachers in the humanities—literature, art, music, philosophy, and so forth—are now feeling the pressure to use scientific methods in their own disciplines.[62]

But is the scientific method the only genuinely reliable path to knowledge in all fields of human life? No, and two arguments we've seen before are effective against this scientistic idea: (1) empiricism can't prove empiricism, and (2) there are no uninterpreted facts.

1. Empiricism Can't Prove Empiricism

The scientific method is a form of the philosophical view called **empiricism**. "Empiricists claim that sense experience is the ultimate source of all our concepts and knowledge."[63] They may use instruments such as microscopes or telescopes to amplify their ability to see, or decibel counters to amplify their ability to hear, but "ultimately, it always comes back to our senses, one way or another."[64]

Presumably, proponents of scientism would insist that you can "know" that our senses are the only reliable way to get truth. But how can you prove through empirical methods that empirical methods are the only reliable way to know? That is a presupposition you must take on faith. In fact, it's circular reasoning.

What authority do Richard Dawkins and Steven Pinker have to tell anyone that "faith," "revelation," and "authority" are bad ways to know and empiricism is a good way to know? It just so happens that they both participated in a roundtable broadcast addressing that question.[65] Everyone in the discussion appeared to agree that if religious people would just get some education and listen to scientific authorities instead of religious ones, such people would be a great deal better off.

But the host of the show, card-carrying liberal Chris Hayes, pushed back. He said that he didn't have time to read up on all of the science in every field and that even if he did he would still be taking the word of the scientists who did the studies he was reading. He doesn't have time to repeat all their experiments, even if he knew how.

peer-reviewed: evaluated by experts in the field before being published

cognoscenti: the smart people; those "in the know"

I consider myself a pretty educated person. . . . I read peer-reviewed* studies. . . .[But] if I am honest with myself I am still at a fundamental level relying on trust to a certain degree, and there's no way of getting around that. And to pretend that "Oh, what we the enlightened cognoscenti* do is so different from what [religious conservatives] are doing who just trust authority" I think is really self-delusional.[66]

Dawkins agreed partially with what Hayes was saying:

Nobody can read up all the scientific literature. The best scientist in the world can't keep up with science outside his or her own field. And so there really is a matter of trust.[67]

But Dawkins insisted that

science has earned the right to trust, because you know that when people are challenged in science they can produce the evidence. They can say, "Look, here's [a study by] Brown and McAllister [in] 2008 showing so and so. You can actually cite chapter and verse.[68]

ence; they argue that observational science is *limited*. (Again, atheists continually misrepresent Christians as if their stance is the former and not the latter.) It's limited because science can only describe the created order or explain how things function. It can't authoritatively declare what ought to be, morally. It can't provide the interpretive lenses. It can't inductively infer all of the laws of logic. Science is dependent on presupposed deductive declarations from philosophy (or, for the Christian, theology).

Professor Heuer, in this brief piece, isn't perfectly clear about what he's combatting. But if we asked him to attempt to prove that rational, evidence-based approaches are the best way to deal with complex ethical issues, what could he do except turn to rational, evidence-based arguments? He could say, "The evidence shows that evidence-based

approaches work best." But that would be begging the question. (And he's sneaking in assumptions when he says the evidence "shows" certain things. Evidence doesn't show anything apart from a philosophical—or theological—interpretive system. [See Activity 4, "The Evangelist Meets an Evolutionist," question 4.] Why should we limit ourselves to merely evidence-based approaches to ethics in the first place? Christians *must* ask (unless they're willing to capitulate to scientism), "What role does faith or trust in an authority source play?" (Secularists already admitted that they have to have faith in others too because they can't do all the empirical experiments themselves.) For the Christian, faith in God's interpretive revelation is necessary for unlocking an understanding of knowledge. Christians can't ignore the fear of God—

In other words, we should trust scientific evidence because of all the scientific evidence for trusting scientific evidence. Dawkins (and Pinker, who said much the same) are using circular reasoning. They are using empiricism to prove empiricism.[71]

A biblical worldview does *not* lead to a radical skepticism which refuses to trust all the work of unbelieving scientists. The great majority of the work of today's scientists, no matter their religious views, is valuable. But the worldview foundation of your knowledge matters. If you're called on to either trust God or trust your own eyes—and those are truly your only two options—the biblical position is clear: "We walk by faith, not by sight" (2 Cor. 5:7) because "the fear of the Lord is the beginning of knowledge" (Prov. 1:7).

The irony here is that scientism can't respond by saying, "We walk by sight, not by faith." They, too, must exercise faith: they must believe that the five senses are the only reliable way to know.

2. There Are No Brute Facts

Much of Unit 1 was dedicated to making the second argument against scientism's preferred way of knowing. That argument is simply that there are no uninterpreted facts. Everyone sees all scientific evidence through the worldview lenses he's wearing. It's not a simple and obvious process to move from the facts on the ground to a theory in your head. People wearing different lenses will come up with different theories.

Did you ever hear Rudyard Kipling's *Just So Stories* as a kid? They're fanciful tales written to explain "How the Camel Got His Hump," "How the Leopard Got His Spots," and other things all well-rounded children need to know. In one of the stories, "How the Elephant Got His Trunk," we discover that a young elephant was too curious and stuck his stubby nose into the mouth of a crocodile. The croc snapped his mouth shut and began a tug-of-war that ended up stretching the elephant's nose into the length it now has.

"How the Elephant Got His Trunk"

unless they choose to capitulate to scientism. God warns that that path only leads to foolishness (Ps. 53:1).

Evidenced-Based Certainty

Even though Stanley Fish is an unbeliever, he eloquently challenges Dawkins's and Pinker's trust in evidenced-based certainty. (Fish is a postmodernist, which explains his motivation for critiquing the overblown confidence of modernists in their scientific certainty.) He does so by noting that their evidence is always interpreted through the lens of their own dogma. They're not more unbiased, just more subtle, than Christians who cite their interpretive philosophical assumptions from the Bible. [Stanley Fish, "Citing Chapter and Verse: Which Scripture Is the Right One?" *New York Times* (website), March 26, 2012]

Just-So Stories

The effort to find evolutionary explanations for human behavior often gets ridiculous.

Why is it, for example, that small children the world over commonly love throwing rocks into bodies of water? (They'll stay at it for a long time sometimes. Given evolution, surely a behavior this universal must have an explanation derived from natural selection.)

Maybe children in hunter-gatherer societies participated in some fish-scaring exercises, throwing rocks in the water so the fish were startled right into the waiting spears of the adults?

Such an explanation couldn't really be proved or disproved. It's a just-so story.

This kind of pure guesswork is common in nature documentaries. The evolutionary lens is the only basis for a particular explanation about nature that they'll make up.

Brainstorm some of your own observations of human behaviors and come up with evolutionary just-so stories to explain them.

The variation in students stories for the same behavior may indicate the impossibility of nailing down any real reason for human activities within an evolutionary schema.

How can you view those same behaviors through the lens of a biblical worldview?

[Students still might not know for sure specific explanations if there are none revealed in Scripture. But the Bible will give them a reliable overarching perspective on human nature.]

Evolutionary explanations for the origin of life are just-so stories. In the documentary, *Expelled: No Intelligence Allowed*, Ben Stein questions some of the prominent critics of Intelligent Design for their own explanations for the origin of life. They responded with just-so stories: life spontaneously appeared on the back of crystals; life was transplanted onto our planet from aliens. They claim, with a straight face, that this is empirical science—in contrast to the explanations given by Intelligent Design proponents or young-earth creationists.

The Meaning of *Unfalsifiable*

The criterion of unfalsifiability was a major focus of the twentieth-century philosopher Karl Popper. His basic principle was that any scientific hypothesis must be inherently testable to be considered scientific.

To call evolution's explanations of modern human or animal behaviors "unfalsifiable" is *not* to say that they are therefore true. What it means is that, even given the evolutionary schema, it is impossible to establish empirically that any given behavior developed as a survival value. Why should survival value become the only controlling interpretation of everything? It's an assumption—one that is unproven and can't be proven. It's like saying, "It will rain at this location on September 18, 2312." It may; it may not. It is impossible to know.

Haidt on Religion

A consistent materialist has a real problem with religion. First, of course, he or she is bound to think it's ridiculous. And indeed, Jonathan Haidt is pretty condescending about religion in his book that claims to explain morality. He basically asks, "Once we realize the truth that religion is merely a group adaptation, why can't we find our morality in some less restrictive and demanding place than the Bible?"

But instead of thinking religion is ridiculous, a consistent materialist is bound to think that religion is necessary. Everything we do is necessary. Religion has been a universal in human experience; apparently it has helped us get this far in the evolutionary battle of survival. Shouldn't materialists fear to kill off religion, lest it kill off the human race?

The Incoming Tide of Science

Even after students are armed with counter-arguments against scientism—and, more importantly, are armed with a truly biblical view of their world—they may still feel beleaguered by the culture. One goal of a Christian worldview book, on the personal and affective level, ought to be to make them feel joyfully, gratefully, humbly *right*, no matter what the majority of educated people in the West say.

Because Christians believe the biblical worldview instead of the default materialistic view of most Westerners, they'll always be in the minority. So why should students be confident? The materialistic worldview that denies God and His revelation is not and never has been satisfying—as a way to *live* or as a way to *know*. This should be no surprise since it's contrary to God's creational norms.

The desire for acceptance, respectability, and affirmation that they are intelligent can be a powerful force for students, especially if they're pursuing higher degrees in a secular university context. Even though peer pressure has so much pull, it's very important for Christian students to understand that the allegations by the adherents of scientism that Christians are unscientific fools are false. The difference between themselves and materialists isn't their own stupidity; the difference is presupposed worldview lenses of interpretation based on different metanarratives of the world. One idolizes finite fallible humans as the ultimate source and authority of knowledge; the other worships God as the ultimate source and authority over human knowledge.

Students should be confident that, even though they are considered foolish by the world around them, they're wise because they fear God and are using the right interpretive lenses (1 Cor. 1:25–31). Their standard of wisdom must be God's Word and not secular academia, which rejects the sure foundation of God's wisdom (Ps. 119:99; Prov. 1:7). Students must not forget that the secular world is under the direction

of Satan, who is battling against God (Eph. 2:1–3; 6:12). They must not forget that the mass of humanity is in rebellion against God and trying to throw off His rule (Ps. 2:1–3). And they must not forget that God's rule will win out in the end (Ps. 2:4–12).

Once children accept the idea that silly events in the distant past explain features of our world today, the possibilities are endless: they can come up with hypotheses for why bananas are yellow (an unfortunate incident involving highlighters), where red hair comes from (a guy who accidentally swallowed fire), and why all children have to go to bed earlier than they want to (because of the monsters under the bed, of course).

The problem with these stories is that they're "unfalsifiable." There is no evidence for them except the power of the overall worldview that generates them. So it's fruitless to argue with a child who accepts that worldview. If you try, he'll just go away thinking, "What more proof does that grown-up need? Highlighters and bananas are clearly the same color!"

Evolutionary theory comes up with plenty of "**just-so stories**" about the world, and particularly about characteristics of human society. Name any major feature of human existence, and educated people will make guesses as to how evolution brought it to us.

Take religion, for example. One of the leading secular moral philosophers of our day, Jonathan Haidt of New York University, attempted to explain the existence of religion from an evolutionary perspective in his book *The Righteous Mind: Why Good People Are Divided by Politics and Religion*. Haidt knows that the standard evolutionary answer is that humans, like other animals, are "hypersensitive to agency."[72] Our brains are trained to detect the difference between movement caused by wind or water and movement caused by an "agent"—a being that can move under its own power and that may therefore pose a threat (or an opportunity). Atheists such as Richard Dawkins argue that humans, because of this capacity, started seeing supernatural agency behind purely natural events. Religion, in other words, was one huge evolutionary mistake.

But Haidt offers a somewhat more positive assessment of religion. In his view, religion is a group-level adaptation. Morality inside a group helps the whole group be more successful. Other things being equal, the group of human animals with the more successful moral rules will beat the one with a worse morality. In other words, survival of the fittest doesn't just work on an individual level, but at a group level.[73]

But this is a just-so story. Where, exactly, is the evidence for it? And what kind of evidence could ever be found for it? The story is unfalsifiable; it draws all of its persuasiveness from the power of evolutionary theory, not from the observed evidence. Only if evolution is true does it make any sense. So Haidt can't turn around and logically claim that the existence of religion is evidence that evolution occurred.

TRUE MYTH

Before C. S. Lewis became a Christian, he was an ardent believer in the myth of scientific naturalism. But, he says, "Long before I believed Theology to be true I had already decided that the popular scientific picture at any rate was false."[74]

> The picture so often painted of Christians huddling together on an ever narrower strip of beach while the incoming tide of "Science" mounts higher and higher corresponds to nothing in my own experience. That grand myth [of evolutionary progress] . . . is not for me a hostile novelty breaking in on my traditional beliefs. On the contrary, that cosmology is what I started from. Deepening distrust and final abandonment of it long preceded my conversion to Christianity.[75]

Back to Materialism and Morality

Ask students to identify which moral convictions are contestable in the following statement made by materialist and arch-promoter of scientism, Steven Pinker:

> In combination with a few unexceptionable convictions—that all of us value our own welfare and that we are social beings who impinge on each other and can negotiate codes of conduct—the scientific facts militate toward a defensible morality, namely adhering to principles that maximize the flourishing of humans and other sentient beings. This humanism,

Lewis mentions another major objection to scientific naturalism—what he calls its "absolutely central inconsistency." This objection may be a little more difficult to understand than the two already presented in this chapter, but it's a strong argument.

He explained that science claims to rely on inferring things based on observations. If the inference is invalid, the whole structure collapses. Lewis questions whether we can be certain that matter in the farthest reaches of the universe behaves according to the principles a scientist observes in his laboratory on earth. If not, or as Lewis puts it, "unless Reason is absolute,"[76] then "all is in ruins." But those who promote this worldview want us to believe that reason is nothing more than the accidental result of unthinking matter in its current phase of perpetual and pointless evolving. What's contradictory about this is that we are expected to accept this proposition but simultaneously reject the very basis of it.

Lewis concluded,

> The difficulty is to me a fatal one; and the fact that when you put it to many scientists, far from having an answer, they seem not even to understand what the difficulty is, assures me that I have not found a mare's nest* but detected a radical disease in their whole mode of thought from the very beginning. The man who has once understood the situation is compelled henceforth

to regard the scientific cosmology as being, in principle, a myth; though no doubt a great many true particulars have been worked into it.[77]

Modern-day writer Francis Beckwith offers an illustration supporting the same point Lewis made. The materialist can only defend his viewpoint by drawing inferences based on reasons. To do that, he has to be able to act as a rational agent—to think. Materialism teaches, however, that thinking is something the brain does entirely in a physical sense; it functions according to the laws of physics and chemistry the same way other bodily organs do and is also affected by natural selection. If thinking is a "nonrational" process, then the results of our reasoning, including the ideas that materialism grows out of, are not trustworthy.

Beckwith illustrates the problem this way:

> If while I'm playing Scrabble, the letters randomly spell "materialism is true," should I change my belief and embrace materialism? Of course not, for this collection of letters is the result of nonrational forces or chance. But if the brain's "reasoning" is like the random string of Scrabble letters, then its apparent [results]—including the claim that materialism is true—are arrived at in no more rational a fashion than the phrase "materialism is true" on the Scrabble board.[78]

mare's nest: a fraud, illusion, deliberate hoax

It's like John Nash, the mathematician who went insane. He only crawled out of madness and back to sanity when he began arguing with the voices in his head. He explained, "I began rejecting them and deciding not to listen." Nash observed that "to some extent, sanity is a form of conformity."[79] He meant that "sanity" in any given culture means going with the flow of what people around you believe about the world.

But what if they're all fallen people who believe foolish things? Even well-educated people actually believe that we all got here from nowhere and evolved from nothing—and they think science proves it. ("That's orthodoxy," says Terrence McKenna.) If you believed that spoiled meat spontaneously generated maggots, they would laugh at you. But they can say "life created itself" with a straight face. Going with that flow is what's crazy. It suppresses the truth evident all around us (Rom. 1:17–32).

Lewis was converted when his friend J. R. R. Tolkien, author of *The Lord of the Rings*, urged him to see Christianity as a **"true myth."**[80] Lewis began to realize that the Bible told a powerful story that explained the world (another meaning of the word *myth*, see second definition on page 309), and he began to believe that it all really and truly happened. Jesus really lived a sinless life. He really died and rose again.

Christianity doesn't ask you to deny the evidence in front of your face, but it does demand that you interpret that evidence through the lens provided by God in Scripture. As one theologian has said, "Any decision to distrust God's words is a decision to trust someone else's."[81]

---

which is inextricable from a scientific understanding of the world, is becoming the de facto morality of modern democracies, international organizations, and liberalizing religions, and its unfulfilled promises define the moral imperatives we face today.

[Steven Pinker, "Science Is Not Your Enemy" *New Republic* (website), August 6, 2013]

Students should learn to ask questions like the following:

- From an evolutionary perspective, why should I care what causes flourishing for other humans as long as I survive?
- What, indeed, counts as flourishing, and how can I know?

A Basis for Inferences

Here is a real-life example of what C. S. Lewis was talking about when he questioned the possibility of the absolutely reliable rationality of human observation in an evolutionary world of random chance. Michael Graziano, professor of psychology and neuroscience at Princeton University, offers something of a just-so story to explain the existence of what we call "self-awareness" from a materialistic perspective. Why are humans self-aware?

In this materialistic worldview, the brain concocts "self-awareness" as a tool for survival, like Hal in *2001: A Space Odyssey*. Says Graziano:

> There is no subjective impression, there is only information in a data-processing device. When we look at a red apple, the brain computes information about color. It also computes information about the self and about a (physically incoherent) property of subjective experience. The brain's cognitive machinery accesses that interlinked information and derives several conclusions: There is a self, a me; there is a red thing nearby; there is such a thing as subjective experience; and I have an experience of that red thing.

[Michael S. Graziano, "Are We Really Conscious?" *New York Times* (website), October 10, 2014]

Although Graziano doesn't spell out this particular implication, it's apparent that in an evolutionary schema, the human capacity for what seems to be self-consciousness is just a survival tool. The brain needs to construct that model in order for the organism to survive and reproduce.

In response to Lewis's argument, Graziano essentially says that humans aren't really deriving inferences, as we're accustomed to thinking of that process. Instead we are machines that have developed to be adept at controlling our environment for our own survival. Whether our inferences are accurate or not is immaterial, as long as they help us survive.

But this whole explanation is a just-so story projected onto the evidence of how the brain operates. It's not coming from the evidence itself. It's coming from the evolutionary worldview that's drawing conclusions about the evidence—forcing the evidence to fit with that presupposed system of belief.

1. Empiricism can't prove empiricism; there are no uninterpreted facts

2. a trusted authority, which is determined by already accepted presuppositions

3. Believers in scientism must resort to circular reasoning to support their fundamental presupposition of empiricism; they can prove only that empiricism provides *some* knowledge. They can't prove that empiricism is the only way whatsoever to know everything. That presupposition, which in itself denies the possibility of divine revelation as another source of knowledge, is based on faith—faith that human knowledge is ultimate.

4. It's an explanation of reality that is unfalsifiable as long as a larger story of reality continues to be presupposed. No evidence can in itself confirm or deny it.

♀5. Scientism demands the conclusion that reasoning is reliable (and that humans can know and agree on what is reasonable or rational—implying absolutes), but that conclusion has no basis in a world (from which reason comes) that is mindlessly random and aimless (denying any absolutes).

THINKING IT THROUGH 20.4

1. Provide two arguments against the view that the scientific method is the only genuinely reliable path to knowledge in all fields of human life.

2. If people don't have the time and expertise to confirm every scientific experiment for themselves, then what must they rely on for their knowledge?

3. Why is it impossible for believers of scientism to deny that they walk by faith?

4. What is a just-so story?

♀5. According to C. S. Lewis and Francis Beckwith, why is rationality incompatible with the worldview of scientism?

CHAPTER REVIEW ANSWERS

Making Connections

1. • frustrated
   • diverted
   • has to study a fallen world
   • mistrusted
   • exalted
   • done by fallen people for fallen purposes

2. empirically discovered knowledge

3. Since there is no ultimate meaning, individuals make up meaning for themselves.

4. because of all the scientific evidence

20 CHAPTER REVIEW

Scripture Memory

Romans 1:25

Making Connections

1. List six ways that science has been affected by the Fall.

2. In scientism's worldview, what is the only kind of knowledge that counts as proof?

3. In scientism's worldview, where does meaning in life come from?

4. In scientism's worldview, why should we trust scientific evidence?

Developing Skills in Apologetics and Worldview

5. How can you go about proving a moral claim (such as that human trafficking is harmful) without using the tools of empirical science?

6. How can you prove that scientism can't justify any moral claims?

Examining Assumptions and Evidence

7. How do wrong worldview models impact the work of science?

8. Is scientism consistently naturalistic? Why or why not?

9. Why is it dangerous to make up your own meaning and morality?

10. Why can't rationality be justified in scientism's worldview?

Becoming a Creative Cultivator

11. Find one current event that exemplifies at least one of the six ways that science has been affected by the Fall. Identify the way in which the Fall has affected science, and explain how it could be corrected with a biblical worldview approach.

10. Scientism can't provide a basis for universal absolutes, which are necessary for reliably rational explanations of reality.

Creative Cultivation

11. Students should apply what they have learned throughout the chapter. For example, students might find an article that discusses the search for water on Mars. Science is diverted in this direction because evolutionists presuppose that water proves the existence of life on another planet, which might explain how life was seeded onto our own planet. However, from a biblical worldview, the mere existence of certain chemicals doesn't prove the evolutionary assumptions or that their model actually works. (Whether on earth or on Mars, they're just shifting the problems of their model from one place to the next.) From the biblical worldview, exploring is good, but motivations and goals can divert that exploration.

TERMS TO REMEMBER

singularity—an unrepeatable, unexplainable event

myth—(1) a widely held but false belief or idea; (2) a traditional story typically involving supernatural beings or events, which may or may not have actually existed or happened

naturalistic fallacy—the *is-ought* problem, which is that science can describe what is but can't determine what ought to be without presupposing a religious worldview or philosophical assumptions that are other than naturalistic

determinism/fatalism—the idea that human freedom is an illusion, that humans don't have wills but are programmed to do whatever the evolutionary machine wants them to do

nihilist—a person who believes in a will to power that crushes anyone in its way

empiricism—the philosophical belief that sensory experience is the ultimate source of all our concepts and knowledge

just-so story—an explanation of reality that is unfalsifiable as long as a larger story of reality continues to be presupposed and through which all evidence is interpreted

true myth—a traditional story typically involving supernatural beings that actually existed and events that actually happened

Developing Skills in Apologetics and Worldview

5. While empirical evidence may come into play to support an ethical claim (the psychological damage, STDs that result from sexual abuse or slavery, etc.), the proof must rest on absolute standards of morality that arise from God's revealed truth about the design of His world and the value of humans. Revelation must be the ultimate source of knowledge that our morality is based on rather than purely scientific empiricism, which can't provide all humans with absolute value if they're just animals trying to survive and trying to pass on their genes.

6. Since scientism excludes all knowledge what is empirical and empirical knowledge is only able to describe what is and not what ought to be, then scientism can't possibly justify any moral claims at all.

Examining Assumptions and Evidence

7. Scientific work will be diverted from solving problems or from using those solutions properly.

8. No, it holds to the unexplained, supernatural event of the big bang—a miracle that can't be empirically explained.

9. Making up your meaning often leads to despondency because of the futility of living up to your self-made dreams. Making up your own morality often leads to injustice toward powerless individuals or groups.

The student will be able to

21.1 Defend the young-earth creationist position.

21.2 Explain why gifted scientists who are Christians, given the opportunity, ought to positively contribute to the good of others and this world.

SECTION OBJECTIVES 21.1

1. Identify the underlying cause of the conflict between young-earth creationists and the wider culture.

2. Outline the major origins models according to their underlying worldview presuppositions.

3. Defend both the historicity of Adam and the absence of death before the Fall.

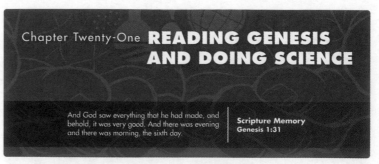

Chapter Twenty-One **READING GENESIS AND DOING SCIENCE**

And God saw everything that he had made, and behold, it was very good. And there was evening and there was morning, the sixth day.

Scripture Memory
Genesis 1:31

21.1 READING GENESIS 1–3 AS FOUNDATIONAL TO A BIBLICAL WORLDVIEW

One of the meanest things today's secular press can call someone is a "fundamentalist." Even the normally gracious *New York Times* columnist David Brooks, for example, complained in one of his regular pieces about "the stupidity of the fundamentalists."

> Fundamentalists are people who take everything literally. . . . They are incapable of seeing that while their religion may be worthy of the deepest reverence, it is also true that most religions are kind of "too weird."[1]

Brooks's columns are actually often friendly to religion[2] (Brooks is a non-observant Jew*[3]). But in this comment about fundamentalists, he's taking the classic liberal line: "Hey, religion is useful for making people nice, but when religious people start *actually believing* that Jesus walked on water or rose from the dead, that's just weird." Brooks isn't talking only about religious weirdos in a cult compound somewhere; his comments are critical of all serious Christians (though he has "fundamentalists" of all religions in mind).

TAKING EVERYTHING LITERALLY

We need to look closely at the leading example of weirdness that Brooks points to, the idea that so-called fundamentalists "take everything literally." There are two major ways you could take this comment. Either he means that fundamentalists take themselves and their world too seriously, or he means that strong religious believers are tone-deaf to literary devices such as metaphor, allegory, and hyperbole. Perhaps he has both ideas in mind.

In any case, Brooks is saying that he knows the standard by which religion and religious reading ought to be judged. He knows which religions count as "too serious," and he knows which interpretations (of the Bible, the Qur'an, the Vedas, etc.) count as "too literal."

And either way, conservative Christians probably don't measure up to Brooks's standards. Conservative Christians believe that countless people around the globe are on what Jesus called the broad way to destruction, and that after their deaths it will be too late for them to find the narrow way that leads to life (Matt. 7:13). Such a worldview tends to make you joyful about God's grace in your life and serious about the fate of others—ten times the New Testament calls on Christians to be "sober."

But let's take up the other possible charge, that conservative Christians are "**literalists**" (i.e., they take the Bible too literally). Most people who make that accusation mean that, according to their worldview, Red Seas don't literally part, big fish don't literally swallow prophets for three days and spit them out, and messiahs don't literally get resurrected.

---

non-observant Jew: *an ethnically Jewish person who does not engage in the religious practices of Judaism*

Lesson Plan Chart—Chapter 21

The Literary Standard

It is indeed possible to read the Bible too literally, as the examples in the text suggest ("I am the door," "Our God is a consuming fire"). But we shouldn't use the phrase *too literally* in a glib way, as if it's obvious to anyone which interpretations count as too literal and which interpretations are just right. How can someone know how to interpret a Scripture passage? The standard for literary judgment isn't something that exists apart from the Bible but is the Bible itself. If the Bible is God's Word (it is) and if God doesn't lie (He doesn't), then the statements of the Bible will fit together logically. The right interpretation will fit with the rest of Scripture. For example, we're told that God is a Spirit, so we know that He's not literally a consuming fire. The context and the rest of Scripture make clear that this is a metaphor.

And most important, universes don't literally get created in six days. The real focus of the common charge that Christians take the Bible too literally is just one passage of Scripture: Genesis 1. In fact, the cultural pressure on Western Christians to abandon a straightforward reading of Genesis 1 is immense. If you don't drop it, you might get called a "fundamentalist" in the *New York Times*.

But Genesis 1 is fundamental to biblical Christianity. If you give it up or change it, you give up (or change) the foundation Creation-Fall-Redemption provides for the entire Christian worldview. Christianity stands or falls with Genesis 1. You can't have your cake and let scientific naturalism eat it too.

REDEEMING SCIENCE

If you're a Christian, you're called to be an agent of redemption, to push the (apparent) conflict between science and religion back into harmony. As part of that calling, you'll have to come to grips with Genesis 1. But the debate over the origins of the universe is so complex, what can you do? Where can you start? We suggest two things:

(1) Recognize the role one's worldview plays in the debate.

(2) Focus on the truly significant theological issues in the area of **origins**,* namely the questions of (a) whether Adam and Eve ever existed and (b) whether there was death before the Fall.

origins: *the study of the beginnings of the universe and human life*

1. Recognizing the role worldview plays in the debate

There's one traditional, straightforward way of reading Genesis 1; there's one totally opposite view—scientific naturalism—in which Genesis 1 is a fairy tale and the big bang is our mother; and there are multiple views in between, all trying to bridge the gap in some way. Some think God guided evolution, others that He got it started and then went on a long vacation.

Christian biologist Gerald Rau has written a helpful book titled *Mapping the Origins Debate*, in which he lays out as objectively as possible the various views on how the cosmos (and life, and species, and humans) came to be. People from all over the spectrum have praised the book; they think Rau was fair to their positions, while recognizing that such a complex issue is hard to summarize. Even the strongly naturalistic National Center for Science Education (the organization that sponsored the "Project Steve" mentioned in Chapter 1) was willing to say that the book "offers a semi-fair analysis of different viewpoints."[6]

Rau begins his book, as we began this unit, by talking about what science and the scientific method are. He argues that every major view of the origins of life and the universe has the same "facts," the same "evidence," to explain. The major models of

READING GENESIS AND DOING SCIENCE | 323

LITERAL OR FIGURATIVE?

The Bible uses countless metaphors; metaphor is a natural feature of every human language. No one could communicate without it. Here's a metaphor you know: "Time is money." Think of all the ways that metaphor shows up in English:

> You're *wasting* my time.
> This gadget will *save* you hours.
> How do you *spend* your time these days?
> That flat tire *cost* me an hour.
> I've *invested* a lot of time in her.
> You need to *budget* your time.
> Is that *worth* your while?
> He's living on *borrowed* time.[4]

These metaphors are so common that we don't even think of them as figures of speech.[5] People are well practiced at metaphor, in other words. So no one is confused when Jesus says, "I am the door" (John 10:7ff.), or when the author of Hebrews says, "Our God is a consuming fire" (Heb. 12:29). No serious Christian takes *everything* in the Bible literally—if seeing Jesus as a literal door and God as a literal fire is what "literally" means.

---

in great doctrinal controversies in the late nineteenth and early twentieth centuries over the truth of Scripture in opposition to liberal modernists. Then, as now, the claims of science about human origins were at the heart of the debate.

Another common denotation of *fundamentalist* is "someone who strictly adheres to a set of basic principles." In that case even secularists could be labeled as fundamentalists. That's not meant to be pejorative; it's simply a recognition of their absolute commitment to their worldview.

Genesis 1 and the Fundamentals

Reading Genesis 1 in its plain sense—as a historical account—is fundamental to biblical Christianity. It's fundamental because reading it as a metaphor undermines a whole host of important biblical doctrines and creational realities.

What is lost if Genesis 1 viewed as primarily a metaphor for God's choice to "anoint" certain evolved hominids as human?

If Genesis 1 is not a historical account, then the metanarrative of Creation, Fall, and Redemption does not cohere.

- Creation can no longer be the standard by which we judge the way things ought to be. Ethics have no creational basis because the nature of reality is redefined. The paradigm of "structure and direction" is undermined. God's character of holiness and goodness is undermined because death, "the last enemy," is present from the beginning.

- The severity of the Fall is mitigated. The groaning of the creation in suffering, death, and frustration (i.e., thorns, thistles, and the like) would become part of God's original "very good" creation.

- Redemption is also affected. If the earth was never a perfectly good place, and if death and suffering are not the result of sin, then redemption is not a promise of restoration to a world as God originally intended it to be. The promise of a new creation without suffering and death ends up being disconnected from the work of Christ to redeem humans from sin.

Some Christians feel pressured to conform the Bible to the latest scientific consensus regarding origins. They fear Christianity will be discredited if they don't. Further, they think they can make this accommodation with little cost. But they lose far more than a few passages that are troublesome for evolution. They lose the entire biblical worldview. Destroy the metanarrative (CFR) and you undermine the beliefs and values that grow out of it. People may still affirm key Christian beliefs, but they have undermined the worldview basis for those beliefs.

It's appropriate and even necessary to ask, "What did Moses mean in Genesis 1?" But it's never appropriate to act as if Genesis 1 stands on its own, as if God hasn't said anything else relevant to the interpretation of that passage. He most certainly has, as the rest of this chapter will show.

The more accurate description of the interpretational approach of conservative Christians is that they hold to the plain sense of Scripture in its historical-grammatical context. The text is meant to be read straightforwardly with clarity. Literary devices are objectively recognizable. Scripture is not meant to be read as if it were encoded. It shouldn't be read entirely as allegory or as mythology.

[For a simple introduction to hermeneutics, see Gordon D. Fee and Douglas Stuart, *How to Read the Bible for All Its Worth*, 4th ed. (Grand Rapids: Zondervan, 2014).]

The Term *Fundamentalist*

Fundamentalist, like *cult*, is generally a derogatory label. When someone uses it pejoratively, as Brooks did, it often has as little content as *cult* usually does. *Fundamentalist* is often a put-down that's used to characterize someone as blindly religious. The term frequently refers to radicalized terrorists.

Even though few people would call themselves "cultists," there still are many American Christians who do call themselves "fundamentalists." Self-described fundamentalists use the term as a way of identifying themselves with a particular theological position in the history of Christianity. They identify with the "fundamentals" of the faith, honoring the heritage of American Christians who engaged

Debating Creation and Evolution

Debating origins is touchy; people feel strongly about their positions. Why? It may seem obvious, but it's worth asking: why is the origin of the universe more controversial than the debate over which grass variety is best for suburban lawns or even the debate over who is the best college football quarterback? The debate over origins is more controversial because people have a deep sense—a sense in their God-given conscience—that their origin says something about their morals. That is, if we were created by a god or gods, we're obligated to them in some important and even daily way. If not, we're free. (Or so we think.)

There are two approaches in most debates:

- The participants are likely to revert quickly to a "modernist" approach to knowledge and evidence. They will argue over the "facts" and ignore the role worldview plays in the interpretation of those "facts."

- One or more of the participants will recognize the role faith plays in knowledge. They will recognize that a worldview lens interprets all of the evidence.

[You may want to show students excerpts from the DVD "Uncensored Science: Bill Nye Debates Ken Ham" (Answers in Genesis, 2014).]

Answering the Charge of Fideism

It's important to distinguish the worldview apologetics approach from the common charge that Christian worldview thinking, is guilty of fideism (i.e., leapfrogging over knowledge into blind faith; see TE note "Fideism in a Nutshell," p. 23).

Are Christians just sticking their heads in the sand and refusing to acknowledge the undeniable facts of science?

[Students should review Chapter 2 to respond to this charge, reasoning according to the following points that were discussed there.]

No, worldview apologetics doesn't ignore or dismiss evidence. It simply notes that evidence must be used in the right way. Just as evidentialists are wrong to discard presuppositions in their search for neutrality, fideists are wrong to rule out evidence in favor of simply appealing to their presuppositions. Both presuppositions and evidence are necessary. The key is to place them in their proper roles. Biblical presuppositions must be the authoritative foundation from which one evaluates the evidence—not the reverse. But evidence does need evaluation. And presuppositions are

falsifiable. The way to falsify a presupposition is to demonstrate that it is self-refuting or inconsistent. The presupposition invalidates itself when the evidence can't even be used in a supportive role to one's admitted presupposition. Every false worldview will be inconsistent with its own presuppositions (Prov. 26:5).

Understanding the Chart

Students need to grasp the basic import of the chart—that God's involvement in His creation increases as you move from left to right. In other words, presuppositions about God determine the interpretation of the evidence. One way to make certain they get it is to display the boxes in the chart in the wrong order and ask students to reorder them as a pop quiz or as a class exercise.

---

how we all got here are different for one reason: "Each [model] flows logically from its philosophical underpinnings."[7] Rau stresses that

each model rests on and is inextricably connected with particular philosophical presuppositions. Apart from that, it is nonsense. Thus, when passing judgment on a particular model, we are usually not judging its logical consistency or ability to explain the evidence as much as its philosophical or religious roots.[8]

As Rau maps out the various models, he notes that the spectrum of major views lines up with "the degree of interaction between the supernatural and natural worlds."[9] The various views can be summarized this way:[10]

NATURALISTIC EVOLUTION	UNDIRECTED EVOLUTION	PLANNED EVOLUTION	DIRECTED EVOLUTION	OLD-EARTH CREATION	YOUNG-EARTH CREATION
There is no supernatural interaction with the natural world because there is no supernatural.	Deism: God started the creation but then let it go its own way.	Deism with a twist: God perfectly laid out the path for evolution in advance but has not been involved since.	God has been actively intervening in the process of evolution from the beginning, but through natural processes.	God jumpstarted major portions of the evolutionary tree at different times throughout history.	God created the entire planet and all life in it within the last 7,500 years in basically the form we see today.

Do you see how God's involvement in His creation increases as you move from left to right in the chart? This observation alone doesn't solve the debate: God can create worlds and run them any way He wants to. But if Rau is right that the various positions all arise out of prior philosophical commitments, the debate becomes a bit simpler. We can focus on the philosophy (or theology) and save the evidence for later. Someone who believes in a deistic God simply won't come to the conclusion that the evidence is in favor of young-earth creationism—or naturalism—until he gives up his deism. Someone who believes that God reigns sovereignly over every detail in His creation naturally will not be interested in the deistic positions on the chart.

World-famous scientist Stephen Hawking is known for his work on black holes and for his best-selling book, *A Brief History of Time*. He's also known for working through the incredible adversity of Lou Gehrig's disease (ALS). He is director of research at the Centre for Theoretical Cosmology at the University of Cambridge in England. He told the *New Scientist* in an interview,

> Science is increasingly answering questions that used to be the province of religion. The one remaining area that religion can still lay a claim to is the origin of the universe, but even here science is making progress and should soon provide a definitive answer to how the universe began.[11]

LIMITS OF HUMAN REASON

In the final paragraph of *A Brief History of Time*, Hawking describes what the goal of scientific naturalism is:

> If we do discover a complete theory [of the universe and its origins], it should in time be understandable in broad principle by everyone, not just a few scientists. Then we shall all, philosophers, scientists, and just ordinary people, be able to take part in the discussion of the question of why it is that we and the universe exist. If we find the answer to that, it would be the ultimate triumph of human reason—for then we would know the mind of God.[12]

Contrast this with Paul's striking statement on knowledge: "'For who has understood the mind of the Lord so as to instruct him?' But we have the mind of Christ" (1 Cor. 2:16).

Rhetorical Strategy with Atheists

Aristotle talked about three major elements of persuasion: *logos* (reason), *pathos* (feeling), and *ethos* (reputation). And when Christians testify to their conversion, they commonly invoke all three. They were persuaded of the truth of the Bible (*logos*); they felt a deep need to have forgiveness for their sins (*pathos*); and they found they were attracted to Christ (*ethos*). Christians are honest about the way persuasion occurred in their lives. But atheists commonly focus only on *logos*. They talk as if they were driven by the evidence alone. They rarely acknowledge the role played by their own attraction to sin (*pathos*) or to society (*ethos*). Christians might bring this up to appeal to the conscience of an atheist: "We're honest about the role things other than reason play in our conversion experiences; why can't you be?"

Stephen Hawking is clearly a person of faith. Everybody is. At the bottom of every model of the earth's origins is a bedrock of belief or trust in some authority.

Just because faith plays a key role in determining your position on the origin of the cosmos doesn't mean any model is OK as long as you really believe it. But the foundational role faith plays in every model cannot be denied either. One key way of living redemptively when it comes to science is helping other people see the role their worldview—their faith—plays in the model they adopt.

THINKING IT THROUGH 21.1A

1. What specific origins position is foundational to biblical Christianity's meta-narrative of Creation, Fall, and Redemption?

2–4. Summarize what differentiates the following positions from one another:
- Naturalistic Evolution versus Undirected Evolution
- Undirected Evolution versus Planned Evolution
- Planned Evolution versus Directed Evolution versus Old-Earth Creation

5. In what way do the major views on creation and evolution correspond to views about the supernatural?

2. Focusing on the truly significant theological and exegetical issues

So which authority do you trust? Which proposed bedrock should your faith rest on? Every serious Christian alive will give the same ultimate answer: you trust God. And God has revealed facts about the origin of the universe in the Bible—specifically (but not only) in Genesis 1.

But interpretations of Scripture themselves arise out of theological presuppositions. Rau says about his chart,

> Each of the six models of origins presented here is intimately wedded to a certain theological interpretation of scripture, so the model and the theology rise or fall together. Since we each have a faith commitment to a certain theology, we also have a faith commitment to a corresponding model. To change our model we also need to change our theology and admit that what we believed is incorrect. This is something few are willing to do, so the conflict continues.[13]

Here are the different views that the major models take on Genesis:

NATURALISTIC EVOLUTION	UNDIRECTED EVOLUTION	PLANNED EVOLUTION	DIRECTED EVOLUTION	OLD-EARTH CREATION	YOUNG-EARTH CREATION
Genesis 1–3 is ancient myth; there is no God.	Genesis 1–3 is ancient myth; there is a God, however.	Genesis 1–3 provides some general theological truths, but Adam and Eve weren't real individuals.	Adam and Eve were real individuals linked to previous ancestors by evolution.	The days of Genesis 1 were not literal twenty-four-hour days. Adam and Eve came from a pre-existing race of hominids but were the first humans.	The days of Genesis 1 were literal twenty-four-hour days; Adam and Eve were created from the dust of the ground.

THINKING IT THROUGH 21.1A

1. young-earth creation with its straightforward reading of Genesis 1

2–4. • While both views consider Genesis 1–3 an ancient myth, **naturalistic evolution** denies the existence and involvement of any supernatural at all, but **undirected evolution** accepts that God initiated the existence of matter and energy.

- While both views consider Genesis 1–3 as nonhistorical and accept God's existence only in a deistic way, **planned evolution** accepts general theological truths from Genesis and posits that, rather than just allowing creation to go its own way, God's original plan is still in force even though He's not directing anything now.

- All three views accept God's hand in creation through evolution.

Planned evolution posits that God is no longer involved and Adam and Eve probably didn't exist as real individuals. Genesis isn't real history.

Directed evolution posits that God is actively involved but only through providential, non-miraculous working. Adam and Eve were real humans, though not necessarily the first two.

Old-earth creation posits that God is not only actively involved but also miraculously involved—making the evolutionary transitions take place. Adam and Eve were the first real human individuals after pre-human hominids.

5. The less people believe in a supernatural being or in God's active and direct involvement in the world, the stronger their belief is in the undirected process of evolution. In other words, a lower view of God and His sovereignty leads to denying the clarity of God's Word.

Scripture as the Final Authority

The Protestant Reformers spoke of Scripture as the "norming norm." They meant that Scripture is the standard that judges all other standards of human knowledge. This even includes the methods of interpretation for understanding Scripture itself.

Someone may challenge: "How can anyone be certain that his own interpretation of Scripture is correct? Human beings are finite and fallen, and some passages are hard to understand (2 Pet. 3:16)."

The answer is:

- God created humans in His image with the capacity for language and logical reasoning. God communicated to humans with the intention that His revelation would be clearly understood. That's why conservative Christians hold to the plain sense of Scripture.

- Scripture teaches people how they should interpret it because they can read how Jesus or the apostles interpreted it.

- While there are different models of interpretation, the basis for those models can be objectively judged.

People who are unaware of the models that underlie variant interpretations often think that the Bible can mean whatever someone wants it to mean. Instead, the validity of the model of interpretation should be examined. Protestants believe that if Scripture is the norming norm, then discovering the sound interpretation is possible when Scripture is interpreted by Scripture. Since the Bible can't contradict itself, passages that are more difficult to understand can be interpreted by passages that make the meaning clear.

The Genre of Genesis

One of the key interpretive issues for understanding Genesis revolves around its genre. Some professing Christians think that they have the solution for making peace with evolution. They say, "Genesis is poetry or metaphor. Once I acknowledged that, then I could accept evolution and keep my Bible."

This is a common argument. But can the historicity of Genesis be so easily swept aside? What is the support for this interpretive model that claims that the creation account is simply poetic and therefore not historical? Other historical accounts in Scripture are set to poetry without compromising the clear acknowledgment of historicity. Psalm 136 is poetry and it accurately describes historical events such as the Exodus from Egypt and the wilderness wanderings.

In addition, other passages recognize the historical reality of God's creative work (John 1:3; Col. 1:16) and the historical reality of

Adam and Eve (Matt. 19:4–5; Luke 3:38; Rom. 5:12; 1 Cor. 15:45–47; 1 Tim. 2:13).

[For further help on interpretational issues with special regard to Genesis, see Jason Lisle, *Understanding Genesis* (Green Forest, AR: Master Books, 2015).]

Framework or History?

One of the most popular figurative interpretations of Genesis today is known as the framework hypothesis. Students should research the young-earth response to this model of interpreting Genesis by using one or more of the following resources. Then they should write a paper that summarizes the framework hypothesis and the young-earth creationist counterarguments.

Robert V. McCabe and Tim Chaffey, "What's Wrong with the Framework Hypothesis?" Answers in Genesis (website), June 21, 2011.

Robert V. McCabe, "A Critique of the Framework Interpretation of the Creation Account," Answers in Genesis (website), June 6, 2007.

Andrew S. Kulikovsky, "A Critique of the Literary Framework View of the Days of Creation," Kulikovsky Online (website), January 5, 2000.

An Unbelievable Lifespan?

While our current experience would lead us to regard any claim of an eight- or nine-hundred-year lifespan as fanciful, Moses treats Adam the same way he treats all the other figures in his many genealogies. He consistently lists their names, their sons' names, and their ages. The details in the biblical text show that the author intends for people to read Genesis as history. For example, "Genesis 1 speaks of years and seasons and days with evenings and mornings governed by the sun, moon, and stars. Genesis 2 describes the location of the Garden of Eden and names four rivers. Genesis 4 names the city that Cain built. Genesis 6–8 describes certain events on specific days of different months of the 600th and 601st years of Noah's life. The eleven occurrences of the Hebrew word *toledoth* scattered through Genesis (in Genesis 2:4, 5:1, 6:9, 10:1, and so on) and translated as 'this the account of' or 'these are the generations of' tie the whole book together as one historical record." [Terry Mortenson, "In Defense of the Historical Adam," Answers in Genesis (website), July 28, 2015.] (Students would benefit from reading the article in its entirety.)

In the case of Noah, the depth of the water is given, as is the location of the boat's landing, the number of sons Noah had, and things he

---

Some disagreements Christians have over the interpretation of Scripture aren't very serious because not every statement in the Bible is equally important. That might sound odd, even sacrilegious. But Jesus Himself said:

> Woe to you, scribes and Pharisees, hypocrites! For you tithe mint and dill and cumin, and have neglected the weightier matters of the law: justice and mercy and faithfulness. These you ought to have done, without neglecting the others. (Matt. 23:23–24)

In other words, the Jews were supposed to give God a tenth of everything, even tiny spices. But pursuing justice, mercy, and faithfulness is more important than counting anise seeds. They weigh more.

How much do you think the creation of man and woman weighs? Is that issue more like counting seeds or more like doing justice and mercy?

We really ought to let the Bible answer that question. We've already argued that Scripture's entire story rests on the creation account in Genesis 1. Now let's discuss some of the evidence, searching out what parts of the creation narrative are most important in the rest of Scripture.

historicity: *historical authenticity; having actually existed or happened in the past*

The two most important elements of Genesis 1, as seen throughout the Bible, are the historicity* of Adam (whether or not he really existed) and the question of death before the Fall. And these two points, as we'll see, are closely related.

The Historicity of Adam

You can't believe in the evolution of humans from earlier, ape-like creatures without turning the Adam story in Genesis 1 into some kind of metaphor (at best). If Adam is the product of evolution, then God didn't take him from the dust of the ground and breathe life into his nostrils. That's all just symbolic. And if Eve is the product of evolution, she wasn't made from Adam's side to be his helper. So maybe "Adam" and "Eve" were just two hominids* to whom God decided to give the gifts of moral conscience and language, or maybe their story is entirely symbolic because the ancient Israelites couldn't understand the big bang. If you reject a straightforward reading of Genesis 1, Adam and Eve can be whatever the latest evolutionary models want them to be.

hominid: *member of a primate family in the evolutionary taxonomy that includes the human species as well as orangutans, gorillas, and chimpanzees*

But Adam and Eve's story is very difficult to read as metaphor or symbolism. For one thing, Adam is given a lifespan that sounds just like those of the other people in Genesis. "All the days that Adam lived were 930 years, and he died" (Gen. 5:5). If Moses (the author of Genesis) intended for Adam to be a mere symbol, that's an odd detail to include. It would be like a stranger at an airport coming up to you and saying, "Excuse me, I'm Sterling Ryznich, and this is my poodle, Sarah, whose mother died last Wednesday. Can you tell me the time?" Why is he giving you all this information? It isn't relevant if his sole purpose is finding out the time.[14] Likewise, if Adam and Eve are mere symbols, why mention Adam's lifespan or Eve's little comments when Cain and Seth were born (Gen. 4:1, 25)?

Granted, Adam's lifespan is nothing like we see today. But it was nothing like what Moses saw, either, and he still faithfully recorded it. In Genesis, lifespans after the Flood are much shorter than lifespans before it.

genealogy: *a record of a person's ancestors*

Several genealogies* in the Old and New Testaments also list Adam, and none of them includes a footnote saying that he didn't really exist. He's treated just like the other people in the family tree of King David and King Jesus (1 Chron. 1–9; Luke 3:38). If Adam didn't really exist as a historical person, did Abraham? Or Joseph? Or anybody else in Genesis? Where does the metaphor stop and the history begin?

---

did after the Flood ended. If we are to reject all the stories of Genesis that don't fit our experience, where do we stop? Did the Joseph story happen? Most slaves in our experience don't rise to second in command of powerful nations. The argument for reading Genesis straightforwardly is the same as the argument for reading the whole Bible straightforwardly: once you start picking and choosing among the parts you find believable and the parts that suddenly can't be taken literally because you find them incredible, you are on the slipperiest of all slopes. God may graciously keep you from slipping any further. But once you admit that the Bible could be wrong, what you find believable becomes the authority standing over the Bible and giving God permission to speak—or not.

Theological Truth and the Historicity of Adam and Eve

Guide students to follow the logic of 1 Timothy 2:12–14. Paul's theological basis for a woman's role in the church is *because* of creational and historical realities—Adam was formed first and Eve was deceived.

Next, guide students to follow the logic of 1 Corinthians 11:7–10. Paul's theological basis for gender roles in the church is reinforced by creational realities that God built into the world historically. The church practice can only make sense precisely because God built a structure into the existence of males and females.

Perhaps even more important, theologically speaking, both Jesus and Paul assume that Adam really existed and that he was created before Eve. As we discussed in Unit 5, Jesus based His whole argument about marriage on the fact that Adam and Eve were "created . . . male and female" and "joined together" by God (Matt. 19:4, 6). Paul makes several points from the fact that "Adam was formed first, then Eve" (1 Tim. 2:13; cf. 1 Cor. 11:9).

Paul also makes an even more significant theological point from the story of Adam, a point about Fall and Redemption. One theologian explained that point very well:

> Paul draws an important analogy [in Romans 5 and 1 Corinthians 15] between Adam and Jesus. Just as the first Adam introduced *sin and death* to all humanity through his disobedience in the garden of Eden (eating the forbidden fruit), now Jesus, the second Adam . . . , introduces *life* through his *obedience*. . . . For Paul's analogy to have any force, it seems that both Adam and Jesus must be actual historical figures. . . . A historical Adam has been the dominant Christian view for two thousand years.[15]

The theologian who wrote that paragraph is Peter Enns, writing in a book called *The Evolution of Adam*. Enns was dismissed in 2005 from the biblically orthodox seminary he taught at because he began to doubt (and later did deny) what he had said in the above quotation. Enns himself laid out the options as he saw them:

1. Accept evolution and reject Christianity. [Enns, to his credit, did not wish to do this.]
2. Accept Paul's view of Adam as binding and reject evolution. [Enns, to his discredit, did not wish to do this either.]
3. Reconcile evolution and Christianity by positing a first human pair (or group) at some point in the evolutionary process. [Back to Enns's credit, he just couldn't make this option work with what the Bible says.]
4. Rethink Genesis and Paul.[16]

LOOKING FOR EVE?

If you search an online Bible for *Eve*, you'll get just four hits. Her name appears twice in the Old Testament and twice in the New. But one app allows you to search for "Person: Eve" and pick up all the references to her in Scripture, even if she's just called "Adam's wife" or "the woman." You'll find more than eighty references to her that way.

RETHINKING GENESIS

Among conservative theologians who profess to believe in the truth of Scripture, John Walton has probably done the most ingenious job of making Genesis fit modern evolutionary theory.

Walton views the passage literally—sort of. In his view it is an account of the origin of the world, but it is not a scientific account—nor one that should be harmonized with science. Instead it is an ancient account full of ancient symbolism. He is confident that *create* means "give function to" or "make useful." In other words, God took the physical stuff already in existence and gave it new functions. Walton says that the seven days of creation reveal what the function of the creation is. Ancient temples were dedicated in seven-day ceremonies. The function of the seven days in Genesis 1 is to take the already existing creation and give it the function of a cosmic temple for God.[17]

But careful readers have raised serious questions about Walton's approach. (1) Other Hebrew scholars doubt Walton's claim that *create* means "give function to." They point to numerous instances in which the Hebrew word is not being used to grant functions and other contexts in which material creation is in view.[18] (2) Walton himself is forced to admit that the dedications of ancient temples were not always seven days in length.[19] The Israelite tabernacle, for instance, was dedicated in a single day (Exod. 40). (3) For Walton's view to be true, he has to be sure that he is correctly interpreting the cultural background information that he insists must shape the interpretation of Genesis 1. But other scholars, who are equally expert in this material, do not always share Walton's interpretation of the evidence.[20]

Unless the way God created the world is the standard by which we judge the way things ought to be, it makes no sense to say that the order of creation (Adam, then Eve) has any bearing on who spoke in church and who wore head coverings. But Paul grounded church practice in the simple historical fact that Adam was formed first.

Rethinking Genesis

Theistic evolutionists have recently argued for a reinterpretation of Genesis 1–2 on the basis of Ancient Near Eastern (ANE) studies. They argue that a straightforward reading of a text is the reading that the original author intended and the original audience would have understood. They claim that in light of the way creation stories in the ANE worked, we should not expect Genesis 1 to

be a literal historical account or even an account of the origins of the material world. Background information is beneficial to the student of the Bible, but note these caveats:

- Our records of what ancient cultures thought is necessarily incomplete and fragmentary; as a result, many reconstructions are disputed even among experts in the field (1 Tim. 1:4).
- Understanding ANE material itself requires interpretation, and these documents are less studied and less complete than the biblical manuscripts.
- While the original recipients of Scripture may well have thought similarly to other people in the ancient world about a whole host of matters, one of the purposes of revelation was to enable them to think differently on matters of theological significance, such as the origin of the world.

Option 4

While those holding to Option 3 try to fit evolution into a traditional conservative reading of Scripture, those holding to Option 4 demand a completely new reading.

In this view, "[Genesis] should be understood figuratively within its own Ancient Near Eastern context. In other words, it is like an ancient story or parable that was originally intended to teach higher truths about God. Thus, it is ahistorical and never speaks to historical or scientific truths." [Jimmy Tuck, "Peter Enns's Hermeneutic of Creation: In Step or Misstep?" *Frontline* 23 (November/December 2013): 6–7]

But in order to defend this interpretation, the inspiration and infallibility of Scripture must be redefined:

> For Enns, inspiration is similar to Christ's incarnation. It is both divine and human [which requires] God's submitting to humans' ways of thinking even if those ways were wrong. Thus, [in Enns's view] God accommodated His message to the worldview of the ancient times, and He used ancient myths or stories to reveal truths about Himself to His people. Furthermore, Enns argues that those who penned God's Word were subject to their own sinful condition and finite perspective, and their culture clouded their thinking and tainted the words they wrote. As a result, claims Enns, Scripture contains errant ideas and mistaken statements that reflect ancient thinking. [Tuck, 6]

How would you respond to these claims? What questions could you ask someone like Peter Enns?

- *If some of the Bible is erroneous, which parts are true and who decides?*
- *Didn't the role of the Holy Spirit prevent erroneous human ideas from being put into Scripture? [John 17:17; 1 Cor. 2:13; 1 Thess. 2:3–4; 2 Tim. 3:16; 2 Pet. 1:20–21]*
- *Why would the erroneous ancient mindset dictate the mindset of the biblical authors? Should the current "scientific" consensus dictate our interpretation today if humans are so prone to error? [1 Cor. 1:17–31]*
- *If Paul's theology of sin and salvation stems from a myth, then what's the basis for still accepting the gospel? [1 Cor. 15:45–49]*

[For further refutation of Enns, see Lee Anderson Jr., "A Response to Peter Enns's Attack on Biblical Creationism," *Answers Research Journal* 6 (2013):117–35, especially 126–27.]

Making Yourself the Authority

Augustine points out the fundamental issue with those who would pick and choose from Scripture. Is the text authoritative, or is the reader authoritative? Proponents of the radical reader response theory believe that the reader is authoritative (i.e., the reader determines the meaning). Conservative Christians believe that the meaning is found within the text of Scripture (i.e., that the reader discovers the meaning). Radical reader response theorists believe that the reader ultimately judges the text. Conservative Christians believe that the Living Word ultimately judges the reader.

All those who read the Bible do so according to a set of expectations and rules—standards that determine what they'll accept, what they'll reject, and how they'll interpret what they read. This is true of Christians as well as non-Christians. The key difference between those two sets of readers is, or at least ought to be, that non-Christians tend not to let the Bible itself be the standard by which they read, whereas Christians always at least attempt to let the Bible be its own standard of interpretation.

Here's an example. In their scientism, modern secularists read about Christ's miracles in the Gospels or the ten plagues in Exodus and conclude that these things either never happened or are embellishments based on coincidences. Why do they interpret it that way? Secularists apply a standard for Bible interpretation based on their presupposition that the order of the cosmos is fixed immutably and that these natural laws can never be stretched, broken, or suspended. They make natural laws an idol and set them above God's revelation of Himself. But this is a faith-based view—how can they know that natural laws are immutable? Christians read about the miracles and conclude that this is the kind of world in which miracles can happen, and this is the kind of God who can cause them. Why? Christians can interpret it this way because of their presupposition that the world was created by an all-powerful God.

Jesus Permits Disagreement?

Ask students to read John 12:44–48.

What does the Student Text mean when it says on this page that "Jesus, in this age, permits you to disagree" with the Bible?

It doesn't mean that Jesus approves. It means that He will delay judgment until His Second Coming. At that time, those who didn't believe will be judged on the basis of the very truth of Jesus' words that they refused to accept.

The final option is what Enns went for, and this is how he did it: he said, "The fact that Paul considered Adam to be the progenitor of the human race does not mean that we need to find some way to maintain his view."[21] Enns said we have to "leave room for the ancient writers [of Scripture] to reflect and even incorporate their ancient, mistaken cosmologies* into their scriptural reflections."[22]

In other words, the apostle Paul was simply wrong.

People like Enns commonly laugh at ignorant "fundamentalists" (there's that word again) who, they say, need to stop reading so "literalistically." But in doing so, they're laughing at Jesus and Paul too.

The best answer to any argument that says Paul (let alone Jesus) was wrong is the question that Augustine of Hippo asked many centuries ago (see sidebar): if you reject one thing the Bible says, what's to stop you from rejecting everything? Either the Bible carries God's authority, or it doesn't. Jesus and Paul say Adam was a historical figure. Jesus, in this age, permits you to disagree. But

cosmology: a theory or model of how the physical universe began and how it works

> **PICKING AND CHOOSING FROM SCRIPTURE**
>
> Augustine (AD 354–430), who lived in the North African city of Hippo, wrote the following to Faustus, a bishop in the Manichaean religion that Augustine himself once followed. The founder of Manichaeism believed that Jesus' revelation was incomplete.
>
> It is one thing to reject the books [of the Bible] themselves, and to profess no regard for their authority, as the Pagans reject our Scriptures, and the Jews the New Testament . . . ; and it is another thing to say, "This holy man wrote only the truth, and this is his epistle, but some verses are his, and some are not." And then, when you are asked for a proof, instead of referring to more correct or more ancient manuscripts, or to a greater number, or to the original text, your reply is, "This verse is his, because it makes for me; and this is not his, because it is against me." Are you, then, the rule of truth? Can nothing be true that is against you?[23]

those who want to live redemptively and bring healing to the world must trust the authority of their Creator. A rock-solid faith in God's Word is one of the best gifts you can give to the world.

Death Before the Fall

The second truly significant theological issue in the origins debate also has to do with Adam, though not with his creation but with his fall. Just as Paul's writings are one of the key reasons Christians are not free to believe that Adam and Eve are mere symbols or metaphors, Paul provides strong theological reasons to believe that a man named Adam truly fell, bringing evil and death into the world. Paul wrote in his rich letter to the Roman Christians,

> Sin came into the world through one man, and death through sin, and so death spread to all men. . . . Death reigned from Adam to Moses, even over those whose sinning was not like the transgression of Adam. (Rom. 5:12–14)

Death came into the world "through sin," beginning with Adam. So how could death have happened for millions of years before that, as in the evolutionary view?

Paul says that death came into the world through the sin of Adam. Some readers say that Paul meant only human death, not animal death. (Even animal death makes some of the six models on Gerald Rau's chart impossible—which ones?) But think about Genesis 3. Clearly, the animal creation was affected by Adam's fall. And a few pages after Romans 5, in Romans 8, Paul details how it was affected. Read carefully, with CFR in mind:

> The creation was subjected to futility, not willingly, but because of him who subjected it, in hope that the creation itself will be set free from its bondage to corruption and obtain the freedom of the glory of the children of God. For we know that the whole creation has been groaning together in the pains of

---

Evolutionary Models Disqualified by Animal Death

Which of the six models on Gerald Rau's chart become impossible to believe even if only animals (and not humans) experienced death before the Fall?

Naturalistic evolution, undirected evolution, and planned evolution are not affected by self-inconsistency because those views don't even claim to believe in the historicity of Genesis or Adam and Eve. Therefore, death of any kind doesn't matter because humans were never historically cursed with death because of sin.

Directed evolution and old-earth creation are inconsistent with themselves. Those views claim to believe in a historical Genesis (in some sense), and they claim to believe in a historical Adam and Eve (in some sense). But they

claim that Adam and Eve were related to pre-hominids or non-human ancestors (animals) that died. Death of any kind matters because the entrance of death into the world was due to Adam's sin, according to Scripture. But how could Adam's animal relatives face the same consequences prior to the Adamic curse for sin?

A Summary of Paul's Argument in Romans 8:17–25

Have students read each verse in conjunction with New Testament scholar Thomas Schreiner's summary of the thought-flow in Romans 8:17–25 shown in the chart on the next page. (The numbers in parentheses indicate the verse numbers in Romans 8.)

[Chiasm adapted from Thomas R. Schreiner, *Romans*, Baker Exegetical Commentary on the New Testament (Grand Rapids: Baker Books, 1998), 6:432–433.]

childbirth until now. And not only the creation, but we ourselves, who have the firstfruits of the Spirit, groan inwardly as we wait eagerly for adoption as sons, the redemption of our bodies. (Romans 8:20–23)

The creation, Paul says, has been "subjected to futility" and is in "bondage to corruption." It's "groaning . . . in the pains of childbirth." And that, to state the obvious, is bad. And yet if evolutionary models of the origin of animal and human life are accurate, this death, futility, corruption, groaning, and pain had been going on for millions of years before Adam and Eve came along.

> *"Why must God the Son become incarnate, live our life, die our death, and be raised for our justification? Scripture's answer is clear: We need a redeemer because Adam as the first man and covenantal head of the human race brought sin, death, and destruction into this world, and it is only by the last Adam, our Lord Jesus Christ, that it can be paid for and reversed."*[24]
>
> —STEPHEN WELLUM

So here's the key question: Could God possibly have called such a world "good," as He does in Genesis 1? Could God have looked at millions of years of dead panda babies and said with satisfaction, "This is very good"? And think about the layers of fossils, every one of them representing the drowning, disease, or dismemberment of an animal. Think about your own dog getting his throat punctured by a wolf and his legs ripped off, his intestines exposed. Think about your grandma, her body eaten away from the inside out with cancer. *Is this good?*

All theories of evolution—all of them—say that death is necessary, if not exactly good. Death at least brings progress. Evolution is time and death, time and death.

Paul, in contrast, says that death came into this world through sin. Paul, under the inspiration of the Holy Spirit, says that the creation itself is waiting, groaning for death to end.

Christians who believe in evolution do have explanations for how God could call the world "very good" in Genesis 1. They say, for example, that God called the world "good," not perfect; they say that sin brought spiritual death to humans, but physical death was already present.[25]

They can say this, but by doing so they create further problems. The impulse to put the Bible together with evolution has always been defended by saying that if

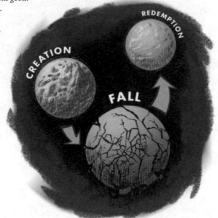

Suffer with Christ in order to be glorified with him (17),
    because present sufferings are minimal compared to our future glory (18),
        and this future glory is so stupendous that all of creation eagerly anticipates the revelation of God's children (19).
            For creation also was subjected to futility by God since the curse of Genesis 3:16–19, and thus it also awaits the day of the liberation of God's children, for on that day it will be freed from corruption (20–21).
                Let me [Paul says] restate the main point of verses 20–21. To this very day creation groans together and suffers birth pangs together, longing for its freedom (22).
            Creation is not the only entity that groans and waits for future glory, but we believers groan and wait for the consummation of our adoption, the future redemption of our body (23b).
        The reason we groan is that we have the firstfruits of the Spirit, and thus we long for our completion (23a).
    We should not be surprised that we have not yet realized all the blessings of our redemption since hope by definition means that future blessings are not yet ours (24).
Thus in the present we wait with endurance for the completion of our hope (25).

Romans 8 makes clear that the whole of creation (animals are part of that creation) was subjected to God's curse when Adam sinned, and the whole of creation (including animals) will be restored to a peaceful existence when God's curse on humanity is removed (Isa. 11:6; 65:25). Those who try to argue that animal death preceded God's curse due to human sin can't reconcile their position with this metanarrative described in Romans 8. In addition, Genesis 3:21 (cf. 3:7) implies that animal death was a consequence of the curse just as thorns and thistles were a new phenomenon (Gen. 3:18). This fits in with the fact that, originally, animals were not to be eaten—even by other animals (Gen. 1:29–30). If all things must be restored because all things have been affected by the Fall, then all things (including animals) were free from the conditions of the Fall (death) before human sin entered the world (Acts 3:21).

For further reading:

Ken Ham, "Was There Death Before Adam Sinned?" Answers in Genesis (website), April 25, 2014.

Simon Turpin, "Did Death of Any Kind Exist Before the Fall?" Answers in Genesis (website), April 3, 2013.

Words Must Reflect Reality

The word *good* in Genesis 1:31 can't mean its opposite. The Student Text isn't intending to be grotesque by describing some of the details of what happens to bring about death and suffering. It's simply trying to confront students with the reality of it. Someone might be able to convince you that something horrible is really good by presenting it to you in the abstract. But the reality of it makes its horridness undeniable.

Good may be *called* evil, and evil may be *called* good (Isa. 5:20). But eventually people snap back to reality when they have an up-close-and-personal experience with the reality of evil. At that point, they can't call evil good. The Bible clearly indicates that death is bad (Ps. 116:3). It's something to be delivered from (Ps. 116:8). And that deliverance is accomplished through the deliverance from sin (1 Cor. 15:55–57).

Making the Problem Worse

Trying to make evolution fit into one's theology creates problems with interpreting the actual text of Scripture—like Paul's and Jesus' comments assuming the existence of a historical Adam. But accommodating evolution also creates distinct problems for apologetics—precisely the kind of problem apologetics is designed to avoid. How? Christians who accept evolution think that they're avoiding a major objection to the

Christian faith from nonbelievers—now they won't scoff at us for not believing in evolution. But by doing so, these compromising Christians have provided an opening for an equally big challenge. If evolution is the biggest *scientific* challenge to the Christian faith, then the problem of evil is the biggest *philosophical* challenge to the Christian faith. Recently philosophers have argued that the severity and scope of animal suffering is incompatible with the goodness of an all-powerful God. Traditionally, Christians have argued that all death and suffering is the result of human sinfulness. The whole creation suffers because its vice-regent sinned. But Christians who embrace evolution are left without a defense to the problem of animal suffering since they must confess that God created and called good a world that contained animal suffering before the Fall.

A Slippery Slope

The slippery slope argument is a fallacy only when the claim is that one misstep *necessarily* leads to the next misstep. However, it is still legitimate to argue that one misstep has often been observed to lead to other missteps. It's *possible*; it may even be *likely*. Denying the straightforward message of Genesis 1–3 is, in fact, that kind of slippery slope. Not every Christian who has accepted theistic evolution has slipped to the bottom. But every Christian who has accepted theistic evolution does have an inconsistent worldview that undermines the gospel he professes to believe. This is just as dangerous as getting smallpox. Sure, you might survive it, but nobody wants to get it.

The Problem of Unbelief

The creation/evolution debate is actually a matter of belief/unbelief. Bible-believing Christians shouldn't be intimidated by the intellectuals of this world or even by ordinary people) who consider belief in creation ignorant (Ps. 119:99; Rom. 1:21; 1 Cor. 1:25; 2 Cor. 4:4; Eph. 4:17–18). "Let God be true though every one were a liar" (Rom. 3:4).

Christians ignore scientific consensus, Christianity and the Bible will be discredited. But evolution isn't the only challenge to a biblical worldview. One of the other major challenges is the question of how an all-good, all-powerful God could create a world with so much death and suffering. Bible-believing Christians have always had a solid scriptural answer: death and suffering came through the Fall of Adam. But theistic evolutionists can't say that; for them, death has always been around. They avoid the error of atheism by disagreeing with much of modern biology and geology, but they have created another problem: blaming God and not humans for suffering and death.

Christians ought to know in their consciences and from their Bibles that death doesn't belong here. Christians should also know that death will one day be "swallowed up in victory" by the work of Jesus Christ (1 Cor. 15:54).

WHAT DAVID BROOKS REALLY MEANT

When David Brooks of the *New York Times* criticized "fundamentalists" for "tak[ing] everything literally," what he really meant was something like this:

> You ought to read the Bible according to a standard other than itself—namely my standard. My worldview standard says that doing justice, loving mercy, and walking humbly are good. So take Micah 6:8 literally. But my worldview standard says that God didn't create the world in six twenty-four-hour days, so don't take Genesis 1 literally.

But if you read the Bible according to the standards the Bible sets for itself—if you let the whole Bible speak—Adam has to be a historical figure; he has to be the person who brought sin and death (for animals and humans) into the world. We have a question of authority: who gets to determine which parts of the Bible we're allowed to believe? Remember, the decision not to trust God's words is always a decision to trust someone else's. And without Creation as the Bible presents it, Fall and Redemption aren't resting on any foundation.

Before Charles Darwin persuaded educated Western people that their great-great-grandparents were primates, no one ever read Genesis 1 to say that Adam was a metaphor for human moral consciousness. They read it to mean that God created Adam, breathing life into dirt.. You're dirt too. The Bible compares us all, in fact, to clay on a potter's wheel (Rom. 9:21). And when the Potter talks, it's a good idea to listen hard—even if other pieces of clay are contradicting everything He says.

THINKING IT THROUGH 21.1B

1. If Adam and Eve are actually the products of evolution, why must their creation in Genesis 1 be reinterpreted as a metaphor?

2. Why is it problematic to reinterpret Adam and Eve's creation as a metaphor?

3. Why must a biblical Christian reject the view that Paul was mistaken about Adam being a historical person?

♀ 4. Could God call a world full of painful animal death "very good"? Why or why not?

THINKING IT THROUGH 21.1B

1. The descriptions in Genesis of their direct creation (how God formed Adam from dust and Eve from his rib) contradict the evolutionary story of development over time from pre-hominids. The descriptions in Genesis have to be explained away somehow.

2. They are given specific lifespans, included in historical genealogies, and identified as historical people by both Jesus and Paul.

3. Biblical Christians believe that the biblical writers were borne along by the Holy Spirit so that the Scripture they wrote is without error. Furthermore, Paul's view was the same as Jesus' view. The Bible's claim to be revelation from the Creator is undermined if its truthfulness is denied at any point.

♀4. God couldn't have declared His creation good in Genesis 1 even if only the nonhuman world was already subject to physical death and futility. According to Romans 8, the whole creation (that would include animals) being subjected to futility is bad. Because this futility is in fact due to human sin, creation awaits its own redemption/restoration at the time of humankind's final redemption.

21.2 CHRISTIANS IN THE SCIENCES

No one is in charge of science. Not the top scientist in the biology department at Harvard or Cambridge or MIT. Not a science czar at the United Nations. Not the author of a book on the *New York Times* list of science bestsellers. No one person sets the "rules" for how science is practiced. And no one can change the rules. They are agreed upon, more or less, by the scientific community. And that community itself has fuzzy boundaries. Who counts as a "scientist"? It depends, to a degree, on which scientist you ask. For all the vaunted objectivity of science, scientists manage to have some pretty heated arguments and even to trade personal insults. "John Christy has made a scientific career out of being wrong," said one prominent scientist about a Christian climatologist (in private e-mails that went public in 2009). "He's not even a third-rate scientist."[26] Why the mockery and the put-downs if science is all about objective data? The reality is that "science is like any other social network. It's a lot easier to go along with the crowd."[27]

And the crowd has made its expectations pretty clear. "No supernatural beings allowed" is right at the top of the list. Second place may go to "The universe is basically the way it has always been." As evolutionary materialist Bill Nye put it to Christian creationist Ken Ham in a public debate viewed by millions, "Natural laws that applied in the past apply now."[28]

Like Ham, many scientists believe that a supernatural being created the world, and that this world is most emphatically *not* the way it's supposed to be—it's fallen. How can such people hope to make it in the world of science?

Sometimes they don't make it, as Chapter 11 in the Redemption unit pointed out. In this age, God promises His people suffering along with whatever victories He chooses to give. It's hard to work, let alone to rise to a place of influence, in a scientific profession that says you don't count as a scientist. It's harder in some fields than in others, depending on how far away from creational norms those fields have been bent. Besides that, Paul informs us,

> We do not wrestle against flesh and blood, but against the rulers, against the authorities, against the cosmic powers over this present darkness, against the spiritual forces of evil in the heavenly places. (Eph. 6:12)

Faithful Christians in Western science will run into opposition of one kind or another. And when they do, they need to push back—nicely.

PUSHING BACK NICELY

That pushback, in fact, needs to be not just nice but full of genuine love—love for God, for one's neighbor, and for the creation. A Christian full of that love and gifted by God to be a scientist can do truly great things. And those great things will be even more effective than pointing out the Christian origins of science. If scientifically trained and gifted Christians let their lights so shine before others that those others save money—or increase the safety of their kids, or experience healing, or benefit from one of the countless other gifts good science and technology can bring—it will be hard to argue that Christianity is antiscience. If you have scientific gifts, use them to serve your neighbor, and see what good will come. Christians should be known more for their good works in science, for positive things, than for saying "no" to the reigning scientific consensus about evolution or naturalism.

SECTION OBJECTIVES 21.2

1. Explain why some gifted scientists may find it harder to take advantage of certain opportunities in the scientific community.

2. Give examples of work done by some scientists who self-identify as Christians that has positively contributed to the advancement of science.

3. Recognize both the imperfection of Christian scientists because of the Fall and the abilities of non-Christian scientists because of God's common grace.

4. Explain why the biblical worldview provides a foundation for doing the work of science.

5. Use their own gifts to actively identify and solve real-life problems for themselves and others.

A Two-Pronged Strategy

In regard to the Ken Ham and Bill Nye debate, Rick Phillips commented:

> It was glaringly obvious that Ham and Nye view the data before them through the lenses of two differing worldviews. While this is obvious to Christians (and Ken Ham freely admitted this), secularists are oblivious to the presuppositions which determine their doctrines. This is why the only approach that can be reasonably fruitful in debates like this is one that subjects the underlying assumptions to critique.

[Rick Phillips, "Lessons from Ken Ham vs. Bill Nye Creation Debate," Reformation 21 (website), February 6, 2014]

Phillips also opined that

> Ham's most effective tactic was showing video clips of creationist scientists who have made important contributions to society. It was hard for Nye to advance his central thesis that American scientific progress requires intolerance to creationism when Ham had just shown a creationist who helped invent the MRI machine. For Christians concerned with reaching the culture, this situation urges us to become more engaged with society at every level. The more that secularists interact with thoughtful, contributing Christians—at the workplace, in the university classroom, or on the Little League baseball diamond—the less secularist despisers will succeed in the strategy of demonization that insulates non-Christians from exposure to biblical truth and Christian love. [Phillips, "Lessons from Ken Ham vs. Bill Nye Creation Debate"]

This is precisely the argument of this section. Christians should use this as part of their strategy. They aren't just attacking evolution but positively contributing to science.

Science Without Evolution

Regardless of whether they were true Christians, many past scientists would have presupposed the biblical metanarrative as they did the work of science. They didn't need to presuppose the evolutionary metanarrative to place the evidence into a successful model for making scientific discoveries and technological advances.

Famous scientists that did successful work without an evolutionary model include Isaac Newton, Gregor Mendel, Louis Pasteur, Johann Kepler, Galileo Galilei, Robert Boyle, Blaise Pascal, Michael Faraday, James Joule, Joseph Lister, and James Clerk Maxwell.

For enrichment, you may have students research and report on the valuable contributions of one of these scientists of the past.

Contemporary Creationists

If you search online for lists of creationists involved in science, you'll find quite a number—a list much longer than the one in the Student Text. Have students look over the list, pick out a figure, and write two paragraphs on his or her accomplishments.

Alternatively, you can have students search for the term *creation scientists* on the Answers in Genesis website. They will find not only brief biographies of creation scientists but also articles that disprove the claims of evolutionists that creation scientists don't do science. Have students discuss their findings.

[Ken Ham, "Bill Nye Program (Unwittingly) Praises Creationist Research," Answers in Genesis (website), March 6, 2015]

A University Cancer Research Lab

Christians can do their small part in taking dominion even in their little corner of the world.

The Bob Jones University Cancer Research Lab opened in 2010 as a result of a large grant from a private donor in memory of her husband who died from cancer. It is housed in the former Barge Memorial Hospital on the BJU campus. Dr. Steve Figard is the research director for the lab, and he has taken students to scientific conferences and conventions to make presentations, such as a poster presentation made at the annual American Institute for Cancer Research (AICR) Conference. The two-day conference, held in Washington, DC, featured nearly a hundred presenters from colleges and universities around the world. Medical schools and laboratories from such schools as Ohio State University, Johns Hopkins University, Tufts University, University of South Carolina, and the University of Paris were all on hand to make presentations to the hundreds of delegates assembled.

"It was an incredible opportunity for Bob Jones University to be featured as a presenter at an international cancer research conference," said participant Danny Machado, a junior biology major from Guatemala. "While what we presented was preliminary work, it was the beginning of putting BJU's Cancer Research Laboratory on the map."

Their research project, "Partial Characterization of the Extraction Method for and Treatment with a Potential Anti-Cancer Agent from Almonds," originally began as a research project while Dr. Amy Tuck, BJU biology faculty member, was serving as the interim director of cancer research. Students at BJU had been working on the project for three years and were able to accumulate sufficient data by 2014 to make their poster presentation. The students designed and executed a set of experiments using almonds in their quest to find a natural substance to eliminate gastric cancer cells.

"From an academic perspective, it was a privilege to interact with health professionals and research directors from medical schools around the world," said participant Anthony Nye, a senior biology major from Indianapolis, Indiana. "This conference brought together international experts in cancer research and it was a privilege for BJU to participate."

Many, many conservative Christian scientists around the world are doing precisely this kind of good scientific work in a wide range of scientific fields. The mere existence of every one of these believing scientists is pushing back nicely against the opposition Christianity faces from much of the scientific community. Here are just a few examples.

John Baumgardner

John Baumgardner, a creationist with a PhD in geophysics and space physics from the University of California at Los Angeles, developed a computer model called "Terra" that predicts how the earth's crust might react under certain conditions. He used Terra to make a model for how Noah's flood may have occurred, and the program is so robust that it is used by geophysicists all over the world. *U.S. News & World Report* called Baumgardner "the world's pre-eminent expert in the design of computer models for geophysical convection, the process by which the Earth creates volcanoes, earthquakes, and the movement of the continental plates." [29]

MRI: (magnetic resonance imaging) a device that produces an image of internal organs

Raymond V. Damadian

Raymond V. Damadian is a good example of a scientist who has pushed back. He developed the science behind the MRI* and built an operational prototype. And he's a committed young-earth creationist.

Danny Faulkner and Ron Samec

Ron Samec and Danny Faulkner are astronomers who have written and contributed to many scientific papers with titles such as "Photometric Study of the Solar Type Pre-Contact Binary, V2421 Cygni." [30] They have done a good deal of work on binary star systems, pairs of stars which orbit around a common center—work which helps us understand the physical forces operating in our universe.

Steve Figard

Steve Figard is a conservative Christian, a young-earth creationist with a PhD in biochemistry from Florida State University. He has made numerous contributions to his field, especially in cancer research. He developed "five immunoassays related to cancer (free and total PSA, CEA, AFP and CA19-9)." [31] In layman's terms, he developed tests that can detect the presence of cancer. Figard directs the Cancer Research Lab at Bob Jones University.

John Hartnett

John Hartnett is an expert in the design of atomic clocks. He has numerous professional publications. His creation research has focused on the development of a creationist cosmology, one using a modified metric tensor coupled with Einstein's general theory of relativity. [32]

Mark Horstemeyer

Mark Horstemeyer is the chairman of computational solid mechanics at the Center for Advanced Vehicular Systems (CAVS) and a professor of mechanical engineering

Doing research and making presentations and papers is how work gets done in science.

["BJU Students Make Presentation to International Cancer Research Conference" Bob Jones University (website), November 17, 2014]

Keeping Evolution Honest

One reason the Christian community needs to keep sending young-earth creationists out into the scientific community is that evolutionists need to be kept honest.

First, instead of pretending that nature figured things out, creationists point out all of the scientific intelligence that directed experimentation to arrive at desired results.

Second, without direction and without an ethical basis, scientific endeavors are prone to abuses. Christian influence in the culture

gives a platform for God's common grace. And secularists are more prone to borrow from Christian ethics because God's creation works best when humans live according to God's structure of the world.

Answers Research Journal

Many students may already be familiar with articles from Answers in Genesis—most of which are written for nonexperts. Those articles need to be written on a more popular level to reach teens and adults who aren't experts in a scientific or theological specialty. But students need to realize that creation scientists and theologians also write at a much higher level—scientifically and philosophically. They deal with technical subjects for experts in their field. (Some students who have gone on to higher education assume that creation scientists are all

at Mississippi State University. He has numerous professional publications and is an expert in the computational modeling of physical materials. He has been an editor for the *Proceedings of the International Conference on Creationism*, which has been very influential in the push to develop rigorous models of science based on Scripture.[33]

D. Russell Humphreys

Humphreys worked for Sandia National Laboratories from 1979 to 2001. His research for Sandia ranged from nuclear physics to superconductors. Later on at the Institute for Creation Research, he worked on the RATE project—Radioisotopes and the Age of The Earth—which challenged evolutionists by proving the presence of helium in zircon crystals, where the evolutionary model predicts no helium. Humphreys has also contributed many papers to peer-reviewed creationist journals. He is on the board of directors of the Creation Research Society, the oldest creationist organization in the United States. He has developed a creationary model for planetary magnetic fields and has made pioneering efforts in creation-based cosmologies.[34]

Georgia Purdom

Georgia Purdom received a PhD in molecular genetics from Ohio State University in 2000; she has worked for Answers in Genesis and has led the Microbe Forum, a group researching the role of microbes in the world before and after the Fall.

Joel Salatin

In the science of sustainable local farming practices, Joel Salatin is a recognized leader. He calls himself a "Christian libertarian environmentalist capitalist lunatic farmer" (and he should add "punchy writer" to the list—the man can write, and he's the author of multiple books and articles). One journalist said of Salatin, "He's not going back to the old model. . . . He is just looking totally afresh at how to maximize production in an integrated system on a holistic farm. He's just totally innovative."[35] Salatin is out speaking a hundred days a year, promoting his farming methods. He says, "What we aspire to is to have the best food available."[36]

John Sanford

Sanford was a professor at Cornell University for more than twenty-five years. His research focused on plant genetics. While a professor, he invented the "gene gun" and contributed to developing better crops. He published a book, *Genetic Entropy and the Mystery of the Genome*, that extends Haldane's dilemma into modern terms. His book clearly demonstrates that the human genome cannot be millions of years old based on mutation rates.[37]

> ### PEER-REVIEWED CREATIONIST JOURNALS
>
> Peer review is the system whereby articles submitted for publication in scholarly journals are subject to blind review by other experts (blind in that those reviewers aren't told the names of the authors whose papers they're evaluating). There are currently three peer-reviewed creationist publications:
> - *Creation Research Society Quarterly*
> - *Journal of Creation*
> - *Answers Research Journal*

---

amateurs who can only write for a popular audience.)

One example of the kinds of articles you can find in *Answers Research Journal* was written by the lead author of the Student Text. Here's the abstract summarizing his article:

> Literary theorist and prominent public intellectual Stanley Fish is a self-described "antifoundationalist"—someone who believes that truth is relative to one's "interpretive community." As such, he provides an as-your-own-poets-hath-said opportunity for Christian apologists. He is particularly helpful in puncturing the inflated claims of Enlightenment secularist liberalism, and along with it the scientism that underlies much public discourse in the West. Fish can be useful to theological conservatives, and creationists in particular.

John Frame's approach to presuppositional apologetics, and in particular his "tri-perspectivalism," are helpful tools making possible a careful Christian appropriation of Fish's work.

[Mark Ward Jr., "The Dwarfs Are for the Dwarfs: Stanley Fish the Pragmatic Presuppositionalist," *Answers Research Journal* (website), July 10, 2013]

The point is that Christians can find helpful allies to critique the overblown absolutist claims of modernists who believe that their scientific (evolutionary) model provides the absolute truth. Stanley Fish is no Christian; he's no creationist. In fact, as an antifoundationalist who believes all truth is relative to one's own community, he's a postmodernist that Christians would disagree with on many issues. But it's helpful to use his critiques of modernists who are self-confident in their

scientism. We can point to someone outside our own community who similarly critiques proponents of scientism and calls them on their bias and their hidden presuppositions.

Some students may be surprised to find how accessible and helpful even some of the more academic writing in these journals can be—especially now that they've had biblical worldview training. They may find the more academic nature of the articles helpful when they start taking university-level classes.

Do Creationists Disagree?

On every question of consequence in this entire globe, there is a spectrum of belief. There is a continuum from denial to avowal on every major proposition. This means that among creationists there is not perfect unanimity, and this may alarm students when they first discover it. (For example, was there a canopy around the earth before the Flood? Should distant starlight be explained by hypothesizing that God created the light in the process of traveling to the earth? Different creation scientists have different theories; they don't all agree on these issues.) There are old-earth creationists and young-earth creationists. There are young-earth creationists who have personality conflicts with others. There are splits, there is acrimony, there is fallenness. All of this is to be expected because it's consistent with a biblical worldview. And if there is a spectrum of belief on different matters among Christians, there is an even wider spectrum when it comes to non-Christians. At least Christians have parameters for thinking guided by Scripture. But autonomous individuals have no such boundaries.

One valuable point can be made about disagreement among professing Christians on the reading of Genesis 1–3. There is only one standard, straightforward, traditional view that has been the orthodox view for thousands of years with very little dissent until recently. But there are many alternative views (including those of John Walton and Peter Enns, mentioned earlier in the Student Text). People who by their own admission can't accept the traditional view of Genesis 1–3 because of the supposed findings of evolutionary biology and modern geology nonetheless have not agreed on what the text is, in fact, saying. That is telling.

The Hippocratic Oath

The Hippocratic oath (mentioned on page 335) has been used for centuries by Western medical doctors and is often discussed. But it's rarely read. Here it is:

I swear by Apollo the physician, and Aesculapius the surgeon, likewise Hygeia and Panacea, and call all the gods and goddesses to witness, that I will observe and keep this underwritten oath, to the utmost of my power and judgment.

I will reverence my master who taught me the art. Equally with my parents, will I allow him things necessary for his support, and will consider his sons as brothers. I will teach them my art without reward or agreement; and I will impart all my acquirement, instructions, and whatever I know, to my master's children, as to my own; and likewise to all my pupils, who shall bind and tie themselves by a professional oath, but to none else.

With regard to healing the sick, I will devise and order for them the best diet, according to my judgment and means; and I will take care that they suffer no hurt or damage.

Nor shall any man's entreaty prevail upon me to administer poison to anyone; neither will I counsel any man to do so. Moreover, I will give no sort of medicine to any pregnant woman, with a view to destroy the child.

Further, I will comport myself and use my knowledge in a godly manner.

I will not cut for the stone, but will commit that affair entirely to the surgeons.

Whatsoever house I may enter, my visit shall be for the convenience and advantage of the patient; and I will willingly refrain from doing any injury or wrong from falsehood, and (in an especial manner) from acts of an amorous nature, whatever may be the rank of those who it may be my duty to cure, whether mistress or servant, bond or free.

Whatever, in the course of my practice, I may see or hear (even when not invited), whatever I may happen to obtain knowledge of, if it be not proper to repeat it, I will keep sacred and secret within my own breast.

If I faithfully observe this oath, may I thrive and prosper in my fortune and profession, and live in the estimation of posterity; or on breach thereof, may the reverse be my fate!

The main point is to do no harm to the patient. This is common grace. Even though the oath is mixed with a metanarrative of mythology, the ethics were borrowed from the creational norms of the biblical worldview.

Inconsistent Worldviews

Every false worldview will be inconsistent with itself—whether ancient Greek mythology or modern secular evolutionism. They can only bend away from God's creational norms so much. Eventually they will have to work according to God's creational norms. They will have to rely on God's common grace. They will have to borrow from the biblical worldview—the only true basis for the reality of the world and thus for scientific work.

Get Involved: Science Fairs

Students may have one last opportunity in high school to get involved in a science fair project. If students have the talents and the interest, then they should have the biblical worldview motivation for working to produce a quality project.

What kinds of needs might you be able to research and begin to address in a science fair project?

[Allow students to brainstorm the kinds of things they're interested in solving or learning about. Maybe they'll come up with a good idea that a team of them can work on together.]

Jonathan Sarfati

Jonathan Sarfati is an intellectually gifted individual. He doesn't know how he does it, exactly, but he is able to play as many as twelve games of chess at once while blindfolded. And he can win (his record is eleven victories and no losses at a chess club in his home country of New Zealand). Sarfati's doctoral work was in chemistry, focusing on spectroscopy. He has worked with Creation Ministries International and has edited the peer-reviewed *Journal of Creation*.

Andrew Snelling

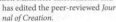

Andrew Snelling's doctorate is in geology, and he's one of the relatively few scientists in the world permitted to take rock samples out of the Grand Canyon. He has written or contributed to nearly three hundred articles in various publications, many of them seeking to popularize the work of creation science.

Kurt Wise

baraminology: *a discipline in creation biology studying the "created" (Hebrew: bara) "kinds" (Hebrew: min) and forming a taxonomy*

Kurt Wise received an MA and a PhD in paleontology from Harvard University; his credentials are undeniable. Even evolutionist and atheist Richard Dawkins said that Wise "may well be creationism's most highly qualified and most intelligent scientist."[38] Years ago when he came to a personal point of crisis over the conflict between creation and evolution, he explicitly chose to believe the Bible's account of human origins. Wise has devoted much time to the discipline of baraminology.*

REMEMBERING THE FALL

These scientists would be the first to tell you that they are far from the only Christians in science—and that they're far from perfect, far from omniscient. Accepting the Bible's authority doesn't automatically make them right about all their scientific claims, any more than it ensures you get an A+ on all your calculus quizzes. These scientists struggle against the effects of the Fall in their own work—and in their own hearts—in countless ways. (And inclusion in this list doesn't mean they agreed to be on it or that BJU Press perfectly agrees with all of them.)

But Bill Nye can relax. He wanted "scientifically literate voters and taxpayers for the future," and "engineers that can build stuff, solve problems."[39] He was worried that creationism would keep that from happening. God forbid. Rather, it's the first chapter of Genesis that calls on us to press God's world toward its ideal and maximize its usefulness. Creationists can be—and many *should* be—scientists.

REMEMBERING COMMON GRACE

No one on the list above would deny that non-Christians can do valuable work, even morally good work, in science. When Jewish physician Jonas Salk developed the polio vaccine, saving and improving the lives of countless children, he was pushing back the effects of the Fall. He was restoring a little slice of the lives of these people to the way those lives were supposed to be. Legs that would have been crooked are now strong and straight. That's good.

And, of course, the list of non-Christians who have made significant and beneficial scientific advances (not all advances are beneficial) is much longer than the list of Christians. That fact is a reason for humility and hard work, not for admitting defeat.

The History of Science

Let's go back to the history of science for a moment. The typical story told by scientism is that science and religion have been at war since the time of the Greeks. Oxford professor and historian of science Peter Harrison says,

> The history of science, on one very common understanding, has three distinct stages. Science is said to have had its origins in Greek antiquity when philosophers first broke away from the myths of their forebears and sought rational explanations for natural phenomena. Science subsequently suffered a setback with the advent of Christianity, going into significant decline in the Middle Ages. But it then emerged triumphant with the scientific revolution of the seventeenth century when it finally broke away from religion and set out on its progressive path to the present.[40]

But Harrison doesn't buy it. The idea that mankind used to believe in myths but has moved on to rationality is "difficult to sustain," he says. The Greek tradition of medicine, for example, began with Hippocrates, the source of the Hippocratic oath (which, historically, Western doctors have taken at the beginning of their medical careers). But this ancient "scientific" tradition coexisted perfectly well with the religious cult of Asclepius, the Greek god of healing. In fact, the Hippocratic oath begins with references to two Greek gods: "I swear by Apollo the physician, and Asclepius the surgeon."[41]

Scientists today, despite their claims to be concerned with "just the facts," still mix reason and myth (remember the "just-so stories"?). The myths scientists believe in today don't seem like myths to them because so many people accept them. But a lot of people believed in Asclepius too. (To this day, we use the word *hygiene*, which comes from Hygiea, Asclepius's daughter, goddess of cleanliness.) Every piece of knowledge has always come with faith attached—for everybody, not just for Christians.

Doing Science Yourself

This historical argument should give Christians gifted in science added confidence that they do belong in the scientific world. But if Christians aren't actually *doing* science, the argument is probably worthless. Christianity is not merely compatible with science but generates it—so if it's your calling, go do some science. Push back nicely against the reigning view that science must be naturalistic. Subdue the earth, and take dominion over it.

Maybe you could be like Michael, a high school student (using BJU Press materials) who made it into *Popular Science*'s list of top teenage scientists and inventors. Michael saw human needs and worked on solving them. First, he noticed his own need: he was always forgetting to turn out the lights and getting in trouble for it. So at age ten he invented a contraption that would turn them off automatically using light and motion sensors. By age sixteen he had moved on to other people's needs, inventing a nasal spray that can stave off dangerous diabetic attacks and save lives.[42]

If you're gifted in science—which is almost the same as saying, "If you love science"—then you may be called to that hard work. And you'll need to do it according to the creational norms for science laid out in Chapter 19.

Get Involved: Science Camps for Christian Students

Former BJU faculty member Dan Wooster works in a cooperative relationship with Answers in Genesis to provide science camps from a Christian perspective through Camp Infinity. STEM camps focus on science, technology, engineering, and math. The camp also trains campers in biblical apologetics. Each week focuses on a different age group from elementary to high school to college-aged campers. Students interested in expanding their horizons or testing out their talents and interests should check into what camps like these have to offer them before or during their higher education.

Career Opportunities

Students need to be encouraged not to limit themselves. The job market can be tough at times. But the sciences and mathematics often open up the best opportunities. Jobs in those sectors frequently have the most needs to fill. Students might be surprised by the wide variety of jobs available that they might actually find interesting. Have each student research and summarize one of the job examples listed below. They should provide an overview of the types of tasks, common skills or other requirements including educational preparation, and projected job growth and median salaries.

Earth and environmental science: Aquacultural manager, cartographer or photogrammetrist, hydrologist, industrial health and safety engineer, meteorologist, soil and water conservationist, surveyor

Physical science: Astronomer, aviation inspector, chemical technician, electrician, food science technician, forensic science technician, nuclear power reactor operator, occupational health and safety specialist, physicist, power plant operator

Life science: Agricultural technician, animal breeder, anthropologist, athletic trainer, biochemist, marine biologist, microbiologist, veterinarian, zoologist

Behavioral and social science: Marriage and family biblical counselor, political scientist, sociologist

Interdisciplinary science: Patent lawyer, technical writer

Engineering: Aerospace engineer, architect, automotive engineer, CAD technician, chemical engineer, civil engineering technician, electrical and electronics engineer, geographic information systems technician, landscape architect, mechanical engineer, nuclear engineer, robotics engineer, transportation engineer

Math and computer science: Computer programmer, computer software engineer, data scientist, economist, multimedia artist or animator, statistician

Human biology and health: Audiologist, biomedical engineer, certified diabetes educator, certified registered nurse anesthetist (CRNA), dental hygienist, dietitian or nutritionist, emergency medical technician and paramedic, neurologist, optometrist, physical therapist, science writer

Genetics and genomics: Bioinformatics scientist, cytogenetic technologist, genetic counselor

And these are only a few of the potential jobs. But many of them require specialized training, which means students need to prepare to be qualified.

Answering a Hypothetical Question

Knowledge requires three major elements: the person who thinks (reasons), the data he thinks about, and the laws his thinking must conform to. While Christians and secularists may agree about the laws of logic to some extent, the model of interpretation will diverge based on the metanarrative they accept and the authority sources they acknowledge. Christians acknowledge God's authority; they acknowledge God's revealed perspective because He is Lord.

> A biblical epistemology will . . . acknowledge . . . three elements. Secular epistemologies have found it difficult to relate sense experience, reason, and feelings in their accounts of human knowledge. They have also been perplexed by the relation of the subject (the knower), the object (what the knower knows), and the norms or rules of knowledge (logic,

reason, etc.). . . . So the three aspects of knowledge correspond to the attributes of God's lordship. The object is the world as God's *control* has made it and maintained it. The norm is God's *authority* for human knowledge. And the subject is the knower, standing in the *presence* of God. . . . Take away one of those, and there is no knowledge at all. . . . So I distinguish three perspectives of knowledge. In the "normative perspective," we ask the question, "what do God's norms direct us to believe?" In the "situational perspective," we ask, "what are the facts?" In the "existential perspective," we ask, "what belief is most satisfying to a believing heart?" Given the above view of knowledge, the answers to these three questions coincide.

[John Frame, "A Primer on Perspectivalism," Frame-Poythress.org (website), June 4, 2012]

THINKING IT THROUGH 21.2

1. positively contributing to the advancement of science and technology in an effort to love and serve their neighbors

2. The MRI takes imagery of internal organs, largely for medical purposes.

   The Terra computer model predicts the reaction of the earth's crust under certain conditions for predicting volcanoes and earthquakes.

   The RATE Project is advancing research for more accurate dating methods.

   The farming methods of Joel Salatin are advancing a more holistic, sustainable, local approach.

   The development of the Cancer Research Lab is advancing the tests that can detect cancer.

   Scientific research on binary star systems furthers our understanding of the operation of the universe.

3. No. Christians are fallen and finite, and non-Christians receive God's common grace to do their work.

4. You'll need to learn to do organized empirical study, and then to build a model that explains the resulting data. You'll need to work to communicate your findings, work according to standards (and adjust existing ones if they need to be adjusted), and work according to norms of truth, goodness, and beauty.

⊘ 5. Every piece of knowledge always comes with faith attached. In spite of a wrong worldview, unbelievers can still discover scientific realities by God's common grace.

A SOMEWHAT HYPOTHETICAL QUESTION

Consider this imaginary scenario. You go to an academic conference full of scientists. You present a historical paper describing how different cultures over time have defined what counts as "knowledge." You take questions. Up pops a hand. The top biology professor from MIT asks: "So what do *you* think counts as knowledge?"

If you were to answer that question with, "I think the fear of the Lord is the beginning of knowledge," you would get a written invitation not to come to next year's conference. You broke the rules of the discipline.

So what *do* you say? What do you think?

You'll need to learn to do organized empirical study and then to build a model that explains the resulting data. You'll need to work to communicate your findings, work according to standards (and adjust existing ones if they need to be adjusted), and work according to norms of goodness and beauty.

Christians who believe the Bible—Adam, Jesus, Paul, all of it—need to set new expectations for funding and research in the sciences. We need more research projects run on creationist presuppositions. We aren't going to solve all difficulties for the creationist viewpoint right away, such as the question of how stars can be millions of light-years away in a galaxy that's only six thousand years old, but creationists are working on it. Secular science takes lots of time and money to get to answers, with a huge number of dead ends along the way. (In fact, one secular scholar wrote a widely read article titled, "Why Most Published Research Findings Are False."[43]) Creation science needs time—and even false starts—too.

Good science from Christians is one of the best apologetics for the Christian faith right now—if indeed creationist scientific models make more successful predictions than evolutionary models. Christianity is ready to tackle the work of science.

THINKING IT THROUGH 21.2

1. Other than just defending the biblical view of origins, what else should Christians who are scientists be doing?

2. Summarize at least three important scientific contributions that demonstrate that creationists are not antiscience.

3. Does the fact that someone is a Christian make him a good scientist or that someone is a non-Christian make him a bad scientist? Explain why or why not.

4. Summarize the creational norms necessary for meeting a particular human need (i.e., for *doing* the work of science).

⊘ 5. What does the coexistence of Hippocratic medicine with the worship of Asclepius in ancient Greece tell us about the relationship of religion and science?

21 CHAPTER REVIEW

Scripture Memory

Genesis 1:31

Making Connections

1. What underlying worldview presupposition will determine where somebody will land on the spectrum of origins views and which model they will resort to in order to explain Genesis?

2. What are two major biblical truths that are often undermined when Genesis 1 is reinterpreted rather than read according to its straightforward meaning?

3. Who sets the rules for how science should be done? Might some of those rules be erroneous?

4. What could perhaps be a more effective way to witness to the truth and substance of the Christian worldview than mere debates over origins?

Developing Skills in Apologetics and Worldview

5. How should you respond to someone who claims that people's view of origins isn't important as long as they believe the gospel?

6. How should you respond to someone who claims that a belief in creationism will negatively affect the work of technological advancement?

Examining Assumptions and Evidence

7. Differentiate a literalist interpretation of "Our God is a consuming fire" (Heb. 12:29) from a straightforward interpretation of that statement.

8. If Christians believe that Genesis is mistaken about origins, how does that necessarily affect their interpretation of the rest of Scripture?

9. Why are the theological truths of humankind's fallenness and God's common grace vital to understanding the quality of scientific work done by both believers and unbelievers?

10. Answer the question in the sidebar on page 336.

Becoming a Creative Cultivator

11. Identify a physical need in your classroom. Hypothesize a technological tool that might solve the problem.

Examining Assumptions and Evidence

7. A literalist interpretation would ignore the genre and context, taking literary devices such as metaphors, parables/allegories, and hyperbole as the literal meaning. In that case, God's essential being (not a theophany) would be literal fire.

A straightforward interpretation takes into account the literary devices according to the genre and context but maintains the historical realities when both the immediate and overall context of Scripture demand it. Scripture's interpretation of itself can't be dismissed and reinterpreted to mean whatever the reader wants it to mean due to preconceived assumptions rooted in autonomous human "knowledge" from sources external to biblical revelation. Scripture declares God's essential being to be Spirit.

8. Scripture is then subject to the authority of human judgment, open to charges of error, and susceptible to endless reinterpretation.

9. Both of these truths are important for understanding why believers can be mistaken in their work even though they have a right worldview and why unbelievers can do good work even though they may have a wrong worldview.

10. Knowledge requires three major elements: the person who thinks (reasons), the data he thinks about, and the laws his thinking must conform to. The model of interpretation will diverge based on the metanarrative people accept and the authority sources they acknowledge.

Becoming a Creative Cultivator

11. Answers will vary.

Examples could include things that have already been invented or something imaginary. For example, twenty-five students need to sharpen three pencils at the beginning of each math class within a few minutes so as not to hold up the class hour. An electric pencil sharpener that could sharpen three or more pencils at one time would speed up the process for everyone.

TERMS TO REMEMBER

literalist—an interpreter who denies literary devices such as metaphor, allegory, hyperbole, and so on

origins—the study of the beginnings of the universe and human life

CHAPTER REVIEW ANSWERS

Making Connections

1. the presupposed degree to which God (the supernatural) is involved with His creation (the natural)

2. the historical reality of Adam and Eve bringing sin into the world; that death entered into the whole world only as a consequence of sin

3. No one person is in charge; the scientific community decides. Any group of finite and fallen humans setting up rules is subject to error.

4. actual contributions to scientific and technological work that will connect Christianity to showing love to one's neighbor

Developing Skills in Apologetics and Worldview

5. While it may be true that a person can still be a Christian and believe in the gospel, a wrong view of origins seriously undermines the foundation that the gospel rests on: the metanarrative of CFR.

6. A belief in creationism doesn't deny the good work of the scientific method used in the present day to recognize present-day needs and solve present-day problems through scientific and technological tools. Rather than attacking that kind of scientific progress, creationism provides a basis for doing that work. Creationists simply question the philosophical and theological assumptions smuggled into the work of science in relation to the model of origins.

8

HISTORY

CHAPTER 22 OBJECTIVES

The student will be able to

22.1 Connect the importance of history to the origin of God's created order and the advance of God's redemptive plan.

22.2 Explain the purposes for studying history.

22.3 Discern the creational norms for how historical study should be conducted.

SECTION OBJECTIVES 22.1

1. Attribute the origin of history to God's created order.

2. Attribute the advance of history to God's redemptive plan.

3. Explain why properly understanding the Bible and how it connects to one's own context demands historical awareness.

4. Explain why the historical development of God's redemptive plan was necessary.

Chapter Twenty-Two **FOUNDATIONS FOR HISTORY**

[God] made from one man every nation of mankind to live on all the face of the earth, having determined allotted periods and the boundaries of their dwelling place, that they should seek God, and perhaps feel their way toward him and find him. Yet he is actually not far from each one of us.

Scripture Memory
Acts 17:26–27

22.1 HISTORY BEGAN

"In the beginning, God created" (Gen. 1:1). A Christian philosophy of history is founded on this creation.

> All things were made through him, and without him was not any thing made that was made. (John 1:3)

Only God is eternal. Everything else, at some point in time, began.

Without the creations of that first chapter, we couldn't have "history" in any meaningful sense. It's not just that God in Genesis 1 provides a model for history by giving us a chronologically ordered list of what happened on seven successive days. It's that in Genesis we meet time divisions in the first place. God set the order in the heavenly bodies "for signs and seasons, and for days and years" (Gen. 1:14). God built the march and measurement of time into His creation in the beginning.

The early theologian Augustine, under pressure from the reigning worldviews of his day, thought it was unworthy of God to take a whole week to create the world. He theorized that God actually created the world instantly and that the seven days of Genesis are only an analogy.[1] But the Bible goes out of its way to specify that God used "days," days with a "morning and evening" like our own days. Humans are often impatient with God's timing (2 Pet. 3:4), but since the beginning God has worked out His will through history.

Creation took time; and so does redemption. God could have sent Jesus Christ immediately to die for the sins of Adam and Eve. But He didn't. He allowed a great deal of time to pass—a great deal of history to transpire—while the Fall worked out its effects all over the planet.

God let sin have increasing reign for a thousand years before He wiped out almost all life on the planet with a flood. But even then, Christ's redemption was still far off in the future. God chose to work out His redemptive purposes through all the many generations of history in one particular family, Abraham's family—until the ultimate coming of Abraham's seed, Jesus Christ. And now for over two thousand years God has unfolded in history the spread of His church over the world.

It should be no surprise, then, that much of the Bible is straight history. Genesis is entirely history, as is the first half of Exodus. Even the Mosaic laws in Exodus, Leviticus, and Deuteronomy are delivered not in a mere list but as part of a long story.

Some of the earliest Old Testament prophets were also historians of a sort, recording God's view of Israel's history from the time of Joshua through the Babylonian exile in the books of Joshua, Judges, Samuel, and Kings. The final book of the Hebrew Bible is Chronicles, a history that spans from Adam to the end of the exile.

THE FLOW OF BIBLICAL HISTORY

Understanding Scripture requires keen historical awareness, something not all readers of the Bible have. You may have heard some people complain

---

Lesson Plan Chart—Chapter 22

Section Title	Pages	Activity Manual	Days
22.1 History Began	340–42		1 day
22.2 Why Study History?	342–45	Activity 38	1 day
22.3 Christian Foundations for History	345–52		3 days
Review	353		1 day
Total Suggested Days			**6 days**

The Importance of History

Some people love history; others hate it. The study of history can be boring when students are only expected to memorize long lists of random names, dates, and bare facts. That's the structure or bones without the meat. But when those names come alive in biographical sketches or the events are colored with the details of riveting action, then the study of history can be fascinating. Teaching history in a more exciting manner makes history interesting. But why is it important? The study of history becomes even more significant and captivating for students when they understand that it answers one of the most basic and most important worldview questions in the CFR metanarrative: "Where am I? Or what is the nature of the world and universe I live in?" History gives context—a broader view of life and where it's going.

that Christians pick and choose which Bible verses they'll follow. They condemn homosexuality, for example, but not eating shrimp—even though Leviticus prohibits both.

The Bible's awareness of history is vital to answering this complaint. The Mosaic law was a historical covenant in force between the time of the Exodus and the time of Christ. Certain laws in the Mosaic Covenant reflect God's moral expectations for all time. For instance, God's condemnation of homosexual desires and actions is rooted in the creation order (Gen. 2:22–24), stated in the Old Testament law (Lev. 20:13), and reaffirmed in the New Testament (Rom. 1:26–27; 1 Cor. 6:9; cf. Matt. 19:4). Other laws in the Mosaic Covenant served as pictures or object lessons for the people. They were valid while the covenant was in force, but not afterward. Jesus "declared all foods clean" (Mark 7:19). Thus, Christians, who are under the New Covenant, not the Mosaic Covenant, do not have to observe food laws (Heb. 8:6–13; Acts 10:15). All of the Bible is beneficial for the Christian, but not all of it is directly applicable. To know which parts are and which are not requires historical awareness.

Historical awareness is important for understanding other biblical doctrines as well. Paul argues very specifically that Abraham was justified by faith before he was ever circumcised, as Jewish law later demanded (Rom. 4:9–12). Paul makes this historical argument to demonstrate that circumcision cannot be a requirement for justification.

God could have written a logically organized systematic theology book with an appendix full of precise, unchanging behavior rules. He could have handed the book to Adam and provided translations for new language groups as they developed. But He didn't.

He unfolded both His creative work and His redemptive work historically, and then gave us a Bible narrating and explaining that work. And that Bible tells us that He didn't create all humans at once (as He may have done in the case of angels) and place them in the new Jerusalem. Instead God began with two individuals in a garden and told them to fill and develop the world. When humans reproduce, they don't bear other adults but children who have a lot of growing and developing to do.

And God brought His people through a period of childlike development too. The Bible itself says that the Old Testament law treated God's people like children; the law was like a "guardian" that we no longer need (Gal. 3:24–25). In the Old Testament, God took His eternal law and applied it in specific ways to Israel's life in the Middle East. The prophets declared precisely what God's will was for the people. But in the New Testament, the apostles reason with God's people and work through lengthy explanations about how God's eternal law should be applied to various situations (e.g., 1 Cor. 8:1–9:27). Why the change? Part of the answer is that God's people had matured. In the Old Testament, they were "children" who needed God to apply His law to their specific situation. In the New Testament era, they're full-grown sons who can look back at the general statements of God's will in the Old and New Testaments, at God's specific Old Testament applications, and can reason through to the right application in their time and place.[3] The point is that God designed even the way His people relate to His law to go through a process of development.

The social structures and institutions that define the horizons of the possible for various cultures—the things that fill history textbooks—have also gone through a process of development in God's providence. In Eden, nations, governments, schools, businesses,

> "I can only answer the question, 'What am I to do?' if I can answer the prior question, 'Of what story do I find myself a part?'"[2]
>
> —ALASDAIR MACINTYRE

The Origin of History

What are two of the major metanarratives through which history can be viewed?

History can be viewed through the lens of biblical creation or through the lens of evolution.

Secular textbooks often begin their discussion of ancient history through the lens of evolution. Christian textbooks should begin their discussion of history through the lens of Creation, Fall, Redemption. The very idea of time having a beginning point has its basis in God. This contrasts with any view that sees matter as eternal, whether in Greek philosophy or in evolutionary theory.

Other than recounting the steps of the creation process, does a creation-based origin of history really matter? How does it affect a person's view of the rest of history?

Yes, it matters! The early days of human history serve as the foundation that the rest of history is built on. History isn't just about what happened; it's also about why things happened. The foundation of CFR influences the explanations for why things happened the way they did.

A large part of historical analysis involves an examination of human nature. Without the foundation of the CFR origin of history, there's no basis for presupposing the basic belief that humans are made in the image of God, that they're fallen, and that there is yet hope because they're redeemable. Apart from those basic beliefs, it's likely that any analysis of human nature will be skewed. When history is examined merely to learn from past human examples, that may lead to a more naive understanding, which in turn leads to a more naive view of the predictability of

where present actions will eventually lead (one of the key reasons for studying history).

Isn't it possible to do the work of history without a larger story of the world or basic beliefs?

No, not if the work of history is being done well. History is more than the mere recounting of events. Good history always involves a selection of events and an interpretation of those events. The interpretation of those events necessarily depends on a worldview lens, based on answers to fundamental questions: Where did the universe come from? Why is it here? Where is this world headed?

These questions can only be answered by faith; the answers are presuppositions because of commitments to a belief system and authority source. Every historian works from a belief system, whether he's aware of or consistent with it or not.

The Bible and Historical Awareness

One of the most difficult matters of biblical interpretation is discerning the Christian's relation to the Mosaic law. A historical reading of Scripture enables Christians to see that they're not directly under the Mosaic Covenant's code of laws but under the New Covenant (Gal. 3:1–3). At the same time, since much of the Mosaic law is the concrete application of creational norms to Israel's situation, New Testament believers are not lawless (1 Cor. 9:21) and can learn much from the Mosaic law about how to live lives pleasing to God (1 Cor. 10:6).

Scripture must be read and interpreted in historical context. The Bible isn't a random collection of stories or moral platitudes like the Qur'an or the sayings of Confucius. So Bible classes shouldn't be taught as if it were. The Bible must be understood as one larger unfolding story of human history. And Christians not only need to know what that story is but also where they fit into it (see Chapter 10 of the Student Text). Bible classes should be taught within that strong theological framework. Then the moral applications can be made properly. Right behavior ought to be grounded on right beliefs.

The Christian and the Mosaic Law

See the TE notes on pages 87–88.

See also Ken Casillas, *The Law and the Christian: God's Light Within God's Limits* (Greenville, SC: Bob Jones University Press, 2008).

Institutional Development

Why did institutions need to develop?

Humans needed to learn how to carry out the Creation Mandate according to the wisdom that God built into the world.

As humans shared their learned wisdom, others were able to build on that knowledge without having to reinvent things from scratch. That allowed the opportunity for further investigation and honing of skills. Eventually, systems and methods became ingrained into a society as the best approach known to humankind. As disciplines became more complex, they became professionalized or institutionalized with specialities developed for experts.

Speculate about how the discipline of history might have naturally developed. How would doing historical study have become more professionalized over time?

Originally, before the Flood, generations of eyewitnesses would have been able to provide, even hundreds of years later, firsthand accounts of the events of the world to the younger generations. The older generations would provide an oral history of the world.

As death began to come at younger ages and events became more numerous, the earliest civilizations began to write down their histories. Humans would have to do research for accuracy. Without direct revelation from God, they would have to interpret the causation and significance of the events for themselves.

The Progress of Redemptive History

In the biblical worldview, history is advancing to a culmination; it's not an endless cycle of meaninglessness in which a person must project or invent his own personal meaning. The progress of human history (and therefore life's meaning) is ultimately rooted in the magnification of God's glory through His redemptive plan for His creation (see Chapter 10). Although there may be some events that are more pivotal or that are high points in the unfolding of God's redemptive plan, no event or no individual life is outside the scope of God's larger plan for the world. God has a sovereign purpose for *everything* that takes place (Job 31:4; Prov. 5:21; 15:3). His intimate involvement is reassuring to the righteous (Ps. 139:17–18) but frightening to the wicked (Jer. 16:17; 32:19).

God's Merciful Purposes in History

Ask students to write an essay explaining why God would providentially plan for the world to be developed by humans with evil in it.

How does viewing history through the lens of redemption resolve this?

God allows evil to persist in this world to give humans a small taste of what they wanted—

---

trade associations, banks, airlines, internet standards consortiums, and a host of other institutions did not exist. These institutions developed over the course of history.

THE PROGRESS OF DIVINE REDEMPTION

Once again, why would God design a world that works by development over time? The Bible does not address this question directly. However, looking at Scripture gives us some clues. The progress of redemption reveals things about God's power, wisdom, and glory that would not have been put on display otherwise. Israel's system of sacrifices, for example, provides us with a richer understanding of Christ's death. Similarly, Christ didn't immediately come as the perfect Prophet, Priest, and King. Instead, God raised up prophets (Moses, Elijah), priests (Aaron, Eleazar), and kings (David, Solomon) so that their successes and failures could provide a background for understanding the significance of Christ's roles.

It's one thing to say, "Sin is bad." It's another thing to make readers feel the injustice and irrationality of sin by putting it on display in the history of the Israelite nation. Likewise, "grace is undeserved favor" is a nice thing to say, but grace is seen to be more glorious when the path to the cross and the resurrection of Christ unfolds over time.

The development of cultures also allows the glory of God to be displayed through the skills of His image-bearers. A world in which humans produce the pyramids, Aristotle's writings, Bach's music, and the Saturn V rocket needs history to develop. One generation builds on the insights and skills of those that preceded it.

THINKING IT THROUGH 22.1

1. What is a Christian philosophy of history founded on? Explain why.

2. Why does God design redemption to unfold through a historical process?

3. Why would God design a world that develops over time?

4. What does a developing history allow humans to accomplish?

♀ 5. Propose an alternative to the seemingly arbitrary application of the Old Testament law by Christians today.

22.2 WHY STUDY HISTORY?

It's good to study history for three worldview reasons: (1) History helps us understand the ways and works of God. (2) History teaches life lessons—as atheist philosopher George Santayana said, "Those who cannot remember the past are condemned to repeat it."[4] Since all knowledge comes with historical background, the opposite of history is amnesia. (3) History provides a sense of cultural identity. That's why schools around the world teach students the histories of their respective nations.

UNDERSTANDING THE WAYS AND WORKS OF GOD

The historical narratives of Scripture are given primarily so that God's people can understand His ways and His works. God has at various points in history acted to further His plan of redemption. But these acts of redemption require interpretation, something provided, in part, by the historical books of Scripture.[5] Christians believe that not only the historical records in Scripture but also those interpretations are inspired by God. The Bible both tells us historical things only God could know—like

---

life without God. God also allows evil to persist in this world to give humans a chance to repent and to be saved from hell. Redemptive history helps us make sense of difficult portions of the Old Testament, such as the warfare against the Canaanites. Instead of destroying the world or societies immediately and entirely, for the sake of His mercy, God delays His wrath for a long time (Gen. 15:13–16). God does this repeatedly in redemptive history (Gen. 6:5–8; Exod. 32:31–33; 34:6–7). Furthermore, if God had not preserved His people (at least a remnant) to attempt to fulfill the Mosaic law (however imperfectly), Jesus could not have been born into a context in which He fulfilled all righteousness for sinners worldwide (Gal. 4:4). In sum, evil persists, under the limitation of God's sovereignty (Job 1:12; 2:6) because of God's goodness. He delays His wrath to provide an opportunity for salvation (2 Pet. 3:3–12).

THINKING IT THROUGH 22.1

1. It's founded on creation because history began when time began and when God built the mechanisms of measurement and chronology into His creation.

2. The progress of redemption reveals things about God's power, wisdom, mercy, and glory that would not have been put on display otherwise or that we would not have fully understood experientially.

3. It is due to the task of the Creation Mandate—humans image God in their creativity and wisdom when they develop social structures and institutions.

4. Since humans are able to build on others' work from the past to advance their skills of taking dominion over the earth,

---

what day man was created on—and explains the significance of those things. Even the order in which Adam and Eve were created was significant, for example, though we wouldn't have known what it meant if God hadn't told us (1 Tim. 2:12–13).

God offers explanations of the foundational acts of redemption. For instance, we know from Scripture what no Roman centurion on Golgotha could have known, and that no scientific measurement, then or now, could ever determine: that a despised and rejected man dying on a cross was bearing the weight of the world's sins on His shoulders.

Though the foundational acts of redemption that need divine explanation have been accomplished, that doesn't mean God is now inactive. He is still actively working out His plan of redemption in the world. He has told us that this is one of His purposes He will accomplish (Gal. 4:4). So Christian historians are called to connect those purposes (as revealed in Scripture) with the events they study. They are also justified in drawing conclusions about what God may be doing in the world.

You just read a statement that's very controversial, even among Christians. Did you see it? The issue is this: can a Christian historian really discern God's purposes in history? At a specific level, he'd better be careful. Speaking for God is not something anyone should take lightly. But failing to speak for Him isn't either.

When the historian sees the gospel spread, he can look to Scripture and see this as one of God's stated purposes in human history. He can look at the ways God prepared people to receive the gospel or historical events and ideas that led people to turn to the gospel. He can suggest that God moved in history in those ways to further His gospel purposes. Of course, even when the gospel faces setbacks, God is still working out His will in the world. In those situations, the historian should turn to what the Bible says about the suffering that His people can expect.

Obviously, the Christian historian who undertakes such study must be humble because he doesn't have the insight into the significance of events that the biblical historians had as recipients of divine revelation. But he does understand something that non-Christian historians refuse to acknowledge: the broad sweep of God's purpose for history.

LEARNING LESSONS FOR LIFE

Humans are finite and fallen—and that's another excellent reason to study history. C. S. Lewis points out that people share "a great mass of common assumptions" simply because they live together at the same time and place. This is true even among people who vehemently disagree with each other.[6] But pick up a book from a bygone era, or begin to study the thought of another time and place, and you'll find yourself in a different world of thought—so different, sometimes, that it can be hard to grasp.

Uncovering your own assumptions is very hard work. Culture is at its strongest when it's most invisible. Breathing the air of another century is one of the best ways to expose your own presuppositions and to force you to evaluate them. You'll find that some of the assumptions of previous eras were healthier than those of the present.

The Merneptah Stele, created in Egypt about 1,200 years before Christ, has the first mention of "Israel" in written sources outside the Bible.

tion of historical significance. The divine viewpoint is often different from what humans might conclude on their own. Christian historians seek to understand the ways and works of God throughout history—because God is working out His plan through all that happens. But that task is very difficult without authoritative revelation. Human models of chronology are often fallible. And moral judgments can be faulty. As such, historical evidence should never be treated as a more foundational or more trustworthy authority than Scripture. While some historical evidence will support the biblical claims, evidence alone will never prove the Bible in the most absolute sense. History needs to be interpreted through a biblical lens to be rightly understood.

 ### Evidence for the Exodus

You may want to show students some excerpts from Timothy P. Mahoney's *Patterns of Evidence: Exodus* (DVD) (Thinking Man Films, 2015). However, be aware that Mahoney largely follows David Rohl's hypothesis for correcting the faulty dating system. But this is only one of the options for correcting that system of dating—an option that has been rejected by other conservative archaeologists who also favor an earlier date for the Exodus, but who interpret the available evidence differently.

  ### God's Purposes for Events

Ask students to read Luke 13:1–4.

Why were the disciples misled in their interpretation of the significance of events?

They evaluated the significance of a historical event through the lens of what they presupposed to be a scriptural evaluation. But their theology wasn't well-rounded. They assumed that really bad things would happen to only the worst kinds of people.

Introduce several major historical (or current) events. Then have the students provide a biblical analysis of the significance of those events. Students may debate what they believe the significance to be. It will likely be harder to discern the precise significance (God's purposeful plan) with as much certainty as they may have initially thought.

Examples of historical events in which God's purposes may not be easy to discern:

- The assassination of Abraham Lincoln
- The failure of attempts to assassinate Hitler
- The failure to stop Pol Pot's reign of terror with the Khmer Rouge in Cambodia
- Any terrorist attack or mass shooting around the world

they're able to build a great variety of complex and quality structures into their societies: schools, businesses, trade associations, banks, transportation networks, nations with governments, and so forth.

5. Christians should recognize that they live under the New Covenant rather than the Mosaic Covenant. They can learn a lot about God's plan of redemption from sacrificial, dietary, and other such norms even though they're not bound by those laws. They can also learn from God's inspired application of creational norms and moral laws so as to apply God's norms to their own situation—even if the applications are not exactly the same. Of course, the Old Testament sometimes states God's moral will directly, and these statements are always applicable in every era.

Discerning the Ways and Works of God

The value of biblical history is that it provides a window into the divine interpreta-

Lessons for Life

Although God's detailed purposes for every event may not be perfectly discernible, most major events in history do have some kind of significance that can be attached to them. Based on Christians' understanding of the events, they should apply biblical principles in order to learn lessons for life.

What lessons can students discern from the following historical people or events (some are negative, others positive)?

- Custer's Last Stand
- The failure of the British defense of Singapore against the Japanese during World War II
- The boldness and sacrifice of the Protestant reformers
- David Livingstone's exploration and missionary work in Africa

What is a major assumption (other than evolution) that our culture embraces that previous cultures didn't embrace (to their credit)?

Answers will vary. One major example would be the blending of roles of men and women in the church, home, and society.

What is another major assumption that our culture embraces (to our credit) that previous cultures failed to embrace?

Answers will vary. One major example would be that race-based slavery is contrary to the equality of all humans.

Cultural Identity

Divide students into small groups. Assign each group to take thirty minutes to research a different culture and come up with a thumbnail sketch of that culture. (Books like *Cultural Geography Fourth Edition* from BJU Press may be useful.)

Based on your thumbnail sketch of another culture, how well do you think you understand these people's assumptions, values, and practices? How should that impact your evaluation of their culture?

A thumbnail sketch may be accurate, but it can only generalize major characteristics. To truly understand another culture, a person must thoroughly study it and/or experience it. Therefore, any evaluation must be done with humility.

How should believers compare and contrast their own culture with other cultures?

Believers shouldn't idolize their own culture, which has been affected by the Fall like every other. Nor should they embrace multiculturalism, which treats all cultures as equally good. Every culture, including one's own, reflects beliefs and values that are either more or less conformed to the biblical worldview.

How would you describe the differences (in assumptions, values, and practices)

---

telos: *the ultimate end of a goal-oriented process (borrowed from the Greek)*

Previous eras, for example, didn't all make reason the source and standard of truth; they made it a tool—among other tools—for finding truth. Previous eras, even non-Christian ones, saw a **telos***** in created things. Where the spirit of this age sees an undirected process of evolution guiding everything to nowhere in particular, past eras have seen inherent purposes in created things.

People of the past also got some things wrong that we get right. They were no less intelligent than people today, but they were just as fallen and finite. Many of them saw a purpose in created things because they lived in what they considered an "enchanted" world where spirits or gods were in the rocks, trees, and rivers.

Mere history—simple description of what people have done and thought—does not really distinguish between old worldviews and newer ones. The Bible is the only ultimate standard for determining what's true and false. That's why Scripture ends up being the key evaluative instrument in the toolbox of a Christian historian.

History can provide insight into the consequences of ideas and actions. Today's bright ideas may have already failed (or succeeded) many times before, and that's worth knowing. History, then, is a well of wisdom. But only when it's interpreted through the lens of the Christian worldview.

ESTABLISHING A CULTURAL IDENTITY

The assumptions, values, and practices of the cultures we live in all have histories. Why do Americans value freedom, individualism, equality, and growth? They value these things in large part because of the history of the development of America.

We can value the economic growth that enabled entrepreneurial Americans to raise the standard of living for millions of others around the world. We can value the equality that allows those from humble backgrounds to develop their God-given abilities and rise to prominence so that they can benefit their community, state, or nation. We can value a culture in which people take responsibility for their actions, in which people are willing to step out and take risks that bring significant gains for themselves and others. We can value a culture in which we have the freedom to worship God as Scripture commands us. And history helps us understand where these values came from—and it gives us Abraham Lincolns, Booker T. Washingtons, and William Bradfords who exemplify these virtues.

But history, when read through a scriptural lens, can also serve as a warning to keep us from making our culture an idol. It can caution us about the pursuit of growth that seizes land unlawfully, about the danger of an equality that refuses to submit to God-given authorities, about an individualism that cares little for family or community, about a liberty that stands on its right to do wrong.

social class stratification: *the establishment of higher and lower classes*

Even though the Fall affects the values of every culture, history can at the same time reveal the positive characteristics of other cultures (perhaps those with longer histories) that may value different things. They may value conformity to the group, social class stratification,***** and the stability of tradition. There is value to be found in every culture because each is constructed by God's image-bearers making something of His good creation.

History, then, should play a vital role in everyone's life. While Scripture is the norm that must be applied to all of life, history gives us a clearer vision of the life that Scripture is being applied to. For this reason, the rest of this chapter will explore how the discipline of history should be pursued.

---

between your own culture and the culture that you have been assigned?

Answers will vary.

What would you evaluate to be a positive difference or a negative difference? Why?

Answers will vary. Believers should be willing to learn to accept differences of other cultures. Not everything that is different is wrong. However, believers must also be aware of the underlying religious worldview beliefs and values that often drive the behavior and practices of a culture. This knowledge shapes what can and cannot be embraced from various cultures.

How would you discover the origin and driving forces behind a cultural identity?

Study the historical backdrop of a people group to understand where they came from, who they are now, and where they're going.

Your Own Specific Cultural Identity

Every person has a cultural identity. That identity isn't just an ethnic or national identity. There are many cultural subgroups.

Ask students to write an essay about their own cultural identity, from its broadest description to the narrowest subgroup that they identify with. How was their cultural identity formed? What beliefs and values drove it? Can they discern any negative aspects in their own cultural identity? What positive aspects do they hold dear—that they wouldn't be willing to give up even if they were persecuted?

Students should reflect that their faith, family, and friends drive their cultural identity within the historical and geographical context in which they live.

THINKING IT THROUGH 22.2

1. What are three worldview reasons for studying history?

2. What often gets exposed when you study a different group of people from a different time period with a different worldview?

3. How can history challenge unfounded contemporary assumptions?

4. What powerful force entrenches assumptions, values, and practices in a specific group of people?

♀5. Why should a Christian historian seek to carefully discern God's purposes in history?

22.3 CHRISTIAN FOUNDATIONS FOR HISTORY

Given that history is so important and that God built history into the way His world works, how should a Christian practice the discipline of history? Another way of asking this question is "What creational norms must the historian conform to?" If God designed His world to unfold historically and if He intends humans to make sense of this historical unfolding, then it is likely that the very nature of the world and the very nature of the human person would require historical investigation to proceed according to a certain structure (see page 123).

But as we noted in the previous unit on science, determining the norms for disciplines such as science and history is not as straightforward as determining the norms of marriage and family life. The norms for studying history are not spelled out in the Bible. Instead, the Christian recognizes that God built the world according to the blueprint of His wisdom (Prov. 8:22–31). To learn the creational norms for wisdom a person needs to bring together fear of the Lord (Prov. 1:7) and observations about the world (cf. Isa. 28:26) and view them through the corrective lenses of Scripture.

Wisdom is God's creation, and it is God who teaches through general revelation. Those who reject God are going to miss some of the basics of how life works. Thus, the Christian historian should expect his approach to historical study to be distinct from the approaches of unbelievers. But since general revelation is given to all people, the Christian should expect unbelieving historians to have discovered much that is right about studying history. Since the Christian is finite and fallible, the unbeliever will in some cases have discovered things that the Christian can learn from. As he does this, however, the Christian needs to continue to run all of this teaching through the filter of a Christian worldview.

FOUNDATIONAL ESSENTIALS

A historian can arrogantly assume (or pretend) that he has a "neutral" perspective, or he can fall in the opposite ditch, despairing that he'll never do justice to his subject matter because of his **situatedness*** within history. Neither option is healthy. Instead, a historian would do well to acknowledge to himself his basic commitments and nonetheless work to be fair and thorough. The Christian historian, in particular, will come to history with some fundamental presuppositions.

In contrast to a **cyclical view of history**, the Christian believes that history had a beginning described by Genesis 1. The Christian believes that history also has a

situatedness: *the inescapable truth that every human views the world from a particular historical, geographic, and intellectual point of view*

THINKING IT THROUGH 22.2

1. History helps us understand the ways and works of God; it teaches life lessons; it provides a sense of cultural identity.

2. your own hidden assumptions and presuppositions that need to be evaluated

3. Since ideas and actions may have already failed or succeeded many times before, history can provide insight into the consequences of today's ideas and actions.

4. the historical development and backdrop of people's forefathers on whose shoulders they stand

♀5. Although Christian historians must be careful not to make dogmatic assertions since they don't have access to revelation outside the Bible, they should attempt to connect what has happened in the past to God's revealed will.

---

1. Defend an approach to historical study that both maintains acknowledged basic commitments and also strives for thorough honesty.

2. Summarize and explain each creational norm for conducting historical study.

3. Explain why conducting historical research should expand the Christian's worldview grasp of the ways and works of God, lessons for life, and cultural identity.

Applying Foundational Concepts to History

Identify some of the foundational concepts from earlier chapters in the Student Text that are being applied in this chapter to the practical discipline of history.

- *Creational norms*
- *Structure and direction*
- *Image of God in humans*
- *Wise dominion through the application of the fear of the Lord to general revelation*
- *Common grace*

Remind students that applying themselves to the work of any discipline always requires working from a presupposed structure of thought—a worldview lens. Therefore, they must always carefully evaluate the worldview commitments of the sources they're learning from—including history.

In the next chapter students will learn about some of the faulty lenses through which people teach or learn their history (naturalism, hyper-nationalism, postmodernism, and class, race, and gender studies). Sometimes the perspective from which someone presents historical interpretation is obvious, but many times it is simply subtly assumed.

The Myth of Neutrality

On one extreme, secular modernists tend to believe that facts are neutral. A historical fact just is. They tend to be blind to the reality that all data must be interpreted through a worldview lens before that data becomes meaningful—before it becomes history. It's only after that data has been interpreted according to a system that a piece of knowledge can be deemed a fact.

For example, the mere death of a person is fairly close to being a bare piece of data. But then a name is attached, his position is known, his death is revealed to be by assassination, his geographical and historical context is filled in, and so on. Then the data surrounding Franz Ferdinand's death begins to be put together into an *interpretation* of who he was, what happened, and why it happened.

On the other extreme, secular postmodernists misconstrue the reality that everyone has a perspective. The error of postmodernism is to assume that all perspectives are either equally right (everyone decides truth for himself) or equally wrong (there is no truth—or nobody can discern it for sure). But there is an objective reality to who Franz Ferdinand of Austria was, what happened, and even why it happened. Even postmodernists would have to agree that a person would be just plain wrong if he were to claim that Ferdinand won the Tour de France and was killed when a piece of cheese broke off of the moon and struck him on his big toe. Reliable sources tell us otherwise.

A historian who follows the biblical worldview approach won't shrink from his presupposed worldview commitments in the futile pursuit of being unbiased. But he also determines to be honest and fair in his assessments. A historian who follows the biblical worldview approach will be willing to evaluate others' perspectives. Since truth is often multifaceted, several perspectives may help him arrive at a more holistic understanding. But he also knows that some perspectives are wrong and that there is ultimately only one perfectly holistic perspective—the mind of God. His job is to think God's thoughts after Him. Such an approach is marked by humility because no fallen and finite human can always do that faithfully.

Similarity Does Not Equal Identity

The statement "Similarity does not equal identity" is used to correct a common error in thinking. It means that just because two ideas or two events are similar doesn't mean that the two ideas or events are identical or the same. This error is made when distinguishing characteristics are ignored. The Student Text is careful to warn against this error: just because the biblical worldview of history progresses in a linear fashion and the evolutionary view of history progresses in a linear fashion doesn't make the two views identical. A person would be misled to accuse a believer of holding to an evolutionary view of history simply because he holds to linear progress in history.

Other people make a similar error when they support a cyclical view of history simply because history may be full of similar events. It seems as if history is repeating itself. But this is due to the fact that the nature of humans is the same, not because the metanarrative of the world is cyclical in nature.

---

this-worldly culmination: "Then comes the end, when [Christ] delivers the kingdom to God the Father after destroying every rule and every authority and power" (1 Cor. 15:24). At the end of earthly history, "the kingdom of the world has become the kingdom of our Lord and of his Christ, and he shall reign forever and ever" (Rev. 11:15). Though human history had a starting point, it will never end because the age to come is an eternal age (Luke 18:30).

The Christian view of history, though linear, is not simply the Enlightenment (and evolutionary) view of continual progress. Christian historians would not agree with what one prominent sociologist said:

> The human march forward has been filled with wrong turns, backsliding, and horrible crimes. But taken in its grand sweep, it has indeed been a march forward. On every dimension, the last half-dozen centuries in particular have brought sensational improvement which, with qualifications, continues to this day.[8]

Christians can certainly acknowledge and praise all the progress that humans as God's image-bearers have made in medicine, science, engineering, and the arts (and in many other fields), but Scripture also reveals that the righteous will suffer persecutions and that evil people will grow worse and worse (2 Tim. 3:12–13). The Enlightenment view is a defection from the Christian view because it replaces the coming kingdom of Christ with scientific and technological advances as the measure of progress.

Christians also know something of their location in history. We live at the end of the ages (1 Cor. 10:11) and in the last days (Heb. 1:2). God hasn't told us how much longer these last days will extend. But this much is clear: Christ's death, resurrection, and ascension make up the defining moment in human history. The kingdom of God has come in salvation, and it is going to come in judgment. It could happen at any time.

CREATIONAL NORMS FOR HISTORY

Nailing down your basic commitments as a historian is essential, but a Christian historian cannot stop there. He must seek out the best practice for his discipline—its creational norms. This section outlines seven such norms.

Problems with the Cyclical View of History

There is a moral order to God's world (creational norms) so that human conformity to God's moral order should produce predictable patterns of success. In addition, the fallen human nature provides patterns of behavior that are predictable—with predictable outcomes of disaster. But analogous patterns in history don't equal a cyclical reality of history. Similar events don't erase the metanarrative of progress to an intended end.

Furthermore, the paradigm of an idyllic past that degenerates into never-seen-before corruption only to be reborn into a golden age tends to be forced. It's easy to minimize the evil in a past age and emphasize the evil in the present age in order to press others to take action. It's also easy to overly emphasize the good in one's own age in order to feel good about one's own success.

Depending on where a person believes he is in the cycle, the cyclical view can lead to an overblown optimism or an overblown pessimism. But "Christian faith, Augustine protested, could have nothing to do with the belief that 'the same ages and the same temporal events recur in rotation.'" [David Bebbington, *Patterns in History* (Vancouver: Regent College Publishing, 1990), 34] The reason for his protest is that, in the biblical view, (1) God intervenes and (2) sovereignly upholds His own plan, which is (3) progressing toward a certain culmination in the Day of the Lord (Bebbington, 43). All three elements, which comprise God's providence, are absolutely necessary; all three elements are generally ignored in a cyclical paradigm.

1. Studying Source Materials

Historians necessarily begin their work by looking at sources. Sometimes these sources are artifacts that archaeologists have recovered. Historians can gain some knowledge of how people lived by looking at the pottery they used, the kinds of houses they lived in, even the kinds of animal bones found in their garbage dumps.

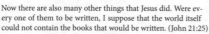

Sometimes sources are traditions that have been handed down from generation to generation or oral histories collected from the participants in historical events. But often the sources are written records that have somehow survived the centuries. The best sources—**primary sources**—are the letters, diaries, official records, and such that provide first-hand accounts of historical events.

Sifting through sources is central to the work of the historian, and that work often looks pretty much the same whether it's done by a Christian or a non-Christian. And yet, even here worldview makes a difference. It can influence a person's evaluation of what source material is significant and worthy of tracking down or of what topics are significant for study.

Historians gather primary sources; they then necessarily evaluate the material and seek to judge the reliability of those sources. These are the pieces of information they use to construct a readable story.

2. Making Models

But when a historian writes a history, he is never simply writing "what happened" because "what happened" is complex, contains many factors, and may not be fully knowable. Even the divine Author in writing Kings and Chronicles or Matthew, Mark, Luke, and John is not simply telling us "what happened." In one sense we get less than what happened:

> Now there are also many other things that Jesus did. Were every one of them to be written, I suppose that the world itself could not contain the books that would be written. (John 21:25)

But in the Gospels we also get more than what happened: we get interpretation of the events that even the people who witnessed them may not have had. This is true both of histories in the Bible and of those outside it. Historians identify and interpret evidence, and, on the basis of this, construct narratives. This is a complicated business because human historical actions are themselves always complicated and impossible to reduce to single causes, intentions, or motivations.[9]

Any time a limited human being tries to summarize or package a large set of complex information, he necessarily forms a model—like the scientific models discussed in the previous unit. Because historians are not inspired, they make their models with limited information (to varying degrees) and with limited understanding (to varying degrees) of the significance of the events they study and write about. A recognition of this human finitude, along with the realization that their own fallenness can affect their judgment, should make Christian historians humble as they make models.

As a result of the biblical view of providence in history, Christians need not be overly pessimistic in spite of the times of suffering, which only increase in measure in the last days before the Day of the Lord. That final Day provides Christians with a stable hope or optimism even though they can't be overly optimistic in a fallen world characterized by depravity.

A final problem with the never-ending cyclical view of the world is that it undermines Creation, Fall, and Redemption. The cyclical view generally leaves the beginning of the world in question. Personal responsibility for sinful behavior can be minimized as the mere cycle of fate. And the cycles are generally considered to continue on forever. Ideas have consequences. And the cyclical view of history undermines the biblical metanarrative out of which values, then actions arise.

Historical Research Project

Divide students into small groups to do a simple historical research project. Allow students to brainstorm which event they would like to research. Events could be from recent history in their own family, school, church, community, or nation.

Choosing an event to research involves:

- asking what types of events occurred
- judging which events are both interesting and significant—in the context of a particular people group (their family, school, church, community, or nation)
- determining which questions need to be answered—not only describing what occurred but analyzing why it took place and evaluating how it was carried out
- deciding whether they have the resources to answer those kinds of questions

Students should make use of all seven creational norms for doing historical study. The first step involves gathering their source materials: eyewitness accounts that are oral or written (primary sources might include pamphlets or minutes from an official meeting, etc.) and artifacts that pertain to the event (pictures, physical objects, etc.). If students are researching events from national history, then a variety of good secondary sources may be used as well (e.g., newspaper clippings). The second step involves selecting the relevant data. As they work through the selection process, they should also have a model by which to interpret the evidence that they have gathered and are selecting. They should evaluate the events by a moral standard, discern God's providence, detect causes, and clarify a timeline. Finally, they should share their findings in a report.

A Distinctive Christian Model

Many Christians wonder whether there is really a distinctively Christian way to go about doing particular disciplines of study, such as history. This is because they presuppose the two-story view, which divides the sacred from the secular. They presuppose that "secular" disciplines are largely neutral. Renowned historian George Marsden responds to this popular but mistaken way of thinking by summarizing three pervasive influences that Christian commitments should uniquely contribute to the study of history: "First, our Christian commitments shape our selection of topic. . . . Second, our Christian perspectives will influence the questions we ask about the subject. . . . The third pervasive type of influence has to do with determining which of the theories that are current we are likely to accept." [George Marsden, "What Difference Might Christian Perspectives Make?" in Ronald A. Wells, ed., *History and the Christian Historian* (Grand Rapids: Eerdmans, 1998), 15–16] In other words, a Christian perspective should affect the analysis, evaluation, and acceptance of a particular interpretation of the data.

Marsden also clarifies that it's not as if Christians will always arrive at different conclusions from those of their secular counterparts, but some analyses will certainly be different. This might be due to any number of factors, including differing views of justice or human nature. In addition, although the Christian might agree with the conclusions of his secular counterparts, the basis for reaching the same conclusion might be entirely different. The biblical worldview may provide the only legitimate justification for such a conclusion.

Models: Interpretive Narratives

Explain how the three ingredients of a worldview lens should influence someone's historical interpretive model.

A biblical model presupposes a particular metanarrative (CFR; linear history, etc.). It also presupposes basic beliefs about the world that arise out of that larger story of the world (human nature, ethical norms, etc.). Based on those basic beliefs, the actions of individuals or groups of people will either be praised or condemned (or, as is more often the case, both praised and condemned).

Should the model come before or after the selection process, moral judgments, and other evaluations?

Both, the model comes before and after. The culmination of the historical study should produce a more refined model. But it would be impossible to begin the process of historical study without a model of interpretation influencing the selection process, moral judgments, and other evaluations.

Provide examples of events in which the narrative dramatically changes based on the perspective or interpretive model being used to select and morally evaluate the data.

One of the clearest biblical examples is when the Pharisees tried to explain Jesus' miracles as satanic. But Jesus refuted their model of interpretation (Mark 3:22–27).

Major examples in American history include differing views on European exploration and colonization of the New World, the religious commitments of the Founding Fathers, whether or not the American Revolution can be biblically justified, the nature of Reconstruction, and evaluation of the 1960s.

Controversial interpretive issues in British history include Oliver Cromwell's protectorate in England, British imperialism in India, and the Opium Wars in China.

Summarizing Events

Ask several students to summarize an event that took place in the previous weeks.

Afterwards, ask them how many details they included and how many details they left out. Did they tell the class *everything* that took place? How did they decide which parts to include and which parts to leave out? Have students ever met people who included too many details in their summary of events? Why might that cause frustration?

Selection and Agendas

Although Christian historians should maintain a biblical commitment to their basic

---

3. Selecting What's Significant

Have you ever read a transcript of a real-life conversation? You can tell immediately that you're reading transcribed speech and not written discourse. Real-life dialogue is full of *ums* and *uhs*, run-on sentences, and awkward pauses that simply don't show up in formal writing. Even if it were possible, no one would ever want to read literally *everything* that was said by every participant in the Battle of Hastings in 1066, for example. It would take forever to read, and it would be impossible to grasp. Nor would anyone ever want to read a precise account of every step, every sword swing, every longbow shot, every horse, every outfit, every blade of grass trampled.

The records we have from that fateful battle already demonstrate one of the key principles of historiography (the practice of history as a discipline): selection. The people who wrote accounts of the battle in letters or books *selected* the stories and events and themes they felt were most important. And so does every historian.

Selectivity is unavoidable, and what a historian deems significant will depend to a great extent on his worldview.

Christian historian Timothy Larsen, for example, noticed a problem with selection in many histories of Victorian England. All historians recognize that this time period was a very religious one. "Yet, somehow all of that religion too often does not find a place in what is written in Victorian studies textbooks, or works of reference, or taught in courses. In such places, although there are laudable exceptions, one not infrequently learns simply that Victorians lost their faith."[10]

Why would secular historians tend to select stories of lost faith when writing about a highly religious age? Perhaps those historians could identify more with people who lost their faith; these people's experiences seemed more rational and normative. Secularism is the direction the world was going at the time they were writing, and therefore it seemed to deserve emphasis in their accounts of the past.

But Larsen, a Christian, was more attuned to the value of Christianity in the Victorian era. There certainly were people who abandoned their profession of faith in Christ in England during the nineteenth century, and their stories are worth telling. But Larsen noticed something secular historians were not interested in: a significant number of these ex-Christians came back to faith in Christ. What secular historians relegated to footnotes Larsen wrote a whole book about. He called it *Crisis of Doubt: Honest Faith in Nineteenth-Century England*. In this case Larsen's Christian perspective enabled him to see what many others were missing.

This does not mean, however, that the Christian historian seeks to make history as Christian as possible. The Christian historian's worldview should include the belief that all people are made in the image of God. Therefore, he should expect to find amazing achievements in non-Christian societies. The Christian worldview also teaches that the Fall has had pervasive effects. So the Christian should expect to find these effects in all cultures. But the Christian also believes that God is working out His redemptive plan throughout history. The Christian historian will be careful not to neglect the historical advance of the gospel. His Christian principles will lead him to select the most valuable information about the period he's studying, and what could be more valuable than the work of God?

---

beliefs and to the overarching biblical metanarrative, they shouldn't skew history to fit a particular agenda. Trying to make biblical Christianity or broader Christendom look good by ignoring mistakes or even sinful choices undermines the Christian historian's trustworthiness. In order to maintain honesty, Christian historians must remain humble. The same applies to recounting one's own national history. No nation has a perfectly clean record. Every nation has been led by and populated by finite and sinful people who have displayed, to varying degrees, their mistaken and sinful choices. Every generation in every place will be filled with examples of human failings and self-interest. However, an overly pessimistic view of all history is characteristic of an off-base agenda too. Every generation in every place will likely be filled with examples of God's

common grace—of human triumph in the face of great difficulty and self-sacrificial care for others. A good historian won't just select the events that reflect one extreme or the other. He will attempt to select that which characterizes history holistically.

Selection: A Case Study

Discuss with students how understanding multiple perspectives is essential for understanding historical events. For instance, if the topic is European exploration and colonization of North America, students should realize that considering the perspective of both Europeans and Native Americans is important for understanding and evaluating that period of history.

How did Europeans of that time view property ownership?

4. Making Moral Judgments

Historians not only recount what happened in the past, but they also often evaluate what happened. Sometimes they're able to do this by pointing to minority voices who raised moral objections at the time the events unfolded. For instance, a historian may point to the resistance that American missionaries gave to the seizure of Cherokee land by Andrew Jackson and the state of Georgia. Or a historian might note that pastor James Waddell Alexander was concerned that the Mexican-American War might provoke God's judgment on the nation,[11] or that the American diplomat tasked with negotiating the treaty at the end of that war sought the fewest concessions possible from Mexico on account of "the iniquity of the war, as an abuse of power on our part."[12]

Sometimes there are no contemporary figures who speak out against moral wrongs because they all share the same moral blind spots. Christians can treat historical figures with moral blind spots fairly by positioning them within the context and assumptions of their times. But Christian historians also have in Scripture a moral standard by which to evaluate the conduct of any time period.

5. Discerning History as Divine Providence

Let's consider now the question introduced earlier. Can historians see God's hand in history?

Scripture teaches that the same God who spoke the universe into existence maintains that existence (2 Pet. 3:5, 7). He controls the clouds, the wind (Ps. 104:3–4), and even the ocean waves (Ps. 107:25, 29). When people or animals eat, the Bible says God is the one who has provided food (Ps. 136:25). Children are born according to God's providence (Ps. 113:9). Not even a sparrow dies apart from God's control (Matt. 10:29). That sovereign rule extends to individual lives and the affairs of nations (Prov. 16:1–9, 33). God determines the boundaries of those nations (Acts 17:26). He sometimes frustrates the plans of nations (Ps. 33:10–11). God looks down from heaven as the King of all the earth. When a king is successful in battle, it's not due to his own power or superior military equipment; it's due to God (Ps. 33:13–17). And God's rule extends so deep that it even shapes the intentions of people's hearts (Prov. 21:1).

So the answer of the Bible is "Yes, God's hand is evident in history because everything that happens is the work of God in some way." Joseph said basically the same thing to his brothers after their father Jacob died: "You meant evil against me, but God meant it for good, to bring it about that many people should be kept alive" (Gen. 50:20). The same event had two distinct sets of planners: (1) the brothers and (2) God Almighty.

Of course, non-Christians cannot accept the existence of two planners or two authors. As the *Stanford Encyclopedia of Philosophy* puts it, "The assumption that there is a divine author of history takes the making of history out of the hands of humanity."[13] But the Bible everywhere insists that God's rule is real and that people's choices are as well. Both shape history and are yet somehow compatible. This is a great mystery, but it must be affirmed by the Christian historian. It means, for instance,

---

• Many Europeans believed that if a person took something that was unowned and made something of it, his labor made that which was previously unowned his property. Thus unclaimed or unused land could become one's property by improving it with one's labor.

• Europeans also believed that property was something that could be possessed in perpetuity, handed down from generation to generation, or sold to others.

How did Europeans view American Indians and their claim on the land?

• Initially, Indians were viewed as wild people, who were part of the wilderness landscape, and Europeans claimed that the Indians had no conception of private property. Some claimed that because the Indians simply traveled from place to place they had no sense of property ownership.

• Eventually, Europeans came to recognize that Indians did recognize property rights even if they did not follow European customs regarding property.

John Smith reported of the Indians near Jamestown, "They all know their severall landes, and habitations, and limits to fish, fowle, or hunt in.' . . . From Plymouth, Edward Winslow reported that every tribe knew its territory, and within that zone, when individuals wished to plant, the sachem 'giveth them as much as they can use, and sets them their bounds." [Stuart Banner, *How the Indians Lost Their Land* (Cambridge, MA: 2005), 19–20]

How did Native Americans think about property?

• American Indians were not simply hunters and gatherers, as Europeans initially thought. Those that practiced agriculture would set up a village with assigned plots of land for growing crops. After the soil wore out, the village would move to a new location and new plots would be allocated.

• Thus property was owned, but not in perpetuity as an asset to be passed from generation to generation.

• Different tribes would also know the boundaries between the land they hunted, fished, and lived on and the land claimed by another tribe.

• Given this understanding of property, American Indians did not sell land in perpetuity to others. When Indians "sold" land to Europeans, they were giving them the right to make use of the land and to act as allies to the tribes. This is why the same land could be sold to differing Europeans. What was being sold was not the land but the use of it.

Moral Judgment: A Case Study

After students have gathered source materials and selected their data for their case study, ask them to feed it into a model of interpretation (in this case a biblical worldview), and make a moral judgment.

For example, what should they conclude about the European settlement in the New World?

For complex questions like this, students need to take into account the wide number of individual incidents that are being summarized under the heading "European settlement," the perspectives of all the parties involved, and an application of a biblical worldview. Any broad-scale evaluation would need to acknowledge:

• Some of the negative effects of European settlement, such as the ravages of disease, were unintentional and unavoidable.

• Some of the conflict between Europeans and Native Americans resulted from misunderstanding.

• The idyllic picture of peaceful Indians who lived eco-friendly lives in an unspoiled wilderness Eden is mythic. As humans who were blessed with the ability to subdue the earth, American Indians actively managed their environment. As fallen humans, they fought with each other before the Europeans came, and after the Europeans arrived their reaction to the threat was often brutal.

• Despite the efforts of some Europeans (such as the Pilgrims or William Penn) to treat American Indians justly, too often Europeans unjustly deprived Indians of their land, either by force or by failure to honor treaties made with them. Christian missionaries who worked among the Indians were at the forefront of noting and resisting these injustices, as exemplified in the case of Andrew Jackson's removal of the Cherokee from their land in the Southeast.

Are Moral Judgments Necessary?

Is it possible to do the work of history without evaluating what happened? Can't historians just recount what happened without any bias?

The purposes of history are understanding the ways and works of God, learning lessons for life, and establishing a cultural identity. None of the purposes of history can be accomplished without moral judgments. If people ignore these purposes or stop short of making moral judgments, then they're not fully studying history. They've only done a halfway job. In fact, they miss the whole point of history.

Point out to students that some historians act like they're simply recounting what happened without any interpretation or judgments. But every accounting will be slanted by selection and emphasis, subtly conveying a point of view.

Present-Day Moral Obligations

It's easy to judge mass populations of the past and wonder why nobody stopped the wrongdoing. But students are a part of the unfolding history of their own time. Even if they're in the minority, they need to stand for what is right. They need to decide what evils their own culture is doing that future generations will judge them for allowing instead of striving against.

Personal Experiences of God's Providence

Describe experiences of God's providence in your own history.

Remind them that everything that has happened in our lives—good or bad—has been due to God's personal care (Ps. 139:17–18) and purposeful plan for our highest good (Gen. 50:20; Rom. 8:28) and His greatest glory (Rom. 11:33–36).

What kind of events are Christians most likely to select to highlight God's providence in their lives?

Christians often cite God's providence when pivotal events change their lives, a series of smaller details all come together, or a difficulty has been clearly used to work out for a never-imagined greater good, and so forth.

What are two major issues that need to be clarified when a believer maintains that God providentially controls everything in history?

- *The problem of evil*
- *The free choices of humans*

Christians must maintain that God is not directly responsible for temptations or evil (James 1:13). Christians must maintain that

---

that the Christian historian studying the Great Awakening will discount neither the Spirit's working in hearts nor the roles played by the social and political conditions of the time and by powerful personalities.

Another objection—and a powerful one—to God's rule over history is that Christians are sometimes selective in their appeal to providence. Christians often point only to instances in which their points of view are favored; they tend to neglect instances in which the tide turns against them. You've heard Christians do this in prayer request time: People praise the Lord for preserving their lives in a car accident, but they generally fail to acknowledge that God allowed the accident in the first place.

At its worst, a selective reading of providence like that can be used to justify wrongdoing. The success of a revolution may lead certain Christians to justify their rebellion against rightful authority—even though the Bible says that "whoever resists the authorities resists what God has appointed" (Rom. 13:2).

Many Americans appealed to the idea of Manifest Destiny to justify the seizure of Mexican and Indian lands in the westward expansion of the United States. Though some Christians opposed this expansion, others argued that it was part of God's providential plan to spread liberty and Protestant Christianity[14]—as if stealing people's land is OK as long as you give them a gospel tract in the process.

But since God is providentially ruling over all, then everything that happens is providential. Sometimes the workings of providence may, with humility, be discerned by comparing events with God's revealed will in Scripture. If the gospel was preserved in England by the defeat of the Spanish Armada, the Christian historian may suggest that God used that military event to preserve the gospel witness in England—a gospel witness that would centuries later spread around the world. Often, the matter is more mixed. Christian missions was aided (though often hindered as well) by the spread of the British Empire. The empire itself brought both benefits (e.g., infrastructure) and problems (e.g., racist treatment) to the peoples it conquered. The purposes of God in such complex situations are most likely varied. Christians shouldn't doubt God's control when evil seems to triumph or when Christianity suffers setbacks. Why did God permit Christianity to take firm root in Europe but to be subdued in North Africa and halted in its early spread into China? To questions like these the Christian must simply answer, "The secret things belong to the Lord" (Deut. 29:29).

The Christian historian, then, must not neglect the providence of God, but he must proceed in such matters with dependence on what God has revealed and with great humility.

6. Clarifying Causation and Chronology

Historical models typically relate events to one another. So whether a historian is writing a history of the Battle of Gettysburg or of the entire Civil War, he's seeking to order events and to see if he can determine causation. These can be complex tasks. For instance, American Civil War expert Allen Guelzo notes how difficult it is to order the events of the Battle of Gettysburg given that the participants had watches set by dawn, dusk, and church bells—and many had no watches. Thus reports about the timing of events varied widely. Guelzo had to weigh the varying reports and organize them into the most coherent model that he could develop.[15]

---

humans are capable of making their own choices; God does not coerce the choices of humans. God does allow Satan and humans to follow the course of their own natures by removing His hand of grace (Exod. 4:21; Job 1:12; 2:6) or allowing them to continue in their own blindness instead of illuminating them by His Spirit (Prov. 14:12; 1 Cor. 2:14). But He never allows their actions to circumvent or undermine His plan (Eph. 1:9–10). All of their actions, which they are personally responsible for, will be used by God to fulfill His wise ends (Rom. 9:14–22).

Causation: A Case Study

Ask a history teacher or another professional historian to discuss the complexities of determining the causation of certain events. Then have him present a particular case study for students to examine. For example, what were all the factors that led up to the sinking of the *Titanic*?

Taking Advantage of Communication

Encourage students to read history on their own. They shouldn't just learn history through a textbook, which can only provide an outline of bare facts. There are fascinating accounts of particular events with riveting action. There is a whole world to explore. Students can be transported to another place and another time because history has been written down for their benefit. Encourage students to take advantage of the rich resources available to them. (Students can ask a history teacher which books or authors they would recommend.) They can expand their horizons by reading. They'll find that the best movies tend to be rooted

Another historian points out that there are numerous proposed causes for that same Civil War, from states' rights versus nationalism, to divisions over the morality of slavery, to differing cultural ideals and economic systems. The plural in the title of his book, *The Causes of the Civil War*, points to the idea that complex events have complex causes. Though slavery stands at the nexus of these causes, that doesn't mean that culture, economics, and politics played no role. Slavery was tied into all of those things, and yet different people may have had very different primary motivations for joining the war effort on either side.[16] In the case of the Crimean War, one historian makes the case that both religious and political concerns provoked the conflict.[17] Causation is complex. The potential causes that stand out to a particular historian as interesting and worth discussing will very likely have a lot to do with his worldview.

7. Communicating Historical Truth

Finally, just as in science, the findings of historians must be communicated in order to benefit others and advance the historical discipline. Sometimes this is done in detailed journal articles that focus on the specifics of a particular incident or aspect of history. Sometimes historians write scholarly monographs* for the benefit of other historians. Sometimes they will instead write for the average interested reader. They might build upon the work of many other historians and put together a sweeping survey that looks at the history of a region, a nation, or even the world.

monograph: *a detailed, scholarly book on one specific topic*

HISTORY AND WORLDVIEW

Historians all do their work looking through worldview lenses. But this doesn't mean that historical research and writing leave a person unchanged. Though the Christian historian should not change his views on biblically rooted matters of doctrine and practice, his historical study should give him a richer view of the world. He should be developing a deeper understanding of how precisely God has worked in the world, a better understanding of the intractability* of sin through a myriad of examples, and a greater ability to understand and evaluate his own culture biblically.

intractability: *difficulty in resolving or eliminating*

Historical research doesn't alter the fundamentals of the faith, but it may alter our evaluations of history. For instance, some think that the Puritans were hypocrites for seeking religious freedom for themselves and then denying it to others. But a student of history will know that modern ideas of religious liberty came later. The Puritans were always looking for the freedom to worship and live in a society governed by Scripture, not simply for "religious liberty" as an abstract value.

Or some might have thought that the American founders were all Christians (since they were clearly not modern secularists). But closer examination reveals that between the First and Second Great Awakenings there was a religious decline in America. Unitarianism and "rational" religion spread, especially among the educated classes. Thomas Jefferson predicted that by the time he died evangelical Christianity would be extinct in America. In reality, even as he spoke, the Second Great Awakening was under way.[18]

Christians who study history ought to look at everything through the lenses of the biblical worldview. But they're looking at something; they aren't just looking at the lenses. They're studying source material, tracking down witnesses, and looking

whole overarching personal and family history. Students can record them.

The students and their relatives will have to be selective. What's significant? What's most important to them? What's interesting? If the interviewee is a Christian, ask him to interpret the ways and works of God in his own life. What would provide a lesson for life? What defines the culture of the family, where he is today, and what makes him tick? How would he interpret God's providence in his life? Can he make any moral judgments about his own actions or that of the culture around him? What caused him to move where he did, participate in the job that he chose? What were some of the chronological benchmarks?

After gathering the source material from the eyewitness account and selecting the most relevant data, students should write out a historical report summarizing the account. How would they present the story of their relative to a future generation? More families should be able to pass on to the next generation an account of their forefathers. The ability to communicate and preserve that record is in our power with all of the tools that we have today.

Revisionist History

Although the term *revisionist history* has become associated with largely negative connotations, it's only negative when people rewrite what truly happened in order to bolster their own agendas. What people believe about the past becomes a powerful tool for motivating them to respond in a certain way in the present. Therefore, "history" has often been manipulated to support particular social and political ends. Some secularists are so bold as to proclaim that the past reality doesn't matter as long as the present agenda is worthy. But this separates truth from goodness. (See an example of this on page 409 in the Student Text.)

But if rewriting history means that the initial knowledge and interpretation of events was, in fact, not accurate and that with further information or better analysis historians can now provide a more accurate account, then revisionist history is a good endeavor. Historians must be willing to revise their models just as scientists must be willing to revise a theory based on new evidence. American Christians are wary of revisionists who hold to a secular model of interpretation that overturns the model of interpretation from past American history—a past model that is often presumed to be built on the Judeo-Christian ethic. There are many cases in which this may be true. But there are also examples in which past generations

in the best stories recorded in real history. Reading may take more time and effort, but it's generally more rewarding than the superficial story lines of most movies. Here are some examples of topics of interest:

Biography

- Athanasius, Augustine, Bernard of Clairvaux
- Alexander the Great, Julius Caesar
- Catherine the Great, Elizabeth I
- Marco Polo, David Livingstone
- Martin Luther, Lady Jane Grey, John Knox
- William Bradford, Anne Bradstreet, Jonathan Edwards
- Billy the Kid, Butch Cassidy, Jesse James
- George Washington Carver, Thomas Edison
- William Carey, Adoniram Judson, C. H. Spurgeon

Regions, Eras, and Events

- South America, Africa, or Russia
- Ancient empires such as Nubia, Greece, and Rome (famous battles, culture before, during, and after the time of Christ, etc.)
- The Industrial Revolution (social conditions and transformation)
- The US Civil War or World War II (battles, weaponry, strategy, politics, espionage)

Ask students to brainstorm what else would fascinate them and why.

Passing on Family History

Ask students to interview one of their grandparents (or a great-grandparent or another elderly relative). They should ask their relatives to provide a firsthand account of one major event that they lived through. Or they can ask their relatives to recount their

of Americans may have been blind to their own failings and viewed almost all events through proverbial rose-colored glasses. A more objective generation, including secularists by God's common grace, can provide a more accurate critique.

Humility Is Key

Revising history demands humility because humans from any country often failed more than past generations of their countrymen may have wanted to admit. However, a more objective present generation should be careful of its judgments of past generations. It's easy to be anachronistic—to use present-day standards to judge past generations of people who didn't have those same standards (especially if those standards or applications of those standards are socially constructed rather than universally absolute creational and moral norms). It's easy to forget that the past generation living through those struggles surely had a different perspective with a more detailed knowledge of the situation than we have. It's easy to forget our own failings in the present and how futile it is for a minority to push back against evil and stop it. Humility is key in the work of historical evaluation and revision.

History Provides Meaning

Ask students to imagine what it would be like to wake up one day with amnesia. What if they couldn't remember who they were, where they came from, who they were related to, or what they'd done in life?

As long as you remained in that state, how difficult would it be to move forward in life?

Answers will vary.

People who have experienced such a problem generally struggle to put into words how horrible the situation was until they could put the pieces back together or build a new life with history. They lost the ability to make sense of life. History is vital for the meaning of your life.

---

at archaeological evidence. They're doing the work of historians. But they do it as Christians.

WRITING HISTORY

Humans are story-telling creatures. We can't help it. We view even the objects we run across in our day-to-day lives as parts of tiny stories. That coffee cup on the shelf has no meaning—it's just a blob—until it's part of a story: "Once upon a time, I poured coffee into that mug, put it to my lips, drank it down slowly, and placed it in the dishwasher." Certain coffee cups mean more because they're part of more significant stories, such as "Once upon a time, my best friend left for Germany and gave me this cup as a parting gift."

The power to tell the story of more significant things—such as a person, a city, a college, or even a nation—is the power to give meaning to those things. History is a powerful tool for bringing glory to the God of history and for helping our neighbors better see the world as He sees it. Only the history in the Bible can give us a true God's-eye view, of course, but history books written according to creational principles can do a great deal to shape God's image-bearers.

THINKING IT THROUGH 22.3

1. Since Christians believe that human history begins at creation and culminates at Christ's return, what philosophy of history must be rejected?

2. Restate in your own words the seven creational norms for conducting historical research.

3. What are generally the best kinds of sources?

4. Why should the Christian historian appeal to God's providence in history? What danger must he avoid when doing so?

♀5. Why are models necessary for the study of history?

THINKING IT THROUGH 22.3

1. the cyclical view

2. • studying source materials
   • making models
   • selecting what's significant
   • making moral judgments
   • discerning history as divine providence
   • clarifying causation and chronology
   • communicating historical truth

3. primary sources or firsthand accounts of the historical event

4. God is always at work in all of history; the Christian can't just select the positive things that occur in order to point out God's providential working—all things are a part of God's plan that He will eventually work together for good

♀5. Every finite historian must select which material to highlight and then interpret it according to a coherent worldview system of thought.

22 CHAPTER REVIEW

TERMS TO REMEMBER

telos
situatedness
cyclical view of history
primary sources

Scripture Memory

Acts 17:26–27

Making Connections

1. How does the fact that God took a week to create the world demonstrate that God works His will through history?

2. How does God's plan of redemption demonstrate that God works His will through history?

3. What are three primary sources that historians use in their research? How does their worldview impact this research?

4. What makes determining causation difficult for historians?

Developing Skills in Apologetics and Worldview

5. How would you explain to an unbeliever why Christians follow some laws from the Old Testament and not others?

6. How could you persuade someone if you disagree with his moral judgments about a historical event?

Examining Assumptions and Evidence

7. What significant difference between the Old Testament and New Testament demonstrates the historical progress of God's people from child to adult?

8. Why is it controversial to claim that historians should connect God's purposes with the historical events they study?

9. How can you prevent your cultural identity (assumptions, values, practices) from becoming an idol?

10. Why is history always more than simply retelling what happened?

Becoming a Creative Cultivator

11. Write a brief history about a significant person or event in your town during the last thirty to sixty years. Conduct an interview of at least one eyewitness to gather oral history.

FOUNDATIONS FOR HISTORY | 353

CHAPTER REVIEW ANSWERS

Making Connections

1. God could have spoken everything into existence instantly; instead He created the world through the chronological time of seven successive normal historical days.

2. God could have sent Jesus to immediately redeem Adam and Eve and the creation; instead He waited to send Jesus until the fullness of time in human history.

3. Primary sources can include artifacts archeologists uncover, traditions or oral histories handed down through generations, and written records of firsthand accounts. The historian must discern which sources are reliably trustworthy and significant.

4. Many times events are complex with varying causes.

Developing Skills in Apologetics and Worldview

5. You would need to explain to him the biblical history through differing covenants of administering situational applications of God's timeless moral principles; once he's aware of the significance of the historical context, then he will have no excuse for continuing to accuse Christians of arbitrary applications.

6. Examine the reliability of his sources, his selection of the facts (the whole context, accurate chronology), accuracy of proposed causes and effects, and his presupposed model or worldview (his standard for moral judgments). Even though Scripture is the ultimate standard, good

Christians who share a similar world-view may still disagree because of a different apprehension of all of the above listed factors.

Examining Assumptions and Evidence

7. God changed from providing numerous specific laws in the Old Testament to providing only general principles in the New Testament because expanded revelation and the New Covenant work of God enhanced His expectations—He expected His children to grow into maturity, making correct applications from general principles. This is necessary because God's people come from vastly different time periods and regions of the world rather than from one nation that's a theocracy.

8. Unless God's specific purposes have been clearly revealed in inspired revelation, the Christians historian can't dogmatically claim to understand all of God's specific purposes in a particular event of history.

9. Evaluate your cultural identity and its historical development through the lens of Scripture, recognizing with humility the failures of the past and how even good values can be applied in a fallen manner.

10. History always involves interpretation (fitting facts into a model) and selecting what's significant for the purposes of learning lessons for life, understanding the ways and works of God, and evaluating a cultural identity.

Creative Cultivation

11. Answers will vary.

TERMS TO REMEMBER

telos—the ultimate end of a goal-oriented process giving purpose to history

situatedness—the inescapable truth that every human views the world from a particular historical, geographic, and intellectual point of view

cyclical view of history—the idea that history is an endless circle of repetition in contrast to a linear progression with a beginning and a culmination

primary sources—firsthand accounts or records of historical events

The student will be able to

23.1 Critique four significant ideologies that distort the work of historians.

23.2 Evaluate how fallenness can affect a historian's selection and moral judgments.

SECTION OBJECTIVES 23.1

1. Summarize the naturalistic view of history, and evaluate its views on determinism and morality.

2. Describe the characteristics of extreme nationalism and summarize its view of history, identifying problems with its demonization of others and minimization of its own shortcomings.

3. Summarize the postmodernist view of history, identifying problems with its skepticism of a larger unifying story, its denial of historical certitude, and its refusal to critique wrong perspectives.

4. Summarize the views of history that emphasize class, race, and gender, identifying problems with single-issue emphases, forced interpretations, and blindness to both good and evil in every race, every class, and every gender.

Chapter Twenty-Three **FALLEN HISTORY**

You are of your father the devil, and your will is to do your father's desires. He was a murderer from the beginning, and does not stand in the truth, because there is no truth in him. When he lies, he speaks out of his own character, for he is a liar and the father of lies. But because I tell the truth, you do not believe me.

**Scripture Memory
John 8:44–45**

23.1 THE FALL, HISTORY, AND IDEOLOGIES

In John 8:44, Jesus calls the devil "the father of lies." The first lie Satan told was about history. And the first lie Adam told was too. When God asked Adam if he had eaten from the forbidden tree, Adam responded with a historical narrative: "The woman whom you gave to be with me, she gave me fruit of the tree, and I ate" (Gen. 3:12). In one sense, this historical narrative is true. God did give the woman to be with Adam. The woman did give Adam the fruit from the tree. And Adam did eat. But Adam selected and arranged the details to tell a story that wasn't true: "This sin isn't my fault; it's God's. He's the one who gave me this woman."

Adam omitted some key information: Eve was created to be Adam's helper; he was given the authority to lead (1 Tim. 2:13). Eve was deceived when she took and ate the fruit; Adam's guilt was greater than Eve's because he was not deceived when he ate (1 Tim. 2:14). But Adam failed to mention the part of the story in which he let the serpent undermine the order of authority in his family. Adam's historical account didn't include his own intentional rebellion against his Creator.

This first historical lie reveals the complex way that the Fall has affected the study of history. Historians today can do the same thing Adam did: they can communicate facts about things that really happened. But they can select and organize those facts to present a false picture.

Historians also never write from a neutral perspective; they're influenced by ideologies similar to those we discussed in the government chapter. Historians can fasten on to truths and exalt them to a role in their theories that distorts their work. Other truths can easily be left out.

This section will focus on four significant ideologies that distort the work of historians. The first one you should recognize from the science unit: it's naturalism. The second is nationalism. The third is postmodernism. The fourth is a fixation on the issues of class, race, and gender.

NATURALISM

Remember that scientism exerts its influence beyond the sciences; it has claimed authority even in the humanities, in disciplines such as history. One proponent of scientism even asked in a major American newspaper, "[When] will the humanities . . . gratefully accept the peace imposed by science?"[1]

Scientific naturalism has definitely put pressure on the practice of writing history. This pressure is an obvious result of naturalism's view of humanity. According to this worldview, humans and their civilizations are merely the products of nature operating according to physical laws of cause and effect.[2]

Why Certain Cultures Dominate History

Jared Diamond's *Guns, Germs, and Steel* is an excellent example of the naturalistic approach to history. This 1997 book is an impressive attempt to bring

354 | HISTORY

Lesson Plan Chart—Chapter 23

Section Title	Pages	Activity Manual	Days
23.1 The Fall, History, and Ideologies	354–64	Activity 40	4 days
23.2 Selection and Moral Judgments	365–67		1 day
Review	368		1 day
Total Suggested Days			**6 days**

The Power of a Historical Narrative

What people believe about the past will direct their behavior in the present. That reality makes history a very powerful tool in the arsenal of social engineers.

Remember, one of the major purposes of teaching people a historical narrative is to give them context. The purpose is to provide a broader view of life—to explain where people have come from and where they're going. Its explanations are meant to clarify why things happened in order to warn against certain social or political agendas or to reinforce one's own social ends.

Some people recognize the great power of the historical tool to shape what we believe about the past in order to manipulate people's responses in the present. Therefore, it

many disciplines together—geography, archeology, botany, zoology, and others—to tell the history of the world and all its major civilizations. The book won a Pulitzer Prize shortly after it was published and still remains a bestseller today.[3]

One of the opening stories in Diamond's book describes the impressive army of the Inca king Atahualpa and its incredible defeat even though it vastly outnumbered the Spanish forces under the command of Francisco Pizarro. Diamond asks why Atahualpa didn't cross the ocean and conquer Spain rather than the other way around. Diamond notes rightly that people around the world are equally intelligent. So why have certain cultures dominated world history while others have remained undeveloped or even primitive?

Why didn't Inca forces cross the ocean and conquer Spain instead of the other way around?

Diamond's answer focuses on environmental conditions. Cultures with fruitful land (and easily domesticated animals and crops) can start towns and cities because not everyone has to be a farmer. They can establish political organizations and develop writing systems for their languages, giving these societies further advantages over hunter-gatherers and subsistence farmers. Diamond notes that these were precisely the conditions in Eurasia, so those peoples had a head start in developing the technologies—like guns and steel—that would eventually help them conquer the world.

A Christian Critique of Naturalism in History

The Christian historian can agree with Diamond that the environment does have an effect on human civilization. For instance, the sophisticated Nubian culture (called "Cush" in the Bible) was destroyed by the encroaching Sahara Desert. The Bible itself affirms the effect of the environment on civilizations. The very way God described the Promised Land to the Hebrews focused on its natural richness: it was "a land in which you will eat bread without scarcity, in which you will lack nothing, a land whose stones are iron, and out of whose hills you can dig copper" (Deut. 8:9). Israel's location at the intersection of continents and bodies of water was also advantageous for trade.

matters little to them if their recounting of history is accurate and their interpretations are truthful (i.e., whether these correspond to reality). The only thing that matters is that the narrative advances their social goals. Lying about the past is justified in their eyes.

A prime example of the manipulation of history to powerfully motivate people to support a sociopolitical cause is exemplified in the popular support of Adolf Hitler leading up to World War II. Because it's so obvious in retrospect that Hitler was an evil person, it's hard to understand why so many of his own countrymen at the time gladly put him into power. Hitler used hyper-nationalism, but he also manipulated historical facts. He convinced his people that Germany had been unfairly dealt with by the Treaty of Versailles, and he came up with a narrative

about the Jews that made them the scapegoats to incite violence against them.

 Historical Oversimplification

Can the environment have a major effect on the course of history?

Yes, especially in the ancient world, the environment would often play a major role. For example, since a water source was vital, cities would form near rivers.

Provide two reasons that explain why interpreting all of history as primarily an environmental response is simplistic.

Technology overcomes environmental factors. This is why ancient people with less technology were more affected by the environment.

Causation is complex; many factors are involved. For example, beliefs and values are

also powerful forces. Spain had values that motivated that nation to explore and conquer. In contrast, Native Americans had developed a lifestyle in keeping with their own values. As a result, they had no incentive to explore the world or to conquer Europe.

Make sure students understand that the environment is a factor in shaping a society—it can be a major factor. But it's never the *only* factor. Humans are always responsible for their behavior in response to their circumstances.

Other questions to discuss:

Geography is an important factor for shaping the course of history, but is it more important than any other factor?

Are humans powerless to resist the inanimate forces of nature around them?

Can't world history be shaped by moral values that become widespread enough to become the cultural values of a whole society?

Are those values only or primarily shaped by the environment? Or can it be the reverse—one's values shape one's response to overcome environmental obstacles?

Because of common grace, cultures advanced by learning to use the natural resources around them to fulfill the Creation Mandate. They overcame the obstacles of the environment around them. They learned creational norms (Isa. 28:23–29). All this was made possible because of God's unconditional covenant with Noah (see the TE note on the Noahic Covenant, page 140).

Naturalism and Morality

What concern does George Marsden raise about naturalism?

It leaves no room for moral evaluation.

Why should people desire to evaluate cultures morally?

Moral evaluation is inescapable. Was Spain's conquest of Central and South American empires moral? Were the human sacrifices of the Aztecs moral? Was the slave trade moral? History is full of moral and immoral actions, and recognizing the morality or immorality is impossible for the historian to avoid.

What does Marsden identify as the basis for naturalistic morality?

He identifies cultural survival as the basis for naturalistic morality. That which promotes a culture's survival becomes part of its moral code, and that which threatens its survival is considered immoral.

Why must this be the basis of morality in a naturalistic worldview?

There is no external standard that morality is based on. Everything must develop naturally.

What does Marsden say the result of this form of morality is and why?

moral relativity because each culture develops its own survival mechanisms

Why is moral relativism a problematic conclusion?

The Spanish could argue that their morality justified their conquest of weaker civilizations, and the Aztecs could claim that their morality justified their practice of human sacrifice. There is no basis to critique a culture's moral code—even if people from other cultures are suffering from the actions of those from different cultures.

 ## Evaluating Cultures

Divide the class in half and allow students to debate whether or not Spanish culture was superior to Incan culture. In other words, was the culture of Spain more or less conformed to biblical values and creational norms compared to the culture of the Incas?

After allowing them to debate, ask the following questions.

Is the superiority of one culture or the other a legitimate question to debate?

From a biblical worldview, it's a legitimate question because there is an absolute and transcendent standard of values that supercedes both cultures. The generalized behavioral characteristics of a culture can be identified and judged (Titus 1:12–13). And there are objective creational norms built into God's creation to which any culture conforms to a greater or lesser extent.

[Note that the question is admittedly stated in such a way as to hide the complexity of the issue.]

How could a Christian historian decide the debated question?

It's actually not a simple question with a simple answer. Both cultures reflect some conformity to God's creational norms because all people are created in God's image and carry out the Creation Mandate to some extent in some way. Both cultures also reflect depravity because all people are fallen. The historian must be careful to select all relevant data about both groups of people and not just emphasize the positives of one culture and the negatives of the contrasting culture. It's wrong to merely present the Spanish as civilized Christians and the Incas as uncivilized pagans. Although Native American cultures can be biblically critiqued as contrary to biblical ethics, Catholic Spain contradicted those biblical ethics in its greed for the land and possessions that it took without justification.

But even though the environment has an effect on civilizations, the environment itself doesn't determine human history. One reviewer said of *Guns, Germs, and Steel,* "Much more powerfully than any other species, we change the environment around us. . . . Human beings do indeed often 'approach limits imposed by environmental constraints' only to find a way to overcome and escape those constraints, as the history of technology repeatedly illustrates."[4] A Christian reading these comments should immediately think of the Creation Mandate. The environment does not determine human history because humans have been given the responsibility to rule over creation and not the other way around.

determinism: *the philosophical view that everything that happens in nature or society is caused by previous events and conditions, not by human choices or divine will*

There is a **naturalistic determinism*** in Diamond's theory that doesn't fit with the Bible's emphasis on the real impact of human choices. "By justice a king builds up the land, but he who exacts gifts [bribes] tears it down," Solomon said (Prov. 29:4). In other words, a just king can make a major difference in his environment—and so can a greedy one. Human righteousness and wickedness change the world and the future of nations. For instance, Mao Zedong's attempt to bring about a cultural revolution in China in the late 1960s and early 1970s brought wide-scale environmental devastation to his country.

Diamond thinks naturalism will prevent racism by showing that all peoples are fundamentally equal—and that is a good desire. But accomplished Christian historian George Marsden notes that naturalism also leads to major problems. Naturalism teaches that humans are the result of evolution and that their cultures result from "natural evolutionary processes." But if cultures have simply evolved naturally, there are no moral absolutes by which to judge cultures. In a naturalistic worldview, morals also evolve; morality evolved as a way for different cultures to survive. If different cultures evolve different moralities, Marsden asks, what right does the historian have to say one method of survival is superior to another? He concludes, "Some sort of moral relativism seems the only consistent option."[5] But this isn't an acceptable option. What if the morality of one culture develops into a form of eugenics*? The Christian has a standard by which he can judge this to be wrong; the naturalist will have difficulty doing so with intellectual consistency.

eugenics: *the "science" of improving the human race by improving its genetic stock and pruning off undesirables*

NATIONALISM

Nationalism is the attitude of lifting up the independence of a nation or ethnic group as a kind of ultimate good. The great evil, in this view, is to be ruled over by another nation. In nationalism, a person's greatest loyalty is to be given to the nation or ethnic group—loyalty even to the point of death. Nationalism is often supported with quasi-religious ceremonies, symbols, and even holy days.

Like other flawed ideologies, nationalism has picked out certain aspects of truth. It recognizes that humans do not live merely as individuals but as communities. They develop shared memories, customs, and values, which bind them together and enable them to do more as a group than they ever could have done as a loose collection of individuals. Often the combination of values in particular cultures is worthy of high praise. Germany, for example, has developed a reputation for highly skilled manufacturing and attention to detail that makes people around the world value its products. Other cultures have developed a respect for close family life and a determination to always do the honorable thing even when that means sacrificing self-interest. The preservation of these cultures is a good thing. People who love their nation's cultural heritage are often worried when immigrants with different cultures threaten to change something they value highly. As a result, the concern to preserve one's culture

---

Students should understand that the Christian historian should be able to step back and biblically critique both cultures or praise both cultures based on *specific behaviors.*

 ## Patriotism Versus Nationalism

The kind of nationalism being critiqued here has often been labeled *jingoism* to differentiate extreme nationalism from a praiseworthy spirit of patriotism.

What characterizes patriotism?

- *thankfulness for the stewardship of forefathers who have entrusted that which they built up to the next generation*
- *love of the unity around the beliefs and values of like-minded people*
- *desire to preserve that cultural identity*

Patriotism is only good to the extent that that stewardship, those beliefs and values, and that cultural identity can be considered good. For Christians, if all those things contradict their biblical worldview, their patriotism will be very limited. They may only praise God for common grace reflected in their country.

What attitudes and behaviors characterize jingoism? In other words, when does patriotism become idolatry?

- *blind commitment to the nation regardless of the morality of its policies*
- *unethical treatment of other people groups*
- *elevating one's own culture beyond its due and failing to recognize the goodness of other cultures*

American Christians have often been tempted toward nationalism because of the

can be twisted, but the desire for cultural preservation is not in itself bad. Also, when a country is threatened by a military invasion, it's typically considered heroic to defend one's nation with one's life.

Nationalistic Idolatry

But nationalism tends toward idolatry, and this idolatry becomes evident when people of other ethnic groups are demonized simply for being culturally different. Nationalist movements tend to evaluate other cultures more negatively than honesty and fairness would allow. In the past, many Americans claimed that immigrants from Ireland, Germany, Italy, and Eastern Europe were drunken, shiftless foreigners who would debase American culture. In fact, most of these immigrants proved to be hardworking folk who assimilated into American life while holding on to the best of their own traditions. The genuine value of other ethnic groups is forgotten when nationalism ignores the fact that all humans are made in God's image and have received His creation blessing. There is something we can appreciate in every culture on earth.

In an effort to preserve something good in its own culture, a nationalist group may do truly wicked things against another culture, from persecution to lynching to outright war.

Nationalistic Salvation

Nationalism is also a powerful force offering an attractive prize to larger minorities within certain nations. The Tibetans in China, the Kurds in the Middle East, the Chechens in Russia, and the South Sudanese in Sudan are all ethnic groups that have sought in various ways to break free and form their own independent nations. The Kurds have achieved some measure of success; they have self-rule within Iraq. The South Sudanese won full independence in a bloody civil war.

But the salvation promised by nationalism is usually hollow. Independence rarely achieves what revolutionaries hope to gain. The great conflicts of the twentieth century, as well as many of the smaller ones, were fueled by nationalism. Nationalism was the flint that created the spark in the powder keg of Europe, leading to World War II. German and Japanese nationalism spawned World War II. And the postwar nationalism fueled various revolutions against colonial powers around the world. While in most if not all cases there was good reason to grant these countries independence, national independence rarely brought salvation. One particularly sad case is Eritrea, which fought for freedom from Ethiopia for many years, only for the revolutionary leader to establish himself firmly as a dictator once his people achieved independence.

German nationalism was one of many nationalisms that shaped the twentieth century.

Christian influence that the United States benefited from. This should become less of a temptation as the United States abandons Christian morality. Allegiance to Americanism must not displace allegiance to Christ.

Preserving Cultural Identity

What is the opposite extreme from jingoism, and why is it dangerous?

Globalism is the opposite of extreme nationalism. Globalists aren't concerned about (and may even work against) national borders, economies, sovereignties, and cultural identities. They promote multiculturalism. (Every culture is good so there is no reason to preserve any one cultural identity.) They work toward a utopian social order. They embrace big government in violation of sphere sovereignty.

When is preserving cultural identity good?

When a cultural identity is founded on worldview beliefs and values that conform closely to biblical values and creational norms, then Christians, conservatives, and traditionalists want to preserve that identity. When a massive influx of people from a different culture with different beliefs and values (based on different religious commitments) desire the benefits of a successful culture but adamantly reject assimilation (a new cultural identity), then conflict will occur. Secularism's pretense of neutrality and tolerance will fail.

What are proper ways to endeavor to preserve a cultural identity?

- *a secure border and a standardized immigration system enforced by the rule of law*
- *education that instills in the next generation the values that built the nation*
- *a social atmosphere that reaches out to help legal immigrants assimilate*

What are improper ways to endeavor to preserve a cultural identity?

- *ethnic cleansing or genocide*
- *racist persecution*
- *unethical or unjust treatment*

Discerning Cultural Appreciation

Sometimes Christians don't understand the underlying influences of cultural differences so they too easily embrace those differences without realizing the roots in false beliefs and values. (They've been influenced by secular ideals of multicultural tolerance). But other times Christians are too particular, magnifying abstruse associations or just plain rejecting anything that is different from their own culture. (They've confused Americanism with Christianity.) It is necessary to apply biblical wisdom to an accurate and thorough knowledge of another culture.

Divide students into small groups and ask them to research and evaluate the following. It is traditional for women from India to paint designs on their palms and feet the night before their wedding. (The practice is called *mehendi*.) Should such a practice be appreciated and embraced? Does such a practice so threaten the cultural identity of a nation that immigrants should be denied entry?

First, Christians must ask why it is a tradition. What does it signify? The religion of Hinduism is so intertwined with the social culture of India that this practice has become tradition. But the tradition is still a Vedic custom that symbolically represents the inner and outer sun. The people in that culture still understand the symbols to communicate an inner awakening or enlightenment. The henna paint that is used represents good luck or karma, based on their beliefs in the spirit world. As individuals, Christians can't appreciate or syncretize their own practices with this false religion.

Second, Christians must ask how significantly the tradition affects society. What implications does it have and in which contexts? If Christians understand sphere sovereignty correctly, the practice isn't a threat to the social order of a nation. Christians would need to keep the practice out of their churches, but not necessarily try to remove it from the nation. This Hindu practice isn't parallel to the religious-political (theocratic) threat of Islamic sharia law.

Idolizing Democracy

Self-rule doesn't necessarily guarantee a free and just society (see pp. 257–59 in the

Student Text). The American Founding Fathers distrusted pure democracy and recognized that even a constitutional republic with a federalist system of checks and balances still needed the foundation of morality to succeed. They predicted that if the people became immoral, the constitutional republic would begin to collapse. Their prediction is coming true.

Responding to the Whig Fallacy

Ways to resist the Whig fallacy:

- Research history with specificity to get a fuller understanding of the errors of even good men from the past. Whig history is generated through generalizations that tend to minimize the errors of flawed people. (Note this contrast between Whig history and biblical history—even the greatest people of the Bible are almost without exception presented as extremely flawed people.)

- A more accurate understanding of the people of the past demands a more thorough understanding of how they thought *differently* from people in the present. One test to see if you truly understand their different thinking is whether or not you are condescending toward them simply for not being modern. Beware of anachronisms—projecting today's understandings on people of the past. Whig history is generated when people try to support their present agendas by too quickly rallying historical figures to their side to agree with them. But the past must be understood in its own context.

- Study the past to understand the *past* accurately. Whig history is generated when a superficial understanding of the past is applied to the present. Lessons for life should be drawn, but only *after* the past has been understood accurately. Beginning with the present application in mind and mining for support in the past leads to twisting historical narratives to fit agendas—conservative or progressive.

- Avoid oversimplification, which results only in caricatures and hasty conclusions about causation. Whig history is generated when, for the sake of touting progress, the whole course of history is simplistically traced as one long uninterrupted line of success from there to here. Because societies of the past were just as complex as societies in the present, determining causation is complex.

[See Herbert Butterfield, *The Whig Interpretation of History* (London: G. Bell and Sons, 1931).]

Two Extremes to Avoid

There are two sides to the one coin. If historians can exaggerate the good of their own party, they also can exaggerate the bad of others. Whig histories may do both, but the

Nationalism in Japan was a major contributing factor to the deadliest war in the history of mankind, WWII.

Nationalistic History

Every nationalist movement necessarily tells a story about itself—a history. And the temptation such movements face is obvious: to spin that history to favor the nation.

Nineteenth-century historians such as Thomas Macaulay in Britain, George Bancroft in the United States, and others in France and Germany wrote national histories that extolled the virtues of their countries and their political views. They selected events to frame a story that made their respective nations look good. They tended to turn history into a story about a progressive march toward the bright day when their nations arrived to grace the universe.

These kinds of boastful nationalist histories largely fell out of favor in the twentieth century as the dangers of nationalism became apparent, especially in light of the role German nationalism played in the two world wars. Historian Herbert Butterfield, in his 1931 book *The Whig Interpretation of History*, famously warned against any view of history that "studies the past with reference to the present"[6] and tends "to praise revolutions provided they have been successful, to emphasize certain principles of progress

THOMAS MACAULAY: A WHIG AND HIS STORIES

Thomas Macaulay (1800–1859) wrote an influential five-volume history of England from the reign of James II through the reign of William III. Macaulay was associated with the Whig party, which favored a constitutional monarchy in England (instead of an absolute monarchy), a strong Parliament, and religious freedom for dissenters from the Church of England. Macaulay wrote as though the history of England was the history of the triumph of the Whigs' ideas. He presented anyone who opposed Whig ideas in a bad light and anyone who supported them in a good light.

It's important to understand that a Whiggish approach to history doesn't necessarily have anything to do with the Whigs as a political party. Anybody with any strong partisan view can write a Whiggish history.

emphasis is usually on the goodness of their own people. The class, race, and gender approaches to history, discussed later in this chapter, tend to demonize people outside their group to magnify their own oppression.

A Christian must be careful to resist both extremes. One political group will want you to believe only in the shining light of your own people; another political group will want you to be shocked at the unmitigated darkness of oppression faced by minorities. Both of these historical narratives incorporate many of the errors of the Whig fallacy.

Creation, Fall, Redemption is the corrective to both extremes. Christians can see God's common grace in people who have been created in the image of God. They can see that every human reflects the innate desire to fulfill the Creation Mandate. But Christians can also identify fallenness even in the best

efforts and causes in history. They also can't ignore the horrendous depths of depravity. Hypocrisy isn't just an individual sin; it can be a national sin. Disappointments in our heroes from the past shouldn't lead to despair though. There are examples of God's justice and God's redemption. He has a larger sovereign plan of redemption that everything fits into so that all will be made right one day (Eph. 1:10–11). When making moral judgments, Christians must be careful not to ignore and/or magnify only one of the three major CFR realities.

Culture Shock

Ask a student who has lived in another country for an extended time—a year or more:

Did you experience culture shock? How did you learn to humbly appreciate the

in the past and to produce a story which is the ratification if not glorification of the present"[7]—what he called a **Whiggish** view of history.

Butterfield warned that the Whiggish approach to history viewed past events through the eyes of present concerns. For example, if people today are concerned about individual liberties, the historian will choose to write about the events that seemingly led to today's conceptions of liberty. But the people of a particular time and place may have had very different interests. Perhaps they focused more on religion or kinship, not liberty. The Whig historian fails to really understand the concerns of people who lived in other times and places. Whig history neglects what people of the past thought was significant and how and why they thought differently from people in the present. Butterfield was also concerned that Whiggish historians made moral evaluations based on a current moral consensus—and then used their moral evaluations to further promote their vision of how life ought to be.

A Christian Critique of Whiggish and Nationalistic Histories

Christians can certainly fall prey to ultranationalist and Whiggish views, but at the very heart of the Bible is a command that ought to keep us away from them: "Love your neighbor as yourself" (Lev. 19:18). You like your nation? Great! Allow others to like theirs. Don't let the value you place on your culture blind you to the values of other cultures; admit it when Germans have cleaner homes, better highways, and a greater mastery of engineering. Admit it when the Chinese and the Brazilians and the South Africans have better food or folk songs or any of a thousand things, huge or almost invisible, that cause cultures to differ from one another.

The people of the past are your neighbors, too, in a sense. And they ought to get the same benefit. They had weaknesses that your culture doesn't have, but they had strengths your culture doesn't have too. It's a very Christian thing to seek to understand others as they saw themselves, to try to put yourself in their shoes and feel their concerns. As a Christian, you have a clear moral standard that sometimes requires you to disagree with the actions and beliefs of others. But to lie about those actions or beliefs by failing to present them accurately isn't biblical.

For instance, the Christian historian may find that he sympathizes with the Puritans rather than with Charles I and the Church of England prelates. But when he tells this part of history, the Christian historian must try to help the reader understand King Charles, his motivations, and his aims. Likewise, though he may be sympathetic to Cromwell and the Puritans, his duty as a historian is to portray them truthfully, warts and all.

"Christian America"

One area in which this is especially pertinent for American Christians is US history. In the face of rising secularism, many Christians have argued for a "Christian America" approach that claims to demonstrate that the United States has always been "a Christian nation." It's true that Christians from the time of the Pilgrims onward have played significant roles in American history. Nor was the United States founded as a secular nation. American political leaders have consistently spoken in religious terms throughout our history. Secularists are wrong to ignore these aspects of the American story.

---

foreign culture and see room for improvement in your own culture?

[You could also ask a special speaker to share an experience of culture shock.]

Usually when people move to a foreign country, they begin to compare and contrast their own culture with that of the country they're trying to adapt to. This experience can be fun; some people love adapting to their new cultural contexts. But almost everyone will also experience culture shock—the feeling of distaste or even abhorrence because of different ways of doing things. Extreme nationalism will only aggravate culture shock. Both sides in a cultural exchange need to be humble about their cultures. Both cultures have differing strengths and weaknesses. Missionaries always have to balance their love for their own country with allowing nationals to love their country.

They can do this by learning to love their new neighbors and by preferring them over themselves (Phil. 2:3–4). The root problem of nationalism is arrogant self-interest.

However, as a Christian, you may also be in a place of government or military service for your own country. God divided people into nations, and there is a healthy self-interest that is inherent in that sovereign sphere. The tasks and responsibilities of government officials include protecting their own people and seeking justice for them.

Historical Culture Shock

The particular views of people from the past will usually be organized into a complex system differing from present-day culture. Some of their beliefs and values might have been wrong, and Scripture is an authoritative, timeless standard by which to judge them. But often good values and views were simply arranged differently because of perspectives that were formed according to a different situational context.

Divide students into small groups to brainstorm examples of different views that they might find difficult to accept today, but that don't actually violate Scripture.

One example might include child labor laws and, in connection with that, the emergence of adolescence bridging the gap between childhood and adulthood. Were past generations wrong for establishing the age of adulthood as twelve to sixteen? Is the present generation wrong for delaying adulthood to age eighteen to twenty-one? Determining the age of adulthood has a major affect on social norms. Whether adulthood begins earlier or later, there are both positive and negative social effects. Neither social order can be completely condemned or completely idolized.

  ### Christian or Secularist?

Divide the class in half and allow students to debate whether famous American presidents such as Washington and Lincoln were biblical Christians.

It isn't necessary to force these great leaders into a mold that they don't clearly fit into. While the biblical quality of their faith does matter in respect to their personal relationship with God and their own eternal life, it doesn't matter as much in respect to their national leadership. They seemed to genuinely believe in the general moral principles of the Bible to guide the nation. In that regard, Christians can appreciate their leadership without having to classify them as biblical Christians. In fact, there's a greater danger in trying to make them out to be something they weren't. That would necessitate minimizing core beliefs of the Christian faith that were not held by these men.

[Thomas Kidd, "The Enigmatic Faith of Washington and Lincoln," Gospel Coalition (website), February 19, 2012]

Avoiding the Two Extremes in American History

American Christians must be careful to resist two extremes. On the one hand, many believers distressed by the secularization of the United States wish to claim that most of the Founding Fathers were indeed Christians. On the other hand, secularists embrace the notion that most of the Founding Fathers were deists because they want to minimize the role of religion in the founding of the nation.

The reality is that while a number of the Founding Fathers were orthodox Christians, many of them embraced rational religion. Nonetheless, the Founding Fathers were not secular. They recognized the importance of morality for the new nation, and they placed a great deal of stock in religion to produce that morality. Thus, though many were not orthodox, neither did they want to exclude Christianity from public life.

THINKING IT THROUGH 23.1A

1. Humans and their civilizations are merely the products of nature operating according to physical laws of cause and effect.

2. The environmental conditions in Spain were more favorable, allowing its culture to advance beyond mere hunting and subsistence farming to develop the technology for conquering other lands.

3. the sovereignty and loyalty to a specific nation or ethnic group; to be ruled over by another ethnic group

4. They demonize opponents and minimize their own wrongdoing in order to present their history as a progressive march toward the triumph of their values.

♀5. All people are created in the image of God. Therefore, they have value and deserve to be treated justly.

The Power of Metanarratives

Remind students of the power of metanarratives and the necessity of them to a worldview (Student Text, pp. 10–13). Postmodernism recognizes the shaping power of metanarratives. Basic beliefs and values grow out of metanarratives (the second ingredient of a worldview). And what people believe about the past will direct their behavior in the present (the third ingredient of a worldview). Postmodernists also recognize the abuse of that power in many cases, but they reject the idea of the metanarrative and not just the abuses.

Because they reject any overarching metanarrative out of which beliefs and values arise, their beliefs and values often seem like a jumble of moral relativity. It only seems like a jumble though because postmoderns can no more resist actually having a metanarrative than they can resist having a worldview. Everyone has a worldview—even though people may not be aware of it and may not systematize it well (Student Text, pp. 15–16). Every worldview has a metanarrative—it's one of the three necessary ingredients that make up a worldview (Student

THEISTIC RATIONALISM

Theistic rationalism is a term coined by Gregg Frazer to describe a moderate form of deism. **Theistic rationalists** tended to believe in a God who did answer prayer and act providentially in the world. They also tended to believe that the Bible contained some revelation from God. But they believed that reason was the judge of what was true revelation and what was myth. They did not believe that Jesus was God, but they tended to believe that he was "a great moral teacher."[8]

HOW CHRISTIAN WERE THE FOUNDERS?

Champions of the Christian America approach are often not careful enough about determining the actual beliefs of early American leaders. The American Founders did believe that religion should play an important role in public life, and they did not hesitate to use religious language in their speeches and writings. Yet, while there were orthodox Christians among the founders, many held to "theistic rationalism." While affirming belief in a god and his providential control, they denied the Trinity, the deity of Jesus, substitutionary atonement, and the inerrancy of Scripture. When Christians today appeal to such figures in support of a "Christian America" view of history, they diminish the vital importance of fundamental doctrines of the faith.

But not all Americans who spoke of God were Christians. Some—such as Jefferson and Adams—were "theistic rationalists" who denied the fundamental doctrines of the faith (see sidebars above). When Christians try to claim them as brothers in Christ, they're not only inaccurate but they may also be unintentionally signaling that those doctrines are unimportant for Christianity.

Another danger of the Christian America approach is that it sometimes seeks to justify immoral national acts. Andrew Jackson, in this view, becomes a hero of democracy; Manifest Destiny is celebrated as God's will; and negative aspects of US history are minimized. This approach to America's past dishonors the memory of faithful Christians who worked hard to prevent or rectify national sins. It also undermines the Christian responsibility to evaluate the events of history from a scriptural perspective. America is not a new and perfect Promised Land; Americans have always been capable of sin.

THINKING IT THROUGH 23.1A

1. Summarize the naturalistic view of history.

2. According to the naturalistic view of history, why did Spain conquer the Inca Empire rather than the other way around?

3. What do nationalists view as the ultimate good? What do they view as the ultimate evil?

4. How do nationalists write history to favor their own country or ethnic group?

♀5. How does Genesis 1:26–28 undermine nationalism?

POSTMODERNISM

French philosopher Jean-François Lyotard is famous for defining *postmodernism* as "incredulity toward metanarratives."[10] *Incredulity* means "skepticism, an unwillingness to believe," and *metanarrative*, as you learned in Chapter 1, means "an all-encompassing story." Postmodernists are skeptical whenever anyone tries to tell a big story that shows how all the little stories relate. Whiggish history provides a perfect example: postmodernists are quick to point out that it seems more than a little suspicious that Whig history manages to make all the little stories in American history point to the vision of America that the writer happens to hold himself.

Text, p. 15). So postmoderns do have identifiable and commonly held approaches or positions (beliefs and values).

But precisely because postmoderns reject a self-conscious recognition of their metanarrative, they're bound to be poor systematizers of beliefs and values—they're often inconsistent. All false worldviews will be inconsistent, but postmoderns tend to be more so. Most false worldviews care when you point out an inconsistency and try to fix it; postmoderns don't usually care. Their metanarrative of reality says that the world is an incoherent place.

Modernism promised that revelation was unnecessary because human knowledge alone could verify all truth. Since human knowledge alone has failed to provide the absolute certainty that modernism promised, postmoderns have become skeptics

instead of welcoming revelation back in. They reject both revelation as the basis of knowledge and modernism's rationalistic empiricism as the basis of knowledge. That means they're left with personal subjectivity and incoherence. The solution is to embrace the revelation that gives the only right metanarrative of the world—CFR.

A Postmodern Approach to History

In a postmodern approach, history isn't so much the recounting of events and the interpretation of those events. The postmodern approach often ignores the contextual factors that guide objective interpretation (e.g., political, social, and economic factors). Instead, the cultures of the downtrodden are listened to more closely so as to criticize the received histories. (This might have value if

The opposite of a metanarrative is a "local" narrative. A historian might write the history of a particular West African village, for example. Postmodernists would want the local narrative to stand on its own rather than being brought into a larger, all-encompassing metanarrative. Postmodernists think that no such narrative exists (or that if it does, no human has reliable access to it[11]). Instead, they want to see multiple viewpoints expressed, especially the viewpoints of the marginalized and oppressed. Nobody gets to take charge and make all the little stories fall in line. Postmodernism reacts to naturalism the same way we did in the science unit—by noting that there are no uninterpreted facts. Truly "neutral," "objective," "impartial" histories are impossible. In a fallen world, this is undoubtedly true. Even primary sources—personal letters, official records, etc.—come with a bias and are not fully reliable.[12]

In a postmodern view of history, there's no way to get at what "really happened." As Alun Munslow says, "The past is not discovered or found. It is created and represented by the historian as a text."[13]

A Christian Critique of the Postmodern View of History

Postmodernists are correct to note that there are often multiple viewpoints about historical events. Consider a historian studying the "Great Game" between Russia and Great Britain over spheres of influence in central Asia in the nineteenth and twentieth centuries. It will likely matter a great deal whether the author is Russian—or British—or Afghan.

And yet postmodernists take their skepticism further than a biblical worldview allows.

Even unfallen humans were limited; if Adam and Eve had never eaten of the forbidden tree, their perspectives on life in the garden would still have been different. If an unfallen Eve at age two hundred, say, had written *A History of Eden* (published by Mesopotamian Books), her history might have focused more on the things that interested her, whether botany or childrearing or artisan guilds. She would have seen things and known things that Adam didn't. And the reverse is true: Adam's history would have been different from Eve's, though not contradictory to it.

There are as many perspectives on a historical event as there are people who know anything about it. Postmodernists tend to throw up their hands and say, "So we can never know what *really* happened; we're lost in this sea of perspectives." And the Christian grants that, unless God reveals some history to be true—as He does in the countless historical records in the Bible, culminating in the history of Christ's incarnation and resurrection—then we can't know that history. But our lack of full knowledge doesn't mean that the work of history is pointless. If human finiteness and fallenness kept us from knowing anything about history, they would also keep us from knowing anything about anything.

God's grace—common grace to all humans and special grace to His children—makes it possible for historians to listen to other people with care, diligence, and respect, even and especially if those people are long dead. The creational norms for the work of history suggested in the previous chapter are the tools Christian historians can use to push back against their own fallenness and finiteness. In other words, the Christian historian studies source materials, selects models with humility, selects significant events according to a Christian worldview, makes moral judgments, looks for God's hand, and carefully considers the possible "causes" for historical events—and then he writes it all down and publishes it. Even if this doesn't seem to work in (postmodern) theory, it pretty clearly works in practice.[14]

these claims were validated and viewed from a biblical perspective, but postmodernism is largely a destructive rather than constructive endeavor.) Gordon S. Wood critiques a 1999 postmodern historical revisionism of King Phillip's War by saying, "Instead of a traditional historical account of the war, [Jill] Lepore reflects on the ways people wrote about it. Hers is a history sparing of events but rich in imagination, in moral ruminations over the meaning and justice of war, and in literary and cultural theory. Indeed, rarely has a work of history stressed the dependence of reality on texts as much as this one. Lepore is less interested in happenings than in their symbolic meaning. . . . Nothing is as it may seem on the surface." [Gordon S. Wood, *The Purpose of the Past* (New York: Penguin Press, 2008), 216] In fact, it's so symbolic that Lepore claims that this war is still going on today.

Resorting to conjecture and symbolism is a trend in postmodernist histories since postmodernists tend to highlight the uncertainties of history. Their selectivity runs in this direction in order to bolster their model of postmodernism. They have a controlling metanarrative to manipulate too.

Wood concludes his analysis of postmodern history with this resounding condemnation: "Postmodern history is meditative and self-reflective history. It often tells us more about the historian than the events he or she is presumably recounting" (Wood, 226).

Presuppositions and Perspectives

Are all perspectives equal?

No, some perspectives are just plain wrong. They don't correlate with reality. The supporting evidence doesn't fit with the presupposed model of interpretation. All true knowledge must reflect reality as God knows it. Contrary to Alan Munslow's claim, history can't just be created by historians' texts; it must be discovered.

While it's true that humans don't have access to God's comprehensive knowledge, even their limited knowledge can be accurate—especially if based on revelation. [See the last paragraph on analogical knowledge in the TE Note, "An Architectural Model," p. 298.]

Can presuppositions be disproved?

Yes. It's a common error for people, once they realize that everyone views things through a worldview lens, to assume that presuppositions are irrefutable—that they're just held on the basis of dogma or blind faith. But presuppositions should interact with evidence. And if the presupposition can't consistently explain all of the evidence (as will be the case with all false presuppositions), then the presupposed model must be rejected. [See the TE note, "The Possibility of Refuting Presuppositions," p. 22.]

Do all differing perspectives contradict?

No, some perspectives are just differently focused. The perspective may emphasize different details or answer a different question.

Can people with the same basic biblical worldview model have different perspectives—even ones that contradict?

The more specific and detailed an issue gets—and the less revelatory information we have—the more likely and the more legitimate it is for believers with the same model to disagree. Specialists in a discipline will often debate ideas and conclusions. And that's OK.

Common Grace and Creational Norms

Make sure students don't miss the biblical worldview basis for rejecting the postmodern approach to history. Even in regard to history outside of that which has been directly revealed by God, a historian—Christian or not—can work hard to reliably discover the truth of what really happened—to some extent for many events. This is due to God's common grace as the historian utilizes the creational norms of the historical discipline. Yes, he is finite, fallible, and fallen. Therefore, inaccuracy is always a possibility that must be worked against. But it *can* be worked against. Every historian will subject his study to a presupposed model of interpretation, but that doesn't mean that he is constrained to reject objectivity. It doesn't mean that evidence doesn't serve to refine the model. Inasmuch as the model correlates with Scripture, the Christian can't throw it out, but evidence can correct the Christian's model to more closely align with Scripture.

Daniel Dreisbach on Jefferson's Letter

I think that what we read in this "wall of separation" statement is not a broad principle that church and state must always be separate. Rather [Jefferson is] reaffirming the principle of federalism. He's explaining why he, as president, cannot issue such proclamations, and yet he, as the governor of Virginia, had issued days for prayer, fasting and thanksgiving.

["Interview: Daniel Dreisbach" *God in America,* PBS (website), October 11, 2010]

What does Dreisbach mean when he says that Jefferson is reaffirming federalism?

"Federalism divides a nation's power among national, regional, and local governments. . . . A constitution rules the nation's various levels of government, delegating powers to each. The federal system guards against tyranny by separating the government's powers." [Tim Keesee, AMERICAN GOVERNMENT, 3rd ed. (Greenville, SC: BJU Press, 2014), 16–17]

So Jefferson was merely reserving the rights of states to address religious matters and keeping the federal government out of those matters. The constitution hadn't enumerated any power to the federal government to interfere.

  ## Pooling Students' Perspectives

Ask students to recount classwide or schoolwide events that they were all involved in a week ago, a month ago, and a year ago. After choosing the events, you can divide students into small groups to write a historical accounting of each event, or you can have them give oral accounts.

How many details do students agree on?

Hopefully students can come to an agreement on things like chronology, a general summary of what happened, who was there, and so on.

How do students differ in their accounts?

Students may interpret, select, or emphasize specific details differently. Their response to the events may differ.

Which of the differing perspectives are legitimate perspectives?

Different subjective responses may be legitimate. Emphasizing details that are true that someone else may recognize to be true but didn't emphasize may also be legitimate.

Which of the differing perspectives are not acceptable?

Suppose a student wasn't at the event, but he or she claims to have been there. That

---

For example, several US historians have set out to construct a historical model that fits the evidence better than the one used by the Christian America movement. Daniel Dreisbach, one of these historians, argues that if American Christians sometimes claim too much Christianity for the American founders, secularists generally claim too little. Secularists take Thomas Jefferson's famous phrase about the "wall of separation" between church and state to mean that all religion should be excluded from public life: no prayers before governmental meetings, no religious symbolism on government buildings, and no public funding for religious charities.[15]

Dreisbach conducted a careful historical study of Jefferson's "wall of separation" phrase. It comes, in fact, from a letter Jefferson wrote to the Danbury Baptist Association in 1802. Dreisbach makes the case that Jefferson was reaffirming that since the states were in charge of religious matters, the national government wouldn't interfere with the free exercise of religion. Dreisbach is a Christian, so he's not neutral when it comes to this issue. But Dreisbach makes use of the tools of historiography* to keep him—as much as possible—from prejudice and bias and to help him listen faithfully to what Jefferson actually said. Other historians, even those who have different biases, recognize the merits of Dreisbach's work.

historiography: *the methods and principles historians use in researching and presenting their findings*

Anyone who expects the work of history—outside the Bible—to do more than listen carefully to the past and establish models to understand it all will be disappointed. But someone who's willing to do hard work with the available tools of historiography will still be doing something valuable.

Even the Gospel writers used the tools of the historical discipline. In the first verse of the Gospel of Luke, the writer comments that "many have undertaken to compile a narrative of the things that have been accomplished among us." In other words, there were written sources that Luke had read. And then he even mentions primary sources: "Just as those who from the beginning were eyewitnesses and ministers of the word have delivered them to us, it seemed good to me also, having followed all things closely for some time past, to write an orderly account" (Luke 1:1–3). Luke's main purpose in this preface is not to teach how the work of history ought to be done, but these statements show that he worked hard at being a responsible and careful historian of the earthly life of Jesus.

The four Gospels, taken as a group, also teach us something about history: the existence of multiple different perspectives shouldn't make us throw up our hands and give up on the possibility of true reports. The Gospels give accounts of Jesus' life from four perspectives. Every perspective is absolutely true, and yet each is different—not contradictory, but different. Each writer sees and emphasizes details that the others don't. Matthew tells stories from Jesus' childhood that no one else includes (2:13–23). Luke highlights the place of women in Jesus' entourage (e.g., 23:55). John focuses on Jesus' deity in a unique way (1:1–3). Mark even notes the color of the grass (6:39)!

Of course, apart from Scripture no human perspective on an event will be absolutely true. Historians must constantly evaluate perspectives, including their own. Even postmodernists do this evaluating; they just don't always admit it. Christian historian Carl Trueman notes that the list of marginalized groups to whom postmodernists try to give a voice somehow fails to include "members of the Ku Klux Klan, Holocaust deniers, serial killers, or collectors of other people's toenail clippings"—all of whom have been "written out of the dominant narratives of this world; but none . . . enjoys the support of a significant postmodern lobby group."[16]

---

student's account of what happened is contradicted by thirty other students who really were there. Historians can't just make up events; their perspectives have to be rooted in reality.

Why might there be more disagreement about things that happened a long time ago?

Generalizations may be accurate, but details can be easily forgotten unless details are written down and verified soon after the event.

Why might there be a lot of disagreement about activities that happened recently?

Students should be able to remember more details of their personal experience. The more details there are to discuss, the more interpretations there could be.

This exercise should confirm that recounting historical events can be complex. But it should also confirm that a lot of things can

be established with a great amount of certainty. And just making something up that isn't rooted in reality is unacceptable.

 ## Compassion for the Oppressed

Is oppression a reality of history?

Yes, in a fallen world many humans mistreat others. They use their power or influence to leverage their selfish desires. Christians can't be blind to these realities.

How should God's people respond to injustice?

God not only requires His people to forgive repentant offenders or to patiently endure their suffering, He also requires His people to defend the helpless by striving against evil, seeking justice (Isa. 1:15–17; Jer. 7:5–10).

Is every claim of injustice valid?

Postmodernists, who say they wish for all local narratives to be heard, don't listen to the KKK's narratives. But they have difficulty giving a reason for this choice. The Christian has one: all stories are not equal because the moral standard of Scripture condemns some perspectives.

CLASS, RACE, AND GENDER

Postmodernists want to bring the oppressed "other" into the mainstream of history. In the Western world, ruled as it has generally been by rich white males, the "other" includes the lower classes, racial minorities, and women. As a result, many historians today focus on class, race, and gender in their studies.

But not all of the focus on these themes arises out of postmodernism—especially the focus on class. Marxist historians have always emphasized the role of class because it's essential to their big story about the world that the lower classes will rise up and conquer the upper ones.

These approaches have brought some genuine benefits. Historian Gordon Wood notes,

> Many historians have absorbed from theories no more than the desire to write about issues of race and gender. And this desire has led to many stimulating and worthwhile contributions to our understanding of the past. Our knowledge of slavery in America, for example, has been greatly amplified over the past forty years; and no one can deny that our appreciation of women's history has been similarly enhanced.[17]

But there are dangers in focusing on race, class, and gender in the work of history. For instance, early-twentieth-century historian Charles Beard—influenced both by relativism and Marxism—wrote an influential book, *An Economic Interpretation of the Constitution of the United States*. Beard argued that the framers of the Constitution weren't motivated by the public interest when writing the document. Rather, as property owners, they wrote a constitution that would protect and benefit their own interests. Beard concluded that the Constitution was thus an instrument of class warfare, or conflict between classes based on differing economic interests.

Later critiques of Beard's work explained that since the majority of American men of the time did, in fact, own property (most were farmers), the interests of the common man and those of the framers were not sharply at odds. In addition, primary sources indicate that average citizens often expressed the opinion that the Constitution would benefit them. Finally, a close look at the Constitution itself reveals that the Founding Fathers were just as concerned about providing protections to persons as about maintaining protections of property. People at that time wanted both.

Thus one critic concluded: "Whether Beard had his thesis before he had his evidence, as some have said, is a question that each reader must answer for himself. Certain it is that the evidence does not justify the thesis."[18] Beard's work illustrates a problem with all strictly Marxist history. The pattern for how history must unfold is already determined by the theory. Yet often the historical evidence simply doesn't fit.[19]

Writing about recent Marxist historian Gary Nash, Gordon Wood observes, "Nash is so bound up in the Marxian categories of class warfare that he can make little sense of what happened." Because of his Marxism, Nash must believe that revolutions arise from dissatisfied lower classes. Wood notes, however, that this stands at odds with

No, in a fallen world many humans will feign mistreatment to manipulate people to feel sorry for them to leverage their selfish desires. Christians can't be blind to these realities.

How might it be beneficial to the study of history to analyze the cultural experience of a particular people group, gender, or economic class?

Their unique experiences can foster appreciation for their contributions to society even in the midst of genuine hardship.

Which Comes First?

Which should come first, the thesis or the evidence? The reality is that the process of historical study runs from hypothesis (a tentative thesis) to research to a finalized thesis. There is always a danger of presuming a conclusion and then amassing evidence to fit with it because the evidence can be forced to fit a preconceived mold. But, as students should know by now, no evidence is ever uninterpreted. It's always selected and evaluated through a presupposed worldview lens or model of interpretation. The problem is not that Charles Beard started with a hypothesis that he set out to prove; it's that when the evidence didn't support his hypothesis, he refused to revise his thesis. The solution isn't for historians to set aside any tentative thesis or presupposed model and start from a position of unbiased neutrality (as if that were possible). The solution is to make sure the research process is rigorous and honest—that the evidence really does support the presupposition.

It's also legitimate for a reader to find out what a historian's preconceived worldview model of interpretation is. That way when the reader researches, he knows how particular historians are interpreting the evidence in accordance with a particular model (one that a Christian might need to reject because revelation is a more authoritative basis). This doesn't mean that a historian with a different model will get everything wrong (due to common grace and the nature of reality). But it does necessitate greater care and stricter critique.

Presuppositions: Good or Bad?

This book has worked hard to demonstrate the value of presuppositions (and the impossibility of approaching data or evidence without them). Examples like Beard's abuse of his presupposition demonstrate how important evidence is too. And the worldview apologetics approach never denies the importance of evidence or the possibility of using evidence to refute a presupposition. Worldview apologetics simply argues that there is a proper way to use the evidence and an improper way. The proper way is to use the evidence to show that the presupposition is self-refuting even when the evidence is viewed through that presuppositional lens or by showing that the evidence is being manipulated and twisted to correlate with the presupposition [see TE note "The Possibility of Refuting Presuppositions," p. 22]. Make sure students understand that Beard's problem wasn't that he had a presupposition. It's that his presupposition was wrong. And he dishonestly tried to support it with twisted evidence.

A Problem of Emphasis

There's nothing wrong with learning more about topics that relate to a particular class, race, or gender. The problem is when that particular emphasis is so selective or when interpretations are forced. What's the motivation for such selectivity? Usually there's a political agenda that underlies the endeavor. Remember, some people recognize the great power of the historical tool to shape what people believe about the past in order to manipulate people's responses in the present. Therefore, it matters little to them whether their recounting of history is accurate or their interpretations are truthful (i.e., to them that they correspond to reality). The only thing that matters to them is that the narrative advances their social goals. Lying about the past is justified in their eyes.

Class, race, and gender studies are notorious, not so much for explicitly lying (although that may occur), but for subtly magnifying the emphasis of class, race, or gender so much that it skews reality. Overreacting to Whig history, which makes the majority class, race, or gender out to be angelic, it goes to the opposite extreme, making them out to be demonic. Neither extreme properly recounts the historical reality.

A Problematic Solution?

Divide the class in half and allow students to debate whether class, race, and gender studies encourage people to unite or to divide.

There are many who would claim that class, race, and gender studies are meant to solve a problem. People need to learn from past injustices so that they can be more compassionate today. There is a great deal of truth in such a claim, and Christians should want to know about past injustices, evaluate them from Scripture, and seek ways to bring about justice. If justice is the primary purpose of government, then learning about past injustices and how to avoid them becomes very important.

Nonetheless, race, class, and gender studies may lead to the conclusion that evil exists because upper classes always oppress lower classes, men always oppress women, and Caucasians always oppress people of color. While these sins do happen, all of these groups commit sin against each other because sin is a human problem not a race, class, or gender problem.

Some would argue further that all inequality between various groups is evidence of injustice. However, a biblical worldview doesn't define justice in terms of equality in every situation. For instance, in Scripture the wealthy are commanded not to oppress the poor (Isa. 5:8), but wealth itself can be viewed as a gift from God (Prov. 10:22). Practically, consider if the teacher gave every student the same grade without regard to either performance in the class or effort invested. The result would be equal but unjust.

In addition, while race, class, and gender studies can perform a service, if only to shed light on groups of people who were previously ignored, they can also create a bias against further study of significant persons and events because they do not nicely fit into those categories.

Finally, while understanding how certain people groups have been oppressed in the past, and while justice should be sought for those who still suffer from the effects of those injustices, these studies can run the risk of creating a grievance culture, which doesn't really work for the betterment of these groups and which harms society overall by hardening lines of division between people. Creating such divisions in an attempt to promote revolution was part of the Marxist philosophy of promoting the study of class. These studies often encourage people to divide rather than encouraging people to integrate and to assimilate around a common cause as humans or countrymen. Marxism purposefully inculcates resentment by dividing people into many smaller contentious groups in order to stir up revolution for the purpose of gaining power. Once Marxists are in power, a unified populace would threaten their tyranny, but a divided populace would be too weak and too focused on attacking one another to stop the tyranny. While it may not be accurate to claim that most of those involved in historical study through the lens of race, class, gender want to divide society through their work of history, special care does need to be taken to avoid such a result.

the fact that "the white colonists in British North America enjoyed the highest standard of living of any people in the Western world" and that they "had the broadest ownership of farm land of any place in the Western world." Nash's Marxist theories force him to see "American society [as] a poverty-stricken, class-ridden place where rich and poor were at each other's throat."[20]

Wood also highlights another problem with these single-issue emphases:

> So suffocating has been the stress on "race, class, gender" issues that sometimes beginning graduate students hesitate to write about anything else. A female historian who wanted to study the eighteenth-century founders told me that she was criticized by other female scholars for wasting her time working on those "dead white males."[21]

The Christian historian should, by contrast, seek to understand, praise, and critique all of God's image-bearers by the standard of Scripture. Studying the plight of slaves and researching the life of George Washington are equally legitimate endeavors for the Christian.

A Christian Critique of the Race, Class, Gender Emphasis

Historical ideologies are dangerous because they tend to find the Fall concentrated all in one place, and they find redemption in the wrong place. Studies that focus on race, class, or gender tend to locate the evil in the world in economic differences, gender roles, or racial divisions. Without a doubt, the wealthy have oppressed the poor, men have oppressed women, and those of European descent have oppressed Africans and Indians. Christian historians must expose these wrongs for what they are—sin.

But Christians also recognize that sin is not just a problem that runs through one certain class, race, or gender. It runs through all people. And trying to remove all inequalities of class, race, and gender won't bring true redemption. Fallen people and cultures will twist any good gift of God.

It was possible for a slave owner such as James Madison to have real moral insight when writing the US Constitution. And it was possible for freed American slaves to go to Liberia and create a stratified society that prospered in certain ways and yet treated indigenous Africans unjustly. Good and evil are found in all races, every class, and both genders—because they're found in every person.

THINKING IT THROUGH 23.1B

1. Explain the meaning of Lyotard's definition of postmodernism as "incredulity toward metanarratives."

2. What limitations do fallenness and finiteness place on the Christian historian?

3. Which group of historians especially emphasize the role of class?

4. Which group of people should the Christian historian seek to understand, praise, and/or critique by the standard of Scripture?

♀ 5. Why is the following statement by Alun Munslow false? "The past is not discovered or found. It is created and represented by the historian as a text."

[Thinking It Through 23.1B answers appear on the next page.]

23.2 SELECTION AND MORAL JUDGMENTS

Every small child understands the principle of selection in the work of history. "He hit me" is almost always the item selected from the list of events in a recent altercation. "I pushed him" is rarely mentioned—unless a perceptive parent prods the child for that information. "He hit me" is most likely true. But why don't four-year-olds tend to mention their own role in fights? Because to do so would violate their principles of selection, which are designed to (1) make themselves look good and (2) make their enemies look bad. By selecting only certain details, even ones that really happened, little kids end up giving histories that aren't really "true."

This is why witnesses in court promise to tell not just the truth but "the whole truth." They can be held in contempt of court if it comes out later that they have omitted certain key details. The legal principles of selection require you to tell the court (1) anything you're asked to tell and (2) anything else that is relevant to the purpose of establishing the innocence or guilt of the defendant.

Historical Selection

Historians look at lots of fights and lots of court cases and countless other events. They, too, must use principles of selection, as discussed in the previous chapter. They can't list *everything* that happened—that would take longer than the events took to happen because so much is always going on at once.

The principle of selection is very clearly at work throughout the Bible. The Gospel of John ends with this comment: "Now there are also many other things that Jesus did. Were every one of them to be written, I suppose that the world itself could not contain the books that would be written" (John 21:25).

But selection can lead to errors—like when certain political and historical ideologies affect selection. For instance, a historian who sees history through the lens of race, class, and gender may tell the story of the American Revolution from the eyes of Indians, women, and the poor to the neglect of the contributions of George Washington, John Adams, and Benjamin Franklin. This wouldn't be a problem if the historian were writing a narrow study investigating neglected aspects of Revolutionary War history. It would be a problem in a general survey of the war, such as you find in a textbook. Likewise, an advocate of the "great men" approach to history may focus so much on Washington, Adams, and Franklin that the significance of average men and women to the war is not mentioned as it ought to be.

Sometimes faulty selection can be a much more personal matter, one perhaps invisible to the historian doing the selecting. We mentioned in the previous chapter Timothy Larsen's book, *The Crisis of Doubt*. While researching that book, Larsen, a twenty-first-century Christian historian of Victorian

The Victorian era was "the golden age of church attendance."

THINKING IT THROUGH 23.1B

1. It means that postmoderns are skeptical of any larger unifying story of the world.

2. While historians can carefully study the past and provide viable models to explain what really happened with a certain degree of certainty, they won't have a comprehensively infallible understanding apart from divine revelation.

3. postmodernists or Marxists

4. all of God's image-bearers without exception

♀5. It may take hard work to discover what really happened from an objective perspective, but the truth and reality of what happened usually can't be completely covered up even by the victors. Finiteness and fallenness can be pushed back against with the historical tools that do allow genuine discovery of past realities.

SECTION OBJECTIVES 23.2

1. Explain how selection can lead to errors in the presentation of history.

2. Compare and contrast the proper and improper uses of moral judgments in historical evaluation.

Honesty Is the Best Policy

By common grace, unsaved people have learned from their own personal experience that God's law is good and upright. They have learned that society runs best according to God's creational norms. Ask students to recount incidents from their own childhood that helped them learn that historical revisionism (selecting only details that would make themselves look good) made their punishments worse.

Challenge students to learn wisdom from those minor experiences. Failing to learn that wisdom can cause deeper scars when they're caught or known for their historical inaccuracy (lying) to get away with things as teens. It only gets worse if adults do it to their employers, to the government, or to other God-given authorities.

Reactionism to Whig History

Can students recognize that class, race, and gender studies in this era represent a reactionary tendency against the Whig histories of the previous era? The Whig histories hurt more than they help. Those promoting class, race, and gender studies get a lot of leverage when they can point to the dishonesty of highly selective Whig histories. They claim to provide the counterbalancing emphasis. But going to the opposite extreme just causes more backlash in society as groups are pitted against each other.

Selection: Good or Bad?

Just as presuppositions are always necessary and often good and helpful, so also selection is always necessary and often good and helpful. Presuppositions can be abused, and the work of selection can also be done improperly. How can a person tell if a historian who is summarizing events has abused selection? There are several ways.

• You could become an expert by studying all of the detailed evidence yourself. But not everyone can or should be that kind of expert. (This is option 3.1, pp. 4–5.)

• You can read the historical critiques of other experts who agree or disagree by providing more correlating or contradicting data or who provide alternative interpretations. Ultimately, you will depend on the strength of your own presuppositions to determine which historians are interpreting the evidence fairly and correctly. (This is option 3.2, pp. 4–5.)

Selection and Ideologies

Divide students into groups and have them read a short summary of a particular historical or current event from different perspectives. Then have students write a paper to identify a particular ideological influence (e.g., one of the historical ones from this chapter or a political one from Chapter 17) and to discuss how selection and moral judgment may have been affected by the ideology. Students should conclude the paper by summarizing the proper interpretation and moral judgment of the historical or current event.

The Limitation of Reason

Hopefully students have had to stretch their reasoning skills in this course about biblical worldview—perhaps more than in most other courses in high school. But one of the most important lessons students need to learn is what John Henry Gordon finally came to realize [see sidebar]. Reason may be a helpful tool to enable humans to correctly understand a lot of things; it's a gift that is a part of the image of God. But human reasoning is *limited*; it can't comprehensively and finally bring anyone to absolute assurance of anything on its own. Humans are dependent on their omniscient Creator to authoritatively reveal absolute truth through His declarations. That's the only sure foundation all human reasoning must be built on (Prov. 1:7).

Narratives and Moral Judgments

The work of history culminates with conclusions of moral judgment. In fact, if a work of history fails to provide this kind of conclusion, its task hasn't really been finished. Some historians would rather leave the hard work of moral judgment for their readers to decide because it's in the drawing of moral conclusions that sharp disagreements become evident. Many of these disagreements end in an impasse. That's because people often argue in circles at the point of moral judgment without going down deeper to critique the presupposed worldview lens. It is the presupposed worldview that makes many moral conclusions seem so obvious. Since values arise out of larger narratives of the world, people's moral judgments will often differ depending on which of the larger narratives they presuppose. It's often difficult to change someone's moral judgment as long as they still hold to the same larger narrative.

However, even people with the same metanarrative, people with a shared biblical world-

---

DOUBTER IN CRISIS

One Victorian who had a crisis of doubt was John Henry Gordon. Once a Sunday school teacher, Gordon became one of the "more abusive and blunt anti-Christian lecturers."[22]

But a preacher that his mother convinced him to hear simply used the Bible, and Gordon was cut to the heart. After he reconverted, he admitted that his unbelief—he was a strict materialist—had never brought him any satisfaction.

He had also noticed that his atheist friends couldn't agree on morality. He questioned "whether or not Secularism provided the intellectual resources for making . . . moral judgments."[23] He began to see atheistic secularism as a "just-what-you-like-ism" in which the ultimate moral authority was self. Gordon called it "a recipe for immoral self-indulgence."[24]

Finally, Gordon came to realize that he had idolized reason to such a degree that almost nothing could be determined to be true.[25] His solution wasn't to dismiss reason or to accept things contrary to reason, but to recognize reason's limitations and to trust reason's Creator.

England, noticed that existing histories of that era (including encyclopedia entries, books, articles, etc.) give heavy coverage to the "crisis of faith" that many Victorians experienced. The discussions center on how Darwinism led to these crises.[26] He further noted that key encyclopedias on the era included entries for the "doubters" but lacked entries about Charles Spurgeon, Thomas Chalmers, or other leading Christian figures. Larsen found one encyclopedia that included entries on "Babism, Bahaism, Spiritualism, the Theosophical Society, Transcendentalism, and Zionism, but none on Baptists, Congregationalists, Dissenters (or Nonconformists or Free Churches), Evangelicalism, or Methodism."[27]

Larsen isn't claiming that these works have an overt bias against Christians, but he says that it can occur. For example, historian A. N. Wilson assumes that atheists are "honorable," that doubters who remain in church are "dishonorable," and that believers have sinned "against the Intellect."[28] But more often, Larsen says, the personal interests and views of scholars in the historical discipline are leading them to a misconception about the Victorian era.[29] They see doubt as a major theme and fail to see the Christian religion in its place in the times.

Larsen notes in his study that doubt is a major theme in the Victorian era *precisely because of the importance of religion*. The Victorian era could be called "the golden age of church attendance."[30] Furthermore, the evangelical emphasis that true religion brought together head, heart, and action (rather than just being something you show up to do as a matter of course on Sundays) was actually an essential part of the reason there were so many doubters. If the dominant religion of the time had been different, the challenges to that religion would not have been intellectual.[31]

Larsen's principles of selection—formed by his Christian faith—allow him to see things that non-Christian historians didn't care to see: not just the reconversions to Christianity of some of the Victorian era's famous doubters, but the reasons for those reconversions. Larsen noticed that the skeptics fell out of love with skepticism because it never offered a positive worldview, one that explained and promoted morality and gave life significance beyond the physical realm. Larsen also noticed that skeptics often found the Bible more compelling when they came to it for a purpose other than trying to find problems in it.[32]

Historical Moral Evaluation

Another area in which the Fall affects historians is that of moral evaluation. A now widely recognized example of this is the early-twentieth-century view of the Puritans. The Puritans were often dismissed as dour, strict, fun-hating people who always dressed in black. These misapprehensions may have lasted so long among scholars and non-scholars alike because many of them disapprove of Puritan beliefs. It took the diligent work of Harvard professor Perry Miller to bring Puritans some respect among scholars.

---

view, can still disagree. There are a number of reasons for this. It may be that their understanding, when they put all the facts together into the biblical worldview, causes them to differ. Or it may be that one or both parties have been unwittingly influenced by ideas from other worldviews. Christians need to be charitable to other believers. They may need to examine their own assumptions to ensure that they're all biblical; they may need to graciously agree to disagree; or they may need to seek to persuade other Christians to abandon unbiblical assumptions that are affecting their judgments

Debating Moral Judgments

Divide the class in half to debate one or two of the following questions of moral judgment according to the larger narrative of the biblical worldview.

- Was the American Revolution justified?
- Was the Mexican-American War justified?
- Was Manifest Destiny justified?
- Was the dropping of the atomic bomb on Japan justified?
- Was the Vietnam War justified?
- Was the second war in Iraq (2003–2011) justified?

Particular political issues are also often debated in current events.

- Is capital punishment justified?
- Will increased gun control prevent crime?
- Is climate change primarily caused by humans?

Failures of Moral Judgment

Wrong moral judgments can be clearly exemplified throughout history:

A more recent example would be popular treatments of Muslims from both sides of the political spectrum. The American left makes a multicultural effort to avoid criticism of Muslim culture. In order for this view to work, they have to translate offensive concepts such as *jihad** into inoffensive ones. Jihad, in their view, becomes a merely spiritual struggle—despite the lack of historical evidence for the claim that this is what the term has meant.[33] The American right, on the other hand, tends to lump together the ancient doctrine of jihad with modern terrorism despite the fact that careful study reveals some important differences.[34] Moral evaluation can bias historical study.

jihad: (gee HOD) the Islamic concept of holy war against non-Muslims

And yet moral evaluation is necessary. A historian's first responsibility in writing about the mass slaughter of Armenians in Turkey in 1915 is to accurately describe the conditions, motivations, and actions of the people in that place and time. He must understand them on their own terms first. But he fails if he never arrives at a moral evaluation—and if he does give a moral evaluation, it should be based ultimately on Scripture and not on other grounds.

COMPLEXITIES AND LIMITATIONS

Understanding past events is a complex task. Humans are so limited that we often make little effort to see things from someone else's perspective. And we're so fallen that we often turn around and exalt our own perspective to an ungodly height. We select the facts that further our own agendas and evaluate actions in history from a perspective other than the one God gives in Scripture. The Fall deeply affects the work of history.

THINKING IT THROUGH 23.2

1. What major influences often guide a person's choices in historical selection?

2. What did Larsen's principles of selection allow him to see that non-Christian historians didn't care to see?

3. Why have many historical scholars erroneously dismissed the Puritans as dour, strict, fun-hating people who always dressed in black?

♀ 4. Why is moral evaluation necessary in the work of history?

Ronald A. Wells, *History and the Christian Historian* (Grand Rapids: Eerdmans, 1998).

THINKING IT THROUGH 23.2

1. political and historical ideologies as well as personal agendas

2. the reconversion of major skeptical doubters to Christianity and the reasons for their reconversion

3. Their moral evaluations were formed by their presupposed disapproval of Puritan beliefs rather than by the factual realities.

♀ 4. Historical study is incomplete if it merely seeks to accurately describe the conditions, motivations, and actions of the people in a place and time but fails to present those facts within a framework of understanding—which demands moral evaluation. The purposes of history listed in the previous chapter (understanding the ways and works of God, lessons for life, and cultural identity) can't be fulfilled without this moral interpretation.

• During the women's suffrage movement, the basis of the opposition to women voting was clearly unbiblical. Many of the opponents of women's voting rights dismissed women as being unable to understand matters of politics. Therefore, many Christians rightly concluded that it was best for women to gain the right to vote.

• At the height of American slavery, black Americans were often said to be ignorant and inferior. Some people were convinced of that lie because it was illegal to educate slaves. Many African Americans, though they lacked formal education, proved that they were not ignorant or inferior.

• The oft-repeated generalizations that government is a necessary evil and that all politicians are dishonest were refuted in the government unit.

• Throughout history stereotypes have presented Jewish people as greedy and dishonest (partly because such a large number of Jewish people were businessmen, bankers, etc.). But a fairer assessment shows them to be hard working and wise.

Ask students to provide other examples of moral judgments that are clearly wrong.

Further Reading

If a student is especially interested in possibly entering into the historical field of study, then you may want to recommend for enrichment Carl R. Trueman's *Histories and Fallacies* (Wheaton: Crossway, 2010).

Other helpful books include:

David Bebbington, *Patterns in History* (Vancouver: Regent College Publishing, 1979).

Gordon S. Wood, *The Purpose of the Past* (New York: Penguin Press, 2008).

CHAPTER REVIEW ANSWERS

Making Connections

1. nationalism
2. postmodernism
3. class, race, and gender histories
4. naturalism

Developing Skills in Apologetics and Worldview

5. If facts are deliberately ignored or exaggerated in order to support or to criticize a particular model of historical understanding, then people are being ideological rather than truthful in their understanding of history.

6. Any framework of understanding that draws conclusions from the facts of history will demand moral judgments. The purposes of history can't be accomplished without moral judgments.

Examining Assumptions and Evidence

7. Environmental factors are only one influence—not the ultimate and only determining factor; humans can adjust to or adjust their environment. Furthermore, naturalism is unable to provide a basis for morality that stands above every culture.

8. Nationalism demonizes other people groups by exaggerating flaws while idolizing one's own people group by minimizing flaws. It looks for salvation in the independence of one's own people group. It has to rewrite history and justify sinful actions to make one's own people group look good.

9. Postmodernism is overly skeptical that anyone can formulate a model of past events with any accuracy or can provide a unifying story of the world.

10. It relies on forced interpretations to support an assumed conclusion about a single issue that is used to interpret all of history. Furthermore, it fails to evaluate every group fairly.

Becoming a Creative Cultivator

11. If students are writing a history that encapsulates the school year for future generations, then they should select the most important events. They may pick out minor details that, from their perspective, support the retelling and interpretation of those major events.

---

23 CHAPTER REVIEW

Scripture Memory

John 8:44–45

Making Connections

1. Which ideology writes history to favor one's own nation?
2. Which ideology denies that the past can really be known?
3. Which ideology allows single-issue emphases to commandeer the interpretation of history?
4. Which ideology teaches that favorable environmental conditions determine a culture's advancement?

Developing Skills in Apologetics and Worldview

5. How could you demonstrate whether political and historical ideologies are inappropriately affecting the selection of historical data?
6. How would you defend the necessity of moral evaluation in the work of history?

Examining Assumptions and Evidence

7. Why is the ideology of naturalism flawed?
8. Why is the ideology of nationalism flawed?
9. Why is the ideology of postmodernism flawed?
10. Why is the fixation on class, race, and gender a flawed approach to history?

Becoming a Creative Cultivator

11. Write a brief history of the school year. Why did you select the details that you did?

TERMS TO REMEMBER

naturalistic determinism—the philosophical view that everything that happens in nature or society is caused by previous events and conditions, not by human choices or divine will

nationalism—the view that the independence of a nation or ethnic group is an ultimate good and that the great evil is to be ruled over by another nation or people group

Whiggish—an approach to history that "studies the past with reference to the present" and tends "to praise revolutions provided they have been successful, to emphasize certain principles of progress in the past and to produce a story which is the ratification if not glorification of the present"

theistic rationalists—people who tended to believe in a God who did answer prayer and act providentially in the world; also tended to believe that the Bible contained some revelation from God; but believed that reason was the judge of what was true revelation and what was myth; did not think Jesus was God but tended to believe He was "a great moral teacher"

Chapter Twenty-Four HISTORY IN LIGHT OF REDEMPTION

Remember the former things of old; for I am God, and there is no other; I am God, and there is none like me, declaring the end from the beginning and from ancient times things not yet done, saying, "My counsel shall stand, and I will accomplish all my purpose."

Scripture Memory Isaiah 46:9–10

24.1 FINDING RELIABLE SOURCE MATERIALS

The brilliant Samuel Johnson (1709–1784) wrote the first major English dictionary practically by himself. It took him only nine years. He was a committed Christian and has been called "arguably the most distinguished man of letters in English history."[1] Besides that, he was a real wit. Once Johnson was conversing with a similarly clever man who argued that matter didn't really exist. Someone else told Johnson, "Though we are satisfied his doctrine is not true, it is impossible to refute it." Johnson immediately kicked a large stone with "mighty force"—kicking so hard that he bounced back when the rock didn't move—and said, "I refute it *thus*."[2] That refutation of an erroneous philosophy appears to have worked, at least in the minds of most people, since the story keeps being repeated nearly three hundred years later.

But refutations of erroneous history are not so simple. Astronaut Buzz Aldrin, the second human to ever set foot on the surface of the moon, once tried to use an argument similar to Johnson's. One day a moon-landing skeptic, conspiracy theorist Bart Sibrel, confronted Aldrin in public and demanded that he swear on the Bible that he really did land on the moon. (Sibrel has made documentaries claiming that the moon landing was cleverly faked.) Aldrin refused to swear, so Sibrel called him "a coward, and a liar, and a thief." Aldrin, who was seventy-two at the time, refuted Sibrel *thus*: he punched him in the jaw.

This action is not the biblically recommended way of dealing with historical disputes, and though

it made the news, it doesn't appear to have worked. There are still many active groups of people online who don't believe that the moon landings ever happened—or that the Holocaust occurred (to name just two prominent groups of history skeptics). Despite all our scientific, archaeological, and information-retrieval capabilities, people still make false and outlandish historical claims all the time.

"HISTORY IS NOT SIMPLY A COLLATION OF FACTS WHICH CAN ONLY BE RELATED TOGETHER IN ONE VALID NARRATIVE." [3]

—CARL TRUEMAN

How can you spot—and refute—false claims about history? You can't kick a rock or punch a conspiracy theorist every time you hear false claims. So what can you do?

A Christian worldview is essential to the answer. It provides assurances that we can know certain things about history, and it gives us the basic shape of that history. We know that the history of the world is the history of what God is doing to glorify Himself by redeeming His fallen creation—and judging His enemies. Without such a framework, the work of studying and writing history becomes aimless—or aims at the wrong targets.

Lesson Plan Chart—Chapter 24

Section Title	Pages	Activity Manual	Days
24.1 Finding Reliable Source Materials	369–72		2 days
24.2 Proposing Historical Models Humbly	373–75		1 day
24.3 Seeing God's Hand in History	376–80	Activity 41	2 days
Review	381		1 day
Total Suggested Days			**6 days**

The student will be able to

24.1 Determine the appropriate means and motivations for establishing or refuting historical claims.

24.2 Explain why data from source materials should be humbly and honestly interpreted according to a viable model.

24.3 Defend the legitimacy of discerning divine providence in human history.

SECTION OBJECTIVES 24.1

1. Explain the appropriate means for establishing or refuting historical claims: scholarly study of legitimate source materials through the interpretive lens of a biblical worldview.

2. Summarize the appropriate motivations for establishing or refuting historical claims: the glory of God and the good of others.

Worldviews and Evidence

Both a proper worldview and evidence are necessary for right historical conclusions. Samuel Johnson's friend didn't believe it was possible to refute the man who doubted the existence of matter because that man's worldview would have constrained him to believe all evidence to be merely an illusion (including Johnson's rebounding off the stone that he kicked). But Johnson was convinced that his own worldview could interpret the evidence, thus confirming a material world. He refused to place his arguments within the wrong worldview; he would accept and demonstrate the common sense of the evidence within the right worldview. Johnson left it up to the observer to decide for himself which worldview was more satisfying.

Buzz Aldrin demonstrated that he was exasperated with someone who had a false worldview. He knew that all the evidence in the world would never satisfy people with Sibrel's worldview. But instead of being satisfied that the right worldview approach to the evidence would be self-evident to the vast majority of observers, Aldrin lashed out with a "might makes right" response.

What approach should a Christian historian take? Obviously, any expert will tend to be frustrated with the denial of clear evidence by ignorant or misled groups. But Christians must not lash out. They must present the evidence in the context of their own worldview and allow God to convince the minds of others who observe the evidence set in the context of the right worldview.

Framework and Details

The historical work process flows as follows:
- presuppose a broad worldview
- gather specific evidence from source materials
- interpret the evidence and determine conclusions according to a *specific* model, which is subject to evidence-based revision

The beginning of this section confirms the necessity of presupposing the right worldview to handle the evidence properly. Then the section delves into the work of gathering specific evidence from sources. The next section will deal with models of interpretation. But first, a few clarifications about worldviews are in order.

Students need to understand that people with false worldviews won't always get specific claims wrong. This is due to common grace, but it's also due to the fact that false worldviews are so inconsistent that they sometimes have to borrow from the biblical worldview (the only true representation of reality). Some false worldviews will be off base in one area but not in another; their belief system can overlap with the biblical worldview. For instance, most secularists would agree with Samuel Johnson that the world really is material and not just an illusion.

In addition, while the correct worldview framework is important, it doesn't automatically provide all of the specific claims within the framework. People who accept the same basic framework still need to do the hard work of gathering the evidence before they can create a specific model to come to conclusions. People who accept the same basic framework may disagree about specifics, but they can try to convince others of their position based on evidence and theories that fit within the same basic framework.

The Fundamental Task

The work of history is primarily a work of studying source materials. Only then can the rest of the work of history be done (making a model of interpretation, learning lessons for life, etc.). Trying to construct a historical narrative without any evidenced source materials or denying a historical narrative by ignoring all of the source materials would make for a very bad historian—one that few people would take seriously.

Why is Holocaust denial an apt example of excessive historical skepticism?

The skeptics' unbelief is patently absurd because of the quantity and quality of source material available.

But a Christian worldview by itself doesn't tell you whether the Holocaust happened or whether Neil Armstrong really took "one small step for a man." A biblical worldview provides the necessary framework, but the Christian worldview also calls on you to act. There really is only one way to build reliable historical models: hard work with the sources. If you want to know history—and especially if you yourself are called to be a historian—you need to learn how to find, sift, and process historical evidence until you have a model to communicate to others.

HISTORICAL EVIDENCE

The fundamental task of the historian is to study the basic source materials of history. Sometimes these sources are artifacts uncovered by archaeology. Historians have to know enough about archaeology to make accurate assessments of that evidence. They have to understand the careful systems used by archaeologists and the complex nature of interpreting evidence from archaeological digs. Ancient cities were often built on top of even more ancient cities; historians who work in ancient eras have to understand the art and science of figuring out what artifacts belong to what historical layer. They have to interpret evidence, such as the fact that some clay pottery in a city appears to have come from somewhere else. Could this mean that there was active trade going on in that place?

And, of course, written materials are often uncovered in archaeological digs—coins, inscriptions, tablets, and (in some dry places in the world) papyri, documents written on an ancient form of paper. The research of some historians means reading countless letters and scraps from which they build a picture of the ancient world. Here's what a wife wrote her husband a century and a half before Jesus was born:

> Isias to . . . Hephaestion; greetings. . . . I am displeased because after having piloted myself and your child through such bad times—and having been driven to every extremity owing to the price of corn—I thought that now at least, with you at home, I should enjoy some respite. But you have not even thought of coming home nor given any regard to our circumstances![4]

Letters provide a good example of primary sources.

On the one hand, this short letter (and so many others like it) provides tantalizing hints about how different life was in ancient times. It's the historian's job to breathe that ancient air and describe it to the rest of us. On the other hand, clearly husbands and wives way back then were people, just like they are today. There is a simple humanity in the letter; wives today still want their husbands to come home.

A good historian enters into his source materials, trying to listen to them faithfully as a neighbor should do—even if that neighbor lives far away in time and space.

Primary Sources

Historians use two major kinds of written sources, whether they study ancient eras or modern times—primary sources and secondary sources. A **primary source** is simply a source that comes from the period being studied. If a historian is studying World War II, then primary sources would include maps laying out guerrilla plans from the French resistance, letters from American generals to US politicians (or from soldiers to their girlfriends), and technical memoranda used by the Nazis to effect the final solution.[5] A biography of General Dwight D. Eisenhower or of

---

What are some of the types of source materials available to refute the claims of the Holocaust deniers?

Primary sources include eyewitness testimony from hundreds of diverse people, thousands of verified photographs, artifacts and ruins from concentration camps, letters, documents, and records. Secondary sources include biographies, textbooks, and so on.

Is there an alternative explanation for all the source materials?

No other explanation is credible. The model of interpretation that attempts to force all of the evidence into a worldwide conspiracy theory is hardly convincing to objective people, let alone to historical experts.

Given that there's no lack of evidence, is there an alternative explanation for why people still want to deny that the Holocaust took place?

Religious or political ideology controls their narrative, usually due to racism.

Hard Work with Rewarding Results

The work of history might be compared to doing the legwork of an investigation like a detective. A detective finds scraps of evidence and works to put it all together to solve a mystery. Doing this legwork is far from easy or glamorous, but the end result can be very rewarding. (You might show students an excerpt from the PBS show *History Detectives*, which exemplifies this reality.)

The work of history could also be compared to putting together a jigsaw puzzle. Students may be used to the dry facts from a bare-

Official documents are primary sources for historians.

Hitler himself wouldn't be "historical" if it didn't delve into archives and ferret out old letters, telegrams, and pay stubs. Such a biography is not itself a primary but a **secondary source**.

Secondary Sources

There are historians whose work it is to take mostly secondary-source material and construct a bigger narrative out of it all. No one could possibly read all the documents written by World War II generals, let alone those by soldiers and mothers and villagers and everyone else affected by the war. But a historian who reads secondary sources such as specialized studies by scholars who have focused on the letters of soldiers or the archives of war departments can make use of that research to write a history.

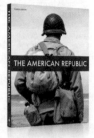

History textbooks pull together the work of many primary and secondary sources to create new secondary sources.

WORLDVIEWS AND HISTORY

Scholarly historical work is to be done primarily on the level of primary sources. This means that the historian has to know the language that the documents are written in. He has to read them for himself. He has to weigh the accuracy of each source. He has to make sure that the document is not a forgery. He may need to compare two primary sources that give conflicting accounts. For all of this work, a Christian worldview is essential. Ideally, having an accurate view of humanity's fallenness should help Christians make careful judgment calls about the validity of someone's statements. Wives missed their husbands in ancient Greece, just like they do today. And, just like today, husbands sometimes lied.

Glorifying God Through History

Even non-Christian historians would agree with us about the value of research in the primary sources. Virtually all practicing historians, whatever their worldview, engage in this kind of research. So what's distinctive about the way a historian with a biblical worldview works?

HISTORY IN LIGHT OF REDEMPTION | 371

What questions might historians generally ask when mining each of the following sources?

- newspapers
  What were the important events? What were the issues of major concern and debate?
- maps
  What was the map's purpose? Who was the intended user?
- artifacts
  What material was it made of? What type of people would have used it?
- documents
  Who wrote it, when, and for whom?

[For more questions with a correlating primary source, refer to Justin Taylor, "How Historians Ask Questions of Primary Sources," Gospel Coalition (website), March 17, 2015.]

Reliable Secondary Sources

Historians who are writing peer-reviewed academic works should base all their basic work on primary sources. Secondary sources should only be used when referring to areas outside of his particular frame of study. For instance, such a historian could use secondary sources when writing an introduction that surveys the history leading up to the period and place he is examining.

Some historians, however, write general histories that cover a much broader scope of history. These can be highly regarded, such as the *Oxford History of the United States*. The authors of such histories must rely on others who have done hard work in the primary sources. Even if they have done primary source research in certain areas, they will need to rely on the research of others for other areas. Such general histories will be reliable as long as the author has based his work on the conclusions of experts who have thoroughly researched the primary sources.

 Worldview and Motivations

A biblical worldview doesn't just guide the work of gathering and interpreting source materials. It should also motivate the work. Why should it be done? What will it accomplish? The answers to those questions should ultimately be traced back to glorifying God and loving others.

How specifically could historical work reflect God's glory?

- *Accurately dating the Exodus provides supportive evidence to refute those who would claim that the Bible is inaccurate.*
- *God's common grace toward a people group can be displayed in a broad sweep of history.*

---

bones textbook recounting of names, dates, and events. They have the puzzle pieces. Those pieces provide a basic picture. But if all students have ever read is bits of data about the event and they have never actually read the story of the event, then they're likely missing the engaging excitement that brings the picture to life.

 Working with Primary Sources

As investigators, historians learn to ask a variety of basic questions. And they learn to find answers to those questions in corresponding primary sources. If historians want to search for anecdotal illustrations of interpersonal relationships in family or society, they will tend to find those answers in letters, diaries, or personal items; they wouldn't normally find that data in maps,

battle plans, or lists of inventory (though an occasional nugget may turn up in an unexpected place).

What kinds of sources might historians normally look into to find out about the following categories of information?

- diet
  stomach or bones, inventory lists from cargo ships or stores, menus
- weather
  almanacs, newspapers, diaries
- economic conditions
  wills, tax records, receipts
- clothing styles and trends
  photographs, drawings or paintings, oral or written histories, statues, actual garments

Historians don't always start with a question in mind. They may start by mining the primary sources available to them and come up with questions as they examine them.

- *God's special grace toward a particular Christian can be displayed in a biographical sketch (e.g., George Mueller).*

How specifically could historical work reflect love for one's neighbor?

- *The historian can correct unjust accusations by correcting faulty moral judgments or caricatures of people from the past.*
- *Historians can influence the sociopolitical goals of their cultures by reinforcing the values of a positive cultural identity or by prophetically warning people using lessons of the past.*

Working for a Greater Purpose

Unbelieving historians don't always work for big sales or academic prestige either. The point isn't that they do, but that Christians certainly ought to have a higher purpose. Many unsaved historians find satisfaction in work that they believe will help better society as well. They believe that the present society can learn from past mistakes.

But unsaved historians really do lack a major motivating purpose for the excellence of their work—God's glory. Believers have the privilege of resting in God's control over all of history. The forces of history are too large and too complex for any group of humans to have manipulated. Unsaved historians who may have optimistically entered their field believing that they could help the present society learn from its mistakes and move on to greater heights of progress may find themselves overwhelmed with discouragement when their work seems futile. But the Christian historian can remain confident that "[God's] counsel shall stand, and [He] will accomplish all [His] purpose" (Isa. 46:10). The Christian historian can marvel at God's wisdom and power to bring all the threads of history together to weave one larger story that accomplishes His ends and reflects His glory and grace—even in a fallen world where humans are never coerced by God.

 Discerning What's Most Important

What themes from history would you select and emphasize? Why?

Any theme selected by a historian should support one of the larger purposes of history (the ways and works of God, lessons for life, cultural identity). This allows for a wide variety of themes, but it also provides a basis for evaluating the strength with which the theme accomplishes the purpose and whether a particular theme has swallowed up all other themes.

On one hand, a Christian historian will be working, ultimately, for a greater purpose than big sales or academic prestige. So he or she ought to work in a truly excellent and diligent way, "as for the Lord, and not for men" (Col. 3:23).[6] Christians shouldn't be sloppy or lazy in their historical work because when they study history, they are—in a very real way—studying the outworking of the plan of God over the course of history:

> Remember the former things of old; for I am God, and there is no other; I am God, and there is none like me, declaring the end from the beginning and from ancient times things not yet done, saying, "My counsel shall stand, and I will accomplish all my purpose," calling a bird of prey from the east, the man of my counsel from a far country. I have spoken, and I will bring it to pass; I have purposed, and I will do it. (Isa. 46:9–11)

If God rules over flying eagles and calls rulers from far countries to fulfill His purposes, then the plan of God lies underneath the surface of every good history book. Christian historians work to glorify God. Many non-Christian historians are careful, diligent practitioners of their craft, but they do not have this highest of motivations.

Benefiting Others Through History

On the other hand, the work of the historian is for other people, not just for the Lord. It's a work of service to one's neighbors, including dead ones. It lets them speak. It also serves living neighbors, of course; history provides wisdom for them. It broadens our understanding so that we're freed from the cultural nearsightedness we have from simply living in our own time and place. It helps free us from conformity to the spirit of the age. The biblical worldview of Christian historians will guide them as they write history. It will shape not only their moral evaluations, but also their principle of selection. They will ask themselves, "What stories do my neighbors need to hear?"

Researching and writing for the good of others is one area where the Christian worldview is pushing back against the direction of the historical disciplines today. In the previous chapter we noted that historians can be so caught up in discussions of race, class, and gender that they miss other important discussions—or twist the historical evidence to fit what they consider to be the flow of history. Ultimately, only your worldview can tell you what's important enough in history to warrant research. Race (or rather, ethnicity), class, and gender *are* important themes. But ideally, a Christian historian will be so rooted in what's truly important that he won't be knocked over by passing fads within his discipline.

THINKING IT THROUGH 24.1

1. What provides a basic historical framework, assuring that we can know some basic things about history and make some basic moral judgments?

2. What is the fundamental task of the historian?

3. Identify and explain the two major kinds of written sources that historians use.

4. What two motivations should direct a Christian's engagement in rigorous scholarly historical study?

♀5. Of the two types of sources identified and explained in question 3, which is more reliable? Explain why.

Does a broader, generalized history warrant your emphases? What would determine your answer?

Historians are led by at least three broad questions: What happened? How do we know it happened? Why did it happen? But historians are also guided by the question of significance: why does it matter?

Your worldview will shape your answer.

Would a specialized history warrant your emphases?

Specialized histories allow for points of detail to be examined. And if the specialized history contributes something to the overall picture, then it can be a valuable asset to the historical discipline. If the point is so minor that it doesn't contribute to the overall picture, then even experts would rarely if ever draw on it for their own research.

THINKING IT THROUGH 24.1

1. the biblical worldview

2. to study the basic source materials—more specifically, to find the sources, sift through the sources (selection), and to process the sources (interpretation), forming conclusions (moral judgments)

3. primary sources (those that come directly from the period being studied)

   secondary sources (those that rely on the historical evaluation and conclusions of others who have already studied the primary sources of a historical era)

4. love for neighbor and the glory of God

♀5. Primary sources are generally more reliable because they are direct sources about the period being studied. Even if they contain inaccuracies, they are inac-

24.2 PROPOSING HISTORICAL MODELS HUMBLY

A bunch of pottery shards buried in dirt don't make a history. Nor do a bunch of ancient letters, or a cache of war plans in a national archive. Somebody—a historian—has to sit down and combine all of the available raw information into a model that explains the data. And that model itself will be built on the backbone of a story the historian tells about what's going on in that period of history.

Human actions don't make any sense unless they're placed in some sort of context. But having a context—or an overarching story—doesn't necessarily make the work of interpretation easy. Christian historian Carl Trueman points out that "human historical actions are themselves always complex and impossible to reduce to single causes, intentions, or motivations."[7]

Think about last Friday night. Why did you spend your time the way you did? Can even *you* give a full explanation for that choice? We like to think we have full control over our choices, but our influences and our opportunities and our desires—and a thousand other factors—play into those choices.

Trueman says, "It is important to realize that forces far larger than any individual agent are at play in the world, and that human beings are not simply shaped by what they read or what they hear, but also by hidden forces of which they themselves might be unaware, such as economic and ethnic factors."[8]

An archaeologist's report will explain what was found in a dig and where. And he will attempt to explain the findings. He will propose, perhaps, that different layers of the dig be dated to the third century BC based on the pottery shards found in those layers. He might suggest that trade with a neighboring region picked up during the fifth century BC based on the artifacts found in another layer. Or he might note that at a certain period the site appeared to be destroyed and abandoned. All of this is a model the archaeologist is constructing from the available information.

Archeologists have developed systematic ways to analyze the various layers of an ancient archeological site.

EXAMPLES OF FAULTY MODELS

Like archaeologists, historians who work from primary sources also make models. They look at the primary source data and construct a narrative from it. Models should be revised as new information comes to light.

Victorian Religion and Skepticism

In Chapter 23, we pointed out that many historians studying the Victorian era have constructed a model that presents that time period as one of a crisis of faith. However, a Christian scholar working on that same time period noted that this thesis excluded some key primary sources. He constructed a model to explain more of the data, arguing that the Victorian era was a highly religious time in which, nonetheless, certain basic tenets of religion were being challenged. Some religious people lost their faith in Christianity, but some of the most prominent doubters actually came to doubt their doubts and returned to faith in Christ.[9]

curacies that reflect a viewpoint from that time period, which may be valuable for the historian. Secondary sources often contain layers of interpretation that can make them less reliable.

SECTION OBJECTIVES 24.2

1. Explain why a model is necessary.
2. Compare and contrast faulty models with viable models.
3. Defend the necessity of humility and honesty in the work of model-making.

Data, Facts, and Models

Many people erroneously assume that facts "just are." Most people are drawn to this assumption and staunchly maintain it be- cause they want to believe that neutrality is possible. But facts are never brute. Facts are always conclusions that have been drawn through an interpretive process. Facts must not be confused with raw data, that is, data that is meaningless until put together into a system of understanding. That system of understanding is a model. Models can be so ingrained into people's thinking that they're unaware that they process the data they receive through models. From the time that people are born, they begin to pick up on how to interpret the world around them. From the time they begin learning in school, their instructors reinforce interpretive methods. So as soon as people receive a piece of data, they process a conclusion through a whole web of presuppositions that they have learned to accept since childhood—unless they stop to rigorously evaluate their own processing of that data all the way down to their fundamental presuppositions. When you live in a society that agrees on principles of rationality, then many of those conclusions seem like common sense; they seem like brute facts. But they are actually interpreted facts. This comes to light only when divergent worldview presuppositions are identified as controlling the diverse opinions of different people evaluating the evidence and coming to different conclusions.

Worldviews and Models

A worldview is the overarching story that provides a framework or context. A model is a more specific system of thinking within that worldview framework. True believers won't reject the biblical worldview, but they may need to more accurately understand the biblical worldview and how it relates to their situational context. Therefore, believers may need to revise their models so that they fit the evidence more consistently and accurately. Admittedly, sometimes the biblical worldview itself is referred to as a model, but it is an overarching model that shouldn't be subject to revision. Only smaller models within its framework may be revised.

Horizons of the Possible

Choices we make today presume a technological context. People from the past wouldn't have been able to make the same choices because they didn't have the same technological or economic possibilities (e.g., transportation). Choices we make today also presume a context of cultural identity.

Were students consciously aware of the massive forces that were underlying the possibility of their choices in the last week?

It's likely that they were not. Most people just engage in the activities of their society, taking for granted the hundreds of years and billions of factors that brought their societal possibilities about. They're reliant on historical precedents far more than they may think.

People from other cultures, even in the present day, would not make the same choices because they don't have the same desires or values—shaped by historical influences.

Ask students to think of examples of historical influences that undergird their nation's cultural identity.

One example: The second amendment rights of Americans—the right to bear arms—is difficult to understand without the historical context. A missionary talking with people from a small city-state where no citizens were allowed to have guns was asked why many Americans support gun rights. Their own city was very safe, but when they listened to news from the United States, they would hear about all of the violence. They couldn't understand why the American government didn't just ban all guns. How could the missionary explain why so many Americans rejected this proposal? He could only do so by trying to explain the larger historical context that undergirds the American constitutional rights and cultural values—a context very different from that of a small, government-controlled city-state. It's necessary to understand data within a historical model.

Multiculturalism: A Flawed Model

Robert Woodberry's findings challenge the model of multiculturalism. The multicultural model purports to protect indigenous cultures by working against interference from outside forces. Change is always construed to be negative. Tolerance and acceptance are the controlling ethic. But Woodberry's research shows the positive impact of missionaries, who not only opposed imperialistic abuses but also introduced changes into the indigenous cultures. Woodberry's model recognizes that some changes were bad—independent missionaries needed to stand against imperialism. But some changes were good—independent missionaries improved political and economic conditions through literacy and the biblical ethic. Missionaries who apply a holistic biblical worldview to all of life will end up both adapting to and challenging cultural norms. It shouldn't be any surprise that calling on people to conform more to God's creational norms would improve their culture.

Students would benefit from reading the whole article: Andrea Palpant Dilley, "The Surprising Discovery About Those Colonialist, Proselytizing Missionaries," *Christianity Today* (website), January 8, 2014.

Use discernment, but the following editorial magnifies how badly the multicultural ethic can corrupt government policy: "Ignoring Sexual Abuse in Afghanistan," *New York Times* (website), September 20, 2015.

Humility Is for Everyone

Humility is fundamental to honesty. Whig histories violate this fundamental ethic. People who hold to those kinds of historical models are likely to spin the evidence whenever anything negative is brought up against their favored people group or institution. But Christians shouldn't react to Whig history by emphasizing the flaws of their predecessors or traditional institutions as viewed through the lens of contemporary values. This is simply another kind of Whiggish history. Christians should account for finiteness and fallibility even in the best of people and institutions and in every generation and subgroup. But they must also account for God's providential common grace. Flawed people

Missionaries and European Colonialism

Another example is the common historical model of the European colonization of Africa, Asia, and the Americas that portrays missionaries as key *partners* in the colonization project. In this model, missionaries sought protection from the European powers, and in exchange, they helped destroy the various native cultures they found—by participating in the "civilizing" project the great European nations were engaged in. Missions, according to this model, was a significant part of the oppression and injustice that nineteenth-century powers like England inflicted on nations such as Kenya.

But sociologist Robert Woodberry has proposed a different model based on extensive research. His research began with the observation that some countries that emerged from colonization were democratic while others were totalitarian. Some of these countries were very similar in natural resources and even in ethnicity. What made the difference in political outcomes?

Woodberry noticed that in some colonies the missionaries were part of state churches. These missionaries did often work closely with the colonial powers. But, he pointed out, many other missionaries served churches that were not state churches. He found that these missionaries tended to oppose injustices practiced by the colonial powers. For instance, it was missionaries of this sort that smuggled pictures of horrible abuses out of the Congo. And missionaries in South Africa spearheaded an agreement that protected the peoples in what is now Botswana from further European land grabs. In addition, Woodberry found that these missionaries invested a great deal of time and effort in teaching the people they ministered to how to read and write. The net effect, Woodberry concluded, was that the countries where these missionaries worked are now more stable and democratic. Those missionaries weren't trying to be social reformers or to lay the foundations for democracy. They were protesting injustices against the people they loved and educating those people in the basics that they needed to read and understand Scripture. But there were unintended, unforeseen positive results. Woodberry's model is a better explanation of the data.[10]

THE NEED FOR HUMILITY

In these two examples Christians come out looking better after a historian and a sociologist made more reliable models, using more of the data. But Christians doing historical research have to remain humble: the best model could result in Christians looking worse than they did before. And a model itself is just a fallible human construction—another reason for humility. Other historians may find gaps, logical problems, or alternative explanations. Christians cannot simply reject alternative models as attacks on their faith (they may be or they may not). Christians have to seek to substantiate their models with the best research available.

In Woodberry's case, he constructed a statistical model to test whether the case studies he had gathered would be confirmed. He then tested other factors, such as "climate, health, location, accessibility, natural resources, colonial power, disease prevalence."[11] These did not statistically correlate to stable democracy the way that the presence of independent missionaries did. Only God knows precisely what role missionaries in Tanzania, Vietnam, and other places played in bringing positive change. But Woodberry presented a useful model with appropriate humility and yet with appropriate confidence because he had followed the best practices of his discipline.

and institutions are used for good. Individualists who reject traditional institutions and authority structures often do so by critiquing hypocrisy of past generations, but they often fail to see the same flaws in themselves.

Evaluating a Model with Humility

One positive result of the Reformation was the freedom for particular groups of Christians to define themselves according to the scriptural convictions of their own consciences. Thus, a multiplicity of denominations formed. Each group was convinced that its own teaching and practices most closely aligned with the standards of the Bible.

As a result, people today love their own denomination and can be very convinced that its positions reflect the original first-century church better than any other denomination.

But supporting those convictions with a faulty historical model is counterproductive. The classic example of this is the model that is often referred to as the "Baptist Bloodline." The evaluation of this flawed model isn't meant as a critique of Baptists generally since most Baptists reject this historical model of their origins.

The Historical Claims of the Model

The "Baptist Bloodline" is a model that claims that Baptists came into existence from the time of John the Baptist (assuming his title referred to his founding of a particular church group rather than his activity of baptizing). The model claims that Baptists were then assured that they would never go out of existence. In Matthew 16:18, Jesus promises to preserve a biblically correct local church—the Baptists. Since a biblically sound local church can never go out of

THE NEED FOR HONESTY

What if Woodberry's research had ended up not supporting his thesis? What if he had found that countries with independent missionaries in the nineteenth century, even controlling for other factors, all ended up being totalitarian dictatorships with abysmally low literacy rates? What should he have done?

This brings us to the important historical concept of **objectivity**, which is not the same as neutrality. As historians use the term *objective* today, they don't mean that people should be neutral—without biases or presuppositions—when they do their research. They don't even mean that historians should put aside their basic worldview commitments. A Christian historian cannot set aside his fundamental belief in the existence of God, God's sovereign control over all things, the accuracy of Scripture, or the work of the Holy Spirit in human hearts. But objectivity does mean that the historian doesn't try to marshal support only for the position he wants to be true. He tries, by God's grace, to find the truth.

> It is actually the duty of a historian, when he postulates a certain thesis . . . to make a special effort to find evidence that would call his theory into question."[12]
>
> —CARL TRUEMAN

For instance, a Baptist church historian might be looking for evidence that in the early centuries of the church baptism was practiced exclusively by immersion. A Presbyterian church historian may be looking for evidence that infants were baptized in the early church. It's not wrong for these historians to look for historical support for their church's doctrinal position. But they have to be sure that they're not selecting only facts that support their case to the neglect of contrary facts. They will actually want to look for evidence that goes *against* their expectations. And they'll want to be sure that they don't interpret texts in ways that support their position while neglecting that alternative readings are possible or even more likely. What is at stake here for the Christian historian are the virtues of honesty and integrity. In fact, Christians haven't always lived up to Scripture's standard. A historian shouldn't distort his model of history to make the facts fit the story he wants to tell.

THINKING IT THROUGH 24.2

1. Once a historian has gathered all of the raw data from source materials, what must he use to explain that data?

2. How did Robert Woodberry demonstrate that his model is superior to existing popular models?

3. Give two reasons why humility is essential in historical work.

4. What is the difference between objectivity and neutrality?

9 5. Why is the work of historical interpretation difficult—even when you have an overarching biblical worldview through which to filter the evidence?

existence, they conclude that Baptist groups should be identifiable in a succession of groups down through the centuries. Those groups would have to be the dissenters from the Roman Church: Donatists, Cathari, Waldensians, and Anabaptists. The model claims that these groups should be identified as Baptists by different names.

A Critique of the Historical Claims

How would you set out to critique such a model as a Christian historian? Even if your knowledge is limited, can you provide some critiques of the claims and groups purported to be Baptists?

First, the presuppositions are theologically flawed.

- *John was associated with his task of baptizing and not with a particular group of people called Baptists, who were baptized for church membership.*

- *Matthew 16:18 simply provides assurance that Jesus would always have a people who would remain His followers. It doesn't teach that only Baptists could ever qualify as true followers, a claim that makes particular denominational distinctives essential for salvation.*

- *The term for "church" is used throughout Scripture in a general way to refer to a variety of assemblies of called-out people. It's a term that can refer generally to the organic church of all believers in all ages and need not always refer to a particular local assembly or institutional church (Acts 9:31; 1 Cor. 12:13; Gal. 1:13; Eph. 1:22).*

Second, the historical evidence is forced.

- *Similarity does not equal identity. The fact that various persecuted groups dissented from the Roman Church just as Baptists did doesn't mean that those groups can be identified as the same as the Baptists.*

- *Evidence reveals that most of the listed groups are more notably different from the Baptists—including biblically unorthodox positions that Baptists reject. (For example, Donatists held to baptismal regeneration.) As a result, the historical model is built on flawed assumptions that are contrary to clear historical evidence.*

Humility for the historian means that he's willing to be corrected by the evidence even if it doesn't favor the group or the position that he desires.

[For reference see H. Leon McBeth, *The Baptist Heritage: Four Centuries of Baptist Witness* (Nashville: Broadman Press, 1987), 49–63.]

Objectivity Versus Neutrality

Just as a person can be honest while holding to a particular position, so a historian can also be objective while presupposing a particular worldview. The discussion above suggests another good example. A survey of both the written an architectural evidence favors the conclusion that immersion was the dominant mode of baptism throughout the period of the early church. Furthermore, in the first centuries of the church those given baptism were adults. It is also the case that baptismal regeneration became the dominant view very early in church history. The former two points would make Baptists happy and Presbyterians or Anglicans less happy. The final point would be avoided by evangelicals of multiple denominations. The historian from any of these denominations is not neutral about what he thinks the Bible teaches about these issues, but he must handle his historical research objectively so that he honestly reports the viewpoints of others.

Incidentally, one aid to objectivity for the church historian is the recognition that true doctrine is established by Scripture rather than by historical practice.

THINKING IT THROUGH 24.2

1. a model that depends on a worldview

2. His model not only proved through case studies that missionaries were known to have confronted abuses, but it also relied on statistical analysis—countries with more independent missionaries tended to lead to a more educated populace and thus to a democratic society.

3. Any model is a fallible human construct that may at some point need to be reworked based on additional information, alternative explanations, or better logical interpretations.

   Christianity (or your own ethnicity or whatever group you're studying) may come out looking worse off with a revised model.

4. Objectivity refers to honesty even while holding to a belief system with its presuppositions; neutrality is a myth that says it's possible to make interpretive conclusions about the facts without any presupposed worldview model.

♡5. Historical events are almost always complex with multiple factors, causes, and influences.

SECTION OBJECTIVES 24.3

1. Define providence and defend its reality in human experience.

2. Explain the objections to discerning divine providence in human history (outside of specific biblical revelation).

3. Explain guidelines and limitations for properly discerning divine providence in human history.

Moral Judgments in Perspective

The parameters of a variety of moral judgments could be illustrated by a series of concentric circles. In the largest circle, the broadest moral judgments knit together the widest group of people with which a person could agree due to a fundamentally shared worldview. For example, this circle might be inclusive of people who have been largely influenced by the biblical ethic and creational norms but don't necessarily accept the biblical worldview. The next circle in would include professing Christians who share the same basic biblical worldview. The next circle in might represent believers who definitively share the biblical worldview *and* quite a similar broad philosophy of applying that worldview. The next circle could represent people who share very particular doctrinal or applicational distinctives. The circles of agreement keep getting smaller until you reach your own familial or personal convictions and standards. The more specific you get, the narrower the fellowship becomes. Deciding which issues fit where in the circles is important because you wouldn't want to limit a kindred spirit with people you could largely get along with in respect to an issue in its particular context. But the more detailed knowledge—the more nuanced a view or the more specific someone gets on an issue—the less kindred fellowship they may be able to have with others. This is why, for example, Christians have broader associations in a network of churches (with a fair amount of disagreement) and local churches (with very specific stances). Unity in any one of the circles must be determined

24.3 SEEING GOD'S HAND IN HISTORY

One of the benefits of studying history is the exposure it brings to other ways of thinking. C. S. Lewis noted that even authors of the past who considered each other enemies actually agreed on a great many assumptions simply because they lived in the same time period.[13] For instance, contemporary American views about democracy, free speech, separation of church and state, and many other topics are views common to many people living in the United States. But these views would seem foreign to people in most other places and other times in world history. Likewise, the ideas that democracy is subversive, that free speech is dangerous, that the state has the responsibility to protect true religion, and that divine law should regulate behavior are foreign to many Americans—but these ideas used to be simply assumed in many places and times in world history.

MAKING MORAL JUDGMENTS

Moralities and political views have differed significantly over time, and this ought to lead to more humility on the part of the historian. It's important to judge historical figures within the context of their times. For example, today someone who favored sending African Americans to Africa or denying them the right to vote would rightly be called a racist. But Abraham Lincoln himself held such opinions even as he signed the Emancipation Proclamation.[14] Yet given the intellectual and political climate of his day, Lincoln clearly deserves great charity for pressing for a position that more closely aligned with Scripture despite retaining some unbiblical views common for his time.

But the Christian historian has a more definite standard than the shifting views of contemporary cultures. A biblical worldview roots all moral evaluations, of course, in Scripture. That standard never changes, and it is applicable at all times and places.

Christian historians share the blind spots of their own eras. They, too, fall short of the standards of Scripture. So the Christlike thing to do when a sinner writes about other sinners, living or dead, is to give as much grace to people as possible. And one way a historian does this is by acknowledging the cultural and intellectual forces that shaped figures of the past. Christian historians should write with the biblical virtues of grace and kindness.

DISCERNING DIVINE PROVIDENCE

providence: *the theological term designating God's control over and directing of human affairs*

How to view divine **providence*** is one of the most controversial topics among Christian historians. Virtually all Christians accept the doctrine of God's providence, however they might define it. The Bible teaches that God is in control of every event in history. He directs all human affairs (Ps. 22:28; Prov. 16:33; Acts 17:26), particularly for the good of His people (Rom. 8:28; Eph. 1:11). Nonetheless, not even the persecution and suffering of God's people are outside the bounds of His providence (2 Tim. 3:12), and the goodness the Lord shows to non-Christians is also included (Matt. 5:45). Sometimes the Bible lets its readers see God at work "behind the scenes" of world history. For instance, God motivated King Cyrus to send some of the exiled Israelites back to Judea. God didn't use a miracle to do this. He worked silently within Cyrus's heart (Ezra 1:1–2). We would not know about this except that God first predicted that He would do it and then did it. But some Christian historians think that, for various reasons, a Christian should avoid discussing providence in histories outside of the Bible.

---

by shared beliefs (the truth) and not just a pragmatic desire for getting along with everybody.

You can apply this paradigm of concentric circles to history and politics. Broad conservatism is inclusive of several smaller concentric circles—traditional conservatism, laissez-faire conservatism, and neoconservatism. Those three groups agree on some broader basics, but vehemently disagree over specific nuances that can be important. Even traditional conservatives often disagree among themselves on a particular strategy.

Judging providence in history is one of those specific nuances. Christians with the same basic worldview and even specific agreement on a philosophy of doing history may disagree with one another.

Defining Providence Properly

God's work of providence is His work of upholding and governing the world. This work of preserving the natural order or working things out through His guidance of natural occurrences must be distinguished from God's work of supernatural intervention, which overrides that natural order—the more precise parameter for defining a miracle. God doesn't perform miracles nonstop, but He does work providentially all the time. God always works in concurrence with the built-in nature of His created order. (*Concurrence* means that God is 100 percent sovereign *and* the created thing or person is 100 percent responsible for its own functioning or actions. As such, both God's sovereignty and human responsibility are entirely preserved—mysterious as that is in its full outworking.) Nothing in

Problems with Saying Certain Events Are Providential

Carl Trueman raises two objections to discussing divine providence in history. First, he says, God's providence stands over all things. *Everything* that happens in the world is providential. Therefore, claiming that providence is the reason something happened doesn't really explain anything. Second, he notes that those who do appeal to providence often do so to promote their own point of view or to claim God for their side in some argument. To say "God did this" ends the argument, often unfairly.[15] John Fea points out the way that this is often done in American history. Some historians point to anything that promotes American freedoms and interests as an example of God's providence, thereby attempting to justify the rightness of the American Revolution or some other event.[16] Fea notes that such claims presuppose the position they're seeking to support; they assume that God approves of their causes. As Christian historian Mark Noll observes, whether you see the Reformation as an act of God for purifying the church depends on whether you're Protestant or Catholic.[17]

C. S. Lewis also raises an objection to finding God's providential hand in history. He warns of the danger of ascribing "our calamities (or more often our neighbours' calamities) to divine judgment."[18] Lewis asks how anyone can possibly know whether a certain calamity is a divine judgment unless God explicitly says so. Lewis also notes, however, that unbelievers are even more prone to this error than Jews and Christians are.

Guidelines for Saying Certain Events Are Providential

There is wisdom in the objections these writers raise. Certainly, we have no right to claim God for our side, while we do have a responsibility to be on His side. But there are also some answers to those objections that we need to think through.

Imagine a prayer meeting at a church when a member stands up and says:

> Last week I was taking a big road trip when my car broke down in the middle of nowhere. I don't have much mechanical expertise, but I got out and started to poke around under the hood. I didn't know what I was looking for, so I started to pray for help. Fifteen minutes later a car pulled over behind me. The driver knew a lot about fixing cars, and he was able to get me going well enough for me to get to a garage for a more permanent fix.

Someone who gives a testimony like this will usually end by praising God for answering prayer and providing help. If you've grown up in church, you've probably heard testimonies like this—or even given them.

But suppose that, instead of praising God, the person who gave the testimony concluded with a statement like this: "I'm not certain this was an answer to prayer; it may just have been a coincidence." Most Bible-believing Christians would think that saying this is somehow wrong because they believe that prayer matters (James 5:16), that God is our Father and cares about what we need, and that He wants us to ask Him for those needs and delights to meet them (Matt. 7:9–11). If God providentially sent the help, He also providentially sent the car trouble itself. He could have kept the water pump temperature sensor from wearing out, but He didn't. Christians' cars break down just as much as non-Christians' cars (maybe even more). And yet Christians are still right to see God's hand behind their automotive experiences.

Given all this discussion of divine providence, what do you think of the following comment in an actual history book about Henry VIII?

God's creation is left to random chance or to fatalistic determinism (Job 37:6–13; Ps. 148:8; Prov. 16:33; Matt. 6:26; 10:29). God hasn't abandoned His creation to work according to natural laws on its own (that's the view of deism). God remains personally and actively involved (Acts 17:28; Col. 1:17; Heb. 1:3, cf. Neh. 9:6). Divine providence includes everything that happens (Eph. 1:11) from historical turning points (Job 12:23; Ps. 22:28; Dan. 4:34–35; Acts 17:26) to ordinary personal minutiae (Ps. 139:16; Prov. 20:24) without attributing guilt to God for the evil He allows (Gen. 50:20; Prov. 16:4; Lam. 3:38; Rom. 8:28; James 1:13).

[Millard J. Erickson, *Christian Theology*, 2nd ed. (Grand Rapids: Baker Books, 1983), 412–35]

 Providence Doesn't Equal Approval

Give examples of erroneous discussions of divine providence in history. That is, can you identify common justifications for the actions of individuals or groups because self-interest was fulfilled or positive results were accomplished all the while ignoring the violation of biblical principles?

The Manifest Destiny doctrine in nineteenth-century America is one clear example.

Those who supported Manifest Destiny claimed that God intended for the United States to have all the western lands to the shores of the Pacific. They claimed that God had spoken when He hadn't (Ezek. 13:7–8). Therefore, they violated the third commandment (Exod. 20:7). Insofar as they promoted taking land from American Indians and Mexicans unjustly, they also violated the eighth and tenth commandments (Exod. 20:15, 17). Manifest Destiny is an example of civil religion—using religious language or concepts out of context to justify political ends. Christians must object to civil religion because (1) it replaces the God of the Bible with a god of the people's own making, (2) common sense or public opinion replaces biblical revelation as the voice of God, (3) it is a step toward secularism, as Americans looked for a common denominator of religious belief that all could agree on. In the end Manifest Destiny was a false gospel of a false god that abused the doctrine of God's providence to justify unjust actions.

Correcting a Misunderstanding

In response to Trueman's first objection, when Christians identify a particular event as providential, what they're really identifying is the significance of that event as it relates to God's larger revealed plan or principles of righteousness. They generally recognize that everything is providential, and they don't deny that truth by picking out certain events to highlight God's providence. When Christians interpret events as providential, they really mean to explain how those particular events, good or bad, might fit into God's moral will as He brings about all things to accomplish His revealed plan. [Wayne Grudem, *Systematic Theology* (Grand Rapids: Zondervan, 1994), 332]

Choosing Sides

Although Trueman's second objection is a legitimate critique, the abuse of a principle doesn't negate the principle. The reason people can identify an abuse is because they have a standard by which to judge the legitimacy of a claim that attempts to justify people's actions based on God's providence. That standard is the moral or revealed will of God in Scripture. It's true that descriptions of events or actions aren't sufficient alone to determine which side is in the right. Only prescriptive revelation has the authority to justify which side is in the right. This is what the oft-quoted phrase refers to when it asks not whether God is on our side but whether we are on God's side.

Lewis's warning is a caution that must be taken seriously. Because both people and events are so complex, causation or correlation are usually more difficult to discern than we tend to think. Retribution theology (assuming that only bad people have bad things happen to them and only good people have good things happen to them) is a dangerous error (Job 42:7–8; Ps. 73:1–28; Matt. 5:45; Luke 13:4–5; John 9:1–3; 2 Tim. 3:12).

Providence Outside the Bible

Ask students to write a paragraph or two describing a recent event from their own lives. Every event is providential, but is there a particular event in which they believe they can see its significance? That is, they can see how God worked things together according to His larger revealed plan or according to principles of righteousness. Is there a particular prayer that God providentially answered? Every prayer is answered (yes, no, or wait). But is there a clear manifestation of God's working to address the situation so that you can see Him working out His will in your life, perhaps in unexpected ways?

Identifying Providential Events

We always understand the significance of events—how what happens fits in with God's overall plan for the world—according to our presuppositions. That doesn't mean that everyone's opinion is legitimized as a viable perspective—that is, people just need to learn to view things through the eyes of other people (the postmodern approach of multicultural tolerance). Some people's presuppositions are wrong; they're based on the wrong foundation of authority or the wrong historical model.

What it does mean is that disagreements must be handled by evaluating the bases for presuppositions or models. Conclusions can only be challenged by doing the hard work of evaluating the substantiation behind the conclusions. Otherwise, discussing differing opinions will simply degenerate into an impasse without any chance of making progress toward a resolution.

God's Sovereign Control over Evil

God uses evil people and their evil actions to accomplish His good purposes without being culpable of any of the evil Himself. In fact, God judges the evil actions of the people He uses to accomplish His purposes (Prov. 16:4). For example, the very enemies God used to judge His people Israel for their wickedness were in turn judged by God for their wickedness against Israel (Obad. 1:15). It would be tempting to question the justice of God in this (Rom. 9:13–23). Instead, Christians understand the outworking of God's sovereignty and human responsibility to be a mystery (Rom. 11:33–36). The best we can know is that humans act freely according to their own sinful natures. Any good they do is due to God's grace. Therefore, if God chooses to allow a person to do evil, He doesn't need to use coercion. God simply removes His restraining hand of grace and gives evil people the freedom to

Had this makeshift political match [between Henry VIII and Katherine of Aragon] not taken place, and prince Henry taken instead a younger, more fertile consort (such as his father's former choice for him, Katherine's niece Eleanor), his subsequent break with Rome almost certainly would not have occurred, in which case any tender young English reformation must have faced the wrath of a ruthless, orthodox monarch and his equally Catholic heirs.[19]

How is a conservative Protestant Christian to respond? To say, "That's a mighty big, world-changing coincidence," doesn't seem to be the right response.

We don't know all of God's purposes in the world. And it's hard or impossible to figure out exactly what God is doing through every situation in your own life—or what He's doing in others' lives through you. Sometimes, you figure out after a decade why God gave you certain experiences. But there's a lot you won't know about even your own life until that day when we shall "know fully" even as we have been "fully known" (1 Cor. 13:12).

Nonetheless, the Bible does reveal quite a number of God's purposes. And when, broadly speaking, those purposes get fulfilled, it's right to point to God's good and powerful hand of providence. If you're convinced that the Protestant Reformation rescued the biblical gospel and other precious biblical doctrines, rooting the church once again in Scripture—if you're convinced that the health of Christ's church depended in large measure on the success of the Reformation—then how could you fail to see God's hand in Henry VIII's choice of a wife? Think of the wide-ranging consequences of that choice. Could it be that one of them was the modern missionary movement launched from English-speaking lands? God says it's not His desire "that any should perish, but that all should reach repentance" (2 Pet. 3:9). He wants the gospel to go to the ends of the earth (Matt. 28:19–20).

In the final chapter of Genesis, Joseph told his brothers,

> As for you, you meant evil against me, but God meant it for good, to bring it about that many people should be kept alive, as they are today. (Gen 50:20)

We don't need special revelation from God to conclude that, though Henry VIII meant to do evil (to divorce his lawful wife), God meant it for good, to bring it about that many people should be evangelized, as they are today.

Of course, if our understanding of biblical doctrine or of God's purposes in Scripture is incorrect, then our interpretation of God's providential purposes in history is bound to be incorrect too. This is why it is the Christian's responsibility to rightly understand Scripture and the purposes of God as stated in Scripture. Given that understanding, it cannot be wrong to examine whether those purposes are actually being worked out in history.

This is the answer to Carl Trueman's argument that since everything is providential, providence is not a worthwhile category for the historian: some events clearly promote God's purposes as stated in Scripture. Since God is providentially in control of all things, as Trueman acknowledges, it is appropriate to point out the connection between God's stated purposes and the events that promoted them. And when events go against God's purposes, it is right to see the hand of the evil one. As in the case of Job, God sometimes gives Satan a long leash.

Dangers to Avoid in Discerning Providence in History

We should note that a "providence" is different from a "miracle." God providentially works through the ordinary operation of human thought and action. He uses what

act consistently with the evil already in their hearts. All of this is under the divine control of God (Exod. 4:21; 7:3; 9:12; 10:1; 14:8), but all evil is the responsibility of human agents freely choosing to act consistently with their own natures (Exod. 7:14, 22; 8:15, 32; 9:34). God's decision to remove His grace and mercy doesn't violate God's justice because nobody deserves God's grace and mercy in the first place.

Case Study: Bloody Mary

The death of King Edward VI at age sixteen left the English throne open for Mary I, Henry VIII's daughter. A devout Roman Catholic, she did all she could to purge England of Protestantism. Her cruelty, including the murder of hundreds of Protestants, caused people to give her the moniker Bloody Mary. If God used Henry VIII, in spite of his wickedness, to forward Protestantism, what was God doing by putting Mary on the throne (Dan. 2:21)? Wasn't this a setback in God's plan?

With all that students know about discerning providence in history, ask them to make a moral judgement about this event. How does it fit in with God's overall plan for the world? Ask students to write a half-page paper relating the event to God's providence.

You may wish to allow students more time to research the history. In particular, you may hint to students to read statements made by Hugh Latimer, one of the men burned at the stake. He reportedly told Nicholas Ridley, another man being burned with him, "We shall this day light such a candle, by God's grace, in England, as I trust shall never be put out."

theologians call "secondary causes." He doesn't have to use His own finger, as it were, to crush His enemies. When the Spanish Armada—a military offensive launched by Roman Catholic Spain—suffered defeat in 1588, keeping Protestant England permanently out of the hands of the pope, the immediate causes for that naval victory included the fact that the English had superior firepower. They had developed a more efficient way of repeatedly firing their cannons.[20] The Christian historian would be irresponsible to simply call the defeat of the Spanish Armada a providential act of God while ignoring the secondary causes at work to bring about its defeat.

Christians should also refrain from appealing to providence to justify the rightness of their own actions. For instance, what if the English appealed to the Armada's defeat as an example of their national righteousness compared to that of the Spanish? What if Henry VIII justified his divorce by pointing to the spreading of the gospel that resulted?

This kind of thinking gets everything precisely backwards. God sometimes uses crooked sticks to draw straight lines. For instance, the assassination of France's leading Protestants in the Saint Bartholomew's Day Massacre didn't mean God favored the Catholics and their doctrine. Nor did it mean that God was more in control of the events in England than of the ones in France. One of the purposes of God in the world, according to the Bible, is that His people will sometimes suffer (Matt. 5:12–13; Heb. 12:7–11; 1 Pet. 1:6).

Not all possible historical examples of divine providence are clear-cut. In fact, most are not. This means once again that Christian historians must be humble. In many cases, they will not know what God's purpose—or, more accurately, His purposes—might be. Historians shouldn't be afraid to confess their ignorance or offer mere suggestions. But neither should this limitation prevent historians from considering the providence of God. God really is providentially controlling all things.

Saint Bartholomew's Day Massacre: A providential reading of history doesn't look at those who are successful and presume that they're the ones God favors. It looks at Scripture to see what God favors, and then it is justified in making interpretations of history.

WRITING AND TEACHING

A historian's task is not complete when he has researched an event, of course. That research must be communicated to others. The two most common ways for a historian to communicate his research are through teaching and writing. Writing can be published in scholarly journals or in books—whether those books are scholarly or popular, that is, written for people who aren't specialists. Some historians look down on writing for a general audience, but the Christian shouldn't. If all people should have a Christian perspective about God's world, then Christians should write histories that

Historians are able to look back at the widespread and long-range impact of Bloody Mary's short reign. Since Mary's reign forced many Protestants to flee to mainland Europe, some historians have concluded that Protestant influences from mainland Europe were inculcated into English Protestants, who soon returned to England with those influences. Mary's five-year reign also reinforced anti-Catholic sentiment so that Elizabeth I was careful to rule with shrewd moderation.

Secondary Causation

The historian's primary task is to examine the means that God uses to unfold the historical narrative of the world. God is always directly involved providentially, but His direct involvement is usually through secondary causation. Trying to pinpoint a miracle in everything that occurs tends to diminish the importance of God's providential work. It takes faith to see God's hand in the natural outworking of providence. That faith is denigrated when people will recognize that God is at work only if He intervenes in a supernatural, miraculous way.

Sinning So Grace May Abound

Some argue that since positive results can sometimes come about because of one's own wickedness, then it follows that that wickedness is justified. This is an example of the effects of the Fall on human logic. This argument is similar to that which is condemned in Romans 6:1–2. It's twisted logic that turns grace on its head (Jude 1:4). If people are truly learning from the grace of God, then they will learn from God's reprieve of judgment by turning away from their wickedness (Titus 2:11–12). Otherwise, God's reprieve will come to an end; presumptuous sin leads to judgment that *must* be carried out (Amos 7:1–6; 8:1–2; 9:8–10).

Research and Writing

If any students are interested in pursuing careers in the historical field, remind them of the interdisciplinary nature of most fields. Some high school students may love their history classes, but they may neglect their grammar and writing classes. They'll find out in college that history majors often have to take a historical research and writing class because much of the work of history relies on researching and writing. Challenge students not to neglect their other classes. If they work hard in all of their classes they will be more likely to succeed in their specialty.

Teaching History

Teaching can be done in a variety of venues. It doesn't just occur in traditional settings such as a school or university classroom. The teaching of history might take place at a national park from a tour guide. It might take place through a political think tank on a blog. It could even be done on a radio show that engages the populace with current events. Historians work for the military. They staff museums and other historical attractions around the nation. They write journal articles. They make documentaries for television. They may even work alongside lawyers as support staff. All of these areas need Christians with a biblical worldview.

Kinds of Research and Writing

Ask students to compare and contrast the two kinds of writing.

Popular General Research and Writing

Focus: the broad sweep of history

Goal: pulling themes together into a narrative

Task: systematizing details

Scholarly In-Depth Research and Writing

Focus: particular and technical subjects

Goal: support broad claims

Task: gathering details

Which kind of writing is more important?

Both kinds are important. Though they serve different purposes, both kinds of writing should be viewed with respect.

---

are accessible to a wide readership. On the flip side, some Christians are suspicious of scholarly histories. They may think that scholarship is elitist or detracts from more directly gospel-related work. But if Christian scholars aren't doing excellent work in the primary sources, then they will be dependent on the work that non-Christians do.

God calls Christian historians to view—and do—their work through the lenses of a biblical worldview. And He calls all believers to view history through those same lenses.

THINKING IT THROUGH 24.3

1. What is divine providence?

2. Give a biblical example of God's providence in human history.

3. Explain two reasons why some historians believe that Christians should avoid discussing providence in histories outside of the Bible.

4. Even though humans can't know all of God's purposes in the world and won't figure out exactly what God is doing through every situation, why should Christians still point to God's providence in history?

♀5. Why shouldn't a providential reading of history look at those who are successful and presume that they are the ones God favors?

THINKING IT THROUGH 24.3

1. the theological term designating God's control over and directing of human affairs

2. God motivated King Cyrus to send some of the exiled Israelites back to Judea just as God had predicted. He did so not through a miracle but by silently working in Cyrus's heart (Ezra 1:1–2).

3. First, everything that happens in the world is providential. Therefore, claiming that providence is the reason something happened doesn't really explain it.

   Second, those who appeal to providence often do so to selfishly promote their own point of view or to illegitimately claim God for their side in some argument.

4. The Bible reveals at least some of God's broader purposes in history, and some situations do seem to point to God's good and powerful hand of providence working out those purposes.

♀5. Scriptural teaching on what is good and evil determines who God favors, not beneficial or detrimental circumstances. God providentially uses all circumstances, good and evil, to eventually work out His plan.

24 CHAPTER REVIEW

Scripture Memory

Isaiah 46:9–10

Making Connections

1. What should provide the framework for historical study?

2. What must a historian do before he can communicate a historical model to others?

3. What is a historical model?

4. What can cause a historical model to be faulty?

Developing Skills in Apologetics and Worldview

5. How would you evaluate the claim that the attack on the Twin Towers on 9/11 was an act of God's divine judgment on the United States?

6. How would you respond to someone who denies that the Protestant Reformation was an act of God's divine grace in world history?

Examining Assumptions and Evidence

7. Why should Christian historians seek to benefit their neighbors through their historical work? Give an example of how they could do this.

8. Why are humility and honesty necessary in the work of model-making?

9. Why is the discernment of divine providence in human history one of the most controversial topics among Christian historians?

10. Why wouldn't it be right to settle the debate over discerning divine providence in human history by viewing all historical events as merely inexplicable coincidences?

Becoming a Creative Cultivator

11. Read a section from a Christian history textbook; then read a section from a secular textbook about the same historical era. Identify ways a model influences each excerpt—affecting the selection of data from sources, the moral judgments expressed, or the discernment of divine providence.

within the framework of the biblical metanarrative.

One example is the historical work that provides a more accurate portrayal of the Puritans.

8. humility because of finiteness and fallenness; honesty for the sake of telling the truth objectively and with integrity

9. Because everything that takes place in human history is in one sense a part of God's providential work to carry out His plan, it's difficult for humans to judge how specific events work together to fit into God's larger plan. Humans tend to identify whatever favors themselves as God's working out of His plan.

10. Knowing about God's complete control over everything and knowing what God has revealed as His purposes in Scripture, believers should be able to discern His good providence in at least some of the events of human history.

Becoming a Creative Cultivator

11. Provide students with copies of several excerpts. Some excerpts should show obvious differences; other excerpts might have subtle but important differences. By God's common grace, some excerpts may not be objectionable or different from Christian treatments. Note that the model underlies the work that went into putting the textbook together and won't always be explicit.

CHAPTER REVIEW ANSWERS

Making Connections

1. a biblical worldview

2. find, sift through, and process the source materials

3. It's the unifying story that is told, making sense of all of the data of historical evidence.

4. a unifying story that's false because it doesn't take into account all of the data or misinterprets some of the data

Developing Skills in Apologetics and Worldview

5. From a biblical worldview, it's possible that God uses the evil acts of others in order to communicate and carry out His divine displeasure (Amos 2:4–5). However, Jesus Himself cautioned His disciples not to jump to conclusions about calamities that happen to other people (Luke 13:4–5).

6. From a biblical worldview, it seems more than plausible that God's good hand of providence was specifically at work in the recovery of God's Word in the common tongue and the doctrines of justification by faith alone in Christ alone by grace alone, which rapidly spread across the globe and impacted the world for centuries after that.

Examining Assumptions and Evidence

7. Historians can give a voice to people from the past so that truth can be known. Historians can provide examples for people in the present so that wisdom can be gained and a larger contextual view of the world can be learned

TERMS TO REMEMBER

primary source—a source that comes directly from the period being studied

secondary source—a source that relies on the historical evaluation and conclusions of others who have studied a historical era

objectivity—an attempt to present the truth honestly regardless of one's own biases

providence—the theological term designating God's control over and directing of human affairs

9

ARTS & CULTURE

The student will be able to

25.1 Explain why people with a biblical worldview must hold to an objective and transcendent standard for beauty just as they do for truth and goodness.

25.2 Defend the idea that a person's subjective apprehension of truth, goodness, and beauty must be developed according to the divine standard.

25.3 Use the creational norms of truth, goodness, and beauty to evaluate various artistic products.

SECTION OBJECTIVES 25.1

1. Detect the fallacies of both the scientistic and postmodern views of beauty.

2. Defend the idea that beauty, inextricably linked to truth and goodness, is objectively based on a transcendent divine order.

3. Analyze what art is, namely human subcreation that either imitates or twists God's divine order.

Chapter Twenty-Five TRUTH, GOODNESS, AND BEAUTY

Whatever is true, whatever is honorable, whatever is just, whatever is pure, whatever is lovely, whatever is commendable, if there is any excellence, if there is anything worthy of praise, think about these things.

Scripture Memory
Philippians 4:8

25.1 BEAUTY AND CULTURE

A man in jeans and a ball cap stands in a Washington, D.C., metro station playing a violin as passersby rush off to their various appointments. A few people toss coins into the open case in front of him. A camera up on the wall catches the action—and the sound, the beautiful sound. If you know music, you know this isn't the kind of sound usually produced by street musicians. It's exquisite.

As it happened—though precisely one out of the hundreds of people passing by recognized it—the music was coming from a 3.5-million-dollar Stradivarius and a world-class violinist, Joshua Bell. Very few people stopped, a few more gave money, and Bell's total take for an hour of Bach and Schubert was $32.17.[1]

It's such a fascinating story. And everybody who reads it seems to realize that it has to be some kind of parable. It has to mean something. Dozens of books have mentioned the event. Some use it to make points about marketing. A Buddhist writer uses it to urge everyone to slow down. But what parable did the original writer of the story, the *Washington Post*'s Gene Weingarten, see in the free-but-ignored Joshua Bell concert?

Weingarten saw a parable about beauty. "What is beauty? Is it a measurable fact . . . or merely an opinion?"[2] If beauty is a fact, then it's a kind of personal defect that almost everybody rushed past this

particular beauty. People are busy, especially at subway stations, but surely more people could've—should've—spared three minutes.

That's especially true if Joshua Bell was right about the music he was playing—"Chaconne" from J. S. Bach's Partita No. 2. The nonreligious[3] Bell described the piece as "one of the greatest achievements of any man in history . . . a spiritually powerful piece, emotionally powerful, structurally perfect."[4] Bell told one interviewer, "A great piece of music gives one the sense of divine order."[5] Bell said,

> Everyone's definition of what God means can vary. But music is something that really takes you to that . . . thing that is greater than we are—the beauty, the magic of the universe. Bach, for instance, [is] probably one of the

Joshua Bell

Lesson Plan Chart—Chapter 25

Section Title	Pages	Activity Manual	Days
25.1 Beauty and Culture	384–86	Activity 42	1 day
25.2 Truth, Goodness, and Beauty in the Eye of the Beholder	386–93	Activity 43	2 days
25.3 Norms for the Arts	393–99		2 days
Review	400		1 day
Total Suggested Days			**6 days**

 ### Joshua Bell and Common Grace

What part of the Joshua Bell quote reflects a wrong worldview?

that anybody can define who God is

What part of Joshua Bell's quote is consistent with the biblical worldview?

He recognizes that the world is structured according to God's design. There are built-in creational norms for every discipline. The creative cultivation of humans in the realm of music is no exception to those norms.

Joshua Bell on Music

Listen to the piece of music mentioned in the Student Text—played by Joshua Bell if possible.

great recruiters to religion . . . because it's when you listen to Johann Sebastian Bach, the music . . . you can only think that there is something, something great out there. There is no other explanation for his music.[6]

SECULAR AND POSTMODERN VIEWS OF BEAUTY

But the secular postmodern West isn't eager to admit that there is something greater than we are, especially if that something makes demands on us. The leading worldviews of our time deny that beauty really exists, or at least that we can reliably recognize it.

For naturalistic materialists, beauty is just an accidental byproduct of evolution. Music, for example, may be an unintended effect of language formation. Or maybe musical males attract more females.[7]

According to postmodernists, for you to make an **aesthetic*** judgment—to call something "beautiful" or "ugly"—is to say something about your individual feelings and not necessarily about any reality outside yourself. For a postmodern, beauty is so deeply stuck in the eye of the beholder that it cannot get out. Beauty is decidedly not fact; it's mere opinion.

aesthetic: *relating to beauty or the experience of beauty*

A Cultural Triad: Truth, Goodness, and Beauty

Christian philosopher Ron Horton has observed that "our age attempts to separate goodness and beauty, but the Bible ascribes both to God."[8] "How great is his goodness, and how great his beauty!" (Zech. 9:17). God unites goodness and beauty—and, of course, truth. Truth, goodness, and beauty make up a **triad**, a collection of three concepts that seem to flow necessarily together. Modern Western worldviews doubt and weaken all three.

This chapter makes a fairly simple argument: modern Western attacks on beauty sound an awful lot like modern Western attacks on truth and goodness. And that similarity is not accidental. Truth, goodness, and beauty stand together. If you don't accept **relativism** when it comes to truth (knowledge) and goodness (morality), why would you agree that beauty is merely in the eye of the beholder?

Perhaps you are, in fact, nervous about ever claiming that someone else's aesthetic judgment is wrong. If your friend loves "Bang Yer Head" by an earsplitting screamo band, but you find it distasteful, who are you to judge?

This relativistic perspective about beauty would surprise people of past ages, especially Christians. Our secular age is the first in history in which people find it easy to believe beauty is what we make of it, and hard to believe that "beauty" is something that exists independently of human judgment.[9]

But we'll discover as we explore culture and the arts that Joshua Bell was right. Beauty points to a **divine order**, and what's more, beauty is part of that order. The arts are full of creational norms. **Art** is a work of discovery and imitation as much as it is a work of creation. A culture that denies that beauty exists outside the eyes of its beholders is a culture that is "revolting against reality itself."[10]

Subcreators of Truth, Goodness, and Beauty

As we've seen in various portions of this book, the Creation Mandate is a call for—and a blessing to—humans to be "creative cultivators." "We take the stuff of creation and shape artifacts and institutions," says Ken Myers. "We build things from stone and steel. We make art by arranging colors and textures, sounds and words." Myers is right: "Culture is what we make of creation."[11] And that's the way God designed things to be.

What causes Bell and others to glory in this piece of music?

The music is purposefully designed to communicate a certain kind of emotion that is transcendent. People are drawn to that kind of emotional communication.

Is Bell's conclusion about this music purely subjective, or could there be an objective element to his evaluation?

While his appreciation for and apprehension of what good music is may be an opinion (subjective), it's an opinion that has an objective basis in a recognizable created order. He's well-acquainted with methods and artistic techniques that underlie a successful piece of music. He knows that music can be designed to evoke certain emotions.

Bell commented to the reporter that music is "both powerful and profound" and "can serve to heighten our emotions and provide a sense of well-being and purpose." He said, "I actually believe that music, along with all art forms, is a basic human need and should be a necessary part of one's education throughout life." [Blair Howell, "Concert Preview: Music of Violinist Joshua Bell 'Feeds Both Brain and Heart,'" *Deseret News* (website), November 9, 2013]

Music is rooted in something objective that evokes particular subjective responses. [See Michaeleen Doucleff, "Anatomy of a Tear-Jerker: Why Does Adele's 'Someone Like You' Make Everyone Cry? Science Has Found the Formula" *Wallstreet Journal* (website), February 11, 2012.]

Why might some people disagree with Bell's assessment of this kind of music?

It may be that they don't desire the kind of emotional response that this music is meant to evoke. They may be drawn toward music that reflects emotions of hard-driving excitement rather than music that reflects romantic, peaceful, and transcendent emotions. The difference of opinion then is not based on a fault of the music or Bell's assessment of it, but on the limited range of musical emotions that they desire. Music education could expand their emotional range in the musical arena.

It may be that the hearers are so unacquainted with the style and what it is meant to communicate that it's like a foreign language. They can't process the music and respond to it emotionally. Their musical knowledge needs to grow to appreciate it.

Learning From Ken Myers

This unit on culture and the arts will be controversial with your students, and perhaps with you! The arts have always been difficult to discuss because the effort to describe them in words can seem like an effort to distill them into a medium they don't belong in. Music and visual art transcend the verbal. Ken Myers, host of the *Mars Hill Audio Journal*, is one of the leading Christian experts gifted to describe, analyze and evaluate, and even *enjoy* the arts—the creative expressions of God's image-bearers. Myers argues repeatedly in the same way this book does, though with sometimes different terminology. He points over and over to the "givenness" of creation, to the divinely created order of the cosmos, as the structure music and the arts should align with. In fact, he often points out that in previous eras, people believed that the creational order was such a given that if they wanted successful lives they needed to find that order and conform themselves to it. This was true in music and art no less than in morality and society. Myers's voice is desperately needed at a time when most Western Christians themselves don't believe that the created order ought to have any influence on their own artistic and musical habits. [Look in particular for videos of lectures Myers delivered in Moscow, Idaho, for Canon Wired; and for lectures and panel discussions given at Southern Baptist Theological Seminary in Louisville, Kentucky. Find excerpts to share with students.]

Truth, Goodness, and Beauty

Although the Bible doesn't explicitly say that there is an interdependent triad of truth, goodness, and beauty, these are biblical categories. In Philippians 4:8, Paul provides basic norms by which all cultural pursuits can be evaluated. Notice that the six virtues ("whatever is ____") can be grouped into three categories. First is *true*. Truth stands as a category of its own. *Honorable, just,* and *pure* can be grouped together under the heading of goodness. *Lovely* and *commendable* can be grouped under the heading beauty. Truth, goodness, and beauty are the biblical norms for evaluating all cultural endeavors. Notice also, that Scripture doesn't permit us to pick and choose our criteria. All three categories must hang together ("if there is any excellence, if there is anything worthy of praise").

Music and Evolution

If there is no divine order for music to conform to, then you're left with evolution. Evolutionary biology tends to boil every human behavior—including music—down to what gets males the most partners and females the most offspring.

The other major evolutionary explanation, the idea that music is an accidental byproduct of human language, also fails to satisfy. Consider the power, the depth, the cultural variety, the universal appeal of music—can it all be explained away as an accident? A. N. Wilson didn't think so. Once an outspoken atheist, he converted to Christianity after listening to Mozart one day. (Not that Mozart is gospel, but it was an apologetic for divine order.) [See TE note, pp. 390–91.]

"Bang Yer Head"

Many students will stiffly resist the key implication of God's created order applied to music, namely that some music is *disordered.* Play for them "Bang Yer Head"—it's a real song you can find online. Ask them to vote by secret ballot on whether they think it's "beautiful." This will give you a barometric reading of your class's inclinations, that is, the predisposed shape of their affections as they have trained them thus far.

Carrying Out the Creation Mandate

Instead of taking an evolutionary view, Christians should view art as a part of the task of carrying out the Creation Mandate. Art is part of culture, and culture is the result of carrying out that mandate. As such, humans are to be subcreators. That is, their creativity is supposed to develop God's creation according to His divine order. As fallen beings, humans will carry out their tasks (including art, music, literature, etc.) in ways that are more or less conformed to God's design. Denying the possibility that music or art might reflect human sinfulness is a denial of structure and direction; it's a denial of CFR.

Humans are "subcreators"—creators under God.[12] The best art—whether it's realistic or abstract painting, comic or tragic theater and film, intense or subtle music—captures the beauty of God's creation and helps us see the beauty of God. The best stories capture something of the great story that that the divine Author is writing, and they help us see that story with clearer eyes.[13]

Good subcreation can't help but glorify the ultimate Creator. When colors, sounds, and words are arranged beautifully, they point beyond themselves as all created things are supposed to. They point to a divine order and a divine Orderer.

Culture is far bigger than the arts, of course. Culture includes science, engineering, business practices, academic research, food preparation, marriage customs, and much more. But in this unit we'll focus on the arrangement of colors and textures, sounds and words. Though we'll reference multiple areas of culture, we'll focus mainly on music, the visual arts, literature, and drama. These are such large categories that we will be able to speak in only a general way.

THINKING IT THROUGH 25.1

1. Identify the aesthetic errors of scientific naturalism. Identify the aesthetic errors of postmodernism.

2. What three concepts fit together in a cultural triad?

3. Identify the source of the triad, which demands that the triad be objective and transcendent.

4. What does it mean to be a subcreator?

5. If cultural creativity is a matter of subcreation, then what purpose should good art seek to fulfill?

25.2 TRUTH, GOODNESS, AND BEAUTY IN THE EYE OF THE BEHOLDER

Without ever reading a philosophy book, average Western people still absorb the doubt in the air about truth, goodness, and beauty. Sociologist Christian Smith, the scholar who coined the term *moralistic therapeutic deism* to describe the religion of American teenagers, recorded comments from many interviews with those teens that demonstrate this doubt about what's moral. One teen said,

I think morals are just a social tool to keep us not killing each other, to keep us in line with our culture, so it can function as a unit.[14]

Another said,

Well, a lot of the times it's personal, it changes from person to person. What you may think is right may not necessarily be right for me, understand? So it's all individual.[15]

Yet another:

You can't say, you feel that something is absolute. You can be like, man, I feel that's ridiculously wrong, you know, you have the right to choose, that's your choice. But, I don't know, *absolute's* such a strong word. Um, I don't know, I really don't. . . . I mean, in today's society, sure, like to murder someone is just ridiculous. I don't know, in some societies, back in time, maybe it's a good thing.[16]

THINKING IT THROUGH 25.1

1. Scientific naturalism (the scientistic view) makes beauty merely accidental or utilitarian. The postmodern view makes beauty entirely subjective rather than objective.

2. truth, goodness, and beauty

3. God and His divine order of creation

4. Humans are image-bearing creators under God and are tasked with imitating or representing God and His divine order of creation.

5. It should seek to reflect the glory of God by appropriately arranging the truth, goodness, and beauty of God's divinely created order.

SECTION OBJECTIVES 25.2

1. Explain why some unbelievers embrace relativism with regard to truth, goodness, and beauty and why believers must reject relativism with regard to all three.

2. Refute the fallacies of both the scientistic and postmodern views of truth, goodness, and beauty.

3. Clarify that, although people's tastes need to be developed, their providential personal and cultural situations may lead them to explore different aspects of God's beauty.

4. Identify the ultimate purpose and standard of beauty.

And one more:

> I guess it kind of depends on the situation. Like taking an extra vacation day, for me it's not going to hurt anyone. In my job, it's not really going to hurt anyone. Is it morally right? Probably not, no. What's a moral rule, though? A personal thing? Well then I would say that sometimes breaking a moral rule might be all right, depending on the situation.[17]

People have been justifying and rationalizing their sin ever since Adam, of course. That's not new. What's new is the "relativistic" rationalization that has become popular in the modern West. The teens quoted above see morality as relative, not to an absolute standard, but to an individual or cultural or situational one. "It's personal" or "that's your choice." "It kind of depends on the situation." Only "in today's society" or "in our culture" is murder bad—or porn, or gossiping online, or software piracy.

Straight-up moral relativism is—one would hope—not as likely to afflict Bible-believing teens. They know there are moral absolutes given by their Creator. And Smith's statistics (he surveyed hundreds of teens in various religious groups) bear this out. Conservative Christian churches generally do a pretty good job of convincing their teens that moral rules are set by God and accessible in the Bible. The same goes for the concept of truth; teens raised in Christian homes mostly accept that the Bible is really true and whatever disagrees with the Bible is false.

But truth and goodness are tied not just to each other but also to beauty. Weakening one of the three weakens the other two. A biblical worldview rests all three on a firm foundation in the triune God. Let's discuss truth, goodness, and beauty in order to cement the relationship among them and, ultimately, build a Christian view of the arts. If Christians do not accept relativism when it comes to truth and goodness, why would they accept relativistic visions of beauty?

TRUTH IN THE MIND OF THE BEHOLDER

"What is truth?" The question is as old as Pontius Pilate and, of course, older than that. Influential thinkers in the West have tended to move in two different but related directions on this question.

- **The scientistic direction:** As we discussed in the science unit, "It is a tenet of scientism that only certifiably scientific knowledge counts as real knowledge. All else is mere opinion or nonsense."[18]
- **The postmodern direction:** "Postmodernism tends to hold that there is no all-embracing, 'totalizing' viewpoint, no 'God's-eye view,' no pure objectivity. . . . There are, according to most postmodernists, only interpretations."[19]

These two directions seem opposed because scientism claims objectivity, but postmodernism, if it's consistent, has to regard science as only one viewpoint among many. But in practice, educated people in the West tend to hold both of these contradictory approaches to truth together. They assume that science is the only way to answer certain questions, and that the answers to other questions are culturally relative. For them evolution is true, but ideas outside science vary culture by culture. They hear biblical truth claims as one person's opinion (and a long-dead person at that) rather than as the testimony of the only Person whose opinion truly matters. Truth outside science is in the mind of the beholder, in this view.

Some Christians respond by insisting that "all truth is objective!" And it is. There *is* a God's-eye view. But we need to be very careful what we claim because we don't have access to the divine view on the specifics of every issue. God hasn't revealed to us His

Moral Relativity

The quotations at the bottom of 386 and the top of 387 reflect several teenagers speaking unmistakably as members of a culture that has thoroughly inculcated relativistic presuppositions by means of the *is-ought* fallacy (see page 312). Their conclusions reflect their metanarrative.

- "I think morals are just a social tool . . ."

How many teens think this way in our culture? How many adults do? Why?

Secular society has deceived the vast majority of people—including professing Christians—because they accept evolutionary presuppositions. Christians sometimes do so without realizing the subtle connection between these kinds of conclusions and the evolutionary basis. [Review the Student Text and TE notes in Chapter 20 if needed.]

If this is an accurate description of what morals are—tools for our culture to get done what it wants to get done—then why should I observe my culture's morals if they get in the way of what I want to get done? Is my failure to follow the rules really going to doom the culture? If not, why should I care? But this utilitarianism (see page 243) quickly leads to injustice to others and antinormative damage to oneself from bending God's creational norms.

- "A lot of the times it's personal, it changes from person to person. . . ."

Have you ever heard people say something like this? Can you tell the story of what circumstances caused them to say it?

Did you both accept the moral (don't steal, don't lie, etc.) and argue about whether or not you were in violation of it? Or did you argue about the standard itself?

People with the same worldview will argue over whether there was a violation of an agreed-upon moral. But people with a different worldview will argue about the justification of the moral itself. Moral relativity leaves everybody to fight over the latter—with no way to resolve any arguments. Might makes right (see page 230). Is personal tyranny the best moral philosophy? Or is the rule of law by a transcedent, absolute standard better?

- "You can't say, you feel something is absolute. . . ."

Find the absolute in this teen's statement.

"You can't say . . . something is absolute" is an absolute. False worldviews self-contradict.

Can you think of a society in which murder is viewed as a good thing?

Modern Western society kills its own babies and defends this as a positive good, liberating women from the shackles of unwanted children. But this doesn't undercut this book's point that morality is absolute, found in God's absolute person. It shows how inconsistent society is with its own agreed-upon morals. Notice that defenders of abortion are careful to claim that what they advocate is not murder even though it involves the killing of innocent human beings.

- "I guess it kind of depends on the situation. . . ."

Does the Bible ever recognize situations in which it's morally acceptable to discern that a law doesn't apply?

Yes, Jesus appealed to David's decision to eat the bread of the presence in the tabernacle in a time of extremity (Matt. 12:1–8). Jesus recognized "weightier matters of the law." If a weightier matter and a lesser matter come into genuine conflict, it is clear which must win. Situational contexts can change the application of laws, especially when those laws are administrative rather than moral. But these exceptions don't support situational ethics, which purports that the underlying morals themselves are relative.

What kinds of laws are relative to the situation, and which aren't?

Laws the Bible says are weightier are more likely to involve moral culpability when broken, while laws that were given just to regulate Israelite society or for some other specific circumstance are more likely to be flexible—such as the law forbidding the Jews to boil a kid in its mother's milk (Exod. 23:19).

 ## Answering Moral Relativism

Ask students to write three paragraphs in response to the following scenario: Imagine that a non-Christian friend gets into a discussion with you about morality. He or she insists that you're too narrow and too worried about morality when you should just go out and enjoy life. What could you say—graciously, winsomely, and wisely—to this person?

Answers should be rooted in the biblical metanarrative of CFR, the gospel, and the wisdom from Proverbs.

Moral Relativism Is Problematic

New York Times columnist Ross Douthat writes:

> In 1970, the Catholic Theological Society released a text called *Human Sexuality: New Directions in American Catholic Thought*, which aimed to provide a guide for Catholics (and seminarians, in particular) interested in the most au courant Catholic thinking on matters of sexuality. Its findings were very au courant indeed. 'At this time the behavioral sciences have not identified any sexual expression that can be empirically demonstrated to be of itself, in a culture-free way, detrimental to the full human existence,' the authors assured their readers. The best theological thinking, they suggested, indicated that Catholic teachings on sexuality were best understood as rough guidelines, to be applied creatively and charitably to the necessarily complicated realities of human sexual desire. Eventually, the institutional Church would grow up and recognize this reality. "Until that day arrives, enlightened and well-integrated individuals might well free themselves of conflicts by simply reflecting on the relativity of their society's sexual ethic and proceed discreetly with their sexual project." (These recommendations were issued at the height of the priestly sexual abuse epidemic, though it would be decades before anyone realized that fact.)

[Ross Douthat, *Bad Religion* (New York: Simon and Schuster, 2013), 100–1]

This example isn't meant to pick on Catholics but to point out that ideas have consequences. In fact, it reveals that *secularist* influences were at the root of the problem. The idea of moral relativity plays out badly in real life.

Responding to the Douthat Quote

What would you seriously expect people to do with such permission? What harm would they do to others and themselves?

People will do whatever they can get away with. And they will try to rig the system to get away with it. The sexual revolution devastates the family structure. Men abuse women;

---

precise viewpoint on the minimum wage in early twenty-first-century America. God knows what the wisest and most successful approach to the issue is, and He has spoken to the issue in a general way in the Bible ("the laborer deserves his wages," Luke 10:7). But there's no Bible with a chart in the back giving us dollars-and-cents figures.

We are finite, and we are fallen. Objective truth really exists, but our access to it is unavoidably **subjective**. You are a "subject." All that means is that you think and feel; you are "subjected" to stimuli from various "objects." You can't stop being a subject because God made you one. You can't detach yourself from reality and become a totally **objective**, neutral, fact-processing machine. Subjective factors color the human apprehension of truth.

The Bible teaches as much. The Bible says that if you want true understanding, you must be a certain kind of person. "The fear of the Lord is the beginning of knowledge," Solomon says (Prov. 1:7). God "stores up sound wisdom for the upright" (Prov. 2:7). You cannot be wise if you will not be good. And Jesus makes this astonishing claim to some of His hearers: "Because I tell you the truth, you do not believe me" (John 8:45). In contrast, Jesus goes on to say, "Whoever is of God hears the words of God" (John 8:47). Of course, in this context, *hears* refers not to properly functioning ear drums but to spiritual understanding (cf. John 8:43). This is why Paul distinguishes between the "wisdom of this age" and the "wisdom of God" (1 Cor. 2:6–7). To those "of this age," God's wisdom seems foolish (1 Cor. 1:18–25). Indeed, they're "not able to understand" it (1 Cor. 2:14). But people who have the Spirit of God can understand God's wisdom (1 Cor. 2:10–14).

So postmodernism is correct about one thing: you aren't born with a God's-eye view of truth. And yet scientism is right about one thing too: there is real truth out there to discover. The Christian view unites these two realities in a way that manages not to be self-contradictory. The Bible says that if you fear God, then you have access to God's view on everything He thinks you need to know to live a wise and faithful life. You have access to all the divine revelation you need. You have truth.

So what is truth? It is a gift of God. The Christian view of truth gives us genuine confidence because truth is not relative to cultures or individuals. But the Christian view also gives us genuine humility because we have to admit we can only know the truth if God opens our eyes.

GOODNESS IN THE HEART OF THE BEHOLDER

As with truth, the major Western worldviews of our time have a particular take on goodness.

adaptive: *able to adjust to differing conditions*

- **The scientistic take:** "Morality is a collective illusion, genetic in origin, that makes us good cooperators. . . . Morality is purely emotions, although emotions of a special kind with an important adaptive* function."[20]
- **The postmodern take:** "There is no standard, not even a divine one, against which the decisions of a free people can be measured."[21]

Neither of these views of goodness and morality is new. Both were alive and well when C. S. Lewis was invited to give religious radio talks to the British during World War II. The very first matter Lewis addressed to a nation at war was moral relativism (although it would not have been called a "postmodern" idea at the time). The second was an evolutionary view of morality.

---

women degrade themselves for men; adults abuse children—and cover it up. Injustice abounds. This has occurred in every sector and every subculture of our society. No group is excluded—not just because of compromise with relativism, but because the Fall has affected everyone. The experiment of moral relativism has already borne its ugly fruit. But how many people will identify the culprit?

Knowing Truth

- In the biblical worldview, truth is absolute because it is inextricably connected to God, who is absolute. To know truth is to know the mind of God. (See the TE note "An Architectural Model" on page 298 about analogical knowledge.)

- In the biblical worldview, truth is knowable. Humans can apprehend the mind of God *insofar as God has revealed it to*

them. God spoke in an accessible Word to humans who have the capacities to understand their world in relation to the Word.

- In the biblical worldview, humans are limited; they can't comprehensively apprehend the mind of God. Furthermore, humans won't take hold of the significance of God's Word without the illuminating work of the Holy Spirit. Thus, the fullest knowledge of the truth is dependent on humbly submitting to the fear of the Lord (Prov. 1:7).

The Means to Apprehension Is Humble Submission

Have students read John 8:31–59. Note how the argument between Jesus and these Jews ends—the way all such arguments must, unless people repent and believe: "So they picked up stones to throw at him." The very best defender of the Christian faith who ever

(Postmodern) Moral Relativism

"I know that some people say the idea of a Law of . . . decent behaviour known to all men is unsound, because different civilisations and different ages have had quite different moralities," Lewis said.[22] That's basically the postmodern argument against the objective reality of goodness.

Lewis used a counterargument that was very relevant at that moment. There was no sense in saying Hitler was wrong, he said, "unless Right is a real thing which the Nazis at bottom knew as well as we did and ought to have practiced."[23]

"There are thousands of cultures, [so] it is hard," said one young American who was recently asked to define morality. "But I am not living in that culture, like here the way we are taught and stuff, I mean there are rights and wrongs, and there are definites in every culture. They may be different in every culture."[24]

But people who proclaim that different cultures are allowed to have different views of morality still generally end up condemning those other cultures when it suits them. For example, when the Iranian leader Ayatollah Khomeini issued a *fatwa*, a formal Islamic death sentence, against author Salman Rushdie, "enlightened," tolerant Western governments rushed to condemn Khomeini's act. Never mind that the *fatwa* was entirely defensible from an Iranian point of view since Rushdie had deeply insulted the prophet Muhammad and therefore all Muslims. "Multiculturalism" never lasts long.[25] People can't live as if morality is entirely relative.

Materialist Moral Illusion

Lewis's second talk on the BBC was about another denial of the objective reality of goodness and morality—the evolutionary, materialist denial. This is the idea that "morality is a collective illusion . . . that makes us good cooperators."[26]

Lewis called this the "herd instinct." And he didn't deny that there is such a thing. We all have instincts to love our offspring or to eat. But that's not the moral law, Lewis said. In order to demonstrate this, Lewis asked his listeners to think about times when their instincts conflict:

> Supposing you hear a cry for help from a man in danger. You will probably feel two desires—one a desire to give help (due to your herd instinct), the other a desire to keep out of danger (due to the instinct for self-preservation). But you will find inside you, in addition to these two impulses, a third thing which tells you that you ought to follow the impulse to help, and suppress the impulse to run away. Now this thing that judges between two instincts, that decides which should be encouraged, cannot itself be either of them.[27]

The moral law, Lewis argued, is that feeling that you ought to choose one instinct over the other, whether you feel like it or not. Everywhere in history and in the world we see evidence that people feel beholden to a moral law, even when they disobey it.

The Bible explains why: God wrote the moral law on the heart of every person (Rom. 2:14–15). These norms are part of the creational or natural law that God has established for His universe and revealed in Scripture, though fallen people suppress them. Different moral systems exist because cultures don't all suppress the same truths (Rom. 1:18).

---

ing human culture) in relation to that Word, and have their affections for God trained to obey the convictions of the Spirit. (Utilize Activity 43 for further explanation.)

God's Word, especially in the New Testament, doesn't catalogue every specific detail of application. But God does expect all Christians to apply His Word to every detail of their lives. Christians are supposed to be mature—they're supposed to apply the principles of God's law to their specific situations by means of submitting to the Spirit's illuminating conviction of the applied Word (Gal. 5:25).

Multiculturalism and the Fatwa

Literary theorist Stanley Fish wrote an essay about what he calls "boutique multiculturalism," a particular brand of moral relativism:

> The trouble with stipulating tolerance as your first principle is that you cannot possibly be faithful to it because sooner or later the culture whose core values you are tolerating will reveal itself to be intolerant at that same core. . . . Confronted with a demand that it surrender its viewpoint or enlarge it to include the practices of its natural enemies—other religions, other races, other genders, other classes—a beleaguered culture will fight back with everything from discriminatory legislation to violence. At this point the strong multiculturalist faces a dilemma: either he stretches his toleration so that it extends to the intolerance residing at the heart of a culture he would honor, in which case tolerance is no longer his guiding principle, or he condemns the core intolerance of that culture (recoiling in horror when Khomeini calls for the death of Rushdie), in which case he is no longer according it respect at the point where its distinctiveness is most obviously at stake. Typically, the strong multiculturalist will grab the second handle of this dilemma (usually in the name of some supracultural universal now seen to have been hiding up his sleeve from the beginning) and thereby reveal himself not to be a strong multiculturalist at all.

[Stanley Fish, "Boutique Multiculturalism, or Why Liberals Are Incapable of Thinking About Hate Speech," *Critical Inquiry* 23, no. 2 (Winter, 1997): 382–83]

In simple terms, Fish is stating that when a tolerant culture is confronted by an intolerant culture, the tolerant culture has two choices:

- Be tolerant of the intolerant in order to be consistent with your own principle.

---

lived, the one with the most love and the one with the best arguments did not persuade them all. When the Word of truth was applied, people were offended.

Subjective Apprehension

Christians will always disagree about applications—especially in a realm like culture and the arts, which depends on a more subjective apprehension of what's really being communicated nonpropositionally through those artifacts. But it's not wise to just throw up your hands and accept relativism. Instead, you should examine why Christians disagree on the applications if they hold to the same biblical worldview. This is what you must examine:

- Is Biblical truth the foundational authority that undergirds cultural evaluation? Or is the myth of neutrality presupposed instead? Or is an alternative authority source presupposed in place of God's Word?

- Is the biblical truth properly understood? Are the interpretations of the biblical passages correct? Have all the biblical passages been considered?

- Has the indicative (the understood truth) been legitimately formed into an imperative (the truth applied)? In other words, is the conviction in the situational context an accurate reflection of both the biblical principles and the meaning of the artifact?

- Do those people with shared convictions actually consistently apply those convictions to the cultural artifacts?

The apprehension of the answers to these questions will depend on how well people know the authority of God's Word, interpret God's Word, interpret God's world (includ-

- Be intolerant of the intolerant in order to oppose those who violate your principle—but in the process violate your own principle.

This dilemma is the inevitable result of relativism. It's a failed system. There must be a transcendent standard for moral evaluation.

Evolution and Religious Beliefs

In regard to the scientist take on goodness—that morality is simply emotional adaptation—Michael Ruse, an atheistic philosopher, called morality a "collective illusion." But can Ruse scientifically prove his theory of emotional adaptation, or does he just presuppose it to make it fit with his metanarrative?

Furthermore, does his theory really work in the reality of the world? There are a hundred thousand little ways in which we all sin against one another—verbal and physical slights, coarse joking, lazy avoidance of problems, and so on. What kind of pressure does it take for someone to strive for maturity by putting these sins to death (Rom. 8:13)? Does the evolutionary view provide that kind of pressure? Or does the Christian view? Merely by naming morality as a collective illusion, proponents of scientism have exerted a kind of authority over morality; they have transcended it. Do we really want educated people thinking that, at bottom, morality is just grease for helping society get along—that we don't really need it? Or do they need to feel an inescapable divine law that transcends herd instinct and self-preservation so that they'll be constrained to make an ethical choice regardless of how they may feel with themselves at the center of the universe?

Perceptions of Objective Morality

Divide the class in half to debate the following question and guide them to the answer.

Is it possible for a person's subjective perception of morality and what is actually objectively moral to cohere (to be one and the same)?

If there is an objective morality (and there is), then it will need to be perceived—people need to become aware of it. How would you know that your awareness of an objective morality is accurate? Only by means of a transcendent authority. This is why knowledge based on revelation is absolutely necessary. The Christian's perception of morality and what is actually objectively moral can cohere when he has a God's-eye view. Scripture can show that a moral perception is accurate. Specific applications must still be subjectively apprehended, but there is an objective basis for working to-

ward that end. That means it will be possible to evaluate a person's subjective apprehension based on an objective standard.

Reject that revelatory authority source, and perceptions of objective morality will be chaotic. But, as C. S. Lewis says, there will always be a basic perception of agreed-upon morality. This is because of the image of God in man—the conscience—and common grace. Believers are in the world to bear witness to the truth. It's through them that the Holy Spirit convicts the world (John 16:8).

The Scientific View of Beauty

To be fair, the quotation of the scientistic view of beauty is given by an opponent of the scientistic view, not a proponent. But what else could a strictly materialist view say? Every feature of human behavior has to either contribute to the survival of the fittest or

be shown to be the accidental byproduct of a behavior that does. Beauty, in other words, cannot be real in scientism. It's merely light waves bumping into atoms and provoking more atoms to go bump. That's all.

This is why many secularists resort to the two-story view. Their scientistic view is unsatisfying in the realm of the fine arts. In this compartment they hold to a postmodern view of beauty—in the beholder's eye.

A. N. Wilson on Music and Atheism

British intellectual A. N. Wilson ["Why I Believe Again," *New Statesman* (website), April 2, 2009] spent twenty years, from almost age forty to almost sixty, as an atheist. Now he is a professing Christian (though his various disparaging references to Noah's ark suggest his wrong view of Scripture). His

---

Subjective and Objective Morality

One of the moral problems people today have is "the inability to distinguish between objectively real moral truths or facts and people's human perceptions or understandings of those moral truths or facts."[28] It's just like truth: because people don't have a God's-eye view of goodness, they think goodness isn't really real.

But this kind of relativism gives rise to injustice. If every culture gets to set its own morality, what right did Britain have to declare war against Hitler's Germany? And moral relativism fails to grasp something else that Lewis argued—there really is basic agreement about morality around the world.[29] "Men have differed as to whether you should have one wife or four. But they have always agreed that you must not simply have any woman you liked."[30]

The Bible says that if you want to find true goodness, you must be a certain kind of person. It requires wisdom to apply moral truth to particular situations in your culture (Col. 1:9–10). "Honor your father and mother" applies everywhere in the world, but in some cultures it means saying "Yes, ma'am," and in others, even within the same country, it doesn't. A foolish person can't make these applications (Prov. 17:24). You've got to refuse to conform to the world before you can discern God's will (Rom. 12:2).

And Christians recognize that the demands of divine morality aren't merely external. Right actions are actually immoral if they're done with a sinful motive (Matt. 6:1–8; 1 Cor. 13:3). The goal of Christian ethics is not simply change in behavior but change in character.

So, as with truth, the apprehension and practice of goodness has a subjective element to it, but what's good or bad is objective, factual, real—a divine norm.

BEAUTY IN THE EYE OF THE BEHOLDER

And now to beauty. "Beauty," says a Christian art and music textbook, "is what makes art, art." To call something "art" at all is to say, "first, that somebody made it (for we don't call accidents 'art'), and, second, that its appearance has the potential to reward those who pay attention to it. That is, it can be appreciated for its beauty."[31]

How do scientism and postmodernism, the main intellectual currents of our time, regard beauty? Basically the same way they regard truth and goodness.

BEAUTY

just-so story: a fanciful and unfalsifiable explanation of how something originated

- **The scientistic view:** "The sense of beauty has emerged through the process of sexual selection. . . . By making himself beautiful the man is doing what the peacock does when he displays his tail: he is giving a sign of his reproductive fitness, to which a woman responds as the peahen responds, claiming him . . . on behalf of her genes."[32]
- **The postmodern view:** Beauty is in the eye of the beholder.

The scientistic view should be recognized immediately for the "just-so story"* that it is. What evidence could possibly confirm or falsify such an idea? Evolutionists who favor group-level selection offer a second fanciful explanation, the idea that beauty unites the community around special objects, conferring on that group an evolutionary advantage over other groups.[33] But recall what Joshua Bell said about the power of music to point to "divine order." And think of your own experiences with beauty—are you willing to write them off as accidental neuron firings? Beautiful things are, to us, significant things: we admire them, we gather them, we treasure them. Materialism strips all significance and meaning from beauty, just as it does with everything else in the universe. But it doesn't work. You can't act as if the beautiful things you treasure are beautiful only by evolutionary accident.

The postmodern view is only slightly different, really. It, too, removes ultimate meaning from beauty by insisting that one person's idea of beauty has no authority over any other person's view.

Once again, you know better. Your experience and, more importantly, your Christian worldview both tell you beauty isn't merely subjective.

A man goes to the Louvre* in Paris to see a famous work of Renaissance art. He stands for some time with furrowed brow, studying the master painter's work. Finally, he comments to a nearby guard: "I don't like it." The guard replies, "Sir, these paintings are no longer being judged; the viewers are."[34]

Louvre: (loov) the most prominent art museum in the world

The guard is exactly right: beauty stands over us and not just in us. It confronts us. And it calls us. That's one big reason sunsets and galaxies and moonscapes were made. "The heavens declare the glory of God" (Ps. 19:1).

> The beauty in creation is all the time saying, "There is a great God of glory and power and generosity behind all this awesome universe; you belong to him; he is patient with you in sustaining your rebellious life; turn and bank your hope on him and delight yourself in him, not his handiwork."[35]

Cultural Variation

As with truth and goodness, beauty has to enter through your senses for you to perceive it. There is a subjective element to beauty. Whole cultures perceive it in characteristically different ways. Even within the boundaries of Western music, Rachmaninoff sounds unmistakably Russian, and Vaughan Williams sounds quintessentially British. But both composed utterly beautiful music. Think, too, of Arabic and Hindi microtonal music: it's almost incomprehensible to Westerners, but it would be arrogant to say that such music is not beautiful—at least without first trying to understand it.

Nonetheless, we must not conclude from looking at the cultural landscape that beauty is culturally relative. There are elements of beauty common among cultures, of course: "Symmetry and order; proportion; closure; convention; harmony, and also novelty and excitement: all these seem to have a permanent hold on the human psyche."[36] But it's OK if two cultures see beauty in different hues: beauty is so massive that new angles of vision are always waiting to be explored.

> [Beauty] is an object bigger than we [are]—infinitely bigger than we [are]—so we all see different aspects of it. And, as we do so, more of God's glory is [seen] than if we all saw the same things. As it turns out, the Christian doctrine of beauty provides the only true basis for diversity.[37]

No Basis for Taste?

If beauty is something real, something solid, then it's wrong to deny it, just as it's wrong to deny truth or goodness. It may even be wrong for you, depending on your gifts and opportunities, to fail to explore avenues of beauty made available to you. You can educate your taste, and you should. To do so is to take dominion and learn more of God at the same time.

And there is an explanation for taste. It can be difficult, but humans made in the beautiful image of God can justify their judgments about beauty by using critical reasoning.[38] If two people disagree over whether or not something is beautiful, the possibility must be left open that one of them may be wrong.

Some students may find the Louvre illustration bewildering—even offensive. Why? Americans tend to be egalitarian. They tend to think that they can judge art based on their own unstudied taste, and they tend to resent the idea that there exists an objective aesthetic standard that can judge their taste.

Nonetheless, a person's tastes may be so underdeveloped that his judgments aren't reliable compared to those of others who have spent many years honing their skills to discover good craftsmanship. The *Mona Lisa* may not be initially attractive, but people who recognize the artistic techniques can see the masterful subtlety. It may be true that most people don't find the woman in the picture to be attractive, but the techniques used to paint the subtle expression is recognizably masterful.

It takes time to gain an appreciation for certain kinds of beauty; certain pieces of music which alienated this writer on first listen have come to be his favorites, to display a depth he never could have known without repeated exposure—without aesthetic education. This is one of the best reasons for students to go to a Christian liberal arts college—education in the beautiful doesn't happen by accident.

Do Christians have to be experts in order to make aesthetic judgments?

Nobody can be an expert on everything, but everybody can learn from experts, and Christians should learn from aesthetic experts so that they make better aesthetic evaluations, just as they should learn from expert historians or scientists so that they can make better historical or scientific evaluations. For instance, media ecologists such as T. David Gordon can use their expertise to raise considerations that have never occurred to many Christians. For instance, Gordon points out the importance of both "form" and "content" to musical meaning. Gordon evaluates various forms of music, the messages they convey, and their fittingness to various texts and communal purposes. [T. David Gordon, *Why Johnny Can't Sing Hymns* (Phillipsburg, NJ: P&R, 2010)] This is expertise that not every Christian will have the time or ability to develop, but some Christians can develop expertise in these areas and serve the church by writing and speaking about what they have learned.

On the other hand, the Christian doesn't have to be an expert in aesthetics to render judgments about the truth or goodness of a work of art, just as a Christian does not need to be a scientist to identify points at

article describing his two conversions—first to atheism and then from it—is fascinating because he says that it was the existence of beauty (love and music and language) that convinced him that the world was more than just material. The world had to have a spiritual dimension to it.

Wilson says that the deaths of numerous friends and family members in a brief period of time persuaded him that "purely materialist 'explanations' for our mysterious human existence simply won't do." Wilson points in particular to human language. He tells a story of how he and a Darwinian materialist were eating dinner and laughing about how increased age brings a decreased ability to remember names. "Eager, as committed Darwinians often are, to testify on any occasion, my friend asserted: 'It is because when we were simply anthropoid apes, there was no need to distinguish between one another by giving names.'"

But Wilson asks for the evidence: what evidence could there possibly be that apes went from grunts to grammar and sentences? "No, the existence of language is one of the many phenomena—of which love and music are the two strongest—which suggest that human beings are very much more than collections of meat. They convince me that we are spiritual beings, and that the religion of the incarnation, asserting that God made humanity in His image, and continually restores humanity in His image, is simply true."

Wilson points to communication—love and music—as reasons for his conversion. Love and music are real; they are such deep experiences for all mankind that they point to the reality of the spiritual realm.

which the theory of evolution is contrary to Scripture. Perhaps a work of art is aesthetically excellent, but the content is false or the morals are bad—or both. A Christian should be able to discern false content or bad morals without even entering into an aesthetic evaluation of a work of art.

Cultural Variation

Do cultural differences, and differences in what various cultures perceive to be beautiful, undermine the proposition that there is an objective aspect to beauty?

No. Consider an analogy with food. Various cultures have developed foods that cater to different tastes. Germans, Indians, and the Chinese all have distinctive cuisine. Some people like some of these tastes and not others. Some people have developed an appreciation for the variety of tastes. The differences are part of the good variety that God built into His creation. But this does not mean that some tastes are not better than others. A person who prefers a burger to an exquisite cut of steak would benefit from developing his taste.

There is room for taste—but only within the parameters of truth, goodness, and beauty. God has given different people different personalities, giftings, and interests.

Developing Taste

Is it sinful to not develop one's taste? Must Christians develop their tastes so they can appreciate a wide variety of music, visual art, literature, and so on?

Different people have different opportunities and abilities, and all people have a limited amount of time. Nobody has the time or ability to develop taste for all that falls within the bounds of truth, goodness, and beauty.

This makes the development of taste a matter of wisdom. Given the variety of responsibilities that a Christian has, is developing a particular taste going to help him better meet his responsibilities and glorify God, or will it hinder him in that pursuit?

Should a Christian avoid developing taste because it leads to pride?

It's true, as the apostle Paul says, that "'knowledge' puffs up" (1 Cor. 8:1). But that doesn't turn ignorance into a virtue. It does, however, place an added responsibility on those who have developed both their intellect and their taste. They ought to keep in mind Paul's earlier admonition: "What do you have that you did not receive? If you received it, why do you boast as if you did not receive it?" (4:5).

Some people like symphonies and other people like sports. Can't Christians just enjoy whatever they are more inclined to?

Christians have liberty to engage in a wide variety of pursuits, and not all of them need to be high culture. The creativity of image-bearers is not only expressed in high culture. The invention of association football, or soccer, was innovative. As rules and talents developed the game became more beautiful—if someone trains himself to recognize it (compare a game in the 1950s to today's game). In addition, participation in sport provides exercise and builds virtues such as self-discipline, teamwork, and endurance.

Nonetheless, some cultural activities have more significance and value than others. Though not all Christians have to reach the same conclusions, all Christians should evaluate their activities in light of long-term value.

Cultivating Folk Culture

Not all art is created by skilled craftsmen. Some art is drawn by children. Some of that art is objectively not beautiful. But parents hang it on the refrigerator anyway. The art of a child is not valued for its beauty. It's valued for familial reasons.

In previous generations—before professional music was recorded and brought into the home—families would often gather to play instruments and sing together. What if someone suggested that the family could enjoy better music if they hired a chamber orchestra to come play for them? That would have missed the point of the family gathering to make music together. Family musicians may not have the skill of professionals, but they have enough skill to create something valuable and shared.

1. Why is relativism attractive to contemporary people?

2. Why shouldn't believers embrace a relativistic view of truth, goodness, and beauty?

3. What justifies Christian confidence in the apprehension of objective truth, goodness, and beauty?

4. Why should Christians be humble when they evaluate the truth, goodness, and beauty in art?

◊5. Respond to the following statement: "Beauty is in the eye of the beholder."

25.3 NORMS FOR THE ARTS

One of the ways you know you're growing as a Christian is that familiar verses and stories from Scripture come to mean more to you. You memorized them, perhaps, as a small child, and they were just words on a page in an activity book. But then they came to your mind when you faced a particular temptation in seventh grade, and suddenly they took on a deeper significance.

Let's try to see that happen with one particular verse (the one you're supposed to memorize for this chapter)—Philippians 4:8.

Whatever is true, whatever is honorable, whatever is just, whatever is pure, whatever is lovely, whatever is commendable, if there is any excellence, if there is anything worthy of praise, think about these things.

Maybe you learned this as a verse about watching TV and movies—and it most definitely applies to those things. But it's much richer and deeper than that.

This is an important statement in God's Word about a vocation some readers of this book are even now being called to. It's a command that all Christians, whatever their calling, ought to embrace their whole lives long. This verse underpins a Christian view of the arts. It provides a biblical reason to take truth, goodness, and beauty as norms.

Lists of virtues like these—truth, honor, justice, purity, loveliness, and so on—are found in the Bible and elsewhere. But Paul doesn't commend just any kind of justice or purity; he's promoting the specifically Christian practice of these virtues. In fact, "truth," "justice," "loveliness," and the other virtues mean something different when they're viewed through non-Christian lenses.

And one of the reasons we know this is that the virtues qualify and modify each other in specifically Christian ways. Not everything that is "true" is also "honorable." If you've ever watched a movie you regret seeing, it's probably because things that truly do happen in this world—graphic violence and sexual immorality—were made even more dishonorable by being turned into entertainment for people in easy chairs. It dishonors sex to take it out of the marriage bed and put it on a plasma screen (Heb. 13:4). It disrespects the sad necessity of the sword in a fallen world (Rom. 13:4) when people watch blood and gore for kicks.[46] The Bible describes sin truthfully, but it does so with respect for its readers, not in a vulgar, base, corrupting way.

Christians are typically alert to questions of truth in the movies or in popular books. They're ready to point out the pantheistic worldview in the *Star Wars* films or

(Incidentally it may be worthwhile for students to consider what was gained and what was lost with the advent of recorded music.)

Families may not gather to make music as often as they used to, but Christians still gather in churches and make music together. What would be lost if someone suggested that the music would be better if the church hired professionals or began to use prerecorded music for worship?

Some Tastes Are Disqualified

Banksy is a popular, talented British graffiti artist and social critic. He's a darling of the art world, a world that loves its darlings like no other. Banksy once constructed a prank by creating a real-life "bemusement park" called Dismaland, featuring a ramshackle castle with a muddy moat, discourteous employees, anti-consumerist slogans, a bumper boat game involving boats filled with fleeing immigrants, and what one blogger called a "demented assortment of bizarre and beautiful artworks," such as Cinderella's wrecked carriage with paparazzi photographing the blonde princess's corpse draped over the door. [Christopher Jobson, "Welcome to Dismaland," Colossal (website), August 20, 2015]

One writer wondered whether Banksy was "profound" or a "snake-oil salesman." She opted for the latter, seeing through the modern art world's disdain for the beautiful: "For all Banksy's contempt for capitalism, the exhibit still exits through the gift store. . . . You get to pay your money and admire." [Andrée Seu Peterson, "Overdrawn Banksy," *World* (website), October 3, 2015]

Good art can recognize the fallenness of this world, but styles or art that glory in the

Fall magnify the opposite of God's character. Tastes for a disordered world reveal affections that are disordered. God didn't create creative cultivators to use their powers of creativity to mirror the destructiveness of a fallen world. A culture that glorifies the grotesque or the violent is antinormative—contrary to creational norms.

Beauty in God

The insight that God is the ultimate standard for all beauty is in some ways so general as to be almost unhelpful. It says so much that it may seem to be saying nothing. The key question is, "What *access* do we have to this divine standard?" But Todd Jones, PhD candidate in musicology at the University of Kentucky, suggests that it is still very important to acknowledge the standard. God is the standard for beauty; and there is a created *order* through which we have access to that standard. Jones says, "The fact that 'creation' unity only gets you so far is no more of a problem than knowing that a 'modesty' agreement only gets you so far. The point is to agree on its importance, not to locate the line in the identical place. If an interlocutor and I both have theologically driven, biblically faithful lines of reasoning, I think there's generally going to be a ballpark we can both fit into—not to mention coming to terms in a Romans 14 kind of way. Limiting your liberty, as they say, can expand your ministry" (private correspondence, September 25, 2015).

1. Humans desire to defend their rebellion (autonomy) against their Creator and the created order.

2. God is the objective and transcendent source and ultimate standard of all truth, goodness, and beauty in the divinely created order that human sub-creators ought to seek to reflect.

3. Christians can be confident because God grants this wisdom and spiritual understanding through the illumination of the Spirit to those who fear Him and seek His guidance for faithful living in the revelation of His Word.

4. Christians must be humble when they seek to apply general biblical truths to their specific situation because they are finite and fallible—they may need to further develop their tastes and/or better understand God's revelation.

◊5. This is a statement of aesthetic relativism. While beauty is subjectively apprehended, it remains an objective reality that excludes some things even if some beholders consider them beautiful.

1. Determine that the creational norms for evaluating a cultural product include truth, goodness, and beauty—and that they must all stand together in harmony.

2. Exemplify the necessity of joining truth to goodness and beauty in various artistic subcreations.

3. Exemplify the necessity of joining goodness to truth and beauty in various artistic subcreations.

4. Exemplify the necessity of joining beauty to truth and goodness in various artistic subcreations.

Clarifying Note

In the "Norms for the Arts" section, the goal in each subsection—"Truth," "Goodness," and "Beauty"—is to offer a smattering of examples from a few categories. It's not possible to be comprehensive. Students should not be confused into thinking that poetry exemplifies goodness, but not truth. We're simply picking from various genres for the sake of illustrating how truth, goodness, or beauty might be exemplified in various ways in various categories.

A Complete Triad

The next chapter will demonstrate more fully why all three parts of the triad must be taken together. Another way to illustrate the triad is to present it as a three-legged stool. If any leg of the stool—truth, goodness, or beauty—is missing, then the Christian can't rest comfortably on it. The cultural artifact has a problem; it shouldn't be accepted without qualification. Some cultural artifacts are so corrupt that they can't even be accepted with qualification (Prov. 14:16).

A Biblical Philosophy of Censorship

Christian thinker Ron Horton has provided an overview of approaches to censorship in his essay "A Biblical Approach to Objectionable Elements in Christian Education" (available on the BJU Press website). The following discussion is based on that essay.

Wrong approaches:

• The ignorant or careless don't think through any approach at all (Rom. 16:19).

• The permissivist defends sordid and salacious elements—usually on the basis of a desire for realism (1 Tim. 6:11; 2 Tim. 2:22; Phil. 4:8; Eph. 5:1–18; Titus 2:11–12).

• The exclusivist is conscientious. Evil is evil; *any* presentation of it is wrong. Only an idealized world without any exposure to sinfulness is allowed.

---

the voyeuristic* violence in *The Hunger Games*, but some Christians are so eager to point out what's true (or not) in art that they fail to give sufficient weight to the honor and purity a work of art is supposed to have. We instinctively cringe at the thought of drinking polluted water but eagerly quench our thirst with clean water. That's the way a Christian should respond when contemplating works of art—recoiling at the impure and being refreshed by the pure.

voyeuristic: *taking pleasure in watching the pain of others*

Truth heads Paul's list in Philippians 4:8. **Goodness** comes next (think on whatever is "honorable," "just," "pure"). **Beauty** follows: we are supposed to think on "whatever is lovely" and "whatever is commendable." By *lovely* Paul appears to mean something that is visually beautiful; *commendable* probably refers to beautiful, well-chosen speech.[47]

Teens who grow up with rules about what they can and cannot watch or read or listen to or play sometimes fixate on the many pleasures they are denied by their parents. "But Sarah's mom lets her watch it!" is one of the more common arguments used by aggravated teens. (And you will always be able to find a Sarah whose mom is not as strict as other moms.)

But don't miss the repeated *whatevers* in Paul's list: whatever is true, whatever is honorable, whatever is lovely. Yes, there are things that don't fit in those categories because of the Fall. But there's a lot that does fit, more than you could experience in a lifetime.[48] This is a big world with lots of artistic and cultural good in it. "Of every tree of the garden you may freely eat," God told Adam and Eve (Gen. 2:16, NKJV); don't repeat their mistake by fixating on the one tree that's off-limits.

What Paul has given in Philippians 4:8 is a set of creational norms by which all cultural pursuits can be evaluated, and they boil down to truth, goodness, and beauty. This triad provides a biblical norm for evaluating all cultural endeavors. Let's look at examples of truth, goodness, and beauty in culture and the arts.

TRUTH

Christ identifies himself as the truth (John 14:6). Satan stands directly opposite to God. There is no truth in him, and his followers don't listen to Jesus precisely because He is telling the truth (John 8:44–47). God's Word is truth (Ps. 119:160). And God exhorts us to delight in the truth (Ps. 51:6). Truth is to be sought after diligently; it's an aspect of wisdom to connect the truth of God's Word with the truth of God's world in a way that enables you to live wisely (Prov. 23:23).

Literature

Good literature helps us do that. The criterion of truth doesn't rule out fiction. Often fiction can help a reader see reality more clearly than plain exposition of the facts can. When Nathan confronted David about his sin with Bathsheba, he first told him a story (2 Sam. 12). The story stunned David with the truth of what he had done—a truth he had until then rationalized away.

Jesus' own parables were, in one sense, fiction. There probably never was a servant who owed his master ten thousand talents but was forgiven his debt—and then went out and choked somebody else who owed him only a hundred denarii (Matt. 18:21–35). But nothing could be more true-to-life than this and the other parables Jesus told. Our sin debt to God really is like a huge bill we could never pay off, and our failure to forgive others really is shameful by comparison.

This third position might be attractive to some, but it is impossible to conform to and contradicts Scripture, which itself presents evil. Every objectionable element can be found in the Bible, but it presents it in the right way.

- Profane blasphemy (John 8:48)

- Scatological realism (Isa. 36:12)

- Erotic realism (Prov 5:18–19; Song of Sol.)

- Sexual perversion (Gen. 19; 2 Sam 13)

- Lurid violence (Judg. 20; 2 Sam 20)

- Occultism (1 Sam. 28)

- False worldview (Job's three friends)

• The pragmatist realizes that the exclusivist position is simply impossible in real life application. Some exposure will happen, so limit it. But there's no objective basis for doing so; it's subjective and inconsistent.

The biblical approach:

"If a work of literature [or a movie, book, etc.] . . . treats evil in the same way that it is treated in the Scriptures, we regard it as not only acceptable but also desirable reading, listening, or viewing for someone of sufficient maturity as to benefit from comparable portions of the Scriptures (with the qualification that visual or auditory effects are more potent than those of reading). If it does not treat evil in the way evil is handled in the Scriptures, its content is not good. Evil in the Bible appears dangerous and repulsive" (Horton).

In addition, the medium is the message (see page 421). The *form* of God's instruction (literature) is purposefully distinct from visual media. A biblical description of immorality given as a warning when depicted in a visual medium provokes lust rather than

Or consider the lessons about the appropriate balance of reason and emotion in Jane Austen's *Sense and Sensibility*, or of the dangers of rash vows in Shakespeare's *King Lear*, or the follies and dangers of sudden wealth in Dickens's *Great Expectations*. Stories should be experienced as stories before we try to reflect on the truths they contain; stories are narratives and not lists of truths. But all stories undoubtedly communicate truth, and a great many of them communicate falsehood too.

Music

Music, by contrast, may not seem to be either true or false. But music does communicate at a deep level. And that communication can be true or false. Two Christians who have thought deeply about art and music have observed,

> Ugly music is ugly because it lies. It suppresses . . . the truth and goodness of creation and providence. Sad music pleases us by speaking truthfully (in tones and rhythms) about the effect of the fall and the law's curse on creation. . . . Happy music moves us the way it does by speaking truthfully about grace and hope in a new creation. Only music's potential for communicating the good and the true explains why we find such succor [assistance, relief] in it.[49]

Visual Arts

Visual arts can clearly communicate truth too—as well as lies. Jacques-Louis David's *Death of Marat* was full of artful lies that served his political cause. Leni Riefenstahl, widely regarded as the greatest female filmmaker of the twentieth century, made her film *Triumph of the Will* as a piece of Nazi propaganda, with Adolph Hitler as the star.

The truth that the visual arts convey may be obvious in the case of realist painting, but even abstract art serves up truth and falsehood to its viewers. Compare, for example, the "drip paintings" of Jackson Pollock to the Nihonga paintings of Christian artist Makoto Fujimura. Both are abstract, but Pollock's work implies that chance rules the universe while Fujimura's art points to a divine order.[50]

Jackson Pollock's famous drip paintings imply that chance rules the universe.

The Death of Marat tells several lies that served the artist's political cause.

warns against it. Thus while the Bible should serve as the model for handling objectionable elements, the difference of medium must also be considered.

Horton provides some criteria for discerning if the material violates a biblical presentation of evil:

- Gratuitousness: Is it a representation of evil for its own sake (e.g., to entertain, to arouse lust)?

- Explicitness: Is the purposeful representation of evil conspicuous, excessive, or vivid?

- Moral tone: Does it encourage the tolerance of sin or portray evil as good?

- Pervasiveness: Are the problematic items too pervasive to easily censor?

- Maturity: If the goal is inoculation and not isolation, spiritual leaders must discern

what is age-appropriate so that the dosage doesn't harm.

Propaganda

Literature violates the standard of truth when it can rightly be labeled propaganda. A story may be masterfully woven together with a beautiful resolution. But its claims are rooted in a lie or in a false worldview. One example of this kind of rewritten history is the autobiography *I, Rigoberta Manchú: An Indian Woman in Guatemala*. It's a defense of Marxism and feminism based on a questionable narrative of her own life. Tyrannical political regimes often make use of stories to inculcate their viewpoints into people's thinking. Furthermore, while historical fiction is generally a fine genre, the readers of it need to realize that the story line and some characters are made up even though

the setting is based in history. But literature that purposefully blurs the line between history and fiction becomes a lie.

Music's Place in Life

An ad for Google Play Music promises listeners that it will provide at any point in their day the music they need, "curated radio stations to make whatever you're doing better. Our team of music experts . . . crafts each station song by song so you don't have to."

Media ecologist and social critic Nicholas Carr ["Music Is the Oil in the Human Machine," Rough Type (website), June 23, 2015] replies that Google Play is making Muzak available to everyone: "Music becomes an input, a factor of production. Listening to music is not itself an 'activity'—music isn't an end in itself) but rather an enhancer of other activities."

But Carr points out that if music is just a factor of production it becomes "an industrial lubricant that, by reducing the friction from activities, makes for more productive lives." The implication is that you should outsource the choice of music to experts instead of spending money and time and interest on it yourself. Choosing your own songs, Carr says, would require you to "develop . . . personal taste in music," and that would be "wasted labor, a distraction from the series of essential jobs that give structure and value to your days." Is that really a Christian way to view music?

Ask students what they think of such a critique. Is music critic, Nicholas Carr, right to oppose such a philosophy of music?

It's not wrong to fill the background with music (that's not Carr's point), but it says something when music only fills the background. The subtle cultural norm can become a lie suggesting that music doesn't exist on its own as art but is only a functional filler. Art should be more than a pleasant background hum, visually or aurally. It is a gift of God for His image-bearers to enjoy by giving it full attention. It says something about a culture that people can't just sit back and relax to feed on the music itself.

The Death of Marat

What lies did the artist put into his painting?

- The lighting makes the painting feel religious to communicate feelings of martyrdom, but Marat was a bloodthirsty and awful revolutionary, not a saint.

- Marat's skin appears baby fresh and beautiful in the painting, but he had a skin condition that caused blisters and other unsightly blemishes.

- Charlotte Corday was admitted to David's bath because she pretended to have the names of enemies of the state. Marat wrote the names down before she stabbed him. By contrast the painting shows a letter from Charlotte Corday which reads in English "Given that I am unhappy, I have a right to your help." The idea is that she was admitted close to him because of his eagerness to help, not because of his eagerness to slander and agitate. Furthermore, there is a completely fictitious letter on the wooden stand (with money) to a widowed mother of five.

Comparing Pollock and Fujimura

Search online for Makoto Fujimura's website, which shows and explains his paintings. Although apprehending the order in his art is subjective, his paintings reflect the orderliness of the universe. They are abstract (nonpropositional communication to the emotions), but he wants to reflect some truths about an orderly reality. In contrast, Pollock's paintings are both abstract and reflective of randomness (chaotic emotions for a chaotic universe).

[For a Christian evaluation of one of Fujimura's paintings, see chapter 4 of Paul Munson and Joshua Farris Drake, *Art and Music: A Student's Guide*, ed. David Dockery (Wheaton: Crossway, 2014).]

Art and Self-Esteem

On the internet discussion site Quora—which collects opinions on various questions users pose and then vets those opinions via public voting—a teenager posted a (frankly amateurish) drawing and asked Quora users, "Is my drawing worth selling?" [Search online for "quora is my drawing worth selling? Am I ready?"]

Take a look at the responses with your class, and see what the students think. Some Quora users said, "Don't let anyone tell you you're no good!"

What's better—receiving constructive criticism to help you improve or simply being told that you're good?

Anyone who truly wants to excel will choose the constructive criticism.

Do Quora users' answers reflect the existence of divine norms for beauty?

No, the answers reflect the importance self-esteem is given in our culture. A culture that prevents excellence from being praised and failures from being evaluated excludes the possibility of developing the virtues of humility and excellence.

At least one user provided detailed, constructive, and courteous criticism. If there were no aesthetic norms, would it be possible to offer such a criticism?

GOODNESS

There is no one good but God alone, Jesus told the rich young ruler (Mark 10:18). And yet nonbelievers can truly do good, as we discussed in the common grace chapter. And Christians are expected both to do "good works" and to grow in "goodness" over time (Gal. 5:22).

Works of art can express goodness, and they can encourage us to pursue it. A beautiful landscape or melody may cause you to so delight in the beauty of God's creation that your heart wells up with a desire to please Him. Every branch of the arts can display goodness.

ART AND WORLDVIEW IN *LES MISERABLES*

In Victor Hugo's novel *Les Miserables*, Fantine is perceived as morally blameless even though she sold her body for money—because the author assumes a world in which she had no choice. The reader swallows a view of sin as a problem with society (which it is in part) but brushes aside a view of sin as a problem with the self (which it always is). This all happens without the distraction of an argument. It happens because Hugo's story assumes a false view of the world, and the (careless) reader absorbs the assumption.

Poetry

"Poetry is the art of using words charged with their utmost meaning," says Dana Gioia, a poet and the former chairman of America's National Endowment for the Arts.[51] Think of the good that can be done through such words, the comfort people can enjoy in sorrow, and the sharp insights people can share to enrich their neighbors.

Fiction

Novels explore human morality with a depth that only God can exceed. Few if any other kinds of writing can make you feel the weight of a moral dilemma the way a novel can or explore the possibilities of human personality or sense the call of goodness. Even insight into human fallenness can be good (and true as well as beautiful) if it is treated the way the Bible treats it.

Drama and Film

American poet Carl Sandburg said in an interview that some people

> think motion pictures, the product Hollywood makes, is merely entertainment [and] has nothing to do with education. That's one of the darnedest fool fallacies that is current . . . . Anything that brings you to tears by way of drama does something to the deepest roots of our personalities. All movies, good or bad, are education, and Hollywood is the foremost educational institution on earth.[52]

Films combine some of the most viscerally powerful artistic methods known to man—close-ups, a swelling musical score, sweeping vistas, emotionally charged acting, romance, action—in the service of whatever story and values the movie exists to spread. If those two things are righteous and if truth and beauty are also present, a film can do powerful good. But if you diminish any member of the triad, the others suffer. If the film isn't true, it's not as beautiful. If it's not good, it's not true. If it's not beautiful, it's neither good nor true. Truth, goodness, and beauty are most fully themselves when they harmonize together. They aren't three independent pillars; they're three strands of a braid.

The classic theater drama *Our Town* by Thornton Wilder braids them well. The play is an insightful and entertaining reminder of the brevity of life—one that's very consistent with the message of a biblical book like Ecclesiastes. *The Winslow Boy* by Terrance Rattigan demonstrates a family's love of truth in their desire to protect their son's reputation against false charges in Edwardian England. Skillful dramas like

---

No, it's only possible to make suggestions for improvement if there is a standard by which to judge that improvement.

Expressing Goodness Poetically

In the poem "Remember" [available online] how does poet Christina Rossetti use the power of poetry to encourage good?

She expresses the feelings of a loved one about to depart in death. It's an encouragement to those who have lost loved ones to reflect on their memories with happiness rather than sorrow.

Expressing Goodness in Fiction

Read an excerpt from Charles Dickens' *Oliver Twist*, a book that was written to critique the corruptness of society's treatment of orphans.

How does the author use the power of the novel to encourage good?

He is able to show the plight of the orphans and the hypocritical excuses of those who "cared" for them. His goal was to encourage positive change.

Entertainment Education

Let students choose several television shows to evaluate according to a biblical worldview. Use the "objectionable elements" guidelines mentioned on page 394. Then ask some additional questions about the education that takes place along with the entertainment.

these can press truth and goodness into human hearts. Those hearts may resist, but they can hardly help but be swept up into the story.

BEAUTY

It's time we clarify something: by "beauty" we do not mean "prettiness." Beauty salons and beauty aids all have their place, and a truly beautiful woman is a marvel of divine design that almost no human being can fail to notice. But beauty is deeper and broader than the female cosmetics industry. Dana Gioia, quoted earlier in this chapter, has observed that beauty means something particular in the Christian tradition. "Beauty," he says, "is the pleasure we get in recognizing the particular manifestation of a broader, universal order."[53]

It's our connection with "the essential harmony of creation," he explains. "The world and the cosmos are intrinsically beautiful. And as God's creation, we have been made to recognize this order."[54] All humans, not just Christians, can recognize this order by virtue of having been created in the image of a Creator.[55] No healthy person is wholly incapable of distinguishing beauty from ugliness or order from chaos.

Music

Leonard Bernstein was one of the most gifted musicians of the twentieth century. He was a creative composer who could write both classical and popular music. His "Chichester Psalms" is a beautiful setting of multiple biblical psalms in the original Hebrew (Bernstein was ethnically Jewish).

Bernstein is also known for a series of videotaped lectures on music he delivered at Harvard, his alma mater. In them he brilliantly demonstrates some of the "laws"—his word—underlying Western music. He shows how one musical interval, the fifth, developed into the full chromatic scale used all throughout the Western tradition.[55]

Bernstein describes that scale as a discovery, not an invention. And this particular discovery of a beautiful creational order for sound is all the more remarkable because it's not the only one. Other musical scales exist besides the Western one. There's a beauty even in the simplicity and mathematical precision of these scales, but so much more beauty is experienced in the apparently infinite variety of musical compositions that can be built on them.

Art

Art likewise relies on the beautiful structures God built into creation, from physical structures like pigmentation to much deeper and more complex aesthetic laws regarding form, proportion, and line.

We need look no further than our Bibles to learn that mere beautiful forms, even without words, can communicate truth. As we've had reason to observe several times in this book, "the heavens declare the glory of God" (Ps. 19:1) and "what can be known about God is plain . . . in the things that have been made" (Rom 1:19–20).

Art communicates through form. Beauty was created to be a medium for communicating truth. And people were created to receive it. But people aren't all healthy; fallen people suppress the beautiful just as they suppress the good and the true.

> "For a Christian, beauty is truthful, pleasurable, revelatory, and transformative. It's our recognition of the deepest tendencies of forms in the universe, the highest and most complete level of understanding."[57]
>
> —DANA GIOIA

Why is entertainment a powerful educational tool?

It indoctrinates subtly and makes ideas appealing so that they're easier to accept.

"But when we ask the question, 'What entertains you?' we are getting closer to the center of the cultural upheaval of the past five decades. We are asking a personal question at the heart of our identities: what delights you? What satisfies you? It is the question of what you—or society more broadly—worship. If you subvert and change the very nature of what entertains people, you can change the object of their worship. That means you change people, because human beings become what they worship. That means you change culture." [Brian Mattson, "The Sexual Revolution, Entertainment, and Christian Art," drbrianmattson.com (website), October 26, 2015]

Part of maturing spiritually involves a willingness to critique even enjoyable things (Eph. 4:17–24). Students should be willing to honestly critique their own viewing habits. If they aren't willing to do so, then they're confirming their idolatry—their worship of entertainment is more important to them than faithfulness to God and His Word.

Do entertainment agendas tend to educate society with Christian or secularist values?

The great majority of shows don't reflect common grace; few remnants of the Christian ethic are left in mainstream programming. The common theme—even in programming directed toward families—is promiscuity.

Megan Basham, "Family Unfriendly," *World* (website), February 28, 2009.

Rebecca Hagelin, "Agenda-Driven Entertainment," Heritage Foundation (website), December 3, 2004.

Does entertainment really affect the viewers' behavior?

Yes, the Bible is clear that Christians are to set their minds on things that are good. Christians are to put off what is bad. They are to renew their minds. Why? Sinful patterns are inculcated by what you feast on. What you feast on reveals what you really desire and believe. Eventually, your behavior will reflect what you really believe.

How should students respond to this education through entertainment?

They should put their worldview into practice by being salt and light. This may mean unplugging from the ungodly entertainment education system and cultivating something that builds others up. Christian film still leaves much to be desired, but it is an attempt to bring goodness back into entertainment education. Some students may be called to the hard work of producing quality stories that reflect a Christian worldview.

Beauty Means Harmony

Prettiness is often superficial, but the beauty in the triad refers to something far more expansive and substantive. It refers to the harmony and order built into God's world by which we can respond with pleasure. It's the opposite of chaos.

 ### Expressing Beauty in Music

How does music display beauty effectively?

Beautiful music is beautiful because it places numerous elements into a designed order for emotional communication. In other words, the music reflects certain laws the composer has discovered that accomplish his desired expression of communication to emotions.

Is it possible for music to be ugly?

Yes, if there are laws for music, then those laws can be violated. Some music clashes.

Admittedly, sometimes this clash is done on purpose by a composer in order to reflect the clashing of emotions (think of a soundtrack). This doesn't necessarily mean that the music is bad; the soundtrack may fit the scene in the film perfectly well. But if the score is only and always continuously clashing, it isn't beautiful.

You may want to have students evaluate musical examples, asking them how well they think a particular work reflects beauty. For example, compare the following two pieces, neither of which is bad. But which one reflects more beauty?

- Jón Leifs' "Hekla, Op. 52" (The music is meant to imitate the explosion of a volcano. The point isn't to say the music is sinful. But is it beautiful?)
- Antonín Dvořák's "Largo from the New World Symphony"

Expressing Beauty in Art

Laws regarding form, proportion, and line give artists guidelines to help them learn how to be successful. These rules shouldn't be viewed negatively; they should be viewed as the means to success. This principle is well understood in sports. The rules don't hinder the game. They help the game to progress. Without the rules there would be chaos and frustration. The same is true in art. Without rules the discipline devolves into chaos. The average viewer looks in frustrated disgust at esoteric art that freely violates the rules. Sometimes esoteric art brings to the forefront the specific technical abilities of an artist—as if the technical skills are the end instead of the means to the end. The beauty is lost when artists pridefully show off their technical abilities to the neglect of presenting harmony and order in a hospitable manner.

The Beauty of Creation

Show students pictures of God's creation similar to the descriptions given in the Student Text. Remind students that this beauty is the remnant of God's good creation marred by the Fall. And yet God's creation still declares His beauty.

The beauty of creation has caused many people to worship the creation rather than the Creator that the creation points to. Christians should be careful not to make the same mistake. They should glory in their Creator when they bask in the beauty of His creation.

Art, Film, and Music Critics

Critics and other specialists can interpret works of art and point out technical details that can enhance our understanding of works of art. But just as Christians can benefit from scientific work done by unbelievers while at the same time needing to filter that work through the lenses of a Christian worldview, Christians should also be discerning about what they learn from art critics.

Elements that are highly objectionable to Christians may register little or no objection from an unbelieving critic. Unbelievers also often operate with different conceptions of truth, goodness, and beauty. Even some Christian sources do a poor job of critiquing cultural artifacts from a biblical worldview.

So the structures of art are regularly twisted in wrong directions. There is no "art for art's sake." Art always serves one worldview or another.[58] Art is the discovery of beauty in the laws of creation, but it's also human communication, with all the possibilities for truth or falsehood and goodness or evil that entails. Art lets you look at some aspect of the world through someone else's eyes. The view can be enlightening or damning.

CREATION COMMUNICATES THROUGH FORM

Paul Munson and Robert Drake write,

We know that God speaks through the Bible. But that same Bible tells us that God speaks through his creation too. How is it, for instance, that the meadows and valleys of Psalm 65:13 "shout and sing together for joy" except through the way they look? Or how is it that in Psalm 148 the sea creatures and deeps and fire and hail and snow and mist and all the other things there listed are to praise the Lord? They can only do so by their forms, since they have no other language. We know that God speaks through design as well as through words. So do artists and composers.[59]

The Divine Standard

Just as God is the ultimate standard of truth and goodness, so also with beauty. This may seem strange since God is invisible. But God's beauty is not invisible. It's a beauty that becomes apparent to His people meditate on His perfections (Ps. 27:4). When God acts, He reveals His beauty (Ps. 90:17, KJV). When He reveals Himself, His beauty shines (Ps. 50:2).

Though God is invisible, He created a visible world. Think of the flaming colors of a sunset sky streaked with clouds of orange, purple, and pink or of the great clear blue dome on a summer's afternoon or of the gossamer grey texture of an autumn evening, low against the red-orange-yellow treetops (cf. Job 26:13). Or consider trees—some of them tower above us like gigantic pillars that seem to hold up the vault of heaven, spreading their branches to create a green-roofed cathedral (cf. Ezek. 31:2–9). Or consider the smell of cedar or pine (cf. Hos. 14:6). Think of walking through a forest carpeted with small white-and-purple wildflowers. Or imagine strolling through a field of waist-high grass that bends under the gentle breeze (cf. Isa. 28:4; 40:6; James 1:11).

God also describes humans as beautiful (Isa. 44:13). And though beauty, when divorced from truth and goodness, can be dangerous (Pro. 6:25; 31:30), within the bounds of truth and goodness, the bright eyes, flowing hair, glowing smile, and the forms of male and female bodies are beautiful (Song of Sol. 1:15–16; 4:1–7; 5:10–16).

What's more, humans can enhance their beauty with clothing and jewelry. A sparkling necklace, a golden ring, a sharp suit, a beautiful gown, hair curled or braided—all can enhance human beauty (Exod. 28:2; Isa. 3:18; Zech. 9:16; 2 Chron. 3:6; 1 Pet. 3:3). Of course, this adornment can be inordinate (1 Pet. 3:3–4). But in cautioning us about elevating external beauty over internal beauty, God is not dismissing the reality of either.

CREATIVE CULTIVATORS

A studied opinion about art or music, and one worth sharing, is hard to come by. It's (ideally) why we look to art, film, and music "critics" to help us know what pieces of art to spend our time and money on.

And we keep bothering about this because of something Dana Gioia, a contemporary poet in the Christian tradition, describes this way: When we see beauty, we "see this beautiful and meaningful pattern unfolding . . . like a vision of redemptive order in a fallen world."[60]

Some reviewers focus primarily on beauty or truth while neglecting goodness. Others focus on goodness while neglecting beauty or truth. All three components are needed for a truly Christian review.

The Divine Standard of Beauty

Determining what is beautiful is difficult because of the subjective element. But the divine standard is accessible to us. God created a world of flowers, trees, landscapes, mountains, and oceans. What makes these aspects of the creation beautiful?

God made his world full of sound: the running of rivers, the sighing of the wind, the chirping of the birds? What makes these sounds beautiful?

By seeking to answer these questions, a Christian can get a feel for God's view of beauty. This doesn't mean that art simply reproduces nature. When the Bible speaks of the beauty of rings, necklaces, clothing, and hairstyles, it shows that one of the purposes of art is to enhance natural beauty. A cut diamond is more beautiful than a diamond in the rough. By observing the beauty God has placed in creation, students can begin to formulate in particular what the creational norms for beauty might be.

No artistic creations in this world are perfectly true, good, or beautiful. But for a piece of art to be truly redemptive and truly worthy of Christian contemplation, no member of the triad can be deeply violated.

When truth, goodness, and beauty come together, we glimpse the God we were all created to love and serve. We gain a vision of how this world is supposed to be. And that is attractive to people, even fallen people. By God's grace they see something in a good story, a good movie, a good painting—they see something good that they can't help but want, at least a little.

This means that true beauty is a powerful message from God. No wonder, then, that sinful people don't want to acknowledge that any ultimate standard for beauty really exists. Munson and Drake, in their book on the Christian view of the arts, argue that people's inherent "attraction to aesthetic relativism suggests an aversion to God's glory." They ask, "Could it be that we hate beauty because we hate God? That we hate real pleasure?"[61]

Christians ought to love real beauty because they know the only real, lasting pleasures available in this world. Christians, who live under the blessing of God's original mandate to mankind (Gen. 1:26–28), ought to cultivate the traditions of beauty they've inherited. And they ought to create more beauty. By doing so, they're displaying something of God's truth and goodness to their neighbors.

THINKING IT THROUGH 25.3

1. When Christians defend a false, bad, or ugly cultural artifact, what common error do they tend to make?

2. Why doesn't fiction violate the *truth* element of the triad?

3. How can drama and film promote goodness?

4. When does beauty become dangerous?

⚲5. Why does art always serve one worldview or another?

1. They look for ways that the artistic product does align with one or two of the prongs in the triad while ignoring or minimizing how it fails to align with the other one or two prongs of the triad.

2. As long as fiction isn't presented as historically true, it can promote the truth in principle and in moral applications to life—as exemplified in the Bible's use of parables.

3. When tied to truth and beauty, the power of the story can be an effective medium to press home to the viewer particular worldview values.

4. when it is divorced from truth and goodness—like the harlot depicted in Proverbs 7

⚲5. Art always communicates truth claims and values by means of its presentation of beauty.

The Next Step

This chapter has made the case that behind the subjective apprehension of truth, goodness, and beauty lies objective reality. But it has not taken the next step of working students through different pieces of literature, film, visual art, or music to show how some pieces are superior to others or to show the different virtues of pieces.

We recommend making use of Paul Munson and Joshua Farris Drake, *Art and Music: A Student's Guide*, ed. David S. Dockery (Wheaton: Crossway, 2014). Munson and Drake write from a perspective similar to the one laid out in this chapter. But they also provide students with concrete evaluations and exercises that prepare the students for these evaluations.

Other Resources

In addition to Munson and Drake and the resources from Ken Meyers suggested earlier, you may want to consult the following resources:

C. S. Lewis, *An Experiment in Criticism* (Cambridge: Cambridge University Press, 1961).

H. R. Rookmaaker, *Modern Art and the Death of a Culture* (Wheaton: Crossway, 1994).

Roger Scruton, *Beauty: A Very Short Introduction* (New York: Oxford University Press, 2011). Scruton is not a Christian but a conservative who makes a case against aesthetic relativism.

Making Connections

1. the scientistic (naturalistic materialist) view

2. the postmodernist view

3. truth, goodness, and beauty

4. God Himself is the source and ultimate standard; God's character is absolute and He transcends His creation and human cultivation of creation.

Developing Skills in Apologetics and Worldview

5. Remind them that beauty is a part of the created order designed by God to reflect His own character. God created a world with great diversity, so there's a wide variety of ways for beauty to be expressed. But it is also possible for artifacts to contravene creational norms for beauty and thus be objectively not beautiful.

6. First, those shows violate some objective standards of morality. Second, claiming that taking a voyeuristic approach to violence doesn't affect you reveals that it *has* affected you. At the very least, it reveals that you're desensitized toward something God hates, which is a dangerous condition to be in.

Examining Assumptions and Evidence

7. point to the divine order by capturing the beauty of God's creation, which helps us see the beauty of God's glory

8. finiteness: limited knowledge of God's Word and God's wisdom or limited knowledge of the art form

   fallenness: worldly and corrupt violations of biblical morality or sensibilities that have not been properly developed

9. Because beauty is diverse, different cultures may emphasize different aspects of beauty.

10. The Christian lens for evaluating an artistic product must keep truth, goodness, and beauty all in focus in order to present an accurate biblical worldview. Any single virtue that's violated presents an inaccurate worldview.

Becoming a Creative Cultivator

11. Answers will vary. This will be a very difficult assignment, but it is one they have already been doing implicitly their whole lives and will continue doing, especially if they are serious Christians, through the remainder of their lives.

TERMS TO REMEMBER
aesthetic
triad
art
relativism
divine order
subjective
objective

25 CHAPTER REVIEW

Scripture Memory

Philippians 4:8

Making Connections

1. Which view denies that beauty truly exists by arguing that what we call beauty is merely accidental or useful?

2. Which view of beauty denies that humans can reliably recognize it, arguing that what we call beauty is merely subjective opinion?

3. What are the three objective and transcendent creational norms for evaluating human subcreations?

4. What is the source of the three creational norms for art? How does that source ensure that the norms are objective and transcendent?

Developing Skills in Apologetics and Worldview

5. How should you respond to Christians who claim that beauty is entirely culturally relative or personally subjective?

6. How should you respond to a Christian who says, "I can see how some people wouldn't be able to handle the *Texas Chainsaw Massacre* films, but they don't affect me"?

Examining Assumptions and Evidence

7. Since humans are subcreators under God, what should their artistic products seek to do?

8. If truth, goodness, and beauty are objectively real, what keeps people from seeing them?

9. If beauty is objectively real, why is beauty viewed differently in different cultures?

10. Why must all three creational norms stand together in harmony in order to be truly redemptive?

Becoming a Creative Cultivator

11. Analyze a picture of a famous work of art or a recording of a famous piece of music. Write three paragraphs of critical analysis explaining how the artistic work conforms either to the triad of creational norms or violates one or more of them. Explain why your tastes are or are not drawn to it and defend that response.

TERMS TO REMEMBER

aesthetic—relating to beauty or the experience of beauty

triad—a collection of three concepts that seem to flow necessarily together

art—something that somebody purposefully makes to be recognizably appreciated for its beauty

relativism—a denial of any absolute standard; any standard is personal, cultural, or situational

divine order—the transcendent design of God's created world that reflects His own character of truth, goodness, and beauty, which all subcreation ought to seek to mirror

subjective—a personal response to (thinking, feeling, etc.) or perception of an objective reality

objective—a factual reality regardless of how a subjective person responds to or perceives it

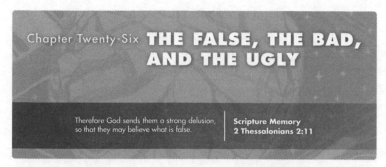

Chapter Twenty-Six **THE FALSE, THE BAD, AND THE UGLY**

Therefore God sends them a strong delusion, so that they may believe what is false.

Scripture Memory
2 Thessalonians 2:11

26.1 UNRAVELING TRUTH, GOODNESS, AND BEAUTY

It takes countless colored threads to produce a beautiful tapestry—such as the imposing, five-hundred-year-old "Hunt of the Unicorn" tapestries that John D. Rockefeller once bought for $14 million.[1] And, obviously, it takes a creative intelligence to design such a piece of art. The threads have to be placed into a relationship with each other—woven, stitched, clipped—every thread in its place.

When God created the world, everything just fit in proper relationship to everything else. With God at the heart and all things properly in submission, the whole creation was rightly ordered. This perfection brought glory to God and joy to mankind. Each molecule and atom of God's creation, every blade of grass and drop of water, was intertwined and woven together into a fabric, and God made the whole into something far more than the sum of its parts. Just as a tapestry is far more valuable than piles of thread, Creation is more valuable than piles of matter.

In the Fall, one of the threads in God's tapestry, mankind—which was, in fact, the chief thread—began yanking itself out of the weave, damaging other threads and marring the picture in the process. In Adam's effort to assert his independence, he caused the creation to begin to unravel. The beautiful tapestry became tangled, marred, and diminished.

Truth, goodness, and beauty form a tapestry in which each thread is necessary.

Lesson Plan Chart—Chapter 26

Section Title	Pages	Activity Manual	Days
26.1 Unraveling Truth, Goodness, and Beauty	401–6		2 days
26.2 The Great Unraveling of Human Nature	406–11	Activity 44	1 day
26.3 Pop Goes the Culture	411–16		2 days
Review	417		1 day
Total Suggested Days			**6 days**

The student will be able to

26.1 Detect when an artistic product idolizes or attacks truth, goodness, or beauty by divorcing one from the others.

26.2 Detect when an artistic product is meant to elicit a response that ignores truth, goodness, or beauty.

26.3 Explain how the sensibilities of pop culture, regardless of the content, tend to attack truth, goodness, and beauty.

SECTION OBJECTIVES 26.1

1. Explain how idolizing truth, goodness, or beauty above other elements in the triad distorts the creation order.

2. Explain how attacking truth, goodness, or beauty is rebellion against the creation order.

A Note About Rhetorical Strategy

As a teacher, you should be aware of the rhetorical strategy of this chapter and the next. The first major section of the chapter examines art that *worships* an individual part of the truth-goodness-beauty triad, ignoring the importance of the other two parts. Then it examines art that *attacks* truth, goodness, or beauty. In the second major section of the chapter, the discussion shows that humans are not merely truth receptors, beauty receptors, or goodness receptors. Humans ought to receive all aspects of truth, goodness, and beauty triad as unified persons.

A secondary rhetorical strategy goes along with the first. The illustrations in the first two sections are drawn from relatively high culture: plays that very few high school readers would be familiar with as well as books and articles that are unfamiliar. This is purposeful; students are less likely to grasp the principles of the chapter if they perceive it as an attack on things they hold dear.

But in section 26.3 the chapter does critique something that may be dear to them: pop culture. But it doesn't zero in on the content—the actual cultural artifacts produced (or rather mass-produced) in that arena of culture—as much as on the sensibilities formed by that whole arena. The idea is to lead students step by step to the point where they're able to question what everyone around them sees as an unquestioned good, what one writer called "the Fifth Freedom that our forefathers fought for." [Fred Sanders, "They Quit Making Good Music When I Turned 30," *First Things* (website), October 21, 2009]

Chapter 27, the final chapter of the book, is a fitting end and culmination to the book because it shows that God's original marching orders to mankind are still the best antidote to human cultural fallenness. Yes, we need sometimes to condemn, sometimes to critique, sometimes to consume, and sometimes even to copy cultural forms around us. But ultimately we should aim as obedient servants of our Creator to cultivate and create—to work and keep the cultural garden we've been given.

We certainly have other incredibly important tasks in this life: to progress in sanctification by God's grace, to disciple the nations, to provide for our own families. But the commands of the Bible are not in conflict with one another. The point of BIBLICAL WORLDVIEW: CREATION, FALL, REDEMPTION is that some of the major world-structuring commands of Scripture (namely those in the Creation Mandate) have been widely ignored. Though, in another sense, the Creation Mandate is always widely practiced anyway—even by lost people—because all humans participate in God's blessing.

Worldview: A Christian Cultural Framework

According to a Christian worldview of culture, or what some call a Christian cultural framework, all of creation is a tapestry of truth, goodness, and beauty. This triad governs, or ought to govern, human creations. People should not produce art, or any other cultural product, that is not true, good, and beautiful. Moderns reject and ignore these constraints, and in so doing they damage culture.

Conservative cultural commentator Rod Dreher summarizes the insights of Jewish sociologist Philip Rieff:

> What makes our own era different from the past . . . is that we have ceased to believe in the Christian cultural framework, yet we have made it impossible to believe in any other that does what culture must do: restrain individual passions and channel them creatively toward communal purposes. Rather, in the modern era, we have inverted the role of culture. Instead of teaching us what we must deprive ourselves of to be civilized, we have a society that tells us we find meaning and purpose in releasing ourselves from the old prohibitions.

[Rod Dreher, "Sex After Christianity," *American Conservative* (website), April 11, 2013]

ART THAT WORSHIPS TRUTH, GOODNESS, OR BEAUTY

If you really love God, then you will feel defensive when God's image-bearers worship His handiwork instead of worshiping Him. You'll be upset when they unweave His beautiful tapestry. (And, of course, you'll want to become an expert re-weaver; but that's the topic of the next chapter.)

In this unit we've been discussing three interwoven things in particular that fallen people are always in the process of unraveling in culture and the arts. Those three things are truth, goodness, and beauty. Ultimately, in the triune God, these three things are united. And just as the personality of an artist always shows up in the style of his work, God imprints truth, goodness, and beauty on His creation. To unweave these three things is to attack the unity of the one, tri-personal God they flow from.

Idolizing Truth

If, for example, truth gets detached from goodness and beauty, the results will be disastrous. People will worship a sort of disembodied reason, mere "facts" disconnected from moral considerations.

Consider the medical experiments of the so-called Unit 731 of the Japanese military during World War II. The Japanese abused Chinese and Russian prisoners for the sake of scientific advancement and medical knowledge. They offered exactly one justification for their painful and immoral research methods: they said they were just following where the pursuit of truth led.

This is truth without goodness or beauty. Yes, the Japanese doctors and scientists, using their God-given faculty of reason, discovered some truths through their work (and Allied governments gave the "researchers" immunity from prosecution for war crimes to get that information). But it was barbaric work, work that led to the degradation of the very thing it pretended to exalt. Who could possibly call it "reasonable" to maim and murder infants, even and especially in the name of knowledge?

The war crimes of World War II are considered sufficiently despicable today that just about no one would defend them. The whole Western world is united, for now, in opposition to conducting medical experiments on unconsenting children and adults. But plenty of educated people are happy to affirm that the pursuit of truth should not be "contaminated" by moral (or aesthetic) considerations.

Embryonic stem cell research (scientific use of human embryos) is another good example: does it destroy human life or not? Many Westerners are impatient with this question. Embryos don't experience pain, they say, and if getting rid of some of them brings medical benefits to others, then religious considerations shouldn't stand in the way.

But biblical religion does and *must* stand in the way when voiceless, powerless people are victimized. No truth is worth having if you must give up goodness to get it.

But TV personality Bill Maher, an atheist, disagrees:

> The plain fact is religion must die for mankind to live. The hour is getting very late to be able to indulge in having key decisions made by religious people—by irrationalists.[2]

Maher is wrong: goodness and beauty don't contaminate reason. In fact, when one of them is unraveled from the others, the result is ugliness and evil.

 ### Idolizing Truth but Ignoring Goodness and Beauty

Mark Snoeberger applies this insight about the modern rejection of cultural constraints on the passions to the realm of music:

> The Church as a whole seems to have reached an alarming watershed—a consensus decision that (1) there is no profit in philosophizing and theologizing about aesthetics, that (2) the threat of being aesthetically "of the world" does not exist, and that (3) the threat of not being aesthetically "in the world" is by far the greater crisis of the evangelical church.

[Mark Snoeberger, "Musing About Music" Detroit Baptist Theological Seminary (website), June 13, 2013]

The church's refusal to allow ethical evaluation of the Fall's effects on music is parallel to secularism's dismantling of the Christian cultural framework. But in a biblical worldview, the Fall requires that ethical evaluation not be detached from aesthetics. The words of a song may be true. That's good as far as it goes. But its not sufficient. To make lyrical truth the sole criterion of musical evaluation idolizes truth while ignoring goodness and beauty.

 ### Idolizing Goodness but Ignoring Truth and Beauty

Students trained in worldview thinking should become adept at cutting through to the presuppositions underlyng public arguments. People in the news and in newspaper editorials use superficially plausible arguments to justify their sins; they're adept at

Idolizing Goodness

Goodness can also get yanked out of the cultural weave. It can be made to stand on its own, without truth and beauty.

Of course, people don't generally think of themselves as doing this yanking. They think that their definition of what's good is true, or they wouldn't adopt it. But think carefully: the very definition of *good* has been adjusted a great deal in Western culture over time. Sexual morality may be only the most obvious realm in which that's the case.

It was in 1996 that a Democratic president, Bill Clinton, signed the Defense of Marriage Act limiting legal marriage to heterosexual, monogamous couples. Ten years later, then-senator Barack Obama wrote in his autobiography, *The Audacity of Hope*, that he was opposed to "gay marriage" though he admitted he might prove to be "on the wrong side of history."[3]

By 2012, President Obama had decided that history had spoken, and he officially announced his support for gay marriage in a *Good Morning, America* interview. The argument that Christian conservatives are, in fact, on the "wrong side of history" has since become increasingly common. Such an argument assumes a great deal, however. As one writer put it,

> Upon inspection, "X is on the right side of history" turns out to be a lazy, hectoring* way to declare, "X is a good idea," by those evading any responsibility to prove it so.[4]

Lots of people—the majority of a culture—can sign on to a view of "good" that isn't true. America is doing this kind of thing with gay marriage; many in the US South did it with their racist views. People who didn't accept phrenology* were on the wrong side of history for thirty years or so during the nineteenth century, but today the idea that bumps on your head predict your personality type is, to say the least, unpopular. Any doctor who used phrenology today could be sued for malpractice; he could do real harm to a patient by missing the truth of his condition. What is good (like marriage or medicine) cannot be divorced from what is true, or it becomes evil. Truth, goodness, and beauty are most themselves when they are together.

Idolizing Beauty

Truth is distorted when it's in isolation; goodness is too. And when beauty gets unwoven from truth and goodness, we get **romanticism**. Romanticism prizes intense emotion and seeks it in ever-concentrated doses. Sensualism, eroticism, and anti-intellectualism generally result.

Nineteenth-century writer and poet Oscar Wilde, whose plays are still performed and whose books are still read today, was an "aesthete."[5] One of his characters, the "New Hedonist" Lord Henry, expressed what appears to have been Wilde's own view:

> Beauty is a form of genius—is higher, indeed, than genius, as it needs no explanation. . . . It cannot be questioned. It has its divine right of sovereignty.[6]

Can you draw a connection between what Lord Henry said here and this next quotation from him?

> The only way to get rid of temptation is to yield to it.[7]

hectoring: bullying, harassing, intimidating through force

phrenology: the "science" of feeling bumps on people's heads and thereby describing their personalities

finding explanations that our culture will accept. And generally speaking, their public defenses will appeal to a genuine good in one area to defend a sin in another area.

For example, Planned Parenthood Federation director Cecile Richards landed on the cultural hot seat in 2015 because of sting videos showing PPF leaders haggling over the sale price of dead baby parts. She argued that "fetal tissue donation . . . is an important, prudent element of healthcare research in this country." She also argued, "Women come to us for . . . breast cancer screenings, cervical cancer screenings, birth control. . . . Half of our clinics are in medically underserved communities in America."

["Planned Parenthood President Says Organization Has Broken No Laws," ABC News (website), July 26, 2015]

How is a good thing idolized in order to justify sin and injustice?

One of the ways abortion proponents attempt to justify this evil is by switching the focus to a good that becomes idolized to such an extent that the evil is ignored. Providing healthcare for impoverished women is good. Scientific research to heal disease is good. But is it ever defensible to achieve that good by means of killing innocent babies? Certainly not! Killing defenseless babies—separate human beings within the bodies of their mothers—is never justifiable because some good can be produced from the evil.

In addition, the revulsion that people feel when they see the tiny parts of a baby torn apart and lying in a petri dish reveals that beauty—or in this case ugliness—can play a role in awakening the conscience to matters of truth and goodness.

Are We Riding Hobby Horses?

Why would this textbook mention homosexuality yet again (e.g., Obama's support for gay marriage) especially right after an illustration about abortion? Are homosexuality and abortion hobby horses? No, these are simply evils that are often in the public eye. Most recently LGBT issues have been in the public eye because their proponents have been seeking to advance their vision in the public square. People who desire to defend the fundamental institutions of culture are thus required to speak on these issues.

Nonetheless, it's important to recognize that people yank goodness out of the cultural weave in many other ways too. Heterosexual divorce has most certainly wreaked more havoc on the American family and the society as a whole than gay marriage has so far. In fact, gay marriage is only the next logical step for a culture that has come to see marriage as all about the love of two adults and not about the covenantal commitment between a man and woman tasked with filling the earth. Abortion serves the same evil twisting operation, yanking the same good—procreation—out of the cultural weave. Abortion and no-fault divorce take specific aim at one of the Bible's stated reasons for the existence of marriage. Clearly, by yanking childbearing/childrearing out of the cultural weave and leaving it dangling, these societal forces have done untold harm.

Idolizing Beauty but Ignoring Truth or Goodness

A female *New York Times* reporter spent an entire twenty-four-hour period watching Brazilian TV. She reported back to her American readers what she learned by watching Globo, the biggest TV channel in Brazil—with a 34 percent audience share.

After the news, "the rest of the evening was filled with soap operas [called *telenovelas*], from which you could learn that women always wear heavy makeup, huge earrings, polished nails, tight skirts, high heels and straight hair. . . ." [Vanessa Barbara, "Escaping Reality with Brazil's Globo TV," *New York Times* (website), November 10, 2015]

This particualr kind of idolization of beauty is warned against in Scripture (Prov. 31:30). Notably, visual mass media has the tendency to idolize beauty to the neglect of goodness and truth in other areas as well. Notice, for instance, that successful politicians now must be handsome or beautiful while the substance of their positions or morality suffers from relative neglect.

What Idolizing Beauty Destroys

Why is any advice to yield to temptation foolish? (Ps. 1:1, Prov. 6:20–29; Rom. 6:16) *Such advice is the exact opposite of God's advice in the Bible (Rom. 6:13). The difficult struggle with temptation itself is far less grievous than the lasting consequences that result from giving oneself over to be enslaved to sin (1 Tim. 6:10). Yielding to one temptation will only lead to worse temptations that lead a person to devolve until greater and greater destruction is done to both himself and others (2 Tim. 3:13).*

Stealth Attacks Against Truth

Christians need to be alert to the dangers of arts and entertainments that subtly attack truth (Prov. 14:16; Eph. 5:10). Typically, Christians focus on explicit content that is sordid (and profanity) and warn against the moral debauchery of that content. But the beliefs and values woven into a work of art can be just as damaging. False worldviews can slowly inculcate false presuppositions that will undermine the truth (see the TE note "Knowledge Is Constructed" on pages 2–3). When certain false ideas are repeatedly assumed in a culture, they affect the plausibility structures of that culture. Even Christians can have truth become implausible for them if they allow their thinking to be shaped by art and entertainment with false worldviews rather than by Scripture.

Goodness in Art: Dealing with Objectionable Elements

Christians have to reckon with portrayals of sin in art. Two different wrong courses of action are tempting to Christians. According to Ron Horton's classic essay, "A Biblical Approach to Objectionable Elements in Christian Education"(available on the BJU Press website), the permissivist justifies art with objectionable elements on two grounds: (1) the aesthetic quality of the work or (2) "the necessity in art of an honest view of life."

The first justification is a classic case of separating beauty from truth and goodness. The Christian worldview insists that good art must keep all three together.

According to Horton,

> The second criterion—the necessity in literature of an honest imitation of life—is the standard defense by modern writers of the sordid and salacious elements in their fiction. But ideas of the world and of life vary widely. Every serious secular novelist invents fictional worlds that vindicate his moral and religious preferences. Moral libertines nurture private worldviews that justify and re-

inforce their licentious lifestyles. Even were there an accurate, biblical consensus of the nature of life and the world, it could hardly be maintained that literature, while imitating reality, need include all of reality. The Bible speaks of some realities we are to flee (1 Tim. 6:11; 2 Tim. 2:22). Moral considerations must override the aesthetic and mimetic in a Christian's perspective on literature and life. That which threatens the moral and spiritual life cannot be justified on other grounds. Permissivism arrogantly elevates human wisdom above divine.

Some may conclude that Christians should simply avoid works in which objectionable elements appear. Horton calls this the exclusivist option. But in the present world it is impossible and actually undesirable to have art that totally avoids any objectionable ele-

ments. By this standard, education and the Bible itself would need to be avoided. In fact, Christians can benefit from art that deals with sin. For instance, Jane Austen's *Emma* explores the contrast between using people and loving people. George Eliot examines the consequences of greed—for money or for a person—in *Silas Marner*. C. S. Lewis's *Perelandra* examines the whole matter of temptation. A final example is Shakespeare's *Macbeth*, which some Christians find objectionable because of the murders and the witches. Ultimately, however, the play asserts the biblical truth, "Be sure your sin will find you out" (Num. 32:23). In these works we benefit from a presentation of sin that may serve to expose and critique our own sinfulness.

How does the Christian practically evaluate works of art and avoid these two errors.

If this chapter is correct—that beauty can become an idol, making truth and goodness drop away—then there is a connection between these two Oscar Wilde quotes. Someone who pursues beauty at all costs, who gives it divine authority separate from truth and goodness, can't hold on to truth and goodness for long. You can't have beauty by itself, or truth by itself, or goodness by itself.

To love God is to love reality as He has ordered it—a reality where truth, goodness, and beauty share a unity in His person. These three things are a tapestry. Trace any one thread, and it will lead to the others—and ultimately to God.

ART THAT ATTACKS TRUTH, GOODNESS, AND BEAUTY

Fallen art and culture can isolate truth, detach goodness, and unweave beauty from the unity they are meant to maintain. Culture can separate three things that were designed to be together. But, of course, art and culture can also attack these three things individually and directly in this fallen world. For this segment of our discussion about fallen arts, we'll focus on one artistic medium: the theater. It's certainly capable of great good, but the following three plays—all winners of major theater awards—attack truth, goodness, and beauty, respectively.

Attacking Truth

You may never have heard of the play *Equus*, by Peter Shaffer, but you may have heard of its biggest star. Daniel Radcliffe, who played the title role in the *Harry Potter* films, took a role in *Equus* in the middle of the filming of the Potter series. *Equus* means "horse" in Latin; in the play, Radcliffe's character, seventeen-year-old Alan Strang, is undergoing psychotherapy for having blinded six horses.

The psychiatrist assigned to help the young man discovers that Alan actually worships horses. But some horses were present while Alan committed immorality with a stable girl. Riddled with guilt and convinced that the horses had witnessed his sin, Strang blinded the animals.

The play ends with the psychiatrist voicing frustration over his job. He feels reluctant to take away Alan's horse-god even though he recognizes the god as false. He fears that treatment will strip Alan of the emotional power of his pagan worship.

The Bible records the lives of messed-up people such as Samson who, today, might wind up in a psychiatrist's office—and who committed heinous sins like Alan Strang's. So *Equus* is not objectionable simply for telling a story about fallen people committing sin; the play is wrong because it promotes an untruth. Whereas the Bible never leaves readers with any doubt that the truth is the only way to lead a good human life, *Equus* ends by shrugging its shoulders: if a big lie makes someone happier, why force the truth on him? The play even goes a step further and suggests that Alan's pagan mental derangement actually makes him more human. The psychiatrist, in contrast, seems to imply that conventional morality makes people less human, somehow emptier.

Attacking Goodness

Sometimes art attacks goodness as well. In *The Real Thing*, a play by British playwright Tom Stoppard, which was recently revived on Broadway, an actress (Annie) and a playwright (Henry), who have an adulterous affair, leave their spouses and marry each other. Annie has taken up the cause of a political prisoner named Brodie, who himself writes a play, but one so obviously terrible that Henry is asked to fix it up.

In one scene, Henry insists that Brodie's play is horrendous and unusable. He uses an illustration to argue the point with Annie. He tells his wife that a good cricket bat will knock the ball two hundred yards while a bad one will barely make it go ten feet. He points to a well-made bat:

> This [bat] isn't better because someone says it's better. . . . It's better because it's better. You don't believe me, so I suggest you go out to bat with this [script from Brodie] and see how you get on.[8]

Good writing makes ideas travel like a cricket ball (American translation: like an out-of-the-park home run). Bad writing, not so much.

Then Annie gets the part of the female lead in a production in another city, where she promptly begins another adulterous affair, this time with her young co-star, Billy. Even though Henry finds out, Annie refuses to leave either Henry or Billy. Henry manages to accept the new arrangement and reconciles with Annie at the end. The audience is left with the feeling that in the search for love, you have to go after "the real thing" at all costs, even if it means sacrificing your marriage or your dignity.

In writing the script for this play, real-life playwright Tom Stoppard marshalled his considerable literary skill to hit a homer with the immoral idea that extramarital affairs are justified if one is in search of true love. You can say it's all just art—that it's all in good fun. But in the original London production, Annie was played by an actress who ended up having an affair with Tom Stoppard in real life. The affair broke up his marriage to Dr. Miriam Stoppard. Sadly, the play was dedicated to Miriam.

Attacking Beauty

Art can also attack beauty, of all things. Some "art" is truly ugly. *Pillowman*, a play by Martin McDonagh, focuses on Katurian, a writer whose short stories frequently describe violence against children. Two detectives arrest Katurian because his stories bear a striking resemblance to some actual child murders that have taken place in his area.

The title *Pillowman*, is taken from one of the stories Katurian tells. The Pillowman is a creature made of pillows, and his job is to help suicidal people. He "helps" them, however, by traveling back in time to when they were children and persuading them to commit suicide early. This way they don't have to suffer so much in life. Such a task takes an emotional toll on the Pillowman, so he goes back in time and convinces his own younger self to commit suicide.

This is not the most gruesome of Katurian's stories. The *New York Times* reviewer offered this "advisory note" to potential theatergoers: "Severed fingers and heads, electric drills, barbed wire and premature burial all figure prominently."[9] And don't forget the crucifixion of a child.

One reviewer was critical of *Pillowman*: "The supreme and only unquestioned good in the play is the preservation of Katurian's stories from censorship and police destruction."[10] But what if those stories are twisted, evil, and ugly?

Pillowman suggests that because we can't know truth, goodness, and beauty, the only way to measure art is to experience its power over us. Whether it makes our flesh crawl with horror or our hearts sing with joy, it's art if it makes us feel.

GLAMORIZING SIN

All three of these plays won mainstream awards. They represent the art of drama today—and that means that attacks on truth, goodness, and beauty are going to be difficult to avoid for anyone who lives on the cultural grid. You will run into fallen pieces of art in one way or another.

list them out), organize your life so you can follow those desires, and then act on them.

It treats discovering and following the desires of your heart as a serious moral duty, something you may need to go to great lengths to accomplish. Once again, the idea that any of your desires might be harmful to yourself or others is not considered. This is again an attack on goodness: you're supposed to assume that all your desires are intrinsically good, even if God calls them evil. In contrast, believers are to reorient their desires (Ps. 37:4). The driving motivation needs to be directed away from self and toward God—the Creator, Savior, and King of one's life (Ps. 24). That driving motivation will produce the desire to fear and love God (Eccles. 12:1, 13–14; John 14:15), bringing about obedient satisfaction that God is glorified. This is what humans were created for.

Attacking Beauty: Horror Movies

Eminent Canadian philosopher Charles Taylor points out in his book *A Secular Age* that medieval man viewed himself as "porous," susceptible to external spiritual influences both good and evil. Modern man, however, views himself as "buffered," set apart from the world and thus the lord of his own interior. He lives as if there's nothing that is transcendent; he himself transcends all.

And yet humans, the Bible says, have had "eternity" placed in their hearts (Eccles 3:11)—people know, at some level, that God exists and a transcendent world does too. So they reach out for the deep feelings that transcendence used to provide. One way they do it is viewing horror movies to get that sheer feeling of terror that they never experience otherwise. Horror films operate as *Pillowman* did, by reveling in the most gruesome elements of human life in a fallen world. Instead of transcendence, however, they give "descendence." Instead of arcing above the circle of the earth and coming closer to God, they reach down below mankind's level into the rotten grave, into what the Bible calls Sheol.

Glamorizing Sin

Pop music lyrics resist in-depth analysis. On the surface, they aren't meant to be taken seriously. But there's always a worldview that's being reinforced by that music. That worldview gets absorbed into the mental bloodstream of a person who listens to pop nonstop. A person's thinking will be molded into the worldview that he or she most meditates on. As a Christian you can't serve two masters (Matt. 6:24). You can't meditate on God's Word in Sunday school and then give yourself over to meditating on the false

Horton provides three criteria that work together: Is it gratuitous? Is it explicit? What is the moral tone? Horton's entire essay is worth reading.

 ## The Destructiveness of Attacking Goodness

A non-Christian woman came to a pastor for counseling. Her life was a mess; drunken one-night stands were the norm. She was run ragged by her promiscuity, but she kept at it. The pastor gave her the gospel and urged her to repent of her promiscuity and drunkenness. Her response: "You mean I don't have to do what I want?"

Her comment was revealing—she saw herself as shackled to sins that were destroying her, and yet she was genuinely surprised to find out that she didn't have to follow her heart, that she could be given a new heart through Christ.

The common refrain of popular culture is "follow your heart." But your heart's desires could be contradictory (like the desire to have a family versus the desire to pursue a very demanding career that takes you away from family), or your heart's desires might be self-destructive. Such cautions are completely ignored. This willful ignorance of the wickedness and fallenness of the human heart is an attack on goodness because it urges people to call "good" what are in fact evil desires—like "the real thing" in Stoppard's play.

You may want to do a web search for "Follow your heart." As of this writing, a WikiHow article is one result. It recommends a three-step process in which you discover what your desires are (you're supposed to

worldviews of pop culture through music that's diametrically opposed to Scripture. God's Word will seem increasingly boring, and the pop music will seem more and more enthralling. It's a ploy of the Prince of the Power of the Air to saturate you with the pleasures of the world, drawing you away from God so that you become "dull of hearing" (Heb. 5:11, cf. 3:7–19; 5:12–6:8).

 ## Applying the Principles

Students need to be trained to actually apply the principles they're learning. They need to try some specific analysis and evaluation using the categories of truth, goodness, and beauty (Eph. 5:10).

For example, make application with regard to pop music just discussed above. It's not just secular pop music that is dangerous. After being trained in a biblical worldview, students shouldn't be so easily deceived by pop music artists who claim the name of Christ but whose lifestyles and teachings are contrary to Scripture. Justin Bieber can serve as a representative example.

Have students consider the unlikely situation that Bieber has asked to meet with one of them to get spiritual counsel. Have them frame their counsel around the lyrics to Bieber's song "Purpose." [We would suggest that you read the lyrics (readily available on the internet) to the students. We do not recommend listening to the song as a class activity.]

Students could appeal to Bieber to embrace the scriptural teaching that salvation is not gained by efforts to improve oneself (Rom. 4:2; Eph. 2:8–9). the gospel offers more hope than resolving to try to do better next time.

Students should also help him understand that Scripture demands a clear confession that we're nothing but sinners until we're rescued from sin. It demands a clear recognition of sin and repentance from it.

Students should contrast Bieber's view of giving himself grace (not being too hard on oneself) with the biblical teaching that sanctification involves both a dying to self and a Spirit-empowered fight against sin (Rom. 6:1, 11–23; Phil. 2:12–13; Gal. 2:20). [You may also refer students to Activity 15.]

Students should encourage Bieber to receive instruction in right and wrong from biblically wise people. They should warn him against following his heart (Prov. 1:7–9; 4:13; 5:12–14; 6:23; Jer. 17:9).

Paul instructed the Corinthians,

> I wrote to you in my letter not to associate with sexually immoral people—not at all meaning the sexually immoral of this world, or the greedy and swindlers, or idolaters, since then you would need to go out of the world. (1 Cor. 5:9)

Every reader of this textbook has been exposed to fallen culture. We have been entertained by works of human art which have unwoven truth, goodness, and beauty from the tapestry. Sometimes we've done this on purpose, sinning "with a high hand" (Num. 15:30). But sometimes we were misled by someone else's recommendation or saw something in a store window we never intended to see. Those images and themes made it into our heads and into our hearts, where sin already lives.

Now what? Try some analysis and evaluation using the categories of truth, goodness, and beauty. If you have seen a film (or listened to music or read a book) you now object to, sit down and think through—even write out—why you object to it. Analysis is a way of distancing yourself from something emotionally, trying to view it from another perspective, hopefully a biblical one. And biblical evaluation measures what you find by God's standards. Ask yourself questions: Was this work of art true? Was it good? Was it beautiful? Did it unite all three qualities, or was one of the three either attacked or worshiped?

Analysis is hard mental work, but what's the alternative? Being swept away by the powerful forces of your culture. "The unexamined life is not worth living"[11] isn't a Bible verse, but it's certainly consistent with Scripture. One of the goals of a Christian should be to have his or her "powers of discernment trained by constant practice to distinguish good from evil" (Heb. 5:14).

THINKING IT THROUGH 26.1

1. What's the problem with trying to keep goodness and beauty from "contaminating" the pursuit of truth?

2. How should goodness be defined?

3. What results when beauty is disconnected from truth and goodness?

4. Instead of idolizing truth, goodness, or beauty, what do some artists explicitly do to undo God's tapestry?

5. Analyze and evaluate the most recent cultural artifact you watched, read, or listened to. Was it true? Was it good? Was it beautiful?

26.2 THE GREAT UNRAVELING OF HUMAN NATURE

People are tapestries too. For a temporary period at some point in the future, our bodies and souls will be unwoven: bodies in the grave, souls with the Lord. But at the beginning of eternity God will weave us back together like He wove His Son. David says we are "fearfully and wonderfully made." He says to God, "You knitted me together in my mother's womb" (Ps. 139:13). We run into difficulties when we try to unweave the knitting—to separate the different "parts" of man. Some people talk as if we humans are controlled by little, separate beings called "mind," "will," and "emotion," each of which is vying for supremacy in our brains . . . or our hearts . . . or whatever organ you want to pick.

THINKING IT THROUGH 26.1

1. Pursuing truth apart from beauty and goodness leads to ugliness and evil.

2. by the truth

3. Romanticism, which often results in sensualism, eroticism, and anti-intellectualism

4. They directly attack truth, goodness, or beauty.

5. Answers will vary. Students should identify the cultural artifact, provide a context for it, summarize its content, and provide specific biblical support for their evaluations.

SECTION OBJECTIVES 26.2

1. Defend the unity of the inner person as the receiver of truth, goodness, and beauty.

2. Explain why truth disconnected from goodness and beauty is irrational.

3. Explain why goodness disconnected from truth and beauty is immoral.

4. Explain why beauty disconnected from truth and goodness is ugly.

The Unity of the Human Nature

One of the best sources on anthropology, the theological study of man, is John Frame's *The Doctrine of the Christian Life* (Phillipsburg, NJ: P&R, 2008). What Frame says—especially in his chapter titled "The Organs of Ethical Knowledge"—underlies this section.

You can't see your inner person, but God can. And God's Word teaches that all our actions arise out of an indivisible mixture of all our faculties. We do have minds, we have wills, and we have emotions, but the Bible never separates them. God never commands our minds to think, our wills to choose, or our emotions to feel. God through Scripture simply gives us commands—as whole beings.

One of the proofs of our fallenness is that we perceive a conflict inside ourselves over what we ought to think, choose, and feel. Sometimes we don't really *feel* what we *think*—we don't feel deep gratitude for the death of Christ or deep hatred for the sin we know is harming us. Sometimes we don't really *think* our *feelings* are right—like when we feel a strong pull to sin, or when we feel no love for God. Sometimes we *choose* something we *think* and *feel* is wrong.

No aspect of man is more fallen than the others. The Fall has tainted every part. So one of the goals of the Christian life is to bring our thoughts, choices, and feelings into righteous unity—to think the truth, choose the good, and feel the beautiful. Psalm 86:11 says:

> Teach me your way, O Lord,
> that I may walk in your truth;
> unite my heart to fear your name.

"Teach me your way, O Lord"—that's our thinking. "That I may walk in your truth"—that's our doing, our choosing. "Unite my heart to fear your name"—that's our feeling. Like a three-note chord, our thinking, choosing, and feeling should harmonize. Our understanding of God's way should lead us to choose to walk in that way with emotions that resonate with the fear of God and love for Him.

The Fall of Adam and the Curse on creation mean that our ability to think, do, and love God's way is impaired. And there are curse-compliant elements in every culture that make thoughtful, loving, obedience to God more difficult. Said one wise pastor:

> There is something more impacting on the soul of a Christian than being tied to a stake and put on fire. And that is to be systematically pressured over his whole lifetime by a culture intent on slowly drawing his heart away from God.[12]

One of the ways fallen culture puts that pressure on us is by unweaving *people*: treating them as if they are just truth-, goodness-, or beauty-receptors.

NOT JUST TRUTH-RECEPTORS

But people are more than truth-receptors or fact-processors. Art woven with truth, goodness, and beauty will reflect this fact.

Pieces of culture that flatten people into mere truth-receptors might be defined by their willingness to look evil and other hard truths in the face. Telling hard truths is regarded as the primary virtue of Cormac McCarthy's 2006 novel *The Road*, for example. *The New York Times* review of the Pulitzer-Prize–winning book ends this way: "*The Road* offers nothing in the way of escape or comfort. But its fearless wisdom is more indelible than reassurance ever could be."[13]

The plot follows a father and his young son as they try to survive in a post-apocalyptic wasteland. The new humanity of that era includes "good guys"—like the father and son—who are "carrying the fire" by trying to hold on to civilization. But the world that the main characters stumble through is full of bad guys that commit

TRUTH ✓

~~GOODNESS~~

~~BEAUTY~~

The Rationalist

Here are some key points Frame makes about the Bible's teaching regarding man:

> It is sometimes thought that reason, emotion, conscience, imagination, will, etc. are more or less autonomous units, battling one another for supremacy in each human life. I believe it is more scriptural to say that the whole person is the one who makes ethical decisions, and that the ethical faculties are ways of describing the person as he makes those decisions. In my view, reason, emotion, and so on are not conflicting voices within us, but are rather different ways of characterizing and describing the whole person. Reason is the whole person reasoning, emotion the whole person feeling, etc. Further, each of these is dependent on the others: reason is dependent on emotions, will, imagi-

nation, etc., and vice versa. The best model, in my judgment, is perspectival. All these faculties are perspectives on one another and on the whole person. [Frame, *Christian Life*, 361]

> Will is our capacity for making decisions. So, by definition, the will is involved in all moral decisions and acts. Traditionally, will is contrasted with intellect (reason) and emotions. So in some accounts, it almost seems as though will, intellect, and emotions are little beings up in our heads who vie for supremacy. Arguments have been made both about which of these three faculties is superior to the others and about which one ought to be superior. . . .

> My own view, however, is that we make decisions as whole persons, and that intellect, will, and emotions are per-

spectives on the whole persons, not subsistent entities. The intellect is the person's ability to think, the will his capacity to decide, the emotions his capacity to feel. We are talking about three abilities that people have, not three independent entities within them. That, I think, is a more biblical perspective, for Scripture never distinguishes these three capacities or makes any general statements about the superiority of one or the other. [Frame, *Christian Life*, 368]

And this comment by Frame is very important: "Scripture never says, as some Greek philosophers did, that reason should rule the emotions, or, as Hume did, that reason should be the slave of the passions. There is no hierarchical relation between the two. Both reason and emotions are equally aspects of the image of God in which we are created. Both are equally fallen, both equally redeemed in Christ's people." [Frame, *Christian Life*, 374]

Frame follows this paragraph with an excellent illustration:

> When we warn young people against fornication, we often tell them not to follow their feelings, for obvious reasons. But their problem is not just a problem of emotion. It is also a problem of reasoning. They are tempted to act according to unsanctified emotions, but also according to unsanctified reasoning. If they reasoned right, they would put a higher priority on glorifying God and a lower priority on their present gratification. So they are wrong, not only in following their wrong emotions, but also in following their wrong reasoning. The remedy is not (as Plato thought) to bring emotions under the rule of reason, but to bring both emotions and reason under the rule of God's word. [Frame, *Christian Life*, 374]

Human beings are not just reasoners, not just choosers, and not just emoters. They are all those things all the time—simultaneously. And all those things at all times are fallen and need to be redeemed/sanctified.

The Nobility of Naturalism

Naturalistic materialists—who are all atheists, naturally—will often talk as if it's noble to admit to ourselves that life has no ultimate meaning—noble and, of course, morally liberating for them (as previously discussed in the Student Text on pages 311–14). We've got to man up, they say, turn against the wind and acknowledge the truth.

It isn't true, of course—the idea that life has no meaning beyond what we humans create.

But atheistic materialists think that it is. And yet what if people—lots of people—really began to think that it was true? What impact would that have on their moral lives and the cultural artifacts they produced—if they were consistent with their belief about the meaninglessness of life? You see, truth and goodness are tied together inextricably. (See again the illustration in the sidebar on page 312 of the Student Text.)

Some naturalistic materialists admit they hold this position for ethical as well as metaphysical reasons. Aldous Huxley wrote:

> The philosopher who finds meaning in the world is concerned, not only to elucidate that meaning, but also to prove that it is most clearly expressed in some established religion, some established code of morals. The philosopher who finds no meaning in the world is not concerned exclusively with a problem in pure metaphysics. He is also concerned to prove that there is no valid reason why he personally should not do as he wants to do, or why his friends should not seize political power and govern in the way that they find most advantageous to themselves. The voluntary, as opposed to the intellectual, reasons for holding the doctrines of materialism, for example, may be predominantly erotic, as they were in the case of LaMettrie . . . , or predominately political, as they were in the case of Karl Marx.

[Aldous Huxley, *Ends and Means* (London: Chatto & Windus, 1941), 272]

Note, however, that atheistic materialists aren't all overtly or obviously bad people. Rebellion need not take the form of raping and pillaging; indeed, intellectual rebellion and even aesthetic rebellion can damage more people than much more obvious sins.

A Vision for Christian Movies

Film is a powerful medium that Christians can use with good effect. Movies tell stories, and a good movie can tell a powerful story that will reshape the way people think.

Nevertheless, telling stories through film has significant challenges. One of these is that Christians sometimes have misguided goals in making films. Some think that films should be used as evangelistic tools. But God has already ordained another means for heralding the gospel—preaching. When movies become preachy, they don't work. God gave preachers the task of explaining Christian teaching precisely through propositional language. It's impossible for movies to be theologically precise without violating the medium.

murder and even cannibalism. At the end of the book, the father dies after being shot with an arrow. As he dies, he urges his son to keep carrying the fire, and the boy does find another family. They claim, at least, to be "good guys," but it turns out that their goal is the same as his father's was: to avoid brutality for as long as possible and then succumb to it.

The book lends some nobility to the idea of carrying the fire of civilization, but it also argues that that decision is irrational. The lives of those who resist the darkness end in the same futility as the cannibals.

Cormac McCarthy is known for his lean prose; this makes the book feel honest. It's true that destruction flows with the current of the world; civilization is always swimming upstream. But the Christian knows that the Fall isn't the end of the story. Redemption has come in Jesus Christ, and the Good Guy will win in the end. He will carry the fire, launching an everlasting civilization and banishing all darkness.

People in court swear to tell the truth, and McCarthy has told it: people really are as bad as he shows. But people in court also swear to tell the whole truth. By lopping off the end of the story, omitting redemption, McCarthy has actually told a falsehood. It would be like cutting off the end of Joseph's story in the Bible. Joseph is the favorite son of his father, and he is given a wonderful coat, which makes his brothers jealous. They throw him in a pit and sell him into slavery. The end. The critics might praise the story as "uncompromising" and "gritty." They might admire the author for resisting the temptation to produce a happy ending. But there was a happy ending, and every little salvation in the Bible—and in the world—is a picture of the big salvation God has brought to His creation.

There is one book in the Bible that, at first glance, seems to say, "Let's be honest. Everything is futile." It's Ecclesiastes. But Ecclesiastes itself doesn't end in despair; it ends with a promise that God will bring justice to the world (Eccles. 12:14).

On the flip side, Christian movies are often too propositional—too preachy. (This sin is not unique to Christian movies; secular ones regularly do it, too). Certain Christian end-times films of the 1970s, for example, were so obvious—and corny—in their attempts to get out the truth that you'd have a hard time watching them without cringing. When a movie features long stretches of dialogue uninterrupted by action, people sense that something is wrong; movies aren't supposed to be sermons. Christian movie reviewer Paul Asay says, "Evangelicals demand so much from their Christian movies: authenticity, biblical accuracy and, often, a clear altar-call at the end. The one thing we're not so much of a stickler for is artistic quality. If we get it, great. If not, well, maybe next time." Asay points to some movies, such as the 1981 Best Picture winner *Chariots of Fire*, which were all about faith but still managed to honor film as a medium.

Many truths in Scripture can be illustrated well in film, but some of those truths are too complex; they need to be *explained*, something movies are not made for. Good movies appeal to people as more than just truth-receptors, but also as image-bearers of a God of goodness and beauty. Truth is most itself when it is interwoven with goodness and beauty. Rationality disconnected from your emotions and ethics is irrational.

THE FOOLISHNESS OF PREACHING

Evangelistic films are often defended by a statement like this: "People won't listen to a sermon—but they will watch a film." Movies can and do communicate truth. But the complex truths of the gospel require explanation, something movies aren't good at. God already ordained an "art form" appropriate for communicating the gospel: preaching. God says that the "foolishness of preaching" is a powerful method for transforming people's lives (1 Cor. 1:21).

So Christian movies should do what movies do well: tell good stories. The stories can be about a whole range of things; they might be about survivors of a shipwreck, mill owners suffering from financial struggles, soldiers and war, or political corruption.

As the stories unfold, elements from a biblical worldview can be baked in. The importance of family could be shown by the way a family in the film pulls together to address a challenge. Instead of being hit over the head with that theme, it's simply woven into the warp and woof of the narrative. A historical film could unpack the problems of socialism through imagery rather than through exposition. A science fiction piece would be an ideal medium for challenging scientism.

By using approaches such as these, Christians who make films are seeking to influence the plausibility structures of their audience. But to be truly plausible, films made from a Christian worldview must be honest about the world as it is. Christians ought to be able to tell a story that isn't simplistic but realistically complex because we're the ones with the all-encompassing worldview that understands all humans as created and fallen—and redeemable. Some Christian stories should be tragedies. They could be stories about how a particular vice brought a person to ruin. These are stories that warn against sin. Some stories should reflect the reality that in the present evil age the righteous suffer for doing right. Some stories should show the simple goodness of righteous living and how it blesses others. Some stories should contain what Tolkein called a eucatastrophe, "the sudden happy turn in a story which pierces you with a joy that brings tears." [Humprey Carpenter, *The*

NOT JUST GOODNESS-RECEPTORS

People are more than goodness-receptors too. They're more than their consciences.

Journalist Sabrina Erdely writes frequently on themes of bullying and assault. Her work has appeared in some of America's most widely read magazines—*GQ, Self, New Yorker, Mother Jones, Glamour.*

And *Rolling Stone.* It was an article in that magazine that catapulted Erdely to national prominence. Entitled "A Rape on Campus," it told the horrendous story of a conspiracy to commit a violent rape at a frat party at the famed, historic University of Virginia.[16] Erdely also accused the UVA administration of sweeping sexual assault accusations under the rug in order to keep up its public image.

UVA is a national symbol of respectable American academia. The story was so terrible, and the actions so criminal, and the accusations so damning that the story exploded into the American twenty-four-hour news cycle.

But the rape never happened, at least not as described. As the story gained prominence, other investigations (including those by the police and by the *Washington Post*) turned up evidence that Erdely's story was largely fabricated. Two weeks after the story ran, it fell apart. She defended herself, saying, "I am convinced that it could not have been done any other way, or any better."[17] But she had not followed ethical journalistic practice. Her article was condemned by the prominent *Columbia Journalism Review* as the worst journalism of the year.[18]

Some people still defended Erdely's piece. They said, "Even if it didn't happen here, it's happening elsewhere." But here's the point: this is journalism asking a reader to be a raw conscience, unwoven from the truth. It's asking people to be outraged over something that didn't happen. A conscience is good. And rape is bad. (And rape does happen.) But by making wildly false accusations, Erdely actually hurt her conscience-raising cause. Now a true victim of on-campus rape may be more likely to be perceived as a girl who's just crying wolf.

Christian art can be guilty of turning people into mere goodness-receptors too. Some Christian artists and writers seem to believe that the Fall never happened and that people can be inspired to be good by viewing pictures or hearing stories in which only good things happen. Thomas Kinkade was the torch-bearer among painters for this sentimentalized view of the world. His paintings were idyllic, meaning they portray an idealized place where every light seems to shine extra bright and everybody is happy, happy, happy. Christian books, too, sometimes take a Pollyannaish view, which—like the best-selling 1913 novel *Pollyanna*—is simply naive about the extent of the Fall.

It's difficult to write a book in which goodness looks truly good, evil looks truly evil, and yet the evil doesn't defile the reader and the good doesn't make him feel like he's eaten too much sugar. The Bible does it (think of the Gospels). And that's the high calling of the Christian writer. The Bible sets an artistic standard or norm, not just a moral one.

The Moralist

GOODNESS

~~TRUTH~~

~~BEAUTY~~

"SENTIMENTALITY IS LOVING SOMETHING MORE THAN GOD DOES."[19]

—R. H. BLYTHE

What does time watching television rob a person of?

time for important things

Particular Lies and General Truths

One of the writers in the public square who (partially) defended the writer of the *Rolling Stone* article was the assistant editor of the University of Virginia student newspaper. Her basic argument was that even if that particular rape didn't happen, the fact that the story proved so believable to so many people was in itself suggestive of the culture at the University of Virginia. In other words, where were the people saying, "This is impossible! This sort of thing doesn't happen here! I know those people!"

Horowitz also used the same argument the Student Text does—that false stories make true ones less believable, overall hurting the chances of rape victims to receive justice. So it's hard to understand why Horowitz would say, "Ultimately, though, from where I sit in Charlottesville, to let fact checking define the narrative would be a huge mistake." [Julia Horowitz, "Why We Believed Jackie's Rape Story," *Politico* (website), December 6, 2014]

Horowitz wants people to be up in arms over rapes on campus (and they should be!)—she wants their goodness-receptors sounding the alarm. But fact checking (that is, the use of truth-receptors) has to define the narrative of the Erdely case, or it will end up doing harm to everyone actually involved. Making false accusations creates victims of a different sort. In addition, false stories about campus rape will lead to a public that may disbelieve future true stories about campus rape. Truth cannot be divorced from goodness, or goodness from truth.

Inexcusable Victimhood

In a fallen world, there will be actual victims of the sinful actions of others. Everyone has been sinned against by others, and many people—especially the weakest people—have been sinned against grievously. These facts, easily seen in Scripture, ought to stir the Christian conscience, and the Bible calls on us to oppose oppression; empty religiosity isn't the solution (Prov. 28:4; Isa. 1:10–17; Jer. 22:3). Wrongdoing must be made right; the repentant person will embrace the consequences to make things right (2 Cor. 7:10).

But people who falsely accuse others in order to achieve their own ends are not victims; they are wicked (Ps. 120:2; Prov. 21:6; 26:8). If there isn't anything truly offensive that someone objectively did wrong, then it's a damaging lie to claim that there is. That divorces truth from goodness by turning

---

Letters of J. R. R. Tolkein (Boston: Houghton Mifflin, 1981), letter 89] The story of this world is one of eucatastophe, a story in which God ultimately intervenes and brings great joy out of evil, suffering, and sorrow.

The Fallenness of Movies and Viewers

One pastor points out that when he watches a movie, he can tolerate a lot of violence and even a lot of profanity but has "zero tolerance for nudity." He explains, "There is a reason for these differences. The violence is make-believe. They don't really mean those bad words. But that lady is really naked, and I am really watching. And somewhere she has a brokenhearted father." [John Piper, "Why I Don't Have a Television and Rarely Go to Movies," *Desiring God* (website), June 25, 2009]

Consider reading to the class the whole article of humble pastoral advice. Discussion points could include the following.

Why does watching movies not make a Christian better able to address the needs of his culture?

If the films corrupt the Christian, he won't be able to help those in the culture who need gospel help, no matter how "relevant" he is.

Is Piper right to have a high tolerance for violence and bad language?

Regarding language, it is significant that what makes the language a problem in some cases is the fact that the speaker means little by it. It is a great sin to use God's name to mean nothing or to speak about serious matters, such as damnation and hell, as if they were meaningless.

people into pure consciences who don't have to check their feeling of offense against a standard of truth. And enforcers who don't check the matter against a standard of truth make themselves complicit (Prov. 18:13).

💻 Victim Culture, Microaggressions, and Truth, Goodness, and Beauty

Bona fide liberals Jonathan Haidt and Greg Lukianoff tell the story of a college student who was disciplined for reading a book with a picture on the cover that offended other students—even though the content of the book was not offensive. Lukianoff, in fact, is the president of the Foundation for Individual Rights in Education. He is no friend to Christianity, and neither is Jonathan Haidt, but both writers are classic liberals in the sense that they see the dangers of a public square free of all dissenting ideas. They believe in the marketplace of ideas, especially on college campuses.

Haidt and Lukianoff are alarmed by the way "social media makes it extraordinarily easy to join crusades, express solidarity and outrage, and shun traitors" (an anarchist mob lynching mentality). They note that even liberal professors are "scared to death" of their students' ability to shout them down and ruin their reputations:

What are the effects of this new protectiveness on the students themselves? Does it benefit the people it is supposed to help? What exactly are students learning when they spend four years or more in a community that polices unintentional slights, places warning labels on works of classic literature, and in many other ways conveys the sense that words can be forms of violence that require strict control by campus authorities, who are expected to act as both protectors and prosecutors?

Because there is a broad ban in academic circles on "blaming the victim," it is generally considered unacceptable to question the reasonableness (let alone the sincerity) of someone's emotional state, particularly if those emotions are linked to one's group identity. The thin argument "I'm offended" becomes an unbeatable trump card. This leads to what Jonathan Rauch, a contributing editor at this magazine, calls the "offendedness sweepstakes," in which opposing parties use claims of offense as cudgels. In the process, the bar for what we consider unacceptable speech is lowered further and further.

[Greg Lukianoff and Jonathan Haidt, "The Coddling of the American Mind," *The Atlantic* (website), September 2015]

The following articles are written from a Christian perspective and are also well worth digesting and discussing with students. They reinforce the idea that people cannot be pure consciences— goodness-receptors—without truth and beauty also playing a role.

- Carl Trueman, "Is Hurt Mail the New Hate Mail," Reformation 21 (website), July 2009.
- Tyler O'Neil, "How C. S. Lewis Predicted Today's College Campus Craziness—in 1944," *PJ Media* (website), December 1, 2015.

You may also want to read excerpts from C. S. Lewis's *The Abolition of Man* (New York: Harper One, 1944).

NOT JUST BEAUTY-RECEPTORS

On February 24, 1970, Mark Rothko was arguably America's most important living painter. On February 25, he was dead. His assistant found his body on the floor of his New York studio. After overdosing on antidepressants, the painter had committed suicide. Rothko, a brainy and articulate theoretician who wrote multiple articles discussing his artwork, left the world with no explanation. There was no note.

Rothko created paintings that the critics labeled "color field" paintings. After casting about unsuccessfully in modernist art, Rothko finally found his niche. He painted large patches of color on canvas. Mark Rothko was an ardent Marxist who felt like people in the 1950s and '60s were vacillating between the threat of the Cold War and consumerist distraction. In order to connect people with their humanity, he sought to give them deep emotional experiences. Instead of painting subjects, Rothko painted only areas of color on his canvases. Rothko said:

> I'm not an abstractionist. . . . I'm not interested in relationships of color or forms. . . . I'm interested only in expressing basic human emotions—tragedy, ecstasy, doom and so on—and the fact that lots of people break down and cry when confronted with my pictures shows I communicate those basic human emotions. . . . The people who weep before my pictures are having the same religious experience I had when I painted them.[20]

One art critic said that if there is a spiritual dimension to Rothko's work, it is aestheticism—devotion to beauty (like Oscar Wilde).[21] These paintings were, in Rothko's view, color and texture harnessed to present raw emotion. Rothko flattened people into beauty-receptors, purely emotional beings. But beauty and emotions without truth are meaningless.

If you shuffle through his paintings, you notice that his palette choices become increasingly dark toward the end of his life. Many of his final paintings were charcoal-colored paint on black backgrounds.

Beauty without truth or goodness leads to its insignificance. As one *New York Times* art critic observed, "Beauty can attach itself to the sublime ([as in painters such as] Titian [and] Rembrandt) or to the merely decorative, and Rothko's pictures have always looked alarmingly good hanging over sofas in [New York City] apartments."[22]

As a Marxist, Rothko, took aim at capitalist consumerism, but even during his lifetime he couldn't protect his paintings from becoming another commodity to buy and sell. (His "Orange, Red, Yellow" sold for nearly $87 million in 2012.) And without truth, Mark Rothko could not direct his own emotions away from the darkness. His depression mirrored his paintings; deep feeling that wasn't *about* anything, just feeling for feeling's sake. Rothko ultimately left the world with nothing to say to us all.

WHY BOTHER?

Some readers of this book are called to be carpenters or mothers or salespeople, and it may not seem apparent to you why careful analysis and evaluation of the truth, goodness, and beauty in drama, art, and literature is worthwhile for you.

An Aesthetic Reminder

This is one of the most challenging portions of BIBLICAL WORLDVIEW: CREATION, FALL, REDEMPTION. Aesthetics is a demanding topic despite the role beauty plays in the daily life of every one of us. We find it difficult to put into words something that we experience in another vein (i.e., in sights, sounds, smells, and feelings).

"To believe in God involves accepting him as the sovereign perfection, not only of truth and goodness but also of beauty, thus establishing the highest possible conception of excellence." [Clyde Kilby, *Christianity and Aesthetics* (Chicago: InterVarsity, 1961), 22]

"The Bible comes to us in an artistic form which is often sublime, rather than as a document of practical, expository prose, strict in outline like a textbook. . . . We do not

But think about it: carpenters, mothers, and salespeople are all creators. Your creations will shape the people those creations touch. This may be most obvious for mothers: the family culture—of food, of bedtime rituals, of cleanliness—that you create will shape your children. What you make of your world will be their world, their entire world. Will it be a world of truth, goodness, and beauty?

Or will you shape your children (or your customers) with a stunted or idolatrous view of the world?

THINKING IT THROUGH 26.2

1. What part of a human receives truth, goodness, and beauty?

2. What's wrong with making the explicit realism of evil into a virtue by "transparently telling the hard truth"?

3. What's wrong with crusading for some good cause if the crusade isn't rooted in the truth?

4. What is the end result of an artist creating something beautiful while ignoring truth and goodness?

♀5. Why is analysis of the arts and culture important for everybody?

26.3 POP GOES THE CULTURE

So far in this chapter on fallen culture and arts, we've analyzed (1) a few offerings of high culture that most people your age don't care about and (2) a few plays that your parents won't let you see anyway. But now we'll use the concepts we discussed—truth, goodness, and beauty—and apply them to the cultural artifacts you actually like (or are *tempted* to like). Let's talk about pop culture.

Popular culture is the commercially driven culture of media and entertainment shaped by the tastes of ordinary people. It is "a culture of diversion" driven by novelty.[23] Pop culture is whatever sells. That doesn't mean it's all bad; it depends on the quality of the culture doing the buying.

If you think this section is going to be a rant about sex, language, and violence on TV, you're about 2 percent right. Somebody needs to rant; Christians just *can't* make peace with a popular culture that entertains people with sins Jesus died to eradicate, or our Christianity offers nothing to anyone. There was a time in American culture, at least, when conservative Christians generally said a unified "no" to vulgar movies and music, but no longer. As Andy Crouch, the evangelical Christian leader we quoted in Chapters 5 and 8, has said, "Evangelical Christians . . . seem to be more avidly consuming the latest offerings of commercial culture, whether *Pirates of the Caribbean* or *The Simpsons* or *The Sopranos*, than many of my non-Christian neighbors."[24]

Attacks on truth, goodness, and beauty are attacks against the God who created them; so the content of the songs, films, magazines, books, and shows of popular culture really does *matter*. And the fact that Christians are consuming as much or more popular culture than their non-Christian neighbors isn't just problematic or unwise. It's sin. Have you ever in your life stopped watching a movie or listening to a song, not because your parents commanded you to but because God did?

Why Bother?

Ask students to try to guess at the relevance of this Student Text material for their own future callings. Try to get them to express for themselves the reason why an understanding of beauty, of culture, and of the arts will be important to their calling as created individuals and as the church of the next generation. For example, someone interested in marketing and advertising may begin to grasp how beauty and truth and goodness have to work together for his work to be something more than mere artful manipulation. A future factory worker may begin to grasp how the arts can be an important means of sanity in a difficult job. A future farmer may begin to grasp how beauty must play a role in plans as a future business owner. A future teacher may begin to see how there are more avenues into a student's soul than lesson objectives, that beauty and goodness can and must play their roles in the shaping of young minds.

THINKING IT THROUGH 26.2

1. The whole unity of the inner person: mind, will, and emotions

2. It ignores goodness and beauty—the redemptive and sanctifying work of God's grace in the world.

3. Falsehood undermines a just cause.

4. Even though an element itself might be beautiful, the end product is warped into something that is detached from significance or goodness.

♀5. Regardless of occupation, all people are made in God's image to be creative cultivators of God's creation, shaping a world of truth, goodness, and beauty.

have truth and beauty [alone in the Bible], or truth decorated with beauty, or truth illustrated by the beautiful phrase, or truth in a 'beautiful setting.' Truth and beauty are in the Scriptures, as indeed they must always be, an inseparable unity." [Kilby, *Christianity and Aesthetics*, 19, 21]

In other words, form and content may be distinguishable but are inseparable. God could have given us a list of propositions to believe:

1. God created the heavens and the earth.
2. In Adam's Fall, we sinned all.
3. Christ is fully God and fully man.
4. Christ died for our sins.
5. Go to church.

Or something like that but much longer!

But God didn't give us such a list. He gave us a beautiful book, which is really a set of beautiful books. The beauties are different. Some of them have the beauty of tightly reasoned argument (such as the letter to the Romans), others have the beauty of a vivid poetic imagination (such as Psalms), others have the beauty of intense invective (some of the prophets), or of compelling narrative (like the Joseph story), or of pithy sayings (like Proverbs), or of incisive and thought-provoking commentary (like Ecclesiastes).

This fact really is remarkable, perhaps especially given that these disparate aesthetic elements still unite to tell a single story of Creation, Fall, Redemption. The Qur'an is not like the Bible; it uses comparatively fewer literary genres and is nonlinear, like a web of disconnected sayings rather than a timeline or story.

SECTION OBJECTIVES 26.3

1. Judge which content is unacceptable for Christian consumption.

2. Summarize the sensibilities that pop culture produces within a culture.

3. Explain how pop culture powerfully reinforces a wrong definition of truth.

4. Explain how pop culture reinforces a wrong definition of what matters in the realm of goodness and beauty.

5. Explain that, while pop culture's sensibilities may be appealing, matured sensibilities are worthy of the effort in order to take dominion over God's world.

Taking Pop . . . Seriously?

Let's return to an analysis of a very popular pop song from Justin Bieber, "Purpose" (chosen because it was the title track on the number-one hottest album as of the moment of this writing, though that status will change numerous times before the first student ever reads this text). This time, instead of evaluating the content, we'll examine the sensibilities—the shaping of tastes.

Bieber's words are theologically inane, and yet they're uttered as if they're profoundly meaningful and personal, even intimate.

What does close, personal exposure to people who constantly utter inanities do to hearers—especially when such lyrics pretend to be theological? What effect does it have on listeners' own thinking, their own values? Pop music is about valuing the now and about getting instant gratification (frequently, but not always, sexual gratification). If Bieber's thoughts had any theological substance, they wouldn't be immediately accessible and couldn't be popular. They would offend the sensibilities of an audience shaped by pop music.

What does it say about a culture that it supports a multi-billion-dollar business dedicated to the proposition that people should love themselves enough to get pleasure now? What does it say about someone that he or she spends significant amounts of money (which can be replaced) and time (which can't) on inanity? These are the sensibilities that pop culture irrefutably cultivates, whether in music, movies, or magazines.

This is not to say, again, that there is no structure in pop—it relies heavily on the created structures of the world, most especially the potentials of music and the human voice. These remain good things. But they are twisted into the service of values that aren't lasting.

Sensibilities and Content

Digging deeper to sensibilities doesn't mean we can safely watch wicked content as long as we have sufficient analytical tools to defend ourselves against bad sensibilities. Some Christians begin to feel that they're smart enough after their biblical worldview training to "handle" objectionable elements because they feel they have achieved a safe critical distance. There is such a thing, but the Fall is ever present both in cultural artifacts and in consumers of culture. The point that we're making in this section is that even among the pop-culture shows, songs, movies, and scores that are free of overtly wicked content, there's still a danger for Christians. There is good as well. There is structure, and there is direction within popular culture.

SENSIBILITIES

So that was your 2 percent, and we're done with critiques of content. Christians need to dig deeper than the level of content, down to the level of **sensibilities**—your ability (or inability) to appreciate some artistic or cultural work, your affections and expectations when it comes to art and culture. Listen again to this comment from another Christian leader you read in Chapter 8:

> I rarely meet the young Christian who needs to be exhorted to engage their culture. They seem to consume what everybody consumes, and are in general agreement with the zeitgeist that a steady stream of entertainment is the Fifth Freedom that our forefathers fought for.[25]

Zeitgeist refers to the spirit of the age, and in our age that spirit makes it not just a right but practically a duty for people to consume the products of pop culture at every available moment. It's top-forty radio in the morning while getting ready, streaming music in the car, TV after school, YouTube and games (or both at the same time) after dinner, and a Netflix binge on the weekend. And your peers expect you to sing along with the top hits and spout the latest catch-phrases. Just listen to how people at school talk, all the way down to the kindergarteners. Pop culture will come up *a lot*. It has become something of a shared religion, the one experience most people in America can relate to.

Some reviewers complained that Emma Thompson was too old to play Elinor Dashwood in *Sense and Sensibility*, but they failed to level the same complaint at her male co-star.

Maybe at your house it's Christian radio, Christian music, Christian TV, God-Tube, and a David and Goliath video game. The content may be different (and that's a step in the right direction), but the sensibilities formed are the same: you begin to expect to be entertained all the time. You don't develop the patience necessary to be rewarded by more difficult artistic forms like painting and poetry and literature. You're never just quiet. Your mind wanders when you read. And you think kids who make it through three years of piano lessons ought to get a medal or something.

A life full of diversion that focuses on immediate pleasure and whatever's cool is not a life of truth, goodness, and beauty. Let's bring out CFR again: diversion is good, and so is immediate pleasure—but not when they're twisted and inflated to fill your life, crowding out better things.

THE POWER OF CULTURE

"The power of culture is the power to define reality,"[26] says Christian sociologist James Davison Hunter. In Chapter 5 we quoted Andy Crouch's observation that culture defines "the horizons of the possible."[27] Your expectations and assumptions and sensibilities are molded largely by the culture you land in as an infant. "All [cultural] institutions are character shaping," says Hunter. And "today, entertainment [is] especially important."[28] The high culture and the pop culture

Neither can be forgotten. Reactionaries have forgotten the structure; permissivists have forgotten the direction. If this book emphasizes the fallen direction at the expense of the created structure, it's because we "rarely meet the young Christian who needs to be exhorted to engage their culture." Very few young people (though they do exist) are unwilling to recognize the good in pop culture, but countless Christian students are unwilling to recognize the bad.

Horizons of the Possible

Ask students to pick one cultural artifact they value and then answer each of the following five questions from Andy Crouch:

If we want to understand culture, then, it's always best to begin and end with specific cultural goods. I've found five questions to be particularly helpful in understanding how a particular artifact fits into its broader cultural story. The first two questions arise from culture's meaning-making function—culture's role in making sense of the world. (1) What does this cultural artifact assume about the way the world is? What are the key features of the world that this cultural artifact tries to deal with, respond to, make sense of? (2) What does this cultural artifact assume about

you "consume" both shape your character. But the high culture stuff typically isn't playing in the background at the mall and isn't getting shared by your friends online. Pop culture is influential if only because it's everywhere. Is it shaping your reality with the truth?

Actress Emma Thompson spent five years writing the screenplay for a movie adaptation of Jane Austen's classic novel *Sense and Sensibility*. It became one of her biggest hits, but some reviewers complained that she was too old for the role of Elinor Dashwood. At thirty-five, she was indeed a good deal older than the nineteen-year-old Elinor in the original story. But oddly enough, no one seemed to have the same complaint about Thompson's male love interest in the film, who in the book was twenty-three but in the movie was played by an actor (Hugh Grant) the same age as Thompson.

The arts both reflect and enforce a cultural narrative in which women are supposed to live up to certain youthful ideals. These ideals, good or bad, affect the sensibilities of the viewers.

Have you ever noticed that pictures of Eve painted in the 1500s to the 1800s make her look, well, a little fat by contemporary standards? In Albrecht Dürer's five-hundred-year-old woodcuts, she's positively corpulent.* But Eve lost a good deal of weight in the twentieth century, as any recent kids' Bible storybook will show.

corpulent: *very large; overweight*

Maybe you've seen one of those videos that demonstrates how Photoshop can be used to alter a woman's picture. Something is wrong with the sensibilities of a culture in which photos of the women admired as truly attractive are doctored by computers.

Television isn't the sole reason that the ideal of feminine beauty has changed over time. We could point to a complex of factors. But what does it do to a culture's sensibilities when its TV shows and movies almost never feature unattractive people—except when gawking at a hoarder or one of the "biggest losers" is the whole point of the show?

Watching one TV show won't make you believe that all dads are stupid and premarital sex has no consequences. And pop culture in the West isn't all lies. But even "reality" TV is heavily edited by producers to tell stories and make points that shouldn't be taken as gospel. Pop culture "ain't necessarily so." It isn't all true. It isn't all good, and it can skew your view of (feminine) beauty.

Your Best Life Now

Christian culture watcher Ken Myers has a great deal of wisdom to offer in his book *All God's Children and Blue Suede Shoes: Christians and Popular Culture*, a book that thinking Christians can profit from. One of his most penetrating insights is that popular culture lulls us into thinking that we can have everything worth having immediately. If you've got the cash (or a credit card that's not maxed out) along with the self-confidence and sex appeal that come from using the right products, then there's no need to delay until you're more mature, wiser, or more perceptive to experience the feelings, think the thoughts, or imagine the fantasies you desire. "There is no distance between you and any good thing."[29]

Pop culture, then, offers a drastically limited definition of good—because, in its view, anything that takes a massive time investment isn't good, or (at least) isn't a good worth having for most people.

And where is the *goodness of God* in American popular culture? Once again, let's set aside content (like the way God gets mocked and cursed on the TV show *South*

the way the world should be? What vision of the future animated its creators? What new sense does it seek to add to a world that often seems chaotic and senseless? Then come two questions that acknowledge culture's extraordinary power to shape the horizons of possibility. (3) What does this cultural artifact make possible? What can people do or imagine, thanks to this artifact, that they could not before? Conversely, (4) what does this cultural artifact make impossible (or at least very difficult)? What activities and experiences that were previously part of the human experience become all but impossible in the wake of this new thing? Often this is the most interesting question of all, especially because so much technological culture is presented exclusively in terms of what

it will make possible. Yet few cultural artifacts serve only to move the horizons of possibility outward and leave the horizons of impossibility unchanged. Almost every cultural artifact, in small or large ways, makes something impossible— or at least more difficult— that was possible before. Finally, because culture inevitably begets more culture, we have to look at the effect of this artifact on future culture. (5) What new forms of culture are created in response to this artifact? What is cultivated and created that could not have been before?

[Andy Crouch, *Culture Making: Recovering Our Creative Calling* (Downers Grove, IL: InterVarsity Press, 2008), 29–30]

Sharing Your Own Testimony

As a teacher, can you give a personal testimony as an adult to the effort and time and maturity it took for you to appreciate something you now love but didn't always? A particular composer, artist, writer, newspaper editorial page—anything? It may be beneficial for your students.

Ugly Women on American Television

Brazilian television isn't the only place where unattractive women are not permitted (they're only allowed in certain narrowly defined circumstances or to make a statement). In American TV, too, unattractive people—especially women—are generally kept out of sight. Even extras are thin, dressed to a T, and have great hair. This phenomenon can be witnessed in the fact that even the "ugly" female characters on certain popular shows are not, in fact, ugly. These shows are not recommended viewing (and this writer has admittedly never seen them), but several writers pointed to Liz Lemon of *30 Rock*, played by Tina Fey, who is repeatedly referred to as "ugly" on the show. "The thing is, Tina Fey fits conventional standards of female beauty almost to a T." [Chloe Angyal, "Pretty Ugly: Can We Please Stop Pretending That Beautiful Women Aren't Beautiful," Feminist Sting (website), 2010]

The author of that comment was writing on a feminist blog, and this is one occasion when conservative Christians and certain feminists have something profound to agree on: American culture's standards for female beauty are unrealistic and even harmful, sometimes leading to anorexia/bulimia or more commonly to a great deal of agnst and fear in many truly beautiful women who are made in the image of God.

Men suffer from the same treatment, though probably not to the same degree. One writer pointed out that, in general, British shows that are remade for American audiences (such as *The Office*) are stocked with female and male characters who are much more attractive than their British counterparts. Men are taller and more striking. The writer noted, however, that this doesn't always fit the show. In this case, American devotion to good looks undercuts what's really central to a good story: plot and character.

[Seth Stevenson, "Life on Mars," *Slate* (website), January 19, 2010]

Subtly Informing Sensibilities

Here's is an illustration of the subtle way pop culture informs sensibilities and determines the horizons of the impossible. A Christian blogger posted this:

My wife and I do allow our children to watch some TV, but we often feel vaguely guilty about it, even though we're super careful in what and how much they watch. Here's one reason why we feel that guilt: my five-year-old son was watching his then favorite cartoon, a preschool version of *Transformers* about a set of rescue robots that live on Griffin Rock, an island town, and most nights he would request that his bedtime story for the evening feature a certain subset of those characters. He would carefully pick out certain ones that had to be in the story I was about to tell, and maybe toss in an archnemesis or two that they had to thwart that night.

One evening I made up a story about how it was raining glue and the Transformers were asked to stop the glue and clean up the mess. Maybe, someone suggested, these rescue robots could make it rain? "Only God can make it rain," replied one of the Transformers—I said. My little son immediately interjected, "There's no God in *Transformers*!" I informed my firstborn that I couldn't tell a story in which God wasn't allowed. He wouldn't hear of it. He was very insistent. We hit an impasse, and I can't remember how I solved it, or if I did! We may have had to call in Mom's wisdom.

I promise this preschool show had never once said, "Repeat after us *Transformers* kids: 'There is no God.'" But after thirty or so episodes in which God and His Word are never consulted for answers, and in which God is never thanked for rescues, my son got the message very clearly: *Transformers* is a secular world, a world where God and religion are not permitted. I checked, and there are churches on the cityscape in the background in some of the shots used in that cartoon. But in a secular place like Griffin Rock, religion isn't ever encouraged, or even allowed, to come out of the buildings it's stuck in.

The assumption is that religion obtrudes, that it doesn't belong out in the public square, that it really ought to stay private—that assumption is more often implicit than explicit. It's just in

the air. Without ever being told in so many words that God doesn't belong, the fact that He's never invited is itself a message that people get loud and clear. And as soon as you push the boundaries of this assumption that God doesn't belong, people will pop up and object like my five-year-old did.

I'm not whining, however, just observing. And I do not think I have uncovered some conspiracy; I don't believe that the secularism of Griffin Rock was fully purposeful. Stories people tell reflect their worldviews, that's all.

[Mark Ward, "There's No God in Transformers!" By Faith We Understand (blog), November 28, 2015]

Eurocentric Examples?

Nearly all the specific praise for cultural artifacts in the Student Text is goes to products of the Western cultural tradition. That is for two reasons: (1) the writers of the book are Western and know Western culture in a way they simply don't know other cultures, and (2) the Western tradition is the only major world culture that has been deeply impacted by the gospel—though the gospel is certainly not its only major influence.

Efforts to displace the Western canon in humanities programs in US universities are so misguided as to be wrong. But the effort to include things of value from other cultures is praiseworthy—as long as the cultural artifacts selected are themselves praiseworthy.

Park) and let's think again about the sensibilities pop culture tends to form. Pop culture doesn't blaspheme God as much as it ignores Him. Living in a pop culture world forms a sensibility, a pervading sense that God doesn't really matter, that someone can live just fine without Him. God does get trotted out to approve of NASCAR races—but then He gets shoved back in His box as soon as the opening prayer is done. The world of pop culture is a secular one where it's assumed we can all, as John Lennon famously sang, "imagine there's no heaven."[30]

And what about the good of heaven itself—if there's no distance between us and any good thing? Jesus said, "The way is hard that leads to life" (Matt. 7:14). So why bother?

Soon, your parents may not have any direct influence over what pop culture you take in. Whether they have been permissive or strict, before too long you're going to have to decide for yourself what role popular culture will play in your life—and in your kids' lives.

One silly pop song, an episode of a sitcom, or a YouTube video won't turn you or your future kids into atheists, but a steady diet will give your sensibilities an atheistic shape. Rather than asking yourself, "What's wrong with this movie/song/show?" ask yourself, "What's right with this?" In other words, "How will exposing myself to this bit of culture help me achieve Christian goals for my life?" Your choices in life aren't always going to be between good and evil but will sometimes involve deciding between what's permissible and what's best. Myers says, "Popular culture . . . specializes in instant gratification. But like most instant things, it may spoil your taste for something better."[31]

High culture, ideally, offers something better, but high culture is still a mixture of good and bad just like pop culture is. But one thing you can say about "the best which has been thought and said"[32] in high culture is that it often stretches you in ways you can't appreciate until after the stretching operation. It takes the purposeful cultivation of your sensibilities, not just passive exposure, to be able to enjoy it. You can't help admiring someone who stuck with piano lessons and now clearly relishes the music he or she has become capable of producing. But the only way you can have that good thing is by recognizing that there's a big distance between you and it, and patiently taking a step or two in that direction each day.

> *"Pop music, largely created by and for commercial purposes, resists serious analysis. . . . Commerce, then, has an enormous interest in our not taking such questions seriously."*[34]
>
> —T. DAVID GORDON

Soaking and Vegging

Everybody's busy. We're tired. We turn to TV or movies because we want to veg, "to relax to the point of complete inertia."[33] And not just physically but mentally. We don't want to have to critically analyze and evaluate; we just want to soak. It takes effort to probe beneath the surface of your entertainment.

Don't soak or veg. (Soaked vegetables tend to get corpulent.) Analyze, using truth, goodness, and beauty. Ask questions like these: Is it true that sports are worth what Americans pay to watch them? Is it good that American news programs focus so much on celebrities? Is the singing on the latest competition show truly *beautiful*?

True, good, beautiful art is worth a lifetime of practice and study. Bad art is simply not worth spending your life on. And neither is mere diversion. The billions of hours Americans spend on it every year isn't *true*. It doesn't give an accurate picture of what diversion is worth and what human lives are for. Diversion *is* worth something: "Popular culture . . . is a part of the created order, part of the earth that is the Lord's, and thus something capable of bringing innocent pleasure to believers," says Ken Myers. "But not everything that is permissible is constructive."[36]

> *"WHO IS SLAIN WHEN TIME IS KILLED?"* [35]
>
> —ERNEST VAN DEN HAAG

What, after all, are you trying to construct in your life? What's your goal? To make it to death without too much pain? Or to lay up treasures in heaven, treasures no moth or rust can ever get to, treasures that will pay out interest for eternity? Good art is entertaining, but it isn't mere diversion—just killing time. It forms the sensibilities in you that are necessary for good dominion over God's world. We are not called to inertia.

THE THINGS WE DELIGHT IN

The stories about early Scottish missionary John G. Paton are amazing—both the stories of failure and of success. On the South Pacific island of Tanna, the cannibals went along with some of Paton's instructions for a while. But they finally drove him off the island, and he was rescued by a ship just in time. The natives of Tanna explained to Paton why they hated him so much:

> We have taken everything your house contained, and would take you too if we could; for we hate the Worship, it causes all our diseases and deaths; it goes against our customs, and it condemns the things we delight in.[37]

The Bible condemns many things American popular culture delights in. It condemns the unspoken assumption of pop culture that a life of diversion and novelty is a good life in the first place. Ken Myers says that attempting to free ourselves from enslavement to pop culture's sensibilities doesn't mean we have to become ascetics, but it does mean that we should get more rather than less out of our experience of culture, namely more of what's true, honorable, just, pure, lovely, and commendable.[38]

There are so many true, good, and beautiful pieces of art, music, and literature available, especially in the Western tradition, and for English-speakers. The category of things that are "true, honorable, just, pure, lovely, commendable, excellent, and praiseworthy" (Phil. 4:8) is not a small one. Whatever you give up to gain these things will not really be a sacrifice.

The 1997 film *Titanic* was one of the most lucrative cinematic productions ever made. Drawing its storyline from one of the twentieth century's most famous events, the movie features beautiful cinematography and beautiful people. It catapulted at least one member of the cast, Leonardo DiCaprio, to international stardom.

The gist of the story is that a young artist saves his rich female counterpart from an arranged marriage. The two unmarried characters commit immorality. The heroine

Film Criticism Up Close

See if you can get a real-live film critic to come speak to your class, perhaps someone from your local newspaper. Such people still exist. Here are some suggested questions to ask the critic:

- What makes your film-watching different from that of the average moviegoer?
- What do you think about the Carl Sandburg quote about movies on page 396?
- What do you think of preachy movies?
- Are you ever surprised that Christians go to or praise a particular movie?

Exemplars of Philippians 4:8

Ask students to write out Philippians 4:8 at the top of a sheet of paper and then proceed to match each of the six adjectives in the list with one film, piece of music, or work of art they're familiar with. Ask them to write out a brief explanation (no more than one paragraph) for each choice. For example, the adjective *true* might refer to *Citizen Kane* because the movie displays the folly of selfish ambition, and *honorable* might go to *Mrs. Miniver* because it shows how British housewives in wartime Britain of the 1940s could contribute to the war effort with honor. *Pure* might be associated with a novel, *lovely* with a Bach piece, and *commendable* with any number of cultural artifacts.

Reading Assignment

Ken Myers' *All God's Children and Blue Suede Shoes* has made numerous appearances in this unit and for good reason—it's packed with insight. If you can get students to read the two introductions (the original and the 2012 introduction), they may come away both with excellent questions and with a desire to keep reading.

The Things We Delight In

It's impossible to anticipate every reaction (and nonreaction) students will have to BIBLICAL WORLDVIEW: CREATION, FALL, REDEMPTION, but most likely there will be students who are put off by this chapter on fallen culture. It's demanding in two senses: it discusses intellectually demanding topics, and it demands that students examine the things they themselves delight in. You should pray—as the authors of this course have—that students will, by God's grace and through the influence of His Spirit, really listen to any genuine wisdom contained in this chapter.

1. because both pop culture's content and sensibilities are often contrary to the Christian worldview

2. the sensibilities that are being shaped— your ability or inability to appreciate an artistic work because of expectations and affections that have been formed

3. It has the power to define your perception of reality and the plausibility structures that define how you live.

4. Pop culture demands a mass audience; thus it tends toward instant gratification rather than producing goods that require investments of time and thought.

♀5. because the criticisms often condemn what they love and delight in

---

survives the marine catastrophe, but the hero dies. The director, James Cameron, sets before the audience a "savior," whose affection for a young woman impels him to rescue her relationally and physically.

Part of the message seems to be that precluding a conventional but unwanted marriage is reason enough to take moral liberties. In fact, *Titanic* offers an inadequate salvation and does so in God-condemned fashion. The sexually immoral who do not repent cannot inherit the kingdom of God (1 Cor. 6:9). This wildly successful film romanticizes a teenage affair in a way that pits beauty against truth and goodness. It strives to capitalize on a disharmony between our emotions, our ethics, and our intellect. Such an endeavor should make us feel the way we do when we look at a false equation: $2 + 2 = 5$. Cameron's movie may have been cinematically impressive, but its morally inverted storyline should seem just as dangerous as basing one's checking account on faulty arithmetic.

1. Why can't Christians just make peace with pop culture?

2. In addition to content, what else should Christians be aware of when analyzing culture and the arts?

3. Why is culture so powerful?

4. Why does pop culture offer a drastically limited definition of goodness?

♀5. Why do people tend to react negatively to any criticism of their consumption of pop culture?

26 CHAPTER REVIEW

TERMS TO REMEMBER

romanticism
popular culture
sensibilities

Scripture Memory

2 Thessalonians 2:11

Making Connections

1. What major event damaged God's tapestry of the world, making it necessary to critique artistic and cultural creations?

2. What's ultimately being attacked when truth, goodness, and beauty are unraveled?

3. What three components of human nature, woven together to make us who we are, should never be separated into isolated compartments?

4. What drives popular culture?

Developing Skills in Apologetics and Worldview

5. How would you describe the dangers of cultivating exclusive pop culture sensibilities?

6. How would you respond to someone who argued that as long as Christians are communicating truth, aesthetic considerations don't matter?

Examining Assumptions and Evidence

7. Christians can't avoid sin in a fallen world—it's already inside them; so why bother avoiding fallen elements of human culture?

8. What is it about the medium of film that makes preaching the gospel through a movie difficult?

9. Why are sensibilities important to evaluate in addition to the actual content of an artistic product?

10. Name one thing about high culture sensibilities that is morally superior to the sensibilities typically formed by popular culture.

Becoming a Creative Cultivator

11. Create a chart with three questions across the top: Is this cultural product true? Is it good? Is it beautiful? List down the side five specific cultural artifacts from a variety of artistic media (movies, literature, painting, music, etc.).

   • Check each box in which the artifact conforms to standards of truth, goodness, and beauty.

   • Below the chart, provide a brief sentence or two defending your choices for each of the five.

   • If the class evaluates the same five artifacts, discuss why your answers differ from those of your classmates.

CHAPTER REVIEW ANSWERS

Making Connections

1. the Fall

2. God's own character, which is imprinted on His creation

3. mind (truth), will (goodness), and emotions (beauty)

4. It's commercially driven.

Developing Skills in Apologetics and Worldview

5. The sensibilities of pop culture tend toward the ephemeral, the immediate, and the banal. Christianity is about eternal, significant realities. To grow as a Christian requires discipline and effort. The sensibilities of pop culture are thus opposed to Christian maturity.

6. Just as it's wrong to justify sinful elements in a work of art based on aesthetic quality, it's not good to justify aesthetic junk just because it's free of sinful elements. Truth, goodness, and beauty are all important.

Examining Assumptions and Evidence

7. God has commanded Christians to grow in maturity, which is evidenced in saying no to the flesh and to temptations from the world. He has given us standards of truth, goodness, and beauty that we are obligated to discern, turning away from what is evil.

8. Propositional explanations rarely work well in movies, which are meant to illustrate rather than explain complex truths. God's chosen medium for communicating the gospel is the expositional preaching of the Word.

9. Every time a person consumes a cultural product, he's shaping his affections/delights to expect and to be appealed to by a certain category of artistic consumption.

10. High cultural sensibilities have to be cultivated so that affections and tastes are developed toward more quality and maturity and so that your own creative cultivation can produce something of substance.

Becoming Creative Cultivators

11. Answers will vary.

TERMS TO REMEMBER

romanticism—a view of art that prizes intense emotion, often resulting in sensualism, eroticism, and anti-intellectualism

popular culture—culture that results from quickly spreading mainstream and widely marketed media for the purpose of immediate gratification and pleasure

sensibilities—your ability or inability to appreciate something because of your expectations and learned affections

The student will be able to

27.1 Summarize four possible responses to cultural artifacts and apply criteria for discerning which gesture is most appropriate.

27.2 Explain why the postures of creativity and cultivation should be the ultimate goals of Christians implementing a biblical worldview as they engage culture.

SECTION OBJECTIVES 27.1

1. Explain why discernment is necessary and how that wisdom can be gained.

2. Construct condemnations of some cultural artifacts or practices.

3. Construct critiques of some cultural artifacts or practices.

4. Evaluate the appropriateness of consuming some cultural artifacts.

5. Evaluate the appropriateness of copying some cultural artifacts.

Chapter Twenty-Seven **CREATIVE CULTIVATORS**

The Lord God took the man and put him in the garden of Eden to work it and keep it. | **Scripture Memory Genesis 2:15**

27.1 GESTURES & POSTURES

Babies aren't born knowing how to make all the gestures they need for day-to-day communication. In India, especially in Gujarat State, babies need to learn a little side-to-side head wobble you'll see all over the place. It means something like "yes" or "OK" or "good," depending on the context. The Western equivalent would be a head nod. [1]

If you want to communicate effortlessly with a Gujarati, you have to pick up this gesture, just like Gujarati babies do. And you have to know when to use it. As a gesture, the head wobble is good. As a posture, not so good—you don't just keep doing it and doing it. Likewise, the gesture of bowing in Japan is an important gesture to master, but it shouldn't become your permanent posture; you'll kill your back if you go around stooped like that all the time.

Christian thinker Andy Crouch has suggested that gestures and postures make a good analogy for Christian approaches to culture and the arts. He suggests four *c*'s that are appropriate gestures, but not good postures:

- Condemning culture
- Critiquing culture
- Consuming culture
- Copying culture

Sometimes you must *condemn* certain cultural artifacts.* That's the appropriate gesture toward child pornography, for example. But condemnation is not an appropriate posture—you can't condemn every **cultural artifact**. You have to *critique* some things, *consume* others, and maybe *copy* yet others.

Since you're an image-bearer tasked with dominion by your Creator, there are two postures you do need to make permanent, two more *c*'s: you need to *cultivate* and *create*. (But we'll talk about those in the next section.).

CHRISTIAN APPROACHES TO CULTURE

CONDEMN
CRITIQUE
CONSUME
COPY
CULTIVATE
CREATE

cultural artifact: *almost anything made by a human being, embedded within a certain culture*

Lesson Plan Chart—Chapter 27

Section Title	Pages	Activity Manual	Days
27.1 Gestures and Postures	418–25	Activity 45	3 days
27.2 Creating and Cultivating	426–33		2 days
Review	434		1 day
Total Suggested Days			**6 days**

Culture Making

Much of this chapter is based on Andy Crouch's book *Culture Making: Recovering Our Creative Calling* (Downers Grove, IL: InterVarsity, 2008). He's the originator of the six gestures/postures, and his book contains real wisdom for students who want to be creative cultivators, but his work also needs to be read with discernment. For example, his dismissal of a straightforward reading of Genesis 1–3 undermines the foundation of a Christian worldview.

Gray Areas?

Assign students to debate the following two questions:

Do gray areas exist?

The idea of gray areas is often misused in a world that supposes no one can objectively

MATURE DISCERNMENT

You're more than old enough to recognize that there is a gray area between the good stuff and the bad stuff in culture and the arts.

- Some cultural artifacts are truly excellent, totally worth your time. The "classics" in art, literature, and music generally achieved that status because so many people over time have considered them to be worthwhile.
- Some products of human culture are less valuable but still worthy. You might read a sci-fi trilogy or watch a Hercule Poirot mystery for the fun of it.
- And some cultural artifacts may be righteous choices for someone else but not for you—or not now. Some of the significant works of the twentieth century—such as *Brave New World* or *1984*—shouldn't be read by high schoolers for the fun of it. They contain sexual and other themes that shouldn't provide entertainment for Christians. And yet these writings are significant enough in Western thought that some Christians believe that they ought to read them with a guarded heart. Other Christians, knowing the weakness of their flesh, know that they ought not to read such works, whatever value they might have. Scripture recognizes that godly Christians, knowing their own hearts, can make different, but correct, choices (1 Cor. 9:1–22; Rom. 14:5).

Choosing among available cultural options in our consumer society can be difficult or even overwhelming. Being a Christian in the modern West involves having to make some tough calls about culture. And you'll never be able to make those tough calls if you won't make the easy ones. **Discernment** is gained through a process of training:

> Solid food is for the mature, for those who have their powers of discernment trained by constant practice to distinguish good from evil. (Heb. 5:14)

And that training is not something you do by yourself. The Bible calls on young people to gain wisdom by listening to their elders (Prov. 2:1–2), by searching for truth like you would for buried treasure (2:3–5), and by becoming the sort of person God grants wisdom to (2:6–7). You're also called to be part of a church community that helps you—and puts pressure on you—to make wise choices (Heb. 10:24; Matt. 18:19–20).

When (by the wisdom of God through His Word and His people) you spot evil, your obligation is clear: you've got to condemn it. But the Bible not only calls you to spot evil and avoid it but also *to discern the good and pursue it.* Peter says that "whoever desires to love life and see good days" (is that you?) should not only "turn away from evil" but also "do good" (1 Pet. 3:10–11).

APROPOS RESPONSES

So don't hear the previous chapter ("The False, the Bad, and the Ugly") as a call to pull out of all the joys of human culture. Music is fundamentally *good*, a gift of God. Painting is good. Journalism is good. Architecture, novel-writing, cinematic production, literary criticism—every legitimate vocation that arises out of the human need to make something of our world (Gen. 1:28) is fundamentally good. Enjoy them. Use them. Create new things yourself within the tradition of your calling. The Bible calls you to get more out of your cultural life, not less—as Ken Myers said—"at least more that is true, noble, right, pure, lovely, and admirable."[2]

discern right and wrong. However, the idea of gray areas can be legitimately used in recognition of the fact that God-fearing Christians who are pursuing sanctification and eschewing worldliness may disagree about the specific applications of the principles that they share. In the context of disputable matters, Scripture advises Christians to charitably allow for differences among themselves, knowing that only God can be the ultimate judge (Rom. 14:5; 1 Cor. 4:4).

If so, how should a gray area be discerned?

Examine why there's a disagreement instead of just assuming that the issue is relative. Is there a source of authority other than divine revelation in play? Is there an unbiblical theology or philosophy at work? Is there a disconnect between beliefs and behavior? Is there disagreement about the interpretation a specific passage of Scripture? If the answer is yes to any of the questions except the last one, then this is not simply a gray area. If there is a disagreement about the interpretation of Scripture, the issue may or may not be gray depending on the clarity of the passage. If an area is gray, Christians should do what is edifying to others, making sure they aren't causing others to sin against their own conscience (1 Cor. 6:12; 8:9).

Maturity and Discernment

Gray areas can also be navigated by recognizing different levels of maturity in different situations. In one context, making use of the cultural artifact would be unwise. But in a different context, with a higher level of maturity, the cultural artifact is acceptable. Parents recognize this factor all the time when they refuse to let their preschoolers participate in things that they or their older children can participate in.

Discernment must not be disconnected from the moral character of knowledge. No knowledge is neutral (see pages 19–20). Christians can't merely consume cultural artifacts as if they're just doing it to become more knowledgable about their culture without any moral effects. In addition, Christians who engage with culture must guard against excusing consumption of wicked culture with the rationalization that they need to better understand the culture they're engaging. The heart is deceitful.

Beside that, the worldview challenges that Christians face are present not only in entertainment that promotes sensuality, graphic violence, or blasphemy. All cultural productions are produced from someone's worldview. Even seemingly light entertainment expresses ideas and values from a worldview. Encourage students to move beyond consumption of entertainment. Encourage them to evaluate the worldviews that stand behind their entertainments. They may even need to examine the assumption that free time is simply time for entertainment.

Putting Off and Putting On

Ask your students a question that they should answer silently: "When was the last time you chose not to consume a particular cultural artifact precisely because of your own fallenness, or even immaturity?" Encourage them, if they can't recall making this choice numerous times, to begin taking the reality of the Fall and its effect on their hearts and the culture around them more seriously.

There is also a corollary question. Ask students to recall the last time they replaced consumption of sinful culture with some good cultural endeavor. Have they ever purposefully picked up a good book in place of a sinful one? Have they ever turned off a movie in disgust and decided to make a better one? What among their daily cultural fare is true? Are the celebrity click-bait articles *true*? Are the songs in their earbuds *noble* or *honorable*? Are the news shows they watch *right*? Are the quotes and funny images they share on Facebook or Snapchat *pure*? Are they *lovely*? What is there in your students' cultural lives that is in any way *admirable*? Urge them not to merely drop the cultural artifacts and practices that violate these biblical norms but to pick up cultural artifacts and practices that meet them.

Thirst for Relevance

Many Christians want to win the culture back to a Christian worldview. They believe that to win the culture, they must attract the culture. To attract the culture, they must be relevant to the culture. To be relevant, they can't condemn or critique it—they must consume and copy it. But this is a failed strategy. It actually makes Christians irrelevant.

Jedd Medefind argues that Christians need to trade in their quest for relevance for prophetic boldness—faithfully standing for righteousness: "The relevant person is simply the one skilled at echoing back to society the things it most values." [Jedd Medefind, "What the World Needs Most Is Not Our Relevance," *Comment* (website), June 1, 2010] But if society's values are formed by an anti-God world system (Eph. 2:1–3; 4:17–20), should we be mirroring those values? "Love of relevance can blind us to things we ought to critique and numb us to things from which we ought to recoil" (Medefind). And why does the world need to be offered something from us that it already has? That makes us irrelevant.

The biblical alternative Medefind advocates is to exchange attempts to be relevant for a prophetic role—speaking to the heart of cultural matters based on a transcendent standard even if it means that the culture lashes back (e.g., the prophet Jeremiah):

> Virtually every moment in which Christians blazed to God's glory came as they accepted a prophetic role over mere relevance: calling for an end to the barbarism of Rome's gladiator bloodfests; nailing ninety-five theses to the Wittenberg doors; pushing tirelessly against the British slave trade; maintaining steadfast Christian witness behind the Iron Curtain. . . . Looking back at historical mountaintops helps us see the stakes in choosing between the prophetic and the merely relevant. But we are misled if we come to assume that we face no such decisions until we are placed before jeering crowds or firing squads. Most prophetic choices are, in fact, small ones. (Medefind)

This prophetic approach means that you stand for what's good, not just for that which stands a chance of success.

Christ and Culture Approaches

Have students choose one of the following journal articles (available for download from the Detroit Baptist Theological Seminary website). They should read the article and then write a one- to two-page summary and review of it.

Mark A. Snoeberger, "Noetic Sin, Neutrality, and Contextualization: How Culture Receives the Gospel," *Detroit Baptist Seminary Journal* 9, no. 1 (2004): 345–78.

Mark A. Snoeberger, "D. A. Carson's *Christ and Culture Revisited:* A Reflection and a Response," *Detroit Baptist Seminary Journal* 13, no. 1 (2008): 93–107.

Alternatively, read and digest the articles yourself, and then present to the students a summary of a good approach to Christ and culture. Understanding these articles is vital.

Is Culture Neutral?

Mark Driscoll, formerly pastor at Mars Hill Church, was known for identifying himself as "theologically conservative and culturally liberal." [*Confessions of a Reformission Rev.: Hard Lessons from an Emerging Missional Church* (Grand Rapids: Zondervan, 2006), 46.] "Culturally liberal" meant being generally affirming of popular culture and making constant references to it in his preaching. He confused people, he admitted, because he preached substantive messages from the Bible while maintaining this very positive stance toward popular culture (particularly that of the Seattle area where he was based). The author of a *Christianity Today* article on Driscoll observed that Driscoll's evangelistic methods utilized "a high degree of cultural assimilation." Driscoll defended himself in his interview with *Christianity Today* by saying that "culture is the house that people live in, and it just seems really mean to keep throwing rocks at somebody's house." [Collin Hansen, "Pastor Provocateur," *Christianity Today* (website), September 21, 2007]

Discuss this last quote with the class after reading portions of the *Christianity Today* article and selected paragraphs from John MacArthur, "Grunge Christianity?" Grace to You (website).

Condemning Culture

And yet, we can't forget the Fall. Sexual trafficking is a significant element within human cultures around the world. The various institutions complicit in this trafficking make a lot of money for their national economies. They employ a lot of people. And many people use their "services." The porn that accompanies this trafficking is also a perverse form of artistic expression. But it is all unequivocally wrong, in every way imaginable. It all ought to be stopped. If only it could be—it seems only Jesus has that power. But that shouldn't stop us from condemning the selling and using of God's image-bearers and from doing what we can to stop it.

Likewise, certain pieces of art are fit only to be *condemned*. When Marcel Duchamp took a urinal in 1917, flipped it over, wrote "R. Mutt" on it, and called it "Fountain," he was purposefully expanding the definition of "art" past the breaking point. "Fountain" was not art; it was not beautiful; it wasn't good or true. It was a slap in the face of Western culture and ultimately of the God who created beauty. Of all places for beauty to be attacked, you'd think the art world would be the last. But it's not.

Christian artist Makoto Fujimura, head of the International Arts Movement and an expert in a shimmering and colorful form of traditional Japanese painting called Nihonga, says, "When I began to exhibit [my art] in New York City . . . 'beauty' was a taboo not to be spoken of in public. . . . The art world still resists this word."[3] Fujimura observes that Western artists of the twentieth century shied away from beauty and instead "produced work aimed at shocking people into recognizing and decrying the horrors of the age."[4] Fujimura actually sees some genuine value in this kind of work. The prophet Isaiah himself was told by God to use a shocking bit of "performance art" to communicate truth to Israel—he was told to walk around almost naked and barefoot as a sign of what would happen to the people of Israel if they didn't repent (Isa. 20; cf. Jer. 13:1–11).

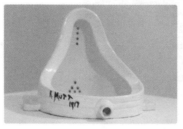 

Marcel Duchamp's "Fountain" (left), and Tracy Emin's "My Bed" (right)

But, Fujimura says, today the mission of artists has been twisted. "Artists have been conscripted . . . as frontline soldiers to defend 'freedom of expression' against tradition and conformity."[5] In other words, now artists shock people for no purpose other than to exercise their freedom to shock people. The result is more and more shocking and degrading pieces of art, such as English artist Tracy Emin's "My Bed," an unmade bed surrounded with trash and stained clothing. Even the non-Christian British public condemned Emin's work and said "good riddance" when a good deal of it went up in flames in a warehouse fire. Sometimes the most redemptive thing you can do is to condemn a particular work of human culture.

Condemning culture can go too far: you're not free to condemn something merely because you don't like it. There is great diversity among beautiful things, and another person or culture may see genuine beauty that you can't (yet) see. To justify condemning a piece of art or other artifact of culture, you've got to do some work to explain to yourself and others how that thing violates truth, goodness, and beauty.

The Christian faith is meant to exist in all cultures. Jesus told His followers to "make disciples of *all* nations" (Matt. 28:19), and that means that dress, music, and other aspects of culture will rightfully differ between Filipino Christians and Canadian ones. The early church recognized that Jesus didn't put Jewish cultural expectations on Gentiles (Acts 15:22–29). But biblical faith also condemns parts of every culture in existence—and it calls them to a divine standard.

That call is why you can't make this particular *c*, condemnation, a posture—only a gesture. You *need* art and music like you need water and food and love. To be human is to love and need beauty. Dogs don't hire interior decorators.

Critiquing Culture

Sometimes the appropriate Christian gesture toward a particular artistic creation will be to *critique* it.

The label "**critic**" is not always a nice one. But, especially in a world full of more cultural experiences than you have time for, critics are necessary for several reasons. They can help you know what to watch or listen to or read so that you don't waste time on comparatively worthless options. And then they can help you process what you just saw or listened to or read.

Help is the key word here. A good critique helps the critic's neighbors. A truly good critique holds up various cultural artifacts to divine standards of truth, goodness, and beauty, something a non-Christian will generally have trouble doing. But even a non-Christian movie reviewer can help his neighbors analyze and understand the message of a particular film, book, play, or painting. And when even non-Christian critics are saying, "This is hyper-sexualized" or "This is luridly violent," what should Christian movie watchers conclude? That the time for critique is over, that condemnation is the only appropriate Christian response.

THE MEDIUM IS THE MESSAGE

When critiquing culture, you may find it helpful to use one key intellectual tool, the famous observation of media theorist Marshall McLuhan: "The **medium** is the message."[6] What he means is that the way one communicates a message significantly affects its meaning. Imagine that there's a romantic comedy about how an unlikely couple gets together. At the climax of the movie, when the man and woman look into each other's eyes and realize that they are meant for one another, the music softly rises.

Then it blares: "Ding dong, the witch is dead!" It's the song from *The Wizard of Oz*.

What does a romantic scene *mean* when accompanied by that music? Something confusing. Movies don't use Sousa marches—or Gregorian chants or "Twinkle, Twinkle, Little Star"—during romantic scenes because the mediums of march music, chant, and nursery songs carry messages, messages that don't fit with romance. *Star Wars* would be a different movie if you switched John Williams's Darth Vader theme and his Princess Leia theme.

Music *means*, cinematic genres *mean*, graphic design *means*—everything humans make carries meaning.

Is it ever appropriate to criticize an ungodly culture? (Eph. 2:1–3; 4:17–20; 5:6–14)

Yes. While every culture will reflect both created goodness and evil twistedness, the evil must be exposed by the light.

What kind of alternative should the Christian church offer to the surrounding cultures in which it finds itself?

a culture that avoids the fallenness and enjoys the createdness of the culture around it

What kinds of Christian condemnation of culture are wrong?

the kinds that fail to recognize any goodness in human culture but speak as if it is completely fallen—and as if the condemners don't themselves have a culture but are noncultural

 Application Can't Be Dodged

There's no point in developing a biblical worldview—in which the Fall plays a prominent role—if you won't actually list out some cultural artifacts that you feel must be condemned. A Bible that is read and never applied is a Bible that isn't really read properly (James 1:22–25). But condemning cultural artifacts in a group setting, especially when that group is still immature, is a dangerous thing to do! If you feel up to leading the discussion that will ensue, ask the students to be specific about which elements and artifacts of culture they feel ought to be condemned. If you don't feel up to that task, then list out some artifacts that will be controversial enough to sustain interest but not so controversial that they'll cause tempers to

---

flare. By now you should have a good idea about what's on that list for your students.

 Culture and Beauty

The point at the top of the page (that condemning culture can go too far) is an extremely important one and can defuse some of the tensions that the invocation of absolute standards of beauty will inevitably bring in nearly any group of Western people. The Christian and biblical worldview does not claim that the works of visual, literary, and musical artistry that make up the Western canon are immune from the effects of the Fall, or that they render all cultural artifacts of other cultures ugly by comparison. Other cultures, by God's grace, can preserve something of genuine beauty in their art. In fact, the export of debased Western culture has sometimes ruined what is good in other cultures. A biblical worldview is willing to praise the good of the Western tradition—the probing fiction, the incredible statuary, the enduring poetry—as well as condemn the bad. A biblical worldview is eager to recognize the good and reject the evil in every image-bearer and in the culture of every group of image-bearers. If the argument carries an unmistakably Western imprint, that is because there is no point in trying to be noncultural; Westerners cannot write as Easterners. It's also because the Western cultural tradition is the one tradition in the world that has been most shaped by Christianity.

[David de Bruyn, "Multiculturalism and Judging Culture," Religious Affections Ministries (website), January 21, 2011]

 The Medium Is the Message

John Dyer writes in his excellent book *From the Garden to the City* (Grand Rapids: Kregel, 2011) that he was an avid tech user, never questioning the value of his technology, until one question set him spinning:

In my final semester of seminary, a professor, who was known both for his brilliance and shocking, out-of-nowhere statements, said something that changed everything for me. In the middle of addressing a variety of current issues in society and culture, he looked straight at all of us and said, "One of the most dangerous things you can believe in this world is that technology is neutral." Wait, what? I thought. Surely, he must have misspoken. After all, nothing could be more obvious than the fact that technology is neutral. What matters is that we use technology for good, right? . . . What could be so dangerous about that? I returned to class the next day prepared to ask the professor about his statement, armed with the best arguments I could muster about why technology is, in fact, neutral. However, when I arrived that day, the professor was not there. He had fallen ill and would not be able to return to class that semester. (Dyer, 15)

Nevertheless, the question remained with Dyer. His book sets out to show how technology itself can influence the horizons of the possible. Technology affects how people view the world and function in it. It affects how people think the world ought to be.

What message does the medium carry if Facebook and Twitter are used to inform about and conduct debate on social and political issues?

One thing to consider is that it reinforces superficial soundbites. The debates often produce more heat than light because internet platforms aren't usually good for deeper, linear thought that follows a logical argument all the way back to its philosophical underpinnings. The medium of a book or a substantive article lends itself to a thoughtful analysis. The author has the space to develop his ideas through dozens of pages of argumentation. The reader also has space to consider the arguments being presented. In contrast, the medium of the internet tends to encourage people to be quick to speak and slow to hear any detailed, convincing arguments from another viewpoint (James 1:19). Facebook and Twitter may still have a place in students' lives for other purposes. But people need to think carefully about the message embedded in the technology itself.

Humble Postponement

What cultural artifacts are you willing to say you're not ready for, but think you might be in the future after receiving a more detailed biblical worldview education at a Christian university?

For instance, there was probably little reason for students to read Dan Brown's The Da Vinci Code when it was released. From both a literary and theological standpoint, there are far better ways to spend their time, and for some it could have been faith-shaking. Yet a Christian scholar might well find it part of his calling to read the book and compose a critique.

[Note that the answers should reflect an understanding that certain things aren't appropriate even for a mature Christian adult. For instance, there is no cause for adult Christians to watch sexually explicit entertainment. As a teacher, you may want to give your own experience. Do you regret having watched certain movies, read certain books, taken certain college courses—all before you were ready?]

You yourself may need to become a critic of sorts in order to help your neighbors or your family. There may be times when it will be appropriate for you to read a book you disagree with simply to be able to discuss it with your Muslim coworker or your agnostic college roommate. Several years ago when Dan Brown's *The Da Vinci Code* reached the bestseller lists, some Christians held their noses and read the novel just because it was actually persuading a lot of people that Jesus had a wife and children, despite the fact that it was simply bad literature.

Not all non-Christian literature is bad, of course. Good literature in general "clarifies the human situation to which the Christian faith speaks."[7] The best of human art provides insights into the human condition that we all find ourselves in. The ability to read a book that you have objections to and come out wiser—that's "critiquing."

The only way you can critique something from the standpoint of a biblical worldview is to have a thorough, head-heart grasp of that worldview yourself. Until then, the more difficult the critique, the more likely you should stay away. Or wait. Tony Reinke, author of *Lit! A Christian Guide to Reading Books*, says that some books demand a certain maturity before they can be read with profit. Reinke and his wife evaluated their own nine-year-old son and decided he wasn't old enough to handle certain books. You don't send boys into battle, says Reinke. They have to develop the instincts of a solider first. Reinke says, "So, too, our children—and those who are children in the faith—need time to grow the deep roots of a biblical worldview before being called to exercise that worldview against the force of culture displayed in non-Christian books."[8]

Reinke says this doesn't necessarily stop him from reading a non-Christian book out loud to his children; when he does that, he has a chance to stop and have discussions along the way. But when his child reads on his own, "choosing what books to read is often not a yes/no decision but a now/later decision. . . . Be cautious of reading literature that you are ill-equipped to read with discernment. Sometimes the proper Christian approach to literature is humble postponement."[9]

Sensitive to the effects of the Fall in his children, Reinke is aware that "critique" is a demanding task not every Christian (no matter his or her age) is ready for. God has probably placed parents and other spiritual leaders in your life—pastors, teachers—who *can't* articulate precisely how a certain cultural artifact twists truth or goodness or beauty. Nonetheless, they've seen the effects of fallen culture on fallen young

---

A MOVIE THAT TEACHES ABOUT TOTAL DEPRAVITY

Many contemporary American Christians have the impression that past generations of believers were "isolationists" who failed to "engage culture." This criticism contains significant elements of truth. Some American Christians have, in practice, denied the goodness of God's created world and acted as if creation were only a stepping stone to heaven. But recognition of this fact has led to many overcorrections. One particular Christian magazine seems to write the same movie review over and over: "This is a culturally significant film you need to know about. Yes, it has plenty of sex and violence, so kids shouldn't see it without their parents' permission and presence. But the on-screen sins help us learn about the fallenness of man and provide bridges for you to talk to your non-

Christian neighbor." One church actually showed the sexually-explicit film version of *Les Miserables* to the congregation in a service, presumably because Victor Hugo's story does contain a memorable illustration of grace.

Admittedly, such films have created a bridge between the Christian community and the world—but which direction are most people on that bridge going? Christian leaders and thinkers such as David Wells have noted that the world's entertainment has had a lot more influence on the church than vice versa. There's a reason for this: Christians still have to contend with their flesh (Gal. 5:13, 17), and the sins portrayed in entertainment too often please the flesh.

422 | ARTS & CULTURE

Practice Critique

Have your students write a brief critique of a few elements of culture that you assign. Choose cultural artifacts from folk, pop, and high culture. Consider selecting things from past cultural eras. This may reduce the tendency of some to defend certain pieces simply because they currently like them. Also pick things that aren't overly egregious. Cultural critique is very demanding work, and your students must not be expected to come up with brilliant analyses and incisive evaluations. However, they will be called on quite soon to decide which elements of culture they'll consume, critique, copy, or condemn. This will give them practice in a setting in which they can receive wise feedback.

Critics That Never Condemn

For all the good that *World* magazine may accomplish in Christian journalism, one of its consistent flaws is its philosophy of movie and television reviews. The reviewers critique the movies and shows, which often include ungodly elements, and then consistently recommend the consumption of them anyway. For example, after recommending a particular show as one of the top three to watch, the reviewer adds that the show includes pervasive and explicit nudity. In the next recommendation, the reviewer recognizes that an attempted rape is so graphically shown that it should have been edited out, but that doesn't keep her from putting it on the top-three recommended list! [Megan Basham, "Three to Watch," *World* (website) October 31, 2015]

people for a long time. The Bible tells us to listen to wise people even if their critiques aren't professional.

Critique is an important gesture available to Christians. If cultures are truly a mixture of good and evil, they're all ready for critique. But you can't make "critique" your full-time posture. Some Christians use cultural critique as an excuse to watch movies they really should just condemn. Then again, there will be many times when it is appropriate for you to simply "consume" the offerings of your culture.

THINKING IT THROUGH 27.1A

1. What is the biblical means for training young people in discernment?

2. According to Proverbs 14:16, how must you respond when you spot evil?

3. What makes condemning a cultural artifact an absolutely necessary response for a Christian? When shouldn't condemnation be the response?

4. For what two reasons is critique a bad posture?

♀5. Why are both maturity and a biblical worldview prerequisites for critiquing art?

Consuming Culture

You eat food, don't you? You use toothpaste, right? The food you eat and even the toothpaste you use are very much products of your culture. A newspaper once published pictures of the breakfasts kids around the world got from their parents; it turns out that kid breakfasts in Japan really are different from kid breakfasts in Brazil and Greece.[10] Even toothpaste differs in various cultures; tea-flavored toothpaste is popular in China.[11]

CONSUME

If your mom puts a plate of steak in front of you, don't critique it. Those are bad gestures when it comes to mom's cooking. Just consume it. And if she buys you a tube of Crest, smear it on your teeth, rinse, and spit.

There is a time for critique, even of food. You should be generally aware of the calories and sugars you ingest, and you'll want to critique your own eating habits on a regular basis. But once you've set up healthy guidelines, you're free to simply enjoy the countless culinary creations available to you inside those lines.

"The earth is the Lord's," Psalm 24 says. God's kids are allowed to open up His fridge and forage for stuff, whatever's in there. If they ask for bread, they don't get stones (Matt. 7:9). "Everything created by God is good, and nothing is to be rejected if it is received with thanksgiving" (1 Tim. 4:4).

Especially since you're a student, trusted people will regularly tell you, "This piece of art is good. Look at it." Or, "This book is good. Read it." You can't know what effect the painting or novel will have on you, but you jump in anyway and "consume" it—because you trust. Maybe you don't feel fully capable of judging the piece of art. You're just taking it in. That's OK sometimes. Good ideas in art can still plow up soil in which truth can later grow.

The classic Western film *Big Country* (and this is one of the few times in this book when *Western* means cowboys) holds profound lessons and a great example of someone "turning the other cheek" out of strength, not weakness. But you may not get that on first watch. And if you stop the movie every time one of those lessons comes up, you'll lose some of the power of the experience of just consuming it.

Divide students into groups to read through Proverbs 2 and answer this question:

How would you summarize this chapter?

If you relentlessly pursue God's wisdom (1–4), then you will fear and know God (5) because the Lord is the source of wisdom (6–7a), providing all these benefits of protection from various categories of people (7b–19) so that you can walk uprightly and obtain God's promised blessing (20–22).

THINKING IT THROUGH 27.1A

1. The biblical means is guidance by godly elders (parents and church leadership) who are tasked with wisely applying Scripture. Young people aren't left to learn discernment on their own.

2. Respond with caution, which is defined as turning away from evil. This is in contrast to foolishly assuming that you can handle it, which is a overconfident and reckless response.

3. It's necessary when something is both unequivocally wrong and its presentation of or support of twisting God's created order is blatant and explicit. But it is never called for merely in response to something you personally don't care for.

4. First, critique can be overbearing because of nitpicking—people should be allowed to consume whatever is basically good. Second, critique can be an excuse to consume blatantly explicit material that should instead be condemned.

♀5. A biblical worldview is necessary for being able to make the right evaluations. Maturity is necessary for discerning what is truly true, good, and beautiful.

Encourage the Rubber to Meet the Road

Hopefully, your students perceive that the tools of analysis in this book, especially in this final chapter, are meant to be aids to them and not strict rules, per se. They're not meant to be abstract concepts memorized and regurgitated for a final exam. Encourage them to use these concepts. Once they have read through the first two sections of this chapter, you may wish to assign them the duty of placing the next ten cultural artifacts they see in their own lives into one or more of the first four categories proposed by Andy Crouch. Does this [song, movie, book, play, etc.] deserve mainly to be condemned, critiqued, copied, or consumed? Have them make a chart leaving space for notes on why they chose the category or categories they did in each case.

Critique Requires a Standard

Help students understand that critique implies the adoption of a standard. Non-Christian critics are fuzzy on this fact. They acknowledge a standard for scientific knowledge: namely, the consensus of the accredited members of the relevant scientific profession. But for moral and aesthetic judgments they formally acknowledge no standard and thus have trouble making judgments. In reality, critics assume standards of truth, goodness, and beauty all the time even though there is no secular basis for these standards. The Christian basis is rooted in love for and fear of God. Those who love and fear God will receive from Him wisdom to discern righteousness. Proverbs 2 explains the standard and how to apprehend it.

A Balanced View of Consumption

Some consuming is good; some is bad. It depends on who's doing the consuming and what's being consumed. And it depends on whether you're consuming the goods or the goods are consuming you. *Consumption* is, in fact, the archaic name for tuberculosis, used because the disease "eats up" the body, causing it to waste away. Consuming too much aesthetic junk can cause one's mind and even one's humanity to waste away. But the fact that people get hungry, as C. S. Lewis once pointed out, is a clue that we are meant to eat. And the fact that we have aesthetic desires is a clue that we are meant to consume some things. There isn't anything inherently wrong with being what practically all humans are—consumers.

Christian Boltanski's work of art "No Man's Land" was an overly cynical display, questioning the modern world's devotion to consumption. (It's an example of conceptual or activist art, discussed on page 429.) Boltanski put thirty tons of discarded clothing into one massive pile for the purpose of pointing to the vanity of life: "You can hold onto the clothes," he said. "But you can't keep anybody." [Dorothy Spears, "Exploring Mortality With Clothes and a Claw," *New York Times* (website), May 9, 2010] The Pixar movie *WALL•E* was also a cynical critique meant to make the same point: massive piles of discarded stuff should cause us to consider the consumption habits of the modern world.

However, it's true that devotion to consumption means that people discard consumer goods before their useful life is gone, which means, in turn, that companies don't build things to last. A cheaply made shirt or blouse is initially appealing, but what is the overall cost to the individual and to society of a lot of cheaply made shirts? Consuming a few quality goods might be better than consuming a lot of cheap goods. This is true in our aesthetic lives too.

Consuming Happens First

As you grow older, you begin to understand the moral lessons or values embedded in the cultural artifacts that you were allowed to consume as a child. Wise parents will be careful about their children's consumption habits because they know that their children are unaware of the values they're learning as they are simply being entertained.

What were some of your favorite books or movies when you were a young child?

There should be some familiar enough ones that you can evaluate along with the students.

What were some of the moral lessons you were unknowingly being influenced by but can now discern?

Hopefully, children's material is teaching them common lessons of morality such as respect, responsibility, kindness, and so on.

How long did it take for you to identify that lesson? Did you get it upon your initial exposure to the piece of art or did it take a while to sink in?

Most likely the lesson wasn't immediately identifiable; they probably didn't see it until they had watched or read the material dozens of times.

Appropriate Times for Copying

The problem with copying isn't with copying; it's with what is being copied. If the general nature of a cultural tradition is twisted, then copying is problematic. But if the cultural

---

C. S. Lewis's Chronicles of Narnia are full of insightful points about human nature, such as the scene when Digory starts to tell Aslan that he sinned because he was under a magic spell—only to have Aslan growl. But the author of *What I Learned in Narnia*, a book exploring those moral lessons, encourages readers to simply consume the stories first, then worry about the lessons later.

Some people view consuming fiction and fantasy stories like Lewis' Narnia books as escapism. But as Lewis pointed out, the people who are normally concerned about escape are jailers—and what matters is what you're escaping from and what you're escaping to.[13] The arts can lead you away from the pain you're facing and into beautiful and complex worlds created by gifted minds imitating their Creator. Sometimes you just go to those places and enjoy them, without too much focus on critique.

> "BY APPRECIATING THE BEAUTY OF LITERATURE, WE HONOR GOD, THE GIVER OF ALL BEAUTY." [12]
>
> —TONY REINKE

Nonetheless, in a world touched everywhere with poison, you can't live in a constant mode of consumption. We can't take a Pac-Man posture and consume anything that comes within the span of our always-chomping mandibles.

Copying Culture

Humans, made in the image of a creative God, often need to put aside the gestures of condemnation, critique, and consumption and adopt another gesture: making things of their own. And that's not easy; it's a process requiring training and growth—a process in which you have to start somewhere. So a fourth necessary *c* is *copying*. If you go to the National Gallery in Washington, DC, you'll often find someone there with an easel copying a masterwork. If you're learning to sculpt, there's hardly a better way to do it than to copy the masters. You'll copy their work and their methods—and even their tools. It probably won't be necessary to reinvent the pottery wheel. But once you've mastered the artistic or cultural tradition you've received, you'll be able to do some creating on your own.

Every act of human creation involves a degree of copying because we can't create completely out of nothing. We are subcreators. We have to use existing materials. When humans tried to copy the flapping motions of bird wings, we failed to fly. But we still ended up using design elements from birds. An airplane wing is very different from a bird wing, but there's some necessary copying in the airfoil design.

Nonetheless, copying can quickly go astray. A kindergartener may prefer tracing a flower to the hard but educationally necessary work of drawing it himself. And though there are many skillful and beautiful things worth copying in culture and the arts, American Christians don't tend to get as excited about those things as they do about copying pop and celebrity culture.

Evangelical Christians have a "deeply neurotic relationship with popular culture,"[14] says secular journalist Hanna Rosin. She says evangelicals in America are like the Old Testament Israelites who began fitting into the culture of the pagans around them so much that it became difficult to tell them apart. It's like we inhabit our own gigantic parallel universe where an evangelical "can now buy books, movies, music—and any-

---

tradition is directed toward good creational norms, then copying is helpful. There is an appropriate place for copying. Learning a craft usually requires copying. In fact, cultivating and creating usually can't happen until an apprentice learns to copy a master first. But once the fundamentals are learned, the apprentice can apply his knowledge and skill to create something wonderful too.

Evangelicalism's Relationship with Popular Culture

Hanna Rosin's entire article is well worth the read (warning: there is one sexually explicit reference in the piece). [Hanna Rosin, "Pop Goes Christianity: The Deep Contradictions of Christian Popular Culture," *Slate* (website), May 5, 2008] Since her criticisms of evangelical copycatting constitute the majority of the "Copying Culture" section, it

will be obvious that we (and, to a somewhat lesser extent, Andy Crouch) take a dim view of a lot of the culture-copying that goes on in evangelicalism. As noted above, cultural copying is not bad if it's part of learning a tradition. But some of it is so bad (and is such a betrayal of everything Christianity can be and has been) that students probably need a stiff dose of Rosin's viewpoint. It is always fascinating to be examined by a perceptive outsider.

Copying Culture and CCM

Have you ever seen one of the classic CCM posters in a Christian bookstore—the one that contains a chart saying, "If you like this secular band, you'll love this Christian band?" Discuss this kind of chart with students in terms of the structure-and-direction model.

thing else lowbrow to middlebrow—tailor-made for his or her sensibilities."[15] That's copying at its worst. It's purposefully being "conformed to the world" despite the command of Romans 12:1–2.

At one point Christians were known for boycotting offensive offerings from popular culture, says Rosin, but in more recent years they've moved from boycotting to co-opting and have begun trying to "enlist America's crassest material culture in the service of spiritual growth."[16] Every artifact of American popular culture seems to have a Christian version, regardless of how incongruous* it may be. Rosin, a secular Jew, compares this phenomenon to living on a different planet where everything's the same as on earth except that it's synthetic and the wrong color.

Her article mentions, for example, "Christian" chick lit and "Christian" Harlequin or "Christian" rappers and "Christian" raves. (Rosin wonders how techno music can be called "Christian" when it has no lyrics; she says that her personal favorite is the "Christian" version of professional wrestling.)[17]

Rosin asks two penetrating questions of this parallel culture: "What does commercializing do to the substance of belief, and what does an infusion of belief do to the product?"[18] In her opinion, when your love song for Jesus sounds just like a ballad for your boyfriend, both your faith and your music may be damaged. By sanitizing the rock lyrics of Jay-Z or Nirvana, you force "a message that's essentially about obeying authority into a genre that's rebellious and nihilistic, and the result can be ugly, fake, or just limp."[19]

Copying can be a worthwhile gesture for Christians to make but a horrible posture for them to maintain.

GESTURING WITHOUT POSTURING

If you were marooned by yourself on a desert island with no technology, you wouldn't need any skills in analyzing and evaluating culture and the arts. But as soon as you add other people, you've got a culture. And you're going to need to develop the ability to detect good and evil—structure and direction—in that culture. Some things you see or read or hear will need to be condemned, others critiqued, others just consumed, and some copied. Never will one of these first four *c*'s be your permanent posture, but a well-educated Christian will know when and where to gesture in these ways.

THINKING IT THROUGH 27.1B

1. List four possible gestures or responses to cultural artifacts.

2. Once healthy guidelines have been set up, what should Christians feel free to do with the cultural artifacts within those guidelines?

3. What's one prerequisite for creating a cultural artifact yourself?

4. What gesture have evangelical Christians tended to overuse, prompting secularists to criticize them? Is the criticism valid or not?

5. Can humans create anything that is untouched by the Fall? Why or why not?

incongruous:
inappropriate; not fitting in with the surrounding context

responses are subject to the Fall, emotional communication is also subject to the Fall. Music that communicates on an emotional level is subject to the Fall. Therefore, music itself needs to be evaluated.

Why isn't "copying" the best posture to adopt toward pop music?

Music reflects the values and attitudes of the musicians. They effectively communicate their worldview to their audience. Christians need to be careful which forms they copy because the forms they copy may well express a worldview that's contrary to Scripture. Christians need to make sure that the values and attitudes expressed by the music, don't reflect a twisted direction (Rom. 12:1–2). They need to make sure the values and attitudes expressed by the music fit well with the verbal message of the gospel. That means Christians will have to be extremely selective about what they copy—copying can't be their general posture.

Boycott or Othercott?

Andy Crouch has an interesting discussion of the effectiveness of boycotts in *Culture Making*. He points out that a proposed boycott of a given Hollywood movie, even if it has massive buy-in from evangelicals who hear about it, is unlikely to make much of a dent in the success of such a film. He proposes engaging in an "othercott." What he means is that we should be creative and support alternatives instead. In some cases Christians may want to support different kinds of activity altogether. For instance, instead of going to the movies, they could attend the symphony or get involved in a community group.

THINKING IT THROUGH 27.1B

1. condemn, critique, consume, copy

2. consume them—enjoy the subcreations of God's image-bearers that fall within the bounds of truth, goodness, and beauty

3. copying—building on what's already come before you

4. Christians are often accused of cheap copying; the criticism is often legitimate because the copying turns out to be ugly and fake: it either forces a Christianized version onto something that would otherwise be a good subcreation without the Christianese slapped onto it, or the forced Christianese melded with an unworthy medium just doesn't correspond to the Christian message.

5. Since the world and the people in it making the cultural artifacts are fallen, then perfection will always be elusive.

Is music structural—a God-created good?

Yes, music as a general category is a God-created good; it's structural. That means that all the elements that go into music were created by God and discovered by humans.

Is every particular musical expression God-created?

No, specific expressions and genres are human cultural creations; they are directional and not neutral.

If a particular musical expression is a human cultural creation, is it possible for music to be nonmoral?

No, when fallen humans and cultures begin to design music by combining the good, God-created musical elements into specific musical forms of communication, then it's always possible for it to go in a fallen direction (i.e., for fallen communication to occur).

[See Albert Wolters, *Creation Regained: Biblical Basics for a Reformational Worldview* (Grand Rapids: Eerdmans, 2005), 93. This is no different than humans using good, God-created language elements to form specific words and sentences. The words and sentences can be formed in either a redemptive direction or a fallen direction.]

Do musicians intend for their communication to be understood? How?

Yes. While the music itself doesn't communicate through propositional language, musicians do make use of objective techniques to communicate subjective emotional cues.

Don't misunderstand the point. Emotions are not inherently wrong. Music is designed to evoke an emotional response. But there is no part of the image of God that hasn't been damaged by the Fall. Since emotional

1. Construct a cultural artifact that displays love for God and neighbor.
2. Explain why the posture of cultivation is necessary: to hone skills for creativity.

The Six C's

Make sure the students understand the rhetorical progression of this chapter so far. The first four *c*'s—condemn, critique, consume, copy—are gestures, things to do when appropriate. They're not appropriate postures the way cultivating and creating are. Creating is the culmination of the six *c*'s.

Instead of Copying . . . Create

Andy Crouch stands squarely in the mainstream of American evangelicalism, but he's actually skeptical of many of its tactics for fomenting cultural change.

In *Culture Making* he argues that lasting cultural change happens slowly, that even the most earthshaking, world-changing event—Christ's resurrection—went unnoticed by most of the world for a long time. And it was, like other revolutionary moments, actually the end product of centuries of other events. Generally, changes that are truly world-changing and quick are changes for the worse. "The only thing you can do with Rome in a day is burn it" (Crouch, 58).

Christians often seem to think that one truly successful Christian hit on top-40 radio (this is Crouch's example) will send people pouring into the church. But good changes don't happen that fast. And changes have unpredictable results: industrialization brought child labor laws—a good change, most would say. But it also took children out of family-run enterprises and disconnected them from seeing their dads work. Christians also seem to think sometimes that giving people the right worldview will usher in lasting change. Crouch wouldn't have written a book if he thought thinking was unimportant, but he urges readers to recognize that there's more to it: you have to *create* culture; "Culture is not changed simply by thinking" (Crouch, 64).

How does culture get changed then? Crouch gives this emphatic answer: "The only way to change culture is to create more of it" (Crouch, 67). It's a rare person who's willing to leave a hole in his cultural life; if you want people to stop listening to bad music or eating bad food, you have to create good music and good food to replace them. "Creativity is the only viable source of change" (Crouch, 73). A tradition is a tradition because it's handed down, then cultivated and developed, and then handed down again. Our

27.2 CREATING AND CULTIVATING

Every senior in high school gets "The Question." Some have a ready answer for it; some grow to dread it: "What are your plans?" Never mind that a large percentage of college freshmen have no major, another large percentage change their major after declaring one, and less than half of college freshmen graduate in four years anyway.[20] How are you supposed to know what your plans are? A lot of things are going to change for you—and *in* you—during the next few years.

But you still have to make some sort of choice, and your options are narrowing. Kids in elementary school are told, "You can be anything you want to be." But by now a career requiring good spelling or calculus skills may no longer be available to you. You've discovered you're not gifted in those areas.

But there are still many options. And in order to choose wisely, you need to know about a raging debate in higher education over two of them: the liberal arts (or the humanities) versus the sciences.

College costs a lot more money than it used to. And it provides less of a guarantee than it used to that you'll actually get a job that pays well enough to justify the expense. The fields where you are most likely to make money at the moment are the so-called STEM fields: science, technology, engineering, and mathematics. Many parents nowadays aren't too excited about laying out tens of thousands of dollars for you to major in art or literature. The return on investment just isn't as likely.

Or is it? Art and literature professors can't deny that their grads typically don't make the cash that engineers and doctors and software developers do, so they tend to point to other values of the liberal arts. One such professor, who teaches literature, tried to distill those values into a list:

> Every defense of liberal [arts] education . . . makes one or more of the following arguments:
> - Studying the liberal arts makes you a better citizen.
> - Studying the liberal arts makes you more empathetic and compassionate.
> - Studying the liberal arts teaches you critical-thinking skills.
> - Studying the liberal arts makes you a capable communicator, in speech and writing.
> - Knowledge is good for its own sake.[21]

These are all good justifications, but they may not be very comforting for parents looking at a $60,000 tuition bill. And none of them is particularly Christian.

Created to Create

Is it worthwhile, from the perspective of a biblical worldview, to study the liberal arts and humanities? Some readers of this book are about to spend four years—or six, or ten, or sixty—doing it. Is it a good idea?

The answer is a definite *yes*. The humanities are *vital* in the most literal sense of the term: necessary to life. The arts are a glorious part of what makes us human. This is not to put down the sciences. They, too, are blessings God gave to mankind in the Creation Mandate. And this is not to say that every single reader of this book should major in the humanities. Some aren't called to college; others are called to the sciences.

But the arts, even when they don't carry clear practical or monetary value, provide you the opportunity to do something truly God-like. They let you *create*.

first job as would-be culture-makers is to be cultivators who have learned some discipline and can therefore develop it in a new direction. This is undeniably what happens in the Western classical tradition of music. It's why we still talk about Plato's ideas in philosophy courses. And it's a humbling reminder that we all stand on the shoulders of giants.

The Decline of the Humanities

Consider the possibility that the decline of the humanities is related to the decline of the human. In an age in which the importance of human rights are a watchword and in which the impression is given that such rights are more honored than they were in previous generations, it may seem odd to say that the overall valuation of humanity is going down. Yet that devaluing is the natural result of defining mankind according to the naturalistic evolutionary story. If all human value begins and ends on this planet with no reference to any supernatural source of value, then there is no supernatural goal toward which humans can point their lives. They are forced, as earlier chapters have argued, to manufacture their own ends, their own goals, their own purposes for life. Wealth and consequent comfort—materialism as a consequence of philosophical materialism—have become the goal almost by default for many Westerners. And therefore (keep following the logic here), only those things that contribute to that goal have value. In jettisoning his connection to the divine, man has made himself a tool of his desire for stuff. The humanities don't make any appreciable contribution to the race for acquiring more stuff, so they are comparatively devalued. That's why, for example,

This is the ultimate *c* in the Christian approach to culture. Condemn and critique when you must, consume when you can, copy when appropriate. But your goal as a created being should be to turn around and do some creating of your own. *Creating* (and, as we'll see, *cultivating*) shouldn't just be a gesture but should be a life-long posture.

American culture, especially, is at war. You will have to battle the fallen elements of culture your whole life. But you weren't created for condemnation and critique. You were created to create.

Think yet again about Genesis 1:26–28:

> Then God said, "Let us make man in our image, after our likeness. And let them have dominion over the fish of the sea and over the birds of the heavens and over the livestock and over all the earth and over every creeping thing that creeps on the earth."
>
> So God created man in his own image, in the image of God he created him; male and female he created them.
>
> And God blessed them. And God said to them, "Be fruitful and multiply and fill the earth and subdue it, and have dominion over the fish of the sea and over the birds of the heavens and over every living thing that moves on the earth."

By the time you get to these verses in Genesis 1, just about the only thing you know about God is that He is explosively creative. Inventing one animal is hard enough, let alone multiple kinds, some of which can fly—*fly*! Would you have thought of that? Some animals can eat four tons of food in a day (the blue whale). Some make light from their bodies (the anglerfish). And at least one eats sunshine (the sea slug[22]). And that's only the beginning of the list of amazing things animals can do.

The only earthly creature that can do more amazing things is man. And one of the things that most sets humans apart from animals is the very creativity first modeled by God. You were created to create.

sea slug

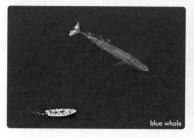

blue whale

anglerfish

work as a professor in the humanities is extremely hard to come by. [Karen Kelsky, *The Professor Is In* (New York: Random House, 2015)] It's the decline of humanity that has lead to the decline of the humanities.

Making Choices for the Future

State the obvious for your students: they should view their choice of a college major through the lenses of a biblical worldview.

Now that they have been told that the Creation Mandate is still in effect, that we were created to create and not merely to consume, that both "sacred" and "secular" callings are given to Christians—what are they going to do with this information when it comes to filling in that looming, intimidating "preferred major" blank on their college forms? If they're walking with God, they should feel free to do what they delight in (Ps. 37:4).

They should, in fact, be sure to do what they delight in—because the strong desire to serve the Lord in a particular calling (from engineering to medicine to preaching to mothering) is in fact part of their calling, a gift given to help them discern that calling. There's no doubt that future salary possibilities need to play a role in their decision about a major, but where there's true gifting from God, there will be true provision from Him. Those who seek first His kingdom, no matter how it is that they do so, will have all the material things they need added to them.

Habits and Hobbies

Many people (some who are not even Christians) have decided that they have something better to do with their evenings than watch TV. They instead pursue avocations, or hobbies. They read about their particular interest, they sew, they build, they write, they sing, they invent. They create and cultivate. The internet can be a vast black hole for time-wasting, a cesspool of sin, or a fascinating place where hobbyists of all sorts can share their ideas.

Which of your enjoyments might turn into professions, and which might turn into constructive hobbies? What can you do to promote your future enjoyment of that hobby now?

[Encourage students to expand the horizons of the possible in their lives by looking for and taking advantage of the many opportunities offered to them through their church, school, and community.]

If you like to sing but don't think you could make a career out of it, what singing opportunities in college might pay dividends for you throughout your life? What electives might you take simply because you love the topic and want a better introduction to it? We are called to cultivate and create; what plans do your students have to answer those callings?

Liberal Arts and a Cup of Joe

Lee was taking a coffee break with Joe, a fellow Christian he'd just met at a conference for conservative evangelicals. Lee was describing the liberal arts training he enjoyed getting in his youth. After several minutes listening to Lee praise his "liberal arts" education, Joe got a puzzled look on his face and said, "You don't sound very liberal."

If your students still don't know what a liberal arts college is, they need to find out. (The term *liberal* in this context isn't referring to a political or religious ideology but refers to the broadening of the whole person.) A liberal arts college is a place that provides general intellectual development in literature, mathematics, philosophy, and social and physical sciences instead of focusing directly on individual professional or technical subjects. Only a liberal arts school is likely to train a graphic design major who studies Spanish extensively and then heads into doctoral work in New Testament studies, eventually becoming a professional writer (which was precisely Lee's career path). There's no vocational or technical school that can impart that particular blend of knowledge and skill.

Some young people have such a strong sense of calling to an individual technical vocation that they may not feel it necessary to take another literature course. And it may indeed be God's desire for them to go to a technical school. Not everyone's situation allows the same opportunities. But some students who go to the local tech school are missing out on experiences that would have enriched them and their families for a lifetime. This is disappointing if they had the opportunity but didn't realize what they would miss out on and turned it down.

College Education for Mothers?

Some people, Christian and non-Christian, have openly doubted that women should spend the time and money (usually their parents') on a college education if they're "just" going to be mothers. And indeed, not all women and not all men are called to go to college. But as this book has pointed out in several places, motherhood requires as much or more creativity and wisdom and skill as any other vocation. Motherhood shouldn't be disparaged. Never underestimate the expansive role and influence of a mother's job in the home. No one in the world has cracked the secret code and figured out how to raise perfect children; the Fall is too strong, and foolishness is bound too tightly in their little hearts. But mothers do have incredible influence on their children, influence that will last far beyond the mothers' own lifetimes. What models of cultivation and creativity will they bequeath to their children? What will mothers know about child development, about biblical counseling, about the fine arts, about storytelling and children's literature, about diet and home healthcare? A good college—particularly a Christian one—can make massive contributions to the work of mothering.

An Exercise in the Difficulty of Creating

Humans have five senses: touch, taste, smell, sight, and hearing. God created each sense, of course, and gave incredible variations of them to His animal creation.

Add a sixth sense. Create one. What would it be? It may prove difficult to even conceive of what other senses a human being could have. Creating is not easy. But God doesn't call humans to create out of nothing. Humans are subcreators. They use the natural resources that God has already provided and turn them into something useful or beautiful.

A Call to Action

Sound homiletical methodology (the practice of preaching) includes an element in which the preacher, having explained and illustrated the scriptural text, must then apply the truth to the lives of his hearers and finally exhort people to go and do what the Bible calls them to do. As this book comes to a close, spend some time exhorting students to live out the biblical worldview (the

third ingredient of a worldview). If they're regenerated people indwelled by God's Holy Spirit, they will have the talents and abilities to do what God has called them to do.

A life of destruction is comparatively easy. Anyone with a little education can be a critic. Complaining comes naturally to fallen people; sniping makes the internet go round. But to build something new with one's life, to be a self-conscious cultivator of the traditions one has inherited, and a new creator within that space—that's hard work. But it's rewarding work.

One pastor and ministry leader complained about those of the millennial generation that they wanted to be trusted and given important jobs without having done anything. These young people are impatient with the idea that they must justify their value to their employers. They like the feel-

ing of having done important things, but they don't like the sweat necessary to get those things done. Whether this is true or not as a generalization, it should not be true of people with a biblical worldview. They know that human life means work because "work" and "keep" were our original duties (Gen. 2:15). You can, hopefully, tell your students from personal experience that hard work in the calling God has given—with the gifting God has provided—has brought you the most rewarding experiences of life (e.g., finishing a degree, guiding a project to completion, teaching all the way through *Biblical Worldview: Creation, Fall, Redemption*).

Flannery O'Connor

In the last paragraph on page 428, the text references Flannery O'Connor, probably the

Love—and the gratitude and joy and hope that spring from it—is the affection best suited to drive Christian creativity, just as truth and goodness and beauty guide and shape that creativity. It's out of the abundance of the heart that the mouth speaks, Jesus said (see Luke 6:45).

Culture and the arts aren't exempt from the two great commandments driving everything: love for God and love for neighbor. That love for neighbor is why sculptor Frederick Hart said,

> I believe that art has a moral responsibility, that it must pursue something higher than itself. Art must be a part of life. It must exist in the domain of the common man. It must be an enriching, ennobling, and vital partner in the public pursuit of civilization. It should be a majestic presence in everyday life just as it was in the past.[25]

SKILL

Frederick Hart (1943–1999) was a sculptor in the Western classical tradition who took that tradition to new heights. Many would say that his *Ex Nihilo* at the National Cathedral in Washington, DC, is utterly astounding. Hart could make life out of stone. But the art world did worse than reject him; it ignored him.[26] Hart sculpted a bronze statue for the Vietnam memorial; same result. Tom Wolfe, one of the critics of the world of art, summarized their view of Hart. Artists like Hart, "used a devious means—skill—to fool the eye into believing that bronze or stone had turned into human flesh. Therefore, they were artificial, false." Wolfe says that the art world created a climate in which "no ambitious artist was going to display skill, even if he had it."[27]

It is peculiarly appropriate, then, that Hart's masterwork was about God's creation of man. We were given our creative skills in order to use them for the glory of God and the good of mankind.

In other words, our neighbors need our creativity. Some thinkers who've explored art have called this others-oriented principle "**hospitality**." When a hostess invites a guest over for dinner, she usually prepares a meal she has made before (new recipes don't always turn out to be "hospitable"). But regardless of whether the lasagna is novel or not, no true hostess tosses in bizarre ingredients—gum drops, walnuts, tea bags—to express her culinary creativity. Her goal is to please her guests, not break their teeth or sour their stomachs. She also sets the table, lights the candles, and plays the background music for the same reason she takes care with the lasagna ingredients—for the good of her guests. Likewise, a carpenter makes doorways the new homeowners don't have to stoop to walk through. A knife maker crafts blades that are sharp and handles that fit smoothly in the hand. One significant measuring stick of worthy art is whether this piece of culture moves beyond mere self-expression to the benefit of others.

THE GREAT WAR IN ART

When a gifted young Christian artist attended the prestigious Savannah College of Art and Design for her Master of Fine Arts degree, she heard about a "great war" between what many there sneeringly called "decorative art" (the kinds of things you would hang in your living room) and "**conceptual art**" (as if decorative art—both realistic and abstract—didn't have any concepts behind it). By "conceptual," they meant "activist." Art was expected to make disturbing statements in support of some cause such as environmentalism or feminism. If art didn't disturb, it wasn't art. There was a definite Marxist theory behind this view. Art had to oppose established ruling norms in order to foster conflict—and therefore, progress.

Christian art is permitted to disturb (the Bible's own literary art is sometimes disturbing, such as in the book of Judges), but Christian art must be driven by love.

The irony is that works of merely "decorative" art produced by that Christian MFA student—driven by love—sold for $5,000 to $7,000 each while nobody would buy the "conceptual art." She paid off her grad school bill with her creativity.

twentieth century's most celebrated—and most read—American short story writer. Her stories are masterful, aiming hard at self-righteousness in Southern culture, no matter where it's found. But her stories are also redemptive. The redemption may come in the final sentence, and in the final moment of the main character's life (as in her famous story "A Good Man Is Hard to Find"), but people recognize their selfishness and arrogance and manage to receive the gift God gives of horror against their sin. While O'Connor may seem primarily to be a critic, she doesn't end with despair, as if self-righteousness is a problem in other people that can never go away; she ends with hope, as if self-righteousness is a problem in us that can be expunged.

Motivations for Engaging in Creative Cultivation

Is it hospitable for Christians to consistently create artwork that looks demonic and then simply defend it by saying it represents the fallen world we live in? That kind of defense isn't reflective of hospitality. A hospitable heart filled with love and gratitude won't consistently direct others to meditate on the twistedness of a fallen world. The reality of the Fall may be recognized, but the Christian focus should be on God's good creation and God's redemptive love that delivers believers from a fallen world. If joy and hope never shine through the darkness, then there's something out of place in the heart of the artist. The overflow out of the heart of a Christian should manifest intimacy with God, and not just meditations on evil. God's goodness and God's good world should be attractively and hospitably displayed by Christian artists.

Thomas Wolfe on Frederick Hart

The footnotes in the "Skill" sidebar point to an article by Tom Wolfe. ["The Artist the Art World Couldn't See," *New York Times Magazine*, January 2, 2000, 16] The article is well worth reading. However, note that Hart did make use of nudes for some of his sculptures, and this fact is referenced in the article. His *Ex Nihilo*, a fantastically stunning and beautiful piece, also makes use of nudes. Searching for his work online will lead you to such images, and you need to be aware before doing so in front of the class. Christians have differing opinions on the acceptability of nudes in art—especially when it's high culture—but since truth, goodness, and beauty should never be unravelled, nudity even in high cultural art should be deemed unacceptable. What is relevant in the article to the purposes of the chapter is what Wolfe says about Hart, namely that he adopted classicism.

Activist Art

Is activist art problematic because it's trying to inculcate or reinforce a worldview and move people to action?

No, every work of art expresses or presupposes worldview ideas and values. And good art can stir people beyond contemplation to action.

What makes activist art problematic then?

The driving motivation to disturb, disrupt, and foment rebellion against a normative society is the exact opposite of being hospitable. It's often based on an unbiblical methodology for change: revolution (see pp. 280–81). Though a Christian may be called to create some art that exposes sin or injustice, this cannot be the posture of a Christian artist.

"The Last Leaf" by O. Henry

This short story can be found in *Explorations in Literature* 4th ed. (Greenville, SC: BJU Press, 2013, 221) as well as on numerous websites. If time permits, you may want to read the story to students and analyze it according to truth, goodness, and beauty. This piece provides an example of hospitable art.

Guidelines for Showing Hospitality

Many in the art world believe that good art must push the boundaries, shock people, offend people, overturn conventions, and perhaps even rouse people to action in favor of this cause or that. It's difficult to reconcile this position with the biblical command to love your neighbor as yourself. While love may, for the other's good, offend or rouse to action, that's not the habitual posture of love.

Hospitable art loves others by inviting them to share in the beautiful. It enables others to experience joys that they wouldn't have otherwise experienced. It draws them to see beauty that they wouldn't have otherwise seen. To do this requires great skill, but the point of the art is not to showcase the skill of the artist. Skill is used in service of others.

If you were setting out to create something hospitable for others, what guidelines would you formulate that would help you accomplish that goal?

- *Align your delights with God's delights.*
- *Purpose to create skillful art but not art designed to showcase your skill.*
- *Strive to help people delight in the goodness of God's creation, hate the effects of the Fall, and long for the consummation of redemption.*

"The greatest motivator to artistic expression is to enjoy something. And you want to share what you enjoy. That should be the governor that shapes your art. If somebody's not feeling what you feel, you try to tailor your efforts in order to get them to feel what you feel. That's hospitable. You think, 'I like this, and I think you should, and I'm going to do whatever I can to help you feel this with me.'" [28]

— ZACH FRANZEN

O. Henry illustrates this self-giving artistry in his short story "The Last Leaf,"[28] in which a budding artist who lives in Greenwich Village catches pneumonia and becomes disillusioned with life. Her roommate tells an older neighbor and fellow artist that the sick woman believes she will die when the last leaf falls off the ivy vine outside their window. In response, the older man secretly spends the next night out in cold rain, painting a permanent leaf on the brick wall. Two days later he succumbs to pneumonia, whereas the younger, temporarily depressed artist eventually recovers. Rarely is the sacrificial nature of artistry so dramatic, but this brief piece of literature demonstrates the power of art to show hospitality, to make a home for people.

Think about the common art form of photography. Many photographs, such as Ansel Adams' famous black-and-white photos of Yosemite National Park, capture a frame of God's glorious creativity. Others, like the ones hanging in your hallway, represent your family's nostalgic past. Such art isn't self-absorbed. It points away from itself to our Creator God or to the importance of human relationships. Its beauty pictures truth and goodness for the enjoyment of others. Even selfies can be used to send Grandma a smile.

Ansel Adams created famous photographs of American landscapes.

Examples of Hospitable Art

Show students more examples of hospitable art, reflecting truth, goodness, and beauty. Discuss with the students how the art communicates each aspect of this triad.

Examples of Inhospitable Art

Using discretion, show students pieces of art that violate hospitality. This would include content that is chaotic, grotesque, or demonic. It would also include art that is self-absorbed, showing off esoteric techniques rather than sharing meaning with an educated viewer.

TO CHANGE THE WORLD

This is the final section of a long book (congratulations if you've made it this far; extra points if you've read all the sidebars). This section isn't so much making an argument as weaving a spell. The argument has already been made throughout the book: you were created to create in all legitimate aspects of human culture, and by doing so to live redemptively in God's world. You may not be called upon by God to change the whole world, but the good cultural creations you come up with *will* make a difference in the circle of "neighbors" God gives you to love: your family, your church, and your community.

American Christians are pretty enamored with the idea of making a big cultural splash. They flock to see celebrities and sports stars who are Christians. They're thrilled when a song by a Christian music group hits the secular Top 40. A lot of Christians were positively ecstatic when Mel Gibson's *The Passion of the Christ* made it to theaters. They were practically ready to build additions onto their churches to prepare for the influx of converts they expected. *Hollywood is evangelizing for us!* But the conversions didn't materialize. The Narnia films didn't bring them in either.

Positive cultural change on a grand scale is possible, but take a lesson from Jesus: He invested in precisely twelve disciples, and only three of them were really close. He didn't make all that big a splash. The great majority of the world's population had no idea that He lived or died. Or resurrected. But that resurrection was a tiny seed that grew into a massive tree. Nothing in the history of the planet has ever had a greater cultural impact. Don't assume that you have to change the world in obvious ways for your life to be faithful and worthwhile.

A homeschooling mother of six started producing a regular podcast that aims to revive the practice of family reading time.[30] No one but God will ever know the good she has done for other families. A dad who didn't care for soccer started a soccer league for his sons so they'd have a place to play and grow. A group of Christian young adults discovered a mutual passion for well-designed board games, and they thought they could do better. So they started their own game-design company, launched a website, and got an online video series going.[31] It's hard to look at these cultural artifacts, these good works, and pinpoint the direct benefits they bring. In a hundred years, no one will ever have heard of them, most likely. Christians don't create because they have the power to bring *permanent* good. Only God can do that. We create because we are created in the image of a good Creator.

CULTIVATING

All those who create art and other cultural artifacts have to go through a period of being horribly bad at their chosen craft before they can make any progress. Every world-famous concert pianist begins by plunking out three-note melodies. Every legendary artist starts with scribbles. Every carpenter starts out bending nails and cutting lumber too short. Every novelist starts with wooden prose. And every artist or musician or writer—every sort of cultural creator—has to take the art he or she has inherited and *cultivate* it before adding to it. The etudes pianists play are "studies," exercises in the craft of music-making with that particular instrument. Cultural creators all have to toil in fields others have plowed before they can grow something new.

CULTIVATE

Perfectionism That Discourages

One of the dangers of encouraging the good pursuit of creativity at a level that masters truth, goodness, and beauty is discouragement. People just beginning a pursuit need to be encouraged; they need to be equipped with the fundamentals to continue honing their skills. Parents and master teachers need to be careful to mentor with constructive criticism. Unreasonable expectations can crush the heart. While the self-esteem movement in the Western world hinders good creative cultivation, the pressures for perfectionism in the Eastern world can be just as unbiblical. Operating according to a biblical worldview means that people who are learning a craft or a job skill should be constructively encouraged and equipped. Each individual is valuable regardless of the level of giftedness. Individuals don't have to be the best; they simply need to be faithful in using the talents that God has given.

Cultivation Ideas

Invite several people from your church or community who are skilled in a variety of ways. Have them explain to the students how they got interested in their art or craft. Ask them what they would advise students to do to cultivate the interest and skill in that art or craft.

Encourage the students to expand their horizons by engaging in something beyond the passive intake of media consumption or video games. How can they positively contribute to the culture around them?

Celebrity or Servant?

In chapter 14 of his book *Culture Making*, Andy Crouch presents a contrast between the pursuit of becoming a celebrity and the pursuit of humble servanthood. (His example of servanthood is problematic, but his overall point is valid.) The latter pursuit is what substantively affects people. For all its glitz and glamor, temporary celebrity rarely provides the mass transformation it promises—without the compromise that's often required of maintaining widespread popular fawning. Instead of seeking power and glory, seek to serve others in need. That's the model we see Jesus portraying (John 13:1–17). That's the model the New Testament exhorts us to follow (Gal. 1:10). That's the path that the early church followed, causing it to spread throughout the Roman Empire even as Christians were being persecuted. At that point they certainly weren't becoming the power brokers of society; later on, when they did, the church soon became corrupt.

After You Condemn Culture

John Dyer is the author of a book on technology with a CFR title—*From the Garden to the City: The Redeeming and Corrupting Power of Technology* (Grand Rapids: Kregel, 2011). Dyer was asked at a conference on faith and technology how he deals with media consumption while raising his young children. He said that he doesn't find it helpful to think of limiting screen time (he's a Christian theologian and software developer) but instead encourages his children to use their technology to cultivate and create rather than just to consume. There are things on screens that must be condemned, critiqued, consumed, and copied. But Dyer reflects the heartbeat of this book when he says that creating needs to fill the void left by condemning. In other words, if you get rid of something bad, you generally need to replace it with the good thing that was being twisted by the evil thing.

Feasting with Babette

Babette's Feast is a fine example of a work of art that can be consumed though it contains some elements that should be critiqued (e.g., playing the lottery). The film also can provoke students to create that which is beautiful, true, and good for the benefit of others.

The story line raises an interesting question for Christians who believe they ought to be creative cultivators. The folks in the movie who are worried that a decadent meal might lead them into sin have concerns that are rooted in the reality of the Fall. God's good gifts can be prized above the Giver. Christians can become so enthralled by the beauty and goodness of the best culture that they forget the God who gave them these gifts. On the other hand, abstaining from food that ought to be received with thanksgiving is sinful as well (1 Tim. 4:3–5). Cultivating love for the Giver, not just the gift, is a lifelong discipline.

You can't be a successful writer, for example, unless you read a lot:

> How do you cultivate an "ear" [for language]? . . . Wide reading. You cannot memorize rules, you will not even want to try, until you have an intuitive knowledge of language, until you have cultivated some taste.[32]

Some upperclassmen in high school, a few, have begun to truly *create* in their fields—they can make utterly beautiful and original paintings or poetry or pastries. But most young people need more time cultivating their skills and studying their disciplines before their God-given creative powers can be given full display. Some skills take almost a lifetime to cultivate.

But when you've toiled in the field, cultivating, and when you've put in your time to gain a creative skill, there's almost no feeling on earth like exercising that gift for God's glory.

In *Babette's Feast*, a 1987 Danish film, a French refugee named Babette arrives in a rural part of Jutland in Denmark. Never revealing her past, she works for fourteen years—for free—as the cook for a pair of spinsters who are members of an austere religious sect. She cooks the bland meals these two buttoned-up sisters expect.

Then she wins ten thousand francs in the lottery—a fortune at that time. She decides to stage a grand meal for the ladies and the small group of graying congregants in their tiny religious assembly. The old folks are afraid that the exotic ingredients Babette is shipping into the tiny seaside town will cause them to sin; will she feed them a decadent meal, leading them into sensuality? They agree not to express any pleasure over the meal but to merely consume it dispassionately, the way they eat their normal pabulum.

One guest at the meal, however, is an outsider who knows good cooking when he tastes it. Astounded by the quality of the food and drink, he regales the other guests with stories of a legendary meal he once enjoyed at the Parisian restaurant Café Anglais.

Babette's amazing culinary artistry wears away the distrust of her austere guests, and "a mystical redemption of the human spirit settles over the table."[33] The power of creativity, borne of love and gratitude, overcomes even the most abstemious* objections as Babette shares her joy through her creative work. It turns out that Babette was once the chef at Café Anglais and that a dinner for twelve at her restaurant used to cost ten thousand francs.

abstemious: *refusing to be self-indulgent*

The simple, rural folk assume Babette will return to Paris, but she has spent every bit of her lottery winnings on the extravagant meal. One of the sisters says, in tears, "Now you will be poor the rest of your life." Babette replies, "An artist is never poor."[34]

CHRISTIAN CREATORS

Christian creators, such as contemporary classical composer Dan Forrest, can express their love for God, for neighbor, and for their art with hearts full of joy. Forrest's work has achieved worldwide recognition. His choral work *Requiem for the Living* has been particularly popular—you can find it online. Forrest's website carries his statement of beliefs, which shows how the Creation-Fall-Redemption worldview drives his work:

> All good things, including any beauty that we encounter, are from God, through God, and ultimately to God. All beauty is God's beauty, wherever it is found.

Foundation for Life

In Chapter 1, students were encouraged to take part in culture based on a solid understanding of their worldview. Students should have a much better understanding of that worldview now. Their appetites should have been whetted for getting involved in many different spheres: education, politics, art, science, music, sports, and so forth. The question still remains whether they will participate in the activities of life based on (a) their own wisdom, assuming the popular thinking of their culture or (b) God's wisdom from a biblical worldview.

What they learned in this textbook should have begun the process of equipping them and encouraging them to participate in every one of those spheres without limiting themselves. They should have been encouraged not to limit the Bible. The biblical viewpoint should guide their participation in every one of those spheres. The Bible is not limited to only a few explicitly religious spheres of life. Students must be salt and light as they apply scriptural wisdom to everything they think and do.

As Abraham Kuyper said, "There is not a square inch in the whole domain of our human existence over which Christ, who is Sovereign over all, does not cry: 'Mine!'" [James D. Bratt, ed., *Abraham Kuyper: A Centennial Reader* (Grand Rapids: Eerdmans, 1998), 488]

Our world was designed to be a place of beauty and goodness, but was marred by sin, and continues to struggle with evil. But one day God will make things fully right again; and in the meantime, beauty and goodness are not totally lost—they still shine through, and point us toward the way things ought to be.

Whatever abilities I have, for creating beauty, are gifts from God. So I will make the most beautiful music I can, not because music making is my ultimate end, but because I want to press my gifts to their maximum potential toward the true ultimate end: glorifying God. This is equally true of my "secular" music and "sacred" music, of my concert music and church music.

Jesus Christ is Lord, to the glory of God the Father. "He must increase, and I must decrease."[35]

Just as going on the offensive and doing good science is one of the best defenses of the Christian faith in the scientific arena, doing good art (including literature, music, and all forms of culture—even if that culture never goes beyond the confines of your immediate family) is one of the best defenses of the Christian faith in the cultural arena.

Christians will never quite feel comfortable in this fallen world until Christ makes all things new. But this is still our Father's world. "He shines in all that's fair."[36] Christians should be on the forefront of creative work, cultivating a culture of transcendence attractive to a broken world.

THINKING IT THROUGH 27.2

1. What posture toward culture should be the ultimate goal of Christians?

2. In addition to critical thinking, what other two elements must be included in a biblical worldview?

3. Why can't the biblical worldview stop with simply destroying those things that are raised up against God?

4. What ought to motivate creativity?

5. Why must every subcreator begin with cultivation?

---

1. creativity because God created humans to be subcreators

2. feeling (affections) and doing (action)

3. Christians were originally created to and are called to positively construct in all fields of human culture. The Fall may impede creativity, but it doesn't remove the responsibility and privilege of the Creation Mandate.

4. love for God and others

5. Every person must study and exercise the practice of their skills before becoming creative on their own.

Making Connections

1. condemn, critique, consume, copy, create, cultivate

2. Discernment is gained through a process of training that brings a person to maturity; this begins under the guidance of those with biblical wisdom (parents, teachers, pastors).

3. Although a biblical worldview must necessarily condemn whatever is set up against God, the goal is to constructively contribute to God's created order positively.

4. Rather than being enamored with the ideal of changing the whole world, we should endeavor to make a difference by living faithfully in our own circle of neighbors: family, church, and community.

Developing Skills in Apologetics and Worldview

5. The Bible is matter of fact about things that happened; it doesn't demand that you imagine all of the details. Movies as a medium, by nature, explicitly show even the sordid details you don't need to meditate on in order to understand the biblical warning.

6. Christians need to discern whether a cultural artifact, by God's common grace, reflects truth, goodness, and beauty. If the cultural artifact stands on its own as true, good, and beautiful, then Christians may be able to copy it and make use of it for Christian purposes too. If it can't stand on its own as true, good, and beautiful, then it would need to be so changed that its transformation couldn't legitimately be called copying. But if it's just copied with Christianese slapped onto it, then it would remain illegitimate.

Examining Assumptions and Evidence

7. You must demonstrate that it violates the standards of truth, goodness, or beauty in some objective way.

8. Critiques must be based on the biblical criteria of truth, goodness, and beauty, which are all rooted in the character of God.

---

27 CHAPTER REVIEW

TERMS TO REMEMBER
cultural artifact
discernment
critic
medium
conceptual art
hospitality (in art)

Scripture Memory

Genesis 2:15

Making Connections

1. List the six possible gestures/postures a person can use with regard to culture and the arts.

2. How can a person gain discernment according to Hebrews 5:14?

3. Is the primary goal of a biblical worldview to be destructive or constructive? Explain your answer.

4. Should you try to change the whole world? Why or why not?

Developing Skills in Apologetics & Biblical Worldview

5. Assuming it's true that "the medium is the message," how would you differentiate between the biblical portrayal of immoral acts (e.g., Gen. 19:30–38 or 2 Sam. 13:1–20) and a movie with scenes depicting similar situations?

6. Based on Romans 12:1–2, how would you differentiate between legitimate copying of and illegitimate blending into the surrounding heathen culture?

Examining Assumptions & Evidence

7. In order to justify condemning a cultural artifact, what must you demonstrate beyond merely disliking it?

8. By what standard should a Christian critique a cultural artifact?

9. When was the last time you simply consumed a cultural artifact without critiquing or condemning it? Do you support or regret that choice?

10. Why is cultivation a prerequisite for creativity?

Becoming a Creative Cultivator

11. Think of the last cultural artifact you created. This could include poetry or a short story, instrumental or vocal music, a painting or a sculpture, a meal or a craft (e.g., woodworking). Write a paragraph explaining how or whether your cultural artifact demonstrates the principle of "hospitality."

---

9. Answers will vary. Just sitting back and consuming a cultural artifact increases one's ability to simply enjoy it. While it's not always good to consume without critique when major or pervasive objectionable elements are present, it's also not always good to spoil something that is largely good by shifting the focus to picky criticisms.

10. Creativity usually results in poor quality and taste without first cultivating the foundational skills.

Becoming a Creative Cultivator

11. Answers will vary. Students should mention objective ways that they were able to show love for others through what they produced.

TERMS TO REMEMBER

cultural artifact—anything made by a human being and embedded within a certain culture

discernment—biblical wisdom

critic—someone helps others know what is worth watching or reading by summarizing the content and helping others process the content

medium—the way one communicates a message, affecting the meaning

conceptual art—activist art meant to make disturbing statements that are often politically motivated

hospitality (in art)—art driven by an others-oriented principle of love, which commonly drives decorative art

ADDITIONAL RESOURCES

ENDNOTES

Frontispiece

1. Theodore Roosevelt, "Chapters of a Possible Autobiography," *The Outlook: Volume CIII* (New York: The Outlook Company, 1913), 403.

Chapter 1: Worldviews

1. Glenn Branch, "The Kilosteve," *Reports of the National Center for Science Education* 29, issue 3 (2009): 35.

2. Bill Maher, interview with Conan O'Brien, *Late Night with Conan O'Brien*, NBC, January 4, 2008. http://www.nationalreview.com/node/155715/print.

3. Stephen Jay Gould, *Leonardo's Mountain of Clams and the Diet of Worms* (Cambridge, MA: Harvard University Press, 2011), 269–84.

4. Real Science 4 Kids (website), http://www.gravitaspublications.com/.

5. Albert Wolters, *Creation Regained: Biblical Basics for a Reformational Worldview* (Grand Rapids: Eerdmans, 2005), 3.

6. Gregg L. Frazer, *The Religious Beliefs of America's Founders* (Lawrence: University of Kansas Press, 2012), x.

7. Kitty Ferguson, *Stephen Hawking: His Life and Work* (London: Transworld, 2011), 129.

8. Brian J. Walsh and J. Richard Middleton, *The Transforming Vision: Shaping a Christian World View* (Downers Grove, IL: IVP Academic, 1984), 35.

9. Based on a comment by Bradlee Dean, quoted in Matt Labash, "What Would Jesus Rap?" *Weekly Standard* (website), May 15, 2006.

10. Richard Dawkins, *The God Delusion* (New York: Houghton Mifflin Harcourt, 2006), 19.

11. Stanley Fish, *The Trouble with Principle* (Cambridge, MA: Harvard University Press, 2001), 33.

12. Brian Swimme, *Journey of the Universe*, PBS, June 11, 2011.

13. Ibid.

14. Carolyn Weber, *Surprised by Oxford* (Nashville: Thomas Nelson, 2011), 124–26.

15. Neil Postman, "Science and the Story We Need," *First Things* 69, January, 1997.

16. Nathan Wilson, *Death by Living: Life Is Meant to Be Spent* (Nashville: Thomas Nelson, 2013), 6.

17. Richard Dawkins, quoted in "The Reading File," *New York Times* (website), November 9, 2003.

Chapter 2: Presuppositions

1. J. Warner Wallace, *Cold-Case Christianity* (Colorado Springs: David C. Cook, 2013), 29.

2. Gary Habermas, William Lane Craig, Paul D. Feinberg, Kelly James Clark, and John M. Frame, *Five Views on Apologetics*, ed. Steven B. Cowan (Grand Rapids: Zondervan, 2000), 95.

3. Ibid., 100.

4. Stanley J. Grenz, David Guretzki, and Cherith Fee Nordling, *Pocket Dictionary of Theological Terms* (Downers Grove, IL: InterVarsity Press, 1999), 48.

5. Stephanie Pappas, "What Preserved *T. Rex* Tissue? Mystery Explained at Last," *NBC News*, November 27, 2013.

6. Thomas Nagel, *Mind and Cosmos: Why the Materialist Neo-Darwinian Conception of Nature Is Almost Certainly False* (New York: Oxford University Press, 2012), 5.

7. Bertrand Russell, quoted in Emily Eakin, "So God's Really in the Details?" *New York Times* (website), May 11, 2002.

8. Thomas Nagel, *Mind and Cosmos: Why the Materialist Neo-Darwinian Conception of Nature Is Almost Certainly False* (New York: Oxford University Press, 2012).

9. Tim Keller, *The Reason for God* (New York: Dutton, 2008), xviii.

10. Richard Dawkins, Richard Dawkins Foundation for Reason and Science (website), http://old.richarddawkins.net/quotes?page=4.

11. C. S. Lewis, *Mere Christianity*, revised edition (New York: HarperCollins, 2009), 62.

12. A. Viberg, "Job," *New Dictionary of Biblical Theology* (Downers Grove, IL: IVP Academic, 2000), 201.

Chapter 3: The Two-Story View

1. Gary Gutting, "Is Atheism Irrational?" *New York Times* (website), February 9, 2014.

2. Lesslie Newbigin, "Certain Faith: What Kind of Certainty?" *Tyndale Bulletin* 44, no. 2 (1993): 340.

3. Adapted from Nancy Pearcey, *Total Truth: Liberating Christianity from Its Cultural Captivity* (Wheaton: Crossway Books, 2004), 20–21.

4. Barack Obama, "Remarks by the President at the National Prayer Breakfast," The White House (website), February 2, 2012.

5. Abraham Lincoln, "Second Inaugural Address of Abraham Lincoln" (March 4, 1865), http://avalon.law.yale.edu/19th_century/lincoln2.asp.

6. "Moving America Forward: 2012 Democratic National Platform," http://www.panly.net.

7. Ibid.

8. Michael J. Sandel, *Justice: What's the Right Thing to Do?* (New York: Farrar, Straus and Giroux, 2009), 261 (emphasis added).

9. Nancy Pearcey, *Total Truth: Liberating Christianity from Its Cultural Captivity* (Wheaton: Crossway Books, 2004), 19.

10. *The Incredibles* (DVD), directed by Brad Bird (Burbank, CA: Walt Disney Home Entertainment, 2005).

11. Herman Bavinck quoted in Jan Veenhof, *Nature and Grace in Herman Bavinck* (Dordt College Press, 2006), 29–30.

12. James D. Bratt, ed., *Abraham Kuyper: A Centennial Reader* (Grand Rapids: Eerdmans, 1998), 488.

13. Stanley Fish, "Why We Can't All Just Get Along," *First Things*, February 1996, 10.

14. List of disciplines adapted from Albert Wolters, *Creation Regained: Biblical Basics for a Reformational Worldview* (Grand Rapids: Eerdmans, 2005), 3.

15. Bob Jones Sr., sermon, September 14, 1948, J. S. Mack Library archives, http://www.markandlauraward.com/blog/2014/01/27/dr-bob-jones-srs-first-use-of-all-ground-is-holy-ground/.

Chapter 4: God the Creator

1. N. D. Wilson, "Myth Wars: C. S. Lewis vs. Scientism" (video), Desiring God Conference, September 27, 2013, http://www.desiringgod.org/conference-messages/myth-wars-c-s-lewis-vs-scientism#full-video.

2. Michael Reeves, *Delighting in the Trinity* (Downers Grove, IL: InterVarsity Press), 21.

3. Ibid., 31.

4. Quoted in J. N. D. Kelly, *The Athanasian Creed: The Paddock Lectures for 1962–3* (London: Adam and Charles Black, 1964), 17.

5. "Muhammad Ali," Wikipedia, en.wikiquote.org/wiki/Muhammad_Ali.

6. Roy Sorensen, "Nothingness," in *Stanford Encyclopedia of Philosophy*, ed. Edward N. Zalta (Winter 2012).

7. Jonathan Edwards, "A Dissertation Concerning the End for which God Created the World" as cited with updated language by John Piper, *God's Passion for His Glory* (Wheaton: Crossway Books, 1998), 247.

8. Roy Sorensen, "Nothingness," in *Stanford Encyclopedia of Philosophy*, ed. Edward N. Zalta (Winter 2012).

9. Michael Reeves, *Delighting in the Trinity* (Downers Grove, IL: InterVarsity Press), 28.

10. Quoted in James R. Boyd, *The Westminster Shorter Catechism with Analysis, Scriptural Proofs, Explanatory and Practical Inferences and Illustrative Anecdotes* (Philadelphia: Presbyterian Board of Publication, 1884), 19.

11. Diagrams based on Wayne Grudem, *Systematic Theology* (Grand Rapids: Zondervan, 1995), 267ff.

12. Carl Sagan, *Cosmos* (DVD), Cosmos Studios, 2002, http://www.cosmolearning.com/documentaries/cosmos/.

13. Ann Druyan, quoted in Brit Mandelo, "Exploring Carl Sagan's *Cosmos*," Tor.com (blog), November 9.

14. Neil deGrasse Tyson, *Cosmos: A Spacetime Odyssey* (DVD) (Los Angeles: 20th Century Fox, 2014).

15. Herman Bavinck, *Reformed Dogmatics*, ed. John Bolt, trans. John Vriend, *God and Creation* (Grand Rapids: Baker Academic, 2003), 2:412.

16. "Are You a Pantheist?" Universal Pantheist Society (website), http://www.pantheist.net/.

17. Christian Smith and Melinda Lundquist Denton, *Soul Searching: The Religious and Spiritual Lives of American Teenagers* (New York: Oxford University Press, 2005), 162.

18. Ibid., 162–63.

19. Robert Bellah, "Civil Religion in America," *Dædalus, Journal of the American Academy of Arts and Sciences* 96, no. 1 (1967): 1–21.

20. Voltaire, quoted by J. I. Packer in *Still Sovereign*, eds. Thomas R. Schreiner and Bruce A. Ware (Grand Rapids: Baker Academic, 2000), 277.

21. Terri Gross, "Seth Macfarlane: TV's 'Family Guy' Makes Music, Too" (interview), NPR (website), October 17, 2011.

22. C. S. Lewis, *The Four Loves* (San Diego: Harcourt Brace Jovanovich, 1960), 127.

Chapter 5: Man and His Mandate

1. "Prime Directive," Wikipedia, http://en.wikipedia.org/wiki/Prime_directive.

2. People for the Ethical Treatment of Animals (website), http://www.peta.org.

3. Brian May, "Life Is Evolution," *New York Times* (website), March 28, 2007.

4. Jeri Taylor, "Nothing Human," *Star Trek Voyager* (season 5, episode 8; DVD), directed by David Livingston (Los Angeles: Paramount, December 2, 1998), http://www.amazon.com/gp/product/B005HEVKSA/ref=dv_dp_ep8#.

5. "Threshold," *Star Trek* episode, http://en.memory-alpha.org/wiki/Threshold (episode).

6. "Carl Linnaeus," Wikipedia, http://en.wikipedia.org/wiki/Carolus_Linnaeus.

7. G. K. Chesterton, *The Everlasting Man* (Radford, VA: Wilder Publications, 2008).

8. C. S. Lewis, *Prince Caspian: The Return to Narnia* (New York: Harper Collins, 1951), 218.

9. Stephen Hawking, televised interview with Kenneth Campbell, *Reality on the Rocks*, 1995.

10. Stanley Horton, *Systematic Theology* (Springfield, MO: Gospel Publishing House, 2013), 373.

11. Gregory Berns, "Dogs Are People, Too," *New York Times* (website), October 5, 2013.

12. Robert Krulwich, *Morality*, NPR radio podcast

(season 2, episode 3), http://www.radiolab.org/story/91508-morality/.

13. Christian Smith and Melinda Lundquist Denton, *Soul Searching: The Religious and Spiritual Lives of American Teenagers* (New York: Oxford University Press, 2005), 173.

14. Gilda Sedgh, "Induced Abortion Incidence and Trends Worldwide from 1995 to 2008," *The Lancet* 379 (2012).

15. Larry Bumpass, "The Measurement of Public Opinion on Abortion," *Family Planning Perspectives* 29 (July/August 1997): 177–80.

16. Janine Latus, "Self-Esteem: The Repair Kit," *O Magazine*, January 2008.

17. Roman Price, lifepulp.com, http://bit.ly/QdAoyZ.

18. Centers for Disease Control and Prevention (website), http://www.cdc.gov/nchs/fastats/leading-causes-of-death.htm.

19. Jonathan Last, *What to Expect When No One's Expecting* (New York: Encounter Books, 2013), 7.

20. "Combined Oral Contraceptive Pill," Wikipedia, http://en.wikipedia.org/wiki/The_pill.

21. "The World Factbook," Central Intelligence Agency (website), https://www.cia.gov/library/publications/the-world-factbook/rankorder/2054rank.html.

22. See "China's Achilles' Heel," *The Economist*, April 2012.

23. Nina Fedoroff quoted in Steven Duke, "Earth Population 'Exceeds Limits,'" *BBC News* (March 31, 2009).

24. Bryan Smith, "BJU Press BI—Story," conference presentation April 12, 2011, http://prezi.com/xxsnfdf17mic/bju-press-bistory/.

25. John Frame, *Systematic Theology* (Phillipsburg, NJ: P&R Publishing, 2013), 1034.

26. "Naples Waste Management Issue," Wikipedia, http://en.wikipedia.org/wiki/Naples_waste_management_issue.

27. Victor P. Hamilton, *The Book of Genesis: Chapters 1–17*, New International Commentary on the Old Testament (Grand Rapids: Eerdmans, 1990), 171.

28. Malcolm Gladwell, *Outliers: The Story of Success* (New York Little, Brown and Company, 2008).

29. Carina Chocano, "The Chef at 15," *New York Times Magazine* (website), March 28, 2014.

30. Ed Panosian, Church History class, Bob Jones Seminary.

31. See Jared Diamond's evolutionary and materialistic, but still valuable, account of human history, *Guns, Germs, and Steel: The Fates of Human Societies* (New York: W. W. Norton, 1997).

32. Based on Andy Crouch, *Culture Making: Recovering our Creative Calling* (Downers Grove, IL: InterVarsity Press, 2009), 41.

33. See Brian J. Walsh and J. Richard Middleton, *The Transforming Vision: Shaping a Christian World View* (Downers Grove, IL: IVP Academic, 1984), 55.

34. Andy Crouch, *Playing God: Redeeming the Gift of Power* (Downers Grove, IL: InterVarsity Press 2013), 35.

35. Andy Crouch, *Culture Making: Recovering our Creative Calling* (Downers Grove, IL: InterVarsity Press, 2009), 23.

36. John Frame, *The Doctrine of the Christian Life: A Theology of Lordship* (Phillipsburg, NJ: P&R Publishing, 2008), 866.

37. Andy Crouch, *Playing God: Redeeming the Gift of Power* (Downers Grove, IL: InterVarsity Press 2013), 201.

38. Peter Gutmann, "The Sounds of Silence," Classical Notes (website), 1999; see also Alex Ross, *The Rest Is Noise: Listening to the Twentieth Century* (New York: Farrar, Strauss and Giroux, 2007), 364ff.

39. This argument about John Cage is based on Andy Crouch, *Culture Making: Recovering our Creative Calling* (Downers Grove, IL: InterVarsity Press, 2009), 73-74.

40. Ibid., 22.

Chapter 6: Everything God Made Was Very Good

1. Albert Wolters, *Creation Regained: Biblical Basics for a Reformational Worldview* (Grand Rapids: Eerdmans, 2005), 48–49.

2. Gregg R. Allison, "Toward a Theology of Human Embodiment," *Southern Baptist Journal of Theology* 13, no. 2 (2009): 4.

3. Frederica Mathewes-Green, "The Subject Was Noses: What Happens When Academics Discover That We Have Bodies," *Books and Culture* (January/February 1997): 14.

4. Zachary G. Smith, "Gnosticism," ed. John D. Barry and Lazarus Wentz, *The Lexham Bible Dictionary* (Bellingham, WA: Lexham Press, 2012).

5. Christian Smith and Melinda Lundquist Denton, *Soul Searching: The Religious and Spiritual Lives of American Teenagers* (New York: Oxford University Press, 2005), 189.

6. Erik Lundegaard, "Truth, Justice, and (Fill in the Blank)," *New York Times* (website), June 30, 2006, A23.

7. Andy Crouch, *Playing God: Redeeming the Gift of Power* (Downers Grove, IL: InterVarsity Press 2013), 45.

8. Rob Lister, *God Is Impassible and Impassioned: Toward a Theology of Divine Emotion* (Wheaton: Crossway, 2012), 163–64 (especially the Feinberg quote).

9. "Making Data Dance," *The Economist*, December 9, 2010, emphasis added.

10. Ibid.

11. "About Abby," Abby Johnson (website), http://www.abbyjohnson.org.

12. Ibid.

13. Albert Wolters, *Creation Regained: Biblical Basics for a Reformational Worldview* (Grand Rapids: Eerdmans, 2005), 50.

14. See Stephanie Coontz, *Marriage, a History: From Obedience to Intimacy or How Love Conquered Marriage* (New York: Viking, 2005).

15. James Fincannon, "Six Flags on the Moon: What Is Their Current Condition?" NASA (website), April 2012.

16. David T. Koyzis, *Political Visions and Illusions* (Downers Grove, IL: IVP Academic, 2003), 185.

17. See review of Carl Trueman's *Republocrat* (Phillipsburg, NJ: P&R Publishing, 2010) at http://byfaithweunderstand.com/2010/10/11/confessions-of-a-christian-conservative/.

18. See Albert Wolters, *Creation Regained: Biblical Basics for a Reformational Worldview* (Grand Rapids: Eerdmans, 2005), 38.

19. "'Nones' on the Rise," Pew Research Center (website), October 9, 2012.

20. Alice Chasan, "On the Frontline of the Mommy Wars" (interview with Linda Hirshman), Belief.net (website), October, 2006.

21. Ibid.

22. Ibid.

23. Brian J. Walsh and J. Richard Middleton, *The Transforming Vision: Shaping a Christian World View* (Downers Grove, IL: IVP Academic, 1984), 156.

24. Ibid.

25. Barba Demick, *Nothing to Envy* (New York: Spiegel 7 Grau, 2010), 220. See also "Famine in North Korea," Wikipedia, http://en.wikipedia.org/wiki/Famine_in_North_Korea.

26. David T. Koyzis, *Political Visions and Illusions* (Downers Grove, IL: IVP Academic, 2003), 197.

27. Colin Kidd, *The Forging of Races: Race and Scripture in the Protestant Atlantic World, 1600–2000* (Cambridge: Cambridge University Press, 2006), 3.

28. Robert Benne, *Good and Bad Ways to Think about Religion and Politics* (Grand Rapids: Eerdmans, 2010), 58.

Chapter 7: Far as the Curse Is Found

1. John Frame, *Systematic Theology* (Phillipsburg, NJ: P&R Publishing, 2013), 851.

2. John Piper, "Nudity in Drama and the Clothing of Christ," Desiring God (website), November 20, 2006.

3. Gregg R. Allison, "Toward a Theology of Human Embodiment," *Southern Baptist Journal of Theology* 13, no. 2 (2009):9.

4. Jeffrey Kluger, "The Evolution of a Narcissist," *Time*, September 1, 2014.

5. Alan Jacobs, *Original Sin* (New York: HarperCollins, 2009), 92.

6. "Fall," MormonWiki, http://www.mormonwiki.com/Fall.

7. J. R. R. Tolkien, *Return of the King: Being the Third Part of the Lord of the Rings* (New York: Houghton Mifflin Harcourt, 1988), 924.

8. "Lun Lun the Giant Panda Gives Birth to Twins!" Zoo Atlanta (website), July 15, 2013.

9. Natalie Angier, "One Thing They Aren't: Maternal," *New York Times* (website), May 9, 2006.

10. Alfred Lord Tennyson, in "In Memoriam A. H. H.," *The Works of Alfred Lord Tennyson* (Ware, Hertfordshire, England: Wordsworth Editions Ltd., 1998), 338.

11. Abraham Kuyper, *Calvinism: Six Stone-lectures* (Charleston, SC: BiblioBazaar, 2009), 174.

12. Gilda Sedgh, "Induced Abortion Incidence and Trends Worldwide from 1995 to 2008," *The Lancet* 379 (2012): 2.

13. Alfred Lord Tennyson, in "In Memoriam A. H. H.," *The Works of Alfred Lord Tennyson* (Ware, Hertfordshire, England: Wordsworth Editions Ltd., 1998), 339.

14. Richard Dawkins, *The Selfish Gene* (Oxford: Oxford University Press, 1976), 2.

15. Carl Sagan, "One Voice in the Cosmic Fugue," *Cosmos* (TV series), season 1, episode 2.

16. John Frame, *Systematic Theology* (Phillipsburg, NJ: P&R Publishing, 2013), 858.

17. Bruce Waltke, *Genesis: A Commentary* (Grand Rapids: Zondervan, 2001), 92.

18. Derek Kidner, *Genesis*, Tyndale Old Testament Commentary (Downers Grove, IL: InterVarsity, 2008), 71.

19. Bruce Waltke, *Genesis: A Commentary* (Grand Rapids: Zondervan, 2001), 95.

20. "Maternal Mortality," World Health Organization (website), May 2014.

21. Nik Ripken with Greg Lewis, *The Insanity of God: A True Story of Faith Resurrected* (Nashville: B&H Books, 2013), 63.

22. Ibid., 118.

23. Ibid., 60.

24. Charles Murray, *Coming Apart: The State of White America, 1960–2010* (New York: Crown Forum, 2012), 167.

25. Stephanie Coontz, *Marriage, a History: From Obedience to Intimacy or How Love Conquered Marriage* (New York: Viking, 2005), 5.

26. "The Holy Virgin Mary," Wikipedia, http://en.wikipedia.org/wiki/The_Holy_Virgin_Mary.

27. Deb Richardson-Moore, "Help, Don't Hurt, the Homeless with Your Gifts," Greenville Online, March 2, 2014.

28. See Steve Corbett and Brian Fikkert, *When Helping Hurts* (Chicago: Moody, 2014).

29. Herman Ridderbos, *Paul: An Outline of His Theology* (Grand Rapids: Eerdmans, 1975), 91.

30. John Frame, *The Doctrine of the Christian Life* (Phillipsburg, NJ: P & R Publishing, 2008), 866.

31. W. B. Yeats, "The Second Coming," in *The Classic Hundred Poems*, ed. William Harmon (New York: Columbia University Press, 1998).

32. Nik Ripken with Greg Lewis, *The Insanity of God: A True Story of Faith Resurrected* (Nashville: B&H Books, 2013).

Chapter 8: Common Grace, the World, and You

1. C. S. Lewis, *Mere Christianity* (New York: Harper Collins, 1980), 56.

2. C. S. Lewis, *The Screwtape Letters* (New York: Harper Collins, 1942), 8.

3. Examples adapted from John Frame, *Systematic Theology* (Phillipsburg, NJ: P&R Publishing, 2013), 863.

4. Herman Bavinck, "Calvin and Common Grace," Princeton Theological Review 7 (1909): 437–65.

5. Kenneth Myers, "Is 'Popular Culture' Either?" *Modern Reformation* 6 (January/February 1997): 9–12.

6. T. M. Moore, *Redeeming Pop Culture* (Phillipsburg, NJ: P&R Publishing, 2003), 9.

7. Kenneth Myers, *All God's Children and Blue Suede Shoes: Christians and Popular Culture* (Wheaton: Crossway, 1989), xiii.

8. Ibid.

9. Ibid., xii–xiii.

10. John Frame, *The Doctrine of the Christian Life: A Theology of Lordship* (Phillipsburg NJ: P&R Publishing, 2008), 866.

11. Cornelius Platinga Jr., *Engaging God's World: A Christian Vision of Faith, Learning, and Living* (Grand Rapids: Eerdmans, 2002), 63.

12. Ibid.

13. Fred Sanders, "They Quit Making Good Music When I Turned 30," *First Things* (blog), October 21, 2009, http://www.firstthings.com/index.php?permalink=blogs&blog=firstthoughts&year=2009&month=10&entry_permalink=they-quit-making-good-music-when-i-turned-30.

14. Andy Crouch, *Culture Making: Recovering Our Creative Calling* (Downers Grove, IL: IVP, 2013), 89.

15. Richard Mouw, *He Shines in All That's Fair: Culture and Common Grace* (Grand Rapids: Eerdmans, 2002), 28.

16. Nancy L. Segal, "The Closest of Strangers," *New York Times* (website), May 23, 2014.

17. Fernando Garibay, Paul Blair, Stefani Germanotta, and J. B. Laursen, "Born This Way," http://www.metrolyrics.com/born-this-way-lyrics-lady-gaga.html.

18. "Born This Way (song)," Wikipedia, http://en.wikipedia.org/wiki/Born_This_Way_(song).

19. John Piper, *When I Don't Desire God: How to Fight for Joy* (Wheaton: Crossway, 2004), 47.

20. Bruce Waltke, *The Book of Proverbs, Chapters 1–15*, New International Commentary on the Old Testament (Grand Rapids: Eerdmans, 2004), 180–81.

21. Ibid., 100–101.

22. M. J. Stephey, "What Came Before the Big Bang?" *Time*, August 13, 2009.

23. Ibid.

24. Ibid.

25. Sinclair Ferguson, ed., *New Dictionary of Theology* (Downers Grove, IL: IVP Academic, 1988), 328.

26. Douglas Wilson, *Collision* (DVD), 2009, http://www.collisionmovie.com/.

Chapter 9: Structure and Direction

1. C. S. Lewis, *Perelandra* (New York: HarperOne, 2012), 161.

2. Albert Wolters, *Creation Regained* (Grand Rapids: Eerdmans, 2005), 66–67.

3. Ibid., 91.

4. C. S. Lewis, *Christian Reflections* (Grand Rapids: Eerdmans, 1967), 33.

5. Laura Sessions Stepp, "Books—*Unhooked: How Young Women Pursue Sex, Delay Love, and Lose at Both*," *Washington Post* (website), February 14, 2007.

6. Ross Douthat, "Conservative and Affirmative Consent," *New York Times* (website), October 16, 2014.

7. Rachel Slick, "The Atheist Daughter of a Notable Christian Apologist Shares Her Story," The Friendly Atheist (blog), July 15, 2013.

8. Albert Wolters, *Creation Regained* (Grand Rapids: Eerdmans, 2005), 57.

9. Laura Sessions Stepp, "Books—*Unhooked: How Young Women Pursue Sex, Delay Love, and Lose at Both*," *Washington Post* (website), February 14, 2007.

10. "Materialism, n." OED Online, December 2014, Oxford University Press.

11. "Affluenza," Wikipedia, http://en.wikipedia.org/wiki/Affluenza.

12. Lily Rothman, "Kids TV Survey: How Much TV Kids Watch," *Time*, November 20, 2013.

13. See Andy Crouch, *Culture Making* (Downers Grove, IL: InterVarsity Press, 2009), 29–30.

14. Vern Poythress, *In the Beginning Was the Word* (Wheaton: Crossway, 2009), 9.

15. Stephen Anderson, *Doctor Dolittle's Delusion: Animals and the Uniqueness of Human Language* (New Haven, CT: Yale University Press, 2006).

16. Vern Poythress, *In the Beginning Was the Word* (Wheaton: Crossway, 2009), 353ff.

17. Jay Hathaway, "NPR Pulled a Brilliant April Fools' Prank on People Who Don't Read," Gawker (blog), April 3, 2014, http://gawker.com/npr-pulled-a-brilliant-april-fools-prank-on-people-who-1557745710.

18. Ronald Horton, *Christian Education: Its Mandate and Mission* (Greenville, SC: BJU Press, 1992), 66.

19. Ibid.

Chapter 10: An Everlasting Kingdom

1. Albert Wolters, *Creation Regained: Biblical Basics for a Reformational Worldview* (Grand Rapids: Eerdmans, 2005), 72.

2. Isaac Backus, *An Appeal to the Public for Religious Liberty Against the Oppressions of the Present Day* (Boston: John Boyle, 1773), 6.

3. Albert Wolters, *Creation Regained* (Grand Rapids: Eerdmans, 2005), 45–46.

4. Bruce Riley Ashford, quoted in Justin Taylor, "An Interview with Bruce Ashford on Christian Cultural Engagement," The Gospel Coalition (website), May 5, 2015.

Chapter 11: Redeemed for Good Works

1. J. R. R. Tolkien, "On Fairy Stories," in *Tree and Leaf* (London: George Allen & Unwin Unlimited, 1964), 62.

2. J. R. R. Tolkien, *The Two Towers*, Part 2 of *The Lord of the Rings*, 2nd ed. (New York: Del Rey Books, 2012), 362.

3. Ibid., 362–63.

4. Ibid., 363.

5. Ibid.

6. C. S. Lewis, *The Last Battle* (New York: HarperTrophy, 1994), 228.

7. D. A. Carson, "Editorial: The Hole in the Gospel," *Themelios* 38 (2013): 354.

8. Cornelius Plantinga Jr., *Not the Way It's Supposed to Be: A Breviary of Sin* (Grand Rapids: Eerdmans, 1995), 16.

9. "Colombia: Pastor Martyred," Voice of the Martyrs (website), October 12, 2009.

10. Personal communication with the lead author of this textbook, March 2013.

11. Richard Lee, ed., *The American Patriot's Bible: The Word of God and the Shaping of America* (Nashville: Thomas Nelson, 2009).

12. "Births: Final Data for 2013," *National Vital Statistics Reports 64* (January 15, 2015): 6.

Chapter 12: The Mission of the Church and Your Vocation

1. Gregg R. Allison, *Sojourners and Strangers: The Doctrine of the Church*, ed. John S. Feinberg (Wheaton: Crossway, 2012), 89, fn 60.

2. Christopher J. H. Wright, *The Mission of God's People: A Biblical Theology of the Church's Mission*, ed. Jonathan Lunde (Grand Rapids: Zondervan, 2010).

3. Kevin DeYoung and Greg Gilbert, *What Is the Mission of the Church? Making Sense of Social Justice, Shalom, and the Great Commission* (Wheaton: Crossway, 2011), 232–33.

4. Alan Jacobs, "Gardening and Governing," *Books & Culture* (March/April 2009): 18.

5. Tim Keller, *Every Good Endeavor* (New York: Dutton, 2012), 70.

6. Martin Luther, *Sermons I*, ed. John W. Doberstein, Luther's Works, ed. Helmut T. Lehmann (Philadelphia: Fortress, 1959), 177.

7. *The Incredibles* (DVD), directed by Brad Bird (Burbank, CA: Walt Disney Home Entertainment, 2005).

Chapter 13: The Man and the Woman in Creation

1. Christin Milloy, "Don't Let the Doctor Do This to Your Newborn," *Slate* (June 26, 2014).

2. Ibid.

3. Ibid.

4. Sarah Wright, "Society Needs to Look Beyond Marriage," *New York Times* (website), July 24, 2014.

5. Wayne Grudem, "Does Kephale Κεφαλη Mean 'Source' or 'Authority Over' in Greek Literature? A Survey of 2,336 Examples," *Trinity Journal* 6:1 (1985): 38–59.

6. Andreas Köstenberger, *God, Marriage, and Family: Rebuilding the Biblical Foundation,* 2nd ed. (Wheaton: Crossway, 2010), 24.

7. Rachel Held Evans, "The False Gospel of Gender Binaries," (blog), November 19, 2014.

8. Michael Reeves, *Delighting in the Trinity* (Downers Grove, IL: InterVarsity Press), 28–29.

9. Andreas Köstenberger, *God, Marriage, and Family: Rebuilding the Biblical Foundation,* 2nd ed. (Wheaton: Crossway, 2010), 25.

10. Thomas Schreiner, in *Women in the Church*, ed. Andreas Köstenberger, Thomas Schreiner, and Scott Baldwin (Grand Rapids: Baker, 1995), 151; Philip Towner, *The Letters to Timothy and Titus*, New International Commentary on the New Testament (Grand Rapids: Eerdmans, 2006), 235; Howard Marshall, *The Pastoral Epistles*, International Critical Commentary (New York: T & T Clark Ltd., 2004), 470.

11. Amy Richards, "When One Is Enough," *New York Times* (website), July 18, 2004.

12. Ibid.

13. Ibid.

14. "Core Beliefs," Council on Biblical Manhood and Womanhood (website), http://cbmw.org/core-beliefs/.

15. "What Is CBE," CBE International (website), http://www.cbeinternational.org.

16. "Core Beliefs" and "Statement of Faith," Council on Biblical Manhood and Womanhood (website), http://cbmw.org.

17. "About CBE," CBE International (website), http://www.cbeinternational.org/content/about-cbe.

18. Rachel Held Evans, "For the Sake of the Gospel, Let Women Speak," (blog), June 7, 2012.

19. Philip H. Towner, *The Letters to Timothy and Titus*, New International Commentary on the New Testament (Grand Rapids: Eerdmans, 2006), 219–20.

20. Rachel Held Evans, "For the Sake of the Gospel, Let Women Speak," (blog), June 7, 2012.

21. C. S. Lewis, *The Lion, the Witch and the Wardrobe* (New York: HarperCollins, 2002), 119.

22. *The Lion, the Witch and the Wardrobe* (DVD), Buena Vista Home Entertainment/Disney, 2005.

23. Andrew Adamson, quoted in Eric Brady, "A Closer Look at the World of Narnia," *USA Today* (website), December 2, 2005, http://usatoday30.usatoday.com/life/movies/news/2005-12-01-narnia-side_x.htm.

24. Marvin Olasky, quoted in David Wegener, "The Impact of Feminism," *Journal for Biblical Manhood and Womanhood* 3 (Winter 1998): 4.

25. Council on Biblical Manhood and Womanhood, *Recovering Biblical Manhood and Womanhood: A Response to Evangelical Feminism*, eds. John Piper and Wayne Grudem (Wheaton: Crossway, 1991), 35–36.

26. Jonathan Parnell in David Mathis, John Piper, et al., *Good: The Joy of Christian Manhood and Womanhood*, eds. Owen Strachan and Jonathan Parnell (Minneapolis: Desiring God, 2014), 4.

27. Rachel Held Evans, "For the Sake of the Gospel, Let Women Speak," (blog), June 7, 2012.

Chapter 14: Marriage Twisted

1. "The Trivializing of Dan Quayle," *Chicago Tribune* (website), May 28, 1992.

2. "I Love the 90's Murphy Brown" (video), https://www.youtube.com/watch?v=pmFTeVNPk1g.

3. "'Murphy Brown' Reunion" (video), https://www.youtube.com/watch?v=KSmY96A6ADA.

4. See Barbara Dafoe Whitehead, "Dan Quayle Was Right," *Atlantic Monthly*, April 1993.

5. William Arndt, Frederick W. Danker, and Walter Bauer, *A Greek-English Lexicon of the New Testament and Other Early Christian Literature*, s.v. *pornos* (Chicago: University of Chicago Press, 2000), 855.

6. Joseph Carroll, "Society's Moral Boundaries Expand Somewhat This Year," Gallup News Service, May 16, 2005.

7. Christopher Ash, *Marriage: Sex in the Service of God* (Vancouver, BC: Regent College Publishing, 2005), 249–52.

8. Andreas J. and Margaret E. Köstenberger, *God, Marriage, and Family*, 2nd ed. (Wheaton: Crossway, 2010), 50–51.

9. William J. Bennett, "Why Men Are in Trouble," CNN (website), October 4, 2011.

10. *Child Maltreatment 2012* (Washington, DC: Children's Bureau of the US Department of Health and Human Services, 2013), 21, http://www.acf.hhs.gov/sites/default/files/cb/cm2012.pdf.

11. John Inchley, *Kids and the Kingdom* (Wheaton: Tyndale House, 1976), 95–105.

12. "Mandatory Reporters of Child Abuse and Neglect," Children's Bureau of US Department of Health and Human Services, 2013, https://childwelfare.gov/pubPDFs/manda.pdf#.

13. "Teenager, n.," OED Online, December 2014, Oxford University Press.

14. Patricia Hersch, *A Tribe Apart: A Journey into the Heart of American Adolescence* (New York: Ballantine Books, 1998), 14.

15. Rosaria Butterfield, *The Secret Thoughts of an Unlikely Convert: An English Professor's Journey into Christian Faith* (Pittsburgh: Crown & Covenant Publishers, 2012).

16. Matt Hastings, "Tampa Students Protest Homophobic Speaker," *FightBack! News* (website), October 12, 2013.

17. "Community Covenant," Wheaton College, http://wheaton.edu/about-wheaton/community-covenant.

18. Anna Morris, "Students Hold Demonstration Before Chapel Speaker," *Wheaton Record*, February 7, 2014. See also http://arealrattlesnake.com/2014/02/20/more-than-a-single-story-at-wheaton-college/.

19. "Gay and Lesbian Rights," Gallup (website), http://www.gallup.com/poll/1651/Gay-Lesbian-Rights.aspx.

20. Brian Ward et al., "Sexual Orientation and Health Among U.S. Adults," *National Health Statistics Reports* 77 (July 15, 2014): 1.

21. Peter Westen, "The Empty Idea of Equality," *Harvard Law Review* 95 (January 1982): 537–96.

22. See, for example, soulfource.org, gaychristian.net, and similar sites.

23. Anna Morris, "Q&A with Dr. Rosaria Butterfield," *Wheaton Record* (website), February 7, 2014.

24. Derek Brown, "Review of *Making Gay Okay*," The Gospel Coalition (website), October 1, 2014.

25. Mel White, *What the Bible Says—and Doesn't Say—About Homosexuality,* http://soulforce.com/wp-content /uploads/2013/09/whatthebiblesays.pdf.

26. See James V. Brownson, *Bible, Gender, Sexuality: Reframing the Church's Debate on Same-Sex Relationships* (Grand Rapids: Eerdmans, 2013), 275.

27. John Allen Jr., "Interview with Anglican Bishop N. T. Wright of Durham, England," *National Catholic Reporter* (website), May 21, 2004.

28. Michael Hannon, "Against Heterosexuality," *First Things* (March 2014).

29. Mel White, *What the Bible Says—and Doesn't Say—About Homosexuality*, 2nd ed. (Lynchburg, VA: Soulforce, 2005?), 18, http://drops.forwarddesigner.net/SAS.

30. One example of current standard pro-homosexual readings of the Bible is James Brownson, *The Bible, Gender, and Sexuality* (Grand Rapids: Eerdmans, 2013), which dismisses the very passage Jesus appeals to when discussing marriage, Genesis 1, saying it has nothing negative to tell us about homosexuality.

31. Luke Timothy Johnson, "Homosexuality and the Church," *Commonweal* (website), June 11, 2007.

32. Albert Mohler, "The Bible Condemns a Lot, but Here's Why We Focus on Homosexuality," The Briefing (podcast), May 22, 2012.

33. Supreme Court of the United States (blog), April 7, 2014, http://www.scotusblog.com/case-files/cases/elane -photography-llc-v-willock/.

34. Richard B. Hays, *The Moral Vision of the New Testament: Community, Cross, New Creation: A Contemporary Introduction to New Testament Ethics* (New York: HarperOne, 1996), 402.

35. John Paulk, "To Straight and Back: My Life as an Ex-Ex-Gay Man," *Politico Magazine* (website), June 19, 2014.

36. Anna Morris, "Q&A with Dr. Rosaria Butterfield," *Wheaton Record* (website), February 7, 2014.

37. Stephanie Coontz, *Marriage, a History: How Love Conquered Marriage* (New York: Penguin Books, 2006), 4.

38. Ibid., 5.

39. Ibid.

40. David Popenoe and Barbara Dafoe Whitehead, "Should We Live Together? What Young Adults Need to Know About Cohabitation Before Marriage," 2nd ed. (Piscataway, NJ: National Marriage Project, 2002), 1.

41. Robert Lauer and Jeanette Lauer, *Marriage and Family: The Quest for Intimacy*, 5th ed. (New York: McGraw-Hill, 2004), 135.

42. Casey Copen et al., "First Premarital Cohabitation in the United States: 2006–2010 National Survey of Family Growth," *National Health Statistics Reports* 64 (April 4, 2013): 1.

43. Sheela Kennedy and Steven Ruggles, "Breaking Up Is Hard to Count: The Rise of Divorce in the United States, 1980–2010," *Demography* 51 (April 2014): 596.

44. David and Amber Lapp, "Alone in the New America," *First Things* (website), February 2014, 30–31.

45. Anjani Chandra et al., "Sexual Behavior, Sexual Attraction, and Sexual Identity in the United States," *National Health Statistics Reports* 36 (March 3, 2011): 26.

46. Mark Pattison, "Study Finds Cohabitation Even More Harmful to Children than Divorce," Umatuna Si Yu'os (website), 2011, http://umatuna.org/study-finds-cohabita tion-even-more-harmful-to-children-than-divorce.

47. Ben Wattenberg, "The First Measured Century," PBS program, http://www.pbs.org/fmc/timeline/ddisruption .htm.

48. "Cohabitation," Wikipedia, http://en.wikipedia.org /wiki/Cohabitation.

49. Christopher Ash, *Marriage: Sex in the Service of God* (Vancouver, BC: Regent College Publishing, 2005), 224.

50. Noah Smith, "Liberals Are Rescuing Marriage," BloombergView (website), July 15, 2014.

51. Ted Olson quoted in Jennifer Rubin, "Why Gay Marriage Opponents Have Lost," *Washington Post* (website), October 13, 2014.

52. Steven Petrow, "Civilities: The President Made History with Three Words Last Night," *Washington Post* (blog), January 21, 2015.

53. Wilcox, W. Bradford. "The Evolution of Divorce," *National Affairs* 1 (2009): 81.

54. Sheela Kennedy and Steven Ruggles, "Breaking Up Is Hard to Count: The Rise of Divorce in the United States, 1980–2010," *Demography* 51 (April 2014): 596.

55. Christopher Ash, *Marriage: Sex in the Service of God* (Vancouver, BC: Regent College Publishing, 2005), 40.

56. Ashley McGuire, "The Feminist, Pro-Father, and Pro-Child Case Against No-Fault Divorce," Witherspoon Institute (website), May 7, 2013.

57. Ibid.

58. Marcia Pappas, "Divorce New York Style," *New York Times* (website), February 19, 2006.

59. Anne-Marie Slaughter, "Why Women Still Can't Have It All," *The Atlantic*, July/August 2012.

60. John Piper, "A Vision of Biblical Complementarity: Manhood and Womanhood Defined According to the Bible," in *Recovering Biblical Manhood and Womanhood: A Response to Evangelical Feminism*, eds. John Piper and Wayne Grudem (Wheaton: Crossway, 1991), 27.

61. Ruth Padawer, "When Women Become Men at Wellesley," *New York Times Magazine* (website), October 15, 2014.

62. Steven Douglas Smith, *The Disenchantment of Secular Discourse* (Cambridge, MA: Harvard University Press, 2010), 29.

63. Rod Snyder, "Love Wins: The Shifting Landscape on LGBT Issues in the Evangelical Church," *Huffington Post* (blog), July 22, 2014.

64. Dashka Slater, "The Fire on the 57 Bus in Oakland," *New York Times Magazine* (website), January 29, 2015.

65. Anthony Esolen, "A Requiem for Friendship," *Touchstone*, September 2005, 27.

66. Ryan T. Anderson, "Marriage: What It Is, Why It Matters, and the Consequences of Redefining It," Heritage Foundation (website), March 11, 2013.

67. "*The Brady Bunch*," Wikipedia, http://en.wikipedia.org/wiki/The_Brady_Bunch.

68. "The Trivializing of Dan Quayle," *Chicago Tribune* (website), May 28, 1992.

69. "Candace Bergen Agrees with Quayle," CNN Entertainment (website), July 11, 2002, http://web.archive.org/web/20080126033326/http://archives.cnn.com/2002/SHOWBIZ/News/07/11/showbuzz/index.html.

Chapter 15: Marriage Redeemed

1. Kurt Eichenwald, "The Bible: So Misunderstood It's a Sin," *Newsweek* (website), December 23, 2014.

2. David Platt, *Counter Culture: A Compassionate Call to Counter Culture in a World of Poverty, Same-Sex Marriage, Racism, Sex Slavery, Immigration, Persecution, Abortion, Orphans, and Pornography* (Carol Stream, IL: Tyndale House, 2015), 152.

3. John Piper, "To a Spouse Considering Divorce," Desiring God (website), July 31, 2014.

4. Katherine Schulten, "How Do You Define 'Family'?" The Learning Network (a *New York Times* website), February 24, 2011.

5. Ibid.

6. Andy David Naselli, "Training Children for Their Good," *Journal of Discipleship and Family Ministry* 3 (2013): 50.

7. http://www.endcorporalpunishment.org/.

8. Paul D. Wegner, "Discipline in the Book of Proverbs: 'To Spank or Not to Spank?'" *Journal of the Evangelical Theological Society* 48 (2005): 715–32.

9. C. S. Lewis, *God in the Dock* (Grand Rapids: Eerdmans, 2014), 301.

10. Stanley Fish, "Two Cheers for Double Standards," *New York Times* (website), March 12, 2012.

11. Thomas R. Schreiner, in *Two Views on Women in Ministry*, eds. John Piper and Wayne Grudem, rev. ed. (Grand Rapids: Zondervan, 2010), 184.

12. Andreas J. and Margaret E. Köstenberger, *God's Design for Man and Woman* (Wheaton: Crossway, 2014), 103–4.

13. Roger W. Gehring, *House Church and Mission: The Importance of Household Structures in Early Christianity* (Peabody, MA: Hendrickson, 2004), 210–11.

14. Ibid., 211.

15. Andreas J. and Margaret E. Köstenberger, *God's Design for Man and Woman* (Wheaton: Crossway, 2014), 16.

16. Doug Wilson, "Sexual by Design," lecture and question/answer session at Indiana University, April 2012, http://www.canonwired.com/bloomington/.

17. Raymond C. Ortlund, in *New Dictionary of Biblical Theology*, eds. T. Desmond Alexander and Brian S. Rosner (Downers Grove, IL: InterVarsity Press, 2000), 652.

Chapter 16: Foundations of Government

1. George M. Marsden, *The Twilight of the American Enlightenment: The 1950s and the Crisis of Liberal Belief* (New York: Basic Books, 2014), 92–95.

2. Ronald Reagan, quoted in Steven Weisman, "Reagan Takes Oath as 40th President," *New York Times* (website), January 21, 1981.

3. James G. March and Johan P. Olsen, "Elaborating the 'New Institutionalism,'" in *The Oxford Handbook of Political Institutions*, eds. R. A. W. Rhodes, Sarah A. Binder, and Bert A. Rockman (New York: Oxford University Press, 2006), 3; Douglass C. North, *Institutions, Institutional Change and Economic Performance* (Cambridge: Cambridge University Press, 1990), 3; Philip Selznick, *The Moral Commonwealth: Social Theory and the Promise of Community* (Berkeley: University of California Press, 1992), 232–33.

4. Charles Dickens, *Great Expectations* (New York: James G. Gregory, Publisher, 1861), 1:86.

5. "Revenge," Wikipedia, http://en.wikipedia.org/wiki/Revenge (disambiguation).

6. Michael J. Sandel, *Justice: What's the Right Thing to Do?* (New York: Farrar, Straus, Giroux, 2009), 19, 261.

7. Ibid., 31ff.

8. Ibid., 37.

9. Michael Slote, "Utilitarianism," *The Oxford Companion to Philosophy*, ed. Ted Honderich (Oxford: Oxford University Press, 1995), 890.

10. This discussion of utilitarianism also drew on Frederick Copleston, *A History of Philosophy* (London: Burns and Oates, 1966), 8:11–42; Richard Norman, "Happiness," *The Oxford Companion to Philosophy*, ed. Ted Honderich (Oxford, OUP, 1995), 332–33; Alan Ryan, *On Politics* (Liverlight, 2012), 696–721; Robert C. Solomon and Kathleen M. Higgins, *A Short History of Philosophy* (New York: Oxford University Press, 1996), 230–31.

11. See also Nicholas Wolterstorff, *Justice: Rights and Wrongs* (Princeton, NJ: Princeton University Press), 93–94.

12. Arifa Akbar, "Mao's Great Leap Forward 'Killed 45 Million in Four Years,'" *The Independent*, September 17, 2010.

13. Frank Dikötter, *Mao's Great Famine: The History of China's Most Devastating Catastrophe, 1958–1962* (New York: Walker Publishing Company, 2010).

14. Carl R. Trueman, *The Creedal Imperative* (Wheaton: Crossway, 2012), 178.

15. Edmund Burke, *Burke's Speeches*, ed. F. G. Selby (London: MacMillan and Co., 1897), 311.

16. Otto von Bismarck, *Bismarck: The Man and the Statesman, Vol. 1* (New York: Cosimo Classics, 2013), back cover.

17. Fred Miller, "Aristotle's Political Theory," *Stanford Encyclopedia of Philosophy*, ed. Edward N. Zalta (Fall 2012), http://plato.stanford.edu/archives/fall2012/entries/aristotle-politics/.

Chapter 17: Political Perspectives

1. Nancy S. Love, *Dogmas and Dreams: A Reader in Modern Political Ideologies*, 3rd ed. (Washington, DC: CQ Press, 2006), 7.

2. David T. Koyzis, *Political Visions and Illusions: A Survey and Christian Critique of Contemporary Ideologies* (Downers Grove: InterVarsity, 2003), 8.

3. Ibid., 13–41.

4. Ibid., 42–68; Nancy Love, *Understanding Dogmas and Dreams*, 2nd ed. (Washington, DC: CQ Press, 2006), 21–47; David Boaz, *Libertarianism: A Primer* (New York: Free Press, 1997), 1–58.

5. See Jonathan Haidt, *The Righteous Mind: Why Good People Are Divided by Politics and Religion* (New York: Pantheon, 2012), 282.

6. David Koyzis, *Political Visions and Illusions* (Downers Grove: InterVarsity, 2003), 60–61.

7. Ibid., 63–64.

8. David Boaz, *Libertarianism* (New York: Free Press, 1997), 28.

9. Murray N. Rothbard, *For a New Liberty: The Libertarian Manifesto*, rev. ed. (New York: Collier, 1978), 46.

10. David Boaz, *Libertarianism* (New York: Free Press, 1997), 57.

11. Murray N. Rothbard, *For a New Liberty: The Libertarian Manifesto*, rev. ed. (New York: Collier, 1978), 23.

12. Nancy Love, *Dogmas and Dreams* (Washington, DC: CQ Press, 2006), 7.

13. Michael J. Sandel, *What Money Can't Buy: The Moral Limits of Markets* (Farrar, Straus and Giroux, 2012), 9–11, 47–51, 113–14, 125–27; Nicole Gelinas, "Review of *What Money Can't Buy: The Moral Limits of Markets*," in *City Journal* (May 2012), http://www.city-journal.org/2012/bc0511ng.html.

14. Jonathan Edwards, *Sermons and Discourses, 1730–1733*, ed. Mark Valeri, in *Works of Jonathan Edwards*, ed. Harry S. Stout (New Haven, CT: Yale University Press, 1999), 17: 403.

15. Isaac Backus, *An Appeal to the Public for Religious Liberty* (Boston: John Boyle, 1773), 8.

16. David Koyzis, *Political Visions and Illusions* (Downers Grove: InterVarsity, 2003), 126; Robert P. Kraynak, *Christian Faith and Modern Democracy: God and Politics in the Fallen World* (Notre Dame, IN: University of Notre Dame Press, 2001), 25.

17. Mark A. Noll, *America's God: From Jonathan Edwards to Abraham Lincoln* (New York: Oxford University Press, 2002), 54.

18. John Cotton quoted in *A Source Book in American History to 1787*, ed. Willis Mason West (Boston: Allyn and Bacon, 1913), 204; Robert Kraynak, *Christian Faith and Modern Democracy* (Notre Dame, IN: University of Notre Dame Press, 2001), 67.

19. Kraynak, 124–27.

20. Hugh Helco, *Christianity and American Democracy* (Cambridge, MA: Harvard, 2007), 7.

21. Mark Noll, *America's God* (New York: Oxford University Press, 2002), 57–58; Helco, 8, 13.

22. Noll, 54.

23. Ibid., 57.

24. Helco, 13.

25. C. S. Lewis, *The Weight of Glory* (New York: Macmillan Company, 1949), 113.

26. C. S. Lewis, *Present Concerns* (New York: Houghton Mifflin Harcourt, 1987), 18.

27. *Inaugural Addresses of the Presidents of the United States* (Bedford, MA: Applewood Books, 2009), 2:182.

28. Mark Henrie, "War Without End," *First Things* (February 2013): 47.

29. Summary based on David Koyzis, *Political Visions and Illusions* (Downers Grove: InterVarsity, 2003), ch. 6;

Nancy Love, *Understanding Dogmas and Dreams* (Washington, DC: CQ Press, 2006), ch. 4; R. N. Berki, *Socialism* (London: Dent, 1975); Joshua Muravchik, *Heaven on Earth: The Rise and Fall of Socialism* (New York: Encounter Books, 2003).

30.   Nancy Love, *Understanding Dogmas and Dreams* (Washington, DC: CQ Press, 2006), 89.

31.   Analysis largely based on David Koyzis, *Political Visions and Illusions* (Downers Grove: InterVarsity, 2003), ch. 6.

32.   H. Evan Runner quoted in David Koyzis, *Political Visions and Illusions* (Downers Grove: InterVarsity, 2003), 93.

33.   See Melvin J. Thorne, *American Conservative Thought Since World War II: The Core Ideas* (New York: Greenwood, 1990), 11–13; Ethan Fishman and Kenneth Deutsch, *The Dilemmas of American Conservatism* (Lexington, KY: University Press of Kentucky: 2010), 2–4; Irving Kristol, "American Conservatism 1945–1995," *Public Interest* 121 (Fall 1995): 80–89.

34.   Edmund Burke, *The Works of the Right Honourable Edmund Burke*, 5th ed. (London: George Bell and Sons,1886), 2:555.

Chapter 18: The Goal of Government

1.   Hugh Heclo, *Christianity and American Democracy* (Cambridge, MA: Harvard, 2007), 20.

2.   Ronald Beiner, *Civil Religion: A Dialogue in the History of Political Philosophy* (New York: Cambridge University Press, 2011), 1.

3.   Ross Douthat, *Bad Religion* (New York: Free Press, 2012), 6–8.

4.   Gregg L. Frazer, *The Religious Beliefs of America's Founders: Reason, Revelation, and Revolution, American Political Thought*, eds. Wilson Carey McWilliams and Lance Banning (Lawrence, KS: University Press of Kansas, 2012), 16–17, 227–31.

5.   Hunter Baker, *The End of Secularism* (Wheaton: Crossway, 2009), 124.

6.   This section draws on ibid.; Greg Forster's *Starting with Locke* (New York: Bloomsbury Academic, 2011) and *The Contested Public Square* (Downers Grove, IL: IVP Academic, 2008); and Steven Smith's *Disenchantment of Secular Discourse* (Cambridge, MA: Harvard University Press, 2010).

7.   Ronald Dworkin et al., "Assisted Suicide: The Philosophers' Brief," *New York Review of Books* (website), March 27, 1997.

8.   Steven D. Smith, *Disenchantment of Secular Discourse* (Cambridge, MA: Harvard University Press, 2010), 53–59.

9.   Ronald Dworkin, *Life's Dominion: An Argument About Abortion, Euthanasia, and Individual Freedom* (New York: Knopf, 1993), 13, 88.

10.   John Locke, *Second Treatise of Government* (Seaside, OR: Watchmaker Publishing, 2011), 9.

11.   Michael J. Sandel, *Justice: What's the Right Thing to Do?* (New York: Farrar, Straus and Giroux, 2009), 243.

12.   See Daniel Walker Howe, *What Hath God Wrought: The Transformation of America, 1815–1848* (New York: Oxford University Press, 2009), 349–51.

13.   Facebook.

14.   Alexander Solzhenitsyn, *The Gulag Archipelago, 1918–1956: An Experiment in Literary Investigation* (New York: Collins Harvill, 1986), 312.

15.   Greg Bahnsen, *By This Standard: The Authority of God's Law Today* (Nacogdoches, TX: Covenant Media Press, 2008), 3–6.

16.   Ibid., 4.

17.   Edwin C. Darden, "The Law Trends Toward Transgender Students," *Phi Delta Kappan* (October 2014):76–77.

18.   See Greg Forster, *The Contested Public Square* (Downers Grove, IL: IVP Academic, 2008).

19.   See D. A. Carson, *The Intolerance of Tolerance* (Grand Rapids: Eerdmans, 2012).

20.   David Koyzis, *Political Visions and Illusions* (Downers Grove: InterVarsity, 2003), 78.

21.   See Edward M. Panosian, "A Church Historical View of a Christian's Responsibility Before Caesar," in *The Providence of God in History* (Greenville, SC: Bob Jones University Press, 1996), 27–35.

22.   Martin Luther, *Luther's Works*, ed. Walther Brandt (Philadelphia: Fortress, 1962), 45:62–64; cf. William Tyndale, *The Obedience of the Christian Man* (New York: Penguin Classics, 2000).

23.   Justin Martyr, *First Apology*, chs. 11, 12, 17.

24.   David W. Hall, *The Genevan Reformation and the American Founding* (New York: Lexington, 2003), 191, 194.

25.   Winthrop S. Hudson, "John Locke: Heir of Puritan Political Theorists," in *Calvinism and the Political Order* (Philadelphia: Westminster, 1965), 108, 113; Greg Forster, *Starting with Locke* (New York: Bloomsbury Academic, 2011), loc. 1661.

26.   Greg Forster, *Starting with Locke* (New York: Bloomsbury Academic, 2011), loc. 1661; Alan Ryan, *On Politics* (Liveright, 2012), 139–40.

27. Edward M. Panosian, *The Providence of God in History* (Greenville, SC: Bob Jones University Press, 1996), 4.

Chapter 19: Science Is Something God Created Humans to Do

1.   *New Oxford American Dictionary*, s.v. "scientism."

2.   Richard Dawkins, Richard Dawkins Foundation for Reason and Science (website), http://old.richarddawkins.net/quotes?page=4.

3. Neil deGrasse Tyson, *Cosmos: A Spacetime Odyssey* (DVD) (Los Angeles: 20th Century Fox, 2014), episode 1.

4. Lawrence Principe, *The Scientific Revolution: A Very Short Introduction* (New York: Oxford University Press, 2011), 37.

5. Ibid.

6. Ibid., 57.

7. Donald Petcher and Tim Morris, "Well Done, Good and Faithful Scientific Servant," in *Science and Grace: God's Reign in the Natural Sciences* (Wheaton: Crossway, 2006), 243–78.

8. "Fierce Curiosity About the Fundamental Nature of Things," Milliken, http://www.milliken.com/en-us/Innovation/Pages/innovation-deep-science.aspx.

9. Alvin Plantinga, *Where the Conflict Really Lies: Science, Religion, and Naturalism* (New York: Oxford University Press, 2011), ix.

10. Lesslie Newbigin, "Can the West Be Converted?" *Princeton Seminary Bulletin* 6 (1985): 32–33.

11. Ibid, 33.

12. Lawrence Principe, *The Scientific Revolution: A Very Short Introduction* (New York: Oxford University Press, 2011), 19.

13. Vern Poythress, *Redeeming Science: A God-Centered Approach* (Wheaton: Crossway, 2006), 28.

14. Rob Dunn, "Painting with Penicillin: Alexander Fleming's Germ Art," Smithsonian (website), July 11, 2010.

15. Prince Philip, as reported by Deutche Presse-Agentur, August 1988, quoted in "His Royal Virus," *American Almanac*, August 25, 1997.

16. Paul Davies, "Taking Science on Faith," *New York Times* (website), November 24, 2007.

17. Ibid.

18. Ibid.

19. Ibid.

20. "Armstrong 'Got Moon Quote Right,'" *BBC News* (website), October 2, 2006.

21. Karen Kaplan, "Did Neil Armstrong Really Say, 'That's One Small Step for a Man'?" *Los Angeles Times* (website), June 5, 2013.

22. Gene Cernan, *In the Shadow of the Moon* (DVD) (Los Angeles: Mirage Productions, 2008), 1:30:00.

23. Chris Krycho, "Speak the Truth in Beauty: A Review of *Echoes of Eden*," Mere Orthodoxy (website), February 11, 2015.

24. Paul Spencer Sochaczewski, *An Inordinate Fondness for Beetles* (Singapore: Editions Didier Millet, 2012), 195.

25. *Owls: Silent Hunters* (video), Incredible Nature Birds Documentary, World of Nature, 2014, https://www.youtube.com/watch?v=19DfrkRECDY.

26. David C. McClelland, *The Achieving Society* (New York: Free Press, 1961).

27. Donald Petcher and Tim Morris, "Well Done, Good and Faithful Scientific Servant," in *Science and Grace: God's Reign in the Natural Sciences* (Wheaton: Crossway, 2006), 6.

28. Duane A. Garrett, *Proverbs, Ecclesiastes, Song of Songs*, New American Commentary, ed. E. Ray Clendenen (Nashville: Broadman, 1993), 108.

29. Thomas Kuhn, *The Structure of Scientific Revolutions* (1962; repr., Chicago: University of Chicago Press, 2012), 17–18.

30. Vern S. Poythress, "Three Modern Myths in Interpreting Genesis 1," *Westminster Theological Journal* 76 (2014): 321–50.

31. Thomas Kuhn, *The Structure of Scientific Revolutions* (1962; repr., Chicago: University of Chicago Press, 2012), 10.

32. Buckminster Fuller, *Critical Path* (New York: St. Martin's Press, 1982).

33. David Russell Schilling, "Knowledge Doubling Every 12 Months, Soon to Be Every 12 Hours," *Industry Tap into News*, April 19, 2013, http://www.industrytap.com/knowledge-doubling-every-12-months-soon-to-be-every-12-hours/3950.

34. "Prototype Kilogram 20, Replica," National Institute of Standards and Technology, http://museum.nist.gov/object.asp?ObjID=38.

35. "History of the Meter," Wikipedia, http://en.wikipedia.org/wiki/History_of_the_metre#International_prototype_metre.

36. Terrance Egolf and Rachel Santopietro, *Earth Science*, 4th ed. (Greenville, SC: BJU Press, 2012), 11.

Chapter 20: Fallen Science

1. *Encyclopædia Britannica Online*, s.v. "Émile Coué."

2. National Institute on Aging, "Prevalence of Alzheimer's Disease," *2011–2012 Alzheimer's Disease Progress Report*, National Institutes of Health (website).

3. Hugh Lofting, *The Story of Doctor Dolittle* (1920; repr., Mineola, NY: Dover Publications, 1997), 39.

4. "Bill Nye: Creationism Is Not Appropriate for Children" (video), August 23, 2012, https://www.youtube.com/watch?v=gHbYJfwFgOU.

5. *CBS News*, *60 Minutes*, and *Vanity Fair*. CBS News/60 Minutes/Vanity Fair National Survey, January 2, 2013. ICPSR34992-v1. Ann Arbor, MI: Inter-university Consortium for Political and Social Research [distributor], 2014-03-20.

6. "83% Say Measles Vaccine Is Safe for Healthy Children: No Partisan Differences in Views of Vaccine Safety," Pew Research Center (website), February 9, 2015.

7. Richard Dawkins, *The Magic of Reality: How We Know What's Really True* (New York: Free Press, 2011), 19.

8. Kurt Vonnegut, *Fates Worse than Death* (New York: G. P. Putnam's Sons, 1991), 117–18.

9. Ibid., 118.

10. Ibid.

11. Richard N. Williams, *Scientism: The New Orthodoxy* (New York: Bloomsbury Academic), 6.

12. "Metaphysical Naturalism," Wikipedia, http://en.wiki pedia.org/wiki/Metaphysical_naturalism.

13. http://www.quora.com/Religion-and-Politics /Why-do-some-people-think-Its-in-the-Bible-is-a-valid -argument/answer/Mark-Ward-11/comment/9138897

14. Ibid.

15. Mark Regnerus, "New Research on Same-Sex Households Reveals Kids Do Best with Mom and Dad," Public Discourse (website), February 10, 2015.

16. Steven Pinker, "Science Is Not Your Enemy," *New Republic* (website), August 6, 2013.

17. Robert Ingersoll, *The Works of Robert G. Ingersoll: Lectures* (New York: Dresden Publishing, 1915), 290–91.

18. Richard Dawkins, *The Blind Watchmaker* (New York: Norton, 1986), 1.

19. Alvin Plantinga, *Where the Conflict Really Lies: Science, Religion, and Naturalism* (New York: Oxford University Press, 2011), ix–x.

20. "Missa Charles Darwin," Gregory W. Brown (website), http://www.gregorywbrown.com/missa-charles-darwin/.

21. Gregory W. Brown quoted in Jan McCoy Ebbets, "We Sing the Theory of Evolution," *Insight*, April 15, 2011, 1.

22. Charles Darwin, *The Descent of Man and Selection in Relation to Sex* (London: John Murray, 1882), 2.

23. Charles Darwin, *The Origin of Species* (New York: P. F. Collier and Son Company, 1909), 297.

24. "Terence McKenna Pokes Fun at the 'Big Bang' Theory" (video), https://www.youtube.com /watch?v=BWv02kYyvo4.

25. Terence McKenna, quoted in Chris Twomey, "Words with the Sham Man," Eye Weekly (website), July 7, 1994.

26. "Terence McKenna Pokes Fun at the 'Big Bang' Theory" (video), https://www.youtube.com /watch?v=BWv02kYyvo4.

27. Ibid.

28. *New Oxford American Dictionary*, s.v. "myth."

29. https://twitter.com/sapinker/status /258350644979695616.

30. Jennifer Schuessler, "An Author Attracts Unlikely Allies," *New York Times* (website), February 6, 2013.

31. Alva Noë, "Are the Mind and Life Natural?" NPR (blog), October 12, 2012.

32. "Terence McKenna Pokes Fun at the 'Big Bang' Theory" (video), https://www.youtube.com /watch?v=BWv02kYyvo4.

33. Elizabeth Kolbert, "The Big Question: What's the Point?" *Intelligent Life* (website), September/October 2014.

34. Charles Darwin, *The Origin of Species* (New York: P. F. Collier and Son Company, 1909), 529.

35. Ibid.

36. Lawrence Krauss quoted in Cara Santa Maria, "Lawrence Krauss: 'A Universe from Nothing,'" *Huffington Post* (website), July 18, 2012.

37. Ibid.

38. Thomas Nagel, *Mind and Cosmos: Why the Materialist Neo-Darwinian Conception of Nature Is Almost Certainly False* (New York: Oxford University Press, 2012), 12.

39. Julian Barnes, *Nothing to Be Frightened Of* (New York: Knopf, 2008), 1.

40. "Neil deGrasse Tyson on the New *Cosmos*" (video), https://www.youtube.com/watch?v=da3G2ezt9R0.

41. Steven Pinker, "Science Is Not Your Enemy," *New Republic* (website), August 6, 2013.

42. Rebecca Grambo, *Eagles* (Stillwater, MN: Voyageur Press, 2003), 32.

43. Kurt Vonnegut, *Breakfast of Champions* (1973; repr., New York: Dial Press, 1999), 266, 270.

44. John Gray, "What Scares the New Atheists," *The Guardian* (website), March 3, 2015.

45. Ibid.

46. Ibid.

47. Ibid.

48. N. D. Wilson, *Death by Living: Life Is Meant to Be Spent* (Nashville: Thomas Nelson, 2013), 20.

49. See page 11.

50. Quoted in Sabrina Tavernise, "Warning: That Tan Could Be Hazardous," *New York Times* (website), January 10, 2015.

51. "Take Me to Church," Wikipedia, http://en.wikipedia .org/wiki/Take_Me_to_Church.

52. Andrew Hozier Byrne, "Take Me to Church," https:// www.musixmatch.com, © The Evolving Music Company.

53. "Hozier Is 'Thrilled' to Be Performing at the Grammys," Grammy.com (video), February 5, 2015.

54. N. D. Wilson, *Death by Living: Life Is Meant to Be Spent* (Nashville: Thomas Nelson, 2013), 20.

55. Steven Pinker, "Science Is Not Your Enemy," *New Republic* (website), August 6, 2013.

56. Richard Dawkins, *The God Delusion* (New York: Houghton Mifflin Harcourt, 2006), 266.

57. John Gray, "What Scares the New Atheists," *The Guardian* (website), March 3, 2015.

58. "Documentary: John Nash, A Beautiful Mind" (video), https://www.youtube.com/watch?v=ctV1C0YpyTU.

59. John Nash, in Mark Samels and Randall MacLowry, "A Brilliant Madness" (transcript), PBS (website).

60. Steven Pinker, "Science Is Not Your Enemy," *New Republic* (website), August 6, 2013.

61. Richard N. Williams, in *Scientism: The New Orthodoxy*, ed. Daniel N. Robinson and Richard N. Williams (New York: Bloomsbury Academic, 2015), 6.

62. Armand Marie Leroi, "One Republic of Learning: Digitizing the Humanities," *New York Times* (website), February 13, 2015.

63. Peter Markie, "Rationalism vs. Empiricism," *Stanford Encyclopedia of Philosophy*, ed. Edward N. Zalta (Spring 2015), http://plato.stanford.edu/archives/spr2015/entries/rationalism-empiricism/.

64. Richard Dawkins, *The Magic of Reality: How We Know What's Really True* (New York: Free Press, 2011), 18.

65. "United in Godlessness: The 2012 Reason Rally" (video), https://www.youtube.com/watch?v=4iiXobOUtEU.

66. Ibid.

67. Ibid.

68. Ibid.

69. "Liberals Are Stifling Intellectual Diversity on Campus" (debate), Intelligence Squared U.S., http://www.intelligencesquaredus.org/images/debates/past/transcripts/022415%20Liberal%20Stifling.pdf.

70. Ibid.

71. Stanley Fish, "Citing Chapter and Verse: Which Scripture Is the Right One?" *New York Times* (blog), March 26, 2012.

72. Jonathan Haidt, *The Righteous Mind: Why Good People Are Divided by Politics and Religion* (New York: Vintage Books, 2013), 292–317.

73. Ibid., 224–25.

74. C. S. Lewis, *The Weight of Glory and Other Addresses* (1949; repr., New York: HarperCollins, 1980), 135.

75. Ibid., 134–35.

76. Ibid., 135.

77. Ibid., 135–36.

78. Francis Beckwith, "What's Upstairs," *First Things* (website), November 2004.

79. John Nash, in Mark Samels and Randall MacLowry, "A Brilliant Madness" (transcript), PBS (website).

80. Walter Hooper, ed., *The Collected Letters of C. S. Lewis* (New York: HarperCollins, 2004), 1:977.

81. Layton Talbert, "The Trustworthiness of God's Words: Why It's Important to God" (Sunday school class), Mount Calvary Baptist Church, Greenville, South Carolina, January 11, 2015, http://www.mountcalvarybaptist.org/Pages/Sermons/Default.aspx?SpeakerID=393.

Chapter 21: Reading Genesis and Doing Science

1. David Brooks, "I Am Not Charlie Hebdo," *New York Times* (website), January 8, 2015.

2. David Brooks, "The Prodigal Sons," *New York Times* (website), February 17, 2014.

3. Christopher Beam, "A Reasonable Man," *New York* magazine (website), July 4, 2010.

4. George Lakoff and Mark Johnson, *Metaphors We Live By* (London: University of Chicago Press, 2003), 7–8.

5. George Lakoff and Mark Johnson, *Metaphors We Live By* (Chicago: University of Chicago Press, 1980), 107–8.

6. Timothy H. Heaton, "Review of *Mapping the Origins Debate*," *Reports of the National Center for Science Education*, November/December 2013, 1–2.

7. Gerald Rau, *Mapping the Origins Debate: Six Models of the Beginning of Everything* (Downers Grove, IL: IVP Academic, 2013), 28.

8. Ibid., 30.

9. Ibid., 38.

10. Ibid., 41 (adapted from Rau's chart).

11. Stephen Hawking quoted in Alison George, "Stephen Hawking's Bedtime Stories," Signs of the Times (website), March 19, 2009.

12. Stephen Hawking, *A Brief History of Time* (New York: Bantam, 1998), 191.

13. Gerald Rau, *Mapping the Origins Debate* (Downers Grove, IL: IVP Academic, 2013), 189.

14. Georgia M. Green, *Pragmatics and Natural Language Understanding* (New York: Routledge, 2012), 96–97.

15. Peter Enns, *The Evolution of Adam: What the Bible Does and Doesn't Say About Human Origins* (Ada, MI: Brazos Press, 2012), xvi.

16. Ibid., xvii–xviii.

17. John H. Walton, *The Lost World of Adam and Eve: Genesis 2–3 and the Human Origins Debate* (Downers Grove, IL: InterVarsity Press, 2015), 50.

18. Raymond C. Van Leeuwen, "ארב," in *New International Dictionary of Old Testament Theology and Exegesis*, ed. Willem VanGemeren (Grand Rapids: Zondervan, 1997), 1:731; Andrew Steinmann, "Lost World of Genesis One: John H. Walton, American Evangelicals and Creation," *Lutheran Education Journal*, May 9, 2012.

19. John H. Walton, *The Lost World of Genesis One: Ancient Cosmology and the Origins Debate* (Downers Grove, IL: InterVarsity Press, 2010), 181–82.

20. Richard E. Averbeck, "A Literary Day, Inter-Textual, and Contextual Reading of Genesis 1-2," in *Reading Genesis 1-2: An Evangelical Conversation*, ed. J. Daryl Charles (Peabody, MA: Hendrickson, 2013), 13.

21. Peter Enns, *The Evolution of Adam: What the Bible Does and Doesn't Say About Human Origins* (Ada, MI: Brazos Press, 2012), 139.

22. Ibid., 95.

23. Augustine of Hippo, "Reply to Faustus the Manichaean," in *St. Augustine: The Writings Against the Manichaeans and Against the Donatists*, ed. Philip Schaff, trans. Richard Stothert (Buffalo, NY: Christian Literature Company, 1887), 4:178.

24. Stephen Wellum, "Debating the Historicity of Adam: Does It Matter?" *Southern Baptist Journal of Theology* 15, no.1 (2011):3.

25. "Did Death Occur Before the Fall?" BioLogos (website), July 9, 2012.

26. Michael Wines, "Though Scorned by Colleagues, a Climate-Change Skeptic Is Unbowed," *New York Times* (website), July 15, 2014.

27. M. J. Stephey, "What Came Before the Big Bang?" *Time* (website), August 13, 2009.

28. "Bill Nye Debates Ken Ham" (video), February 4, 2014, https://www.youtube.com/watch?v=z6kgvhG3Akl.

29. Chandler Burr, "The Geophysics of God," *U.S. News & World Report*, June 16, 1997, 55–58.

30. Robert L. Hill, et al., "Photometric Study of the Solar Type Pre-Contact Binary, V2421 Cygni," *American Astronomical Society Meeting Abstracts* 222 (June 2013): 115.

31. "Steve Figard" (faculty information page), Bob Jones University (website).

32. "Dr John Hartnett," Creation Ministries International (website).

33. "Mark F. Horstemeyer" (faculty information page), Mississippi State University (website).

34. "D. Russell Humphreys, Ph.D.," Creation Ministries International (website).

35. Todd Purdum, "High Priest of the Pasture," *New York Times* (website), May 1, 2005.

36. Ibid.

37. "Dr John Sanford, Ph.D.," Creation Ministries International (website).

38. Richard Dawkins, "Sadly, an Honest Creationist," Scepsis (website), 2005.

39. "Bill Nye: Creationism Is Not Appropriate for Children" (video), August 23, 2012, https://www.youtube.com/watch?v=gHbYJfwFgOU.

40. Peter Harrison, *The Territories of Science and Religion* (Chicago: University of Chicago Press, 2015), 22.

41. James Copeland, ed., *The London Medical Repository, Monthly Journal, and Review* (London: Thomas and George Underwood, 1825), 258.

42. Blaire Briody, "Real Genius: Eight Brilliant Inventors Still in High School," *Popular Science* (website), August 24, 2009.

43. John Ioannidis, "Why Most Published Research Findings Are False," PLOS Medicine (website), August 30, 2005.

Chapter 22: Foundations for History

1. Augustine, *On Genesis*, ed. John E. Rotelle, trans. Edmund Hill (Hyde Park, NY: New City Press, 2006), 266–77.

2. Alasdair MacIntyre, *After Virtue: A Study in Moral Theory*, 3rd ed. (Notre Dame, IN: University of Notre Dame Press, 2007), 216.

3. See T. D. Bernard, *The Progress of Doctrine in the New Testament* (London: Macmillan, 1864), 154, 157–58; Albert M. Wolters, *Creation Regained: Biblical Basics for a Reformational Worldview* (Grand Rapids: Eerdmans, 2005), 40–41.

4. George Santayana, *The Life of Reason or the Phases of Human Progress* (New York: Charles Scribner's Sons, 1906), 284.

5. Geerhardus Vos, *Redemptive History and Biblical Interpretation* (Phillipsburg, NJ: P&R, 1980), 7–8.

6. C. S. Lewis, "Introduction," in Athanasius, *On the Incarnation* (1944; repr., Crestwood, NY: St. Vladimir's Seminary Press, 1996), 5.

7. David Bebbington, *Patterns in History: A Christian Perspective on Historical Thought* (Vancouver: Regent College Publishing, 1990), 21–22.

8. Charles Murray, *Human Accomplishment: The Pursuit of Excellence in the Arts and Sciences, 800 B.C. to 1950* (New York: Perennial, 2004), xviii–xix.

9. Carl Trueman, *Histories and Fallacies: Problems Faced in the Writing of History* (Wheaton: Crossway, 2010), 106.

10. Timothy Larsen, *Crisis of Doubt: Honest Faith in Nineteenth-Century England* (New York: Oxford University Press, 2006), 1.

11. John Hall, ed., *Forty Years' Familiar Letters of James W. Alexander* (New York: Charles Scribner, 1870), 2:74.

12. Virginia Trist correspondence, *Nicholas Philip Trist Papers, 1765–1903* from the Southern Historical Collection, Wilson Library, University of North Carolina at Chapel Hill, collection 02104, folder 225, scan 24, http://dc.lib.unc.edu/cdm/singleitem/collection/02104/id/56196.

13. Daniel Little, "Philosophy of History," *Stanford Encyclopedia of Philosophy* (website), ed. Edward N. Zalta (Winter 2012).

14. Daniel Walker Howe, *What Hath God Wrought: The Transformation of America, 1815–1848*, Oxford History of

the United States, ed. David M. Kennedy (New York: Oxford University Press, 2007), 704–5.

15. Allen C. Guelzo, *Gettysburg: The Last Invasion* (New York: Knopf, 2013), xii.

16. Kenneth M. Stampp, *The Causes of the Civil War* (Englewood Cliffs, NJ: Prentice-Hall, 1965).

17. Orlando Figes, *The Crimean War: A History* (New York: Metropolitan, 2010), 1–60.

18. Gordon S. Wood, *Empire of Liberty: A History of the Early Republic, 1789–1815* (New York: Oxford University Press, 2009), 587–88.

Chapter 23: Fallen History

1. Armand Marie Leroi, "One Republic of Learning: Digitizing the Humanities," *New York Times* (website), February 13, 2015.

2. George M. Marsden, "What Difference Might Christian Perspectives Make?" in *History and the Christian Historian*, ed. Ronald A. Wells (Grand Rapids: Eerdmans, 1998), 17.

3. "*Guns, Germs, and Steel*," Wikipedia, http://en.wikipedia.org/wiki/Guns,_Germs,_and_Steel.

4. William H. McNeill, review of *Guns, Germs, and Steel* in *New York Review of Books* (website), June 26, 1997.

5. George M. Marsden, "What Difference Might Christian Perspectives Make?" in *History and the Christian Historian*, ed. Ronald A. Wells (Grand Rapids: Eerdmans, 1998), 17.

6. Herbert Butterfield, *The Whig Interpretation of History* (London: G. Bell and Sons, 1931), 11.

7. Ibid., v.

8. Gregg L. Frazer, *The Religious Beliefs of America's Founders: Reason, Revelation, and Revolution* (University Press of Kansas, 2012), 19–20.

9. For example, see David Barton, Liberty University Convocation (video, 2:30–3:09), September 9, 2011, http://youtube.com/watch?v=dybHrSi4Now.

10. Jean-François Lyotard, "The Postmodern Condition," in *The Postmodern History Reader*, ed. Keith Jenkins (New York: Routledge, 1997), 36.

11. Stanley Fish, *There's No Such Thing as Free Speech* (New York: Oxford University Press, 1994), 7–8.

12. Keith Jenkins, ed., *The Postmodern History Reader* (New York: Routledge, 1997), 1–30.

13. Alun Munslow, *Deconstructing History* (New York: Routledge, 1997), 190.

14. Carl R. Trueman, *Histories and Fallacies: Problems Faced in the Writing of History* (Wheaton: Crossway, 2010), 27–28.

15. For example, see Ian Millhiser, "The Supreme Court Just Blew a Gaping Hole in the Wall of Separation Between Church and State," ThinkProgress (website), May 5, 2014.

16. Carl R. Trueman, *Histories and Fallacies* (Wheaton: Crossway, 2010), 53, fn 16.

17. Gordon S. Wood, *The Purpose of the Past: Reflections on the Uses of History* (New York: Penguin, 2008), 5–6.

18. Robert E. Brown, *Charles Beard and the Constitution: A Critical Analysis of "An Economic Interpretation of the Constitution"* (Princeton, NJ: Princeton University Press, 1956), 196; cf. 195–200.

19. Cf. Mark T. Gilderhus, *History and Historians: A Historiographical Introduction*, 5th ed. (Upper Saddle River, NJ: Prentice Hall, 2003), 56–60.

20. Gordon S. Wood, *The Purpose of the Past* (New York: Penguin, 2008), 281, 286–87.

21. Ibid., 292.

22. Timothy Larsen, *Crisis of Doubt: Honest Faith in Nineteenth-Century England* (New York: Oxford University Press, 2006), 113.

23. Ibid., 122.

24. Ibid., 123.

25. Ibid., 124.

26. Ibid., 1–9.

27. Ibid., 5; cf. 2–5.

28. A. N. Wilson quoted in ibid., 245.

29. Ibid., 5.

30. Ibid., 1.

31. Ibid., 11–13.

32. Ibid., 15–17, 242–43.

33. David Cook, *Understanding Jihad* (Berkeley and Los Angeles: University of California Press, 2005).

34. Ibid.

Chapter 24: History in Light of Redemption

1. *Oxford Dictionary of National Biography*, s.v. "Samuel Johnson."

2. James Boswell, *The Life of Samuel Johnson, LL.D.*, (Philadelphia: Claxton, Remsen, and Haffelfinger, 1878), 1:375.

3. Carl R. Trueman, *Histories and Fallacies: Problems Faced in the Writing of History* (Wheaton: Crossway, 2010), 17.

4. From Charles Barrett, ed., *New Testament Background: Selected Documents*, rev. ed. (New York: HarperOne, 1995), 28 [translation slightly adapted].

5. Mark Ward Sr., *Deadly Documents: Technical Communication, Organizational Discourse, and the Holocaust* (Amityville, NY: Baywood Publishing, 2014).

6. Andreas J. Köstenberger, *Excellence: The Character of God and the Pursuit of Scholarly Virtue* (Wheaton: Crossway, 2011), 33–54.

7. Carl Trueman, *Histories and Fallacies* (Wheaton: Crossway, 2010), 6.

8. Ibid., 107.

9. Timothy Larsen, *Crisis of Doubt: Honest Faith in Nineteenth-Century England* (New York: Oxford University Press, 2006).

10. Andrea Palpant Dilley, "The Surprising Discovery about Those Colonialist, Proselytizing Missionaries," *Christianity Today* (website), January 8, 2014.

11. Ibid.

12. Carl Trueman, *Histories and Fallacies* (Wheaton: Crossway, 2010), 99.

13. C. S. Lewis, "Introduction," in Athanasius, *On the Incarnation* (1944; repr., Crestwood, NY: St. Vladimir's Seminary Press, 1996), 5.

14. Allen C. Guelzo, *Fateful Lightning: A New History of the Civil War and Reconstruction* (New York: Oxford University Press, 2012), 375.

15. Carl Trueman, *Histories and Fallacies* (Wheaton: Crossway, 2010), 166–67.

16. John Fea, *Why Study History? Reflecting on the Importance of the Past* (Grand Rapids: Baker, 2013), 76–78.

17. Mark Noll quoted in Tim Stafford, "Whatever Happened to Christian History?" *Christianity Today* (website), April 2, 2001.

18. C. S. Lewis, "Historicism," in *God, History, and Historians: An Anthology of Modern Christian Views of History*, ed. C. T. McIntire (New York: Oxford University Press, 1977), 226–27.

19. James McDermott, *England and the Spanish Armada: The Necessary Quarrel* (New Haven, CT: Yale University Press, 2005), xii.

20. Colin Martin and Geoffrey Parker, *The Spanish Armada*, rev. ed. (New York: Palgrave, 1999), 184–205.

Chapter 25: Truth, Goodness, and Beauty

1. Gene Weingarten, "Pearls Before Breakfast," *Washington Post Magazine*, April 8, 2007.

2. Ibid.

3. George Robinson, "Violinist Joshua Bell Walks in the Footsteps of Masters," *Jewish Journal*, October 12, 2006.

4. Gene Weingarten, "Pearls Before Breakfast," *Washington Post Magazine*, April 8, 2007.

5. Blair Howell, "Concert Preview: Music of Violinist Joshua Bell 'Feeds Both Brain and Heart,'" *Deseret News*, November 9, 2013.

6. Bob Faw, "Interview with Joshua Bell," *Religion & Ethics Newsweekly*, October 10, 2014, www.pbs.org.

7. Paul Munson and Joshua Farris Drake, *Art and Music: A Student's Guide*, ed. David Dockery (Wheaton: Crossway, 2014), 83.

8. Ronald Horton, "Aesthetics" (class lecture), Bob Jones University, September 1, 2011.

9. James K. Smith, *How (Not) to Be Secular: Reading Charles Taylor* (Grand Rapids: Eerdmans, 2014), 22–23.

10. Paul Munson and Joshua Farris Drake, *Art and Music: A Student's Guide*, ed. David Dockery (Wheaton: Crossway, 2014), 22.

11. Kenneth Myers, *Mars Hill Audio* 78, audio journal, January/February 2006 (00:08–00:57).

12. J. R. R. Tolkien, "On Fairy Stories," in *Tree and Leaf* (Boston: Houghton Mifflin, 1965), 37.

13. Ibid., 71.

14. Quoted in Christian Smith, *Lost in Transition: The Dark Side of Emerging Adulthood* (New York: Oxford University Press, 2011), 28.

15. Ibid., 22.

16. Ibid., 29.

17. Ibid., 30.

18. Richard N. Williams and Daniel N. Robinson, *Scientism: The New Orthodoxy* (New York: Bloomsbury Academic, 2014), 6.

19. Robert C. Solomon and Kathleen M. Higgins, *A Short History of Philosophy* (New York: Oxford University Press, 1996), 300.

20. Gary Gutting, "Does Evolution Explain Religious Beliefs?" *New York Times* (website), July 8, 2014.

21. Richard Rorty, *Achieving Our Country: Leftist Thought in Twentieth-Century America* (Cambridge, MA: Harvard University Press, 1998), 16.

22. C. S. Lewis, *Mere Christianity* (San Francisco: HarperSanFrancisco, 2009), 5.

23. Ibid.

24. James K. Smith, *How (Not) to Be Secular: Reading Charles Taylor* (Grand Rapids: Eerdmans, 2014), 36.

25. Stanley Fish, "Boutique Multiculturalism, or Why Liberals Are Incapable of Thinking About Hate Speech," *Critical Inquiry* 23 (Winter 1997): 383–84.

26. Gary Gutting, "Does Evolution Explain Religious Beliefs?" *New York Times* (website), July 8, 2014.

27. C. S. Lewis, *Mere Christianity* (San Francisco: HarperSanFrancisco, 2009), 9–10.

28. James K. Smith, *How (Not) to Be Secular: Reading Charles Taylor* (Grand Rapids: Eerdmans, 2014), 61.

29. R. W. Hepburn, "Relativism, ethical," in *The Oxford Companion to Philosophy*, ed. Ted Honderich (New York: Oxford University Press, 1995), 758.

30. C. S. Lewis, *Mere Christianity* (San Francisco: Harper-SanFrancisco, 2009), 6.

31. Paul Munson and Joshua Farris Drake, *Art and Music: A Student's Guide*, ed. David Dockery (Wheaton: Crossway, 2014), 15.

32. Roger Scruton, *Beauty: A Very Short Introduction* (New York: Oxford University Press, 2011), 31. [See also Charles Darwin, *The Descent of Man, and Selection in Relation to Sex* (1871; repr., New York: Penguin Classics, 2004), 114–15.]

33. Ibid., 29.

34. Story told by Mike Bullmore, "Feeding on God: Cultivating a Fruitful Life in the Word" (sermon), New Attitude Conference, 2006.

35. John Piper, *The Pleasures of God: Meditations on God's Delight in Being God*, rev. ed. (Colorado Springs: Waterbrook Multnomah, 2000), 86.

36. Roger Scruton, *Beauty: A Very Short Introduction* (New York: Oxford University Press, 2011), 119.

37. Paul Munson and Joshua Farris Drake, *Art and Music: A Student's Guide*, ed. David Dockery (Wheaton: Crossway, 2014), 26.

38. Roger Scruton, *Beauty: A Very Short Introduction* (New York: Oxford University Press, 2011), 6.

39. "Tate Egg Protester Faces Life Ban," BBC News (website), December 12, 2001; Martin Creed, "Work No. 227," Museum of Modern Art, New York, 2000, http://martincreed.com/site/works/work-no-227.

40. Martin Creed, "Work No. 79," 1993, http://martincreed.com/site/works/work-no-79.

41. "Tate Egg Protester Faces Life Ban," BBC News (website), December 12, 2001.

42. Roger Scruton, *Beauty: A Very Short Introduction* (New York: Oxford University Press, 2011), 85.

43. Ibid.

44. Philip Yancey, interview with Steven Curtis Chapman, "Listening In . . . .," Today's Christian Music (website), n.d.

45. Paul Munson and Joshua Farris Drake, *Art and Music: A Student's Guide*, ed. David Dockery (Wheaton: Crossway, 2014), 35.

46. Mark Minnick, "Characteristics of a Christlike Mind" (sermon), Mount Calvary Baptist Church, Greenville, SC, August 25, 2013.

47. Markus Bockmuehl, *The Epistle to the Philippians*, Black's New Testament Commentary (Grand Rapids: Baker Academic, 1998), 253.

48. Gordon D. Fee, *Paul's Letter to the Philippians*, New International Commentary on the New Testament (Grand Rapids: Eerdmans, 1995), 416.

49. Paul Munson and Joshua Farris Drake, *Art and Music: A Student's Guide*, ed. David Dockery (Wheaton: Crossway, 2014), 85.

50. Francis A. Schaeffer, *The Complete Works of Francis A. Schaeffer: A Christian Worldview* (Westchester, IL: Crossway Books, 1982), 5:200.

51. Dana Gioia, "Can Poetry Matter?" *Atlantic Monthly*, May 1991, 94.

52. Carl Sandburg, quoted in Robert Konzelman, *Marquee Ministry* (New York: HarperCollins, 1971), 13.

53. Dana Gioia, "Beauty's Place in the Christian Vision" (chapel sermon), Biola University, La Mirada, CA, February 8, 2012, www.youtube.com/watch?v=xmEbg36_IDY.

54. Ibid.

55. Kenneth Myers, *All God's Children and Blue Suede Shoes: Christians and Popular Culture* (Wheaton: Crossway, 1989), 35.

56. Leonard Bernstein, *The Unanswered Question: Six Talks at Harvard* (DVD), Kultur Video, 2001.

57. Dana Gioia, "Beauty's Place in the Christian Vision" (chapel sermon), Biola University, La Mirada, CA, February 8, 2012, www.youtube.com/watch?v=xmEbg36_IDY.

58. Douglas Wilson, *Wordsmithy: Hot Tips for the Writing Life* (Moscow, ID: Canon Press, 2011), 20.

59. Paul Munson and Joshua Farris Drake, *Art and Music: A Student's Guide*, ed. David Dockery (Wheaton: Crossway, 2014), 40.

60. Dana Gioia, "Beauty's Place in the Christian Vision" (chapel sermon), Biola University, La Mirada, CA, February 8, 2012, www.youtube.com/watch?v=xmEbg36_IDY.

61. Paul Munson and Joshua Farris Drake, *Art and Music: A Student's Guide*, ed. David Dockery (Wheaton: Crossway, 2014), 30.

Chapter 26: The False, the Bad, and the Ugly

1. "*The Hunt of the Unicorn*," Wikipedia, http://en.wikipedia.org/wiki/The_Hunt_of_the_Unicorn (adjusted to 2014 dollars).

2. Bill Maher, *Religulous* (DVD), director Larry Charles, 2008.

3. Barack Obama, *The Audacity of Hope: Thoughts on Reclaiming the American Dream* (New York: Crown, 2006), 350.

4. William Voegeli, "The Redskins and Their Offense," *Claremont Review of Books*, Spring 2014, 17.

5. Leonard Cresswell Ingleby, *Oscar Wilde* (New York: Mitchell Kennerley, 1907), 335.

6. Oscar Wilde, *The Picture of Dorian Gray* (1891; repr., Mineola, NY: Dover Publications, 1993), 16.

7. Ibid., 13.

8. Tom Stoppard, *The Real Thing* (London: Faber & Faber, 1984), 52.

9. Ben Brantley, "A Storytelling Instinct Revels in Horror's Fun," *New York Times* (website), April 11, 2005.

10. John Simon, "Exquisite Corpses," *New York* magazine (website), April 25, 2005.

11. Plato, *Apology* 37e–38a.

12. Mark Minnick, sermon at Mount Calvary Baptist Church, Greenville, South Carolina.

13. Janet Maslin, "The Road Through Hell, Paved with Desperation," *New York Times* (website), September 25, 2006.

14. Nick Schager, "*Courageous*: Subtle as a Chastity Ring," *Village Voice* (website), September 28, 2011.

15. Frank Scheck, "Courageous: Film Review," *Hollywood Reporter* (website), September 30, 2011.

16. Sabrina Rubin Erdely, "A Rape on Campus: A Brutal Assault and Struggle for Justice at UVA," *Rolling Stone* (website), November 19, 2014.

17. Ravi Somaiya, "Magazine's Account of Gang Rape on Virginia Campus Comes Under Scrutiny," *New York Times* (website), December 2, 2014.

18. David Uberti, "The Worst Journalism of 2014," *Columbia Journalism Review* (website), December 22, 2014.

19. R. H. Blythe, quoted in Kenneth Myers, *All God's Children and Blue Suede Shoes: Christians and Popular Culture* (Wheaton: Crossway, 1989), 85.

20. Mark Rothko, in Selden Rodman, *Conversations with Artists* (New York: Capricorn, 1961), 93.

21. Michael Kimmelman, "Rothko's Gloomy Elegance in Retrospect," *New York Times* (website), September 18, 1998.

22. Ibid.

23. Kenneth Myers, *All God's Children and Blue Suede Shoes* (Wheaton: Crossway, 1989), 56.

24. Andy Crouch, *Culture Making: Recovering Our Creative Calling* (Downers Grove, IL: IVP, 2013), 89.

25. Fred Sanders, "They Quit Making Good Music When I Turned 30," *First Things* (blog), October 21, 2009, http://www.firstthings.com/index.php?permalink=bl ogs&blog=firstthoughts&year=2009&month=10&ent ry_permalink=they-quit-making-good-music-when-i-turned-30.

26. James Davison Hunter, "The Backdrop of Reality: James Davison Hunter in Conversation with James K. A. Smith," *Comment* (Fall 2013): 37.

27. Andy Crouch, *Culture Making: Recovering Our Creative Calling* (Downers Grove, IL: IVP, 2013), 28.

28. James Davison Hunter, "The Backdrop of Reality: James Davison Hunter in Conversation with James K. A. Smith," *Comment* (Fall 2013): 39.

29. Kenneth Myers, *All God's Children and Blue Suede Shoes* (Wheaton: Crossway, 1989), 114.

30. John Lennon, "Imagine," Chappell Music, 1971.

31. Kenneth Myers, *All God's Children and Blue Suede Shoes* (Wheaton: Crossway, 1989), xiv.

32. Matthew Arnold, *Culture and Anarchy: An Essay in Political and Social Criticism* (1896; repr., New York: Cambridge University Press, 1993), viii.

33. *New Oxford American Dictionary*, s.v. "veg."

34. T. David Gordon, *Why Johnny Can't Sing Hymns* (Phillipsburg, NJ: P&R, 2010), 26.

35. Ernest van den Haag, *Passion and Social Constraint* (New York: Stein and Day, 1963), 332.

36. Kenneth Myers, *All God's Children and Blue Suede Shoes* (Wheaton: Crossway, 1989), xiii.

37. John Gibson Paton, *John G. Paton D.D.: Missionary to the New Hebrides: An Autobiography*, ed. James Paton (London: Hodder and Stoughton, 1891), 218.

38. Kenneth Myers, *All God's Children and Blue Suede Shoes* (Wheaton: Crossway, 1989), 183.

Chapter 27: Creative Cultivators

1. Devdutt Pattanaik, "East vs. West—The Myths That Mystify," Technology, Entertainment, Design (TED) website, November 2009.

2. Kenneth Myers, *All God's Children and Blue Suede Shoes: Christians and Popular Culture* (Wheaton: Crossway, 1989), 183.

3. Makoto Fujimura, *Culture Care: Reconnecting with Beauty for Our Common Life* (New York: International Arts Movement, 2015), 9.

4. Ibid., 18.

5. Ibid., 19.

6. Marshall McLuhan, *Understanding Media: The Extensions of Man* (1964; Cambridge, MA: MIT Press, 1994), 8.

7. Tony Reinke, *Lit! A Christian Guide to Reading Books* (Wheaton: Crossway, 2011), 128.

8. Ibid., 61.

9. Ibid.

10. Maria Wollan, "Rise and Shine: What Kids Around the World Eat for Breakfast," New York Times Magazine (website), October 8, 2014, http://www.nytimes.com /interactive/2014/10/08/magazine/eaters-all-over.html.

11. "Tea-Flavored Toothpaste Is Helping Chinese Brands Edge Out the Competition," Shanghaiist (website), July 29, 2014.

12. Tony Reinke, *Lit! A Christian Guide to Reading Books* (Wheaton: Crossway, 2011), 122.

13. C. S. Lewis, On Stories and Other Essay onLiterature (Orlando, FL: Harcourt, Inc., 1982), 63.

14. Hanna Rosin, "Pop Goes Christianity," *Slate* (website), May 5, 2008.

15. Ibid.

16. Ibid.

17. Ibid.

18. Ibid.

19. Ibid.

20. "Why Create a College and Career Plan?" http://www.mymajors.com.

21. Alan Jacobs, "On Defending Liberal Education," *The New Atlantis* (website), September 25, 2014. Used by permission.

22. Catherine Brahic, "Solar-Powered Sea Slug Harnesses Stolen Plant Genes," *New Scientist* (website), November 24, 2008.

23. Stephen Altrogge, "A Solid Worldview Won't Save My Kids," The Blazing Center (blog), January 2015.

24. Flannery O'Connor, *Mystery and Manners: Occasional Prose* (New York: Farrar, Straus and Giroux, 1970), 34.

25. Frederick Hart quoted in "Hart Cathedral Collection," Angela King Gallery (website).

26. Tom Wolfe, "The Artist the Art World Couldn't See," *New York Times Magazine*, January 2, 2000, 16.

27. Ibid., 17.

28. O. Henry, "The Last Leaf," in *The Trimmed Lamp, and Other Stories of the Four Million* (Garden City, NY: Doubleday, Page & Company, 1907), 198–208.

29. Zach Franzen, personal communication, June 17, 2015.

30. "Read-Aloud Revival," http://amongstlovelythings.com.

31. Tantrum House, http://www.tantrumhouse.com.

32. Richard A. Lanham, "The Abusage of Usage," *Virginia Quarterly Review* 53, no. 1 (Winter 1977):32–54, http://www.vqronline.org/essay/abusage-usage.

33. Mark O'Connor, "The Kingdom Is a Feast," *Kairos* 24, issue 20 (October 27, 2013): 19, http://www.cam.org.au/Portals/0/kairos/kairos_v24i20/files/assets/basic-html/page19.html.

34. Kim Hammond and Darren Cronshaw, *Sentness: Six Postures of Missional Christians* (Downers Grove, IL: InterVarsity Press, 2014), 88–89.

35. Dan Forrest, "What I Believe," http://www.danforrest.com/bio/what-i-believe. Used by permission.

36. Maltbie Babcock, "This Is My Father's World," *Rejoice Hymns* (Greenville, SC: Majesty Music, 2011), 147.

MEMORY VERSES

1: Worldviews

2 Corinthians 10:4–5 For the weapons of our warfare are not of the flesh but have divine power to destroy strongholds. We destroy arguments and every lofty opinion raised against the knowledge of God, and take every thought captive to obey Christ.

2: Presuppositions

Hebrews 11:3 By faith we understand that the universe was created by the word of God, so that what is seen was not made out of things that are visible.

3: The Two-Story View

Colossians 1:19–20 For in [Christ] all the fullness of God was pleased to dwell, and through him to reconcile to himself all things, whether on earth or in heaven, making peace by the blood of his cross.

4: God the Creator

John 1:1–3 In the beginning was the Word, and the Word was with God, and the Word was God. He was in the beginning with God. All things were made through him, and without him was not any thing made that was made.

John 17:24 "Father, I desire that they also, whom you have given me, may be with me where I am, to see my glory that you have given me because you loved me before the foundation of the world."

5: Man and His Mandate

Genesis 1:26–28 Then God said, "Let us make man in our image, after our likeness. And let them have dominion over the fish of the sea and over the birds of the heavens and over the livestock and over all the earth and over every creeping thing that creeps on the earth."

So God created man in his own image,
  in the image of God he created him;
male and female he created them.

And God blessed them. And God said to them, "Be fruitful and multiply and fill the earth and subdue it, and have dominion over the fish of the sea and over the birds of the heavens and over every living thing that moves on the earth."

6: Everything God Made Was Very Good

Proverbs 3:19 The Lord by wisdom founded the earth; by understanding he established the heavens.

7: Far as the Curse Is Found

Romans 8:19–21 The creation waits with eager longing for the revealing of the sons of God. For the creation was subjected to futility, . . . in hope that the creation itself will be set free from its bondage to corruption.

8: Common Grace, the World, and You

1 Peter 2:11–12 Beloved, I urge you as sojourners and exiles to abstain from the passions of the flesh, which wage war against your soul. Keep your conduct among the Gentiles honorable, so that when they speak against you as evildoers, they may see your good deeds and glorify God on the day of visitation.

Proverbs 1:7 The fear of the Lord is the beginning of knowledge; fools despise wisdom and instruction.

9: Structure and Direction

Ephesians 5:10–11 And try to discern what is pleasing to the Lord. Take no part in the unfruitful works of darkness, but instead expose them.

10: An Everlasting Kingdom

Genesis 3:15 (NKJV) And I will put enmity between you and the woman, and between your seed and her Seed; He shall bruise your head, and you shall bruise His heel.

11: Redeemed for Good Works

Matthew 5:14–16 You are the light of the world. A city set on a hill cannot be hidden. Nor do people light a lamp and put it under a basket, but on a stand, and it gives light to all in the house. In the same way, let your light shine before others, so that they may see your good works and give glory to your Father who is in heaven.

12: The Mission of the Church and Your Vocation

Acts 2:42 And they devoted themselves to the apostles' teaching and the fellowship, to the breaking of bread and the prayers.

13: The Man and the Woman in Creation

Genesis 2:18 Then the Lord God said, "It is not good that the man should be alone; I will make him a helper fit for him."

14: Marriage Twisted

Genesis 3:16–17 To the woman he said, "I will surely multiply your pain in childbearing; in pain you shall bring forth children. Your desire shall be for your husband, and he shall rule over you." And to Adam he said, "Because you have listened to the voice of your wife and have eaten of the tree of which I commanded you, 'You shall not eat of it,' cursed is the ground because of you; in pain you shall eat of it all the days of your life."

15: Marriage Redeemed

Proverbs 18:22 He who finds a wife finds a good thing and obtains favor from the Lord.

16: Foundations of Government

2 Samuel 23:3b–4 When one rules justly over men, ruling in the fear of God, he dawns on them like the morning light, like the sun shining forth on a cloudless morning, like rain that makes grass to sprout from the earth.

17: Political Perspectives

Psalm 82:1–4 (NASB) God takes His stand in His own congregation; He judges in the midst of the rulers. How long will you judge unjustly and show partiality to the wicked? Vindicate the weak and fatherless; do justice to the afflicted and destitute. Rescue the weak and needy; deliver them out of the hand of the wicked.

18: The Goal of Government

Revelation 11:15b The kingdom of the world has become the kingdom of our Lord and of his Christ, and he shall reign forever and ever.

19: Science Is Something God Created Humans to Do

Psalm 111:2 Great are the works of the Lord, studied by all who delight in them.

20: Fallen Science

Romans 1:25 They exchanged the truth about God for a lie and worshiped and served the creature rather than the Creator, who is blessed forever! Amen.

21: Reading Genesis and Doing Science

Genesis 1:31 And God saw everything that he had made, and behold, it was very good. And there was evening and there was morning, the sixth day.

22: Foundations for History

Acts 17:26–27 [God] made from one man every nation of mankind to live on all the face of the earth, having determined allotted periods and the boundaries of their dwelling place, that they should seek God, and perhaps feel their way toward him and find him. Yet he is actually not far from each one of us.

23: Fallen History

John 8:44–45 You are of your father the devil, and your will is to do your father's desires. He was a murderer from the beginning, and does not stand in the truth, because there is no truth in him. When he lies, he speaks out of his own character, for he is a liar and the father of lies. But because I tell the truth, you do not believe me.

24: History in Light of Redemption

Isaiah 46:9–10 Remember the former things of old; for I am God, and there is no other; I am God, and there is none like me, declaring the end from the beginning and from ancient times things not yet done, saying, "My counsel shall stand, and I will accomplish all my purpose."

25: Truth, Goodness, and Beauty

Philippians 4:8 Finally, brothers, whatever is true, whatever is honorable, whatever is just, whatever is pure, whatever is lovely, whatever is commendable, if there is any excellence, if there is anything worthy of praise, think about these things.

26: The False, the Bad, and the Ugly

2 Thessalonians 2:11 Therefore God sends them a strong delusion, so that they may believe what is false.

27: Creative Cultivators

Genesis 2:15 The Lord God took the man and put him in the garden of Eden to work it and keep it.

SCRIPTURE INDEX

VERSE	PAGES	VERSE	PAGES	VERSE	PAGES
Genesis		3:19	72	32:32	141
1	14, 63, 67, 81	3:20	185, 188	48:4	43
1:1	10, 48, 138, 340	4:1	326	50:20	349, 378
1:2	63	4:1–16	105	**Exodus**	
1:14	340	4:4–7	225	4:22	226
1:21	77	4:7	101	9:29	41
1:22	67	4:16	150	18:21–22	240
1:26	63, 132, 186	4:21	263	19:5	41
1:26–28	62–63, 65, 67, 186, 238, 258, 282, 399, 427	5:5	95, 326	20:8, 11	39
1:27	6, 40, 186, 206, 289	5:16	150	20:12	79, 190, 203
1:28	14, 67, 79, 96, 139, 150–51, 186, 190, 206, 287, 290, 295	4:19	105	20:13	246
		4:21–22	72, 239	20:14	127
		4:21	239	20:15	244, 262
1:31	322	4:23	225	20:17	244
2	69	4:22–24	105	21:15	190
2:5–6	177	2:24	83	21:16	244, 279
2:7	63	4:25	326	21:33–33:14	262
2:9	95	4:26	225	22:16–17, 21–27	244
2:10	177	5:3	190		
2:11	239	6	140	23:1, 6–9	244
2:18	77, 184, 186–87, 206, 239, 256	6:5	97	25:18–20	40
		6:6	80	28:2	398
2:19–20	186	8:20–22	140	31:1–5	216
2:20	101, 187	8:22	83, 288, 296	40	327
2:22–23	186	9:1–7	140, 240	**Leviticus**	
2:22–24	341	9:2–3	290	19:9–10	256
2:24	127, 185, 187, 190, 192, 206, 212, 246, 256	9:2–4	290	19:13	244
		9:3	62	20:10	277
3:1, 3, 4–5	94	9:6	66, 190, 244	20:13	341
3:7	95, 200	11	132	23:22	247
3:10–12	96	11:4	150	**Numbers**	
3:12	200, 354	11:6–8	109	15:30	406
3:15	74, 101, 138–39, 144–46, 150	12:1–3	140	**Deuteronomy**	
		12:3	226	1:16	242
3:16	101, 202, 394	12:7	147	1:17	242
3:16–19	186	18:19	191	4:6	248
3:16–17	200	19:30–38	434	4:9	192
2:17	94, 109	20:6	110	6	229
3:17–19	101, 303	29:31	67		

TOPICAL INDEX

A

Abimelech 110
abortion 189, 279
Abraham 22, 140–42, 146, 340
Abrahamic Covenant 140, 143
Abraham, Nathaniel 32
abuse 126
action 6, 13, 17, 44, 71, 110, 171,
    243, 247, 261, 344, 347, 359, 366,
    373, 378–79, 390, 407, 428
Adam 8, 12, 14, 42, 64, 69, 74, 81,
    94–98, 100–102, 141, 185–87,
    194, 200, 225, 263, 300, 326–28,
    343, 354, 361, 401
Adam, second 98, 147, 161, 327
Adams, Ansel 430
Adamson, Andrew 195
adultery 201–2, 213, 224, 277
aesthetic, aestheticism 34, 385,
    392, 397, 399, 410
"affection drives cognition" 116–18,
    120
Ahab, King 110
Aldrin, Buzz 369
Ali, Muhammad 53
Allberry, Sam 209
already 155–57, 160
ambassador 115
Apollo 11 292
aristocracy 248
Aristotle 23, 86, 248, 342
Armstrong, Neil 292, 370
arts 3, 43, 70, 104, 124–25, 151,
    174, 300, 385–87, 393–99, 402,
    411, 418–23, 428–33
asceticism 115
Asimov, Isaac 138
atheism 57, 100, 127, 290, 312–14
Augustine 220, 328, 340
Austen, Jane 395
autonomy 37, 188, 238, 256, 313

B

Babel 109, 132
Babette's Feast 432
Babylonian exile 340
Backus, Isaac 256
Bahnsen, Greg 276
baptism 171–72, 174, 176, 375

Baptist, John the 201, 274
Barr, Adam 209
basic beliefs 6, 15, 119
Bathsheba 394
Baumgardner, John 332
Beard, Charles 363
beauty 34, 49, 95, 109, 111, 113,
    115, 178, 222, 292, 300, 311, 336,
    384–85, 390–92, 394–98, 402,
    404–5, 410–11, 415, 429
Bebbington, David 346
Bechwith, Francis 319
Bellah, Robert 59
Bell, Joshua 384, 390
bending 95, 122–25, 130–31, 134,
    296, 331
Benerito, Ruth R. 294
Bentham, Jeremy 243
Bernstein, Leonard 397
biblical theism 56, 59
big bang 7, 11, 118, 124, 309, 323
biology 4, 290, 308, 312, 330
bisexuality 211
Bismark, Otto von 246
blaming authority 79
blaming emotion 80
Boaz, David 255
"book of nature" 286
Bradford, William 344
Brooks, David 322, 330
Brown, Gregory W. 308
Brown, Murphy 200, 217
Bruno, Giordano 286
Buckley, William F. 263
Bulverism 229
Bunyan, John 115
Burke, Edmund 246, 263, 265
Bush, George H. W. 200
Bush, George W. 259
Butterfield, Herbert 358
Butterfield, Rosaria Cham-
    pagne 205, 209

C

Cage, John 74
Cain's murder of Abel 105
Calvin, John 166, 281
Cameron, James 415
cannibals 415

capitalism 84–85, 261
caricature 130, 134
causation 350
Cernan, Gene 292
Charlemagne 271
child abuse 188, 203, 246
childlessness 67, 201
children 190–92, 195, 203, 227–28,
    233
China 245
Christian Reconstructionists 154
Christians for Biblical Equality
    (CBE) 194
chronology 340, 350
church 168–74, 226–27, 250
church and state 270–72, 274
Citlau, Ron 209
civil religion 59, 271–72
class, race, and gender 363–65, 372
Clegg, Brian 118
Clinton, Bill 403
cohabitation 210–12
common grace 108–12, 115–16,
    120, 123, 202, 277, 304, 312, 334,
    361, 396
commonwealth 248
communication 129, 132–33, 298,
    351, 418
complementarianism 193–97, 214
condemn 201, 207–8, 242, 261,
    341–42, 363, 389, 415–16
condemning culture 418, 420–21
conservatism 253, 258, 262–65
Constantinianism 271
consuming culture 418, 423–24
consumerism 164, 410
conversion 10, 278, 314, 318, 366,
    431
Coontz, Stephanie 210
Copernicus 298
copying culture 418, 425
cosmic effects 100–102
cosmology 10, 118, 311, 318–19,
    328, 332
Cotton, John 259
Council for Biblical Manhood and
    Womanhood 194, 196
Covenant, Davidic 142

Fedoroff, Nina 68
fellowshiping 172
feminist 214, 217, 232
Figard, Steve 332
finite 22, 53, 249, 343–44, 346, 361, 388
Fish, Stanley 9
Fleming, Alexander 290
Flood 6, 67, 97, 139–40, 225, 332, 340
folk culture 113
fornication 201
Forrest, Dan 432
Frame, John 95, 100
Frazer, Gregg 7, 360
free market 84, 255, 265
Friedan, Betty 212
Fujimura, Makoto 395, 420
fundamentalist 322, 328, 330

G

Galileo 286
Garrett, Duane 296
Gaza 259
gender 185–86, 188, 193, 195, 197, 215, 232
Gibson, Mel 431
Gioia, Dana 396–98
Gladwell, Malcolm 69
glory 51–52, 54, 88
God's goal 52–53, 174
goodness 389–90, 394, 396, 398, 402–5, 409, 411, 413, 429
Gordon, John Henry 365
Gould, Stephen Jay 3, 291
government 238–43, 245, 248–50, 254–55, 257, 259–60, 275, 282
Gray, John 312–14
Great Commission 73, 175
Great Famine, The 245
Great Leap Forward 245
Great Society, The 264
Guelzo, Allen 350
Gujarati 418

H

Haeckel, Ernst 305
Haidt, Jonathan 318
Haldane, J. B. S. 292–93
Hamas 259
Hannah 268

Harrison, Peter 335
Hart, Frederick 429
Hartnett, John 332
Hawking, Stephen 7, 64, 324–25
Hayes, Chris 316
head system 6
head-heart system 6, 10, 13, 21, 44, 120
heart system 8
heliocentric model 298
Henry, O. 430
hero 168, 309, 409
Hersch, Patricia 204
high culture 113, 411–14
Hippocratic oath 335
Hirshman, Linda 86–87
history 340–46, 351–52
Hitchens, Christopher 313
Hobby Lobby 36, 276
Holmes, Sherlock 217
homosexual 40, 117, 201, 205–9, 211, 214, 216–17, 259, 276, 341
honor 190, 227
Horstmeyer, Mark 332
Horton, Ron 133, 385
hospitality (in art) 429
Hozier 314
Hugo, Victor 396
Hume, David 312
Humphreys, D. Russell 333
Hunter, James Davison 412
husband 186–88, 192, 195, 202, 206, 221–24, 239
Hussein, Saddam 259

I

identical-twin studies 116
ideology 252, 259
image 63, 65, 97, 128, 138, 186, 244, 289, 391
image of God 63–64, 66
image-bearer 37, 63–70, 75, 77, 94, 96, 101, 128, 132, 193, 196, 230, 232–33, 239, 244–46, 258, 263, 278, 287, 342, 344, 357, 364, 408
immanent 59–60
individualism 79, 256, 262, 344
Ingersoll, Robert 307
institutions, cultural 33, 44, 58, 74, 79, 83, 103–6, 112, 124–25, 166, 170, 174, 184, 210, 238–39, 241,

249–50, 256, 259, 262, 270, 275, 341, 385, 412
instruction 228
intelligent design (ID) movement 277
International Arts Movement 420
internationalism 264
inventors hall of fame 294
Iraq 259, 357

J

Jackson, Andrew 274
Jacobs, Alan 97
Jefferson, Thomas 271
Jeremiah 274
John the Baptist 37, 156, 201, 268, 274
Johnson, Abby 80
Johnson, Luke Timothy 207
Johnson, Lyndon 264
Johnson, Samuel 369
Jones, Bob Sr. 44
Jones, David W. 213
judgment 154, 156–57
Just So Stories 317–18, 390
justice 242–45
justification 24, 177, 328, 341

K

Kepler 298
Khomeini, Ayatollah 389
Kidner, Derek 101
King, Martin Luther Jr. 36–37, 242
kingdom 145, 155, 238, 268
kingdom of God 38, 145–47, 149, 151, 154–57, 159–61, 170, 176, 238, 270, 346, 416
Kinkade, Thomas 409
Kipling, Rudyard 317
kitsch 113
knowledge 8–9, 19–20, 22, 25, 28, 32, 35, 52, 62, 94, 96, 117, 298, 305–6, 313, 315–17, 324, 336, 342, 387–88, 402, 426, 428
Kolbert, Elizabeth 311
Kostenberger, Andreas 213, 232
Krauss, Lawrence 311
Krulwich, Robert 65
Kuhn, Thomas 297
Kuyper, Abraham 5, 41

308, 340–41, 354, 384–86, 390–91, 395, 397–98, 401, 404

organism 170, 174

original sin 97

origins of the universe 311, 323–25, 328

Owen, Robert 260–61

P

pandas, giant 99, 101, 329

pantheism 56–59

Patton, John G. 415

Paul 23, 26, 30, 112, 146–47, 173, 179, 194, 201, 327–28

penicillin 290

People for the Ethical Treatment of Animals (PETA) 62

Perelandra 122

Philemon 278

Phillip, Prince 290

Philospher's Brief, The 273

pilgrim 115

Pillowman 405

Pinker, Steven 307, 310, 312, 314, 316

pirates 108, 110

Planned Parenthood 80, 189

Plantinga, Alvin 289, 308

playground bullies 32

pole metaphor 124

political ideology 252

Pollock, Jackson 395

Pollyanna 409

polygamy 83, 105, 200, 201, 278

Pontius Pilate 387

popular culture 107, 112–13, 203, 411–15, 424–25

postmodernism 12, 229–30, 354, 360–61, 387–88, 391

poverty 247

Poythress, Vern 132, 289

praying 40, 173, 275–76

presupposition 18, 20–22, 28,–29 289, 291, 324–25, 336, 343, 345, 375

primary source 347, 370

primitivism 346

Principe, Lawrence 286

Priscilla 232

progressivism 254–55

Project Steve 2, 5, 10, 14, 16, 119, 323

pro–LGBT 211

proof 21

providence 204, 209, 258, 341, 349–50, 376–79, 395

prudence 280

Ptolemaic model 297

Purdom, Georgia 333

Q

Quayle, Dan 200, 217

queer theory 205

R

Radcliffe, Daniel 404

rape 409

rationalism 9, 25, 271, 360

rationality 63, 81, 288, 342, 408

Rattigan, Terrance 396

Rau, Gerald 323

Rawls, John 277

Reagan, Ronald 161, 238, 249

Real Thing, The 404

reason 25

redemption 42, 138, 141, 146, 148–49, 343

Reeves, Michael 54, 187

Reinke, Tony 422

relativism 363, 385, 389–90, 399

restoration 43, 147–49, 151, 181, 220

resurrection 8, 19, 22–23, 39, 42–43, 73, 106, 117, 145–46, 149–50, 221, 231, 271, 342, 346, 361, 431

Revelation 147

revelation, general 59, 89, 296, 345

revelation, special 59, 89, 378

revenge 105, 242

revolt 280

Richards, Amy 189

Riefenstahl, Leni 395

Ripken, Nik 103, 106

Rockefeller, John D. 401

romanticism 403

Roosevelt, Franklin 264

Roosevelt, Theodore v

Rosin, Hanna 424–25

Rosling, Hans 80

Rothbart, Murray 254

Rothko, Mark 410

Rushdie, Salman 389

Russell, Bertrand 25

S

Sagan, Carl 57, 60, 100

Salatin, Joel 333

Salk, Jonas 334

salt and light 13, 16, 165

salvation 145, 154, 156–57

Samaritan woman 231

Samec, Ron 332

same-sex marriage 37, 40, 83, 89, 159, 207–8, 276–77, 307

Sandburg, Carl 396

Sandel, Michael 37, 243, 273

Sanford, John 333

Santayana, George 342

Sarfati, Jonathan 333

Satan 59, 67, 94, 97, 101, 110, 113, 115, 122, 125, 128, 138, 145–47, 159, 160, 238, 354, 378, 394

scaremongering 217

Schweitzer, Mary 20

science 287–88, 290–92, 294–96, 300, 302–5, 308, 312, 315

scientific method 4, 24, 28, 287, 304, 307–8, 315–16, 323

scientific naturalism 307, 310–11, 313–15, 318–19, 323

scientism 286, 289–90, 306–8, 313, 315–17, 387–88

Scruton, Roger 392

secondary source 371

secular Western goodness 87, 90

secularism 11, 34, 38, 43, 124, 272–73, 277, 291, 348, 359, 365

secularization 3, 272

seed 138, 141–42, 146–47, 226, 340

selection 348, 365–66, 372

self–esteem 65

sensibilities 412–15, 424

sex 126–28, 163–64, 186, 211, 216

sexual abuse 203

Shadrach, Meshach, and Abednego 281

Shaffer, Peter 404

Shakespeare 57, 113, 125, 395

sin 130, 154, 202, 224

singing 174, 415

singleness 128, 196, 198, 201
singularity 309
Slaughter, Anne Marie 214
Smith, Adam 253
Smith, Christian 58, 65, 386
Smith, Steven D. 273
Snelling, Andrew 334
socialism 253, 259, 261–62
Solomon 19, 117, 127–28, 133, 142,
179, 201, 242, 246, 298–99, 342,
356, 388
Solzhenitsyn, Alexander 275
Somalia 103
South Korea 85
Soviet Union 85
standardization 299
standards 86–88, 113, 150, 264,
278, 299–300, 322, 330, 336, 376,
406, 421
Star Trek 62–64, 302
STEM 426–27
Stepp, Laura Sessions 126
Stoppard, Tom 404–5
structure 123, 127, 132, 133, 165,
287
Stylites, Simon 115
subdue 14–15, 63, 67–72, 81, 90,
94, 139, 146, 148, 177, 190, 287,
306, 335, 427
submissive 85, 188, 191, 194, 202,
221–22, 224, 227, 280–81
suffering 6, 109, 149, 153–54, 159,
162, 164, 223, 276, 315, 330–31,
343, 376
Superman 79
supernaturalism 14
Swimme, Brian 10

T

T. rex soft tissue 20
tapestry 401, 406
teaching 2, 165, 172, 174, 194, 374,
379
technology 73, 123, 131–32,
164–65, 287, 292, 302–3, 331, 356
teenager 58, 65, 203–4, 224, 227,
386
Tennyson, Lord Alfred 99
theistic rationalist 7, 360
theocracy 276
theological motivations 286

theonomy 276
Thompson, Emma 412
Titanic 415
Tolkien, J. R. R. 138, 153, 319
total depravity 110
totalitarianism 250, 258, 374–75
traditional conservatism 263, 265
transcendent 59–60, 392
Trinity 50–51, 54, 63, 132, 185, 187,
239, 271, 293, 360, 402
Trueman, Carl 362, 369, 373, 375,
377–78
truth 7, 9, 18–19, 21, 24–30, 34, 50,
56, 79, 80, 83–89, 96–97, 387–88,
111, 115, 117–19, 125, 160, 165,
172, 230, 232–33, 256, 292,
297–98, 307, 315, 328, 344, 351,
365, 375, 390, 394–98, 402–5,
407–8, 411, 415, 429
truth, goodness, and beauty 111,
115, 299–300, 384–99, 401–16
Tucker, Mary Evelyn 10
Twin Towers 292
two-story view 32–35, 37, 41–44,
168, 272, 309–10
Tyson, Neil deGrasse 57, 312

U

Unit 731 402
Unitarianism 259, 351, 360
University of Virginia 409
USSR 85
utilitarianism 242–43

V

visual arts 386, 395
Voltaire 59
Vonnegut, Kurt 305, 312

W

Wallace, J. Warner 18
Walton, John 327
Washington, Booker T. 344
Weingarten, Gene 384
Wellesley College 215
West Africa 304
Whiggish 358–60
Wilberforce, William 166, 274
Wilde, Oscar 403–4
Wilder, Thornton 396
Williams, John 421

Williams, Richard N. 315
wisdom 10, 23, 52, 85, 125, 166,
176, 185, 232, 247, 248, 263,
296–97, 344–45, 372, 388, 390,
400, 413, 419
Wise, Kurt 334
witness 160–61
wives 186–87, 192, 195, 197–98,
202, 206, 221–24, 239
Wizard of Oz, The 421
Wolfe, Tom 429
Wolters, Al 6, 81, 123
Wood, Gordon 363
Woodberry, Robert 374
world 106, 113
worldliness 113–15
worldview 5, 15, 25, 32, 44, 49, 64,
252, 288, 311–12, 317, 344–45,
351, 385, 387, 428
worldview apologetics 21
Wright, Sarah 184

XYZ

Yeats, William Butler 106
Yosemite National Park 430

DEBATE RUBRIC

	MESSAGE

Identification of Apologetic Approach

3 Accurately identifies the overall approach of the Christian debater by providing support and illustrations from the debate for such an identification

2 Accurately identifies the overall approach of the Christian debater but fails to provide relevant support or illustrations from the debate for such an identification

1 Fails to identify the overall apologetic approach of the Christian debater

Evaluation

3 Provides a thorough evaluation of the benefits and drawbacks of the approach and offers additional arguments the Christian could have used

2 Provides some evaluation of the benefits or drawbacks of the approach with no additional arguments

1 Fails to provide an evaluation of the benefits or drawbacks of the approach

Organization and Development

3 Provides a logical flow and unity of thought with clear conclusions

2 Demonstrates some logical flow but lacks unity or clear conclusions

1 Demonstrates poor overall planning and organization

_____ **Message Score**

	MECHANICS

Grammar and Usage

3 Writer displays a command of grade-level skills (e.g., agreement, verb and pronoun usage, sentence structure).

2 Writer displays a basic knowledge of grade-level skills (e.g., agreement, verb and pronoun usage, sentence structure).

1 Writer displays little or no knowledge of grade-level grammar skills.

Spelling

3 Writer uses and spells words above grade level.

2 Writer spells words on grade level.

1 Writer misspells grade-level words.

Capitalization and Punctuation

3 Writer demonstrates a command of grade-level capitalization and punctuation.

2 Writer demonstrates an understanding of grade-level capitalization and punctuation.

1 Writer misuses grade-level capitalization and punctuation.

_____ **Mechanics Score**

_____ **Total Score (Message plus Mechanics)**

A 16–18	B 14–15	C 12–13	D 10–11	F 6–9

PHOTO CREDITS

Key: (t) top; (c) center; (b) bottom; (l) left; (r) right

Unit 1

7 Karwai Tang/Getty Images Entertainment/Getty Images; 25 © iStockphoto.com/harmatoslabu; 29 John Chillingworth/Stringer/Picture Post/Getty Images; 34 (sky) © 2006 Jesse Larson, (church) © iStockphoto.com/stu99, (house) Norman Pogson/Shutterstock.com

Unit 2

53 Library of Congress; 56 "Selznick Kimball Young"/Wikimedia Commons/Public Domain; 64l Ultima_Gaina/iStock/Thinkstock; 64r Agency-Animal-Picture/Getty Images News/Getty Images; 66l © iStockphoto.com/Avatar_023; 66cl © iStockphoto.com/Britta Kasholm-Tengve; 66cr © iStockphoto.com/SensorSpot; 66r © iStockphoto.com/afhunta; 69t lightphoto/iStock/Thinkstock; 69b © iStockphoto.com/Fenykepez; 79t Hulton Archive/Getty Images; 79b "Vietnam Protestors" by US Army/National Archives/Wikimedia Commons/Public Domain; 85t tupungato/iStock Editorial/Thinkstock; 85b Guido Koppes / age fotostock / SuperStock

Unit 3

97 kursaltunsal/iStock/Thinkstock; 99 AP Photo/Atlanta Journal-Constitution, Jason Getz; 103 AP Photo/Jerome Delay; 111 © iStockphoto.com/Tarzan9280; 115 JACQUELYN MARTIN/AFP/Getty Images; 119 © iStockphoto.com/Pauline S Mills; 130l "Abraham Lincoln Caricature" by DonkeyHotey/Flickr/CC By-SA 2.0; 130r "George Washington - Caricature" by DonkeyHotey/Flickr/CC By 2.0

Unit 4

139 © iStockphoto.com/Sasha Radosavljevic; 157l © iStock-photo.com/georgi1969; 157r © blickwinkel / Alamy; 158 AP Photo/Juan Bautista Diaz; 164 © iStockphoto.com/trekandshoot; 177t, b © iStockphoto.com/ZU_09

Unit 5

189 Dr. Najeeb Layyous / Science Source; 192 © iStockphoto.com/RonTech2000; 205 AP Photo/Mark Humphrey

Unit 6

240 "Mich. Guardsmen inspect water wells in need of repair in Iraq" by Petty Officer 1st Class Carmichael Yepez, Joint Combat Camera Center Iraq/Flickr/CC By 2.0; 242 AP Photo/File; 245t Universal Images Group / SuperStock; 245b Keystone-France/Hulton Archive/Getty Images; 253 © iStockphoto.com/TarpMagnus; 257 Architect of the Capitol; 260l © Alan Wylie / Alamy; 260r The Granger Collection, New York; 261 © Georgios Kollidas - Fotolia; 263l Royal Albert Memorial Museum, Exeter, Devon, UK / Bridgeman Images, 263r Bachrach/Archive Photos/Getty Images; 269l AP Photo/Mary Ann Chastain; 269r jhans/Bigstock.com

Unit 7

287 © iStockphoto.com/ookawa; 293tl © iStockphoto.com/Grafissimo; 293tr © iStockphoto.com/Volodymyr Goinyk; 293bl © iStockphoto.com/MajaPhoto; 293br © iStockphoto.com/kuch3; 308 Cover art for Gregory W. Brown's Missa Charles Darwin. Design and Illustration by Brett Picknell (2013). Courtesy of Navona Records, LLC.; 317 "Illustration at Cover of Just So Stories (c1912)"/Wikimedia Commons/Public Domain; 332t Courtesy of Dr. John Baumgardner; 332b BJU Photo Services; 333t, 334l © AnswersinGenesis; 333b Greg Kahn/The Washington Post/Getty Images; 334r Creation Ministries International (US) CREATION.com

Unit 8

343 DEA / S. VANNINI/De Agostini/Getty Images; 355 "Millais, John Everett (Sir) - Pizarro Seizing the Inca of Peru - Google Art Project"/Wikimedia Commons/Public Domain; 357 Past Pix / SSPL / Science and Society / SuperStock; 358 © TopFoto / THE IMAGE WORKS, INC.; 365 North Wind Picture Archives via AP Images; 370 "Vmail letter" by NathanBeach/Wikimedia Commons/Public Domain; 371l "Dad-pow-postcard-wwII" by Steven Keech/Wikimedia Commons/CC By-SA 3.0; 371r "Mauthausen Ausweis from WWII - front"/US Army/Wikimedia Commons/Public Domain; 373 imageBROKER / SuperStock; 379 Private Collection / © Look and Learn / Bridgeman Images

Unit 9

384 Joe Kohen/WireImage/Getty Images; 395l Fine Art Images / SuperStock; 395r "The Death of Marat" by Jacques-Louis David/Royal Museums of Fine Arts of Belgium/Wikimedia Commons/Public Domain; 401 AP Photo/Paola Crociani; 412 © AF archive / Alamy; 420l Geoff Caddick/PA Wire URN:8988422 (Press Association via AP Images); 420r Rex Features via AP Images; 427t "Elysia-chlorotica-body" by Karen N. Pelletreau et al./Wikimedia Commons/CC By 4.0; 427bl Mark Carwardine/Barcroft Media/Getty Images; 427br Peter David/The Image Bank/Getty Images; 428 © iStockphoto.com/Lisa-Blue; 429 Raymond Boyd/Michael Ochs Archives/Getty Images; 430 "Adams The Tetons and the Snake River" by Ansel Adams/National Archives/Wikimedia Commons/Public Domain

EXPLAINING THE GOSPEL

One of the greatest desires of Christian teachers is to see their students repent and believe in Christ. Relying on the Holy Spirit, you should take advantage of the opportunities that arise for presenting the gospel. You may find the following outline helpful, especially when dealing individually with a young person.

1. The Lord God is king over all His creation (Rev. 4:11).
   - God created all that there is (Gen. 1–2).
   - God created the world with laws about how His world is to work and the way people are to live.

2. All have sinned—including me (Rom. 3:23).
   - Since Adam first sinned, all people are born rebels against the rule of God (Rom. 5:12).
   - God has made me in His own image so that I might declare His glory by being like Him (Gen. 1:26–27).
   - But I am a sinner. I disobey God's Word. The Bible teaches that I am to love God more than anything or anyone (Mark 12:30). It also teaches that I should love other people at all times (Mark 12:31). But I don't enjoy doing what God wants me to do, I don't delight in obeying my parents, and I don't like being kind to other people.
   - God will punish me for my rebellion and sin (Rom. 6:23). God hates sin, and there is nothing I can do to get rid of my sin. I can try to change my behavior, but I can never change my heart.

3. Jesus died and rose again for me (Rom. 5:8).
   - God loves me even though I am a sinner.
   - He sent His Son, Jesus Christ, to live a perfect life and to die on the cross, suffering the punishment for my sin.
   - Three days later, God raised Jesus from the dead and has made Him the ruler of His eternal kingdom. Jesus is alive today. This is the gospel of Jesus Christ: the fact that He died on the cross and has been raised up to be God's appointed King (1 Cor. 15:1–4).

   - God desires to restore me to bearing His image by making me like His Son, the perfect image bearer of God (Rom. 8:29).
   - God gives a new heart—new loves and desires—to every one of His children (Ezek. 36:26–27).

4. I need to put my trust in Jesus (Rom. 10:9–10).
   - I must repent (turn away) from my sin and let Jesus control my life. I must also believe what God has done through Jesus (Mark 1:15).
   - If I repent and believe in what Jesus has done, I am putting my trust in Jesus.
   - Everyone who is trusting in Jesus is forgiven of sin.
   - Everyone who is trusting in Jesus submits to having Him as his King.
   - Everyone who has been saved by God will continue trusting and obeying Jesus for the rest of his life (Heb. 3:14).

When talking individually with a young person, ask questions to discern sincerity or any misunderstanding. (What is sin? Are you a sinner? What is the gospel? What does it mean to repent?) Read the verses from your Bible. If the student shows genuine sorrow for sin and a sufficiently accurate understanding of the basics of the gospel, encourage him to call on the Lord as you listen. Perhaps he will pray something like the following:

> "God, I know that You hate sin. But I also know that You love me. I believe that Jesus died for me and rose from the dead for me. I want to follow Him wherever He leads me. I now turn away from my sin, and I am trusting in Jesus to forgive me and to be my King forever."

Show the student the Bible's command that believers unite together in regular fellowship (Heb. 10:24–25), and encourage him to get involved right away in a sound church. Tell him that whenever he sins, he will be forgiven as he confesses those sins to God (1 John 1:9).